LION
· IN THE ·
LOBBY

Clarence Mitchell, Jr.'s
Struggle for the Passage
of Civil Rights Laws

DENTON L. WATSON

William Morrow and Company, Inc.
New York

Recognizing the importance of preserving what has been written, it is the policy of William Morrow and Company, Inc., and its imprints and affiliates to have the books it publishes printed on acid-free paper, and we exert our best efforts to that end.

Library of Congress Cataloging-in-Publication Data

Watson, Denton L.
    Lion in the lobby : Clarence Mitchell, Jr.'s struggle for the
passage of civil rights law / Denton L. Watson.
        p.   cm.
    ISBN 0-688-05097-2
    1. Mitchell, Clarence M. (Clarence Maurice), 1911–1984. 2. Afro-
Americans—Biography. 3. Civil rights workers—United States—
Biography. 4. National Association for the Advancement of Colored
People—Biography. 5. Afro-Americans—Civil rights. 6. United
States—Race relations. 7. Civil rights movements—United States—
History—20th century. I. Title.
E185.97.M63W37 1990
323'.092—dc20
    [B]   90-30797
                                                                                              CIP

Printed in the United States of America

First Edition

1 2 3 4 5 6 7 8 9 10

BOOK DESIGN BY BILL MCCARTHY

To my father, Audley Granville Watson,
and my late mother, Ivy Louise Watson

Foreword

One of my first experiences on the importance of the First Amendment came during the Depression in the 1930s when I witnessed a demonstration by some of the leading white ladies in Baltimore against the mistreatment of welfare clients.

It was unforgettable to see these high-minded, neatly dressed, and purposeful people hoist their picket signs, form their line, and begin marching in front of the welfare office building. Soon, the police escorted them to a waiting patrol wagon. The door closed behind them, and they were taken off to the police station. Picketing was then unlawful in Maryland.

Many years later, I drove past a police station in the same city where a number of patrolmen in uniform were picketing over unsettled grievances. One sign said, IF YOU SUPPORT OUR EFFORT, HONK YOUR HORN. I honked my car horn. A protester who was white turned and, as an expression of appreciation, raised a clenched fist in the black power salute that became popular in the 1960s. Although I do not favor code words or signals that have implications of color, I was pleased to see the picket line. It showed that in the years between the thirties and the seventies, at least some people in the law enforcement field have learned that the Constitution of the United States touches their daily lives and is their best shield against unjust treatment.

The forty-plus years between those two scenes represent the primary period of my life's work to make the Constitution a meaningful document for all people. I began this job by, first, trying to make the executive branch of government work properly. We needed not only just laws but also right national policies. Second, we had to get Congress to enact laws for the protection of our rights. Third, we had to make sure that these laws were properly enforced. Without enforcement, it would not have been worth getting the laws in the first place.

Even in the darkest period of America's history, when lynch mobs ran rampant throughout many parts of the country killing and maiming black men, women, and children, my faith in the democratic process as a means for achieving freedom and equality for all has never waned. I have spent most of my life hoping for and working for the right of all men to share in the blessing of our Constitution. I, too, am a law and order man. I am a man who has sought the kind of order that makes freedom grow instead of stifling it.

As a people whose society is governed by the rule of law, Americans have over the years developed various processes and institutions for bringing pressure on the system to achieve change. It took black Americans many painful attempts to develop their own institutions that could provide the cohesive framework for developing the strategies that were required to bring sufficient pressure on all three branches of government to win the enactment of the civil rights laws. One of the main institutions is the NAACP. As director of the NAACP Washington Bureau, I proudly served as an instrument in this process.

Now as I look back at the history of the fight we have been waging, I feel a sense of inspiration because I am privileged to live in a time when we have gotten all three branches of our national government to work for civil rights.

The NAACP, of course, could not have won those great victories by itself. On the Supreme Court, we had Chief Justice Earl Warren. In Congress we had the Charles Mathiases, the Joseph Tydings, the Hugh Scotts, the Hubert Humphreys, and a host of other staunch supporters and lukewarm allies. There were also many bitter foes like the James Eastlands, the Strom Thurmonds, and the Samuel Ervins. Nevertheless, we did win enactment of the most comprehensive set of civil rights laws this nation has ever known. In the process, we were able to bring about one of history's greatest social revolutions in a peaceful manner. How this fundamental change in social and institutional attitude was accomplished is the story I plan to tell.

—CLARENCE MITCHELL, JR.

Author's note: Mr. Mitchell had prepared this introduction for a book after his retirement from the NAACP in 1978, but he never told his story himself. Instead, he entrusted me with the responsibility.

Acknowledgments

During an interview in early December 1983, Clarence asked me when I expected to complete this work. Optimistically, I said in about a year. He looked me straight in the eyes and said, "You, know, I won't live to see it." With an awkward smile, I mumbled, "Oh, yes, you will."

On Sunday evening, March 18, 1984, when his son Michael called to inform me that "Daddy has just passed on," I therefore could only bang my desk in anguish and cry out, "Oh, no." I had not visited with him for about three weeks because I was preparing questions for another of our numerous interviews, and was ready to do so the week he died.

His loss, though profound, did free me to proceed with this work wholly on my own. Previously, despite the vast reservoir of materials I had collected on his work from the NAACP General Office and Washington Bureau files at the Library of Congress, the Truman, Eisenhower, Kennedy, and Johnson libraries, the National Archives, and the Moorland-Spingarn Research Center at Howard University, I was very dependent on him. Juanita, her fragile health, notwithstanding, was determined to live to see me finish the book and filled the void her husband had left.

I was first drawn to Clarence soon after I joined the NAACP national public relations staff in 1971, when I visited his office in Washington to learn about his activities. After about forty-five minutes, as I was leaving that evening, he asked me how I planned to get to National Airport. "By taxi," I responded. "I will take you there," he objected. As I looked at his desk covered with telephone messages from senators and other important personages in Washington, I thought it was only fair for me to decline his offer. But Clarence insisted. The fact that I was only a junior executive did not matter to him. He took me to the airport then and, subsequently, every time that I met with him at his office. His humility and warmth strengthened my love and respect for him. When he finally agreed in 1978 to cooperate with me in writing this book about him, I knew I could not have had a better subject. The following year, I embarked on that mission

9

when I interrupted my NAACP tenure to live and work in Baltimore for two years.

I am indebted to Juanita Mitchell for her encouraging Clarence to set aside time for interviews with me, for giving me access subsequent to his death to the personal papers and to her own rich collection of materials, and for her warm friendship and confidence. I am similarly grateful to the other members of the Mitchell family for their support, especially to "Uncle George," who was the first to open up to me his collection of news clippings and memorabilia.

Had Roy Wilkins not hired me, however, and given me carte blanche to travel and to learn about the NAACP, none of this would have been possible. To him and to my other NAACP associates and friends—notably, Henry Lee Moon, Maybelle Ward, Gloster Current, Nathaniel Jones, Ruby Hurley, Kelly Alexander, Sr., and Dr. Aaron Henry—I am thankful for their lessons on civil rights. I am equally indebted to Yvonne Price, once the NAACP liaison at the Leadership Conference on Civil Rights, who steered me to sources on Clarence's activities in Washington, and to the many people who granted me interviews. Similar appreciation is expressed to the archivists at the Truman, Eisenhower, Kennedy, and Johnson libraries, the National Archives, the Moorland-Spingarn Research Center at Howard University, and the Schomburg Library in New York for their dedicated help.

Eunice Riedel, my editor at William Morrow who set me on course, did not live to see me more than halfway through. Words cannot express my appreciation for her lessons on writing a book. To my friend Paula Giddings, I am grateful for steering me to Eunice. Indispensable were the insights, comments, and encouragement from Joseph Rauh; Robert Weaver; Joseph R. L. Sterne, editor, editorial pages of the *Baltimore Sun;* Ramsey Clark; Juanita Mitchell; and John A. Davis, who read all or parts of my manuscript. Davis and Weaver were especially helpful with their firsthand knowledge of the Fair Employment Practice Committee period. Rauh was proud that, next to Mitchell, he knew more than any person about the struggle to pass civil rights legislation.

To my wife Rose and children, Victor and Dawn, I express my deepest appreciation for their enduring with me the sacrifices that were essential for fulfilling this mission.

In the end, none of this would have been possible without the grants I received from the Ford Foundation, which enabled me, first, to begin research and, second, to leave the NAACP staff in 1985 for a second time to devote full time to this mission. To my program officer, Lynn Walker, thanks. I am also thankful for the interest shown in the book by Anheuser-Busch, the AFL-CIO, the General Motors Corporation, and for a research grant from the Lyndon Baines Johnson Library.

Contents

CONTENTS

Introduction

"In those days, Clarence Mitchell was called the 101st Senator but those of us who served here then knew full well that this magnificent lion in the lobby was a great deal more influential than most of us with seats in this chamber."

Senator Howard Baker, Jr., of Tennessee, in paying this tribute to Mitchell following his death on March 18, 1984, had not worked with him for as long as many of his colleagues, who had come to recognize the lobbyist as "the 101st Senator" because he had spent more time on Capitol Hill than most of them. But, as the son-in-law of Everett McKinley Dirksen, the incomparable Republican Senate minority leader from Illinois, Baker had absorbed enough of the esteem in which the civil rights lobbyist was held to have been able to portray with the southerner's flowery eloquence Mitchell's genius for influencing lawmakers of all shades of ideology.

Dirksen's predecessor as Republican leader of the United States Senate was gruff, conservative William F. Knowland of California. Knowland's support was crucial for passage of the 1957 Civil Rights Act, the measure that broke the psychological barrier to such legislation that had existed since the end of the Reconstruction. Their counterpart for a while on the Democratic side of the aisle was Lyndon Baines Johnson, followed by Mike Mansfield of Montana.

In the White House, a fully converted Johnson used the immense power of the presidency to translate the mighty folklore of southern race relations into an enduring political passion play in Congress in order to cap the most critical phase of the modern civil rights movement. Johnson himself, in recalling Mitchell's confidence in pushing for the 1968 Fair Housing Act when other civil rights leaders wanted him to issue an executive order instead, said, "He didn't have the highest title in the room, but all in all he had forced down my door more than any other person," and had gotten what he wanted.[1]

As director of the Washington Bureau of the National Association for the Advancement of Colored People from 1950 to 1978 (previously, he was labor director for four years), Mitchell was a civil rights leader who served the public interest by seeking enforcement of the Constitution to protect the rights of minorities. He was a top NAACP policymaker and its mouthpiece on Capitol Hill. There, in addition to working with the White House and executive agencies, he spent three quarters of his time in direct contact with Congress, attempting to implement NAACP policy. The NAACP, by the same token, was his most important instrument, providing him with organizational support, spiritual nourishment, and essential resources from its immense cultural reservoir. He enhanced his NAACP base with his position as legislative chairman of the Leadership Conference on Civil Rights—a coalition of civil rights, civic, labor, and religious organizations that vastly extended the NAACP's political reach.

Mitchell's battlefield also extended throughout the entire federal bureaucracy. He was at the same time defender of the little people, those who all too often found themselves under the heel of oppressive state and local governments and with no other defender than the NAACP.[2]

Mitchell's embrace of humanity led him to defend individuals with the same fervor that he would himself or his kin. So much so, John A. Davis recalls, that during their tenure with the Fair Employment Practices Committee, Ernest G. Trimble, another associate, used to complain, "Clarence, you just want everybody to do right, and that's hard." Robert C. Weaver, whose friendship with Mitchell dated from the same period, noted a resulting contradiction: "Clarence was very quick to criticize other people's morals, and here was Adam Clayton Powell—amoral"—serving as his closest ally in Congress for much of the 1950s.

Those qualities set Mitchell apart from a second category of lobbyist who represented selfish monied interests—those who evoked the hired-gun image and led one senator battling for regulatory legislation to brand them a gang of ineffectual mercenaries, a nuisance to Congress. Mitchell, as Weaver was so well aware, represented the cause of justice. To advance those interests, he organized political support in Washington and throughout the nation—an activity that was reinforced by a broader strategy to direct national and international attention to America's racial problems. Mitchell could thus arouse passion for battle where few people thought it was possible.

A third group of lobbyists representing organizations like labor unions served narrower, bread-and-butter causes in the interests of workers and a less privileged segment of society. Public interest lobbyists like environmentalists, representing a tradition that extended back to the prohibitionist, peace, and pacifist movements, made up a fourth group.

Although the basic practice of lobbying is the same, influencing law-makers to support a particular bill or cause, the scope of the issue with which a lobbyist is concerned determines the lobbyist's strategy or approach to his job. As Mitchell explained:

> When I began working for the NAACP, we had periods of great financial difficulties. It was usually after some awful crime that our finances would improve. Someone observed that the persons who believed in civil rights were not moved to fight or work except in times of emotional distress. I think this is true of many humans. When we make appeals for the community chest, we like to talk about the problems of little children. When we are troubled with wars and natural calamities, we tend to make greater sacrifices than in times of peace or when we have no problems.
>
> In this respect, the leaders of great movements must be different from others. Those who are willing and able to change the social structure so that our fellow humans may have better lives must be willing to give their time and attention to the tedious and to things that lack glamour in order to have complete success.[3]

Congressman Richard Bolling of Missouri was all too well aware that in the bitter two-year struggle for the 1957 Civil Rights Act,

> the formulation of strategy was often the critical factor. For, while the combat may be compared to a chess game, it is one in which the chessmen constantly change value. And there are many steps from the conception of a strategy to its successful conclusion. There are skirmishes and battles, victories and defeats, all manner of crises. Each of these engagements is integral to the process of passing the bill.

Mitchell was central to the development and execution of this strategy for the passage of civil rights legislation.

Andrew J. Biemiller, the AFL-CIO's lobbyist, marveled at another of Mitchell's legendary qualities: "I never remember a time going up there [on Capitol Hill] that I didn't bump into him. I am not talking about by design now. I just mean when I was going up there on other matters. He was a very busy guy. I don't know where he got all that energy."

In fulfilling his mission, Mitchell corralled such mighty, contending egos as Knowland, Dirksen, and Johnson into a resolute phalanx standing against both historical forces and human passion, and moved the legion of other similarly independent-minded lawmakers whose support was indispensable for breaking the southern stranglehold on Congress, especially in the Senate. He did this not just once, in 1957, or on those innumerable occasions when he had to marshal forces to defeat harmful legislation, but also in 1960, 1964, 1965, 1968, and subsequently in those instances where additional legislation was needed to strengthen the landmark laws. Mitchell accomplished such seemingly impossible feats in part by enlisting conservative-minded leaders to goad straddlers off the fence. His ability to find support where others thought none existed was a cause of wonderment among supporters and opponents alike. His most salient qualities were his integrity and his ability to transcend skin color to appeal to the better nature of lawmakers in influencing them to uphold the Constitution. He created a sense of confidentiality with those officials by never taking notes during meetings. Immediately afterward, though, he would write a memo- randum to the files or other notes.

Among the basic rules by which Mitchell functioned were the follow- ing: (1) Be fair and honest. (2) Do not exaggerate your position. (3) Do not threaten, or the lawmaker will get on a high horse and be impossible to work with. (4) And remember that some lawmakers vote on principle while others serve their political interests.

Mitchell firmly believed that lawmakers should be praised when they did the right thing and damned when they didn't. His position contra- dicted long-standing NAACP policy, which was that public officials should not be commended because they were obliged to serve the public good. Mitchell felt that public praise encouraged them to do better. As an exam- ple, he pointedly noted that in his autobiography, John Ehrlichman recalls the Nixon administration's experience with Vernon Jordan, then president of the National Urban League. He "was happy to take the millions of dollars we pumped" into his organization, said Ehrlichman, but he main- tained "that he'd lose his credibility with his constituency if he openly praised the Nixon administration." Mitchell explained that that was not his style. He praised the good deeds and criticized the bad.[4]

At the peak of his influence in 1965, Mitchell ranked among the most successful lobbyists in U.S. history—a profession that began before the founding of the Republic when the Colonies kept representatives in London. He symbolized the spirit of the Founding Fathers, who, remem- bering that King George of England had rejected their protests, took great store in the guarantee that every citizen with a grievance had a constitu- tional right to petition the Congress for redress.

The NAACP, for its part, first realized the power of kings in 1915 when it began pushing for legislation to protect African Americans against descrimination. More menacing than opposition to any such measure, how- ever, were the antiblack bills that the southerners were pushing with the help of northerners who were trading for votes for their own measures. But as the NAACP's official organ, *The Crisis,* reported, the organization was on its guard: "It employs in each branch at Congress a man whose duty it is to keep it informed by mail and telegram of all proceedings affecting colored people." The NAACP had helped defeat several hostile bills the previous year and was anticipating many more.

The widening scope of the federal government's programs following World War II gave rise to a significant increase in lobbying activities. This expansion had begun much earlier, but it was given a giant boost by the New Deal and the war. The increasing complexity of the national economy made local and state governments much more dependent on Washington and multiplied the need for legislative "liaisons" and "consultants."

Though essential, the art of lobbying was little understood until recently, thanks to regulations that were enacted following a near success in 1936. (At that time the House, unhappy with the product of a conference committee that had sought to resolve differences in versions of a bill that had been introduced by Senator Hugo L. Black and passed by both houses of Congress, rejected it.) In fact, for most of its history, the practice of lobbying has been confined to the shadows of public esteem, dating from the time when special-interest pleaders began filling the lobbies of the Athenian senate.[5] On this side of the Atlantic, tools of the trade were considered to be booze, broads, and black bags—a rogue's saga. Kenneth Crawford's *The Pressure Boys* documented this picture of lobbying in the United States in the 1930s. More recently, the phantoms of the U.S. Chamber of Commerce, the National Association of Manufacturers, the banking and power utilities industries, and the hundreds of trade associations have been replaced by the representatives of the defense-industrial complex with megabucks to spend on steering votes in Congress. Lobbying has been defiled by a new spirit of venality employing sophisticated forms of influence peddling that skirt the law but are clearly unethical.[6]

Despite the sometimes unsavory connotations, lobbying is an essential practice. Few major bills are ever passed without some influence being exerted to win votes. There are, too, legitimate ways for a lobbyist to wine and dine a lawmaker. Mitchell avoided such practices. "I have never bought anyone a drink," he explained, "and I don't think I've ever paid for a congressman's lunch or dinner. Most of them want to pay for lunch for me, but I try not to let them do it."

Mitchell made sure his personal life was beyond reproach by taking absolutely no chance that would leave him open to charges of hanky-panky or legal wrongdoing, or that would in any way besmirch the family name. His one and only love was his partner in combat, Juanita Jackson Mitchell.

Joseph L. Rauh, Jr., a founder of the Americans for Democratic Ac-

tion, who was his closest lobbying partner, followed a similar path of survival, and to such an extent that, he said, he actually paid more than his
fair share of taxes. Rauh recalls one occasion when he and Mitchell were
about to cross a Washington street. As Rauh stepped off the sidewalk
against the light, he felt a firm hand on his arm holding him back. Mitchell had him wait for the green light before they crossed. That habit of
toeing the line was for the best, because, from his arrival in Washington in
1946 to work for the NAACP until his retirement thirty-two years later, J.
Edgar Hoover's Federal Bureau of Investigation kept a very close watch on
Mitchell, down to his performance in evening classes at the University of
Maryland Law School, where the worst they could discover was that he
maintained a C average, although this was due to his attending school
without any letup in his lobbying activities.

Mitchell's rectitude, could cause problems, as Rauh recalled:

"Being Clarence's fellow traveler down the corridors of Congress for
thirty years hasn't been so damn easy. First, this guy walks so fast and so
far, I can't keep up with him. Around noon I get hungry and he doesn't
eat; at about late afternoon I want a drink and he doesn't drink. Not only
does he not rest, eat, or drink, but you get called names just for sitting
beside him in the galleries.

"Back in 1957, Clarence and I were sitting there on the voting question and up jumped Senator Harry Byrd, the one who used to own the
State of Virginia. He looks up in the gallery, points at Clarence and me
and says, 'There they are, the NAACP and the ADA—the Gold Dust
twins.'

"Then in 1964, a senator named Spessard Holland from Florida looked
up and said, 'There they are, those vultures of the gallery.'"[7]

Mitchell normally was a courtly man, a statesman who was ever ready
to seek out that kernel of human goodness in even diehard segregationists
as he worked for passage of civil rights legislation or to kill a harmful
measure. He could never match the racists on the House or Senate floor in
name calling, but he was no slouch. Angered by Senator James Eastland's
goadings, he publicly lambasted the Mississippian for having a "stinking
albatross" around his neck and was as a result hurting the Democratic
party. As Mitchell recalled this acerbic relationship with Eastland, "I used
to have to stand outside Eastland's office and ask Senator Philip Hart [of
Michigan] to go in and present whatever it was I wanted to the chairman of
the Judiciary Committee." Most times when Mitchell appeared before Eastland's committee, he would pointedly absent himself.

As for working with Mitchell, David L. Brody of the Anti-Defamation
League is proud that "Clarence taught me how to lobby." A staff member
recalls, "The thing about Mr. Mitchell is that he was always so cool. You

felt confident working with him. He wasn't rivaling anybody. Everybody liked him. He always stayed in the background. But for a while it appeared that he and the executive director [Roy Wilkins] were on the same level." For fellow staffers, he was the undisputed authority on legislation. "He never hemmed or hawed. He was able to give a straight answer. What he didn't know was that his was the last word on the matter after everybody else here, including Wilkins, had gotten tired of trying to figure out a position."

Seen through the eyes of twenty-five-year-old Jane O'Grady, fresh out of the University of California at Berkeley with a graduate degree in political sociology, Mitchell's lobbying operation was at first mystifying. She had come to Washington to work for what later was expanded to the Amalgamated Clothing and Textile Workers Union, one of the members of the Leadership Conference on Civil Rights, and was immediately thrown into the thick of battle for the 1964 Civil Rights Act. She knew nothing about what was going on. But as one of the labor lobbyists under the direction of Andrew Biemiller, the gruff former two-term congressman from Wisconsin who was the third member of the Leadership Conference's legislative directorate, she had the best of teachers.

To O'Grady, Mitchell and Biemiller were like a "Mr. Nice Guy and Mr. Bad Guy" combination. "Clarence was the soul of graciousness and diplomacy." He had a velvet touch and the "patience of a saint." He knew the names of everyone in the room, even those of the eleven-year-olds who came to stuff envelopes. Leadership Conference meetings were democratic forums to which the leaders brought issue papers that were the result of considerable study. Mitchell listened to all the contending forces. Biemiller looked big and tough on the outside, but he was a marshmallow underneath. Rauh was sharp and smart, capable of capturing the essence of an hour's discussion that had rambled all over the room and framing a consensus that accurately reflected the many viewpoints. O'Grady also respected Rauh for having a good sense of what would work with Congress and knowing how to proceed on an issue.

O'Grady sat in awe during those strategy sessions with a roomful of trench lobbyists, many of whom were as green as she. Arnold Aaronson, secretary of the Leadership Conference, and Marvin Caplan, his assistant, officially presided, but it was Mitchell who was really in charge. In the back would be the spitball throwers, dashiki-clad radicals like Marion Barry, a leader of the Student Nonviolent Coordinating Committee who later became mayor of Washington. O'Grady simply sat with her eyes wide open as those who supposedly represented the grass-roots folk challenged the establishment folk—those who believed in the legislative process. The generation gap added to the tension. So firm was the hold of Mitchell,

Rauh, Biemiller, and others on the meetings, however, that they remained in control of the policy-making process. Little wonder, therefore, that the student radicals did not attend meetings regularly.

Marshaling all available forces for the 1964 battle, Mitchell placed O'Grady in charge of a team of young lobbyists from organizations like the League of Women Voters and the U.S. Catholic Conference. The O'Grady Raiders, as Mitchell called them, were responsible for rounding up friendly lawmakers during the long process of voting on the bill, and subsequently on other civil rights bills. This strategy served to let the congressmen know they were being watched. Mitchell also placed other watchers in the galleries to conduct similar vigils.

The Leadership Conference's temporary headquarters was at the nearby Congressional Hotel, where a master chart of lawmakers' offices was kept. Gallery watchers relayed alerts through this office whenever a member was off the floor too long, a situation that could slow debate because of lack of a quorum. Also, because there was no electronic voting then, it took literally thirty-five minutes for the votes in the House to be counted by roll call. So many lawmakers simply waited twenty minutes in their offices before rushing over to the floor to cast their vote at the last minute, thus increasing anxiety. O'Grady and her team were assigned to all thirteen floors of the two House office buildings. On each floor two "raiders" were stationed at a phone in the office of a cooperating lawmaker to receive calls from the Capitol about impending action.

O'Grady was surprised at the good-naturedness with which those lawmakers usually took the badgering. One reason was that her team avoided potentially hostile members. Even the friendly lawmakers, however, sometimes got tired of being hounded and became grumpy. After a while, upon seeing a raider approaching down the hall, some would shout, "We're going, we're going." As the youngsters became part of the scene, they found they could slacken their vigil because the lawmakers were remaining on the floor and responding promptly to calls for quorums and votes. "We teetered precariously on the borderline of being major annoyances and were sort of objects of good fun," recalls O'Grady.

Despite the hazards, O'Grady found that the system was ideal for getting a young lobbyist known on the Hill. "Clarence probably didn't even realize the extent to which he was helping all of us get to be the kind of lobbyist he was, not that any of us would ever reach his stature. But he was training us, in a sort of fundamental way. We were there, people saw us, they knew us, they knew the organization." That was the first step in lobbying, getting to be known. Ironically, because the black student radicals scorned the legislative process, they missed this training.

Later, O'Grady realized that older professional lobbyists would not have stooped to such badgering. Had she been more experienced, she would have cringed at the thought of doing such a thing. But "we were as pure as the driven snow." They "didn't know any better, and it was a useful device for letting members know there was a concerned constituency out there watching them." So the system worked. Furthermore, when Mitchell asked you, "any time, to do anything, no one ever said no to him. It would have been like saying no to the President of the United States. So it was an adventure, it was good fun, and, as I look back on it, what better training for me."[8]

Rauh himself, who developed a reputation in Washington befitting the pronunciation of his name (*row*), with a temper to match, had a more intimate picture of Mitchell as "the ideal lobbyist in the sense that he never boiled over. But he was able to boil over when the situation called for boiling over. He had the patience of Job, but knew when the right moment had come to substitute eloquent anger for patience. His job thrust him into the middle of the fight but it was his character and personality that happened to come out on top." He "would put anybody who was arguing against him on the defensive" by showing "what had happened and was still happening unfairly to blacks. He would have examples out of his own life."

As close as Mitchell and Rauh were, working as an inseparable team for more than a quarter century, there were meaningful differences in their approaches to constitutional and civil rights issues, which sometimes led to spirited discussions between them; it, however, was a healthy tension necessary for executing the complex operations they had undertaken. Mitchell, of course, typified the outlook of a black rights advocate who saw the world against a backdrop of racial oppression; Rauh was the white liberal incarnate who was driven much more by the epochal experiences of a people persecuted for their religious and ethnic differences, as manifested in a sense of moral outrage over all forms of racism and bigotry, than by the actual scars of discrimination.

Mitchell was basically a conservative, a trait that was common to most blacks like himself who were seeking an end to second-class citizenship. He wanted change—not the overthrow of the system, but removal of degrading racial barriers so that he and his people could enjoy its benefits with full equality. Rauh used to tease him, "Clarence, if you were white you would be a reactionary." Mitchell would only laugh. Rauh's impression was that his being a civil rights leader gave Mitchell "a certain radicalism. But it was more a radicalism in civil rights than in anything else." Consequently, Rauh found that Mitchell "was a little bit skeptical of me."

Jews were never officially second-class citizens in America even though they did suffer discrimination. Coming from a more socially secure background, Rauh not only was a radical civil libertarian, but as a lawyer he had no fear of taking on cases that others might have avoided as too controversial or left-wing.

While Mitchell believed that the struggle to uphold the Fourteenth Amendment's equal protection clause of the Constitution was the overriding priority, Rauh believed there were times when protection of First Amendment rights should take precedence over Fourteenth Amendment ones. For example, during the desegregation of the Charleston Navy Yard in 1953, Mitchell thought it outrageous that whites were permitted to demonstrate outside the base's cafeteria because blacks for the first time were eating there. Rauh thought that that type of freedom of expression was protected by the First Amendment.

Rauh was particularly concerned about abuses to the freedom of association that led to the blacklisting of individuals and organizations by the Justice Department and the professional "security corps" in the House Un-American Activities Committee, which was adept at destroying its victims with the Communist smear. Mitchell was guided by the NAACP policy of supporting any legitimate effort to root out communism but which carefully avoided any action that would endanger "the historic liberties of citizens" in the process.

The 1975 struggle over extension of the 1965 Voting Rights Act provided another example of Rauh's and Mitchell's different outlooks. Despite his undying belief that all citizens were entitled to equal protection under the law, Mitchell's emotions got the better of him when Hispanics began pushing for coverage by the voting law. They, too, were suffering discrimination in Texas, California, and a few counties elsewhere. Mitchell did not want them included because they were demanding a "national origins" provision in the bill for themselves in addition to the "race, color, or creed" designations. He and Rauh disagreed strongly but in a friendly manner on this issue. Owing to Mitchell's views, the Leadership Conference could not take a position, because, as Rauh recalls, "By God, if anybody had a veto, he had a veto."

Rauh therefore wrote a separate provision for covering the Hispanics, which Birch E. Bayh, Democrat of Indiana, introduced as a separate title even though it was part of the same bill. Adamant that the bill should be limited to blacks, Mitchell still was not satisfied. Bayh, nevertheless, pushed the provision through and Hispanics won coverage in the 1975 extension of the Voting Rights Act.

Afterward in a meeting between representatives of the Leadership Conference and major Hispanic groups, everyone sat dumfounded as Mitchell lost his temper. Seared in Rauh's brain are Mitchell's words, "Blacks were dying for the right to vote when you people couldn't decide whether you were Caucasians."

The issue for Mitchell was much more than racial philosophy. It was a question of ethnic attitudes toward blacks, and Mitchell fiercely resented the Hispanics' sense of superiority, which was demonstrated by their unwillingness to work with blacks. While Jews did not mind working alongside African Americans in the struggle for equal protection of the laws and other forms of constitutional justice because they regarded the causes of both groups as one, Hispanics, in contrast, were aloof. For example, Kivie Kaplan, a Jew who was president of the NAACP, knew all too well that once in his native Massachusetts, there had been signs on lawns that read, DOGS AND JEWS KEEP OFF THE GRASS.[9]

Rather than dividing them, however, the differences between Mitchell and Rauh strengthened their relationship and reinforced their work on the Hill. This was particularly evident in 1958 when their personalities and weltanschauungs led them to adopt different approaches in attempting to beat back a slew of attacks on the Supreme Court, which had resulted from the 1954 *Brown* v. *Board of Education* school desegregation ruling and other decisions protecting the rights of blacks and other minorities. An important factor in determining their strategies was their perception of Lyndon Johnson. Regarding the Senate majority leader as a cynical, self-serving politician, Rauh worked with the dominant liberal Senate bloc* to frustrate Johnson's maneuvers to mollify southern supporters in order to win support for a foreign-aid measure he wanted to get passed, and to avoid a filibuster that would have prolonged adjournment. Mitchell developed a relationship with the Texan and teamed up with him to defeat the more important anti–Supreme Court bills with the help of NAACP branches, which were mobilized by Roy Wilkins, executive director.[10]

When Mitchell fell to the floor of his kitchen from a massive heart attack in the early afternoon of March 18, 1984, he was carrying as always a copy of the U.S. Constitution in his wallet. With Juanita, he had just completed the short walk from Sunday morning service at the Sharp Street Memorial Methodist Church. He was setting the table for the lunch Juanita was preparing when death came.

His end symbolized his life. Next to the Bible, he treasured the Constitution most as a living compact of freedom that made possible the creation of laws to guarantee equality for all citizens; he was at peace with his Maker

*Hubert Humphrey (D-Minn.), Paul H. Douglas (D-Ill.), Thomas C. Hennings (D-Mo.), John A. Carroll (D-Col.), Wayne Morse (D-Ore.), Joseph S. Clark (D-Pa.), Jacob Javits (R-N.Y.), and John Sherman Cooper (R-Ky.).

following the service; and he was with his only love at home. The sturdy, attached brick building at 1324 Druid Hill Avenue had been Mitchell's personal base of security and assurance throughout his professional life in Washington.

Once characterized by stable black middle-class families, the neighborhood was now racked with high unemployment, abysmal poverty, and decay. As the area's most notable resident, Mitchell waged a continual battle to keep it stable and forced the city to maintain the little park across the street facing his home. Such efforts did not spare him the experiences of inner-city crime. As he was approaching the steps of his home just after ten o'clock one early spring night in 1974, two youths approached him. One pulled out a handgun and demanded his wallet. Instead of handing it over, he grabbed the gun. It fired as he tried to wrestle it from the youth's grip, wounding him in two fingers.

He fell to the ground along with the gun, giving one of the youths a chance to retrieve it and again point it at him. Rather than surrendering, Mitchell reached to his back pocket as if he too had a gun and told the youths he would blow their heads off if they did not leave. Frightened, they fled as he grabbed one's sunglasses and watch. The youths were later arrested.

The following year, Mitchell carried his messianic zeal onto the world stage to the United Nations as a member of the U.S. delegation headed by Daniel P. Moynihan. The new assignment was his first respite from the NAACP, one he earned by trading in his fifty-eight days of accumulated vacation time. Exposed as a student at Lincoln University to Africans studying there who had a strong pride in their heritage, Mitchell had vowed that he would never go abroad, and never did, until his people were free at home. So, like Moynihan, whose oratorical excesses in extramural pursuits had made him a lightning rod at the UN Building in New York's Turtle Bay, Mitchell was soon embroiled in controversy for speaking bluntly. He incurred the wrath of legions of blacks at home by defending Moynihan for his labeling Uganda's President Idi Amin a "racist murderer" because he had denounced Zionism and called for the extinction of Israel. Mitchell diplomatically likened Amin to Hitler and declared, "When we are assailed with cruel and degrading words, we feel, and are, free to express our indignation."

African Americans were disappointed that, given his status as "the 101st Senator," Mitchell was serving as merely a member of the UN delegation rather than as its head. Subsequently, some of his more vocal critics also began expressing their own outrage at Amin's butchery. One of these was a former black ambassador to the United States who, in a 1977 meeting in Kenya, challenged then Vice President Daniel Arap Moi for not using his influence to curb his neighbor's excesses.

Despite a partial disability in later life resulting from an extended hernia, Mitchell never slowed down or shunned public activity. His forbearance of his physical condition was modeled after Lillie Carroll Jackson's long service through the NAACP despite a distorted face caused by a mastoidectomy that almost took her life. Mitchell would have preferred to correct the hernia, but a physical examination he underwent in 1979 in preparation for an operation showed he had a badly damaged heart. He remembered that five years earlier while speaking at a church function in North Carolina, he had suffered a terrible pain in his chest that forced him to sit down. The pain quickly passed and only later did he realize that he had suffered a "silent" heart attack. Advised that he stood only a fifty-fifty chance of surviving the anesthesia, he took his doctor's advice to forgo surgery.

He nevertheless assumed a "retirement" program that included the practice of law along with Juanita and son Michael in the family firm, writing a weekly column for the *Baltimore Sun,* a highly visible role in the state higher education system as a member of the University of Maryland's board of regents, and several other civic projects such as being a member, and later chairman, of Senator Mathias's Judiciary Selection Committee.

Mitchell's departure from the NAACP in 1978 was unpleasant, unbefitting his lifelong devotion to the organization and his monumental contributions to the struggle for racial equality and justice that benefited even his most severe critics on the NAACP national board of directors. No stranger to the rough-and-tumble of NAACP politics, he accepted his lumps and begged for no quarter.

As an expression of appreciation for his service, the board should have named him executive director to succeed Wilkins upon his retirement two years earlier. Wilkins himself offered no help even though Mitchell, because he thought his associate was being treated unfairly, had incurred the board's unforgiving wrath in his defiant defense of the NAACP leader during an extremely bitter retirement battle. It would have been impossible for the board to pass over Mitchell had Wilkins named him as his successor. Although his family maintained he had wanted to succeed Wilkins, Mitchell denied any such desire. There was no doubt that had he been offered the job he would have accepted it, but he would never ask or apply for it.

Another possible role for Mitchell could have been as an elder statesman–lecturer. Few living individuals were renowned as "walking civil rights archives." His knowledge and experience were central to understanding the epic quest for the protection of constitutional liberties for blacks through the enactment of laws. Yet, in this regard too, the opportunity to benefit from his dying love for the NAACP was lost.

Fortuitously, given the debilitating nature of NAACP politics, the denial of the distinction of NAACP executive director no doubt prolonged Mitchell's life by sparing him the frustrations of the top office. His departure from the NAACP also enabled him to share the remainder of his life with his hometown, Baltimore, where the extent of his dedication to ending racial injustice was not well known. The day after his death, the *Sun* published an editorial describing his monumental contributions and proposed a physical memorial so that the city could express its appreciation. Mayor William Donald Schaefer then appointed a commission and accepted its recommendation that the historic downtown courthouse be renamed for Mitchell. On March 8, 1985, his first posthumous birthday, the building where he had covered the Donald Gaines Murray desegregation case in 1935 was dedicated the Clarence M. Mitchell, Jr., Courthouse. [11]

Like so many black leaders who had devoted their lives to the civil rights struggle, Mitchell died poor but relatively oblivious of his financial condition. He had subsisted during his entire NAACP career on a salary that Wilkins kept low by his own self-denial in order to keep the association solvent. Mitchell turned down offers from Johnson, his friend Robert Weaver, and others for higher-paying jobs. He preferred instead to amass his riches in the archives of freedom.

Juanita, in similarly dedicating her life to the struggle in her hometown and state, stoically endured Mitchell's sacrifices with him and treasured the "quality time" he spent with her, their four sons, Clarence III, Keiffer, Michael, and George, and fifteen grandchildren. A painful awareness as she looked back on life was that "we are poor because he gave so much, and I gave so much." The love that united them in youth burned as intensely throughout their lives despite the ravages of work and time. Self-consciously, Juanita once complained of her septuagenarian obesity, only to be comforted by the tender warmth emitted by her now heavy-set Clarence: "Oh, darling, you are beautiful." Typically, in their advancing years they had discussed inevitable death, vowing that neither would leave the other alone to suffer the travails of life. But fate was the controlling force.

As legal counsel and president of the Baltimore NAACP branch and legal redress chairman of the Maryland NAACP state conference, Juanita dedicated her professional talents to the struggle for racial justice. She and Lillie Carroll Jackson, who was president of the state NAACP operation until shortly before her death on July 5, 1975, became major historical figures in Maryland.

Under their leadership, the NAACP desegregated several units of the University of Maryland between 1935 and 1950; desegregated public schools in the state, with Baltimore becoming the first southern city to obey the Supreme Court's 1954 decision; won equalization of teachers' salaries in Maryland, a development that spread to other states where such discrimination existed; challenged the judicial enforcement of racially restrictive covenants in property deeds and thus contributed to the Supreme Court's *Shelly* v. *Kramer* decision in 1948 that held such contracts could not be honored by the courts; began major voter registration campaigns and the political empowerment of blacks; desegregated municipal swimming pools, tennis courts, state parks, the Fort Smallwood Municipal Beach, and the Sandy Point State Beach, establishing national patterns; waged a continual struggle for jobs for blacks in the public and private sectors; and supported the sit-in demonstrators and freedom riders by providing legal defense and bail.

Mitchell was involved in some of those activities, especially when the local and state NAACP needed support from Washington. For those contributions, his and Juanita's reward was the knowledge that they were leaving an unparalleled legacy of civil rights laws and policies for their nation. Their services had been totally selfless. In addition to the NAACP's Spingarn Medal, Mitchell's most prized recognition of his service was the Medal of Freedom that Carter awarded him in 1980. Recalling the festivity that followed the program on the White House lawn, Juanita reminisced, "He certainly gave us some wonderful moments. My darling. He couldn't give us money. . . ."

PART ONE

Journey Toward the Promised Land

CHAPTER ONE

Trauma of a Lynching

G eorge Armwood, 22, who was murdered by Eastern Shore whites on Wednesday night was an old offender, according to some of the town's prominent residents.

Some years ago, Armwood is said to have raped a woman of our race, but escaped penalty of the law when white people for whom he was working declared that he was a "good boy" and they would be responsible for him.

He was generally recognized as a feeble-minded person.

After the crime, a civil officer called John M. Dennis, prominent Princess Anne undertaker, and asked him to take care of the mutilated body of Armwood. The request was met with a refusal on the grounds that it was the city's duty to remove the murdered man.

The final way of meeting the issue was to toss the body into a lumber yard owned by Mrs. D. M. Dougherty, white, who registered violent protest against this in the morning.

Silent groups of our people on their way to work or with nothing in particular in view, solemnly gazed at the horribly-mangled corpse which had been stripped of all clothing and was covered with two sacks.

"The skin of George Armwood was scorched and blackened while his face had suffered many blows from sharp and heavy instruments. A cursory glance revealed that one ear was missing and his tongue between his clenched teeth, gave evidence of his great

31

agony before death. There is no adequate description of the mute
evidence of gloating on the part of whites who gathered to watch
the effect upon our people.

Some of the school children who were bold enough to venture
out carried a reporter to the high school and explained on the way
that most of the people were afraid to come out during the night
but a few of them had been seen darting through alleys and dark
streets when the activity of the mob was at its height.[1]

Clarence Mitchell, Jr., was on his first assignment as a cub reporter for
the weekly *Baltimore Afro-American* in October 1933, and had great difficulty containing his revulsion. The schizophrenic nature of Baltimore's
racism had made it possible for him to have spent all his twenty-one years
in the city without being dehumanized by the ever present Jim Crow, so
the trauma he experienced that sunny morning on the Eastern Shore was
especially profound—so much so that it set the course of his life in the
struggle for freedom and equality for his fellow black Americans. He had
recently been graduated from Lincoln University in Pennsylvania during
the throes of the Great Depression. He was very grateful for the fifteen-
dollar-a-week job, which he got through the New Deal's National Recovery Administration "Blue Eagle" campaign to generate employment. The
national economic crisis, however, was far from his mind as he witnessed
the demonic expression of human hatred.

The advent of the lynching had been well advertised throughout Maryland, neighboring Washington, D.C., and northern Virginia. In Princess
Anne members of the fire department sounded the alarm and brought out a
fire truck as a signal for the mob to gather. Everyone, including newspaper
reporters, had ample time to attend the event. No one was surprised by the
news; the Eastern Shore's reputation was such. Less than two years earlier,
on December 4, 1931, Matthew Williams, a black man whose mental
capacities were believed to be less than normal, shot and killed his white
employer in Salisbury because he felt his wages were too low. Williams
then turned the gun on himself, attempting suicide. But he botched the
job. From the hospital in Salisbury, where he lay that night critically
wounded, a mob of about two thousand hauled him from his bed, hanged
him on the courthouse lawn, then dragged his body to the edge of the
town's black business district, where it burned the mangled, lifeless hulk.
The Williams lynching was thought to be the first in Maryland since 1911
and the first on the Eastern Shore in an even longer period; the Armwood
lynching brought the number since 1882 to thirty-three, thirty of whom
were black.

Eastern Shore men were incited to lynch Armwood by their frustration over the handling of another case involving Euell Lee. This black man was arrested seven weeks before Williams and charged with murdering an Eastern Shore farmer, his wife, and two daughters. Not until March 30, 1933, did a court in Towson, just outside Baltimore, convict him, owing to his lawyer's dogged fight to protect his rights by appeals and other legal maneuvers. Then those clamoring for Lee's execution could not get their satisfaction because Lee's lawyer, in the inevitable last, desperate effort, appealed to the U.S. Supreme Court. Impatient over the slow process of justice, a group of whites sought a scapegoat. He was George Armwood.

From the moment word of an attack on seventy-one-year-old Mary Denston, wife of a Somerset County farmer, reached Salisbury, law officers and armed civilians began a thorough search for a black man. The men spread out, covering both Somerset and neighboring Wicomico counties. Denston said she did not know who had attacked her sometime after eleven o'clock that Monday morning as she was returning home after spending the night with her daughter. But, based on the finding of a hat near where the white woman was allegedly attacked, the searchers began looking Monday night for twenty-two-year-old Armwood.

Armed men methodically tramped through the woods and swamplands in neighboring counties. Guards posted at bridges and highway check-points kept watch on all possible escape routes. Later that night, Armwood was found in the home of John Richardson, brother of the man for whom he had worked. Armwood was charged with felonious assault, a relatively minor crime; Richardson was charged as an accessory after the fact because he allegedly took Armwood in his car from the area of the crime to his home below Pocomoke in Somerset County. Richardson claimed he did not know Armwood had committed a crime when he came running to him and begged to be saved from some undisclosed danger.

Armwood's arrest electrified the town. People immediately demanded the death penalty even though the crime for which Armwood was charged would not have drawn more than a short term in jail. Eastern Shore men were not interested in justice. They wanted vengeance against a mythical enemy created by their prejudice.

No place on the Eastern Shore was safe enough for the hapless man. After keeping Armwood in the Salisbury jail for three minutes, the state police spirited him up to Baltimore city, about a three-hour drive, for safekeeping. But if the Eastern Shore was the economic backwater of the state, it was not politically impotent. Expediency was now more important than justice and human life. As the uproar for Armwood's blood grew, shortcuts to justice became the inevitable course. State's Attorney John B. Robins and Judge Robert S. Duer of the First Judicial Circuit of Maryland exercised their authority over that of the governor and attorney general and ordered that Armwood be brought back to Princess Anne.

The convergence of large crowds and the press on the town that Tuesday confirmed the certainty of a lynching. Mitchell, two other reporters, and Paul Henderson, a photographer, all from the *Baltimore Afro-American,* set out at nightfall for the Eastern Shore. Driving the publisher's big Lincoln car, the group couldn't take the much shorter route from Baltimore, which was a ferry linking the Western and Eastern shores at Annapolis, the state capital, because it had stopped running for the night. Instead, they took a northerly route through Havre de Grace above the headwaters of the Chesapeake, swung east to pick up the old Maryland Route 13, and traveled southward through Delaware.

It was an uneventful trip except for the excitement caused by smoke billowing from underneath the car as they set out. The problem, they discovered, was not serious. It had been caused by failure to release the emergency brake. Once that was done, the group settled in for an all-night ride over dark country roads down to the southernmost tip of that isolated segment of the state. All the way they picked up reports on what was happening in Princess Anne. Somebody gave Mitchell a pistol. He had never fired one before. He stuck it in the upholstery and forgot about it.

Journeying through the dark, sparsely settled countryside, Mitchell passed the time by contemplating the circumstances of Armwood's fate on the Eastern Shore. That region, a jagged isolated strip of land between the Chesapeake Bay and the Atlantic, is unique in many ways. First, its strong identity with the Chesapeake Bay, from which it draws its economic and physical character, makes the region famous for its abundant supply of top-grade blue crabs, fat luscious oysters, and meaty, juicy terrapin. The Chesapeake Bay itself, which not only dominates the Eastern Shore but Baltimore as well, allows Maryland to boast of having more water frontage than any other state in the Union. An inland sea, the Great Bay, as it is often called, is composed of an enormous body of water flowing to and from the Atlantic upward for nearly two hundred miles to the head. The jagged nature of the bay gives it its special character and beauty. The name *Chesapeake* is wrapped in the Algonquin Indians' folklore and roughly means "the Great Shellfish Bay."

The whole social and economic structure of the Eastern Shore in the 1930s reflected the region's history as a principal slave-trading center. It was not known precisely when slavery was first introduced in Maryland, but the state in 1664 became the first English colony to legalize it. By the time the federal Constitution was adopted in 1789, there were more than one hundred thousand slaves in the state. Maryland, though, in 1783 prohibited the African slave trade—everywhere except on the Eastern Shore, where slaves were kept more for their economic value than for laboring in the fields. That practice not only drove up the price of slaves within Maryland as a valued commodity by making them scarce, but it also gave the state, together with Virginia and Kentucky, the dubious reputation of a "Negro-raising state" or "stud farm"; slaves were now bred strictly for commerce. Slave breeding ranked with seafood as the principal income producer. Isolated from the industrial and liberalizing currents stimulating the rest of the state, the Eastern Shore thus doggedly clung to the slave trade long after it was evident that slavery would have to end. The political consequences were enormous.

Only in southern Maryland, on the Western Shore, was the white population outnumbered by slaves and free blacks up through and beyond the Civil War. Tobacco was a major industry there. For every four blacks laboring in the fields, there was only one white. In contrast, only one fifth of the Eastern Shore residents once lived in slavery. A slightly larger proportion of blacks before the Civil War was free.

Given the opprobrium attached to its principal business, it was little wonder that the Eastern Shore became known for its "slave counties."* Although blacks represented a small portion of the population, whites of this largely rural area regarded them as a major economic threat even while their number was steadily declining. This trend began around 1880, when the saturation point of black labor was reached, and continued for thirty years as the surplus of black births over deaths was drained off by migrations from the area, primarily to Baltimore. Although white migration was also continuing at a steady pace, the black migration, not surprisingly, was greater.

Mitchell was well aware of the Eastern Shore's economic desperation in the 1930s. He returned home to Baltimore from college to find that although soup lines and other evidence of hardship were everywhere, whites in the more culturally advanced Baltimore did not vent their emotions as savagely as on the Eastern Shore. There, whites considered themselves one hundred percent patriots. Most of those white families were of Scottish and English heritage, their ancestors having settled in the region as early as 1650. Historic landmarks from Revolutionary and pre-Revolutionary periods were ubiquitous, proudly confirming their Americanism. The first Presbyterian church built in America was located in Princess Anne. Portraits of George Washington hung in public buildings; the George Washington Hotel in Princess Anne, with its card room where slaves were lost

---

*Somerset County, whose main town was Princess Anne, was one of the six principal slave-trading centers. It far outranked its competitors in the number of traders doing business there. The other principal trading centers were Centerville (Queen Anne County), Cambridge (Dorchester County), Snow Hill (Worcester County), Easton (Talbot County), and Salisbury (Wicomico County). By 1930, blacks represented 3.4 percent of Somerset's and 2 percent of Wicomico's population. Only seven towns on the Eastern Shore had a population of more than 2,500 in 1930. The largest was Salisbury with 10,997.

and won "before the war," was graphic evidence of the townsfolk's pride in their national hero, who, though a slaveholder, was considered a gentleman and good Christian.

On the economic front, the Eastern Shore's Americanism boiled down to an almost primitive struggle for survival that often resulted in whites' taking out their frustrations on or expressing their fears most violently against blacks. The Eastern Shore certainly did not have a monopoly on such conditions or emotions. They were commonplace throughout the southern, border, and some midwestern states, especially in rural areas, where the benefits of President Roosevelt's New Deal programs and philosophy had little immediate effect. Even so, most Eastern Shoremen never lost faith in Roosevelt's desire to help them. Their faith was based more on the promise of improved wages and a better life than on actual results. That was the general attitude. But when it came to the National Recovery Administration, Eastern Shoremen had every reason to be doubtful about quick progress. In Crisfield, for example, which was a major seafood center about twenty-five miles from Princess Anne, there was a strong feeling among jobless oystermen that the NRA, rather than providing jobs and higher wages, had further knocked the bottom from under the local economy.

The problem was that the NRA sought to increase the purchasing power of workers by establishing minimum wage standards for industry based on a forty-hour week. The NRA, among other things, sought to promote collective bargaining and advocated ideal labor standards based on conditions existing in the more progressive industrial states. Thus, where industry existed, the NRA offered strong possibilities for social reform. Since oystering and other forms of the seafood industry, as well as farming, were not covered by NRA codes, the dilemma for Crisfield and the Eastern Shore as a whole was obvious. Not only did the shirt factory in Crisfield, where girls had been making as much as eighteen dollars a week, shut down, but workers in an oyster-packing house saw their earnings drop to ten dollars a week for a sixteen-hour workday.

If whites were frustrated by the lack of social and economic progress under Roosevelt's recovery program, Eastern Shore blacks were downright bitter. For, not only was their deprivation during the Depression totally unrelieved, but they also became the scapegoats in an economic situation tailor-made for exacerbating class and racial tensions.

The Eastern Shore was the South in microcosm. The fierce conflicts between poor whites and oppressed blacks who were forced to compete for the economic crumbs of the region reflected similar struggles occurring on a wider scale throughout the South and increasingly in the North and Midwest. As an Eastern Shore editor said, "A lynching is bread and meat to me." Lynchings provided gruesome relief for those trapped in the system while sparing prison guards from violent explosions of frustration. Those benefiting most were the Cotton Kingdom barons of the antebellum South and the nineteenth-century czars of the industrial North. They were replaced by corporate empire builders whose unfettered rampages brought down the economic system on their heads in the Great Depression. The problems of poverty for poor whites and blacks were now aggravated by competition for New Deal jobs and benefits. This problem, of course, was not unique to the Eastern Shore. It existed wherever there was a sizable number of blacks. Blacks, as always, were kept in line at the bottom of society by white laborers who feared the economic threat they represented.

The inextricable relationship between economic interests of blacks and their social and constitutional rights was evident to those who understood the history of slavery and the struggle for civil rights. The primary factor underlying racial oppression and discrimination, like that underlying colonialism, is economic. Booker T. Washington's program for uplifting the blacks contained strong economic planks to support what he saw as primarily a working-class struggle to overcome the effects of slavery. The NAACP from its founding in 1909 began expanding on this vision by fashioning a civil rights philosophy along the lines of the eighteenth-century liberalism that inspired the abolition movement. This philosophy held that the "individual's economic freedom consisted in his right to state protection in the acquisition of property and in the employment of it for his private ends and profits." The NAACP saw as a first priority for making this capitalistic dream a reality the need to create the proper conditions under which blacks might rise from the depths of poverty. Still totally shut out by the private-capital system and state governments in the 1930s, blacks now saw a ray of hope in the federal government.

A major step in the direction of economic advancement was taken when the NAACP investigated working and living conditions for blacks on the Mississippi Flood Control project in the Delta. Two of its investigators, Roy Wilkins, the NAACP's newly hired assistant executive secretary, and George Schuyler, a well-known black writer, confirmed the prevalence of cruel economic exploitation. "It is no exaggeration to state that the conditions under which Negroes work in the federally financed Mississippi levee construction camps approximate virtual slavery," Wilkins reported in *The Crisis,* the NAACP's journal. With the Roosevelt administration launching one program after another to rescue the national economy, blacks became increasingly vocal in protesting discrimination in federal programs.

As an avid reader of *The Crisis,* Mitchell found intriguing the heated debates over suggestions for a subminimum wage for blacks ostensibly to ease the accelerated displacement of black workers caused by the NRA's minimum wage standards. Long before inauguration of the New Deal, the South had been displacing blacks with whites in higher-paying or upgraded jobs. To avoid paying the NRA's newly mandated minimum wages, southern employers began suggesting a subcategory to save the jobs of blacks. But radical black intellectuals, notably John P. Davis, executive secretary of the Washington-based Joint Committee on National Recovery, and Robert C. Weaver, a young, Harvard-trained economist, were vehemently opposed. Weaver, for example, argued that the suggested wage differentials "would brand black workers as a less efficient and submarginal group." It would increase animosity and friction between black and white workers and destroy many of the advances blacks had made in the industrial North. Furthermore, it would prevent labor unity and thus damage the developing collective bargaining movement. Rather than relegate blacks to a low-wage caste and give this form of blatant racial discrimination federal government sanction, Weaver suggested, all workers should be paid at standard rates according to their qualifications.

The Eastern Shore in 1933 was light-years away from the concepts of social progress based on economic growth that were embodied in the NRA philosophy. The region was its own private world. What Mitchell saw there made him realize how American racism functioned. The cancer, though confined to certain areas, still had a malignant and destructive effect on the rest of society. Silence about the disease was tantamount to full acceptance by major institutions. Maryland bore responsibility for the Eastern Shore's transgressions as much as the nation was accountable for the South's treatment of African Americans.

The Eastern Shore, like the South, was completely locked out of the industrial North's economic system even as Baltimore was reaping considerable benefits through its bustling harbor. Consequently, blacks were paying the double penalty of being workers and being black. Between 80 and 90 percent of the basic labor supply in Somerset County was black. As superfluous labor, their earnings were down to as low as 25 to 50 cents a day. "Negro wage differentials" had been a historical fact of their lives as well as for blacks throughout the South. They did not need, as Weaver and Davis were correctly arguing, the NRA to enshrine that reality in governmental code. As if blacks were not suffering enough from social and economic disadvantages, whites also resented the relief they received. But all that blacks could do was grin and bear the resulting terror and economic discrimination. Every day some 200 to 300 blacks gathered at the Crisfield docks waiting for the arrival of oyster boats. A few lucky ones would get jobs hauling or shucking, while whites got the better-paying dredging jobs.[2]

*   *   *

Armwood was already dead when the *Afro-American* group arrived at midmorning in Princess Anne. Revealing his fearlessness as well as his innocence, Mitchell immediately moved out on his own to pursue his first assignment as the group split into two teams. "The curious thing about that period was I had a romantic notion that newspaper reporters were somehow immune to attacks," he remembered. "I had my press card in my hat and other reporters were milling around. But at the time that was the worst thing I could have done because the crowd was very much annoyed with the whole press." The lynchers, though, for the time being wanted the mutilated corpse to serve as a lesson to other blacks in the town so they left the reporters alone to cover the crime and spread the word about their demonic behavior.

"As Paul Henderson was taking pictures of the body, a white man came over looking at it. Paul very carefully tried to get him in the picture. I think he did get him. Anyway, he said afterwards, 'I bet he was one of those who helped to do it.' The crowd, of course, was all around on the street corners—a pretty tense situation. By that time the bloodlust had satiated to some extent, because nobody bothered me and we went about interviewing them, asking what they knew about it, all of them insisting that the people who had participated had come over from Virginia. But the potential for trouble was greater than we realized."

Mitchell discovered that Princess Anne was not much of a town. Main Street, with its few stores, gasoline stations, and eating places, was the principal thoroughfare. Because there had not been a lynching in the town for thirty-eight years, this one was an especially big event. People gathered on the street that night, calmly and jovially discussing the event in little groups. "Well," said one man as he drew on a stogie in front of the Washington Hotel, "it would have cost the state $1,000 to hang the man. It cost us 75 cents." Lynching souvenirs, such as a bit of rope and spent tear gas canisters, were prized and proudly displayed. Mitchell did not have to editorialize to portray the stark bestiality of Armwood's fate—"When you see a fellow human with a rope around his neck and skin coming off his body, you don't need to add any touches of horror." The *Baltimore Afro-American* and the state's two leading newspapers, the *Baltimore Sun* and *Baltimore Evening Sun,* covered the event in great detail.

Princess Anne was eerily calm in the wake of the lynching. The heightened frenzy of the mob in the moments preceding and during the event that had replaced the earlier atmosphere of haunting expectation, one that at times had seemed nervously festive, had dissipated after the climax of the elaborate torture-murder.

Another report by Mitchell noted:

> No extra precautions were taken to prevent the curious persons
> from looking at the body, and from sunrise until the time of its
> impromptu burial the corpse of George Armwood was the object of
> the entire town's attention.
>
> The main street of the town was crowded all day following the
> lynching, and many versions of it were openly discussed by spec-
> tators. Some described how the leaders of the mob helped to drag
> the body through the streets. Others forcefully insisted that Arm-
> wood had gotten what he deserved.

The *Afro-American* reporters dutifully informed the victim's mother,
Etta Armwood, and the rest of the family, who lived in a dilapidated two-
story home in Jamestown, about fifteen miles below Princess Anne, of the
lynching. Mrs. Armwood, who hardly ever visited Princess Anne, had
made a special pilgrimage during the previous afternoon and had been assured that her son would be safe.

Mitchell thought it queer that Sheriff Luther C. Daugherty of Somerset
County, a symbol of law and white authority, "admitted that he was standing in front of the jail when the mob came for Armwood." Daugherty said
he saw the mob batter down the jail door, yet he could not recognize any of
the men holding the pole. "He also insisted that other members of the mob
filed by him as they were going for Armwood and although he counted
nearly 75 persons he did not recognize any of these."

That was another aspect of what he came to understand as southern-
style justice that shocked Mitchell. The Armwood lynching and his subsequent coverage of one of the epic trials of the century, involving nine black
boys in Scottsboro, Alabama, who were charged with raping two white
prostitutes, awakened his interest in the fight for antilynching legislation
in Congress and the need for extensive social and judicial reforms in the
country. A black man's life was very cheap, he discovered, cheaper than
when he was a slave because then he was chattel, property with a set value,
and was considered a part of the plantation owner's wealth. Mitchell began
to discern the political implications of society's prejudiced attitude toward
citizens of African heritage; to learn about the official dereliction of duty by
the government and about how county and state officials fostered racial
strife and violence to further their political careers. It was easy for Mitchell
to read extensively about the Armwood and other lynchings because the
National Association for the Advancement of Colored People's campaign
had made the problem one of national concern.

The NAACP's antilynching campaign had been launched in the wake of the bloody 1908 race riots in Springfield, Illinois, Abraham Lincoln's hometown. Before forty-two hundred militiamen could quell the violence, 2 blacks were lynched, 6 killed, over 50 wounded, and more than 2,000 were forced to flee the city while hundreds more had to take refuge in militia camps. That perverse demonstration of historical debt to the Great Emancipator for saving the Union led a group of white liberals and black freedom advocates to preserve his memory in a humanistic manner. They founded the NAACP on Lincoln's birthday on February 12, 1909, launching a new chapter in the struggle against racial oppression.

The conversion of Thomas Dixon's novel *The Clansman,* romanticizing the Klan, into the notorious film *Birth of a Nation* in 1915 was one of the best symbols of the NAACP's epic challenge to end the dehumanizing manifestations of white southern hatred. The film helped spread the passion of hatred of blacks. Lynchings subsequently increased. The increased competition for employment caused by blacks fleeing southern farms for the urban centers during and especially after World War I added another volatile ingredient to this tinderbox racial atmosphere that was frequently exploding with tragic consequences for blacks. James Weldon Johnson, the NAACP's executive secretary, raised this struggle to a new level by seeking antilynching legislation in Congress, thus also laying the foundations for a broader program for pursuing civil rights laws later on. Succeeding Johnson as executive secretary in 1931, Walter White expanded on that drive. Despite White's success in reducing lynchings, as Armwood's murder showed, a black citizen's life still had little value in the 1930s.[3]

Upon returning to Baltimore, Mitchell received another rude lesson on racial injustice, this time involving Maryland's political and judicial systems. There, he saw crass, self-centered politics playing to a national audience. The racial undercurrents that had been so violently thrust to the surface by the specter of a black man abusing white American womanhood were much less troubling to him than the glaring weaknesses he now realized characterized those systems. Mitchell could live with the race-sex bugaboo, despite the threat that it posed to every black male. He had done so until now without any real awareness that it existed. The wanton abuse of human life in so bestial a fashion as he had witnessed on the Eastern Shore was sickening. But was it possible that officials sworn to uphold the law and to be arbiters of justice and fair play could also be so disrespectful of the hallowed principles upon which the American system of government was established?

Governor Albert C. Ritchie, a presidential hopeful a year earlier in the 1932 election, was being sharply criticized for his inept handling of the events immediately leading up to the lynching. He was blamed for not

calling out the National Guard to protect Armwood from the lynch mob
when he had known full well the volatile character of the Eastern Shore and
the prevailing racial attitude there. Rather than facing the political heat, he
stayed in the background so that Judge Duer and other county authorities
would be held responsible for the crime. Stormy reaction around the state
and nation grew when it was disclosed that the crime could easily have
been prevented. Buck passing and recriminations became the order of the
day as each layer of bureaucracy blamed the other for Armwood's murder.

The structure of Maryland's judicial system gave extensive powers to
circuit judges like Duer and made them subject to the sentiments of local
voters, to whom they owed their jobs. The state's attorney, who was also
the chief prosecutor in state court, was another important official in the
administration of justice in each county. Duer was also elected and was
even more susceptible to public pressure because he and State's Attorney
Robins were up for reelection that year. At the other end of the spectrum
was the attorney general of the state, whose political base was not as
provincial but who also depended on public sentiment. That was the dilemma William Preston Lane, Jr., Maryland's attorney general, faced as he
assumed responsibility for building a case against the accused lynch mob
leaders.

The climate on the Eastern Shore was much different when Mitchell
returned there in November to cover the trial of four men who had been
arrested for participating in the Armwood lynching. Shore men had gone
on a rampage in neighboring Salisbury against two hundred National
Guardsmen to protest the arrests. In contrast to his previous visit, newsmen and photographers were now being ferociously attacked as a result of
the bad publicity the region had gotten. Just before he returned, an angry
crowd chased several white reporters into a hotel and set it afire. Fortunately, no one was injured.

If Mitchell had held any doubts about the extent of lawlessness on the
Eastern Shore, the current climate disabused him. In the first place, it took
extreme pressure from Governor Ritchie and Attorney General Lane to get
nine of the lynchers identified. Furthermore, instead of State's Attorney
Robins or the local sheriff arresting the four who could be found, as Lane
had ordered, the attorney general himself had to do so with the help of
Ritchie, who ordered the National Guard into action. Even so, a mob
seeking release of the four men made the National Guard beat a hasty
retreat, and local officials again outmaneuvered the top state officials to
make sure the accused received most favored treatment. To prevent the
mob of three thousand from freeing the men, the state hastily transferred
them to the Baltimore jail. But the political heat was so intense that they
were just as speedily returned the following day to Princess Anne—in tri-

umph, riding on the running board of the car that brought them back to the welcome of several thousand residents.

Outside the Princess Anne courthouse where the hearing was being held following the men's arrest, Mitchell saw a group of blacks talking. One of them said, "If I could just get one person to go in there with me, I'd go in." Without hesitating, Mitchell said, "I'm going in." Then, according to Mitchell, "one of them, a man named Monk went in with me. When we went in, he had the misfortune of stepping on a white man's foot. This man turned to him and said, 'Nigger, I'll kill you. You stepped on my foot.'

"These whites for the most part were roughly dressed. I guess they were fishermen or something. But there was one white man in there who had on a white shirt and tie. He looked like he might have been a businessman of some importance in the community. He recognized Monk and said, 'Monk, I have a package over at the station. Would you go over and pick it up?' Monk said, 'Yes, sir.' That immediately left me by myself. It was kind of an uncomfortable situation. A jammed courtroom. You couldn't tell really what was happening. Whatever they were trying to do to these people who were arrested didn't amount to much, because they all walked out. And that was that.

"Another thing that was interesting to me was the attitude of the community. I stayed overnight in order to be there at the time the hearing started. I stayed at the home of Dr. Thomas H. Kiah, who was principal of Princess Anne Academy. I did not know my way around very well, so he agreed to take me to the downtown section where the hearing was being held.

"As we were walking down the street, the sheriff came up. He recognized Dr. Kiah. The principal said, 'You know, our town is getting a very bad reputation because of these things that are happening. Many of the fellows tell me that if you want to get a job up the road somewhere and those who are hiring find out you are from Princess Anne, they won't take them on.'

"The sheriff said, 'You know, we've got a nice town here. If it just wasn't for these damn newspaper reporters. They are the people who are creating the problem.' He didn't know I was a newspaper reporter, and I didn't think it was proper to enlighten him at all."

The three county judges presiding over their hearing quickly released the four men, holding that they had been arrested without warrants. Mitchell realized that it remained a mere formality to have whatever indictments were brought against the four dismissed and the case closed. A grand jury was impaneled in Princess Anne in late January 1934, to hear evidence against the lynchers. This denouement was not without further wrangling between the county officials and Lane. The attorney general refused to participate. Why bother? He knew exactly what the results of the charade would be. Besides, on his last visit to the Shore, when the four prisoners were taken into custody, he himself had almost been lynched. As Lane was driving away from the armory where the National Guard held the men, a large rock crashed through the roof of his car, just missing him. As he now told State's Attorney Robins, "There [is] nothing that I can accomplish by being present at the hearing." That left the proceedings solely in the hands of county officials. The case was then effectively brought to an end after the indictments were dismissed owing to insufficient evidence against the men.

But if the county had closed the Armwood case so undramatically, repercussions at the state and national levels could not be dismissed as easily. It was well known that the Eastern Shore had its backers. Dr. John J. Bunting, one of the outstanding members of the Wilmington Conference of the Methodist Episcopal Church, for example, decried the strong criticisms of the Eastern Shore. He deplored "the riot and the crime that inflames it," and took strong "issue with those metropolitan papers and persons that refer to the four counties of the First Judicial District as being sparsely settled and backward." Such opinions notwithstanding, outrage against the lynching was overwhelming. Eastern Shore men, in gala spirit, hailed dismissal of the charges as a "victory over Ritchie." Mitchell thought he deserved the opprobrium because he had waited until it was too late before moving to protect Armwood.[4]

Mitchell, in part, shared the view of a commentator in *The Commonweal* magazine that "Governor Ritchie is caught in the shell fire from both sides: he is damned if he does anything and he is equally damned if he does nothing. [Armwood's murder] may result in the political lynching of a governor down in Annapolis, but, in the meantime grease from the political pig may serve to ease through a few adequate legal measures for the future." The writer concluded, "Maryland is on trial and the country is watching."

Ritchie, though, when he was compared with Governor James Rolph of California, came out smelling like a rose. Rolph brought down a hornet's nest on his head by going against the national current when he defended the lynchers of two white men being held in the San Jose jail as "patriots." The storm that erupted across the nation was unprecedented and ironic. Contrary to the support Rolph had hoped to arouse, he only helped to strengthen the drive for antilynching legislation. So did the Armwood lynching. Ritchie, by publicly placing himself in the corner of the crime's opponents, won widespread praise. It was Attorney General Lane, however, who played his political cards best as a strong foe of lynching. Maryland eventually would reward him by electing him governor.

Mitchell next got an opportunity to describe the Armwood lynching the following February in Washington when he testified in support of an antilynching bill, sponsored by Senators Edward P. Costigan of Colorado and Robert F. Wagner of New York, that was before a subcommittee of the House Judiciary Subcommittee. Costigan and Wagner had picked up where the struggle by Congressman L. C. Dyer of Missouri had petered out a decade earlier. Mitchell explained:

> The mob action on the Eastern Shore of Maryland gave evidence of a breakdown in law and order for many reasons.
> One of the state policemen actually said, "We were not going to kill anybody for the carelessness of officials who permitted Armwood to be brought back here." State Police Lt. K. Ridgely declared also that he made no attempts to use his pistol and would not permit any of his men to do so.[5]

Mitchell's appearance before the House Judiciary Subcommittee, which was headed by Frederick Van Nuys of Indiana, had been arranged by Walter White, whose respect the young man had won during the NAACP leader's numerous visits to Baltimore. Mitchell's sweetheart, Juanita E. Jackson, added her voice to the crescendo of outrage by testifying before the Van Nuys subcommittee in support of the Costigan-Wagner bill. Juanita was then president of the Baltimore City-Wide Young People's Forum; Mitchell was vice president of the civic group. Others who testified included Arthur B. Spingarn, chairman of the NAACP's national legal committee; Charles Hamilton Houston, then vice dean of Howard University Law School before becoming NAACP special counsel; Herbert K. Stockton, another member of the NAACP's legal committee; and Walter White. They expressed opinions on social and legal questions as well as on the constitutionality of antilynching legislation.

In 1922, working closely with the NAACP, Congressman Dyer had won passage of his bill by a two-to-one margin after trying for four consecutive years. But final passage was blocked in the Senate by a filibuster led by southerners waving the red flag of federal intervention. Like the Dyer bill, the Costigan-Wagner bill passed the House by a wide margin, but was defeated by a Senate filibuster led by Huey P. "Kingfish" Long, Sr., of Louisiana. Mitchell was not surprised, since he had received a preview of Senate obstruction when he testified on the bill:

> The most vivid recollection I have of the experience is that while I was waiting to testify, Senator Huey Long, Sr. came to me, and in my dual role as newspaper reporter and witness, it occurred

to me that it would be a good story if I could get his opinion of the anti-lynching legislation. He stood in the doorway of the Senate Caucus Room and, in a loud voice, said, "I do not think much of this bill, but I think some of those senators in there conducting the hearing should be lynched." And he said that at least three times to make sure they would hear.

I think the attitude of the opposition was that whether or not this lynching was the work of people acting outside the law, you couldn't invade the rights of states in order to do anything about it. And, of course, there were others who had stories just as gruesome, so by that time, I think, the country had become a little hardened to what took place in lynchings. People were revolted by it and wanted to do something about it, but the full horror did not come through, because it was not portrayed as atrocities would later be on the television screen. We had some horrible pictures of lynchings and yet they could reach only a limited audience, because you had to see them in the papers (and many wouldn't even print them) or at a meeting, where the whole terrible part wouldn't really come through. Still, a considerable part of the public was determined to control such things by having a law by which lynchers could be brought to justice.

Unfortunately, there was an equally strong group that felt that lynching was a means of keeping blacks in their place—that if they did not have such a weapon, blacks particularly in areas where they were numerically strong, would take over—and therefore they were attacking the bill.[6]

Studying Arthur Raper's work, *The Tragedy of Lynching,* Mitchell also learned that "of the Negroes lynched outside the South ninety-three, or more than two-thirds, were in the six states—Maryland, West Virginia, Ohio, Indiana, Illinois, and Kansas—which lie immediately North of the Southern states." He saw how "blacks and whites united in making appeals to Congress for a federal anti-lynching law"—an experience that helped ease the pain of the Armwood lynching. He also learned how national protest movements were organized.

Mitchell himself was a featured speaker at an antilynching rally at Baltimore's Lehman Hall following the Armwood murder. Other principal speakers were Roger Baldwin, founder and head of the American Civil Liberties Union; Roy Wilkins, assistant secretary of the NAACP; and Professor Selby V. McCasland of Goucher College.[7] Many of the protesting voices quickly went silent as the shame of the moment faded. But years later, Mitchell recalled how other prominent Marylanders joined the struggle against all forms of civil rights violations:

In the list of the early years one finds such names as W. Ashbie Hawkins, a black lawyer, and complementing him is the name of Charles J. Bonaparte, one of Maryland's most distinguished white members of the bar. The stern determination of Rev. Harvey Johnson, a black Baptist minister, who worked for freedom of his people, is matched by Rabbi William Rosenau of Baltimore who, in 1911, preached a sermon attacking the "reprehensible attitude of the white man, which would go the lengths, not merely of depriving the Negro of his constitutional franchise, but also of limiting his educational advantages."

As these names faded from the news because of age or death, new personalities emerged to carry on the struggle. The Rev. A. J. Payne, Sidney Hollander and Father John Lafarge were heard with increasing frequency as they spoke out or acted against unjust treatment of Maryland's blacks.

The Rev. Mr. Payne, pastor of Enon Baptist Church, could well take the prize for having more than half a century of identifying with the leadership in constructive civil rights and civic affairs. Not only did he enjoy the reputation of being one of Baltimore's most eloquent preachers, but he is usually admired for his cooperation in providing the use of his church auditorium and his personal participation whenever important problems required his attention.

Some like Edward S. Lewis made attacks on segregation in public parks. Some, like Dr. J.E.T. Camper, were determined to work for jobs and voting rights. Others, like the remarkable versatile lawyer, Juanita Jackson Mitchell, appear in a wide variety of roles—sometimes as counsel, sometimes as witness, sometimes as fund raisers and leaders of mass actions and sometimes as top executives of civil rights organizations.

Perhaps the best example of a united team that worked together in harmony for the good of the state was the combination of Dr. Lillie M. [Carroll] Jackson [Juanita's mother], NAACP leader, and Dr. Carl J. Murphy, crusading editor of The Afro-American newspaper."[8]

The most far-reaching accomplishment of the antilynching crusaders at that time was making lynching a national political issue. Lynchings between 1930 and 1934 were occurring at the rate of one a month, thanks in large measure to the bitter competition for jobs during the Depression when blacks were mercilessly driven from their traditional areas of employment. But even while denouncing the crime, President Roosevelt thought it best not to jeopardize his legislative program by supporting the struggle for an antilynching law. Thus did Mitchell again see how little value was placed on a black man's life.[9]

CHAPTER TWO

Covering the Scottsboro Trials

Mitchell got another perspective on weaknesses in the American judicial system when, upon his return to Baltimore after his first trip to the Eastern Shore, his editors sent him in November 1933 to Decatur, Alabama, to cover the third series of the trials of the nine Scottsboro Boys. The Scottsboro saga epitomized the depth of racism in American society and foreshadowed the tortuous nature of the struggle that lay ahead for Mitchell—a struggle that would be not so much for equality as against racial oppression; for only through the absence of discrimination could African Americans be assured full citizenship. The Scottsboro experience was particularly wrenching because it demonstrated so graphically one of the lifelong obstacles that blacks were forced to encounter.[1]

"Slavery in America," observed W. E. Burghardt Du Bois, the twentieth-century sage of the black struggle for freedom, "is a strange and contradictory story." It could not be regarded as mainly a theoretical problem of morals or a scientific problem of race. "From either of these points of view, the rise of slavery in America is simply inexplicable." As a practical matter, the basic motivating force was economic, "a question of income and labor, rather than a problem of right and wrong, or of the physical differences in men." So was its offspring lynching, which the rulers of southern society encouraged to pit poor whites against blacks to keep both exploited groups in subjugation.[2]

Mitchell's journey deep into the southland enabled him to realize that lynching took more than one form—that there was *legal* lynching, as the nine Scottsboro Boys were experiencing, as well as literal lynching like

Armwood's. Both forms inflicted torture, one mental, the other physical, on victims who were most often black. Legal lynching, though, left open the way for appeals and the possibility that victims would ultimately go free. Legal lynching in the 1930s was a popular substitute for literal lynching, as national pressure against this torture-murder increased.[3]

At the Scottsboro trials Mitchell got a glimpse of the bared roots of racial injustice, which were entrenched in the South but were protected by the rest of the nation. He recalled that "while I have always been poor and came up in real poverty, I wasn't quite prepared for what the poverty level was down there in Alabama." Furthermore, "I wasn't quite prepared for the rigidity of segregation as it struck you in that situation." His extensive study of the trials revealed to him many troubling similarities as well as interesting contrasts between the Eastern Shore and the rural South. The Scottsboro saga also helped him to better understand the extent to which the Depression had exacerbated the historical economic conflicts between blacks and whites.[4]

The drama began unfolding in Alabama on March 25, 1931, when nine black boys were arrested after they had gotten into a fight with a group of white boys. Because they had received the worse of the encounter, the white boys, upon discovering two white girls on a Memphis-bound freight train traveling between Stevenson and Paint Rock, vindictively accused the blacks of raping them. The severity of the sentences meted out within two weeks of the arrests guaranteed widespread attention and alarm. Only the youngest was spared the death penalty. As a *Birmingham Age-Herald* correspondent wrote, the sentencing of eight persons to death on the same day for the same crime was "without parallel in the history of the nation, and certainly in Alabama."[5] The involvement in the case and exploitation of it by the Communists also ensured that Scottsboro would become an international symbol of racism.

Mitchell thought that an interesting sidelight of the trials in Alabama was that, following the arrests, the Scottsboro sheriff warned that he would shoot to kill if the growing mob outside the Jackson County jail made a move against his prisoners. That was in sharp contrast to Princess Anne sheriff's connivance with the mob that had lynched Armwood. Mitchell discerned dramatic parallels in mob emotions and found that determined public officials could, if they wanted to, preserve law and order and protect the lives of those in their custody. While Governor Ritchie had deferred to local officials, Governor Benjamin Meeks Miller of Alabama, who had been elected on a strong anti-Klan platform, assumed full control of events. His no-nonsense stand had been transmitted down to the sheriff's level and played a large part in saving the lives of the Scottsboro Boys the night of their arrest and during the many subsequent months while they were tried repeatedly. But if physical violence had been avoided, events that unfolded in the courtroom were a travesty of justice.[6]

His experiences on Maryland's Eastern Shore and of the Scottsboro trials awakened Mitchell to the extent of racial brutality and pushed him to reconcile his idealistic notion of the world with the base realities of American society. He believed in people of all colors and social classes. He wanted to embrace roughnecks who composed lynch mobs as fellow human beings as much as he did those who respected him as a person; instead, he was repulsed by the undercurrents of the irrational emotions that characterized racial conflicts and mob violence. Consequently, as had the brutalities of the Eastern Shore, the Scottsboro case aroused in him a passionate interest in sociology and politics. He realized that he had to learn more— much more—about human social structures and behavior and about the forces that not only impelled them but also made them work. His first concerns had to be self-preservation and survival. But to save his own neck, Mitchell was beginning to realize, he first had to save America's soul.

Mitchell, an outsider with no previous experience of life in the Deep South, could not have become fully aware during such a short visit of the groundswell of protest against lynching that was developing in Alabama. But he did sense a strong agitation in the air. Protests against lynching were growing, not only in Alabama but also across the nation, with the help of the Scottsboro debacle. A mass rally was held in May that year in Washington to seek President Roosevelt's involvement in the case. About one thousand, mostly black, New Yorkers on their way to the nation's capital stopped in Baltimore in trucks and buses. They spent a night at the Tom Mooney Hall and in friendly homes. Mitchell did not go with them to Washington, but he joined a crowd of five thousand people who attended a meeting in Baltimore where Ruby Bates, one of the former Scottsboro accusers who had changed her story, declared that the accused were innocent victims of a frame-up.[7]

When Mitchell arrived in Decatur, the third series of trials under Judge William Washington Callahan was just beginning. Decatur, a once-busy railroad junction that served as the seat of Morgan County, was almost fifty miles west of Scottsboro and also fifty miles to the south of Pulaski, Tennessee, birthplace of the original Ku Klux Klan of the Reconstruction period. There was not much difference between Scottsboro, site of the first trials, and Decatur. Defense lawyers had requested a change of venue owing to the volatile climate in Scottsboro. They felt that nearby Decatur was just as objectionable, but Callahan ruled that in the interest of economy, it was the best alternative. This nebulous concern for economy over justice was another reminder for Mitchell of the small worth of a black man's life.[8]

Mitchell was a bold reporter and, above all, curious. He missed few

details. He alighted from the train and asked the black man he saw working on the platform to direct him to a place where he could stay. Decatur's
sole hotel was jam-packed, so much so that a long-closed wing had to be
opened to accommodate the many guests who had come to witness the
trials. Mitchell, though, could not stay at the hotel because of his race.

Without asking any questions, the man took Mitchell to a private
home. "It was a comfortable place. It was not anything luxurious, but I
was used to that kind of condition, because I had grown up in it. I had a
clean bed. At that time, although it was fall, it was quite warm. I remember it was sort of a new experience in some ways because in our family
we did not eat certain things for breakfast, like chicken, for example. The
man's wife, however, prepared a sumptuous breakfast that included chicken
and other kinds of things, much more food than I was accustomed to.
Apparently, whatever I paid—it certainly was not too much—was a lot of
money for this family. I must say that I admired them because I don't
believe they would have been too popular with the whites, having a black
newspaper reporter staying with them."

Another thing struck Mitchell. He was a total stranger, yet he was
taken into a private home at a mere request. That sort of hospitality "implied a great deal of trust, because you could be taking almost anybody into
your home." Mitchell was also aware that "I could have been going into
almost any kind of situation where I might have been in difficulty."

The unhappy results of the two previous trials had made more astute
elements of the community wary on the eve of the third trials. The state
had selected Callahan for the current series in the county court because of
his conservative, no-nonsense reputation. Nevertheless, the *Birmingham Post*
found it necessary to warn him that "critics of our courts will now charge,
inevitably, that the State Supreme Court permitted Attorney General
Knight to shop around until he found a judge who combined some of the
qualities of a prosecutor with those of a jurist." So the situation "makes it
doubly obligatory upon [the judge] to proceed with strict judicial impar-
tiality . . . equally as well as did the preceding judge."[9]

Mitchell found the mood of the people around the courthouse ugly. "I
thought it resembled to a great extent the atmosphere in Princess Anne.
Accordingly, I went up to the judge and said, 'Things look rather tense
around here. I wonder whether you would think of calling out the National
Guard.' Callahan had just stepped down from the bench while the court
was in session. He blew a sharp breath of air and said, 'Oh, we're not
going to have any trouble around here unless people like you start it,' and
he went back on the bench." Someone, probably Ted Poston, a black reporter from the New York *Amsterdam News,* warned Mitchell that he had

"better stop asking the judge questions, because first thing you know they will put you in jail for contempt or something like that."

Afterward, someone told him that the judge had actually toyed with the idea of finding him in contempt, but he let the matter rest. "I guess he was conscious of the possibility of making something out of nothing. But, in any event, one of the interesting things about my life is that in every kind of extreme situation I run into somebody decent."

This salutary experience developed when he met a law enforcement officer as he was leaving the courtroom. "He had two very big pistols, one on each side, and a cartridge belt. He stopped me and said, 'Are you a newspaper reporter?' I said, 'Yes.' He was white. He said, 'Well, the only reason I asked you—I don't mean any harm—but I have never seen a Negro newspaper reporter, nor have I ever seen a press card that came from a paper.' He said, 'I just was curious and wanted to see. I didn't mean any harm.'

"I can't tell you how much that did by way of reassuring me as to the role of these people who were there to preserve the peace. I thought they were just totally hostile, ready to shoot you down, you know, at the slightest provocation. But here was a man who seemed really civilized, and it was very reassuring."

Mitchell discovered that Callahan was hell-bent on upholding Alabama's honor by disposing of the case as expeditiously as possible. That meant guarding against any unfavorable publicity or eventuality. In contrast with the second trials in the spring, Callahan established an atmosphere of tense confidence around the courthouse by replacing the National Guard contingent that had been used to maintain order with nineteen armed deputies recruited from around Birmingham. No African Americans besides the three out-of-town reporters could be found anywhere near the building. Cameras and typewriters were forbidden inside and outside the courtroom. When two photographers took a picture of the courthouse, Callahan had the sheriff confiscate the cameras and bring the men before the bench. Mitchell saw him advise them sternly that "there ain't going to be no more picture snappin' around here."

Mitchell realized that the lapse of time between the first two series of trials and the third did have a "kind of dampening effect." Consequently, he found that the "trial was really a kind of entertainment for the town's people," even though he could not remember seeing any women there. He thought that the atmosphere was a "good indication of what poverty does to people." He found that "the persons who were present at all times were the white people. They dressed in dungarees and other rough clothing. They filled the courtroom. It was supposed to be segregated, but [during the session] at night there was no segregation because the whites filled up all available places. The only segregation that continued was of newspaper reporters." Callahan had rescinded the newsmen's privilege of reserved seats inside the rail enclosures. The three black reporters, Mitchell, Poston, and a female reporter from the *Birmingham World,* sat at a separate table. Even so, they were not entirely separated, "because our table, as was the white table, was right in front of the benches where the spectators sat." So "at night, with white spectators over in what was supposed to be the black section, the whites were all around us." [10]

The game was being played out, on one side, by colorful Thomas G. Knight, Alabama's attorney general, son of the state supreme court's chief judge who had written the opinion upholding the original convictions and sentences of the Scottsboro Boys. Slightly crippled, Knight would lean dramatically on his cane to make a point in a voice that sounded to Mitchell like a hangman's. He was pitted against charismatic Samuel S. Liebowitz, a scholarly New York criminal lawyer. Mitchell saw Knight do "everything he could to arouse the prejudice of the jurors. He had a way of speaking quietly." At one point, Liebowitz jumped up and objected to Knight's detailed description of the dangers to white women from sexual attacks as "an appeal to prejudice and passion." Like a skilled actor, Knight spun around to face the jury and declared, "I meant it to be an appeal to prejudice and passion." There was an electric response from the packed courtroom. In later life, Mitchell always wondered what the impact of Knight's performance would have been on a television audience. [11]

Mitchell was impressed by Liebowitz's legal maneuvers as he made another attempt to win freedom for the defendants. Unhappy with the surroundings in which the trials were taking place, Liebowitz again requested a change of venue. Callahan dismissed his motion, so Liebowitz moved once more to quash both the Morgan County venire and the Jackson County indictments on grounds that the jury commissioners had systematically excluded African Americans from the petit and grand juries. Scottsboro was the county seat of Jackson County.

At the second series of trials, Liebowitz had won from Judge James Edwin Horton, Sr., a ruling that there existed a prima facie case of exclusion on racial grounds in violation of the Fourteenth Amendment. Knight had shown that some of the local black citizens whom Liebowitz had presented to the court as potentially qualified jurors did not know the meaning of such terms as "moral turpitude." But Liebowitz had proved that they were far more qualified for jury service than many whites. The blacks testified that many of their friends were equally qualified, yet none were known to have ever served on any jury in the county. Now Liebowitz attempted unsuccessfully to win a similar ruling from Callahan in Morgan County, which had a similar history.

The Horton ruling had been a very important victory. Lawyers knew that no actual proof of exclusion had ever been offered before. Instead, litigants previously relied on contentions and affidavits. That was the basis on which the Supreme Court earlier had held that blacks could not be excluded from jury service because of race. For the first time, however, Liebowitz, won the right to inspect the role from which jurors were chosen in Morgan County to prove that all two thousand—plus names on it were those of white men. [12]

This bold attack against the Alabama jury selection system was central to Liebowitz's defense strategy—an issue that for a time overshadowed all other factors in the cases. Newspaper headlines in the region screamed that the time-honored jury, which they considered necessary for preserving white supremacy below the Mason-Dixon Line, was under attack. Battling to save his own state's honor, Knight argued, "When you challenge the right of jury commissioners to exercise their discretion in the selection of veniremen, you challenge the jury system, not only of Alabama but the whole United States." Alabama's jury law, he maintained, "provides equal protection to all in theory, and it does also in practice within the decisions heretofore handed down by the Supreme Court of the United States." The state's contention, he said, was that "Negroes are not systematically excluded from service because of race or color."

The noisy entry into the Scottsboro cases of the publicity-hunting Communist Party of the United States through its arm the International Labor Defense, by upstaging the NAACP in winning the right to represent the defendants, distorted this struggle over fundamental human rights and constitutional issues and sharply focused attention on the attitude of black Americans toward the Communists. Du Bois notably regretted that their "senseless interference" had an even more damaging impact than blocking the freeing of the "poor victims of Southern justice." Without the Communists' interference, he believed, the NAACP's "tried and successful pattern" of defense would have succeeded. Their interference also made Du Bois's idea of "economic reform as the immediate method of attacking the Negro problem" suspect because of parallels in dogma. The Communists, Du Bois complained, through their agitation to forward "the Revolution," staged the issue "as property rights and race, and spread this propaganda all over the world." His approach, however, differed profoundly from the Communists' in that his espousal of economic reform had a humanistic rather than a political foundation. The Communists were advocating *revolution* to ad-

vance the interests of the state; Du Bois was seeking *reform* for the liberation of his people from what he regarded as industrial tyranny.

The NAACP was upstaged by the Communists because, based on William H. Hastie's advice to Walter White that the Scottsboro case was
weak, it was too slow in recognizing the underlying issues. Mitchell was
one of the many people who were upset by that development. "As the case
now stands," observed the *Baltimore Afro-American* in the initial stages of
the fight in 1931, "the Communists have the National Association for the
Advancement of Colored People licked." What made matters worse for
the NAACP was that while the Communists were ahead, they posed the
danger of winning over blacks as members. Mitchell was very concerned
not only that the Communists would siphon off the NAACP's membership
and thus its primary fund-raising base, but also that there was a real danger
of their undermining the civil rights struggle.[13]

Attempting to control the damage, Executive Secretary White threw
the NAACP's limited legal resources behind the defense of George Crawford, an African American who was accused of murdering two white
women in Virginia. For Mitchell, White's experience showed the dangers
of becoming emotionally involved in such situations.

White sought to justify the NAACP's assumption of Crawford's defense
by downplaying the historical significance of developments in Alabama. In
a letter to Daisy Lampkin, NAACP membership secretary, in April 1933,
he maintained that it was "no disparagement" of the Scottsboro cases "to
say that the issue being fought for," namely the right of blacks to serve on
juries, "has already been determined favorably in at least four cases by the
United States Supreme Court." Now the NAACP was trying to go further
by doing "a most daring thing." The NAACP was contending "that when
a state violates the Fourteenth Amendment to the Federal Constitution by
barring Negroes from grand and petit juries, that state should not have the
right to demand the return of a Negro for trial from a state where his
Constitutional rights are not abridged or denied." That state was Massachusetts, from which Virginia wanted Crawford extradited. But this argument missed the point of the Scottsboro cases. For one thing, as Liebowitz
proved, the issues of the southern states' barring blacks from serving on
juries had not been settled. Second, were the Alabama judicial system permitted to railroad the Scottsboro Boys and to deny them a fair trial without
any challenge, the NAACP's own cause would have been jeopardized. All
black people in the South then would have been defenseless before rednecks
wanting to persecute them.[14]

The jury trial issue long outlived the Scottsboro and Crawford trials
and subsequently became an important aspect of Mitchell's work. As a
result of those two trials, he was able to see that the question of black

representation on juries was relevant not primarily to those who were excluded but to the defendants—that is, to the fairness of their trial. Not
seeing that was the mistake White had made, though Hastie was partly to
blame because of his advice. As history would show, the Crawford case
paled in importance by comparison with the Scottsboro Boys cases. Seeking
to compensate for that mistake, White elevated the extradition issue above
the interests of the defendants. That this was a misplaced priority became
evident when an all-white jury convicted Crawford, who had been extradited back to Virginia for trial. It was only through the brilliant summa-
tion to the jury by Charles Hamilton Houston, Crawford's attorney, that
he was spared the death penalty. The scope of that victory subsequently
became clear when Crawford confessed to the killings to Houston while
serving a life sentence. White had feared such a development when he
initially contemplated entering the Scottsboro cases.[15]

Mitchell sought escape from what seemed to him to be interminable
arguments by the defense, the prosecution, and the court over various issues by taking mental photographs of the scene around him. "Red-faced
bums, fuzzy-haired farmers, and a long line of questionable looking persons
were paid to serve on the two juries needed" for separate trials of the Scottsboro Boys, he subsequently reported in his "Observations and Reflections"
column in the *Afro-American*. "They took many hours to carry on their
alleged deliberations and in the meantime expenses for their board and
lodging mounted to such proportions that bills couldn't be paid in full."
Furthermore, he discovered, "sheriffs and court officials, prosecutors and
jailers, all shared in the financial virtues of the trial." So the most he could
say was "that the whole thing resolved itself into a side show for a crowd of
citizens who were so broke that they could not pay taxes due several years
ago."[16]

The Decatur jury found Haywood Patterson and Clarence "Willie"
Norris, the two lead Scottsboro defendants, guilty once more and sentenced
them to death in the electric chair. Mitchell's faith in the nation's judicial
system was reaffirmed when in 1935 Supreme Court Chief Justice Charles
Evans Hughes ruled in *Norris* v. *Alabama* that the exclusion of blacks from
juries deprived black defendants of the right to equal protection of the law
under the Fourteenth Amendment. Without actually ordering a new trial
on technical grounds, Hughes remanded the Patterson case to the Alabama
Supreme Court, implicitly indicating that a fourth set of trials was required. Although the Alabama Supreme Court quashed the existing indictments, the state was rigidly hostile, so the defendants faced a bleak future.
At least, though, the *Norris* decision was a major advance to end the exclusion of blacks from state juries.

Charges against four of the group eventually were dropped under what was called "the compromise of 1937," ending the Scottsboro trials. Clarence Norris and the other four Scottsboro Boys were again sentenced either to death or to long prison terms.[17]

Norris would spend fifteen years in prison, five of them on death row. The Board of Pardons and Paroles finally released him and another Scottsboro boy in January 1944. But instead of permitting them to go to Cleveland, where Roy Wilkins had found forty-dollars-a-week jobs for them, the parole board insisted that they work at a lumber company near Montgomery. The pay was so low and living conditions so bad that one of the men said life was "no difference than prison." So they fled to the North briefly. They were persuaded to return, but only ended up in prison again. Finally, through the dogged efforts of the Scottsboro Defense Committee, a group that had been formed to help the victims, Norris and the others in prison were released between 1946 and 1948. In 1976, the NAACP, which had helped them from time to time, was finally able to win pardon from Alabama for Norris, the only known survivor.[18]

James Harmon Chadbourn's detailed study *Lynching and the Law* authoritatively confirmed for Mitchell his impressions of the social crosscurrents that were swirling throughout society. Common economic social factors were woven "into the pattern of the typical 1930 lynching community," Chadbourn explained. Those conditions were not limited to the Eastern Shore but were typical of rural southern counties. Such counties were

> below the state average in per capita tax valuation, bank deposits, income from farm and factory, income tax returns, and ownership of automobiles. Educational facilities are also below the state average. The church membership is seventy-five percent Southern Baptist and Methodist. There is generally prevalent a supposed necessity for protecting white women against sex crimes by Negroes. All these, plus emotional and recreational starvation and fear of economic domination by enterprising Negroes, create the complex of "Keeping the nigger in his place." Periodic lynchings are the result.[19]

Arthur F. Raper, like Chadbourn, was hired by the Southern Commission on the Study of Lynching, a creation of the Commission on Interracial Cooperation that had begun its work in 1920, to conduct a comprehensive examination of the crime. Raper's work *The Tragedy of Lynching* was a study of the turbulent history of mob violence, while Chadbourn looked at the underlying factors that contributed to the breakdown of the legal system.

Raper chronicled the breakdown in the moral fabric of communities such as the Eastern Shore and Scottsboro, realities that Mitchell also understood. That breakdown was a common determinant of mob violence, whether it was expressed by a rope and accompanying sadism or by a judge and jury in the courtroom. According to Raper:

> After being kept from the overt act of killings, the mob members have successfully demanded of public officials that the accused person be tried in the local county, that the death sentence be imposed, and that no delay of execution be sought by the defendant's counsel—in most cases a local lawyer appointed by the court. This means that when the mob cannot have its murderous way in defiance of law, it openly attempts to force the constituted authorities to do its bidding. Mobs do not loiter around courtrooms solely out of curiosity; they stand there, armed with guns and threats, to see that the courts grant their demands—death sentences and prompt executions. Such executions are correctly termed "legal lynchings," or "judicial murders."[20]

Lynching, Mitchell saw in Princess Anne, had its devastating economic cost through loss of job opportunities, adverse publicity, and a numbing effect upon citizenship and government. But it was a cost of which lynch mobs and their supporters were totally oblivious. A reason for this blindness was the socializing effect that lynching also had on the community. It brought together white plantation owners and white tenants, mill owners and textile workers, Methodists and religious practitioners of whatever persuasion. Fortunately, though, lynching also had the corollary effect of shocking responsible elements in the community into expressing a desire to prevent expressions of such lawlessness in the future.

As events surrounding the Scottsboro Boys cases showed, the judicial system was perverted for the same bonding purpose. Consequently, in addition to the tension that accompanied trials of this nature in a southern town, the legal procedures following the arrests of the nine boys were normal for those areas and went as expected. The dominant motif in the Princess Anne and Scottsboro tragedies—as in similar ones—was the psychological need of white men to scapegoat blacks by charging them with raping white women. As Attorney General Knight declared, "And when you do protect the womanhood of the state of Alabama, it does not lie in the mouth of any man to tell you what's best for your commonwealth." Regarding one of the accusers, a spectator similarly told a *New York Herald Tribune* reporter that she "might be a fallen woman, but by

God she is a white woman." Judge Callahan likewise, in his instructions to
the jury at the end of Patterson's third trial, said:

> Where the woman charged to have been raped, as in this case, is a
> white woman there is a very strong presumption under the law that
> she would not and did not yield voluntarily to intercourse with the
> defendant, a Negro.[21]

At the same time, the Communists exploited the Scottsboro tragedy
until propaganda and fund-raising opportunities faded. The NAACP then
had to pick up the pieces. Mitchell saw parallels between the Communists'
operations in the Scottsboro Boys cases and in Baltimore. They moved into
any situation that seemed ripe for turmoil. And during the period of recovery from the Depression under the New Deal, when the nation was adjust-
ing to the new concept of government's expanded social responsibility,
there were many such opportunities. Administering public assistance programs was complex, and the staffs at government offices often were neither
sensitive nor compassionate. So they aroused considerable hostility, especially when they denied benefits to applicants. Ever present Communist
orators exploited the discontent around government offices in northwestern
Baltimore.

Mitchell found one instance particularly disgusting: when the Communists brought up an eighty-year-old man among a group of people from the
Eastern Shore to describe his poverty. As the old man concluded his tale of
deprivation, "this crowd just tore him up." They shouted, "You can fight
[back]," when he said, "And there's nothing we can do about [the alleged
exploitation]." Mitchell "thought this was so bad—eighty years old—what
could he do against that crowd?" He discovered, furthermore, that the
Communists never attacked the police, who were always nearby, even
though they were haranguing the crowds to attack social workers, who
were all white, as tools of a capitalist society. "After all," he concluded,
"the police were just workers like ourselves." But they wore guns.

Mitchell believed the Communists were just as patronizing and oppressive as the upper-class whites whom they attacked. He felt the only
probable difference between the two groups was "that whites in control
could carry out anything they intended to do—and often that was bad."
Consequently, despite the bombast of the Communists, Mitchell was satisfied that they would never gain a real foothold in the black community. He
knew, however, that that was little comfort to blacks suffering the brutality of racial oppression.[22]

CHAPTER THREE

A Star Is a Small Reward

C larence Mitchell, Jr., was born on March 8, 1911, in Baltimore, son of Elsie Davis and Clarence Maurice Mitchell. He was their third of ten children. One had died before he was born, and two died while he was very young. Among the living, he followed Evelyn Mary, the oldest of the three girls. Next after him was George Albert, then Lorenzo William and Anna Mae. Parren James followed Clarence eleven years later. Finally there was Elsie Julia.

In five-year-old Clarence's eyes, the two-story row house on Stockton Street near Pressman Street in West Baltimore, where he was born, seemed big. Yet, typical of the city's poor neighborhoods, the cobblestone street was one of the narrowest in a municipality characterized by quaint little thoroughfares and connecting alleyways. The neighborhood fascinated the youngster. One reason was "the big lumberyard right across from where we lived. We had all these mules, piles of lumber and that kind of thing."

Even more exciting was the family's next home at 553 Bloom Street, not far away. The rented house was a little bigger, more able to accommodate the growing family. Clarence slept in what was supposed to be the third bedroom. This was also the bathroom—a sufficiently spacious convenience with indoor plumbing. The neighborhood was even more exciting than Stockton Street because the house was just a few doors down from the corner of busy, commercial Pennsylvania Avenue with its rows of clothing and dry goods stores owned by white merchants. These kept the area's blacks from going downtown to the fashionable department stores, where they often could not even try on clothes. "There was a stable in the middle of the block. They not only had horses, including racehorses, but also from time to time, they'd bring cattle in. Every so often the cattle would escape and there would be a great uproar. They would be trying to catch all these cows running around on the streets, and goats."

Despite the area's lower-class characteristics, the compactly built row houses were comfortable and neat. The main source of heat in the house was a large coal-burning stove in the kitchen. Flues were supposed to distribute heat throughout the house, but they did not work well. The family supplemented this heat with a Latrobe, or "Baltimore," stove, which fitted into the fireplace.

Christmas was a particularly memorable time for Clarence; his parents had a special talent for spreading happiness that made their home a scene from Bethlehem. The Stockton Street house remained throughout his life the symbol of the family's strength, no doubt because he spent his earliest years there. His parents converted the front room, which they euphemistically called a parlor, into a delightfully scented pine forest with a tree that took up half the space. Beneath it was their traditional "garden," with sawdust dyed green for grass. An assortment of animals, angels, street-lamps, and a crèche of ornaments Clarence suspected his parents had saved from their childhood provided the sacred setting. Two miniature tramp figures, with sad faces and patched clothes, were placed prominently; perhaps to remind the children how blessed they were.

The atmosphere was enhanced by a special decorated oil lamp treasured through the years, with a fat, round, colored-glass shade that was lit only at Christmas. Its glow provided much more than physical warmth; it gave the appearance of chasing away their privation. During the year, plain glass lamps were carried from room to room. An additional kerosene space heater was lit in the parlor to supplement the Latrobe stove's losing battle against the cold.

A sturdy round oak table with enormous lion's paws for legs covered with a spotless white tablecloth completed the setting. At the center was his mother's cherished cut-glass punch bowl with little cups hooked on its rim. Decorating the table were her cakes—two fruit (one light and the other dark), two layer (one chocolate and the other with white icing covered with freshly grated coconut), one rich-butter pound cake, and sugar cookies. His father made trips to the colorful Lexington Market, with its open stalls and bustling activity, from which he lugged home a heavy straw basket full of candy, nuts, oranges, and bananas for the table.

Clarence enjoyed the aroma of Prince Albert pipe tobacco and cigars and the good humor of his parents' friends and neighbors gathered to celebrate the season. The youngster marveled as the atmosphere became more joyful as the guests helped themselves from the punch bowl. But no one ever got boisterous.

Clarence never missed the extra source of Christmas heat during the rest of the year. Looking back, he thought it amazing. Perhaps that was because he enjoyed spending so much time at the old Carey Street Elementary School, which was warmer and more comfortable than home. Even so, the joys of Christmas were always increased by the lighting of the space heater. The family looked forward to this event as much as wealthier ones anticipated the lighting of a Christmas tree.

Clarence's fondness for school was nourished by his elementary school teachers, who were devoted to excellence. "I had very good teachers who didn't stress so much what our handicaps were. They taught more in terms of the world in which we lived and the history of the country so that I really never felt that I wasn't an American by right." George B. Murphy, the school principal, a respected member of the family that owned the *Baltimore Afro-American,* tried "to get the children advised on things that had to do with race." Teachers "from time to time would talk about the role of blacks in our country" or of "having seen Frederick Douglass, for example, when he came to Baltimore to speak on something."

Other teachers indelibly imprinted on his mind and in his heart included Norma A. Marshall, mother of a lively youngster three years older than himself named Thurgood—who in later life became the first black justice on the United States Supreme Court. Mrs. Marshall taught Clarence in kindergarten. She helped build his appetite for learning by her personal warmth and natural ability to awaken young minds.

Clarence and Thurgood did not know each other then though they both attended the Carey Street school. A difference of three years in age between children so young can keep them far apart. A more important reason, though, was the difference in their social status. Thurgood lived "on the other side of the tracks" in western Baltimore. His home was on prized Druid Hill Avenue, commonly dubbed by some lower-class whites as Bread and Tea Avenue. They thought that the black residents there were having such a difficult time making ends meet, in their effort to live up to their new social status, that they could hardly afford more than bread and tea for food. That, of course, was a misconception created by racial jealousy. Druid Hill Avenue was the place where upper-crust blacks lived and to which up-and-coming ones aspired. Consequently, it was not until both boys were in the old Douglass High School at Calhoun and Baker streets that the athletic and studious Clarence had a chance to meet the popular, outgoing Thurgood. They later developed a close friendship while both were students at Lincoln University in nearby Pennsylvania.

Its lower social status notwithstanding, Bloom Street had advantages that Druid Hill Avenue lacked. Bloom Street provided an opportunity for cosmopolitan living and for young Clarence to become aware of racial differences and the many ethnic customs that characterized Baltimore. The city was particularly unique in having more identifiable ethnic neighborhoods than perhaps any other similar medium-sized city in America. It had the usual African American, Jewish, and Italian neighborhoods plus clearly defined concentrations of Germans, Irish, Poles, and other European immigrant stock. Unlike hyphenated European ethnic groups, however, whose neighborhoods served as avenues of individual and group development, the city's African Americans found their ghettos to be constantly expanding traps from which they could never escape.

Blacks lived in rigidly defined, overcrowded ghettos. Even Druid Hill Avenue was no exception. There were West Baltimore, South Baltimore, and East Baltimore ghettos; West Baltimore was the largest. Blacks did not dare venture onto places like Eutaw Street, Fulton Avenue, and Broadway or into other white neighborhoods without the danger of being arrested and held on suspicion of some crime. On Eutaw Street, where wealthy Jews lived, for example, they entered the mansions only through the back gates to welcomed jobs. They were barred from sitting on the green park strips dividing Eutaw Street, except when accompanying the sick, the elderly, or children of area residents for whom they worked.

The restrictions on their existence were an unmistakable badge of caste, which also extended to the stores they patronized. In these, they could not try on the garments they wanted to buy; what was worse, they could not even enter some stores at all. In fact, segregation was sometimes worse than in many Deep South cities. Clarence, though, was spared some of the more demeaning aspects of residential segregation, because throughout Baltimore there also existed some neighborhoods in which poor whites and blacks lived side by side, in full harmony, and Bloom Street was one of these.

On one corner of his street lived a German family. Their house was right next to their large butcher shop. On the other corner, near Pennsylvania Avenue, was a Greek family who ran an ice cream parlor. They had a poolroom in the basement of the building and lived upstairs. The Dutch family next to them owned a saloon. Next door to the Mitchells the Sandlers, a Jewish family, lived right above their grocery store. Across the street from them was a second German family, the Reeses, who also owned a grocery store. "I have a clear recollection of those people. Mrs. Reese was such a nice, wholesome person." There were constant fights between Reese and Sandler, "fist fights and that kind of thing." Reese used to accuse Sandler of undercutting him. The German did not welcome the competition from the Jew. "Our family had beautiful relationships with all of them. We just were one big family in the neighborhood and knew all about" Dutch, Greek, German, and Jewish customs.

Their only problem was the black family next door, which was headed by a caterer. They resented having the Mitchells as neighbors and called them "alley niggers," because they came from Stockton Street. Yet the caterer's family, reflecting a limitation of vision and narrowness of mind, deteriorated. The children never amounted to anything. The senior Mitchell, by contrast, was a symbol of manly strength for his family. He was a good musician, playing the piano, violin, and guitar, and might have made a name for himself had he lived in a big city like Chicago, New York, or New Orleans where opportunities in entertainment were much better. Despite its size, Baltimore was not much more than a big country town, very rural in character and provincial in outlook. To survive, the elder Mitchell gave up his dream of music and fame to work as a waiter at the stately Rennert Hotel at Saratoga and Cathedral streets.

Young Clarence did not grow up aware of his poverty because of the quality of his home. His parents had married young. How they managed to clothe and feed the first set of children was always a marvel to him. They often talked about the hardships caused by his father's loss of a job following the great Baltimore fire of 1904 as a reminder that things could be worse. Pride was the Mitchells' calling card and self-confidence their rudder. These values were instilled in Clarence as his parents shielded him from the possible demeaning aspects and the resulting psychological scars of financial privation. There was always enough food on the table for everyone, and his mother ensured that her family's clothes were clean and neatly pressed. She was good at improvising in the kitchen. Whenever she was unable to afford a turkey for Thanksgiving, she would prepare spareribs in such a way, with ample amounts of spicy stuffing, that Clarence never knew the difference. She was also able to stretch pigs' feet for both the main course and dessert by using the gelatin that comes from boiling to make a tasty, sweet dish.

As the oldest boy, Clarence functioned as a secondary breadwinner from as early as he could remember. In those years there were still no electric refrigerators, making ice an important commodity. So was coal. Worry about the cost of gas or fuel oil in Clarence's neighborhood was unknown, since no gas lines ran there, and none of the houses had central heating. Consequently, there were ice and coal yards in the area. A few families were able to buy a bushel of coal all at once, but most had to settle for a peck at a time.

Clarence had a little business delivering ice and coal during the school year—"ice in the summer and coal in the winter." He also had a job in a bakery, which he enjoyed very much. During the summer, he worked at the Tin and Decorating Company on the waterfront, starting the day there at seven o'clock in the morning. "Then, after I left work, I would go to a place on Pennsylvania Avenue and McMechan Street which was known as Grebs. It was a confectionary store, and I would work there from about six until about three in the morning." The streets were safe—"Nobody ever bothered me in going back and forth to my home. In that way I was able to save money, although there came times when we had a really rough sledding with respect to getting money to go to school." Clarence and his brothers also earned extra change in the summer when a neighbor went away on vacation by cleaning her yard and cutting the grass.

Between work and school, the youngster found time for play in the backyard. Clarence enjoyed making wagons for himself and his brothers. With a set of wheels and an empty crate of appropriate size, he fashioned a movable contraption that was the match in speed and durability of any of the sleek, factory-built wagons that wealthy youngsters on Druid Hill Avenue or Eutaw Street had.[1]

As the children got bigger, feeding and clothing them placed much more of a strain on the family than the meager incomes of the elder Mitchell and Clarence could sustain. His mother began taking in clothes to wash and iron at home. His sister Anna Mae, always playing in the backyard—protected by the whitewashed fence—amid the colorful snow-on-the-mountains, milkweeds, and black-eyed Susans planted by her father—fondly watched as Clarence, in addition to everything else, helped their mother by picking up and delivering the laundry in a large wagon with iron wheels. The squeaking, crunching wheels heralded his approach. Anna Mae's bouncing greetings blended in the air with the chirping sounds of birds and other neighborhood children playing. That type of manual labor was so taxing of his mother's strength that memory of her slaving over the wet, heavy, dirty clothes and struggling in the heat of summer, ironing load upon load of laundry, made Clarence sick. He never talked about this bitter part of his early life, except to those closest to him. He even stopped eating cabbage and fish because their smell reminded him of those days when his mother boiled clothes on the stove to make them white while at the same time cooking those dishes.

His dog Knox, which he loved to walk, was an added enjoyment in a life where simple pleasures were especially valued. After Knox died, Clarence gave Anna Mae another dog, appropriately named Claus, as a Christmas present. Although Clarence was closer to her than to his other siblings, there was so much love in the family that his fondness for her "caused no problem," she proudly recalls. Anna Mae lost the birthday card on which he wrote a poem to her after keeping it a long time, but she never forgot the words.

Little sister will you know
I will always love you
So when your cloud in life appears
God help me to be near.[2]

Parren fondly remembers how protective his brother was of him. The six-foot-two Clarence was an excellent athlete who often walked to Druid Hill Park with Parren on his shoulder to go running. While Clarence exercised around the reservoir, Parren stayed under a tree guarding sandwiches.

Clarence was respected for his flash-point temper and his amateur boxing skill; he trained at the YMCA, where he was known as the Shamrock Kid, signifying his toughness, and was a very fierce opponent. As he was fierce, so was he independent. Once in a street fight, when he was getting the worst of a pummeling, he waved away his brother George when he attempted to assist him. Clarence believed in finishing what he started, even if he lost the fight—a trait he carried through life. For him there were lessons in defeats, but his pride forbade him from surrendering to adversity.

His agility, strength, and love of competition made other athletic activities seem effortless. Sister Anna Mae used to admire his prowess at skating back and forth from Caroline Street to Bloom Street. There were few cars then, so it was safe for him to do so. Skates were also his favorite means of transportation for speeding downtown to his job as a night elevator operator at the Rennert Hotel, where he could at least get a few more glimpses of his father working in the dining room.

Somehow he managed to excel in high school, which he attended during the days, despite his arduous schedule. After working from 11 P.M. to 8 A.M., he had just a half hour to be at school. He once tried getting a permanent late pass, but the vice principal, while marveling that he was working so hard, denied his request without hesitation. That was another lesson for Clarence in discipline and punctuality. Douglass High School was made outstanding by its high-caliber teachers. Because it was the only high school in Baltimore blacks could attend, the brightest students were placed in separate classes. Mitchell was in this category.

School, however, was not all work. His sister Anna Mae never forgot the comic picture he made as "Daddy Long Legs" in a play presented by the Douglass High School Mask and Wig Club. He was so eager to go out onstage that he put on his spats backward. Nevertheless, he performed superbly. He was her hero and her worship of him was increased by her female classmates' admiration for him.[3]

Even though he was always correcting everyone's English, the girls loved him madly. He could make his classmates bend over in stitches and often had the teacher in tears. He would also cause the girls to be detained after school by waiting outside the classroom door until after the teacher had gone in, and then mimicking her, sending his friends into convulsive giggles. Angered by such silliness, the teacher would sternly punish everyone except him because he had kept a straight face.

His antics were one way Clarence fought fatigue. Nevertheless, away from school, fun was truly fun; no matter how hard he worked, he still found time and energy to join the Saturday night "hops" at a female schoolmate's home. Contemporary social customs were obvious—the girls were the expert dancers, thanks to the lessons their parents allowed them to take; the boys, regarding dancing as effeminate, never tried to learn until they got to the hops. That gave the girls a welcome opportunity to teach them—all except Clarence, who extended his unusual grace and agility to the floor, where he was unmatched as a dancer.[4]

Given his popularity, not only Parren, but also his other brothers George and Lorenzo tried to emulate "Bill," as the family affectionately called Clarence. The youngsters all looked up to him because he was such a strong figure. George admits, "I tried to imitate him, even though I knew I couldn't emulate him." Parren, as the youngest boy, more fortunately escaped his awesome shadow by the distance of his years.

Sundays were another matter, a day of religious devotion. Hops or no hops, Clarence joined the family in worship at St. Katherine's Episcopal Church to hear their pastor Father Divinish. In his early years, Clarence's Sunday school teacher, Joseph Briscoe, for whom Baltimore named a school, and Father Divinish helped mold his character. A devoted altar boy, after assisting at the first mass at seven, he remained for the eleven o'clock morning service, and then ended the day with the night service. Duty also required him to be present on special occasions. The special Good Friday services at Easter, which among Episcopalians are ritualistic marathons, were challenges for the young Clarence that he could never endure without falling asleep. He was nevertheless rewarded for his faithful service with a promotion to crucifer. Parren, equally devoted, followed in his footsteps at St. Katherine's, rising still higher to become a vestryman.

Little Parren regarded Clarence as such an idol that he almost followed him to Lincoln University—though prematurely. On the day Clarence was packing to leave for the university, the six-year-old boy slipped into the car trunk. Fortunately, someone found him when he went to put in Clarence's luggage.[5]

By the 1930s the border state of Maryland was a recognized wellspring of radical black leaders. W. Ashbie Hawkins, an illustrious lawyer, launched a vigorous challenge to Baltimore's residential segregation ordinance shortly after Mitchell's birth. Earlier black notables included Benjamin Banneker, free born in Baltimore County, who as an astronomer and mathematician served on the commission that laid out the District of Columbia; Harriet Tubman, an escaped slave from Dorchester County who became the "Moses" of the underground railroad; and Frederick Douglass, born a slave in Talbot County, who fled to freedom from Baltimore to become the dominant voice of his day in the abolition movement. Maryland served not only as a transfer point for escaped slaves but as a window that allowed intellectual currents from abroad to enter through its port city, Baltimore; and was a catalyst in the national movement for freedom and human dignity.

Baltimore was especially attractive to blacks because it had a plentiful supply of low-skill jobs. Blacks helped build the city's international reputation as a ship-building and -repairing entrepôt. During slavery and afterward, until the ugly Jim Crow curtain was drawn over the southern region in the 1890s shutting out the spreading ray of hope for full access to the country's economic mainstream, blacks had excelled as shipbuilders, caulkers, and mechanics. Baltimore's blacks, furthermore, won fame for their corporate ownership of the Chesapeake Marine Railway and Dry Dock Company. Through the prestige and organizational skills gained from this enterprise, a number of the company's leaders won recognition at the Philadelphia Labor Congress of black delegates in 1869. This group subsequently formed the National Colored Labor Union in Washington, D.C. Frederick Douglass, before becoming the preeminent black abolitionist spokesman, worked with the Chesapeake Marine Company as a caulker. Even more than the Civil War, World War I dramatically transformed the whole social and economic structure of Baltimore, making it a center of racial ferment.[6]

Mitchell was not sure of any prominent role his forebears played in this history, but he suspected that someone on his paternal grandfather's side had some association with the famous Enoch Pratt of Maryland. Whatever the specifics of the family's early history, his grandfather, George Albert Mathias Mitchell, was born around 1819 and after Emancipation became a farmer in Montgomery County. The farm provided an existence of sorts, but merely surviving was not his idea of living. He gave up that livelihood and migrated to Baltimore, where he did much better at the profitable job of whitewashing fences. His sisters Martha and Cassandra joined him in search of a better life, settling on Stockton Street, a few blocks from where Clarence was born.

One brother, however, did not follow Grandfather George to the city. He was Uncle John, whom Clarence thought was a wonderful old man. Every so often, he would find his way from the country into town for a visit, bringing a large basket of apples, corn, and other produce for the family. Clarence always greeted Uncle John with delight. His white, thick hair made him look so distinguished. It impressed Clarence that he was always clean and neatly dressed, despite the farmer's never ending struggle to make ends meet.

Clarence thought Aunt Martha was "a typical maiden lady." She wore long black dresses and left a favorable impression on the youngster. She was a good cook and made her living by that endeavor. He loved her corn bread and her variety of pies and other pastries. She was especially good at baking what was called "beaten" biscuits. The more patriotic called them "Maryland" biscuits. They were round, thick, and hard, with the diameter of an average-size apple. Clarence could hardly wait to match the strength of his jaws against them. As for Aunt Cassandra, the youngster never managed to find out exactly what she did. Whatever it was, though—probably one of the many unpleasant factory jobs in Baltimore that were reserved for blacks—it was hard work; occasionally when she visited the family she would arrive in a state of collapse.

Uncle John, Aunt Martha, and Aunt Cassandra were all peripheral to his life. Yet the involvement of the granduncle and grandaunts with his family, their continuing ties and affection, played an important role in reinforcing his own sense of belonging and awareness of a strong family unit.

Clarence was less aware of relatives on his mother's side. Elsie Davis Ruff was the daughter of Grace Davis Ruff and Charles Ruff, a Richmond, Virginia, handyman who died in either 1912 or 1913. Grace Ruff died in 1912. He strongly believed there was a Portuguese branch in his mother's family tree. His mother was a light-brown-complexioned woman. Color gradations on her side of the family ran from dark to almost white. Further reinforcing his suspicions were the Portuguese-sounding expressions she often used and some of the dishes she cooked.

The combined strengths of his parents were enough to keep Clarence on a straight and even path throughout his formative years. It is hardly likely that his parents had envisioned Clarence's meeting with U.S. Presidents on civil rights legislation or holding the feet of senators and congressmen to the fire in later years on issues involving the constitutional rights of African Americans. But they wanted him to be something and to make a name for himself, his family, and his race.

Ambition without moral and spiritual fortifications, however, can be like a house built on sand. His parents lacked material wealth, but in their ultimate wisdom realized that with spiritual strength and character, their children could survive whatever adversity they encountered in life. Elsie Davis was the dominant force in this regard. At home with the children while Clarence, Sr., eked out a living downtown at the white man's behest, the stoutly built woman instilled in her children what no man could ever take from them: an understanding and appreciation of their individual worth, a pride in their heritage, and belief in God.

She always made sure that the children kept the yard clean. Its gleaming white fence was like a lifelong beacon to Mitchell. Inside the house, the children dared not stay idle. There was a vintage model hand-wound Victrola that worked well enough for the family to play records of classical and other good music. She also insisted that they study poetry. For recreation, they spent many evening hours at the Pitcher Street Library poring over books and magazines. A moment of great excitement occurred when the family's first and only piano arrived at their Bloom Street home. To get the big instrument through the narrow hallway, they had to take it apart and reassemble it inside. Wherever they moved, the piano followed.

Their subsequent move to 712 Carroltton Avenue in 1929 was a great occasion for celebration. This was the first home the family ever owned, and it made everyone very happy. The three-story house with six bedrooms and a dining room was bigger than their previous homes. It even had central heating, and sat elegantly near historic Lafayette Square, with its uniquely Baltimorean three-, four-, and five-story brick-and-stone structures. The move was an indication of the family's improving social and economic status. But life for the family was still far from easy street. Evelyn, the oldest child, helped her parents scrape together the down payment against the $7,500 price of the house. Elsie Mitchell was now supplementing her husband's income by taking in "table boarders" to make up for the absence of Clarence's contributions. She served meals to teachers from the nearby school and from the Metropolitan Methodist Church at Lanvale Street and Carrolton Avenue. Mitchell was then in his second year at Lincoln University in Oxford, Pennsylvania. He was most excited when he returned to see the new home. With sister Anna Mae on his shoulders, he made a grand inspection tour. His room—his first real room—was on the third floor.

Good luck, though, was not the family's best friend. Unable to meet the second-mortgage payments, they lost the house after living in it ten years. The ensuing struggle mattered little, for the family had seen worse times. Elsie Mitchell survived this loss as well as she had previous calamities. When she died in November 1959 at her final residence at 1602 Druid Hill Avenue, Mitchell celebrated her gift of life with a heartfelt ode, "A Star Is a Small Reward," in the *Baltimore Afro-American*. It read, in part

Mothers are very durable. Mine was one of a kind. A Spartan with a sense of humor and a love of life, she was no stranger to privation, sickness or adversity.

There came the brief recollection of her as a determined and vigorous young woman holding my hand as we sloshed through the wet snow late one Christmas Eve—looking for a tree. This was ordinary you say? Yes, it was, except that she had gotten out of the bed during a serious illness just to be sure that her brood had a Christmas tree.

The year 1959 "was something" for Mitchell—first, Lorenzo, forty-two, who had attended Morgan State College and was now making his living as a chef, was killed in March when his convertible crashed into a tree as he sped along one of Baltimore's scenic avenues. Mitchell was especially close to Lorenzo and deeply grieved his loss. Though bedridden, his mother was determined to attend the funeral, but not in a wheelchair. So Mitchell carried her into St. Katherine's Church. His father, age eighty, died of cancer in June.[7]

Clarence's family welcomed his decision to go to college as a strategic way out of poverty. They also valued education for its intrinsic worth. Clarence would have preferred to go to the University of Maryland in his home state, but that was a Jim Crow institution even though it was supported by everybody's taxes. He chose the next best alternative—Lincoln University, in Oxford, a small town approximately halfway between Philadelphia and Baltimore, nestled among the hills and rich farmlands of Chester County. The tranquil atmosphere was ideal for scholarship, with air as pure as the water that was drawn in abundance from artesian wells.

Lincoln once had served as a refuge for runaway slaves from Maryland. At that time it had been called Ashland Institute. Founded in 1854 by the Reverend John Miller Dickey, a white Presbyterian minister from Oxford, as "an institution of learning for the scientific, classical and technological education for colored youth of the male sex," Lincoln was proud of its tradition of public service. Its promotional newspaper listed doctors, judges, legislators, and diplomats among its many illustrious graduates whose "mission is to serve humanity."

Another factor that led Mitchell and other black Baltimoreans to regard Lincoln as a spiritual reservoir was its links to the Sharp Street Methodist Church and Liberia. Jehudi Ashmun, another white founder, was sent to Africa by the American Colonization Society in 1822 to help free blacks who had settled in what became known as Monrovia, the capital of the African nation. The old location of the Sharp Street Methodist Church had

been an assembly point for those who had gone to Liberia and founded
Maryland County in the new republic. That was one reason why many
Baltimoreans regarded Liberia as a window to their past and identified so
strongly with it.

By the time Mitchell arrived in 1928, Lincoln had a reputation as "the
black Princeton"—a reputation it unabashedly fostered by imitating its
white namesake in neighboring New Jersey. Lincoln's predominantly white
faculty tended the intellectual interests of an all-black student body that
was composed of the cream of the race, what W.E.B. Du Bois called the
"talented tenth." Lincoln drew students like a powerful magnet from more
than half the states of the Union, especially from large metropolitan centers
around New York, Philadelphia, Baltimore, and Washington, as well as
from countries in Africa, the West Indies, and South America.

Despite its atmosphere of intellectual elitism, most of Lincoln's students were from poor families like Mitchell's—only a few came from middle-class families. Yet classism was the furthest thing from those bright
minds. They all received an equal chance to perform in the classroom and
flourished accordingly. Mitchell benefited richly from Lincoln's stress on
scholarship and excellence. He also welcomed the well-earned respite from
working, an opportunity that enabled him for the first time to devote full
time to serious study. To make ends meet he still had to work during
summer vacations, on the waterfront and at soda fountains in Baltimore.
One summer he worked as a busboy at the fashionable oceanfront Gibson
Island Club southeast of Baltimore, where Thurgood's father, Will
Marshall, was head steward. Young Marshall, three years ahead of Mitchell
at Lincoln and now one of his good friends, also worked there as a waiter.
It impressed Marshall that despite the Mitchell family's obvious want and
the always present opportunities for Clarence to join other busboys and
waiters in sneaking home food from the kitchen, his friend refused to avail
himself of what he had not earned. Similarly, Mitchell refused to eat the
food his employers served.

Raymond Hatcher, a close friend who entered the freshman class with
Mitchell, recalls his striking honesty and strong character. Mike, as Mitchell's Lincoln classmates called him, "lectured us one morning on the trashy
materials we were reading, and he held up in his hand what now would be
considered *Playboy* or *Penthouse,* as an example."

He was a "rabbler," or prankster, a carryover from his high school days.
"If you were doused with water and didn't see where it came from, it would
have been either Jim Byrd or Clarence Mitchell who threw it." They were
"the only two guys on campus who could throw water around corners." He
had a "grand sense of humor and an infectious laugh." When "he laughed, it
sounded as though he was laughing from his heels all the way up."

Lincoln strengthened this ability to enjoy and treasure life. Not only was the institution highly respected for producing graduates who went on in life to make something of themselves, but it was also well known for motivating its students to serve their community. That was another reason why Mitchell found the atmosphere at Lincoln so congenial and rewarding. Another was "very fine persons" like Professor Robert M. Labaree, "the man who really got me interested in things like sociology, anthropology, comparative religion and things of that sort." Labaree, a white man, had served as a missionary in Persia. "His children had grown up, and he more or less considered me a son. He was very interested in trying to see that I stayed on the right track." As a result of his teachings, Mitchell could later tell a Lincoln University commencement class, "Much of what I know about the dignity and worth of my fellow men, I learned from him. He really helped to prepare me to live in a world which knows that all civilizations and cultures are not Anglo-Saxon. He was firm in his Christian faith but mindful that our religion has no exclusive option on morality, kindness, and justice. I am certain that when the complete goal of the NAACP is achieved it will correspond to many of the blueprints that he gave to me and to others in his classroom and home."

There being no limit to his hunger for education, Mitchell took "everything they offered" at Lincoln. That meant even comparative religion—"I think as I look back on it, that was really what a liberal arts course is supposed to be, and I must say I enjoyed it." Whatever Labaree taught "really brought home to you the social concepts and the problems of our times as we were experiencing them." That was 1929, a year after he had entered the college—the great stock market crash that year wiped out many fortunes and jobs and sent thousands of people onto bread lines—so those courses "were very pertinent at the time." He learned to speak Greek and Latin fluently. What he really wanted to study more than anything, though, was medicine, so he took all the requirements. But the Depression killed that dream.

This enjoyment of life and study helped Mitchell ease his continuing anxieties over survival. Those closest to him knew he "had real rough sledding" getting money to continue school. During his second year, he thought the end had come. He had used up his savings. But a friend told him, "Don't think of dropping out. The people who are in charge of the business of this school understand what's going on." So he went and talked with Labaree and another professor. They told him to continue school. "You can pay as you get money to pay."

He finished owing Lincoln money and as a result could not participate in all the graduation ceremonies. Three years earlier, the college would have been more lenient. But the Depression had crippled its finances, shrinking the budget from $9,000 to a difficult to believe $2,000 in 1932. Faced with this impending reduction, the university in 1931 began demanding full tuition payment as a requirement for graduation. Despite his disappointment over being left out, Mitchell was glad to have made it through college. As a justly deserved consolation, he was awarded the 1932 undergraduate Class of 1900 prize for outstanding intercollegiate debating.

His mother, that dominant spiritual force "who had set great store by the graduation," made sure she was on hand to share in Clarence's triumph by getting a ride up to Lincoln with the Reverend C. Y. Trigg, pastor of the Metropolitan Methodist Church on Lanvale Street and Carrollton Avenue, where she now worshiped. She attended Class Night activities and watched her son serve as valedictorian even though he could not march in the graduation procession or collect his diploma—"So my mother came up and had all of the flavor of graduation with the students in their robes and watching my classmates get their diplomas." She also heard a graduate read the class poem her son had written, and everybody sang the class song he composed:

> Before the royal line is cast the gauntlet of the world
> So men begin to loose the cords and let the flags unfurl
> The trumpets to the lips are raised and play a martial
>   tune.
> Our time is spent—we must be off—'Tis fragrant Lincoln
>   June.
> The fathers who have gone before now smile upon their
>   sons
> And we ourselves are touched with pride to think of
>   coming ones.
> To east and west we scatter, far to the North and South we
>   stray,
> But we will one day come again, our debt of love to pay.

> *Chorus*

> Fond mother of our plastic youth, who brought us thru
>   the years,
> Take up the Chalice of thy soul and fill it with our tears.
> Do thou high-priestess of our hearts keep memory's flame
>   ablaze;
> For now we rise to give a toast to passing college days.[8]

Finding a permanent job during the Depression was a demanding challenge, so much so that it was hardly worth the effort to study for a

profession. So Mitchell abandoned any thought of studying medicine, since
doctors had to be supported by their wives' teaching school. Moreover, so
many people had scrambled to become teachers that this field too was now
closed to new entrants. Mitchell might have considered becoming a lawyer,
but from all appearances most of them were not managing to make a living, because they were dead broke. So his becoming a journalist was a turn
of fate in his life—thanks to Roosevelt's Blue Eagle program under which
companies were encouraged to hire people. In the tradition of John Russwurm, the nineteenth-century founder of the black press, Mitchell began
using the *Baltimore Afro-American* as a vehicle of protest.[9]

Juanita Jackson was one of Mitchell's contemporaries who was destined
to play a paramount role in his life. She, like an older sister Virginia, and
Marion, who followed her, was "born on the road," in Hot Springs, Arkansas, on January 2, 1913, daughter of Keiffer Albert and Lillie May (Carroll)
Jackson, and in her very early years lived the life of an itinerant. Her
brother Bowen Keiffer, last of the Jackson siblings, was born in Baltimore.
Her father, who could easily have passed for white had he wanted to, made
his living showing religious and educational motion pictures in churches
and schools from town to town. His pioneering endeavor provided blacks
with a welcome alternative to the generally demeaning depictions of the
race that were then prevalent in the movies.

One day while visiting Baltimore he met Lillie May Carroll, a multi-
talented, deeply religious, strong-willed woman and a gifted young teacher
in the Baltimore public schools. For Keiffer Jackson, winning Lillie May
Carroll was worth the effort of courtship. Any doubts he might have had
about pursuing her and winning her love were quickly dispelled when he
heard her singing "The Holy City" in her resonant soprano in what was
then the Sharp Street Memorial Methodist Episcopal Church. They were
married on September 8, 1910. She worked with her husband, singing and
performing other duties to round out the entertainment provided by the
movies.

Traveling throughout the South was often more than a wearying experience for the young couple—it could be a travail. Because Keiffer Jackson
looked white and his wife was evidently of African descent, southerners
constantly challenged him for openly pursuing what appeared to be an
interracial friendship. One reprimand from a sheriff was "You know that a
white man is not supposed to go with a colored woman in daylight," forcing Keiffer once more to produce his birth certificate to reveal his race.
Only after their children were born and provided him with an easily identifiable passport was the couple spared such challenges.

Eight years on the road, though, began taking its toll on the family.

The three little girls needed a real home and proper schooling, so her husband yielded to Lillie Jackson's complaints. They settled in Baltimore at 1326 McCulloch Street. From this point on Keiffer Jackson played a less dramatic role in the upbringing of the children, although he remained a strong, positive father figure. The dominant force, however, was Lillie Jackson, an able businesswoman who ran the family's rental properties, which provided them with a decent source of income. Her husband found much to keep him occupied by helping manage the properties, which had increased in number through recent acquisitions.

Heritage was always a dominant source of inspiration for the family; it was a force that drove them to become commanding leaders. Born on August 30, 1883, in Carrollton, Mississippi, Keiffer Jackson was one of nine children. His father George was white and his mother Jennie Jackson was part Indian. Keiffer experienced the trauma of lynchings at the age of six when the Ku Klux Klan shot and killed thirteen blacks in the Carrollton County courthouse as they awaited the trial of a black neighbor who had been falsely accused. Three years later, he saw three prominent black residents hanged on a tree on the courthouse lawn, where their bodies were left as a message. Rather than intimidating him, these experiences awakened within him a passion for equal justice that he instilled in his children. Those experiences reinforced his determination to be identified as black.

Lillie Carroll Jackson was equally aroused by the climate of injustice around her. She was born on May 25, 1889, in West Baltimore, the seventh of eight children, proud in the knowledge that her father was born and reared in the "great house" on the Douregan Manor plantation in Howard County, Maryland. He was the grandson of Charles Carroll of Carrollton, a signer of the Declaration of Independence. His mother was a black servant—such unions were a common occurrence in those days. The white women of the household taught him to read and write. He refused to marry while his mother was alive and in a condition of servitude. When she died, he was made commissioner of Negro schools in Howard County.

Lillie's mother Amanda was the granddaughter of John Bowen, an African chief who came to the United States in 1810 as a free man and settled in Montgomery County. Because a black woman's children would have been slaves, he married an Englishwoman so that his offspring would be free. Now the Reverend Bowen, Amanda's father established the Ebenezer African Methodist Episcopal Church in Sandy Springs in the county. The Bowens owned a lot of property, enabling the Reverend Bowen to give an expanse of land to his church. According to Juanita, Amanda Bowen became a schoolteacher and aggressively built on this property-owning tradition by buying buildings in Baltimore, forever singing the refrain, "Bricks and mortar. Get bricks and mortar so you can own property. Get independent and pay taxes," in order to instill in her children similar business values. Her daughter Lillie May Carroll showed the benefit of these teachings as well as of her pride in the nobility of her African heritage. Not only did she own property, but, like her mother, she also became a teacher. She was educated in Baltimore public schools and was graduated from the Colored High and Training School.

McCulloch Street, on which the Jacksons settled, was comparable in status to Druid Hill Avenue—both streets were lined with solid, three-story brick and brownstone row houses. Baltimore's whites had attempted to halt the encroachment of blacks onto such streets by enacting the nation's first residential ordinances in 1910. Legal challenges from local blacks led by the pioneering attorney W. Ashbie Hawkins and the NAACP resulted in the U.S. Supreme Court decision that declared them unconstitutional. The racial transition on McCulloch Street, despite the fears of whites, proceeded, even if slowly. For four-year-old Juanita, who enjoyed sitting on the marble front steps of her house, the sight of white girls going across the street in their starched white blouse and blue skirt uniforms to the segregated Western Female High School only tickled her infant fancy—the full significance would come many years later. The stately red-brick school, imposing in the quiet residential neighborhood, was an architect's dream. Among its most striking features was a multisectioned roof, steeply pitched, that was made all the more distinctive by a cupola over what could have been an enclosed brick bell tower. An unusual architectural tension was provided by the juxtaposition of a quadrangle cap rising to a point. The black school, a typically run-down structure, was within three blocks of Western Female High, providing a bitter reminder of the inequality of education in Baltimore.[10]

Clarence Mitchell and Juanita first met at Douglass High. She was two years younger than he. The social class difference that placed her on a better street posed no insurmountable problem. Her mother was strikingly unique among the black bourgeoisie in realizing that social status without substance—that is, constitutional freedom in its ultimate sense, education, and financial security—was an empty shell. People were what mattered to her—all kinds of people. She demanded that her girls maintain a very high standard of decorum. "Boys and books don't go together" was her refrain. That was Clarence's sad discovery in high school—"Juanita's parents had an iron-clad prohibition against her socializing with boys. I knew her but I kept my distance." Were that not so, Clarence would have gone after her despite the demands of school and his jobs. But Juanita's mother made it clear that the girls could not dare look at boys until they were out of college.

They were first brought together by the school's production of the play

Sleeping Beauty, which was performed in French. Clarence was the king, father of the princess, played by Juanita. The prince, who was supposed to kiss the sleeping beauty and wake her up, had to be a girl—Juanita's mother did not want a boy playing that role. The closest Clarence got to her in the play was when he found her "falling out," or fainting while eating an apple. He then ran up to her and said, *"Ma fille, qu'as-tu?"* ("My girl, what's wrong?") She answered, *"A forte vite, de l'eau . . ."* ("Very quickly, water . . .") Obeying the command, the prince ran out and got the king's daughter a glass of water. The scene shifted. The "prince" came in and kissed the princess as Clarence watched longingly.

The next time their paths crossed was in Mitchell's senior year at Lincoln when he returned home on mid-semester vacation. Hearing about a newly created City-Wide Young People's Forum, he went to one of the Sharp Street Church's regular Friday night meetings. There he saw his childhood dream, Juanita Jackson, presiding at the podium: "The spark struck, and from then on that was the big objective: how to get this girl." The occasion was so striking that "I couldn't think of any much else." Getting her, it turned out, was not an insurmountable challenge. The young woman was equally love-struck the first moment she again set eyes on the dashing young man.

Like Mitchell, Juanita Jackson had to go outside Maryland to get a good college education. Her mother saw to that. Devotion to formal study was the consuming passion. Again the awareness that education was the surest passport out of the cycle of poverty was reinforced by the reality of a totally segregated Baltimore. But even though their society was segregated, Clarence and Juanita did not begin to understand the nature of the barriers they were up against until they were leaving high school and wanted to advance their studies. Both sets of parents preached the importance of a first-class education. They disciplined their children to pursue excellence in learning, and the children responded with determination to study hard.

The only possible alternatives within the state to the University of Maryland were Princess Anne Academy on the Eastern Shore, Morgan State College, and Bowie State College, later to be named Coppin State College. Lillie Carroll Jackson enrolled Juanita at Morgan, a Methodist school. Juanita remains grateful: "The Church did all over Maryland what it did in the South. It established schools and colleges. It did what the state wouldn't do. We owe a debt to the Christian Church that we can never repay."

Morgan was founded in the latter half of the nineteenth century primarily as a theological institution. It was subsequently upgraded to a liberal arts college and moved to its permanent location. Juanita remembers how Dr. John Oakley Spencer, a white Methodist missionary and minister who was Morgan's president, "fought to get that college land and buildings at its location where it is now"—in northeastern Baltimore. Neighborhood whites bitterly opposed bringing blacks to the school. They lost a lawsuit, and Morgan was allowed to expand. The old administration building, Washington Hall, with a cafeteria, was then Morgan's principal structure. There were also a chapel and a dormitory. Despite the availability of Princess Anne Academy, Bowie State, and Morgan, all segregated, black parents with a little more wealth, or with relatives in other cities, sent their children outside Maryland to get a good education because those institutions were not accredited. In 1927, during her second year, Juanita's mother withdrew her and took her to Philadelphia to register in one of the white institutions there, where Jim Crow was not so blatant. Her older sister Virginia was already in Philadelphia, living with an aunt and studying at the Pennsylvania Museum School of Art.

Lillie Jackson first attempted to enroll Juanita at the prestigious all-girl Temple University. But Temple balked at giving her credit for her courses at Morgan. That meant Juanita would have had to start all over, a prospect she did not welcome. Her mother therefore demanded, "There's a college Ben Franklin founded. Where is it?"—and off she went with her daughter to enroll her at the University of Pennsylvania. As they had expected, Dean John H. Minnick had no problem accepting the young woman into the Bennet School of Education for Women, though he too hesitated to give her credit for the Morgan courses. Lillie Carroll Jackson was forced to bring her persuasive genius into play. Penn was her last stand, and she would not be deterred. Recalls Juanita, "My mother challenged him. Or rather, he was challenged by my mother's faith in my ability and what I had gotten from Morgan. He relented and agreed to give me credit for every course I had but Bible at Morgan." Entering the university on an accelerated schedule as a senior, she wound up on the dean's list the following February. She graduated with honors in 1931, a year ahead of Mitchell—but not too far ahead to place herself out of his ready reach.[11]

CHAPTER FOUR

Neither North nor South

The Baltimore to which Clarence Mitchell and Juanita Jackson returned from college was as mean as the one they had left. "Mean" was Jackson's way of describing the segregation and discrimination that characterized her hometown. Hence, the apt and popular description: "Baltimore is neither North nor South." Or, as Thurgood Marshall would say, "up-South Baltimore."

W. Ashbie Hawkins, the black attorney who began the fight against Baltimore's residential ordinance soon after it was enacted in 1911, said:

> This law, briefly stated, provided a penalty for any black man who would move into, or attempt to occupy, a house in a block where 51 percent, or more of the houses therein were occupied by whites, and vice versa. It undertook to punish the owner or agent of the property renting it. Exception was made in the case of servants. No attempt was made to restrain the sale or purchase of property anywhere or to anybody.[1]

If a black person dared to buy property in a prohibited neighborhood, he would be punished by the possible loss of his investment because he would not be able to occupy it. Other cities followed Baltimore, especially later in response to the increased immigration of southern blacks seeking jobs in industries deprived of their usual cheap labor supply during World War I. Mitchell's experience as a youngster at a band concert in the city's Druid Hill Park was typical of the city's racial attitudes.

Trained by his mother to love good music, he always sought to avail himself of the free open-air entertainment the city provided. At one of these concerts, he inadvertently took a seat beside a white woman. Suddenly, there was a great commotion as she jumped up shouting, "I'm not sitting by no coon tonight." Her husband unsuccessfully tried to hush her. The sideshow in the aisle ended with the woman walking out, shaking her finger at Mitchell and saying, "I'm going to get the police and have you arrested. Sitting down beside me." Then he felt a hand on his shoulder, patting him, and he heard a white man say, "You were a perfect gentleman in this situation." The whole incident happened so fast that Mitchell was not aware of what it was all about until, as he reflected on it, he remembered the woman's words. He had not been aware of her when he sat down. Because he thought the man who had reassured him had made a "wonderful gesture," Mitchell never stopped wishing he had turned around to find out who he was. Then and throughout his life, he had only sympathy, not hatred, for people like the abusive woman.

Mitchell grew up unaware of the economic and social exploitation his family and people were suffering because of their race. He did not know that in the eyes of society his skin color represented a badge of inferiority. His parents and schoolteachers in Baltimore had shielded him from the ugly reality of racism and the stigma of second-class citizenship. Thus he had always seen himself as an American without qualification. Both his mother and his teachers inculcated in him the importance of citizenship, of study, and of preserving beauty. At an early age he learned self-esteem and an appreciation of beauty. These values were crucial to his proper adjustment to a society in which, as W.E.B. Du Bois explained, "the problem of the twentieth century is the problem of the color-line,—the relation of the darker to the lighter races of men in Asia and Africa, in America and the islands of the sea."[2]

Mitchell's job as a reporter provided him with many dramatic episodes similar to the Druid Hill Park experience. They were not usually accompanied by a reassuring hand. His main assignment for the *Baltimore Afro-American* was covering the life of the city, particularly at the police station. He found it a rewarding experience, seeing the legal system functioning at its most basic level, on the streets and at the precinct house. There he got a graphic picture of how people regarded the police and of how the police treated blacks. He became aware of the myriad nuances of human behavior. The *Afro-American* soon raised his pay to twenty dollars a week, but it did not provide carfare, so he walked everywhere. Not only did he see what others normally overlooked or took for granted, but he was also required to interpret those events and situations for his readers.

The law did not require segregation on city buses, streetcars, or taxicabs, but at night while riding streetcars Mitchell would hear whites complaining, "If this were Virginia, they'd be sitting in the back." This Jim Crowism did not particularly bother him; as an indication of his self-esteem, he never thought "they" was a reference to him. Those whites, who oftentimes were no better off than the blacks from whom they were setting themselves apart, were certainly no better than he. This self-esteem and self-assurance would later be an ingredient of his success.

A double-decker bus ran up the very elegant Charles Street, Baltimore's version of Fifth Avenue. The downtown section of the street was characterized by three-story, attached brick-faced buildings with a few ornate stone structures here and there in between. For some inexplicable reason, blacks were not supposed to ride the double-decker even though there was no ordinance prohibiting them from doing so. One day Mitchell's editors assigned him to desegregate it. As he recalled, "I was a pretty good runner in those days. The driver saw me coming and kept going. So I ran and caught up with him after four or five blocks. He, needless to say, was trying to tell me I shouldn't ride it. But I did." When the *Afro-American* complained, the transit company insisted it did not have a segregation policy. Thereafter, that form of segregation ended, but on cold days drivers still slammed their bus doors shut on blacks and sped away.

Similarly, white taxi drivers were in constant conflict, and sometimes in physical combat, with blacks seeking transportation at the railroad and bus stations. Railways were not segregated, except the intrastate B&O line from Annapolis to downtown Baltimore. Segregation was so rigidly enforced on this line that a white man got six months in jail for sitting in the black section. The ferry plying the Annapolis to Eastern Shore route became a symbol of resistance against efforts to end state-imposed segregation. To an extent, Maryland's Jim Crow adherents won because that segregation law was never repealed. It merely died with the passage of the 1964 Civil Rights Act.

Segregation downtown, the bastion of white commercial interests, was so bad that the majority of blacks only ventured there when it was absolutely necessary, usually to go to work. But in the heart of West Baltimore, the city's largest and most thriving black district, segregation was rubbing salt in the wounds of area residents. Baltimore had the fourth-largest black population in the United States. Nevertheless, whites owned the stores that depended on black patronage.[3]

Blacks could not go near the cash register or behind the counter as clerks. The insult was too much for Mitchell, who was especially galled that whites "even had the effrontery to have a restaurant for whites only" next door to the *Afro-American* building. Before the business was expanded into a restaurant, the white store owners welcomed the trade from black patrons as long as they bought their sandwiches and refreshments there and carried them out. Business got so good that the owners put in tables in little booths, but they refused to allow blacks to sit there and eat. It was a big fight ending that problem, but the *Afro-American*'s staff did desegregate it.

The police department was another bastion of racism. It required a long, bitter fight before a dent could be made in the department's armor. According to Mitchell, "The system of justice in Baltimore was at its worst at the police station level. Blacks were herded into such stations if they happened to be walking by when there was a lineup. Hundreds were arrested on 'suspicion' and held for days without bail. It was awfully easy to get arrested for nothing." Furthermore, for the police, "the third degree was more or less standard operating procedure." Mitchell never saw a white person abused in police stations, while blacks were almost routinely. "And my experience included some of the poorest and most crime-ridden sections of the community where many of the offenders were white." He did not mean that whites were never abused, but, when such offenses occurred, there was always so much publicity that "I would be safe in saying that if there was abuse of whites, it was minimal."

Mitchell thought it strange that rather than teaching poor African Americans respect for the law, police stations fostered racial hatred and cynicism. The mere sight of an African American coming out of a police station often fostered the belief that he had done something wrong. Consequently, most blacks stayed away from police stations as much as possible. Mitchell found this situation downright amusing one day while he was covering one station. As he was leaving, some former schoolmates, upon seeing him, asked, "What did you get arrested for?" Such light moments offered welcome relief from the "terrible brutality" he often witnessed or learned about on the police beat.

Another manifestation of Baltimore's southern outlook was the refusal of whites to address blacks by courtesy titles. Mitchell was most offended one day when the desk sergeant, who could have had no more than a fifth-grade education, demanded of a highly respected, well-dressed black school principal, "Well, boy, what do you want?" A black woman, of course, would have been "girl." Not even the stature of Methodist Bishop W.A.C. Hughes could protect him, while he was a patient at the Johns Hopkins University, from being addressed by a white cleaning woman: "Well, Alfred, how are you today?" That lack of respect was not necessarily hospital policy, but the institution tolerated it.

Once, Mitchell saw a black woman who probably had been drinking but was not drunk come into the station to swear out a warrant. For no apparent reason, a policeman grabbed her and a fierce fight ensued. Finally, the police managed to shove her into a cell. Instead of getting the warrant she had come for, she wound up getting arrested. Mitchell figured she had failed to say, "Yes, sir," or something like that.

In another tragicomedy a white man filed a complaint claiming that black prostitutes had "rolled" him downtown in the red light district. The local magistrate hearing the case arranged for the man to get back his money. As the prostitutes were about to leave, the judge called over the one whom he assumed to be the madam, and said, "Listen, you keep those white men out of the house [brothel]. Don't let them in, or you're going to get into a whole lot of trouble if you do." She agreed to do so. Then, as she was leaving, Mitchell heard the magistrate declare, "Those niggers're getting above themselves."

He could never understand how so many blacks could accept such demeaning treatment. In the courts, too, where segregation was not required by law but still existed by custom, blacks and whites reinforced the pattern by sitting in the accustomed areas. Mitchell actually told a judge he was wrong to tolerate the practice—an initiative that made the jurist apoplectic and Mitchell very unpopular around the courthouse. Eventually, however, even though the judge had trembled, Mitchell found that by his challenging the system, segregation was ended.

In some areas of Baltimore, segregation was indeed required by law. The city's naturally beautiful, hilly, semirural character provided ample space for public tennis courts and golf courses, but African Americans were barred from most of them. One night while covering a meeting of the city parks commission in a poor neighborhood, Mitchell heard the white residents express fears about possible racial incidents if blacks were permitted to use the community's golf course. The whites said that, owing to the tendency of blacks to "colonize," they would begin moving into the neighborhood once the golf course was opened to them. The commissioner responded, "Well, I can't do anything about that. They have a right to play. You have to let them do it." One person then demanded, "You wouldn't let them swim in the same pool with white people, would you?" Finally, as a token gesture the golf course was opened to blacks, but only on special days.

The fact of life was that there were nice swimming pools for whites and inferior ones for blacks, beaches for whites and beaches for blacks. Baseball fields were segregated. Mitchell recalled that one man who in later life became a city judge was arrested for playing with a white partner on a segregated tennis court.

The YMCA and YWCA were similarly segregated. Attempting to be fair, Mitchell thought that "YWCA officials were far ahead of their male counterparts in their efforts to end racial segregation." Also segregated were lunch counters, hotels, theaters, bars, restaurants, and drugstores. Office buildings did not rent to black tenants—not even to federal employees. In some hotels, blacks could not ride on regular elevators.

Mitchell realized that only organized protest could end this Jim Crow system. Juanita Jackson, who, from as early as her high school days, had begun rebelling against racial caste, was very much a part of this struggle. The light-complexioned woman and some of her classmates enjoyed probing the system's racial armor by putting on turbans and going downtown to some of the finest department stores that barred African Americans. There they would speak French and, as expected, were welcomed as foreigners. "That was how we got our kicks in high school, those of us who had the courage to do it," she recalls. She was further angered because "we couldn't be social workers. We couldn't drive streetcars or the taxicabs. We couldn't be telephone operators. We couldn't read meters for the gas and electric company. We couldn't do a large number of things you normally expect to do in a community."[4]

Despite the difficulty of ending such segregation, change was imminent. African Americans like Clarence and Juanita who had gone out of state for a good education and a taste of freedom had awakened to these tremendous deprivations at home and were determined to make Baltimore a better place for their race.

Pennsylvania was far from being the promised land. Mitchell found that blacks could be policemen and firemen in Philadelphia, but they were barred from becoming conductors, operating streetcars, or driving buses. There were other examples of racial discrimination in the state, but, overall, Pennsylvania was better than Maryland. So were other states like Massachusetts and Connecticut, where institutions like Harvard, Amherst, and Yale accepted black students. Juanita similarly welcomed the opportunity to associate freely with whites at the University of Pennsylvania. A catharsis resulted:

> Here at Penn, I was able to lose my fear of white people, I made friends across the board. Gradually, I shed the shell I had brought with me to Pennsylvania, which had made me reticent, afraid to venture, afraid to speak up because of anticipated insults (which were not forthcoming), expected rejection (that did not happen). I have feared no man since.
>
> Again at Pennsylvania, in this first-class educational environment, I developed the security that comes from competition with the best and being able to meet it. It gave me confidence in my own ability. It did something for me that has lasted all my life. I

might be denied equality of opportunity but I knew I was not inferior.

I believe that what happened in Philadelphia ought to happen in Baltimore—my home. Exposure to democratic practices in Pennsylvania strengthened my faith that democracy could work in Baltimore.[5]

The "climate was pregnant with change," recalls Juanita. But the changes that Mitchell and Juanita wanted were reforms, not a displacement of the American democratic system. Their goal was to strengthen it by entering it. So they began serving as catalysts and dedicating their lives to the civil rights struggle. They became nonviolent revolutionaries, returning home determined to use the education that their parents had provided them through great sacrifice for the benefit of their race. The inconsistency that existed in Maryland's system of segregation encouraged their challenge. If integration was permitted in a few instances, why not in all others?

The Baltimore NAACP branch, founded in 1913, had fallen dormant after a long period of aggressive leadership. Mitchell, upon returning from Lincoln University in 1932, joined what remained of the branch. He was immediately designated head of the unit's publicity program, elected to the executive committee, and swamped with a host of civil rights assignments. Craving a still broader activist role, he became even more involved through an opportunity Juanita provided.

Out of college a year ahead of Mitchell, Juanita had initiated her own crusade against segregation. With the support of about two hundred other youths, she founded the City-Wide Young People's Forum in October 1931, a few months after her graduation. The Forum was much more than an organization of concerned young adults; it was a consciousness-raising vehicle, a movement for liberty, and an inspiration to activism. As president of the group, she made Mitchell vice president, assuring his official as well as personal closeness to her. That was the beginning of their lifelong relationship, one that was built on unfading love and dedication to carrying the gospel of human justice beyond the borders of their hometown and state to the far corners of the nation.

Of medium height, brainy, precocious, and stunningly beautiful, Juanita recognized nobility and a passion for freedom in Clarence: "That's what I liked about him. He didn't tolerate any second-class citizenship. He was one handsome young man. He used to dress in those days. He used to wear those blue serge jackets and white pants and white shoes. O-h-h-h, coming down the street, he was something. He was a handsome young man. He was so tall and thin, and he always kept his head so high. But his head wasn't high because he wasn't looking at people. It was a nobility in him that I saw. Because he at the same time was kind to people. He liked people, the humble as well as the great."

Mitchell swept her off her feet with his "silver-tongued oratory." He not only was a smooth talker in private, one who knew how to hold an intelligent woman's attention, but was also a forceful and eloquent public speaker. Juanita could never hear enough of his "handsome oratory," a gift that he used to demolish many a gifted debater in high school and subsequently. He did so well at Douglass High that the students carried him on their shoulders from the auditorium like a victorious gladiator.[6]

Once he headed the Lincoln University debating team against Cambridge University in an electrifying session at Bethel AME Church in Baltimore. For other debates, some of which were held at Grace Baptist Church, challengers were from Oxford University, the University of Edinburgh, and institutions in New Zealand. A page-one announcement in the *Afro-American* on April 21, 1934, heralded the final in a series of such events: "For the first time in the history of Baltimore six outstanding colleges will vie with each other" in a contest at Bethel. They were Howard University, Lincoln University, Morgan College, Hampton Institute, Virginia Union University, and Cheney State Teachers College. No admission was charged the standing-room-only crowd, but when the plate went around, the audience never hesitated to contribute generously for what was a form of enlightening entertainment.

Debate topics included hot New Deal issues like social security and unemployment compensation. Equally thought producing were the unending list of racial issues.[7]

Mitchell demonstrated not only a powerful mental agility, but also a fiercely independent line of thought. Even Du Bois once drew Mitchell's anger because of a blasphemous *Crisis* editorial that questioned with his uniquely bitter sarcasm God's sincerity and ability to protect blacks from the ravages of the Depression, poverty, and racial exploitation. Mitchell, a college senior, responded in less eloquent but fiercely devout language, "Anyone who believes that God fills the rich and the white with good things and sends the poor and the black, empty, away, shows himself to be a jackass of no mean degree." Instead of despair, he said, African Americans should reaffirm their faith by saying, "Lord. I will follow Thee, but I am weak and fear that the bubble of my faith in Thee will burst. Help me to see that our religion is indeed a vision, without which we perish."[8]

Mitchell joined Juanita and the other youths in reaching out to Lillie Carroll Jackson and other patrons like Carl Murphy. "I'll never forget my mother. She undergirded us. She was so happy we were so active doing what she thought we ought to be doing. Coming back with our education to help our people." Had they not started the Forum, she said, "we'd have been missionaries." Her mother had "a messianic view." She preached, "You are here to help your fellow man. She believed in our keeping busy in constructive activities." The "hops" that young Mitchell and others had once attended were now ruled out. "She disapproved of dancing and card playing." The children's social activities were centered around the Church and other endeavors their mother regarded as constructive. Many years later Juanita could still hear her "mother preaching so about the waste of time, 'sitting there playing cards,' and 'the things you could have been doing with your talents.'"

Juanita welcomed ties to the adult committee that Lillie Carroll Jackson organized to guide the Forum. "It made us respectable, because we were bringing in these radicals. We brought in everybody." So much so that Juanita was upset when the Sharp Street Memorial Methodist Episcopal Church, where she was a member, "refused permission for the Forum to use its premises because the pastor considered the Forum too radical." The Bethel AME Church then took them in. In addition to the regular Friday night events, the Forum sponsored talent nights and "Youth at Their Best" symposiums. There was no competition from television, so the sessions were always packed.

Those roots in the Church made it easier for the Forum to win moral and financial aid from other black institutions. Forum speakers came from the upper crust of black intellectual protest thought. Du Bois, Walter White, Roy Wilkins, and William Pickens, the NAACP's firebrand field director, were among the favorites. They also heard every member of Howard University's elite—leaders like sociologists E. Franklin Frazier and Emmet Dorsey, political scientist Ralph Bunche, and poet Sterling Brown, who were contributing to the racial ferment. Equally inspiring Forum speakers were black firemen and policemen from Philadelphia and Washington, who showed Baltimoreans the type of progress being made elsewhere.[9]

Speaker after speaker sang the praises of the City-Wide Young People's Forum. George S. Schuyler, an acerbic critic and author, thought the Forum was "unquestionably the most important in the United States. Your feat of getting together the young people of a great city like colored Baltimore and uniting them behind a program of advanced adult education, is one of the finest achievements in the history of our group." Nannie H. Burroughs, president of the National Training School for Women and Girls in Washington, D.C., felt that the Forum was "the best, most progressive and analytical organization of Negro young people in America." David O. Jones, president of Bennett College for women in North Carolina, regarded the group as "not only inspirational, it is powerful." Sidney Hollander, a member of the Urban League's executive board, was convinced that "the group had done a swell job and seems to have started something really worthwhile." [10]

One of the Young People's Forum's primary concerns during that period of the Great Depression was finding jobs for blacks. The Forum took the movement into the streets with buy-where-you-can-work campaigns that struck at the heart of one of the most glaring forms of economic discrimination. The boycott movement, also known as the Jobs for Negroes campaign, began in the late 1920s in Chicago with total support in the black community. The principal leaders of the movement were the *Chicago Whip,* an aggressive black newspaper, and the powerful Pilgrim Baptist Church. The protest then spread to Baltimore, New York, Washington, and other cities with large black populations. Mitchell was sure that had it not been for the Depression, people would not have paid it much attention. Because of the scramble for jobs, the movement developed and became a catalyst for other protest activities. [11]

The Forum's first target was the neighborhood A&P food stores, which, before the age of supermarkets, dotted the black northwest Baltimore community. Though the stores depended on blacks for 100 percent of their business, they hired only whites. Initially, the Forum had selected just one A&P for protest, but picketing only one store when a whole group was discriminating seemed illogical to Prophet Kiowa Costonie, a young minister from New York who that year was in Baltimore conducting evangelistic services at the Perkins Square Baptist Church. He suggested that the Forum instead picket the whole group of white-owned stores in the area. So the Forum joined forces with Costonie, who organized a group of young men wanting jobs in those stores.

Lillie Carroll Jackson headed the adult advisory committee, whose members accompanied the youths picketing the first A&P store. As expected, the store manager initially rejected their demands to hire black clerks with a curt "It isn't our policy." "Who else buys in this neighborhood?" she countered. Only blacks, the manager responded as expected. The manager's unacceptable excuse was that his white sales clerks would leave if he hired blacks. So Lillie Carroll Jackson replied, "Let those sales clerks buy all those cans on your shelves." Her group marched out, and the picketing began. The picket lines quickly spread to the other A&P stores. Mothers, joined by their children and even a few dogs, ignored tired feet to march for jobs for blacks. Baltimore had never seen a more unified response to blatant discrimination. The Jacksons and other neighborhood residents opened their homes to the picketers, providing them with a place to rest and meals. Against such an onslaught of community outrage, A&P soon caved in and began hiring blacks. [12]

Further testing its strength, the Forum picketers next went to the white-owned retail stores on the 1700 block of Pennsylvania Avenue, which also hired no blacks though they depended on the area's residents to stay in business. Those store owners were much tougher as a group than the A&P management. Solidly opposed to hiring blacks, they moved in court for an injunction to bar the picketing.

Outraged, Mitchell fired back in his weekly *Afro-American* column, "Observations and Reflections," which he began writing soon after joining the newspaper's staff:

> After being present at some of the court sessions, I think that even the merchants ought to be willing to admit that the case should have been settled out of court.
>
> Aside from the fact that the claim of the members of the movement is a just one the case is an unfortunate one because it represents conflict between minority groups in which petty prejudices have frequently gotten the upper hand.
>
> At one point, attorneys for the merchants kept bringing up the question of the right of a colored man to employ white women, which in my opinion was simply catering to Maryland prejudices.
>
> A colored witness said, "Excuse me for saying this, but the policemen said to me, 'that dirty Jew has counter pickets out here,' and I went home to get a sign then." An attorney for the merchants reddened at the words "dirty Jew," and I do not blame him. [13]

Judge Albert S. J. Owens of the circuit court of Baltimore only inflamed passions more, near the end of March 1934, when he signed an order making his temporary injunction against the pickets permanent. He struck down the picketers' demands, holding that their actions represented "criminal conspiracy." He observed that in the A&P case, the picketers did not cease their protest after winning the first round against those stores. Instead, they increased their demands for "every story operated in colored neighborhoods to have all colored employees except Manager." At a set date, furthermore, the picketers demanded that "in 3 stores we want colored managers." They also went beyond merely calling for the hiring of black clerks to demanding that "all boys who were hired" by A&P stores the Saturday after the demonstrations had begun "be dismissed entirely." Owens held that the evidence sustained the merchants' complaint, in that about two hundred picketers marching day and night were disrupting the merchants' business. He found no fault with the quality of picketers. They "are colored persons of the highest type; they are in every way respectable; are well educated and essentially religious and it is inconceivable that they could have been misled into the belief that for any cause, no matter how commendable it might seem to them, they could justify their actions in this case."[14]

Mitchell, however, thought differently:

Baltimore stepped back into the stone age of economics when Judge Albert S. J. Owens made permanent an injunction which forbids picketing of stores in the 1700 block of Pennsylvania Avenue by members of the "Buy-Where-You-Can-Work" movement.

I have always respected the judge as a rather kindly old gentleman, who listened to cases with a great deal of patience and was capable of giving a fair decision.

I am forced now to place him in the pigeon-hole of persons who are hampered from free activity by prejudices and stereotypes.

He is not so much a victim of race prejudice, although he apparently has his share, as he is of economic prejudice that causes him to lean strongly in favor of what represents organized business in the community.

Judge Owens has seen only one thing as the major factor in the movement and that is, "has a man the right to break up another man's business when the latter does not act as the former wants him to?"

The jurist has seen only the fact that business with its legal right to squeeze money from persons under what sometimes amounts to savage and ruthless methods, was being threatened by a group of citizens whose major fight was not a legal, but rather a humane cause.

In making his decision, he could deal only with an equation that had two factors. He could conceive of how a businessman was entitled to run his business any way he chooses, so long as that way was within the law.

He could see how an employee had the right, although a rather feeble right under our laws, to voice a reasonable request for better working conditions or higher pay, but the right of a customer in the determining of employment policy was an unknown and fearsome factor in his equation, one which he finally decided had no place there at all.

He did not administer justice in the case, but I do believe that he tried to administer the law. His knowledge of the law, however, is apparently not such as teaches him to weigh the forces of hunger, moral decay, idealism, and lack of employment opportunity when making a decision.

His honor, the judge, seated in a downtown court where the heat is turned on all winter, couldn't get a mental picture of Pennsylvania Avenue with its high school students wearing white shoes in snow storms, ostensibly because it was a fad, in reality because they had no work and couldn't get money to buy others.

Judge Owens pays for what he gets, and he expects only the thing that he has purchased in return for his money. He, therefore, could not be expected to appreciate the necessity of symbiotic business that not only gives the poor man what he purchases but also gives him work. [15]

Mitchell's disappointment was only short-lived. Four years later, in the Washington, D.C., case, *New Negro Alliance* v. *Sanitary Grocery Company*, the U.S. Supreme Court upheld the right of blacks to picket. The Supreme Court held that the picketing was the result of a labor dispute, so the alliance had a right to picket. Representing the NAACP were attorneys Edward P. Lovett, James M. Nabritt, Jr., Theodore M. Berry, and Thurgood Marshall. Mitchell in later years would become closely associated with those pioneers of civil rights law as well as with John A. Davis, a young political scientist and resident of Washington, who one day suddenly decided to picket the Sanitary Grocery Company store, thus setting in motion events that resulted in the landmark case. [16]

The ruling opened the way in the struggle. Mitchell recalled, "Somebody suddenly realized that blacks couldn't get jobs as street cleaners and as social workers in welfare programs. These also became targets." Street-cleaning jobs were awarded through "blatantly political" and "highly discriminatory" systems. Mitchell, as well as other members of his generation and an increasing number of older strategists, realized that "it was possible to surmount what at that time seemed insurmountable." Though blacks could find work in the construction industry before the stock market crash in 1929, they were confined to the most menial and low-paying jobs. Blacks encountered such discrimination even on government-financed housing projects. So, many other battles were launched during the 1930s to get work for black carpenters, bricklayers, painters, plasterers, plumbers, electricians, and workers in other trades. [17]

The limited gains that were made caused Mitchell to realize that if they were to be permanent, he and his generation would have to fight even harder to preserve them while also improving on them. Rather than being lulled into a false sense of security, he became more vigilant. Most important, despite his notable difference with Du Bois on religious grounds, he and other blacks shared the sage's view that the real emancipation of the black race in America has not yet been accomplished. Emancipation means: first, a chance to earn a living under modern conditions, and afterwards, a consequent freedom of spirit and effort for life itself. It meant that in 1863. It means it even more today when the economic snarls of civilization are far greater than ever before. Whether we think of politics or art, of religion or education, we have got to think of income, of wages and salary, and rents. And until Negroes in America have an assured and permanent place in American industry, they will still be serfs; they will still be disfranchised. They will still be inefficient with only limited powers of spiritual expression.[18]

As a product of Maryland's Jim Crow public school system, Mitchell took a strong interest in the epic desegregation struggle. He eagerly watched as Maryland, under the direction of Charles Hamilton Houston, formerly vice dean of the Howard University Law School, and his protégé Thurgood Marshall, became the successful testing ground for the NAACP's assaults on segregation in public education and discrimination in teachers' salaries. As Houston stressed, those actions were "indissolubly linked with all the other major activities of the association." Those, notably, included the antilynching fight, the NAACP's broad economic program, and the other civil rights programs involving suffrage, free speech, jury service, and transportation facilities. As Houston maintained:

> The N.A.A.C.P. recognizes the fact that the discriminations which the Negro suffers in education are merely part of the general pattern of race prejudice in American life, and it knows that no attack on discrimination in education can have any far reaching effect unless it is bound to a general attack on discrimination and segregation in all phases of American life.[19]

The jump in black college enrollment from 5,231 in 1922 to 22,609 in 1932 increased pressure from blacks for entry into graduate and professional schools in the border states and the South, where they were barred. Houston, as the NAACP's chief counsel, launched the attack on the South's Jim Crow college system in 1935 by suing the University of Maryland in an attempt to gain admission for Donald Gaines Murray to that institution's law school. Houston's ultimate goal was the abolition of segregation at all levels of public education, from nurseries to universities.

The case was a cause célèbre for oppressed minorities and began Houston's practice of using Maryland as the locus for filing lawsuits; he felt that Baltimore's vibrant, courageous NAACP branch and fighting press were important allies and improved his chances of winning such cases. The Murray case also represented the first of Houston's great victories in combatting pervasive legal segregation in other areas such as housing and labor. Houston's approach was a systematic one, based on selecting cases with clear legal issues, overturning negative precedents, and developing strong community or mass interest in each case. Consequently, the courtroom during the trial of the Murray case was packed. Juanita recalls, "He would call Mama. 'Miss Lillie, I'll be over. Get me a crowd. We'll be in so and so courtroom.'" Then Lillie Carroll Jackson would get other NAACP branch activists to begin making telephone calls. Houston also worked variations of this approach. For example, he encouraged Baltimore's NAACP leaders, whom he especially admired, to file other antidiscrimination suits and the NAACP made its resources available to him.[20]

Assigned to cover the Murray trial in the Baltimore City Court, Mitchell, learning of the decision on June 18, 1935, ran a tortuous, uphill twelve-block route all the way from the courthouse to the *Afro-American*'s office to write that history had been made when Judge Eugene O'Dunne granted a writ of mandamus requiring the regents of the university to admit Murray at once. His page-one story gave a clear and detailed account of the courtroom drama and the constitutional issues at stake and revealed Mitchell's joy over the victory. "From the beginning, in the early hours of the morning, to the close at 5 p.m.—past normal closing time—the case was a sharp interchange of legal argument and court wit." Mitchell brimmed with pride upon witnessing the superior conduct of the three black lawyers handling the case. From the opening of the hearing, it was clear that Charles T. LeViness III, the white assistant attorney general, was no match for them.

Judge O'Dunne asked LeViness, "Does the State of Maryland establish the reason of race as a cause for barring Mr. Murray from the University?" LeViness responded, "Yes. It is public policy of this state to exclude colored from schools attended by whites and to maintain a separate system of education."

Mitchell was astonished to hear LeViness contend that until recently, there had been no demand for higher education by blacks. He personally knew otherwise; demand had long existed. It was just that blacks like himself and Marshall had known it was futile to apply, so most potential students never bothered to try getting into the state-funded university. LeViness told the court that the legislature had passed the 1935 law creating a Commission on Higher Education for Negroes in response to "growing demand." In addition to Princess Anne Academy, the other higher education facility for blacks was Morgan College. Although Dr. Raymond A. Pearson, president of the University of Maryland, maintained that Princess Anne provided equal education, he was forced to acknowledge inequalities in the teaching staff, equipment, and general administration. "Finally," Mitchell reported, "under a cross-fire of questioning by Dr. Houston, Dr. Pearson said that he—when denying Mr. Murray entrance— knew that the applicant had little more than a hope of getting any financial assistance for education from the state." The most damaging admission from university officials, however, was that the state provided no alternative in- stitution for black applicants like Murray who wanted to study law.

Mitchell proudly reported that Marshall during the arguments before Judge O'Dunne had raised one of the central issues of the *Gong Lum* v. *Rice* case. There, in denying Martha Lum's plea for admission to a white school, Chief Justice William Howard Taft had taken special pains to point out that the Court was bound to assume that there was a school to which a nonwhite girl might conveniently go. Had her petition mentioned that she had no alternative school in her neighborhood, the outcome would have been different. Marshall also cited the *Piper* v. *Big Pine School District* case in which a fifteen-year-old Indian girl in California won admission to a white state public school because no provision had been made for equal Indian education. Such disparity was ruled to be a violation of the Fourteenth Amendment.

Without leaving the bench, Judge O'Dunne that same day ordered the University of Maryland to admit Murray because his Fourteenth Amend- ment rights had been violated. As Marylanders saw it, freedom bells were ringing loudly. Mitchell spoke for many blacks, no doubt the majority, when he said that he previously had thought such a decision impossible. But from that time, he later recalled, "I could see tremendous significance for the law and I could see countless situations where injustice could be corrected by application of the law."[21]

The *Afro-American,* while celebrating Donald Gaines Murray's victory, the same day also underscored another prevailing sore point, involving une- qual teachers' salaries. The editorial revealed publisher Carl Murphy's im- patience with blacks who were afraid to challenge discrimination by sharply criticizing the Maryland State Colored Teachers Association. Murray's vic- tory, the editorial said, "should make every thinking citizen boil with concern" that the Colored Teachers Association had not challenged the une- qual salary system on behalf of its members. "Like the five foolish virgins, the association slumbers and sleeps. The citizens are still interested, the money is still available" for the teachers wishing to make the challenge. Thurgood Marshall the following year took charge of the NAACP's legal drive for equalization of teachers' salaries. The resulting victories in Mary- land and throughout the South further served to strengthen Mitchell's faith in the law: "Inexorably, the blacks of Maryland and many of their friends of other races and religious faiths worked to end these injustices."[22]

CHAPTER FIVE

A Man Is Molded

L ike many others of his race who were looking for answers to the social and economic plight of African Americans during the 1930s, Mitchell saw politics as an appropriate field for involvement and action. But neither the Republicans nor Democrats accepted black candidates. So Mitchell turned to the Socialist party, running on the state ticket in 1934 for a seat in the Maryland House of Delegates.

Mitchell was never a Socialist, but he considered himself "closer to the Socialists because they represented the best people in town." Those he admired were intellectual humanists, "all very nice people," he felt. He knew Norman Thomas, having met the Socialist party standard-bearer when he spoke at a City-Wide Young People's Forum meeting in Baltimore. But it was Elisabeth Coit Gilman of Baltimore who encouraged him to run for office. She was a fearless political reformer, a mugwump in the tradition of her father, Daniel Coit Gilman, the first president of Johns Hopkins University. They represented the old intellectual gentry and might have been Republicans had they not been so independent.

During the early part of the Depression, Gilman had established the Open Forum for the airing of ideas and concerns in discussion sessions at her home, and the Community Workshop for the Unemployed, a self-help group. She had won notoriety in 1928 when she presented a dinner for Oswald Garrison Villard, editor of *The Nation* and one of the founders of the NAACP, in celebration of the tenth anniversary of his liberal publication. Because no hotel would permit the sixteen white and six black guests to dine together, she had held the dinner at her home in the oldest section of Baltimore's stately Park Avenue. She personified her motto: "When you see a thing that's right, do it." America, however, was not ready for such a happening. She was pilloried from Baltimore to the farthest corner of the nation. Mitchell greatly admired her boldness and integrity. Gilman was like Lillie Carroll Jackson in those qualities. Furthermore, in Mitchell's view the Socialists under Norman Thomas had adopted a strong pro-civil-rights stand. They were poor vote getters, however. Gilman had received 3,059 votes when she ran for governor of Maryland in 1930. Thomas got 10,489 votes in Maryland when he ran for President in 1932.

Mitchell, nevertheless, welcomed the opportunity to run for public office because, he later recalled, "I couldn't get the Democrats or Republicans to give me any support," and the Communists were "very repulsive. Their arrogance always turned me off." Even while using the Socialist party label, "I was just running independent." He did not want to be identified too closely with the Socialists. Consequently, some people "got very angry with me," because he refused fully to support the ticket headed by Dr. Broadus Mitchell, a well-known Johns Hopkins University professor running for governor, and Gilman, a candidate for the U.S. Senate.

Mitchell's rebellion against racial discrimination by political parties was in good tradition. Angered because the Republican party gave no patronage to blacks and demonstrated no other form of appreciation for their faithful support, W. Ashbie Hawkins, the prominent black Baltimore lawyer, had run as a spoiler in 1920 against Republican party boss Ovington Weller for the U.S. Senate. The 6,538 votes Hawkins received were insufficient to prevent Weller from beating the Democratic incumbent because he was crippled by an overpowering challenge from another Democratic party member. But Hawkins made his point. Seven years earlier, Arthur E. Briscoe, a black attorney, had lost a bid on the Republican ticket for a seat in the fourth legislative district by a mere 30 votes out of a total of 9,300. Now after staging a strong primary challenge in 1934, Briscoe was again running in the fourth district against the regular GOP candidate.[1]

Border state Maryland was as racially schizophrenic in politics as in any other area. Blacks comprised 17.7 percent of the population between the two world wars, giving the state the fourth-largest minority population in the nation. They could, in some districts and in close state elections, represent the balance of power. Yet "blacks were not too highly regarded by other blacks if they were Democrats," Mitchell recalled. That reality got him into trouble in 1932 when he voted Democratic. He found that the "general feeling" among blacks was "that anybody who wasn't a Republican was somehow or other a kind of questionable character." Consequently, "I had a Republican ward committee wait on me because I voted for President Roosevelt—my first vote at age twenty-one" after graduating from

Lincoln University. In Mitchell's precinct, "somehow or other, they had a way of finding out how you voted," and the committee wanted to know his reason for jumping ship. He discovered that what he had done "was something akin to treason."

Despite the opprobrium he suffered, Mitchell and a few other independent-minded blacks signaled a growing revolt against the party that had been identified since the Civil War as the friend of blacks. That snowball would become an avalanche by 1936. Furthermore, abandonment of Republican ranks by blacks was a clear message that they no longer could be taken for granted. Lincoln's legacy alone could not hold them. They wanted meaningful responses to their economic and social needs. They saw the period of intense social ferment of the early 1930s as opportune for direct action. By running as a Socialist, Mitchell was registering a protest not only against the Republicans but also the Democrats.[2]

His campaign was an appeal to conscience. He welcomed assurances from Harry W. Nice, the Republican gubernatorial candidate, that he was for the abolition of Jim Crow laws and the establishment of higher education facilities for blacks. But Nice angered him at a meeting by telling a group of blacks in the same breath that he did not believe in social equality. Some other blacks who were present applauded Nice. Mitchell, chastising them in his *Baltimore Afro-American* column, said they were supposed to be intelligent, yet they did not seem to realize that "social equality means having the right to share as an equal citizen all of the privileges to which Americans are entitled." He was outraged when John Webster Smith, another GOP contestant, said that he did not want black policemen and firemen. He similarly questioned the assertion by Mayor Howard D. Jackson of Baltimore that he did not know blacks could not attend the University of Maryland—and Jackson was challenging Governor Albert Ritchie, a fellow Democrat, for the governor's mansion. Ritchie himself had proved that "he is not going to run counter to the Eastern Shore mob spirit or any other kind of spirit that suppressed colored people."

Mitchell concluded that "the Democrats are a lot of high pressure artists, who will tolerate gambling dens, drinking dives, and houses of prostitution, but refuse to support anything that means uplift and justice." In contrast, he lambasted the Republicans as "a bunch of shilly-shallying reprobates who need to undergo a complete metamorphosis." He urged his readers to vote, "but let the persons for whom votes are cast know that the only reason they get support is because the ballot caster takes the least objectionable from a field that is all bad." When he saw that he could not abide by his own advice to others, he presented himself as a protest choice.[3]

The *Afro-American* announced Mitchell's candidacy along with that of seventeen Marylanders that October in a column abutting Mitchell's on the editorial page. Mitchell, meanwhile, continued presenting his regular weekly "Observations and Reflections" column right through the election while campaigning from an office that Lillie Carroll Jackson had given him. The newspaper's undeviating support for him and the two other Socialist candidates was another measure of the publication's crusading spirit.

"How much longer," he demanded in his typewritten campaign flyer, "shall we, the colored people of Baltimore, stand for the gross injustices which are daily being forced upon us?" He cited as examples the state's appropriation of over $1 million a year to the University of Maryland, while Morgan College received "a pitiful $26,000." Furthermore, the flyer claimed, "our colored boys are beaten, shot and hired out like slaves" at Cheltenham, the state reform school. "We have no state Sanatorium for the Feebleminded and Insane. And we suffer from many other injustices." The root of the problem, he felt, was that "in the three hundred years [sic] history of Maryland we have had no colored representative to plead our cause in the Maryland Legislature." He counseled that blacks "can correct this evil by voting for a representative of their own race." He maintained that he was the "only colored candidate" in the fifth district for the legislature and urged residents to register, providing the address, date, and time for doing so. He concluded with a plea for support and promised that "I shall at all times prove worthy of your trust." He signed off with, "Yours for JUSTICE, Clarence M. Mitchell."[4]

Predictably, Mitchell and his Socialist running mates lost. His only regret, and it was echoed by the *Afro-American* in an editorial, was that black Baltimoreans missed "the best opportunity in the history of the city to send a representative to the House of Delegates," all because they voted a straight Republican party ticket. There were more than 16,000 black voters in the district. Arthur Briscoe, the likely black winner, lost by a mere 549 votes out of 10,925 that were cast. At the same time, Mitchell found consolation in the opportunity to say a caustic farewell in his column to Ritchie as he relinquished office to the Republicans following his defeat by Nice:

> Ethics, feelings and friendships were sacrificed on the altar when Democrats of Baltimore marched in the parade that was being reviewed jointly by Nice and Ritchie carrying signs announcing their wish to "crush the Ritchie machine."
>
> Ritchie must be a gentleman because through it all he never changed color nor winked back a tear. His house of cards came tumbling down about his ears, but he met the collapse like a colonial landlord.[5]

Comparing the destruction of black Baltimoreans' economic base to the national scope of the Depression, Mitchell found no comfort. Indeed, he and other blacks had cause for alarm over the volatile national atmosphere. Until the Depression, blacks were the principal source of common labor in Baltimore. They held a virtual monopoly in fertilizer and chemical factories, in steel mills, on road work, on street railroads, and as servants, janitors, and waiters because those were the least desirable forms of work. Normally, 676 out of every 1,000 blacks ten years of age and older were gainfully employed compared to 543 of 1,000 for the remaining population. In March 1934, however, 40 percent of black families were on relief compared to 13 percent of white families. Of the total population, 42.2 percent of families on relief were black, even though blacks were only 17.7 percent of the population. Whites had displaced blacks in every job category, even as domestic servants. Furthermore, New Deal programs, like the National Recovery Administration, were helping to institutionalize racial discrimination in the South and other regions by accepting the differential or prevailing wage systems under which blacks were paid less than whites for the same work.

The unemployment crisis was compounded by the white worker's view of blacks as a threat. By early 1935, only a few short weeks after President Roosevelt had won a resounding vote of confidence in the midterm elections, euphoria had turned to frustration. A forthright President had suddenly become indecisive. The magic of governmental action had disappeared. The country was faced with economic, political, and constitutional stalemates. Despite the New Deal's initial success in saving the nation from disaster and moving it forward, 10.5 million workers were still jobless.

The national mood was one of rebelliousness; the old order had been discredited, and no one was certain about the form or shape of its replacement. The New Deal was being consumed, as it were, by its own success in saving the nation from disaster. The climate was thus ripe for exploitation by local fascist demagogues spouting their social and economic nostrums to the ignorant and insecure. The best known of these were Father Charles E. Coughlin, radio priest of Detroit with an audience of at least ten million and founder of the National Union for Social Justice; Governor Floyd Olson of Minnesota, who preached "the gospel of government and collective ownership of the means of production and distribution" for the "happiness of the masses"; Dr. Francis Everett Townsend, the old-age pensioner; and Louisiana's Senator Huey "Kingfish" Long, who saw his Share Our Wealth movement as an alternative to the programs of the major political parties. Long was the unmistakable leader of the "swelling thunder on the left." Complementing the political mélange were several renowned intellectuals, led by such social theorists as John Dewey and Reinhold Niebuhr, and the "revolutionary conservatives," or "radicals of the right," who were certainly not fascists but were nonetheless agitating against established mores.

Mitchell was convinced that "we were on the verge of a revolution." So were other blacks, who expressed their fears about a fascist takeover in such publications as *The Crisis,* the NAACP's monthly journal. The *Pittsburgh Courier* found it "significant that neither the priest nor the senator has had anything to say of particular interest to the Negro." Long had "talked about 'niggers,' but even that is more than Coughlin has said."

As one celebrated academician revealed many years later during a symposium on the Roosevelt administration, not everyone appreciated the danger. Mitchell, though, had no doubt American democracy was in trouble. He said, "Anyone who heard Governor Floyd Olson up in Minnesota saying that, 'if what we are seeing now is evidence of capitalism, I hope it goes right down to hell,' would know we were on the brink of upheaval which probably would have destroyed this country as we know it." Furthermore, he went on,

> when I think of the speeches that I heard Huey Long make, when I think of Father Coughlin coming on the radio talking about the South, saying "the darkies are no longer singing in the cotton field," when I think of all the rhetoricians who were stirring up the discontented, it certainly [did] not require any great stretch of the imagination to know that if Mr. Roosevelt hadn't done something to give people relief, the farmers who were being faced with mortgage foreclosures and stood in the way of sheriffs executing orders [would have rebelled].

The danger, of course, was not lost on Roosevelt. In an allusion to fascism in Germany and Italy, he expressed fears that the American "people are jumpy and very ready to run after strange gods."[6]

Mitchell was never one of those running after strange gods, so he rejected revolution. He and other young black leaders felt that despite the strong emphasis during the Depression on jobs, their struggle encompassed much more than economic survival. While still a Lincoln University senior, Mitchell, at a seminar sponsored by Elisabeth Coit Gilman, had declared, "It is quite plain that if we are to eliminate prejudice, fighting is not the way to do so. We must 'Americanize' ourselves to a greater degree than we have already done."

Self-assured and determined, his generation was eager to assume responsibility for its destiny. Mitchell felt the problem was that "we have not organized our forces." He was challenged by the ironic reality that a Reverend Mr. Becton, who was conducting evangelistic meetings at Bethel AME Church, could "with a message of religious nature . . . get enough crowds and money to support himself and his followers in luxury, but our schools depend on white philanthropy and our children must seek livelihood under menial conditions." Blacks, he observed, "cry for stores and business; we wrangle over railroad segregation in the South; and we never stop to ask where is the money, that is necessary for business, coming from; or if the colored race was responsible for a large part of the railroad's income, would the attitude change?" He urged blacks to "organize in politics and in farming; in business and in education." Then "America (which is just as much ours as it is the property of the descendants of those white convicts in Georgia brought over by James Oglethorpe) will recognize that its sleeping black tenants are awake and must be reckoned with."

At the same time, Juanita Jackson, as president of the City-Wide Young People's Forum, declared, "I believe that our way to a firm foundation in the economic, intellectual and social fields of America does not lie through radicalism [that is, communism] . . . [or] physical rebellion." She believed first in God. "We must fight—yes! But our Arms must be those which I believe the Christ, who has been acclaimed the leader of all ages, would use." Those weapons were education, economic stability, and self-sufficiency. Looking back many years later, she explained, "We liked the NAACP as a channel . . . [because of its] approach for working within the system, working within the law."

Mitchell's and Juanita's attitudes reflected a confidence and hope in the American democratic system of government that was held by most of the principal black leaders. In contrast, the liberal *New Republic,* in a June 1935 editorial, expressed the despair that was widely shared by many of the ideologues of the period: "Either the nation must put up with the confusions and miseries of an essentially unregulated capitalism, or it must prepare to supersede capitalism with socialism. There is no longer a feasible middle course." Most blacks, however, were more sober and sought friends, with the NAACP's help, among the administrators of the New Deal. Voicing blacks' overriding fear in his widely reported speech at the NAACP conference in St. Louis, Walter White warned that "unless justice is given the Negro, he may be driven to desperation and the use of force." In the same breath, however, he prayed to God "that this may never happen, as we know all weapons are in the hands of those who deny us a chance."[7]

As second-class citizens, blacks had learned from birth to cope with adversity. Economic catastrophe now only reinforced their faith in their ability to meet temporal crises, no matter how severe, and strengthened their belief in God and their own ability to control their own destiny with the help of the Church and organizations such as the NAACP. The black press and predominantly black institutions provided blacks in all walks of life with leadership and a sense of society and of protection from adversity resulting from race.

Thus life for Mitchell, as he contemplated his future, was a philosophical chess game. He had seen enough to describe himself as "the only human barometer in the world." With that instrument, he judged the weaknesses and strengths of others. What he had seen was not comforting. The great challenge, he concluded, was not to dream but to meet the inevitable disillusionment that follows the fulfillment of the dream. In short:

> Every poor man dreams of how he might be a king, but in attaining his end discovers that beneath the crown is a thorn and under purple robes pulses the unsatisfied heart.
> Numerous fools want to be wise, but each, as he acquires wisdom, discovers that the new possession brings with it the companionship of responsibility—and the jester in a philosopher's garb, sighs for the cap and bells.[8]

Had she not found a national forum for venting her passion for human dignity, Juanita Jackson was certain she would have become a missionary. Her dedication to serving humanity was as strong as Mitchell's, and that shared ideal was the foundation of their love. He had captured her heart just before she returned in 1934 to the University of Pennsylvania to work for a year for her master's degree in sociology.

Jackson was an active member of the Sharp Street Methodist Episcopal Church. The Methodist Church, still suffering from the debilitating conflicts that had occurred within its midst over how it should regard the slavery issue that had racked it from its establishment in the United States in 1784, was divided into three branches—the Methodist Episcopal Church, the Methodist Episcopal Church-South, and the Methodist Protestant Church—as a means of satisfying those who wanted to uphold the institution of human subjugation and those who opposed it.

During three successive summers beginning in 1933 Juanita traveled extensively throughout the country for the Bureau of Negro Work and the Department of Young People's Work of the Methodist Episcopal Church, speaking and teaching courses on race relations. That work was a welcome respite from teaching in Baltimore's public schools, which she did between 1931 and 1934. She was invited to attend a 1934 conference of the Church's Department of Epworth League and Young People's Work in Evanston, Illinois, where the National Council of Methodist Youth was being organized, and she was elected vice president of the new group. Even though only 18 of the 1,012 youths attending were black, she set the conference on fire by encouraging the youths to work against lynching, Jim Crow, and other forms of discrimination. The youths "went right down the line and supported everything the NAACP was doing to break down racial discrimination and segregation."

The Methodist youths took a strong stand against the war that was then brewing in Europe, many being conscientious objectors who were "unalterably opposed to all types of military training, voluntary or compulsory," as well as to actual combat. Juanita thought the turmoil "was hell benevolent" as the youths, also demonstrating their very strong social concerns, conducted direct action campaigns against Jim Crow in Evanston. "We actually boycotted restaurants which refused to serve [blacks]. We weren't afraid," recalls Juanita. The tiny group of blacks won support from the large body of white students on the surrounding Northwestern University campus where they were meeting. Their militancy was fueled by the contradictions between America's war propaganda about freedom and its flagrant violations of democracy here at home.

The activities of the Methodist youth group presaged the founding of the Congress of Racial Equality (CORE) in Chicago in 1942 by members of the Christian pacifist Fellowship of Reconciliation and other young radicals with an ideological commitment to "interracialism" and the Gandhian principles of nonviolent direct action protests. Several of CORE's founders, including James Farmer, who would become a prominent civil rights leader in the 1960s, had very strong roots in Methodism. Others in the CORE vanguard would also be disillusioned NAACP youth leaders and Urban League supporters who believed, like one Methodist theology student, that discrimination "must be challenged directly, without violence or hatred, yet without compromise." (Another characteristic of the group was the belief that civil rights was a "human problem," as opposed to a "racial or black problem"—a belief that differed from the predominant view accentuated in later years by Bayard Rustin, another CORE founder, when he, too, reached prominence.)

While Church elders might have forgiven Juanita and her cohorts for their pacifism, they could not countenance their brazen attack on Jim Crow within the Church. The youths became a Trojan horse, with Juanita as the leading general, on the race issue. They boldly opposed a plan to unify the three branches of the Church, because the plan, which was an olive branch to the South, would only formalize segregation throughout the entire Church by setting aside a separate jurisdiction for blacks.

In 1936, with her stature considerably strengthened by having been appointed the NAACP's national youth organizer, Juanita took her crusade to the second conference of the National Council of Methodist Youth,

which now represented eighteen thousand Church groups, at Berea College
in Kentucky. Two thirds of the 750 conferees were youths, although not
everyone participated in the voting process. Black delegates had increased
to 26. Once more, the youths expressed strong opposition to Church unification and voted against it 466 to 16. When they demanded that the
adults, too, express their views on the plan, their elders voted against it 97
to 20.

The Church hierarchy was ready, nevertheless, for Juanita Jackson and
her radical cohorts. "Wherever I went," she recalls, people "would talk
about my being vice president of the National Council of Methodist
Youth." That popularity and esteem were "too much for the Methodists to
take." They kicked out not only Juanita, but also the two white leaders—
Dr. Blaine E. Kirkpatrick, secretary of the Department of Epworth League
and Young People's Work, and his assistant, Dr. Owen Geer—who had
discovered her and encouraged her rebellion. So, even though the youths
slowed unification and won their war of conscience—the spiritual contest—their elders won the political battle. Unification was approved in
1939. Segregation was extended officially within the Methodist Church for
another thirty years, well past the peak of the later phase of the civil rights
movement and after Jim Crow barriers had fallen in the South.

The lessons of that struggle were not lost on Mitchell. Afterward, he
had a better understanding of the difficulty of bringing about racial change
even within his Church. Furthermore, although Juanita's immediate campaign involved segregation among Methodists, she was also concerned with
the broad realm of Christian churches, which, with few exceptions, were
reinforcing society's racial attitudes. Had she been able to achieve a definite
commitment from the Methodists to end Jim Crow, that action, in conjunction with the creation of the series of Catholic Interracial Councils that
began in New York City in 1934, would have helped to speed awakening
within other denominations to the problem of racial oppression.

Juanita's ties with the NAACP were cemented in 1935, when Walter
White won the NAACP national board of directors' approval to hire her as
his special assistant in order to help develop the association's national youth
program. After spending two months in New York learning the operations
of the national office, she began filling speaking engagements; developing a
fund-raising program among wealthy contributors, churches, clubs, and
other organizations; and organizing junior NAACP branches and college
chapters throughout the country.

The NAACP's national office was in a loft in downtown New York
City, at 69 Fifth Avenue, near Fourteenth Street. Juanita occupied the
same office that had been used by Mary White Ovington, one of the founders of the NAACP. Next to her were the association's legal strategists,

Charles Houston and Thurgood Marshall, who shared an office. William Pickens's and Walter White's offices were on the same floor, as was *The Crisis*'s office, which had been occupied by Roy Wilkins since Du Bois's departure. Juanita was the youngest member of that top echelon of NAACP leaders.

She won support from other black leaders by helping them build their own organizations. Notably, that December, she joined Mary McLeod Bethune, mother confessor of the movement, in the founding conference of the National Council of Negro Women. She was a good friend of the older woman, whose dynamic personality ensured large crowds every year when she addressed the City-Wide Young People's Forum in Baltimore.

Juanita found eager constituencies wherever she went. Junior NAACP branches had existed for many years, but not as a coordinated national network with a clear and comprehensive program. Walter White further demonstrated his genius for leadership by giving her a full mandate not only to expand the NAACP's youth memberships to include ages twelve through twenty-five, but also to create a formal division for that age group with its own constitution, which Juanita wrote. White wanted to involve youths in social issues that affected their lives, obtain their insights and energies, and train them as citizens and future leaders. He also saw great political advantage in utilizing their vision. Their radicalism, properly harnessed and channeled, was essential to awakening the more conservative adults and pushing them to be more progressive.

At the twenty-seventh annual NAACP convention in Baltimore in the summer of 1936, Juanita translated the mandate White had given her into a triumph. Working that spring in the national office with youth council representatives, she developed plans for a separate youth program that would be held in conjunction with the adult convention. From Baltimore, Mitchell conducted a vigorous publicity program through *The Crisis,* which was featuring a "Youth Council News" column for its national audience, and the *Afro-American.*

Juanita presented a program to the 217 delegates that was centered on four basic problems: education, jobs, civil liberties, and lynching. She charged the youths with developing strategies for implementing clearly established goals in these areas. "We are ready," she said, "to plunge into the struggle for the equal right to learn, to work, to live." A formal pledge of the youth division declared its awareness "of the type of society in which we live—an order governed by the ruthless profit motive—which, for its continued existence, pits race against race, foments bitterness and hatred between them, and whips up fierce occupational competition for the further exploitation of both." The youths regarded Jim Crowism and political, educational, and economic inequalities as "simply methods for enforcing racial exploitation." They pledged to work through the NAACP to achieve fundamental rights for the nation's twelve million black citizens.

Juanita capped her development of the NAACP youth movement by gaining acceptance of the Reverend James H. Robinson, a young activist, as a member of the NAACP national board of directors, thus establishing a tradition. Her activities were also influencing Mitchell's choice of a career.[9]

Mitchell and Jackson told no one about their engagement in 1934 because the young man first wanted to get a job in order to be able to support a family. Juanita recalls, he began "working on" winning her heart the previous year. "Everybody kept telling him, 'You will never get her.'" He was determined to make her as proud of him as he was of her. His job as an *Afro-American* reporter and columnist had given him a sound professional start, but he wanted a better-paying and more challenging job.

He was at this time also a member of the executive boards of both the NAACP and the Baltimore Urban League. Aware of his professional ambition, the executive secretary of this local league advised him to apply for an Urban League fellowship. He did so and in 1937 won one for a year's graduate study at the Atlanta School for Social Work. This was his third objective, which he welcomed as "a great opportunity." His first objective, of course, was winning Juanita. ("I did that slowly but surely," he later admitted in a letter to Juanita outlining his plans, "and now you are all my own") His second objective was getting his transcript from Lincoln University. That was a problem since he still owed the school money. Nevertheless, he accomplished it "through God's good love and the simple statement of facts." He was confident, he told Juanita, that with her love and support "we will win."

Because she believed in him, he told her, he found himself "thinking and doing things I would never otherwise dream of doing." His ultimate dream, he said, was to "be able to hold you in my arms, kiss your lips when I want to and be all that you could wish to love." For such a beautiful dream to "come true, one had to work hard and suffer much." He loved the challenge. For he had found that "when one dreams one beautiful dream" and had found the one whom he wanted, nothing should stop him from winning her heart. "So whatever else there is before me now is your dream not mine—I will work in Atlanta." He promised to "take all available honors, and all by fair means." On the Sunday before he left for Atlanta, "I want to go to church with you and after that to our hill to talk and take a tender farewell together, for I love you with all my heart." While away, "my prayers darling, will always be able to leap the space from wherever I am to God—and he, my sweet, always grants the worthy ones."

Once more, Mitchell was venturing into the heart of the Old Confederacy, into "an environment I hate cordially." This time, his stay would
be much more prolonged than his first visit to the South in 1933 to cover
the trials of the Scottsboro Boys in Decatur, Alabama. His year-long experience in Atlanta would harden his resolve to fight for the total obliteration
of racial discrimination. He would study sociological principles that would
help him understand what W. J. Cash meant in *The Mind of the South* when
he said that the relationship between whites and blacks in the region was
"organic." There, said Cash, "Negro entered into white man as profoundly
as white man entered into Negro—subtly influencing every gesture, every
word, every emotion and idea, every attitude." But, although both races
were debased and dehumanized by the process, it was the black man who
suffered more, from the anguish of second-class citizenship.

Mitchell rebelled most forcefully against attempts to transform him
into the caricatured southern Negro. For the whole year that he lived in
Atlanta, to prove himself superior to those who had created and maintained
the Jim Crow system, and to avoid suffering the humiliations of racism, he
walked rather than ride the streetcar. The world in which he lived was
small. It was composed primarily of the home where he boarded and the
rich society of the Atlanta School of Social Work. Eventually he extended it
to include the Atlanta NAACP branch.

His rebellion against Jim Crow won national attention when he single-
handedly challenged a group of American Legionnaires and Ku Kluxers
who disrupted a meeting of the southern regional conference of the
NAACP in Atlanta. As the leader of the more than thirty whites who
broke into the NAACP meeting began the usual black-baiting attacks,
charging the organization with being Communist, Mitchell strode forth
and verbally challenged and chastised the group. Startled and nonplussed,
the invaders departed.

"Maybe what the South needs is more of the kind of courage and plain
speaking which Mr. Mitchell demonstrated," the *Afro-American* observed
back in Baltimore. "There used to be an old saying: 'Speak up, you're not
in Georgia now.' Maybe it should be changed to: 'Speak up, you ARE in
Georgia now.'" Walter White wrote Mitchell to express his thanks and
admiration. Having witnessed the unbelievable violence that accompanied
the riot of 1906 in his hometown, White understood the full extent of
Mitchell's daring. "It is that kind of courage and intelligence which makes
the N.A.A.C.P. the power that it is, and God knows, as you have probably
learned in Atlanta—perhaps also in Baltimore—we need a great deal more
of it." He featured Mitchell's action in the NAACP's national press releases
so that the young man's "fine stand will be an inspiration to others."

As Mitchell was bold, so was he intolerant of cowardice in others. "Since I have become a resident here," he wrote Juanita,

> I find that many people do a lot of big talking but few, if any, stand up in the face of a real crisis.
>
> On Friday a little boy of fourteen was given twenty years on the chain gang for being in a children's argument which had a fatal ending. I expected that *The Atlanta World* would blast the matter editorially, but it did not. Instead, it just let the opportunity pass, so to speak.
>
> You see, darling, I have a deep-rooted sense of newspaper ethics. I believe that papers really mold a community and its opinions. For that reason, I divide all papers into two classes: those which are papers and those which are not. Atlanta has no newspaper. None of those here print the real truth and write truly justice-loving editorials.

In contrast to the crusading *Afro-American,* which he admired, Mitchell was sorry to find the *Atlanta World* "especially complacent." He felt that "colored people of this city will never be fighters unless they get a policy at *The World* which will be one of fearlessness and fair-play." He was similarly disgusted with the Atlanta NAACP branch after seeing it almost drop a legal case "because of a jelly-back expression on the part of the branch lawyer" who had advised the local leaders to withdraw. What Atlanta needed, he told Juanita, were people who voted and a Lillie Carroll Jackson to awaken them. "Gee, things would really be constantly hot."

To try to transform that dream into reality, he entered the election for president of the Atlanta NAACP branch, despite his earlier promise to himself not to become involved in any activity other than his studies. Juanita was his inspiration in this cause. She encouraged him to run, and spent several days in the city helping him generate enough support and new memberships to win. An added reward was that they had a rare chance to spend an evening alone together before the fire. Moreover, because their betrothal was secret, Mitchell spent some amusing moments after she had returned to Baltimore listening to other young men's longing discussion of her.

The Atlanta School of Social Work was created in 1920, the result of an idea first sown by Jesse O. Thomas, director of the Southern Regional Office of the National Urban League. Although Thomas was the catalyst, the school's roots dated back to the 1890s when Atlanta first attempted to build a black social welfare system based on the concept of neighborhood unions or cooperatives, and self-help. The founders maintained these cooperatives were needed because the city government was unconcerned with the needs of blacks. The resulting Atlanta Neighborhood Union conducted surveys based on models created by Du Bois for his classic study *The Philadelphia Negro*. The surveys documented the debilitating effects of white oppression on blacks and showed the need for a training facility, which became the Atlanta School of Social Work. E. Franklin Frazier, the prominent sociologist, served as the school's second director, thus helping to ensure its permanence. When Mitchell arrived there, the school's third director, Forrester B. Washington, was in the ninth year of his twenty-seven-year tenure. Washington, a black sociologist, understood that as a result of segregation, "black people have a different social background which has nothing to do with heredity and a great deal to do with environment." He forthrightly maintained that while there was no such thing as "black" social work, in the black community there were "some points of departure from social work among white people, other than the fact that it is done among people of a different color." Social workers in black communities needed to be aware that color itself was the cause of many maladjustments. Thus, the special programs that he was offering at the school were "apart from and in addition to the regular techniques" of social work.

Mitchell found Washington's insight priceless. After relating to Juanita a series of encounters with poor blacks on one of his regular field trips, which were filled with humor and pathos, he concluded:

> Through it all there was the conflict between the old and the new, the clean and the dirty, the glad and the sad. Darling, we just don't know our people—we're too educated. We can't feel the things they feel and learn the agonies they go through.
>
> We want luxury and comfort—while they freeze in alleys and count themselves lucky if they can dip out of a pot of stew. We talk about school or lack it. Why, darling, some of those people I talked with didn't know how to read their insurance policies. One woman found for the first time, when I told her, that she was paying for a $100 policy which she thought was for $250.

The poverty he encountered in Atlanta was, as in Alabama, much worse than anything he had experienced while growing up in urban Baltimore.

In addition to having considerable admiration and respect for Washington, Mitchell also found him interesting. "Today," he wrote his "Juanitalet," "in a meeting of the N.A.A.C.P., Mr. Washington introduced me as 'a brilliant radical young man who is one of the reasons why the first year class is outstanding.'" He begged Juanita to keep that news to herself ("I tell you about it only because it is just one of those little things modesty would permit me to share with *you only*").

The school year, with the exception of a rare visit or two from Juanita, had been for him one of endless longing. "I find all that I have ever dared to hope for flitting across your face in one tender smile. I have found all of the force a man could aspire to lying before me when I know that YOU love me." On occasion, his longing became so severe that he complained: "I feel so disorganized and unable to get myself together. I just can't study or anything. I don't know what's wrong with me—and, gee, I do have so much to do." He nevertheless endured, "so insufficient and incomplete." As June approached, he became increasingly anxious about job prospects. Getting a job so they could be married is "my whole concern and interest—not even school work claims as much attention as that."

It was natural, therefore, that he was crushed when Eugene Kinkle Jones, director of the National Urban League, informed him the organization had no suitable opening for him. "Be brave my own darling, for we shall yet win our objective," he consoled "My own Soldier Princess." "Darling, little captain—you, perhaps will think it strange that I write a letter to comfort you when it is I who have been defeated." But he wanted her to know that rather than giving up, he was determined more than ever to fight for their future. He told her that "from the very beginning, I have put God into this far more than I have told you." Even before he had gotten the fellowship, he had prayed not for that opportunity but "that God would show me the right way and give me the path that would lead our wedded life most quickly and surely." He had answered him then, and He would now in his present crisis. "I can do anything—God helping." Life, he said, was "good to me in many ways. I am alive and well in mind and body. I have perspective of the things beyond and things that have been—I can do anything that is good—and I shall."

He also told her, "I want God to act through you this time because I want you to know Him as I know Him. Darling, He is so real to me and so different from the way other people talk about Him." He assured her that "I love you enough to let you point out my destiny, when, perhaps, my mind is already made up on the way I shall or should go."

His prayers were answered when Mary McLeod Bethune, chairman of the New Deal's "Black Cabinet," an informal group of advisers, hired him to work for the National Youth Administration. Bethune was head of the NYA's Office of Negro Affairs. "Our job," Mitchell told his fiancée, "begins July 1." His salary was to be $100 a month, but in August it was raised to $150. Although he initially did not have a formal title, it soon became director of the Maryland office of the Division of Negro Affairs of the NYA. Bethune, who admired him considerably, told him, "You are to hold the most significant social work job in the state. Mitchell, I know that you can make good but keep your feet on the ground." Mitchell regarded this job only as a temporary assignment pending a better opportunity with the National Urban League.

Just before beginning the NYA job, he met with Eugene Kinkle Jones in Washington. Jones assured Mitchell unequivocally that there were "possibilities" for him in the Urban League. "Keep in touch with me," Jones told him. Faith was indeed moving mountains for him. He had risen from poverty through the love of his family, by the strength of confidence that others had in him, and through his trust in the God he never failed to serve. He had survived his biblical test in the wilderness, and now he was ready to do the work of his Father. His would be a mission of total dedication, supported by his only and true love, Juanita Jackson.[10]

Clarence Mitchell was beside himself with joy. He had asked Lillie Carroll Jackson for consent to marry her daughter, "AND SHE SAID 'YES,'" he wrote his fiancée. "Darling, she smiled and seemed just so much of a mother that I was supremely happy. I could have shouted." He said, "She thinks we ought to be able to get along well if we are thoughtful about the little things."

Their next big day was that Saturday, when he, his bride-to-be, her mother, and her father Keiffer Bowen Jackson would meet at Lillie Carroll Jackson's house for Mitchell to make his request formally. He could hardly wait to see her on Saturday with her engagement ring. But, most important, "PRECIOUS, WE'RE GOING TO BE MARRIED!!"

His last major hurdle was finally crossed. Throughout the two years that he had worked closely with Lillie Jackson in the Baltimore NAACP branch, Mitchell had faithfully supported her as she rebuilt the unit into a fighting machine. She, in turn, had respected him. But, like Mitchell, she wanted to be sure he found a job that would enable him to support a wife and family. Eventually aware that he and her daughter were in love, Lillie Jackson had extracted a promise from both of them that they would not consummate their relationship until they were married. "We had our very high moral standards," recalls Juanita. "She gave us moral guidance. We honored our commitment to ourselves and to her."

Mitchell's steady stream of love letters now reflected confidence about the future. That November, he had finally gotten the Urban League job as executive secretary of its St. Paul office in Minnesota. He was especially grateful for the "splendid letters of approval" that one unnamed Urban League official had sent in his behalf to the organization's board of directors. "This makes me grateful and eager to do the kind of job which will meet with the approval of the national office," he said. To Mary McLeod

Bethune, he submitted a warm letter of resignation from his position as director of the Maryland NYA office. She was not surprised that he was leaving so soon and welcomed his advice on how to strengthen the state NYA office he had been directing for less than six months.

Having won Juanita's love, he now proceeded to gain her total commitment to his philosophy of life. He included her so totally in his life that she became the focal point of his existence. His work and his destiny would be hers. He devoted the few months before their marriage to ensuring that their lives would become one. "The most powerful drive in my religious life is you," he told her. "When I first saw you, you were the unattainable." Her education, family, and standard of living, her appearance, her expectations—"everything was so far above me that sometimes I questioned myself on the wisdom of falling in love with you." But when she seemed so impossible to win and he was ready to give up, "there would always come the admonition, I say from heaven, telling me to pray." On countless nights, he wrestled with the torment of "allowing a fire to grow in me which seemed ready to consume me because the person it was to warm would not give it attention." Now it was such a glorious reality to realize "that you love me," so much so that "I predicate my entire life" and dreams "on you." To himself, he said, "if God has given me Juanita he will give me all else if I pray and it is good for me."

He expected that "St. Paul will be a hard field but then, darling, where is there an easy place?" He was "out to make a reputation" for himself. That would have been a difficult challenge even in Baltimore where he was liked. The problem, he felt, was that many people did not understand the Urban League, which was a social organization, in contrast to the NAACP, which was a legal and political activist organization. St. Paul would be a bigger challenge because "I will have the problem of living above the gossip of small town life." He still would be opening up opportunities in labor unions and "selling Negroes themselves on the unions." He was confident, nevertheless, that his social work training would enable him to overcome all obstacles. Somehow, he said, acknowledging his admittedly competitive nature, "I feel stronger in the face of a difficult situation than I do when the going is easy." As in his childhood, "people who oppose me arouse my fight—not physically necessarily but mentally and there are few things which please me more than outwitting opposition." He reminded her, however, that he never undertook any mission without first praying to God: "There must be something God wants us to do, and we are going to do it."

As their wedding date approached, Mitchell, who had set up bachelor's residence in St. Paul, learned the marriage vow by heart. "I repeat it whenever I feel lonesome," he told her. He thought about the meaning of marriage, and summarized it in the following letter—"By your Husband to Be":

As an ancient institution, marriage has figured widely in shaping the course of human lives, the destiny of empires and the growth of civilization. But, if there had never been a wedding before this, which we are now about to enter, I should still regard it as a profound and romantic occurrence in my life which will be unrivaled by any other single experience or group of experiences in my life either now or in the hereafter. I include the hereafter because marriage is not merely a physical union, but it is also a spiritual phenomenon.

In the physical sense, marriage will first mean the bestowal of my love, protection and honor on one woman—and on her only. It is impossible to live in company with other human beings without at some time having to face a choice of loyalties. For me the choice of loyalties is at the marriage altar. At that place I pledge my loyalty to my bride and no matter what the costs of this loyalty in the future it is hers forever and I will not permit a single act or work of mine to betray it. I will not permit a single friend, relative or institution to question the rightness of it. I shall place it before God when I place the ring on the finger of the woman I love and there it shall remain inviolate.

Further, I assume the responsibility of living in a way that my physical self will always be in a condition which will enable me to work and earn a living for my wife and our children. Since health is one of my tools, I must preserve it [so] that I will always be capable of defending my family from outside aggression of any kind—so long as I have life to do so.

I also assume the responsibility of doing all in my power to have children and to care for such children in a way that will give them every opportunity to enjoy a life better than that which I have had myself, not because my life has been so unpleasant, but because every father should presume that the generation which follows him will have more to build on than he had and for that reason should be offered higher objectives than he had at which to aim.

I must always keep my temper under control in my relations with my wife and I should never do anything which is calculated to annoy or to embarrass her. This should never be difficult because I love her and I sought her love of my own free will. I wooed her when she had no thought of loving me, I planted in her heart a seed which has grown into a rich flower of great beauty. Surely, then, the hand which planted a glorious rose, will not abuse it if growing thereon is some small thorn which pricks my fingers when I touch it. Rather, I shall rejoice that there is such rare fragrance from the petals, such glory in its hue and that some part of my very life's blood flowing from the wound shall find its way to the roots of my flower to make the soul richer and lure the plant to be more beautiful.

Finally, I shall even strive to perfect our spiritual union for therein shall I find the key to eternal life with her, to whom I have given the keeping of myself in my entirety. Surely in the midst of great and breathless beauty I have seen written the promise of immortality. Though there be foolish men who will "eat, drink and be merry because tomorrow they die," I *know* that there is God and the promise of eternal life to such as will have it. Having accepted this eternal life, I desire to spend it with her whom I have persuaded to union with me in this earthly life. But, as I have wooed her for the wedding at the altar, so must I woo her for the life hereafter. I do not know where lies the realm of those who leave this mortal plain but I do know that wherever it be I could never call it heaven without her, who is my Juanita to whom I give myself with every fibre, every nerve, every muscle and every part of me inscribed with her name and proudly wearing the insignia which names me as her possession.

Nothing have I said of what I expect in return, for truthfully I ask nothing more than that which has been given—which gift being her love. In having her love I have all that there is to be had of that which is worth having.

During the six months prior to his going to St. Paul, Mitchell had enjoyed a glorious round of courtship with Juanita one weekend a month in New York. There they took sightseeing trips on a double-decker bus down Fifth Avenue and enjoyed cuisines in Russian, Arabian, Japanese, and other ethnic restaurants to widen their horizons.

They were consumed with anticipation, and also with the feeling of a great pending historical moment that was shared throughout Baltimore and the nation by their many friends. The black press displayed its adoration of Juanita by heralding the announcement of the wedding date, September 7, 1938. None, however, could match the earlier prose of the *Afro-American:* "She is the original breaker of the old maxim that beauty and brains come in separate packages, for not only does she uphold Baltimore's tradition for producing beauteous maidens, but is one of the most brilliant of the country's young career women." They were to be married on the wedding anni-

versary of Keiffer and Lillie Carroll Jackson in the same Sharp Street
Methodist Episcopal Church where the older couple had exchanged vows in
1910. Dr. W.A.C. Hughes, director of the Bureau of Negro Work of the
Methodist Episcopal Church, who had performed her parents' marriage,
would do the same for her.

Juanita's friends and relatives celebrated her betrothal by treating her to
a round of parties in New York and Baltimore. She had submitted her
resignation from the NAACP to Walter White the latter part of June,
effective August 31. "I want you to know from the depths of my heart
what a privilege, what a wonderful experience it has been to work side by
side with you in the glorious activity of the Association," she said. In her
three years with the NAACP, she had tried to justify White's faith in her
and had given her best "to the greatest cause the Negro has in America."
White similarly regretted her departure, for his own career and the cause he
was serving had benefited immeasurably from her spiritual and professional
devotion. He offered her a chance to resume her career after her wedding.
But she would not be persuaded, because "I resigned to marry my prince"
and to raise a family. Her service to her people would now be conducted
primarily through Clarence and the NAACP. She would devote her life to
supporting him so that he could establish his place in history as a great
American. The lifelong partnership with someone who was as dedicated as
he to the struggle for racial justice would be crucial to Clarence's success.

At the home of Roberta Bosley on St. Nicholas Avenue in New York's
Harlem, Juanita received stockings filled with presents that spelled "B-A-
L-T-I-M-O-R-E: Best Always . . . Let Time Increase Money, Offspring,
Respect . . . Everything." From her hostess's collection of exquisite hand-
kerchiefs, the bride-to-be selected her borrowed item, one of delicate lace,
for her wedding day. Other friends gave her a breakfast party, and a dinner
at a Fifth Avenue restaurant. In Baltimore, an aunt gave her a linen shower;
the City-Wide Young People's Forum, which ended its activities that year
because no one else felt capable of following in Juanita's footsteps as the
organization's leader, celebrated her contributions with a good-bye party;
and, finally, on the wedding's eve, her parents entertained the bridal party;
Mitchell and Juanita exchanged presents and gave their bridal attendants
and ushers gifts.

Although Lillie Carroll Jackson had dedicated her life to serving the
masses of the oppressed, the elaborate wedding she gave her daughter revealed her aristocratic qualities. She used Juanita's wedding to further consolidate her place among a segment of the black elite which, like her, was
serving the struggle for freedom. The fifteen hundred guests, from as far
away as California, who filled every seat in the church, comprised the
cream of the NAACP middle class, a collection of leaders that transformed

Baltimore into a glittering national stage during the ceremony that took place at dusk that Wednesday. Lights from hundreds of candles flickered romantically from bowers of palms and lilies that banked the historic Sharp Street building. As the City-Wide Young People's Forum Trio sang "Liebestraum" and "At Dawning," and Anne Wiggins Brown, star of Broadway's *Porgy and Bess,* sang "Oh, Promise Me," the bridal party swept down the aisle. Juanita's innocent beauty sparkled against a gown of white slipper satin and Schiaparelli sleeves, a tight basque bodice that buttoned to a heart-shaped neckline, and a full skirt that drifted into a sweeping train. She wore the veil that had crowned her sister Marion during her wedding earlier that year to Karl E. Downs, another Methodist Episcopal Youth activist. It was a bridal illusion attached to a coronet of tulle and accented by a bouquet of Madonna lilies that filled her arm.

The gowns of her matrons of honor were of turquoise taffeta, with bodices that matched the bride's and Colonial hoop-style skirts. The other attendants wore similarly styled gowns, but in varying colors—trumpet gold and candle flame yellow. They all wore poke bonnets to match their frocks with rust tulle veils. While the bouquets of the matrons of honor were of talisman roses, the bridesmaids carried old-fashioned bouquets of mahogany pompon chrysanthemums. The flower girl wore a ruffled frock of turquoise taffeta with hoop skirt and a poke bonnet.

From the moment the triumphant Juanita entered the church on the arm of her father, her eyes and smile never left those of her prince until she took his arm at the chancel. The glowing candles commanded the atmosphere as the church lights were dimmed. Bridesmaid Louise "Pokey" Woodward could never forget the ceremony. Dr. Hughes's eyes filled with tears as Mitchell spoke the first line of the marriage vow, his eyes captured by his bride's, and solemnly completed his lifelong pledge of fidelity and love. Juanita similarly needed no help with hers. From wherever they sat in the church, every one of the fifteen hundred guests could hear the distinct ring of each word.

After the ceremony, more than two thousand people gathered at the Jacksons' home at 1216 Druid Hill Avenue for the reception. Many waited outside on the sidewalk in a steady downpour for more than an hour to pass through the greeting line. So dense was the gathering that Walter White and many other guests never got near the newlyweds.

Leaving for their honeymoon in New York, Clarence and Juanita were treated to a forty-five-minute farewell party at the train station. "Never before had Pennsylvania Station witnessed such a wedding," reported Lula Jones Garrett. Juanita Mitchell tripped into the station on Clarence's arm dressed in a pale yellow wool suit, chic doll hat, and a wine-colored veil with matching shoes, gloves, and bag. They were followed by two hundred guests who showered them with several pounds of rice. Then Anne Wiggins Brown transformed the railroad station into a *Porgy and Bess* setting as she swung into "Summertime," belting out, "Yo pappy's rich and yo ma is good-looking," with the melody echoing throughout the building. Attendants and other workers deserted their booths and stations to participate in the revelry. The City-Wide Forum Trio provided the accompaniment. Wilson Brown, baritone star of radio, crooned "Old Man River," while Maceo Howard, a Forum vice president, and the trio sang "Nita Juanita" and other love songs. Then, as the couple descended onto the lower platform to board the train, the crowd serenaded them with songs, smiling and waving. They continued until the locomotive passed into the distant night. After spending three delightful days at the Hotel New York, Clarence and Juanita sailed on the S.S. *Monarch* for ten days in Bermuda.

Juanita and Clarence were Baltimore's dream couple. Although their betrothal and marriage were in the tradition of the finest black middle-class culture, Clarence and Juanita were the diametric opposite of E. Franklin Frazier's "black bourgeoisie," who, "having their social heritage" linked to a culture and institutions founded in a rigidly segregated society, "and being rejected by the white world," had "an intense feeling of inferiority." Frazier's bourgeoisie constantly sought "various forms of recognition and place[d] greater value on status symbols" in order to compensate for their inferiority complex. Consequently, the black bourgeoisie dissipated a considerable amount of energy on building facades and in living an illusion. Success thus was a chimera, an unsatisfying existence that required increasing investments in time, money, and energy merely to maintain the vacuous imitation.

In contrast, Clarence and Juanita were blessed with nobility of spirit and ideals if not of birth. They represented a generation of their race that had pledged their lives to the service of their people. Thurgood Marshall, Roy Wilkins, William Hastie, and a host of other brilliant and well-trained blacks were among the leaders of their generation. Clarence and Juanita emerged into public life belonging to the same community. "We were their young people because we were giving of ourselves to help transform the community," said Juanita Mitchell. The older generation supported them as they developed a new blueprint for freedom. From the beginning of their professional careers, their existence was built on a foundation of service to the downtrodden black masses, and guided by the teachings and admonitions of Lillie Carroll Jackson. "When you get married, you should not set yourselves aside with the intelligentsia," she taught them. "Your education is a trust. Share it with your people."[11]

• CHAPTER SIX •

The FEPC Grail

Mitchell arrived in Washington in May 1941, with a mission that had become clearly defined during his service as executive director of the St. Paul Urban League. In Minnesota he had tested his intellect and political acumen against racial barriers to employment, and his record of victories in various discrimination battles, such as in opening up new job and other economic opportunities for blacks, was unsurpassed. St. Paul had provided a sharp contrast to Baltimore, giving him the different perspective of a region that was still reeling from the Great Depression, and had served as a perfect testing ground for his leadership abilities.

In Minnesota, Mitchell had become aware of the lingering ghost of Dred Scott and the miasma of slavery that had so charged the mid-nineteenth-century debates that resulted in the 1850 Missouri Compromise and the 1854 Kansas-Nebraska Act. He would later discover in Washington that that ghost, symbolic of the Midwest's attitude on race, was quietly but firmly reinforcing the South's Jim Crow system. Minnesota had been a part of the Louisiana Purchase but was now linked to the Deep South by only the remotest currents of the Mississippi River. The state might have been spared the agony of racial strife had the controlling branches of the national government been more constructive in their attitudes toward blacks.

Mitchell was the St. Paul Urban League's first executive secretary. The St. Paul unit, created in 1937, was an outgrowth of the Twin Cities Urban League, which had been organized in 1913. Mitchell thought that St. Paul was the "strangest place." He often found the city's racial flexibility, which far surpassed Baltimore's, amusing. On one occasion when he was setting up his office there, although they generally were opposed to racial intermarriage, many were insisting that he hire a white secretary. He, nevertheless, hired a black one. At the same time, St. Paul gave him an opportunity to create programs that showed the practical value of his training in social work in Atlanta. He also established solid friendships with people like Father Francis J. Gilligan, a staff member of the St. Paul Roman Catholic Seminary, who was widely respected as a champion of black causes and of labor. The black *St. Paul Advocate* and the *Minneapolis Spokesman,* which were both owned by Cecil Newman, championed his cause and heralded his accomplishments.

Another token of the respect he won even from former foes was the letter he received from St. Paul's school superintendent, Paul Amadan, against whom he had waged a lively struggle to require the city to hire its first black high school teacher. "I want to congratulate you upon the fine promotion you have received," Amadan told Mitchell. "We shall be very sorry to lose you since you have done an exceptionally fine job here. We have enjoyed very much your fine cooperation and splendid attitude. I hope that if you are replaced, your successor will do as good a job and will cooperate as well as you have." [1]

Mitchell's departure from St. Paul was timely, coming at the peak of his accomplishments. His years in Minnesota had helped prepare him for greater challenges; his confidence was reinforced. Now David was ready for the Goliath of the federal bureaucracy.

Unable to find an apartment in Washington because housing was scarce, he settled Juanita, who was pregnant with their second son, Keiffer, and Clarence III, who had been born in St. Paul, back in Baltimore. That suited him perfectly because he and Juanita already had a firm political base there. They moved in temporarily with Juanita's mother on Druid Hill Avenue. Soon he and Juanita would buy their own three-story, red-brick row house on the next block at 1324 Druid Hill Avenue. It would be his home for the rest of his life.

Hitler's blitzkriegs throughout Europe in late 1939 and 1940 precipitated even more fundamental challenges than those that had preoccupied the nation during the Depression years. Survival of not just an economic system but also of Western democratic values and America's system of government was now at stake. The intertwining of international with domestic currents, notably the dramatic migration of blacks and poor whites from southern and rural farms to urban industrial centers, created new social pressures and political realities, which in turn led to new employment opportunities for minorities that surpassed those of any period since Reconstruction. Thus the three developments most beneficial to civil rights activists were (1) the increasing political strength of blacks outside the South; (2) the critical manpower shortages that forced the use of all available labor in important defense industries; and (3) the increasing assertiveness of a group of well-educated blacks in Washington who, with the support of dedicated white allies, carried the civil rights struggle into the federal bureaucracy and even into the hallowed halls of the White House.

Despite the nation's significant recovery from the Depression and the new employment opportunities being created, blacks were in a dismal economic state owing to the disproportionate loss of jobs they suffered during the Depression. There were fewer blacks in manufacturing jobs in 1940 than in 1910. For blacks, therefore, the battle lines were drawn at home as clearly as abroad. Many companies had no black workers at all even though they were increasingly benefiting from publicly financed defense contracts. Discrimination was rampant in the vast vocational training programs for defense industries. Equally serious were the widespread barriers that skilled black workers faced in craft unions. Finally, beaten by the system, many blacks had lost hope. [2]

Mitchell had encountered these problems on a smaller scale as executive director of the St. Paul Urban League. Now, however, he was better positioned to begin attacking those forms of racial discrimination nationwide as well as that within the federal government from its doorsteps. Because of the war, black employment no longer was merely a question of social reform and responsibility, but was a strategic imperative. Overnight, the labor market had switched from one of massive surplus to one of severe shortage. Blacks seized the opportunity to demand that they be given jobs on a nondiscriminatory basis.

In 1941, the Office of Production Management replaced the National Defense Advisory Commission, which President Roosevelt had created early the previous year to coordinate the nation's defense program in preparation for entry into World War II. Robert C. Weaver, who had been administrative assistant to the chairman of the NDAC, was chosen to head the OPM's Negro Employment and Training Branch. At the NDAC, he had worked in the Labor Supply Division for equal opportunities for blacks in the defense program and for racial integration in all nonmilitary phases of the national war effort. The Negro Employment and Training Branch as well as the coequal Minority Groups Branch, which served Mexicans and other ethnic citizens, were part of the OPM's Labor Division. As the unit representing the largest, most visible, and most assertive minority group, however, the Negro Employment and Training Branch was more important.

A common discriminatory practice during that period was for employers to ignore the pool of local black and other minority group workers and bring in whites from other parts of the country for available jobs. The Negro Employment and Training Branch was charged with ending that practice by ensuring that all available local labor was used before other workers were recruited from outside the community. It developed training programs for blacks in federal agencies, the defense industry, and other critical areas of employment. The unit during its short life set the tone and scope of the struggle for economic opportunities for all minority groups. It was an embodiment of Weaver's philosophy and vision of the achievement of black economic equality.

Weaver was a native of Washington who followed other renowned black contemporaries through Dunbar High School and into Harvard University. By the time Harvard awarded him his doctorate in 1934, he and a former roommate, John P. Davis, had created the Negro Industrial League, which soon became the Joint Committee on National Recovery. That lobbying organization was supported by twenty-four civil rights and religious organizations. The NAACP, one of the member organizations, was then demanding the appointment of blacks to boards, committees, and commissions dealing with NRA programs, but it was neglecting the more important issues relating to NRA regulations. The two radical intellectuals filled the void by testifying and presenting briefs at scores of hearings by government agencies and congressional committees concerning every industry that employed significant numbers of blacks. They challenged representatives of such well-organized industries as lumber, steel, coal, leather, construction, hotel, and laundry.[3]

In fall of 1934, Weaver joined the federal government as associate adviser on the economic status of Negroes in the Department of the Interior. Within a year, he became a full adviser. Under his direction, his division conducted a comprehensive study and issued a report entitled "A Survey of White Collar and Skilled Workers." The most important study of its kind to date, it provided the foundation for subsequent government programs against employment discrimination. Next Weaver, in his own words, "more or less" appointed himself consultant on public housing in the Housing Division of the Public Works Administration. That agency was administered by Harold L. Ickes, who was also secretary of the interior. At the PWA, Weaver established criteria for defining employment discrimination and worked to provide protections for the economic rights of blacks.

Weaver regarded public housing construction as the guinea pig for experiments in reducing discrimination against skilled black workers on publicly financed projects. Until 1929, black workers were almost totally excluded from the building industry. But after 1930, this situation began to change as extreme competition developed for any type of construction work. In 1932, pressed by civil rights groups to end discrimination against black workers on public works projects, Ogden Mills, secretary of the Treasury, issued a directive to construction engineers to end such practices. The following year, on September 21, Harold Ickes, as administrator of the PWA, followed the precedent and issued an order to state engineers that there should "be no discrimination exercised against any person because of color or religious affiliation." The orders, however, were not effective because they contained no definition of discrimination, and thus no criterion for proving that such practices existed or for dealing with contractors and labor unions who engaged in them. Weaver found, for example, that in cases where discrimination was obvious because of the lack of black workers on a project, in order to satisfy the government's requirements all the employer had to do to correct the problem was to hire a few minority workers. That action did not end the problem of discrimination against a class of people.

At Weaver's urging, the PWA's Housing Division adopted as a prima facie basis for proving discrimination the failure to pay skilled blacks a minimum percentage of the payroll for white skilled workers. The percentage was based on the most recent occupational census. This new policy was next adopted by the U.S. Housing Authority when it was created in 1938. It was also the prototype of the "goals and timetable" principle of the affirmative action programs of the 1960s.

Weaver explained the meaning of that principle in his seminal work, *Negro Labor:*

> This mechanism for defining and enforcing non-discrimination in employment was a significant development, although not a definitive solution of discrimination on public financed construction. It almost lost its usefulness by being pushed too far. The minimum percentage clauses were designed to meet a peculiar situation. Their objective was to retain past occupational advances for Negroes in the middle 1930's—a period of slack labor demand. They were frankly a device to regain lost ground; they were not designed to open new types of employment. But as a matter of fact it would have been unrealistic to have attempted to secure significant occupational gains for a minority group in a period when there was mass unemployment.

Supported by the NAACP, Weaver also got the Department of the Interior to oppose the use of all-black labor forces on Subsistence Homestead developments in black areas. Many blacks, especially in the South, had welcomed that prospect, but the NAACP and Weaver felt that accepting all-black work forces would have set a dangerous precedent at a time when an all-out attempt was being made to outlaw racial segregation. The NAACP and Weaver feared that accepting such segregation would have denied blacks justification for demanding work on the bulk of PWA projects, which were being constructed in white areas.[4]

Weaver, furthermore, had foreseen considerable employment benefits for blacks as union members. The New Deal's National Labor Relations (Wagner) Act had provided unprecedented support for the right of workers to organize. Examining in 1936 the impact of the PWA's vast construction projects on employment opportunities for skilled workers, Weaver noted that the federal government through such agencies as the U.S. Postal Service had long been engaged in extensive building programs. In recent years, however, owing to the size, scope, and complexity of such projects, only large construction companies capable of operating over large areas were capable of bidding on such jobs. Most of those companies were by their nature union contractors, because they operated in "closed shop cities," where union membership was a prerequisite for getting a job.

"Thus, as a general rule, the larger projects" were union jobs, Weaver explained. In addition, he said, the administration had "upheld consistently labor's right to organize. As far as Negro labor was concerned, the problem was complex. It was one of maintaining job opportunities for Negroes, using contractors who were often 'union contractors,' and not allowing the employment of colored workers to result in its usual consequence" of using blacks as strikebreakers to weaken organized labor.

Weaver was the most persistent advocate outside of the labor unions themselves pushing for blacks to become full-fledged union members. His copious studies and analyses of union seniority and other requirements helped develop a better understanding of the problems blacks were encountering in various areas of employment. One strategy he utilized for breaking down racial barriers was to press the PWA to obtain cooperation from union locals in getting work permits and acceptance for blacks on the agency's vast construction projects.

Weaver's vision extended well beyond the defense program. He saw the need for blacks to be trained in skills not only for immediate employment but also for jobs that would be available after the war. As he said in *Negro Labor*:

> The urbanization of Negroes involves new occupational patterns. It calls for new skills, and new expressions of old ones. It implies entrance at the bottom of the industrial ladder, and the perfection of methods which will facilitate advancement. These circumstances demand an expanded approach to the problem of preparation for gainful employment. Such an approach requires a

thorough understanding of occupations and comprehension of the
industrial labor problem.

He told Walter White, in discussing the immense challenge of getting
companies to hire blacks at the beginning of the defense program, that "the
big problem as I see it is not to get the first Negro employed, but to get an
equitable proportion of employment in these plants for colored workers,
and to secure an opportunity for trained colored men now both inside and
outside the industry to perform skilled functions."[5]

Blacks hailed Weaver's appointment to the National Defense Advisory
Commission in 1940. His elevation gave them an opportunity to have a
complete picture of developments in training and labor recruitment programs and an opportunity to participate in manpower planning. The
NAACP, through *The Crisis,* welcomed his appointment as "a growing
realization on the part of the federal government that colored Americans
must be given the serious consideration they demand, and that their interests, along with the interests of other Americans, must be faithfully
guarded in the current period of national emergency."

At Weaver's insistence, the commission included a statement against
age, sex, race, or color discrimination in its labor policy. That nondiscrimination policy was undergirded by a training program that, the
commission stressed, was markedly different from "the usual vocational
training courses." It was designed to provide greater employment opportunities than any existing vocational program. He also got the commission
to obtain from the American Federation of Labor and the Congress of Industrial Organizations a firm commitment that affiliated trade unions
would adhere to the government's nondiscrimination policy. That accomplishment took a lot of effort and was the beginning of the long fight to get
unions to end discrimination.[6]

Weaver's historical role in the struggle for black economic opportunity
is comparable to that of Charles Hamilton Houston, the Howard University Law School dean who in 1935 created the NAACP's legal department.
Houston's protégé, Thurgood Marshall, subsequently expanded and developed the strategy the law school dean had established for attacking the
"separate but equal" doctrine into a whole new realm of constitutional law.
Mitchell too would continue to develop and expand, through administrative and legislative processes, on the foundations that Weaver had laid,
and would seek to make permanent those protections that had been won
against discrimination in employment and other areas through the adoption
of regulations and the enactment of laws.

Mitchell respected Weaver as a brilliant intellectual and professional.
He also admired Weaver for not being "the type who went around brag-

ging" about his considerable influence in Washington. Mitchell found him always constructive: "I had observed him when he was in housing, years before I had thought about going into government." He was impressed by Weaver's creation of policies that were adopted by the various agencies, including the U.S. Housing Authority, which resulted in employment of many skilled black workers—"he was always trying to develop some kind of statement for the President to use in his speech." Clearly, as Mitchell noted, "prior to the issuance of Executive Order 8802 the major thrust towards establishment of policies under which we worked could be traced to Bob Weaver." That order, issued by President Roosevelt less than two months after Mitchell had arrived in Washington, prohibited discrimination in defense industries and created the President's Committee on Fair Employment Practice. In addition to influencing the federal bureaucracy, Weaver was the most effective and articulate expert on black economic development.

Weaver was a young, confident intellectual, like W.E.B. Du Bois, so not surprisingly some people found him haughty. But not Mitchell, who observed that, unlike some people who rise to prominence, Weaver "was always conscious of his origin and his early friendships." He recalled an occasion in Minnesota when Weaver, entering a hall to speak at a dinner, saw a shabbily dressed man standing outside. "Dr. Weaver greeted him warmly and respectfully. It turned out that this man had once been his schoolmate. When I complimented him on his cordial manner towards the individual, he remarked that, 'After all, I could be in his place and he in mine.'"[7]

The other major influence on Mitchell during this period was Mary McLeod Bethune, for whom Mitchell had worked in 1938 when he was state director of the National Youth Administration in Maryland. As a result of her extensive influence in the executive branch, she was the esteemed leader of an informal interagency network of racial advisers known as Roosevelt's Black Cabinet, and of the much wider association of persevering leaders called the New Deal's Black Brain Trust. The Black Cabinet was a New Deal phenomenon that came into existence after the midpoint of Roosevelt's first term. The name reflected the attainment of positions of significant influence in the federal government by an appreciable number of blacks for the first time in history. It pressed for more jobs and fairer treatment for blacks in government administration as well as in New Deal programs. Among the more prominent Black Cabinet members were Weaver; William Hastie, who in the Roosevelt administration was, successively, assistant solicitor in the Department of the Interior, the first black appointed to the federal bench as U.S. district judge of the Virgin Islands, and civilian aide to the secretary of war; and Frank S. Horne, another black housing expert. Mitchell was a very junior member of the Black Cabinet.[8]

Bethune's power came largely through her considerable influence with President Roosevelt, with whom she met frequently, and Eleanor Roosevelt, her friend. Mitchell could not recall how much she participated in the Black Cabinet's day-to-day planning, but he suspected that some of the ideas generated by the group went through Bethune to Eleanor Roosevelt and finally to the President.

Mitchell was struck by Bethune's deep sense of identification with her people. A generation later, he found it "amusing to hear people talk about black being beautiful, because Mrs. Bethune was one of the chief exponents of that idea." In many of her speeches, she would declare, "I'm black and I'm beautiful." And nobody disagreed with her. Mitchell recalled:

> I remember one of her speeches about the Cincinnati railroad station. At that time segregation in railroad stations was rampant in the South. Cincinnati was the point at which northern-bound Negroes from Mississippi, Alabama, and other places would come en route to points North. Many of them getting off the trains were so used to Jim Crow stations that they would come into the Cincinnati station and be uncertain where they should go. As she put it, she would stand there, very black and very striking, in the middle of the main waiting room or near the rest rooms, and as people came in her direction, '[she] would say, "Come on children, this is where you belong." And sure enough, her mere presence reassured them that there was no segregation. To me, for a woman who had access to the White House, who had a really close friendship with Mrs. Roosevelt, to do this showed a sense of identification with the masses of her people.
>
> She had a following because of her personality and her ability to speak. She also had her objective, getting everything that Americans ought to have for Negroes.

Because many people knew she had access to the White House, they would respond to a telephone call or a letter from her. She influenced not only blacks but also many whites.

She, somehow, was able to find in government people who would be responsive to pleas for decency and some who zealously wanted to correct wrongs. She had large numbers of people she could call on in many, many places. Then there were some who acted out of sheer fear that she might report them to the President and get them in trouble. They always responded when she called.

Bethune's ability to find and work with trustworthy and committed whites reinforced Mitchell's own faith in humans.

I think that people who are honest and fair to themselves, when thrown into contact with members of other racial groups, tend to find honest and fair people, and they tend to work together. Mrs. Bethune had the advantage of doing that on a very high level. In addition, she was absolutely sure of herself. She was not a weakling. She had no qualms about being black in a white situation.

Mitchell always welcomed and valued her advice and guidance, which she frequently gave him. "She had a way of making the male ego feel very secure because she always did something to remind you that you were a man and that a man is supposed to be a great, superior creature." There was no doubt, though, that "she was far superior to you."

Mitchell was not surprised that she aroused jealousy in some assertive black males, who resented her long shadow over their "little kingdoms." Aware of that growing resentment, "she called a meeting which was held at a church in Washington. Just about everybody who was of any importance in the Negro leadership came from around the country. Before the meeting, many had grumbled, 'What does Mrs. Bethune want now?' 'Why did she call this meeting?'"

She answered them. "I understand that there are some of you who say that you don't think that I should call these meetings. You want to know what I called you to Washington for. Well, I want you to know I have called you to Washington because I wanted you here. And I will call you to Washington whenever I feel like calling you here. I may not even want you to do anything. I just want you to be here." Her audience applauded. Most of them were aware of her demand for deference. Out of respect, they accommodated her. She kept them in suspense for a long time. Mitchell and other young blacks benefited from her self-confidence, which led her to praise them publicly.[9]

In the Negro Employment and Training Branch, Mitchell was one of a dozen or more highly trained professionals on Weaver's staff. He began as regional representative of OPM's Labor Division for Pennsylvania, Delaware, and New Jersey, where there was an enormous concentration of industry. So familiar did he become with his region, he recalled, "that I knew where every industrial or training plant was located."

Weaver thought so highly of Mitchell that he quickly made him his deputy. He thus shared responsibility for all of the Negro Employment and Training Branch's activities in every state and every municipality, with public agencies as well as private defense contractors, in areas with a sizable black population. Mitchell traveled extensively, meeting with employers and union leaders in an effort to persuade them to hire blacks and admit them into training programs.

As Weaver's associate, Mitchell lost some of the independence he had enjoyed in St. Paul. But this was a much more important job because it involved not only the struggle to develop comprehensive measures for protecting the rights of minorities through government leadership, but implementing existing national policy.

It was a period of making bricks without straw. Despite the newness of the work and a lack of presidential commitment, Mitchell and his coworkers found that "you could go as far as you wanted" in pressing employers to hire blacks because Roosevelt was preoccupied with the war. When Mitchell did encounter obstructions from "underlings," as he referred to subordinates, he went over their heads to top company executives. "The presidents didn't know I was not authorized to do so, and I wasn't sure I would have gotten authorization." Fortunately, Weaver "was very, wonderfully supportive." He encouraged Mitchell and never said, "Don't do that because you might get into trouble." Mitchell welcomed the freedom and support as well as the authority and feeling of security that the experienced and confident Weaver gave him. He admired Weaver's ease in conferences with top industry and labor officials. His boss was always "frank without being obnoxious or arrogant." He also was prepared for open hostility toward fair employment programs. He coolly handled these situations. These meetings also required knowledge of job requirements in each occupation, and Weaver discussed training programs for welders as comfortably as he did the skills needed by tool and die makers or for carpenters. Weaver welcomed Mitchell's loyalty and was in turn well served by Clarence's experience in working with employers, local politicians, and others.

Typical of the critical situations and problems Mitchell encountered was the case of the Sun Shipbuilding and Drydock Company in Chester, Pennsylvania. Unlike many other firms, it had a policy of employing blacks, but only in certain categories. Though some of those positions were skilled, they were not necessarily better paying than unskilled positions. Mitchell recalled a conversation he had with an official of that company, who told him, "Well, in all the years that I've been in the shipbuilding industry, I've never seen any Negro shipfitters." Mitchell knew for certain, though, that there were black shipfitters, "but they weren't called that because it meant paying them a decent wage. We had some pretty rough going in some of those plants."

The Sun Company also had a separate shipway for blacks, imitating the prevalent practice in the South. Mitchell vigorously opposed that type of workplace segregation, oftentimes with good results.

On another occasion, the vice president of the Goodyear Rubber and Tire Company in Akron, Ohio, concluded a long meeting about the importance of ending discrimination in defense plants by asking Mitchell, "Do you know where I could find a good cook?" At a similar meeting in Portland, Oregon, an official of the International Brotherhood of Boilermakers exploded, "Goddamit, don't come in here waving the American flag." Such encounters only bolstered Mitchell's resolve. He sought labor's cooperation in getting blacks accepted as union members and in not opposing their employment. He worked on important policy questions and shared the administrative work with Weaver, deploying forces in the field and supervising their activities.[10]

President Roosevelt's issuing of Executive Order 8802 on June 25, 1941, was the most celebrated act in the battle against discrimination in war industries. That date marked the launching of the modern civil rights movement. The struggle for the executive order was led by A. Philip Randolph, president of the International Brotherhood of Sleeping Car Porters. Walter White, since early 1940 had been mobilizing the NAACP's branches to fight discrimination in the defense program, but Randolph became the driving force in the movement. The idea dated back to 1917–18, when the NAACP began calling for equal opportunity in employment. Randolph threatened to lead a march on Washington of ten thousand blacks (White increased the number to one hundred thousand) if Roosevelt did not issue the order barring discrimination in the armed services and defense industries. Roosevelt issued the order to stave off the march, which was to have been held on July 1.

An important historical coincidence was that the order was drafted by Joseph L. Rauh, Jr., who, a decade later, would become Mitchell's inseparable lobbying partner. Rauh's watchword was "No discrimination on grounds of race, color, creed or national origin."[11]

Executive Order 8802 was a compromise that left untouched discrimination in the armed services, but Executive Order 8802 met Randolph's basic demands and created the Fair Employment Practice Committee (FEPC) as an administering agency to implement the directive. The executive order represented the first concrete presidential step since the Civil War to protect the rights of black citizens. Little wonder, therefore, that some people called it a second Emancipation Proclamation. Blacks were jubilant, but they knew that, like the Emancipation Proclamation, Executive Order 8802 was only a partial victory. The FEPC was regarded as merely a handle, albeit an important one, on the door to equal opportunity. The creation of the FEPC signaled the government's awakening to the problem of the color-biased occupational system.

The FEPC throughout its short life, from 1941 to 1946, reflected the tumultuous circumstances that had led to its creation. It was besieged by attacks from its enemies. The first committee was composed of a chairman and six members, who were unpaid, and a paid executive secretary. Its overall responsibility was to receive and investigate employment discrimination complaints and to take "appropriate steps to redress grievances which it finds valid." Mitchell, although he was not involved in the struggle that led to the creation of the FEPC, was immediately drawn into its work and, subsequently, the effort to save it.

The new agency's first major problem was its structure. It was established within the Office of Production Management and was required to share the staffs of the Negro Employment and Training Branch and the Minority Groups Branch. The FEPC served as a board of appeal for those two units, which certified cases to it. The arrangement exposed the FEPC to unavoidable competition. Prior to its creation, the principal person in government to whom discrimination cases were referred was Robert Weaver. Now, the FEPC had been invested with this responsibility, and the role of Weaver's unit, the Negro Employment branch, was merely that of a facilitator. It was natural, therefore, for Weaver, whose authority was cut because of the power he was amassing, to feel some resentment toward the new agency and to protect as best he could his own political and professional base. However, out of commitment to the common cause and the need for survival, he and his staff, despite their unhappiness, cooperated closely with the FEPC on the central mission of attacking job discrimination.[12]

The FEPC's second problem was that it had no independent authority, and could not enforce its orders. It was merely an investigating agency. A third problem was that the committee reflected Roosevelt's ambivalence about the idea of equal employment opportunity for blacks. Complaining about the difficulty of getting Roosevelt's support, Walter White wrote a southern journalist:

> On numerous occasions we have pleaded with the President to break his silence and to speak out against this discrimination which not only was doing an injustice to the Negro but was definitely jeopardizing our national security through reduction of our productivity by approximately ten percent. The first time I urged him to do this was at a conference at the White House last September 25 [1940] at which were present Secretary of the Navy Knox, Under Secretary of War Patterson, A. Philip Randolph, and others. On

that occasion and on several others the President gave as a reason for not taking definitive action against this discrimination that "the South would rise up in protest." On several occasions I have said to him "What South are you talking about, Mr. President? The South of Bilbo and Cotton Ed Smith, or the South of Frank Graham and Mark Ethridge?" . . . I assured the President that apparently I had more faith in the inherent decency of Southern white people than he did in that I was certain that at least on an issue like this far more Southerners would approve his taking an unequivocal stand than would disapprove. . . . Discontent and bitterness were growing like wildfire among Negroes all over the country.

Despite White's faith in Ethridge's liberalism, however, when the southerner, who was publisher of the *Louisville Courier-Journal,* was named the first chairman of the FEPC, he professed his sympathy for civil rights and equal employment opportunity for blacks, but also reaffirmed his belief in segregation. He said that Executive Order 8802 was "a war order and not a social document."[13]

The FEPC and its two companion OPM antidiscrimination units, nevertheless, were able to make progress in the very uncertain period during which the defense program evolved in a makeshift manner. On January 26, 1942, while Mitchell was in Philadelphia meeting with a contractor, the man held up a newspaper with a headline indicating that the Office of Production Management had been abolished and its functions transferred to the newly created War Production Board. Pearl Harbor had established new, overriding priorities for the nation. During his short tenure in the dual role of field assistant of the Negro Employment and Training Branch and OPM field representative, Mitchell opened up skilled jobs for blacks in such firms as the Camp Shipbuilding Company, Bendix Aviation Company, the Wright Aeronautical Company, Western Electric, RCA, and Westinghouse. He was promoted to assistant chief of the Negro Employment and Training Branch in the War Production Board.[14]

Next, on July 30, 1942, Roosevelt abruptly transferred the FEPC and the other two antidiscrimination units to the newly created War Manpower Commission to frustrate efforts to make it effective. Mitchell and other staff members were assigned to work with the FEPC, but not Weaver or Will Alexander, because they had taken their jobs seriously and were, indeed, challenging standard job discrimination practices. They were denied "control over any policy or operation of the Committee." Neither could they "perform any function within the scope of the Committee's jurisdiction." The action was directed more at Weaver than at Alexander owing to the black leader's skill, determination, and accomplishments. Even with his effectiveness impaired, however, he remained the government's leading employment integration expert and advocate.

Weaver was now chief of the Negro Manpower Service of the War Manpower Commission; Mitchell was his assistant even though he was working for the FEPC. Mitchell's duties included supervision of field staff, visits to industrial plants and unions, and training government employees. His goal was the full involvement of blacks in war industries and job training programs.

In January 1943, Mitchell was assigned to work full time for the FEPC as senior fair practice examiner. Weaver regretted Mitchell's departure: "But I felt he would have a much wider opportunity in the FEPC. Also, I wanted to get somebody in the FEPC who knew the hell what he was doing. He was one who did. He didn't have too much company, I might add." No doubt, too, Mitchell was relieved that he was free of divided loyalties. The FEPC provided him with the type of leverage that no black government employee previously had ever had. Weaver and other black bureaucrats, for example, as race advisers could only express their authority through white liberals.

Blacks bitterly protested that the FEPC's unprecedented authority was threatened by Roosevelt's abrupt transfer of the FEPC to the WMC. As a subsidiary of WMC, Walter White wrote Roosevelt on August 18, 1942, the FEPC

> will have to get its funds in the future from Congress. The very bitter attacks upon the Fair Employment Practice Committee by certain southern members of Congress and by such men as Governors [Frank Murray] Dixon of Alabama and [Eugene] Talmadge of Georgia, following the recent Birmingham hearings, are an ominous portent of the treatment which will be accorded to a budget for the work of the FEPC which the War Manpower Commission may submit to the Congress.

Previously, the committee had enjoyed a protected status, receiving its funds through the President's emergency war budget. Roosevelt himself drew much opposition heat as a result of that arrangement.

Other indications of how much the FEPC was being hamstrung were that all matters involving racial discrimination were now considered "the joint problem" of the WMC and the committee; WMC's field personnel had to be included in working out solutions to those problems; and the WMC was given power to fire FEPC field staff.

The FEPC's work was now markedly slowed. The WMC, however, overplayed its hand in January 1943 by abruptly canceling hearings the

FEPC had scheduled on the Southeastern Carriers Conference Agreement of February 18, 1941, between the twenty southern railroads and the Brotherhood of Locomotive Firemen and Enginemen. That agreement had been designed to restrict and eliminate black firemen and trainmen from the railroads. The heat of the resulting protests was so intense that Roosevelt abolished the old FEPC on May 27 and that same day reconstituted it under Executive Order 9346.[15]

The FEPC's eventual doom, however, was confirmed by its successes, particularly in focusing national attention, more than in any other period of history, on the problem of racial discrimination in employment. The agency thus became the symbol for blacks of their frustrations in the struggle for economic equality that they had been waging since slavery. As Walter White had told the FEPC at a hearing in New York on February 15, 1942:

> Most vicious of the existing discriminations against the Negro is that which precludes him from rising above the marginal security level at which he exists. This discrimination is effected largely by the policy and practice of industry in entirely excluding or specifically limiting to the lowest job classifications Negro workers. This discrimination policy and practice works to the detriment of the American people in that it (1) creates a social problem among Negroes, directly related to the economic insecurity of the group; (2) deprives our present defense production effort of an available reservoir of labor; and (3) is contrary to our fundamental democratic principles and concepts of fair play and equality for all.[16]

Mitchell remained insulated from the political battles by the layers of bureaucracy above him. He thus continued his work without interruption. One problem he encountered that illustrated the difficulty of his mission was a case of discrimination against a Jewish applicant for a federally subsidized Engineering Science Management War Training course at Northwestern University. Because of the circumstances that led to the complaint, Mitchell suggested that the FEPC direct its attack at the "employer angle." The university had stated as its reason for refusing to accept the applicant that "if we had a very large proportion of any one race or group we could not operate successfully since our cooperating companies demand diversity of background among the students they hire."

Mitchell drafted an FEPC response to the university that said, "By honoring what you infer is a prejudice against Jews on the part of the companies, you become an accessory in the hands of those who violate the President's Order." The letter noted that the U.S. Employment Service, then an agency of the War Manpower Commission, listed all companies that refused to accept people because of race or other prejudicial factors. It suggested that the university provide the FEPC with the names of companies that refused to accept Jewish applicants. "When you furnish us with this information we will take the necessary steps to correct the attitudes of the companies." He successfully urged that meanwhile, owing to the national need for engineers, the university should accept the applicant and inform the FEPC of its action. [17]

During his extensive travels for the FEPC, Mitchell eased his loneliness by reliving the tenderest moments of his marriage in letters to Juanita. He made his mission hers by intertwining aspects of his work with torrential expressions of his love:

> Darling, I want the mental companionship of our love. I am here in Portland on a great experiment—the importation of Negroes to work in the shipyards. I am planning the states from which they will be drawn, the way they will come and what will happen when they get here. It is a great thrill. I can hardly sit still and think about it. I need you to point out the flaws in my thinking. I need you to show me where the short circuits are likely to develop and you are three thousand miles away where I cannot speak to you each time I want to. . . .
>
> Soon I will be on the way home and that will be a great time. I leave Portland tonight and go to Seattle, then I come back to Portland on Wednesday for a meeting on the immigration question. That night I leave for Denver, Colo. I expect to spend Friday and Saturday in Denver and get into Omaha on Monday morning. I'll stay in Omaha until Wednesday and then go to Kansas City. From Kansas City I come home. And will I be glad to get there. Write to me in Omaha, my darling.

Another time, en route on a B&O Railroad train, he devoted his thoughts to his two young sons:

> Above all things, I want to have them respect the human personality wherever they find it and no matter how it is garbed. They will live such rich lives if they can break out of the narrow shell of race and national identification so that all of the people of the world are regarded as fellow humans—even the people who do not wish to be so regarded.
>
> There is great promise in the future. We will see our sons and

others like them "behold with their eyes the things we have
dreamed."[18]

Under Executive Order 9346, the FEPC was placed within the Office
for Emergency Management in the executive office of the President, and its
organizational structure was revamped. There were two important changes:
First, while the original FEPC had an unsalaried chairman as well as a paid
executive director, the new agency had a paid chairman who was the top
executive; second, there was now a divisional structure, and the field operation had been expanded and organized into thirteen regional and five sub-
regional offices. The previous six field representatives were increased to
sixty-three.

Mitchell was appointed associate director of the Division of Field Operation, the heart of the agency. It was responsible for administering the
FEPC's regional offices and for negotiating operating agreements with eight
other wartime and civilian agencies with which it worked, as well as with
the United Automobile, Aircraft and Agricultural Implement Workers of
America.

Mitchell was boxed in by two high-level whites, his immediate superior
Will Maslow and the committee's salaried chairman Malcolm Ross. He
nevertheless operated freely. Maslow and Ross came from the National Labor Relations Board, and Mitchell had to train them because they were not
experienced in the FEPC's work. In addition to helping them develop policy, Mitchell implemented programs. He supervised the regional offices
and maintained a close watch on the hundreds of cases the FEPC handled.

There were other influential blacks in the agency, most notably John A.
Davis, a political scientist who headed the division of Review and Analysis,
and George Johnson, the deputy chairman, who was a carryover from the
first FEPC as well as a former dean of Howard University Law School.
Davis recalls that Johnson made sure that no one ran the FEPC but blacks,
and "he kept fire under Mike's [Ross] butt." Other bright blacks included
Mitchell's Baltimore schoolmate Elmer Henderson, an attorney who ran the
regional office in Chicago, and George Crockett, a member of the legal
division who four decades later would be a member of the Congressional
Black Caucus. Weaver continued to have considerable input through Maslow, whom he assisted in working out operational agreements with the
other agencies.[19]

Although some of its functions were more clearly defined and strengthened, the second FEPC still reflected extensive conflicts and hesitancy
within the administration over the idea of equal employment opportunity
for blacks. The FEPC was now responsible for all discrimination complaints, thus ending a serious problem that had existed in the first agency.

Its primary weakness remained the lack of enforcement powers. To gain compliance with the President's order, it still had to rely mainly on public hearings to expose discrimination. At least, though, it now had the help of a more involved President, and the agencies with whom it signed agreements assisted somewhat in enforcing its orders. The raging war helped Roosevelt lessen opposition by draping the FEPC with the flag. Hiring workers regardless of race, creed, color, or national origin became a patriotic duty that was essential to victory.[20]

The FEPC's weakness was demonstrated by a problem Mitchell encountered with the WMC, the most important wartime agency. The WMC had overall responsibility for coordinating manpower supply between military and essential civilian needs. It formulated plans and programs and established basic national policies for assuring the most effective mobilization of manpower. Not surprisingly, therefore, Mitchell devoted considerable attention to the implementation of the President's nondiscrimination directives by WMC's regional offices. Most of the WMC's regional directors cooperated with the FEPC. But when one refused to give the FEPC access to its discrimination reports, Mitchell found he had no recourse after the war agency's chairman ignored his complaints. He was similarly frustrated when the U.S. Employment Service, the nation's largest job placement agency, refused to file discrimination reports in various regions. In response to his complaints, Maslow conducted a survey among the FEPC's regional offices to see how many of them had had problems with the USES. Unfortunately, the FEPC was dismantled before anything could be done with the results.

Despite such problems, Mitchell's tenure with the new agency was much more rewarding than with the previous one because he had more authority and support. The bulk of the committee's cases were routine, settled with little difficulty. But others required considerable struggle before any agreement was reached, and many remained unresolved.[21]

The second FEPC's first order of business was to hold hearings against the twenty railroads and thirteen unions* covered by the Southeastern Carriers agreement that the WMC had canceled back in January. Ten carriers and one union previously had settled with the agency. Often called the "ultimate in discriminatory agreements," the master pact, as it was commonly known, not only was designed to eliminate black firemen and trainmen from jobs they long had held with the railroads, but restricted new blacks from being hired. Since most of those black workers had been hired

*The railroads involved in the hearings included the Brotherhood of Locomotive Engineers, the Brotherhood of Locomotive Firemen and Enginemen, the Brotherhood of Railroad Trainmen, the Brotherhood of Railway Carmen of America, the International Association of Machinists, and the International Brotherhood of Boilermakers.

before World War I, they had been able to accumulate more seniority than whites and were therefore entitled to better jobs. Consequently, a reign of terror was launched against them that resulted in the death of ten firemen and trainmen and the wounding of twenty-one others between September 7, 1931, and July 10, 1934. Subsequently, the Railway Labor Act (1934) was used for pushing that kind of economic discrimination against blacks.

Explaining the abuse of the Railway Labor Act, Herbert R. Northrup wrote in *Organized Labor and the Negro:*

> Under it the National Mediation Board designated as exclusive bargaining agents for Negroes unions which exclude Negroes or afford them only inferior status. It assists parties to reach agreements which result in the displacement of colored workers. It has refused to take the racial policies into consideration in determining appropriate bargaining units, thus consigning smaller groups of Negroes to the domination of discriminatory unions.

The National Railroad Adjustment Board's denial of even a hearing, much less justice, to black railroad workers had an even more devastating impact on the group's status. The result of the collusion among the railroads, the unions, the National Mediation Board, and the National Railroad Adjustment Board was that blacks were denied entry or promotion in the industry or were pushed out altogether. First, for example, black firemen, who had to shovel coal into open locomotive furnaces, represented a nonpromotable class who could not be advanced to engineers—the upper and better-paying category, which included only whites. Second, most southern railroads had ceased hiring blacks as early as 1925, but ejection of the group subsequently increased with introduction of cleaner and more desirable automatic-feed and diesel engines. The Southeastern Carriers Conference Agreement accelerated that process.

Following the hearings, which were held in September 1943, the FEPC ruled that the agreement violated Executive Order 9346 and therefore must be set aside. Although the ruling produced no further decisive action from the White House, the hearings did expose to public opinion the horrendous problem of racial discrimination and segregation in employment. Along with hearings in other industries, they also helped increase awareness of and sympathy for the plight of the black worker.

Charles Houston's landmark struggle against the railroads in the companion cases *Steele* v. *Louisville and Nashville Railroad Company* and *Tunstall* v. *Brotherhood of Locomotive Firemen and Enginemen* hit sharply at the exclusion of blacks from closed union shops under the Southeastern Carriers agreement. Houston had been special counsel to the FEPC for the railroad hearings and so knew the full background of the problem. In those cases, the U.S. Supreme Court ruled on December 18, 1944, that in enacting the Railway Labor Act, Congress had not intended that a labor union, representing the majority of workers in situations where it was the exclusive bargaining agent, could exclude the minority of workers from its protection. The union, the Court declared, had a duty to "represent the interests of all its members" regardless of their color. Neither, the Court said, could the union negotiate a contract that deprived a minority worker of his seniority or job privileges in favor of white firemen.

The Court's ruling left no doubt about the illegality of the Southeastern Carriers agreement. But such pacts had become so numerous that to eliminate them by litigation against individual railroads would have been extremely costly. Furthermore, the *Steele* and *Tunstall* cases touched only on the rights of blacks after they had been hired and did not affect minorities who had been barred altogether from employment. In Mitchell's view, those two cases established the fairness doctrine that would become the guiding philosophy in future civil rights programs such as affirmative action. The concept epitomized the concerns Mitchell had voiced as executive director of the St. Paul Urban League about the exclusion of blacks from membership in closed shops.[22]

Discrimination against a class of workers also existed in many other areas. In another railroad job category, blacks could be dining car waiters but not stewards, the more desirable position. Those supervisory jobs were for whites only. Blacks who were determined to challenge this restriction would lose their seniority accumulated as waiters.

Another big problem during World War II involved factories, where blacks were frozen in helper categories. They earned more than apprentices, but if they wanted to advance to skilled mechanics, or master craftsmen, they had to start all over as apprentices, losing their seniority. In other areas, such as carpentry, blacks would be classified as rough carpenters, qualified to lay heavy planks and build scaffolding, but fine carpentry work, the higher-paying category involving hanging doors and installing window frames, was reserved for whites.

Among the boilermakers, another form of conspiracy existed, primarily in West Coast shipyards, that kept blacks as a class out of higher-paying skilled jobs. That problem arose at the beginning of the war emergency when there was a great demand for workers. Under a "master agreement," most of the yards gave the International Brotherhood of Boilermakers, Iron Ship Builders, Blacksmiths, Forgers and Helpers (AFL) closed-shop rights covering about 65 percent of workers. Blacks were relegated to auxiliary unions in which they paid full dues but had few of the rights of full-fledged members. The Supreme Court of California in *James* v. *Marinship Corp.* and

Williams v. *International Brotherhood of Boilermakers* ruled that (1) the auxiliaries were discriminatory; (2) a closed shop from which blacks were arbitrarily barred was illegal; (3) denial of equal membership to blacks represented total exclusion from the union; and (4) an employer could be enjoined from assisting a union in enforcing a discriminatory closed shop agreement. Nevertheless, the Boilermakers found other ways to continue segregation.[23]

Despite the long-range constitutional issues the above problems posed, Mitchell's immediate concerns were basically the same as before: (1) employers and/or unions unwilling to obey Roosevelt's nondiscrimination directives; (2) strikes by white workers who refused to work with blacks or to permit their upgrading, or by blacks protesting workplace discrimination; and (3) uncooperative government agencies, such as the WMC and USES.

As senior FEPC examiner, Mitchell in early May 1943 had helped work out solutions at the Timken Roller Bearing Company, in Canton, Ohio, when white workers refused to train twenty-seven blacks who were being upgraded. He encouraged the black workers to stay on the job while he tried to resolve the problem. He discovered, however, that while the Navy readily agreed to cooperate with the upgrading program, the Army, which had a greater stake in the plant's operations, refused to cooperate. Greater challenges lay ahead at which he would be more successful.[24]

In Alabama, where racial problems in the extensive shipyard and war industry facilities had long been a festering sore, the committee had exposed these problems during the Birmingham hearings in June 1942. That was why Roosevelt had submerged the committee in the WMC. As everyone discovered, however, silencing the FEPC did not solve the problem.

A confidential report, "The Community Emergency in Mobile, Alabama," issued on January 12, 1942, by the National Resources Planning Board Field Office, had warned about existing tinderbox conditions in the area:

> A four-fold expansion of shipyard and other war employment from the month of the 1940 Census to the present date has sufficed to fill this far-from-modern city bank-full; the population has grown from 114,000 to conservatively 130,000, which represents maximum capacity even though an estimated 6,000 workers and their families still reside out of town.

Consequently, the city was out of living space for more workers.

Whites in that southern city, therefore, were in even less of a mood for talk about racial equality than they would have been normally. The *Anniston Times,* priding itself on being a "progressive semiweekly," tried to foster understanding for the Birmingham hearings by expressing its belief that "most Southerners want to win the war the quickest and surest way, and know that this requires the complete mobilization of resources and manpower." That meant, the *Times* said, "the use of Negroes wherever their strength and skill is most valuable." It warned that "failure to utilize the manpower in our 13,000,000 Negroes is inviting defeat and that is something no true American courts today." Alabama's political leaders, however, as their subsequent attacks on the FEPC showed, were nowhere near as statesmanlike as the *Anniston Times*.

Little wonder, therefore, that whites at the Pinto Island yards of the Alabama Drydock and Shipbuilding Company on May 25, 1943, attacked scores of black workers with iron pipes, wrenches, bricks, and clubs because twelve blacks had been upgraded to welders. The disruption lasted four days. Most of the twenty-six thousand workers were induced to return to their jobs after the Alabama National Guard and federal troops had been called out to restore calm and by a settlement the NAACP called "disgraceful" because it provided for continued segregation of blacks. The settlement was devised by the War Manpower Commission, the FEPC, the Navy, the shipbuilding company, the Maritime Commission, and the Marine and Shipbuilding Workers of America. Fearing for their safety, however, the yard's twenty-one hundred black workers refused to return.

To begin implementing the May 29 strike settlement plan, the FEPC dispatched Mitchell to Pinto Island. Mitchell's first job upon arriving at the shipyard the following day was to get the black workers to return to their jobs. At a meeting with the striking workers that was called by the Industrial Union of Marine and Shipbuilding Workers of America (a member of the CIO), Mitchell assured them that he would be at the shipyard the following morning to make sure they were protected. "If you do your best, Uncle Sam will do the rest," he promised. He was present at six o'clock the following morning, when all of them returned.

Mitchell thought the situation was interesting since the President's authority in calling out the Army was not as clearly defined as it had been in other labor disputes. The immediate question in a matter, which was within state jurisdiction because Alabama's governor and local officials had not declared the matter was beyond their control, was how the Army would proceed to quell any further disturbances. Mitchell thought it fortunate that the colonel in charge of the troops was friendly. He offered to begin moving the soldiers from one point to another so that everyone would see them—thus giving an impression of authority and determination. Thus, there was no further trouble. While walking around the yard, which was patrolled by National Guard forces, Mitchell heard a white worker yell to his friend, "What you gonna say?" The other man responded, "What the hell can you say with all these fellas with these guns." Mitchell thought that "it was a very impressive sight, very early in the morning." He received "wonderful support" from the community, and was accompanied to the shipyard by several local leaders. To guarantee continued protection for the blacks, Mitchell recommended that federal troops, who had been positioned with mounted machine guns, be kept in place for the foreseeable future because he did not believe the company guards and the Alabama National Guard could maintain peace.

Mitchell subsequently testified before a House Subcommittee on Shipbuilding Plants hearing on a resolution authorizing investigation of the national defense program; the need for such a hearing showed that the situation at the Alabama shipyard was not unique. He was one of the FEPC's staff members with a record of settling strikes. Based on discussions with him and others, John. A. Davis recommended to Malcolm Ross that the agency make a general statement of policy that it was opposed to strikes in industry that had a racial basis "as a violation of public policy and of labor's pledge to the Government and as dangerous to the war effort." Davis noted that the "FEPC's value in racial strike situations lies in the fact that it has the confidence of the Negro workers." Consequently, he said, when the FEPC encouraged blacks who had struck because of unbearable discrimination to return to work, the agency should be sure that it could devise a solution for their grievances. The FEPC's response to future strikes showed that it accepted the urgency of Davis's recommendations.

A walkout similar to the Alabama one occurred in July 1944 at the Bethlehem Steel Company in Baltimore at Sparrows Point. Once more, the Army had to be called out as a peacekeeping force. Mitchell explained that the problem in Baltimore as elsewhere was that although large numbers of blacks were employed at several shipbuilding yards, "certain customs and regulations" barred them from some jobs. Those discriminatory practices, he indicated, were supported by international labor unions. Mitchell made recommendations that were accepted, and so he helped devise a solution.[25]

White workers for local streetcar companies staged similarly violent demonstrations against the upgrading of black workers. Since transit companies were deemed "essential employers" by the WMC, they were covered by its national edict barring discrimination against any "qualified employee." Mitchell helped provide the FEPC with one of its most celebrated successes in this area during a strike that involved the Philadelphia Rapid Transit Company.

Philadelphia was classified by the WMC as a Group 1 labor market owing to its critical wartime role, so the WMC had another reason beyond wanting to eliminate racial discrimination, for its involvement. The area produced radar, heavy artillery and ammunition, military trucks, incendiary bombs, flame-throwers, and other critical supplies needed for the war. When "flying squads," or provocateurs, staged a wildcat strike on August 1, 1944, and "persuaded" six thousand employees to stay away from their jobs because the Philadelphia Rapid Transit Company was training eight black men to be streetcar operators, one third of the people who worked in war plants could not get to work. The War Department said that the tie-up was particularly serious because of the urgent needs on the fighting front.

Maslow dispatched Mitchell to Philadelphia the following morning to assist the FEPC's regional office there. Upon arriving, Mitchell promptly obtained a full report from the regional director, G. James Fleming, another highly respected black FEPC staffer. Then he began a round of meetings with city and company officials as well as with the Army, Navy, War Labor Board, War Production Board, and interested citizens in an effort to settle the dispute. Without hesitating, he rejected the company's proposal, which would have ended the strike by returning to its former system of discrimination. Discovering that strike leaders were using the company's car barns for meetings to incite workers, Mitchell had them closed. He maintained pressure on related government agencies by proposing that they meet to discuss the problem.

Late that Tuesday night he met with the mayor and various government representatives at city hall. Afterward they issued a joint statement saying that they had "concluded that nothing effective can be done locally to end the transit stoppage." The stage was thus set for President Roosevelt to call out the Army. Mitchell returned to Washington Wednesday night after rejecting another "face-saving" plan, this time proposed by the War Production Board's regional director, to get the strikers back to work by having the black trainees call in sick and stay "off for a few days until things cooled down." Mitchell suggested that such "loyal union men as could be found" return to work and the "full force of the Philadelphia police system back up such action." That prospect, deemed futile, was nevertheless tried just before Mitchell returned to Washington. Only one old police captain showed up to protect the few workers who ventured out. So the predicted futility was verified. The following evening at about eight o'clock, on Roosevelt's orders, the Army took command of the transit system and announced that it would operate it for "purposes connected with the war emergency as long as needful or desirable." By Saturday evening, five thousand fully equipped troops were in Philadelphia operating and guarding every bus and streetcar. The strike leaders were arrested based on evidence gathered by the Federal Bureau of Investigation. Faced with a War Department threat that strikers would be drafted or barred from work for the duration of the war with no unemployment compensation, the workers returned to their jobs by Monday morning.[26]

Mitchell worked on the Philadelphia strike simultaneously with another involving the Los Angeles Transit Company. Like the Philadelphia Rapid Transit, the Los Angeles company, with the support of one of two rival unions, refused to obey the FEPC order to upgrade blacks even though there was a shortage of workers. In both cases considerable pressure was exerted on the government to weaken its demands.

Meeting with Jonathan Daniels, a powerful presidential aide who handled all labor problems for the White House, right after returning to Washington, Mitchell had him reaffirm his pledge to enforce fully Executive Order 9346. Daniels's hesitancy revealed his nervousness over the fact that he was already out on a limb because it was he who had urged the President to call out the Army in Philadelphia. "My God," he protested, "the FEPC has just hurt the war effort in Philadelphia, the most important production area, now it is creating trouble in Los Angeles, the second most important."

Daniels showed Mitchell a lengthy telegram from the mayor of Los Angeles pleading that the War Labor Board cancel a forthcoming hearing on local transit discrimination. According to Mitchell: "Mr. Daniels asked my opinion on what should be done. I informed him that the Los Angeles hearings had been postponed twice at the request of the mayor. I also stated that in this instance the attention of the nation had been focused on the Philadelphia situation, [so] if the government retreated in the Los Angeles Street Railway, it would appear that we had become frightened because of irresponsible opposition. This, I informed him, would greatly weaken our position with employers all over the country and would have a dangerously adverse effect on Negroes."

Daniels suggested that a closed hearing might be better because the newspapers were hostile. But Mitchell countered that such hostility would be helpful "so that from at least one source our story would not be garbled." Daniels "then asked whether it would be possible to hold in abeyance the issuance of directives for a few weeks." Mitchell reminded him that such directives normally are never issued immediately after public hearings. "He seemed somewhat reassured at this point" and requested that the FEPC's chairman inform the Los Angeles mayor about the committee's procedures. This unique exchange showed the type of authority that the FEPC had given blacks during the wartime emergency.[27]

The federal government's firm handling of the Philadelphia strike had a dramatic impact on the Los Angeles conflict. Mitchell was considerably helped on the Coast by Harry L. Kingman, a white regional FEPC director. Kingman had lived briefly in China and, demonstrating his commitment to human justice, had taken a leave of absence from his job as director of Stiles Hall, the University of California at Berkeley's campus YMCA, to

guide the equal employment effort. He instituted affirmative action programs with the help of influential military and civilian officials in the defense industry.

Kingman contributed evidence of discrimination to the FEPC hearings
that proved the discrimination charges against the Los Angeles transit system. The results, which caused the company and union to ask for a strong
directive from the government requiring blacks to be hired as streetcar and
bus operators and upgraded to other platform jobs, left those who had
counseled delay breathless. The government order that was issued relieved
the union and company of the onus of that decision, and it enabled blacks
to begin filling the new positions before the end of August.

Upon returning to Los Angeles, Mitchell had an experience in human
relations that he always enjoyed telling about. A black driver, beckoning
him to the front of the car, said, "There are some ladies about to get on. Be
sure to give one of them your seat." He thought "how wonderful it would
be if all who get jobs after great controversies over whether they should be
hired could be as perceptive as that man in building good will.[28]

Discrimination practices in the Philadelphia and Los Angeles transit
systems were typical of national patterns, providing ideal opportunities for
such goodwill. Blacks were barred from platform jobs—as streetcar conductors, motormen, and bus operators. As a first step in forcing the employment of blacks, the WMC had refused to permit the importation of
workers into those cities until all available labor supplies had been used.
The WMC also supported fully the FEPC's request to enforce the President's Executive Orders 8802 and 9346. Breaking the discrimination practices of such civilian employers was especially important to blacks because
local transportation systems offered considerable postwar job opportunities,
to which they were now looking.

The Philadelphia Rapid Transit Company case was a perfect example of
management-union collusion to perpetuate discrimination. For Mitchell,
the important lesson in that case, as well as those involving the Los Angeles
Transit Company and the Alabama shipyards, was that white workers' resistance to the hiring of blacks for jobs from which they had been barred
could be ended when the government stood firmly behind orders to end
racial discrimination based on historical occupational patterns.[29]

By late 1944, employers in most war-related industries had accepted
the FEPC's jurisdiction, but not the Post Office Department, which Mitchell found through the years to be the worst discriminator within the government. That department's resistance was worsened by the prospect that
the war would soon end, and with it the FEPC's authority. The Philadelphia postmaster had challenged the FEPC's authority. To address the problem, Mitchell arranged for a meeting between the FEPC's chairman and the

U.S. postmaster general in late November 1944. "We discussed pending cases against Post Offices in Philadelphia, Los Angeles, Dallas, Houston, and Seattle. One important result of this conference was acknowledgment by the Post Office Department of the committee's jurisdiction." The FEPC, said Mitchell, "also resolved a question of whether Post Office laborers who accept War Service appointments as carriers or clerks [were] entitled to reinstatement to their old jobs at the close of the emergency period," when former employees serving in the war would expect to return to their jobs. Postal officials "agreed that, as a matter of national policy, such persons" were "entitled to reinstatement" to jobs they, too, previously had. Because there would be a surplus of postal workers, Mitchell had ample reason to fear that the department would exclude blacks from rehiring after the war. Despite progress at the meeting with the postmaster general, he reported that all points were not resolved, so "we will have to undertake further and lengthy negotiations with postal officials." These negotiations were never held because the FEPC was disbanded. But Mitchell, as a member of the NAACP staff, would continue to pursue relentlessly discrimination within the Post Office Department.[30]

Hitler's armies were not alone in facing defeat as spring approached in 1945. While the forces of democracy and freedom were winning in Europe, in the United States racists and reactionary standard-bearers were prevailing in Congress.

Executive Order 8802 had been the first fundamental civil rights victory since the Civil War. The primary forces aiding blacks during the war years were (1) the national desire to win the war; (2) the need to use all sources of available labor; (3) the fear of urban riots, such as those that had swept the country in 1943 (the most spectacular one occurred in Detroit and was sparked by intense competition between whites and blacks for very scarce housing and jobs); and (4) international pressures to portray the American system of government as the antithesis of Nazism and fascism.

The FEPC was the most promising symbol of hope for equal economic opportunity that African Americans had ever had. It gave African Americans their first opportunity in history to be line officers in the federal government. Though small, that group of African Americans extended their influence by maintaining a close-knit network of interrelationships. Previously, they could rise to no higher position than racial adviser to white liberals—a stricture that limited their effectiveness and contributions. The FEPC established a well-defined program by means of which the government attacked racial, ethnic, religious, and other forms of discrimination in employment. It expanded considerably the indicia of discrimination that Robert Weaver had developed and set a precedent for government enforcement of its nondiscrimination orders by issuing directives and getting other agencies to seek compliance.

A central component of the FEPC program was the creation, under the direction of Will Maslow, of a compliance form for the U.S. Employment Service that enabled the government to measure progress among contractors in hiring and placing a substantial number of blacks in skilled positions. The program avoided identifying workers by race while requiring employers to maintain records on the numbers of minorities they had working for them, intended to hire, or had hired after the program went into effect. These principles of accountability and referrals by race were based on the concept of fairness that would also be built into future affirmative action programs.

The best proof that the FEPC was opening doors of opportunity was the increase in the number of minorities employed in war industries, from less than 3 percent in early 1942 to more than 7 percent two years later, and 8 percent by the end of the war. Eighty percent of those benefiting from Executive Order 8802 and the FEPC were black; 14 percent were mostly Mexican Americans, and the remainder primarily Jews.

Under the leadership of the NAACP, African Americans gained their second fundamental civil rights victory on April 3, 1944, when the Supreme Court reversed its ruling from an earlier case and held, in *Smith* v. *Allwright,* that qualified blacks could not be refused the right to vote in Democratic primaries. By affirming again the constitutional right of minorities to the ballot, the Court removed whatever legal doubts might have remained after two earlier rulings.[31]

Developments in the courts like the *Smith* v. *Allwright, Steele,* and *Tunstall* decisions, as well as the NAACP's advancing legal campaign to overturn the "separate but equal" doctrine, strengthened the struggle for a permanent FEPC. The movement was joined by the National Council for a Permanent FEPC, led by A. Philip Randolph, and the NAACP. They, however, were no match for the FEPC's enemies in Congress. Senator Theodore G. "the Man" Bilbo of Mississippi and other southerners led a fight to kill the FEPC by gaining control of the committee's funding in 1944 through an amendment sponsored in the Senate by Richard B. Russell, Democrat of Georgia. That measure barred the use of appropriations for any agency established by executive order and in existence for more than one year without congressional approval. On his deathbed on April 12, 1945, Roosevelt pleaded for Congress to renew the FEPC's funding. Instead, the lawmakers signed the committee's death warrant by appropriating only $250,000—half of the funds the agency had requested—and set June 30, 1946, as the deadline for the FEPC to end its operations. But even with sharp cuts in staff, that sum was not enough to allow the committee to vouchsafe its few remaining employees their termination pay. So, after being denied a request for an additional $27,600, the FEPC closed its doors on May 30, 1946.[32]

In its final days, the FEPC received a gratuitous slap from President Truman. He ordered the committee, which was now frantically using its rapidly waning authority to open a few more opportunities for minorities in anticipation of the reconversion period after the war, not to issue a directive to the Capital Transit Company requiring it to end racial discrimination and hire blacks as platform workers. Capital Transit's discrimination policies were similar to those that the FEPC had ended in Philadelphia and Los Angeles.

Seated before a stack of directives that were about to be sent out when Truman's order arrived, Mitchell looked at George Johnson, and the deputy chairman looked at him. "You know, we can't send these out," Johnson told Mitchell. "But if somebody would happen to take one and give it out it might be a good thing." Several years later Mitchell explained that because he was new to Washington, he missed the hint to leak the FEPC and Truman orders to the press. Houston needed no such hint. He submitted his resignation to Truman to protest the President's Capital Transit order and publicly explained his reason.

Mitchell had the unpleasant task of closing the agency's field division in its final six months after he succeeded Maslow. As a government employee he could do little more than go through the motions of running the division. Afterward, however, he had much to say.

The FEPC, he complained, "had been the victim of the most cynical political short-changing ever since it was established." Nevertheless, it had many impressive accomplishments, such as sharply increasing nonwhite employment in war industries and ending segregation in the Philadelphia and Los Angeles transit companies. He continued in an article in an NAACP bulletin:

It was also this agency, in cooperation with other groups, which brought about the hiring of colored operators in the telephone companies of New York and New Jersey. A graphic sample of its success was shown in a check-up after its hearings in Birmingham, Chicago, Los Angeles and New York. Thirty-one companies cited at these hearings had employed 4,000 non-white workers. A little over a year later these same companies employed a total of 23,000 non-whites.

Many of its successes, however, were accomplished without hearings. Sometimes by the simple action of writing a letter or making a visit, the representatives of the agency could correct a discriminatory practice. At other times negotiations required months before a settlement could be reached. At the peak of its activity, FEPC had handled 12,000 cases and settled satisfactorily more than a third of them. It was receiving approximately 300 new cases each month.

Although the high priest of falsehood, Senator Bilbo, has accused FEPC of stirring up trouble, most of its settlements were accomplished peacefully. During the period between July, 1943 and December, 1944 less than 2 percent of all strikes in the country were due to racial issues. More than half of these were started by colored workers themselves as protests against discriminatory employment policies.

The successes would have been more if the agency had enjoyed the support of the important war agencies, such as the War Department, the War Production Board and the War Manpower Commission. All too frequently, these agencies crippled the action of FEPC.

With the FEPC's death, Mitchell noted, many firms began returning to their old discriminatory practices. "We are where we were at the beginning of the defense program." A "crazy quilt pattern of employment" under which recruiting agents were sent scouring the country for skilled workers while ignoring blacks, Mexicans, and Jews at home was again being practiced. President Truman's forbidding FEPC to issue the nondiscrimination directive against the Capital Transit Company was a painful example of future prospects. By not acting against the company's refusal to hire blacks in platform positions, Truman "strengthened the opposition in the industry" to employment desegregation "and scared off forward-looking officials who possibly would have changed their hiring practices."

Truman blocked the FEPC order because he feared the power of Congressmen Martin Dies, Jr., a Democrat from Texas, and John E. Rankin, Democrat of Mississippi. They charged the agency was influenced by Communists who planned to start a race war in Washington. Dies was then championing an antisubversion crusade and Rankin was a virtuoso at using parliamentary tactics to dominate House action.

But Mitchell still found considerable reason for optimism. The Capital Transit case illustrated "how a few misguided planners and high strategists muffed the ball." They "thought that we could have a Permanent FEPC only if we did not create any trouble by insisting that Negroes be hired as platform men." He did not "know who presented this rubber check," but it became "clear that neither in the White House nor in Congress was there a real intention to establish a strong, permanent FEPC if it could possibly be avoided." The "dramatic resignation" of Charles Houston, formerly the NAACP's special counsel and now a private attorney in Washington, from the FEPC's board of directors, to protest Truman's action in the Capital Transit case, and the "militant fighting of the National Council for a Permanent FEPC" forced a showdown in the Senate early in 1946. Then, a second attempt to pass a permanent FEPC bill, S. 101, sponsored by Senator Dennis Chavez of New Mexico, was killed by a Senate filibuster. That defeat in the Seventy-ninth Congress ended the first major drive to pass a FEPC measure.

Mitchell explained that had Houston and the Council for a Permanent FEPC not held their ground,

> the agency would have been put to sleep with the issuance of some dehydrated reports. The lesson to be learned from this is that in the fight for economic justice, minorities should never exchange immediate possibilities for real progress or for mere promises of future action. Anyone who means to be fair will give both. The people must scrutinize closely those who profess to have liberal convictions to be sure that the spoken word will be followed by concrete action.

That was no swan song. Mitchell had taken up the challenge of the FEPC grail. His experiences in the federal government were now his compass for the rocky course ahead in the struggle for full racial equality. Mitchell was well aware that, whatever the causes of and theoretical adjustments to periodic depressions, the federal government was the only institution with adequate powers to institute proper remedies for the social problems and economic collapse that followed in their wake. The Great Depression had finally forced the federal government to confront this issue and aggressively intervene in the economic affairs of the nation. Blacks benefited from the resulting change in the national attitude about the legitimate role of the federal government in extending its functions and responsibilities. Mitchell's goal now was to harness the forces released by that new attitude into the creation of laws for the protection of the constitutional rights of black Americans.[33]

CHAPTER SEVEN

NAACP Labor Secretary

"A few days ago, I was in Union Station in Washington amid the vast throng of visitors who had come to the capital for President Truman's inaugural," Clarence Mitchell told his audience at a mass meeting for a permanent FEPC in Chicago on January 30, 1949. "I saw a friend from Chicago who asked me whether I was leaving town. When I said, 'Yes,' he could hardly believe me. 'Why, you won't be here for all of the celebrations,' he said. My reply was, 'The only celebration I am interested in is that which we shall have when the civil rights program becomes law."[1]

When the President's Committee on Fair Employment Practice sank in 1946, Mitchell carried with him an idea whose outer frame might have been destroyed but whose soul had now become inseparable from his own. The FEPC experience proved that discrimination could be eliminated. Mitchell's hope for resurrecting the dream was strengthened by Walter White's expansion of the NAACP staff. That May, White reported happily to his budget committee that "we have finally succeeded in obtaining an admirable person" for the newly created position of labor secretary. That person was Mitchell.

Creation of the labor department was the NAACP's first programmatic attempt to address employment discrimination and seek black economic equality for blacks. That attempt would eventually be overshadowed by broader civil rights goals, but for Mitchell the FEPC grail loomed larger than ever. White's other important addition to the staff that year was

Gloster B. Current as director of branches. Current had previously been executive secretary of the Detroit NAACP branch, a job to which Juanita Mitchell had lured him from a promising music career when she had been director of the association's youth program a decade earlier. Along with White, NAACP officers Mitchell, Current, Roy Wilkins, and special counsel Thurgood Marshall, as well as A. Philip Randolph (though he was not associated with the NAACP), were now the principal architects of the modern civil rights movement. Within the next two years, White would add to the team Henry Lee Moon, a veteran reporter and publicist, as director of public relations.

The NAACP Washington Bureau was created in 1942 as "a watchdog in the national capital." Such a program had been tried back in 1917, when the NAACP hired "a trained newspaperman to watch both houses of Congress and report all hostile legislation immediately" to the national office. It had been discontinued for lack of funds. Reviving the idea, George S. Schuyler, the acerbic African American writer, wondered twelve years later "how many Negroes have considered the necessity for lobbyists for the Colored people of this country." White at that time was leading the fierce struggle for antilynching legislation in Washington and was himself a de facto lobbying bureau. But he needed help and acknowledged that reality. The NAACP was still unable to afford the expense of a Washington Bureau, so White continued to divide his time between his national duties and work on Capitol Hill.

Increased competition from other African Americans like Randolph and the obvious need for a more effective program in Washington soon enabled White to win approval from the NAACP national board of directors to create a Washington Bureau. The expectations of blacks were significantly increased by the strengthening of the presidency under the Reorganization Act of 1939, which enabled the Chief Executive to coordinate policy more effectively and facilitated the institutionalization and centralization of long-range planning. If blacks were to make bricks without straw, the federal government was central to their struggle for an end to racial injustice. With strong support from the black press, White immediately launched an aggressive national drive to raise $6,000 for the salaries of an administrative assistant and secretary, rent, and other bureau operating costs.

When Mitchell joined the Washington Bureau, White was its director. White was devoting at least three days a week in the nation's capital to the NAACP's drive for a permanent FEPC, and for antilynching, anti-poll-tax, and other civil rights legislation. Working with him in the bureau were Leslie Perry, an attorney who was his administrative assistant, and Jesse O. Dedmon, Jr., secretary of veterans affairs. White was also being assisted by an advisory committee.

Mitchell welcomed the new opportunity; it "promises to be as challeng-ing as FEPC work." He moved into his new office at the NAACP Wash-ington Bureau on Massachusetts Avenue, two blocks from bustling Union Station and a short walk from Capitol Hill, and immediately began setting up his operation. He requested from White and was granted a week in August for a long-overdue vacation—without pay.

Mitchell began the evolutionary process of becoming a civil rights lob-byist by launching a comprehensive program geared to meet the challenges of employment discrimination that were made more complex and difficult by the nation's rapid reconversion from a wartime to a peacetime economy. About twelve million people had served in the armed forces and another eight million had been working in war production industries. Most of them needed jobs and housing. Between V-E Day and V-J Day, unemployment doubled to one million and then continued to increase as defense contracts were canceled and factories closed. For blacks the problem was critical be-cause most of them had been working in defense industries, for example in munitions plants. Adding to their plight was the unchecked revival of racial discrimination and segregation in those industries. Though the FEPC's jurisdiction during the war was limited to defense-related industries and contracts, blacks had also made considerable progress on the civilian front owing to the severe manpower shortage. Now there was a sizable labor surplus, especially in the northern industrial cities to which blacks had migrated in large numbers from the South.

The resulting competition for jobs between whites and blacks inten-sified racial tensions and fears among many people about outbreaks of riots similar to those that had followed World War I. Two of the most notorious were the 1917 riots in Houston by members of the 24th Infantry, which had led to the summary execution of nineteen black soldiers for violently protesting discrimination, and in East St. Louis, Illinois, where blacks, who represented the majority of workers in giant manufacturing plants like Swift and Armour, were driven from their homes. To protest this wide-spread lynching and mob violence against blacks, the NAACP that year led a silent parade with muffled drums down New York's Fifth Avenue.

Racial and social tensions were further aggravated by massive inflation fueled by the ending of price controls, price wars, and the wage squeeze following the termination of wartime employment perks, such as consider-able overtime. The FEPC anticipated the disproportionate impact of these problems on African Americans. In its *Final Report* to the President, it made three basic recommendations: that he "continue to urge upon the Congress the passage of legislation which will guarantee equal job oppor-tunity to all workers without discrimination because of race, color, re-ligious belief, or national origin"; that the government "take steps not only to promulgate its policy more widely, but to enforce it as well," because the "mere existence of a Federal policy of nondiscrimination will not in itself result in fair employment practices"; and that appropriate government agencies report more widely statistics on "employment and unemployment by race and by sex within industries and occupations" in order to make the public more aware of the handicaps of minority-group workers.

Mitchell had helped prepare those recommendations when he was with the FEPC, and his seven objectives for the NAACP's labor program reflected that same sense of mission. His extensive knowledge of the federal bureaucracy and its pitfalls made him the association's expert on how to achieve social changes through the administrative process of government. To bring about those changes, he proposed the enactment of state and federal FEPC laws.

Although the FEPC no longer existed as an administering agency, the wartime Executive Order 9346 that Roosevelt had issued to strengthen it was still in effect. Mitchell's seven objectives were the elimination of all forms of employment discrimination, greater participation of blacks in trade unions as well as an end to segregation and discrimination by unions, passage of legislation creating effective state and federal agencies such as the FEPC, inclusion of nondiscrimination clauses in state and federal laws covering government contracts, joining labor unions in their struggle for legislation affecting their interests, and expanding and improving vocational training opportunities for blacks. He tailored his program to utilize the NAACP national branch structure as a massive lobbying machine.

Mitchell created a Labor Committee to assist him. The group of distinguished and influential persons he chose served to strengthen his program as well as his political position within the organization. Half of the committee's members were top officials of the American Federation of Labor and the Congress of Industrial Organizations. Among the others, who were mostly NAACP board members, were Charles Houston, whom Mitchell respected for his independent judgment and integrity as well as for his legal genius, Eleanor Roosevelt, and Randolph.

Mitchell's heavy emphasis on labor and the nature of his seven-point program revealed how much he had embraced Weaver's belief that union membership was essential to economic progress by blacks. No one was more aware than Mitchell of organized labor's history of discrimination—it was a record rooted in the ideological foundations of the racial and class consciousness of European immigrants like Samuel Gompers, the first president of the American Federation of Labor. Gompers regarded Chinese, Japanese and later African Americans as "unassimilable," hence they were proscribed from the labor movement. Mitchell's strategy for change on the labor front was more one of inducement than of chastisement, an effective stance he had adopted throughout his professional career. An even more important reason for developing such an alliance was his awareness that labor had amassed considerable political and financial resources under the protective National Labor Relations Act of 1935, popularly called the Wagner Act. He recognized that labor's new clout was essential to gaining passage of civil rights legislation in Congress.

With the demise of the FEPC, Mitchell assumed Weaver's role as the principal national recipient of employment discrimination complaints. Those were funneled mostly through the NAACP's national branch network. He instructed the branches to establish labor committees, preparing and distributing to the most active ones a comprehensive manual as a guide for handling discrimination problems. Although his stated goals weighed heavily on labor unions, a concern heightened by the mass of individual complaints he received, his primary focus quickly became that of educating the nation about the systemic nature of discrimination within the federal government, the injustice of such practices, and the strong and urgent need for effective federal laws to protect the constitutional rights of minorities.

Franklin Roosevelt's administration was dominated by southern influence, but he had been more positive and helpful to blacks than any President since Abraham Lincoln. Now blacks had to deal with Harry Truman, who had a fairly liberal civil rights record as a U.S. senator. But, seeking to balance civil rights demands against fierce opposition from southern lawmakers, he began his presidency on a negative note with blacks by forbidding the FEPC to act in the Capital Transit Company case in Washington and by helping to assure the agency's demise. Truman was a forthright advocate of "equal opportunity for everybody, regardless of race, creed or color," but when it came time for him to translate words into deeds, he ducked. Blacks, whose political influence was still relatively weak, found it much easier to exert pressure on the executive branch than on Congress, so they intensified demands for Truman to use his powers to end discrimination and segregation in federal employment and in the armed services.

Mitchell found that without an administering FEPC agency and enforcement powers, Executive Order 9346 was inadequate for ending discrimination. Authority for administering the order rested with certain agencies, but for all practical purposes that authority was too narrow, he complained. The order had no effective enforcement provisions; more important, it imposed "no obligations upon agencies to cooperate with the [primary] administering agency either in the formulation of personnel policies and programs" or in their implementation.

In developing his new program, Mitchell was guided by his intimate knowledge of the FEPC's weaknesses. He was particularly aware of a complaint in the FEPC's *Final Report* that "policing the non-discrimination policy was an extra chore to agencies who already felt they had more than enough work to do in their old specialized war activities. Officials too often by-passed the issue." Because the FEPC had no effective authority for backing up its recommendations and findings of discrimination, other agencies usually gave it the runaround. Mitchell, furthermore, felt that the old executive order was seen as "inadequate and ineffectual," so that any effort to enforce it "would be of little political significance and in fact might prove to be a political boomerang."

Mitchell's first order of business was to remove racial barriers in the federal government's massive construction program. Meeting with the labor director of the National Housing Agency, he expressed his desire that non-white labor should be used on the agency's projects. He was optimistic that the director would be "cooperative in handling the problems which arise." But, at the same time, he saw in the bureaucracy "very little evidence of action to insure the full use of colored skilled craftsmen in this field." Aware that the U.S. Employment Service offices in Virginia, North Carolina, and California had large numbers of unfilled orders for workers, he documented the availability of approximately fifty-six thousand nonwhites who had been employed in wartime shipyards. Many of them, he pointed out, had skills that were suitable for construction work.

He obtained information on projected federal construction projects in various communities throughout the nation and distributed it to NAACP branches with the suggestion that they prod appropriate local government agencies to use all available workers. One of the most useful pieces of information he circulated was a letter to Walter White from Frank S. Horne, who had succeeded Robert Weaver as the federal government's top black housing expert, detailing a program for the branches to seek construction jobs in the Veterans Emergency Housing Program in more than eighty large cities with labor shortages.

By the end of 1946, Mitchell was working along four clearly defined lines: mobilizing a broad-based attack on employment discrimination in the federal government; leading the struggle for the creation of a permanent FEPC and calling for passage of similar measures by states; developing the strategy for obtaining a strong presidential executive order barring discrimination in government employment; and combatting attacks on labor, which he regarded as also damaging to the interests of blacks.[2]

Common to all aspects of the struggle against employment discrimination were the issues of racial designations on records of government workers, and employment quotas. Mitchell's attention was first drawn to those issues in 1941, when Walter White began raising questions with the FEPC about the Navy Department's requirement that its employees in Navy yards wear racial identification tags. White thought that such a policy served no useful purpose and only fostered discrimination. He pointed out to the FEPC that Nazi labor camps required similar types of identifications.

In the draft of a letter that Mitchell proposed White send to the secretary of war, in September 1946, Mitchell noted that the War Department, despite sharp reductions, was one of the nation's largest employers, with 148,608 black workers. He therefore suggested that "any constructive action" the secretary of war took "to meet discrimination before" it occurred would "have a healthy effect upon both government and private employment." One problem that had been encountered in postwar cutbacks, he noted, was that blacks did not have an opportunity for reemployment equal to that of white workers. Furthermore, he said, investigations by the FEPC and the NAACP had shown that "many colored employees received suspiciously low efficiency ratings when reductions in force were made." Agencies also flatly refused to hire displaced black workers for available jobs.

Consequently, he proposed a series of safeguards "to keep discriminatory lay-offs at a minimum." One protection would have permitted the government to obtain a reliable count of blacks being released in employment reduction programs but at the same time barred the indication of race on personal records. Another would have barred any agency that specified race in filling job vacancies from recruiting workers through the War Department. Strict instructions would be issued to all department heads to follow Civil Service antidiscrimination regulations. Mitchell also proposed that the War Department urge the President to obtain the Civil Service Commission's cooperation in setting up a central hiring register in which proper consideration would be given to everyone with good government employment records. Although the government stubbornly resisted the NAACP's protests against racial identification, Mitchell ensured that the association's policy was well and widely known and would be continuing.

Subsequently addressing the suggested establishment of racial quota systems in layoffs by a state in 1949, Mitchell expressed grave concern when an NAACP branch indicated that it believed "at one time" the association had supported such practices. In his long relationship with the NAACP, he said, he had not known of any policy endorsing a quota system. He said the NAACP was also opposed to any special consideration in giving jobs to blacks. Mitchell proposed a policy statement for adoption by the NAACP national board of directors that unequivocally reiterated the association's opposition to employment quota systems. He also proposed that the statement be distributed to all the branches. The board approved both of these recommendations.

But such protestations against the use of racial quotas still had little effect on the practice, especially in the armed services, where the companion struggle to establish a racial identification system that would not be harmful to blacks was one of the best indicators of the persistence of the military's continuing policy of discrimination. But, at least, the battle lines were as clearly drawn. That meant the NAACP would never cease prodding the military until it resolved those issues and ended racial discrimination.[3]

Mitchell's concern with the employment practices of the federal government centered on its being one of the nation's largest employers; and it was also funded by the public treasury. Agencies that increasingly commanded his attention were the U.S. Employment Service, the Post Office Department, the Atomic Energy Commission, the Veterans Administration, the Bureau of Printing and Engraving, the Bureau of Old Age and Survivors Insurance, the Agriculture Department, and the Civil Service Commission. Discrimination in these agencies, Mitchell found, was made "more serious than ever" in 1947 by revisions in civil service administrative procedures approved by President Truman that gave more latitude to the agencies in sharply cutting wartime employment rolls.

Through the U.S. Employment Service, a New Deal creation, the federal government was also the nation's largest job placement agency for the private sector, finding jobs for masses of workers not only in construction but also in such labor-intensive industries as textiles, public transportation, telephone companies, and, most notably, the railroads.

Initially, USES offices were run by the states, but they had been placed under federal control during the war. Subsequently, Congress voted to return the offices to the states. Mitchell, who had had considerable trouble with USES when he was with the FEPC, viewed the renewed state control with extreme foreboding. It was well known, he said, that "under the states there was incredible injustice" in the USES. There had been some improvement when the federal government took control, but even then "only the greatest amount of policing and the most vigorous follow up" kept some of the states from discriminating. In others, historical discrimination practices continued unabated.

Rather than helping to end discriminatory employment policies, he knew, the state offices would perpetuate them:

It is very clear in Washington that unless great pressure is exerted, the states intend to get back to their former practices as quickly as possible. This means that in the housing program, the state offices will say that they need to import or train skilled workers in the building trades although colored carpenters, plumbers, electricians and bricklayers are unemployed.

In a letter to Secretary of Labor Lewis B. Schwellenbach in August 1946, Mitchell stated that since the USES offices were federally funded, his agency had "an obligation to see that the standards, rules and regulations of the new arrangement give adequate protection to minority group workers using the employment service facilities." He proposed to Schwellenbach "minimum standards" that should be required of state offices before they received federal funds. He called for protections that would assure full utilization of minority groups in local employment and training programs, the assignment of qualified personnel to prevent discrimination, and a prohibition that no office accept discriminatory orders or provide employment service to employers who did not guarantee that they would hire all workers on a nondiscriminatory basis. Segregated offices were also to be abolished.

The following month, at Mitchell's request, Schwellenbach met with the NAACP labor director and a delegation from the National Urban League, the American Jewish Congress, the American Council on Race Relations, the Fraternal Council of Negro Churches, and the CIO and agreed to end segregation in the District of Columbia USES office. This victory was especially significant in that Mitchell had underscored the principle that the federal government should not use tax dollars to support discrimination. But he was extremely disturbed when, at the same time, the Department of Labor bowed to the states and adopted a new policy for operating USES that was "so bad that I am recommending that the [NAACP] study some legal method for challenging the dispensing of $42 million to the states without proper safeguards against discrimination."

Mitchell wrote to the governors of thirty-nine states asking them to adopt the standards he wanted. A few of them, in liberal states like New York, Washington, and Wisconsin, provided encouraging responses, but the attitudes toward discrimination were so diverse that Mitchell saw "little benefit from the employment service under state operation unless state branches of the NAACP insist that the Service be operated for the good of all persons." More far-reaching was his conclusion that only a law that would place the employment service under federal control again would solve the problem.[4]

Mitchell became fully aware in 1941 of how badly the Post Office Department was treating blacks when the FEPC ordered key government agencies to end their discrimination and begin hiring them. The Post Office Department was consistent in passing over eligible blacks for whites with lower qualifications, so he was not surprised by the increasing number of complaints he was now receiving. Owing to the great manpower needs during the war, the FEPC had gotten the Post Office Department to hire blacks as clerks—but they had received only war-service appointments. Mitchell now found that the department wanted to revert to its old practice of restricting the number of black workers. Another continuing problem was the department's practice of promoting workers on the basis of color rather than merit. In early 1947, the New Orleans post office provided him with an ideal opportunity to challenge the agency's racial policies when it denied seventeen temporary black workers permanent employment as clerks. Mitchell was especially angered by this case because fifteen of the men were veterans who were entitled to special preference.

Working closely with the National Alliance of Postal Employees, he filed an appeal in April against the New Orleans post office action with the Board of Appeals and Review of the Civil Service Commission. He charged that the men were denied employment solely because of their race. In October, Jesse M. Donaldson, first assistant postmaster general, informed Mitchell that a departmental investigation had found no evidence to sustain the charges of racial discrimination. Mitchell had expected such a conclusion but the tone of the response angered him. As he promptly complained to David Niles, administrative assistant to the President, "It is startling to receive such a bland self-exoneration" from Donaldson. He therefore requested an opportunity to discuss the matter personally with Niles, with whom he was working on a broad civil rights program. Whether or not the meeting occurred mattered little.

Mitchell was stung even more in November 1947 by the manner in which the chairman of the Board of Appeals and Review of the Civil Service Commission threw out the NAACP's painstaking documentation of discrimination, declaring that there was "no proof that non-selection was because of race." Mitchell then requested a hearing before the full commission. This struggle would continue for many more months. On December 9, Mitchell took his case to the Senate. President Truman had promoted Donaldson to postmaster general, and Mitchell welcomed the opportunity to present evidence of systemic discrimination within the department to the Senate Civil Service Subcommittee as he gave reasons for opposing Donaldson's confirmation.

During the hearing, Juanita Mitchell, who had been supporting her husband's activities in Washington, was present when the Senate subcommittee chairman, North Dakota Republican William Langer, buckled under pressure and indicated he would support Donaldson's appointment. Without hesitating, Mitchell recalled, Juanita began "jumping on" Langer "for going along," causing the senator to rush over to the lobbyist to ask that he inform "this lady over here that I am your friend, that I had called the hearing, and I am going to be working with you." When Mitchell told Langer that Juanita was his wife, the senator got angry, and remained so. A few weeks later, Capitol Hill police ousted Juanita from a stormy House Labor Subcommittee hearing when she protested that the chairman had not

given her husband a chance to answer questions during a session investigating a strike—a conflict the lobbyist labeled a "real disgrace"—by the Cafeteria Workers Union, an affiliate of the United Public Workers of
America.[5]

Though the Senate confirmed Donaldson's appointment, as a result of
Mitchell's complaints it launched an investigation early in 1948 into the
racial policies of the Post Office Department. For the first time, Langer
appointed a black man, John T. Risher, as chief investigator. Mitchell
immediately established a solid working relationship with the investigator.
In conjunction with NAACP branches throughout the country and the
National Alliance of Postal Employees, Mitchell made sure that complaints
and affidavits were properly filed with the investigating subcommittee.

On the eve of his retirement from the Senate at the end of 1948, Langer
submitted a report to his colleagues recommending the establishment of a
full-time tribunal empowered to seek out discrimination in federal employment rather than awaiting complaints. He also recommended the adoption
of a clear definition of racial discrimination, the requirement of quarterly
reports documenting rejections of blacks for employment, and dismissal of
officials found guilty of practicing discrimination. "There are thousands of
individuals throughout the country who have new reasons to be hopeful
because your report has put the official stamp of government on evidence
which cannot be refuted," Mitchell wrote Langer.[6]

Mitchell had again asked for Schwellenbach's help in pressing the administration for civil rights legislation. During a meeting in December
1946, Schwellenbach told Mitchell that he had sent his recommendations
on legislation to the President and expected to have a conference with him
soon. Schwellenbach said the President believed he would have more success if he left out specific recommendations in his message to Congress.
Mitchell, however, suggested "that it would be very disappointing to minorities and harmful to FEPC legislation, if there is no mention of FEPC in
the message." Schwellenbach said that a new FEPC was about third or
fourth on his list of recommendations to the President. He did not know
what the President would think of that priority, but he promised to call
Mitchell after he had conferred with Truman. Mitchell stressed that it was
especially important that the administration offer a strong FEPC bill to
Congress because that was the only kind that minorities would support. "In
addition, I mentioned that this time the generalship of the bill should be
studied carefully, because in the previous session of Congress the hand of
the Administration was not always as evident as it should have been."[7]

Truman, as was clear when he announced the creation of the President's
Committee on Civil Rights on December 5, 1946, was not eager to press

the FEPC issue. In his State of the Union Message the following month he merely reiterated in a brief mention his concern for the "numerous attacks upon the constitutional rights of individual citizens as a result of racial and religious bigotry." A resurgence of lynchings and other forms of racial violence had enabled Walter White to convince the President that forthright leadership was needed to protect the rights of blacks. Truman, faced with the worldwide decolonialization movement and aggressive competition from the Soviet Union during the developing cold war, was eager to avoid racial embarrassments at home and wanted to portray the United States as a truly democratic nation.

While White maintained pressure on the President, Mitchell met with White House and other government officials and enlisted support from allies. At Mitchell's suggestion, the United Public Workers of America submitted three proposals to the committee during its hearings in early 1947. The most important one, which was Mitchell's idea, called for the immediate establishment of a government agency with "power to compel the hiring of persons who have been discriminated against because of race, creed, color, or national origin. This would be a temporary agency to function until an FEPC is established by law. It would serve as an arm of the president in seeing that there is enforcement of no-discrimination policies in government."

Mitchell was overly optimistic in expecting Truman to issue such an order. The distinguished representatives of business, religion, labor, education, and the legal profession on the Committee on Civil Rights, as their historic report, To Secure These Rights, would reveal in October 1947, were not bound by the narrow political considerations that were restraining Truman. The report went well beyond Truman's mandate and for a while, at least, placed him in a bind. The Republicans captured both houses of the Eightieth Congress in the November 1946 elections, so Truman was thrown on the defensive and the civil rights report proved to be a godsend.

The committee's ten basic priorities were: elevation of the Civil Rights Section of the Justice Department to a division and the creation of a special unit for civil rights investigations within the Federal Bureau of Investigation; establishment of a permanent Commission on Civil Rights in the executive office of the President; legal protections against lynching and other forms of violence; abolition of the poll tax as a prerequisite for voting, and the enactment of federal legislation to protect the rights of qualified persons to participate in federal primaries and elections; ending detention and discrimination against people based on race or ancestry, notably the Japanese; enactment by Congress of legislation establishing local self-government for the District of Columbia and extending suffrage in presidential elections to residents in the nation's capital; ending discrimination in the armed forces; providing Alaska and Hawaii statehood and greater protection for the rights of residents in island territories; enactment of laws outlawing discrimination and segregation; and passage of a federal Fair Employment Practices Act prohibiting discrimination in all forms of *private* employment and the issuance of an executive order by the President barring discrimination in *government* employment as well as the creation of an agency to enforce that order.

Truman's historic civil rights message to Congress on February 2, 1948, reaffirming the committee's ten points as national priorities only intensified Mitchell's eagerness for an executive order. In a letter to White discussing the NAACP's strategy on this matter, Mitchell had written:

> As you know, the FEPC legislation may run into some rough water in this Congress and there is a strong possibility it will not get through. We shall be in a very bad position if we have no Federal body working on employment discrimination. Hence, this order can serve two purposes, (1) it may spur the Republicans into some positive action on the legislative FEPC, and (2) it will keep the idea alive if the Congress fails to act.[8]

Truman was still more a ward politician than a national leader as he played for the black vote in November. He had challenged the Republican-controlled Eightieth Congress to take the initiative on the broad civil rights package he had outlined and was content to let it bear the onus of its certain failure to enact such legislation. After due assessment in the spring, both White and Mitchell went along with Truman's strategy because they had more faith in him than in the Congress or any of his potential challenges in the next presidential election. Mitchell noted that despite several minuses, the Truman administration had a number of civil rights pluses, one of which was the filing of a brief by his solicitor general before the U.S. Supreme Court the previous December supporting the NAACP's successful fight against restrictive housing covenants in the *Shelley* v. *Kraemer* case. Oscar Ewing, administrator of the Federal Security Agency, had also set a "fine example" in working to end discrimination in his agency, and his actions "undoubtedly would meet with President Truman's approval."[9]

Meanwhile, Mitchell had begun working to get the states to pass FEPC laws similar to those that existed in New York, New Jersey, and Massachusetts. Their laws prohibited discrimination and provided for committees to enforce them. Mitchell abandoned that strategy, however, after "first-hand meetings with branch officials" and a visit to Colorado, where he met with legislators. He concluded that "the outlook for state fair employment practice legislation is very bad." Not only were few legislatures inclined to pass such laws, but those that might have done so were not interested in strong measures. He therefore redirected his energies to getting a national bill through Congress. The first step toward such a law, he was more than ever convinced, had to be the issuing of a presidential executive order prohibiting discrimination in government employment. He nevertheless urged the NAACP's branches to make the most effective use of whatever state fair-employment-practice laws existed. [10]

On July 26, 1948, Truman granted Mitchell his wish. With nothing to lose and everything to gain after the Democratic National Convention had adopted a more far-reaching civil rights plank than his own, and which had spurred the Dixiecrat bolt from the party, Truman issued not one but two executive orders. The first, Executive Order 9980, was what Mitchell had sought. It reaffirmed the prohibition against discrimination in federal employment and created a Fair Employment Board to review discrimination complaints by federal employees. The second, Executive Order 9981, created the President's Committee on Equality of Treatment and Opportunity in the Armed Forces and, despite its vagueness, heralded a more determined effort to lower all racial barriers in the military.

There was historic irony in these orders. The NAACP had been leading the struggle for desegregation of the armed services since World War I, especially during World War II. But White, acknowledging Mitchell's wisdom in giving the FEPC issue first priority, made that the main focus of the civil rights struggle after the war, while A. Philip Randolph, a descendant of slaves from John Randolph's plantation in Virginia, assumed leadership in militantly demanding that Truman, as commander in chief, end military segregation. Randolph and Grant Reynolds, his dapper associate, had led a group of black leaders in a meeting on March 28, 1948, with Truman, when the elder man exploded: "Negroes are sick and tired of being asked to shoulder guns in defense of democracy abroad until they get some at home. They are prepared to resort to civil disobedience and refusal to register for the draft if it means serving in a Jim Crow Army." He followed up the warning by personally pledging at a Senate Armed Services Committee hearing "to openly counsel, aid and abet youth, both white and Negro, in an organized refusal to register and be drafted." In addition to mounting the soapbox to carry out the threat, he sold "Don't Join a Jim Crow Army" buttons before the White House and continued his protests at the two political party conventions that summer. An NAACP poll showed that 71 percent of all draft-age black students sympathized with his call.

As founder of the FEPC movement, Randolph still was the recognized leader of this struggle, having in September 1943 been the driving force in the creation of National Council for a Permanent FEPC. White in 1941 had been his principal and indispensable supporter when Roosevelt issued

Executive Order 8802. But now White had a different strategy in mind. By October 1946, White and several NAACP board members had become disillusioned with the National Council because of its ineffectiveness. For example, Randolph at one point suggested that the council accept a watered-down FEPC bill sponsored by Senator Robert A. Taft of Ohio in order to salvage something of the 1946 legislative drive. But White and James B. Carey, secretary-treasurer of the CIO and president of the International Union of Electrical Workers, vigorously rejected the proposal. White was also fearful that the "left wing" was planning to take over the fight for the FEPC because of weaknesses within the council. He regarded the issue as much too vital for the NAACP to be "average" in its response to the threat. So White suggested to his board that the NAACP take over the struggle and obtain the cooperation of other groups already working toward that goal.

Mitchell, therefore, promptly made sure that the NAACP got full credit for the employment discrimination order. He prepared an extensive "Chronological Account of the NAACP's Fight" for the order, which studiously highlighted his contributions, and this was widely distributed to the NAACP's branches by Dr. Louis T. Wright, chairman of the NAACP national board of directors, with White's blessings. Mitchell had functioned as White's surrogate in this struggle, drafting letters for his boss to the President, and acting as his mouthpiece in meetings with agency and White House officials.

Mitchell was pleased with Executive Order 9980. He felt that it would indeed be "an important tool" in eliminating discrimination and that it would "greatly aid in keeping alive the importance of having a national" FEPC. Always confident that Truman would issue an order creating some kind of regulatory agency, he had devoted much attention to that agency's composition as well as to its enforcement powers. Early drafts of the order, which Mitchell had helped prepare, had sought "positive" steps "against discrimination in federal employment."

Mitchell had discovered that, to get around restrictions imposed by the 1944 Russell amendment barring funds for the FEPC and similar wartime bodies created by presidential executive orders, Congress began designating them as "intergovernmental committees" rather than independent ones. That enabled them to receive budget authorization through related agencies like the Department of Labor and the Civil Service Commission. He adopted this approach for the antidiscrimination unit. The problem now was to get the Fair Employment Board placed in a supportive rather than a hostile agency.

Initially, Mitchell had proposed that the independent administering unit he wanted be placed within the Bureau of the Budget. "There is nothing in the past history of the Bureau to indicate that its policies on race relations could be considered either friendly or liberal," he felt. However, because it was in the executive office of the President and also controlled the internal operation of government agencies, he thought the bureau would be the best location. Subsequently, however, he was advised that the Bureau of the Budget would oppose any executive order that made it an instrument of enforcement. Despite attempts to discourage him from pressing for a specific administering unit, Mitchell had insisted not only on having one, but also on establishing a policy that addressed patterns of discrimination rather than individual cases. This approach was designed to make the major function of the proposed board one of taking "positive steps to ensure the full use of all persons in government without discrimination because of race, creed, color, or national origin."

Mitchell remained adamantly opposed to placing the enforcement unit in the Civil Service Commission because it "consistently contended that in cases of discrimination it was hampered by certain legal restrictions in effecting redress for compliance." Instead, he attempted to have it placed in the Department of Labor. That agency would have given the Fair Employment Board access to the Labor Department's wage-hour investigators, who could have supplied information on discriminatory hiring practices. The investigators' primary job was to ensure that the minimum and going wage laws were being upheld.

Some of the FEPC's friends went as far as to suggest that employment discrimination be made an offense punishable by a jail sentence in extreme cases. They felt that the FBI should be used to investigate complaints because the FBI's great prestige would frighten employers into complying with the law. Mitchell rejected the idea as impractical. He found, however, that many people who were opposed to placing the FEPC in either the FBI or the Department of Labor were simply against the government's intervening to end job discrimination. Feelings like these helped determine the administering agency's fate.[11]

Executive Order 9980 "was a far cry from the text we had submitted to the White House," Mitchell acknowledged. It was "by no means adequate." Rather than providing the strong central unit and sanctions he wanted, it gave administering responsibility to the heads of each department, who were required to appoint fair employment officers. The order created a Fair Employment Board as a review mechanism and, despite Mitchell's objections, placed it within the Civil Service Commission. He found consolation, though, in the fact that Executive Order 9346 also had not been perfect. Nevertheless, it was "of tremendous value to minority groups." If the new order was "administered by competent people," he conceded, it would have a far-reaching effect on federal service similar to those of the wartime measure. More important, the new order would keep the FEPC idea alive.

The next hurdle was the composition of the Fair Employment Board. Mitchell adamantly opposed the naming of former Civil Service Commission members to the unit because of their record of prejudice and won on that question, but when he submitted his recommendations for the seven-member board, he came up against a stone wall.

The commission, he learned, was opposed to having clearly identifiable representatives of the labor movement, ostensibly "because it would promote rivalries between the AFL and CIO as well as between business and labor." Mitchell attempted "to make a strong case" for his recommendations, especially to have Robert Weaver, who was now with the American Council on Race Relations, appointed to the board, but to no avail. He left the meeting at which his list was discussed with no concessions but only sympathy from the commission members for his concern that "the committee function not only as a body to hear, but also as a group which would initiate action even without complaints."

He submitted to the Fair Employment Board recommendations "that its major function be the prevention of discriminatory practices in Federal employment rather than the mere correction of such individual complaints as may arise." He urged that segregation be considered discrimination since they were intricately related; that quota systems, which were widely used against blacks, be abolished; and that positive action be taken against discrimination.[12]

Time would prove the board's ineffectiveness. Mitchell was, however, considerably encouraged by his progress with the executive branch. The President repeatedly had gone on record as expressing his support for civil rights. With Truman owing his razor-thin 1948 election victory to the overwhelming support of black voters, Mitchell was confident that blacks had a dependable ally in the White House. He felt that blacks also had won other allies to their cause, including Supreme Court justices and ordinary working men who "are convinced that now is the time for our country to erase all distinctions based on race."

This assessment was reinforced by such developments as the strong cooperation he had received from Oscar Ewing in reaching an agreement to end segregation and discrimination in the Bureau of Old Age and Survivors Insurance (for which Ewing, as administrator of the Federal Security Agency, was also responsible). Ewing instructed the agency to follow recommendations Mitchell had helped prepare for ending discrimination; next, he provided for a follow-up meeting with Mitchell to review progress. "This is the kind of approach to the problems of government discrimination we hope the President's Fair Employment Board will follow," said Mitchell. Furthermore, although discrimination in federal service was continuing despite the order, eighteen agencies had established procedures for handling complaints.

Other major accomplishments of the Fair Employment Board during this period included a ruling by the Civil Service Commission in Winston-Salem, North Carolina, that even though the list on which the names of two black applicants appeared had expired, those men were entitled to appointment in the city's post office because they previously had been wrongfully denied their jobs. Also, "an outstanding result" of a Senate investigation in 1948 was "the cracking of the 20-year-old practice of the Post Office Department branch in Memphis of not appointing blacks as clerks." The following year, the Fair Employment Board ruled in the New Orleans post office case that a complainant was entitled to the job he had been denied because of his race and also to seniority accruing from the date on which the discrimination had occurred.[13]

Truman's creation of the loyalty review program in March 1947 to ferret out Communists and their sympathizers from the government placed Joseph Rauh on a path parallel with Mitchell's as he embarked on projects to help protect civil liberties and to expand the social and economic promise of the New Deal. Although Mitchell's work touched briefly on the serious discrimination issue presented by the hysteria over national security of the McCarthy era, that remained Rauh's area of commitment, one that set him on an inspired course that would strengthen the Bill of Rights as much as Mitchell's would strengthen protections against discrimination under the Fourteenth Amendment. The Truman loyalty program was hastily conceived and lacked proper safeguards, so it was rife with abuse. Mitchell received numerous requests for assistance from people in such cities as Cleveland, Minneapolis, Philadelphia, Los Angeles, and St. Louis. He found that federal agencies such as the Post Office Department and the Government Printing Office were using the program to dismiss NAACP members and blacks who filed discrimination complaints.

Various investigating agencies, notably the FBI, were also charging whites and blacks with disloyalty for associating with members of the other race. Mitchell was concerned that among the lists of persons compiled by the House Committee on Un-American Activities were included those of activist blacks with no record of subversive activities. In addition to working with NAACP lawyers and NAACP branch leaders to resolve such complaints, as well as those involving people associated with non-Communist civil libertarian groups, Mitchell proposed to Roy Wilkins, NAACP assistant executive secretary, that either he or White write Truman and urge him to support an effort to revise the loyalty program in order to end abuses. The NAACP board of directors also voted, in

November 1948, to intervene in cases of people charged with disloyalty where racial discrimination or membership in "coordinating," or inter-racial, groups like the NAACP appeared to have been the motivating factor.[14]

Mitchell next began mobilizing the NAACP's branches and outside supporters for protracted legislative battles in Congress. On April 11, 1949, the NAACP board of directors reaffirmed his strategy by making an FEPC law its number one legislative objective. "This was not an easy choice," Mitchell acknowledged, "because all civil rights bills are of great importance." But an FEPC law would "strike at job discrimination in the North and the South," which he and the association clearly regarded as the overriding priority. If a fair employment practice bill was enacted, he was certain, other civil rights legislation would "have an excellent chance for passage." So, having established himself as the key civil rights legislative strategist in Washington, Mitchell was now searching for ways to break through the Senate coalition of Republicans and southerners, the group that had used the filibuster to kill every civil rights bill that had reached the Senate since the House passed the first antilynching measure, the Dyer antilynching bill, in 1922.[15]

During the struggle that gave rise to Executive Order 9980, Mitchell had enlisted the support of several groups in an informal coalition. His actions were in addition to the quadrennial mobilization of black voters that the NAACP had initiated in 1940 in order to intensify pressure on the executive branch, political parties, and presidential candidates in response to complaints of injustices in the military and civilian areas of the defense program. In 1943 and 1944, the NAACP expanded its base by sponsoring a conference of leaders whose organizations represented more than six million blacks. Mitchell recalled that White "originated" the idea of getting groups like Phi Beta Sigma and Alpha Phi Alpha fraternities and Phi Lambda Sigma sorority to testify at congressional hearings. "Walter was the greatest recruiter of support that you could want. And whenever he had some idea of legislative objective, he would . . . go out and recruit various groups—the Elks, the Masons, the fraternities. Anything that had a crowd connected to it."

Those unprecedented political conferences first produced in 1943 and then reaffirmed in 1944 a six-point "Declaration of Negro Voters" that served as a yardstick for measuring parties and candidates that "by words and deeds" showed their "determination to work for full citizenship status for thirteen million American Negroes and to better the lot of all disadvantaged people in this country." Their voting strength in seventeen or more states with at least 281 electoral college votes gave blacks "the potential balance of power in any reasonably close national election and in many state and local elections," the conference of twenty-seven representatives from twenty organizations said. The concerns and agendas of those conferences were much broader than that of A. Philip Randolph's single-issue National Council for a Permanent FEPC. Indeed, the NAACP was one of the most important members of the National Council's seventy constituent organizations. On January 20, 1944, also, the NAACP was represented at a meeting of the interracial Conference Against Race Discrimination in the War Effort. But this group ceased to exist in December.[16]

As in 1944, the people drafting the "Declaration of Negro Voters" on March 27, 1948, were all black. They were from Greek-letter, civic, political, and labor organizations as well as from the International Longshoremen's Association and the National Maritime Union of America, the AFL, and the CIO. Their nonpartisan statement was resoundingly reaffirmed and considerably strengthened on July 22 by a much broader interracial Conference of Cooperating Organizations composed of nineteen groups seeking to have a special session of the Eightieth Congress called by President Truman to pass civil rights legislation. In organizing that "conference," White instructed Wilkins to invite groups like the Southern Regional Council, white women's church units such as those of the Methodists, and notable liberal organizations, in order to get as much as possible "decent white southern sentiment to counteract the professional southerners who are now so much in the news." Wilkins apparently did not succeed in getting any white southerners to participate, but there was a fair representation of established liberal groups. Present were Paul Sifton, a well-known activist for the United Automobile Workers, Herman Edelsberg for the Anti-Defamation League of B'nai B'rith, Alex Brooks of the American Jewish Committee, Mary Alice Baldinger of the American Civil Liberties Union, Charles Zimmerman of the International Ladies Garment Workers Union, and Sanford Bolz of the American Jewish Congress. While the earlier conferences were specifically geared to awakening black consciousness and to punishing anti-civil-rights lawmakers at the polls, the group at the July meeting represented the next step, following creation of the National Council for a Permanent FEPC, in the establishment of a permanent civil rights coalition.[17]

The effectiveness of the NAACP's political mobilization was well demonstrated in the 1948 election when Truman defeated his Republican opponent Thomas Dewey by a hair breadth with the help of bloc voting by blacks. But even with a swing back to strong Democratic majorities in the House and Senate in 1949, the Eighty-first Congress showed itself no more likely to pass FEPC legislation than its predecessor.

The early coalition movement had exerted pressure primarily on the executive branch of the government. The NAACP now discovered how much more difficult it was—compared with Truman, whose gratitude to blacks had made him a civil rights standard-bearer—to mobilize pressure against lawmakers, especially senators, from a national base. The NAACP shifted its primary focus to Congress, its first concern to lessen the obstruction of Senate cloture Rule XXII (establishing the procedure for cutting off what previously had been unlimited debate) as it launched the second major effort to enact FEPC legislation.

In preparation for the coming struggle, White had organized a conference of twenty-one national organizations that was held at the Wendell Willkie Memorial Building in New York on February 5, 1949, to work out an effective and unified strategy for the forthcoming hearings by the Senate Rules Committee on cloture and for removing other obstructions to the passage of civil rights legislation in Congress. That conference set up a Joint Committee on Civil Rights to coordinate the work of participating groups. It created a thirteen-member executive committee as well as a legislative strategy committee to be based in Washington. The conference (1) urged both parties to amend Rule XXII to permit cloture on all preliminary motions as well as on pending legislation "by a majority vote of senators voting in order to stop dictatorial control of the Senate by one-third of its members and restore majority rule to the Senate and people of the United States"; and (2) insisted on the application of cloture should an attempt be made to block adoption of such a rule by a filibuster. [18]

Encouraged by Truman's victory in 1948 and the election of such avowed liberal Democrats to the Senate as Hubert H. Humphrey of Minnesota, Clinton P. Anderson of New Mexico, Paul H. Douglas of Illinois, and Estes Kefauver of Tennessee, civil rights supporters in Congress heeded the NAACP's call to reform Rule XXII. Truman promised in his January State of the Union Message to "stand squarely behind" his civil rights proposals to Congress. Civil rights forces initially regarded the filibuster only as an obstacle to passage of civil rights laws but not as an issue unto itself. Most nonsoutherners, including many senators who supported civil rights, instead saw the issue as one of protecting the institution's integrity and norms against encroachment by the President on their legislative authority. Thus the struggle over the filibuster rule went to the heart of the Senate itself, to its institutional integrity and how it conducted its business. Therein lay another lesson for Mitchell.

Prior to the adoption of Rule XXII in 1917, making it possible for two thirds of the Senate to invoke cloture, senators could hold the floor in totally unlimited debate. Now reformers embarked on a struggle to allow the Senate to invoke cloture by a simple majority. Many senators feared that such a prospect threatened not only the minority's right to be heard but also the Senate's independence and autonomy. The challenge for many nonreformers, therefore, was how best to strike a balance in order to legislate more effectively on civil rights while protecting an effective parliamentary tool.

For the NAACP and Mitchell, the question was much simpler and thus loaded with potential conflict given the inherent limitations on either political party, led by the Senate majority leader, to impose its will on the total body—the willingness or ability of the President to exert his leadership to fulfill his legislative mandate. A skillful President like Franklin Roosevelt could impose his will on Congress without seeming to threaten its integrity; Truman was not as effective.

In the vanguard of those advocating the NAACP's demand for cloture by a simple majority was Majority Leader Scott Lucas of Illinois. Lucas, at the same time, was faithfully pushing Truman's other legislative initiatives. To some he seemed a White House pawn; others saw him as a supporter of the southerners. He was thus in a no-win position—one that was most untenable for a majority leader, whose effectiveness depended on his ability to mold a consensus. Whether Lucas could control the debate on Rule XXII was in question from the beginning. This was one instance when the President's embrace of the NAACP's cloture position ironically was a disaster for civil rights.

At the end of February, following a meeting with Truman, Vice President Alben Barkley, and House Speaker Sam Rayburn, Lucas revealed that the President wanted the cloture issue settled forthwith. "We are going to stay here from now on until we get a disposition of this matter one way or another," Lucas announced, intent upon fulfilling his party's 1948 campaign pledge. That, in the postwar conservative climate, was Lucas's real mistake—openly advocating the President's position on an issue in which many of his colleagues saw the Senate's independence as paramount.

Lucas promptly launched the drive for approval of his Senate Resolution 15, designed to provide for the invoking of cloture by two thirds of the senators present and voting (as against two thirds of the entire Senate) on any motion or measure. The resolution was meant to change a precedent handed down in 1947 by Michigan Republican Arthur Vandenburg, then president pro tempore of the Senate, that cloture could not be invoked on a motion to call up a bill or resolution in the Senate. Vandenburg's rule made it all but impossible for the substance of civil rights legislation to be considered since any opponent could wage unlimited debate on a procedural motion.

To overcome the solid opposition from southerners, Lucas needed at least twenty Republican votes for his petition to invoke cloture on a filibuster against his motion to consider S.R. 15. But Robert Taft, chairman of the Minority Policy Council and de facto Republican leader, while promising the NAACP to support a rule by Barkley to overturn the Vandenburg precedent, refused to commit his party on the issue. A noncommital Vandenburg also publicly absolved fellow Republicans from any obligation to sustain his precedent, leaving them free to vote as they wished.

At the height of this maneuvering, when Lucas was desperately considering his options, Truman at a March news conference embraced so faithfully the NAACP's demand for invoking cloture by a simple majority that he threw a monkey wrench into the works. The timing and manner of Truman's sudden announcement was disastrous and severely undercut Lucas. Because Lucas had not been forewarned, the President prematurely forced his hand. The victory of Truman's unequivocal support was thus painfully Pyrrhic for the NAACP.

Gleefully, Georgia's Richard Russell, the southern Democratic leader, declared, "The President has now justified every statement that we have made that all this campaign was but a step toward simple majority cloture." From the beginning, he reminded his colleagues, he had maintained "they were opening a Pandora's Box. It is now clearly opened." With the bipartisan effort severely strained, the next day Minority Leader Kenneth S. Wherry of Nebraska shouted on the Senate floor, "This Democratic effort to break this filibuster is a phony effort." He maintained, "The President has done the cause of sensible two-thirds cloture serious harm, which raises the question whether he really wants a practical cloture rule or is insisting upon the impossible in order to have a bogey man for political purposes."

With the skids well greased, Russell raised a point of order against Lucas's petition to invoke cloture on the filibuster against his motion to consider S.R. 15. Technically, Lucas's attempt contravened the Vandenburg rule. Barkley overruled Russell's objection, maintaining that the petition was in order and should be voted upon. Vandenburg was livid. A majority of senators was now needed to sustain Barkley's ruling on Russell's appeal of his ruling.

During the bitter debate, Walter White called an emergency conference in Washington of representatives of fifteen NAACP branches and other organizations in the Joint Committee on Civil Rights. After meeting at the NAACP Washington Bureau, they met with their senators, managing to sway two or three votes in the NAACP's favor. Those were not enough to avoid a stunning defeat.

On March 11, the Senate voted 41 to 46 on Lucas's motion to table Russell's appeal. The vote against, composed of an equal number of Democrats and Republicans, not only showed how much Lucas's ability to lead had been damaged, but also upheld Vandenburg's 1947 ruling. The fate of civil rights legislation was therefore set for the foreseeable future. Had Lucas been able to win this relatively minor procedural battle, the Senate, despite the difficulty of obtaining support from two thirds of the senators, might have gone on and modified Rule XXII in some small detail, making Mitchell's job easier.

Instead, California Republican William F. Knowland, a highly respected conservative, quietly lined up thirty Democrats and twenty-two Republicans to support his proposal to make Rule XXII more stringent by requiring two thirds of the entire Senate (as opposed to two thirds present and voting) to invoke cloture on all motions and measures—in effect, keeping in place the old rule. He completed his coup de grâce by adding a provision *barring the right of cloture in all future attempts to change the standing rules.* Mitchell complained that without support from Republicans and Midwest Democrats, the southerners would not have been strong enough to block action on civil rights.

After the Senate voted 78 to 0 to consider S.R. 15, Knowland offered his package as a substitute. Then on March 17, led by a coalition of Republicans and southern Democrats, the Senate adopted, 63 to 23, the Knowland-Wherry substitute amendment.

All chances in 1949 were dead for passing not only the FEPC, but also the anti-poll-tax, antilynching, and omnibus bills in the comprehensive civil rights package that Truman had submitted to Congress. Committees in both the House and Senate, in fact, approved and reported out FEPC bills to the full bodies, but they were laid over until 1950. Not only was Truman blamed for much of this imbroglio, but he was also accused of jeopardizing other Fair Deal legislation he wanted badly. [19]

The sticking point in Congress from now on remained the NAACP's insistence on getting an FEPC law with enforcement powers or none at all. Harking back to the fears aroused during the filibuster battle, Wherry complained that FEPC supporters had selected "the one civil rights bill that they know will be the hardest to pass. They hope it will fail, and they hope they can go to the country in the campaign of 1950 to claim that it was the Republicans who blocked it."

Wherry misunderstood the principle involved in the FEPC fight. Civil rights leaders made this a lightning rod issue in order to set a standard for all future civil rights legislation. As Mitchell had made clear when FEPC legislation was killed in 1946, he felt it was better to hold ground for a strong bill than to accept the shadow of one, which would only increase the difficulty of getting other measures creating any meaningful powers passed. [20] He underscored this philosophy in another sharp struggle against the Taft-Hartley Act, formally called the National Labor-Management Relations Act of 1947—an effort that though unsuccessful, helped cement his ties with organized labor. That restrictive law superseded the prolabor National Labor Relations Act of 1935 (the Wagner Act).

In his February 20, 1947, testimony before the Senate Committee on Labor and Public Welfare, Mitchell maintained that the antilabor bills and other similar measures under consideration, represented "a throwback to a period of industrial strife which would gravely affect the welfare" of not only black but also white workers. He said the bills "put labor on notice that the power of the government of the United States will be used to crush the wage earners seeking to safeguard their rights and deprive them of their civil liberties." In addition to the NAACP's interest in "all wage earners," he said, "we are mindful of the stake that over one and a half million colored persons have in this matter because of their membership in the AFL and the CIO." Mitchell was also aware that the millions of unorganized black agricultural workers who were being encouraged to join labor unions would be hurt by any law that curtailed the freedom of labor to organize and conduct its business.[21]

Not even Truman, however, could halt the postwar avalanche of conservative reaction that gave the Republicans control of the "do-nothing" Eightieth Congress. Extremely anxious Americans made labor a scapegoat for many of the country's ills, such as skyrocketing inflation and the severe wage-price squeeze. Labor exacerbated that anger by its record number of strikes and numerous excesses, such as failing to bargain in good faith and abusing its closed-shop privileges. But, Mitchell noted, while labor was being attacked, no legislation had been proposed to curb those business interests that had "combined to destroy price control," or the meat industry, which had withheld meat from the market to drive up prices. The basic tragedy of the Taft-Hartley Act, he explained in an article in *The Crisis,* was that it had "established a legislative pattern for whittling away valuable social legislation." Mitchell worked with organized labor to try to turn this tide, but the attempt was futile. The NAACP and labor had no trouble getting Truman to veto the Taft-Hartley Act, but Congress easily overrode the veto. The reasons for this antilabor sentiment were that (1) Congress was reflecting more the interests of the powerful and better-organized rural, middle-class, and business segments of the country than the urban, racial, and ethnic communities of northern industrial centers; (2) the key committees in the House and Senate were controlled by southerners; (3) southern senators were not only antiblack but also antilabor; and (4) Truman lacked the popular support that had been the basis of Roosevelt's New Deal coalition strength.[22]

Those events confirmed beyond any doubt for Mitchell the nature of the common cause that bound labor to civil rights. As a senator explained in early 1949 after the Republican-Dixiecrat coalition had blocked moves to liberalize the Senate filibuster rules, "The votes on the Taft-Hartley repeal [that was being considered] is the payoff the Republicans will exact for the assistance the GOP senators gave the Dixiecrats in the civil rights fight.[23] He could not have been more correct, as events proved.

Mitchell was also well aware that it was through the joint efforts of the NAACP and the AFL in 1930 that opponents of President Hoover's appointment of Judge John J. Parker, a North Carolina racist, to the Supreme Court had been able to block his confirmation in the Senate. The AFL, after initially opposing the struggle for a permanent FEPC, by mid-1945 had adopted a more progressive policy. Working through the National Council for a Permanent FEPC, it began urging its affiliates to support this movement. It was the CIO, however, that really showed a deep interest in the FEPC from the beginning, staging a lobbying blitz in Washington during the first major push for an FEPC law in September and October 1945. Though unsuccessful, that effort revealed to Mitchell the extent of organized labor's resources and considerably increased power. Moreover, the growing white middle-class liberal movement, which was also bitterly opposed to Taft-Hartley, passionately identified with labor. By joining forces with organized labor, Mitchell knew, he would one day achieve his dream of getting Congress to pass strong civil rights legislation.

At the same time, Mitchell saw in the developing labor-black alliance an opportunity to push for an end to segregation and discrimination in the unions and thus also attack the type of institutional racism practiced by the National Labor Relations Board. During the attempt to repeal the Taft-Hartley Act in 1949, Mitchell urged Congress to include safeguards against racial discrimination and segregation in any legislation that was adopted. The proposals, which he submitted as amendments to the Wagner Act, would have prevented a union from being certified as the bargaining agent if it segregated or discriminated against employees because of race, religion, or national origin. Mitchell also called for decertification of any union conducting those unjust practices; adoption of a principle that would not have required an employer to bargain with a discriminating union; and denial of the closed-shop privilege to such unions.

Under the original Wagner Act, Mitchell told the House Committee on Education and Labor, the NLRB could have gained the results he was now seeking. Instead, the NLRB "gave its blessing to segregation and exclusion" in a case involving the Larus and Brother Company. The Taft-Hartley Act, he said, incorporated the Larus doctrine into law. It had been contended in that case that the company's black employees could not be represented properly by a union that segregated them into a separate Jim Crow local. The NLRB had ruled that it had no power to order the union to admit the blacks. Previously, Mitchell explained, the NLRB had held, in a case involving the Atlanta Oak Floor Company, that the bargaining agent could segregate its members into separate locals. "A principle was then evolved from these cases under which unions could exclude persons from membership because of race, or segregate them and still remain within the law," he said.

Mitchell noted that the framers of the Taft-Hartley Act had made it clear that racial segregation would be "perfectly legal and proper." Those lawmakers, he said, "tried to make it appear that they were giving minorities a pat on the back." But in reality they "were pinning a donkey's tail of second class citizenship on all of the colored people in the labor movement of this country." The NLRB, he went on, had quickly used its "continued license for immoral conduct" to confirm this practice.

There was, Mitchell told the committee, a growing realization among trade union members that segregation undermined the unions' strength. There had also been "a tremendous growth of democracy" within both the AFL and the CIO. In a characteristic display of diplomacy, he said that the NAACP wanted to show that "the wise leaders of labor are uncompromising foes of segregation and discrimination." But there were those among employers and labor unions who, "by conspiracy and collusion, with or without closed-shop agreements, exclude" qualified black workers. Only court action and fair employment practice legislation in some states had helped in dealing with those problems. Mitchell explained that the pattern of discrimination was varied and not based on geography. Congress, he stressed, had the power to correct this problem by passing legislation "to throw a mantle of dignity and protection over the shoulders of the working man."

Mitchell was especially encouraged by Walter Reuther's unequivocal response to a question from Senator Allen Ellender of Louisiana, an ardent foe of civil rights and fair employment practice legislation, at a hearing of the Senate Committee on Labor and Public Welfare. "I am opposed," Reuther told the senator, "to segregation and all forms of discrimination because they are contrary to all the principles that have made America great. I am opposed to them regardless of geography because I don't think geography changes basic principles." Many people, explained Mitchell, had made similar declarations, but only a few of them had had an opportunity to put their beliefs into practice on the scale that Reuther, who was president of the powerful United Automobile Workers of the CIO, was able to.[24]

Congress, however, was light-years away from enacting civil rights safeguards. But Mitchell had made his point. Despite the problem of segregation in the unions, the interests of organized labor and of black Americans were parallel in many respects. Labor and civil rights groups therefore had a common cause, which was the strengthening of economic opportunity for all workers. Selling Congress on the goal of nondiscrimination, however, would be as difficult as getting it to tip the scale of labor-management relations back in labor's favor or to a point where government's involvement in that area would be more evenhanded.

A spin-off of the struggle over Taft-Hartley was the establishment of an ongoing ideological contest between Mitchell and Oregon Republican Wayne B. Morse, a dedicated but often acerbic liberal. In February 1947, Morse challenged Mitchell before the Senate Labor Committee to agree to a compromise: "I'm trying to be a coldblooded realist. You're going to have some labor legislation. I'm going to vote for it, and if the choice is voting for none or voting for that which goes too far I'm going to vote for that which goes too far."

Mitchell responded, "I would say, Senator, that that would be a very unfortunate position to take. I don't see how you'll remedy anything by just voting for any legislation. It is being initiated in an atmosphere of national hysteria."[25]

Even though Truman had set a historical precedent with his civil rights legislative package, the Fortieth Annual NAACP Convention in Los Angeles in mid-July 1949 not only passed a resolution castigating the Eighty-first Congress for having "betrayed the mandate given it by the American people in the last election in the field of civil liberties," but it also felt that the President "must share responsibility for this betrayal." The NAACP was certainly not ungrateful for Truman's leadership on civil rights; it was merely holding his feet to the fire. The benefits of that strategy, at which Mitchell was now one of the nation's top experts, was demonstrated when Truman, adhering to the NAACP's position, told Georgia's Richard Russell, the most skillful and resourceful opponent of fair employment practice legislation in the Senate, that a proposal advanced by Congressman Brooks Hays of Arkansas was unacceptable. Hays's proposal consisted of a voluntary FEPC without enforcement powers, a constitutional amendment providing for the abolition of the poll tax, and an antilynching bill giving much more power to the states than would Truman's bill. In addition to seeking an FEPC with enforcement powers, the NAACP wanted an anti-poll-tax law instead of a constitutional amendment, because the latter not only would have had to undergo a lengthy adoption process, but its chances of success were also doubtful. The NAACP was also opposed to giving the states power in antilynching cases because experience had shown that they would not enforce the law.[26]

On June 2, 1949, in preparation for the next round in the struggle, White and Wilkins, at a dinner meeting in Washington, had outlined for Hubert Humphrey and Clark Clifford, adviser to the President, the NAACP's program and strategy with a view to influencing the administration. Humphrey, a representative of the Americans for Democratic Action, was a new NAACP ally. Mitchell had not met Humphrey in Minnesota when he was executive director of the St. Paul Urban League, but he learned from a former Lincoln University classmate, whom Humphrey had helped, about his strong liberal credentials as a staffer with the Minnesota office of the Works Progress Administration and as mayor of Minneapolis. While mayor, at the landmark 1948 Democratic National Convention in Philadelphia, Humphrey set a new course in national politics when he, Rauh, and Andrew J. Biemiller, an old-line socialist who was then a Democratic congressman from Wisconsin, got the party to adopt the bellwether civil rights plank that led to the Dixiecrats' walkout. The following year, after entering the Senate, the very first legislation Humphrey introduced was an antilynching bill. In addition to Rauh, other newcomers present at the dinner meeting who would be playing key roles in future battles included Herman Edelsberg, representing a group of Jewish organizations; and James B. Carey, secretary-treasurer of the CIO, and his assistant, George L. P. Weaver, civil rights veterans who had been working with Mitchell and the NAACP.

The close alliance that would develop between Mitchell and Rauh would in many ways symbolize the expanding quest for universal brotherhood. Rauh's father had been part of the wave of European Jews who began immigrating to the United States in the 1890s. Rauh was born on January 3, 1911, in Cincinnati, Ohio. His father found special inspiration from the Ohio River, which aroused in him strong memories of the Rhine in his native Germany. From his modest income as a shirt manufacturer, the elder Rauh made sure his two sons received the best education possible.

Upon being graduated from Harvard Law School, Rauh served his clerkship under Supreme Court Associate Justices Benjamin N. Cardozo and Felix Frankfurter. He followed his indoctrination into civil rights in the war preparedness agencies with service as staff officer under General Douglas MacArthur in the Pacific—a tour of duty that won him the Legion of Merit and the Philippine Distinguished Service Star. His 1946 appointment as deputy to the housing administrator made him the youngest top aide in the Truman administration—a brief experience that subsequently served him well in private law practice. A year after he helped found the ADA in 1947, he began a twenty-year tenure as chairman and vice-chairman of the Democratic Central Committee of the District of Columbia. In 1948 he also began a thirty-two-year span of active participation on the Democratic National Committee.[27]

The group attending the June 2, 1949, dinner meeting was markedly different from Mitchell's regular allies. Six months earlier, for example, while discussing with Wilkins a possible meeting with Truman, he had said that "the most important people" in the delegation should be Phillip Murray of the CIO, William Green of the AFL, Mary McLeod Bethune representing women, and others from black groups. He felt it was better to get people from denominational groups, notably the two wings of the Baptist Church and the African Methodist Episcopal churches, rather than from the National Council of Churches. Also represented should be the Roman Catholic Church, which he regarded as the second most important group, after labor, in the NAACP's early coalition, thanks to the sincerity of supporters like Father Francis Gilligan of St. Paul. He suggested inviting a member of the National Catholic Welfare Conference Board as well as Archbishop Robert E. Lucy of San Antonio.[28]

By now it was evident that if the Republican-Dixiecrat alliance in Congress was to be beaten, the NAACP had to expand its base to involve other established black and white organizations. Wilkins, in accordance with a resolution that he had introduced, and which the NAACP convention had adopted, held a meeting on the weekend of October 14 and 15 in New York with NAACP branch representatives as a first step in mobilizing grass-roots support. The conference, at which Juanita Jackson Mitchell was a notable participant, made plans for the observance of a civil liberties month," highlighted by conferences on January 15–17, involving branches more closely in the civil rights legislative program, and creating an Emergency Civil Rights Committee composed of NAACP board members and branch and state conference presidents. The committee invited other groups "to join with us in demanding affirmative action by the 81st Congress." Wilkins was now acting executive secretary and was moving aggressively to take command of the legislative struggle. An ailing White had been granted a year's leave of absence after the convention so he could get badly needed rest.

The October weekend conference called on the NAACP's sixteen hundred branches and twenty-nine state conferences to formulate plans for the observance of a National Emergency Civil Rights Mobilization from November 15 to January 17. Branches were urged to send delegations to meet with members of Congress during the Christmas recess and to solicit the cooperation of trade unions, churches, fraternal groups, and other organizations as well as to hold mass meetings. They were also urged to send delegates to the National Civil Rights Mobilization conference on January 15–17 in Washington. Thirty-eight organizations, including most of the twenty-five members of the Civil Liberties Clearinghouse in Washington, sent representatives to the NAACP's second meeting on November 10.

The National Council for a Permanent FEPC, the first interracial coalition, became a driving force in this new movement. The delegates adopted the plans the NAACP had outlined, drew up a policy and plan of operation for the NAACP state conferences, and agreed to cosponsor the mobilization. Wilkins was named general chairman. The seventeen-member steering committee that was formed at the November 10 meeting included representatives of the American Jewish Committee, the American Jewish Congress, the Catholic Interracial Council, and Americans for Democratic Action. That core group was expanded into a much larger planning conference in December to include representatives of sixty organizations, which made up the nucleus of a permanent lobbying organization called the Leadership Conference on Civil Rights that was organized in 1950.

Among the organizations represented at the January 1950 National Emergency Civil Rights Mobilization in Washington were three railroad car loads of NAACP members from Maryland who had been brought by Juanita and her mother Lillie Carroll Jackson. Wilkins led a delegation from the conference that met with President Truman and obtained his support for the pending FEPC bill in Congress.

Gaining the full and sustained involvement of a broad range of white liberal organizations in the civil rights movement would have historically beneficial consequences for African Americans and other minorities. Even though White would be named chairman of the coalition, the moving force remained Wilkins. The creation of such a coalition would become one of his most important contributions to the struggle for racial equality. The mobilization was attended by 4,218 representatives of one hundred national church, labor, civil rights, minority group, fraternal, and professional organizations from thirty-three states. The size of the gathering surprised the NAACP and was the best indication of how much the nation had been aroused over the civil rights struggle. The mobilization launched an intensive lobbying campaign on Capitol Hill for the passage of fair employment practices, antilynching, and other civil rights measures. [28]

Mitchell's contribution was evident in the emphasis the mobilization gave to the proposed FEPC bill. His other major contribution was in getting organized labor to regard that proposal as integral to its interests, through a concerted educational program and consistent courtship, highlighted by the NAACP's embracing labor's fight against the Taft-Hartley Act. That support helped win over organized labor as the most powerful and important member in the NAACP's legislative coalition.

▪ CHAPTER EIGHT ▪

Taking Command

J ust as the fifty-six-year-old Walter White was about to depart in June 1949 on a world tour and a year's leave of absence from his position as executive secretary of the NAACP, a bitter controversy erupted within the black community over news of his divorce from Gladys, his wife of twenty-seven years and his secret marriage to a white woman, Poppy Cannon. A three-time divorcée with children from each of her marriages, Poppy was food editor for *Mademoiselle* magazine and a public relations executive attached to the Haitian Information Bureau in New York.

White had submitted his resignation on May 10, but the NAACP national board of directors had refused to accept it. Mitchell was among those mentioned as White's possible successor, but the contest was really with Wilkins, who had actively campaigned to replace White when he was acting executive secretary. Wilkins had been White's deputy for eighteen years. Now a transition in leadership had begun, and he was eager to begin directing the NAACP. But White, though wounded, was still politically powerful. Quiet and intensely persuasive, Wilkins was respected for his skill in running the NAACP's business affairs and as a writer. He had survived surgery in 1946 for stomach cancer and now faced another critical test, this time political.

At the meeting in May 1950, in preparation for White's return, the NAACP board devised a temporary solution to the still explosive issue of White's personal affairs. It relieved White of his administrative duties while allowing him to retain his title as executive secretary. His former office functions, including the hiring of junior executives and most personal secretaries, were added to those administrative functions that Wilkins previously had as assistant executive secretary. White was still regarded as the "top executive." He retained authority over executives above the junior level, and Wilkins was the "second-ranking executive." Wilkins gave up his position as editor of *The Crisis,* which he had held since replacing Du Bois in 1934.

Only White had been appointed by the board; all other staff members had been hired by the executive secretary and reported to him. Now, in addition to Wilkins, the NAACP board took responsibility for appointing Marshall and Henry Lee Moon, director of public relations, and assigned them new functions. The Big Four, as they were called, were jointly responsible for running the association. All that arrangement did, however, was create a White-Moon versus a Wilkins-Marshall division on the staff for the rest of White's tenure—even though White, his prestige still great, quickly regained command of the organization.

Insulated by distance in Washington, Mitchell had remained apart from and above this turmoil. He supported White fully and shared his boss's feelings that a person's true worth should not be measured by the color of the skin, but he studiously avoided internal politics. He realized that the allegiances of staffers to either camp were determined by the persons with whom they happened to speak or associate. He refused to be drawn into such pettiness and, when in New York, would freely associate with people at either end of the hall where White's and Wilkins's offices were located, on the fifth floor of NAACP headquarters at 20 West Fortieth Street, the historic Freedom House.[1]

Wilkins, sensitive and insecure in his position, did not trust Mitchell. Given their closeness, it is possible that White would have preferred to have Mitchell rather than Wilkins as his successor. One reason Mitchell was not considered seriously for the secretaryship was that his mother-in-law, Lillie Carroll Jackson, was not popular with the NAACP board, and Mitchell was known as her fiercest defender. Furthermore, Wilkins was politically stronger. In preparation for his leave of absence, White had recommended that Mitchell be made Wilkins's assistant, but Wilkins blocked that move. The board supported him, saying it preferred to keep Mitchell in the Washington Bureau because he was doing a superb job there. That was true enough, but the explanation could not mask the real motive. Mitchell, meanwhile, was happy with the decision and content to remain in Washington—except that Wilkins began slighting him and he began clashing with Leslie Perry, the Washington Bureau's administrative assistant, over turf. Part of the problem resulted from Mitchell's moving increasingly into Perry's area of work. White had encouraged that, but not Wilkins.

While he functioned as White's surrogate, Mitchell had begun assuming more of White's duties as director of the Washington Bureau. Meanwhile, Perry had been expanding his sphere of influence from merely watching over Congress to initiating and guiding legislative activity. In addition to leading the struggle for anti-poll-tax legislation, Perry since 1945 had been directing the association's drive for adoption by Congress of civil rights safeguards in public housing, slum clearance, and federal aid to education bills. He had been working with such friendly congressmen as Adam Clayton Powell, Jr., New York Democrat, and Jacob Javits, New York Republican, to ensure that the NAACP's position on various bills was represented.

Mitchell's problems with Perry seemed also to have resulted in part from Wilkins's treating Perry as "my representative" in Washington. Wilkins did not use Mitchell the way White would have. For example, in preparing for the January 1950 National Emergency Civil Rights Mobilization, Wilkins delegated the key assignment for on-the-spot arrangements in Washington to Perry. Yet the mobilization had crystallized over Congress's failure to pass FEPC legislation, and FEPC legislation had been Mitchell's pet project for the past four years.[2]

White by contrast, had made it known in Washington that Mitchell was his man. "Clarence speaks for me. Clarence represents me," he told government officials. White had also expressed his affection and respect for Mitchell in a letter to Oscar Ewing, administrator of the Federal Security Agency, during the height of the struggle for a fair employment executive order in 1948. Mitchell, White said, "has a particular gift in being able to talk with all types of people and to gain their confidence." That attribute, White added, was complemented by "a very sound judgment and ability to sift the false from the true." Consequently, "I personally give very thoughtful consideration to any statement which he makes." Little wonder, therefore, that Mitchell told associates that without White's help and keen interest in him, he could never have made it in Washington. White, however, lacked confidence in Perry's judgment.[3]

Just before White returned from his leave of absence, Mitchell gave Wilkins a polite but firm two-week deadline to resolve conflicts between him and Perry in the Washington Bureau. He seems to have suggested to Wilkins that he would leave if that was not done. But Wilkins told him that since White was due back on June 1, it would be better if the executive secretary handled the matter. Mitchell, Wilkins informed White, had complained that he could not "continue to work under the strain of uncertainty and confusion" that currently prevailed in the bureau because the situation was causing "embarrassing cross-action or duplication."

Perry, ironically, was at the time also involved in a romance with a white woman who was a lawyer for the National Labor Relations Board. His affair became a full-blown scandal. In contrast to White's situation, Perry's wife was bent on making her victorious competitor, a vivacious blonde, pay dearly. She filed suit in the federal district court in Washington in January 1950, charging that the white woman had alienated her husband's affections and asking for $50,000 in damages. The suit also charged that the woman had had a son by Perry eighteen months earlier.

Perry's personal problems, his alliance with Wilkins, plus White's lack of confidence in him rendered his continuance with the NAACP untenable. One of the NAACP board's reorganization steps at the May 1950 meeting was to provide for the appointment of a full-time Washington Bureau director; it did not name one. White, in reconsolidating his position, pushed out Perry to make way for Mitchell.

Perry submitted his resignation on July 31 effective August 31. White appointed Mitchell director of the Washington Bureau effective August 1. Mitchell at once turned his full attention back to his program. He brought to the Washington Bureau a cohesion, coherence, and single-minded focus that the program had never had: He had clear authority as "the director," as well as White's total support.[4]

By 1950, the first round in the second major battle for FEPC legislation in Congress had concluded with another trouncing for supporters—a reality that sparked the NAACP's National Emergency Civil Rights Mobilization in Washington that January. Mitchell's broad-based civil rights campaign in Washington was capped by his resolute drive for a presidential executive order to bar discrimination in work under government contracts. The NAACP's epic struggle to overturn the "separate but equal" doctrine established by the Supreme Court's 1896 *Plessy* v. *Ferguson* decision was at a critical stage—one that would enable the association three years later to bring together the many complex currents of history in its elaborate brief, which provided the basis for the Supreme Court's landmark 1954 *Brown* v. *Board of Education* judgment. That brief centered on the origins and meaning of the Fourteenth Amendment, particularly the equal protection clause.

Mitchell was as much inspired by the NAACP's campaign to end segregation in the public schools through the courts as by the promise inherent in the power of Congress to pass laws to protect the constitutional rights of the racially oppressed. The interdependent relationship between the judicial and legislative branches was obvious. Yet, as was equally evident from a comparison between the post-Civil War Thirty-ninth Congress that produced the Fourteenth Amendment and the Eightieth and Eighty-first congresses that were so hostile to the rights of black citizens and labor, the very conservative post-World War II climate was but a shadow of the humanitarian spirit that moved the legislature in 1865—a spirit providing additional manifestations of the lingering Age of Enlightenment.

The great humanitarian reform movement that had flowed from the eighteenth century had had its most dramatic expression in Thomas Jefferson's proposition that "all men are created equal" and "are endowed by their Creator with certain inalienable Rights"; the same revolutionary spirit had driven the Abolitionists to protest the defilement of that dream through slavery—a travesty that was enshrined in even the Constitution under the principle that valued blacks as having only three fifths the worth of whites. It was that type of outrage that had led Frederick Douglass to scoff at the Great Document, "What is it? Who made it? For whom and for what was it made?" However, unlike Douglass and William Lloyd Garrison, the noted Abolitionist who similarly expressed disdain for the Constitution—saying it was "conceived in sin and shaped in iniquity"—Mitchell revered the national charter for its promise of democratic government and freedom for all citizens. The Great Document had been remarkably strengthened during Reconstruction to embrace unequivocally all citizens without regard for race or color.

So much had the legendary radical Republicans, under the leadership of giants like Charles Sumner in the Senate and Thaddeus Stevens in the House, instilled in Congress in the 1860s the spirit of humanitarianism that no outside force was needed to drive them on to seek unconditional legal, economic, political, and social equality for all citizens regardless of color under the Thirteenth, Fourteenth, and Fifteenth amendments. It was a paradox of history that the executive branch then had played a blocking role, with vetoes, dilatory maneuvers, and pleas for caution, while the judiciary nullified legislative radicalism with nihilistic opinions and consolidated the revolt against humanitarian ideals of equality in constitutional terms.

The South, returned to ascendancy by the rapprochement among regional economic interests that culminated in the 1877 Republican-Democratic compromise assuring President Rutherford B. Hayes's election, ensured that Congress would join the other two branches in fully reversing the post-Civil War humanitarian gains. Repeal of some Reconstruction civil rights laws was accompanied by a broad sweep of repressive actions. The former slaves in the one-party Democratic South were again deprived of their humanity and all constitutional rights, notably the right to vote, by the grandfather clause, the white primary, gerrymandering, complicated election procedures, and unabated intimidation through violence and economic repression.

The reversal in congressional imperatives between 1865 and 1950 meant that pressure for reassertion of national democratic principles now had to come from outside rather than from within the Congress. Clarence Mitchell, treading in the footsteps of James Weldon Johnson and Walter White, was the leader of that external mobilizing force. His greatest ally was an increasingly progressive judiciary that was responding with uncharacteristic resoluteness to the NAACP's unfolding strategy of sociological jurisprudence and a sympathetic presidency heeding the message of new political realities.[5]

But if the nine men on the Supreme Court, the President, and a handful of Cabinet officers represented the avant-garde, seemingly oblivious to the popular will but correctly divining the future course of history, the Congress, especially the Senate, which was dubbed "a southern institution," remained Neanderthal in outlook and action. A primary reason was that the power of the southerners, assured seniority and rank by virtue of the one-party Democratic South, was greatly enhanced by House and Senate rules. An attempt was made with the Reorganization Act of 1947 to restructure the Congress, but that legislation preserved the seniority system that gave control of key committees to the southerners and the filibuster rule favoring unlimited debate.

So during this first decade of the "second Reconstruction"—that is, between 1941 and 1951—Congress debated and held hearings, but took no action on antilynching, anti-poll-tax, and other civil rights bills. Nevertheless, demand continued to mount. In the Seventy-sixth Congress, which preceded Pearl Harbor, fourteen bills to advance minority rights had been introduced; in the next, thirty-five such bills were offered; in the Eightieth Congress there were fifty-one bills; in the Eighty-first Congress, there would be seventy-two. Subsequent Congresses would be swamped with large numbers.

Despite its monolithic front on racial questions, it was clear that the South could not alone withstand the changing political currents and block those initiatives. To reign unchecked on civil rights and other liberal issues, southern Democrats since about 1938 had been relying on help from conservative Republicans. That tacit interparty, interregional coalition had provided the Republicans with reciprocal support for tax measures and for blocking unfavorable economic legislation. The coalition's roots dated back to the end of the first Reconstruction, when it was used to kill that humanitarian experiment. Now it was strengthened under the leadership of Senator Robert Taft.[6]

Though the coalition was holding firm, Congress was changing, if only at a glacial pace. The most notable demonstration was the Senate's traumatic removal of one of its members, Theodore Gilmore Bilbo, the archsegregationist from Mississippi who was the most eloquent example of the corrupting influence of racism. Bilbo's fellow senators, at the urging of the

NAACP, charged him with misusing his office to violate the Constitution and federal laws by flagrantly perverting the electoral process in his state. Walter White submitted to the special Senate Campaign Investigating Committee an exhaustive report showing how Bilbo had won renomination in the July 2, 1946, Mississippi primary by intimidating black voters. That such a charge could have been upheld against a member of the one-party South showed how much progressive thought was seeping into the Congress—causing changes that were emphasized by the stinging rebuke of Glen H. Taylor, Democrat of Idaho, on the Senate floor: "What a hypocritical and blasphemous gesture we would witness today, if Mr. Bilbo were to stand in our midst and place his hand on the Holy Bible and swear fealty to democratic institutions, to free elections, to the rights of citizens."

Taylor added: "He has toured the length and breadth of his state stirring up racial hatred, inciting white to hate black and causing black to hate white. To whites who are themselves poor, ill nourished, ill clothed, and ill educated, he does not offer prosperity, nourishment, clothing, food and education. No; he offers to them the delicious sense of feeling superior to someone else, the cheap thrill of membership in a master race, the joy of kicking someone else around." He said that was "the same sort of cheap thrill that was peddled in Germany by an ambitious house painter some 10 years ago."[7]

Bilbo was replaced by John Stennis, an equally rabid but smarter racist. He moved in tandem with James O. Eastland, the senior senator from Mississippi, who faithfully reflected the racial sentiments of his backwoods Sunflower County cotton kingdom. Other notable counterparts in the Senate were Harry Flood Byrd, Jr., a diminutive figure who for much of his life was the single most magnetic force in Virginia politics; and Lister Hill and John Sparkman, both of Alabama. Sparkman was one of a group of liberal populists to come out of the South, which was proof that representatives of the region were not all conservative, except on race. Though he would not be moved on racial issues, Sparkman could be reasoned with; Hill was obtuse.

The southerners presided over the Senate under the august leadership of Richard Brevard Russell, Democrat of Winder, Georgia. Mitchell was particularly aware that it was he who had sponsored the infamous "Russell amendment" in 1944 that had killed the FEPC. But times were changing. Russell had the melancholy task of reigning during a period when victory often was measured not by unquestioned defeat of opponents but by how much he could slow the impending social changes in the South. A tall, patrician, hawk-faced politician with neither wife nor child and not an ounce of the gregariousness that was characteristic of others of his profession, he was condemned by demeanor and ability to become a striking example of the aphorism that most men lead lives of quiet desperation.

In the House, Sam Rayburn, a staunch conservative who was as earthy as he was companionable, conscientious, and sincere, gently and discreetly wielded more cold power as speaker than any comparable figure in recent memory. The Texan, whose commanding presence was the result of his nearly thirty-eight years in the House, controlled the fate of much of President Truman's Fair Deal program. So well did he get along with colleagues of all ideological persuasions that he functioned as an amiable buffer between factions. The paradox of Rayburn's old and intimate friendship with Truman, which developed during the years that the Missourian was in the Senate, was that, loyal to his constituents' interests, the Speaker opposed the President's civil rights program and efforts to repeal the Taft-Hartley Act—key Fair Deal items. Rayburn could determine which bills reached the House floor—although that power was increasingly being challenged by the archconservative House veteran Howard W. "Judge" Smith of Virginia, who maintained a stultifying grip on the House Rules Committee.

Therein lay Mitchell's challenge in 1950—how to mobilize the comparatively weak progressive forces in Congress for the enactment of laws that were needed to protect the rights of the racially oppressed. The philosophical question still remaining after the Civil War was how far the federal government should go in guaranteeing every citizen economic and social equality.

Among Mitchell's most faithful allies in the Senate were men like Hubert Humphrey of Minnesota and Irving M. Ives and Herbert H. Lehman of New York. Ives beat Lehman in a spirited race in 1946 for the Senate. Ives, a Republican, was the former majority leader of the State Assembly and was best known for his coauthorship of the Ives-Quinn bill, passed by the New York legislature in 1945, creating the State Committee Against Discrimination (SCAD). That fair employment practice law, which made the Empire State the first to adopt such a measure, and a similar one in Minnesota were national models. A tall, energetic former insurance dealer in Norwich, New York, Ives began his political career in 1930 by helping to unseat the established Republican organization in Chenango County. In the U.S. Senate, he often acted as spokesman for a small clique of Republicans whose thinking was slightly less conservative than the party line. And he was notably progressive on civil rights and labor matters.

Lehman became one of the Fair Deal's leading spokesmen after he won election to the Senate in 1949 to fill the unexpired term of Robert H. Wagner, who resigned because of ill health. An 1897 graduate of Williams College, he started work as a five-dollar-a-week cotton goods salesman, but later became a partner in Lehman Brothers, the investment banking house founded by his father Mayer, which became Shearson Lehman Hutton. Lehman's career was notable for his long span of dedicated public service, which included ten years as governor of New York, and his strong liberal record.

In the House, Jacob K. Javits, the standard-bearer for the Republican and Liberal parties from New York, representing the Twenty-first District, which included both the Upper West Side and the entire northern tip of Manhattan, quickly won recognition as a public servant of remarkable fortitude and energy. Javits was the image of his district, one composed largely of European refugees chasing the American dream. As a lawyer and a political unknown, he benefited from a couple of lucky breaks in 1946. First, the Democrats fielded an uninspiring candidate against him; second, the American Labor party entered its own candidate in the race, enabling Javits to score a surprising victory in what was formerly a Democratic stronghold. He quickly established himself in Washington as a very unorthodox Republican—"the cross of the GOP," some called him—favoring agencies like the Office of Price Administration against such big-business lobbies as the National Association of Manufacturers. When he voted with fellow Republicans he did so only on noncontroversial legislation.

The dean of the liberal forces in the House was New York Democrat Emanuel Celler, an urbane Brooklynite who first entered the House in 1923. Throughout his years there, he harbored a rage against poverty and discrimination that were as intense as his hatred of communism. The keynote of his public life and the best indication of why he would be such a valuable ally to Mitchell was his comment that "my guilt crawls inside of me because I have not done enough, because I can never do enough, for people whom society punishes for no reason but the color of their skin. I have no room in my heart for any temperance toward the degradation, or despoiling of human dignity."

While Mitchell would rely increasingly on "fighting liberals" like Javits and Celler, and on the quieter New Jersey Republican Clifford Case, in the House, one of his closest and most dependable friends in the 1950s would be Democrat Adam Clayton Powell, Jr. Powell's political base was firmly rooted in the Abyssinian Baptist Church, a celebrated Harlem landmark whose pulpit he inherited from his father. Noted for his toothy smile, which he flashed with disdainful arrogance, Powell was the epitome of flamboyance. He was a bane to whites and a source of pride to his black constituents and other minorities throughout the country. He found vindictive pleasure in jousting with white institutions that seemed invincible to most blacks, and in the process considerably boosted his popularity at home. Inspired by Marcus Garvey and Emperor Haile Selassie of Ethiopia, he galvanized the deep despair of the Depression, through such activities as preaching on a Harlem street corner and organizing protest demonstrations and boycotts of department stores, bus lines, the telephone company, the New York World's Fair, and others, into a crusade to obtain jobs for blacks, creating a movement that landed him a seat in Congress in 1945. Immediately, he began working for an FEPC bill and a national civil rights law.[8]

The second stage of the battle for a permanent FEPC in the Eighty-first Congress commenced in January 1950, with an initial skirmish in the House over the twenty-one-day rule. That parliamentary procedure had been adopted the previous year at the beginning of the first session of the Eighty-first Congress in order to limit the power of the Rules Committee to bottle up legislation approved by other committees. Under House rules, all legislation except revenue and appropriation bills and measures from a few minor committees first had to be acted upon by the Rules Committee before they could be considered on the floor. The rules provided for alternative means for bringing a bill to the floor, but they were cumbersome. The twenty-one-day rule was a simplified approach. It permitted a committee chairman whose bills had been bottled up for more than the stipulated number of days to bring the measure before the House on the second and fourth Mondays of each month upon recognition by the speaker. FEPC backers were now looking to the twenty-one-day rule as a means of getting their bill to the House floor. Recognizing the possibility that such a move might succeed, the opposition moved to rescind the rule.

Mitchell countered with a vigorous lobbying campaign and won the expressed support of several Republican congressmen. When the House voted 236 to 183 to retain the twenty-one-day rule, Mitchell saw that success as the "first concrete evidence of the effect" of the NAACP's National Emergency Civil Rights Mobilization.[9]

The House now turned its attention to the FEPC issue. Two effective measures with enforcement powers, one introduced by Harlem Democrat Adam Powell and the other by Senator J. Howard McGrath of Rhode Island, had been reported out of committees in the House and Senate, respectively, in 1949 and were up for consideration. Congressman John Lesinski, Democrat of Michigan, who was chairman of the House Committee on Education and Labor, which had approved the Powell bill, petitioned the Rules Committee for a "rule" to get the measure onto the House floor. As had previously happened in 1945 when Congresswoman Mary T. Norton, Democrat of New Jersey, attempted to bring her FEPC bill to the floor, a coalition of Republicans and southern Democrats refused to vote the requested rule. When he attempted to use the twenty-one-day rule to bring the bill to the floor on January 23, Lesinski ran into another problem.

Instead of recognizing Lesinski, House Speaker Rayburn recognized J. Hardin Peterson, a Florida Democrat who was chairman of the Public Lands Committee. Peterson moved for consideration of a bill on statehood for Hawaii. Rayburn bypassed Lesinski because he feared there would have been a political backlash against the seven members of the Texas delegation and twenty-two other southern congressmen whose vote he had obtained for the twenty-one-day rule. He felt voters would see this vote as indirect support for an FEPC bill. [10]

Seeking to get around the roadblock, Mitchell began "pinning some hope" on forming bipartisan liaison committees of senators and congressmen who were willing to work with the NAACP for a law against employment discrimination. Reporting to Wilkins on that strategy during a February 10 meeting, Mitchell proposed a bipartisan FEPC committee of ten Democrats and ten Republicans. The meeting was attended by congressmen from both parties as well as representatives of interested organizations. (Those most likely attending, because Mitchell specifically identified them as participating in an April 6 meeting with Majority Leader Scott Lucas, were Thomas Harris, an attorney for the CIO; George Weaver, assistant to the secretary-treasurer of the CIO; Charles LaFollette, national director of ADA; Violet Gunther, ADA legislative representative; Elmer Henderson, director of the American Council on Human Rights; Arnold Aaronson, secretary of the Commission on Law and Social Action of the American Jewish Congress; and Lewis Hines, AFL legislative representative). The group agreed that Jacob Javits would be responsible for getting the Republicans, and Biemiller the Democrats.

Mitchell next sought to persuade Hubert Humphrey to set up a similar bipartisan group in the Senate. Humphrey agreed to discuss the suggestion with Scott Lucas to make sure it did not conflict with the majority leader's plans to bring an FEPC bill to a vote in the Senate. It was agreed that the Senate would take up the issue after the House had acted.

Based on the plans that were discussed, Mitchell said, the House was scheduled to act on February 22 or 27. On the first date, Lesinski was to use the "Calendar Wednesday" provision to bring the bill to the floor. Then supporters would call for a vote to keep the House in session since it was expected that opponents would move for adjournment in observance of Washington's Birthday. (Under the Calendar Wednesday rule, committees whose chairmen wanted to bypass the Rules Committee could be called up alphabetically by the House speaker.) The drawback to the Calendar Wednesday rule was that consideration of the measure had to be concluded on the same day. FEPC supporters remembered that when Congresswoman Norton had used Calendar Wednesday to bring her FEPC bill to the floor in 1945, fifteen minutes after the House session began, a Mississippi congressman had moved for the House to adjourn, and his motion had carried. As a contingency, supporters of FEPC legislation planned that should the current move to invoke the Calendar Wednesday rule fail, another effort would be made on February 27 to have Congressman Lesinski recognized by Rayburn under the twenty-one-day rule.

A snag developed. After the GOP had made its interim policy statement, Javits told Mitchell that the Republicans would not join the nonpartisan effort in the House. Instead, Javits said, he expected to get major party support for an FEPC bill after February 27 and before March 6. Javits never told Mitchell what form that support would take, "although there was an implication that it might be the mass signing of the Powell discharge petition" that was being undertaken by the Harlem congressman. The discharge petition, signed by 218 House members indicating their desire to have a bill released from the Rules Committee, was another means of getting a measure to the floor for consideration. The situation was further complicated by the fact that New York Democrat Franklin D. Roosevelt, Jr., was also circulating a discharge petition for the same Powell bill.

Mitchell learned that Lesinski did not wish to force consideration of the bill on February 22. As the situation became more tangled, he decided that it was time for another meeting with his supporters in Congress, and Biemiller agreed to arrange a session on February 14. Republican Clifford Case was also to attend the meeting of Democrats. About the same time, Mitchell learned that Javits was supporting this effort independently by sending a letter to the sixty-four Republicans who had voted to retain the twenty-one-day rule urging them to be present for a possible Calendar Wednesday vote on February 15, a week earlier than had been planned. FEPC supporters, he said, feared that the House District Committee would use most of that day for handling tedious local business and leave only enough time for the Committee on Labor to be called "at a very late hour." To Mitchell, there was only one clear course of action. "If we have the chance, we should bring FEPC to the floor on the 15th and dispose of it on that day, even if it takes until midnight. However, the meeting on Tuesday, February 14, will give consideration to what should be done if the District Committee follows the anticipated plan [of being heard that day]." A decision evidently was made to press for a vote a week later.

Powell obtained even fewer signatures than Roosevelt for his discharge petition. Following the failure of that effort, Lesinski finally got the bill to the floor on February 22. It was defeated in a marathon session that lasted until 3:00 A.M. Opponents killed the Powell bill by voting for a weak alternative that was sponsored by Congressman Samuel McConnell, Republican of Pennsylvania.

Mitchell reported that the "hard working group of young Republicans as well as Democrats" who supported the Powell bill "were under the impression that they had enough votes to pass it." But a well-organized coalition of conservative Republicans and southern Democrats "shoved the McConnell bill through" in the closing hours of the floor fight. There was so much confusion that many members did not realize they had attached to the McConnell bill an amendment exempting the Atomic Energy Commission or any contractor or licensee of that agency from the measure's antidiscrimination coverage. The coalition, through a "Declaration of Policy," sought to make the watered-down bill palatable by prohibiting discrimination because of political affiliation, sex, and physical handicaps. That meant, Mitchell explained, that the commission could argue that it was required to handle only complaints on race, creed, or color, but could not enforce its decisions even though it was given powers under the McConnell bill to investigate and issue subpoenas. Furthermore, Communists and members of organizations cited by the FBI or the attorney general as Communist front groups were excluded from coverage.

The stage now shifted to the Senate. Senator Lucas assured Mitchell that the McGrath bill would be taken up before April 1, but only after four other pieces of legislation had been acted on. The uncertainty in that schedule made Mitchell nervous. He was also troubled by the prospect that the FEPC bill could be faced with three cloture votes. The first would be on the motion to take up the bill; the second, on the bill itself; and the third would be on the House-Senate conference report that would be made to iron out differences between the two bodies. There was also the fear that Taft would seek to introduce in the upper chamber a McConnell-type bill, with no enforcement authority. As the days dragged on into April, with no action in sight, Mitchell and his legislative strategy group worked on means for obtaining cloture against the expected filibuster. When the anticipated fight finally broke out on May 12, it was, as expected, not over the FEPC measure itself, but merely on a motion to take up the bill. The motion was soundly defeated, on May 19, 1950, when 52 senators voted to impose cloture while 32 were opposed. So once more, as in 1946, the full Senate never had a chance to vote on FEPC. Concluded *The Crisis* after examining the vote, "Neither the Republicans nor the northern Democrats can blame the Dixiecrats. Cloture on FEPC was blocked by northern and western senators of both parties, nine Republicans and twelve Democrats." With the failure of a second attempt on July 12 to impose cloture by a vote of 55 to 32, Majority Leader Lucas gave up, but Mitchell did not.[11]

The struggle for FEPC legislation reaffirmed the reality that while the South bore the onus of rank racism, the North strongly reinforced those attitudes. Without widespread support for Jim Crow and employment discrimination, southerners alone could not have blocked attempts to protect the rights of minorities in Congress. While Republicans and Democrats blamed each other for the FEPC failure, the truth was that both parties as well as the White House were responsible. During the most intense stage of the planning of the legislative fight in the spring, for example, Truman vacationed for a month in Florida. Following a meeting with him upon his return to Washington, Lucas reported that the President was "pretty well satisfied" with the progress of his program. Lucas also said he expected that before Congress recessed for the summer, it would have passed the foreign economic and arms aid programs, increased Social Security benefits, reduced some excise taxes, extended rent control, and increased the borrowing power for the Commodity Credit Corporation. Not a word was said about FEPC or other civil rights legislation.

The charade incensed Mitchell and Rauh. They charged that the lawmakers acted as though something had been done when nothing had. Mitchell nevertheless found much room for hope. In both attempts in the Senate, he noted, a majority of senators had voted for cloture. "The Southern senators understand arithmetic. They know that while we would lose some votes because certain senators do not agree with specific features of proposed civil rights laws, we do have enough to win by a comfortable majority. Hence they fight desperately to protect the one weapon that they have. That is endless talk."[12]

Before Mitchell would turn his attention again to changing the Senate filibuster rule, he wanted to be sure that the FEPC idea was kept alive. Once more, a raging war, this time in Korea, had opened the door of employment opportunity for blacks. He began working to get Truman to issue a second executive order, one that would cover defense contractors.

Following a strategy session on July 14, 1950, at Howard University Law School with George Johnson, his former FEPC coworker; Frank Reeves, the Washington Bureau's legal representative; George Weaver, who, in addition to his official title, was also minority affairs director of the CIO; and Herman Edelsberg of the Anti-Defamation League of B'nai B'rith, Mitchell reported to Wilkins that an attempt might be made to get some fair employment language into proposed war powers legislation for the President. Such language "would not mention an executive order FEPC specifically, but it would provide a legal basis for issuance of such an order by the President," he said. Based on Mitchell's recommendations, a week later White wired W. Stuart Symington, chairman of the National Security Resources Board, the top planning agency for the civilian economy, asking him to meet with an NAACP-led delegation "for the purpose of discussing 'methods by which minorities can make maximum contributions to mobilization.'" Symington along with the secretaries of defense and state formed the triumverate of the President's war cabinet.

At the meeting on August 10, the NAACP called for (1) creation by a presidential executive order of a "manpower resources board," which would have broad authority to subpoena records, obtain testimony from witnesses, and take other necessary steps to implement the nondiscrimination clauses of the World War II Executive Order 9346; (2) measures to ensure that the U.S. Employment Service functioned without discrimination; (3) provision of training and retraining courses so that all available manpower might be utilized as rapidly as possible; (4) equal housing opportunities for all workers commensurate with overall manpower needs; and (5) the appointment of an assistant to the chairman of the National Security Resources Board. [13]

The scope of the proposed executive order was much broader than of previous ones. Mitchell sought to strengthen Truman's 1948 order, which applied only to government agencies, by having the new one cover private employers as well. He remained adamant that the order should apply to all recipients of government aid related to the defense program, that the new agency be independent, and that it be given strong enforcement powers.

As in the past, Truman showed no enthusiasm for issuing any order at all. To get him to do so, on December 3, 1951, required intensive political pressure from the NAACP. This success showed that although blacks were making progress in the courts in whittling away at the legal foundations of segregation and had won the active support of some important allies in the civil rights struggle, the nation was still not prepared to accord them equal citizenship. The outbreak of the Korean War, as well as the Red Scare that had been whipped up by Republican Senator Joseph R. McCarthy of Wisconsin, had also deepened the national anxiety and severely aggravated a conservative mood.

The setbacks in Congress in the 1950 midterm elections only caused Mitchell to reaffirm his original program because he firmly believed that the course he had chosen was the best one. For Truman, of course, the results were not any more encouraging. Only by increasing the number of Democratic supporters—and that would have been a long shot even for a popular President, which he was not—could Truman have hoped for more favorable treatment of his Fair Deal programs by the Eighty-second Congress than had been given them by the Eighty-first, whose continually shifting bipartisan coalitions blocked his most important proposals. His narrow victory in 1948 had been made more reassuring by the Republicans' loss of the one Congress they had controlled in eighteen years. Even so, factionalism among the Democrats had been debilitating. If Truman could not influence enough members of his own party to guarantee him a simple majority for his domestic initiatives, including repeal of the Taft-Hartley Act, what chance was there for civil rights? The conspicuous casualties in the 1950 elections underscored the apparent hopelessness of this cause.

Target number one for Truman and his supporters from organized labor was Robert Taft, leader of the militant GOP opposition. Taft's resounding victory in the face of organized labor's extraordinary campaign against him made him a much more formidable opponent than before and a leading GOP standard-bearer in 1952.

Taft's stunning victory epitomized the national Republican—and conservative—trend. The Democrats retained control of the House, but their number was sharply reduced from 261 to 234. The Republicans' capture of 47—a net gain of 5—of the Senate's 96 seats gave them all but arithmetic control. The Democrats' troubles were compounded by the astounding defeat of two of their most powerful members, Scott Lucas, the Senate floor leader, and Millard E. Tydings of Maryland, chairman of the Senate Armed Services Committee. Tydings lost in a sweeping upset in a state where Democrats outnumbered Republicans by two and one-half to one. Lucas, Truman's faithful ally, was defeated in Illinois by, of all people, former Congressman Everett Dirksen, an orthodox Republican conservative like Taft who would soon be taking over his party's leadership in the Senate. In effect, the biggest loser was Truman because the Eighty-second Congress would be controlled by the southern bloc, which was overwhelmingly against the Fair Deal, and conservative Taft Republicans.

Equally ominous for Truman was the election to the Senate of Richard M. Nixon, a two-term congressman from California who had won prominence in 1948 as a member of the House Un-American Activities Committee during the investigations of the Alger Hiss Communist conspiracy case. Despite his chameleon qualities, Nixon gave most news analysts the impression that he leaned more toward the Republican "Old Guard" than toward any other faction of his party. One of his former roommates at Duke Law School probably summed up his personality best by describing him as stamped by "middle-class, almost Puritanical mores on a Quaker religious background, a basically conservative outlook from the standpoint of having the middle-class Quaker mentality."

For Mitchell, one of the few salutary developments was Herbert Lehman's capture of a Senate seat for his first full term. With his election, in January 1951, to the NAACP national board of directors, Lehman would join Humphrey, Douglas, Ives, and the small group of Senate liberals as an undisputed ally. [14]

Against that background, Mitchell told White that "so far as numbers are concerned, our position in the 82nd Congress will not be greatly different from what it was in the 81st." He believed that the "chief problems will be in key committees of the House and Senate and also with the Senate leadership." Consequently, he urged that NAACP branches be mobilized to exert pressure on lawmakers during the recess to block the election of

Richard Russell, Ernest W. McFarland of Arizona, or Lister Hill of Alabama as Senate majority leader. He was as much opposed to Russell's becoming chairman of the Armed Services Committee, where he would wreck any program to integrate the armed forces. "He came very close to doing this in the 81st Congress." Mitchell also urged that the NAACP work against the appointment of Graham A. Barden of North Carolina as chairman of the House Labor Committee, since in that position he could block FEPC legislation.[15]

When the new Congress convened on January 3, 1951, Mitchell faced a bleak political landscape. McFarland was the new Democratic majority leader, and first-term Senator Lyndon Baines Johnson of Texas, who had moved up from the House, was the new majority whip. Both men were opposed to FEPC legislation and to any major liberalization of Rule XXII, Mitchell's second priority. Southerners controlled both houses of Congress, and Russell was given control of the Senate Democratic Policy Committee, which determined legislative priorities. The House offered no more hope. It rescinded the twenty-one-day rule, which had trimmed the power of the conservative Rules Committee.

Despite Mitchell's reservations about McFarland, he found the majority leader ready to meet with him on February 21, 1951, for an informal talk about the administration's civil rights plans. Reporting to White, Mitchell said that McFarland felt that several southerners, "particularly Senator Holland of Florida," were "anxious to dispose of the civil rights controversy in some way because they believe it is giving the South a very bad name," and that such men as Senator Russell did "not want to see any civil rights legislation passed." Nevertheless, they were "willing to refrain from filibustering if they can stipulate the kind of civil rights program that will be passed in the Senate." McFarland asked Lehman, who was also at the meeting, whether civil rights groups would accept a constitutional amendment on the poll tax repeal. McFarland felt that such an amendment might pass without a filibuster. "I told him that, in my opinion," said Mitchell, "the Administration would be wasting its time if it tried to get a constitutional amendment through on the poll tax repeal because no responsible organization would consider that again."

Mitchell also reminded McFarland that blacks, who had supported Truman overwhelmingly in 1948, clearly were now unhappy with the Democrats. That did not necessarily mean that blacks had withdrawn support from Truman, he said, but that the rest of the Democratic ticket could suffer. In effect, blacks remained committed to Truman because of his exemplary civil rights program, just as they had been loyal to FDR because of the New Deal, but they were astute and selective voters. Mitchell used the surprise defeats of Senators Tydings, a strong civil rights opponent, and

Lucas as evidence of that. He told McFarland that "it appeared that even if the President got reelected in 1952, he probably would not have any real strength in the House and Senate because minority groups in key states were fed up with the failures in Congress."

Mitchell suggested that McFarland "could take a dramatic step in the civil rights field if he would make a statement or speech on the floor of the Senate indicating that if the President issued an executive order setting up an FEPC it would get the full support of Congress when it seeks appropriations." McFarland told Mitchell that he had always voted for appropriations for the wartime FEPC and "would explore this suggestion further." Mitchell reminded McFarland that lynching was still a problem, and it was much more important than the poll tax. "I advised him that favorable action on a good anti-lynching bill would be a real forward step in the civil rights field." Mitchell told White that he "got the impression" that McFarland "has had considerable pressure from Senator Lehman." Consequently, he felt, "our meeting with Senators Lehman, Humphrey, Douglas, and others, will be very significant."[16]

Mitchell's legislative program for the Eighty-second Congress beginning in 1951 anticipated Truman's issuing a fair employment executive order. When he did that, said Mitchell, "we must carefully follow the appropriations of this agency and turn the spotlight on any committee members in the House or Senate who fail to give it their full support." He advised that the NAACP should be prepared for the usual stonewalling in both houses through the manipulation of parliamentary rules. "The Administration must take the responsibility of getting favorable rulings and we must be fully advised on when these rulings will take place in order that we may be prepared to rally supporting votes." The administration would also be held responsible for tying the FEPC appropriations to vital defense legislation in the Senate to forestall a filibuster. "We, in turn, must be prepared to rally supporting votes to prevent FEPC appropriations from being set aside for separate consideration."

With the issuance of an executive order, he felt, civil rights organizations would be free to make an all-out fight for a change in Senate rules. As a result of the filibusters that also killed statehood for Alaska and Hawaii in 1950, "it may be possible to get support from organizations not necessarily friendly to FEPC if the issue is on" changing the rules. If the attempt to change the rules failed, an attempt should be made to embarrass Republican leaders who had maintained that it was possible to impose cloture with sixty-four votes on antilynching legislation. In that event, he continued, the NAACP should get Truman to call a bipartisan meeting of the Senate and House leaders.

At that time, the White House could issue a press statement saying that the President had sought to implement the civil rights program as far as it was within his power by setting up an executive order FEPC. The statement could then point out that the President had requested the leaders of both parties to attempt to get an anti-lynching bill through the 82nd Congress. I suggest the anti-lynching bill because if the anti-poll tax bill is called, undoubtedly, there will be an attempt to substitute a constitutional amendment for it. [17]

Working in tandem with White, Mitchell lined up powerful support in the Senate through Humphrey, Douglas, Lehman, and Ives. Humphrey, in a strong letter to Truman on January 15, 1951, urged the President to issue an executive order similar to that during the World War II to create a new FEPC in order to eliminate discrimination in the current defense industry. On that same day, during his speech to Congress on the budget, Truman complied with the demand and called for the passage of FEPC legislation. That month Ives introduced legislation in the Senate to create the FEPC that Mitchell wanted. In a letter to Ives, Mitchell said he was especially thankful to him, Humphrey, and Lehman for their support because he expected "formidable opposition from a minority of senators." Because of that, he said, he was pinning his hope on an executive order "to fill the gap between the present and that day when legislation is passed establishing an FEPC with enforcement powers applying to all industry subject to Federal jurisdiction." It was to be hoped, Mitchell said, that this executive order would be patterned after the Ives-Quinn bill. "It is significant that you and Senator Humphrey, who have done so much for FEPC legislation in your home state and city, are now working to extend this principle nationally." [18]

The Department of Labor approved the draft of an executive order in January, which it forwarded to the Bureau of the Budget, noting that "it is unthinkable that the Government should permit" billions of dollars in defense "funds to be expended without imposing on those favored with government business the obligation to refrain from discriminatory employment practices and without providing effective means of enforcing such an obligation." Around the same time, Mitchell sent a draft of his own proposed executive order to Charles E. Wilson, director of the Office of Defense Mobilization. In his cover letter, Mitchell told Wilson that he understood that the Bureau of the Budget was considering an order that would create an FEPC with a nonsalaried chairman and a full-time executive secretary. Because past experience had shown that such an arrangement was ineffective, he said, he hoped that the administration would consider having a full-time chairman. Subsequently, in a meeting with Mitchell and several other black activists, Wilson replied that he would support the issuance of an executive order creating an FEPC, but "he was told to keep his hands off the matter because it would be handled 'across the street' [i.e., at the White House]."

Particularly important was a meeting with the President on February 28, 1951, where black leaders presented a six-point program. The meeting was structured to give blacks an opportunity, apart from their white coalition supporters, to communicate their concerns directly to the President. In addition to the expected demand for an executive order setting up an FEPC with enforcement powers, the leaders also urged the President to "abolish segregation immediately in Washington," appoint blacks to administrative and policy-making positions in government, integrate all new agencies established during the Korean War, appoint blacks to foreign and diplomatic service, and eradicate racial segregation in the armed forces. Those items were the main planks in the NAACP Washington Bureau's program.

On March 1 at the fourth annual conference of the Civil Liberties Clearinghouse, Truman made another appeal for FEPC legislation. Clearly, he was playing for time. By April, blacks were demonstrably restless about Truman's inaction on the executive order, despite his calls for passage of FEPC legislation. "It has been nearly 10 months since the National Council for a Permanent FEPC wired the President urging him to issue an executive order similar to President Roosevelt's 8802 . . . as an integral factor in the mobilization of manpower against North Korean Communist aggression," *The Crisis* complained. In addition to Symington and Wilson, White, Mitchell, and other coalition leaders had met with Secretary of Labor Maurice Tobin and other government officials in an effort to win support for the order.[19]

Next, under the NAACP's banner, sixty-seven representatives from thirty-one national organizations met in Washington on May 22 and 23. They were very much concerned that Congress was taking no action on the civil rights proposals that Truman had again submitted in January with his budget message, or on segregation in veterans' programs or plans to change the Senate filibuster rule. Truman's lukewarm support for civil rights—what *The Crisis* called "a trend toward appeasement of discredited Dixiecrats and other reactionaries"—had also alarmed them. The real importance of the Washington meeting was that it resulted in a consensus that wider civil rights activities were required before the next election.

Greater effort, such as a call by the NAACP convention in June for the association to spearhead a pre-presidential-election civil rights mobilization in Washington in early 1952, would be needed to get Truman to act.

Truman's dilemma was that he was eager to hold black votes while also trying to heal the Dixiecrats' split in the Democratic party. Mitchell and White were determined to get him to give presidential leadership to the civil rights struggle. The Washington conference renewed "the request that has been made so often to President Truman since the Communist attack on South Korea, that he issue an executive order establishing an FEPC in defense employment, and that he obtain the same integration in the Army, that is being established in the Air Corps, Navy, Marine Corps, Coast Guard, in veterans hospitals and in military cemeteries around the world."[20]

Prior to the national conference on civil rights in May 1951, White had charged that Congress was engaged in a "willful sit-down strike against civil rights." That assessment was based on a report by Mitchell showing that forty-one civil rights bills and four resolutions had been introduced in the House. Five of them were FEPC bills. The others were proposals for outlawing lynching, omnibus civil rights bills that would eliminate the poll tax, and antislavery and antipeonage bills. Also, Congressmen Case of New Jersey and Franck Havenner, Democrat of California, had introduced bills to protect members of the armed services against assault and other violence by civilians or peace officers. Those were all serious problems on which Mitchell was also working. Mitchell felt, however, that the fate of those bills was "sealed because they have been referred to the Labor Committee headed by Barden of North Carolina." In the Senate, prospects for civil rights bills would have been brighter were it not for the filibuster. There, seven bills and three resolutions to liberalize the cloture rule had been introduced. Also, Senator Lehman and his group had introduced an antifilibuster resolution in the Senate. Other proposed civil rights legislation included abolition of segregation on common carriers, prohibition of discrimination in the National Health Insurance Program as well as in the area of educational finance, a fair housing practices bill, and an equal rights act for the District of Columbia.

As Mitchell had also anticipated in his memorandum to White, Humphrey four days later introduced in the Senate a comprehensive civil rights package of eight bills. They were the same as those that had been introduced in the House.

Mitchell was hard pressed to keep pace not only with civil rights legislation that was being introduced by friendly and not so friendly lawmakers, but also with the southerners' "vigorous segregation program." Gloster Current, after spending three days in April in the NAACP Washington Bureau, wrote Mitchell that "I got the distinct feeling of being on a treadmill and found myself unaccustomed to the pace and rather tired in the evening."[21]

On December 3, 1951, Truman finally issued Executive Order 10308 creating a Committee on Government Contract Compliance, which would ultimately assume a permanent place within the Department of Labor as the Office of Federal Contract Compliance. It was a far cry from what the NAACP had wanted. A few days before it was issued, Mitchell had alerted White that a draft had been circulated and discussed at meetings of the Manpower Advisory Committee and the Interdepartmental Manpower Committee. At Mitchell's suggestion, White and Philip Randolph wired the President that they understood that the proposed order contained no enforcement powers and requested on behalf of the organizations working with them a copy to study. But the only response they received was news that the order had been issued. Mitchell's action on the order revealed his delicate maneuvering style. While alerting White about the order's weaknesses, Mitchell didn't tell his boss until after it had been issued that he had actually seen a copy dated November 27 and had helped to edit it, because he did not want to take any chance that would have exposed or embarrassed his allies in the administration. At Mitchell's request afterward, White informed the NAACP board that the order did not contain the "suggested method of enforcement" that the NAACP had wanted. However, he said, Mitchell believed "that a strong committee could get it adopted as a part of the regular operating procedure."

Mitchell's public response masked the depth of his unhappiness: "We are disappointed because of the weaknesses and lack of enforcement power in this Executive Order. However, we must work to make the most of it, and at the same time seek ways of strengthening it."

The Government Contract Compliance Committee was given much less power than the World War II FEPC had possessed. The order created a committee of eleven members; six were to be appointed by the President, and five were to be chosen by the Departments of Defense and Labor, the Atomic Energy Commission, the General Services Administration, and the Defense Materials Procurement Agency. The order placed the primary responsibility for compliance with the nondiscrimination clause—which was the same clause that had been provided in 1943 under Executive Order 9346—with the heads of federal government agencies. Instead of having enforcement powers, the Government Contract Compliance Committee could only investigate and recommend. The committee could deal only with contractors and subcontractors, while the World War II FEPC had had authority over transportation, labor unions, and many other areas of economic activity. Nor could Truman's committee police any other aspect of government contract-compliance besides hiring practices, such as wages, hours, or product quality.

More than ever, it was obvious that the President who had found the will to fire a politically popular General Douglas MacArthur because of his mishandling of the Korean War and who was capable of engaging the mighty Soviet Union in a burgeoning cold war could not find the courage to emulate his predecessor in protecting the rights of African Americans to earn a living without discrimination. Yet, overall, Truman, because of his rapport with Walter White and his general civil rights stance, encouraged more hope among blacks than any previous President. The conclusion of the FEPC's *Final Report* in 1946 that "unsolved cases show that Executive authority is not enough to secure compliance in the face of stubborn opposition" had an increasingly haunting ring. "Only legislative authority," the report said, "will insure compliance in the small number of cases in which employees or union or both fail after negotiations to abide by national policy of nondiscrimination."

Mitchell wrote in the January 1952 *Crisis* that the only practical thing to do now was to follow White's suggestion that "whatever good may come out of this order depends almost entirely upon the quality of the personnel appointed by the President." White, Mitchell said, put "a finger on the 'switch' which the President can use if he really intends to have the new agency do a good job." The next step was to "get member agencies to assign enough personnel from their staffs to make real investigations of discrimination." He suggested that the Contract Compliance Committee could "set the stage for member agencies to establish hearing panels to determine whether a complaint against a given company is bona fide" by, for example, having a panel of its members obtain and review evidence in a case. He provided a detailed procedure for the committee to follow in handling complaints.

The committee's second job, he continued, was to establish "rules that would convince employers and contracting agencies that [the] mere volume of colored people on the payroll does not prove that there is no discrimination." He pointed out that the words "equal treatment" have "an ominous ring" for blacks. "We fear that some White House advisers still think it is possible to have segregation in employment without discrimination." But the "great truth that segregation in employment inevitably leads to discrimination was dramatically established during the War." Employers discovered then, as school officials were also finding out in response to the NAACP's legal struggle against dual educational systems, that it was much too expensive to attempt to comply with nondiscrimination orders by building "separate but equal" facilities. Invariably segregated facilities perpetuated racial discrimination in hiring, promotion, and transfers of staff. A third responsibility, he suggested, was for the committee to obtain through agencies under its jurisdiction sufficient personnel to do the job. He warned that it must avoid the mistake of the currently functioning

President's Fair Employment Board, which was operating out of the Civil Service Commission with "a minuscule staff of whites only."[22]

Mitchell soon discovered that even the presence of "outstanding people of integrity" on the committee was insufficient to change racial attitudes within the bureaucracy. The public members were Dwight Palmer, president of General Cable Corporation, which during World War II was a top example of how management could cooperate with the FEPC in ending opposition by whites to racial integration in the workplace; James Carey, president of the International Union of Electrical Workers as well as CIO secretary-treasurer; Irving Engel of the American Jewish Committee; Oliver W. Hill, former Richmond, Virginia, city councilman and a member of the national NAACP Legal Committee; Dowdall Davis, editor of the *Kansas City Call;* and George Meany, AFL secretary-treasurer.

Attending a closed meeting of the committee on June 9, 1952, Mitchell complained that since Executive Order 10308 was issued, no action had been taken to fill its requirements. He asked the committee to take "concrete action" to eliminate employment discrimination, beginning with the telephone company in Washington, which, even though it had a government contract, was openly practicing employment discrimination. He reported to the NAACP board of directors that he had suggested to the committee that some method be found to enforce nondiscrimination clauses in government contracts. The committee asked him to submit language that would strengthen the current clause.[23]

Mitchell's continuing attempts to get FEPC legislation through Congress were equally frustrating. Because this was a critical election year, lawmakers again stonewalled on civil rights. The only visible impact Mitchell had on Congress was to keep the civil rights issue alive with the help of such friends as Humphrey and Powell.

Humphrey, chairman of a subcommittee of the Senate Labor and Public Welfare Committee, held hearings on April 18 on fair employment legislation (the Ives-Humphrey bill) with enforcement powers and reported out a bill, S. 3368, which was now to be named the Federal Equality of Opportunity in Employment Act. Notably voting against that bill were Congressmen Taft and Nixon, who was running for Vice President, and Lister Hill. Mitchell was very disturbed about public perception of the bill. Because "FEPC" was such a red flag to so many people, Mitchell had agreed in 1950 with Congressman Roosevelt that if they were ever going to get any employment discrimination bill through Congress, they would have to use a name other than FEPC. Ives and Humphrey, in keeping with discussions they had had with Mitchell, also agreed it was best to adopt a new name when they introduced the bill. However, as soon as S. 3368 was reported out, some newspapers labeled it "a watered-down FEPC bill."

Actually, Mitchell explained, the measure was "a combination of the original FEPC bills" that had been introduced by Humphrey, Ives, and other senators in 1951.

The fact that even some of the friends of FEPC thought the bill was weaker just because the name was changed shows how little attention friends or foes have paid to the actual provisions of this legislation.

Southern opponents use the letters FEPC to conjure up visions of all anti-Negro stereotypes ever known in Dixie. Friends have sometimes pictured FEPC as a means of ending all racial discrimination in one fell swoop. Therefore, it was natural that when the Senate Committee reported out the real bill with the magic letters omitted there was talk on both sides of the civil rights battlefront about the bill being a compromise.

The Ives-Humphrey bill (S. 3368) covered companies engaged in interstate commerce who employed fifty or more people. It would have established a commission to hear fair employment complaints, issue directives to halt discrimination, and enforce its directives through federal court where necessary. A new feature permitted, but did not require, the commission to cede jurisdiction to fair employment agencies in states with laws that the commission considered adequate. The latter provision was an attempt to lessen opposition from some states.

Another important feature of the bill made quotas illegal by barring dismissal of workers on the basis of race, color, religion, national origin, or ancestry. The bill did not require the firing of an employee to make room for another person. It required employers to hire on the basis of qualification only. S. 3368 would not have guaranteed everyone a job. It would only ensure that a person had a fair chance to get a job in 2 percent of the nation's companies.

Because the effort to liberalize the rule under which sixty-four votes were required to end debate again failed, action on the FEPC bill, as well as on anti-poll-tax, antilynching, and other civil rights legislation involving housing, education, and the armed services was blocked by the threat of a filibuster. In the House, the Labor Committee, under its chairman Graham Barden, smothered a similar FEPC bill. Mitchell, nevertheless, was assured of future attempts to pass legislation he wanted because of the increasing number of firm civil rights supporters in Congress.[24]

During that time, Mitchell was also engaged in a noteworthy battle over the Winstead amendment to S. 1, the universal military training (UMT) bill—an idea first proposed by President Roosevelt in 1945 to correct deficiencies in the Selective Service program. Mitchell thought the Winstead amendment was so significant that he devoted an entire Washington Bureau newsletter to it as well as an article in *The Crisis* in May 1951.

Events leading up to that battle in the House had first occurred in the Senate. At the NAACP's urging, a group of senators led by Lehman and Humphrey had introduced an amendment to the UMT bill to protect black members of the armed forces against violence and brutality by civilians and law enforcement officers. Federal protection was already given to federal law enforcement officers, such as U.S. marshals, FBI personnel, Secret Service agents, Post Office inspectors, and Coast Guard members. (A similar proposal urged in 1943 by Henry L. Stimson, then secretary of war, was never adopted.) An example of such brutality had been reported in the *Memphis Press-Scimitar,* on February 16, 1951:

Corporal Jonathan Thomas, colored, a member of the Air Force was beaten in the Greyhound Terminal Restaurant in Memphis by police officers. Witnesses say that Thomas failed to say, "Sir," in answer to the officers' questions.

Thomas was on his way to Tinker Field when police officers approached him from behind and asked if he was going somewhere. Thomas answered, "Yeah," without turning around. The police officers beat Thomas and arrested him for disorderly conduct and resisting arrest.

The Senate nevertheless knocked out the Lehman amendment on March 1 by a vote of 57 to 30. Mitchell said the vote was important because it was the first time that new senators in the Eighty-second Congress had been given a chance to vote on an important civil rights question. He listed all those who "voted right" and "voted wrong" in his newsletter, which was circulated to NAACP branches.

In the House, the battle over the UMT bill began with a simple question from Congressman Arthur Winstead, Democrat of Mississippi, to Mitchell during a hearing before the House Armed Services Committee on March 8: "Would you have objections to the various people, when they register, stating a preference [in effect, as to whether they wanted to serve with a particular racial group] and, as nearly as possible, the military following it out?"

By a 21 to 12 vote, the committee a week later quickly approved an amendment offered by Winstead to S. 1 (which had passed the Senate and was now H.R. 2811). It sought to restore segregation in the Navy and Air Force and to end the Army's faltering integration program by permitting servicemen to choose the units in which they wanted to be trained and serve. It bothered Mitchell that although there were only eleven members from the Deep South on the House Armed Services Committee, twenty-four were from northern and border states, and "hence, the southerners did not have enough votes themselves to get this amendment out in committee, but they were supported by Republican members, "and the measure went to the floor for a vote. When Mitchell asked GOP leader Joseph W. Martin, Jr., of Massachusetts to request that the Republicans, as a matter of policy, vote against the Winstead amendment, the congressman replied that he would "see what might be done about it." He added, "Well, anyway it could be knocked out in the conference between the House and Senate." Mitchell took that last comment as a "storm warning."

To defeat the Winstead amendment, Mitchell, after some effort, got Congressman Melvin Price, an Illinois Democrat, to carry the fight against the measure, and lined up twenty-five other congressmen to join in planning floor strategy. The nation's only two black congressmen, Adam Clayton Powell, Jr., and Democrat William L. Dawson, were important members of that group. Dawson, a conservative who was the undisputed political boss of the five Chicago South Side districts that made up his congressional base, won considerable applause with his impassioned plea for defeat of the amendment. "How long, how long, my confreres and gentlemen from the South, will you divide us Americans on account of color?" he declared in reference to his Georgia birthplace. "Give me the test that you would apply to make any one a full-fledged American and by the living God, if it means death itself, I will pay it—but give it to me," he told the hushed House. The sixty-five-year-old lawmaker told his colleagues that he had been too old to be drafted in World War I but, nevertheless, had volunteered and been commissioned an infantry lieutenant. He led troops in battle against the Germans "trying to save this country." His style of pleading, characteristic of an older generation of blacks, was a dramatic contrast to Powell's flowery bombast. "This mark you see here on my forehead," Dawson said, "is the result of German mustard gas and this left shoulder of mine is today a slip joint. That would have been a good joint if I had not been a good American Negro."

The opposition, unmindful of such patriotism from blacks, remained resourceful. They not only introduced an amendment designed to get rid of the UMT bill altogether, but when that move failed, got the House to consider the Winstead amendment as "the Committee of the Whole," a parliamentary procedure under which congressmen's votes were not recorded.

Through White and Current, Mitchell brought to Washington forty-four NAACP branch leaders from eleven key states. They spent three days lobbying more than one hundred congressmen and maintained vigilance from the galleries to let the lawmakers know that even though their votes were not being recorded officially, they were being watched. The effort succeeded. On April 13 the House knocked out the Winstead amendment by a narrow 107 to 101 vote.[25]

The Winstead amendment battle was just one small skirmish in what would be a long struggle by Mitchell against segregation in the military. He had begun the year by offering on January 24 a three-point program before a subcommittee of the Senate Committee on Armed Services. He called for inclusion in any new Selective Service law provisions to (1) organize all new units without racial segregation; (2) bar the use of privately owned Jim Crow housing and restaurants by the military; and (3) eliminate racial designations from all forms and records of military personnel. That effort was in addition to his work with Lehman to get an amendment to the UMT bill that would protect black servicemen from violence, and to accomplish that goal by having friendly congressmen introduce separate measures. He next began a series of meetings with defense officials hoping to win their support for his three-point program. He vigorously opposed a proposal by Democratic Congressman John Rankin, Democrat of Mississippi, to construct a segregated veterans hospital at the birthplace of Booker T. Washington in Franklin County, Virginia. The bill was soundly defeated after organizations attending the May 22–23, 1951, conference wrote to 315 members of the House opposing it.[26]

On a much broader scale, Mitchell was fighting against what he called "the irrelevant and childish restrictions" of segregation like those that the U.S. Supreme Court had just set aside in *McLaurin* v. *Oklahoma State Regents of Higher Education,* which had been prosecuted by the NAACP. In that case, the Court had gone beyond *Sweatt* v. *Painter* and held that having admitted a black to its law school, the University of Oklahoma could not deny him free use of all the institution's facilities, including the library and lunchroom. Additionally, Mitchell's battles covered all areas of the military including Veterans Administration programs and the rights of black veterans to burial in national cemeteries, as well as such other areas where discrimination still existed as various aspects of life in the District of Columbia, airport use in several states, immigration to the United States, schools on military posts, and the Federal Housing Administration's lending policies.

Just before the first session of the Eighty-second Congress ended, a bill was passed that provided for aid to schools in areas heavily impacted by the defense industry. This program was originally instituted under the Defense Housing and Community Facilities Act, which contained a provision that required schools on federal property to conform to the laws of the states in which such installations were located. That requirement was diametrically opposed to what Mitchell had been fighting for all year—namely, the prohibition of discrimination and segregation in federally funded programs. Truman vetoed the bill. But, again, it troubled Mitchell that "in all of these bills, we are confronted with an unwillingness on the part of Congressmen and senators to introduce non-segregation amendments." Many lawmakers, he said, who could contribute to the civil rights fight by providing "good leadership feel that the need" for such schools in defense impacted areas is so great that "even if Federal funds go to support segregation, in the long run the schools will be improved." Despite a perceptibly greater understanding and sympathy for civil rights by an increasing number of lawmakers, not enough of them saw the need to join the vanguard of the struggle. Mitchell planned to intensify the NAACP's branch program to convince lawmakers of the importance of supporting non-segregation amendments.[27]

Mitchell, along with White and Wilkins, did better in 1952 on the political front. It was a presidential election year in which the crisis of race relations was sharpened by a new weapon called the hate bomb.

For the first time since the NAACP began keeping track of lynchings, none was recorded that year. By sheer force of publicity, the NAACP had completely changed the nation's thinking on the crime. Once it had been defended in the Senate and even in the pulpit; now clandestine violence had taken its place. The news that a dynamite bomb on Christmas night, 1951, had destroyed the home of Harry T. Moore, coordinator of the NAACP's Florida branches, and killed him shook the organization. His wife, Harriett, died a few days later from injuries received in the blast. Individual Ku Klux Klan members had begun to use this new weapon of hate in other areas of the South as well, notably Birmingham, Dallas, Atlanta, and Nashville, and even in California.

One of the Klan's main goals was to stifle black political aspirations in the South, but it was that very power that Mitchell and others were determined to develop in order to help combat the atmosphere of terror. Mitchell joined Kelly Alexander, Sr., president of the North Carolina State Conference of NAACP Branches, in leading the first of a series of voter mobilizations that January in Atlanta. Mitchell prepared summaries of important issues and of the voting records of congressmen and senators for the three hundred delegates attending the conference. "At first the delegates were not able to see how bad their particular congressmen were," Mitchell reported. "But when the district representatives were permitted to stand up and speak about the voting records of their representatives," everyone got the picture.[28]

Early in the year, White also mobilized the NAACP's branches, held a conference with leaders from fifty-two organizations in Washington, and held his quadrennial gathering of black groups, in each case stressing the need for a strong federal civil rights program. Those activities had no more visible impact on Congress than letting lawmakers know that civil rights was very much alive. Neither did they have any noticeable effect on the choice of presidential candidates, even though that was one of White's goals during the time that he, Wilkins, Mitchell, and Henry Lee Moon spent at the Republican and Democratic National conventions in July working to influence both the platforms and the selection of standard-bearers. [29]

Discussing presidential prospects at a Detroit NAACP branch meeting in January, Mitchell praised Truman for having "established a high standard on civil rights." Against Truman's record, he found the likely candidates weak. For example, Senator Estes Kefauver of Tennessee, despite seeking the Democratic nomination in the primaries, announced that he was opposed to FEPC legislation. He also said he was against the filibuster. A review of his record showed that although he had supported the March 11, 1949, ruling that would have limited debate in the Senate, he switched his position and on May 19 and July 12, 1950, voted with the old South against changing the filibuster rule. Senator Russell, another candidate, was even worse on civil rights. His 1950 amendment, which would have required segregation in the armed services and which Kefauver supported, was the one that Mitchell managed to get defeated on June 21, 1950. The problem with Kefauver, Mitchell said, was that upon seeing liberal Senators Claude Pepper of Florida and Frank Graham of North Carolina defeated by rabble-rousing southerners in their bids for reelection, he "threw away his coon-skin cap and flintlock rifle and ran like a rabbit back to the woods of reaction."

Among the Republicans, Senator Taft had always voted for cloture and was on record as opposing the filibuster. But in his speeches throughout the South, Mitchell thought, "he sounded more like a candidate running for Governor of Mississippi than an Ohian seeking the Presidential election." Dwight Eisenhower, another possibility, had yet to live down his statements, made before the Senate Armed Services Committee in hearings on universal military training on April 2, 1948, that if blacks were fully integrated into the services they would never get promoted "because the competition is too tough." Mitchell countered that already the Air Force had shown "how ridiculously false" Eisenhower's statement was. He noted that an encouraging number of blacks had earned their places as commissioned officers in "fair competition with white" candidates.

Mitchell, furthermore, termed as "sheer demagoguery" Eisenhower's statement "I do believe that if we attempt merely by passing a lot of laws to force someone to like someone else, we are just going to get into trouble." Mitchell explained that no laws were being considered that would force people to like others. He charged that by making such a statement, Eisenhower was merely bowing to southern sentiment. Overall, Mitchell concluded that

> on their present records, Eisenhower, Kefauver, and Taft would be wholly acceptable to the Dixiecrat elements, and, if they were to be elected at this time, the northern bank of the Potomac River would be an outpost of the resurrected Confederacy. In other words, what General Lee could not accomplish with the force of arms, these three, on the basis of their present stand, would accomplish by a surrender on civil rights.[30]

Had White had his wish, Truman would have run again in 1952. But Truman, bitterly opposed within his party by such barons as Harry Byrd, Richard Russell, and Governor James F. Byrnes of South Carolina as well as being unpopular in other regions because of the Korean War and domestic problems, decided against repeating his 1948 gamble. When the President announced his decision not to run on March 29, White lamented:

> No segment of the voters was more startled by President Truman's abdication from the presidential race than the Negro. Although he has appeared to soft-pedal the civil rights issue during recent months, no occupant of the White House since the nation was born has taken so frontal or consistent a stand against racial and religious discrimination as has Mr. Truman.[31]

The NAACP, nevertheless, was happy with the Democratic party's civil rights plank and choice of Governor Adlai Stevenson of Illinois as the presidential candidate, although it had strong reservations about his running mate, John Sparkman. In his report of a conference with Stevenson on August 7, Wilkins found him "a charming person, brilliant, witty and keenly analytical in conversation." One immediately got the impression, he said, "that here is a man who understands the whole broad background on civil rights, who needs no kindergarten explanation of philosophy and objectives." Wilkins's ebullient appraisal of Stevenson could easily have been White's. This evaluation was shaped by practical considerations—based on the candidate's expressed support for a change in the Senate filibuster rule "in accordance with the party platform." His view reinforced the NAACP's call for an improvement in "Congressional procedures so that majority rule prevails and decisions can be made after reasonable debate without being blocked by a minority in either house." Stevenson also "looked with favor on the Humphrey-Ives Bill" (S. 3368). It was evident from Wilkins's report, however, that the NAACP could have encountered problems with Stevenson in the future owing to the governor's hints that he might be willing to compromise on civil rights.

In contrast, the NAACP regarded Sparkman with foreboding. Following his nomination, White said, "It will be difficult, if not impossible, for the Democratic Party to sell to Negro voters, as well as to many other civil rights advocates, any nominee whose voting record has been one of consistent opposition to the civil rights objectives of the Democratic Party."

The NAACP similarly would have been much happier with a more outspoken friend of civil rights than the GOP's Dwight Eisenhower and his running mate Richard Nixon. Eisenhower's attitude on civil rights was about the same as Stevenson's. But, influenced by Truman and a strong party platform, Stevenson began his campaign well ahead of Eisenhower among black voters. White and his teammates deserved much of the credit for keeping the Democrats firm on civil rights. At both party conventions, White had presented a nine-point civil rights program to the platform committees. He reported to the NAACP national board in September that he, Wilkins, Mitchell, and Henry Lee Moon had worked "indefatigably" to secure strong civil rights planks and suitable candidates. As a member of the Democratic Platform Committee, Senator Lehman "waged an uncompromising fight" for a strong civil rights plank. He beat back "determined efforts by southerners to evade the issue," particularly the call to amend the Senate's Rule XXII allowing filibuster, and for FEPC legislation. The Democratic civil rights plank, White said, "is stronger than any ever taken by a political party." White attributed much of that success to Lehman.

Carrying the ADA banner, Joe Rauh also ensured that the Democratic platform was within the 1948 liberal pale. He performed his usual peripatetic role in influencing the convention's tone by serving as campaign manager to Averell Harriman, a veteran New Deal official who was then director of the Mutual Security Administration, in his try as a presidential candidate. Harriman's only victory, in the District of Columbia primary, made him exude the refrain, "By golly, I can do it." But Rauh's influence was not as effective elsewhere, so Harriman's presidential ambitions fizzled. Rauh really was for Stevenson, the much stronger prospect, but he found Stevenson difficult to work with. "He was like a Hamlet. He never would say whether he was going to run." Finally, he submitted to a convention draft.

Less identified with either party than was the ADA, the NAACP sought a similarly sympathetic ear at the GOP convention. But, after hearing White and representatives of cooperating organizations, the Republicans only appointed a subcommittee on civil rights. "None of the members," White said, "were at all well known or at all informed on" civil rights. In fact, one "member in particular was exceedingly hostile in his questioning." White felt that the Republican Platform Committee was merely going through the motions and had no intention of adopting a forthright plank on civil rights.

When Eisenhower told Wilkins that he "could not support" what he called "compulsory" FEPC legislation, the NAACP leader urged him to change his position. He informed the candidate that a bill without enforcement powers was "merely good advice," lacking "force and effect." Eisenhower wholeheartedly supported the concept of a commission to study employment patterns and to obtain facts, expose conditions, and advise states. "He said he thought it was unfortunate that FEPC had become such a symbol that a candidate's good intentions and sincerity were judged solely by his attitude toward FEPC." The general "vigorously declared himself in favor of ending segregation in the District of Columbia," saying it should "be wiped out" in the nation's capital. But on the question of providing the District of Columbia with self-government, another issue on which Mitchell was working, Eisenhower was not sure what the future political structure of the nation's capital should be. Eisenhower promised to eliminate discrimination "wherever it exists in Federal employment" and "told of his mixing Negro troops with whites during the Battle of the Bulge in World War II." He also supported his party's platform on abolishing the poll tax and lynching, but he would not promise to do anything about changing the Senate filibuster rules.

Overall, Wilkins found Eisenhower friendly and gracious.

> He appears honest and sincere in his declared opposition to discrimination, but he speaks always in general terms. He sees nothing inconsistent, apparently, in his opposition to a Federal FEPC and the sponsorship of such a bill by leading Republican senators, including Senator Ives of the key state of New York. Eisenhower wants merely to survey discrimination in employment, not enact a law to correct the condition.

Based on the reports from Wilkins and White, the NAACP national board adopted a statement commending Stevenson for "the clarity and courage of his pronouncements" on strong civil rights. The NAACP also praised Eisenhower for his "forthright statements on the abolition of segregation in the nation's capital, in the Armed Forces, and his concern for equal employment opportunity for all." However, the NAACP expressed

regret that the general had failed to support an effective FEPC with enforcement powers and to see the need for an amendment to Rule XXII to
abolish the filibuster. The board also sharply criticized the presence of
Nixon and Sparkman on the national tickets because both "have unsatisfac-
tory records."[32]

The NAACP's criticisms threw Sparkman and Eisenhower on the defensive. Mitchell informed White right after the convention that he found
Sparkman eager to portray himself as a progressive on civil rights, and that
he "would welcome an opportunity to talk at length with leaders in the
civil rights field" and believed he could "explain his position to their satisfaction." Sparkman, said Mitchell, told him that he "supports the civil
rights plank fully because he helped to write it." He regretted that some of
his critics had overlooked his contributions in shaping the plank. "He believes that more and better civil rights legislation will be passed because of
this platform pledge than would have been possible if the words FEPC and
filibuster had been used specifically."

Sparkman was disappointed that the *Baltimore Afro-American* had rated
him below Nixon, whose civil rights record then was no better. An important thing to remember, he said, was that a vice presidential candidate
"must appeal to an electorate that is vastly different from" that to which a
senator must appeal in Alabama.

Sparkman alerted Mitchell to the possibility that southern states would
support Eisenhower in retaliation against the Democratic civil rights plank.
Oil interests, he said, were "spending a considerable amount of money
against the Democrats in Louisiana and Texas, but the possibility of holding Louisiana seems better than the possibility of holding Texas at this
time."

On the Senate filibuster rule, Sparkman offered Mitchell helpful guidance on strategy for the Eighty-third and subsequent Congresses:

> Senator Sparkman believes that any attempt to change the Sen-
> ate rules must be made on the opening day of Congress. If the
> attempt is made at that time the ruling on whether the Senate may
> adopt an entirely new set of rules will be made by Vice President
> Barkley, because the new vice president will not be sworn in at that
> time. If the challenge is not made on the opening day, it would be
> necessary to go through the regular procedure of having the Senate
> rules committee report out any curb on the filibuster, in Senator
> Sparkman's opinion, although he said that he could be wrong on
> this conclusion. He expressed the opinion that precedent might
> require a ruling that the Senate is a continuing body and therefore
> bound by previously adopted rules. Here again, he said that this

would be a question that would require considerable study. He said that he had not heard of the plan to seek a rule change by declaring that the Senate is a new body until it was mentioned at the hearings before the Democratic Platform Committee in Chicago.[33]

In October, the journalist Drew Pearson reported on his radio program that Eisenhower had decided "to come out 100 percent for civil rights." That decision was based on the assessment by "the Republican high command" that the GOP would not carry a single southern state, and that 90 percent of the black vote would go to Stevenson. The unstated message was that to compensate for the expected loss of the white vote in the South, Eisenhower would have to take a stronger civil rights stand to win the black vote.

The 1952 elections returned the Republican party to power for the first time since 1928, confounding some of the earlier assessments. White's viewpoint was more conservative than the NAACP had anticipated. He said race, tidelands oil, and opposition to the liberal social and economic policies of the national Democratic party were the three issues that played a decisive role in the Eisenhower landslide and the GOP's capture of Texas, Florida, Virginia, and Tennessee and both the House and Senate. The schism that had developed among the Democrats in 1948, and had led to the walkout by the Dixiecrats because of their opposition to the strong civil rights plank remained in 1952, weakening the party. But, at the same time, the schism enhanced the balancing power of the black vote, which compensated for the loss of white Democratic votes to Eisenhower and helped keep Arkansas, Kentucky, Louisiana, North Carolina, South Carolina, and West Virginia in the Democratic column. Mitchell, White, and Wilkins prepared the NAACP's pledge to work with the President-elect and the new Congress "to implement the acceptable parts of the party platform and the subsequent pledges made during the campaign." Immediate prospects for success were unclear. For twenty years the dominant political power in the United States had been the great coalition of labor, farmers, city machines, and the South.

On December 4, Mitchell met with Henry Cabot Lodge, Jr., Eisenhower's "liaison in charge," to inform him of key issues that concerned the NAACP and on which he expected the new administration to provide leadership. Those were:

• Strengthening of the Fair Employment Board, created under Executive Order 9980 within the U.S. Civil Service Commission, responsible for eliminating racial and religious discrimination in the Federal service.

• Preserving and strengthening the Committee on Government Contract Compliance established under Executive Order 10308 to assure minority groups of fair treatment by employers holding government contracts.

• Elimination of racial segregation of children of military personnel in Army schools on military posts, of segregated facilities for civilian workers in Navy shore establishments, and segregation in the Department of Defense. [In this connection, Mitchell found the following statement made by President-elect Eisenhower in a meeting with Walter White on November 28, 1952, significant:]

"Recently, I have talked with several Southerners about the abolition of segregation in our schools. I told them that I would not attempt to dictate how they should run their schools, but that as President of the United States, I could not conscientiously appropriate Federal funds for segregated schools."

• Establishment of a policy giving no Federal assistance to rental or sale of private or public housing through the Housing and Home Finance Agency and its constituent agencies that exclude qualified persons on the basis of race or religion. This policy continues despite Supreme Court decisions that racial restrictions in housing are against the public policy of the United States. This can be accomplished by the Executive Branch without the aid of Congress. [Mitchell had previously proposed that Truman issue such an executive order.]

• Continuation and strengthening of the U.S. Department of State program to employ a consultant to help identify and eliminate factors that have prevented the employment and upgrading of qualified minority persons.[34]

Mitchell's demands and the confidence with which they were made signaled the coming of age of the modern civil rights movement. Undergirding the movement's quest for equality and reaffirming Mitchell's faith in his country's system of democracy were the creation of the 1947 President's Committee on Civil Rights, the adoption of a revolutionary civil rights platform by the 1948 Democratic National Convention over Truman's strong objections, and the 1948 executive order desegregating the armed services. He welcomed promises from lawmakers for early action on FEPC legislation in the new Congress. Taft, notably, who would be chairman of the Senate Labor and Public Welfare Committee and whose power now was surpassed only by that of the President, assured Mitchell, "I have in mind hearings on the Taft-Hartley law as soon as we get organized, but after that I know of nothing that will take priority over the FEPC."

Mitchell was further encouraged by the leadership of people in Birmingham, Alabama, like W. C. Patton, attorney Arthur D. Shores, and Dr. Joseph A. Berry, all NAACP activists whom the lobbyist respected. They were on the front line of the civil rights struggle in the South, challenging more openly through the NAACP the very concept of segregation. Mitchell zestfully assisted them from his Washington base. "The day is not distant when you will be duly recognized as those who helped to save the world from a return to human slavery by making the torch of freedom burn more brightly than the fiery crosses of the Ku Klux Klan," he told the Alabama State Conference of NAACP Branches in November 1951. He knew of no nation that could beat the United States in war because of its arsenal of atomic weapons, "yet our democracy faces its gravest threat from a weapon more fantastic than any yet devised by our scientific minds. It is a weapon more costly than a hundred battleships and more paralyzing than the most noxious gas. That weapon, conceived by diseased minds, and fastened in place by some of the most ignorant as well as some of the most intelligent people in this country, is discrimination based on race."

Mitchell warned that Americans paid "uncounted billions of dollars to create segregation." But, because the South cannot bear the cost of Jim Crow without help, more and more it "seeks funds from the Federal Treasury." He cited Aiken County, South Carolina, as an example. On February 28, 1951, representatives from Aiken's Chamber of Commerce, the State Health Department, the South Carolina legislature, and many others appeared before the Senate Committee on Banking and Currency to state that the county was broke and made such demands as $20,000 for white parks and an additional $20,000 for black parks. They also asked for money to build segregated jails and separate schools. "Each of the witnesses who appeared and made this staggering demand on the Federal Treasury said that he wanted the money, but he did not want any Federal control. One witness even insisted that it would be unfair for the Federal Government to ask that the state, county, or city match any of its contributions."

Mitchell noted that some people maintained that the federal treasury belonged to all the people, so all regions had a right to ask for Washington's financial help. But the disparities among the contributions of different states to the national treasury were revealing. For example, in the fiscal year ending June 30, 1951, eight northern states—Massachusetts, Connecticut, New York, New Jersey, Pennsylvania, Indiana, Illinois, and Ohio—paid more than 50 percent of the federal revenue. Ten southern states—Alabama, Arkansas, Florida, Georgia, Louisiana, Mississippi, Oklahoma, South Carolina, Tennessee, and Texas—paid only 9 percent of the national revenue. All ten states combined paid just about one half as much as New York. Mitchell reasoned that every tax dollar that was used to support segregation in the South placed a greater burden upon those states that were already carrying more than their share: "Every American citizen, who thinks of this great country as one united whole, wants to see the South become a land of plenty and a place of economic security. But we in the National Association for the Advancement of Colored People shall launch a campaign in those states where we have political strength to shut off the flow of all Federal funds unless the wasteful practices of spending for segregation is abandoned."[35]

Mitchell's confidence was boosted by the progress that the NAACP under its special counsel Thurgood Marshall was making through the courts to end segregation of schools by the states and to extend the equal protection clause of the Fourteenth Amendment to descendants of former slaves. Marshall hailed the Supreme Court's decisions in the *Sweatt* and *McLaurin* cases as strong indications of the Supreme Court's conviction that segregation was a denial of equality. Using those decisions as "potent weapons," he and his associate attorneys argued four key cases before the Supreme Court that had originated in Clarendon County, South Carolina; Farmville, Virginia; Topeka, Kansas; and New Castle County, Delaware. A fifth case involving the District of Columbia schools had been filed by the late Charles Hamilton Houston and was being carried forward by the Consolidated Parents Group.

The involvement of liberals like Humphrey, Lehman, Ives, Wayne Morse, Paul Douglas of Illinois, and William Benton, a Connecticut Democrat, in the Senate, and Javits, Case, and Celler in the House, also gave Mitchell reason for hope. They, unlike liberals of the New Deal and early 1940s, were committed not just to ending lynchings and employment discrimination but to the concept of racial equality. Humphrey's declaration of faith was symbolic of the new awakening:

> Our conscience in America has become corroded and encrusted with a bitter feeling of guilt because we profess a belief in justice and equality, but we practice injustice and discrimination in every one of these United States. *The outlawing of injustice in employment by adequate and effective legislation is a major step in lifting the burden of guilt from our American conscience.* [Italics Humphrey's.]

Progress toward racial equality during World War II was achieved as a result of the need for national survival and to project a positive image abroad; now the civil rights movement had assumed a life of its own.[36]

▪ CHAPTER NINE ▪

All-Out Attack on Segregation

T wenty years ago, the Negro was satisfied if he could have even a half-decent school to go to (and took it for granted that it would be a segregated school) or if he could go to the hotel in town or the restaurant maybe once a year for some special interracial dinner and meeting. Twenty years ago much of the segregation pattern was taken for granted by the Negro. Now it is different.

That observation by Mitchell in 1953 anticipated the Supreme Court's May 17, 1954, school desegregation decision in *Brown* v. *Board of Education*. His program prior to that landmark date was defined within the context of the 1947 report of the President's Committee on Civil Rights *(To Secure These Rights)*. That remarkable document gave political strength to the struggle for civil rights of all citizens regardless of race, color, or national origin. "Civil rights, after all," said the committee, "are statements of aspirations, of demands which we make upon ourselves and our society."

The committee noted that the national strength was based on the pride Americans had in their freedom and individual differences and that each citizen's aspirations and achievements should be limited only by his or her own talents and energies: "We can tolerate no restrictions upon the individual which depend upon irrelevant factors such as his race, his color, his religion or the social position to which he is born."[1]

In short, 1947 was the year in which the national government led by the President went on record as being officially opposed to racial segregation and stopped just short of declaring that blacks were entitled to equal protection of the laws under the Fourteenth Amendment. Yet the implication was very strong.

To Secure These Rights was a logical outgrowth of the revolutionary climate of the New Deal and the moral outrage generated by Nazi atrocities in Europe. The refocusing of the struggle to a state of heightened political activism, and the shifting of the top civil rights priority from lynchings to economic issues that began in the New Deal, had gained spiritual force during World War II. Subsequently, when the new focus was more sharply defined, as the institution of segregation, and the activities of civil rights groups had considerably broadened, the President's Committee on Civil Rights sanctioned, crystallized, and gave its enormous prestige to the expanded civil rights movement, which sought full citizenship in every respect. The committee considered the entire spectrum of racial injustices and humiliations of a Jim Crow society to be bona fide civil rights grievances. The committee's recommendations were sympathetic to the NAACP's all-out attack on the legal foundations of the "separate but equal" doctrine, which was now widely recognized as being morally indefensible. By the same token, this new climate of understanding nurtured an unprecedented form of liberalism surrounding civil rights issues.

During earlier twentieth-century progressive movements, extending from Theodore Roosevelt's Progressive party through the Woodrow Wilson era and into the New Deal, liberals, with few exceptions, shared the racism of the period. *To Secure These Rights,* however, revealed that by 1947 an increasing number of white Americans regarded racism and segregation as wrong, which signaled the beginning of a new era of progressivism in which the struggle to end state-sanctioned segregation and discrimination became paramount national concerns.

The new social awareness among mainstream Americans was paralleled by the revolutionary concept of sociological jurisprudence that Thurgood Marshall was developing through the courts in order to abolish once and for all the "separate but equal" doctrine of *Plessy* v. *Ferguson.* According to Marshall:

> The obligation to furnish equal protection of the laws does not establish abstract uniformity applicable alike to all persons without regard to circumstances or conditions. Equal protection requires that all persons be fairly treated in their relations with the state. But the concept makes allowance for dissimilarity of circumstances in order that legislation may fall with evenhandedness upon all persons. Special burdens and duties may be imposed upon a particular group or class for the benefit of the public as a whole. Arbitrary discrimination alone is prohibited.

For Marshall the Constitution was a living document with a comprehensive scope that provided for affirmative remedies for legal and social wrongs in progressive stages of history. Marshall, whose argument, based on enforcement of the Fourteenth Amendment, was sustained by the Supreme Court in *Brown* v. *Board of Education,* was confident that once the Court cleared away the constitutional obstacle of the "separate but equal" doctrine, society would take other steps to protect the rights of blacks. Marshall's argument was supported by the wealth of precedents that the courts had established. The forthright manner in which the executive branch was beginning to join the courts in confronting segregation contrasted sharply with the stalemate in Congress over civil rights legislation.

Even though Eisenhower was an avowed states' righter, Mitchell saw the possibility of his providing more positive leadership on civil rights after he assumed office. Eisenhower had won over the civil rights leaders with his sincerity. Unlike those of other politicians, his pronouncements on the subject were not influenced by political considerations but came from the heart. Perhaps most revealing was his speech in Harlem a few days before the election in 1952.

His true regard for blacks was characterized by a "let me say to you people" approach that betrayed an incompatible distance. Eisenhower was not a segregationist, because he believed such practices were wrong and harmful to the nation, but neither was he an integrationist. He was certainly more progressive than Franklin Roosevelt. Like Truman, Eisenhower was somewhere in the middle. Eisenhower recalled that while he was Supreme Commander of Allied forces in Europe and desperate for fighting men on the front lines, he had welcomed in the fall of 1944 the services of twenty-six hundred black volunteer troops. By "coming forward so determinedly, so promptly and operating so effectively, they gave me again a renewed lesson that devotion to America is not determined by any such inconsequential factors as color, religion or origin." Therefore, he said, "I worked for this business of reducing and working toward elimination of segregation." Another demonstration of his attitude on race was an account of an order he had distributed to every officer in England pointing out that the British attitude on race was different from the Americans'. He said that attempts to end associations between black American soldiers and British citizens, which were causing conflicts, "by official order or restriction was unjustified and must not be attempted."

Eisenhower, however, still suffered from inner conflicts. He thought his "political crusade" to avoid another depression and strengthen and expand Social Security programs should merit a higher priority among blacks than the humiliations of segregation and the hardships of discrimination. His promise to end Jim Crow in Washington did not arise so much from a genuine concern for blacks as from embarrassment over the problem. He felt that segregation was "the poorest possible example given to those of other lands of what this country is, and what it means to each of us."

Eisenhower's practical, amoral approach was best demonstrated by his declaration that "wherever the Federal government has responsibility; wherever it collects taxes from you to spend money, whether it be in a contract for recreational facilities or anything else that it does for a citizen of the United States, there will be no discrimination as long as I can help it in a private or public life based upon any such thing as color or creed or religion—never." Mitchell knew only too well that the full implementation of such a commitment could have revolutionary consequences.[3]

As Eisenhower made clear in his first State of the Union Message, he believed in the "ideal of equality of rights" for all citizens. His problem was the limit he placed on the means for achieving that goal. In effect, he was like other moderate progressives on the race question and was bending just enough with the political winds to place himself a step ahead of the majority of Republicans in the Congress who remained aligned with the southerners on civil rights. "Much of the answer," he said, lay "in the power of fact, fully publicized," in "persuasion honestly pressed," and in "conscience justly aroused." By example, "and by the leadership of the Office of the President exercised through friendly conferences with those in authority in our states and cities," he said, "we expect to make true and rapid progress in civil rights and equality of employment opportunity."[2]

Even though he recognized the limitations of such an approach, Mitchell thought the President's promise to end segregation in the District of Columbia, as well as in the federal government and the armed forces, was a step forward. Eisenhower urged Congress to support the proposal to provide "an effective voice in local self government" for the District by passing appropriate legislation. He called for an immediate increase in the size of the capital's governing Board of Commissioners from three to five to broaden representation of all segments of the population. He promised that that was "a first step toward insuring that this capital provide an honored example to all communities of our nation."

The roots of segregation in Washington, D.C., were deep. After President Woodrow Wilson had established the new Jim Crow policy in government agencies, NAACP Secretary May Childs Nerney in 1913 found that blacks were "regarded as a people apart, almost as lepers," and that "the seal of government approval in some cases" had created a caste system "where it did not exist" earlier. A generation later, as the President's Committee on Civil Rights noted, those conditions still existed.

The Department of the Interior under Harold Ickes in 1933 began to desegregate Washington by declaring that there was "no legal way to prevent law abiding citizens from using the parks" under its jurisdiction, "regardless of their race." But it was the denial of the use of Constitution Hall to the singer Marian Anderson in 1939 by the Daughters of the American Revolution that ignited the desegregation movement in Washington. Subsequently, local residents, working through the NAACP and the National Committee Against Segregation in the Nation's Capital, launched a sustained struggle to desegregate the city. The committee's 1948 "Report on Segregation in the Nation's Capital" documented and brought further attention to the problem.[3]

Mitchell, when he came to Washington, thought the capital "was not morally ready to fight for democracy." He found he could not dine in most restaurants in the city including those in the Congress building; the sight of a black clerk, stenographer, or assistant in the Capitol's legislative halls "was a figment of the imagination"; and neither could he ride in the Capitol's "white" elevator. But the wall of segregation was cracking. He became aware of that while working in the Office of Production Management when his boss Robert Weaver and three other black coworkers challenged segregation in the building's cafeteria simply by insisting on eating in the main facility rather than in the smaller dining area used by the kitchen crew and black staffers. There was no violence or need for Weaver to take his case to court. Weaver won the battle because the time was ripe for change, but because other blacks were afraid of reprisals, it took them awhile to follow his example.[4]

As NAACP labor secretary, Mitchell's first opportunity to aid in desegregating Washington came in 1947 when he challenged a proposal by the Public Buildings Administration to bar black District of Columbia taxi drivers from servicing the Pentagon and to award the concession to a white Virginia company. That struggle lasted until 1953, when the Eisenhower administration finally established procedures to protect the rights of the black drivers. Mitchell's efforts included filing a series of protests with top federal officials, enlisting the help of Congressman Adam Clayton Powell, Jr., and creating an informal taxicab association for the fifty to sixty drivers servicing the Pentagon to help them supervise their own activities and thus reduce criticisms. Mitchell's contribution toward desegregating Washington, D.C., also involved the creation of programs to end job discrimination by the Capital Transit Company and the Chesapeake and Potomac Telephone Company.

Mitchell was especially perplexed by the coexistence of both segregation and integration in the city's recreation facilities. The Department of the Interior operated swimming pools, picnic areas, golf courses, tennis courts, and many other facilities without racial distinctions, which, he complained to one official, "demonstrates every day that there is no reason, except racial prejudice" among Recreation Board executives why the playgrounds and programs operated by the city should be segregated. The board tacitly admitted as much by complying with the Interior Department's desegregation requirements in operating federal facilities. Mitchell concluded that all that was needed "to correct this evil condition of racial segregation" was the political will.[5]

In addition to working with the local NAACP branch, Mitchell joined forces with the Leadership Conference on Civil Rights in order to develop a comprehensive program and to prepare a legal document demonstrating that the President's powers allowed him to end the city's Jim Crow practices. At the same time, the administration took its first official step in March 1953 to carry out the President's pledge when Attorney General Herbert Brownell, Jr., in the famous "lost laws" case of *District of Columbia* v. *the John R. Thompson Company, Inc.,* asked the Supreme Court to uphold two statutes forbidding restaurants to refuse to serve blacks. The Court did so on June 8. For some inexplicable reason, the 1872 and 1873 laws were omitted from the District Codes of 1901, 1929, and 1940 and were not brought to public attention until Charles Hamilton Houston, through diligent research, as he himself termed it, discovered them "locked" in a safe in the District Building. The statutes provided for a fine of one hundred dollars and forfeiture of license for one year against owners of certain places of public accommodation who refused service to "any respectable well-behaved person," regardless of race. Brownell also asked the Court to remove questions raised by a lower court over the constitutional power of Congress to grant home rule to the District. Mitchell had been attempting to achieve that since 1950, with many setbacks, but the Court now strengthened the home rule movement by declaring that Congress could grant the District as much self-government as it had given such territories as Hawaii and Alaska. A few weeks later, Mitchell and White asked Brownell to assign a staff member to explore how the President could speed up desegregation in the District.[6]

Finally, in November, the Eisenhower administration, after repeated proddings by Mitchell and the Washington NAACP branch, got the District of Columbia Board of Commissioners to order all its agencies to hire and discharge employees without regard to race, creed, or color. The order established a nondiscrimination policy for the use of city government institutions, facilities, and services, but it exempted for the time being the fire department, the schools, and city-operated recreational facilities. The order put an end to the segregation that remained in movie theaters, many of which had already been admitting blacks, and speeded up integration in public housing. The Board of Commissioners' chairman, whom Eisenhower had appointed, reported to the President that the order "constitutes an important milestone in reaching" the objective he had outlined in his State of the Union Message.

Mitchell, however, was far from satisfied with the order. He felt that "a piecemeal approach might be worse than none at all." District residents and *The Washington Post* also strongly criticized it. The *Post* said it doubted that "this kind of compromise contributes any more to expediency than it does to principle. Piecemeal abandonment of discrimination entails a repetition and prolongation of the wrench away from outmoded patterns of behavior. The only way to abandon discrimination is to abandon it."

Joining the growing movement against racial injustice, the Justice Department in December (thanks to Attorney General Herbert Brownell) argued in an amicus curiae brief submitted to the Supreme Court in the school cases that would culminate in *Brown* v. *Board of Education* that not only did the Court have the right to strike down segregation in public education, but it should do so immediately. (The Truman administration had first thrown the federal government's weight behind this movement by submitting a memorandum supporting the NAACP's position in 1951.)[7]

On the eve of the *Brown* decision, Mitchell saw several other signs that a new door was opening in the civil rights struggle. Channing Tobias, chairman of the NAACP national board of directors, reflecting the new mood of rising expectations among black Americans, electrified the association's convention in 1953 when he announced a ten-year program to achieve the goal of full freedom and equality by the centennial of the Emancipation Proclamation on January 1, 1963. In keeping with this spirit of "Free by '63," which was now the NAACP's slogan, Mitchell that fall presented to Walter White the Washington Bureau's ten-year program for what was then thought to be the final phase of the struggle. Mitchell projected that he would accomplish his goals—passage of civil rights laws and the ending, through executive leadership and edict, of segregation in all federal programs, agencies, and establishments. Mitchell's optimism was fed by other steps Eisenhower took during his first year in office to fulfill his campaign promises about civil rights; among these actions was the implementation, on September 18, 1954, of the long-planned integration of the District of Columbia Fire Department that had been blocked by the Truman administration. Furthermore, the District government now required contractors to sign a nondiscrimination clause similar to that contained in federal contracts, and steps had been taken to end discrimination in hiring by city agencies.

Mitchell had been worried because Truman's Committee on Government Contract Compliance was about to be dissolved. Reestablishing it would have been very difficult. Recognizing the danger, he had moved, after the November elections, to get a commitment from the incoming

Eisenhower administration to continue the committee. Following his December 4 meeting with Henry Cabot Lodge, he wrote the Truman committee's chairman, Dwight Palmer, informing him of his discussions with the
senator. Palmer replied that his committee had submitted its report to
President Truman on January 16, the same day he tendered his resignation,
and that he expected the remaining members to indicate their desire to
terminate their service subject to the President's convenience. Mitchell realized that because executive orders remain in effect until they are rescinded
or canceled by a President, the way was being kept open for the new President to revive the committee. President Truman reaffirmed his support for
the committee by sending his successor a copy of Palmer's report.[8]

When after a few months in office the new administration still had not
reconstituted the committee, Mitchell initiated a series of maneuvers involving Walter White and the NAACP's allies to force Eisenhower's hand.
One of Mitchell's ploys was to get Alice Dunnigan of the Associated Negro
Press to ask Eisenhower during his April 2 news conference what plans he
had to appoint a new chairman for the Government Contract Compliance
Committee or to revitalize it. Eisenhower responded that he was not familiar with the subject but promised to answer it at a later conference. Three
weeks later, when Dunnigan raised the question again, he replied that the
appointment of a new chairman could be expected. Dwight Palmer wrote
White to urge him to follow up and get a commitment from the President
regarding his intentions. Mitchell and White discussed the need for action
with Attorney General Herbert Brownell. In May, following a meeting
Mitchell had arranged for the Leadership Conference on Civil Rights with
Brownell and presidential aide Maxwell Rabb, whose title eventually became associate counsel to the President in charge of civil rights, both officials assured Mitchell that an order regarding the committee would be
issued. Still bird-dogging the administration's progress, Mitchell submitted to it the results of an NAACP survey showing widespread discrimination among firms holding government contracts in twenty-four cities.[9]

The highlight of the summer of 1953 for Mitchell was the President's
announcement in Denver on August 13 that he had established a Committee on Government Contracts to replace Truman's Committee on Government Contract Compliance. A few days later, Mitchell received a small
package from the White House. It contained the pen that the President
had used to sign Executive Order 10479, creating the new committee.
Though the committee was not given the enforcement powers Mitchell had
wanted, the door was still open for improvements later on. Mitchell and
White jointly praised the President for his action and said it was a "challenge to Congress to erase discrimination in all other major industries by
passing a Fair Employment law."

Eisenhower's Government Contracts Committee was very similar to its predecessor. The main difference was that while the Truman committee could only survey and recommend, the Eisenhower committee could receive complaints of alleged violations of nondiscrimination provisions in government contracts and forward them to the appropriate contracting agencies. The agencies were directed to report back to the Eisenhower committee on actions they had taken to resolve complaints. Other functions of the Eisenhower committee included developing educational programs to eliminate discrimination and maintaining cooperative relations with state and local governments as well as with nongovernmental groups, but it had no review authority over agencies. [10]

Mitchell regarded Eisenhower's appointment of Vice President Richard Nixon as the committee's chairman as historic even though as a senator he had voted against FEPC legislation. The appointment, despite Eisenhower's lack of enthusiasm for the FEPC idea, implied the President's strong imprimatur. In fact, Eisenhower carefully spelled out his philosophy regarding his role in upholding the Constitution in an exchange of letters and telephone conversations with Governor James Byrnes of South Carolina, and in his directive to Nixon concerning his chairmanship of the Government Contracts Committee.

"We who hold office," Eisenhower told Byrnes, who was opposed to both the FEPC idea and the President's desegregation of the Charleston Navy Yard,* "not only must discharge the duties placed upon us by the Constitution and by conscience but also must, by constructive advances, prove to be mistaken those who insist that true reform can come only through overriding Federal law and Federal police methods." His oath of office as well as his own convictions, Eisenhower explained, required him to eliminate discrimination "within the definite areas of Federal responsibility." Regarding nondiscrimination clauses in federal contracts, Eisenhower said he expected his actions to "run counter to customs in some states." But the President still hoped that by discussing the matter candidly with Byrnes, they would not only "reach fruitful understanding in this matter—but also that, in so doing, it can be shown that progress does not depend on Federal fiat." Regarding the committee, Eisenhower emphasized that "states should cooperate in, and never impede, the enforcement of Federal regulation *where the Federal Government has clear and exclusive responsibility in the case*" (italics Eisenhower's).

Explaining his views in a letter to Nixon, however, Eisenhower said that "a so-called Federal FEPC law" would not work because undoubtedly it would create "antagonisms" and "set back the cause of progress by a

---

* Mitchell had been battling to desegregate the Charleston Navy Yard since his tenure with the wartime FEPC.

good many years." The committee's functions were to be limited to determining "facts pertinent to the general purpose of promoting economic and political equality, and to bring these facts to the attention of the government and the public." He did not conceive the committee as an agency to usurp the legislative powers of Congress:

> It looks to me that, if we apply to this whole problem standards and criteria that are dictated by decency and fairness, we will not go too far wrong. The Commission [sic] will be an agency that will not only find out whether existing laws are being enforced (and this we must be always concerned with if for no other reason than that we are sworn to defend the Constitution) but will also point out those paths in which people in official and private activities can be helpful in assisting progress toward economic and political equality, regardless of race.

Eisenhower thus was much more concerned about "quieting the fears" of committee critics like Byrnes than with attacking the roots of racial injustices.[11]

It is highly unlikely that Mitchell knew of Eisenhower's observations to Nixon, but in any case he was far less concerned with the personal views of politicians than with their actions. He requested a meeting with Nixon to discuss work left pending by the Truman committee on claims of discrimination against the Chesapeake and Potomac Telephone Company in Washington and the Atomic Energy Commission facilities in Aiken, South Carolina, and Paducah, Kentucky. Mitchell felt that "the solution of these problems would pave the way for highly effective work in other industries" by the committee. Both facilities, which were operated, by the Du Pont and by the Carbide and Carbon companies, respectively, had made considerable progress in hiring blacks. But blacks were still barred from their large training programs. "A victory on this front" in South Carolina especially, Mitchell felt, "would be significant" because the problem was "on the doorstep of Governor Byrnes."

Mitchell, soon impatient with the committee's slow progress, suggested to White a number of steps to pressure it to "get on the ball."[12] By November it began to move. The Eisenhower Committee on Government Contracts was the first body that had ever been established outside the context of a national manpower mobilization for war to deal with private employers. Its work was therefore particularly important; its performance in a noncrisis atmosphere would be a good guide in drafting FEPC legislation. That was evident when Jacob Seidenberg, the committee's executive director, invited the NAACP to participate in a conference to study a range

of questions concerning the committee: the extent and scope of employment discrimination, the manner in which such violations were practiced,
ways to achieve effective compliance with Executive Order 10479, the ade-
quacy of the order's nondiscrimination clause, possible sanctions to be imposed on offenders, and ways in which to use publicity to further this
work.

At that meeting, at which the Government Contracts Committee was
represented by a subcommittee composed of J. Ernest Wilkins, its vice
chairman, Secretary of Labor James P. Mitchell, and presidential aide Maxwell Rabb, and which was attended by several of the NAACP's allies,
White and Mitchell presented recommendations for expanding and accelerating the agency's work. The NAACP leaders warned that if the committee
was "to win and hold public confidence," it had to produce "specific accomplishments" soon. They especially urged speedy action on complaints
against the Chesapeake and Potomac Telephone Company and the Atomic
Energy Commission, and also against the Capital Transit Company in
Washington, which the President's Committee on Fair Employment Practices had tried to desegregate in 1945. The leaders' clear strategy was also
to "keep the public and the Congress aware" of the committee's limitations
and effectiveness "and the need for legislation" to create a permanent
FEPC.[13]

Between that November 30 meeting and a follow-up session on June
16, 1954, a report declared that the Committee on Government Contracts
had "acted affirmatively in whole or in part" on twenty-three of thirty-six
recommendations. An unimpressed Mitchell maintained, however, that the
committee's only meaningful accomplishment had been clarifying the
wording of the nondiscrimination clause. Despite a strong appeal that
Eisenhower and Nixon had made in a letter included in a pamphlet entitled
"Equal Job Opportunity Is Good Business," which was sent in September
1954 to heads of major companies with government contracts, Mitchell
found it necessary to complain about the committee's ineffectiveness. In a
January 15, 1955, statement cosigned by Adam Clayton Powell, Mitchell
said that there was "a considerable amount of skepticism about" the committee's role. Mitchell and Powell presented the statement to Nixon in a
meeting to discuss ways to strengthen and speed the committee's work.
They recommended an announcement of promising steps the committee
had taken regarding the telephone companies in Washington and Baltimore, the Capital Transit Company, and the AEC facilities in South Carolina and Kentucky; the creation of a centralized information bank listing
companies with government contracts; steps to determine hiring policies of
government contractors; and a clear-cut system of enforcing the committee's discrimination findings.

The committee responded that it had not officially closed the Capital Transit Company case, but that the company had already upgraded several qualified blacks to the long-sought category of platform operators and was training them for those jobs. The committee assured Mitchell that it "intends to keep this situation under review for a period of time" and would inform him when the matter was finally settled. Concerning the case involving the Chesapeake and Potomac Telephone Company in Washington, negotiations were continuing. Progress had been made, but "a great deal remains to be done and our committee does not at present regard this matter as being satisfactorily resolved." The Chesapeake and Potomac Telephone Company in Baltimore was also being investigated.

Mitchell was confident that the committee would resolve the telephone company discrimination cases. He would still have to maintain steady pressure to keep the committee moving, but he was satisfied that at least a sympathetic person was handling the case.[14] He found still more reason for encouragement in Executive Order 10590, which Eisenhower issued on January 18, 1955, creating the President's Committee on Government Employment Policy, a watchdog committee having oversight of federal agencies and replacing Truman's Fair Employment Board, which had been functioning within the Civil Service Commission. That the new committee would report directly to the President was a major improvement over its predecessor. Department heads still were responsible for carrying out the order's nondiscrimination policy, but the Government Employment Policy Committee had the authority to conduct investigations and to advise the President on the extent to which agencies were complying with his policy. The White House, rather than the Civil Service Commission, with which Mitchell remained very unhappy, was now the authority of final appeal.

Three months later, Mitchell presented a detailed set of recommendations to the committee. Among other things, he called for the prompt settlement of unresolved cases; establishment of procedures that would permit interested persons to inspect pertinent employment documents such as Civil Service registers; the elimination of racial designations on employment forms and personnel records; verbatim records of oral examinations in order to establish the qualifications for employment, transfer, or promotion; development of specific steps for redressing complaints, which would include disciplinary action against federal employees who violated the new executive order; and immediate "broad investigations" of government employment policies in order to correct current discrimination.

Mitchell had adopted the type of class action approach to employment discrimination complaints that would in the future be widely used by the courts in civil rights cases. In calling for "broad scale action," he said that "the necessity for continually filing individual complaints as we are now doing in the Norfolk, Virginia, Navy Yard would be eliminated if this committee would attack the problem of discrimination on a department-wide basis and require full compliance with the executive order by all units of government."

He cited a complaint being filed against the Department of Agriculture that indicated widespread departmental indifference to discrimination. He stressed that while

> resolving complaints of specific individuals and groups is an indispensable part of any nondiscriminatory program, [it did] not solve the problem of the employee who may not realize he is the victim of discrimination, or may not have access to the facts to show that he is, or is too timid to complain. Nor does it reach the overall unitwide or even departmentalwide pattern of discriminatory personnel practice.

Mitchell's proposed "bold new approach" was modeled after the program now at work in the armed forces, by which every responsible federal officer and designated administrators would implement the nondiscrimination employment policy. The most dramatic evidence that such an approach was possible was the successful implementation, in the years since 1948, of President Truman's Executive Order 9981 calling for equal treatment and opportunities for blacks in the services. There were three factors that were largely responsible for integrating the military: namely, the postwar evolution of a military that was dependent on the recruitment of a large number of blacks; the Truman and Eisenhower administrations' strong support of civil rights; and bold leadership from within the Department of Defense and in the services that established integration as an imperative for obtaining the most effective use of military manpower.

Persons responsible for administering antidiscrimination job programs, Mitchell said, "must be designated on the basis of interest, knowledge of the field, and a willingness to make the program work," and not "just because they are in top positions." Only by "ensuring the program is administered by qualified personnel," he concluded, "can we hope for any major improvement in existing personnel practices."[15]

That Mitchell's message was getting through to the administration was evident from Labor Secretary James Mitchell's appeal to businessmen for cooperation with the President's nondiscrimination policy at a conference in October on equal job opportunities sponsored by the President's Committee on Government Contracts. Among those attending were the presidents and chairmen of corporate giants like the Boeing Airplane Company, the National Gypsum Company, Dreyfus Properties, and the Packard Manufacturing Company. "Virtually everyone is against discrimination just as everyone is against sin," the secretary of labor declared. Nevertheless, "we know there are many sinners." The businessmen, he said, were aware of "a great deal of job discrimination in the United States." Studies documenting the widespread existence of job bias, he said, "were legion." For example, recent surveys conducted by a government agency in four states in order to determine if there was compliance with the nondiscrimination clause in government contracts indicated "that we have a great deal more progress to make." The labor secretary added that the government was still receiving job orders with discriminatory provisions.

He explained that discrimination in hiring was not the whole problem, and that "it may not even be the major part of our problem." The nation, he felt, might have passed from simple employment discrimination to a new problem "more difficult to detect, harder to eradicate, and more challenging." That new problem, he felt, might be "primarily discrimination in promoting, demoting and transferring—the closing of certain classifications or types of jobs to members of particular groups."

The secretary of labor stressed that "nondiscrimination in employment means qualitative as well as quantitative equality." That was the principle Robert Weaver had first enunciated some twenty years earlier during the New Deal and which Mitchell had finally gotten the government to understand. "I am sure," said the secretary of labor, "you will agree that it is not enough, for example, to have 5 percent of your labor force Negro if they are all in the lowest job levels." The secretary invited the businessmen to look at "the levels people have reached, their classifications and the kinds of jobs on which they are employed." That approach was "a prerequisite to doing the job effectively and completely"—and a further expansion of the affirmative action concept.

While acknowledging that the first priority for businessmen had to be profit, the labor secretary stressed that many businessmen had demonstrated over the years that they were also interested in social progress. Consequently, they had undertaken obligations, such as establishing scholarships for the needy, that, although they were not immediately profitable, would help the country later on. Such commitments were "good business, both in the short run and over the long run." He reminded the businessmen that "satisfied employees are more efficient and more productive than disgruntled ones." Nothing destroys morale and efficiency more quickly than a person who feels discriminated against because of characteristics, such as race, "over which he has no control."

Finally, the secretary explained that elimination of employment discrimination had long-term profits in strengthening America's democracy and economy and making the nation more impervious to communism and other totalitarian ideologies. "Elimination of discrimination based on race or religion would strengthen the position of the United States in relation to the two-thirds of the world which is not white."[16]

An example of the increasing awareness of the harmful effects of discrimination was the racial slights suffered by Montague Cobb, a young black doctor from Washington who was a member of the NAACP national board of directors, when the U.S.S. *Missouri,* on which he was a guest during a midshipmen's cruise, docked in Halifax, Nova Scotia. When Cobb, along with the other guests, went as instructed to obtain tickets for the officers' ball that night, only he was denied one. Instead, a naval officer introduced him to the president of the Halifax Colored Citizens Improvement League, who gave him a list of entertainment events scheduled for blacks. Cobb informed the naval officer that he was acting contrary to Navy policy, which was in keeping with steps to abolish segregation throughout the armed services. Instead of permitting Cobb to attend the functions for whites, however, the ship's commanders gave him another list of events that included those for blacks. The "official Navy memorandum," concluded Cobb, placed "a different light on the situation."

Cobb's experience aboard the U.S.S. *Missouri* coincided with Mitchell's increasing involvement with racial problems within the military. He spent considerable time in the fall of 1950 combating discrimination by the Selective Service and working to implement a resolution adopted by the NAACP board of directors on October 9 authorizing him to proceed with that program.

Even though African Americans had fought and died in every war since the founding of the nation, they were suffering the same denials of their constitutional rights while in uniform as in civilian life. Mitchell joined other blacks in welcoming the integration of the Air Force and the Navy in 1949. (The Navy had pioneered the process with partial integration four years earlier, with the exception of its all-white Marine Corps and the nonwhite Stewards Branch.) But neither the Air Force nor the Navy pretended that those were more than beginning steps—an effort primarily concerned with efficient manpower usage.

Mitchell's principal goals were to (1) defeat efforts to reintroduce segregation in the Air Force and Navy; (2) end all segregation in the armed services; (3) obtain a ban against the use of Jim Crow housing and dining facilities for blacks; (4) eliminate the use of all racial designations on personnel records, which was one of the most persistent problems; and (5) protect black servicemen against violence by law enforcement officials and civilians. In addition to seeking the support of military leaders for uprooting the above practices, he reaffirmed his demands that Congress incorporate relevant safeguards in universal military training (UMT) bills under consideration.

The Army's announcement in 1951 that it would integrate troops in the Far East—beginning the most protracted phase of the struggle—was another victory for the NAACP, one in which Mitchell rightfully claimed a decisive role. Mitchell had arranged a meeting on March 15 between six senators and Department of Defense officials. The senators would not agree to sponsor the nonsegregation amendment in the UMT bill that Mitchell wanted, but they obtained a pledge from Defense that there would be no segregation in the UMT program. Mitchell considered the announcement involving Far East troops as a direct result of that meeting. Walter White and Thurgood Marshall, nevertheless, were the unsung heroes of that struggle, bringing the full weight of the NAACP to bear on the Defense Department. White conducted investigations and exposed the extensive discrimination against black GIs by serving as a war correspondent between 1943 and 1945 in the European, North African, Italian, Middle East, and various Pacific theaters of war. His book *A Rising Wind* was based on his observations in Europe. Marshall personally investigated discrimination complaints during the Korean War. Their documentation of racial discrimination against black servicemen abroad was irrefutable evidence of the extent of the crisis within the military.

To avoid a recurrence of Dr. Cobb's experience, Navy Secretary Francis P. Matthews on August 4, 1950, reaffirmed unequivocally the Navy Department's policy of "equality of treatment and opportunity" without regard to race, color, religion, or national origin covering itself and the Marine Corps. The fact that Matthews had to reissue the order just fourteen months after the Navy had announced a specific series of measures to implement earlier initiatives showed the difficulty of the task. The policy applied to housing, dining, and other shore facilities. Matthews said that "the Navy must not be a party to racial or partisan developments by incident or accident." The Navy, he went on, would not "officially participate in endorsing, sanctioning, promoting or subsidizing affairs of local sponsors in extending hospitality which involves, implies restrictions, segregation or discrimination of racial or other groupings, at variance with [this policy]."

Despite such dramatic progress, severe segregation problems remained off-base in surrounding communities and in related military establishments. Early in 1951, with the new policies in mind, Mitchell obtained reassurance from the NAACP's legal department that the principle enunciated by the Supreme Court in *McLaurin* v. *Oklahoma State Regents* also applied to another segregation case involving the Air Force: When the government assumed control of a private facility for use by its armed forces, the installation became a public facility for the duration of such use and thus was subject to the equal protection clause of the Fourteenth Amendment. Mitchell welcomed the opportunity to test that principle that fall when the presidents of NAACP branches in Norfolk, Virginia, and Charleston, South Carolina, asked him to help them fight a Navy order that black and white civilian workers at the Norfolk and Charleston naval shipyards use separate drinking fountains, restrooms, and other facilities. The problem was caused by a January 1952 order from the chief of the Office of Industrial Relations that absolved Navy installations from requirements of Executive Order 9980 governing employment practices within the federal government. The order, as it became clear, left little doubt that segregation would be the norm in most instances.

Supported by White and other civil rights leaders, Mitchell appealed up the chain of command to President Truman. Anna M. Rosenberg, assistant secretary of defense for manpower and personnel, was sympathetic and had been working with Mitchell on this and other problems concerned with desegregating the armed forces. But two days after she left the Pentagon on January 20, 1953, Francis P. Whitehair, then acting secretary of the navy, responded to Mitchell:

> Although our concern over this problem is mutual, the approach of a military establishment will naturally differ from that of the officials of the NAACP. . . . A direct order from the Secretary of the Navy, no matter how forceful, would not only fail to eliminate the basic social causes of the problem but would only antagonize the opposing forces involved.

That, in effect, was now official Navy policy. Adamant that the question had been carefully studied, the Navy reiterated its policy that "common as opposed to segregated facilities should be provided on naval stations," unless local custom or laws required segregation. Mitchell angrily replied that he knew of no law or regulation that would require any federal agency to enforce racial segregation. Following community customs and mores, he told the Navy, could not justify wasting public funds on dual facilities. What made the Navy's reponse all the more infuriating was that, as a result of his detailed complaints, the Air Force had informed Mitchell that month that it had ended segregation on January 1 at noncommissioned officers clubs, swimming pools, and in barracks at the Turner Air Force Base in Albany, Georgia. The Air Force further informed him it would take action on charges that blacks had been unable to obtain housing in an FHA development called Turner City near the base.[17]

The NAACP continued its prodding and got Eisenhower, in his first real test on the issue, to repudiate such racial injustices during his March

19, 1953, press conference. Nevertheless, Robert B. Anderson, the new secretary of the Navy appointed by Eisenhower, still responded to a White House query on May 28 that segregation had been "followed over many years" and was a "practical answer to the problem which the department cannot correct by edict." Not to comply with "local practice," he reaffirmed, "would inevitably lead to disruptive employee relations, poor community relations and an ultimate breakdown of efficiency accompanied by lower production." He reiterated this policy to Mitchell, telling him that the Navy would "measure the pace of non-segregation by the limits of what is practical and reasonable in each area."

Mitchell protested the policy to Maxwell Rabb, the White House minority affairs liaison. He said he understood that Marvin J. Ottilie, in the Office of Industrial Relations of the Navy Department, was the "real author of the various Navy communications endorsing segregation at these yards." Mitchell continued, "What we are faced with is an individual who uses his personal prejudices to formulate policies that are the exact opposite of the policies of the Chief Executive." Powell, who along with William Dawson, the other black member of the House of Representatives, had responded to Mitchell's plea for help by sending a telegram of protest to Eisenhower, also charged that Anderson was guilty of insubordination for disobeying the President's desegregation order. The Navy's policy was made more glaring in that the Army and Air Force had ended segregation among their civilian and military personnel. Eisenhower responded by ordering Rabb to supervise the executive agencies in their implementation of presidential racial policy, and on August 13 he appointed a fifteen-member commission with Vice President Nixon as chairman to study discrimination in industries holding defense contracts—a clear message to the Navy.

Finally, on August 20, 1953, Anderson made a public announcement that naval commanders "have been requested to proceed steadily and expeditiously toward the complete elimination" of all racial barriers in those naval establishments, from Virginia to Texas, where segregation existed. The verbal, and thus highly informal, manner in which Anderson "requested" base commanders to end segregation underscored resistance within the Navy. Not surprisingly, the Norfolk and Charleston base commanders said they would not act without a written directive; two days later Anderson put his order in writing.

The navy secretary directed the commanders to provide progress reports every sixty days. The order was aimed particularly at Norfolk, with about fifteen thousand employees, and Charleston, with eight thousand workers. Mitchell's reponse that the order was "long overdue" reflected his exasperation with the struggle. "Even 60 days is too long to keep segregation anywhere, but especially on U.S. property," he said. Nevertheless, Mitchell welcomed the Charleston Naval Shipyard's desegregation of its water fountains on September 14, and its cafeteria on October 19, 1953. He hoped that "in the near future" the Navy would also end segregation in restrooms. For him these steps were indications "of what will happen in the South when segregation is eliminated in other more extensive aspects of community life." He was encouraged by the fortitude of the few pioneering black and white employees who challenged prevailing regional customs and braved threats of violence to uphold principles of human decency.

Mitchell drew the following conclusions from the Charleston Naval Shipyard success: First, the Navy erred seriously by eliminating segregation gradually. Had Charleston ended all segregation when it banned Jim Crow water fountains, it would have avoided the opportunity for opposition that arose over subsequent desegregation of the cafeteria and that almost erupted into violence. Second, the prominence that a local newspaper gave his letter sharply criticizing the state and its political leaders for upholding segregation encouraged him that such favorable channels of public opinion would be available when further integration occurred. And third, a newspaper saying that ending segregation was an Eisenhower initiative rather than a continuation of policies of the Roosevelt and Truman administrations was "a healthy sign." Mitchell observed that "those who wish to promote race prejudice in national elections may find that their schemes backfire after the election is over" if they cast their ballot hoping their candidate would support segregation.

Removal of most forms of segregation by the Navy only highlighted other Jim Crow customs and the difficulty of establishing a standard federal policy without a national nonsegregation law applicable in all areas of society. Although the President at his November 11, 1953, news conference justifiably pointed to his administration's "record of accomplishment of which we are all proud" in ending all but a few types of segregation by the Navy, Mitchell learned that the federal government still followed local custom when it used privately owned buildings or property. "If the federal government bows to those local requirements," he maintained, "inevitably it becomes a party to the most terrible kind of racial discrimination." Notwithstanding the Supreme Court's removal of constitutional underpinnings for segregation in *McLaurin*, the Navy still told Mitchell that in such cases it was "subject to the laws" of the state. He therefore turned to William P. Rogers, deputy attorney general, and requested an "informal" meeting so that they might together search for a way to "keep the government free of such unfortunate entanglements." Mitchell said that he felt the precedent set by circumventing federal policies was extremely bad.

Despite the above problems, the Department of Defense was eventually able to report that as of August 31, 1954, there were "no longer any all-

Negro units in the services." A few Army units still carried racial designations in the records, but Defense explained that they involved nonblack personnel, and that this distinction was being eliminated. In areas such as that of Navy stewards where racial concentrations existed, no formal barriers prevented transfers without regard for race.[18]

However, there still remained problems within the military. For example, in 1954 Mitchell had to protest the Navy's capitulation to local custom when the U.S.S. *Midway* visited Cape Town, South Africa. The ship's captain and the U.S. consul in Cape Town had agreed to a South African requirement that blacks and other nonwhite personnel (Japanese and Filipinos) aboard the ship be segregated ashore. Mitchell urged the Navy to cancel the visit and asked for a conference with the secretary of navy. He was told that the Navy would send him a telegram in response to his complaint. When he did not receive it, he traced the telegram through the Navy Communication Center and learned that it had been sent but with a notation that it be delayed until the following morning, when the aircraft carrier would already be in Cape Town.

Mitchell was equally disturbed because the Navy had claimed it had to dock at Cape Town for reasons of logistics when his investigation showed that the ship's mission was "a so-called good will visit." The Navy next blamed State Department diplomats for having "arranged for the visit." The President ducked a question on this issue at his next news conference. Mitchell was further disappointed that *The New York Times* and at least one other newspaper carried "glowing stories about the success" of the visit.

Mitchell continued to embarrass the Navy by having Powell obtain a copy of its previous policy statement that had barred the *Midway* visit because of local segregation customs. The Navy now claimed that part of that document could not be released. Mitchell thought this was "an incredible blunder" because the NAACP Washington Bureau had a copy of the statement. The Navy's final explanation, that its crews had to "abide by the accepted local laws and customs" of foreign ports, only reinforced Mitchell's determination to get an unequivocal national commitment covering all the armed services abroad as well as at home. He enlisted the support of Senators Lehman and Humphrey, and they began an investigation. Senator Case also expressed an interest in the matter. The Navy's embarrassment over this incident demonstrated how much the military's attitude had changed since World War II, when the armed services often attempted to get foreign countries to follow U.S. Jim Crow practices in dealing with American servicemen.[19]

Another facet of the military segregation problem involved seating of spectators at sports events sponsored by the services. The NAACP on one occasion had persuaded the U.S. Naval Academy to insist on nonsegregated seating among its spectators when it played in the Sugar Bowl. In a meeting on March 10, 1955, with the secretary of defense, Mitchell urged him to adopt a policy for all the services barring participation of the military in sports events where segregation of spectators was required. Defense refused to do so, preferring to follow a hands-off policy. Mitchell did not give up, however, even though, in November 1956, he ran into another stone wall when the U.S. Military Academy refused a similar request to bar segregation during its game with Tulane University in Louisiana. The following year, the Naval Academy agreed to play the University of Virginia at the Oyster Bowl in Norfolk even though the game's sponsors said that local segregation laws would be strictly enforced. Only after the NAACP protested did the Navy convince the sponsors to reverse the requirement.

Along with Dr. Montague Cobb of Washington and Dr. E. B. Henderson, former president of the Virginia State Conference of NAACP Branches, Mitchell, on October 8, 1957, met with the secretary of the navy and again urged adoption of a broad antidiscrimination policy that included a prohibition against any participation in athletic events unless local authorities provided assurances against segregation. Cobb recalled that as a result of his experiences aboard the *Missouri* the Navy had adopted a similar policy covering entertainment events. The navy secretary, however, replied that such a policy must first be adopted by the Department of Defense covering all the services.

Additionally, the NAACP Washington Bureau continued to receive complaints about discrimination against black servicemen by lower-ranking officers within the services. The chief complaints from blacks, Mitchell continued to find, were about the lack of promotional opportunities, failure to utilize their skills properly, and unequal disciplinary procedures. The NAACP presented evidence to the Department of Defense to support such complaints as well as others about the continued use of racial designations in military orders and on personnel forms, the use of quotas in assignments, and the recruitment of only whites for special overseas assignments or projects. The continued discrimination was inextricably tied to the broader fabric of America's race relations, constant reminders of the systemic nature of racism within the military that would continue to merit the NAACP's vigilance into the 1970s. Mitchell saw desegregation of the armed services and the Supreme Court's *Brown* v. *Board of Education* decision as "two important milestones" in fulfilling the NAACP's goal to end segregation by 1953.[20]

Another major problem area was the continuing segregation of schools attended by military dependents. The Truman and Eisenhower administrations were guided by Public Laws 815 and 874, enacted in 1950, which provided federal assistance for school construction and to school districts in federally impacted areas (which had to educate substantial numbers of children of federal employees living on nontaxable government property). The schools fell into three categories: (1) those operated by the U.S. Office of Education for the Defense Department abroad or on military bases in this country;* (2) those operated by local districts on military bases or adjacent federal lands with federal support; and (3) off-base community schools attended by large numbers of military dependents. Congress considerably restricted desegregation initiatives by stipulating that "no department, officer or employee of the United States shall exercise any direction, supervision or control over the personnel, curriculum or program of instruction" of any local school or school system. Truman had ended segregation in the schools controlled by the Department of Defense—except at Fort Benning, Georgia, where integration was still being implemented—but many bases avoided integration by sending black children to off-base schools. That enabled the Army, in response to complaints about segregated schools in Texas, Oklahoma, and Virginia, to use the stock answer that schools operated by state agencies as part of the state school system were subject to state law.

Parents at Fort Bliss and Fort Sam Houston, Texas, sought Mitchell's help in the fall of 1952. He asked the secretary of defense to end that agency's practice of sending black children to schools off military posts while white children were educated on the bases, usually with transportation and hot lunches provided, and in new buildings. That practice, said Mitchell, was another illustration of how the Army's integration policy was being delayed and sometimes even set back by persons in policy-making positions who were determined to thwart the President's desegregation program.

The Department of Defense contended that it was legally required to follow local segregation practices. Mitchell maintained that no such legal requirements existed and got Senators James H. Duff of Pennyslvania, Robert C. Hendrickson of New Jersey, Ives, Morse, Humphrey, and Lehman to join him in urging the Department of Defense to end such segregation. Finally, as a result of the protest, Defense and the U.S. Office of Education admitted that there was no legal barrier to desegregating the military-base schools even though they were run by local authorities. Mitchell had tried to get a very supportive Anna Rosenberg to issue an order implementing that conclusion, but she did not have a chance to do so before leaving office. Mitchell admired Rosenberg for her interest in a difficult situation. In March 1951 he had also called her attention to the mistreatment of black servicemen and their families by the police and civilians

---

*The U.S. Office of Education was established within the Federal Security Agency, which later became the Department of Health, Education and Welfare.

in communities surrounding military bases—a problem for which Mitchell was seeking legislation, and one whose remedy by such a law was more than a decade away.

Then the waffling began. In early 1953, Earl J. McGrath, commissioner of education assured Mitchell and Humphrey, who was a member of the subcommittee that had guided Public Law 874 through Congress, that the decision whether or not to adhere to segregation was entirely up to the Defense Department. At the same time, the commissioner informed the Department of Defense that he had "neither authority nor responsibility to direct the type of education" that was provided where local authorities were operating schools on federal property. The commissioner stated that although he would be guided by Defense's nonsegregation policy, the federal government would have to bear the full cost of education as help from state and local governments would cease in areas where segregation was required by law. The Bureau of the Budget estimated that the additional cost for absorbing black children into schools on the bases or for upgrading the poor condition of black schools so they would be fit for white children, would be one million dollars a year, not counting funds for constructing new facilities.

Robert T. Stevens, secretary of the army, made the problem seem more difficult than it was. He maintained that the government would have to "duplicate existing school facilities." After discussions with NAACP representatives and federal officials, Stevens promised that the Army would "consider initiating appropriate action" as soon as its commanders completed a survey of what "suitable arrangements" could be made with local authorities for integrated schooling. He stressed, however, that "should the Department of the Army prod the Commissioner of Education to set up duplicate facilities" at posts with segregated schools in Virginia, Oklahoma, and Texas, the government would be opening itself up to attack "for needlessly spending public funds." (By implication, the Air Force and Navy would also have to set up duplicate facilities on their bases in the South.) Furthermore, he maintained, the government could not compel states to grant teaching certificates to instructors hired for the integrated schools.

The Bureau of the Budget's position was that school policy was discretionary. It said that "no authority" required schools on either federal or nonfederal property and operated by state and local governments to be nonsegregated, because such schools were run under their laws. The Federal Security Agency, which was responsible for administering PL 874, proposed an extension of the law to June 30, 1956, to "continue the present situation with respect to segregation." The Bureau of the Budget found Eisenhower's statements unclear as to whether payments to all segregated schools should be stopped. The assumed answer was no. The second question was whether he wished to stop payments to segregated schools on federal property. That could have been done "either by amending the draft bill" to include a nonsegregation requirement or by presidential action under the discretionary authority of the existing law. Clearly, the President could end segregation in all schools on federal property, whether operated by Washington or state and local governments. Mitchell saw the dilemma as one for the President to resolve, but Eisenhower remained hesitant.

Eisenhower was pressed to take a public stand during his March 19, 1953, news conference when Alice Dunnigan, at Mitchell's suggestion, asked him what he was doing about this problem. Eisenhower replied that "whenever Federal funds are expended for anything, I do not see how any American can justify—legally or logically, or morally—a discrimination in the expenditure of those funds as among our citizens." All must share equally in the benefits of those funds, he maintained. He promised to look into the matter.

Mitchell felt that all the President had to do was issue the desegregation order. To spur him, Mitchell prepared a memorandum giving reasons for issuing such an order and had Powell send it to the White House right after the news conference. Mitchell's contention was based on the then common NAACP position that it was a waste of taxpayers' money to support segregated schools. He recalled that when the Atomic Energy Commission began building its Savannah River Works Project, officials from South Carolina and Georgia had visited Washington to plead for money to construct new schools for the expected population influx. Many requests were made for funds to build schools for black children. Mitchell insisted:

> The problem of inadequate schools for colored children had been there all of the time, but these state officials apparently decided that while everybody was excited about spending money with which to make the H-Bomb it would be a good time to raid the Federal Treasury to do a job that they should have been doing all through the years out of their own state and local taxes.

The memorandum noted that families of servicemen from Pennsylvania, New York, and Minnesota, who were forced to send their children to separate schools outside military posts, complained they were being made to pay a penalty for serving their country. The memorandum concluded that not only was segregation wasteful, but by funding such systems the federal government was supporting the "undemocratic treatment of our own citizens at a time when we are trying to sell democracy to the rest of the world."

Eisenhower promptly took the political bull by the horns. On March 25, 1953, he announced that all schools operated by the Army would be integrated by the beginning of the next school term. That, of course, meant just one: the elementary school at Fort Benning, which had remained all-white at the request of the local school board. The others had been integrated and were being run by the U.S. commissioner of education. An effort would also be made to integrate schools run by local authorities. Mitchell greeted the news with relief but foresaw the need for "a considerable amount of follow-up action." With continuing support from Humphrey and Powell, Mitchell, under the heading, "Faith and Custer in Georgia," was able to report in October:

> Early in September, a group of little colored children left home for school in Georgia. They arrived at the school building where white children were also present. Classes started. An observer would not have been able to tell the difference between this school and one like it in New York or Boston. By a quirk of good fortune, the school was named Faith. The incident took place at Fort Benning, where, because of the NAACP's long campaign, Jim Crow was ended this fall. The last stand of segregation in the Custer School, too, also on the post, is now in the past. Both schools are integrated.
>
> Elsewhere in the U.S., the picture is not as cheerful. Segregation still persists in 21 schools located on posts but operated by local authorities. This month, at a press conference, Assistant Secretary of Defense John M. Hannah, was quoted as saying that segregation would be abolished in the fall of 1955. In response to a protest from the Washington Bureau, Mr. Hannah said he was not quoted correctly and that:
>
> "We have insisted that the military services eliminate segregated schools 'not later than' September 1, 1955.
>
> "My attitude on racial integration is firmly fixed and well known and I do not expect to vary from it. However, it is a little discouraging to be criticized by your organization when we are trying to accomplish the objective that you seek, and to which I subscribe."
>
> In Temple, Texas, Brigadier General Edward G. Farrand of Fort Hood denied that the Bureau was right in saying that he was ignoring the President's program for ending segregation. He has leased land to local school authorities to operate a Jim Crow school. His explanation was: "Negotiations to [lease the land] were started long before the President's policy was announced." The unanswered

question is: who gave the authority to continue the negotiations after the President spoke?

Mitchell again praised Eisenhower for following through on the NAACP's demands. He found it particularly significant that the Fort Benning schools were integrated "peacefully and successfully despite opposition from Governor Herman Talmadge." But it bothered him that, while the U.S. government was paying most of the cost of the twenty-one segregated schools operated jointly with local authorities on military posts, "we are encountering stubborn resistance from local officials and sabotage by some Federal officials."[21]

That resistance was obvious in November 1953 when the *Sherman* (Tex.) *Democrat* announced in a page-one story that a new school for whites only would be built at Perrin Air Force Base. Mitchell vigorously protested those plans as well as the Army's dedication of another segregated school at Fort Hood in the hometown of Oveta Culp Hobby, secretary of health, education and welfare, an opponent of integration. Earlier she had suggested delaying action on the twenty-one segregated schools. She pleaded for more time to see how the Supreme Court would rule on the subject and to study the effects of converting to federally operated schools.

On January 12, 1954, the internal impasse was finally resolved when Secretary of Defense Charles E. Wilson ordered that the twenty-one schools too be integrated. Mitchell blamed Hobby in particular for this delay, because the secretary's home state of Texas was "the leading contender for the new national air academy."

Mitchell welcomed the news but was still concerned. He disputed the White House's earlier contention that extra funds would be needed from Congress to implement the President's order. Since several local school officials had told him that a very small amount of state funds was being spent to operate schools on military posts, it was the NAACP's belief that all those schools could be integrated by September 1954 without much cost to the federal government. Seeking to offset efforts to frustrate the administration's integration program, he recommended in a memorandum to the White House that all leases for school property on military posts be voided if local authorities refused to comply with the desegregation order. Delay in carrying out the order, he said, would only cause unnecessary confusion, especially since many local communities were ready now for integration.

Mitchell's belief that the armed services continued "to be one of the greatest forces for good or ill in racial relations in the United States" was supported that September when schools in the Canal Zone; at Craig Air Force Base, in Alabama; and at Fort Belvoir, Virginia, were integrated. Two others, the Naval Air Station school at Pensacola, Florida, and Reese

Air Force Base, in Texas, had been closed; the remaining seventeen would be fully integrated by the September 1955 deadline. The change in attitude that Eisenhower's experience with black soldiers induced in him had occurred with others who had had similar experiences. One was a white principal, who said in a letter to the superintendent of Baltimore's public schools: "My step-son found the colored boys who fought in Korea beside him to be first-class fighting men, who neither asked for nor received special favors. He learned that the colored skin received enemy bullets with the same bravery that the white skin received them."

In his article on "The Status of Racial Integration in the Armed Services" in the *Journal of Negro Education* in 1954, Mitchell explained that the two primary channels of public opinion against the "entrenched evil" of segregation in the military were the NAACP and the black press. Other groups, he said, from time to time attacked that wrong, but "these two institutions have never relented in their protests." One important lesson Mitchell learned from this struggle was "the necessity for continued vigilance."[22]

Despite the Supreme Court's *Brown* v. *Board of Education* decision, Navy brass at Bainbridge, Maryland, signed an agreement with Cecil County officials to provide a school for white children only, and Washington actually supported this defiance. Mitchell's call for the "strongest condemnation" of this resistance soon ended the problem.

A year later, the Department of Defense, in a reversal of previous assurances, reported that it had granted an extension of the September 1955 desegregation deadline to schools at Fort Meade, in Maryland, and the Pine Bluff Arsenal, in Arkansas. The Army claimed it was bound by long-term leases (seventy-five years at Fort Meade and twenty-five at Pine Bluff Arsenal) both signed with local authorities in July 1951. Not surprisingly, Defense interpreted the Supreme Court's "with all deliberate speed" qualification of its *Brown* decision as sanction for extending the September 1 deadline. However, Mitchell pledged to press for integration of all the holdout schools "at the earliest practicable date." Toward the end of the year, a United Press survey showed that the only schools, apart from the above two, that were still segregated, were those at Algiers, Louisiana. The following fall, Mitchell learned that the remaining schools at Pine Bluff, Fort Meade, and Algiers were also integrated at the beginning of the 1956 school year. In less than four years Eisenhower had fulfilled that part of his promise.

Additionally, Mitchell regarded as a good omen the Army's refusal in 1956 to permit southern colleges to continue conducting segregated off-duty extension courses at Fort Gordon and Fort Benning, Georgia, and Fort Jackson, South Carolina. Courses at Fort Rucker, Alabama; Fort Campbell,

Kentucky; and Fort Bragg, North Carolina, previously had been inte-grated. Because HEW refused to withhold funds from segregated schools, however, the problem persisted at off-post facilities. Segregated public schools in communities outside military bases were an even more difficult challenge, which Mitchell felt Congress would have to resolve.[23]

Cold-war clouds provided a glimmer of hope for the NAACP's efforts to desegregate other areas of the military, notably the National Guard and reserve forces. Eisenhower's answer to the challenge from the East was to propose a "New Look" to the nation's defense strategy that would combine an expanded military reserve, to provide for instant mobilization if neces-sary, with a strong atomic deterrence capacity. National military reserve plan was the euphemism for an alternative to the controversial universal military training proposal, which had been rejected by Congress. A top priority for Eisenhower was to build a 2.9-million-man ready reserve force by 1960. At the beginning of the Eighty-fourth Congress in January 1955, the administration had sought to submit as one package proposals for re-newing the Selective Service law, which was due to expire in June of that year, with proposals for expanding the military reserves. They were, how-ever, separated into two proposals in order not to jeopardize the draft law.

After conferences with military experts in January, Mitchell urged the Department of Defense to include safeguards against segregation in the proposed reserve plan. Under the plan volunteers trained in the reserve program would have an option of serving in the National Guard in lieu of the regular services. Defense advised him that integration would be assured only in that section of the reserve program controlled by the federal govern-ment but not in the state-operated National Guard, which offered partici-pants the opportunity to serve without lengthy breaks from home or job.

Mitchell felt that the federal government was about to let an oppor-tunity to integrate the National Guard slip away. Expressing his strong concerns to the House and Senate Armed Services committees, he noted that, owing to segregation, blacks were barred from serving in units in at least seventeen states. He said the implications of adopting the reserve program without requirements for integration that covered the states could be seen from the fact that at least 70 percent of blacks who had served in World War II had been from states where the National Guard was segre-gated.

The first reserve training bill reported out by the House Armed Services Committee contained two features that Mitchell found objectionable. One would have enabled state governors to request assignments to the National Guard. The other would have allowed persons to serve in the National Guard in lieu of the national military reserves.

Mitchell had Adam Clayton Powell introduce two amendments that had been prepared by the NAACP Washington Bureau. One would prevent Defense from assigning reservists to segregated National Guard units. The other required that as a condition for participating in the reserves program, a state must eliminate segregation in its National Guard. Those amendments, considered as one, were approved by a 126 to 87 vote on May 18. Immediately afterward, their opponents, including the White House, launched a vigorous campaign to defeat them because of fears that southerners in the Senate would kill the entire reserve program rather than integrate what they considered state militia units.

The following day Carl Vinson of Georgia, chairman of the House Armed Services Committee, offered a substitute amendment that retained the safeguard barring Defense from assigning persons to segregated National Guard units, but it did not contain the provision requiring the ending of segregation in the National Guard as a condition for participation in the reserve training program. The Vinson alternative was soundly defeated, and the reserve training bill was withdrawn.

As intensive efforts to revive the bill were launched, Eisenhower said at a press conference that he was opposed to the nonsegregation provision because it was extraneous. Others, including newspapers, joined in a chorus of attacks that Mitchell found incredible. *The New York Times* claimed that the intention of some who supported the nonsegregation "rider" was to block passage of the full bill by creating an alliance of regional opponents. Bowing to those and other objections, the House Armed Services Committee reported out a new bill that eliminated the provision that would have forced draftees to serve in segregated National Guard units against their will. The bill also did not mention the National Guard; but it contained a provision amending the Universal Military Training Act, which included the National Guard. So, in effect, the National Guard would still be a part of the existing ready reserve program and would be able to receive reservists who did not want to enter regular service. The NAACP contended that, if whites were offered that opportunity, blacks should have it too. Despite a personal appeal from Eisenhower, Powell introduced another amendment proposed by the NAACP that would have desegregated the National Guard. In response to Eisenhower's complaint that he was pressing "extraneous" matters into the military reserves bill, Powell on June 9 told the House that he would "not retreat one inch" on the amendment.

Mitchell watched from the gallery on July 1 as the House, by 105 to 156, defeated the second Powell amendment. It then passed the new reserve bill and sent it to the Senate. Thanking William Dawson for his support, Mitchell said he was shocked to see Majority Leader John W. McCormack vote against the amendment. He likewise expressed those sentiments to McCormack. Such forthrightness no doubt pricked the conscience of the austere congressman from Massachusetts and would help win his support in later key battles.

Still trying, on the night of July 13, Mitchell, Joseph Rauh, and John Gunther, also of the ADA, met with liberal senators to urge them to introduce the nonsegregation amendment to the House bill, which it was now considering. The attempt failed, and the Senate passed the bill without a ban against segregation in the National Guard. That left Maryland as the only southern state where the National Guard was open to all races. Mitchell took particular note that the black population where the Guard was for whites only ranged from 17 to 49 percent. Yet, he was thankful that the NAACP had succeeded in blocking the provision in the Senate that would have required draftees to be assigned to segregated units against their will.

The Reserve Officer Training Corps also presented special problems, but in that case it was not the Department of Defense that was at fault but colleges and universities with Jim Crow admission policies. Mitchell recognized that correction of all of the racial problems outside the immediate control of the federal establishment would have to await passage of comprehensive civil rights laws and a more favorable national climate.[24]

Mitchell, working in concert with other related organizations, found it was much more difficult to get the executive branch to help end segregation in housing than in the armed services. Eisenhower was no more willing than Truman to tackle that hot political issue. For blacks the issue was one of survival because segregation intensified the housing crisis for them— a crisis of scarcity that was compounded by the Federal Housing Administration's discriminatory mortgage insurance policies for remodeling and new construction.

During the time that Congress was working on the Defense Housing and Community Facilities and Services Act of 1951, Mitchell tried to get lawmakers to incorporate an amendment barring discrimination and segregation. Despite an initial promise, that effort failed. Consequently, none of the constituent units of the Housing and Home Finance Agency had antidiscrimination provisions. (The HHFA, under which the various housing programs were consolidated, was established in 1946. By 1951, in addition to the Defense Housing and Community Facilities program and the FHA, the other principal units were the Public Housing Administration and the Division of Slum Clearance and Urban Redevelopment.) The problem was further exacerbated by the clearance of blacks from more desirable inner-city properties under the guise of urban renewal—a program that was properly damned as "Negro clearance."

Responsible agencies, following the advice of their lawyers and White House officials, maintained that federally funded housing did not preclude segregating buyers and tenants solely on the basis of race. The NAACP, however, refuted those claims in a lengthy memorandum* on the grounds that the Fifth Amendment, public policy, and national laws forbade distinctions based on race or color. Mitchell, White, and Weaver, now a member of the NAACP's national board of directors, gave the memorandum to Raymond Foley, administrator of the Housing and Home Finance Agency, on January 11, 1952. The NAACP maintained that Washington had a constitutional obligation to see that the right of citizens to be protected by their government was "not interfered with either directly" or indirectly by the federal government itself by its "giving effect to private racial discrimination."[25]

Although the Supreme Court in *Shelly* v. *Kraemer* had knocked the last legal props out from under residential segregation in 1948 by declaring that housing covenants violated the equal protection clause of the Fourteenth Amendment, the Truman administration refused to budge, and the federal government continued to perpetuate and expand discrimination and segregation against blacks, most notably through the FHA's administrative and financial policies. Now the Eisenhower administration was reinforcing those policies.

Mitchell repeatedly reported problems in such places as Aiken, South Carolina, where federal housing was being built for workers at the Atomic Energy Commission's H-bomb project. Although some local residential neighborhoods were well integrated, the housing agencies were construct-

---

*The January 11, 1952, NAACP memorandum refuting those claims was submitted to the Housing and Home Finance Agency. The NAACP maintained that not only did the Defense Housing Act provide for the creation of housing for certain classes of people but that the law also made it permissible for the HHFA administrator to bar discrimination and segregation. The National Housing Act of 1949 contained no provision that expressly prohibited the FHA from fostering segregation. In general terms, the act only authorized the FHA commissioner "to make such rules and regulations as may be necessary to carry out the provisions" of the National Housing Act.

However, the memorandum said, "it is completely unnecessary for an Act of Congress to contain an expressed prohibition against discrimination including segregation for the reason that any Act of Congress is proscribed by (a) the prohibitions of the Fifth Amendment; (b) the public policy of the United States; and (c) the laws of the United States." The Supreme Court's decisions in *Hirabayshi* v. *United States,* 320 U.S. 81 (1943); *Korematsu* v. *United States,* 326 U.S. 214 (1944); *Steele* v. *Louisville and Nashville Railroad Company,* 323 U.S. 192 (1944); *Tunstall* v. *Brotherhood of Locomotive Firemen and Enginemen,* 323 U.S. 210 (1944) were based on the argument that the Fifth Amendment expressly imposed prohibitions against distinctions among citizens that were based solely on race or color. The national public policy that governed administration of the National Housing Act "also prohibited any Federal agency from enforcing or giving effect in any way to *private racial discrimination*" (italics added). That policy was established in the Supreme Court's decisions banning restrictive covenants in *Hurd* v. *Hodge,* 334 U.S. 24 (1948) and *Urciolo* v. *Hodge,* 334 U.S. 24 (1948), as well as in other cases in which it was held that a state may not constitutionally prescribe that black and white families must be segregated in different residential areas: *Buchanan* v. *Warley,* 245 U.S. 60 (1917); *Harmon* v. *Tyler,* 273 U.S. 668 (1927); *Richmond* v. *Deans,* 281 U.S. 704 (1930); *City of Birmingham* v. *Monk,* 185 F. 2d 859, cert. denied 341 U.S. 940 (1951). This policy was also supported by *Hurd* and *Urciolo.* Title 8 of the U.S. Housing Code, Section 42, also required that all citizens "shall have the same right in every state and territory as is enjoyed by white citizens thereof to inherit, purchase, lease, sell, hold and convey real and personal property."

ing separate developments for blacks. In Savannah, Georgia, the Old Fort area, where blacks had lived for years, was being cleared by the public housing program for a whites-only project.

Similarly, in Mitchell's hometown of Baltimore, plans were unveiled for clearing two black neighborhoods with federal support. Blacks were to be excluded from one project, and only a few minorities were to be permitted in the vicinity of the other, the rebuilt area around Johns Hopkins Hospital. While the federal government was funding two thirds of the cost, the city's redevelopment commission was paying displaced whites more than blacks were receiving for their homes and charging whites less than blacks had to pay for new properties elsewhere. The result was that on the average a black family was paying $2,000 more than a white one for relocation. Similar situations existed in such cities as Nashville, Tennessee, and Birmingham, Alabama.

Such blatant injustice made Mitchell increasingly bitter. At one point he complained to the Senate Banking and Currency Committee:

> Perhaps the most colossal illustration of FHA's sins is up in Bucks County, Pennsylvania, where an enormous new city known as Levittown, which will have a thousand homes, is being built soley because it is getting FHA financing. The owner of that development says that it is going to be exclusively for white people. He is willing to let dogs in but no Negroes.

Furthermore, he complained, blacks "are cheated out of their property." For example, in Oklahoma an appraiser offered a black man $4,000 for land that was worth $12,000. The appraisers said they had lowered their offer because "there was just a bunch of coons living out there and we, therefore, thought the land was not of much value."

In Savannah, Mitchell knew a pastor forced out of the Old Fort area who was first offered $8,000 for the church property. Later the city offered $13,000. Finally, after the minister contested the transaction in court, he was awarded $40,000. "So it is a very horrible thing," Mitchell concluded, "that not only do we get excluded from these areas, but when they start clearing the land they cheat us out of our property values."[26]

Mitchell thought Eisenhower's espousal of responsible executive leadership while doing everything possible to avoid the housing discrimination issue demonstrated gross cynicism. Eisenhower confirmed Mitchell's fears about his intentions when he appointed former Congressman Albert Cole as the new HHFA administrator. Mitchell saw that as a signal of an important, though not necessarily positive, shift in national housing policies. Addressing the appointment on March 2, 1953, Mitchell cited the former congressman's record of opposing public housing. He urged the Senate Banking Committee to find out whether Cole intended to junk those federally funded projects that the NAACP regarded as essential to meeting national needs—especially public housing, which was benefiting blacks considerably more than FHA programs. He also asked the committee to determine whether Cole would honor the Supreme Court's decision that racially restrictive housing covenants could not be enforced.

Mitchell noted that in its amicus curiae brief to the Supreme Court on the restrictive covenant case, the Justice Department properly had supported rulings that "judicial enforcement of racial restrictive covenants real property is incompatible with the spirit and letter of the Constitution and laws of the United States." Justice said it was "fundamental that no agency of the Government should participate in any action which will result in depriving any person of essential rights because of race, creed, or color." Cole was noncommittal on housing segregation despite Mitchell's proddings. Mitchell concluded, "It is not extravagant to say that his testimony could even be interpreted to mean that the [public housing] program may be abandoned. On segregation, he was personally opposed, but he surrounded his personal view with enough qualifications to leave the door open for continued segregation."

Right after the Senate approved Cole's appointment, in what Mitchell called an "informal" meeting on March 13, 1953, he promised the lobbyist that he would follow the President's policy of not allowing segregation in federally funded programs. Mitchell welcomed the Senate's restoration of cuts in appropriations that would have killed the public housing program and also severely reduced the HHFA's Race Relations Service. At another meeting on May 7 when Mitchell submitted a memorandum to Cole on how the housing agencies could abolish segregation, he remained noncommittal. Mitchell had representatives of seven major organizations join him in a meeting with Cole on July 22, 1953. Cole responded later that summer by holding a series of "shirt sleeve conferences" in several cities ostensibly for the purpose of developing the administration's new housing policy. Hoping that some good might come out of them, Mitchell helped NAACP representatives to prepare for those meetings. But, as he feared, the conferences were only a public relations gimmick.

A few weeks later, at the invitation of the housing agencies, Mitchell submitted a set of recommendations to the President's Advisory Committee on Housing. He called for an adequate supply of dwellings at reasonable sale and rental rates that would be open to all persons without racial discrimination; implementation of that policy by one agency with final authority to resolve differences; and the establishment of a more centralized housing administration under the direction of an impartial person who would consider the program in its totality. Mitchell by now had no doubt that Cole was a major obstacle to eliminating discrimination. The HHFA in December confirmed his fears by approving a loan for the Birmingham redevelopment project even though the city had not resolved relevant racial issues.[27]

During a meeting with the President on January 13, 1954, Mitchell mentioned the housing problem. Eisenhower brushed aside the complaint with an "I understand that Al Cole has taken care of that" response. Following up on the President's suggestion, Mitchell met with Cole right after the session and submitted a statement for inclusion in Eisenhower's message on housing that was to be sent to Congress on January 25.

The NAACP draft noted that the Supreme Court had prohibited legislative and judicial enforcement of segregation and would have had Eisenhower again express that it was legally and morally wrong to use federal funds to extend such practices. The statement would also have had the President instruct "the housing agencies to formulate policies which will guarantee that no housing built with the assistance of the Federal Government will be denied eligible renters or buyers solely because of race."

Cole dutifully forwarded the statement to the White House, but it was never used. Instead, Eisenhower "acknowledged that many members of minority groups, regardless of their income or their economic status, have had the least opportunity of all of our citizens to acquire good homes" and urged administrative remedies that were wholly inadequate. Even this statement, Mitchell lamented, was not acted upon.[28]

Cole had added fuel to the fire when he said during a subsequent news conference that his agency would be guided by local views on race in certain redevelopment programs. He angered Mitchell by referring to a statement from a black official calling for what amounted to a housing quota for blacks to undercut the NAACP's drive for congressional legislation barring segregation in federally funded programs. The proposed amendment provided, "The aids and powers made available under the several titles of this Act are not to be conditioned or limited in any way on account of race, religion, or national origin of builders, lenders, renters, buyers, or families to be benefited." Each time the amendment was submitted, Mitchell complained to White, it was defeated because of a strong belief among many liberals that the provision would defeat housing legislation, which, like the school aid bill and the military ready reserve program, they wanted to see enacted under any circumstances; and because of misleading assurances from the housing agencies that discrimination could be ended without legislation.

Mitchell pointed out to the Senate Banking Committee chairman that

Cole had tried to confuse the issue by using the proposed housing quota to support his contention that his agency would have very real difficulties administering "the insured mortgage program on the basis of this or any similar formula." Cole not only denied that the FHA fostered segregation, but added his "firm belief" that providing adequate housing for blacks and other nonwhite citizens would best be achieved by administering federal policies on the basis of equality. "If we were to attempt to develop a special program for the benefit of minority groups, we should be recommending what is essentially class legislation."

Tacitly acknowledging the futility of getting any support from the Eisenhower administration, Mitchell redoubled his appearances at hearings like those held by the Senate Banking Committee. Most often they were sparsely attended, but over the years the hearings enabled him to establish a legislative record for action. They also served to help him mobilize support.

More than ever, Mitchell welcomed the head-on confrontation with Cole; he distributed widely copies of Cole's letter along with his own news release countering the official's self-serving claims. He challenged as "thoroughly dishonest" Cole's assertion that the FHA now made no distinction as to race, creed, or color on applications for mortgage insurance. Every housing official, he said, including Cole, knew that FHA-insured projects were designated "as white or for colored at the time lenders agree to advance funds." Consequently, although policy forbade restrictive written covenants, the FHA promoted "exclusion from new housing through other types of agreements." Under Cole's stated plan, Mitchell said, federal funds would finance an all-white Levittown in Pennsylvania, plus an all-black community for those who were excluded from it because of race. (The Levittown situation was a new problem, which the NAACP national convention in Dallas deplored in a July 3, 1954, resolution.) "This is the doctrine of appeasement and expediency," he said. "It is totally unworthy of our country." It particularly angered him that the builder could not have created a whole new community without help from the federal government. The builder might have been a successful one to many, he charged, "but in the eyes of minority group members who are denied housing by him solely because of race, he is a symbol of the encroachment of police-state methods in America."

Even more disturbing to Mitchell was that despite Eisenhower's "fine pronouncements," the President was not much better than Cole. At his news conference on April 7, 1954, Ethel Payne, a *Chicago Defender* correspondent, at Mitchell's urging, asked the President what he had done to implement his housing message. The President, as usual, promised to look into the matter. When the question was repeated at his May 5 conference,

Eisenhower suggested that Payne check with the housing agencies. Fortunately, said Mitchell, the President never went on record as endorsing a "weak and utterly unacceptable suggestion" that the housing agencies had sent to the White House for its adoption as official policy. The best response Eisenhower could give when he was again asked that question on August 4, according to *The New York Times,* was that "he had tried as hard as he knew how to have accepted this idea, that where Federal funds and Federal authority were involved, that there should be no discrimination based on any reason that was not recognized by our Constitution. He would continue to do that." A week later, Mitchell won support from a very unlikely source, the National Association of Real Estate Brokers, which asked Eisenhower on August 11, 1954, to instruct the housing agencies to revise their racial policies. But, while effectively conceding that Mitchell was right in attacking housing segregation, the real estate brokers did not support the more meaningful struggle for legislation.

Cole, on solid political ground, supported by powerful real estate interests and by the White House, bobbed and weaved in his encounters with Mitchell, and he also feinted. One such pretense was Cole's White House-sponsored Conference on Minority Housing Problems on December 9 and 10. Mitchell again presented the NAACP's goals and was not surprised to receive no satisfactory response. Cole only aggravated the problem by endorsing a percentage program for blacks that the National Association of Home Builders had proposed. Mitchell rejected it, first because it was a quota, and second because the home builders had proposed that the black 10 percent be built on "suitable sites." That meant, Mitchell feared, that the housing would not only be segregated, but it would also be built on land nobody else wanted. It usually meant "that it would be close to a rendering plant, the city dump, or an abandoned grave yard."

Mitchell concluded that "the Court has said that you can't enforce segregation through the courts, and it is not being enforced through the courts. It said that the legislators may not have segregation, and the legislators do not have segregation in the laws, but the [executive branch] contends that as an administrative arm of government it is not reached by these court decisions and, therefore [it continued to segregate]. I am sorry to say that there is a considerable volume of evidence to indicate that not only is the action of the Housing and Home Finance Administration acceptable to the White House, [but] I don't believe there is a scintilla of evidence to show that the White House supports the program saying that the Federal Government must not be used to promote segregation in housing."[29]

As if to confirm that conclusion, Cole on August 5, 1955, dismissed Frank Horne, head of the HHFA's Race Relations Service, and his assistant, Corienne R. Morrow. A black housing-expert, Horne had first joined the Roosevelt administration as assistant to Mary McLeod Bethune in 1935 when she was director of the Division of Negro Affairs of the National Youth Administration.

Subsequently, Horne became Robert Weaver's assistant in the U.S. Housing Authority and succeeded Weaver when he left to head the Negro Employment and Training Branch in the OPM. Horne was a symbol of the struggle by blacks for equal opportunities in housing and construction work. Cole claimed that Horne was dismissed for budgetary reasons, but after widespread protests, he offered him a newly created job as special assistant on the International Housing Activities staff. Horne rejected the offer. Mitchell and other supporters charged that Horne was dismissed because of his insistence on nonsegregation clauses in government-assisted housing.[30]

Especially revealing was a memorandum from Ruby Hurley, the NAACP southeast regional director, complaining about the intense political pressure that she and other local leaders of the association were getting to end their protest against the Birmingham slum clearance project. In the early stages, Hurley reported, Birmingham's mayor had asked her to withdraw her opposition. After she persisted and had exhausted all political avenues in her effort to protect the rights of the black residents in the area, and had begun to develop a court challenge with the NAACP legal department's help, the city really turned on the heat. But, said Hurley, "we are not in politics." The NAACP, she said, was only "trying to protect the rights" of blacks. "Our enemies are powerful interests in real estate and otherwise. Our worst are some of the Negroes themselves."

Mitchell's uncharacteristic response to this appeal for continued help from the NAACP's national office betrayed his own frustration: "I know that you must find it discouraging at times, but you may derive some comfort from the knowledge that in each city there is some issue that will evoke the reaction that you are now witnessing. Fortunately, the tide of progress moves in spite of the opposition."

Despite the obstacles, Mitchell felt that federal policy was advancing to recognition "that physical segregation is discriminatory." The District of Columbia's fire department was integrated on September 18, 1954. The Navy ended civilian segregation at its shore facilities, not only in Virginia and South Carolina, but also in Alabama, Florida, Georgia, Maryland, and North Carolina.

The armed services were the first American institution officially to make prohibition of Jim Crow a *fait accompli*. In September 1953, the Veterans Administration launched a program to end segregation in all its hospitals and related facilities. Nine months later the VA announced that the program was completed. Mitchell asked NAACP branches to inspect

VA facilities and most were indeed found to be integrated, though a few recalcitrant outposts still remained.

Mitchell's fight against segregation in the federal government was still hampered by Congress's unwillingness to pass civil rights measures. But with the Supreme Court having outlawed the "separate but equal" doctrine in *Brown,* the most formidable obstacle had been removed. His proclamation that, thanks to a campaign also directed primarily at the executive branch, segregation was "on the run or completely eliminated in the armed services, defense establishments that employ civilians, schools on military and naval posts, veterans hospitals, atomic energy installations, government reservations and many other federal establishments" heralded sight of the promised land. "Free by '63"—except for massive resistance in the South—thus seemed more a realistic objective than a dream.[31]

Elsie Davis Mitchell,
Clarence Mitchell's mother

Clarence Maurice Mitchell, Sr.

Clarence and Juanita Mitchell

The bridal party

Mitchell with his four sons on the Atlantic City boardwalk

The Salisbury, Maryland, armory. Accused lynchers being taken away. *THE BALTIMORE SUN*

The Princess Anne jail from which the lynch mob took George Armwood
THE BALTIMORE SUN

Juanita Mitchell, Walter White ("the Little Warrior"), and Senator Edward P. Costigan at a Senate hearing on the antilynching bill, 1934

Mitchell *(seated, third from left)* with the wartime FEPC field staff, 1943

Gloster B. Current, Mitchell, and W.E.B.
Du Bois, 1946

A delegation from the National Emergency
Committee Against Mob Violence meets with
President Truman, 1946. LLEWELLYN
RANSOM NEWS FEATURES

Philip Murray, Monsignor Francis J. Haas,
Otto Seyferth, and Clarence Mitchell, 1947

Mitchell stages a one-man picket line
supporting school desegregation in Baltimore,
1954.

President Truman addresses the 1947 Annual
Convention of the NAACP at the base of the
Lincoln Memorial. NATIONAL PARK
SERVICE—ABBIE ROWE; COURTESY OF THE
HARRY S TRUMAN LIBRARY

President Eisenhower meets with an NAACP delegation, 1954.

Clarence and Juanita attend the Atlanta Southwide Conference, 1955, on the Supreme Court's school desegregation decision. REESE

Mitchell accompanies Mrs. Beatrice Young of Jackson, Mississippi, who was beaten by a local sheriff, in a meeting with Senator Sam Ervin of North Carolina, 1955.
MAURICE SORRELL

Mitchell and other NAACP representatives meet with Senator Thomas C. Hennings, Jr., on questions of constitutional rights, 1955.
MAURICE SORRELL

Mitchell and a delegation from Minnesota meet with Senator Hubert Humphrey about segregation in the armed services.

Mitchell with his staff

Mitchell meets with the Baltimore NAACP voter registration committee.

Senators plan an offensive against the filibuster, 1957. AP/WIDE WORLD PHOTOS

Mitchell and a delegation from Mississippi meeting with Representative Adam Clayton Powell, Jr., on strengthening the 1957 Civil Rights Act, 1959

Mitchell standing outside the Capitol after an all-night filibuster by Senator Strom Thurmond, 1957

CHAPTER TEN

Confronting the Agony

No one rejoiced more than Mitchell over the Supreme Court's judgment in *Brown* v. *Board of Education* in 1954. Some newspapers like the *Atlanta Constitution* tried to avoid alarm and advised, "It is a time for Georgia to think clearly. Our best minds must be put to work, not to destroy but to arrive at constructive conclusions." The *Jackson* (Miss.) *Daily News,* however, set the tone that would become the pattern in the South: "It means racial strife of the bitterest sort. Mississippi cannot and will not try to abide by such a decision." *The Crisis* was understandably realistic: "We are at that point in our fight against segregation where unintelligent optimism and childish faith in a court decision can blind us to the fact that legal abolition of segregation is not the final solution for the social cancer of racism."

Speaking in Charleston, South Carolina, Mitchell said the Court had "brought the nation to the border of freedom's promised land"; Americans "will cross over into the spirit of brotherhood and understanding." For him it was "unthinkable that any responsible public official or community leader will be childish enough to pretend that anyone may successfully defy the highest court of our great democracy." He noted that "loose tongued demagogues" like Senator James O. Eastland of Mississippi "will give forth with sound and fury," while others will "try to promote confusion by falsely linking the cause of civil rights with the Communists." Fortunately, however, he thought, "neither of these points of view will be held by the majority of the people, North or South." He expressed the NAACP's confidence "that the colored and white people of the South will get together on

DENTON L. WATSON

the basis of the court's decision and jointly formulate plans to carry it out in their local communities."

Mitchell's optimism was premature. He doubtless underestimated the depth of the South's emotional attachment to segregation, so he did not initially perceive the social and psychological trauma into which the *Brown* decision had thrown the region. The government's manner of enforcing the law to protect the rights of minorities would now become paramount for him.

Juanita Mitchell, as chairman of the NAACP's state legal redress committee, immediately began using the law to desegregate the public schools, enabling Maryland to become the first state to do so.[1]

While the District of Columbia, along with the border states of Delaware (with the notable exception of Milford), West Virginia, and Missouri, were taking the lead in promptly complying with the Supreme Court's mandate, the old Confederacy, especially the Black Belt, became a hotbed of rebellion. Mississippi assumed historically dubious prominence in this regard. Organized and unorganized resistance came from political leaders in and out of state legislatures and Congress. The White Citizens' Council, also called "manicured Kluxism," composed of judges, businessmen, and other professional elites, was the most virulent of the host of resistance movements that was born throughout the southern and border states. It was formally organized in the heart of the conservative Delta region in impoverished Indianola—within Senator Eastland's Sunflower County— less than two months after the Supreme Court's May 17, 1954, judgment. Almost overnight, Citizens' Councils sprang up in every southern state and spread into neighboring ones.

The WCCs intensified the traditional tactics of the moderates of applying economic and political pressure, and welcomed support from the Ku Klux Klan. The Klan was the enforcing arm of the Citizens' Councils. Dormant because of public opposition and anti-Klan laws in such states as Georgia, Florida, Alabama, and South Carolina, the Klan sprang back to life, using terror to punish blacks and whites who subscribed to the principle of racial equality. The WCC's bête noir was the NAACP, which southerners were determined to punish for bringing the school desegregation cases and fearlessly leading the struggle for black political power and equality.

Underscoring the new trend of terrorism for the President and the Justice Department, J. Edgar Hoover submitted a comprehensive report during a top-level Cabinet meeting in March 1956, entitled, "Racial Tension and Civil Rights." The FBI said, "The men bonding together in Citizens' Councils 'want to persuade first but are determined to use force if necessary.'" Hoover's assessment of the southern climate had been based on such developments as the Citizens' Council rally the previous month in Montgomery, Alabama, where Eastland told a crowd of twelve thousand, "The Anglo-Saxon people have held steadfastly to the belief that resistance to tyranny is obedience to God."[2]

Mitchell was discovering that although the Supreme Court had settled the basic legal question, factors of law, social custom, and dollar costs of implementing the ruling were much harder to resolve. National attention was especially focused on the seventeen southern and border states and the District of Columbia, where separate schools had been mandatory either by law or state constitutions. But few states could claim that they had never at some time in the past legally required segregation. Furthermore, it was no secret that de facto segregation existed in the North in cities like Chicago, Detroit, and New York, based on residential patterns and the discriminatory actions of property owners and landlords. Other Americans besides those in the South were also determined to use any means possible to prevent implementation of the Brown judgment, compounding the national social trauma.

Mitchell became painfully aware of this reality in September 1954 when he enrolled his second son, nine-year-old Keiffer, at the Gwynn's Falls Junior High School in northwest Baltimore. Juanita, by that time having joined the ranks of constitutional lawyers following her graduation in 1950 from the University of Maryland Law School, was embarked on a crusade to "sue Jim Crow out of Maryland." She was carrying the battle into the counties to make them comply with the Fourteenth Amendment equal protection clause. She and her mother were bent on changing Maryland from a lynching state to a land of equal opportunity—one that would provide a progressive climate for accelerated business development and economic prosperity. In the tradition of Charles Houston, Mitchell too regarded Maryland as a civil rights laboratory, and regarded the mission of his wife and mother-in-law as his own.

Mitchell's oldest son, Clarence III, had helped to integrate Gonzaga College High School in Washington, D.C. Michael, the third son, under Baltimore's freedom of choice program, was helping to integrate Pimlico Junior High School. (The fourth son George was then too young but would later integrate Boys Latin School.)

The peaceful beginning of integration in Baltimore in which Keiffer was involved was misleading. On the last day of September, whites began picketing an elementary school where twelve black children had enrolled in kindergarten in a section of south Baltimore called Pigtown, characterized by high unemployment and other social problems. As Keiffer was about to enter Gwynn's Falls Junior High School, two white men approached him. One of them asked him the time. When he replied that he did not have a watch, the man struck him in the face. Both men then ran away. Mitchell reported the incident to the police, but Keiffer was unable to identify either of the men in a lineup. At the same time, the *Baltimore Sun* was giving extensive coverage to anti-integration demonstrations in Milford, Delaware, while the Baltimore NAACP branch monitored local events.

Not surprisingly, picketing spread the next day to four other schools, all in south Baltimore. Previously both black students and teachers had been accepted peacefully in the high school in that section of the city, but now white students began picketing with signs bearing such messages as NIGGERS GO BACK TO AFRICA, and GIVE US OUR SCHOOL BACK. Those demonstrations almost turned into a riot when whites began threatening physical attacks and blacks responded in kind. Throughout the weekend, inflammatory phone calls were made to white parents with children in integrated schools spreading false rumors that a black boy had stabbed a white girl to death, that schools had been burned down, that black people were assembling to attack whites, and that white gangs were ready to engage blacks in pitched battles.

Over the weekend, Mitchell, Juanita, Lillie Carroll Jackson, and other local NAACP leaders met with the Baltimore city solicitor to discuss getting an injunction against the pickets. He was unwilling to do so because he was preparing for a case in which a so-called National Association for the Advancement of White People was seeking (unsuccessfully as it turned out) an injunction against the Baltimore City School Board for allegedly illegally integrating the system before the Supreme Court's ruling in the *Brown* case.

Picketing spread to the Gwynn's Falls Junior High School that Monday. Mitchell, accompanying Keiffer, saw white women on two corners outside the school with crudely lettered picket signs similar to those displayed at the other schools. He thought it ironic that those whites, children of Polish, Czech, Slavic, and other Middle-European immigrants—mothers of Keiffer's schoolmates—were telling blacks to "go back to Africa." Because of the presence of adults and teenagers with no connection to the school carrying pointedly political signs reading WAKE UP, MR. POLITICIAN, WE WANT OUR RIGHTS, and LET THE PEOPLE DECIDE, Mitchell concluded that much of the protest was inspired by professional out-of-town agitators. He suspected that they were from the National Association for the Advancement of White People.

Several cars serviced the picket lines with refreshments like soft drinks and apples-on-the-stick. Mitchell recorded the license plate numbers of those cars, obtained the names and addresses of the owners, and later gave them to the police. After rushing back home and calling the police, he quickly made his own picket signs. He then returned to the school and began a one-man demonstration with signs that read, on one side, I AM AN AMERICAN TOO, and on the other THIS IS MY COUNTRY TOO.

When the police arrived they merely stood aside while the demonstrators continued to threaten Keiffer, who remained in his classroom. Increasingly, however, Mitchell's daring was driving the whites into a frenzy. Faced with a possible riot because of the lone demonstrator, the police commissioner told the picketers that they were violating the law by interfering with the school. Threatened with arrest, some left. The following morning the police dispersed the few remaining picketers and Keiffer encountered no further problem. Also helping to restore calm was the ruling by the Baltimore city court judge hearing the NAAWP's anti-integration case that the city school board had acted legally in abolishing segregation in the schools. One NAAWP member told an associate that the judge "just cut our throats."

Similar anti-integration protests in the Anacostia area of Washington made Mitchell suspect that there was a conspiracy to create racial friction. The *Washington Star,* however, reported that there were demonstrations at only 8 or 9 out of 169 schools. Mitchell, reassured, concluded that the reason the demonstrations in Baltimore and Washington had not spread was that school officials moved promptly and city leaders supported them. The officials made public appeals over radio and television for students and parents to cooperate in ending the disorders. Although Mitchell thought the Washington police were more alert than those in Baltimore, both arrested troublemakers. Furthermore, several private groups, notably churches, held meetings to discuss the situation. Consequently, the public was determined to prevent trouble.

His experiences with these demonstrations would help guide Mitchell in developing an approach for dealing with rapidly spreading violence, especially in the South. He felt that the best remedy for inflammatory newspaper stories and organized agitation was prompt enforcement of the law. The trouble was that in Jackson, Birmingham, Little Rock, and other cities in the South, law enforcement officers and political leaders were all too often a part of the mob.[3]

When the Supreme Court seemingly encouraged foot-dragging by its follow-up "with all deliberate speed" order for implementing *Brown,* Mitchell complained bitterly to the *Chicago Defender* that U.S. Solicitor General Simon E. Sobeloff had encouraged it by advising the Court that the Justice Department had no objection to a one-year deadline to achieve integration. Sobeloff said that "the court should not lump the five cases in one decree as 'no single formula could be devised' to take care of all the conditions found in the states involved." Sobeloff suggested that the Supreme

Court issue a decree ordering the school board to file a desegregation plan with the district court within ninety days, but also said that the high court should leave it to the discretion of the lower court to decide how long it would take for a school district to achieve integration. Concluded Mitchell:

> A nation linked by air, by bus, and rail travel such as we are, sounds silly when it talks about delaying law enforcement in deference to local customs. An air traveler may start a nap in New York and wake up in Miami. What does he care about the customs when he gets off the plane? When people know that they must obey the law they will accept integration whenever the court tells them they must. This applies to Mr. Soboloff's home state of Maryland as well as to South Carolina.[4]

Brown v. *Board of Education* was Walter White's crowning achievement. He provided the organizational structure and inspiration that enabled Thurgood Marshall to fulfill his dream. He built an institution, the mighty NAACP ship, that Roy Wilkins would guide, and that was also Clarence Mitchell's vehicle for freedom in Washington. The ailing White would not live to see the decision fully implemented.

"Not owning or being capable of using a camera, I was not able to take the photographs you asked me to take in Haiti," he wrote Mitchell on March 21, 1955. "But I was able to do something much better, namely to purchase at the Galerie du Centre d'Art in Port-au-Prince five beautiful reproductions of paintings done by five of the best Haitian painters." With his heart acting up on him again, White was unable to resume his killing work pace. He visited his New York office only occasionally upon his return from his Caribbean vacation. After chatting with Wilkins and others, he dictated the letter to Mitchell and returned to his apartment. He died shortly afterward of a heart attack.

Mitchell thanked the editors of his hometown newspapers, the *Baltimore Sun* and the *Baltimore Evening Sun,* for their tributes, noting that during the twenty-two years he had known and worked with White, "it never occurred to me that his race was important." White's life had given the lie to all theories of racial superiority.

"Thousands in our own country and foreign lands thought of him as the champion of a just cause. They did not seem to care about his ancestry." Mitchell noted that White was equally at ease with the President of the United States or a garrulous taxi driver. Among White's warmest admirers were southerners in and out of Congress. His spectrum of friends included people like J. Edgar Hoover, director of the Federal Bureau of Investigation, with whom Mitchell was having a running battle. "They differed with him violently on the race question but, nevertheless, understood that his objectives were wholly in keeping with the American tradition," Mitchell said.

Among the black press, he was called "The Little Warrior." "If anyone in American history has come close to occupying the mythical position of 'president of the Negroes,'" said the *Chicago Defender*, "it is the Atlanta-born, blond-haired, blue-eyed Negro who, in his 61-year-span became the foremost contemporary champion of civil rights." Governor Averell Harriman of New York; Paul Robeson; Helen Rogers Reid, chairwoman of the board of the *New York Herald Tribune*; James B. Carey, national secretary-treasurer of the CIO; author John Gunther; and composer Oscar Hammerstein II were among the three thousand who paid their last tributes to him at St. Martin's Protestant Episcopal Church in Harlem.

White's legacy was monumental. He influenced an era and radically changed the nature of human relations in American society for the better. Among his most important contributions were (1) leading the successful national campaign against lynching; (2) creating the NAACP legal department with its highly skilled staff, which provided the groundwork for the prosecution of the school desegregation cases; (3) getting President Truman to create the President's Committee on Civil Rights and serving as a key adviser to it; (4) developing a formal civil rights lobbying program through the Washington Bureau; (5) transforming the NAACP from an elite organization to one representing all blacks, with a membership that had reached 240,000 in 1954; and (6) leaving a staff of experienced professionals in their prime of productivity.[5]

For Mitchell, "it was never a contest" to be White's successor, so he did not regard it as a loss when the NAACP national board of directors unanimously named Roy Wilkins executive secretary. Mitchell felt that had he wanted to mobilize support on the board he could have done so. Fellow Baltimorean Carl Murphy, for one, discussed that question with Lillie Carroll Jackson. "But I made it clear I did not want it." He also told Wilkins he did not want the position.

Mitchell was concerned about getting along with Wilkins. Relations between the two had hit a particularly rough spot the previous October, when White was away from the office following his first heart attack. Wilkins, eager to consolidate his position, used that opportunity to sharply reprimand Mitchell for bypassing the national office in sending out his own press releases, distributing his annual report to the press, and not coordinating his activities more closely with him. Wilkins's main concern was that no one become confused about who spoke for the NAACP.

Wilkins was particularly upset by Mitchell's aggressive protests of the aircraft carrier *Midway*'s visit to Cape Town, and especially for moving onto the acting secretary's turf by upbraiding *The New York Times* for its sympathetic editorial toward the Navy. His reprimand revealed a significant difference between the styles of the two men. Wilkins, born in St. Louis, and reared in St. Paul, where racism did not leave as deep a scar as in Maryland, tended to react less violently to discrimination than Mitchell did. Wilkins was willing to accept the Navy's excuse that it had no alternative but to dock at Cape Town; Mitchell, in contrast, brooked no compromise on questions of rights; neither would he accept any excuse on segregation. Furthermore, once Mitchell took a stand on principle, he stubbornly held to his position. He would repeatedly make references to the Navy's insensitivity toward its black servicemen, emphasizing its institutionalized racism, notwithstanding Wilkins's strong displeasure.

On office procedure, however, Mitchell respected Wilkins's wishes. Shortly after White's death, Wilkins indirectly got the NAACP board of directors to tell Mitchell to stop sending out press releases from the Washington Bureau even though the lobbyist considered them an essential part of his program. Wilkins's style of initially getting more involved in the bureau's work also annoyed Mitchell. Asserting himself, Wilkins informed Mitchell that he, instead of the Washington Bureau director, would testify before a particular congressional committee. Wilkins instructed him by letter to draft a statement for him, and Mitchell complied. Had it been White instead of Wilkins, such an arrangement would have been determined more informally and by means of a suggestion. Despite this uneasy beginning, Wilkins supported Mitchell on the principle of his program, which was what mattered most. A team player, Mitchell made every effort to get along with Wilkins in the interest of the NAACP, so Mitchell never lost a step in settling into the new routine.

In subsequent years, Rauh would notice that when Wilkins visited Washington for strategy sessions, Mitchell oftentimes would not be there. Mitchell considered Washington his domain and so would absent himself. Another reason was that Mitchell found it difficult to openly disagree with his boss, who was not always as well informed as Mitchell was or else had different views on a subject. Wilkins, as head of the NAACP, served as the lobbyist of last resort, and Mitchell welcomed his presence when his prestige counted. Walter Reuther, the United Auto Workers president, served a somewhat similar function. When there were issues before Congress that needed the support of lawmakers who could be swayed by labor, Reuther's presence would be requested. Mitchell would never take orders from New York that were not issued by Wilkins and told Rauh so in no uncertain terms. Rauh considered Mitchell as neither the number one nor number two man at the NAACP; he was more like number one and a half.[6]

Roughly a year before White's death, Mitchell had submitted to him a proposal for increasing his staff to help him cope with the additional work load in the Washington Bureau. He had an assistant, Earle Fisher. Now, he was asking for four new professionals and three new secretaries for a total added cost of between $25,000 and $41,000.

Because of a limited budget and the demands of national politics, Mitchell was fortunate to get approval to hire one additional person as bureau counsel, who would also share Fisher's duties as legislative representative. He hired J. Francis Pohlhaus, a white graduate of Western Maryland College and Georgetown University Law School, formerly from Baltimore. Pohlhaus took a $748 pay cut from his $5,948 position as an attorney in the Civil Rights Section of the Justice Department so that he could team up with Mitchell beginning in 1954. Previously, he had spent three years with the Justice Department and with the Bureau of Old Age and Survivors Insurance (Social Security) in the Federal Security Agency. A Roman Catholic with a deep sense of social mission, he helped organize the Catholic Interracial Council of Baltimore and served as an officer. He was also active with the St. Peter Claver Center, the Washington branch of the Friendship House movement. Soon Fisher would leave the bureau, and Mitchell's staff for the rest of his tenure with the NAACP would be composed of Pohlhaus and two secretaries.[7]

Sheer numbers represented the certainty of black voter strength in the South. In Black Belt states like Mississippi, blacks outnumbered whites by as many as seventeen thousand to seventy-five hundred in Humphreys County, for example. Despite the murder of Harry Moore and his wife Harriett in 1951, the NAACP continued to brave the terror in order to register blacks and convince them to vote. Since 1951, Mitchell had been trying without success to get the Justice Department to stop the killings, which were especially prevalent in Birmingham and elsewhere in Alabama.

In 1955, Mississippi entered the national spotlight. On the night of May 7 the left side of the face of the Reverend George W. Lee was blown off by a shotgun blast as he drove his car through Belzoni; on August 13 Lamar Smith, a sixty-year-old farmer, was shot to death on the Lincoln County courthouse steps in Brookhaven before a crowd of witnesses that included the sheriff; in late August fourteen-year-old Emmett Till, visiting from Chicago, was sadistically murdered near Money in LeFlore County, and his battered body was found in the Tallahatchie River. Both Lee and Smith, ignoring death threats, had refused to remove their names from the registration lists and to cease their political activities. Smith was also distributing circulars to blacks telling them how to vote by absentee ballot and thus avoid probable violence at the polls. Till was killed because he allegedly whistled at a white woman.

Killing Till was the biggest mistake his murderers could have made. Mississippi blacks had desperately wanted to call national attention to their plight. The deaths of Lee and Smith had hardly caused a ripple outside the state. As Dr. Aaron Henry, who later became president of the Mississippi State Conference of NAACP Branches, put it to Mitchell several years later, "Black boys were being killed and dropped into the Mississippi River every day. But the Till thing, by the stroke of God, or something, became a nationally known incident that captured the heart of the world." The brutal slaying of a child, for no other reason than that he might have acted fresh, showed that Mississippi's white supremacists would employ any means to uphold their doctrine. The case also proved the extent to which Mississippi blacks were powerless to change the system of oppression as well as the ineffectiveness of the federal government and federal laws in protecting citizens from such violence.

Mitchell found that attention from the wire services and sympathetic newspapers like Hodding Carter's *Democrat Delta-Times* helped to publicize this case. So did a visit to the state by Congressman Charles Diggs of Michigan—the first such visit by a member of Congress—and the organized strength of Mississippi's black activists, most notably under the NAACP.

Mitchell labeled Till's murder a lynching, charging that "mob action" was involved. The NAACP published a scathing booklet, entitled *M Is for Mississippi and Murder,* which, among other things, recounted widespread calls in the state for massive resistance and defiance of the Supreme Court's desegregation order. One white man, for example, was reported to have said " 'a few killings' would be the best thing for the state just before the people voted on a proposed constitutional amendment empowering the legislature to abolish public schools."[8]

Mitchell became fully aware of the growing oppression during a visit to Mississippi in the fall of 1954. At the November 8 NAACP board of directors meeting in New York, he reported attempted intimidation of blacks involved with the NAACP. Those acts included the sudden cancellation of a businessman's automobile liability insurance, which was required by state law; demand for earlier payments for supplies; threats by a local banker to "tie up" an NAACP branch president's bus and store because he would not turn over the association's membership list; and the issuing of grand jury subpoenas against an NAACP delegation because the group had submitted an integration petition to a local school board.

Mitchell, as a manner of inspiring bravery among NAACP branch leaders in the South, sometimes recounted a legendary confrontation when a school board chairman singled out a young member of the delegation submitting a school integration petition. "There is a nigger back there who is a sharecropper. Nigger," he shouted, "don't you want to take your name off this petition that says you want to send your children to school with white children?" The young man was badly frightened. He shook all over, but when the shaking reached up to his head, "he shook that, 'No.'"

Violence and economic pressure, despite a black population of 986,000, cut the number of black voters in Mississippi from 22,000 to less than 8,000 in 1955. Progress that had been made in the Deep South after the 1944 Supreme Court ruling banning white primaries was all but nullified.[9]

Demands for protection of the right to vote in the South thus became a burning issue—even more than school desegregation. Despite the violence, the number of NAACP branches in Mississippi increased by ten to twenty-one during the year, while membership jumped 100 percent. Mitchell reported that the NAACP "leadership in Mississippi is supplied by bold men and women who will not turn back." Notable among them were Drs. E. J. Stringer and A. H. McCoy, leaders of the NAACP state organization, and Medgar Evers, newly hired NAACP field secretary, who was conducting investigations into the increasing number of cases of brutality and murder. Mitchell urged the national NAACP to investigate the methods of intimidation and to seek ways to help those victims.

In December, the NAACP board voted to deposit up to $20,000 in the Tri-State Bank of Memphis. That money, together with deposits from other organizations, churches, and labor unions, was meant to increase the bank's own reserves in order to allow it to make more loans to embattled blacks. The board also called for an investigation of the "surplus commodities situation in Mississippi" to see how it functioned and whether the program, directed from Washington and providing food to the destitute, discriminated against blacks. It also directed the national office staff to meet with the Mississippi Power and Light Company to ascertain if overcharges for restoration of power was customary or "a part of the economic pressure being exerted on Mississippi businessmen known to be active with the NAACP."

Mitchell urged the White House and Congress to act, not only against the violence, but also to adopt his many recommendations for ending black second-class citizenship. Early in 1955, he won assurances from the Selective Service that Dr. Stringer, threatened with induction because of his civil rights activities, would not be drafted. He unsuccessfully sought to block the appointment of a Mississippian to the U.S. Court of Appeals for the Fifth Circuit because the man was one of the leaders of those obstructing enforcement of the *Brown* decision. Mitchell urged the U.S. attorney general not to appoint any of the eleven hundred Mississippi attorneys similarly opposed to school desegregation to federal judicial posts. Mitchell and Pohlhaus met with the director of the Farmers Home Administration on complaints that the agency was denying loans to civil rights activists, and the problem was resolved promptly.

That May, he enlisted the support of the Fraternal Council of Negro Churches. He prepared a statement for the council demanding that President Eisenhower direct the U.S. attorney general to begin an intensive investigation in order to prosecute those persons in Mississippi found guilty of repudiating the Constitution and violating the civil rights of others. Among the council's complaints were the state's passage of laws limiting voting by blacks and its defiance of the *Brown* school desegregation order. The statement charged that the White Citizens' Councils had created a pattern of public behavior that promoted violence. "The evil of an election based on appeals to prejudice," it said, had reached the Senate, where James Eastland called for an investigation of alleged Communist influences on the U.S. Supreme Court. Eastland, the statement charged, as chairman of the powerful Internal Security Subcommittee of the Judiciary Committee, had openly sought reelection in 1954 on "a platform of race hate."

Mitchell, charging that the Mississippi violence was a manifestation of the broader pattern of opposition to the civil rights movement, urged the President to demand that Congress pass civil rights laws to erase federal support for "un-American practices of racial discrimination." He called for protection against mob rule and federal action to ensure that all citizens could get jobs on the basis of qualification rather than race, an end to segregation in interstate travel, abolition of the poll tax as a requirement for voting, and the "guarantee by law for our citizens at home all of the noble objectives we seek to preserve throughout the free world."[10]

The Justice Department told Mitchell it lacked authority to prosecute suspected murderers and civil rights violators in what it claimed were state jurisdictions. That condition particularly galled Mitchell because all too often, in the rare instances when prosecutions occurred, all-white state and local juries refused to convict clearly guilty people. In the Till case, for example, a petit jury acquitted of murder charges the two men who had admitted taking the boy from his residence by force, and a grand jury refused to indict them for kidnapping. Subsequently, *Look* magazine quoted both men on exact details of the murder, but they could not be tried again for that crime.

Thurgood Marshall refuted the Justice Department's position, maintaining that as a result of *Sweatt* v. *Allwright* and *Terry* v. *Adams,* he was "unable to see any difference between federal and local elections, insofar as the Constitution and laws of the United States" were concerned. Marshall said that those cases gave the federal government all the authority it needed to get involved when a citizen's voting rights were denied in any election, implying that Washington could enter areas other than those covered by the cases.

Seeking a solution, Mitchell arranged a meeting for an NAACP delegation with Warren Olney III, assistant attorney general, on September 7. Also present were Wilkins; special counsel Thurgood Marshall; Ruby Hurley, the southern regional secretary; and Medgar Evers, field director for Mississippi. The delegation reviewed the eight-month reign of terror in Mississippi, especially the activities of the Citizens' Councils, the Lee, Smith, and Till murders, and the summer's vitriolic gubernatorial campaign.

During the campaign, the NAACP noted, "all the candidates ranted and raved against Negroes, threatening them and telling what they would do if elected to 'keep the Negro in his place.'" The daily newspapers were inflammatory, inveighing against all civil rights supporters, including the Eisenhower administration, the Supreme Court, the NAACP, the CIO, and Eleanor Roosevelt. "Race hatred was fanned white-hot with Negroes as targets so that any dullard could understand that the authorities and responsible people of the state were prepared to do nothing if violence occurred," the NAACP complained. The political forces gave the green light "to hoodlums to demean, to persecute and to kill Negroes, with or without provocation." The NAACP repeated its call "for prompt and effective action by the Federal government." It said that every moment of delay in halting "the jungle fury unloosed in Mississippi" compounds the national shame.[11]

In a December 2 memorandum to Attorney General Herbert Brownell that provided the basis for a lengthy meeting with him, Mitchell said that other states would adopt Mississippi's pattern of "revolt against the government of the United States" unless Washington took a firm stand. Mitchell said it was "obvious that existing civil rights statutes must be strengthened and new legislation enacted" to protect individuals against physical violence and to protect their right to vote. Mitchell urged Brownell to call a conference of senators and congressmen whose names he provided to obtain passage of civil rights legislation that had been introduced in Congress.

Brownell responded that the conference was a good idea and he promised to let Mitchell know whether he would call it. Brownell said that Eisenhower was so concerned about the Mississippi situation that he was considering commenting on it in his 1956 State of the Union Message to Congress. Brownell asked Mitchell whether it would be better for the President to instruct the attorney general to hold the conference, and Mitchell replied that because prompt action was needed, it would be better for Eisenhower to refer to the conference in his message. Mitchell promised to help get some of the lawmakers on his list to attend the meeting. (However, Eisenhower never did mention it, so the conference was not held.)

Mitchell's and Brownell's confidence in each other was reflected in other matters as well. Mitchell urged Brownell to accept an invitation from students to speak at the University of Mississippi even though he might be picketed. Mitchell reasoned that if the state permitted the attorney general to be insulted it "would show how completely Mississippi" was opposed to law and order. The two men discussed news stories that said Mississippi would try to bar FBI agents from operating in the state as well as reports that Hugh White, the state's governor, allegedly stated that he was expecting serious trouble from the federal government unless all possible action was taken to find and prosecute the would-be assassins of a local civil rights leader. Brownell told Mitchell he had not seen the stories, but he had been in touch with Governor White on that and other matters. Although Brownell felt that the Justice Department did not have authority to enter the Till and other cases, he reassured Mitchell of his sincere concern.

A few days later in a letter Mitchell drafted for Wilkins to send to the President, he wrote that while trouble was greatest in Mississippi, in Georgia, Louisiana, and South Carolina violence and economic pressure were also used to deny blacks the right to vote and to a fair trial. Virginia had even passed legislation to abolish its public schools rather than desegregate them. "Not even religious freedom is safe," the draft explained, giving examples of black and white clergymen being driven out of states because of their pro-civil-rights views. In one case the governor and a federal judge were members of the white clergyman's church. The letter urged the President to call on Congress to pass legislation that would preserve law and order and basic civil rights. It also asked the President to deny further aid to trouble states unless they ceased their defiance.[12]

At the same time, Mitchell called for Congress to unseat the Mississippi delegation. In a legislative memorandum, Washington Bureau counsel Pohlhaus presented precedents and legal reasoning and examined ways by which Congress could rid itself of members who did not represent the state or were dedicated to the suppression of the federal Constitution. The memorandum argued that the "increasing tempo of warfare" brought the nation to the stage where "the Federal government must assert the Constitution as the supreme law of the land or surrender to the forces of anarchy in Mississippi." The Fourteenth and Fifteenth amendments had been virtually nullified, resulting in disfranchisement of over 45 percent of the state's population. Furthermore, state officials encouraged the suppression of constitutional rights, and the legislature had officially taken action to violate an order of the Supreme Court and the Constitution. The memorandum said that "the necessity and duty of determining if it can countenance the sending to its halls representatives of a group of white supremacists" belonged to Congress.

The Washington Bureau suggested five ways in which Congress could punish Mississippi by acting against its elected delegation: (1) expel the delegation by a vote of each house because its members no longer represented a state with a republican form of government within the meaning of Article IV, Section 4, of the Constitution; (2) exclude the delegation on the same ground; (3) exclude the delegation under each house's power to judge the elections, returns, and qualifications of its members (Article I, Section 5) (fraud, intimidation, and coercion of voters or potential voters which resulted in failure to conduct free elections would be the basis for exclusion); (4) reapportion the state to conform to the Fourteenth Amendment, Section 2; or (5) replace the state government and establish a new republican form of government under Article IV, Section 4. This effort failed.[13]

Clearly lacking was a national will. The Eighty-fourth Congress had not passed any of the one hundred civil rights bills that had been introduced in the first session that would have given Mississippians and other southern citizens some chance of obtaining redress through the federal courts for violations of their rights. For example, S. 900 and H.R. 3563, antilynching bills, would have been applicable to the Till case. Passage of that law would have removed all doubt about federal jurisdiction. Such a law would have enabled a balky FBI to gather evidence and make scientific tests where necessary. Local officials would have been unable to attribute their inaction to the lack of trained investigators. However, under existing civil rights statutes, even if the FBI had secured enough evidence to support prosecution, the Department of Justice would still have had to prove "specific intent" by the killers under the *Screws* doctrine in the Smith case, which it was investigating. That doctrine required not only proof that the defendants killed the victims to keep them from voting, but also that they did so with the specific intent of depriving them of a constitutional right. The bills would remove that obstacle and allow for civil remedies in the courts.

Also introduced were measures to protect the right to vote by extending federal protection against intimidation and coercion in primary elections (the only ones that mattered in Mississippi) and anti-poll-tax bills. The measures would also grant the U.S. attorney general the right to seek injunctive or other relief for disfranchised voters, thus placing the burden of protection on the federal government rather than on individuals subject to local pressures. Other measures would have provided FBI help in gathering evidence for civil suits, protected servicemen, and eliminated racial discrimination in interstate commerce.

Mitchell charged that instead of acting on that legislation in 1955, northern Democrats "were busy making plans for winning the White House in 1956." Consequently, "they made a peace pact with southern" party members not to act on civil rights. Meanwhile, "Republicans looked to the White House for their cue on whether to push for civil rights bills. But the White House considered other matters were more important."

No one was less afraid to walk the southern gauntlet than Mitchell. With very few exceptions, lawmakers in Washington knew him as gentlemanly and calmly persuasive, but he could erupt like Mount Vesuvius when pushed. Addressing the fifteenth annual convention of the South Carolina State Conference of NAACP Branches in November 1955, he challenged local politicians on their home turf by charging that they were "willing to destroy the state" and even the country rather than obey the law. But the NAACP, he told his audience in Columbia, was "determined that they shall not succeed." The NAACP, he said, had "a program of fighting for civil rights on all fronts and with all the weapons that the United States Constitution provides." He explained that that program, which, among other things, was designed to meet economic pressure, was built on political action for passage of civil rights legislation. As for weapons, the boycott was one. He said there were thousands of Americans who would "be happy to stop eating whatever you say you have stopped eating" and would "stop wearing or using whatever you say that you cannot buy because of your views on civil rights."

While the Republicans and Democrats were sidestepping civil rights in hopes of gaining at the polls in 1956, Mitchell was targeting candidates for defeat. He warned that blacks would support or oppose candidates based on how Democrats and Republicans behaved in the next session of Congress— whether they were willing to "tolerate rebellion against law and order" or to "give American citizens at home the same protection we give to the humblest citizens of ex-Nazi Germany and Imperial Japan," that is, whether, the United States guarded "the right to vote for all." Thus, it would "not mean much to the human race," he admonished, "if Congress permits civil rights that have been won in the Far East to be lost in the near, near east—meaning South Carolina."

A few days later on December 1, Rosa Parks, a black seamstress, left work at the Fair Department Store in Montgomery, Alabama, and boarded the bus on her way home. She refused an order from the bus driver to give up her seat to a white man who was standing and was arrested for violating the city's segregation ordinance. A new phase of the civil rights struggle was thus launched as the Montgomery Improvement Association led by a twenty-six-year-old Baptist minister named Martin Luther King, Jr., launched a twelve-month bus boycott to challenge the South's racial system. Like tributaries flowing into a mighty river, African Americans were joined by their passion for freedom in an irresistible movement.[14]

*   *   *

While blacks in Montgomery walked and formed car pools rather than
ride the city's buses, Mitchell grabbed an opportunity to punch a hole in
South Carolina's segregation dyke that promised benefits to blacks throughout the region. The differences in the strategies that King and Mitchell
were using reflected the MIA's more limited scope in contrast to the
NAACP's broader program for obtaining far-reaching changes in the nation's laws. On the night of February 27, 1956, after he had spoken at the
First Baptist Church of Sumter, Mitchell, accompanied by the Reverend
Horace P. Sharper, the church's pastor and president of the Sumter
NAACP branch, went to Florence to catch a train to Washington. At the
railway station, a policeman told them they had used the whites-only door
and ordered them to use the side door to the colored waiting rooms. Mitchell refused, and he and Sharper were arrested. Both men posted the $17
bail that night. Normally, police were not posted at the station, but the
White Citizens' Council knew who Mitchell was and the railroad was aware
of his travel plans because he had confirmed his reservations. The police had
planned a confrontation with Mitchell. "I had a feeling that they expected
us to give in so that they would not have to recall us in, but we didn't.
They then piled into the front seat and drove us to the police station,"
Mitchell explained. The following morning the courtroom was so jammed
with spectators that Mitchell and Sharper had to enter through the judge's
chamber. Supporters came with cash should they have had to pay a fine.
One man, he learned, brought $645; another had collected $3,000. The
money was not needed.

Mitchell knew that such segregation had become illegal on January 10,
so the Jim Crow signs in the railroad station had been removed. In 1953,
he had filed a petition with the Interstate Commerce Commission that
resulted, on November 25, 1955, in the order banning segregation in interstate travel, which included not only the railroads, buses, and planes but
also the stations and airports. The city attorney informed the judge that his
investigation of the legality of the arrest had disclosed that "a conviction is
unlikely since we do not have a city ordinance covering the case." He
moved for dismissal of the charge against Mitchell and Sharper, which was
failure to obey an officer.

A white newspaper reporter drove Mitchell back to the railroad station
after he left the courtroom. Awaiting him were fifty black South Carolinians who trooped into the formerly whites-only waiting room for the first
time in their lives.

One South Carolina politician subsequently upbraided the Florence police for not "bashing" Mitchell's head, which "would have had a highly

salutary effect on integration philosophy in the Florence area." He condemned the "jelly-fish" manner in which Mitchell's "flagrant violation of
South Carolina segregation customs" was handled. "A few cracked heads
here and there would avert bloodshed on a larger scale later on," he said.
Mitchell challenged the man to come to Washington so that they could
visit the Supreme Court "where you can observe for yourself the expressions
of respect" that were accorded to "your fellow citizens of all races who come
to see that great tribunal."

Mitchell did not consider the matter closed. On Mitchell's request,
Charles C. Diggs, a black congressman from Detroit, sent a telegram to the
President and the Interstate Commerce Commission charging that the arrest of Mitchell and his companion was "part of a developing pattern of
terror tactics." He called for an investigation of the arrest, which the FBI
promptly began, to see whether federal civil rights laws had been violated.
Mitchell made political capital of the incident: "Justice," he noted of the
case, "will prevail only when people make use of their constitutional rights.
When they don't, they permit others to continue violating the law."

After he left Florence, Mitchell became concerned that many people
thought he would never go back. When the Florence NAACP branch again
invited him to speak on April 22, he quickly agreed to do so. In a small
way, he said, that speaking engagement helped to demonstrate that no city
in the United States "should use fear and intimidation to bar Americans
who wish to make a lawful public appearance." Between seventeen hundred
and two thousand people attended the meeting. Owing to bomb threats,
the Florence police cordoned off the streets around the church. The police
chief himself, who attended the meeting, told Mitchell, "If they blow you
up, they've got to get me too. I believe in being fair to both races. That's
why I am a member of the NAACP and the White Citizens' Councils."
The police chief also explained that had he been in Florence on February 27
Mitchell would never have been arrested. Mitchell realized that the chief's
attitude was one common throughout the South. Law enforcement and federal officials in the region "could not see that sympathy for anti-civil rights
organizations was improper. Under strict orders from Washington, they
might act to halt violence, but such orders were rarely given."

Mitchell pressed the NAACP to file a civil suit against Florence for
violating his civil rights, not in order to be vindictive, but to send a message to the South that the rights of blacks must be respected. Immediately
after the charges against him were dismissed, he sought "to make it clear
that I bear no ill will toward white people per se, and I certainly bear no ill
will toward the city officials involved in my arrest and trial." But, he
stressed, he believed that the police officer who arrested him, and the judge
and city attorney who were involved in his case, were "all victims of an

abominable system that must die if we are to vindicate democracy in the eyes of the rest of the world."

Wilkins, not wishing to focus more attention on Mitchell, whom the black press had made a national hero, did not act on Mitchell's request to file a civil suit. When Mitchell, pursuing the matter, filed a complaint against the Florence police with the U.S. Justice Department, he was informed that the case had been closed. Mitchell, expressing to Warren Olney his "deep dismay," said he understood that in many instances the department was unable to act because no one was willing to file a complaint. "I am ready to testify in any action that the department may bring." He had learned through an article in a Florence newspaper that the city's mayor had promised the White Citizens' Council that "a new policing policy will be put into effect" at the railroad station so officers could handle any situation that might arise. The news story reported that the city council was considering a segregation enforcement ordinance, which would be contrary to the federal government's position. Mitchell told Olney, "It is very disheartening to be confronted with flagrant violations of the federal law and to have the government refuse to act." In the Florence case, he said, it appeared that Justice's inaction would encourage "other incidents at this particular depot." He thought it tragic that blacks might be arrested and possibly beaten for using the whites-only waiting room, as some southern legislators had advised they should be, in order to make examples of them. "It is my opinion," said Mitchell, "that the failure of the Department of Justice to act in my case will increase the possibility."

The Department of Justice assured him that should Florence reintroduce segregation at the railroad station, the federal government would take "appropriate and vigorous action." Mitchell won another point, but the matter did not end there. He quickly followed up with another complaint to Olney that a policeman periodically was seen at the station directing black passengers to use the formerly colored waiting room. He hoped that the department would investigate his complaint and seek an end to those practices.

Never surrendering, Mitchell kept hammering away at the problem. Reporting to Wilkins, he cited the Florence case among other matters on which he was working with the Justice Department as examples of how problems worsen when action is delayed. "I pointed out that there seemed to be a real need for making certain that senators and congressmen fully understand the department's problem on civil rights matters."

Since nothing had been done about his suggestion to Attorney General Brownell that the Eisenhower administration call a conference of Republicans and Democrats to enlist support for a comprehensive civil rights bill, Mitchell now convinced Olney to work on it. Mitchell told Wilkins that he aimed to win over lukewarm supporters of civil rights who were in key positions, especially those from areas where the black vote was not important to them personally and who needed to be prodded by the Justice Department.[15]

Two other symbols of bravery whom Mitchell used to reinforce his struggle for legislative protections were Gus Courts and Beatrice Young, both of Mississippi. Young's travail, which Mitchell described as "something as brutal as Nazi and Soviet prison tortures," began on November 26, 1955, when a deputy sheriff in Jackson came looking for her niece at the woman's house. When Young asked him if he had a search warrant, he threatened to kick down her door, so she let him in. Then, although she was pregnant, he beat her with a club and his fists. Next he took her to jail, where the beatings resumed. At one point, Young begged the jailor, another man, not to hit her on a particular spot on her head because she had been injured there previously. The jailor told her to show him where. When Young did, the jailor struck her on that spot with a bunch of keys.

Mitchell was especially moved by Young's sufferings. Her attitude was representative of that of other Mississippi blacks who were looking to the NAACP to get the federal government involved. He invited her to Washington to tell her story to the House Judiciary Committee, to which he submitted her affidavit. When she arrived in early February, still showing signs of the brutality, he attempted to arrange rudimentary comforts for her, but she responded, "I don't need no entertaining." Her only concern was to get federal help and protection for black citizens in Mississippi. Young's audience at the committee hearing was stunned by her testimony.[16]

Testifying before the Senate Subcommittee on Constitutional Rights in Washington two years later, Gus Courts explained, "Just like those Hungarian refugees from Russian oppression, you see before you an American refugee from Mississippi terror." He, his wife, and thousands of Mississippians like them "had to flee in the night" merely because they wanted to vote.

As president of the Belzoni NAACP branch, he had been working to get blacks in Humphreys County to pay their poll taxes and to register to vote. In that county, no blacks since Reconstruction, including himself at age sixty-five, had had the vote. "That's all I wanted," he said. Courts led a group of blacks to pay their poll taxes, but the sheriff refused to accept their money. After a few blacks signed an affidavit and had him brought before a federal grand jury in Oxford, the sheriff said he would not block their path to the polls. Consequently, Courts in 1955 got about four hundred blacks to pay their poll taxes, but only ninety-four of them were allowed to register: The registrar threw another roadblock in their way by saying, "We are busy today, come back tomorrow." The next day, the registrar told them to return the following week. At that time, the state legislature was preparing to pass a bill to tighten the registration law, and subsequently, no matter how much education a black had, he could not meet registration requirements.

Courts told the senators that he believed the White Citizens' Council was responsible for killing the Reverend George Lee, who was the first black in Humphreys County to register to vote. The day after Lee was killed, Courts said, a Citizens' Council member came to his grocery and told him, "They got your partner last night." Courts said, "Yes, you did." The man said, "If you don't go down and get your name off the register, you are going to be next. There is nothing going to be done about Lee because you can't prove who did it."

Courts told him he would do the same as Lee: "I'd as soon die a free man than live a coward. I was not going to take my name off the register." A few days later, the man returned to Courts's store and ordered him to do two things. First, he must take his name off the register, and, second, he must resign as president of the NAACP branch because they "weren't going to let it operate there." If he did not do as ordered, Courts would be put out of business. Three days later the landlord told him, "I've got another use for the building." Courts moved his store across the street into a building owned by another black man who also refused to take his name off the voter list. Next, his wholesaler, after first cutting off his credit, refused to sell him any groceries, even when he offered to pay cash. Then Courts had to go to a supplier 150 miles away in Memphis to buy some goods. Afterward, he found a supplier in Jackson, which was much closer to his home, who was willing to do business with him.

On November 25, 1955, while Courts was in his store, a car drove by and someone in it fired a shotgun blast through the window, wounding him in his left arm and stomach. As the blood flowed, he called the sheriff, who was not in town. The chief of police arrived and ordered him to go to the Humphreys County Memorial Hospital just two blocks from his store in Belzoni, where doctors had falsely identified the buckshot that killed George Lee as dental fillings. Instead, Courts got a friend to drive him to the black-owned and -staffed Mound Bayou Hospital, eighty miles away. Courts's wife later told him that thirty minutes after he had left the store, the sheriff came and wanted to know where he was. The sheriff said he had been at the Belzoni hospital waiting for Courts. He told Mrs. Courts that he disapproved of her husband's going to the other hospital. Courts concluded that "they would have finished me off if I had landed up in Belzoni Hospital."

Despite reports that the governor of Mississippi feared punitive action from the federal government unless Gus Courts's would-be assassins were brought to justice, nothing was ever done. Instead, Courts had to leave his $15,000-a-year grocery, as well as his trucking business and his home, and flee for his life to Chicago. The shooting left him with a nervous condition and an impaired heart, and rendered his left arm partly useless. [17]

Inevitably, the diehards would make a public show of force against enforcement of the *Brown* ruling—at Little Rock, Arkansas, in early September 1957. The NAACP traced the roots of this uprising to the comfort the U.S. Supreme Court had given segregationists by its "with all deliberate speed" implementation ruling in its second decree on *Brown* on March 31, 1955. Governor Orval D. Faubus of Arkansas welcomed it, saying that the Court had "recognized the local nature of the problem." He said that he had maintained for some time that "the best solution" to school segregation could "be worked out on the local level according to the peculiar circumstances of each school district." Now in 1957, he drew the national spotlight by calling out the Arkansas National Guard and ordering it to bar the entrance of any black student into Central High School, in defiance of a federal court decree that had been first handed down on August 28, 1956. Central High was Faubus's Fort Sumter. He opened a new chapter in the desegregation struggle by using military force to defy a federal court, in the ultimate expression of the southern theory of nullification. His defiance was a concrete expression of the theory of interposition.

To uphold the Constitution, President Eisenhower was forced to federalize the Arkansas National Guard and call out the 101st Airborne Division. Virgil T. Blossom, superintendent of the Little Rock schools, who was trying to steer a very moderate course in keeping with his interpretation of the Supreme Court ruling to implement its landmark 1954 desegregation decision, was thus paradoxically caught in the middle. Leading the battle was Daisy Bates, the NAACP's spiritual force in Little Rock, who was exemplifying in word and deed her concept of what she called the South's "New Negro."

Previously, Bates said, Little Rock had given the impression that it represented the so-called New South that was peaceful, quiet, and progressive. Fooled by the mirage of tranquility, she said, Faubus had called out the troops to halt civil rights progress. "He did not know that the Negro would not run; he did not know that he would shock the conscience of the nation." But Faubus quickly learned, she said, that the New Negro had made a stand for his rights because he had faith in God and the Constitution.

For Mitchell, the basic problem was President Eisenhower's attempt to appease Faubus and the diehards through negotiations, in an attempt to find an acceptable solution to the crisis they had created. Blossom himself echoed Mitchell's feelings when he complained that "the Department of Justice at Washington . . . failed to indict or prosecute a single individual involved in mob action to thwart integration, although more than 50 were arrested by local police. A Federal judge failed to provide United States marshals to help enforce integration at a critical time. The governor of Arkansas failed to use his powers to uphold the law." In fact, Faubus "used his office in a demagogic and opportunistic manner that brought about a breakdown of law and order."[18]

Mitchell's praise of Eisenhower for "the solemn and firm manner in which" he upheld the Constitution was as much an act of diplomacy as of relief. Every gesture was a step forward. He told the President that his actions would "live as a glorious moment in our country's ever brightening future," hoping Eisenhower would exercise the leadership essential for protecting the rights of all citizens.[19]

CHAPTER ELEVEN

Shifting Strategy

Mitchell's determination to incorporate nonsegregation amendments in bills concerning defense-impacted areas, military reserves, and federal housing resulted from his acceptance of the fact that FEPC-type legislation was a red flag to Congress. This aspect of the struggle was a direct continuation of efforts that had begun in the 1930s.

During the New Deal, powerful opponents succeeded in deleting from the National Labor Relations (Wagner) Act a section forbidding discrimination by labor unions. Mitchell doubted that, "whether by informal agreements between members of the House and Senate" or because of other obstacles, Congress would pass any civil rights legislation in 1955, so he decided that the best strategy was to push for such amendments. His most effective weapon became the 1954 *Brown* decision, whose underlying philosophy, based on the equal protection clause of the Fourteenth Amendment, was universally applicable and much more powerful than the principle of economic equality underlying the FEPC struggle. He also sought to help implement the *Brown* decision by expanding his effort at educating lawmakers, blacks, and sympathetic whites that segregation was wrong and a violation of moral principles underlying Western democracy.

Mitchell had forcefully enunciated this strategy of introducing amendments during the 1949 struggle to amend the Taft-Hartley Act. The following year, he saw another opportunity to use it during the effort to amend the Railway Labor Act to permit establishment of the union shop (the right of workers to organize and bargain collectively) and dues check-off. In urging inclusion of an amendment to bar discrimination by railway unions, he had an effective ally in Joseph Waddy, general counsel for the International Association of Railway Employees, the Association of Colored Trainmen and Locomotive Firemen, and the Colored Trainmen of America. Waddy was a law partner of Charles Hamilton Houston, who died in early 1950. Houston and Waddy had won opinions* from the Supreme Court establishing the principle that unions representing a class of employees cannot join in collusive agreements with employers to exclude employees from membership because of race.

In joint testimony on May 18, 1950, before a subcomittee of the Senate Committee on Labor and Public Welfare, Mitchell and Waddy affirmed their belief in the union shop as a matter of principle. They told the committee that if the bill in question (S. 3295) was passed in its present form, it would place blacks at the mercy of discriminating unions and hostile employers.

Under the Railway Labor Act at that time, the majority of a craft or class could choose their union, and the railroad companies were forbidden to negotiate collectively with any other organization or representative. No provision compelled the chosen representative to permit the minority of workers to become members in the union or to otherwise engage in collective bargaining. Waddy urged that those weaknesses be corrected as a "necessary concomitant to any amendment providing for a union shop and dues check-off."

Railway labor organizations, particularly the "Big Four" (Brotherhood of Locomotive Firemen and Enginemen, Brotherhood of Railroad Trainmen, Brotherhood of Locomotive Engineers, Order of Railway Conducters) and the Switchmen's Union of North America, then had provisions that barred blacks from union membership and from collective bargaining. Whites made collective agreements that covered blacks even though blacks could not participate in negotiations because they weren't in unions. The white unions used those provisions to discriminate against black members of the crafts, to eliminate minorities from their jobs in the industry, and to avoid hiring more blacks. Other railroad unions had shunted blacks into Jim Crow auxiliary locals, allowing minorities only indirect, inadequate, and pro forma participation in union affairs. To comply with state fair employment practices laws, some unions had amended their constitutions to remove racial restrictions, but only in jurisdictions where prohibitions applied. Since only ten states (none in the South) had FEPC laws, the problem was national. Even in states where FEPC laws existed, Waddy explained, there was "always the blackball."

---

*Steele v. Louisville and Nashville Railroad Co. and Tunstall v. Brotherhood of Locomotive Firemen and Enginemen.

A member of the committee asked whether the force of law was necessary to bring about social change and then reluctantly responded to his own question that "the practices of our country seem to show" that without law such changes do not occur. Mitchell explained that such concern was overriding for people like himself, for, "as we sit in the gallery and listen to the statements that are made on the floor of the Senate about the tremendous progress that has been made in the South as a result of voluntary efforts, we shudder to think how the truth is being misused"—not always consciously, he added. He stressed that no major change in race relations in the South had been achieved except through court action in litigation brought primarily by the NAACP. That included equalization of teachers' salaries, and the winning of the right to vote in the Democratic primaries in South Carolina and Texas. "We could cite cases of instances in which the door of opportunity has been closed in the face of every single colored applicant and it was only opened when the FEPC law which made it a legal requirement was put on the books."

Another "terrifically important problem," Mitchell explained, was that in the South, as long as the locomotive firemen's job had been dirty and backbreaking, requiring workers to shovel coal into hellishly hot furnaces, it was deemed appropriate for blacks. But when industrial advances made that job more attractive, discrimination had become a problem as organized groups of white workers began colluding and using force, and even murder, to displace blacks. As a result of those practices, since 1920 approximately nine thousand black firemen, brakemen, switchmen, and flagmen had lost their jobs. "We traced the loss to a plan of strategy devised by the Railroad Brotherhoods." Concerning the South, the prevailing fiction was "A colored man can do almost any kind of work, no matter how skilled it is, as long as he is classified as a helper, wearing blue overalls, as the helpers do, but when he changes to white overalls and is considered a master craftsman, then discrimination enters into the picture and they said, 'We don't want him as our fellow employee.' That is the thing that must be corrected by law."

Opposition from southerners to the safeguard Mitchell sought against this kind of discrimination was expected. Segregationists usually had a field day whenever an attempt was made to attach civil rights amendments to important legislation, but he was more distressed upon hearing the standard cry of liberals: "Let's not kill the bill by adding civil rights features." Underlying such reticence was the still relatively weak commitment among many liberal organizations, influential individuals, and powerful lawmakers in Congress to the idea of black equality. Lawmakers who usually championed civil rights legislation frequently denounced even the mildest form of safeguard amendment for housing, labor, education, and, subsequently, hospital construction bills. Thus, very few members "of the liberal bloc will even sponsor much needed amendments."[1]

The Railway Labor Act amendment (S. 3295) the Senate passed on December 11 did not contain the language the NAACP wanted.* As a compromise, the Senate Labor and Public Welfare Committee expressed in its report the intent of Congress to end segregation and discrimination. The House, too, passed the bill overwhelmingly in an unusual session on January 1, 1951, without the amendment. But the Washington Bureau interpreted a clause** in the bill as providing a basis for the NAACP to attack Jim Crow auxiliaries. Soon after the bill became law, Mitchell asked the National Mediation Board for commitments to ensure that black workers would not be required to join Jim Crow auxiliaries under the new union shop provisions. The board refused the request on grounds that it did not have a specific case before it. Mitchell therefore asked Senator Lehman to help in getting this commitment from the board since such a ruling would have reduced the need for the NAACP to engage in future costly legal action in order to enforce the provision. But Lehman could not bend the board.[2]

Toward the end of 1951, Mitchell had his first opportunity to test the new law when employees with the Baltimore and Ohio Railroad in Baltimore sought to join Local 511 of the Brotherhood of Railway and Steamship Clerks and were told to join the segregated Local 6067. Mitchell assisted Lillie Carroll Jackson in negotiations with the union president. After they failed, the NAACP filed a lawsuit in the District of Columbia. The union assured the court that it would not require black workers to join a separate local as a condition for keeping their jobs. Although the three workers who sued remained on the job, they were still denied membership in the white local. But two other black men were permitted to join Local 511, thus setting a precedent.

---

*The amendment read: Notwithstanding any other provisions of this Act, or of any other statute or law of the United States, or of any territory thereof, or of any State, or any union, labor organization or labor representative that segregates members into separate or auxiliary locals or excludes any member of the craft or class from membership therein on the grounds of race, creed, color or national origin, or denies membership therein to any member of the craft or class upon terms or conditions not generally applicable to all members of the craft or class; or excludes any member of the craft or class from participation in the collective bargaining process; or that uses its position as a collective bargaining representative under this Act to discriminate against members of the craft or class on the grounds of race, creed, color or national origin; or that uses its position as such collective bargaining representative to bar the employment by the carrier of any person because of his race, creed, color or national origin, shall not act as representative under this Act of any craft or class, and shall not be entitled to any of the provisions of the Act.

**Paragraph 11 (a) provided that an employee otherwise eligible for membership but denied it only for reasons not applicable to other members, could not be forced out of his job for failing to join a labor organization. Furthermore, an employee denied membership, or expelled from membership, for any reason other than his failure to tender uniformly periodic dues and initiation fees and assessment, could not be forced out of his job for failing to join or remain a member of a labor organization.

In another breakthrough, Mitchell advised a black worker at the Washington Terminal to apply for membership in the white Local 364 of the Brotherhood of Railway Carmen. As expected, his application was denied and he was threatened with dismissal. At a hearing on January 28, 1953, Mitchell and Waddy argued that the workman's dismissal would violate the Railway Labor Act as amended in 1951 through the Senate Labor Committee's "sense of Congress" report (language that, while not in the law, explained Congress's intention). "After a lot of negotiations, back and forth," the Brotherhood's lawyer told Mitchell the worker would not be fired and would be admitted to the white local. But the absence of a nondiscrimination law meant that the problem was far from solved. The union never abolished the black local. The Senate Labor Committee's "sense of Congress" report also never explicitly barred segregation. So the NAACP continued to receive many complaints from blacks who applied for membership in the white Local 364 and were handed a receipt for 716, the black local. Another problem, Mitchell found, was that workers who did not pay the full application fee at once got only a receipt but no guarantee that they could not be fired. So, he concluded, without explicit barriers, "we will have a serious problem."[3]

Mitchell in 1950 had correctly assumed that the AFL and the CIO would support the proposal to amend the Taft-Hartley Act to bar discrimination in unions not covered by the Railway Labor Act. Although he won their backing, the act was not amended. His hope was renewed when Eisenhower, upon assuming office in 1953, moved to keep his campaign promise to seek removal of features that were repressive to labor. One provision of the act, for example, could be used to get rid of a union even though that had not been Congress's intention. Mitchell felt that there was a good chance of success in getting the nonsegregation provisions included in the law because of the breakthroughs in Baltimore and Washington.

Testifying before the House Committee on Education and Labor on March 31, 1953, Mitchell noted that Walter Reuther had said a condition for merger of his Congress of Industrial Organizations with the American Federation of Labor would be ending segregated unions. George Meany, president of the AFL, while appearing before the House Labor Committee, in effect had given such assurances when he told Congressman Adam Clayton Powell that he favored a Taft-Hartley amendment barring discrimination. Thus Mitchell had won two very important allies. He explained that many other labor leaders in the mining, steel, meat packing, and clothing industries were working to eliminate discrimination from all union activities. However, he stressed, "Membership in a union and full representation by it should not depend on the personal honesty and courage of the leaders of organized labor." He said that to the extent that unions were "protected by law in exercising collective bargaining rights, there must also be protection for the individual against unreasonable discrimination based on race." The NAACP therefore offered amendments to achieve that objective. Among the problem unions that Mitchell listed were those of government employees, boilermakers, bookbinders, electrical workers, stereotypers and electrotypers, typographical workers, wireworkers, and the plumbers, pipe fitters, roofers, and dampproofing and waterproofing workers.

Racial discrimination, Mitchell explained, was most acute in the construction industry "because, there, if you are not a member of a labor union, you cannot work on the job." For all practical purposes, he said, a closed shop—a job or plant in which a person cannot work unless he is first a union member—still existed in the construction industry, although the Taft-Hartley Act outlawed such shops. (In a union shop, a non–union member would be hired on condition that he join the union.)

Explaining the difference between a closed shop and racial discrimination for the House committee, Mitchell said that the problem was "having willing joiners, but no one admitting them" because of their race. Professional variations of the closed shop, he explained, were the bar and medical associations, which required individuals to meet certain criteria before being admitted to practice. He felt that unions should be allowed to do the same to protect wage and working conditions, provided that membership was not restricted by arbitrary factors like race. He said that even Senator Taft, the Ohio Republican who coauthored the Taft-Hartley Act, had supported the tacit closed shop existing among construction unions at an atomic energy plant in South Carolina. At Mitchell's request, Taft, the majority leader and a member of the Senate Labor Committee, had agreed to help in ending discrimination on that project because the senator was apparently convinced that, practically, it was best for workers to go "to a union and be referred from the union to the job." That practice, Mitchell stressed, was a closed shop. While Mitchell was not opposed to that exclusionary practice, he felt that where an employer made a closed shop agreement, the union had no right to bar from membership a qualified person who sought to join because of race.[4]

Powell was the Taft-Hartley amendment's sponsor in the House. In the Senate, New York Republican Irving Ives led twelve other Labor Committee members in introducing the provision to make racial discrimination by employers and unions an unfair labor practice. Unions that discriminated would be deprived access to the election and administrative services of the National Labor Relations Board, which adjudicated conflicts. Employers who failed to end discrimination would face a court injunction. Unalterably opposed was Alabama Democrat Lister Hill. Mitchell still hoped that Taft, the only other member of the committee who did not cosponsor the amendment, would later express his support.

Mitchell still lacked the administration's backing. On August 3 he wrote asking Eisenhower to urge Congress to adopt the NAACP amendment introduced by Senator Ives along with other changes that the administration reportedly was planning to seek. "This amendment would give needed protection for minority groups in matters under the jurisdiction of the National Labor Relations Board." But as the fate of the NAACP amendment and other antisegregation proposals showed, this particular struggle yielded no easy victory. The proposed Taft-Hartley revisions foundered in fatal wrangling between prolabor and conservative forces in both sessions of the Eighty-fourth Congress.

Mitchell, however, never lost hope. His optimism was buttressed by the Selective Service Act (Public Law 783) prohibition (enacted by the Seventy-eighth Congress) "that in the selection and training of men under this Act, there shall be no discrimination against any person on account of race or color." That provision and progress made with the Railway Labor Act, Mitchell felt, were precedents for comprehensive legislative safeguards for civil rights.[5]

James Weldon Johnson, NAACP executive secretary, had begun the original struggle in 1923 for a nonsegregation clause in federal aid to education bills, and Walter White intensified it during the New Deal as a result of the significant increase in federally funded programs. The President's Committee on Civil Rights sanctioned the nonsegregation principle by recommending that Congress condition "all Federal grants-in-aid and other forms of Federal assistance to public or private agencies for any purpose on the absence of discrimination and segregation based on race, color, creed, or national origin."

In 1940–42, although very few funds from the national treasury were being spent directly on elementary and secondary education, the federal government was still providing more than $400 million for related programs, such as vocational education and land grant colleges. But the diversion of resources away from schools during the New Deal and war years, and the postwar boom in school-age children, created political pressures for expansion of funding for education. This problem was further aggravated by the inability of states adequately to finance public elementary and secondary schools and by the severe inequalities in educational opportunities because some states were much poorer than others. In 1950 the Census Bureau estimated that by 1960 there would be 10.5 million children in school. Various studies indicated that they would require 480,000 new and replacement classrooms and 375,000 new teachers. The classrooms alone would cost approximately $14.5 million. Blocking passage of a comprehensive aid program were fears that federal control of public schools would follow the federal dollars, and that federal funds would be allocated for private schools, compromising the principle of separation of church and state, which outside the South transcended the racial bugaboo.

When a federal aid to education bill came before Congress in 1943 for the first time in sixty years, opponents guaranteed that it would not pass by attaching a nondiscrimination provision to it, ostensibly to safeguard minority rights. But that only sealed the bill's fate by confirming a third fear, of federal control of education. Still, with millions of children leaving school as illiterates or not getting schooling at all because of inadequate financing of education, the issue remained a burning one. One attempt prior to *Brown* to circumvent this impasse involved eliminating references to racial minorities but setting minimum spending for schools by all states so that federal per pupil payments would meet the "separate but equal" doctrine. But the NAACP was opposed to such a measure since it was embarked on a campaign for full removal of black second-class citizenship in the developing school cases.

Mitchell joined this struggle in 1950, when efforts were renewed to get a federal aid to education bill through Congress. He argued that the South could not "possibly maintain even an approximately equal system of separate education" for black and white children without federal funds. "Hence, any appropriation from Congress that underwrites the cost of the dual school system postpones the day on which all children will have access to existing school facilities without regard to race, creed, or color." The National Education Association, the primary mover behind the drive for federal aid to education since World War I, and other important supporters of that campaign, opposed the NAACP's demands because they feared that an antidiscrimination amendment would surely kill any legislation. Both Wilkins and Mitchell stood pat on withholding operating or construction funding for schools from states having segregated school systems. So Mitchell was confronted with a dual need: educating liberals on the moral justification of the NAACP's stand, and getting the nonsegregation amendment past southerners in Congress.

One early convert was the Congress of Industrial Organizations, whose initial position was tantamount to an endorsement of gradualism, calling "for a progressive equalization of school plant facilities between the races before receiving Federal grants." But Mitchell told his friend James Carey, secretary-treasurer of the CIO, that such a plan "would not be adequate" and soon the organization changed its position to match the NAACP's. Acknowledging the change, Mitchell said, "I like to think that we did play some small part in bringing it about." Not many organizations followed and cooperated. Mitchell that year, and subsequently, also failed to get an antisegregation amendment included in Public Law 874 authorizing payments for schools, or in PL 815 providing grants for school construction, both in federally impacted areas.

In a statement to the National Conference on Federal Aid to Education in November 1950, Mitchell asserted that it was "immoral to ask" black citizens "to accept a condition which results in white schools worth $250 per pupil and colored schools worth $48 per pupil." Without proper safeguards against segregation, he said, federal aid to education "would underwrite and extend this kind of inequality," since education was a state function. Thus, apart from seeking through courts a prohibition of segregation in public education on the ground that segregation was a denial of equal protection under the Fourteenth Amendment, the NAACP's only alternative was to have Congress include nonsegregation safeguards in federal funding programs. Mitchell promised the conference that the NAACP would challenge in court any bill passed that was racially discriminatory.

Lester B. Granger, executive director of the National Urban League and a member of the National Citizens Commission for the Public Schools, agreed with Mitchell that "the logic of your position can't be argued against on more than its moral grounds." Biracial and unequal education in the South, Granger acknowledged, was one of the most serious public school issues. But it was difficult for the National Citizens Commission "to grab hold on a handle on the issue as long as we operate on our present base," which was a commitment to stimulating local citizen interest and action in support of the public school system. "We have carefully refrained from either laying down a hard-and-fast blueprint for local action or taking responsibility for local leadership when action has been initiated," he said.

The Citizens Commission assumed that local community leadership was necessary for "a strong public school system or an enlightened watch-dog interest on the part of the public." But segregation posed a barrier to local citizen participation since blacks were shut out of the school system and prevented from understanding it.[6]

The intense soul-searching that this liberal coalition was undergoing further showed why Mitchell's drive for an effective FEPC and his struggles for nonsegregation protections in other federal programs continued, with few exceptions, to run into dead ends. Not enough Americans were socially or psychologically ready to acknowledge the far-reaching injury that segregation and discrimination were causing blacks. Even those who were aware of that injustice were not willing to support effective remedies. Neither did blacks, despite their increasing voter strength, have the necessary political power to achieve their goals in Congress.

Consequently, although seventeen southern states, in the school year 1952–53, received $220 million for educational purposes, the National Education Association and the Council of State School Officials, nearly a year after *Brown,* argued that it would be inconsistent to include a non-segregation amendment in federal aid to education and school construction programs when such safeguards were not contained in statutes authorizing grants for colleges of agriculture and mechanical arts, for vocational education, and for school lunches, or in federally impacted area programs. (Prohibition against segregation in federally funded schools on military bases, already discussed in Chapter 9, was an exception, imposed by the White House.) Nor was there any such language prohibiting segregation attached to the funding programs for public hospitals or airports, even though some states practiced segregation in these facilities. NAACP special counsel Thurgood Marshall responded to the NEA's argument that the earlier legislation had been passed before the Supreme Court's 1954 judgment, and before the NAACP's contention that segregation was unconstitutional had been "unequivocally declared as the law of the land." The situation was different now because the "separate but equal" doctrine had been declared unconstitutional.

Nevertheless, rather than complying with the Supreme Court's 1954 *Brown* ruling, by the end of January 1955 legislatures in Georgia, Louisiana, Mississippi, and South Carolina were preparing under the guise of the states' rights doctrine, to abolish their public schools or to preserve segregation by using state police powers. Similar acts of massive resistance had also been proposed in Alabama and Tennessee, while Virginia was preparing to sidestep the desegregation order by allowing public funding to be used for newly created private schools.

Mitchell proposed that Congress adopt what seemed to be a fairly simple amendment stating, "[Each state plan shall] *certify that school facilities of the state are open to all children without regard to race in conformity with the requirements of the United States Supreme Court decisions*" (italics added).* Adam Clayton Powell, by working closely with Mitchell and introducing the amendment year after year lent his name to it. (Although civil rights safeguards to such measures as the military reserve and housing bills were also often dubbed the "Powell Amendment," the one involving federal aid to education became permanently identified by that name. Henry Cabot Lodge, Jr., a moderate conservative Republican, was the amendment's sponsor in 1949; subsequently, after he entered the Senate, Herbert

---

* In phrasing that amendment, Mitchell and the NAACP legal department were handicapped by not knowing what deadline the Supreme Court would impose in its supplemental ruling on May 31 for implementing the May 17, 1954, school desegregation order. The NAACP could not wait for the ruling because lawmakers were working on the school aid bill. Though the wording would be changed, the thrust remained the same.

Lehman was Powell's counterpart in faithfully offering the provision in the
upper chamber.)

Moving to head off renewal of a congressional initiative that had been
launched the previous year, Eisenhower on February 8, 1955, a week earlier than he had planned, sent Congress his educational message calling for
a $7 billion school construction program. The President's plan gave pri-
macy to state and municipal responsibility for the quality of public school
education. Since neither the plan nor the administration's bill (S. 968)
submitted to Congress said a word about protection against segregation,
Mitchell feared that the measure would fuel attempts to continue racial
segregation in public schools. That criticism also applied to five other bills
before the Senate Labor and Public Welfare Committee. In fact, one bill (S.
686) actually provided for grants-in-aid under a "separate but equal" distribution formula.

During one of a series of hearings before the Senate Labor and Public
Welfare Committee, and the House Education and Labor Committee,
Mitchell pointed out two loopholes in the administration's bill. One could
have allowed Georgia, through its State School Building Agency, to get
federal aid even if it flouted the *Brown* decision. Another would have enabled states to set up redistricting plans or policies in order to continue
segregation.

As an example of problems that could develop without the safeguard,
Mitchell cited "gross discrimination" in federal spending for hospital con-
struction under the Hill-Burton Act, which recognized the right of states
to practice racial segregation. The position of the Department of Health,
Education and Welfare, which administered those funds, was that it was
powerless to correct the problem. Mitchell recalled that when the Medical
Facilities Survey and Construction Act, an amendment to the existing Hill-
Burton Act, was being considered in 1954, he had urged the Senate Labor
Committee to include protective language. Because he did not get it, the
NAACP was forced to wage a long and tedious remedial battle in the
courts. He had almost no doubt that the school construction funds "would
be handled in a similar manner."

But if an attack from Agnes Meyer, wife of *The Washington Post*'s publisher, perplexed Mitchell, another from the Council of State School Officials really angered him. Meyer called Mitchell to warn him that if the
antisegregation amendment killed the bill, she would "personally demolish" him. Mitchell was not sure what she meant by the threat, but he
nevertheless followed her instructions to convey her sentiments to the
NAACP board and made sure that her threat to him was well advertised
elsewhere before congressional committees or wherever he spoke. Such op-

position only increased his determination to fight harder for a law barring discrimination in federal aid-to-education programs.

The Council of State School Officials, whose political weight he feared more, charged in one hearing that the NAACP's demands for an antisegregation provision was a "red herring" pushed by "extremists on both sides getting together, just like the Communists and Fascists sometimes get together," to kill the bill. That charge, Mitchell said, was "one of the most cruel, reprehensible and dishonest things I have ever heard." Mitchell denied being an extremist. "If we had been extremists, I think things would have been much hotter in some sections of this country than they have been in the last hundred years or more."

Congress had a "clear duty to require that any state receiving assistance must conform to the requirements of" *Brown,* Mitchell said, since local will was not enough or was easily frustrated by officials for political or personal reasons. As an example, he cited a case in which Arlington County officials were about to agree on desegregating schools, and the Virginia attorney general stepped in, defying local autonomy, and blocked the effort. As for the argument that antisegregation protection was not in other legislation, Mitchell replied that that dereliction was "to the everlasting shame of this country." But, anticipating the inevitable, he added that the southern members of Congress could not alone be blamed if the committee failed to report out the amendment he wanted, because, except for its chairman, Alabama Democrat Lister Hill, all other twelve members were from the North.

Mitchell's exchange with Michigan Democrat Pat McNamara during a Senate Labor Committee hearing in January had served as a curtain raiser for the emotional debate that would rage around this issue. The dialogue also showed the lobbyist's increasing impatience with antisegregationists like McNamara who found it easier to compromise on the rights of blacks, ostensibly in the interest of the general welfare, than to insist that southern states obey the Supreme Court.

McNamara claimed that his own state, Michigan, had never had segregation in schools and that he was a staunch antisegregationist. But, he continued, attaching the amendment to the bill would kill federal aid to education in the North as well as in the South. Mitchell countered that the charge about killing bills was raised against every constructive piece of social legislation that came before Congress, from housing to labor. Was it "too much to ask that as a condition of receiving" assistance "the whole country agree to abide by the highest court in the land"? He saw nothing unreasonable about protective amendments and concluded that "the time has come to attach" them to all federal activities.

Although he did not say it then, Mitchell felt that McNamara was a perfect example of northerners who were doing the South's dirty work. To repeated questions of whether he would prefer Congress not to pass a public school construction bill without the safeguard, Mitchell responded: "I think that would be the ultimate position that we would be required to take if a bill came out of the committee without such a provision in it. I think it is important for me to say that we are mindful of the fact that a great number of the people who would suffer if this legislation did not pass Congress would be colored people who live in the South, who presently go to dilapidated, rundown, wornout schools. There are some things that are more important than material things. One of those things is the right of a child to feel that he is the equal of his fellows, and that he can go to school with dignity as an American, rather than going to school as a Negro, or a person who is set apart from his fellows, simply because of his race."

Mitchell left no misunderstanding about who was responsible for the bill's fate: "Our position is that if people come to the Congress of the United States and ask for Federal aid they ought to be willing to accept that aid under the terms of the United States Constitution." One South Carolinian said he did not expect his state to end school segregation until the year 2015. So Mitchell said that the record should show that it was not the NAACP but the opponents of desegregation who would kill federal aid to education.

Mitchell suggested that many of "these bill killers" are from states that pay the least federal revenues. To avoid any dispute, he used figures compiled by Senator Barry M. Goldwater of Arizona showing that ten southern states, "which presumably would deal the fatal blow to a bill with an antisegregation provision, all combined do not pay as much into the Federal treasury as New York." They paid about 9 percent of the federal revenue, and New York paid about 18 percent. Other states that paid a high percentage were New Jersey, nearly 8 percent; Ohio, about 7 percent; Illinois, almost 9 percent; and Pennsylvania, 9 percent. Their representatives all served on the Senate Labor Committee, as did California's—another state that paid a high percentage.[7]

Many people did not buy these arguments. Graham A. Barden, the North Carolina Democrat who was chairman of the House Education and Labor Committee, waited until Mitchell had left the witness stand to take a cheap shot at the amendment: "My colored people are not out of line with me, as far as that is concerned. When one tells you all of this stuff about how much misery, etc., there is, I know more about my district than anybody I know up here in Washington . . . I do not ascribe any of the things to them some would say they believe and some would say they demand, etc." Congressman Cleveland M. Bailey, a West Virginia Democrat who also opposed the amendment, told Mitchell that "you, by the position you are taking here, insisting upon a qualification going into this legislation, are going beyond the basis of equality and asking this committee to look upon your group as someone separate and apart and even higher than the average American citizens." But such attitudes were expected from segregationists.[8]

Of seven of the thirteen-member Senate Labor Committee expressing support for the amendment during the early maneuvering, six, including Colorado's Gordon Allott, were Republicans. Graham Barden's opposition did not surprise Mitchell. He was hurt, however, when he asked Allott to introduce the amendment in the Senate and the Coloradan replied that while he would vote for it, he was inclined not introduce it because the administration was opposed to it.

Mitchell's discussions with Allott revealed some of the reservations about civil rights issues that the lobbyist would continue encountering from lawmakers. Allott said that his unwillingness to introduce the amendment was caused by the lack of support he received from his state's black voters. He said that while he wanted to support certain measures on principle, he had to take into consideration the source of his votes. Mitchell explained that the NAACP's lack of expressed support for him was due in part to its policy of being a nonpartisan organization. It did not endorse candidates. Another problem, Mitchell explained, was that because Republicans often did not support civil rights, blacks were very suspicious of them. Mitchell recalled that when the Eighty-third Congress took up the proposed antisegregation amendment to the Taft-Hartley Act, the NAACP had had enough votes in committee to include the amendment in the bill, but the administration opposed it, "and all of our supporters on the Republican side deserted us." Mitchell told Allott that a similar situation was taking shape in the Labor Committee on federal aid to education. Many people had pledged to vote for it, but nobody wanted the responsibility of introducing it, and that was "almost the equivalent of voting against it." It also bothered Mitchell that Allott's position was shared by Senator Irving Ives of New York, a normally strong civil rights supporter. Because the GOP controlled the White House, Mitchell would have preferred to see the Republicans carry the ball on this issue. But the Democrats posed an even more serious problem, because even fewer of them supported the measure, or they were noncommittal. Normally stalwart liberals like Paul Douglas and Wayne Morse withheld commitment.

Other more threatening hitches quickly developed in the Senate over strategy. One was whether the amendment should be attached to any bill reported out of the committee, or be withheld and introduced on the Senate floor. The latter course would avoid embarrassing the Senate Labor Committee chairman, Lister Hill, and thus hurting his chances for reelec-

tion in 1956. Worse, some Democrats wanted to omit the amendment
from the bill and substitute a written committee report on the intent of
Congress to bar segregation in school construction. But the proposal would
not have been legally binding.

Very concerned about this waffling, Roy Wilkins, on April 20, 1955,
sent an impassioned, lengthy letter to Senator Lehman, an NAACP board
member, to make sure he upheld the association's do-or-die attitude toward
the amendment. Still searching for a Senate sponsor for the amendment,
Mitchell a few days later urged that he and Wilkins see Lehman "to pin
him down definitely on offering our amendment or some variation of it."
Getting Lehman's support might ensure Morse's, who at one point had
indicated he would take the same position as Lehman.

Wilkins's letter was timely because opposition was developing within
the NAACP's ranks. The next day two powerful NAACP board members,
Eleanor Roosevelt and UAW president Walter Reuther held a long private
discussion with Wilkins on the amendment, which was preliminary to
their formally requesting in a jointly signed letter that the NAACP reconsider its plans for getting the safeguard adopted. Eleanor Roosevelt was like
Mary McLeod Bethune in many ways. Always busy, she would pop into
NAACP board meetings briefly but long enough to make her presence felt.
She told Wilkins that although she had voted to reaffirm the NAACP's
position on the amendment, she had not understood clearly the filibuster
threat that loomed in the Senate. She feared that the NAACP's stand would
only spark a filibuster over whether the amended bill should be brought
up, instead of a debate on the substance of that measure itself. After informing Thurgood Marshall about this development and apparently getting
his advice, Wilkins turned the matter over to Mitchell.

In their letter to Wilkins, Roosevelt and Reuther said that they wanted
the NAACP board of directors to reconsider its effort to attach the antisegregation amendment to the bill in the Senate Labor Committee and
instead have it introduced and debated on the Senate floor. Otherwise, they
believed, the amendment would deny any opportunity for substantive arguments over ending school segregation, and the NAACP would fail "to
awaken fully the conscience of the American people because the discussions
will revolve essentially around technical and procedural matters instead of
the principles involved." But if the Senate debated the issue, NAACP allies
could present to the nation "the complete case for insisting that such language is desirable and necessary in order to comply with" the Supreme
Court's ruling on *Brown*.

Two underlying considerations that had been brought out in the April
21 meeting were not mentioned in the letter. One was politics. The Republicans were eager to embarrass the Democrats by voting for the NAACP

language. So the last thing Lister Hill wanted was the NAACP amendment. Eleanor Roosevelt, faithful to her late husband's New Deal heritage, certainly did not want to see the Democrats come up short on this one. Furthermore, those Republicans who did not want to see the school construction bill passed, deviously looked to the safeguard to help kill it. A second consideration involved priorities. Labor wanted the Senate to act promptly on a minimum wage law, but this was bottled up in committee by the school aid bill.

Wilkins said that labor "did not want to go contrary to NAACP and have a public split with us, but they have projects of their own, including school construction." The NAACP, Wilkins warned, could be sure that the bill would never reach the floor if it stood pat. Yet, if the association agreed to introduce the amendment on the floor, possibly nothing more would be accomplished than to have it well debated. Clearly he was being guided by Mitchell.

Given the final say in this matter, the NAACP Washington Bureau director maintained that "nothing would be gained and something might be lost" if the bill was not amended in committee. If the NAACP strategy was followed, said Mitchell, school construction aid advocates would pressure the Senate leadership to take up the bill, eliminating the possible stumbling block of a lack of momentum. The other question was one of political advantage. At the beginning of the first session of the Eighty-fourth Congress in 1955, the Democrats had been eager to get the school aid bill passed early so that they could take credit for it. Mitchell figured that, having committed themselves to it, failure by the Democrats to act on the bill because it contained the antisegregation amendment would place the Democratic leadership "in the position of willfully denying aid to school children because" the legislation called for obedience to the Supreme Court and the Constitution. Another advantage of insisting on action now, he felt, was that all groups favoring the aid program would be forced to work together to defeat a filibuster.

From another vantage point, Mitchell felt the extended debate centering on the issue itself, rather than on parliamentary procedure, would enlighten the public by letting the country "see that the ruthless supporters of the filibuster would use it against any humanitarian cause—even the welfare of school children." He saw the debate as an opportunity to kill two birds with one stone: In addition to exposing the true killers of federal aid to education, it "would undoubtedly generate tremendous pressure for a change in the Senate rules curbing talkathons," as a result of the public reaction against those conducting the filibuster.

However, if the amendment was not attached to the bill in committee, he explained, opponents could always move to table it when an effort was made to bring it up on the Senate floor. Because of the division among liberals, "such a motion would ultimately prevail." Amendment supporters and not opponents would then be subjected to public pressure to abandon their drive. Furthermore, the NAACP's withdrawal from its position "would be a surrender to those who were trying to blackmail supporters by threatening to block the full bill before action could be taken on the floor. Mitchell noted that those threats were similar to those Congressman Barden was making in the House, to block fixed minimum-wage protections from the Davis-Bacon Act covering federal construction contracts. "We believe that in both instances the American people will be able to judge those who attempt to sabotage the bills on their true motives."

Mitchell similarly had to defend his strategy against a forceful attack from Congressman Stewart L. Udall of Arizona, another liberal Democrat. Udall acknowledged that there was room for differences, particularly since he, as a politician, was "schooled in the art of the possible, while principle is the central thing in your work—and rightly so." In an effort "to get half-a-loaf" sometimes, Udall said, "our principles hang on the brink (and sometimes go over) but generally we have found that a modest program is better than none." The lawmaker urged Mitchell to approach the matter in a "liberal spirit."

Responding on July 7, 1955, Mitchell told Udall he regretted "exceedingly" that he had to face him as an opponent, "primarily because I believe with all my heart that we are right." It was tragic, he said, that "those who would rather wreck the school construction program than agree to a fair amendment are able to escape blame for their misdeeds." Mitchell said he was convinced that if liberals who wanted federal aid to school construction "would devote their energies to supporting rather than opposing our amendment, the southern opposition would collapse and the bill become law." Again he said that the public should see a list of those congressmen "who love segregation so much that they would forgo the benefits of the school construction program," rather than accept the amendment. But it would never be possible to produce such a list, he said, since liberals continued protecting the prosegregationists so that the question could not come to a vote.[9]

That the NAACP was struggling up a very steep hill was most forcefully demonstrated by Eisenhower himself. He charged in his July 6 news conference that the antisegregation amendment would be extraneous "for the simple reason that we need the schools." That statement led Mitchell to observe that, a month earlier, the President had said much the same thing about the military reserves bill—"I want a form of compulsory service set up to build our military reserve, segregation or no segregation."

Expressing how much the NAACP had been hurt by both blows,

Wilkins wrote Powell that it was "shocking for the Chief Executive to brush aside the question of racial segregation in the military reserves as being 'extraneous.'" Furthermore, "the President was so ill-advised as to imply strongly in his weekly press conference of June 8, 1955, that those who supported the nonsegregation amendment were placing their personal desires above the security of the nation." Wilkins told Powell that "manpower alone does not make for a strong reserve, and that inequality in sacrifice on the part of young men, due to the accident of color, is not likely to produce in the whole body of fighting men that morale which is the surest defense of the American way of life." Wilkins said the President had joined opponents engaged in a flanking maneuver to evade the Supreme Court ruling.

Wilkins, of course, was merely commiserating with Powell, because the congressman had responded to Eisenhower's June 8 conference by saying that he would "not retreat one inch" on his amendment. In a prepared statement, Powell said that Eisenhower had been misled and misinformed by both Republican and Democratic leaders and "maneuvered" into a position where all of the good he has done for civil rights is in danger of being lost." Powell repeated that because of "road blocks," there was no way to get a civil rights measure through Congress on its merits, except by the amendment route, so he was only following the President's 1953 policy. He urged Eisenhower to send a strong message to Congress calling for passage of civil rights measures on their merit.[10]

The House Labor Committee on July 15, 1955, approved the school bill (H.R. 7535) 21 to 9. Seeking to rally support for the amendment, Mitchell sent out an urgent advisory stating that the White House and leaders of both parties were making a last-ditch effort to kill it. It was therefore no surprise when, five days later, the committee defeated the Powell Amendment 10 to 15. Mitchell figured that "only three of those who supported our amendment were against the bill." Six of those who voted against the Powell Amendment, he said, were also against the school bill—a point he repeatedly stressed to support his contention that the Powell Amendment could not be blamed for the school bill's ultimate fate.

Following the defeat, Mitchell drafted the committee's minority report for Powell, stressing the need for the amendment. The committee reported out the unamended bill eight days later to the Committee of the Whole House (by way of the House Rules Committee), where the vote on it would be unrecorded. This was the first step by the full House in acting on the bill. As Powell took the fight to the House floor, Mitchell told him in a telegram, "May your heart be stout, your voice strong and your victory overwhelming."

Udall was one of the five nonsouthern Democrats who voted against the Powell Amendment. Several lawmakers said they opposed the amendment only to be sure that the school aid bill would clear Howard Smith's House Rules Committee. But the committee held up the bill anyway. Powell, therefore, planned to offer the amendment during the next session. Mitchell emphasized that the main reason for the amendment's defeat was White House pressure on Republicans, so that GOP leaders did not prod fellow members to support it. Mitchell also learned that Barden was peeved that the school construction bill, as it was reported out of his House Labor Committee, carried the Davis-Bacon minimum wage provision. Some opponents of the Powell Amendment zealously pushed for the Davis-Bacon provision to win labor's support. Mitchell felt that the provision was much needed, but not more than "our amendment."

Mitchell compared the fate of the Powell Amendment and the school bill with the ongoing struggle to attach similar provisions to the reserve training and public housing bills. In those instances, the leadership of both parties also opposed him. "In the case of housing, some of the Republicans who stood up for the [antisegregation] amendment on the first count were waved down" by Minority Leader Joseph W. Martin, Jr., of Massachusetts. The Senate Committee on Labor, which was considering similar funding bills that had no antisegregation provisions, took no action on the measures. Consequently, in 1955 the first session of the Eighty-fourth Congress ended in suspended animation on the issue.[11]

Mitchell found an opportunity to call national attention to his cause at the White House Conference on Education in November, which was attended by eighteen hundred delegates. The conference had been called by Eisenhower to obtain recommendations on the education problem. Despite the *Brown* decision, the agenda omitted any mention of public school segregation. Mitchell brought up the matter forcefully by making an impromptu demand during a plenary session that the federal government not pay the travel expenses of delegates to the conference from southern states that had taken steps to defy the ruling and the Constitution. The South Carolina delegation, which sparked his outburst, had submitted a report to the conference that said:

> By far, the most important problems in the educational field confronting the people of South Carolina are those which have arisen as a result of the decisions of the Supreme Court of the United States involving the school cases. . . . We report that it is our carefully considered judgment that the public schools will not be operated in South Carolina on a racially integrated basis.

The administration rejected Mitchell's demands at every turn. Rather than discouraging Mitchell, opposition from important agencies like HEW and from the comptroller general only gave him more ammunition to submit to Congress in support of his demand that it pass the Powell Amendment.[12]

Seeking a way out of the impasse over who was responsible for enforcing *Brown,* Walter Reuther in January 1956, obviously having shifted his position, urged the President and the attorney general to relieve current confusion by stating unequivocally and immediately whether the adoption of a federal aid to education bill without an antisegregation amendment would permit the government to allocate funds "only on condition" that states comply with the *Brown* order. If so, then the amendment obviously was unnecessary. But, he said, if the administration maintained that without the amendment it lacked authority to withhold funding to the problem states, then the President and the attorney general were "morally obligated to make" their positions known so that the badly needed aid bill could be "enacted to insure every American child his rightful educational opportunity without regard to race, creed or color." Without a clarifying statement, he promised, the UAW would urge enactment of the school construction bill with the NAACP safeguard.

This request seemed to be a last-ditch effort by Reuther to stave off growing opposition within the labor movement to the amendment. Several unions, eager to profit from the construction jobs the aid program would create, were not interested in the amendment. A notable exception was the United Electrical, Radio, and Machine Workers of America, which remained one of Mitchell's most faithful allies throughout the years. In addition to the UAW, Mitchell had also won support for the Powell Amendment from what was now a united AFL-CIO. Both the Electrical Workers and the AFL-CIO, however, shifted back to their previous positions after their counsel Arthur J. Goldberg said that the amendment was "unnecessary." Based on *Brown* and the companion case *Bolling* v. *Sharpe,* in which the Supreme Court ruled that the due process clause of the Fifth Amendment prohibited segregation in the District of Columbia public schools, Goldberg said that "all public schools in the states must be operated on a nonsegregated basis." So "it necessarily follows that public schools built with Federal aid constitutionally can only be operated on a nonsegregated basis." What Goldberg overlooked, however, was the key question of who was responsible for enforcing the decisions.

White was now more vocally attacking the NAACP's unyielding demand as unreasonable. The National Education Association remained opposed to the Powell Amendment, believing "that the benefits from Federal assistance for emergency school construction for children of all races far outweigh the temporary disadvantages that arise from the unwillingness of

a few states to comply at once with" *Brown.* Mitchell responded that the
NEA overlooked the fact that in the South a few public officials were
bravely seeking to uphold the Constitution. In Tennessee, for example,
Governor Frank Clement refused to call a special session of the legislature
to block public school integration. Mitchell said, in appealing to House
Majority Leader John W. McCormack for understanding and support, that
if states defying the order still received federal grants without safeguards
against discrimination, there was little incentive for Governor Clement to
continue his exemplary behavior. Mitchell felt that "aside from the clear
obligation of Congress to support the Powell Amendment, it also seems to
be a matter of plain common sense."[13]

Eisenhower, running for reelection, was joined by his Democratic opponent, Adlai Stevenson, who had returned to the campaign trail, in openly
opposing the NAACP approach. The school integration issue posed the
greatest test of Eisenhower's leadership since the threat of war in the Tai-
wan (Formosa) Strait. Former President Truman, however, showed them
the type of leadership Mitchell was seeking by expressing support for the
amendment. Mitchell regarded Truman's stand as most important because,
despite his good civil rights record, many people still regarded him as
conservative and somewhat of a southerner. But Truman had undergone
considerable change during his years in the White House. In addition to
taking other strong civil rights stands, Truman had also opposed unequivocally a provision in an amendment to a bill to complete federal assistance
under the Defense Housing and Community Facilities and Service Act of
September 1951, which would have required already integrated schools to
segregate by conforming to the laws of the states in which they were located.

Eisenhower, by personality and design, was following a less confrontational approach on the desegregation issue. Intent on strengthening his
popularity in the South, he used the immense prestige of the White House
to bolster a philosophy of moderation even during his first two years in
office when Republicans controlled Congress. He insisted on his "devotion
to the decisions of the Supreme Court" and to "the equality of opportunities for every citizen." He maintained that the question was not "quite
as simple as that"—meaning, demanding that the states uphold the law of
the land. He said he was approaching the issue from "the other end,"
because "I believe that every law, every important bill, and every important purpose from Congress should be in a bill of its own, so that we don't
get a confusion of issues, and therefore, don't know for what we are voting
or what we are not voting for." The President believed the Supreme Court
opinion on school segregation "specifically provided [that] there be a gradual implementation, and referred it back to the district courts, so that it

should be gradual"—that was because the justices recognized "the deep ruts of prejudice." He stressed that American children needed schools "right now, immediately, today," and that he thought nothing should delay the school construction bill.

Eisenhower was equally assertive about, and sympathetic toward, southern defiance. Regarding the "Southern Manifesto," signed in March by one hundred lawmakers in Congress, which called the Supreme Court decision "illegal," he acknowledged that "we are probably going to be busy" on that question "for a while." Eisenhower, in fact, was a states' righter himself—more so than Truman ever was—so, as he said, he did not interpret the manifesto as an attempt at "nullification," a position he regarded as politically wise. For by being considerate toward the South, he was giving himself breathing room in cases where states were openly defying the decision—because that "would be a place where we get to a very bad spot for the simple reason" that he was sworn to uphold the Constitution. "I can never abandon or refuse to carry out my own duty," he said. For him, though, the important thing was that the Supreme Court had said that "progress must be gradual." He noted as progress that more than a quarter-million black children in border and some southern states already had been integrated into previously all-white schools, and the Texas Supreme Court had recently declared that any law or provision in the state constitution that contravened the U.S. Constitution was null and void.

"So let us remember," Eisenhower said, "that there are people who are ready to approach this thing with the moderation, but with the determination to make progress that the Supreme Court asked for." This was the time, he stressed, "when we must be understanding without being complacent, when we must be understanding of other people's deep emotions, as well as our own." He not only gave further comfort to the diehard segregationists, but he also took a swipe at the NAACP by declaring that "extremists on neither side are going to help this situation." Americans should "remember this one thing, and it is very important. The people who have this deep emotional reaction on the other side were not acting over these past three generations in defiance of law. They were acting in compliance with the law as interpreted by the Supreme Court of the United States under the decision of 1896." It was therefore "going to take time for them to adjust their thinking and their progress to" the reversal of that position.

Mitchell was especially bothered that Eisenhower's philosophy contradicted his 1953 position of upholding the law regarding the desegregation of the armed services and schools in federally impacted districts. Why could he not take a similarly firm stand now, when the issues were truly national and more far-reaching? Mitchell wanted to know. The problem was that 1953 was political light-years from 1956; Eisenhower was now thinking more like a candidate than President.

Mitchell was equally troubled that Stewart Udall, a liberal whom he admired, "would criticize those who disagree with the Stevenson and Eisenhower positions on this amendment." In a telegram to the congressman, Mitchell noted that the NAACP had condemned the presidential candidates' equivocation "on this vital issue." Hurt because Eisenhower and others had labeled the NAACP leaders as extremists, he complained to Udall that it was "most unfair to equate those who are struggling to preserve democracy with the Eastland camp of anarchists who are seeking to destroy orderly government."

As Mitchell had feared, the President's philosophy of moderation encouraged defiance. In the wake of the *Brown* decision in 1954, the Louisiana legislature had passed a bill to maintain segregation under state police power to protect "health, morals, better education, and peace." Another bill that the legislature passed provided for cutting off state financing to any public school that eliminated racial segregation. That year, the Mississippi legislature, in a special session, approved a constitutional amendment that would give the state power to abolish public schools. The Georgia legislature also adopted a constitutional amendment to permit the establishment of private schools to maintain segregation. "Come hell or high water," Georgia Governor Marvin Griffin said, "races will not be mixed in Georgia Schools."

Now at a meeting in Richmond in January 1956, governors Thomas B. Stanley of Virginia, Griffin of Georgia, James P. Coleman of Mississippi, and George Bell Timmerman of South Carolina took a united stand against school integration. They agreed to have their state legislatures adopt a resolution of interposition, request congressional action supporting their position, and use "legal measures" to prevent school integration. Governor Luther Hodges of North Carolina, who attended the meeting as an observer, did not join in the plan, but he said that he found the discussion "substantial."

The following month, students rioted and stoned Autherine Lucy after she was enrolled at the University of Alabama. She was then suspended. A federal judge ordered her readmitted, but university officials expelled her, claiming that she had made baseless charges against them. The Alabama legislature passed a resolution praising this, and the Eisenhower administration did nothing to protect Lucy's constitutional rights.* The Southern

---

*The celebrated Lucy case, *Adams* v. *Lucy,* did not arise from the Supreme Court's 1954 and 1955 decisions, because Lucy had sought admission under the earlier Supreme Court's decision of *Sweatt* v. *Painter,* handed down in 1950.

Manifesto was adopted in the wake of this defiance and was the highpoint of reaction.

Next, several southern states went after the NAACP itself. The attorney general of Louisiana, invoking a 1924 anti–Ku Klux Klan law that had not been used previously, demanded the NAACP's membership list. The NAACP refused to give it to him, so the attorney general obtained a court injunction barring the association from operating in the state. In June, the attorney general of Alabama obtained a similar injunction, and a judge imposed a $100,000 fine on the organization because it refused a similar demand for its membership list. Texas and Georgia made the same demands on the NAACP. Georgia even jailed the Atlanta NAACP branch president because he did not respond promptly to a charge that the organization had failed to pay income taxes. The Virginia legislature, at a special session in September, passed a law prohibiting the NAACP or any lawyer representing it from challenging racial discrimination in the courts.

Mitchell responded to the attacks by intensifying his efforts in Washington to get Congress to uphold the *Brown* decision and to protect other constitutional rights of minorities. He welcomed the Supreme Court's determination to uphold the equal protection doctrine enunciated in *Brown,* which was demonstrated when, on March 5, 1956, it reaffirmed the ruling of a lower court that had ordered the University of North Carolina to admit three black students. A week later, the Court ruled in a case involving the University of Florida that its order for the gradual elimination of segregation in public schools in *Brown* "had no application to a case involving a Negro applying for admission to a state law school," and that therefore the university had to admit at once a black student who had been seeking admission for seven years. [14]

Testifying before a subcommittee of the House Committee on Education and Labor in April 1956, on bills to amend public laws relating to federal aid to education and school construction in defense-impacted areas, Mitchell explained that the difference between attitudes on the nonsegregation amendments—such as those that had been included in the Selective Service and the Hill-Burton acts—during the period prior to *Brown* and subsequently was that discrimination was now clearly defined to mean segregation. Consequently, Powell Amendment–type safeguards were now, much more so than in the past, political hazards for some southern politicians, because they could not hide behind the "separate but equal" doctrine.

Given Eisenhower's moderate approach to upholding *Brown,* it was clear to Mitchell that the principal "remedy available to the victims of injustice" would remain costly court action. Furthermore, Mitchell re-

minded the subcommittee, some southern judges—notably in Virginia—
"were actively working to prevent those who seek their civil rights from
being represented by counsel of their own choosing." He maintained that it
was only when residents of those states realized "that Federal benefits and
obedience to the law of the land go hand in hand" that much of the opposition to discrimination would end.

On January 24, the House Committee on Education approved the
school construction bill (H.R. 7535); but, by a vote of 17 to 10 the same
day, it rejected an amendment from Congressman Powell that would have
required the giving of federal aid only to states that complied with *Brown*.
In the House Rules Committee, where it had been sent on its way to the
full House, the bill became stalled by intense maneuvering for several
months, as opponents of the antisegregation safeguard attempted to have a
bill reported out with a closed rule that would have prevented the addition
of the Powell Amendment on the House floor.* Failing to get the closed
rule, opponents mapped plans to defeat the Powell Amendment at the next
opportunity, in a Committee of the Whole House, when the congressman's
votes on the House floor would not be recorded. But, Mitchell told Powell,
because so many members supported the amendment "and are anxious to
let their constituents know where they stand, we will make every effort" to
see that there was a recorded vote. To accomplish this, he promised that
"we will be certain that proper observations are made from the gallery."[15]

After several false starts, supporters forced the bill out of the Rules
Committee in June. As debate on the Powell Amendment was about to
begin, Mitchell was encouraged by the support he had received the previous week at the NAACP convention in San Francisco from the delegates,
who passed a resolution declaring that those who opposed the Powell
Amendment were, "in reality, voting to give money for what they know
will be more segregation." He concluded that when "all the fine words and
lofty statements" were stripped away, the reality was that

> some are for the school bill for political reasons. Others are for it
> because they sincerely want to see the children of the nation go to
> classrooms in better buildings. In both instances, however, they are
> willing to sacrifice the civil rights of colored people in order to
> obtain these ends. No amount of editorial writing or speech mak-
> ing will change this dreadful truth.

* At the same time, within the House Rules Committee, Congressman Graham Barden of South Carolina, chairman of the House Committee on Education and Labor, had asked for an *open* rule because he
wanted to introduce an amendment to remove a provision of the bill that incorporated the minimum
wage requirements of the Bacon-Davis Act, which organized labor supported. Mitchell found it interesting that Barden "was much more vigorous in his attack of this than he was on the Powell Amendment, although he announced his opposition to both."

*   *   *

Back in May, the NAACP national office in New York had expressed
similar dismay over an editorial in *The New York Times* opposing the Powell
Amendment. The NAACP had said that the Supreme Court in *Brown* had
in essence placed the responsibility on federal courts for determining
whether schools were being desegregated in a manner consistent with "all
deliberate speed." The Court had urged "a start in good faith." But, the
NAACP had said, the South on the whole had adopted an attitude of
defiance. The NAACP had said that "the knowledge that moral support for
integration" in other parts of the country was widespread and wholehearted
was comforting, but that did not "desegregate a single school." So the
burden of forcing compliance was placed on black parents in the South and
organizations to which they turned for support. The NAACP therefore continued to regard the Powell Amendment as a legislative means for alleviat-
ing that burden. [16]

Preliminary debate on the federal aid to school construction bill began in
the Committee of the Whole House on June 28. The Powell Amendment was
offered on July 3. Mitchell's hopes were buoyed when lawmakers approved it
that day by a vote of 164 to 116. But two days later, the amendment was
dropped amid parliamentary confusion. Upon realizing the mistake, lawmakers voted the amendment back in by 177 to 123. Neither of those votes
was recorded. But, as unmistakable proof for Mitchell that a majority in the
House supported the Powell Amendment, on the third vote on the measure,
which was recorded when the bill went from the Committee of the Whole to
the House proper, a solid majority of 225 to 192 approved it.

Now the lawmakers worked to approve the school construction bill
(H.R. 7535) and to resolve differences over the level of funding, among
other things. The crucial vote was on a motion from Congressman Samuel
McConnell, Republican of Pennsylvania, to recommit the entire bill to the
Education and Labor Committee in order to add amendments that would
have included the major portion of the Eisenhower administration's federal
aid program. Had McConnell's motion carried, the Powell Amendment
would have been passed by the House. But the McConnell motion lost by
a vote of 262 to 158—with most of the Democrats voting against it.
That ended any hope for passing not only the school construction bill that
year, but also the Powell Amendment. Of course, had the Republicans
been willing to accept the Democrats' bill, there would also have been no
problem.

Mitchell concluded that it was partisan politics and not the Powell
Amendment that killed the School Construction Bill in the House on
Thursday, July 5, 1956. He nevertheless was heartened by the clear-cut

votes in which the House refused to provide funds to states that were defying the U.S. Supreme Court school decision.

Examining in a partisan light, 148 Republicans and 77 Democrats favored the amendment on the roll call vote, while 146 Democrats and 46
Republicans were opposed. On the final vote (194–224) on the bill (H.R.
7535), 75 Republicans and 119 Democrats voted for it; 119 Republicans
and 105 Democrats opposed it. *Congressional Quarterly* noted that more than
90 Republicans voted for the Powell Amendment and then turned around
and voted against the main bill to which they had attached the safeguard.
Despite the setback, the protracted battle for what would eventually become Title VI of the Civil Rights Act of 1964 was well launched.

Mitchell was consoled that the House had thrice passed the Powell
Amendment. He knew that many liberals had to be properly educated
about the true meaning of the civil rights struggle before he could succeed
in his mission. He and Wilkins had retained Herbert Lehman's firm support. But Lehman did not run for reelection in 1956, so the New Yorker
would no longer be the bill's sponsor in the Senate at a time when Hubert
Humphrey and other potential supporters were tied up with the struggle
over other civil rights legislation. It was Richard Bolling's telling observation that the bill's fate reminded him of Voltaire's statement "The best is
the enemy of the good." Bolling concluded:

> It is not pleasant to consider how effective a tool in the hands of
> reaction the issue of civil rights may become unless liberals in both
> parties in Congress and in the country recognize the manner and
> purpose of its use. The passage of civil rights legislation as such is
> the way to assure to all our citizens their rights, but we may de-
> prive all our citizens of better educational, medical, economic and
> other opportunities if we allow the cause for which we fight with
> all our skill, energy and conviction to be used to defeat the other
> "goods."

Two days later, the House passed extensions to PL 875 and PL 815
providing federal aid to schools in federally impacted areas and for school
construction, without adding antisegregation safeguards. Mitchell was
pleased, though, that the program to eliminate segregated schools on military posts had been completed and the effort to end racial designations on
orders and records was progressing.[17]

But this success was offset by the President's policy of moderation toward ending segregation in public schools and other civilian areas. Mitchell
thought the period at times resembled the Civil War era. President Lin-

coln, he observed, was so reluctant to move on freeing the slaves that Frederick Douglass

> referred to him as the slow moving train in Washington. There were times when Lincoln seemed to believe that merely letting sleeping dogs lie would solve some of the problems of that day. But Lincoln found that he had to come to grips with the question of human slavery. The constant outcry of the people who believed in just solutions helped him make up his mind.
>
> Somehow, both President Eisenhower and candidate Stevenson seem to be under the impression that those who want the U.S. Supreme Court decision in the school cases upheld are extremists. They seem to think that if these people would just shut up there would be no problem.

Encouraged by the debacle in Congress over school construction aid in 1956, Mitchell noted, South Carolina began firing black teachers because they refused to sign a pledge to support segregation. That was in addition to the efforts to drive the NAACP out of business in several states. This defiance continued to spread in the South even as Eisenhower submitted another request to Congress on January 28, 1957, for $1.3 billion in school construction aid. Mitchell provided more testimony for Congress on the difficulties of getting the South to comply with the law of the land.* Perhaps, Mitchell said, the clearest statement of resistance had been provided by Governor Marvin Griffin of Georgia in his state address on January 15: "More than two and a half years have passed since the United States Supreme Court, in its decision of May 17, 1954, sought to usurp from state and local governments the administration of school affairs. The effect of this unconstitutional and unlawful decree has not been felt in Georgia as yet. That fact is no mere accident. The determined and cooperative efforts of a dedicated people, a steadfast general assembly, and an administration committed unequivocally toward preservation of our cherished institutions—all of these working together have stemmed the tide."

---

* Mitchell testified before the House Subcommittee on General Education on February 26, 1957, about southern legislatures' opposition to implementing the *Brown* decision. Typifying the spreading pattern were South Carolina's passage of a law forbidding employment of NAACP members by the state, counties, school districts, and municipalities; Mississippi's establishment of the State Sovereignty Commission, which announced that it would use secret investigators to halt public school integration; North Carolina's adoption of the so-called Pearsall Plan in order to permit the state to maintain segregation through private tuition payments and local-option school closings; and Virginia's passage of twenty-three laws, including measures giving the governor authority to take over an integrated school, to reassign its pupils, and to reopen it on a segregated basis. Those Virginia laws were in addition to one that permitted the state to sidestep the desegregation order by allowing public funds to be used to educate children in private schools.

But, on the question of federal aid, Mitchell noted, the governor had this to say: "Georgia has forged into the lead in the southeast in many other fields. One of the most important of these is the fact that she stands first in the seven-state area in the total amount of Federal funds brought into this state in benefits for our people under various matching programs. An alert state administration, taking advantage of all that is due Georgia, brought in $91,800,000 [in] federal grant payments in 1955, exceeding neighboring states in amounts ranging from $15 million to $47 million."

That statement, Mitchell said, was a "beautiful illustration of the philosophy of Gimmie and Git. When funds are being passed out, the governor of Georgia says, 'Gimmie the lion's share.' When it comes to obeying the law, he wants the Supreme Court and everyone else who favors integration in schools to 'git out of the state.'"[18]

CHAPTER TWELVE

At the Crossroads

"As an officer of the NAACP, which is non-partisan," Mitchell wrote former President Truman, "I am not identified with either party." (He was a registered Independent and would remain so for the duration of his lobbying career.) He told Truman, "I am happy to say that I voted for you as President and would vote for you again if you were running for any office in any state, territory, or city in which I could cast a ballot." History, Mitchell said, showed "that you were a far better judge of the American sense of fair play than those who opposed your civil rights program."

Mitchell's complimentary letter was prompted by Truman's criticism of the attitude of the Eighty-fourth Congress toward civil rights, that "some people are so afraid of rocking the boat that they stop rowing." Mitchell heartily agreed with Truman's observation that "you can't cure a moral problem by ignoring it." Truman's "forthright declaration on civil rights made it possible to talk about the evil of segregation openly," he said. Truman had placed the federal government at the head of the fight against segregation. "Previously many people seemed to regard it as a subject that was taboo in polite society." He felt that President Eisenhower had "supported and carried forward the heritage left by you in the Executive Branch of government." However, Mitchell regretted that Congress, whether under Republicans or Democrats, was "still a haven for pussyfooting, compromise and sabotage of civil rights."

Mitchell did not believe that Truman had seen the "ultimate dimensions" of what was needed to remedy racial injustices. For example, "he might not have believed that you could peacefully achieve desegregation in hotels and restaurants of the South." Mitchell felt with forthright presidential leadership that was possible. Nevertheless, he thought that, relative to prevalent attitudes, Truman was a giant on civil rights—a vast improvement over Roosevelt, who had not only been slippery but had always protected his flanks. Even though he had created the FEPC, Roosevelt never supported the NAACP's fight for antilynching legislation, the most important civil rights issue of that time. Mitchell felt that Truman had displayed more courage than Roosevelt in bucking the South on such issues as his civil rights executive orders, employment programs for blacks, and his appointment of William H. Hastie as a judge for the U.S. Court of Appeals for the Third Circuit, and in his attempt to implement the report of the President's Committee on Civil Rights through legislation.

Mitchell shared White's belief that neither legislation nor litigation could by itself cure any evil. But, said White on *America's Town Meeting of the Air* broadcast in 1951, "both of them, and particularly legislation, are among the most potent methods in a democratic society to create public acceptance of the basic principle of Democracy; namely, the right of every citizen to live, to work, to play and to pray as a free person in a free society." No American, he said, "as reasonable and intelligent human beings" could or would deny that right to another individual "if we honestly believe in Democracy." So it "was imperative that our Congress, our state legislatures, and our city governments swiftly and unequivocally enact whatever legislation is wise, effective, and equitable to wipe out now America's greatest menace to unity, health, and national prestige, and that is the ghetto."[1]

With the filibuster in mind, Mitchell saw little hope for success as he assessed prospects for civil rights legislation in the Eighty-third Congress in 1953. There were 48 Republicans and 25 Democrats outside the Deep South in the Senate. Along with Wayne Morse, an Independent, they represented a total of 74 potential votes for civil rights. That was probably why, Mitchell concluded, some northern senators were stoutly maintaining that the present cloture rule was not insurmountable. He knew, however, that at least 9 Republicans from states like Colorado, Kentucky, Nevada, New Hampshire, North Dakota, and Wyoming were likely to continue opposing curbs on the filibuster. That meant he could count on only 39 Republican votes. Since Democrats from such states as Arizona, Colorado, Kentucky, Nevada, and Oklahoma were also expected to continue their past opposition to curbs on the filibuster, he expected support from only 19, for a total of 59, including Morse. That was a solid majority, which, with the 332 Republicans and Democrats in the House outside the Deep South, could pass civil rights legislation. He was nevertheless skeptical. As he had begun to realize back in 1949, the South could no longer be blamed as "the chief stumbling block" to civil rights legislation. He said, "We must continue to turn the spotlight on the members of Congress from northern and Border states who have the power to act if they want to do so." Those legislators, he charged, could no longer pretend "that the tropical zone of prejudice is in Georgia and Mississippi," because, as the records showed, South Dakota's Karl E. Mundt was just as much against civil rights as South Carolina's Olin Johnston.

Furthermore, on January 3, the House adopted its old rules, thus continuing the power of the Rules Committee to block civil rights and other liberal legislation. The chairman of the Rules Committee derived his power from the House procedure under which chairmen of standing committees that favorably reported out bills first had to obtain a rule stating the terms of debate on the House floor. The chairman of the Rules Committee could sit on a bill unless his colleagues forced him to report it out. To reduce the power of conservatives on the Rules Committee to block legislation they did not favor, the House in 1949 adopted a "twenty-one-day rule," which enabled standing committee chairmen, upon being recognized by the Speaker of the House, to request that the bill be brought directly to the floor if a rule had not been granted within the specified number of days. Two years later the conservatives got the House to repeal the twenty-one-day rule.

Mitchell was concerned that even though all the key committees were now controlled by Republicans, alibis would still be manufactured for inaction. What was worse, such excuses would be supported by "a handful of colored politicians who have graduated to a kind of country club status in American life"—clearly an allusion to Chicago's Dawson, one of three black members of the House (the others were Powell and Diggs). Mitchell hoped that they would "remember that on the social measurement scale, the distance between owning a Cadillac and pushing a janitor's broom may be just one little depression. We also remind them that as long as humans are cruel enough to roll bombs inside a New York tavern because those inside are Spanish-speaking, the lynch spirit is not dead in the United States." (Despite his occasional jabs at the conservative Dawson, whom he regarded as "an interesting person," Mitchell grew to like him because he recognized him as a shrewd—if overly cautious—political operator. One such demonstration was Dawson's observation to Mitchell that "you are going to get that [Powell] amendment through because they don't want federal aid to education." Dawson opposed the Powell Amendment because he felt the aid was more important.)[2]

As was the practice in each session of Congress since 1949 when Senator Howard McGrath, a Democrat from Rhode Island, introduced the first omnibus civil rights bill, Adam Clayton Powell sponsored one in the Eighty-third Congress. The NAACP Washington Bureau found that combining the Powell bill with another submitted in the Eighty-second Congress by Emanuel Celler would provide an even stronger measure. The Powell bill had sections relating to lynching, fair employment, housing, and education. Both bills provided for establishment of a Civil Rights Commission to study racial discrimination continually and to make recommendations to the President (an idea proposed in 1947 by the President's Committee on Civil Rights), and for establishment of a Civil Rights Division in the Department of Justice. While the Celler bill called for additional FBI agents to investigate civil rights cases, the Powell bill provided for an investigative staff under the direction of the Civil Rights Division. The Celler bill would have created a Joint Congressional Committee on Civil Rights. Both bills would have amended and strengthened various federal codes to protect better the rights of blacks, including the right to vote, and would have eliminated segregation and discrimination in interstate commerce and established criminal and civil sanctions against the persons and carriers guilty of such offenses.

With the omnibus and several other civil rights bills that had been introduced in 1953 sitting dead in the water, Mitchell concluded toward the end of the year that if the Republican leadership was convinced that it must act on this area, it might move to pass a weak antilynching bill, a good anti-Jim Crow travel bill, an acceptable plan to reorganize and strengthen the functions of the Department of Justice in the area of civil rights, or possibly worthwhile legislation to protect members of the armed services against assault and violence by civilians. At the same time, the Republican leadership might accept a constitutional amendment to repeal the poll tax (which Alabama, Arkansas, Mississippi, Texas, and Virginia still required) in place of the "good law" that Mitchell preferred to remove that obstacle to voting in Dixie.

Mitchell wrote Republican party leaders urging them to put civil rights on the agenda when they met with Eisenhower on December 17–19. He reminded them that during the 1952 presidential campaign, the GOP had published a pamphlet entitled "The Republican Party and the Negro," which said that a GOP administration would "not be tied down by a southern anti-Negro bloc in control of Congress and committees." The current committee chairmen, he pointed out, were all from northern states. As examples, the chairman of the Senate Labor and Public Welfare Committee— which controlled the fate of fair employment practice legislation—was from New Jersey; the chairman of the Senate Judiciary Committee—which would consider antilynching and other related civil rights legislation—was from North Dakota; and the heads of the House and the Senate Interstate and

Foreign Commerce committees—which would pass on legislation to supplement Supreme Court decisions in this area—were from Ohio and New Jersey, respectively.

Mitchell sent the lawmakers a review he had prepared to show "that our organization is eager at all times to give the public a full and fair picture of progress no matter which party is in power." Although the document listed several important gains achieved through executive action by the President, it concluded that "we cannot report a single positive action in the Congress." The President would not be running for office in 1954, but several senators and representatives came from states where civil rights could determine the election. Mitchell therefore hoped that the GOP leaders would urge the President to join them in working for the passage of civil rights laws.

The Eighty-third Congress closed as it began—with a record of failure on civil rights. The strongest effort was one to end Jim Crow practices in interstate travel. This attempt centered in the House on H.R. 7304, which would have imposed a fine of $1,000 on carriers that separated passengers according to race. H.R. 7304 was a combination of bills introduced by Democrats Powell and Dawson and Massachusetts Republican John Heselton. Its counterpart in the Senate was S. 2672, introduced by Irving Ives and another Republican, John M. Butler of Maryland. The Senate, however, refused to act on the bill until the House passed it.

The House Interstate Committee did not hold hearings on H.R. 7304 until May 1954. Mitchell complained that some committee members delayed to see "what the Supreme Court would do in the school cases," then after the *Brown* decision they said that "it would be a good idea to let the dust settle before bringing up any other civil rights proposal."

On July 21, 1954, the committee finally reported out H.R. 7304 by a 19 to 7 vote. Leo E. Allen of Illinois, chairman of the House Rules Committee, to which the bill had been referred, maintained that he could not act on the measure because the House leadership thought it was too late in the session. To force action, on August 3, Heselton attempted to have the rules suspended so that the House could pass the bill. That maneuver required the consent of Majority Leader Charles Halleck of Indiana and Minority Leader Sam Rayburn of Texas. Halleck agreed, but Rayburn adamantly refused. Until Congress adjourned, Mitchell kept urging Republican leaders and the White House to induce Allen to reconsider his opposition and give the bill a favorable rule, to no avail.

In the Senate, Illinois Republican Everett Dirksen's bill to establish a commission to investigate discrimination was generally regarded as an attempt to avoid creating an FEPC with enforcement powers. As a result of the NAACP's opposition, the Senate Judiciary Committee, where the

Dirksen bill (S. 1) was sent, did not report it out. The measure that Mitchell considered a bona fide FEPC bill was S. 692, introduced by Ives, Humphrey, and others, that was reported out of the Senate Labor and Public
Welfare Committee with only Alabama's Lister Hill opposing it. An FEPC
with enforcement powers was supported by all the Democrats on the Labor
Committee and opposed by Republicans, with the exception of Ives. But
the Senate did not bring up the bill for debate. Throughout the session,
Mitchell thought the administration might support H.R. 7304, but at no
time did it appear to him that the administration would give FEPC and
other civil rights measures, including antisegregation safeguards to various
bills, even mild support.

Neither did efforts to attach antisegregation amendments to various
bills get anywhere in the House or Senate that year. Mitchell gained small
comfort from the defeat of proposed constitutional amendments to set aside
the Supreme Court decision in the school cases sponsored by Senator James
Eastland and, in the House, by James Bell Williams, both of Mississippi.
Mitchell also managed, with Powell's help, to modify the sweeping powers
that the revised Organic Act of the Virgin Islands would have given the
governor: While the governor was given power to reorganize the current
executive branch in the Virgin Islands without the consent of the legislature, all future reorganization would have to be done with the legislature's consent. Mitchell was disappointed, however, that the House and
Senate killed bills to give statehood to Hawaii and Alaska, which would
likely have added four pro-civil-rights votes in the Senate. Not considered
were antilynching, anti-poll-tax, and other civil rights bills. In listing the
civil rights record of the Eighty-third Congress, Majority Leader William
Knowland, drawing on the record of Eisenhower's Republican-led administration, mentioned the Supreme Court decision against public school segregation, the ending of segregation in the armed services, action against
segregation in the nation's capital, appointment of blacks to government,
and other actions of the executive branch. But his report did not mention
FEPC, anti-Jim-Crow travel, and the other civil rights bills on which Congress had failed to act. So, Mitchell said, it appeared that the members of
the Eighty-third Congress would run in November on civil rights records
made by the Supreme Court and the executive branch.

Mitchell warned that the voters would have the last word on the civil
rights issue.[3] Earlier in the year, he had challenged the lawmakers to act by
noting that the Republican party's most effective force "for winning back a
substantial part of the Negro vote" was President Eisenhower, who had "repeatedly spoken and acted against segregation and discrimination based on
race." But, Mitchell said, "let no one be fooled by the applause given to"
the President, for he would not be running for office in 1954. He chided

the Republican lawmakers for being "content to ride on the President's coat-tail," letting him carry the civil rights ball by way of executive action. "The great leaders of the party have been content in the Congress to strangle and destroy important civil rights bills." The Democrats, the louder advocates during the last campaign, now were "signing peace pacts with anti–civil rights forces for the purpose of soft-pedaling civil rights." Mitchell was also very unhappy that Eisenhower had ignored all pleas for support on civil rights legislation. He blamed the administration and leaders of both parties for Congress's failure to pass such measures. [4]

Election Day, 1954, brought a change in Congress, but without the expected Democratic sweep. The results were nevertheless portentous for civil rights. The elections made Eisenhower the third President in the twentieth century—the others were Wilson and Truman—to face opposition majorities in both houses at midterm. Mitchell struggled to fathom the swirling political crosscurrents, and his only certain conclusion was that prospects for the passage of civil rights legislation in the Eighty-fourth Congress were dimmer than previously.

The first problem was that Eisenhower would have to tread gingerly to win bipartisan support in Congress for his legislation. Even more serious, some powerful southerners controlled Congress at a very critical time. In the House, Sam Rayburn was returned as speaker. North Carolina's Graham Barden again became chairman of the Labor Committee, which handled FEPC bills. Virginia's seventy-one-year-old Howard Smith, a bitter enemy of Roosevelt-Truman liberalism and a diehard segregationist to boot, now headed the Rules Committee. One of the few consolations was that Emanuel Celler became chairman of the House Judiciary Committee, which handled antilynching legislation.

In the Senate, the chances for changing Rule XXII were about the same under the Democrats as they had been under the Republicans. William Jenner of Indiana, chairman of the Senate Rules Committee under the GOP, was replaced by Democrat Carl Hayden of Arizona, a filibuster supporter.

Former Governor J. Strom Thurmond of South Carolina, who had been National States' Rights party candidate for President in 1948 and an open Eisenhower supporter in 1952, now joined the Senate after staging the unprecedented coup of winning election as a Democratic write-in candidate by a two-to-one majority. James Eastland, too smart to be a "rootin'-tootin'" race-baiter like Theodore Bilbo, as many called this deposed senator, through seniority moved within a hairbreadth of the chairmanship of the Senate Judiciary Committee as its second-ranking member.

Lyndon Johnson, reelected for a second term, moved into the cockpit of power as majority leader of the Senate. He remained an avowed advocate of states' rights and local control, reflecting the backward attitude of his constituents. Mitchell was at first ambivalent toward Johnson. He was aware of Johnson's humanitarian record in Texas during the New Deal when, as an official with the National Youth Administration, he had demonstrated sympathy for blacks and Mexicans. He was then known in Washington as Mary McLeod Bethune's fair-haired boy, and Mitchell and other blacks like Robert Weaver and William Hastie accepted her high opinion of him. Mitchell's favorable regard for him was also strengthened by Johnson's having helped his brother-in-law Carl Downs when the latter was president of Sam Houston College. As a congressman, Johnson had arranged for a World's Fair building to be moved to the Houston campus, where it was converted into a dormitory. When Johnson ran for the Senate, Mitchell formed a little cheering squad with other blacks. Johnson thus came to the Senate with the aura of a moderate.

It was Missouri's Stuart Symington who introduced Mitchell to Johnson. Mitchell found him to be a typical contemporary Democrat with an overriding concern for holding the party together that was shared by others like the black conservative William Dawson. Their watchword was "Don't get in a fight in the Senate over civil rights." They were willing to do battle over that issue in the House but argued that to do so in the Senate was divisive and hindered progress on other programs with broad advantages for the party. They strongly supported court decisions barring segregation, and antidiscrimination executive orders. Johnson's acknowledgment to Mitchell that this, too, was basically his position set them on a collision course that quickly became acrimonious.

Mitchell knew that Johnson was an astute politician. His knowledge of Johnson's penchant for background wheeling and dealing was supported by Drew Pearson's December 1954 report in his nationally syndicated "Washington Merry-Go-Round" column telling how masterful a job the Texan did keeping Democratic forces united during the wrenching debate over the anti-Communist smear campaign of Wisconsin's Senator Joe McCarthy and his cashing in on commitments obtained backstage. Johnson wanted to make Eastland chairman of the Senate Internal Security Subcommittee of the Judiciary Committee, which was responsible for investigating hate groups, where Eastland could continue the harmful work of his now-discredited friend McCarthy. Harley M. Kilgore of West Virginia, chairman of the Judiciary Committee, was flatly opposed. Johnson got his way by proposing to appoint to the Judiciary Committee two archreactionary Democrats—Price Daniel of Texas and Alan Bible of Nevada, who would have voted with the opposition and thrown control of the committee to the Republicans. Kilgore's power as chairman would have been nullified, so he agreed to have Eastland forced on him. With victory in hand, Johnson appointed Daniel and Bible, as well as Thurmond, to the Interstate and Foreign Commerce Committee, which controlled the fate of legislation Mitchell wanted in this area.

Mitchell adopted a strategy of persuasion rather than confrontation while he considered his options. He declared that the election in both the North and South "sharply emphasized the sophistication of voters who favor civil rights legislation." The results were "a warning to both major parties that they will never get a comfortable margin of control in Congress until they show that civil rights pledges made at campaign time are adopted as party policy in the legislative caucuses." He said that the NAACP Washington Bureau's experience was that when neither party had a good legislative record, voters in key states scrutinized closely the records of individual candidates in order to make a choice.

Republicans in North Carolina and Maryland won reelection even though their Democratic opponents had tried to use the Eisenhower administration's civil rights accomplishments against them. Mitchell also thought the victories of Senators Estes Kefauver of Tennessee, John Sparkman of Alabama, and W. Kerr Scott of North Carolina were "living proof that appeals to race prejudice" had lost their potency in the "new South." Newly elected Governor Theodore R. McKeldin of Maryland was another symbol of how injecting racism into a political campaign could backfire, since his opponent had received support from segregationists. Kefauver was under unrelenting attack for supporting the Democratic party's strong civil rights platform in 1952. Sparkman was similarly under fire because despite his anti-civil-rights record he had helped to write that platform; Scott was accused of supporting the Supreme Court decision outlawing public school segregation. "No one," Mitchell said, could pretend "that all of these men are great exponents of civil rights." But "each took all of the fire that the promoters of Jim Crow could pour on them and each was able to get elected." Liberal Democrats like Paul Douglas and Hubert Humphrey easily won reelection to the Senate.

Douglas, a Quaker, was one of the more colorful of Mitchell's allies. He entered the Senate with a great sense of tradition, in the footsteps of giants like Henry Clay, John C. Calhoun, Thomas H. Benton, Daniel Webster, Stephen A. Douglas, Charles Sumner, John Sharp Williams, "Fighting Bob" La Follette, and George Norris. He was actually filling the seat occupied a century earlier by Stephen Douglas, a realization, he acknowledged, that "humbles a freshman." Mitchell found Douglas especially valuable because he was a living embodiment of his own credo: "Support one's party in all procedural matters everywhere. Argue substantive programs within party councils in the hope of gaining a majority within the party. But when the chips are down in the Senate, a senator should vote his profound individual convictions on substantive matters regardless of who is with or against him."

Based on the trend, Mitchell predicted that Eisenhower would have the edge in the 1956 presidential election because the most influential Democrats "have shown a fatal tendency to sacrifice civil rights in the interest of party harmony"—a clear reference to Johnson. He concluded that the national elections had "strengthened the cause of freedom."

The obviously reactionary lineup of the Eighty-fourth Congress was a test for Mitchell's faith in the essential goodness of his fellow humans. He saw signs that the South's rebellion against *Brown* was strengthening rather than weakening the nation's moral fiber and commitment to the protection of the rights of all citizens regardless of race or religion. Furthermore, Americans were aware that America's race relations were the "Achilles' heel of our foreign policy."

An even more important source of inner strength for Mitchell was the Christian Church, which he felt was "perhaps the most revolutionary force" in American society despite its weaknesses. With the World Council of Churches, the Catholic Church, and a host of other faiths declaring that the Supreme Court's school segregation decision was "right and just," he said, "church leaders have at last discovered that Christianity must be more dynamic if it is to challenge Communism successfully." An example was the Catholic Church, which was leading the way in the South. He noted that Archbishop Francis Rummel of Louisiana had "dared to call segregation a sin" and Bishop Vincent S. Waters of North Carolina had ended segregation in a local church. "When the event took place, he was on hand in person to preach the sermon and to interview those who objected." Mitchell believed that Jesus would have done the same thing. He was certain that segregation could not survive "because it is contrary to every decent concept that Americans are taught from the time they leave the cradle until they are lowered into the grave."

Given these and other signs of change, Mitchell concluded that the racial convulsions in Mississippi and other parts of the country might "continue for a short time in the future, but the separation of races as a way of life in the South no longer has any practical value for those who have supported it in the past."[5]

The question of time, however, was relative. Although Mitchell believed that Congress would one day pass civil rights legislation, he knew that whether that occurred sooner or later depended on the amount of political heat Congress felt. Toward the end of February he launched, in Amityville, New York, a sustained, intense campaign to politicize and educate local black leadership through NAACP branches. His main target was the national Democratic party, which he charged had "traded its proud banner of civil rights that it waved in 1952 for the rebel flag of the Old South." Because of the abundance of goodwill in the country, he said, "we sometimes forget that the termites who have consistently tried to eat away the foundations of freedom and democracy are still at work." He reminded the Democrats that the Republicans learned the importance of civil rights the hard way. The GOP for many years ran on the memory of Abraham Lincoln. "Its leaders failed to realize that colored voters could honor the Great Emancipator in their hearts, but they could also be practical enough to cast their ballots against those members of his party who departed from his principles." Similarly, he said, "hundreds of thousands" of black voters loved Franklin D. Roosevelt. "But they are smart enough to detect and vote against Dixiecrats who try to cover anti-civil rights wolf fur with a harmony sheepskin."

Mitchell was particularly angry because in nearly two months the only hearings the Democrats had held were on a bill to restore segregation to the District of Columbia Fire Department. The hearings were conducted by Georgia's James C. Davis, chairman of the Subcommittee on Police, Fire and Traffic of the House Committee on the District of Columbia. Assisting Davis "as a kind of straight man" was John Bell Williams of Mississippi. Mitchell said the sessions sounded like an *Amos 'n' Andy* episode in which "the script was prepared by the Ku Klux Klan." Davis, he charged, knew that his bill could not pass, so his purpose was not to get a law enacted but to provoke racial incidents and turn back the civil rights clock in Washington. Mitchell's repeated denunciations of the bill showed his anxiety over the sharp increase of anti-civil-rights action. It deeply hurt him that Davis enjoyed the power of chairman because black voters in northern states had helped to elect a Democratic Congress.[6]

Equally disturbing for Mitchell was the myopia of normally faithful liberal allies in supporting an attempt in the Senate by Henry Cabot Lodge to change the constitutional provision of awarding the winning presidential candidate all electoral votes in a state to a system of proportional allotment matching the popular vote. Thus, for example, in Pennsylvania in the 1948 election, Republicans, who won the state, would have received approximately 19, the Democrats 16, and the Progressives 1 vote. If a candidate received less than 40 percent of the popular vote, the Lodge proposal, cosponsored in 1950 by Congressman Ed Gossett, Democrat of Texas, would have required lawmakers to vote as individuals rather than in blocs representing their states in a joint session of the House and Senate. Some liberals thought that the proposal was much more democratic than the current electoral system, which they considered archaic because it enabled a candidate with a minority of popular votes who had an electoral majority to become President.

Mitchell had an uncanny ability to smell a rotten situation. The drawback, as John A. Davis, Mitchell's former FEPC associate, showed in a
memorandum prepared for him, was that the Lodge proposal would have
drawn the political eyeteeth of all independent voters including blacks,
who could swing elections in big pivotal states like New York, New Jersey,
Pennsylvania, Ohio, Indiana, Michigan, Illinois, California, West Virginia, Kentucky, and Tennessee. Davis suggested that the timing of
Lodge's proposal was based on the view that the Republican party would be
a large minority entity in the pivotal industrial states, and he hoped to gain
a proportional share of votes for the GOP by adding those states to traditionally Republican ones in the North and West. Lodge also expected the
Democratic party, which he regarded as a "liberal" party, to be plagued by
splinter groups like the Dixiecrat, liberal, and labor factions of the party;
but while splitting northern electoral votes, the South would remain solidly
Democratic. Dixie would regain hegemony, driving out liberal and independent Democrats. These divisions would destroy the Democratic party,
assuring the GOP of 40 percent of the electoral votes in several states. Thus
the Lodge proposal would reduce the North's political influence. John
Davis maintained that the proposal would create a multiparty system and
destroy the President's effectiveness in foreign affairs.

As proof of the accuracy of Davis's analysis, which he circulated widely,
Mitchell noted that Senators Price Daniel and Karl E. Mundt, Republican
of South Dakota, had expressed views similar to Gossett's, to the effect that

> the electoral college permits and invites irresponsible control and
> domination by small organized minority groups, within the large
> pivotal states. It aggravates and accentuates the building up and
> solidification within these states of religious, economic, and racial
> blocs; small, definable, minority groups, organized along religious
> or economic or racial lines, by voting together, can and do hold a
> balance of power within these pivotal states. As a result, the politi-
> cal strategists in both parties make special appeals to those various
> groups as such. These groups have become more and more politi-
> cally conscious. They know their power.

Because few nonsoutherners recognized the danger, the Senate, reflecting the dominant influence of rural and small-population states, overwhelmingly approved the Lodge-Gossett Resolution with the help of
liberals like Hubert Humphrey. Protesting Humphrey's position, Mitchell
said that he respected the Minnesotan's belief that the Lodge-Gossett proposal represented "the next best thing to your own proposal of a direct
election of the President by the people." But, said Mitchell, Humphrey's

testimony before the House Rules Committee supporting the proposal had been misused by others with less progressive motives to show that liberals were divided on the issue. Furthermore, Mitchell complained, Humphrey "did not give sufficient weight to the views of the NAACP, CIO, and other persons such as Mr. Charles LaFollette, national director of the ADA."

As Davis suggested, Mitchell engineered the proposal's defeat in the House, where representation reflected a largely urban population, by organizing, almost overnight, a core group of about thirty congressmen to lead the struggle against the resolution. Mitchell was especially disturbed that, when he sought White House help, he was told that the President wanted to see the measure pass.

During the House debate, Clifford Case, leading the struggle, explained that had the proposal been in effect during the 1948 election, Georgia alone would have had more influence in determining the outcome than the much more populous states outside the South. Had the House not killed the proposal, Davis was certain, the states would have approved it with southern Democrats and Republicans voting as solid blocs. Rural areas also would have supported it in order to lessen the influence of the great urban states. The 1950 battle, however, was only a rehearsal for more concerted and expressly antiblack attempts at passage in 1951, when another measure, initially cosponsored by Daniel and Humphrey and subsequently by Mundt and Daniel, was again defeated, and in 1955–56, when the third proposal finally lost by 37 to 48 only because, as a constitutional amendment resolution, it required a two-thirds vote. Helping tip the scales against the resolution was a letter to *The New York Times* cosigned by Davis and nine eminent political scientists and historians.*

This time, in 1955, protesting more sharply Humphrey's cosponsoring the resolution with Daniel,** Roy Wilkins told the senator that the NAACP was "somewhat bewildered and distressed" over his action. But the NAACP was not being unfriendly toward him, as Humphrey had complained. The NAACP, Wilkins lectured him, did "not see the Hubert Humphrey of 1955 as the Hubert Humphrey of 1948," although the senator still was not a person to be denounced. "His record has been a good one and his basic convictions are similar to ours. He has wandered off the track a bit, but we view this wandering with sorrow rather than with

*Wallace S. Sayre, professor of public administration, Columbia University; David B. Truman, professor of government, Columbia University; Arthur Schlesinger, Jr., professor of history, Harvard University; Arthur W. McMahon, Eaton Professor of Public Administration, Columbia University; Samuel H. Beer, professor of government, Harvard University; Peter H. Odegard, chairman, Department of Government, University of California at Berkeley; Harvey C. Mansfield, chairman, Department of Political Science, The Ohio State University; Stephen K. Bailey, professor of public affairs, Princeton University; and Wilfred Binkley, professor of political science, Ohio Northern University.

**Other senators sponsoring the 1955 resolution (S.J.R. 31) were Alexander Wiley (R-Wis.), Wil-Mont.), Mike Mansfield (D-Mont.), and Richard L. Neuberger (D-Ore.).

anger." Mitchell turned the tide again in 1956 only after the most strenuous battle yet by convincing enough lawmakers of the antiblack motives of sponsors like Daniel. As an alternative, Mitchell supported direct election of the President, but such proposals were also defeated.[7]

Mitchell saw these political battles as demonstrations that unless blacks did "something about them, they could suddenly find themselves going backward instead of forward." After another major attempt in 1956, Mitchell became less concerned with this threat as the danger of its success diminished in succeeding years. Other problems were more persistent. He maintained that blacks could not rely on the courts or the executive branch alone to protect their rights. "We must exercise our political power so that the Congress of the United States will keep pace with the progress made by the executive and judicial branches of Government."

At the NAACP's 1954 Freedom Fulfillment Campaign in Washington, Mitchell had declared, "All of us are convinced that we shall reach our goal of full emancipation before 1963." Although NAACP leaders rejected the limits Eisenhower had placed on federal action in the civil rights area, by March 1955, at an NAACP meeting in New York on legislative aims, Mitchell questioned "whether the Democrats could be entrusted with national power during the transition of the United States from segregation to integration."

By June 1955, Mitchell's patience had completely worn out. "Republicans and Democrats," he charged in a blistering attack at the NAACP annual conference in Atlantic City, "have united in a bipartisan program of smothering civil rights legislation in the 84th Congress." Senate Majority Leader Johnson stood at one end of Pennsylvania Avenue "ever ready to douse the smallest spark of positive action with a bucket of harmony," while at the other end "the President maintains complete silence on much needed civil rights bills but becomes very vocal in opposing vital civil rights amendments." Owing to the complicated legislative maneuvers used to kill civil rights legislation, he said, it was imperative that the NAACP have a nationwide team of technicians who could move into action on short notice whenever home districts and states needed help with members of Congress.

Mitchell earlier had distributed to the branches a lengthy, detailed suggestion list with three basic goals: getting civil rights legislation passed; adoption of NAACP-endorsed nondiscrimination amendments to broad legislation, such as the federal aid for school construction bill; and defeating anti-civil-rights legislation. Additionally, the statement listed the civil rights bills before Congress and all the committees to which those bills had been referred. It also identified legislation that was hostile to civil rights. Now he suggested organizing a warning system "so perfect that overnight we can blanket the country with information on what individual members of Congress" were doing on civil rights.

"We must become students of double-talk," he said, in order to identify and vote against those who use it. "It is not enough for northern lawmakers to introduce and make speeches on civil rights bills. We also want them to work for hearings and votes on these bills." The rallying cry of Eisenhower Republicans and northern Democrats was "We don't need legislation because the court has settled everything." The Democrats' slogan was "A full dinner pail but no civil rights"; they asked "that we shut our eyes to injustices such as discrimination in employment, segregation in housing and monumental dishonesty in the spending of federal grants for schools and for other purposes"; they believed that as long as they passed minimum wage laws and expanded Social Security and health programs, blacks in the North would continue to vote for them even though they ignored legislation that would halt acts of violence in the South.

Mitchell said the NAACP supported "the great programs that improve the lot of the common man," and "we want them enacted into law." But blacks also wanted "an FEPC law to guarantee that we can get jobs in those plants where the minimum wage is a dollar or more." Blacks wanted to "walk in the front door of hospitals that receive Federal grants instead of having to sneak in through the back door and ride up on the freight elevator to the wards or clinics." Blacks wanted to be doctors, nurses, and medical technicians in those hospitals. "We want enough civil rights bills passed to make it possible for us to enjoy the great benefits of social welfare laws without the threat of being shot down or bombed just because we also want to vote and enjoy the full rights of American citizenship in Atlanta, Georgia, as well as Atlantic City, New Jersey."[8]

In a rousing speech in Jackson, Mississippi, the previous fall, Mitchell had declared, "No matter what demagogues may say, no matter what state legislatures may do, we are fortified by the knowledge that freedom from racial segregation is God's plan; we fear no storm or opposition, and we know that neither we nor the nation will ever turn back." The "groundswell of opinion" against segregation that Mitchell saw everywhere, and which was clouded by the "new weapons of hate," namely dynamite bombs and economic pressure, only made him work harder for the passage of the NAACP's legislative program.

This was the resolute spirit that he was continuing to inspire in his audiences a year later. He told an NAACP conference in Columbia, South Carolina, that blacks were learning a valuable lesson. "Progress is a glorious thing, but it does not come easy. Some people risk their money, some people risk their reputations, and others risk their lives, but that is the

chance every American has been taking in one way or another since the
Pilgrims landed at Plymouth Rock. Now the odds are much more on our
side and the only way we can lose is to give up ourselves." One of the first
tasks that blacks had to undertake, he said, was "to make registration and
voting as dear to you as your religion." He called for a boycott of national
products whose local distributors were refusing to make deliveries to black
businessmen. Regarding one case involving a popular soft drink, he said,
"If need be, just stop drinking everything except water."

At the close of the Eighty-third Congress, members of the House Committee on Interstate and Foreign Commerce had agreed to give early consideration during the next Congress to a bill to prohibit segregation in
interstate travel, another NAACP priority. Democrats reneged on the commitment in 1955—a failure, Mitchell complained, that was characteristic
of their attitude on civil rights. His determination, nevertheless, was buttressed by the nearly one hundred civil rights bills introduced before the
first session of the Eighty-fourth Congress adjourned in 1955. Many of the
bills were redundant. The House Judiciary Subcommittee No. 2, after
being prodded by the NAACP and sponsors of the bills, held hearings on
fifty-one of them. The bills covered fair employment practice, as well as
providing for protections of the right to vote. They were against violence,
segregation in interstate travel, and Jim Crow housing and education programs that received any form of federal assistance. They would create a Fair
Employment Practice Committee with enforcement powers, amend existing
civil rights laws, and strengthen the functions of the civil rights section of
the Justice Department.

On July 28, 1955, the full House Judiciary Committee favorably reported out a bill sponsored by Celler to protect servicemen from abuse and
violence—legislation that Mitchell had been pushing since 1951. Subcommittee No. 2 of the Senate Judiciary Committee also began preparing recommendations on other bills. Legislation similar to that being considered
by the House was before the Senate Judiciary Subcommittee on Constitutional Rights headed by Missouri's Thomas Hennings, who would play a
crucial role in the developing fight. A former St. Louis trial lawyer, he was
noted for his high principles and aloofness from petty partisan controversies. Neither that nor any other Senate committee held hearings on these
measures. Mitchell thought it ironic that the Department of Justice, which
had frequently asserted that existing laws gave it no power to enter many
civil rights cases, did not accept an invitation to testify at the House hearings.[9] The likely reason was that Eisenhower had not yet expressed support
for such legislation.

To break the stalemate caused by Republicans standing on one side and
Democrats on the other with neither proposing a mutually acceptable legis-

lative program, Mitchell enlisted Herbert Brownell's help. Their meeting occurred after the September 7 meeting between Assistant Attorney General Warren Olney III and NAACP leaders, when administration support was sought for laws to combat violence in Mississippi. Although Justice was not then actively supporting any of the initiatives in Congress, it had begun searching for an appropriate legislative program after the *Brown* decision was handed down. Mitchell presented Brownell with a copy of *To Secure These Rights* and suggested that he develop a legislative package from its recommendations. Brownell himself said he was considering provisions for protecting voting rights, for creating a Civil Rights Commission, and for an assistant attorney general in charge of civil rights. Brownell also said he was considering a provision that would become known as Part III to provide the attorney general with authority to seek injunctions in civil suits to protect Fourteenth Amendment rights in cases involving civil rights violations.

Toward the end of September 1955, Mitchell held lengthy discussions with members of Senators Lehman's and Hennings's staffs on plans for legislation for voting rights, school construction, and other matters to be considered by the next session of Congress. Hennings had won election in 1952 despite Truman's strong opposition. In further defiance of countervailing currents, he quickly won a seat on the powerful Senate Democratic Policy Committee, whose chairman was Lyndon Johnson. It was agreed that if the House and Senate actions were to be coordinated, the Hennings Subcommittee on Constitutional Rights would have to hold hearings early on the omnibus civil rights bills and related matters. That could be done in connection with the hearings that the subcommittee was then holding on constitutional rights, or separately. Mitchell suggested that the subcommittee consider holding hearings in Mississippi. He offered to go there in advance to assist in selecting witnesses on violence, intimidation, and denial of the right to vote because of race. That idea was quickly abandoned because it would have inspired reprisals within Congress against the subcommittee.

Prospects for positive action on civil rights legislation grew dimmer with each passing week and would almost vanish by December as both Democrats and Republicans began looking toward the coming presidential election. The two tough issues that normally generated intense election-year heat, and which faced lawmakers upon their return to Congress in January 1956, were civil rights and revisions to the Taft-Hartley Act. The middle-of-the-road southern Democratic leadership led by Sam Rayburn and his protégé Lyndon Johnson was not eager to touch either issue. Mitchell found that while liberal Republicans hoped to promote a split in Democratic ranks over civil rights, they themselves wanted to avoid a showdown.

Using the 1955 Mississippi murders of the Reverend George Lee, Lamar Smith, and Emmett Till as a spur, Mitchell invited several congressmen to a bipartisan strategy conference on December 9 in the House Interior and Insular Affairs Committee room. He emphasized the urgency by expressing his appreciation to Emanuel Celler for his agreeing to attend and citing the experiences of Dr. A. H. McCoy in Jackson, Mississippi. Someone had fired a shot into a room of McCoy's home where his eighteen-month-old daughter lay asleep, he explained. The police had refused to protect McCoy even though he was being attacked daily in the press for his civil rights activities. "Obviously," said Mitchell, unless Congress acts, "people like Dr. McCoy will be subjected to this kind of mistreatment indefinitely."

Mitchell's invitation was an outgrowth of an agreement that Democrats Powell, James Roosevelt of California, and Charles Diggs, as well as Republicans Hugh Scott of Pennsylvania and John Heselton of Massachusetts, had made toward the end of the first session to try for better teamwork on civil rights. Forty-seven congressmen (fourteen Republicans and thirty-three Democrats) promised to attend, but only four did so: Many had returned home or were prevented from showing up because of bad weather. Those who were there were all Democrats—Emanuel Celler, Charles Diggs, Edna Kelly of New York, and Richard Bolling of Missouri. Some others sent staff members in their stead; Powell sent a position paper. The meeting, nevertheless, was productive, with the group serving as advance planners.

In addition to agreeing on the need for antisegregation safeguards for grants-in-aid to states, the group concluded that no further hearings on civil rights bills were required. Celler felt that the House Judiciary subcommittee, which had held hearings, would act favorably on the legislation, but that the full committee needed prodding. It was agreed that this was a job for civil rights groups. Diggs thought the most important measure was the bill to protect the right to vote. If that bill passed, he felt, Congress would have to strengthen the Department of Justice to investigate and prosecute civil rights complaints, such as the murders in Mississippi. Bolling felt strongly that with their right to vote protected, blacks would have the political power necessary to gain legitimate goals. As terrorism in the South had aroused public opinion, Bolling preferred to concentrate on legislation to protect personal security and the franchise rather than to conduct a broader fight. Mitchell would continue to meet regularly with Celler.[10]

The following month in his State of the Union Message, Eisenhower, for the first time, called for civil rights legislation in order to create a bipartisan commission to investigate charges of the denial of the vote to blacks in some areas. Mitchell was lukewarm to the idea of having that as the administration's legislative program.

The previous February, Mitchell had written to James Roosevelt thanking him for introducing a resolution to establish "a joint Congressional Committee on Civil Rights." But he had warned that to be effective, committee members would have to be interested in, and dedicated to, a program extending civil rights to all citizens. "It would be a mockery," he told Roosevelt, "to include known opponents of civil rights." Moreover, such a committee should not be "considered an end in itself, but only an instrument to assist in this expansion of citizens rights." Discoveries of civil rights violations, Mitchell went on, "would be fruitless unless preceded, accompanied, and followed by passage of legislation to remedy the evils" that were so readily apparent. Morever, the proposal, he concluded, would not be acceptable if Congress were to approve it merely as a substitute for substantive legislation.

An effective committee that Mitchell cited to Roosevelt was a previous, late-1930s Congressional Committee on Civil Liberties, headed by Senator Robert M. La Follette, Jr., Progressive of Wisconsin, that publicized grave civil rights violations and prepared the way for constructive legislation. *

The NAACP welcomed Eisenhower's proposal but said it did not go far enough. The State of the Union commitment was the best, to date, that blacks had gotten from him on civil rights legislation. Mitchell then astutely used it as an opening for working more closely with sympathetic members of the administration, chiefly Brownell. In a meeting with Brownell, Mitchell suggested that he and the attorney general meet regularly in order to keep Brownell informed about NAACP progress on the Hill. Mitchell told Brownell that the bipartisan group would work to get congressmen to support the administration's recommendations after they had been submitted to Congress—provided that he and the attorney general agreed on the contents of the administration's recommendations. Mitchell said that there was always the possibility that amendments to the administration's proposals would be offered. Having obtained Hennings's pledge to support the struggle for an effective program, Mitchell suggested that Brownell himself might testify in support of the recommendations. Mitchell also urged the Hennings Subcommittee on Constitutional Rights to hold very brief hearings "in order to get action as quickly as possible."[11]

Mitchell regarded as a bit of good fortune the House's passage on Janu-

---

* A subcommittee of the Senate Committee on Labor and Public Welfare, the La Follette Civil Liberties Committee was authorized to "investigate violations of right of free speech and assembly and interference with right of labor to organize and bargain collectively." Through its hearings, begun in 1936, the committee helped bring to national attention grave injustices and paved the way for establishing the Civil Rights Section in the Justice Department in 1939.

ary 16 of the bill to protect servicemen against violence, which he felt might be used as a vehicle for more important civil rights legislation.

The death of Harley Kilgore, chairman of the Senate Judiciary Committee, on February 27, cast a dark cloud over Mitchell's hopes for getting civil rights legislation passed in 1956. Eastland was the ranking committee member. Four days before Kilgore's death, Mitchell had requested that the chairman of the Senate Rules and Administration Committee hold hearings on charges of misconduct by Eastland. Mitchell's request was refused. He had previously called Eastland the "'chief microbe' poisoning the blood stream of the nation." Now he intensified his attack. The press reported that he branded Eastland a "stinking albatross" around the neck of the Democratic party, which "might have to kiss our votes goodbye" if it did not do something about the senator.

Actually, drawing on his love and knowledge of classical poetry, Mitchell had evoked the theme of Samuel Taylor Coleridge's *The Rime of the Ancient Mariner* to castigate the Democrats. Because the Mariner unthinkingly killed the albatross, a good omen following the ship at sea, the crew initially was alarmed—"Ah wretch! said they, the bird to slay,/That made the breeze to blow!" But during the interim that conditions remained favorable, they switched their tune to commend the Mariner, thus implicating themselves in the sin: "'Twas right, said they, such birds to slay,/That bring the fog and mist." The crew, in effect, became accessories after the fact and would not live to see the end of the voyage. As the seas became dead calm and the hot sun beat down on the unmoving ship, water and food ran out. Before all two hundred of them died, the crewmen tied the rotting albatross around the Mariner's neck. The Mariner had a chance to live by doing penance, but not they, because their crime had been deliberate while the Mariner's had been unthinking.

Mitchell drew a few criticisms from those who were unable to appreciate the symbol of the albatross—one from a poem whose theme is concern with man's rejection of love through his own irresponsible actions and his need to recapture a loving spirit for his salvation. Mitchell forcefully defended his attack. He informed one critic that after he had cursed Eastland, the senator agreed to his request to meet with an NAACP delegation from Mississippi—the first time Eastland had ever done so. As a demonstration of how the baron of backwoods Sunflower County thrived on his record of reprehensible behavior, Mitchell recalled Eastland's brazen bragging to a Mississippi audience about how he had broken the law in the Senate in order to block action on civil rights. Not only did he not call a meeting of the Judiciary Subcommittee on Civil Rights for the three years he was chairman, but to prevent anyone else from using the rules behind his back to do so, he "had special pockets put in my pants and for three years I carried those bills around in my pockets everywhere I went and every one of them were {sic} defeated."

The lonely cries of opposition from Herbert Lehman and Wayne Morse to Eastland's elevation were swamped by the unanimous approval of the Democratic Steering Committee. Lehman berated Eastland as "a symbol of racism in America" and as a "symbol of defiance to the Constitution of the United States as interpreted by the Supreme Court." Mitchell asked many senators to vote against Eastland's appointment, but they either declined or absented themselves during the vote. Seniority prevailed, and Eastland became chairman on March 2.

Except for the two senators who opposed Eastland, Mitchell complained, "all others who were present when the vote was taken are guilty of looking the other way when a mad dog is loose in the street of justice." He blamed both parties. Had they wanted to do so, the Republicans could have, with the help of Lehman and Morse, overlooked the tradition of seniority and elected a Republican to the post. By bowing to party policy and tradition, he told Thomas Kuchel, Republican of California, the Republicans had helped the Democrats put Eastland in a position to "do extensive damage to the country as a whole." Tradition, Mitchell said, was much less important than protecting human freedom.[12]

That same day, the Senate Judiciary Subcommittee on Constitutional Rights favorably reported out bills to put an end to lynching, to create a Civil Rights Division in the Department of Justice, and to protect voting rights, as well as a bill to protect servicemen against violence that was similar to the one the House had approved. Another favorable development was that on March 21 Subcommittee No. 2 of the House Judiciary Committee reported out an antilynching bill, and an omnibus civil rights bill (H.R. 627) that Celler had introduced and that would become the main one under consideration.

The arrest of Martin Luther King, Jr., and other bus boycott leaders in Montgomery had now elevated King to a national symbol as reporters from all over the country added fervor to what previously had been a local event. Mitchell was oblivious to those developments because he did not believe they had an important bearing on the legislative struggle in Washington. Not so the White House, which was trying to deflect the South's wrath from the administration for, first, Eisenhower's appointment of Earl Warren as the Chief Justice of the Supreme Court, and, second, the Court's decision in the Brown case. After a delay caused by intense wrangling between the White House and the Justice Department over how strong the legislative proposals should be, Brownell on April 9 finally sent Congress the administration's first civil rights recommendations that significantly went beyond the President's call in his State of the Union Message for a bipartisan commission and were generally similar to the attorney general's proposals of the previous fall. The principal thrust of his package was protection of the right to vote, regarded as a means for safeguarding other constitutional rights.

The administration called for (1) the creation of a six-member, temporary, bipartisan Civil Rights Commission with authority to hold public hearings, subpoena witnesses, take testimony under oath, and obtain necessary data from any executive department or agency; (2) provision of a new assistant attorney general to head a full-fledged Civil Rights Division of the Justice Department thus taking civil rights enforcement out of the Criminal Division (that action would permit the placement of more emphasis on civil remedies); (3) protection of the right to vote by considerably expanding existing statutes to include civil remedies, so that violations would "not necessarily be treated as a crime." (The existing statute protecting the right to vote provided only for criminal remedies and limited coverage to law enforcement officers; it did not cover private individuals.) The proposal would cover private individuals to correct this weakness. The attorney general would be authorized to seek injunctive relief or other civil remedies to protect Fourteenth Amendment rights and he would be able to speed the process for preventing violations; (4) Giving the attorney general power to initiate civil action to prevent conspiracies interfering with Fifteenth Amendment rights.

Eisenhower stayed in the background while his attorney general carried the ball. Brownell's proposal to broaden the functions of the Civil Rights Section of the Justice Department beyond its original 1939 scope, to include protection of individuals' rights from violations by other private citizens, was the type of historical initiative that merited recognition of the President. Until the creation of the Civil Rights Section, the only actions government had taken in defense of individual liberties had been during Reconstruction. Even after Reconstruction, government was still regarded as the chief enemy of liberty. That concept underlay the Bill of Rights and the Fourteenth Amendment. But the revelations of the La Follette Civil Liberties Committee, the NAACP's lengthy campaign for an antilynching law, and now the association's efforts to prevent the types of violence (initiated by private individuals, in contrast to the state's action through its representatives "under color of law") that took the lives of civil rights activists in the South had demonstrated that federal authority to protect individual rights needed to be broadened.

Brownell, in effect, was pressing Congress to reassert its former vigor in protecting Fourteenth and Fifteenth amendment rights, which had been lost by the last decade of the nineteenth century owing to adverse Supreme Court rulings on the constitutionality of the civil rights laws adopted during Reconstruction, repeal by Congress of many civil rights laws that had not been annulled by the Supreme Court, and adverse public and political reaction to those laws. Because the Supreme Court and the executive branch had already taken dramatic steps toward reversing those post-Reconstruction rollbacks of civil rights, the pressure was increasing on Congress to act.[13]

Reaction among lawmakers to the administration's proposals was, as expected, mixed. Hubert Humphrey, for example, at first called the proposal "lip-service by leap-year liberals"; then the following day he tempered his comment, saying he was "delighted to have this belated administration support." Emanuel Celler said that the program was like "using a bean shooter where you should use a gun." Richard Russell accused the administration of "cheap politics" and said that Brownell had "perverted the office of attorney general more than any man in history." Most important, though, Minority Leader Knowland, signaling a change of attitude that was needed for bipartisan support, predicted that Congress would act on just two of the administration's proposals: for a Civil Rights Commission and the creation of a Civil Rights Division in the Justice Department. Eisenhower told those Republican legislative leaders who complained that the package was too strong that he had reviewed the proposals very carefully and did not see how they could have been more moderate or less provocative.

The administration's initiative was a badly needed boost for Mitchell, although he evidently felt it was inadequate. Mitchell's lobbying strategy was to push for the maximum and accept less when there was no alternative. He knew that he had a sincere ally, Brownell, within the administration, so until Congress voted on the legislation, there was always hope that he could get more.[14]

Mitchell's political campaign through the NAACP branches reached a feverish pitch in 1956. It received a boost early in the year from the Leadership Conference on Civil Rights's March 4–6 National Delegates Assembly for Civil Rights in Washington, whose purpose was to drum up liberal support, and which was led by Wilkins. Knowing that liberal organizations outside the Congress were supporting him reassured Mitchell. He was also encouraged by his own philosophical outlook on racial attitudes in the North, which he expressed to Powell near the end of April:

No sensible person in the North would advocate that racial segregation should be enforced by law. There are, of course, a few northern people who believe that certain aspects of racial segregation should be retained. Some want it in housing, some in skating rinks, a few want it in schools, and far too many want it in churches. Fortunately, whenever there is an open clash between those who want segregation and those who oppose it, the latter usually win overwhelming public support in northern communities.

Newspapers, the NAACP, labor groups, political leaders, some churches, and many other community forces have combined to make it physically, economically, and socially safe to speak up for integration. This is the main difference between the North and the South. I am convinced, by personal experience, that there is substantial support for integration in the South. I venture the opinion that the pattern of thinking on this subject is almost the same as in the North. There is even an added factor in the South's favor. Southern white people who have employed colored people in their homes or lived side by side with them as neighbors know that propaganda about crime, disease, and lack of intelligence among colored people is utterly false. In contrast, some northern white people, who have no personal contact with colored people, are sometimes gullible enough to accept vicious slander as facts.

Regrettably, an organized minority of whites in the South is able to exert physical, economic, social, and political pressure on the hardy souls who dare to assert that all men are equal regardless of race. Securing the right to vote, greater economic opportunity and protection against physical violence will do much to overcome the present barriers to truth and progress in the South. Perhaps the greatest single mistake being made in the North today is the support of so-called gradualism.

When northern people support this term they are giving a breathing spell to those who are determined to do nothing at all to make the South obey the requirements of the U.S. Constitution. In addition, while the North is preoccupied with debates on "go-slow warnings" the opposition to civil rights is actively working to destroy and stamp out even the smallest expression of liberal thought in that region.[15]

Eastland, dragging out the process, was holding hearings on similar measures rather than accepting the bills the Hennings subcommittee had approved. "Stepin Fetchit, in his prime," observed Louis Lautier of the *Baltimore Afro-American,* "had nothing on the slow-motion paces through which Eastland is dragging the Senate Judiciary Committee in the ludicrous civil rights hearings." Consequently, Lautier predicted that the Eighty-fourth Congress would end before the hearings were concluded. Obviously, said Mitchell, "if we are to get action in the committee," Eastland "must be outmaneuvered by members who support civil rights."

In addition to Eastland, Mitchell was facing twenty other Senate committee chairmen from the South. Reactionary southern senators alone controlled nine standing committees.* Mitchell welcomed as a good omen developments in the House.

To avoid having to hold hearings on the administration's proposals, Celler substituted the Justice Department's language in the civil rights bill for his own. The revised bill still bore Celler's name as author and the original number, H.R. 627. That maneuver enabled both parties to support it and the Judiciary Committee to report out the bill promptly, but it was immediately apparent that Smith had no intention of holding hearings and was going to pigeonhole it in the Rules Committee. James Roosevelt initiated a discharge petition, which required 218 signatures, to force the bill onto the floor. Because Roosevelt was unable to get enough signatures before the deadline, forty-year-old Richard Bolling moved to seemingly commit political suicide by dropping the legislative equivalent of an H-bomb in the House Rules Committee. The very junior congressman (a relative freshman, in his fourth term) made a motion in the Rules Committee to take up H.R. 627.

Bolling, a liberal, was elected to Congress in 1948, after resigning from the Army as a lieutenant colonel. He had tried to persuade a dozen people to run for the seat of the fifth district in Kansas City against the entrenched machine. When no one would, he himself ran. He began his service on the powerful Rules Committee with the blessings of his fellow Missourian President Truman and Sam Rayburn. Soon members discovered he was an astute student of the House rules, on which southerners were the acknowledged experts. Chairman Smith, for one, when he did not delay or kill a bill in the committee, could tie up his adversaries on the House floor by invoking little understood rules. Once when he announced he was going home to look after his cows on his farm and did not know when he would return to hold a meeting on a pending civil rights bill, Bolling forced him to return by threatening to use a rule that would have permitted the committee to hold the session without the chairman's consent.

Bolling had other advantages. He knew he had the votes to win his fight. His ace was an elder statesman on the committee, Republican Clar-

---

* The other unyielding southern foes who controlled standing Senate committees were Allen J. Ellender of Louisiana, Agriculture and Forestry; Richard B. Russell of Georgia, Armed Services; J. W. Fulbright of Arkansas, Banking and Currency; Harry F. Byrd of Virginia, Finance; Walter F. George of Georgia, Foreign Relations; John L. McClellan of Arkansas, Government Operations; Lister Hill of Alabama, Labor and Public Welfare; and Olin D. Johnston of South Carolina, Post Office and Civil Service. Border state moderates were chairmen of two other standing committees: Carl Hayden of Arizona, Appropriations; and Matthew M. Neely of West Virginia, District of Columbia.

ence Brown, Sr., a veteran conservative like Taft who came from a district
in Ohio that had a history of participating in the Underground Railroad.

When Mitchell first thought about enlisting Brown's help, some people
told him, "Oh, there's no use trying him. He's conservative. He wouldn't
go along with it." But, said Mitchell, "it just so happened that I took the
trouble to talk with him very carefully and to ascertain what he would do
and wouldn't do" in a given situation. In what he recalled as a moment of
"youthful enthusiasm in their meeting," Mitchell was hammering away
that the country needed antilynching legislation to prevent killings, and
FEPC legislation "to keep our fellow citizens from starving to death."
Brown agreed with Mitchell on the need for an antilynching bill, but he
challenged him to prove that people would starve if an FEPC bill was
not passed. Nevertheless, after discussing the merits of the FEPC bill, he
told Mitchell he favored it too. "From that time on," Mitchell explained,
he tried to keep his "advocacy of legislation free from the tempting but
easily disproved assertions based on speculation rather than hard facts."

Brown enjoyed spreading confusion among the Democrats, so he
backed Bolling—a former lieutenant and legman for Sam Rayburn who
had maintained his considerable influence with the House speaker.
Rayburn, too, wanted not only the civil rights bill, but also to see Smith's
wings clipped because the Rules Committee chairman had usurped the
speaker's role of dictating the flow of legislation.

Helping Bolling and Brown win by 6 to 4 were Republican Harris
Ellsworth of Oregon and three Democrats: Ray J. Madden of Indiana,
James J. Delaney of New York, and Thomas P. "Tip" O'Neill, Jr., of
Massachusetts.

Finally, reported *The New York Times* on June 28, an impatient Smith
told a long line of waiting witnesses who were trying for the second time to
stall approval of the bill: "See if you can't get together and shorten your
testimony. I haven't encouraged any shortening in the past, but the jig's
up. I know it."

The debate on the House floor was another wrangle. Mitchell was
amazed at having to answer such questions during intervals in the debate as
whether H.R. 627 "would give powers to the attorney general that he
might abuse by directing them against such matters as the refusal of citizens in Montgomery, Alabama, to ride on segregated buses." Nothing in
the bill, he told Pennsylvania's Hugh Scott, gave the attorney general authority to prosecute persons who refused to ride on a segregated bus. [16]

Eighteen days after it had killed the federal aid to school construction
bill with the Powell Amendment, the House (on July 23) passed the civil
rights bill 279 to 126. (This vote further supported Mitchell's conclusion
that it was partisan politics and not the Powell Amendment that killed the

school construction bill.) A relieved Mitchell issued a statement for the NAACP saying, "Passage of the civil rights bill is a stern warning to Mississippi and other defiant states that the nation abhors control of elections with blackjacks, cross burnings and murder." The NAACP therefore urged leaders of both parties to keep Congress in session until the bill became law.

The back of the Republican-Dixiecrat coalition in the House that had developed from early in Roosevelt's first administration was finally broken—for the time being, at least. In the upper chamber, Mitchell began working with New Jersey's Clifford Case, who narrowly won election to the Senate in 1954, to take up the bill immediately. Case, a liberal Republican, was another close civil rights ally. For Mitchell the problem in the Senate was that while Democrats and Republicans could similarly have joined to defeat Eastland's choke hold on the Judiciary Committee 11–4, the "southern" states of Indiana, Utah, and Idaho refused to go along.

To avoid getting caught in a partisan crossfire, and to keep the Senate action properly aligned with the House's, Mitchell asked the Senate Judiciary Committee to report out H.R. 5205, the House bill to protect servicemen against violence that had already passed the lower chamber, and another measure that would exactly fit H.R. 627. Eastland was no more favorably disposed toward H.R. 5205 than to the civil rights bill, so he kept it bottled up also, and it died in his committee.

There was a comical interlude during the hearings that recalled one that had occurred in 1920 during the struggle to pass legislation safeguarding the right to vote. At that time, a man had attempted to photograph James Weldon Johnson and Walter White with a Louisiana congressman. The lawmaker strode from the room saying he did not want his picture taken with niggers. Now, Mitchell got caught in a flap when a *Jet* magazine reporter photographed the lobbyist conversing with South Carolina's Olin D. Johnston during a break in the hearings. Up for reelection, he ordered a guard to seize the photographer's film, allegedly because the man had violated Senate rules. Mitchell charged that Johnston objected because the photographer was black. Another obvious reason was that Johnston feared he would be damaged politically if the photograph was published back home.

Mitchell told the white reporters, "This is an outrage. You all should protest, because nobody should have the right to confiscate a photographer's pictures." The reporters then formed a line behind Mitchell and began marching to see the sergeant of arms in order to retrieve the plate. The *Jet* photographer immediately told Mitchell that he had surrendered only a blank plate, not the exposed one. To give the photographer a chance to get out of the building, Mitchell halted the procession and lamely explained to the nonplussed reporters that the situation had changed. Mitchell later recalled, "Do you know that *Jet* was afraid to publish the picture?"[17]

In a second desperate attempt to recall the House bill from the Senate Judiciary Committee, where it had been sent with unusual speed and was now firmly bottled up, Paul Douglas, supported by Lehman, moved to get it onto the Senate floor through a parliamentary maneuver called the "morning hour" by which the Senate would have "adjourned," contrary to Lyndon Johnson's plans to recess, and thus been allowed to continue the session the next day but as part of the same "legislative day." Any motion to call up the bill was out of order as long as the Senate had merely recessed. The ill-fated maneuver only antagonized Johnson more. He had previously threatened that the President's foreign aid program would be doomed if Republican civil rights supporters dared to push for H.R. 627. (Mitchell charged that the GOP meekly surrendered, but he blamed the Democrats more for the failure.) Johnson now growled that the Douglas-Lehman move was a challenge to his leadership, and his GOP counterpart Knowland agreed that the motion was a vote of no confidence in both leaders. Determined to crush Douglas, Johnson got Karl Mundt to ask for a roll call on Douglas's motion. It lost by a 6 to 76 vote. Afterward in the elevator, the humiliated Douglas ordered Howard Shuman, one of his assistants, "Howard, let us punch the bell three times and pretend that I am a senator."

Only three Republicans, North Dakota's William Langer, Irving Ives, and Ohio's George H. Bender, and two Democrats, Lehman and Hennings, had supported Douglas. Hubert Humphrey, quietly backing Johnson, voted against Douglas. (Humphrey was also influenced by Stevenson's quiet promise that he wanted the Minnesotan as his vice presidential running mate.) The vote meant that the bill was dead for 1956. The defeat was a glaring example of how practical politics could overwhelm principles. Uppermost in Johnson's mind was that southerners would have filibustered the bill and prevented action, revealing the Democratic party to be badly divided on the eve of the national convention.

As senators berated one another, Mitchell came down from the gallery and asked Clifford Case, whom he had called off the floor for a quick meeting, to get a commitment from Johnson and Knowland that the civil rights bill would be the first order of business in the new Eighty-fifth Congress. In his typically quiet manner, Case gained the floor and engaged the leaders in a temper-cooling colloquy. Both of them openly agreed that if either remained a leader in 1957, no matter which party was in the majority, he would press for action early.

"Once Johnson made up his mind he was going to act," Mitchell knew, "there was no turning him around, even though he was up against some very formidable opposition from his southern supporters," to whom he owed his position as majority leader. Mitchell thought it especially significant that Johnson had said he would clear such action with the nine-member Majority Policy Committee, which controlled legislation. Johnson was the chairman of the committee. Mitchell discounted the vote of Carl Hayden of Arizona, who usually sided with southern bloc members Lister Hill and Richard Russell. He was confident that Johnson could get a committee majority because the other members were moderates.

Mitchell now realized that Johnson was challenging Russell's leadership of the southern Democrats by asserting for the first time his influence over a group of senators independent of his native region. That required a lot of strength, but Johnson carried it out.

Afterward, Douglas told Mitchell that although the results of this fight were discouraging, he believed that "it did serve to point up again the inflexible character of the Senate rules when it comes to seeking consideration for civil rights bills," again underscoring the need for revisions. That the confrontation was not futile, he felt, was revealed by "the strong elements of bi-partisanship in resistance to civil rights legislation."

Rubbing salt into Mitchell's wounds, Eastland went back to Mississippi in August and bragged to his constituents about how he finally dealt with the civil rights bills before the Judiciary Committee:

> The liberals had a schedule calling for committee approval on bills important to them by May 1; one was the appointment of [Simon] Sobeloff [who as solicitor general argued the administration's school integration position before the Supreme Court] to a Circuit Court of Appeals judgeship. I had committee staff prepare a lengthy brief on Sobeloff, and in the committee meetings recognized Senator Johnston, who spent five weeks of our committee sessions reading it. I told them they could have him [Sobeloff] as long as no further civil rights measures were offered, and on July 1 we agreed. We couldn't meet on July 9, the next scheduled date, because I had to learn about a new irrigation system on my farm at Doddsville; while I was in Doddsville, Senator Johnston got unanimous consent for the Senate to begin sessions at 9:30 a.m. daily, which eliminated Judiciary Committee meetings except by unanimous consent.[18]

Pressing ahead, Mitchell won from Warren Olney implied agreement to continue pressing for the principle (Title III—historically, "Part III") that would become a major bone of contention in the approaching battle over the 1957 Civil Rights Act—authority for the attorney general to seek injunctions against persons who sought to deprive others of their civil rights. Olney told Mitchell that the Justice Department was conducting an analysis of arguments made against the bill in the first session of the Eighty-fourth Congress and intended to press for passage of H.R. 627, apparently with that controversial feature, if Eisenhower was reelected in 1956.

Mitchell again urged the administration to call a conference of Republicans and Democrats "during which there would be a full and frank explanation of why prosecutions had not been undertaken in specific cases." That meeting, he told Olney, "should convince members of Congress that action" was necessary and win over lukewarm supporters in key leadership positions. He was certain that there were lawmakers from areas where the black vote was not important to them personally who needed prodding from the Justice Department. Olney promised to work on the meeting, while Mitchell would help in getting members of Congress to attend.

Mitchell was now at the crossroads to the gates of the "Promised Land"—the one that Walter White had dreamed of in his book *How Far the Promised Land?* Legislation represented indispensable keys to those gates. He was all too well aware that, unlike the courts, whose decisions were based on reason and law, Congress acted on the basis of public opinion, so he increased political pressure on Congress. He knew that most important to holding lawmakers to their word was their perception of the self-interest of their constituents, of the economic costs of segregation, the increasing moral outrage over terrorism in the South, the awareness of the extent to which blacks were being denied the right to vote in the South, and international embarrassment over racism.

Mitchell proudly noted that each of the three blacks (Powell, Dawson, and Diggs) in Congress in 1956 "in his way makes a contribution to the greatness of our country." Whether Republicans or Democrats were in office, he said, progress "was made in the past because of the political power of the people. Those who have sought to turn back the clock have been busy under all administrations. They have failed to place the stamp of final approval on segregation because the NAACP has met them at every crossroad and alley-way."

The NAACP's confidence in its political power was further buttressed with the encouraging increase in black voter registration. In 1940 there were 140,000 black voters registered in the entire South—a scant 10,000 more than were registered in Louisiana in 1896 before disfranchisement. Four years later, when the Supreme Court outlawed white Democratic primaries, the South still had fewer than 200,000 registered black voters. In 1948, the number had risen to 1.3 million, and the goal for 1956 (which would not be realized) was 3 million. The association had marked "the beginning of the Negro's political coming of age" and the time when "the Negro himself recognized his political power" with Walter White's successful campaign to block the appointment of Judge John Parker in 1930 to the Supreme Court. Now Mitchell was leading a national effort through NAACP branches to expand this power to gain passage of civil rights legislation.

The political climate for much of 1956 was clouded with uncertainty, owing to Eishenhower's health problems, over whether he would run again, and charged by the intense contest between Adlai Stevenson and Estes Kefauver for the Democratic presidential nomination. The two Democratic contenders, to counter Eisenhower's favorable civil rights ratings, strove to outdo each other in appealing for the black vote until Stevenson slipped badly by calling for the removal of the integration issue from the campaign. Since Stevenson's civil rights views were similar to Eisenhower's, the Illinois Democrat's ultimate capture of his party's nomination presented blacks with only alternatives of moderation.

Mitchell blamed Stevenson for the NAACP's difficulty in getting the two most recent Democratic National Conventions to adopt strong civil rights planks. He thought the conventions "were doing a whole lot of pussyfooting on many things" and were not giving blacks the opportunity they needed to shape party policy. Indeed, had it not been for organized labor's help, he said, "I think those conventions would have come through with some rather weak commitments of one kind or another." Mitchell therefore concluded that as President, Stevenson would not have been forthright on civil rights. He believed he would have followed his party's traditional approach of "moving where you could politically, but if you ran into" any strong resistance, "don't touch it." So, despite the increasing militancy of blacks, Mitchell did not think Stevenson "would have been a flaming standard bearer." In 1952, he felt stronger toward the bid by Senator John Sparkman for the vice presidency. He knew him well and felt that Sparkman, coming from Alabama, would have represented "a forward movement." But even though he regarded himself as a Stevenson supporter, Mitchell was not sure how well he would have performed on civil rights as President. Mitchell believed that civil rights legislation would have passed if Stevenson had thrown his weight into the battle, but also that Stevenson would have taken too long to make important civil rights decisions and would have done so in a manner making nobody happy— especially since the main roadblock in Congress was "the abject surrender of some liberals in Congress."[19]

Mitchell saw the 1956 political contest as one between anarchy in the South and well-being in the North. He thought there were "naive persons so busy watching the fires in the Middle East and Hungary" that they did not realize they were "sitting on a hot seat right here in the United States." He considered the Southern Manifesto and the Democrats' "double talk in their civil rights platform promises" at their 1956 national convention to be seeds for "home grown rebellion." He felt that the Democrats knew the document would be subject to double interpretation, yet incredibly, "the platform drafting committee willfully refused to include language that would condemn the use of violence by anti-integration groups in the South." Charging that the platform was designed to assure southerners that the federal government would not use force to back up the Supreme Court decision, he called it the "biggest pile of fertilizer outside the stockyards." As for the Republicans, "they walked up to the brink of equivocation and fell in."

The NAACP concluded that the GOP platform seemed only "a shade better than that of the Democrats," but both platforms were undeniably weaker than in 1952. The 1952 Democratic platform had called for legislation to secure, for all citizens, equal employment opportunity, personal security from violence, equal participation in the nation's political process free from arbitrary restraints, and the strengthening of the administrative machinery to enforce existing civil rights laws better. The 1952 Republican party platform had reaffirmed the right of all citizens to full, impartial enforcement of federal laws for the protection of civil rights. Although the GOP believed that it was the primary responsibility of each state to regulate and control its own institutions, the platform said that the federal government should take "supplemental action" under the Constitution to oppose racial, religious, and national-origins discrimination. The 1956 Democratic platform pledged that the party would continue its efforts to eliminate racial discrimination of all kinds, and to seek federal protection for the full right to vote, to "engage in gainful occupations," to enjoy personal security, and to education in all publicly supported institutions. The Republican platform expressed support for the civil rights program announced by the President and acceptance of the Supreme Court's 1954 school desegregation decision. Mitchell and Wilkins urged NAACP branches to redouble their efforts to ensure that candidates considered the association's interests.

Lawmakers at all points along the political spectrum with an interest in civil rights, from liberals like Herbert Lehman to southerners like Richard Russell, regarded Mitchell as central to the legislative struggle. Bolling recalls that "he not only had physical strength, a strong mind, and a good mind, but he also had the capacity to conceptualize and to understand the legislative process. Thus he had a major role in pulling people together." At the same time, Bolling recalled, Mitchell was "looking at the country to see how you could put it together" in order to gain passage of the first civil rights act since 1875.[20]

Steadily courting lawmakers, Mitchell thanked them through letters for their support and, in his speeches before hometown audiences, took pains to praise those who had good civil rights voting records or who had been particularly helpful on an issue or in a battle. For example, while he told Thomas Kuchel that he had enumerated to a member of the NAACP board of directors from California the senator's "valuable vote" and other forms of support for legislation in Congress favored by the NAACP, he also complained to Kuchel about his not having tried to stop the confirmation of Eastland as chairman of the Judiciary Committee. However, Mitchell let Kuchel know that, in light of the senator's positive actions, "it would be very foolish for me to imply in any way that your action on Senator Eastland's confirmation" was "based on any racist principle."

Another Republican whom Mitchell praised warmly and repeatedly was Hugh Scott, who represented a strongly conservative district in Pennsylvania but had a considerable interest in civil rights. (Scott, once a Republican National Committee chairman, knew Brownell well and helped Mitchell communicate with the administration through the attorney general.) Similarly, Mitchell minced no words in denouncing lawmakers who were anti–civil rights, and he made sure that NAACP branch leaders knew about their records. "I am sure," he told a New Jersey NAACP audience in October, that "it is shocking to be told that your congressman was on the same team with John Bell Williams of Mississippi and other anti–civil rights operators" in voting against H.R. 627.

Outside Congress, Mitchell's most important working base was the NAACP branch structure, through which he reached his primary, predominantly black constituency. Overall demographics led the *Congressional Quarterly* to conclude in 1956 that "Negroes may be said to hold a theoretical balance of power in those districts" where the population percentage of the group was "larger than a winning candidate's margin of victory." That margin had been an important factor in the 1952 elections, and as the Republicans tried to build a two-party system in the South, they sought to attract blacks back to the party of Lincoln. Despite Eisenhower's personal popularity, the Republicans were still the underdogs. Only twice since 1932 had they controlled Congress, and they very much yearned to do so again beginning in 1957. To succeed, the GOP needed black support. In the thirty-odd speeches he made during the year, Mitchell played on that reality to the hilt.[21]

Mitchell's distinction as the most effective civil rights lobbyist in Washington, plus his educational program among blacks, had made him one of the most influential national black leaders in the country. He was

not as well known as the other leaders outside the NAACP and the civil
rights community, but the program he was developing and implementing
in Washington was the goal of all other civil rights organizations. As head
of the NAACP and chairman of the Leadership Conference on Civil Rights,
Wilkins, of course, had much broader influence than Mitchell or Martin
Luther King. The development of the Leadership Conference coalition, in
addition to Wilkins's drive to build the NAACP into a much stronger
machine of organized activism, was crucial to Mitchell's success.

Mitchell's legislative priorities were determined by the complaints of
civil rights abuses that he received primarily through the NAACP branches.
He sought no new rights for blacks, only that they should be extended the
same rights accorded to others under the Constitution. The moral and political justifications for the safeguards he sought were given political weight by
the fact that his proposals to Congress and the executive branch were based
on actual circumstances, rather than on social and political ideology or on
philosophical concepts. (Even though the Montgomery bus boycott had
elevated King's stature, it would not be until the 1963 Montgomery demonstrations that he would consolidate his role in the movement.)

As November drew closer, Mitchell's blows became harder. He charged
that Democratic party leaders had been misled if they believed that the
black "vote was in the bag." Although they had made Eastland chairman of
the Judiciary Committee, that senator, Mitchell repeatedly stated, was the
Republicans' best vote-getter. He concluded that the Democrats had presented friends of civil rights with a dilemma that had only two solutions.
The first, and most obvious, was to switch to the Republican column in
November—"that would automatically eliminate 21 southern chairmen
from the key committee posts they now hold." The second alternative was
to initiate a "tremendous reform" within the Democratic party by those
members who supported civil rights. The type of reformers he had in mind
were those who "were determined to defy tyranny," like Richard Bolling,
Thomas O'Neill, Ray J. Madden of Indiana, and James Delaney of New
York, all of whom had demonstrated on the House Rules Committee that
southern committee chairmen were not invincible. As for the Republicans,
Mitchell felt that their chief virtue was that most of the better-known race-
baiters in Congress were Democrats. That was regrettable, "because the
party of Abraham Lincoln ought to have also a dynamic, positive civil
rights program."

Eisenhower added fuel to this fire in the fall, when he reaffirmed his
states' rights policies in the South:

> Four years ago I pledged that as President of all the people, I
> would use every proper influence of my office to promote for all

citizens that equality before the law and of opportunity visualized by our founding fathers. I promised further to do this with conviction that progress toward equality had to be achieved finally in the hearts of men rather than in legislative halls. I urged then, as I urge now, the handling of this question to the greatest possible extent on a local and state basis.

By now, however, Mitchell was depending more on Eisenhower's attorney general than on leadership from the chief executive to get legislation through Congress. Mitchell hailed Brownell's calling U.S. Attorneys to Washington to instruct them to enforce the Supreme Court's decision barring segregation in interstate travel. He urged Brownell to expand enforcement to include "all of the decisions and national policies on civil rights."

Mitchell was confident that 1957 would be the turning point for civil rights: "We believe that it will produce more progress and more victories." Most dramatic, he said after the elections, was the "definite pledge" from the victorious Eisenhower administration that it would move to protect the right to vote. [22]

CHAPTER THIRTEEN

Breakthrough

Mitchell was not alone in seeing the 1956 election as a bellwether for black voting patterns and power, another manifestation of the second Reconstruction. He regarded the vote as the key to the "race problem": Once the African American's right to the vote was assured, he felt, it would "no longer serve as an issue on which to win elections. When that happens other issues will assume their true perspective and white and Negro alike can vote on them in national fashion." He long had warned that African Americans would punish any political party that, as a whole, did not seem sufficiently sympathetic to their interests in Congress, and the results confirmed the NAACP's strategy of political mobilization of black votes through its branches.

On November 6, 1956, African Americans registered their most dramatic political shift since 1936, when they had demonstrated their independence by deserting the party of Lincoln. They did not now abandon the Democratic party as overwhelmingly as they had the Republicans earlier, but with their votes they sent a very clear message indicating that, more than ever, blacks held the balance of power. By defecting from the party of Franklin Roosevelt in such significant numbers, they showed that Adlai Stevenson's pursuit of party unity with a rebellious South had been illusory at best. The Republicans scored heavily as blacks contrasted Eisenhower's civil rights record with the nonperformance of the Democratic-controlled Eighty-fourth Congress.

Vice President Nixon had carried that message to Harlem during the campaign by declaring that the Republican party was "solidly behind" the

President's civil rights program, "which means that if you support him and elect a Republican Senate and House of Representatives you will get action, not filibusters."

That was the message that Mitchell had been urging NAACP branches to send Congress. Hammering home this note, he declared in November that "seldom in the long political history of our country has a man been so helpful in defeating members of his own party" as Eastland. Returns in states like Louisiana, Texas, North Carolina, and Florida showed that "in addition to helping Republicans get elected in the North, the Eastland speeches and atrocities" were enabling the opposition party to make inroads in the South.

Unmistakably contributing to the trend was the encouraging increase in black voter strength—even though it was considerably short of the goal of three million the NAACP had set for 1956. The number of African American voters registered was only 25 percent of their voting potential—compared to 52.5 percent of whites registered—but the increase since 1944 augured substantial progress and strengthened Mitchell's game plan.

While in 1952 black voters in the South had supported Stevenson more strongly than anywhere else in the nation, in 1956 southern blacks switched more sharply to the Republican ticket than did northern blacks. Consequently, even as blacks helped the Democrats carry key wards in the North and to again deny the GOP control of both houses of Congress, their increased support of the popular Eisenhower led to a resounding reelection victory. The challenge for the GOP now was to accelerate the shift of African American voters; the Democrats wanted to halt that trend and at the same time remove the stigma that had resulted from the deep divisions within its ranks over civil rights.

A Gallup poll conducted in January 1957 supported the conclusion that there had been an abrupt shift in the nation's political base. The Gallup report observed that "of all the major groups of the nation's population, the one that shifted most to the Eisenhower-Nixon ticket last November was the Negro voter." Gallup found that the vote for Republican candidates in black districts had increased by 18 percent above the 1952 vote, when only one fifth of blacks had voted for Eisenhower. Samuel Lubell, the political analyst, placed Eisenhower's gain among blacks at 11 percent; while the NAACP's survey of election returns from predominantly black areas in sixty-three cities in all sections of the country showed a gain of 19.9 percent for Eisenhower. That meant that Stevenson had received only 62 percent of the identifiable black vote, a drop of 17 percent from 1952.[1]

Mitchell told the *Congressional Quarterly* that Democratic leaders had said in 1956, "We can't make progress on civil rights or we'll destroy our good men in the South. They won't get reelected. So we will do what we can to put pressure on the Executive Branch to push civil rights legislation. We have to keep the party together so we can keep up its social progress." The election results, he observed, jolted both the Democratic and Republican parties out of their complacency. Mitchell felt that the Democrats "learned they will have to do something to make up for their anti-Negro southern committee chairmen while the Republicans found out they can win Negro votes away from the Democrats." Mitchell believed the constant reminder of that fact represented a "refinement of our previous approach." Before "we talked too much in terms of cliches about the alliance of certain northern Republicans and southern Democrats." Now the message was that if either party wanted to win, it could not ignore the black vote.

Similar conclusions were drawn by congressional leaders of both parties. Back in April 1956, for example, anticipating the national party convention, a staff member alerted Lyndon Johnson to impending changes in attitudes within the northern wing of the Democratic party. He had learned that the consensus among the press was that the Democratic party could no longer afford the luxury of cooperating with the South. At the same time, southern whites had to be induced not to bolt the party again over civil rights. A considerably weakened civil rights plank had induced many whites not to do so and ensured the Democrats' continued control of Congress. The message was that the Democratic party had to carefully balance its interests in black and white votes in the South. The hemorrhage that the region was causing among white, as well as black, voters was regarded by Democrats as a grave threat to their majority status.

Mitchell's assessment was forcefully reinforced by Senator Richard L. Neuberger, a freshman Democrat from Oregon, in an article in *The New York Times* entitled "Democrats' Dilemma: Civil Rights." He examined the election results in terms of the impact the civil rights issue had had on white voters rather than on blacks (as Mitchell had done) but came to the same conclusions: "The civil rights dilemma loads down the Democrats in the North, as the Old Man of the Sea sat athwart the shoulders of Sinbad the Sailor."

Neuberger had awakened to that conclusion during the weeks preceding the election when he joined Wayne Morse on his reelection campaign and was hard pressed to explain Eastland throughout Oregon, a state where African Americans represented less than 2 percent of the population. Eastland, it was clear, was having the harmful effect on the Democratic party about which Mitchell had been warning. Neuberger therefore urged that for the Democrats to overcome the dilemma, Congress had to pass the civil rights bill in 1957. Like Mitchell, Neuberger had an open mind toward some southern lawmakers. He differed with northern Democrats who wanted a leader in the Senate further left than Johnson. Neuberger felt that at least until the Democrats' number in the Senate was "appreciably greater than at present," his colleagues should accept someone like Lyndon Johnson who represented a composite of their group "on the issues which move them most emotionally." Johnson, after all, along with Sam Rayburn, was one of the few southerners who did not sign the Southern Manifesto.

Mitchell, too, disagreed with the popular assumption that the South was solidly conservative. To the contrary, he understood, there was a tradition of liberalism in the region. He noted that many southerners had challenged McCarthyism, and voted to censure the senator. Many of them like Lyndon Johnson took the lead in supporting the Rural Electrification Administration and the Tennessee Valley Authority. Congressman Frank E. "Cotton Ed" Smith of Mississippi had sponsored the original farm price support legislation that became a big issue in the 1956 campaign; John Sparkman was a leading public housing advocate; Richard Russell had led the fight for the free school lunch program; Lister Hill was a main proponent of federal aid to education and was coauthor of the Hill-Burton Act for hospital construction (with its segregation provision); and Olin Johnston was very prolabor. The South, Mitchell concluded, was split evenly between liberals and conservatives. Although most lawmakers from the region were diehard segregationists, he felt that given the national political picture, they could be made, one way or another, to bend on civil rights. The bottom line, though, was that most Republicans would very likely support civil rights in order to increase their support among blacks.

Few in Congress could match Mitchell's knowledge of national politics or parliamentary rules. He had found that to counter the wiley southerners, who were using the rules with devastating effect on civil rights, he had to know them at least as well as they. He received much help from Congressman Adam Clayton Powell, who gave him his parliamentary rule book, and from Richard Bolling. He learned the Senate's rules by observing proceedings from the gallery.[2]

In the wake of the 1949 filibuster-rule-change debacle, reformers had shifted their focus from the need to liberalize the cloture rule to the majority's right to adopt standing rules at the beginning of each Congress. The Knowland-Wherry substitute amendment barred that right. Signaling the beginning of a new battle on the eve of the Eighty-third Congress, Herbert Lehman summed up the reformers' unhappiness by demanding, "Why should it be considered that rules adopted by majority vote, in the 1st session of the Senate in 1789, are binding and in effect in the Senate, without affirmative, majority action on the part of the Senate of 1953?" The reformers regarded the Constitution as the authority on the issue, with its provision that a majority of "Each House may determine the rules of the proceedings."

The civil rights forces in 1953 had a true conservative to contend with as majority leader. Mitchell was therefore not surprised when, on the opening day of the Eighty-third Congress, Robert Taft bluntly rejected the pleas of a civil rights delegation led by Walter White from the fifty-three national organizations then comprising the Leadership Conference on Civil Rights to help curb the filibuster by adopting new rules for the Senate. Taft said that upon his recommendation, the Republican party caucus had voted against any change. Holding to the traditional opposition line, he told the delegation that the Senate was a continuing body so it was not required to adopt rules at the beginning of each new Congress as was the House. Taft acknowledged that the current requirement of 64 votes to invoke cloture was too stringent and needed to be reduced, but he was not willing to try to change the filibuster rule at that time. Not surprisingly, Taft was supported by Richard Russell, leader of the Dixiecrats. Wiser by Truman's experience, Eisenhower announced a hands-off policy. He stressed that the Senate should decide its own business free of outside interference. Taft maintained that despite the stringent cloture rule, if the senators were "sincere and interested," the 64 votes needed to cut off talkathons on civil rights measures could be obtained.

Joseph Rauh, who since 1950 had been walking the halls of Congress with Mitchell without a major victory, challenged Taft's argument that the Senate was a continuing body with an exhaustive brief for lawmakers he prepared to show otherwise. Rauh maintained that the Senate could not be a continuing body since all bills that were not enacted into law died at the end of each session of Congress; unconfirmed presidential appointments similarly died, as did all unratified treaties. But such arguments were to no avail. Four days later, at the end of the second day of debate, the Senate voted 21 to 70 to table a motion that had been offered by Clinton Anderson to consider the adoption of rules for the Eighty-third Congress. Had that move prevailed, Irving Ives, as the southerners feared, would have introduced a motion to revise the filibuster rule. Supporting Taft's move to table Anderson's motion were 41 Republicans and 29 Democrats. Five Republicans, 15 Democrats, and one Independent (Wayne Morse, who later became a Democrat) voted against Taft. The Republicans indicated that they might consider an antifilibuster resolution in the spring, but it was one the NAACP thought least desirable. The pretense only increased Mitchell's frustrations.[3]

Four years later, with prospects for action on civil rights legislation brighter than ever, the first battle line remained the filibuster, not the bill itself. The politics, though, were markedly different. First, with the Democrats again controlling the Senate, by a slim 49–47 margin, Lyndon Johnson occupied the majority leader's chair. Second, those with eyes on the 1960 presidential election—mainly Johnson, Minority Leader Knowland, Vice President Nixon, and Hubert Humphrey—were already preparing on the opening day of the Eighty-fifth Congress for the campaign. Not long after the November elections, Johnson's office quietly made it known that a civil rights bill would be passed in the next session of Congress. He told southerners in no uncertain terms that they had better drop their customary "corn and pot liquor" arguments and address themselves to the merits of the issue. He informed one reporter, "It was realized that there could be no 'compromise' in the sense of an empty and evasive deal. The bill that was going to emerge had to have meaning and substance."[4]

Less than an hour after the Senate convened on January 3, 1957, Anderson once more moved to consider adoption of the rules. He was joined by 14 Democrats and 11 Republicans, many of whom were stalwart liberals. They repeated arguments that the Senate was not a continuing body, so that at the beginning of each Congress members had a right to adopt rules unhindered by the filibuster. The liberals encouraged Nixon, as president of the Senate, to rule favorably on their motion to reverse the Knowland-Wherry provision. Nixon granted their request by offering an advisory opinion, but he cleverly referred the motion to the Senate, forcing it to make the decision. He said the Senate could adopt new rules "under whatever procedures the majority of the Senate" approved. Voicing the liberals' line, he maintained that the Senate could not be bound by any previous rule that denied its membership the power to exercise its constitutional right to make its own rules. To do otherwise, he argued, was unconstitutional. But the conservatives ruled the day. The Senate immediately approved 55 to 38 Johnson's motion to table the Anderson motion. That action kept in place the old 1949 rule. Both Johnson and Knowland, who also opposed the Anderson motion, thus won time for subsequent further maneuvering. The skirmish was a good indication of how the senators, especially the Republicans, would vote on civil rights in this session. A hopeful development was that 17 more senators than in 1953 now supported the reformers.[5]

Nixon, too, won points with the civil rights forces. Furthermore, because the rejection was only temporary, Nixon's opinion could easily be converted from an opinion to a ruling at the beginning of the Eighty-sixth Congress unless the senators acted before that date to head off the next likely challenge. Based on an assessment of the vote on the tabling motion that was done for Johnson by his staff, a majority of senators would uphold the Nixon ruling in the next Congress. That would open the way for a simple Senate majority to adopt new rules for a majority cloture, which was what the NAACP wanted. Consequently, Russell began working quietly with Johnson to offer a resolution to change the cloture requirement from two thirds of the entire Senate to two thirds of senators present and voting. That was recognized as only a technical change since it was expected that an attempt to impose cloture would find the full Senate assembled. By giving the impression of having made a concession to the liberals, Johnson was able to end further demands for change. The modification would benefit the South because Rule XXII had really not been changed. In cooperation with Knowland, Johnson also began taking steps that would repeal the Knowland-Wherry provision barring clotures on resolutions amending the standing rules. Johnson's office felt that the question of permitting cloture on a motion to take up the rules was a concession that had to be made or the northerners would oppose the more important step, which was "a specific measure stating the rules continue from Congress to Congress." Johnson's strategy was guaranteed to defeat alternative proposals and to protect himself against the type of isolation that destroyed Scott Lucas in 1949. He yielded a little to the reformers, but only enough to protect his authority without weakening what he perceived as the Senate's institutional integrity. Neither did he injure his prospects for 1960.[6]

Mitchell's main concern, however, was not 1960 but the struggle over the civil rights bill itself. As he later explained, although most people assumed that it was impossible to pass civil rights legislation under the 1949 rules, he never thought so. Rule XXII only made the job more difficult. Neither did he believe that Eastland could continue indefinitely bottling up civil rights bills in the Judiciary Committee. In fact, Mitchell said, the unsuccessful filibuster fight had given new strength to those who insisted that the Senate should be able to limit debate by forcing them to concentrate their energies on passing civil rights legislation. More important for him was guiding the struggle through the shoals of conflicting personalities and treacherous political waters. One memorable difficulty for him was the acrimonious conflicts between Herbert Brownell and Thomas Hennings, both of whose support was crucial to success. Because of personality differences that were obvious in early 1957, Mitchell could never get the attorney general and the chairman of the Senate Committee on Constitutional Rights to cooperate.

His ace in the hole was the conservative Knowland, who announced in January that he would retire at the end of his current term in 1958 to give more attention to his job as assistant publisher of the *Oakland Tribune,* the family newspaper in California. Many people knew, however, that he wanted to seek his party's nomination for President. Knowland first came to the Senate in 1945 when then governor of California Earl Warren, who was now Chief Justice of the U.S. Supreme Court, appointed him to fill the vacancy created by the death of the previous occupant of that seat. Knowland until now, in addition to being opposed to filibuster reforms, had not been a civil rights supporter. He was Robert Taft's handpicked successor as majority leader and had joined in maintaining the southern Democratic–northern Republican coalition that had been strengthened by Taft and Senator Eugene D. Millikin of Colorado to assure votes for the tax and fiscal policies of business and banking backers of the Republican party. While Taft and Millikin reciprocated as usual on civil rights, Nixon began building his presidential strategy on the black vote, forcing Knowland to abandon the coalition and follow suit. Knowland unequivocally promised Mitchell that he would lead the struggle to end the almost certain filibuster of the civil rights bill.

Knowland confidently told the *Congressional Quarterly* that the Senate would approve civil rights legislation in 1957 regardless of the filibuster. Minority Leader Joseph W. Martin, Jr., a conservative from Massachusetts, also felt that there was "no question" that the House would approve the administration bill in "about two days."[7]

Members of the Leadership Conference on Civil Rights joined the struggle full force as a coalition and as individual groups, with respective leaders assuming prominent roles in enlisting support for civil rights legislation in Congress. The challenge was to use the rearranged political setting to advantage. A more formal working relationship between the NAACP and the conference had been adopted, with Arnold Aaronson serving as secretary. Most of the organizations agreed to speak with one powerful, unified voice through Roy Wilkins, chairman of the coalition.

Aaronson coordinated activities among the Leadership Conference's members and acted as Wilkins's deputy to those groups. This arrangement enabled Mitchell to work with Wilkins, not in tandem and as an equal as he had with Walter White, but along clearly established lines of responsibility in a situation where the Washington Bureau director was the principal legislative strategist for the NAACP as well as for the coalition, and the chief civil rights lobbyist. Wilkins, during the key debates on the Senate floor, would spend two thirds of his time in Washington testifying on the Hill and rounding up support from allies to impose on lawmakers the full prestige and influence of the NAACP and the Leadership Conference. Wilkins and Mitchell displayed considerable respect for each other and worked closely as a team.

Mitchell and Francis Pohlhaus, bureau counsel, attempted as much as possible to have face-to-face contacts with lawmakers in their Capitol Hill rounds and made a special effort to get members of the Judiciary and Rules committees to attend meetings. With Wilkins's help, Mitchell continued to encourage local NAACP leaders to call or write their senators and congressmen urging them to act favorably on civil rights legislation. Mitchell was being helped by the *Congressional Quarterly,* which not only devoted considerable attention to him and the NAACP but also to the importance of the black vote.[8]

The drive in Congress for passage of civil rights legislation proceeded with the introduction of numerous bills in the House and Senate and was given a somewhat forceful push by Eisenhower in his State of the Union Message. Once more, Attorney General Brownell called on Congress to correct what he regarded as a major defect in the law by approving the administration bill. Parts I, establishing the Civil Rights Commission; II, creating the Civil Rights Division within the Justice Department; and IV, giving the attorney general authority to seek injunctions in court to protect Fifteenth Amendment rights, were based on recommendations by the President's Committee on Civil Rights. Part III, Brownell's brainchild, provided the attorney general with authority to seek injunctions in civil suits to protect Fourteenth Amendment rights in cases involving civil rights violations.

Brownell was particularly concerned about rebuilding the GOP's strength and evidently saw an opportunity to do so in the bill. When he became chairman of the Republican National Committee in 1944, there was a prevalent opinion among party members "that the Republican Party was finished and that it would never again be the majority party." It was weak in governorships and in both houses of Congress. The reluctance of voters "to change horses in the middle of the stream" during the war meant that the GOP was "merely going through the motions of fielding a candidate for President." Brownell's goal was to reestablish the two-party system as a functional reality, and he was responsible for beginning the comeback of the modern Republican party. The revival was obvious in 1948, when the general feeling "among Republican leaders around the country was that there was an opportunity to win." Therefore, Brownell in 1948 found that it was much harder than in 1944 to get the GOP presidential nomination for Governor Thomas Dewey of New York because he was now considered merely a stalking horse. Brownell evidently believed that giving the GOP a high civil rights profile would help correct this weakness.

The catalyst that led Brownell to devise Part III was the murder of Emmett Till, after which the Justice Department received thousands of letters demanding action. After a very careful study of the laws, he was concerned that "we could never find any evidence that would allow us to act under any federal statute." The Till murder dramatized for Brownell "the lack of power of the attorney general and the Department of Justice to act in matters of this kind to enforce the constitutional promise that had been made to our citizens."

The administration bill had critical weaknesses. Private suits, long, drawn out, and costly, would have to be filed before the government could intervene. The poor and disadvantaged would have to bear the grave burdens of seeking protection for their rights even with the NAACP's assured support. Remedy would also be slow and would be limited to the individual in a given community—there would be no class action benefits for a whole group of people. Nevertheless, the bill promised to end the government's neutrality when citizens were denied the right to vote.[9]

An important concern for Mitchell and among liberals was to get the bill through the House as quickly as possible so that there would be enough time in the Senate to overcome the filibuster and to forestall opponents who wanted to prolong the hearings so they could "press for all kinds of weakening amendments." That strategy would avoid a problem experienced in the Eighty-fourth Congress when the administration submitted its proposals so late that there was not enough time for the Senate to act on a bill before adjournment. Recognizing the dangers of election year politics, Congressman Bolling surreptitiously helped to stall action on the bill so that it wasn't torn to shreds in the inevitable Senate filibuster just before the Democratic National Convention was to begin on August 13. When, however, Emanuel Celler, chairman of the House Judiciary Committee, and Thomas Hennings, chairman of the Senate Subcommittee on Constitutional Rights, attempted to get the bills reported promptly out of the Judiciary Committee in 1957, they met opposition. Though unwelcome, this delay, gave the NAACP and its allies time to document more fully the level of racial oppression in the South.[10]

The committee hearings were crucial because they were the only opportunity outside the House and Senate chambers for private individuals to have their views put on record. Second, the committee hearings provided a record of the intent of Congress. Their third and most important function was to shape a basic bill for consideration by the full House and Senate. The going was particularly rough as the hearings began Thursday, February 14, because Congress had not passed any civil rights legislation since Reconstruction.

Mitchell was assured favorable action by the House Judiciary Committee. In addition to Celler, its members included stalwart supporters like Peter Rodino, Democrat of New Jersey, and Republicans Kenneth Keating of New York and William McCulloch. Mitchell was impressed by McCulloch, from Piqua, Ohio, because there were only a handful of blacks in his district. Despite this lack of political incentive, he had few equals in his consistent support for civil rights.

The manner in which the cream of the old South's segregationists appeared before the committee to deny fiercely the need for a civil rights law made Mitchell wonder whether they intended to stage a second attack on

Fort Sumter. The cast of characters included former and future governors, state attorneys general, celebrated orators and other naysayers, but the stars were Sam Ervin, Herman Talmadge, and Strom Thurmond. Mitchell marveled at the patience with which Celler and cochairman Keating heard them. George Corley Wallace, then a minor circuit judge in Alabama, was cordial: "I enjoyed my service with the distinguished chairman in Chicago on the platform committee at the Democratic National Convention. We differed on many matters there, especially on the matter of civil rights, but I found the chairman fair and willing to listen to arguments of us people from the South."[11]

Resigned to the inevitable, the southerners adopted a strategy of weakening the bill by attacking its most vulnerable parts. Mitchell saw another opportunity in the committee hearings to outflank opponents who were attempting to undercut the NAACP by charging that much of the testimony from its leaders about abuses in the South was "hearsay." For the Senate hearings he brought up Gus Courts of Belzoni, Mississippi, the Reverend William Holmes Borders, pastor of the historic Wheat Street Baptist Church in Atlanta, and other witnesses from the South who could provide firsthand experiences of oppression.

Mitchell never counted on Sam Ervin's obfuscatory tactics, which he used to test Brownell's temperament and knowledge during three days of wrangling and needling. Ervin's adversaries frequently found themselves not only up against the Senate's acknowledged best raconteur but also confronted with a host of folk heroes like Job Hicks, Uncle Ephraim, or Old Jim, who were all endowed with the eternal wisdom of the senator's native Morganton Hills of North Carolina. As Dixie's handsome sixty-year-old knight-jester, he contrasted sharply with the rough hill people he so often fondly spoke of. Ervin was as suave in his recitation of constitutional precepts as he was in dress—highly polished shoes, fine fabrics, and tasteful cravats.

Most of the controversy between Ervin and Brownell centered on the 1957 Civil Rights Act's deleted Part III provisions giving the attorney general authority to seek injunctions or other civil remedies for suspected violations of civil rights. Ervin said he disagreed with the attorney general on the "fundamental proposition" that the federal government should be empowered to bring suits on behalf of individuals who alleged that their rights had been violated. It was Brownell's unwavering position that "if there is a public right involved, that is the obligation of the government official."

On a provision giving federal courts authority to take jurisdiction of right-to-vote cases before all appeals to state administrative and judicial authorities had been exhausted, Ervin objected to what he saw as the federal government's passing upon and making "the final determination both as to" the voter's "possession of the qualifications prescribed by state law and his qualifications under the 14th and 15th Amendments." Brownell explained that the federal government would not be empowered to act unless a person's rights had been violated and that would be "no more so than under present law."

Ervin's third objection—and southerners made it one of the most controversial by saying that the provision was a power grab by the attorney general—concerned the proposed use of injunctions and other civil remedies—as opposed to criminal ones—to protect the right to vote. Ervin demanded to know whether Brownell would "give a remedy which for all practical purposes would supplant existing remedies which give" the election official a *right* to be "indicted by a grand jury and tried before a petit jury and be confronted and have the right to cross-examine his accusers." Brownell responded, "You would rather have us send him to jail than to get an injunction against him?" He knew that the southerners preferred this alternative because the status quo made it all but impossible to get a jury to convict such officials on criminal charges.

Because Ervin, for three days, spent so much time putting Brownell through the constitutional wringer, Mitchell found himself in the unhappy position late that Saturday afternoon of pleading with a normally sympathetic Hennings for his witnesses to be heard. "The great tragedy is that these people pay their own expenses" to come to Washington, Mitchell explained. With Ervin in mind, Hennings could only respond, "I feel very strongly that it is our duty to hear every witness who wants to be heard, but I do not feel it is our duty to stay all day and all night and Saturdays and Sundays in order to listen to lengthy cross examinations and get into that." Enjoying his command performances, Ervin refused to give Hennings any indication of when his examination would end.

Under those circumstances, Hennings could not even allow Mitchell to submit the prepared testimonies of his witnesses because Ervin wanted extended time to rebut them. Said the unflappable North Carolinian, "Having looked at the nature of these statements, it is going to be an impossibility to finish with a single one of these witnesses this afternoon, because there are some lengthy charges without specifications." He insisted, "I am going to cross-examine." A weary Hennings welcomed a motion to adjourn some time after 4:00 P.M. Mitchell sent an angry night letter to several subcommittee members who had been absent urging them to attend a meeting of the full Judiciary Committee the coming Monday and support an effort by Hennings to limit the hearings in order to prevent the civil rights bills from being killed "by unfair delay." He informed them that the witnesses who could not testify would have to return that Monday at their own expense to do so.

They did so, but then Mitchell ran into another problem. Because of his wife's illness, Courts had to cut short his testimony before the committee and hurry back home to Chicago. During a break in the hearings, Senators Johnston and McClellan approached Mitchell in the hallway, where he was talking to a group of reporters, and hinted at their plans to discredit the witnesses. Said Johnston, "We are going to get some of these boys for perjury; coming up here talking about bodies in rivers and things" of that sort. Mitchell felt Courts was particularly vulnerable to those threats because of possible conflicts with his income tax returns as they pertained to his business losses when he fled Mississippi, so he never brought him back.[12]

Wilkins, however, was under no pressure when he appeared before House and Senate committees along with Mitchell. Testifying with a low-key, forceful eloquence, he provided a wealth of detail on the oppression of blacks in the South in order to justify the need for the Eisenhower administration's proposals. His basic position, he maintained, was that although the executive branch had taken several steps to end segregation and discrimination in various areas, Congress had not passed any similar legislation in more than eighty years. To halt practices denying blacks the right to vote in the South as well as to break the legislative stalemate, the approximately twenty-five organizations for which he was speaking were willing "to compromise our demands, though without relinquishing our principles." He pointed to weaknesses in the administration's proposals, noting that the legislation in question "took no account of the problem of discrimination in employment; it made no reference to segregation in interstate transportation; it did not deal with the poll tax or with violence directed against members of the armed services or with several other pressing issues." The supporting organizations were "willing to accept much less at this time than we believe to be justified," he said, because they wanted a civil rights bill to pass. But in accepting a *"minimum"* bill, he stressed, "it must be a *meaningful* bill" like H.R. 627, which the House had passed in 1956. The administration's bill was now represented by H.R. 1151, which was introduced in the House by Republican Kenneth Keating of New York. In the Senate, the administration's proposals were contained in S. 83, which was introduced by Everett Dirksen, minority whip, and thirty-six other senators.

Buttressing Wilkins's call for legislative protections for the right to vote, the NAACP submitted to the Senate Subcommittee on Constitutional Rights an article, among other exhibits, from the December 10, 1956, issue of *Life* magazine documenting the painful travail of a family in Choc-

taw County, Alabama, which was driven out of the area by economic pressure because the wife of the black businessman was quoted in an earlier
issue of the magazine as saying, "Integration is the only way through which
Negroes will receive justice. We cannot get it as a separate people. If we
can get justice on our jobs, and equal pay, then we'll be able to afford
better homes and good education." That was a simple enough demand,
but it was death to the southerners' way of life—the central issue of the
struggle.

Not only administrative devices (such as literacy tests and inconvenient
registration days and hours), Wilkins stressed, but also economic reprisals
and open violence had been used to bar blacks from voting and seeking
their constitutional rights. He referred to Mississippi's Sovereignty Commission, a Gestapo-type operation established by opponents of civil rights
legislation who feared that the passage of measures safeguarding the constitutional rights of black citizens would "doom their empire of thought-
control and secret police." Then, as Ervin was about to begin his prodding,
Wilkins took his stand: "There have been inflammatory speeches by persons in responsible positions of government, local, state, and national.
There have been shootings and bombings of homes and churches. There
have been mobs and threats of bodily harm. There have been economic
pressures. Special statutes, selective, discriminatory, and punitive in
nature, have been passed by state legislatures."

Despite their outrage, blacks had been patient "because they felt that
they were on the side of the law and the Constitution." They had not
succumbed to despair or to the great temptation to defend themselves in
kind. They had hoped "that the Congress, the Chief Executive, and the law
enforcement officers of government would protect their rights." But they
were now being discouraged by "the incredibly lengthy discussions of technical language which, they are told, is necessary to protect the constitutional rights of those who have made careers out of denying Negro citizens
their constitutional rights."

The system of injustices the pending legislation was designed to correct
had "been in open operation for decades. No one, least of all an officeholder
who is the beneficiary of such practices, pretends not to understand their
function. No one suggests, soberly and with a straight face, that these
procedures are, in the real sense, constitutional."

One injustice was the blatant denial by local registrars of the rights of
blacks to register and vote. When those practices were challenged, "some
of the representatives elected under that system function in faraway Washington as attorneys for the defense, secure in the knowledge that they will
not be answerable to the victims at the ballot box."

Wilkins demanded, "Are our great traditions of freedom to be traduced in this transparent manner? Is there no hope for frustrated and beleaguered citizens beyond the despotism of local overlords? Is there a United States of America? Does it have a Constitution and does that document have meaning for more than the cunning and the strong?"

These victims, he said, were merely asking for "a minimum safeguard of the constitutional rights which have been so long denied them. But in the face of this patience, in the face of these provocations, even this minimum is being challenged."

Wilkins warned that he could not predict the mood that these outrages that had existed for eighty years would inspire. "I know only that it is a terrible responsibility for any man or men in high office to destroy the hope of any people that fair and orderly government will secure to them their just heritage as law-abiding citizens."

Ervin was undeterred by such lectures and attempted to drag Wilkins into the quagmire of the fine points of constitutional law. Wilkins calmly disarmed him by maintaining that he was a layman, not a lawyer. Then he proceded to beat Ervin with simple logic.

Wilkins: Senator, I believe, and perhaps because I am a layman I am not able to follow these things exactly, but what confuses me is, is this injunctive procedure about which you speak, which you describe as a new process, is that now not presently in the law in criminal procedure and civil procedure?

Ervin: Not in civil rights cases nor in the generality of criminal cases.

Wilkins: But it is in the law. I mean the injunctive procedure is allowable in the law; it is not?

Ervin: In a comparatively minor number of cases, the Congress has passed laws creating things which are both criminal offenses and civil wrongs, and in limited classes of cases, they have authorized injunctive relief against acts which fit both of those categories.

Wilkins: Senator, the reason I ask you this is because we have as an organization a special concern about it, because we have recently been in the courts in an injunction procedure, and we have not had any jury. We have been hauled in, as you say, summarily, but we have not maintained that this injunctive procedure, in itself as a procedure, has done us an injustice.

If you say this is a new procedure which violates all of these guarantees that you speak of, then I am genuinely alarmed, not only generally, but for myself personally. [13]

Mitchell, who provided backup testimony, had his day in Ervin's court and got considerable unwitting help from such diehard segregationists as the Louisiana attorney general and Governor James P. Coleman of Mississippi. Not only did the attorney general insist that there was no widespread denial of the right to vote in his state, but he also maintained that the extensive purges that had occurred in Ouachita Parish had been corrected. Mitchell joined Olney in refuting those claims by obtaining a statement from his sources in the state showing that the voters had not been returned to the rolls.

Mitchell reiterated his contention that blacks were tired of being studied and that remedies did not exist in southern state courts for racial injustices. Blacks were "bitterly disillusioned." He maintained that the civil rights bill would remedy "the most pressing aspects of this problem." Furthermore, the Civil Rights Commission would conduct scientific studies that would establish guidelines for other remedies.

In response to Ervin's persistent clamor for a jury trial amendment, Mitchell recalled the intellectual contest between Ervin and Brownell: "As an observer on the sidelines, I would say that if I were sitting in a jury and heard these two magnificent lawyers contest that issue, when I retired to the jury room I would be inclined to give the verdict to the attorney general because I respectfully submit, Mr. Chairman, that these questions which you have raised are not really a part of what we have to fear in the country." Mitchell said that the greater fear was that while the United States was "engaged in very laudable excursions to all parts of the world for the purpose of defending democracy, there is a serious problem right here at home that we do not seem to have the means of correcting under present law."

Mitchell also sought to have Governor Coleman confirm the intention of the Mississippi state legislature in creating the State Sovereignty Commission. In response to his questioning on this point, Coleman replied:

"In 1954 before I was governor of Mississippi and as soon as the Supreme Court decision was handed down . . . the Governor then called a special session of the legislature and an amendment was proposed to the constitution which would abolish any public school if it were to be integrated. That was submitted to the people and they ratified it at the polls and it is now a part of the constitution of the State of Mississippi. It is utterly legally impossible, it is legally impossible to integrate a school in Mississippi. If the U.S. Supreme Court were to order one integrated they would just be closed up and those who sought to have it integrated would be like Samson who pulled the temple down on his own head.[14]

This was exactly what Mitchell had wanted the Mississippi governor to state for the record. His position supported the NAACP's claim that without meaningful federal civil rights laws, the South would continue defying the Constitution and undermining the American system of democracy.

To counter the jury trial amendment threat, Mitchell began an extensive campaign of disseminating information aimed at unmasking the hypocrisy behind Ervin's arguments. He was fully aware that progressive forces in the South were increasingly restive, as the *Carolina Times* made clear in a bitter editorial: "Either Senator Ervin is an inveterate liar or he is grossly ignorant of what is going on in North Carolina, too ignorant to represent four million of its citizens in the U.S. Senate." The newspaper was especially upset that Ervin had said that "until today I never heard of a single individual in my state that's been denied the right to vote." It was of great concern to the newspaper that

> when one hears or reads of such ignorance on the part of southern representatives in Congress and the legislatures of southern states, there is no wonder that this section of the nation can produce no men of presidential caliber, or such few leaders in other fields. There is also no wonder that North Carolina stands almost at the bottom of the ladder in education, value of public school property, amount of weekly wages paid for all employment. Only Arkansas and Mississippi rank lower. It is utterly impossible to raise the educational standards, the economic level and develop a great state, otherwise, when its leaders in public office, both federal and state, are of the caliber so plainly disclosed by Senator Ervin.

As in other cases, Mitchell used detailed documentary evidence, prepared with the help of Washington Bureau counsel Frank Pohlhaus, to refute his opponents' claims that there was no need for civil rights legislation or for a particular provision. Ervin's own words, from his days as a judge on the North Carolina Supreme Court, were among Mitchell's best weapons: "[I]n this state a contempt proceeding is authorized by statute. . . . This court has described it as *sui generis,* criminal in its nature, which may be resorted to in civil or criminal actions. . . . And it is held that persons charged are not entitled to a jury trial in such proceedings."

The NAACP's position, established as a result of the committee hearings, would enable the association's allies to prepare better for the extensive debates, especially on the Senate floor.

Under the North Carolina statutes on which Ervin's opinion was based, the NAACP Washington Bureau said, a person charged with contempt of court did not receive a jury trial. Neither did he have a right of appeal if the contempt was committed in the court. "In this respect," the NAACP explained, "the North Carolina law grants less protection than comparable federal law." The NAACP explained that the statute granted the power to find contempt to any court, justice of the peace, referee, commissioner, clerk of court, county board of commissioners, utility commissioner, or industrial commissioner. Yet Ervin was now the chief spokesman for those who alleged that a jury trial in contempt cases was necessary to preserve the American form of government. Citing cases and penalties, the NAACP stressed that while he had served on the North Carolina Supreme Court, the senator strictly applied state law that recognized the contempt principle of punishment—although in Ervin's case the strict application of the law meant doing so only against labor unions and their members.

The NAACP found that during Ervin's tenure on the North Carolina Supreme Court, he had participated in thirteen contempt cases. The court had nullified nine of them but upheld four involving injunctions or restraining orders against unions and their members that limited picketing during the course of strikes against textile mills. Although Ervin was "now inveighing mightily against alleged dangers" he saw in the proposed civil rights legislation because of the lack of the jury trial provision, the NAACP charged, there was found no "dissent or expression of opinion as to the undesirability of these features of injunctive relief, though all" were present in those cases in which he participated. The NAACP suggested that the lack of dissent was attributable to Ervin's acceptance of another principle enunciated by the North Carolina Supreme Court: "Without the ability to require obedience to its mandates . . . or to perform any other act the court is competent to require to be done—many of its most important and useful functions would be paralyzed." The NAACP said that as a judge on the state's highest court, "Ervin was bound to realize the validity of this principle, and the necessity of upholding it if the judicial power of the state was to be validated."

It was because Ervin recognized the importance of the contempt principle, which made a jury trial unnecessary, the NAACP Washington Bureau said, that he had embarked on his present course, which was part of the program of "massive resistance" to the judicial power of the federal courts. The NAACP warned that if he succeeded, it would undermine the authority of the judicial branch and raise defiance of the courts to a "respectable national pastime." Mitchell welcomed confirmation of this assessment from nationally syndicated columnist Roscoe Drummond, who wrote that "much of the opposition to the civil rights bills" was "based on the fear" that, if enacted, they would be successful in protecting the right to vote.[15]

Action in both the House and Senate became interrelated, with the main battle shaping up in the Senate, first in the Judiciary Committee, and next on the floor, where the bill faced a filibuster.* As with the Eighty-fourth Congress, it was evident that the House would easily pass a civil rights bill. The strategy was to get the strongest bill possible through the House and fight against weakening amendments in the Senate. This bill became H.R. 6127, a "clean" bill with only minor amendments bearing Celler's name that the House Judiciary Committee quickly approved on April 1 and sent to the Rules Committee. To head off the ever present threat of the bill being bottled up by hostile chairman Howard Smith, James Roosevelt again introduced a resolution in the House in preparation for initiating a discharge petition on H.R. 6127 in the event that that action was needed.

The chances of a rerun of the 1956 scene in the House Rules Committee were small, because no one now doubted that Chairman Smith could be beaten. Congressman Richard Bolling, the David of the Eighty-fourth Congress who had led the attack against Smith, despite a recent operation, faithfully attended committee sessions and fought filibuster tactics by the bill's opponents. House Majority Leader John McCormack promised that the bill would be passed "at least 2 to 1" by the end of May. That forecast might have been overly optimistic, but it was not too far off the mark. Three weeks after Congress returned from its Easter recess in May, the Rules Committee voted 8 to 4 to send the Eisenhower administration's four-part bill to the House floor under an open rule permitting four days of debate and unlimited amendments.

Earlier, Ervin and South Carolina's Olin Johnston had failed to stop the Hennings Subcommittee on Constitutional Rights from favorably reporting the civil rights bill (S. 83) to the full Judiciary Committee. Both the House Judiciary Committee and the Hennings subcommittee defeated attempts to adopt jury trial amendments. Only the day before the House Rules Committee's favorable action, the Senate Judiciary Committee had rejected by a 4 to 6 vote a proposal by Ervin to strike from the bill all but the last section with the voting rights protections. Hennings was blocked in his attempt to get the full Judiciary Committee to act promptly on the bill as opponents tried another maneuver.

The goal was to wear down the bill's supporters, but the opposition did not figure on Mitchell's stamina. Right after the Senate Judiciary Committee on April 29 adopted a motion to make S. 83 the "pending business," a

---

*The last civil rights bill cleared by the Senate Judiciary Committee, which had jurisdiction over such measures, was an antilynching bill in 1949. Despite Eastland's record, there was no indication that there would be an uprising similar to the one that had occurred in the House Rules Committee in 1956. Because there were no published rules governing individual congressional committees, precedents favored the chairman's authority. With such broad authority, Eastland could continue sitting on civil rights bills for as long as he wanted because the committee met at the chairman's call even though it was supposed to meet every Monday. *Congressional Quarterly Weekly Report*, February 15, 1957, p. 205.

majority agreed to halt consideration of the bill at any time for action on other items. Then, to use labor and the civil rights groups as foils against each other, Arkansas Democrat John L. McClellan sponsored a so-called right-to-work amendment to the bill. The measure would outlaw closed shops by making the right to work a federal concern. This development caused Mitchell to send out an "urgent communication" to NAACP branch leaders urging those whose senators were on the Judiciary Committee to pressure the lawmakers to oppose the amendment. Although the branch leader's senator might be pledged to support the civil rights legislation, Mitchell wrote, if he voted for the right-to-work amendment, liberals, who would normally back the civil rights bill, would vote against it "in an effort to defeat any threat to the rights of organized labor." Mitchell said it appeared that there would be enough votes to defeat not only the jury trial amendment but also the right-to-work amendment. Hennings and Dirksen had agreed on a substitute bill exactly like H.R. 6127 and planned to introduce it if needed. Events outside the Senate Judiciary Committee and in the House were helping to determine the bill's course.[16]

Mitchell found another strong voice in Edward P. Morgan, commentator for the American Broadcasting Company, who observed that Congress had "refined its buck-passing on civil rights to a kind of political ping-pong game, tossing responsibility for key legislation on the subject aimlessly back and forth between the House and Senate." On the "right-to-work," or "union busting" gambit, he said, one was "forced to examine the consistency if not the sincerity of men like Senator McClellan." As chairman of the committee investigating labor-management racketeering, Morgan continued, the senator no doubt would urge new restraining laws, "but he had counseled caution against tossing in punitive measures prematurely." Now McClellan had come up with what was clearly a "transparent attempt to block the civil rights bills." Furthermore, if there had been any fear that the Senate Democratic leadership would carry the civil rights fight, "Lyndon Johnson dispelled it" by his statement that there was "no point in raising deep divisions." Concluded Morgan: "If the senior senator from Texas is not careful, he may find himself sued for plagiarisms by President Eisenhower who is plainly in no mood to raise deep divisions on the subject either. His last recorded opinion was expressed April 24 to an interracial conference in Nashville. He urged new plans and effective programs to make service of God and neighbor meaningful."[17]

An anxious Mitchell was on the attack. He told the New England Regional Conference of NAACP Branches that the pending civil rights bill was "a test of whether our country really believes in safeguarding the right to vote." He explained that when the "fake arguments" of opponents were stripped away, it became clear that they really did not want blacks to get the vote in the South. He voiced his "shock and dismay" that northern senators like Joseph C. O'Mahoney of Wyoming and party whip Mike Mansfield of Montana, both Democrats, had joined southern lawmakers in attacking parts of the bill. "Their support of arguments offered by Senator Harry Byrd of Virginia and Senator Sam Ervin of North Carolina against court enforcement of lawful decrees, when voting rights have been denied, is one of the biggest political surprises since Harry Truman defeated Tom Dewey."

He said that the Republicans could not expect those who believed in civil rights "to accept a supine surrender to a renaissance of the confederacy in Congress." Although the forces of the South were "able, resourceful, and intelligent," they simply did not have the votes to beat civil rights unless New England, midwestern, and border state Republicans allowed them to do so. He gave backhanded praise to Massachusetts Senators John F. Kennedy and Leverett Saltonstall for having risen to "positions of respect and power" in their parties. Both, he said, were deeply concerned about foreign affairs and military problems, and so he hoped that local NAACP leaders would "call upon them to bring their great skill and persuasive powers to bear on the home front problem of civil rights."[18]

Mitchell welcomed increased activity by the White House on pending legislation that was apparently generated by the President's continuing fuzzy responses in his press conferences to questions on the civil rights bill. At this May 15 press conference, for example, Eisenhower had caused considerable uneasiness among the bill's supporters by saying he was not prepared to comment on the jury trial amendment, and suggesting that the reporter discuss the issue with the attorney general. Mitchell felt better after Deputy Attorney General, William P. Rogers, subsequently briefed Eisenhower and legislative leaders on the bill. The President then demonstrated a better understanding of the issues at his June 5 press conference, when he unequivocally expressed his opposition to the jury trial amendment. He forcefully noted that when William Howard Taft had been President, he "stated that if we tried to put a jury trial between a court order and the enforcement of that order, that we are really welcoming anarchy."

Senators leading the fight had begun to draw up careful plans to get the civil rights bill through the upper chamber. On April 29, the day Congress returned from its Easter recess, Paul Douglas, the bill's floor manager, proposed that the Senate move to "discharge" the Judiciary Committee if it did not act on the measure by the middle of June. That same day, Knowland's office telephoned Mitchell to let him know that the senator had returned to Washington sooner than expected. Because Knowland wanted to meet with the NAACP leaders promptly, Mitchell asked Wilkins to keep his calendar "reasonably clear" that week so there would be no problem in setting up the appointment. Next, Mitchell recommended to Wilkins that the NAACP discuss the following points with Knowland: (1) opposition to the jury trial amendments; (2) opposition to the right-to-work amendment; (3) the question of whether Knowland would support a move to discharge the Senate Judiciary Committee if necessary; (4) the question of timing (when the Senate should take up the bill after the Senate Judiciary Committee had reported it out and it had been placed on the calendar); and (5) the question of whether Knowland would insist that the Senate remain in session beyond its regular adjournment date if necessary. Mitchell sought assurances on this last point in the hope of heading off a possible move to carry the civil rights bill over into the next session of Congress in 1958, when it would have become an election issue.

Knowland further encouraged Mitchell by announcing that he was opposed to including disruptive amendments in the bill. On May 2 he also assured a civil rights delegation including the NAACP that he favored keeping the Senate in session during the summer, if necessary, to pass the bill.

Lyndon Johnson announced that the Senate would not take up the bill until after the House had acted, a subtle expression of support since the House had the votes to pass not only a civil rights bill but also a strong one. It was well known that Johnson wanted a compromise. Knowland was the key to Mitchell's strategy; the more important individual from the standpoint of partisan politics was Johnson, although Johnson's influence was often less obvious. Unless Johnson favored the bill, it could not pass the Senate, just as it could not get through the House without Rayburn's approval. The most important consideration for Johnson, therefore, was to avoid a filibuster. On that question, he obtained the cooperation of Richard Russell, who subsequently worked out an agreement with the southerners to forestall a talkathon. Having won House Majority Leader McCormack's agreement to schedule debate on H.R. 6127 early in June, Mitchell was well on his way to achieving the long-sought legislative breakthrough.[19]

Another important conference on technical aspects of the bill involved Mitchell; Pohlhaus; Harry Kingman, the Hubert Humphrey–type liberal from California; a representative of Senator Clifford Case's office; and several Justice Department lawyers. Kingman founded his private Citizens' Lobby organization after retiring as general secretary of Stiles Hall, the University of California at Berkeley's campus YMCA. He went to Washington to contribute his efforts through the Leadership Conference on Civil Rights and helped establish a solid relationship between Mitchell and William Knowland.

Although Knowland was a conservative, Kingman explained, the senator had been very sympathetic to the plight of the Japanese Americans who had been forcibly evacuated from California during World War II. In the fall of 1956, Kingman wrote Knowland to express his interest in civil rights and began working to get the senator to meet with Mitchell. Kingman's efforts, as it turned out, were unnecessary since Mitchell had on his own initiative already approached and met with Knowland; but the humanist Kingman's written compliments to Knowland had helped cement his friendship with Mitchell. Following the conference with Justice Department lawyers, Case and Thomas Kuchel wrote to Brownell to inquire about technical points that had been discussed, and again got the attorney general on record. In his June 3 response to the senators, Brownell drew substantially on an American Civil Liberties Union statement that had been included in the *Congressional Record* and thus demonstrated that his position on the jury trial amendment was identical with that of the NAACP and its allies.[20]

Immediately after the Rules Committee reported out the bill, the House approved the four-day debate rule by a vote of 290 to 117. The following day it agreed by unanimous consent to reduce debate to three days, ostensibly so that Rayburn could participate in a Navy function, but the Speaker really wanted to accelerate the debate. Rayburn further helped by overruling a point of order raised against the bill by Rules Committee chairman Smith that would have sent the bill back to the Judiciary Committee because of alleged technical imperfections. That parliamentary maneuver was among the many traps the bill still faced. Although southerners raised points of order in the House to stall action on many bills, Mitchell found that they prevailed only on civil rights legislation, because this was given "a different kind of treatment" from other bills, and not because the southerners were "such parliamentary wizards." He expected that the southerners would launch their major attack on the bill with three or four amendments, but it appeared to him that there were sufficient votes to defeat them. Once more, Mitchell called on the NAACP field troops to lobby their congressmen.

The Supreme Court's blockbuster rulings on June 17 in three milestone internal-security cases, which rebuked the government for abuses of individual freedoms, struck chords of liberalism that resounded throughout the executive branch and Congress. Joseph Rauh argued the most important of these, which involved John T. Watkins, a UAW official who was convicted of refusing to provide the House Un-American Activities Committee with the names of Communists. Speaking for the majority in overturning Watkins's conviction, Chief Justice Earl Warren declared that "we have no doubt that there is no Congressional power to expose for the sake of exposure." In another case in which the court freed five California Communist leaders who had been convicted under the Smith Act (outlawing advocacy of the violent overthrow of the government), the Court upheld the right to advocate the forcible overthrow of the government, provided that action to achieve that end was not advocated. As Justice John Harlan said, the essential distinction "is that those to whom advocacy is addressed must be urged to do something, now or in the future, rather than merely to believe something." The third case involved John Stewart Service, an ex–Foreign Service officer, who the court held had been wrongfully dismissed from a government job as a security risk.

These and other dramatic decisions led Rauh to note that in the past three years there had been significant progress in strengthening the Bill of Rights. Other observers found marked significance in the balance of power now existing in the Court and in the court's relationship to the other two branches of government. President Eisenhower's appointments to the Court had established a new majority that was extremely sensitive to defense of civil liberties as well as to civil rights. Justices Warren, Hugo Black, William O. Douglas, and William Brennan provided the core of that majority, with Justices Harlan and Felix Frankfurter often sustaining their judgments on civil liberties cases. Instead of repeatedly overturning progressive legislation, as it had during the first Roosevelt administration, the Court was now asserting that the legislative and legislative and executive branches of govenment and the lower courts must be more sensitive to procedures affecting citizens' liberties and reputations.

On June 18, the House passed the civil rights bill, H.R. 6127, by a 286 to 126 vote with only two minor amendments and sent it to the Senate. The first gave the bipartisan Civil Rights Commission authority to investigate alleged deprivations of the right to have a person's vote counted, and the second provided that anyone charged with contempt of court under the act would have a lawyer or be provided with one if he could not afford the expense.

Part I of the bill gave the commission subpoena powers and a two-year life span. In addition to investigating violations of voting rights because of color, race, religion, or national origin, it would study legal developments concerning the denial of equal protection under the Fourteenth Amendment and submit reports and recommendations to the President, and it would appraise federal laws and policies regarding equal protection. Significantly, the House reinserted in the bill authority that had been deleted earlier in committee for the commission to investigate "unwarranted economic pressure." Part II of the bill provided for an additional assistant attorney general who would, as the attorney general had pledged, head the newly created Civil Rights Division. Part III gave the attorney general authority to obtain preventive (injunctive) relief against civil rights violators to protect Fourteenth Amendment rights. Part IV also gave the attorney general authority to obtain preventive relief in cases involving voting rights violations because of race in federal and state elections. Most important, the attorney general was relieved of the necessity of exhausting state administrative remedies before seeking injunctions.[21]

The next step for civil rights supporters in the Senate was to beat Eastland at his own game, and H.R. 6127 became the perfect vehicle for doing that. On June 3, when the Senate Judiciary Committee had been scheduled to vote on the right-to-work amendment, Ervin pulled a switch. He moved to substitute his jury trial amendment for what he opportunistically called that "union-busting" measure sponsored by McClellan, and the maneuver prevailed, setting the stage for one of the greatest battles waged on the Senate floor over civil rights since the nineteenth century. Mitchell was unhappy that Ervin had succeeded in modifying the bill because three midwestern and border state senators (Estes Kefauver, O'Mahoney, and Republican John Butler of Maryland) teamed up with the southerners. Studying ways to repair the damage, Mitchell was somewhat reassured by the knowledge that the committee had defeated other hostile or weakening amendments.

Even though Hennings and Dirksen had a substitute bill ready, because Ervin had succeeded in attaching the jury trial amendment to S. 83—which Eastland had bottled up in the Judiciary Committee—under normal circumstances the substitute, too, would have had to go through the same graveyard. On June 20, to prevent that, Knowland and Paul Douglas of Illinois made a motion, under the rarely used Rule XIV, that the Senate proceed to consider H.R. 6127—in effect stopping the bill at the desk and placing it at once on the calendar. They resorted to the use of Rule XIV because they figured it was the most expeditious means for getting the bill onto the Senate floor. An alternative would have been a motion to discharge the Senate Judiciary Committee from further consideration of the bill. Such a motion would have been open to a debate and a filibuster that would have required three or four cloture votes—what Russell euphemistically said would have been "a lengthy educational campaign." The Rule XIV maneuver, which succeeded the same day, automatically prevented Eastland from bottling up the bill in his committee. The bill then could be called up anytime by a majority vote. (See Appendix 1 for Pohlhaus's explanation of the parliamentary procedure.)

The extensive debate on the key vote on whether to uphold a point of order raised by Russell against the use of Rule XIV, because it was obvious that he was being outflanked, revealed the historical importance of the battle—one in which Mitchell was the principal leader outside the halls of Congress. It was ironic that Russell's long and illustrious career should now be put to service that he knew was a lost cause, but, determined to preserve what he perceived as the South's honor, he continued the charade, which could do no more than slow the pace of imminent change. The irrevocable course of history was Mitchell's powerful ally as his skilled, committed supporters combatted the very determined opposition on the Senate floor. As Missouri's Hennings complained, they raised all kinds of "bogies under the bed which might befall the states of the late Confederacy of which my late departed ancestors were all a party," and reminders about repressions imposed by King George III upon the colonies, to ward off enactment of a law that would authorize the attorney general to require immediate integration of public schools in the South.

Hennings struck a strong underlying chord of urgency when he declared, "I believe, of course, not only in full justice to all citizens of the United States, as provided by the Constitution, but I believe that we must tell the Free World—indeed, the uncommitted nations of the world and even those committed now to the Communist bloc—that we of the United States of America do not judge men's rights to full participation of first-class citizenship in these United States by the color of their skin or their place of national origin." Jacob Javits similarly warned, "The whole world is watching us, not only our country. This is the time to act."

Wayne Morse and some other liberals succumbed to a troubling tendency that always annoyed Mitchell by choosing to battle for adherence to the principle of parliamentary procedure despite the reality of an intransigent opposition. Morse's unpredictability had already been demonstrated in 1952 when he bolted the Republican party to support Adlai Stevenson over Eisenhower. He had been one of the first Republican senators to back the general for the presidency, but later, becoming disillusioned, he criticized Eisenhower for his record and campaign promises. He remained an Independent for more than two years before joining the Democratic party. His betrayal of what Mitchell considered the senator's own liberal tradition still shook the lobbyist, though it should not have. Morse had signed Douglas's statement in the current battle that the Senate should bypass Eastland's committee, but he switched and urged that the bill be referred to the Judiciary Committee for seven days. His action caused the wire services to flash the news that the "Democratic liberals are breaking up." *

---

* Mitchell and Douglas charged that Morse switched sides to win southern votes for a bill that would authorize the federal government to contract for a big power dam at Hell's Canyon on the Snake River, between Idaho and Oregon. The bill passed the Senate but it failed in the House. Eventually, Congress authorized a drastically scaled-back project. Douglas explained in his memoirs that Morse was all too well aware that in 1955 the southerners had helped pass the Colorado River storage bill over the strong objections of Knowland and Kuchel, who had feared an adverse impact on California. Both were strong civil rights supporters, but they willingly paid the price for their convictions. Morse testified before a Senate committee that a southerner had told him that support for changing the filibuster rule would cost him votes for the Hell's Canyon project. Liberal Democrats, for the most part, favored the plan, but Republicans like Arthur V. Watkins of Utah opposed it, preferring smaller dams lower down the river built by private power companies.

Five northern liberals joined five southerners in voting to send the civil rights bill to the Judiciary Committee. Lyndon Johnson backed Morse's stand as a political sop to the diehards by saying it would "save time." Mitchell found Morse's demand for changes in Rule XIV in order to avoid future attempts at circumventing committees, and the refusal of many liberals like him to support modification of Rule XXII, to be a troubling contradiction.

An avowed stickler for following parliamentary procedure and "long-established custom," Morse insisted that the House bill be sent to the Judiciary Committee in order to afford witnesses an opportunity to comment on it. He maintained that such an opportunity was "a part of the democratic rights of the people of the United States." In the interest of affording proper consideration of this "great" and "momentous issue" that had divided the country, he said, every effort should be made to resolve all doubts in favor of procedure. The resulting committee hearing would also help iron out conflicts between the bill bottled up there and the House version. Bypassing the committee, he stressed, was simply a "procedural shortcut" that would set a bad precedent by capitulating to "parliamentary expediency." He charged further that the move was to "discipline a committee before the committee has had a chance to act on the bill."

Proudly proclaiming that he was an honorary vice president of the NAACP, Morse directed some of his remarks to that organization and the ADA—in reality to Mitchell and Rauh—because they were pressing for the bypass maneuver. He declared, "I think you are proposing a great injury to sound civil rights programs in the United States."

Mitchell and his allies were adamant that five and a half months were ample for the Judiciary Committee to have held hearings, marked up a bill, and reported it out. It had not done so with any of the fourteen bills that were introduced in January. As Michigan Democrat Pat McNamara advised Morse, having agreed that that "was too long a time for the Senate bill" to be held hostage, "his argument falls." Humphrey was similarly effective in making his point. The debate, he said, was not over liberalism or conservativism, or over action or inaction, but over whether a valid procedure should be used in the interest of justice and fairness.

Mitchell, too, was a stickler for parliamentary procedure—when it was fairly applied. When that procedure was used to frustrate the quest for constitutional rights, as was now happening, he believed that morality should take precedence. He subsequently wrote Morse about "some of the things that were on my mind as I listened to your speech against the use [of Rule XIV]." Saying that it was "a good thing to possess a long memory and a sense of gratitude," he recalled Morse's "strong, uncompromising fight" for funding to keep the Fair Employment Practice Committee alive during the war, and other support such as his opposition to the approval of Eastland as chairman of the Judiciary Committee. Mitchell said that the maneuver Knowland and Douglas had used "was a vital boost to the chances of overcoming the terrible dilemma" that was posed by the Judiciary Committee's obstruction. Mitchell believed then, he said, "and [I] am more strongly convinced now, that had the Russell point of order prevailed it would have been a disaster for civil rights." Mitchell saw no reason to question the propriety of the Rule XIV approach. Despite their disagreement on that, he appealed to Morse to use his skill and influence to help pass the bill in the present session. Not only would Morse not budge, he remained unpredictable.

Owing in large part to Mitchell's strong influence, liberals like Humphrey, Douglas, Hennings, and Javits, in addition to conservatives like Knowland, were leading this determined battle for the civil rights bill. Those senators pushing to bypass the Judiciary Committee were faithfully reflecting his impatience and views that the rightness of the civil rights cause should take precedence over parliamentary procedure. Humphrey reminded his colleagues that in the Eighty-second, Eighty-third, and Eighty-fourth Congresses, he had introduced bills similar—"word for word"—to the current House measure, all of which had suffered the same disastrous fate in the Judiciary Committee. As for the proposed President's Commission on Civil Rights: "That is just about as new as Ben Franklin's Almanac. I introduced that bill in 1949." That, too, was not acted on.

Humphrey denied charges he was being pressured by the NAACP and the ADA—"not one bit." As the Lord was his judge, he declared, "not once has either organization written to me or telephoned me within the last three months, much less the last three days." That was because they knew he would do exactly what he was now doing. He admitted to their strong influence: "As a matter of fact, I have taken more heat from both organizations in recent months than have many other members of the Senate." He suggested he might "have taken a lot of it because I have been their friend. Sometimes friends have a way of punishing one another." So, he declared, "I say to the National Association for the Advancement of Colored People that if their patience has run out, I can well understand why. Many of their fine members have suffered indignities which no American citizen should have to suffer." If the NAACP "thinks Rule XIV ought to be applied, I can understand why."

Humphrey, Douglas, Hennings, Javits, and Knowland were the "radical Republicans" of 1957. Despite the bipartisan label, they were serving their nation in the same democratic and humanistic spirit. Humphrey, in fact, was so close to Mitchell that he often sounded like him on the Senate floor: "The Senate must realize that its procedures come into disrepute when they completely nullify the taking of action. The procedures which senators should be worried about are those which make it impossible for the Senate to have an opportunity to act, or those which make it impossible for a majority of the members of the Senate even to have an opportunity to vote on a measure of this sort."

Once more it was Richard Nixon, presiding over the Senate, who saved the day for the civil rights forces. He decided that Russell's point of order was inapplicable to this situation. He said that the basic issue was not a procedural but a substantive one, and left it up to the Senate to make the final decision. The Senate then voted 39 to 45 against Russell's point of order, which was against an objection to referring the administration civil rights bill to the Judiciary Committee. The final action had the effect of placing the bill on the calendar, where it could be called up at any time by a majority vote. Notable among those who lined up with the southerners in support of Russell were John Kennedy, Kefauver, Mansfield, Johnson, and, of course, Morse. Johnson did not fight to sustain Russell's point of order, so its defeat was not interpreted as his own loss. Everett Dirksen, emphasizing the partisan stakes involved, lent the Douglas-Knowland forces invaluable support by recalling the history of the Reorganization Act of 1947—a central factor in the debate over the provisions of Rule XIV. He voted against the Russell maneuver. Dirksen and Russell had both served on the Joint Committee on the Reorganization of Congress.

Mitchell was especially thankful for the firm stand taken by Knowland and Douglas. Those who sought to "water down H.R. 6127," he told Knowland, were "paying the highest tribute to your skill and determination." They knew they could not win in a frontal attack, so they were "trying to move in through the back door of compromise." Opponents still had three opportunities to filibuster: first, when the bill was called up for consideration; second, if that failed, during debates on the bill and on amendments; and third, after the House-Senate Conference Committee had agreed on a compromise bill.[22]

Mitchell discerned two basic deep-seated historical realities underlying the struggle for passage of civil rights legislation. First, Americans in the North were so concerned with conflicts in the Middle East and in Hungary that they were oblivious to potentially explosive racial conditions here in the United States; while in the South, blacks were increasingly challenging the system of state-imposed oppression, but whites were refusing to heed the warning signs and thus causing anarchy. He regarded the supplanting of Georgia's Walter F. George by Herman Talmadge in the Senate as a tragedy that reaffirmed the South's intention to stick to its unconstitutional way of life. The tall, highly personable Talmadge represented the new-style segregationist, an advancement of sorts over the crude, race-baiting demagoguery of his red-gallused father, Eugene, who had once occupied the Georgia governor's mansion for eight years. In Mitchell's book, Talmadge was "a wimp" and an unabashed racist compared to George, who was a "mighty oak," a southern gentleman in the tradition of Richard Russell and Sam Rayburn. The battle lines were drawn.

Leading the southern forces in the Congress was "General Russell." A subtle dramatist, he launched his offensive with astounding effectiveness—not with a direct broadside, but with an oblique maneuver that promptly threw the Knowland-Douglas forces onto the defensive. "Mr. President," he declared on July 2 while unsuspecting colleagues were engrossed in a totally unrelated debate, "for the first time" in the twenty-four years since he had first become a member of the Senate, "I respectfully request that I be not interrupted in the course of my prepared discussion." Then, with attention riveted on him, he unleashed a barrage on H.R. 6127 from which the civil rights forces would not recover until 1964. At last, Russell had a perfect opportunity to vent with volcanic fury the sectional bitterness that had been bottled up inside him for so long—feelings that the South was a victim of "conscious hate." The wounds had been reopened in a most personal manner during his 1952 quest for the Democratic presidential nomination, when all he could poll at the national convention was 292 votes out of a total of some 1,200. That evidence of sectional prejudice was confirmed by one powerful Democratic leader, who told him: "Dick, I would support you—if I could. We just can't put a southerner on top of this ticket."

Russell's move also revealed why this normally urbane gentleman of legal distinction was such a highly respected master strategist. He astounded not only the civil rights forces but the entire nation with his "exposé" that this was not a voting rights bill, as was popularly assumed, but a measure "cunningly designed to vest in the attorney general unprecedented power to bring to bear the whole might of the Federal Government, including the armed forces if necessary, to force a commingling of white and Negro children in the state-supported public schools of the South."

Part III, the section providing the attorney general with authority in civil rights suits to protect Fourteenth Amendment rights, was especially vulnerable because, as Russell revealed, it was the "heart of the bill"—not the voting rights section, which he charged was only "a smoke screen to obscure the unlimited grant of powers to the attorney general of the United States to govern by injunction and federal bayonet." The agony of sectional injury heightened his complaint that the provision was "the ultimate in the technique of legislative draftsmanship to obscure purpose while executing and conferring power." His attack was devastating because it was meant, first, to do severe psychological damage, and to set the stage for subsequent

offensives. Russell tried to undermine much of the moral authority underlying arguments for H.R. 6127 by maintaining that those claiming it was
a "moderate" voting rights bill were engaged in a "campaign of deception." He felt that even President Eisenhower, who the day before had
again said there was no reason for alarm because the bill was designed only
to ensure the constitutionally guaranteed right of every qualified citizen to
participate in elections, had been deceived. He charged that the bill's framers were maintaining that this was a voting rights bill because Americans
generally frowned on denial of the right to vote. The true purpose of the
legislation, he maintained, was to enforce "judicial law," law handed down
by the Supreme Court that declared segregated schools unconstitutional.
He was particularly concerned that

> the social order of the South, with the separation of the races in the
> South, was accepted and protected by the laws of the land for
> nearly a hundred years. It is the only system the present generation
> has ever known. It was overturned in the twinkling of an eye, not
> by an act of Congress, after debate and explanation, but by action
> of the Supreme Court in striking down long-established law.

Furthermore, H.R. 6127, he explained, would give the courts "a much
firmer base" to outlaw segregation of all public eating places, swimming
pools, and hotels in the South that were licensed by the state—thus opening up another opportunity for the use of military force.

Russell invoked the fearsome ghosts of Charles Sumner and Thaddeus
Stevens by recalling their brutal rampages through the South—conducted
from the halls of Congress—as he appealed to the national sense of guilt
over Reconstruction. The true intention of this "actual force bill"—as humiliating as that enacted in 1866—was "to put black heels on white
necks." He said that the bill had such powers even though they were "more
cunningly contrived than the forthright legislation aimed at the South in
the tragic era of Reconstruction." He warned that this "studied misrepre-
sentation" was designed to camouflage the bill's "sweeping powers" in
order to punish the South.

The nefarious intention of this "potential instrument of tyranny and
persecution" was clear, Russell declared, from the cunning manner in
which Part III was tied to Section 1985 of Title 42 of the U.S. Code—a
Reconstruction statute that authorized the attorney general to bring suit
against anyone conspiring, or about to conspire, to deprive a person of the
equal protection of the laws. Its scope was adequately broad to protect
against the segregation in schools and other institutions that had been rendered unconstitutional by the Supreme Court's 1954 ruling. Section 1985

automatically invoked Section 1993, which empowered the President or the attorney general to use the armed forces "to aid in the execution of judicial process." Russell correctly charged that this was done by "amending one statute or existing law by reference and taking this statute or law and incorporating it, by reference to a number, into another law, without anywhere spelling out the total effect of the proposed law in express terms."

After Russell had paused in his pounding of the "Reconstruction laws" and the humiliating origins of Sections 1985 and 1993, in the years 1866 and 1871, respectively, the other southerners jubilantly rushed for vengeance. Olin Johnston demanded, "Senators, do you want to be responsible for a second Reconstruction era or a second pillaging of the South?" That the "horrors" of the "Tragic Era" were highlighted by three generations of southern racial nightmares was irrelevant. The concerns of the southern senators were for "our people," the "white people of the South," not oppressed black citizens. Congress was not the place for objective critiques of history. Russell knew that "there are millions of people in this country outside the South who would not approve of another Reconstruction at bayonet point of a peaceful and patriotic South."

Many who should have known better did indeed fear the ghost of Reconstruction. America had undergone profound changes over the past ninety years. Russell was all too well aware that this was no longer a divided nation, but one that had been unified by the blood of southern sons fighting in two world wars and through other sacrifices. Said Russell:

> The South was finally freed of the bayonet rule of Reconstruction days through the efforts of northern men. There was less bitterness and hate between the soldiers than between the civilians in the War Between the States. Northerners who had been subjected to the waving of the bloody shirt came South in the forces of occupation. They found the truth about the South, and their hearts were touched with compassion at the treatment accorded their late enemies during the Reconstruction era. It was really the veterans of the war and those who served in the forces who occupied the South for 12 years who finally broke the chains forged for the South by Sumner and Stevens.

The Hayes-Tilden Compromise was the result. It was a manifestation of the beginning of this national unification—one that required a forgiveness of the South's racial past, no matter how morally unsound. Subsequently, the world wars, continuing rapid industrial development, a revamped and expanding economy, a communications revolution, and the massive migration of blacks and whites from the South to the North had brought a

greater sense of national identity and purpose to all areas. Racial attitudes—except for the most glaring abuses—that had for so long been the
hallmark of the South were now a national phenomenon. Southern whites
moving to other areas had carried their old hatreds and phobias with them;
northern whites who once had thought themselves immune from those passions, with so many blacks now living among them—and threatening their
way of life—openly manifested similar prejudices in defense of their own
cherished social homogeneity. Mitchell had been troubled for a long time
by this northern attitude, which had compounded the difficulty of overcoming archaic congressional rules in the struggle for civil rights legislation. Here now was "General Russell" inscribing this sectional animosity
toward a group of Americans in the tablets of the *Congressional Record* with
baronial elegance, as he underscored the reality that the interests of the
southern archetypal racists and northern whites were one.

With a victorious flair, Russell concluded his magnificent performance
by calling for a national referendum—"before the outrage possible in this
bill is inflicted upon a helpless people"—to demonstrate the unity of the
American people.

The bill's supporters accused President Eisenhower of pulling the rug
out from under his attorney general in his news conference the following
day, July 3, when he answered questions in response to Russell's charges.
To a question on Part III, he replied that he was just reading the bill and
did not understand all its provisions. That response was later interpreted as
a deliberate attempt to signal his willingness to jettison Part III to save the
bill. That meant Eisenhower had deliberately nailed the Part III coffin
shut. That impression was reinforced by the President's lengthy meeting
that same day with Russell, after which the Georgian gave every indication
that he had won this fight.[23]

Scrambling to recover, the NAACP Washington Bureau distributed a
detailed chronology of earlier discussions of Part III on the Hill, in a futile
attempt to refute Russell's charges that Brownell had led a sneak attack on
the South's way of life. Mitchell wrote to Knowland that during the hearings before the House Rules Committee in the Eighty-fourth Congress, and
in debates on the House floor, Howard Smith and other congressmen had
frequently referred to Part III. Again in the Eighty-fifth Congress, Mitchell
attested, although opponents had concentrated on the jury trial issue during the House Rules Committee hearings, the Part III issue had been raised
during the daily sessions, all of which Mitchell had attended.

Ervin himself acknowledged that he had raised questions on Part III
with Brownell during the February hearings, when the attorney general
had appeared before his subcommittee. He complained that Brownell had
stonewalled. Mitchell concluded that after losing on the jury trial issue in

the House, opponents had shifted "to another ground" to create confusion among the supporters of the civil rights bill. Working to convince an evidently nonplussed Knowland of the falseness of Russell's claims that the administration and the civil rights forces had deceived the nation into believing this was only a voting rights bill, Mitchell called Knowland's attention to the record of the Senate hearings, in which the Reverend William Borders of Atlanta had testified that he had been jailed for sitting at the front of a Georgia city bus. Mitchell maintained, "Surely, no one would be foolish enough to assume that this testimony was related simply to the right to vote. Obviously, it is the kind of problem that would be reached under Section [Part] III." Mitchell told Knowland that the bill would not end all racial discrimination, but it would give much-needed support to basic civil rights, and that had been its intended purpose from the beginning.[24]

Convinced by Mitchell's explanation, Knowland worked to regain the momentum. Debate on Knowland's motion to take up the bill that would become the Civil Rights Act of 1957 began on July 8, with most of the time during the eight days that followed being consumed by opponents' speeches. Russell and his southern cohorts were a study of rectitude. They had captured the high ground during the propaganda battle outside the Senate, so they could appear to be cooperative. They therefore worked to hold the psychological advantage by disavowing any intention to filibuster. By and large, they kept their promise to limit their arguments to the merits of the bill—but while these arguments were generally devoid of irrelevant matter and emotionalism, they played to their audience of lawyers with abstruse points of constitutional history, intent on confusing all but the most astute.

Meanwhile, Mitchell feverishly mobilized his forces. During a strategy session with a small group of allies on July 12, suggestions for saving the bill were made in conjunction with a Leadership Conference meeting that was scheduled to be held five days later, to coincide with final debate on Part III in the Senate. Suggestions included a meeting at the Capitol with a bipartisan group of senators to discuss the status of H.R. 6127 and to make additional plans for winning complete victory. Mitchell and Hyman Bookbinder, an AFL-CIO civil rights lobbyist, had won assurances that Democrats Douglas, Humphrey, and John O. Pastore of Rhode Island and Republicans Case, Ives, Javits, and Kuchel would attend. It was agreed that there would also be a meeting with Knowland, and Mitchell would make the arrangements. Suggestions were also made for a possible meeting with the President. A list of senators who were "very much in doubt on such matters as the jury trial amendment," Part III of the bill, and subpoena powers for the Civil Rights Commission was also prepared, with the intention of working to sway them.

On July 16 the Senate made the civil rights bill the pending business. Conferring at their planned July 17 meeting, at about the same time that Eisenhower was again demonstrating his ignorance of Part III in another news conference, a group of six pro-civil-rights senators (Douglas, Humphrey, Pastore, Javits, Ives, and Case) frankly acknowledged that there just were not enough votes to save that provision. Knowland had been invited to attend, too. When the meeting was about to begin and he did not show up, nobody wanted would agree to go for him, believing that he was too conservative to be of much help. Without hesitating, Mitchell walked over to Knowland's office, persuaded him that his presence was essential, and escorted him into the meeting. Mitchell was rewarded by hearing the minority leader urge courage as he tried to find an alternative. But the effort was to little avail because Part III was already doomed.[25]

Shortly before the vote on an amendment to remove Part III that was sponsored by Clinton Anderson and Vermont Republican George D. Aiken, both liberals, Wilkins observed that the situation in the Senate outwardly was "still fluid." But, he said, "from all realistic sources and observers," it had to be concluded that "we will lose the vote on the Anderson-Aiken motion by not less than 10 votes." The most support he said he could count on was 35 or 36 votes. That meant opponents had 57 to 60 votes against Part III.

Wilkins said that he had gone with Mitchell to see the Massachusetts delegation's members, John Kennedy and Leverett Saltonstall, in their offices. The interview with Kennedy "was pleasant as he will vote with us on Part III" and, Wilkins mistakenly thought, the jury trial amendment. But the interview with Saltonstall "was with a stubborn man who had made his choice and had to stick by it, especially in the face of his press pronouncements." Saltonstall repeated to the NAACP group southern clichés, for example about the federal government's "interfering" with local government. The best the delegation could get from him was a promise that he would vote for Part IV as it stood. Wilkins said that letters to senators from NAACP supporters were "woefully short in total," even though there had been some pickup. "They just do not seem to understand the value of writing." Douglas told the delegation he was getting one hundred letters a week, more than half of which were from opponents. Wilkins's estimate was close.

Acknowledging the distortions and the psychological damage that had been caused by the horrendous specter of having the armed forces and the Navy invading the South, and in a desperate attempt to get the debate back on track, Humphrey declared: "I do not like to have the American people reminded in however well meaning a way of the dark and sad days of Reconstruction. It is a bad chapter." He and Knowland then cosponsored an amendment to repeal Sections 1989 and 1993 of the Reconstruction statute, which gave the President authority to use federal troops to enforce civil rights laws. Thus, on July 22, the Senate exorcised the ghost of Thaddeus Stevens and Charles Sumner by approving by a vote of 90 to 0, the amendment offered by Knowland and Humphrey to repeal the offending 1866 statute.[26]

But Part III still posed a threat to the southern way of life and was a lingering reminder of the "Tragic Era." Two days later the Senate approved, 52 to 38, the Anderson-Aiken amendment deleting the main feature of Part III, which would have authorized the attorney general to institute civil action for preventive relief in civil rights cases. H.R. 6127 now truly became a voting rights bill.

Mitchell called the effective removal of Part III a "direct hit amidship." At an emergency civil rights meeting in Boston, he drew another picture of the Senate, one that looked "like the scene at a bathing beach when the cry of help sounds from the deep waters off shore." Imagine, he said, "what it would be like if on a hot Sunday afternoon, in the presence of thousands of spectators, the life guards, before undertaking the rescue, should get out a rule book to check on whether the person who needed help was wearing the proper type of bathing suit." The civil rights bill, he said, was in such a situation, "in the deep waters of southern opposition."

Mitchell praised Javits's painstaking defense of the bill on July 18 in a protracted debate, not with the southerners, who knew they had already won, but with undecided moderates from midwestern and border states, as one of the greatest legal explanations he had ever heard. Javits listed twenty-four specific civil rights protected by the Constitution and federal laws, which the attorney general had cited earlier during the hearings before the Hennings subcommittee "as a specification illustrative of the voting rights with which he wishes to be able to deal under Part III." Thus, if the Justice Department could have been entrusted with those powers for so long, why should there be now such an overriding fear that the attorney general would abuse the implied discretionary powers provided in the bill in other areas, like school desegregation? That fear was now the animus of the attacks on Part III. Javits refused to yield ground: "I think if we seek to write statutes which would deprive our executive officials of all discretion, then we would be writing legislation involving tyranny at least as bad—no worse, but at least as bad—as the tyranny of the executive or the tyranny of the judiciary. So we must leave the executive officials an area for the exercise of discretion."

Mitchell found it "most startling" that the major opposition to the bill was coming from an alliance between southern and western senators, both Republicans and Democrats. This was not the first time that had happened to the civil rights struggle, he noted, quoting from Walter White's auto-biography:

> One of the most inexplicable but interesting phenomena to me has been the extraordinary attitudes of several western senators who were regarded as liberals on economic questions but who have been most injurious to the Negroes' cause. Chief among the latter number was the late Senator William E. Borah of Idaho, who per-sistently and consistently used his oratory and reputation as an au-thority on constitutional law to oppose federal anti-lynching laws and other legislation of that character.

Two of those persons whom Mitchell had in mind were O'Mahoney, born in Chelsea, Massachusetts, and South Dakota Republican Mundt, who had always joined with southerners against civil rights.

Concerned more about Dred Scott, Harry T. Moore, and Emmett Till than about Reconstruction phobias, Mitchell regarded Part III as merely "the restraining hand which the government of the United States would place on the shoulder of any state, city or local official who would arrest or intimidate a colored person for exercising his constitutional right to take the seat of his choice on a public bus." Part III, he said, was the key the government might use to unlock jail doors and set free ministers protesting Jim Crow.

He knew that, having scored these two crucial victories of weakening the 1866 statute and all but killing Part III, the southerners would stage their next battle over the jury trial amendment. Mundt and O'Mahoney were two of the principal jury-trial-amendment advocates. Mitchell was less surprised by the Republican's stand than by the Democrat's. He sug-gested that O'Mahoney was politically motivated. He said it was well known that the Democratic leadership's objective was to get a bill that would be acceptable to the northern wing of the party, while also giving the least possible offense to the southern wing. "Senator O'Mahoney's views, perhaps merely by coincidence, help to reach that objective."

Now was the moment when Mitchell began to tell true friend from foe, genuine supporters from those who swam with the tide only when the issue was academic. But, said Mitchell, "Even the true friends of civil rights do not have a blank check on our gratitude and affections. In this present crisis when the courts, the state legislatures, and all of the power of the South are being massed to crush the aspirations of colored people by force, intimida-tion, and even murder, it is impossible to understand the actions of our friends who turn their backs on this horrible scene and go off into flights of legal philosophy."[27]

One person he clearly had in mind was Wayne Morse, who ominously announced that he could not "reconcile himself to voting for" a bill that was so narrow and limited in its scope that "I fear it will bear naught but a label so far as its practical" effects were concerned. Whether or not he was being deliberately vindictive, Morse seemed to be throwing back at Mitchell the lobbyist's admonition to the senator during a hearing on the Taft-Hartley amendment in 1947 that he could not conceive of a person honestly voting for any legislation when he knew it did not serve the full purpose for which it was intended. More precisely, Morse was continuing to betray an ambivalence on race that was not dissimilar to O'Mahoney's.

Rauh tried to throw additional light on Morse's behavior. He saw Morse as a "maverick, a loner," a point man who was "way out there ahead" of Humphrey, Douglas, Hennings, Case, and Javits. Rauh felt that "any good fight needs a Morse, but it also needs a Humphrey and a Douglas." They were sure bets. Despite his differences with Morse, Rauh considered him a friend. Rauh remembered another situation in which Morse "blew up" at both Mitchell and him, complaining that they were trying to persuade him to accept a compromise he did not want. Rauh accepted Morse's idiosyncrasies because he felt that it "was very valuable to have somebody to your left." He never wavered as Humphrey sometimes did during this period, owing to his quiet alliance with Johnson.

Mitchell, the idealist, who no doubt most often saw himself in Humphrey, the politician, was not this sympathetic toward Morse. He regarded Morse's behavior as "mutiny among trusted friends," but he was certain the civil rights ship would sail into port in meaningful form because "we have an able captain, William Knowland." Beside Knowland stood "the white-thatched towering leader of civil rights, Paul Douglas." Mitchell said that those who professed "to find the Knowland-Douglas partnership strange showed they did not understand the American concept of democracy." He maintained that the concept was broad enough to include persons of varying political affiliations, different economic views, and a wide variety of opinions. Knowland, according to Mitchell, had known from the beginning "where he intended to go in this fight." He had not swayed "with every passing breeze," nor had he "switched strategy for the purpose of expediency."

Two other stalwart supporters who drew Mitchell's ringing praise for their "unqualified support" were Hennings and Stuart Symington. However, all of them were up against Richard Russell, whom Mitchell called "a master magician" who had "pulled a host of Civil War rabbits out of the hat." On both Part III and the jury trial issue, Mitchell said, Russell had "added a new twist to the act by telling the audience that each little furry creature that he displayed was a ravenous, dangerous wolf." Mitchell was not surprised by Russell's tricks, but he was disturbed that "so many of his colleagues believed him," or pretended to do so. Therein lay his challenge—to deprive the South of enough of this moderate support to assure the civil rights forces victory.[28]

Kefauver and Idaho senator Frank Church, encouraged by Johnson, joined O'Mahoney in carrying water during the next crucial battle over the jury trial amendment. They crafted the provisions' wording and gingerly got it through the Senate. Johnson would later say that there was no "hocus-pocus in the way the jury trial amendment" was prepared. "Everything that happened, short of technical drafting work, took place right on the Senate floor in plain sight of the press and public," he said. Those who were "looking for backstage directions and shrewd deals" were wasting their time. "Whatever maneuvering took place was solely and simply to break the ironclad 'monolithic' type of thinking which has always ruined the prospects of civil rights legislation in the past." The truth was, nevertheless, that O'Mahoney, a western liberal in the George Norris tradition, had been willing to accept the jury trial amendment that the Judiciary Committee earlier had actually adopted.

As Johnson joined in rounding out what was appropriately called "Johnson's Compromise," he tipped his hand on June 19 when the Senate began discussion on how to proceed with H.R. 6127. When Russell announced that he intended to have the bill sent to the Judiciary Committee, Johnson, usurping the role of the presiding officer, called the attention of Knowland, Douglas, and Russell, in that order, to what was about to happen. The presiding officer was supposed to recognize the senators in the order in which he wanted them to address the chamber. Johnson's move instantly gave Knowland the opportunity to announce that he was delaying his motion to place the bill on the calendar until the following day. Johnson's ruse was not lost on Russell, who was placed in the position of having to respond.

Johnson's no-filibuster agreement was reaffirmed in order to avoid splitting the Democratic party; also, Russell did not want to alienate African Americans by totally defeating them. It was very noteworthy that while Mitchell could hardly find strong enough language to denounce O'Mahoney, other nonsoutherners, and so many of the southerners, he was judiciously silent about Johnson. That was because he knew that the Texas leader had made a deal with the southerners to keep them from filibustering the bill and he did not want to take him on at this juncture.

Johnson himself had told Mitchell that he knew some Texans would not understand his vote on the 1957 Civil Rights Act, but that he was going to cast it anyway. He promised to get fellow Texas Democrat Ralph W. Yarborough to go along with him, even though Yarborough could have been defeated. It appeared to Mitchell that Johnson was thinking more about the social relevance of his action than about its political consequences. Mitchell also got the impression from their conversations that Johnson felt he could vote in Congress in any way he pleased and still get reelected. One reason for this belief was that Texas's population was changing, with a large influx of African Americans and Mexicans.

Johnson was helped considerably by his aide George E. Reedy, who provided the senator with a series of observations and assessments regarding the prospects and implications of the civil rights battle. Reedy's political evaluations were based on the observation that the Republican party had been captured by the Nixon-Rogers-Brownell axis, which was determined to "sell itself completely to the key minority vote" in such states as New York, Pennsylvania, Illinois, New Jersey, and California. He told Johnson that the "South must cold-bloodedly assess the situation" presented by the current debate. Noting differences between the past and present, he said that previously it had been "possible to kill off all legislation simply because the Republicans were willing to cooperate." That was no longer the case, he said—bearing out Mitchell's own evaluation—because *the Republicans have made a calculated decision to build their party by appealing to the minority vote. The South is now completely without allies"* (italics Reedy's).

Reedy said that the only way the South could stave off disaster was to appeal to those senators who wanted to see a civil rights bill enacted, but who were willing to listen to reason—in other words, to compromise. He said that that meant some sort of bridge to such men had to be maintained at all costs. That opportunity was presented by the O'Mahoneys, the Andersons, the Mansfields, and others who were "willing to beat their brains out in the interests of reasonable and prudent legislation." But if the South totally rebuffed them, he said, they would "retire from the field," leaving civil rights leadership to the Douglases and the Javitses. "And if the moderates retire from leadership, they will then follow the extremists of the North because they have no place to go. They *must* vote for a 'civil rights' bill and if they are not put in a position to shape one themselves, *they will vote for a bill written by Brownell, Douglas, and Javits"* (italics Reedy's).

Reedy said that, unfortunately, the only picture that the public had was one of "the North making concessions and the South remaining adamant." That was a false picture, he said, "because all the Northerners (such as O'Mahoney and Anderson) have conceded so far is that they are willing to give up obviously vicious features of the measures. *This is the same thing as a man giving up the right to contract cancer."* Evidence, he said, should be "presented to the public that the appeals to reason have had an impact on

both North and South" (italics Reedy's). Johnson's maneuvers indicated that
he was following Reedy's recommendations closely.

After a process involving four transformations, the O'Mahoney amendment to Part IV that was finally accepted provided that there would be no
requirement for a jury trial in prosecutions for civil contempt (where the
court was coercing a defendant to cooperate), but there would be jury trials
across the board in cases involving criminal contempt (where the defendant
was being punished for disobeying an order). The amendment also provided
that there would be no bar to African Americans' serving on juries. With
Knowland still adhering to the NAACP position on the issue, the battle
came down to a contest between two men: Knowland and Johnson.[29]

Declaring, "Lets have it now and fight it out," an impatient Knowland
made his big mistake of challenging Johnson openly, when on July 31 he
offered three separate motions for unanimous consent to set a time for a
vote on the O'Mahoney amendment. Knowland told a reporter that he
intended to force a vote later in the week by moving to table the O'Mahoney amendment, even though he knew he would lose a few supporters in
the showdown. The result was a disaster for civil rights forces. The following morning, Johnson seized the initiative by calling up Knowland's unan-
imous-consent request. Just after midnight that Wednesday, the
amendment passed 51 to 42. The partisan nature of the final battle was
shown by the 39 Democrats and 12 Republicans who voted "aye" and the
nine Democrats and thirty-three Republicans who voted "nay."

In the crush, the northern liberal Democratic coalition split wide open.
Pastore, one of the three leaders who had struggled so hard to save Part III,
became an advocate to amend Part IV. John Kennedy joined a small group
of normally pro-civil-rights senators to vote for the amendment. Knowland, who had counted 39 Republican votes, wound up with just 33. The
rest was anticlimax.

Although Knowland and the administration had come up short in this
battle, when Mitchell met with the senator in his office that night, he found
Knowland "deeply moved by what had happened, but he was equally determined to carry the fight to the finish." Mitchell recalled that Knowland had
"really fought right to the bitter end" for the full bill, "and when they lost,
"that big, strong, brusque, Knowland actually broke down and cried" in his
office as he, a staff member, and the lobbyist commiserated. Seeking guidance, Knowland asked Mitchell whether he thought it was worthwhile to
continue the fight. Without hesitating, Mitchell told him yes.

Douglas, too, was determined "to carry on." The White House reported the following morning that Eisenhower was "damned unhappy" and
"bitterly unhappy" with the Senate action. Regardless, he had to take
much of the blame for this fiasco. While the power of the presidency

should have resulted in more influence over senators, a very lukewarm and often hesitant Eisenhower had allowed the Democrats to get the better of the Republicans. Eisenhower himself would be credited with the fact that the first civil rights act passed by Congress in this century came during his administration. It was Brownell, though, as Mitchell explained in later life, who really deserved credit for that breakthrough. Mitchell felt that Eisenhower merited credit only for being distracted enough to permit his attorney general to lead the administration on this issue.

Furthermore, the Democrats now had the upper hand over Republican leaders with eyes on 1960, which led GOP strategists to try to stall the bill's final passage. White House officials sent telegrams to African American leaders throughout the country saying that the bill was no good. Nixon suggested that the civil rights forces "ought to consider whether the best strategy wouldn't be to hold the bill in conference until next year and then make an all-out fight for a stronger bill." Morse, too, for different political reasons, continued hoping that Congress would "reject this bad bill."

Mitchell had felt that way, too, right after the vote, but the following morning Joseph Rauh had hardly opened his eyes when his telephone rang and he heard Mitchell saying that the civil rights forces had to support what was left of the bill before people got the idea that the legislative process could not work in the field of civil rights. Mitchell was certain that this was the best he could get from Congress, and it was much better than anything he could have gotten in the past. He was the first to realize the psychological and historical importance of this development. Congress was about to pass its first civil rights law in eighty-seven years. At long last the veil of *Scott* v. *Sanford*—which the Thirteenth, Fourteenth, and Fifteenth amendments had been designed to remove, but which subsequently had been strengthened in *Plessy* v. *Ferguson,* and which, despite *Brown,* had continued to blind the national legislature to the injustices of second-class citizenship for African Americans—was being raised. And Congress's role in this social achievement was as great as that of the Supreme Court in declaring the "separate but equal" doctrine unconstitutional.

Unlike critics, Mitchell was well aware that all he had asked for originally had been the voting rights provisions, the Civil Rights Commission, and the assistant attorney general in charge of civil rights. Even though he felt that Part III "was a tremendously important thing," it was "clear that none of us who were working for this would have said the bill was emasculated" without it.

This meant, explained Rauh, that "we didn't buy our own propaganda. We kept saying it wouldn't be worth passing if we lost those fights" for Part III and against the jury trial amendment. "But we knew it would be worth passing, and we had a lot of words to eat. Clarence ate a lot of words. I ate a lot of words" in order for the bill to become law. Rauh was gratified that history had proved them right. "I believe Clarence was the kind of wise human being" who saw the importance of accepting the compromise. "It was a lot easier for a white man to compromise than for a black man. It was a lot easier for me to say: 'I'll be philosophical. Forget this. We will get a better bill next time,' than it was for Clarence." Rauh went on: "Nobody could call me an Uncle Tom; but they could call Clarence an Uncle Tom because he was black. So I found Clarence's performance remarkable. I don't think Clarence then or elsewhere ever thought about the consequences to himself of something he was doing. He thought about whether it was right, and he did it." Mitchell's actions confirmed Rauh's impression that "he could fight like a tiger. But he could take his lumps and then come back and say, 'Let's pick up the pieces. Let's get something going, and we will go on.'"

Rauh was torn by Mitchell's frustration. He recalled an occasion when Mitchell and he were pounding the corridors "with tails between our legs," trying to get someone to offer an amendment to bar discrimination in the National Guard. Humphrey, Douglas, and Morse "all turned us down." Mitchell then looked at Rauh and said, "There will never be real civil rights out of the Senate until we have a black senator." Rauh told Mitchell he was wrong in thinking so. "We are going to get it, and I believe we are going to get good civil rights legislation before we get a black senator because I don't think he will make that much difference." Rauh felt that the issue was "going to be how the public feels."

Rauh saw Wilkins take a "terrible, terrible pounding from the militants in the NAACP and elsewhere to reject the bill." The American Civil Liberties Union opposed it, too, saying it was worse than nothing. Mitchell, however, argued strongly that the compromise was better than nothing. Rauh took his position; so did others like Hyman Bookbinder of the AFL-CIO.[30]

With the decision made, Wilkins on August 7 led a civil rights caucus of sixteen organizations in declaring that although the bill was "a bitter disappointment," it did contain some potential good. The caucus urged supporters in the Senate to vote for it "in the hope that some means would be found to strengthen it in the House." The caucus said that any bill passed would be "the beginning, not the end of the struggle." Rauh, meeting with Congressman Bolling and a core group of other liberal activists during what they dubbed "swimming pool weekends," followed up this decision by working for passage of the strongest compromise bill they could get.

A triumphant Johnson, after proudly announcing that "I shall vote for this bill" because it was effective legislation, went into the Senate to steer the measure through 24 days of debate—including a marathon final debate that lasted 121 hours and 31 minutes without any further amendments, because there was an agreement that there would be none in exchange for the southerners' getting the amendments they wanted. Finally, the Senate passed the Civil Rights Act of 1957 by a roll call vote of 72 to 18.

As the NAACP had hoped, the formula that House and Senate leaders had agreed on for the jury trial amendment greatly increased the effectiveness of the bill. The revision, which Mitchell got the Justice Department, with Brownell's help, to shape to ensure a better amendment, provided that no jury trial would be required even in criminal contempt cases if the sentence by the judge was not for more than forty-five days in prison and a $300 fine. There would be a jury trial only if the sentence and fine were greater and the defendant demanded one. This revision was another indication of how Mitchell worked—he always looked for positive ways to ease the damage of defeats.[31]

When the House returned the bill to the Senate for the final vote on August 27 after approving the compromise version, it was supposed that it would sail through. But Dixiecrat standard-bearer Strom Thurmond broke the no-filibuster agreement and made one final gesture of defiance for the benefit of the folk back home in South Carolina. Late the following day he launched a filibuster that lasted twenty-four hours and eighteen minutes— a record for a one-man talkathon. That record for endurance was matched only by Mitchell, who remained in the gallery through the long night after the sprinkling of hangers-on had left. Thurmond's wife, Jean, sat through much of the night, until she got tired and also left. Mitchell maintained his vigil until the South Carolinian had clocked his last word at 11:00 P.M. the following evening, as if in penance for the sins that others had wrought against his people.

Chicago Defender reporter Ethel Payne, one of the black reporters who were close to Mitchell, recalled seeing a very intense and sensitive man during "the heat of the battle on Capitol Hill go day after day without sleep and food to endlessly haunt the corridors, the cloakrooms and the offices of representatives and senators, urging them to support the civil rights measure." She watched him "sitting in the visitor's section of both houses, listening to abuse of the NAACP, the Negro people, and assaults upon the bill both from the North and the South. We all sat watching while Senator Lyndon Johnson, the most astute maneuverer on the Hill, cracked his whip and marshalled his forces to cut the guts and the heart out of the bill." During the long debate over the jury trial amendment when the galleries were packed, "you could count the Negroes on one hand" because they did not appreciate the importance of having the senators seeing them there; but Clarence and Juanita Mitchell were there. Payne became deeply embarrassed when a white reporter turned to her and asked, "Where are the Negroes? Aren't they interested in their own rights?"

Rauh found it delightful at one point during the long series of debates when old Senator Harry Flood Byrd looked up at the gallery and shouted angrily, "There they are, the NAACP and the ADA—the Gold Dust Twins," in a reference to a popular cleanser trademark.

Clarence Mitchell was a very relieved man when the Senate, by a vote of 60 to 15, on August 29, brought to reality that moment of which he had dreamed for so long. The victory was a great psychological breakthrough: for the first time since the Civil War, the President and Congress had intervened jointly to protect the rights of blacks. Despite his disappointment that the bill was not as strong as he had wanted, Mitchell regarded the provisions creating the Civil Rights Division of the Justice Department, establishing the Civil Rights Commission, and protecting the right to vote as historic achievements. The Civil Rights Division and the commission, especially, were the heart and soul of the machinery for protecting the constitutional rights of blacks. One represented the mighty arm of federal enforcement; the other was the conscience and moral rudder of the nation.

In a fierce meeting of the Georgia delegation after the Thurmond filibuster, when charges and countercharges were flying, Russell told his southern colleagues that if he had not taken a conciliatory position possibly they would have gotten a "worse" bill. That was also Johnson's response to the stream of angry letters he received from segregationists back home. Johnson maintained that he'd had to play the role he had to protect their interests—that is, in order to defeat Part III. Doing some Monday morning quarterbacking, Mitchell believed that, despite its importance, Part III might have unglued the bill. He figured that the Republicans who voted for this section would have turned around afterward, as they had done so frequently on other issues, and refused to support cloture if that had been necessary.[32]

Among the people who Mitchell felt deserved most credit for passage of the act, after Knowland, was another Republican, Richard Nixon. Mitchell said that Nixon's ruling on June 20, upholding the Knowland-Douglas maneuver to bypass the Senate Judiciary Committee and place the bill on the calendar, "opened a door that long had been closed to civil rights legislation." He thanked Congressmen Joseph Martin, the minority leader, and Kenneth Keating, and Senators Knowland and Johnson just as fervently for their help. An indication of Mitchell's keen sense of politics was his telegram to Johnson right after the Civil Rights Act was passed, expressing his appreciation for the senator's leadership. Mitchell, hinting at the political benefits, told him that the bill represented a late birthday present for the majority leader. Its passage, he said, "revealed that there are far more Americans who think of the welfare of the whole country than there are servants of sectionalism." Johnson responded that he agreed with Mitchell "that when the chips are down," members of the Senate "think of the welfare of the nation."

As important as the passage of the 1957 Civil Rights Act was in making Lyndon Johnson a national political figure and in paving the way for his nomination for the vice presidency three years later, so also did this victory unequivocally establish Mitchell as an equal to Wilkins and King, the two major civil rights leaders of the period. That in the NAACP's organizational structure Mitchell ranked as a subordinate to Wilkins was immaterial. On Capitol Hill, at 1600 Pennsylvania Avenue, and throughout the rest of the executive branch, Mitchell was recognized as a leader to be reckoned with.

Mitchell was confident that the Senate's final approval of the 1957 Civil Rights Act represented the beginning of a new era in American race relations: "At last the Congress has assumed some of its responsibility in the field of civil rights. I predict that the constructive results and continued effort by all of us will encourage the nation's law making body to carry on the good work until the full job is done."[33]

CHAPTER FOURTEEN

The Undaunted Optimist

P resident Eisenhower could have increased considerably his contributions to the civil rights struggle following passage of the 1957 Civil Rights Act by calling on the South to obey the new law and the *Brown* decision. Instead he signed the act without public ceremony on September 9, shortly before heading for the Newport Country Club for another round of golf, just as Governor Orville Faubus of Arkansas was leading whites in violent rebellion against the federal court order to desegregate Little Rock Central High School. Many people like Mitchell and Joseph Rauh thought Faubus had been inspired by southern lawmakers who went home bragging that their success in deleting Part III showed that Congress did not support *Brown*. The deleted Part III, which would have given the attorney general authority to protect the Fourteenth Amendment rights of Arkansas's citizens, became the rallying point for stronger civil rights laws just as FEPC had galvanized the struggle for legislation against employment and other forms of racial discrimination after World War II.

Despite passage of, or plans for, more than one hundred state laws to cripple the NAACP and nullify Supreme Court civil rights decisions, Mitchell was confident that "law, logic, morality and all other American concepts of decency" were "on our side" and would help African Americans win. The setback over Part III notwithstanding, he felt that the climate in Congress was "warming up in our favor" as a result of Little Rock, which had led people like Congressman Kenneth Keating of New York to call for passage of constitutional protections for blacks against mob violence.

Properly enforced, Mitchell believed, the new law would enable more blacks in the South to register and elect pro-civil-rights representatives to Congress. There would be "no more flummery about how many bubbles" there were in a bar of soap when blacks sought to register. "After the stern restraint of a Federal injunction has been applied, those who use force, economic restrictions, and deception to keep the voting lists lily white will realize that the vote must be given to all without regard to race." Mitchell had "the unshaken conviction that by 1960 some of the congressmen from the Old South will be colored." He found that many people did not realize that the new civil rights statute (Public Law 85-315) covered state and local as well as federal elections (by amending Section 1971 of Title 42 of the U.S. Code), so he began educating them. Without Part III, the victims of injustice still had to initiate action, and the courts continued to have the principal burden for protecting their Fourteenth Amendment rights.[1]

Another problem was lack of will within the administration to enforce the new law and to push for more civil rights legislation. Herbert Brownell, who had spent two thirds of his five years as attorney general working on civil rights issues, remained in office long enough to put a cap on the Little Rock uprising. After one month in office, his successor, William Rogers, formerly deputy attorney general, announced his intention to enforce civil rights laws "the same as in other areas, with no more belligerence and no less." He suggested that "we ought to give the Little Rock matter a chance to rest," and that from the standpoint of public interest no more statements should be made about the matter. "The Little Rock people seem to have been handling the matter pretty well," he said; "I am trying to avoid saying anything that will aggravate" the problem. In response to calls for new civil rights laws, he said that the country "should have a little more time to see how the law works and to enforce it." Little wonder, therefore, that the Little Rock school board filed a petition in court to postpone its desegregation program in a further attempt to nullify *Brown*. The Supreme Court, however, forcefully rejected those plans.

Mitchell thought differently. "We say to the U.S. Department of Justice: You know the facts of voting discrimination; you have a new law; in the name of the Constitution that we all hold dear, stop talking about 'cooling off' and put the heat on those who are trying to destroy our government from within by sabotaging free elections." He charged that some Republican leaders were so fearful that Democrats would embarrass them for alleged defense program failures that they wanted to sacrifice civil rights to appease southern leaders in Congress. He said that that was the reason Rogers had called for a cooling-off period, and why Democrats like Montana's Mike Mansfield had joined "the brigade that is trying to put the drive for human freedom in the ice box."[2]

When Labor Secretary James P. Mitchell suggested to the National Newspaper Publishers Association's "Summit Meeting of Negro Leaders" in Washington in May 1958 that "so-called professional civil righters were responsible for the passage of a weak bill" because they did not insist on the House version, the NAACP leader protested. Mitchell was very upset that the labor secretary had repeatedly made those charges in public meetings and to visitors in his office, but not in the presence of himself or Wilkins. Now, openly challenged at a crowded conference of influential people, Mitchell felt obligated to respond. While remaining in his seat beside Juanita and his mother-in-law, he said so that everyone could hear, "That simply is not true."

The presiding officer sent an official to urge Mitchell not to embarrass their guest. Mitchell replied that he had no intention of doing so, but that he had to keep the record straight. At the end of his address, the labor secretary invited Mitchell to discuss the matter with him. Although Mitchell had met with the labor secretary "many times before," the two previously had never discussed that particular matter.

Mitchell then approached the secretary at the platform as he was preparing to leave. While they were talking, William O. Walker, NNPA president and a Republican strongly sympathetic to the administration, rushed up and rudely demanded, "Who is this man? We don't know him." Never before had any black leader treated Mitchell that way. Like most of the other publishers present, however, Walker knew Mitchell very well. Many of them had commended him for having gotten the 1957 Civil Rights Act through Congress. Carl Murphy, publisher of the *Baltimore Afro-American,* who regarded Mitchell with pride, tried to intercede, but here, too, partisan politics got in the way. Murphy was a Democrat, so in this situation he had little sway with Walker, who was trying to make points with the Republican administration. In fact, Walker was so furious that he would not listen to anyone. Mitchell had found the secretary willing to talk, but, since Walker prevented him from doing so, the lobbyist asked for a chance to explain the matter over the microphone. He was barred from doing so.

As he left the platform, he attempted to address the conference anyway. Walker, who had been following him, seized him and called for help to remove him from the room. No one moved to help Walker as Mitchell persisted. Despite such a promise and the eagerness of several persons at the conference to hear his story, the opportunity was never given. The confrontation became so heated that it almost, in Lillie Carroll Jackson's words, "busted up" the conference as the publishers took sides, many of them calling Walker "an Uncle Tom for the Republicans." Finally, Mitchell left the conference.

Mitchell felt that black publishers like Walker lacked courage and were holding back the movement by letting government officials get away with lies. Murphy had invited Juanita and Lillie to the conference. As they always had done at forums in Washington where Clarence was speaking, they brought along a few friends to show hometown interest—in this case, in Murphy's activities. Mitchell told Juanita that he was upset not only because he thought the black press was failing in its duty to challenge people like the labor secretary, but also that Walker was unfair in not permitting him to speak.

Much of the black press upbraided Mitchell for his conduct. The *Pittsburgh Courier,* for instance, sympathized with Eisenhower's repeated calls for "patience and forbearance" and his stated "truism" that "laws themselves will never solve problems that have their roots in the human heart and human emotions" so "we must depend on more and better education than simply on the letter of the law." The *Courier* felt that the President, in addressing the conference on May 12, "could easily have resorted to demagogic remarks that would have perhaps stirred" the emotions of the four hundred people attending the luncheon at which he spoke, but, being a "responsible head" of the nation, he tempered his remarks. Another black newspaper called Mitchell's response at the NNPA meeting regrettable and worried that blacks "can't win friends by resorting to bad manners or losing their heads." Black reporters like Alice Dunnigan and Ethel Payne thought otherwise. Dunnigan reported that Walker had attempted to "gag" Mitchell; Payne said the NAACP leader's experience was "a bitter lesson of the high cost and toll of fighting for a cause virtually in a one-man campaign."

Roy Wilkins defended Mitchell just as stoutly, telling one critic that the NAACP Washington Bureau director was "one of the most skilled, best informed, and most dedicated legislative workers in Washington." Wilkins said that Mitchell and every staff member of the NAACP and other organizations who had worked for the 1957 act were galled by the charges the labor secretary had persistently made. Clarence "felt duty bound to object then and there—and publicly" when he repeated them in his presence.

But Mitchell's frustrations ran deeper. In his statement to the publishers conference, which was included in their report, he noted that when a mob in Lima, Peru, spat on and stoned Vice President Nixon, "he was getting a South American version of what colored Americans experience in the South"—with "one important difference": The Peruvians were not bound to respect the U.S. Constitution. But in this country, those who had taken an oath to uphold the Constitution were often leading forces that opposed equal treatment under law. Furthermore: "When the rocks fly and mob hysteria rises, there is always a cry for a halt to progress. The timid run for cover. The dishonest try to blame the victims and accuse them of being agitators or trying to move too fast." He thought the nine children who braved the mobs and entered Central High School in Little Rock gave the world a magnificent demonstration of courage similar to that shown by the Vice President "when he walked into a hostile crowd to tell our country's story. We must support the courage of the children and the courage of the Vice President by making sure that the American story is one that inspires the world to follow this nation's example in protecting human freedom."

Mitchell was using the national sense of outrage to make a point, thus overlooking the inappropriateness of his comparison—an indication of his lack of expertise in international affairs. The rioting Peruvians felt that they were protesting U.S. injustice just as much as blacks at home were doing.

Despite his disappointment with Walker, Mitchell never held the incident against him. A quarter of a century later, Juanita would marvel at how gracious Mitchell was to Walker during a dinner party at the home of a mutual friend. The compassion that he demonstrated to the publisher, now in his eighties, was a typical example of Mitchell's tolerance for the weaknesses in others, a quality that he passed on to his children, especially Clarence III, who easily forgave personal wrongs.

Mitchell's first challenge of 1958 was to overcome the Eisenhower administration's we've-done-enough tendency. Even though some congressional leaders were inclined to act on the NAACP's demands, without initiative from the administration, everything was more or less at a standstill—at least until after the 1958 midterm elections. Roy Wilkins warned that unless the government maintained a firm stand "over the whole desegregation front, mobs, and their back-stage managers will continue to mock law and order," causing more, not fewer, Little Rocks.

Through the 1957 Civil Rights Act, Congress had partly shorn away the hypocrisy of the South's contention that black political equality would lead to social equality and, combined, to miscegenation. It was now demonstrated that the nation was willing to grant blacks some political equality, but the fulfillment of this constitutional right did not necessarily lead to social equality. The Supreme Court in *Brown* never ruled that the Preamble to the Constitution gave the federal government power to procure the objects (life, liberty, and the pursuit of happiness) of the American democratic system for its citizens, so many lawmakers saw no reason to fulfill that obligation, even though the Thirty-ninth Congress in shaping the Fourteenth Amendment had authorized subsequent Congresses to do so.

The Fourteenth Amendment did at least three things. It provided that all persons born or naturalized in the United States were full-fledged citizens and equal under the law. It said that "no State shall make or enforce any law which shall abridge the privileges or immunities of citizens of the United States; nor shall any State deprive any person of life, liberty or property without due process of law; nor deny to any person within its jurisdiction the equal protection of the laws." And it provided that "Congress shall have power to enforce, by appropriate legislation, the provisions of this article."

Senator Paul Douglas was painfully aware of this mandate. "We should never forget," he would declare upon introducing the civil rights bill, "although some would have us do so, that the 14th Amendment is an organic and integral part of the Constitution of the United States, which all public officials have sworn to uphold." Congress's responsibility was "to put our moral house in order—for the benefit of citizens now denied their rights and for the benefit of the whole nation in its difficult position as a leader of the free world."

Having come a step closer to the goal of equality, Mitchell more than ever was determined to codify those ideals underlying the first Reconstruction. *Brown* reasserted the legal right for blacks to be equal citizens. Congress through legislation had to provide the federal government with as much power as was needed to protect that equality. In Mitchell's words:

> No man enjoys liberty if he is consigned to a special status because of his race, his religion or his national origin. The 1954 decision of the court has established forever that there is no legal justification for separating Americans on the basis of race. Legal decisions are not self-executing. We enjoy their benefits only to the extent that we are willing to work and sacrifice for what is rightfully ours. We are now at the place where our civil rights come with our birth certificate. We are also at the place where those rights can be lost or diminished unless we press for all of them now.[3]

Passage of the 1957 Civil Rights Act again proved to Mitchell that having a law was one thing, but enforcing it was another. During his long struggle for the law, rather than despairing when the quest so often seemed hopeless, he made a conscious effort to pave the way for expected results by continually raising the segregation issue in the congressional forum. That was another benefit of committee hearings. For example, he told Wilkins,

there was a "definite connection between" the Jim Crow hospital bill sponsored in 1951 by Congressman John E. Rankin of Mississippi and realization by the Veterans Administration that it could begin desegregation
without fearing congressional reprisal. By demonstrating a determination
not to extend segregation in these hospitals, Congress sent the executive
branch a message of support. Rankin's bill would have established a segregated hospital in Booker T. Washington's name. Had he not engineered the
bill's defeat with the help of Adam Clayton Powell, Mitchell felt, segregation would have "increased everywhere" in the Veterans Administration. In
other instances where he did not achieve an end to segregation, he at least
halted its spread.

Now Mitchell found that the same people who had been opposing public school desegregation were against enforcing the voting rights law. Their
response, he said, was the answer to northerners who worried that blacks
were moving too fast and to those who had said that "the South would be
more willing to obey a law passed by Congress than a Supreme Court
decision." Progress, therefore, meant not the complete solution of problems
but incremental advances toward the goal of equality and full citizenship
rights. Mitchell was encouraged by the reduction from seventeen to seven
(Alabama, Florida, Georgia, Louisiana, Mississippi, South Carolina, and
Virginia) of the number of southern states with totally segregated public
schools and called for redoubling efforts to wipe out that injustice. He
noted the success of George Holland of Minnesota, whom, as executive
secretary of the local Urban League, Mitchell had helped get a milk delivery route in St. Paul, who was now a top official with the Veterans Administration. "We must never forget, however," he said, "that there are
hundreds and thousands of other young men like Mr. Holland who do not
get an opportunity and who in spite of their hard work cannot use their full
talents simply because they are not white."[4]

Not only was Mitchell faced with recurring as well as pending challenges in various areas, including the military, recreation, transportation,
public facilities, education, and housing, but his effort to strengthen the
1957 act was also very quickly superseded by other battles. Two of these
involved gaining confirmation for the appointments of W. Wilson White as
assistant attorney general for the Civil Rights Division of the Justice Department, and of Gordon M. Tiffany as staff director of the Civil Rights
Commission. Filling these offices was necessary to assure the enforcement
powers mandated by the act.

The work of the two new agencies was slowed first because their creation had occurred between sessions of Congress. Next, early in 1958,
James Eastland buried the appointments in what Mitchell called a "parliamentary deep freeze" in the Senate Judiciary Committee. To release them,

William Knowland promised Mitchell that the Republicans would "take the matter in hand themselves" if there was no prompt progress. On May 5 the committee sent the Tiffany appointment to the full Senate, where it was soon approved. But the committee continued to sit on White's appointment, so the Senate did not approve it until August 18.

Meanwhile, Mitchell won a promise of continued cooperation from the FBI. The Justice Department assured him that although White had not been confirmed, plans were being made to take a number of civil rights violation cases to court. He was encouraged that White felt "a heavy responsibility to support the legal justification" for using troops in Little Rock, which was one of the reasons why Eastland and company opposed him.

The Civil Rights Commission was especially important because it was the first such fact-finding agency since Truman's Committee on Civil Rights, and it was intended to be permanent. It was created by Congress rather than by executive order, so its mandate was much broader, and so were its objectives: to "appraise the laws and policies of the Federal Government with respect to equal protection of the laws." As Johnson said in endorsing it, the commission "can sift out the truth from the fancies" and "return with recommendations which will be of assistance to reasonable men." Eisenhower conformed to the law's requirement for a bipartisan commission by selecting three fairly conservative southern Democrats, two northern Republicans, and a priest—all guaranteed to cause him little trouble. They were John Battle, former governor of Virginia and leader of the Dixiecrat walkout at the 1948 Democratic convention; Doyle Carlton, former governor of Florida; Robert Storey, dean of the Southern Methodist University Law School in Texas; John Hannah, president of Michigan State University; J. Ernest Wilkins, an assistant secretary of labor; and the Reverend Theodore Hesburgh, president of Notre Dame.

Determining that the major problem with the commission was lack of complaints on voting discrimination, Mitchell suggested that, to "cover more ground in a shorter time," the commission review discrimination complaints that had been submitted to the Justice Department from Mississippi, Louisiana, Alabama, Florida, and Georgia. Owing to fears of violence, which discouraged complaints, Mitchell urged the Justice Department to provide protection for several blacks in Alabama after they had testified at the commission's first hearing in December lest others be discouraged from appearing in the future.

One reason for this difficulty was that nearly all the commission's investigators were white; blacks were reluctant to talk to them. But upon being convinced that the strangers were, indeed, earnest in protecting their rights, an old Alabama black woman, rocking silently on her porch, declared, "You mean the Big Government has come? The Big Government has really come all the way down here to help us? The Big Government is finally doing something to let me vote?" For the first time in sixty years, she said, the federal government had shown an interest in black Alabamians.

In January 1959, Mitchell followed up an earlier complaint to the commission on voting discrimination in Mississippi with several others aimed at barring segregation in federally funded programs. Regarding leases of federal land, he said, there appeared to be no overall regulation requiring a nondiscrimination clause, so each agency could freely adopt or reject the safeguard. At Mitchell's insistence, the Departments of Agriculture and the Interior and the Army Corps of Engineers had adopted such clauses for programs involving recreational uses of land. Nevertheless, he had received complaints about discrimination at the Redstone Arsenal in Alabama on lands the Army leased from the Tennessee Valley Authority. Because access to thousands of publicly owned acres was involved, he asked the commission to conduct an investigation in order to determine a remedy.

With Congress still blocking the Powell Amendment to federal aid to education programs despite the continuing segregation of students in the South and at various newly constructed schools serving military personnel, Mitchell urged the commission to express concern on the problem as well as in the area of hospital construction. The problem with hospital funding assistance was that the Department of Health, Education and Welfare still followed the "separate but equal" formula in the existing nondiscrimination clause of the Public Health Service Act (Hill-Burton Act) although *Brown* declared that principle unconstitutional. (The Mississippi Sovereignty Commission caved in when faced with the loss of an $11 million Veterans Administration hospital because of the nonsegregation requirement. "We've got the tiger by the tail," said Governor James Coleman. "We either accept the integrated facility, or we deny our Mississippi white veterans medical services they need." Only one member dissented as the Sovereignty Commission voted to donate the land for the hospital.)[5]

The Civil Rights Commission's first report in September 1959 was not as revolutionary as *To Secure These Rights,* but it was nonetheless significant. Eisenhower said that it "holds up before us a mirror so that we may see ourselves, what we are doing and what we are not doing, and therefore makes it easier for us to correct our omissions." Noting that the 1957 act was an outgrowth of the Truman Committee on Civil Rights's 1947 recommendations, the commission stressed that by any measurement that law was inadequate to assure all qualified citizens the right to vote. It said that there existed a striking "moral gap" between reality and ideal that spilled over into and vitiated other areas of society. The problem ran "counter to our traditional concepts of fair play" and was a "repudiation of our faith in the democratic system." The commission's recommendations were based on its hearings in Alabama and Louisiana on voting and other racial abuses, and investigations of complaints from five other southern states. The commission therefore called for new legislation to correct the many weaknesses it had found in the voting rights law, particularly its failure to prohibit the destruction of ballot records following elections.

Among the commission's recommendations in the area of education was one that the President call on Congress to adopt legislation authorizing the commission to serve as a clearinghouse for information and programs concerned with implementing the Supreme Court's 1954 desegregation decision. Another recommendation that would echo loudly in the 1960 elections was for the President to issue an executive order directing all federal agencies to strive for equal housing opportunities and to strengthen other procedures for combatting discrimination, such as in programs like those operated by the Housing and Home Finance Agency.

The comprehensive nature of the commission's report removed any lingering doubts that Mitchell might have had about the agency's value. It was clear that the civil rights forces now had an independent federal agency that not only faithfully supported the NAACP's goals, but also was serving as the national moral arbiter, documenting problems for future executive and congressional actions. The commission's housing recommendations, for example, were based on the complaint that Roy Wilkins had submitted at a February 3 hearing in New York.

To ensure that its priorities would continue to be relevant, the NAACP had to maintain vigilance. Wilkins had found that the commission was interested "in doing a good job," but it was "greatly hobbled in thinking and acting by the ever present political threat" from vocal, powerful southern Democrats and, subtly, from "indifferent, lukewarm, or secretly hostile northern Republicans." This pressure was aggravated by impatient blacks who were "under the hammer" but ignorant of the commission's legal and technical limitations. When the commission, extended in September by Congress for another two years, began planning for new hearings in Los Angeles and San Francisco, Mitchell promptly resubmitted a complaint on airport segregation in the South that the agency earlier had said it could not investigate because of limited time and personnel.

The complaint involved threatened arrests of Gloster Current, director of NAACP branches, and former baseball star Jackie Robinson, now a member of the NAACP board of directors, at the Greenville, South Carolina, airport for sitting in the main waiting room. Mitchell also recounted his own arrest at the Florence airport three years earlier in order to demonstrate that neither the Civil Aeronautics Administration nor its successor the Federal Aviation Agency had enforced adequately the Federal Airport Act. Furthermore, just as it had refused to act on his arrest, the Justice Department had ignored several other complaints he had submitted on segregated waiting rooms in Tennessee, Georgia, and Alabama. In fact, despite Justice's promise to act against any airport resegregation in 1956, South Carolina had adopted a new segregation law covering Florence County public transportation facilities. But, Mitchell said, as evidence of the capricious enforcement of the law, he and several South Carolinians who had used the main waiting room in 1956 had not been challenged, even though the "colored" sign had been put up again at a nearby area. The fact that the law was enacted after Mitchell had protested so strongly to the Justice Department and could be enforced at any time was another example of the South's defiance of *Brown*. During the hearings on the 1957 civil rights bill, Sam Ervin and other senators had maintained that no legislation was needed to correct the problem, but the Charlotte, North Carolina, airport was still segregated at the time. Mitchell submitted other complaints from blacks in Mississippi alleging discrimination by the Internal Revenue Service and the Social Security Administration, their employers. Both agencies, Mitchell said, denied the charges; consequently, as with airport segregation, he requested the commission to conduct investigations, which it eventually did.[6]

If the Watkins case established Rauh as an unquestioned constitutional authority on civil liberties, his defense of Arthur Miller, the Pulitzer Prize–winning playwright and husband of the voluptuous Marilyn Monroe, made him the envy of Washington's social elite. Rauh defended Miller against charges that were a carbon copy of those in the Watkins case, for refusing to reveal to the House Un-American Activities Committee the names of men who had attended a Communist-sponsored writers' conference in 1947. The district court convicted Miller on the charges in May 1957, but Rauh won the appeal in 1958 on strictly technical grounds. He was never able to get the courts to decide the underlying constitutional issue.

During Miller's trial in 1957, when his actress wife stayed at Rauh's home in the elegant Northwest section of Washington, the army of encamped reporters and television camera crews, in Rauh's words, "made my lawn look like Sherman's march to the sea." When people extended their sympathy to him about the hardships of being a human rights lawyer, his happy response was "Well, if you can think of anything nicer than having Marilyn Monroe in your home for a couple of weeks, it doesn't matter what you get paid." His sixteen-year-old son, Carl, provided the quote of the week. On his way home from school one afternoon, he responded to a reporter who wanted to know what he thought of having the actress as a guest: "Well, ain't quite like having your brother at home." Many in Congress, though, were not as happy about the Supreme Court's rulings in the internal security cases or, especially, the school desegregation cases.

Consequently, in 1958, conservative lawmakers—led in the House by Virginia's Howard Smith and in the Senate by William Jenner, the high-volume Republican orator from Indiana, and Maryland's John Butler—launched a series of attacks on the Court. Others like Eastland, sitting earlier as a one-man internal security subcommittee, had been pushing bills to nullify the Court's 1956 ruling that the government's internal security program must be limited to sensitive positions. The hostility of Karl E. Mundt of North Dakota, Barry Goldwater of Arizona, and Carl T. Curtis of Nebraska, during the six-week Senate Rackets Committee investigation in 1958 of the long, bitter UAW strike against the Kohler Company of Wisconsin, caused Rauh to characterize these Republicans as "dwarfs from the last century" who had seized authority and turned the hearing into a "disgusting performance."[7]

At the center of the attacks on the Court was a bill sponsored by Jenner and amendments to it that Butler offered. The Jenner-Butler bill would have prohibited the Supreme Court from reviewing state regulations of lawyers' admission to the bar and thus threatened with disbarment those who handled civil rights cases. This bill also would have made advocating violent overthrow of the government a crime regardless of whether the intention was to incite action, permitted states to prosecute subversive acts unless expressly forbidden by Congress, and prohibited federal court review of congressional committee investigating powers.

Rauh's first concern was that the measure would undermine the Bill of Rights and end the independence of the judicial branch of the government. That, he said, would have been tantamount to "legislative dictatorship." The NAACP, by contrast, was alarmed by the threat to its ability to represent civil rights victims in court.

Mitchell called the bill "one of the most incredible attacks on the court" in the last one hundred years. Many doubted the bill would pass, and even if it did, Mitchell said, the President would veto it. Regardless, he thought the propaganda effect "would be devastating in many parts of the South" and "hang like a Damocles' sword over the heads of every federal judge and every member of the United States court."

Virginia had heightened the fear that constitutional rights were being eroded by passing a law forbidding lawyers to handle civil rights cases unless they were paid only by plaintiffs or close relatives. Although a federal court had thrown out the Virginia law early in 1958, Tennessee and Mississippi still had similar laws and other states were considering them.

Texas, Alabama, Florida, Virginia, Georgia, Louisiana, and Arkansas also had laws giving their interpretations of barratry and other similar types of illegal lawsuits. If the Jenner-Butler bill was passed, the impact on the NAACP and its constituents would be devastating, especially since state judges were elected and thus easily subject to public prejudice.

Rauh was intrigued that August by the southerners' strategy. He said that even though they did not believe "this ripper bill" would be enacted, the southerners increased their demands for it to be brought up. Their maneuver pushed Johnson to substitute a three-bill package that was supposedly less harmful. One bill would have overruled the Supreme Court's decision in *Pennsylvania* v. *Nelson* barring states from passing legislation in the "antisubversive" field; another would have overruled, wholly or in part, the *Mallory* v. *United States* decision preventing the use in evidence of confessions obtained while federal officers unnecessarily delayed arraignment; and the third would have prohibited federal review by habeas corpus of state criminal trials—an essential constitutional protection for detained persons, which civil rights lawyers valued.

Johnson believed that his maneuver offered everyone something. The southerners could claim they had scored a triple court overruling. The Communist-bashers would get the bill overruling *Nelson*, and states would be free to look for subversives; the law-and-order people would get the bill overruling *Mallory* and the habeas corpus bill. Even the Justice Department, the Judicial Conference (the federal court system's top policy-making group), and many northerners who maintained it was not anti–civil rights supported the habeas corpus bill, which would have made it impossible for a person in state custody to appeal to the federal courts for release.

Mitchell, as well as Rauh, feared that the *Mallory* confession overruler bill would enable overzealous or prejudiced law enforcement officers, seeking to obtain a confession, to detain unlawfully those persons, most likely minority group members, least able to protect their rights because they were poor or illiterate. Mitchell also protested that in the current climate of repression, state judges would abuse their new powers that allowed them to detain people. As an example, he noted that in *NAACP* v. *Alabama,* a case brought by people determined "to put the NAACP out of business," a $100,000 state judgment against the organization was only overturned in 1958 after the Supreme Court had assumed jurisdiction and ruled the fine unconstitutional.

Unlike Mitchell, Rauh and the liberal Senate bloc that was led by, among others, Hubert H. Humphrey of Minnesota and Paul H. Douglas of Illinois did not hesitate to seek ways to back Johnson into a corner. Humphrey and Douglas let Johnson know they intended to counter the anti–Supreme Court strategy with a strong defense of the desegregation decisions. They then not only shattered the majority leader's three-bill strategy but, with support from the NAACP network of branches, which was mobilized to put pressure on lawmakers to defeat the measure, also tabled the Jenner-Butler bill by a 49 to 41 vote. Johnson himself led in executing the maneuver to kill the Jenner-Butler bill, which he knew had no chance of passing, in the hope of getting action on the other bills. He did this by bringing up a noncontroversial bill on federal appellate procedures and immediately yielding to Jenner, who offered his bill as an amendment. After only a few hours' debate, the Senate approved a motion from Hennings to kill the bill Jenner had modified.

The debate then reached its most dramatic moment, when Douglas offered for himself and Senators Humphrey and Wayne Morse of Oregon an amendment to the pending bill overriding *Mallory* that would have Congress express "its full support and approval of the recent, historic decisions of the Supreme Court of the United States holding racial segregation unlawful." Douglas's strategy was to force Johnson to abandon the other anti-Court measures and to make clear that "the real issue is the Supreme Court." His measure, he said, put it "out in the open, right here on the floor of the Senate." The southerners now had a counterthreat on their doorstep.

Johnson, with the filibuster threat in mind, deftly substituted the *Nelson* overruler for the Douglas amendment. Senator John McClellan of Arkansas then moved to amend it with H.R. 3, a tougher states' rights bill, sponsored in the House by Virginia's Howard Smith, that would render future federal laws invalid when they conflicted with state laws unless the latter were specifically preempted by Congress. The Smith bill would have crippled civil rights groups and rendered statutes sanctioned by the Constitution illegal under state law. Mitchell observed that William M. Colmer, Democrat of Mississippi, had said of the Smith bill: "It attempts to raise the 'Halt' sign—the 'Stop, Look and Listen' sign—for the Supreme Court to see." The bill sailed through the House 241 to 155, with the help of 141 Republicans and 100 conservative Democrats.

Mitchell welcomed that first opportunity to be part of Johnson's battle plan. Laboring feverishly to defeat the Smith bill, Johnson even frightened some senators with a threat to offer the Douglas amendment if they did not vote against H.R. 3. During the fight Mitchell learned a very valuable lesson from Johnson about the importance of counting votes in a way that left no margin for error. He was aware that most liberals kept their distance from the Senate majority leader, but some, like Missouri's Stuart Symington, who had introduced them, had established a relationship with Johnson based on mutual respect. John Carroll of Colorado, who had been chosen to lead the Democratic forces, offered a motion in the Senate to recommit the Smith bill to committee. Mitchell's assignment from Johnson was to verify the Democrats' strength and to work with other groups outside the Senate to win support for the Carroll motion.

Senator J. Glenn Beall, Jr., of Maryland, for whom Mitchell had much respect because he had always been a consistent civil rights supporter, agreed to help. But Mitchell was disappointed that Butler opposed the Carroll motion. Mitchell discovered, during his visits to the offices of senators with small black constituencies, that many of those senators said they would vote for the measure. Others, he found, promised their support because they wanted to be fair.

One western senator, who supported giving states more power, nevertheless was opposed to the negative implications of the bill. So he agreed to pair his vote with that of an absent senator and refrain from voting. The effect was to cancel out his own vote. Mitchell passed on that information to Earle Clements of Kentucky, an assistant whip. Clements hurried onto the floor and relayed the information to Johnson, who immediately called for a vote. They won by one vote—41 to 40. Mitchell was especially proud that Carroll recently had been appointed to the Senate Judiciary Committee because Mitchell had insisted that a liberal fill the opening, and his intuition had been rewarded.

Rauh had other reasons to rejoice. Had the tough H.R. 3 not been tabled, he felt, it would have been extremely difficult for the liberals to defeat the *Nelson* overruler, because many senators did not want to risk the charge of being soft on communism.

That now left the *Mallory* overruler. The bill, which was supported by the Justice Department and many northerners in the House and Senate, was barely defeated during the final stages in conference when Vice President Nixon upheld a point of order raised by Carroll at four o'clock one morning, and supporters were too weary to fight back.

In the final analysis, Mitchell gave the major share of credit for victory in defeating the attack on the Supreme Court to Johnson. Rauh, too, welcomed Johnson's help on that issue, but he objected to his heavy-handed style; the majority leader had pushed the three-bill alternative as a lesser evil. So Rauh credited the liberal bloc with having defeated Johnson as well as the anti–Supreme Court group. Mitchell, though, was more impressed by Johnson's ability to maneuver through the political shoals. Besides, he saw much greater benefits accruing from this battle over H.R. 3. He would use the attacks on the Supreme Court and the close margins of victory to reinforce his struggle for stronger civil rights laws.

More effective civil rights legislation in such a climate was foredoomed, even though the Supreme Court was undeterred by the threats. The significance of Mitchell's struggle in the Eighty-sixth Congress was not the toothless 1960 Civil Rights Act that Congress passed, but its continuing refusal to support the Supreme Court desegregation decision by protecting Fourteenth Amendment rights of black citizens. The enormity of that problem would be underscored by the violence that greeted the student demonstrators in the South a few months later.[8]

Early in 1959, four principal civil rights bills were introduced in the Senate: a Javits bill (S. 456), which was a revision of the Part III deleted from the 1957 Civil Rights Act and would enable the Justice Department to initiate suits in behalf of people whose rights were threatened or denied for racial reasons; a Johnson bill (S. 499) that would create an independent Community Relations Service for conciliating disagreements over constitutional issues or that threatened to affect interstate commerce; a Douglas bill (S. 810) that would provide financial, legal, and technical assistance for school desegregation and a version of the 1957 act's Part III; and a seven-point administration "package" introduced in separate bills by Dirksen and Goldwater that would make fleeing a state to avoid prosecution for anti-civil-rights offenses a crime, protect voting records, extend the Civil Rights Commission for two years, create the Commission on Equal Job Opportunity Under Government Contracts, and provide various forms of antisegregation safeguards for federal aid to education. In the House, several bills similar to the Javits bill were introduced. Congressman Emanuel Celler introduced one that, for the first time, endorsed *Brown,* restored Part III, and provided financial aid for school districts undergoing desegregation. Congressman William McCulloch of Ohio introduced the administration's bill in the lower chamber, but there was nothing like Johnson's bill.

The NAACP strongly favored the Douglas, Javits, and Celler bills because of their Part III–type features. For similar reasons, although the association welcomed the administration's package as positive, it felt that the principal drawback was the failure to endorse the Part III protections as had been done in the original 1956 proposal. That omission was deliberate, which particularly upset the NAACP; Attorney General Rogers claimed that enough laws already existed for protecting minority rights and that any more would aggravate racial tensions. Because of the ADA's cool relations with the Eisenhower administration, Rauh had to prod Rogers to drum up more support, through the use of pressure groups, for civil rights programs in the formative stages. He complained that the administration's failure to enlist that type of support was in marked contrast to the approach of the Roosevelt and Truman administration's.

Another indication of the executive branch's lack of commitment to effective protections of Fourteenth Amendment rights was HEW's position that it should not be required to withhold federal funds from segregated school districts unless they disobeyed a desegregation order by a court. But, Wilkins asked the Hennings Subcommittee on Constitutional Rights during hearings in the spring, if the government did not initiate court action and HEW did not proceed until court action had begun, who would take the first step? The answer, Wilkins suggested, was private citizens already bearing the burden of seeking to have the law enforced. He explained, however, that the federal government's position ignored defiant action by the states, such as a recent Georgia law making it a crime for any public official to provide tax funds for desegregated schools, or for other interracial practices proscribed by the state.

Furthermore, because the NAACP was barred from operating in several southern states, it was obvious that the objective of those states was to render blacks helpless and to make it impossible for the association to represent them. "It is not fair, not decent, not American that parents who seek integrated education for their children in accordance with law should find arrayed against them the massed powers of the states including the treasuries composed in part of their own tax money," Wilkins said.

Mitchell believed that the Johnson bill was worse than nothing because it threatened civil rights advances by suggesting a willingness to bargain away constitutional rights. The idea for the Conciliation Service (later called Community Relations Service) first surfaced in Johnson's office during the struggle for the 1957 Civil Rights Act, but it was not offered then. Although Mitchell subsequently learned that the idea had been first offered by someone from Harvard University as a constructive means of promoting intergroup relations, he contended that it was proposed by former Secretary of State Dean Acheson in order to promote harmony within the Democratic party. It was a concept of the North, not of the South, and one that Mitchell felt was inadequate.[9]

Another face-off in the Hennings subcommittee between Wilkins and Sam Ervin was now more narrowly focused on provisions for federal protection of Fourteenth Amendment rights of blacks in the Douglas, Javits, and Celler bills. The federal government, Wilkins maintained, could "ill afford to be neutral" in this struggle between those who obey and those who defy the law. Attempting to trick Wilkins into supporting the South's "freedom of choice" philosophy for evading *Brown,* Ervin demanded to know whether the NAACP's goal was to deny children of different races, whose parents wished them to attend separate schools, the right to do so. He noted that federal judge John J. Parker, following the Supreme Court's reversal of his decision in a school desegregation case,* had interpreted *Brown* as deciding

---

* *Briggs* v. *Elliott,* covering Clarendon County, South Carolina, was one of the five cases included in the *Brown* umbrella opinion.

"that a state may not deny to any person on account of race, the right to attend any school that it maintains."

The southern interpretation of *Brown* was that if state-supported schools "are open to children of all races, no violation of the Constitution is involved, even though the children of different races voluntarily attend different schools, as they attend different churches." Parker lent judicial weight to the new resistance strategy by concluding that neither the Constitution nor the Supreme Court had taken "away from the people the freedom to choose the schools they attend"; they forbade discrimination but did not require integration.

Carefully avoiding Ervin's web, Wilkins explained that the NAACP did not deny parents the right to make any choice they wanted: "But we say this, that the State or the school district or the governmental unit involved has no right under the Supreme Court decision to say to a Negro parent that he cannot send his child to this school because he is a colored child and he therefore has to go to that school over there." Rather than hindering, Wilkins stressed, state power should facilitate and induce compliance with the Supreme Court decision. Wilkins held that if states followed Judge Parker's interpretation of *Brown,* and if they removed restrictions, there would be peaceful compliance, goodwill between the races, and equal opportunity in the schools. "Do not deny parents or children the right to attend the school of their choice," he said, "and when you say a free choice, mean Negro parents as well as the white parents." But the NAACP had found that most people quoting Judge Parker meant "white people should be free to send their children anywhere they please, but not the colored parents."

Outflanked but far from surrendering, Ervin changed tactics, accusing Wilkins of seeking preferential treatment for blacks through civil rights legislation—a charge that predated by a dozen years subsequent attacks on another type of civil rights program called affirmative action. The NAACP, Ervin said, "says it is unwilling to have members of your race seek the enforcement of their rights by the same laws by which the rights of other Americans are enforced." By seeking power for the attorney general to bring suits in behalf of blacks in order to "strike down state laws prescribing administrative remedies which were enacted by the states in the undoubted exercise of their constitutional power which apply to all other Americans," the NAACP was "asking for superior rights" over those granted to other Americans. "There has never been any other group in American history which has had the privilege of having the taxpayers' money used to bring civil suits to enforce their private constitutional rights."

Ervin, of course, was deliberately blind not only to America's history of slavery, but also to current racial oppression, and Wilkins strenuously told him so. He capped his rebuttal by declaring that he could not accept the charge of preferential treatment, "because if I accepted that we would have to eliminate the 14th, 15th, and 13th amendments of the Constitution. Any reasoning which arrives at preferential treatment assumes that the citizens, by reason of their race, color, or religion, or national origin have no protection in the Constitution and they do have such protection now."

Wilkins subscribed totally to the "color blind" constitutional principle enunciated by Associate Justice John Harlan in his vigorous *Plessy* v. *Ferguson* dissent. But, because segregation and discrimination were "color conscious," as the Thirty-ninth and Fortieth Congresses recognized, a central part of Wilkins's philosophy was that the Civil War amendments—organic features of the Constitution—were remedies essential for correcting the effects of slavery on society. To enforce those amendments, Congress was required to enact "appropriate"—that is, "color conscious"—legislation. As Senator Paul Douglas said in introducing his bill, it was intended "to put our moral house in order—for the benefit of citizens now denied their rights and for the benefit of the whole nation in its difficult position as a leader of the free world."

The NAACP, of course, did not have the last word on Fourteenth Amendment protections; opponents of enforcing the Constitution did. From his seat beside Wilkins during the hearings, Mitchell predicted that opposition to civil rights legislation would be as strong as in 1957, when Hennings, in order to help ensure that the motion to bypass Eastland's Judiciary Committee succeeded, left his sickbed to cast his vote in the Senate. Mitchell was confident that with similar support the civil rights bills would pass. But Senator Carroll disagreed with Mitchell that the bypass strategy would succeed a second time because he doubted that, unlike in 1957, the civil rights forces had the administration's strong support.

Not only was the 1960 presidential election an overriding concern for Republicans and Democrats alike, but it was suspected that the administration, in an attempt to win congressional support for a balanced budget, had decided not to antagonize potentially favorable votes by pressing for the main civil rights legislative features: getting Congress's express support for the Supreme Court's desegregation decisions and for the Fourteenth Amendment equal protection principle embodied in the 1957 bill's Part III.

A three-way division was more apparent than ever, with southerners maintaining their traditional opposition to any civil rights legislation, the more numerous northern moderates favoring the administration's proposals (minus Part III), and liberals supporting the NAACP's program. In effect, moderates and liberals both agreed that more civil rights legislation should be enacted, but the South would guarantee that it was weak by blocking strengthening amendments—in the House with support from Sam Rayburn, the seventy-eight-year-old patriarch serving his seventeenth year as speaker, and Minority Leader Charles Halleck, and, in the Senate, from Majority Leader Lyndon Johnson and Minority Leader Everett Dirksen. The irony of this prospect was that the 1958 elections had given the Democrats a commanding majority in the Senate, 64 to 34, with 12 to 15 of those new seats held by members who favored a more active role by the federal government in combatting racial discrimination. [10]

On July 15, the Hennings subcommittee, in an attempt to get the measure past Eastland, reported out a "skeleton" bill that merely provided for a two-year extension of the Civil Rights Commission and required preservation of voting and registration records for three years. Hennings, Javits, Keating, Douglas, and other civil rights supporters planned to fight for strengthening amendments on the Senate floor. But the Judiciary Committee still bottled up the bill despite strenuous efforts to gain approval and even after the Senate, by amending another bill, had extended the Civil Rights Commission for two years. As Congress raced to adjourn in 1959, both majority and minority Senate leaders pledged that they would make civil rights legislation the pending business in the second session of the Eighty-sixth Congress on February 15. That schedule would enable them to dispatch the issue well before the national political conventions.

House Judiciary Subcommittee No. 5, by contrast, reported out a bill (H.R. 3147)* endorsed by the NAACP's annual convention in July, but the full Judiciary Committee the following month reported out an amended version of the administration's proposals (H.R. 8601)—minus the 1957 bill's Part III, and two other important features. Those were Title VI, giving congressional sanction to the President's Committee on Government Contracts Compliance, and Title VIII, providing financial and technical help to communities willing to desegregate, and stating that "the Constitution as interpreted by the Supreme Court of the United States is the law of the land."

After Emanuel Celler on August 27 had filed a resolution to discharge the House Rules Committee from consideration of H.R. 8601, Mitchell, uncertain the resolution would succeed, urged Rayburn in a confidential meeting to permit a group of liberal Democrats to begin the process of overriding Congressman Howard "Judge" Smith, the Rules Committee chairman. Rayburn at first hesitated, doubting that committee members would challenge their chairman in that manner. Mitchell, however, con-

---

*H.R. 3147 incorporated the enforcement provisions of the Douglas, Javits, and Celler bills (Part III) and the seven-point administration program.

vinced him he could win support of Democrats, after which he could enlist
the committee's Republicans. Rayburn consented on condition that the
faster discharge petition effort failed. It was not necessary to implement the
override plans; after the discharge petition had gained 211 signatures (two
thirds of them of Democrats), just 8 shy of the number required to place it
on the House calendar, Smith began hearings in February and reported out
the bill the following month. Mitchell worked closely with Majority Whip
McCormack and Minority Leader Halleck to get it over the final hurdle,
but when the House passed it on March 24 it contained glaring weaknesses.[11]

Meanwhile, the focus in January had shifted to voting rights in the
South, thanks to documentation of the problem by the Civil Rights Commission. The two basic proposals that were the center of debate were, from
liberals led by Humphrey, for the appointment by the President of federal
registrars, and, from the attorney general, for court-appointed referees.

The bill introduced by Humphrey and several Democratic cosponsors
was a refinement of the commission's recommendations. It provided that
following the certification of complaints by the commission, the President
would appoint a federal registrar to ensure the registration of all qualified
voters. If that procedure was challenged by local or state officials, the Justice Department would seek a court order to end this objection.

The basic thrust of the administration's bill was to invest responsibility
for guaranteeing voting rights in the courts. This bill, introduced in the
House by William McCulloch, would authorize the Justice Department to
seek a court injunction under the 1957 act on behalf of anyone who was
denied the right to vote. If the suit was successful, the attorney general
would ask the courts to find that a pattern of discrimination existed. The
victim would then ask the court to have him or her registered. A court-
appointed referee would then determined whether the complainant was
qualified to vote. If there were no reasons for disqualification, and if the
referee's report was not challenged within ten days, the judge would then
certify the person.

A third position involving appointment of federal enrollment officers
was offered by Hennings as a compromise, but it quickly died because it
was identified as a Democratic bill.

NAACP Washington Bureau counsel Pohlhaus had begun pushing the
registrar idea in early 1959 after he, Rauh, and Vince Doyle, a lawyer in
the Congressional Research Department of the Library of Congress, had
spent some time developing it. The idea was first dreamt up in the early
1950s by Rauh and Doyle, who both felt that, as a last resort, it might
help if the federal government went into the South to help blacks to register and vote.

There were other versions of this idea, one of which was incorporated in a bill that Clayton Powell introduced, calling for a "Federal Voter Registration Commission." A similar proposal in the Senate called for a Congressional Elections Commission with discretionary authority to register voters for and conduct congressional elections. These plans would enable citizens to register merely by proving their qualifications.

Mitchell thought that the chief advantages of Rogers's proposal for federal referees was that it applied to federal as well as state elections and would protect the rights of voters already registered—provisions omitted in some voter registration bills. But, by calling for a judicial hearing, requiring additional evidence of discrimination, before the appointment of a federal registration official, the Rogers plan would not simplify the process but increase red tape.

The most favorable feature of the commission's recommendation, Mitchell felt, was that it provided a quick, easy method of registration. Anyone could vote by proving his qualifications under the protection of an official appointed by the President.

Mitchell's alternative proposal combined the best of all ideas in a program providing for a judicial hearing and appointment of federal registrars to process "quickly and simply" all qualified voters. Rogers's pursuit of the moderate plan opposed by the NAACP showed how crucial Brownell's role had been in the passage of the 1957 Civil Rights Act. Brownell offered ideas to strengthen the NAACP's proposals; Rogers sought to weaken them. Furthermore, following the abrupt departure of Sherman Adams, assistant to the President, in the wake of the scandal that had erupted following his acceptance of a vicuna coat as a gift, Mitchell felt that his replacement, General Wilton B. Persons, had become the chief influence in the White House and held him responsible for the administration's lukewarm attitude toward tough civil rights legislation.

In the House, Judiciary Committee chairman Celler switched his support from the registrar to the referee plan introduced as an amendment to the civil rights bill by New York Republican John V. Lindsay, a liberal freshman. That move opened the way for southerners promptly to jump on the moderation bandwagon and win further weakening changes in this proposal. Mitchell's only consolation was the "victory" scored by Michigan Democrat James G. O'Hara in gaining approval for a provision restoring some of the referee's authority by permitting blacks to vote "provisionally" in contested cases. [12]

Another highlight of the 1960 House action was the use of the "germaneness" rule by opponents to block strengthening amendments. Mitchell charged that there was "not a scintilla of merit" to the germaneness arguments. That attack, he said, represented a "carefully engineered sellout"—

or a ruse to avoid supporting a strong bill—and showed that its leaders were "completely incapable of acting in good faith" on civil rights. In vain, with the support of his allies, he argued that the rule did not require an amendment offered as a separate paragraph to be germane to the preceding paragraph. It was sufficient that it was germane to the subject matter of the bill as a whole. But with the bipartisan leadership agreeing to the arbitrary use of the germaneness rule to block any amendments, contrary arguments were futile. Democratic principle surrendered to political expediency as opponents prevailed in their claims that the 1957 bill's Part III was not germane to H.R. 8601 titles dealing with obstruction of court orders or schools in impacted areas, and that a voting registrar provision was not relevant to the title requiring preservation of voting records. They similarly killed a Celler amendment that would have established a permanent Commission on Equal Job Opportunity Under Government Contracts and prohibited adoption of the registrar provision even though, in sending H.R. 8601 to the House floor, the House Rules Committee had specifically provided for addition of a registrar *or* referee amendment to the bill. In subsequently adopting its own rules for consideration, the House barred the stronger voter referee principle.[13]

Wilkins charged that a bipartisan coalition was "tearing the pending bill to pieces." He said that "some members made speeches for the printed record and then voted in opposition to their speeches because the vote was not on roll call." However, the main problem for proponents of civil rights legislation, it became clear during the debate, was not so much the opposition of old Republican–southern Democratic coalition but that southerners were taking advantage of the various splits among them; and the opponents' moves to weaken further the referee proposal coincided with the GOP desire to embarrass the Democrats in an important election year.

Senator Carroll's warning to Mitchell during the Hennings subcommittee hearings that the administration had withdrawn support for the 1957 bill's Part III was confirmed when Rogers used developments in Virginia early in 1960 to buttress his earlier claim that the provision was not needed because conditions in the South had improved. The Virginia Governor's Commission in a March 31 report urged the legislature to authorize local communities to sell public school property in order to avoid compliance with desegregation decisions. Mitchell challenged Rogers's assertion that that was an improvement over Virginia's previous position by explaining that the Virginia commission had in mind only a moderation, not an abandonment, of massive resistance to the *Brown* v. *Board of Education* decision.

So Rogers's contention was the reverse of reality—resistance in the South had hardened, as was shown by the halting of school desegregation.

Southern School News, an independent publication of regional newspaper editors, reported that only 10 new school districts in the South had desegregated in the current school year—the fewest since 1954. Of 2,880 southern biracial school districts, only 762 had begun desegregation, and most were in border states. Five states were still totally segregated, and four had only token desegregation. Four had segregated institutions of higher education. Furthermore, Jim Crow remained the South's hallmark, as the spreading civil rights tactic of nonviolent protest was showing.[14]

In the Senate, Johnson kept his word that he would begin action on February 15 by calling up a minor, unrelated House-passed bill and inviting senators to add civil rights amendments to it. But two weeks later, opposed to both the procedure and substance of the legislation, which was now incorporated in an administration bill (S. 3001) introduced by Dirksen, southerners began a thirty-seven-day, round-the-clock filibuster. At 5:00 A.M. on the second day of the talkathon, Johnson called Mitchell down from the gallery, where he was manning the "graveyard shift," in order to explain his strategy. Betraying a southern nervousness about being seen conversing with the lobbyist, Johnson quickly ushered Mitchell into his office lest the wife of Senator Olin Johnston of South Carolina, who was descending the gallery steps behind Mitchell, see them together. Johnson told Mitchell that if he was challenged on the Senate floor about their meeting, he would explain that as majority leader he had to confer with everyone. As Mitchell confided to Wilkins, at that hour he did not care about that "technicality," so they immediately began their discussions, first on Johnson's amendments strategy, which the lobbyist too found novel.

Despite Johnson's opposition to the bill's Part III provision providing that the U.S. government would protect citizens whose rights were denied by state and local officials, Mitchell insisted that it could win. Johnson said that civil rights forces would need 67 votes for cloture and at least 51 to pass the Part III amendment. Mitchell reminded him that the current cloture rule (provisions under Rule XXII for ending a filibuster), adopted in 1959, was the majority leader's idea—one that he still maintained was a step forward. He felt that Johnson did not have as clear a picture as he because the senator had not spoken with Republicans to get their views of cloture prospects, which were negative.

They next discussed extensively the need for closer coordination on civil rights proposals between Johnson and Senate liberals. Again, based on his personal contacts, Mitchell felt he had a better grasp of sentiments among these lawmakers. Johnson maintained he was open to requests for meetings, but Mitchell had to warn him that "some senators might think he was trying to get them to come to him with hat in hand." Upon Johnson's request, Mitchell suggested that "a good beginning" for such a meeting would include Hubert Humphrey, Paul Douglas, Michigan Democrat Philip A. Hart, Joseph S. Clark, Democrat of Pennsylvania, and Wayne Morse. But Johnson was not eager to meet with either Morse, whom he termed "very individualistic," or Douglas, who had repeatedly challenged his authority.[15]

Events quickly overtook their discussion, but at least the two understood each other. Determined to get a bill, Johnson held round-the-clock sessions in the Senate as a filibuster developed in an attempt to wear out the opposition. Cots were set up in offices, cloak rooms, and even in the Senate baths. Russell's well-organized team of eighteen Democrats, divided into three teams of six for about six hours of floor duty at a time, won the contest.

Observing Mitchell conducting his faithful, lonely vigil, NBC correspondent Robert G. Abernethy commented, "It is ironic but true that, aside from the Senate clerks, the one man who has heard more of the southern filibuster than any other is a Negro—often the only person in all the Senate gallery." Mitchell felt it was important to show friends of civil rights that if they were willing to lose sleep to answer quorum calls at all hours, the NAACP had to demonstrate its moral support, but he found the boring, almost inaudible speeches less than edifying. He protested that the "smell of perfumed words" from the Senate floor was "laced with the odor of garbage." Florida Democrat George Smathers "was squirting the perfume atomizer" while South Carolina's Olin Johnston "was laboriously hauling the refuse." As Mitchell reported in the *Baltimore Afro-American:*

> Slim, well-dressed and soft-voiced Senator Smathers was telling the nearly empty chamber about how much progress colored people were making in voting. Here and there one caught the scent of honey suckle and lavender as he sweetly complimented his opponents, gently chided a questioner, or related the glories of Florida race relations.
>
> Near the end of his speech, Smathers was overcome by his own flow of language. He turned to the rows of empty seats, where his colleagues should have been listening with profound attention.
>
> He walked from his own desk to drive home a point to a chair standing in respectful virginal emptiness. Soon he was addressing a whole row of shiny wooden desks.
>
> Huddled in a few spots on the Senate floor were people like Senator John McClellan, D-Ark., and a captive audience of clerks.

In a final flight of exuberance Smathers eloquently described his feeling of joy when he came through Washington's worst snow storm of the winter.

Perhaps it was because he was in a world of whiteness at the time. . . .

This was the United States Senate, the blue ribbon branch of the national legislature on round the clock sessions because an arrogant band of small-minded men was determined to talk a civil rights bill to death.[16]

Over Johnson's objections, the pro-civil-rights forces pushed for a cloture vote. The attempt on March 10 failed 42 to 53—21 votes short of the required 63. Douglas, revealing the underlying bitterness, then suggested that had there been a real threat that liberals might gain the required votes, Johnson would have supported the South to ensure defeat. Mitchell was partly consoled by Douglas's other observation that the 42 who voted for cloture represented 60 percent of the U.S. population and 70 percent of voters in a presidential election. He therefore concluded that, based on what appeared to be firm evidence of popular sentiment, the majority of Americans probably did not share the reluctance of some senators to protect the constitutional rights of blacks. However, the "unwillingness to see the colored man as a full equal" was the "real cause of frustration" in the Senate over the lack of support for civil rights. His conclusion was confirmed that same day when the Senate approved a motion to table another amendment based on the 1957 bill's Part III.

On March 24, right after the House had voted for H.R. 8601, the Senate approved a Johnson motion to refer it to the Senate Judiciary Committee with instructions to report it out March 29 (See Appendix 1 for Pohlhaus's explanation of the parliamentary procedure). Assured that there was nothing to fear in H.R. 8601, which the Judiciary Committee had further weakened with amendments, Richard Russell induced his regional colleagues, after the bill was watered down once more on the Senate floor, to end their talkathon on April 8. Cloture was not invoked. The Senate promptly passed the bill 71 to 18. Thus, unlike previous Congresses, where the fate of civil rights legislation had been determined by votes on procedural questions, moderates and liberals were now both agreed that more civil rights legislation should be enacted, while the South guaranteed that such legislation would be weak by blocking, with the approval of Johnson and Dirksen, all strengthening amendments.[17]

On May 6, as Attorney General Rogers and his deputy Lawrence E. Walsh looked on, President Eisenhower signed the Civil Rights Act of 1960. It was the second such law he had signed, so he was correct in hailing it as a "historic step forward." But the moment was overshadowed by the international crisis caused that March by the Sharpville massacre, in which South African police killed seventy-two demonstrators and wounded scores more who had been protesting the hated pass laws; and by the Soviets' downing of the American U-2 spy plane the previous day, an incident that gave Premier Nikita Khrushchev ammunition to heighten cold-war tensions. In the course of the U-2 crisis, Americans lost their innocence of the cynical intrigues of international relations. First, their President had to acknowledge to the world that he had lied when he claimed that the U-2 was a weather aircraft that had strayed over Soviet territory; second, their government was forced to admit that it, just like the Russians, was engaged in the dirty business of spying. Even though the new law was nothing to crow about, it was evidence to the world that the United States was attempting to assure the type of freedoms at home that it was accusing the Communists of denying their people. But the attempt fell far short of the promise of full constitutional freedom.

The 1960 Civil Rights Act strengthened the 1957 voting rights legislation by providing criminal penalties for impeding the exercise of rights under a court order as had happened in Little Rock; criminal penalties for burning or bombing of homes, churches, schools, or other buildings; the preservation of registration and voting records in federal elections for inspection; education of children of military personnel in states that had closed schools in order to obstruct implementation of the 1954 school desegregation decision; and the attorney general's voter referee program.

Confronted once more with the challenge of whether a heterogeneous and free people could bridge the gap between the ideal of democracy and its actual practice, Congress again had muffed the opportunity to do so. South Carolina's Strom Thurmond boasted to his constituents that the Senate action indicated "a pattern of defeat for the NAACP and its spokesmen"; while Roy Wilkins, in describing the referee plan, said, "The Negro has to pass more check points and more officials than he would if he were trying to get the United States gold reserves in Fort Knox. It's a fraud."

Mitchell repeated his belief that the difficulty in achieving strong civil rights legislation in the Senate was due to the unwillingness of many lawmakers to view the black "as a full equal." The majority of Americans, he felt, probably did not share such reluctance, but he was deeply troubled by the views of senators like New Hampshire Republican Norris Cotton, who stated, "I shall vote against any provisions of the proposed law which at this time would strengthen or make more rigid or more harsh the rules affecting schools, education, and the social privileges of any group in the

country. I believe such a provision would do more harm than good."
Mitchell agreed with a newspaper reporter who said that the measure
should be known as the "1960 Russell Civil Rights Law," because Russell
"was the major force persuading" his southern colleagues to end their resistance without the necessity of invoking cloture. "This alone," Mitchell
concluded, "shows that knowledgeable southerners of the House and Senate" believed they had little to fear from the bill.[18]

Seeking political capital, a group of Republicans led by Dirksen early
in August offered a bill to create a permanent President's Commission on
Equal Job Opportunity and provide federal monetary assistance to areas
desegregating their schools—two provisions omitted in the 1960 act. That
maneuver drew a sharp protest from Wilkins "against the use, by Republicans or Democrats, of the civil rights issue as a purely political weapon."
After the Democrats quickly tabled it, Mitchell emphasized that their
action revealed a fundamental weakness of the Democratic party—that
it had a liberal base, appealing to such groups as labor and minorities in
cities like New York, Chicago, and Philadelphia, but was controlled by
southerners. He felt that unless the Democrats revised the seniority system,
which gave Dixie control of key committees, the party would "be unable to
deliver on programs that they have suggested they would like to espouse."
Because they missed an opportunity to unite and pass a meaningful civil
rights bill, they could be hurt at the polls in November. But he also felt
the Republicans had a lot of weaknesses that were similarly hurting them.

Assessing Eisenhower's role in the civil rights struggle, Mitchell reaffirmed his conclusion that he "was more valuable than he knew or intended." Mitchell's opinion never changed following a meeting he and
other NAACP leaders had had with the President in 1953, soon after he
took office. Then, as he had concluded during the presidential campaign,
Mitchell believed that Eisenhower was sympathetic to the problems of
blacks, but that he was not inclined to take any action to aid them that
would make it appear he was forcing whites to change their previous racial
attitudes. Mitchell thought that "he really was concerned about stirring up
a situation that would cause" racial confrontations by acting to give blacks
their full citizenship rights. Eisenhower knew that blacks were entitled to
those rights, Mitchell felt, "but only at a pace which would not cause
whites to resort to physical violence to keep them from getting the things
that they were entitled to have." Given that attitude, Mitchell thought,
Eisenhower "was misjudging the possibilities," as subsequent events
proved. When the federal government demonstrated its determination to
enforce the law in protecting the rights of blacks, as had happened in Little
Rock, racist opponents always backed down in a confrontation. Conse-

quently, he believed that Eisenhower could have acted more forthrightly without any political damage to himself or his party.

It was no secret that Eisenhower was uncomfortable with blacks, an attitude that reflected the sparsely populated middle-America ranges around Abilene, Kansas, his hometown. Blacks were not feared or despised; they were objects of curiosity. Mitchell regarded as evidence of that racial attitude Eisenhower's formal White House stag dinners to which he invited blacks. "I'm sure, according to his lights, that represented a great step forward—to have blacks and whites eating together at the White House— but it was more or less stilted." Mitchell guessed that Eisenhower feared he might have problems if white women attended social gatherings with black men.

In 1960, with Eisenhower a lame-duck President with less interest than previously in civil rights, the problem was that the individual interests of lawmakers outweighed the common goals of the party. Without executive leadership, lawmakers had to face even more the likelihood of challenge from anti-civil-rights opponents, so survival, not moral issues, was their overriding concern. Paradoxically, there was more civil rights progress during Eisenhower's eight-year watch than in the preceding eighty-plus years. Jim Crow, nevertheless, was still entrenched in society, not just in the South—a reality that led the NAACP to express "deep concern and regret" that an institution like the Methodist Church had recommended continuation of its racially segregated central jurisdiction and urged predominantly black Methodist denominations to organize social action departments.

Mitchell was only too aware that race remained the most deterministic force in the American psyche. It had been ingrained there since the first slaves landed at Jamestown in 1619 and was even more powerful now than it had been then. Rather than being discouraged, he was optimistic that the NAACP would achieve its goal because more voices like Senator Kuchel's were sounding the trumpet for action in Congress: "Mr. President, the treatment of these fellow citizens serves to remind us how difficult it has been, how difficult it is to achieve the ideals to which we officially and traditionally aspire. We must believe that we must accord to all Americans of whatever racial origins the rights to which they are entitled simply as citizens of the Republic."

Other friendships like that of Congressman Brooks Hays, a moderate Arkansas Democrat who was defeated in a racist campaign in 1958, were also reassuring because they confirmed Mitchell's belief that there were lawmakers who would stand by just principles despite the political risk. Their relationship began soon after Mitchell became a lobbyist and visited Hays in his office. At the conclusion of the meeting, as Mitchell was leaving, he saw a tape recorder behind the lawmaker's chair. Embarrassed, Hays explained that the recorder had not been turned on, and Mitchell believed him and told him so. On another occasion, during the Little Rock crisis, Mitchell attacked Hays so strongly for proposing a solution the lobbyist thought unacceptable that Ralph Bunche chided him for being too harsh. Just as Mitchell began feeling he had been unfair, Hays assured him that his complaint was well-taken. In his autobiography, *A Southern Moderate Speaks,* Hays expressed agreement with Mitchell's Little Rock proposal. As Governor George Wallace of Alabama began displaying interest in running for the presidency, Mitchell worked with Hays and Ralph McGill of the *Atlanta Constitution* in developing a "truth squad" on the governor's record in office.

Mitchell was further encouraged by the Supreme Court decision on February 29, 1960, in *United States* v. *Raines* upholding the constitutionality of the 1957 Civil Rights Act. That case was based on a Justice Department challenge to the Terrell County, Georgia, practice of giving blacks more difficult voter registration qualification tests than whites. The 1957 act had also been used to restore blacks to Louisiana voter rolls in *United States* v. *Thomas* and to bar other forms of discrimination in Tennessee in *United States* v. *Fayette County Democratic Committee.* Mitchell pointed to those successes to demonstrate the need for more court challenges to enforce the 1957 act, as well as for more legislation. Experience, he said emphatically, also showed that the Justice Department "must be given additional authority to file civil suits to protect other constitutional rights that are now being denied colored citizens, including the right to attend desegregated public schools."[19]

In 1952, when the Republicans first nominated Eisenhower, he was the symbol of the new postwar world, the man who had presided over the European war victory and was pressing for new policies against Taft Republicans and Truman Democrats. Now, eight years later, the overriding issue of the presidential campaign was which candidate and party could best deal with the tumult of change at home and abroad. The preamble of the Republican platform succinctly expressed the concerns of both parties: The lives of men and nations around the world were undergoing such transformations as history had rarely recorded before. The birth of new nations, the impact of new machines, the threat of new weapons, the stirring of new ideas, the ascent into a new dimension of the universe—"everywhere the accent falls on the new." Consequently, both parties chose young men as their standard-bearers and defied southern Democrats and northern Republican conservatives by the liberal tone of their platforms. Civil rights was a pivotal issue in that new balance.

In 1960, the NAACP and the Leadership Conference on Civil Rights led in winning adoption of the strongest civil rights planks since 1948 by both parties. Mitchell thus used the opportunity to focus on the records of presidential contenders, which he publicized widely, and to obtain their pledges, based on questionnaires he submitted to them, for stronger legislation. He concluded that there was very little difference on civil rights between John Kennedy, the Democratic contender, and Richard Nixon, his Republican opponent. Both wanted advances. But he felt there was "a wide gulf between the vice presidential candidates," who were Lyndon Johnson and Henry Cabot Lodge.

His ideal choice for President would have been Hubert Humphrey. Next would have been Missouri's Stuart Symington, who also had a solid civil rights record. Mitchell felt that, as President, Symington would have done much to eliminate segregation. Mitchell's relationship with Symington began during the FEPC period, when the senator, as head of a Midwest company, adopted a plan to end segregation among his employees. Subsequently, Mitchell also found Symington, as secretary of the air force, fully committed to the cause of racial justice. But Kennedy was chosen as the Democratic party standard-bearer.

Mitchell first met Kennedy one day in the late 1940s when Powell, standing beside a very slight young man, said, "Clarence, I want you to meet Congressman Kennedy from Massachusetts." Then, as Mitchell walked away with Powell, the New Yorker suggested, "You ought to keep an eye on Jack because he's going to be a very important person one of these days."

Mitchell's next recollection of Kennedy was during the 1952 campaign when he was running for the Senate against Henry Cabot Lodge, who had been very cooperative on civil rights. Mitchell always tried to balance his civil rights interests between both major parties. Because he did not want to weaken Republican support in Congress, he hoped that Kennedy would lose—which did not occur.

Despite Kennedy's liberal aura, Mitchell had questions about the extent of his commitment to civil rights. He was concerned that although Kennedy reportedly was the first senator in New England to have a black staffer in his Massachusetts office, he had none in Washington when Mitchell first visited him. Mitchell also recalled a meeting he had had with Kennedy during the fight for the 1957 Civil Rights Act, when he escorted a Boston civil rights delegation to Kennedy's office. He had found the senator characteristically charming. After receiving the senator's commitment to vote against the amendment to delete Part III, Mitchell asked, "Well, what about the jury trial amendment? How do you stand on that?" Slapping Mitchell on the back and chuckling, Kennedy replied, "Oh, you don't have to worry about me on that. I'm all right." Following this evasive response, Kennedy helped weaken the 1957 act by supporting inclusion of the amendment.

In his evaluation, Mitchell reported that Kennedy had opposed the filibuster the three times he had an opportunity to do so. His running mate Lyndon Johnson, in addition to having been a leading architect in the struggle for the jury trial amendment, had a "one hundred percent record of tolerance" for filibusters. Kennedy voted with Johnson on the jury trial amendment and twice with the majority leader to send the civil rights bill to Eastland's Judiciary Committee. Kennedy, though, supported Part III, while Johnson opposed it.

Richard Nixon, the Republican presidential candidate, had upheld the Senate's right to bypass Eastland's Judiciary Committee, thus ensuring that the 1957 act was passed. But Nixon and his running mate Henry Cabot Lodge earlier had voted in the Senate for the constitutional amendment to give greater power to the South by changing the electoral college system. Kennedy was absent the first time the House voted on the issue, but in the Senate he opposed it strongly. Kennedy had expressed support for the Powell Amendment, although he was twice absent when the Senate voted on the issue. Nixon supported the amendment. Kennedy initially had opposed a strong Democratic civil rights plank. But, at the convention in Los Angeles, succumbing to the drumbeat from Wilkins, Mitchell, King, Randolph, and Powell, evidently with his brother's approval, Robert Kennedy asked Rauh to frame it. So the final plank was much stronger than the weak version that had come out of the committee. Nixon, pressed by Governor Nelson Rockefeller of New York, whom he regarded as an archliberal, had supervised and approved the GOP plank. Added incentive was provided by demonstrations the NAACP and other civil rights leaders organized in Chicago that drew twice as many as the twenty-five thousand people that had assembled in Los Angeles. A key section of the GOP civil rights plank declared:

Equality under law promises more than the equal right to vote and transcends mere relief from discrimination by government. It becomes a reality only when all persons have equal opportunity, without distinction of race, religion, color or national origin, to acquire the essentials of life—housing, education and employment. The Republican Party—the party of Abraham Lincoln—from its very beginning has striven to make this promise a reality. It is today, as it was then, unequivocally dedicated to making the greatest amount of progress toward that objective.

432   DENTON L. WATSON

Johnson, a civil rights opponent until he supported the weakened 1957 act, had consistently voted against the Powell Amendment, while Lodge had sponsored an amendment to a school construction bill and had voted for Powell's racial safeguard three times and twice against.

Records on fair employment practice legislation were similarly varied, with Kennedy supporting an FEPC with enforcement powers in the House in 1949, and Nixon voting for an FEPC without such powers. Lodge had twice voted to invoke cloture against anti-FEPC filibusters, while Johnson had voted for them to continue. As chairman of the President's Committee on Government Contracts, Nixon had also helped the Eisenhower administration achieve significant breakthroughs against discrimination in white-collar and skilled industrial positions. Overall, except for Johnson's, the civil rights records of the candidates were favorable—although Nixon had helped Mitchell much more than Kennedy had.

Despite their generally adversarial relationship, Mitchell continued to have cordial sessions with Johnson. During one of those, while relaxing in his majority leader's office, Johnson invited Mitchell to join him in a drink. As both men enjoyed pleasantries, Johnson said, "Now, you see we've made progress in this country. Who would think that you as a representative of the NAACP would be in here having a drink with the majority leader, who comes from the State of Texas?" Mitchell responded, "If my mother-in-law were to come in here—you know, she is a teetotaller and doesn't want anyone to drink—both of us would be in much more trouble than we'd be if the Ku Klux Klan saw us together."

A politician playing a delicate balancing act with his vocal southern constituents, Johnson's basic strategy was to allow passage of bills he felt would create the least internal trouble for his party. Mitchell believed that Johnson was convinced that racial discrimination, segregation, and all other badges of servitude among blacks should be eliminated. "I felt that way about him even when I didn't agree with some of his legislative positions," he recalled. According to Mitchell, very often Johnson said to him, "Clarence, you can get anything that you have the votes to get. How many votes have you got?"

Mitchell's yardstick in judging lawmakers was whether they voted for civil rights measures. The most important of Johnson's actions, which confirmed for Mitchell that he was not a diehard segregationist, were his opposing legislation to punish the Supreme Court, his refusal to sign the Southern Manifesto, and his voting for the 1957 Civil Rights Act; although the other candidates had done those things also. In 1958, Mitchell realized that Johnson, after "reading the handwriting on the wall," had shrewdly shifted his position from "no civil rights legislation" to sponsoring the "bargain counter" conciliation bill to mediate civil rights conflicts.

Mitchell admired the senator's skill, but he was not deceived by his program. So, because he was a southerner and had a net anti-civil-rights record, Mitchell felt that the Democrats had given the GOP a Christmas
present by placing him on the ticket.

He did not, however, regard this development as hopeless, because
Presidents were amenable to political pressure. Also, he noted, neither the
President, his party, nor the state was all-powerful and could pass civil
rights legislation without bipartisan support. Therefore, those who intended to strengthen the struggle's moral position by supporting civil
rights must place this issue ahead of party. Expanding on this philosophy,
Mitchell declared:

> It is not enough to say that the hearts and minds of men will
> change and on this we shall rely for progress. We cannot, we need
> not, and we shall not wait for the bigots and the apostles of racial
> segregation to get religion and voluntarily hit the saw dust trail.
> We have a duty to protect the citizens who are being denied their
> rights. If their state and local officials insist on trying to turn back
> the clock, as they are now doing, and no doubt will continue to do
> until stopped, it is mandatory that the Federal Government act.
> We do not need a Democratic Congress nor do we need a Re-
> publican Congress. What we need is a Congress that will pass civil
> rights legislation.

Despite the Democrats' lopsided control of Congress, the new lineup
offered Mitchell anything but hope. He regarded Senator Hennings's death
with double sadness, first, because he had lost a warm personal friend, and,
second, because next in line to succeed him as chairman of the Senate
Subcommittee on Constitutional Rights were Olin Johnston, John Mc-
Clellan, and Sam Ervin. As Mitchell suggested to an NAACP audience,
"You guess which one of them will be the best man to have in charge of
implementing the civil rights pledges made in party platforms." Ervin succeeded Hennings, Eastland was continued as chairman of the Senate Judiciary Committee, and Alabama's Lister Hill became chairman of the Labor
and Public Welfare Committee—developments Mitchell felt would make it
necessary "to use special tactics to pry bills from their legislative vaults."
He was happy that, in the House, Adam Clayton Powell survived attacks
by southerners and others who did not want him in that powerful position
with the NAACP's strong support to become chairman of the Education
and Labor Committee.

With Kennedy's capture of the White House, Mitchell, suspecting that
civil rights was still a secondary priority to the new President, began

searching more closely for indications of the direction he would take in this area. Mitchell thought the debates between the Republicans and Democrats during the campaign had helped raise national concern for civil rights. For example, he felt that Nixon might have fulfilled his promise to include a black in his Cabinet even though many within his camp were strongly opposed. Kennedy's promises, such as to end housing discrimination with the stroke of a pen, were also deliverable, and would have to be acted on if the Democrats intended to hold the black vote. But Mitchell did not think the high price he suspected Kennedy would have to pay for the South's support, though good for the Democratic party, would necessarily be good for civil rights. The balance of the equation, of course, depended on Kennedy's own convictions. Kennedy, in Mitchell's view, demonstrated no singular desire to do more for blacks than other great Democratic leaders would do through executive action or by favoring progress through the courts. Dating from his earliest encounters with Johnson, who had always claimed that the struggle for civil rights legislation jeopardized social welfare measures, Mitchell had known that that was the standard Democratic position. He feared that under Kennedy there would be no action on civil rights, and neither would there be any on important social welfare legislation, because he did not believe the young President had the ability to get it through Congress. Mitchell's assessments jibed with the general perceptions among blacks of the candidates. However, developing events were also crystallizing public opinion in support of civil rights much more sharply than Mitchell could have done and would help boost the NAACP's struggle for passage of civil rights laws.[20]

There had been four earlier phases of the relationship of blacks to the political parties and government. The first was characterized by Republican party complacency, from the Civil War to the Hoover administration. During this period, blacks primarily supported Republicans as a result of gratitude for Abraham Lincoln's ending of slavery. Blacks dramatized the close of this phase by showing that they were a significant political force in 1930, when the NAACP defeated President Herbert Hoover's nomination of Judge John J. Parker to the Supreme Court.

The second phase, one of Democratic opportunism, developed in the middle 1920s. It was characterized by pockets of black Democrats who were active in the New York Tammany and Kansas City Pendergast machines, and in the unsuccessful 1928 presidential campaign of Alfred E. Smith, governor of New York. In places like Kansas City, black voter registration swung from being 78 percent Republican to 68 percent Democratic. Those pockets were created by the opportunities provided under the free-enterprise system and local options made available by the white political structure by encouraging the participation of blacks. There were not enough black Democrats to elect Smith—a product of New York City sidewalks and the first Catholic ever to receive the presidential nomination of a major party—but they had been positioned to benefit from his victory had it occurred.

The collapse of the economy in 1929 provided unprecedented economic and political options, as blacks saw an opportunity to swing en masse to the Democratic party under the banner of Franklin Roosevelt's New Deal. Those opportunities created during the 1930s began the third phase, one of Democratic realism, which extended through the Truman administration. Even though they found opportunities in the alphabet agencies—like the National Recovery Administration (NRA), Works Progress Administration (WPA), National Youth Administration (NYA), and Civilian Conservation Corps (CCC)—blacks had to accept Jim Crow customs.

The fourth phase, one of Republican resurgence, was marked by the swing of black votes to Eisenhower in 1956, encouraged by his strong executive initiatives in advancing civil rights.

Thanks to the support of labor, religious, and liberal allies in the Leadership Conference on Civil Rights—thus signaling the fifth phase, bipartisan moral awakening—the party conventions in 1960 not only endorsed the 1954 school desegregation decision, but also condemned all forms of segregation and discrimination, and pledged concrete action to end such injustices in all areas of community and national life. Among the factors contributing to this advance were the spreading independence movements in Africa, an increasing awareness of the adverse impact that the country's race relations were having on foreign affairs, the civil rights protests in the South, and the strategic distribution of the black vote caused by migration to the North. Also helping were rallies that the NAACP sponsored on the eve of the conventions and that were attended by about six thousand people.

The benefits of coalition support, when mobilized behind a comprehensive and detailed set of proposals, were further shown when, for the first time, Leadership Conference representatives were in the majority at all stages of the 1960 Democratic platform-drafting process. There was thus no chance that a minority report could have succeeded on a roll call vote. At the Republican convention, it was discovered that planners had grossly underestimated the turnout of civil rights forces. That type of mobilization won approval for a plank that was in line with the more liberal proposals from Richard Nixon and Nelson Rockefeller, governor of New York. The alternative Republican plank was designed to build an ostensible "two-party" system in the South—one that was similar to the position of the southern Democrats. Both the Republican and Democratic platforms, recognizing the need for strong legislative and executive action in voting, housing, employment, and education, thus considerably strengthened Mitchell's hand as he worked on Capitol Hill to benefit from the national civil rights crisis.[21]

Notably contributing to this new awareness was Juanita Jackson Mitchell. "Charles Houston said you can sue Jim Crow right out of Maryland," she recalled, "so we just began to sue and sue and to file lawsuits." Her mission also undergirded her mother's political and moral activism—Lillie Carroll Jackson's labors had resulted in a mass movement with the buy-where-you-can-work demonstrations of the 1930s in Baltimore expanding dramatically into all areas of social intercourse. With unflagging support from Carl Murphy and his *Baltimore Afro-American,* she had won the black clergy's support. Not all of them helped, because "some of them refused to follow a woman's leadership," Juanita explained. But she was able to get a few of them involved because "she was totally committed to the idea that freedom was ours; we had to reach out and get it." As she made her rounds among the churches on Sunday mornings for funds, each minister would interrupt the services to announce, "Here's Mrs. Jackson," and take up a special collection for the NAACP. And off she would go to another church.

The results of this combination of Lillie Jackson's activism in the "political courts"—city, county, and state governments—with Juanita's battles in the courts of law were manifested in the profound changes occurring in Maryland's social structure. It was activities like these in Baltimore, Harlem, and Chicago that inspired the third phase of black political awakening. Through Juanita, Lillie Jackson, and Murphy, Mitchell was very much a part of this movement—a movement that made Maryland the first state south of the Mason-Dixon Line to comply with the Supreme Court's 1954 school desegregation order. True to form, however, the state battled the NAACP on several fronts in an attempt to preserve segregation until it saw no alternative but to surrender. The NAACP followed the same strategy that Houston and Marshall had used in the school desegregation cases when it challenged segregation in the courts. The NAACP in Maryland had first moved for the equalization of educational and recreational facilities under the "separate but equal" doctrine, thus making the cost of maintaining Jim Crow prohibitive. After the *Brown* decision was handed down, the Maryland NAACP fought to end segregation under the equal protection clause of the Fourteenth Amendment.

Although segregation would not be ended in Maryland until Congress passed the 1964 Civil Rights Act, the NAACP's repeated legal victories and the relentless protests by Juanita and her mother would make the Mitchell name a legend in Maryland. Juanita received considerable help from the NAACP national office through Thurgood Marshall and his assistants Robert L. Carter and, especially, Jack Greenberg. Because of the repeated court victories, Juanita recalled, "the people began to think that the NAACP was God Almighty." Her mother regarded the NAACP as "God's workshop" because "He doesn't want us to suffer discrimination. He's a spirit, and He's got to work through those of us who will give of ourselves and let Him work through us." Faithful to this call, their children, Clarence III and Michael, joined the army of student revolutionaries in launching the second phase of the modern civil rights movement with protest demonstrations in the South that directly challenged segregation.[22]

PART TWO

Fulfilling
a Dream

CHAPTER FIFTEEN

Challenge of the New Frontier

D espite its dominant role as leader, a role characterized by virulent hatred and attacks from diehard segregationists that had forced it to suspend operations in Alabama, Texas, Tennessee, and Virginia and to be especially wary of similar threats in Florida, North Carolina, and Georgia, the NAACP was regarded by impatient young black and white activists as "conservative," too "legalistic," and too slow to act. That perception, ironically, was fostered in large part by the NAACP's successful campaign to overturn the "separate but equal" doctrine and the association's subsequent reliance on the courts to build on the unprecedented opportunities that had been provided by the *Brown* decision to use the Fourteenth Amendment to achieve full citizenship. Yet, as Robert Weaver made clear in his keynote address as chairman of the NAACP's Fifty-first Annual Convention in 1960 in New York City, it was due in large part to this success with school desegregation cases that southerners had targeted NAACP leaders for economic reprisals, violence, social ostracism, and hostile state action. An NAACP leader in the South was a marked person, Weaver reminded his audience, as he contrasted the courage that had been required of the older generation of freedom fighters with the daring of the four North Carolina Agricultural and Technical College students who, on February 1, demanded service at a segregated Woolworth lunch counter in Greensboro. Weaver regarded the tactics of confrontation that black American students were using to challenge the South's Jim Crow system as similar to those which black South African youths had begun to use in Sharpeville to challenge the apartheid system that the white minority

441

rulers had created to oppress them. Weaver's message was reinforced for the convention by the showing of the film *Come Back, Africa,* a documentary on apartheid. Another unmentioned parallel between Sharpeville and Greensboro was that the struggle against the pass laws had been organized by Robert Mangaliso Sobukwe through the newly created Pan-African Congress because he was impatient with the slower African National Congress, founded in 1912. His American counterpart was Ezell Blair, Jr., chairman of the student Committee for Justice in Greensboro and leader of what were called the "sit-downs."

Like many young Americans, Sobukwe was not unmindful of the ANC's past contributions. He was at once a Gandhian and a Methodist who believed in passive resistance, but he was impatient for change. The NAACP's dilemma was similar to the ANC's. The NAACP's battles in the Congress for adoption of the Powell Amendment, for FEPC and other civil rights legislation, and for the right to vote and basic human dignity in the South had shown that its activities were much broader than its detractors were willing to admit. In fact, the Greensboro sit-in demonstrations were spawned by the NAACP. Blair and Joseph McNeil, another sit-in leader, were former officers of the Greensboro NAACP youth council. They had conducted their sit-in in consultation with Dr. George Simpkins, president of the Greensboro NAACP branch, and Ralph Jones, president of the branch's executive committee. The NAACP's activism and successes helped to intensify impatience among blacks for full equality.

It was, after all, the NAACP that had set the ten-year goal of "Free by '63" in anticipation of winning by that year the full rights of citizenship for America's oppressed minorities. The student demonstrators were impatient because the NAACP had chosen to wage its battle through established, mostly constitutional, channels—ones that took into consideration concerns of survival and the protection of the lives and properties of older NAACP leaders. In attempting to stamp out the NAACP in the South, the segregationists sowed the wind and reaped the whirlwind. The students had only their lives to lose. The problem was that fulfillment fell far short of their expectations.

Little Rock was a watershed in the history of black frustrations. Aroused by the excitement of Martin Luther King's MIA movement and the national attention it had drawn, young blacks more than ever regarded progress as too slow and blamed the NAACP in painful terms. Louis Lomax, a forty-one-year-old black journalist, complained, "The Negro masses are angry and restless, tired of prolonged legal battles that end in paper decrees. The organizations that understand this unrest and rise to lead it will survive; those that do not will perish."

No one believed more firmly than Mitchell that the NAACP was the

most important vehicle blacks had for ending segregation and discrimination. The NAACP gave African Americans a considerable base of security,
psychologically if not actually, from which to challenge Jim Crow. Furthermore, no other organization could have provided Mitchell with the extensive political network and institutional support system that the NAACP
did; its branches extended from the less conservative West to the conservative Midwest through the progressive Northeast and into the reactionary Deep South. The most spectacular example to date of the NAACP's
effectiveness was the success of the Montgomery bus boycott. All the principal players in this struggle, including King, were NAACP products.
Furthermore, without the NAACP lawsuit that led the Supreme Court to
conclude that intrastate segregation was unconstitutional, the MIA's year-
long bus boycott would have collapsed. The boycott, of course, had a much
larger meaning for southern blacks than the constitutional issues involved.
It awakened them as much as the buy-where-you-can-work campaign had
signaled the coming of age of Maryland's blacks in the 1930s. "We can't
tell what's going on in white people's hearts," said a woman contemplating
the effects of the boycott. "But we know it changed *our* hearts. We aren't
afraid anymore."

Now, the Greensboro sit-ins had set the stage for the launching of the
second phase of the modern civil rights movement, and reinforced Mitchell's determination to press ahead with the NAACP's legislative program.
The unyielding demands by the North Carolina A and T students, and,
subsequently, waves of other students, to be served at lunch counters
throughout the South were reminiscent of the earlier struggles by Juanita
Mitchell and the NAACP youth movement and Methodist Youth Council
that had desegregated restaurants in Evanston, Illinois, and of "sit-downs"
by NAACP youth members in 1957 and 1958 in Wichita, Kansas, and
Oklahoma City, that had ended Jim Crow at more than sixty lunch counters in those cities. In 1959 the NAACP college chapter at Washington
University in St. Louis also conducted sit-ins at local segregated lunch
counters. The NAACP youth movement Juanita had founded came into its
own during the 1960 NAACP convention. There, 347 youth delegates
from thirty-nine states planned to intensify their struggle against discrimination from their bases on college campuses and within adult NAACP
branches. When Roy Wilkins read a United Press International dispatch
stating that segregation had ended at lunch counters in Arlington, Virginia, youth delegates hoisted him on their shoulders and paraded around
the ballroom singing "We Shall Not Be Moved" and "Freedom."

The sit-ins and the interracial "freedom rides" of the Congress of Racial
Equality, which had been revived from its dormant state, were antithetical
to Wilkins's style of exerting political pressure through traditional channels

for change. The considerable financial, moral, and other support the student activists received from veteran freedom fighters and the churches were,
nevertheless, indispensable to their success. Mitchell supported the students' involvement, but, although he welcomed their zeal, he tended to
downplay the importance of nonviolent direct action protests—a practice
common to NAACP leaders of his generation. Yet the poignant live theater
that such protests, with their passive resistance tactics, were presenting
nightly on television was essential to the success of the next stage of Mitchell's work in Washington. (One reason for this Old Guard ambivalence was
that until 1960 the NAACP was the civil rights movement; now it had
messianic competitors.)

The new protests molded a national consensus in a manner that the
NAACP's legal, legislative, and other carefully targeted programs alone
could not have done. They gave the struggle the emotional appeal that had
been lost with the waning of lynching. One of the benefits of Walter
White's antilynching crusades had been to arouse national consciousness to
an awareness of the inhumanity of racism. Mitchell recalled that Arthur
Spingarn, National President of the NAACP, had once observed that the
NAACP must develop a strategy that, while not emotional, was just as
effective. The Emmett Till murder occurred soon afterward, "electrifying
the nation." Mitchell recalled that NAACP revenues increased because
many people "thought there was some way you could take the case to
court. We explained again and again there was no way we could do it. The
Justice Department had to do it. But people anyway thought their contributions were going to make it possible to take the Till case to court." And
they continued sending in money.

Mitchell's frustrations with Congress had convinced him that unless
politicians were pushed by an overpowering popular force, lawmakers
would not enact the full scope of antidiscrimination laws that were clearly
needed. Thus the student demonstrations were indispensable. They were a
popular response to government power, an effort to make the engines of the
legislative and executive branches work in concert with the front-running
judicial branch. The year 1960 marked the beginning of a decade in which
there was a culmination of forces and an extraordinary confrontation between popular mass protest and government power. Mitchell, as leader of
the legislative forces, was pivotal to this struggle.

Combined, the 1954 *Brown* decision, Martin Luther King's MIA movement, and the passage of the 1957 Civil Rights Act had an enormous
catalytic effect on the thinking of black citizens. The victories galvanized
them into mass action much more than at any time in history. Futhermore,
these civil rights victories reverberated not only in the courts and political
corridors of the nation but in the mass media as well. Especially important

for Mitchell, the 1957 act removed any doubt that Congress could be pressured to pass civil rights laws.

Of itself, King's Montgomery victory was limited even though the open challenge by the black masses, in the heart of Dixie, to the South's Jim Crow system was unprecedented. King, through the force of his personality, his eloquence and ready access to church pulpits and other forums across the country, by 1960 had emerged as a national symbol, the charismatic purveyor of a new style of dynamic leadership. But there were other new players as well. The founding of CORE in 1942, and its testing—with very limited success—of Gandhian principles of nonviolent direct action protests in Chicago, St. Louis, throughout New Jersey, and in the upper South, demonstrated the value of such techniques by those who wished more directly to challenge Jim Crow. The birth of CORE, the Southern Christian Leadership Conference, and the Student Nonviolent Coordinating Committee all showed an open rebellion against the NAACP, with its carefully structured program. As Thurgood Marshall, who had led in cautioning against the dangers of CORE's direct action tactics in the South, later acknowledged, "The young people are impatient . . . and, if you mean, are the young people impatient with me, the answer is yes."

The students, serving as shock troops, continued to move outside the framework of the NAACP but, as a rule, with the association's blessings. Though the NAACP and the younger organizations (CORE, SCLC, and SNCC) were geared to different strategies, and were in obvious competition for membership, media attention, and financial and political resources, their goals were the same. Their relationship was more than symbiotic; it was one of interlocking support. The NAACP vanguard in the South could not afford to have the students and younger organizations too far ahead, and the students could not afford to reject the NAACP's legal and institutional protections. In this regard, Mitchell benefited considerably in Washington from the shock among lawmakers about the students' daring challenges in the Deep South and the resulting sympathy they aroused throughout the nation. The reverberations of the demonstrations were felt in Washington more indirectly than directly, through the awakening of the body politic to the grave moral cancer of racism within the nation. Without the student movement, which made more Americans than ever before aware of the destructive quality of racism and aroused unprecedented moral concern, it is doubtful that either the Kennedy administration or Congress would have gone as far as each did to end second-class citizenship for African Americans.

King himself emphasized the differences in strategies. He regarded civil rights as primarily a moral issue, while the NAACP saw it as a constitutional issue. He acknowledged the need for legislation by explaining, "It may be true that morality cannot be legislated, but behavior can be regulated. The law may not make a man love me, but it may keep him from lynching me." Legislation and court orders "can control the external effects of bad internal attitudes." He saw the struggle as "a three-lane road with some emphasizing the way of litigation and mobilizing forces for meaningful legislation, and others emphasizing the way of nonviolent direct action, and still others moving through research and education and building up forces to prepare the Negro for the challenges of a highly industrialized society." The type of nonviolent direct action he was advocating

> does not minimize works through the courts. But it recognizes that legislation and court orders can only declare rights; they can never thoroughly deliver them. Only when the people themselves begin to act are rights on paper given life blood. A catalyst is needed to breathe life experience into a judicial decision by the persistent exercise of the rights until they become usual and ordinary in human conduct.[1]

To that Mitchell said, amen. There was no stronger advocate than he of giving "rights on paper" their "life blood" through enforcement of the laws. But first the laws had to be enacted, and the courts had to uphold them. Exhortation could never achieve those goals; only through the implementation of carefully structured programs could they become realities.

Mitchell continued to remain deeply involved in the new protests through the activities of his family. In addition to other civil rights work, the family, as already described, had a continual history of political activism, typified by Lillie Jackson's preaching to her followers, "Every day, a voter registration day." Juanita had directed the NAACP's first voter registration campaign in 1942 following the massive protest demonstration in Annapolis and continued to lead this program. She got the ministers in each precinct to appoint someone from their parish to be responsible for conducting door-to-door registration campaigns. She admonished local blacks that "in Baltimore we don't have to die for the right to vote," as was happening in Mississippi; all blacks had to do was go downtown and register. Mitchell helped Juanita develop this program in Baltimore by organizing adult voter registration committees and letting blacks know that they could gain their civil rights more quickly if more of them were registered to vote.

Clarence III, who had led protests against segregated swimming pools and restaurants in Baltimore, headed the third generation of Mitchell freedom fighters. As a Morgan State University student, he had contributed to those demonstrations by organizing busloads of his classmates to go downtown to protest segregation. His mother gave support by organizing cadres of black and white civil rights lawyers to free the demonstrators from jail and to represent them in court. That August, Clarence III journeyed to Atlanta to become a charter member of SNCC. His father had urged him to try to get SNCC to direct its energies onto voter registration campaigns, because he believed that acquiring political power was a more effective means of achieving their goals. "Why don't you get them to sit in at the city councils and state legislatures?" he urged. The students initially did not appreciate the value of that advice and rejected it in favor of the more popular kinds of protests at public facilities.

Just two weeks before the Greensboro sit-in, Mitchell had thanked Attorney General Rogers for his office's successful defense of the rights of blacks to vote in Georgia in *United States* v. *Raines,* in which the Supreme Court also upheld the constitutionality of the 1957 Civil Rights Act. But he expressed impatience with the pace of progress in the area of civil rights. By that point in history, he said, African Americans should have had full equality under the law and their status should not have been any worse than that of the Irish, Poles, Jews, or Catholics. Those groups, Mitchell explained, often had "just complaints," but their problems, unlike racial discrimination, did "not arise from laws enacted by state legislatures or unfair acts of oppression on the part of state law enforcement officers."

Mitchell continued to watch as his son, the "young black man who had been lionized for his civil rights contributions at an NAACP national convention in St. Paul, Minnesota, where he was born," established his name in history in the struggle to desegregate Baltimore. Upon returning to St. Paul for the convention, Clarence III had been struck by the sharp contrast between the lack of racial barriers in Minnesota and the segregation that existed in Maryland. Some of those barriers, like segregation in restaurants, were causing the State Department considerable embarrassment because not even African diplomats could enjoy public services on Route 40—then the main artery between New York and Washington. Minnesota's hotels, restaurants, and other public facilities had all been open to NAACP delegates, most of whom were black, but in Baltimore the invisible Jim Crow sign was real. So "Little Clarence" had returned to Baltimore more determined than ever to continue protests against such injustices.

A week after the NAACP convention in St. Paul, Clarence III was arrested in Baltimore for refusing to leave the Miller Brothers Restaurant. His father thought it interesting that the restaurant "had a huge sign painted on one of its outside walls advertising that it was on the site of what was once a slave auction house." Clarence III was only one of hundreds of young blacks arrested for such "trespassing." The sign was eventually removed.

At that time, according to Mitchell, the hotels and restaurants were going "back and forth on their racial policies." Some announced that they were ending their policies of racial exclusion, only to bow to pressures from their competitors and resegregate. Americans once more were caught in the wrenching moral and constitutional crisis that had almost destroyed the nation a century earlier.

Mitchell urged Juanita on when she, Tucker R. Dearing, and Jack Greenberg, through the NAACP Legal Defense and Educational Fund, Inc., challenged the arrest of Robert Mack Bell (who would later become a city judge) and other young blacks, in *Bell* v. *Maryland,* for sitting in at Hooper's Restaurant. The Supreme Court in 1964 would effectively reverse the convictions by remanding the case to the Maryland Court of Appeals, noting that the convictions contravened the subsequently enacted Maryland Civil Rights Act.[2]

Mitchell expressed his ambivalence toward the new student activism by saying it was a good development and "a thing that was long overdue." He had been concerned that students of more recent times were not sufficiently interested in civil rights. His problem was with their nonviolent and passive-resistance strategies. Mitchell believed firmly in the constitutional right of self-defense. His third son, Michael, however, one day reminded him that there were limits to this right when Mitchell attempted to turn the garden hose on a group called Fight American Nationalists that was picketing the Baltimore NAACP branch. Grabbing his father's hand, Michael reminded him, "Daddy, you can't do that. They've got a right to picket." So Mitchell "did the next best thing." He made a sign with black shoe polish that read, FAN IS MADE UP OF HUMAN SKUNKS and led a counterpicket for as long as the group remained.

Mitchell maintained that a collision of two philosophies was occurring—the NAACP's belief in the constitutional process versus King's belief in moral law, which he held to be higher than man's law. Mitchell, like King, was a devout Christian, but he could not overlook the secular consequences of this competition. One of these involved the competing groups' raising funds from the same sources. For example, in April Mitchell had been informed by Omega Psi Phi fraternity that it had thousands of dollars to donate to the sit-in demonstrators in the South and wanted to know where to send the money. Mitchell responded that there were many costs incurred by the demonstrators, such as transportation, picket signs, rental of meeting places, and bail for those arrested. Currently, NAACP branches were providing most of the bail for the waves of protestors, so he told the fraternity, if it wanted to help free the students from jail, it should send its donation to the NAACP national office.

Mitchell noted that a 1959 NAACP convention resolution had firmly rejected violence but upheld the right of "collective self defense against unlawful assaults." He maintained that, "at this late date in our history," the NAACP could not "encourage our people to follow a philosophy which deprives them" of that basic right.

Rather than opposing those who advocated passive resistance or non-violence, Mitchell recommended that the NAACP provide them with full legal, political, moral, and financial support. He also recommended that the NAACP (1) assist in selecting cities for demonstrations where blacks had a significant political base and thus better assurance against violence; (2) create a financial pool for bail and legal services; (3) assign NAACP personnel to help lead such demonstrations; (4) develop a system of targeting national chains for economic reprisals and protests; and (5) promote an extensive program to show the relation among sit-ins, registration and voting, the civil rights legislative struggle in Congress, and the desegregation of all public facilities, including schools.

Mitchell said that the best illustration of the value of the sit-ins was that they showed the need for political action. The vicious police commissioner of Birmingham, Eugene "Bull" Connor, would not have been in office had blacks exercised their full voting potential in the recent city election. He stressed that he was not blaming apathy or intimidation for the failure of Birmingham's blacks to register and vote. The problem, he said, lay with the need for community leaders to work harder in this area. He recommended that the NAACP immediately assume that responsibility.

Mitchell also observed that NAACP branches had been engaged in direct action campaigns for some thirty years, beginning in 1915 with the picketing of the racist film *Birth of a Nation*. In 1917 James Weldon Johnson and W.E.B. Du Bois had also led the NAACP's dramatic silent parade down Fifth Avenue to protest lynching and other forms of mob violence. Unlike the current sit-ins, the freedom rides, and the related jail-ins, those earlier demonstrations had not been mass protests.

Mitchell said that the NAACP would cooperate with "other organizations now becoming active in the civil rights field" as long as they consulted with the organization's branches in advance and there was mutual respect for joint goals. The organizations also had to have an identifiable membership base, demonstrate a willingness to share in fund-raising, and accept the Constitution as the highest law of the land. He recognized the right of jailed demonstrators to refuse bail as a manner of protest, but "we do not adopt this as the policy of our organization." Like other NAACP leaders, he stressed the point, often overlooked by the organization's increasing number of critics, that, in addition to providing bail and legal assistance for arrested demonstrators, the association would continue fighting in the courts for total vindication of the demonstrators' complaints, since it was through the courts that the objectives of King's Montgomery bus boycott had ultimately been achieved.

The brush-fire spread of the student demonstrations diverted attention from Mitchell's recommendations. The NAACP national office was called upon to provide ever increasing amounts for bail and legal services for the young activists, just as it had been providing economic and other forms of assistance for African Americans targeted by the White Citizens' Councils. Despite the differences in strategies, the NAACP repeatedly noted that many of these young activists were NAACP youth council members. The students' common cry was the same as the NAACP's: "Full equality— nothing less." The difference now was that that demand, more than ever, caught the attention of the national news media and so was heard every- where, along with thundering chants—"Everybody wants . . . Free-ee- dum! Free-dum! Free-dum!"—as demonstrators openly dared to defy the Jim Crow system. Awareness among opponents that the new militancy was no temporary phenomenon only intensified diehard white resistance.[3]

John F. Kennedy, with the help of 80 percent of the black vote, won the presidency by the narrowest margin in modern times. Upon assuming office in January 1961, he not only faced a troubled economy, a rapidly changing world that was made more tense by the cold war, and an intracta- ble Congress; he was also confronted with questions of how well he could meet expectations aroused among blacks by his ringing promises for un- precedented executive action—promises that led black Americans to be- lieve he would fulfill their dream of full equality. The national atmosphere was further heightened by the administration's moral tone and policy of liberalism, which produced a revolution of rising expectations. John Ken- nedy's New Frontier symbolized, as he said, the passing of the torch "to a new generation of Americans" of whom he was the best example. Kennedy himself was as different from the older generation as were the sit-in demon- strators from older civil rights leaders like Mitchell. The inherent tensions between the two generations, between advocates of profound social change and those (not only southerners) clinging to old racial attitudes, also heightened the prevailing sense of impending, profound national turmoil.

The topics covered by Mitchell in a September 1960 meeting with Harold Tyler, who succeeded the frustrated Wilson White as assistant at- torney general, and Maceo Hubbard, deputy chief of the general litigation section (whose relationship with Mitchell dated back to the FEPC period), showed that the NAACP's priorities as the transition period approached were the following: (1) the status of a federal lawsuit attempting to deseg- regate the beaches around Biloxi, Mississippi; (2) a voting suit in Mississippi; (3) federal desegregation action against off-base schools in military-impacted areas; (4) the continuing problems of segregated travel, especially in airports; and (5) the Justice Department's hiring practices.

Tyler was impressed with Mitchell from their first meeting, which occurred soon after he took over the division. He discovered that Mitchell "knew exactly what was going on on the Hill," and in those days when civil rights was not yet popular, he found that reassuring. Many times when Tyler thought he was all by himself with only "a small band of friends," Mitchell dispelled the unease with "his great compassion and humor." Mitchell was normally serious, but Tyler found that "he had a way about him that was so marvelous." One quality that Tyler never forgot was that Mitchell "always had a ready smile for everybody even when his heart was bleeding. He knew how to cope with these guys in human terms. But Clarence was also brighter than most people, too. Let's never forget that." Consequently, his confident, reassuring manner "taught whites and others that color made no difference at all. Clarence was Clarence, and it didn't matter what color his skin was. He was one heck of a guy. That helped a lot." Additionally, Tyler found him very persuasive and very articulate. They talked about ways to strengthen the division, which included the need for personnel. At first, there were only eighteen lawyers. "But Clarence was sufficiently world-wise and practical to understand that just throwing bodies at a problem was not the way to perfectly solve that particular problem." They concentrated on priorities. From their first meeting, Mitchell began having regular sessions with Tyler every two weeks to review progress.

Tyler knew that Mississippi's John Stennis was not "all anti-anything on civil rights" as others like James Eastland and Olin Johnston were. "He was willing to listen to anything within reason. That's why he was important. That's why Clarence put the finger on us to make sure that we supplied meaningful information to the senator" during consideration of the 1960 Civil Rights Act. The strategy worked not only for Mitchell but also for Tyler, who found that "thereafter, Stennis was always very nice to me personally."

Mitchell initially felt assured that African Americans would benefit through executive action more under the New Frontier than in any previous administration, but he knew that there were real limits to how much Kennedy by himself could or would do. He saw evidence of the new President's personal commitment to fair play in his criticism of the U.S. Coast Guard for having no blacks among its members in the Inauguration Day parade, and in his appointments of blacks to top positions in the White House and other parts of the administration. He was also convinced that while President Kennedy would not necessarily be seeking "flaming civil rights" advocates for judicial appointments, he would be selecting more open-minded people for the bench.

Kennedy's expressed concern for the plight of the racially oppressed; his strengthening of the President's Committee on Government Contracts and the President's Committee on Government Employment Policy by combining them, under Executive Order 10925, into one President's Committee on Equal Employment Opportunity; his early directive to executive departments and federal agencies upholding the administration's non-discrimination employment policy for firms holding government contracts—exemplified by the long-range "Plans for Progress" agreement between the government and Lockheed Aircraft Corporation for a voluntary affirmative action program that increased black employment by 26 percent—all brought more ringing rounds of applause from African Americans. The administration's agreement with Lockheed was made under Johnson's leadership after the NAACP had repeated its complaints that the plant was "operated on a rigidly segregated basis."

Among his many other actions, Kennedy barred any department or agency from permitting the use of its "name, sponsorship, facilities, or activity" in connection with any employee recreational group practicing discrimination—a policy readily implemented by Attorney General Robert F. Kennedy. He and other top administration officials resigned from Washington's prestigious Metropolitan Club because it did not accept African Americans as members, and the President endorsed their action.

Also drawing praise was the attorney general's forthright speech at the University of Georgia calling for respect for the law and declaring that the administration would uphold the 1954 Supreme Court desegregation decision. Not since Reconstruction had the South heard such bold talk from the nation's top law enforcement official. The NAACP expressed its "profound appreciation." But Mitchell's optimism soon turned to disappointment when he realized that the President's strategy was to downplay civil rights legislation in order not to jeopardize his numerous other legislative priorities, which included unemployment compensation and assistance to depressed areas, and to issue only executive orders he felt would not ruffle feathers in Congress. His very strong interest in foreign affairs also, especially Cuba, Berlin, and Southeast Asia, provided overwhelming competition for civil rights. Another drawback was the administration's reliance on voluntary initiatives by government agencies, private corporations, and labor unions in ending employment discrimination. In urging employers and workers' representatives to take affirmative initiatives to assure equality of opportunity, Kennedy and Johnson said that they should do so in order to avoid the government's becoming "a police agency." Long experience had taught the NAACP that such a policy of voluntary compliance yielded only limited benefits. Mitchell therefore charged that the New Frontier "looked suspiciously like a dude ranch with Senator James Eastland as general manager and Representative Howard Smith as foreman."[4]

Having been beaten soundly by the southerners in the struggle for the 1960 Civil Rights Act, Mitchell now found his legislative program being challenged from within the NAACP's top hierarchy. Dr. John Morsell, then assistant to the executive secretary and Roy Wilkins's designated heir apparent, was one of those, Mitchell recalled, who maintained that Congress would never pass legislation the NAACP wanted, and that therefore the association was wasting time and resources in that effort. Mitchell also was concerned that "Roy was not very interested in legislative matters. He felt it was not that important." But rather than directly confronting the source of growing unrest in the South, as Mitchell had subtly suggested in his comments on the sit-in demonstrations, Wilkins began asserting his leadership more aggressively in the area of the executive branch in an attempt to set a new course that was based in part on ideas that had been developed for him and Morsell by Washington Bureau counsel Pohlhaus. Although Pohlhaus's position was basically in sync with Mitchell's, it was predicated on the existence of ideal circumstances, which neglected the political realities of which his boss was always aware.

The NAACP's call for more forthright executive leadership was rooted in a faith in the President's prestige and moral leadership—a power implicitly emphasized by Kennedy during the campaign whenever he criticized Eisenhower for not expressing support for school desegregation; the broad authority vested in executive agencies; and the President's constitutional mandate to faithfully execute the laws.

Pohlhaus argued in a memorandum to Wilkins that the school desegregation cases, by rendering unconstitutional state-fostered segregation, made it possible for the President to withhold funds for any federal project wherever discrimination was practiced. He repeated that various courts had upheld the right of the chief executive to refuse to expend funds where such action had been deemed unconstitutional. Pohlhaus took a position between Wilkins and Mitchell, which was that under the doctrine of the separation of powers, the President had a constitutional duty to take action to implement the judgment in *Brown*. Article II, Section 1, under which he had taken his oath of office, conferred on him the responsibility to "preserve, protect, and defend the Constitution of the United States"; Article II, Section 3, authorized him to "take care that the laws be faithfully executed." It was therefore Pohlhaus's opinion that this "duty precludes him constitutionally from allowing the expenditure of Federal funds for purposes that are unconstitutional." Pohlhaus said, furthermore, that the issue involving the "right of the Executive Branch to refuse to expend funds authorized or appropriated by the Legislative Branch on the ground of un-constitutionality of the expenditure" had been decided in many cases by American courts.

In a subsequent letter, Pohlhaus informed Wilkins that there was a legal loophole in the 1944 Russell amendment, which had barred funding for an independent FEPC created by an executive order, "through which you can drive the proverbial Mack truck." By approaching the discrimina-tion problem from the viewpoint of the unconstitutionality of federal sup-port wherever discrimination existed, Pohlhaus said, the goal of an FEPC could be obtained by using the due process clause of the Fifth Amend-ment.[5]

Wilkins and Leadership Conference on Civil Rights advisers, by con-trast, to get around the roadblock in Congress, tended to blur the line separating the executive and legislative branches by demanding that Ken-nedy issue an omnibus executive order that was much more comprehensive than any that had been issued in the past. Recalling in an LCCR paper prepared for him that during the campaign Kennedy, with whom had de-veloped a close friendship, had stressed the integral relation between eco-nomic growth and foreign policy, Wilkins declared that civil rights was "the third leg of the stool." It was, he said, an increasingly important aspect of foreign relations as a criterion for measuring America's professions of democracy in many parts of the globe. The LCCR paper noted that the worldwide movement among the darker races for emancipation and self-determination had "given a momentum to the civil rights cause" in the United States—a momentum that would rapidly accelerate during the next four years. To ensure that the domestic civil rights effort was accelerated correspondingly, the LCCR said, there had to be "a breakthrough in prac-tice comparable to the breakthrough in principle represented by the Demo-cratic platform." This breakthrough had to be accomplished by executive action, since Congress had been derelict in fulfilling its constitutional re-sponsibility.

The LCCR paper noted that both Kennedy and the Democratic plat-form had

> properly emphasized that the protection and advancement of civil
> rights is a shared responsibility among all branches of government.
> It is not necessary nor even possible to choose as between executive
> and legislative actions. Neither alone is adequate to accomplish the
> goal: both are indispensable to it. Only as the legislative power of
> enactment and the purse is joined with the administrative and en-
> forcement power of the executive, in thoroughgoing support of the

LION IN THE LOBBY

constitutional interpretations of the judiciary, can the platform
planks of the Democratic Party be fulfilled.

Among the Democratic platform pledges that required legislative action, the LCCR noted, were those calling for elimination of the poll tax
and literacy tests for voting; extension of the life and broadening of the
powers of the Civil Rights Commission; empowering the attorney general
to file civil injunction suits in all civil rights cases; granting technical and
financial assistance to districts seeking to comply with the Supreme Court
desegregation decisions; and initiating first-step compliance in all school
districts by 1963. The LCCR felt that school desegregation legislation
should include provisions for a comprehensive Part III mechanism that had
been removed from the 1957 civil rights bill, as well as for technical and
financial assistance. The LCCR noted that to date the only comprehensive
stand that Congress had taken on school desegregation was adoption of the
Southern Manifesto—"and the strength of the resistance movement continues to derive in large part from the argument that the Congress has
refused to declare desegregation the law of the land." By adopting that
negative position, those in Congress who had signed the Manifesto had
shown the hopelessness of seeking the passage of civil rights legislation.

Possibly, the LCCR said, the executive branch could utilize the proposed Title III power to protect the Fourteenth Amendment rights of
blacks without legislation, so the LCCR suggested initiating a case to test
that authority. But the LCCR felt that even if that authority was upheld, it
would require a case-by-case approach in order to fix responsibility. The
LCCR, nevertheless, called for enactment of legislation in 1961 to end
within two years segregation in more than two thousand school districts in
the South.

Rather than wait until that time, or until the courts ruled all forms of
segregation unconstitutional, the LCCR felt, the President should provide
"affirmative assistance" through executive and administrative actions to assure all citizens their full rights. It exhorted the President to issue a "Federal Civil Rights Code" barring discrimination in employment of federal
personnel, in all federal facilities and programs, and in all federal grant-in-
aid programs. The LCCR felt that the federal emphasis "should not be so
much on what goverment can do directly as on how it can serve as a re-
source and catalytic agency to encourage the assumption of community
responsibility for the fostering of mutual acceptance with respect for differences among all groups in the community." To facilitate this goal, it
urged establishing within the President's office an agency similar to the
National Security Council or the Council of Economic Advisors.

On February 6, seeking to hold the administration to its commitment to executive action, Wilkins and Arnold Aaronson, secretary of the Leadership Conference, held a conference at the White House with Theodore Sorensen, special counsel to the President, and several other top aides. Wilkins stressed the need for "effective moral and political leadership by the whole executive branch" to make equal opportunity a reality for all Americans. Subsequently, Wilkins and Aaronson submitted to the White House a detailed memorandum entitled "Program to End Federally Supported Segregation and Other Forms of Racial Discrimination," which proposed executive action in the areas of the military, education, employment, housing, health services, and agriculture. That impressive catalog was prepared under Pohlhaus's supervision. The administration's weak response to this study as well as to a report on a wide range of unresolved problems that Mitchell submitted to Vice President Johnson, chairman of the Committee on Equal Employment Opportunity, was yet another reason why blacks were growing frustrated and restless.[6] The administration's response helped to shift the focus within the Leadership Conference back to the type of civil rights legislation Mitchell said the nation needed.

Mitchell's demands for a strong equal employment policy became the first area of conflict with the Kennedy administration. A serious weakness with President Kennedy's EEOC executive order, the LCCR noted, was that it did not cover grant-in-aid programs. The conference's complaints, reflecting Mitchell's order of priorities, again underscored the continuing difficulty of getting a strong FEPC-type structure under an executive order. The Kennedy order broadened the powers of the President's committee to combat discrimination in employment by government agencies and private contractors but that did not satisfy critics. The LCCR noted that past programs had been weakened by the failure of individual agencies to implement them fully. More important, though, was that previous administrations had relied on complaints alone—rather than initiating their own investigations—to correct discrimination. But the complaints process was seriously limited because of fear of reprisals and the ignorance of many claimants of their rights. A third reason for failure, owing in part to staff limitations, was that administering agencies relied on other departments from which complaints originated to investigate racial injustices. Other reasons included friendships among agency heads, lack of interest by administrators, and the secrecy of findings that prevented complainants from knowing the results of investigations and how they might proceed. The Leadership Conference urged that the President's EEO committee or some other impartial agency conduct investigations with the help of adequately trained personnel.

Vice President Johnson took seriously his responsibility as chairman of the EEOC. Even though all the Leadership Conference's complaints were

not met, he worked hard to make the committee effective, personally calling up members of the Cabinet and urging them to improve the federal
government's employment of minorities. The President held a Cabinet
meeting on this problem.

The wide gap between promise and fulfillment, between the power to
act and the fear or unwillingness to do so, was emphasized graphically that
April when the first major event of the four-year observation of the Civil
War Centennial was shifted, under President Kennedy's orders, from local
hotels and restaurants to the Charleston Naval Station in order to avoid
embarrassment over the fact that these hotels and restaurants were still
segregated. The gap was also evident in the executive branch's failure to
enforce the 1957 and 1960 civil rights acts. For example, with respect to
voting, the Justice Department had used sparingly its new authority
to inspect voting records and file suits on behalf of disfranchised blacks in the
South. The Kennedy administration's first desegregation suit in the area of
voting rights was filed on April 13 against the Dallas County, Alabama,
registrars. The Eisenhower administration had filed ten suits between 1957
and January 20, 1961. Although only two of them had been completely
settled before the change of administration, Mitchell welcomed the success
that Justice had so far enjoyed under the 1957 Civil Rights Act in attacking
voter discrimination in Alabama, Georgia, Louisiana, and Tennessee.

Mitchell was especially encouraged that he had been able to persuade
Justice to help blacks in Fayette and Haywood counties, Tennessee, win the
right to vote for the first time since Reconstruction. In 1940, NAACP
leader Elbert Williams in Brownsville suffered what people in the area
called an off-the-record lynching, and his body was thrown into a nearby
river when he tried to register other blacks during an NAACP voter campaign. Many other NAACP leaders had been run out of town for making
similar attempts. Consequently, nineteen years later, not one black was
registered to vote in either Fayette or Haywood county, even though they
both had black majorities. A second test of the constitutionality of the
1957 Civil Rights Act had led the Supreme Court in 1960 to affirm a federal court order that 1,377 black voters should be returned to the roles in
Washington Parish, Louisiana. The White Citizens' Councils had forced
the removal of 90 percent of blacks from the roles under a Louisiana law
that permitted any two registered voters to challenge another person's right
to vote. But less than one tenth of 1 percent of white voters had been removed through such challenges.

Working with the Memphis NAACP branch, which filed voter discrimination complaints with the Justice Department and the Civil Rights
Commission in May 1960, Mitchell urged Justice to use this same provi-

sion of the 1957 act in the suit that had enabled it to win the vote for blacks in Fayette and Haywood counties.

The Justice Department sent John Doar and four other attorneys into the area to help spur registration. When a local sheriff arrested them, Harold Tyler immediately informed J. Edgar Hoover, who was shocked that something like that could happen to his men. The lawyers were then released. From then on, Tyler found that the FBI director began taking more, if still limited, interest in racial problems in the South.

But Justice's interest did not spare the fewer than one hundred blacks who had registered, and others who had made similar attempts, from economic reprisals and expulsion from their tenant farms. As the long legal battle continued in the courts, blacks erected a tent city—"Freedom Village"—for the evicted farmers and their families and sent in money and supplies that included food, clothing, bedding, and gasoline. The national NAACP and its Brownsville and Memphis branches worked with the Fayette County Civic and Welfare League to provide such aid. At the same time, the Justice Department, again using the 1957 act, won restraining orders against the evictions. Mitchell praised Tyler as "the prime strategist" who brought the cases into court. He said he particularly admired Tyler's "resiliency in handling fair criticisms or at least criticisms that the person making them honestly" believed were fair. Tyler welcomed such openness, because Mitchell "just wasn't an ordinary critic" who complained that "we were wrong all the time." Instead, he suggested solutions, "and he would cheer us on if we did something serious." That rapport, like Brownell's sincerity, heightened Mitchell's expectations and increased his impatience with the Kennedy Justice Department.[7]

Responding to the suggestion that his brother the President had the power to force compliance with *Brown,* which involved Fourteenth Amendment rights, Robert Kennedy said, "I don't believe that we do." He, too, in apparent reference to the 1957 act, felt that adequate legislation was available, "which gives us ample authority to take major steps to help and assist where there is discrimination"—chiefly regarding voting rights. Kennedy added that it was "incumbent upon the Justice Department to move in there vigorously" to end voting discrimination. Like members of the previous administration, he believed that having the vote would help blacks open up other opportunities. Mitchell maintained that the vote was not enough: "The right to vote is the cornerstone of freedom, but here in America we do not stop with a cornerstone when we build democracy. We need a lot of other materials to finish the job."

In seeking compliance, the attorney general said, "I have made it a practice that where we intend to take some action . . . in the field of civil rights, that I will contact the top officials of the various states where it involves them or their deputies, and inform them that there is a potential violation of the law, and that we feel it is our responsibility to take certain action. If they take action voluntarily and clear up the situations, or straighten it out, then it is no longer necessary for the Department of Justice to take action. If they do not, then we will move in." For Mitchell, that stand was a capitulation to the states' rights doctrine and only invited more delays.

A third point of contention was Kennedy's campaign promise to issue with the "stroke of a pen" the executive order long sought by the NAACP barring discrimination in housing. Owing to the President's procrastination, doubts soon arose over whether he had the political will his predecessors lacked.

In the area of employment rights, the military continued to block cancellation of defense contracts where racial discrimination was practiced, and the administration resisted demands to end that discrimination.[8]

The call by the Civil Rights Commission for the government to withhold federal funds from public colleges practicing racial discrimination added to the pressure for stronger executive action by the new administration. The commission charged that the federal government had been a "silent partner" in maintaining "separate and unequal" higher education opportunities for southern blacks. Sensing the political dangers, the administration refused to withhold such grants-in-aid.

The issue of withholding federal funds under proposed positions like the Powell Amendment flared up once more when President Kennedy, on February 20, sent Congress his proposals for a three-year program of general assistance to public elementary and secondary schools. Kennedy was all too well aware that any President who dared unilaterally to utilize his authority to end segregation in education was subject to violent reprisals from powerful southern committee chairmen in Congress. In the struggles for the 1957 and 1960 civil rights acts, lawmakers had twice refused to give the attorney general specific authority to initiate school desegregation suits (as opposed to filing suits based on plaintiffs' complaints).

Mitchell stressed that restriction upon the attorney general during his March 10, 1961, testimony before the Senate Subcommittee on Education as he continued his struggle for the antisegregation amendment to the proposed education funding program. He refuted claims that blacks preferred segregation by noting that the NAACP annual convention, comprising a cross-section of blacks from everywhere in the country, had called for the antisegregation amendment. He stressed his belief that there was no "fundamental difference between the people of the United States, whether they live in Mississippi or New York." He felt that "leadership has a great deal to do with the extent to which people comply with the law."

Abraham Ribicoff, the new HEW secretary, said flatly that the administration would not withhold any education aid funds from segregated school districts if Congress passed such a discrimination safeguard. This was an intentional reassurance for southerners that the administration would not initiate that action unless Congress ordered it to do so. Ribicoff maintained that federal aid to education was imperative because many states and localities had exhausted their tax resources for new school construction and improved teachers' salaries. Ribicoff opposed a nonsegregation amendment to the measure being considered, saying it would "do this bill in." He said that the *Brown* decision was "legally and morally correct," but still maintained, "I can imagine no greater tragedy than to place every problem facing America on the back of education."

Mitchell responded that Ribicoff's argument was an attempt to persuade "the colored citizens of our country to forget" the Supreme Court desegregation decision. He was concerned that despite some progress, the federal government was still "busily extending racial segregation in schools" through the impacted-areas program.

Mitchell submitted correspondence from the previous year with Arthur S. Flemming, then secretary of HEW, to the committee to document the futility of trying to end school segregation by administrative means despite discretionary power conferred on the Justice Department by earlier laws and in the 1960 Civil Rights Act. In response to his complaints that black children in Prince Georges County and at Fort Lee in Virginia were barred from attending schools in defense-impacted areas that were funded under Public Laws 815 and 874, Mitchell explained, a sympathetic Flemming had said that where Congress had not spelled out its intention to require desegregation, the executive branch did not believe it had any power to withhold funds. Mitchell concluded that that was also the Kennedy administration's policy on federal aid to education based on Ribicoff's statements.

On March 29, 1962, Mitchell and representatives of other organizations, in a meeting with Ribicoff, pressed his demand for the antisegregation policy covering all grant-in-aid programs and defense-impacted-area schools and urged that a similar policy be adopted covering aid to states for hospital construction under the Hill-Burton Act. Ribicoff at first insisted that he did not have authority to promulgate such policies. Toward the end of the meeting, responding to the pressure, he announced that, beginning in September 1963, the administration would withhold federal funds from segregated school districts serving children who lived on military bases. Ribicoff thus had reversed Flemming's policy and confirmed Mitchell's belief that the administration could just as easily have issued a broader policy covering all schools.

In his correspondence with Flemming in 1960, which Mitchell considered the climax of the NAACP's struggle for school desegregation thus far, he asked HEW to rule that the word "suitable," in statutes affecting education of children of military personnel, would be interpreted to mean "desegregated." Then, HEW had refused to agree with the NAACP. Now, Ribicoff, on March 30, announced that segregated schools in defense-impacted areas would not be considered "suitable." The federal government would therefore begin constructing its own schools if segregation was maintained, thereby lessening Washington's funding contributions to local school districts.

As in the past, Mitchell could not understand the delay in implementing the new HEW policy. Mitchell wanted it to be implemented right away in 1962, rather than a year later. He thought it particularly upsetting that, after the NAACP had gotten President Eisenhower to adopt a desegregation policy for schools on military posts, HEW and the Justice Department had evaded the order through subterfuge. Congress too refused to help. For example, Mitchell informed Congress that in 1958 the Army transferred 21 acres of land from its Redstone Arsenal to the Huntsville, Alabama, school district, which built a segregated school. In Pulaski County, Arkansas, a new school costing $600,000 was constructed for whites only. As Mitchell then battled to save an antisegregation amendment to an extension of the law providing funds for construction and operation of public schools in defense-impacted areas, he noted that prior to 1958, the federal government had spent $192 million for segregated schools. The House still defeated the amendment offered by Congressman James Roosevelt. Now, in 1962 Congress further dampened Mitchell's hopes by killing the Kennedy school construction aid bill.[9]

Mitchell's criticism of the leadership from the executive branch did not extend to the administration's reliance on court action to achieve public school desegregation. President Kennedy's attitude toward the *Brown* v. *Board of Education* decision, which his attorney general reflected, was much more positive than had been his predecessor's. President Eisenhower's position had been that it would be improper for him to comment on the May 17, 1954, school desegregation decision and that implementation should be left to the localities. In contrast, Kennedy promised, "Moral and persuasive leadership by the President to create the conditions in which compliance with the constitutional requirements of school desegregation takes place: this is the kind of leadership I intend to give, the kind of action we shall take." As his actions were proving, he intended to give this leadership only in the area of his executive authority.

Attorney General Rogers had advised a federal judge to postpone the matter when the judge had asked the Eisenhower administration for support during the bitter political battle over desegregation in New Orleans schools. This support from the executive branch was now provided, on February 16, when Attorney General Kennedy filed a suit to compel Louisiana officials to release federal funds to the desegregated New Orleans school district. On March 11, the Justice Department filed another suit to restrain Louisiana state legislators from interfering with the school board in carrying out its duties. Next, on March 17, the administration filed amicus curiae briefs in four other Louisiana school desegregation suits with the expressed aim to "enable the U.S. to act promptly to head off critical situations before they occur." Three weeks later, however, after having taken these encouraging steps, Attorney General Kennedy rejected demands by civil rights groups for a more direct attack on segregation. Kennedy opposed the contention that the government itself had the authority to file desegregation suits. (Only private individuals then could bring such suits.) Kennedy said that the administration had not made "a final determination as to exactly what we will do" about proposals for legislation to give the government that power. He promised that the Justice Department's emphasis would be on voting rights. Mitchell opposed the suggestion because he felt that it placed a much more restrictive limit on the Justice Department's powers to intervene in local jurisdictions than the law should permit.

Finally bending to the NAACP's demands, the Justice Department on September 17, 1962, became bolder and filed its first lawsuit in which the U.S. government was a plaintiff against Prince Georges County in an effort to end racial segregation in public schools receiving federal aid. In order to serve Fort Lee, a major Army post, Prince Georges County had received more than $2.5 million between 1950 and 1962 under the defense-impacted aid program for school construction and maintenance. Fort Lee had angered the NAACP in 1962 by announcing that white children would be educated in Virginia at Fairfax County schools and black dependents would go to Petersburg. That August, Fairfax schools refused to enroll blacks. The NAACP had also submitted to the Justice Department and HEW complaints about continuing segregation of military dependents at Fort Belvoir, Virginia, and Sheppard Air Force Base in Texas. The NAACP urged Justice to file a lawsuit in order to establish a precedent of direct government intervention to desegregate such schools. The NAACP Washington Bureau said that although the lawsuit did not go as far as the action that had been proposed under the original Part III of the 1957 civil rights bill, it was a "long step in that direction."

Mitchell welcomed the attorney general's announcement of the suit and said it "sounds a high note in the field of human rights." He explained to an NAACP branch meeting in Portsmouth, Virginia, that the Prince Georges County suit was "an action in equity" meant to protect the government's interests involving civilian employees and armed forces dependents. Significantly, it went beyond the government's previous action to enjoin unconstitutional state action. But it still did not go as far as the authorization that was sought under Part III (the section that had been deleted from the 1957 Civil Rights Act) or commit the government as much as Mitchell wanted. Nevertheless, Mitchell felt, it was "a long step in that direction." He was convinced that the government's interest in seeing that its funds were spent constitutionally exceeded the lawsuit's asserted, limited goals.

The suit differed from that against Prince Edward County, Virginia, where the government merely sought to intervene rather than to file a lawsuit in behalf of a plaintiff—a request that a federal district court judge subsequently rejected. For two years, white children in Prince Edward County had been attending private schools supported largely by public funds. Blacks, who had spurned an offer to set up similar schools, had to do without formal education. The district court judge argued that the NAACP's request to cut off funds for Prince Edward County could "jeopardize the education of several thousand Virginia children." [10]

Another attempt by Mitchell in 1963 to have antisegregation amendments included in all bills reported out by the House Committee on Education and Labor also failed. Mitchell was still optimistic that he could win this battle because the Committee for Negro Participation in the National Defense Program, a private group, had succeeded in getting an antidiscrimination provision included in the National Selective Service Act of 1940. Based on discussions he had had with Selective Service officials who had participated in the struggle for that provision, Mitchell learned that because no one else would sponsor it, Representative Hamilton Fish, Jr., was asked to do so, and the New York Republican agreed. Fish, a vigorous opponent of the Selective Service, had delayed passage of the bill to bring it into being for several weeks. Fish offered the antisegregation amendment in the hope of killing the Selective Service bill, but Congress instead passed it along with the racial safeguard. Mitchell felt that the lesson of this struggle was that the actions of lawmakers were more important that their motives, as long as whatever they did helped to strengthen constitutional freedoms. [11]

Continuing to develop strategy based on the civil rights bills that had been introduced by supporters at the administration's request (but that the White House subsequently disowned because Kennedy did not want to jeopardize passage of other bills he thought were more important), and to keep interest alive in Congress, Mitchell in July 1961 organized a "Freedom Train" to Washington during the NAACP's Fifty-second Annual Convention in Philadelphia. Of the 1,600 registered delegates, 1,250 crammed into a 22-car train bound for Washington in order to meet with agency heads, their congressmen and senators. Although he had arranged for a delegation to meet with the President, Mitchell, foreseeing that a charming Kennedy would provide his guests with good entertainment but make no commitments on civil rights, did not join in the visit to the White House.

"Sure enough," he said later, the President received the delegation "very cordially." He personally took the members on a tour of the White House, shared pleasantries with them, "and just generally kept everybody very happy, but he didn't make any promises to do anything on civil rights legislation." When the delegation returned to the meeting headquarters and reported the warmth of the reception but nothing else, there was an uproar of criticism during which one person shouted: "We're not interested in Abraham Lincoln's bed. We want to know what happened on civil rights legislation." Curiously, Mitchell realized, Kennedy "did not lose a single friend" by that meeting, and it was "entirely possible that he gained some." Mitchell felt that no other recent President, except perhaps Franklin Roosevelt, could have scored as well. In fact, African Americans would have been outraged had they been so treated by Truman, Eisenhower, or Lyndon Johnson.

Another hurdle was lack of knowledge among African Americans of significant aspects of the legislative struggle. Mitchell recalled that Vice President Johnson, when once addressing a largely pro-civil-rights audience, had said that his ability to enlist the support of a group of young senators had been crucial to his success in attaching the jury trial amendment to the 1957 Civil Rights Act. When he mentioned Kennedy's "great courage" in being one of those supporters, the audience applauded wildly—a spectacle that perplexed Mitchell because it was the opposite of what should have occurred. He knew that the NAACP had to expand its educational program beyond its members. Also, according to Mitchell, "there was one almost humorous twist" to Kennedy's ability to win black support, especially for his advocacy of executive action: Kennedy "had so charmed a lot of Negroes that they not only thought this was a good idea, but they also vigorously opposed anybody who thought otherwise." Mitchell had in mind appointees like Carl Rowan, deputy assistant secretary of state for public affairs. Rowan charged that blacks "were so busy crying" to the President for new legislation "that their tears hide the really fantastic progress that is possible because of appointments and executive action." [12]

Mitchell impatiently accused President Kennedy of ignoring the Democratic platform's civil rights pledge. "If the present administration had dared to run on its current record," he charged in 1961, "it would not have been successful in attracting some of the people who voted for the Democrats in November." Mitchell noted that the Democrats pledged legislation to advance school desegregation, employment opportunities, and to protect constitutional rights of African Americans, but the administration's policy was in truth based on implementation by executive action. "This is incredible," he said, "because it is pretty obvious that executive action, while good, is not going to be good enough." He continued to regard that approach as merely a temporary solution dependent on each new administration's commitment to the particular program until Congress had expressed the nation's political will through legislation. He was supported in this belief by Senator Javits, who stressed that executive action alone would not produce the kind of progress in civil rights both parties had pledged. "Only Congress can make laws," he said, "and laws are essential not only to deal with recalcitrants but, as importantly, to establish a high standard of conduct for the community."

As for claims that African Americans were shifting away from civil rights legislation because they preferred a broad welfare program, Mitchell warned that "the Negro vote is essentially a civil rights vote." He predicted it would go to "whichever party makes a vigorous fight to get it." But protest was the most he could do while waiting for political pressure to build.[13]

The defeat of Kennedy's proposal to create a Department of Urban Affairs and the protracted delay lasting nearly a year in gaining confirmation of Thurgood Marshall as a judge on the U.S. Court of Appeals, Second Circuit, like the demise of the Fair Employment Practice Committee in 1946, were other demonstrations of the limits of presidential executive power. During the 1960 campaign, vice presidential candidate Henry Cabot Lodge was the first to suggest that a black person would be named to the Cabinet if Nixon won. Kennedy then made a similar pledge and he now wanted to fulfill it.

Robert Weaver, with his extensive background in government, was an ideal person for this distinction. In February 1961, after strong opposition from southerners owing to Weaver's advocacy of integrated public housing, the Senate confirmed his appointment by Kennedy as administrator of the Housing and Home Finance Agency, making him the first black to hold such a high-level post. Weaver had been chairman of the New York City Housing and Redevelopment Board and chairman of the NAACP national board of directors. Mitchell felt that the opposition to Weaver's appointment could have been defeated sooner had it not been for the administration's tendency "to find out first which way the wind was blowing before acting." He believed that the real problem was the desire to see whether civil rights leaders who supported an executive order on civil rights really felt strongly about the appointment and also whether naming Weaver would have been acceptable to the country.

Instead of gaining ready approval on Capitol Hill, Kennedy's subsequent announcement of plans to create a Cabinet-level Department of Urban Affairs and Housing quickly ran aground because it was correctly believed that Weaver would be named as its head. A second reason why some lawmakers opposed the Kennedy plan was that they feared the new department would considerably increase the concentration of federal power and impinge upon local authority. A third reason was political, which helped to explain Kennedy's timing even though there was the strong likelihood his plan would have been defeated. Mitchell pleaded with House Republicans not to join the southerners in blocking creation of the new agency. Nevertheless, on January 24, 1962, the House Rules Committee by a 9 to 6 vote refused to send the Urban Affairs Department bill to the House floor, killing it. Mitchell charged that the action by House Republicans, like that of at least eight senators who blocked a discharge motion in the Senate Committee on Government Operations on a similar Urban Affairs Department measure, was a cynical display of racism. But he was also clearly aware of Kennedy's political motivations, which were to embarrass the Republicans.

He said that by joining Rules Committee chairman Howard Smith's southern cohorts in killing the bill, the Republicans had triggered a booby trap that exploded in their faces. The Republicans had maintained that their votes had not been influenced by the rumors a black man would get the HUD secretaryship. But Mitchell felt their action nevertheless gave the President the opportunity to jerk the rug out from under them by confirming that he would name Weaver to the position: "No matter what happens from this point on, any Republican who opposes the Urban Affairs Department will be known as the man who voted to keep the national cabinet segregated. This is a title GOP leaders richly deserve. It may help them get candidates in office in Alabama or Mississippi, but it will be a heavy load in the more civilized areas of the nation."

Following his announcement that Weaver would head it, Kennedy submitted to Congress a more compulsive proposal to create the Department of Urban Affairs and Housing as part of his reorganization plans. But the House on February 21, by a vote of 264 to 150, adopted a resolution disapproving the proposal. Thus the Rules Committee's votes on January 24 had accurately reflected the sentiment of the full House. Mitchell noted sardonically that the fifty-two midwestern congressmen who helped kill the proposal had tacked a "whites only" sign on the door leading to Cabinet meeting rooms. He said that the author of the plan to kill the proposal was Michigan Republican George Meader, who had a record of publicly sup-

porting civil rights but chopping and emasculating such bills in committee. Were it not for congressmen like Meader, he said, "the South would be
powerless in its effort to stem the national tide of civil rights."

Mitchell drew a parallel between the rejection of Kennedy's proposal
and the blocking of Truman's attempt to transform the Federal Security
Administration into the Department of Health, Education and Welfare because some lawmakers did not want Oscar Ewing, a liberal who headed the
FSA, to assume a Cabinet post with HEW. But subsequently, Congress
speedily approved Eisenhower's proposal to create HEW when the candidate for the Cabinet post was Oveta Culp Hobby, an anti–civil rights
Texan.

The problem with the Thurgood Marshall appointment was that Olin
Johnston had feared that if his Senate Judiciary Subcommittee approved it
before the South Carolina primary and sent it to the full committee, Governor Ernest Hollings, who was challenging him for his Senate seat, would
accuse him of cooperating with ultra-liberals. (Hollings did, anyway, even
though Johnston had sat on the nomination.) Next, James Eastland bottled
up the nomination in the full Judiciary Committee until Philip A. Hart,
Democrat of Michigan, and Kenneth Keating of New York pried it loose.
On September 11, 1962, the full Senate, after a four-hour debate dominated by southern opponents, confirmed Marshall, 54 to 16.

Mitchell particularly praised Senator John Carroll of Colorado for helping in this struggle by challenging the dilatory tactics that the opposition
was using. He joined Hart and Keating in declaring an intention to take
the unusual step of moving on the Senate floor to discharge the committee
if the opposition continued, and successfully sought to have misstatements
about Marshall's record corrected. [14]

Economic and legal persecutions also took a new twist in 1961 when
federal agencies connived with local officials to silence NAACP leaders—a
development that embarrassed the Kennedy administration. The most notorious case involved Wesley W. Law, president of the Georgia State Conference of NAACP Branches and a letter carrier for the Savannah Post
Office. Mitchell's campaign against persistent discrimination in the Post
Office Department and to exonerate Law demonstrated the difficulty he was
still experiencing with federal agencies as well as another limitation of executive action.

Law, a twelve-year Post Office veteran, continued to register African
Americans to vote and to lead a successful fifteen-month boycott of local
businesses who practiced racial discrimination despite his earlier having
been the target of an unsuccessful administrative charge concerning his personal conduct and a related departmental investigation. In the 1960 con-

gressional campaign, G. Elliott Hagan, a candidate, referring to Law, promised that "if I was a member of Congress, there is one particular NAACP bigwig right here in Savannah who would cease to work for the United States Post Office." Elected, Hagan was named to the House Post Office and Civil Service Committee and kept his word. Law was charged with five counts of administrative misconduct such as loitering on his route. The Civil Service Committee staff director admitted to Mitchell that despite being advised that the charges against Law "were so flimsy they would be thrown out by the Civil Service Commission," Hagan directed that they be filed.

Mitchell's early appeals to Post Office officials in Washington and other attempts to save Law's job were to no avail. Law was dismissed on September 15, intensifying the struggle through the press and in the Senate. While Law appealed his dismissal to the Civil Service Commission in Atlanta with the help of NAACP attorneys, Mitchell, who thought Law's dismissal was "an incredible abuse of federal authority," enlisted the support of his friend New Jersey Republican Senator Case. The NAACP board of directors also urged President Kennedy to rescind the dismissal. The NAACP told Kennedy that African Americans had suffered "savage economic reprisals" in the South for their campaign for full constitutional rights, "but it has remained for a department in the executive branch of the Kennedy Administration to permit the employment of the might of the U.S. Government in such mean endeavors." The NAACP said that if the federal government had become a partner in economic reprisal against one of its employees exercising his right to seek redress of "notorious grievances suffered by his racial group then we have come, as a nation, to a low estate, indeed."

Addressing the National Alliance of Postal Employees, Mitchell called for Kennedy to halt immediately Law's "persecution" and for reforms to prevent such abuses. A good place to begin, he said, was with the Postal Inspection Service. He felt that that was "one of the most discriminatory of all government agencies." He noted that all of the department's nearly one thousand inspectors were white. Elsewhere, there were a few black supervisors and "a very light sprinkle of colored employees in top jobs, but the great majority of" blacks were still letter carriers, clerks, or custodial workers, "even though many of them are more capable of running local post offices than some of the people who hold those positions." He was "glad to see the ice broken here and there" in big cities like Chicago, Cleveland, New York, and Baltimore. "But this is the atomic age, not the ice age. We not only want a crack in the glacier that has frozen most of the colored people in the lower jobs, we want it melted completely so that our government can get the full benefit of services by all of its citizens."

Responding to a bland reply from the postmaster general to Senator Case's complaint about Law's dismissal, Mitchell told the Post Office head that, based on the documented evidence, "you have become a kind of partner in the system that grants special privileges to those who wish to wreak economic reprisals on pro-civil rights colored citizens who are employed in the Federal Government." Not only had the Post Office Department not acted in good faith, he said, but it was also guilty of deception in its handling of the case. It seemed to him "that the Postmaster General should be deeply ashamed that this kind of disgraceful happening" had soiled the record of the agency he headed.

After Law was reinstated, Mitchell told the *Washington Star* that had his ouster stuck, no federal employee in the South advocating civil rights would have been safe from "smear and dismissal." The following year, the Post Office Department further bowed to NAACP demands pressed by Law and ended Jim Crow restrooms in Savannah post offices. Mitchell also won assurances that Law's participation in picketing a local baseball stadium to protest segregation violated no regulations. Those capitulations were no more than dents in the department's discrimination armor, but at least the administration was made more aware of another side of the racial problem. [15]

In no other area during the Kennedy administration's early months was executive leadership tested more severely than in that of racism in the south, as, through the Justice Department, it responded to the horrendous deprivation of basic rights of blacks and to the brutal repression of non-violent direct action demonstrations. The national NAACP office directed all such complaints requiring federal help to Mitchell, thus placing the Washington Bureau at the center of this struggle.

The pressure to enforce Reconstruction-era civil rights laws and the 1957 and 1960 Civil Rights acts had intensified during the final year of the Eisenhower administration. Mitchell thought that the Civil Rights Division had gotten off to a bad start under Assistant Attorney General Wilson White, who had become disillusioned because the Senate Judiciary Committee had held up his nomination, but he was much encouraged by the dedication of White's successor Harold Tyler in the few months before Eisenhower left office.

Mitchell complained, in a speech delivered to the staff of the Civil Rights Division of the Justice Department on May 17, 1960, the sixth anniversary of the *Brown* decision, that African Americans in the South not only had no faith in the region's law enforcement machinery, but they were also losing faith in the federal government's willingness to protect them. He said that that need not have been so because there were many southern whites who were willing to accept the doctrine of equality under the law. Because very few of those whites held office, he stressed, the Justice Department was "the chief bulwark between law and chaos" in the region.

As an example, Mitchell recalled that one recent Sunday while he was in Meridian, Mississippi, attending an NAACP meeting at a church, someone suddenly announced, "It has happened in Mississippi. Blood is flowing in Biloxi because blacks are trying to use the beach." They were attacked by whites with clubs, blackjacks, and chains when they challenged segregation along the Gulf of Mexico. When it appeared that the blacks, regrouping, might defend themselves, law enforcement officers, who had been standing by passively, moved in and arrested several of the victims. The NAACP group was very tense.

To provide immediate assurance that help was imminent, Mitchell went into the pastor's study and called Washington. He managed to reach a top FBI official who promised to take action at once against the violence. The following day upon returning to Washington, he began working with Tyler to end segregation at public beaches. Tyler discovered that the handle to that problem was an agreement with Mississippi that the beaches would be open to the public without segregation. The agreement had been adopted during the New Deal when the federal government provided Works Progress Administration funds to help rebuild a twenty-four-mile stretch of beach along the Gulf of Mexico after a devastating hurricane. The Justice Department announced on the same day that Mitchell addressed its staff that it had filed a lawsuit against Harrison County and Biloxi charging breach of contract because they had violated the terms of New Deal agreement by failing to desegregate the beach. Eastland delayed a decision on the suit by having a Mississippi judge place it at the bottom of the docket. Nevertheless, Tyler discovered, "the fact that we filed suit down there had a great impact." Eastland, Tyler says, gave him "hell, Columbia." Despite the delay, the suit had an enormous impact, because the federal government to date had done so little to protect the rights of blacks. Mitchell assured Tyler that although he might not yet have won, the fact that the suit had been initiated was good progress. Again Tyler sang his praises. "I just don't want to underestimate that quality of his."

Mitchell redoubled the attack. He obtained from the Department of Agriculture a list of recreational areas in the South that had been built with federal assistance and distributed it to NAACP branches so that they too could initiate desegregation action. The Leadership Conference on Civil Rights later recommended the use of that approach to end segregation at airports receiving assistance under the Federal Airport Act. But, in reality, the process was much too slow. In 1963 the Biloxi and Gulfport NAACP branches, impatient that the beaches were still segregated, would have to stage another wade-in that would be just as violently resisted and cause more injuries.

Mitchell told his Justice Department audience that in 1955 the NAACP Washington Bureau had suggested that the biggest obstacle to federal action in the South was Justice's adherence to outdated civil rights policies. Where there was a concurrent jurisdiction, Justice deferred to states and thus got no action. The department was reluctant to initiate a civil rights case unless there was a reasonable assurance of success. Civil rights cases were begun only by indictment, which meant that most cases were "washed out in the secrecy of a grand jury room." He said that it was possible under the law to prosecute a nonfelony case "on information," thus bypassing the grand jury. Even if the case was dismissed in open court, at least an honest attempt to convict would have been made and the facts disclosed. Although use of the "on information" approach in civil rights cases was rare, he said, it had been used in *Catlette* v. *United States,* a case in which the Justice Department had won conviction against a West Virginia sheriff for having permitted violence against a group of Jehovah's Witnesses.

Tyler's cooperation notwithstanding, Mitchell said, the Kennedy administration was continuing its predecessor's outmoded policies. He believed that it was ironic that the "great barrier to protection" of minorities by the federal government was the jury system, which was supposed to be a shield against unfair convictions and false imprisonment. "Instead, throughout almost one third of the nation it has been used as an umbrella to protect wrongdoers against the storms of public indignation that arise when there are flagrant violations of civil rights such as the murders of Emmett Till and Mack Parker." (Parker, accused of raping a white woman, was seized from his Poplarville, Mississippi, jail cell by a mob forty-eight hours before he was scheduled to go on trial in 1959. His bullet-riddled body was found in the nearby Pearl River. A grand jury refused to consider the FBI's voluminous report or to acknowledge that a lynching had occurred within its jurisdiction.) On the other hand, Mitchell told the Justice Department staffers, the most positive results of the NAACP's strenuous demand for federal action had been the call from the U.S. Civil Rights Commission for appointment of federal registrars to supersede state officials who refused to register black voters.

From the time he had first come to Washington in 1941, Mitchell went on, the Justice Department's policy had been to refrain "from prosecuting certain civil rights cases under the criminal law because it was thought that grand juries would not indict no matter who was the victim and no matter how terrible the crime." If "by some miracle a grand jury returned an indictment in a civil rights case," it was thought that a trial jury would not hand down a conviction. Administrations might change, he said, "new faces may appear on the law enforcement scene," but Justice's policy on criminal prosecutions for civil rights violations "was still tied to the same old hitching post on the New Frontier."[16]

The agenda that Mitchell had outlined to Harold Tyler and Maceo Hubbard in their September 1960 meeting, plus the concerns the lobbyist had expressed to the Civil Rights Division's staff in his May 1960 speech, set the stage for an early 1961 comprehensive review by the Leadership Conference on Civil Rights of the Justice Department's role in protecting African Americans and civil rights demonstrators in the region and in promoting equality of opportunity. Justice's responsibility involved enforcing existing laws; drafting new legislation and executive orders; advising other agencies and setting the tone for the executive branch on civil rights; and leading the struggle in the courts to vindicate the constitutional rights of the oppressed.

The Leadership Conference's review noted that segregation continued despite *Brown* and several subsequent cases* in which the Supreme Court left no doubt that laws requiring racial separation were unconstitutional. Yet less than 7 percent of black children were attending integrated public schools in segregated jurisdictions, blacks were being arrested in Georgia and Mississippi for refusing to ride in the back of public carriers, and they were also being attacked with clubs and police dogs for using public libraries.

The Leadership Conference, in addition to applauding the administration's earlier school desegregation initiatives, called for more voting rights suits in an effort to increase dramatically the number of African American voters before the 1962 primaries; the strengthening of the department's Civil Rights Division's staff and procedures; and adoption of new techniques, such as those used in Biloxi and in the Prince Edward County case where the government, narrowly interpreting the law, sought to protect the dignity of the federal court by enforcing the desegregation decision. The LCCR also suggested using the landmark theory upheld in the 1895 case brought against Socialist Eugene V. Debs and labor leaders to end a railroad strike that had disrupted mail service. The Supreme Court ruled in In re *Debs* that the federal government had inherent authority, despite the absence of a statute, to intervene to protect the general public interest before violence developed.[17]

The Kennedy administration's weak responses to the vicious May 14,

---

*Those cases barring segregation were *Holmes* v. *City of Atlanta,* 350 U.S. 879 (1955) (recreational facilities); *Detroit Housing Commission* v. *Lewis,* 226 F. Supp. 180 (1955) (public housing); *Browder* v. *Gayle,* 352 U.S. 903 (1956) (transportation); *Burton* v. *Wilmington Parking Authority,* 365 U.S. 715 (1961) (restaurants).

1961, Mother's Day attacks on the two busloads of CORE freedom riders in Anniston and Birmingham, Alabama, underscored the NAACP's and the LCCR's concerns. The following day, Wilkins and Mitchell, in a meeting with Robert Kennedy, stressed the need for massive government intervention against racial segregation in interstate travel and called for new civil rights legislation, especially resubmission of the 1957 Civil Rights Act's deleted Part III, in order to protect Fourteenth Amendment rights in the South. President Kennedy was then busy preparing for his approaching face-off with Premier Nikita Khrushchev of the Soviet Union and concentrating on potential sources of East-West tension and did not welcome the well-staged distraction. "Tell them to call it off," he ordered Special Assistant Harris Wofford. "Stop them," he said of the freedom rides. Wofford knew the futility of trying. Rather than providing the requested federal protection for demonstrators the NAACP had requested, the attorney general merely sent his administrative assistant John Seigenthaler to represent the federal government in meetings with Alabama officials about the tinderbox situation there and to observe the demonstrations. Robert Kennedy wanted the state and local police to assume their responsibility to protect the demonstrators and thus avoid the use of federal force. At the same time, Burke Marshall, Tyler's successor, tacitly conceded that new legislation was needed when he acknowledged that the Justice Department was unable to prevent the Mississippi police from arresting the freedom riders. "The legal limitations of the federal system are not understood by the civil rights leaders," he said. "The effect of that lack of understanding on their part and a corresponding lack of ability to act effectively and immediately on our part is going to create a series of problems over a long period of time until segregation is eliminated." Only after Seigenthaler was severely beaten in Montgomery did the administration order six hundred U.S. marshals and other armed officials to Alabama to protect the demonstrators. Mitchell said that the attack on Seigenthaler, a white southerner, was "a dramatic reminder that mobs do not show any discrimination in choosing their victims."

One precedent "that really set things back in Alabama a great deal," Burke Marshall discovered, "was the fact that the mob had been permitted to thwart" Autherine Lucy's constitutional rights in 1956 when she attempted to enroll at the University of Alabama. The Eisenhower administration had done nothing about it. Marshall discovered that many blacks in Alabama were very concerned that the federal government not repeat such a mistake because it would have meant the death of the civil rights movement.

Seeking protection for the demonstrators, the Justice Department had filed a federal lawsuit to enjoin the Ku Klux Klan, the National States

Rights party, and other persons from interfering with interstate travel. It also petitioned the Interstate Commerce Commission to issue regulations against segregation in interstate bus transportation. Attorney General Kennedy said that the lack of such rules had caused "confusion on the part of motor carriers as to their duty to their passengers" as well as contributed to unrest and disorder. Thus the South had continued to defy the Constitution as much in the area of interstate transportation as in education, despite Supreme Court rulings, in 1946 (*Morgan* v. *Virginia*), that a Virginia statute requiring segregation on carriers could not be applied to interstate travel; in 1956 (*Browder* v. *Gayle*), affirming a three-judge federal appellate court decision that intrastate bus segregation in Alabama violated the due process clause of the Fourteenth Amendment, thus clearing the way for a triumphant end of the Montgomery bus boycott; and in 1960, that the Interstate Commerce Act prohibited segregation in bus terminal restaurants serving interstate passengers. (The 1955 Interstate Commerce Commission ban against segregation of passengers on trains and buses and at railroad terminals had omitted bus terminals.)

Furthermore, while acknowledging the state's responsibility to cope with violence, Governor John Patterson of Alabama incited resistance by denouncing the freedom riders as "rabble rousers," threatening to arrest the U.S. marshals who had been assigned to protect the demonstrators, and obtaining an injunction in state courts in conflict with the federal injunction.

Had Mitchell not successfully opposed repeated efforts by the southern states to nullify the 1954 *Brown* decision with legislation making federal laws inapplicable in cases of concurrent jurisdiction where the federal laws did not specifically overrule state statutes, the South now would have had the upper hand. (Commenting on the most recent states' rights attempt in Congress that spring, Mitchell wrote Congressman Kenneth J. Gray that already there was evidence of "bizarre possibilities" of such efforts: *"Alabama concocted a procedure that resulted in the daily arrest of a bus station manager because he obeyed the federal requirement. Mississippi segregated the public sidewalks in front of terminal buildings. Any colored person using the sidewalk to enter what was formerly the white waiting room was subject to arrest, fine and imprisonment. Similar treatment was given to white persons who attempted to enter the former colored waiting room"* [italics Mitchell's]. Thus the administration had been more than forewarned about the level of resistance in the South.)[18]

The Kennedy administration's sending of six hundred federal marshals into Birmingham in response to the crisis that Governor Patterson had helped to create compared hauntingly with Eisenhower's confrontation with mob violence during the 1957 desegregation of Little Rock Central High

School. The administration used the same 1871 statute that Eisenhower had employed as the basis for its action. The statute provided for the President to use the armed forces or other representatives of his authority to suppress insurrection and anarchic behavior that deprived a class of citizens of their constitutional rights. Mitchell, with the NAACP's legal victories like that which ended segregation on buses in Montgomery in mind, defended the freedom riders by explaining that they were merely doing what the Supreme Court "said they have a right to do."

Inherent in Mitchell's stand, which was reinforced by the Leadership Conference on Civil Rights, was a serious difference with the Kennedy administration's priorities and strategy that went well beyond legislation. The crux of this difference was that Mitchell felt strongly that the demonstrations in the South demanded forthright, aggressive leadership from the executive branch in order to protect the rights of minorities, and the administration was not prepared to give such leadership. One reason, of course, was the administration's unfamiliarity with the depth of southern racism, and the equally deep determination of blacks to end the injustices bred by that racism. Attorney General Kennedy, for example, had confessed to a newspaper reporter that he had not been lying awake at nights thinking about racial issues. It was a new subject for him. As with much of the nation, the sit-ins and freedom rides had opened the administration's eyes for the first time to the endemic nature of the South's caste system.

A second reason was that, anxious about preserving his political ties in the South, an insecure President Kennedy studiously attempted to negotiate solutions with political leaders like Governor Patterson, who had supported him in 1960. In so doing the administration depended on political negotiations with leaders more sensitive to local emotions than national imperatives. The President and attorney general wanted local political leaders to assume responsibility for resolving racial problems. Officials like Patterson, however, when they were not race-baiting and exploiting the turmoil, were looking for the least costly way out of their problems. Mitchell wanted the administration to employ political negotiations to garner support for strong, no-nonsense executive leadership.[19]

The dynamite bombings of three black churches in Birmingham in January 1962 caused Mitchell to intensify demands that the Justice Department use the 1960 Civil Rights Act to protect civil rights workers in the South. When Burke Marshall at first responded that "matters of this kind fall within the primary jurisdiction of local law enforcement authorities," and that Justice would only provide the "technical facilities" of the FBI to the Birmingham Police Department, which was conducting the investigation, Mitchell told him that his interpretation of the law was incorrect. Mitchell said the 1960 act specifically established concurrent jurisdiction and made it a federal crime to transport explosives across state lines in order to damage buildings.* Those provisions, which could be used in the Birmingham-area church bombings, created a presumption of violation of federal law similar to that found in the effective statute on kidnappings.

As proof that Marshall's interpretation was not supported by the law's legislative history, Mitchell recalled for him Kenneth Keating's explanation on the Senate floor that if another series of racially inspired bombings developed, "under this amendment we would be certain that the full resources of the FBI would be brought into action against such offenders in whatever community such an incident occurred." The Senate had adopted the Keating amendment without debate, Mitchell explained. Had Congress intended only the limited use of the FBI that Marshall suggested, Mitchell said, the statute created by the Keating amendment "would have been an empty gesture," since the FBI's technical facilities were already available to local authorities. Mitchell further noted that Attorney General Rogers, in his testimony in 1959, explained that in cases of hate bombs, the FBI had cooperated fully with local authorities when requested. Rogers had referred to a section† of the 1960 act that covered interstate flight of persons participating in bombings. Congress then went a step further and adopted the Keating amendment to grant the Justice Department full authority to deal with those crimes.

Marshall promptly responded that he had intended to state it was his department's "practice to initiate Federal investigations in appropriate circumstances." But that assurance was much too little and too late. By then, other bombings were occurring with sickening frequency—in February alone, against religious leaders in California, and in Mississippi against NAACP activists.

Mitchell felt that the Justice Department also was not using available Reconstruction-era statutes‡ "any more vigorously" than had previous administrations in cases of police brutality against African Americans. In most cases, no attempt was even made to prosecute. He believed that the problem remained one of the FBI's deferral to local authorities (especially since many agents were from the areas to which they were assigned), a process that sometimes even permitted the release of information so that defendants could plan their defense.[20]

In terms of the social climate, Mitchell was troubled that Kennedy was

---

*Title 18 of the U.S. Code, Section 837, was added to the Criminal Code by Section 203 of the 1960 Civil Rights Act. Subsection (b) of Section 837 made it a federal crime to transport by interstate commerce explosives with intent to use them to damage any building used for religious or other purposes. Subsection (c) provided that the use of explosives to damage any building created a presumption of interstate transportation.
†Section 201.
‡Such as Title 18, Section 242 of the U.S. Code.

not much ahead of Eisenhower on civil rights. Since the Roosevelt administration, Truman, Eisenhower, and now Kennedy had taken progressively stronger steps on civil rights. Each President felt encouraged by his predecessor's actions to move more forthrightly ahead. Under Kennedy, a desegregation trend in social areas was more firmly established and pushed in 1962. But neither Eisenhower nor Kennedy was willing to take any action that matched the political risks of Truman's initiatives. Eisenhower had, indeed, permitted his attorney general, Herbert Brownell, to lead the administration on civil rights legislation. That initiative was within specific limits. Now, not only was Kennedy dragging his feet on legislation, but he was also doing so in the area of executive leadership. To its credit, the administration showed no hesitancy or weakness in providing such leadership in situations where it felt secure. Those included court actions involving voting rights and school desegregation, and filing the petition with the Interstate Commerce Commission that resulted in the ruling that bus companies could not use segregated terminals. Then in city after city the Justice Department took steps to remove Jim Crow signs at railroad, airport, and bus terminals. That was a significant victory for the freedom riders that was similar in impact to the SCLC's Montgomery bus boycott.

Mitchell knew that there was no doubt within the Justice Department that the mass arrests of freedom riders in Jackson, Mississippi, following the violence in Alabama in 1961 were unconstitutional. They were a police action aimed at enforcing segregation, which was prohibited by federal law; thus they violated the Constitution's supremacy clause, and the Fourteenth Amendment. Nevertheless, Justice acquiesced in their arrest. Robert Kennedy told Senator James Eastland that "my primary interest was they weren't beaten up." Based on the federal process, arrested demonstrators still had to contest the validity of the police action through a lengthy court process. Once more, had the administration demonstrated a willingness to confront southern officials over the protection of the demonstrators by stationing federal marshals in Jackson from the time the first bus arrived, Mississippi authorities probably would not have so brazenly violated federal laws and the Constitution. Robert Kennedy was angry that James Farmer and Martin Luther King had spurned his request to call off the freedom rides and a proposed arrangement to get the demonstrators out of jail. Their determination to use their bodies to right a wrong, he told King, "is not going to have the slightest effect on what the government is going to do in this field or any other."

Mitchell complained that President Kennedy still chose to act "in a way which will maintain a consensus" on the issue. It was obvious that the administration, in consideration of "the public interest," did not plan to move too fast—that is, Kennedy did not want to hurt other programs in

Congress he thought were more important to the nation. The President's foot-dragging caused Congressman John Lindsay of New York to deplore the President's "abandonment of solemn pledges" and to urge immediate issuance of the executive order in housing that he had promised. Kennedy still maintained that within his first twelve months in office he had made more progress on civil rights than had been achieved in the previous eight years—a pace that he felt would "advance this cause." Whether that was so or not, Mitchell was convinced that he did not understand the urgency of the problem.

Mitchell continued to urge the Justice Department to change its policy on protecting civil rights activists so that it would at least expose violence like that involving the beating of Vera Pigee, an NAACP leader, by law enforcement officers in Clarksdale, Mississippi, in December 1961, for using a service station restroom. Despite the dismal "no jurisdiction" or "no prosecution" responses from Justice, he persisted in submitting complaints in order to build a record of inaction to help his drive for civil rights legislation. Furthermore, he felt that the Justice Department should promptly rectify its failure to use the then nearly two-year-old voting referee provision of the 1960 Civil Rights Act in the interests of southern blacks.[21]

Joseph Rauh, hammering on the administration just as much, typically provided a different perspective on the battle by suggesting that Kennedy could "go to bed and thank goodness for the fact that there was an ADA and there were people who were criticizing him from the liberal side." He said that "Kennedy might wake up one day and be the most liberal element in the country. That would be the most difficult position for a President— to be far-out liberal." Criticism from both ends of the spectrum, he said, left the President somewhere in the center where he could obtain broader support.

The extremely volatile confrontations in 1962 in Albany, Georgia, that resulted in arrests of more than three hundred demonstrators in the last three weeks of July, bringing the total in custody since the previous October to over eleven hundred, became the topic of another meeting on August 2 of Robert Kennedy with Marshall, Wilkins, Mitchell, and SCLC and CORE representatives. The mass demonstrations, demanding an end to segregation and the denial of voting rights, were led by the Reverend Dr. King and the Albany Movement. The NAACP leaders told the Justice Department officials that the Albany violence was merely symptomatic of problems elsewhere in Terrell County, Georgia; Spartanburg, South Carolina; and throughout Alabama, Louisiana, and Mississippi. Each case was a "potential powder keg." It was only happenstance that Albany was now making headlines. The NAACP leaders said the time had come "to stop dousing individual blazes" and to institute "a program of total fire preven-tion." Nonviolent direct action had failed to break down racial barriers in Albany because it was confronted with an unyielding power structure.

In a memorandum submitted at the August 2 meeting, the NAACP recommended that (1) because "a great part of the trouble" in the South was due to the "unmitigated contempt" of local law enforcement officers for the rights of African Americans, the Justice Department seek to bypass grand juries when taking actions against such persons as the Albany sheriff, who had boasted of his brutal assault on a black attorney representing civil rights defendants, a strategy that would hopefully arouse the public's con-science and increase convictions; (2) the Justice Department help prosecute private suits filed locally by the NAACP on behalf of victims in Albany; (3) the administration seek ways around the impasse over the 1957 Civil Rights Act's deleted Part III and file suits based on that principle in order to protect constitutional rights and desegregate public facilities in Albany, gain release of jailed demonstrators, and bar future arrests; (4) where Justice found that it could not implement any of these goals, the attorney general inform the President of the need for additional laws and urge him to bring the problem to the nation. Because Albany derived considerable economic benefit from a nearby Air Force base and Marine Corps supply center, the NAACP also recommended that the President withdraw those facilities un-less civil rights demands were met.

Only when Mitchell bitterly criticized the Justice Department did the youthful, boyish-looking Kennedy, with his shirt sleeves rolled up as he sat ill at ease and very distracted with the group of blacks in the elegant office that appropriately symbolized his power, show some animation by respond-ing sharply, "You know as well as I do, Clarence, that we have done what we can do under existing law. We could do a great deal more if our hands weren't tied."

The day before Mitchell and Wilkins had met with Kennedy, ten law-makers representing the heart of Mitchell's bipartisan coalition in the Sen-ate had met with Burke Marshall on the Albany problem and requested that the Justice Department conduct an investigation "into any offense against the persons of those involved." They were Republicans Javits, Keat-ing, Case, Kuchel, and Hugh Scott, and Democrats Paul Douglas, Joseph S. Clark of Pennsylvania, Philip Hart and Pat McNamara of Michigan, and Humphrey.

Mitchell subsequently wrote to Javits and the other senators discussing the meetings that he and the senators had had with Robert Kennedy. Re-garding point 1 of the August 2 NAACP memorandum, he reported that the assistant attorney general had informed him that the Justice Depart-ment had just filed an "information suit" in a New Orleans case to implement the recommendation he had made in his address on May 17. Even though he received no pledge that the administration would do the same in Albany, Mitchell felt it was encouraging to see Justice using that procedure, which bypassed the grand jury.

On point 2, Mitchell, not wanting to appear presumptuous, assured the senators that the NAACP's recommendation, which was similar to one the lawmakers had made to Justice in their meeting on August 1, was not meant to overshadow their initiative and take credit for "any action that the Department has taken or may take in this respect." He said he hoped they would "give careful consideration" to the NAACP memorandum's points 3 and 4 concerning the need for civil action by the Justice Department in order to protect constitutional rights in addition to the right to vote. He referred them to a book by Robert Carr, *Federal Protection of Civil Rights,* which documented "an historical built-in reluctance to take action under the existing criminal statutes." He stressed that there was "nothing to indicate that this policy of being highly selective and extremely cautious in using the criminal statutes has changed."

In his letter, Mitchell also commended the Kennedy administration for accelerating, though insufficiently, civil action on voting complaints and gave it "an accolade for its efforts in attacking racial segregation in transportation and other fields." There was considerable agreement, he said, among civil rights lawyers that the President had authority under existing executive powers to direct the attorney general to protect basic constitutional rights in the courts without specific legislative authority. The attorney general in their August 2 meeting had indicated that the Justice Department was "at least exploring its chances for successful application of this theory to specific cases." However, he went on, "there was a flat refusal to apply it" as the NAACP had suggested in its memorandum. He cited a very recent case of a white Mississippi lawyer representing four black college students who was detained with his clients by the police for nineteen hours. "When we reported this matter to the Department, we were advised that it had no authority to move to compel the release of the prisoners."

Similarly, he found "it impossible to see how any rational observer of the American scene could understand why the National Government tolerates the illegal arrest and continued imprisonment of the Reverend Martin Luther King" in Albany. Even though King was promptly released on bail, Mitchell felt that such an injustice to the internationally recognized leader only stirred up new anti-American feelings abroad. The NAACP's records, he explained, contained many more examples of similar constitutional violations. He cited as another example his own arrest without specific charge in Florence, South Carolina, in 1956.[22]

President Kennedy's response to calls that he do something about the

Albany crisis was merely that he found "wholly inexplicable" the Albany City Commission's prolonged refusal to negotiate with black leaders in the southwest Georgia city. "The United States government is involved in sitting down at Geneva with the Soviet Union," he said. "I can't understand why the government of Albany—the City Council of Albany—cannot do the same for American citizens." He pledged "to attempt as we have in the past to try to provide a satisfactory solution for the protection of the constitutional rights of the people of Albany, and we will continue to do so." The President refused to meet with more than one hundred white and black ministers who marched to the White House demanding "a positive official stand on the moral and ethical issues" in the Albany conflict. Thus, he had tied his own hands even as he wanted sincerely to see the problem resolved.

Meanwhile, Albany officials sought a federal injunction banning mass civil rights demonstrations, contending that they had created an explosive situation. Besides responding that it was "in constant touch" with the situation, the Justice Department filed an amicus curiae brief opposing Albany's request for the injunction. But the federal judge granted it anyway.

From the obvious failure of the Albany protests, Mitchell learned an important lesson—that those who wished to obtain justice must plan their strategy "in terms of final solution in the courts. It may be that common sense will prevail and the diehard opposition will yield without a showdown in a given situation, but all must consider what will be done in the usual situation, where the opposition does not crumble until it is ordered to do so." He prayed that Kennedy would help end the crisis and called for African Americans to increase their political might so that they could combine legal strength with the power of the vote. He observed that the election of liberal officials usually meant that the courts would also be liberal.[23]

Mitchell's subsequent expression of outrage over the Justice Department's posturing in the face of "anarchy" in LeFlore County, Mississippi—the "worst offender"—was equally applicable to Albany. "I think Justice has its political theory mixed up," he said of its resistance to protecting civil rights demonstrators. A federal system of government was supposed to provide for division into national, state, and local governments. "But in LeFlore you don't have government," he charged. Neither was any being provided by the state. So it had to come from the federal government.

Martin Luther King subsequently showed with his demonstrations in Birmingham that moral force, when it was sufficiently aroused, could provide a powerful political incentive for action. But Mitchell believed that nonviolent direct action provided only temporary results. Ultimately, Albany and Birmingham reaffirmed for Mitchell the need for permanent protections for the rights of minorities through "uncompromising and persistent legal action in the courts" and effective legislation in Congress.

In another letter to Keating, whose help Mitchell had also enlisted in an attempt to push the administration to investigate the beatings of blacks trying to use the public library in Jackson, Mississippi, Mitchell noted that the Magnolia State led "a charmed life," as far as the Justice Department was concerned. Owing to Justice's position that the wanton brutality that had occurred at the Jackson library (and in countless other instances) failed "to establish violation of civil rights statutes," Mitchell urged Keating to use his position on the Senate Judiciary Committee to have Congress "demand that the Department state what additional legislation it needs to meet this kind of disgraceful occurrence."

Mitchell was equally incensed when Governor Ross Barnett "and a supine Mississippi legislature" declared war on the United States" that September by blocking the admission of James Meredith to the Jim Crow University of Mississippi at Oxford in 1962. Medgar Evers, NAACP field secretary for Mississippi, who eight years earlier had tried unsuccessfully to enroll there, received vicarious satisfaction from meeting this unyielding challenge as he counseled Meredith.

The physical confrontation was the climax of an intense legal struggle that had begun on May 31, 1961, when Constance Baker Motley, one of Thurgood Marshall's sharp young NAACP Inc. Fund attorneys, filed a federal suit to have Meredith admitted. Barnett's personal obstruction set the stage for another bloody federal-state confrontation after his secret negotiations with President Kennedy broke down. The crux of the problem was that Barnett believed the Constitution stopped at the Tenth Amendment, which reserved to the states all powers not specifically delegated to the federal government. So he maintained: "Mississippi, as a sovereign state, has determined for itself what the federal Constitution has reserved for it." Bloody warfare was therefore inevitable as Barnett made a last-ditch stand to maintain "our way of life." He called on "every public official and every private citizen of our great state to join with me in refusing in every legal and constitutional way, and every manner and way available, to submit to the illegal usurpation of power by the President of the United States." With this flourish, he ignited the segregation pyre that Eastland, Vardaman, Bilbo, and all the other fire-breathing race-baiters had built throughout the state's history.

Mitchell praised Senators Keating and Douglas for introducing a resolution showing "the world that our government is united in defending the judicial process" being used to integrate the university. He urged lawmakers in all the former Confederate states except Mississippi to cosponsor the resolution. At the same time, Attorney General Kennedy finally acknowledged that the blocking of Meredith's enrollment was "one aspect of our largest and most important domestic problem—the problem of assur-

ing the civil rights of all." Like Eisenhower, President Kennedy this time
was pushed to use troops to uphold a court order to advance desegregation
rather than taking the initiative himself. While doing so, he made his first
nationwide appeal on civil rights.[24]

Rauh then was celebrating another civil liberties victory. Three days
before Christmas, Robert Kennedy called to inform him in what Rauh
remembered was "a weepy conversation," that "your boy's on a bus on his
way home" from Lewisburg penitentiary. That referred to Junius Scales,
the son of a former South Carolina governor who was the last Communist
left in prison under the Smith Act. He had been convicted for being a
member of the Communist party. Right after Scales had received a six-year
prison sentence on October 2, 1961, Rauh launched a campaign for his
release. He would have succeeded earlier, but J. Edgar Hoover had objected
because Scales refused to reveal the names of others whom he had brought
into the Communist party. Scales had renounced his red ties after the Soviets invaded Hungary, but that was not enough for the FBI and the House
Un-American Activities Committee. Rauh kept after the attorney general,
however, until he obtained a Christmas commutation from the President.
His release without his "cooperation [by] 'naming names' is a repudiation
of the loyalty test," trumpeted Rauh. For the first time since the advent of
McCarthyism, he said, "the attorney general has refused to treat a man's
unwillingness to inform on others as a ground for withholding favorable
governmental action in his case." Further underscoring a style that differed
markedly from Mitchell's, Rauh would campaign in New York for Robert
Kennedy in the Senate race against Keating to show his gratitude for the
attorney general's opposing Hoover. Mitchell would continue supporting
Keating because of his strong civil rights record.

In January 1963, the "Report on Mississippi" by the Mississippi Advisory Committee to the U.S. Commission on Civil Rights vindicated
Mitchell's concerns for justice in the South. Despite the considerable progress that had been made under the Kennedy administration, the committee found, the extent and manner of denials of equal protection of the law
to African Americans was "a profound shock." It confirmed that in all
important areas of citizenship African Americans in the state received substantially less than was due them. It reinforced the complaints of local
NAACP leaders like Medgar Evers, that the federal government was not
protecting everyone equally. Although the Justice Department had acted in
good faith, it said, its interpretation of the Civil Rights Division's role was
"unduly and unwisely narrow and limited." That weakness, which resulted
in police officers rarely being tried for civil rights violations, had led the

public to believe that few serious charges were ever made. The belief was also reinforced among peace officers that they could mistreat blacks at will.

The committee therefore recommended that the President direct the Justice Department to conduct more thorough investigations of brutality allegations and to institute criminal proceedings regardless of prospects for conviction. It also recommended further exposure of denials of equal protection of the law in the state through hearings and that the Civil Rights Commission recommend that Congress pass more legislation to protect citizens from the abuses it had found.

The report confirmed Mitchell's belief that the major problems with the Kennedy administration were its limited perception of the nature of black oppression in the South and its inability to understand the true meaning of the civil rights movement, which was now just reaching its prolonged peak and would continue to overshadow many of the President's priorities.[25]

Mitchell's general impression of President Kennedy was that his eagerness to "do things for a great many people in the country in the area of social problems" took precedence over civil rights "in any form." So "he was reluctant to do anything" on civil rights legislation. But "we were going to create a furor either in legislation or in executive action," as was demonstrated by the long struggle over the executive order on housing. Mitchell never thought that Kennedy "was reluctant because of the merits" of the order. Furthermore, Mitchell agreed that when pressing foreign policy issues confronting Kennedy were weighed against domestic problems, "you couldn't quarrel with his judgment" in giving so much attention to external problems at the expense of civil rights, because "he had all the facts" before him and was duty-bound to act in the best interest of the country. But Mitchell still felt "that the Democratic Party is a kind of a close confederation of warring tribes, some of whom are ready to fight and die about the race question." President Kennedy, too, was acting in the "interest of party harmony."[26]

CHAPTER SIXTEEN

Honing Political Support

The following is one of Mitchell's "From the Work Bench" columns in 1961.

Jackson, Miss.—When the visitor's plane is a speck in the sky bound for civilization again, Medgar Evers, field secretary of the NAACP in this state, returns to his strange world where policemen would rather club colored heads than hit golf balls. Dogs are trained to bite colored preachers instead of crooks.

Thinking of Mr. Evers and his fine family makes the blood pressure rise when some high placed public official or some demagogue trying to please a crowd makes the charge that colored people of the South are not showing enough interest in civil rights.

Mr. Evers is a walking illustration of what happens when one attempts to live a normal life in Dixie. About a year ago he rode a bus from Georgia to Mississippi. He sat up front. At Meridian, Miss., the local police threatened to put him in jail. When he ignored the threats a hoodlum taxi driver boarded the bus and assaulted him. The taxi driver "got away and cannot be located by police" [was the subsequent explanation for not arresting him].

[On another occasion, when] a local judge handed out a fantastic sentence to a civil rights advocate who was arrested under what appeared to be trumped up charges, Mr. Evers expressed his indignation in a public statement. The judge promptly sentenced him to jail for contempt and that case is now on its way to the Mississippi Supreme Court. *

The simple visit by Tougaloo College students to a public library in Jackson on March 27 [1961] provoked a series of events that underline the unbelievable problems in Mississippi. Most American cities are working hard to get young people to use public libraries. But in Jackson, the students were jailed for "disturbing the peace."

The judge who later convicted them said he realized the evidence showed that the students were quiet, but he felt their presence created the possibility of trouble.

Mr. Evers had to stand on the sidewalk across from the court house during the trial because inside the colored section was filled and the police barred him from the white area. When he joined in applauding the students as they arrived, the police, regarding their support as a breach of peace, rushed into the crowd with swinging clubs.

Mr. Evers, one of the first persons they sought, was clubbed, and only a miracle saved him from being torn to shreds by a pair of police dogs.

Undaunted, that night he held a protest mass meeting. As blacks vented their grievances, the police, massed outside in front of the building, waited threateningly in a drenching rain.

The striking display of bravery by the blacks was reinforced by the unfazed conduct of Medgar and his wife Myrlie. They refused to be discouraged. Mr. Evers is a reminder that the South has many potential leaders with similarly great courage. If the government and the country back them up, they will succeed in cleaning up Dixie and making the region presentable for the eyes of the world.

"Under pressure of federal bayonets, urged on by the misdirected sympathies of the world," intoned Governor Benjamin G. Humphreys on November 20, 1865, "the people of Mississippi have abolished the institution of slavery. The Negro is free, whether we like it or not; we must realize that fact now and forever. To be free, however, does not make him a citizen, or entitle him to social or political equality with the white man."

Mississippi was Medgar Evers's home, the South his world: "It may

---

* The Mississippi Supreme court reversed Evers's $100 fine and twenty-day jail sentence.

sound funny, but I love the South. I don't choose to live anywhere else. There's land here, where a man can raise cattle, and I'm going to do that someday. There are lakes where a man can sink a hook and fight bass. There is room here for my children to play and grow, and become good citizens if the white man will let them." Therefore, rather than follow fellow blacks who left Decatur, the town of his birth, for the slums of Chicago and other northern cities, Medgar Evers reinforced his roots in the region. He was a World War II veteran who had survived the invasion of Normandy and was now engaged in a different kind of warfare. He was a member of the new generation of young, messianic civil rights leaders, and chose not only to improve life for his family and himself but also to lead the struggle against racial oppression, when to do so in Mississippi was tantamount to signing one's own death warrant.

Aptly dubbed the "closed society" by James W. Silver, the eminent University of Mississippi professor of history, the Magnolia State brooked no challenge, from whites or blacks, to its racial caste system. Roughly a quarter century after Mitchell and his generation had shaken Baltimore from its lethargy, Medgar Evers, as one of the tiny handful of Mississippians who dared to challenge his state's racial practices, assumed his place among the elite of elites. As the state field director for the NAACP, a member of the association's national, full-time staff, he symbolized at one and the same time the hope of Mississippi blacks for freedom and the white fear of racial change. Medgar Evers lived at the eye of the storm that centered on the orthodoxy of white supremacy—a powerful, degenerate force that was buttressed by religious fundamentalism and rationalized by the states' rights doctrine.

In personality and circumstance, Medgar, the third of four children of James and Jessie Evers, was an extension of Clarence Mitchell—hence their personal closeness. Mitchell was fourteen years older. Both men came from poor families but were never destitute. Like Mitchell, Evers was brought up in a home with love, where he learned early to respect hard work and to be God-fearing. Unlike Mitchell, he was not shielded by his parents and school from virulent racism. Medgar had to bear the hurt of hearing his father called "boy" by white men and to suffer similar insults as he grew older. He had to learn the art of surviving in a society where the wall of racial separation was forever reinforced by the likes of Senator Theodore Bilbo and his heir James Eastland, archetypal white supremacists.

For Evers, surviving did not mean surrender. To the contrary, the daily injustices he witnessed, such as the lynching of a friend's father when he was twelve years old, only increased his outrage. As a young salesman for the Magnolia Mutual Insurance Company, traveling from the palm-lined

Gulf Coast to the cotton-rich Delta, he became fully exposed to the system of human degradation throughout the state and witnessed the abject poverty and oppression of blacks on the plantations. An admirer of Kenya's Jomo Kenyatta and his Mau Mau anticolonial freedom fighters, he toyed for a while with the idea of using guerrilla tactics to spread terror. Friends counseled him against using such counterproductive tactics, but his son Darrell Kenyatta became in name his living reminder of the legendary leader and a symbol of the cause for which he was fighting. Soon after graduating from unaccredited Alcorn Agricultural and Mechanical College, he was drawn into the NAACP. He was converted to utilizing democratic means to achieve change, although, like Mitchell, he never forswore the right of self-defense.

Magnolia Mutual was created by T.R.M. Howard, who was also founder of a medical clinic in the all-black Mound Bayou township in the Delta, as well as of the United Order of Friendship, a fraternal group, and of the Regional Council of Negro Leadership, a civic group. Through the Regional Council, Evers met and began working with Dr. Aaron Henry, a young pharmacist from Clarksdale who was the group's secretary. It was then that Henry, with the council's help, organized the Clarksdale NAACP branch as his civil rights power base.

During his tenure with Magnolia Mutual, Evers sold NAACP memberships to instill hope in the oppressed and fulfill his desire to wage holy war against Jim Crow. His ties with the NAACP were formalized after a meeting in early spring 1954 with Henry and Roy Wilkins in the home of Dr. Emmett J. Stringer in Columbia. Stringer was a dentist who was president of his hometown NAACP branch, as well as of the Mississippi State Conference of NAACP branches. At that time, it was difficult to find anyone who was willing to accept the job of NAACP Mississippi field secretary. Evers, a lanky, sandy-haired six-footer, a few weeks earlier had demonstrated the type of bravery that had won him two medals in World War II for participating in the Normandy invasion and the campaign in northern France, when he challenged one of his state's sacred institutions. NEGRO APPLIES TO ENTER OLE MISS, ran the chilling headline across the front page of the *Jackson Advocate*. The following day, the state Board of Trustees of Institutions of Higher Learning announced that nothing would be done about the application, so Evers was never admitted. That setback, which ended his chance to enter the University of Mississippi School of Law, only strengthened his resolve. He never relinquished his dream of lowering all racial barriers in the state. That was why he later encouraged and counseled James Meredith as he braved the raging violence to desegregate Ole Miss. Evers's watchword was "We have to make sacrifices to make progress."

He joined the NAACP staff just as the struggle was entering its most dangerous and prolonged stage, as a result of the South's uprising against the Supreme Court's *Brown* v. *Board of Education* decision. For the first time, Mississippi blacks were forced to choose sides in the new battle against segregation. Blacks wanted to know where other blacks stood.

Three elements symbolized this regrouping. One was composed of Evers and other people like Henry, Stringer, Howard, and another indomitable NAACP activist, Dr. A. H. McCoy. They were the kind of front-line leaders Mitchell admired most. The second group was composed of people like Dr. Laurence C. Jones, founder of the historic Piney Woods Country Life School twenty-one miles south of Jackson, which symbolized the daring struggle by blacks for an education. Decades later, the poorly preserved one-room dirt-floored log cabin, which was the original school built in 1909, stood among the expanse of modern classroom and dormitory buildings on some two thousand acres of prime farmland amid several lakes. Jones was a Booker T. Washington–type personality who revealed the radicalizing effects of the struggle in a different age.[1]

On January 23, 1955, the same day on which the NAACP held opening ceremonies for the new field office headed by Evers, the white power structure held a testimonial lionizing Jones as a man of great accomplishment. Jones, who took no salary for his work and plowed back every penny into the school, had recently received $5 million from the state for expansion. Standing up to acknowledge the accolades of his well-wishers, Jones said: "Ladies and gentlemen, you've talked about how great I am, and how much I can contribute to my state, and what a wonderful position the Negroes of our state are in to help carry forward this day. As you praise me, the only thing that bothers me in my heart today is, I can't say the same for you." He then reeled off a litany of complaints: "You've denied me the right to vote, and you won't let my folks vote," and down the line he went. Whites in the audience walked out. That, said Henry recalling the incident, was "a lot of man." Mitchell agreed. Until then, Henry had had little respect for Jones, whom he had regarded as an accommodationist. Now he admired him.

At the other end of the spectrum was Percy Greene, editor of the *Jackson Advocate,* who Mitchell thought was a "good example of how the power structure could force people into corruption." Mitchell recalled that when Greene had worked for the *Baltimore Afro-American,* he was a civil rights crusader and a hard-bitten newspaperman. He later went to Mississippi and founded the *Advocate,* but it became an advocate for segregation. Early in April 1955, in an editorial on the state's newly launched "school equalization program," which was an attempt to lure blacks into accepting voluntary segregation, Greene urged rejection of the Supreme Court's desegregation decision. He concluded: "Insofar as Negroes in the South are concerned, the NAACP is an enemy of the Negro race."

Mitchell recalled that one day, in a long talk, Greene "explained to me his financial situation was such that he could not keep up." But he not only sold out to the segregationists, he also joined them on the staff of the State Sovereignty Commission, which purchased a subscription to the *Advocate* for every school in Mississippi. Mitchell found him very emotional and eager to arouse sympathy for his predicament, but all Greene got from him was pity.

Evers was proud that "I was robbing the cradle" when, at age twenty-six, he married the eighteen-year-old Myrlie Beasley of Vicksburg in 1951. "The idea," he said, "is to get them young, while they're still green, and then bring them up the way you want them." Mitchell's affection for the couple was like a messianic bond that transcended their immediate beings. Medgar did not reveal himself easily to others. But Mitchell knew and understood his agony—a painful existence caused by the never-ending fear and frustration that came with the NAACP job. From the beginning of Medgar's tenure, Myrlie found that the strain of trying to carry out her job as his secretary in addition to being his wife, a mother, and a housekeeper was physically and emotionally wrenching. Myrlie desperately wanted to give up the job and be a real mother to her children, but the family needed her small pay to make ends meet.

Furthermore, the fear of violence made Medgar perpetually taut, because he could not shield Myrlie and the children—Darrell Kenyatta, Rene Denise, and James Van Dyke—from it. Unable to escape, Medgar tried to adjust and to instill courage in his family. When Myrlie reacted with exasperation to one of the incessant crank calls from red-necks, Evers lectured, "Myrlie, don't ever do what you did. If you can't take it, just put the phone down. But don't curse at them. You can sometimes win them over if you are just patient." Mitchell would have reacted the same way.

Caught in the middle of intergroup competition for recognition in the state, Evers found his life was made even more hellish by an often seemingly unsympathetic national NAACP office, which itself was being buffeted by multifaceted civil rights turbulence. The Mississippi field secretary had to endure the anxiety of seeing personalities—from Roy Wilkins down through Gloster Current, national director of branches, to Ruby Hurley, regional director and Evers's immediate supervisor—fighting to maintain steady leadership of the struggle and not to be drowned out by the cacophony from impatient younger protesters. Myrlie believed that a major problem was that Medgar did "not think that all the decisions about" Mississippi should be made from New York. "Nothing's going to be right until our own people are in the driver's seat," he believed. Myrlie felt that "the expectations of him, in terms of operating the office, providing information and everything else was unreal. One person just couldn't do that." As Medgar's only staff member for three years, until the pressures of caring for their children kept her at home full-time, Myrlie was aware of her husband's seven-day-a-week, twenty-four-hour-a-day routine.

A second problem was caused by Medgar's belief that the NAACP alone could not do the job. Myrlie found that the tide began to change in Mississippi on March 27, 1961, when nine black students from Tougaloo Southern Christian College who were members of the NAACP youth council sat down in Jackson's white public library and began to read. The police arrived within minutes to demand that they leave. They refused and were arrested. Other demonstrations and arrests quickly followed. A week after Meredith had filed his federal lawsuit seeking admission to the University of Mississippi, Roy Wilkins launched "Operation Mississippi" at a mass meeting in Jackson, to wipe out segregation in the state. In July, three black Jackson businessmen filed a lawsuit in federal court challenging state laws that required segregated transportation facilities, and the Department of Justice filed another against voting registrars in Clarke and Forrest counties to end discrimination. Next, four members of the intercollegiate NAACP chapter at Jackson State and Campbell College sat in the front of a Jackson bus. Other students were arrested for sitting in at the city zoo. As college and public school students intensified the pace, the Reverend Robert L. T. Smith, a black grocer, that December became qualified to run against Congressman John Bell Williams, a stalwart racist. These assaults opened up a steady propaganda campaign that in turn presaged other assaults, like the lawsuit from the NAACP Legal Defense and Educational Fund the following January to desegregate Jackson's public recreational facilities. With Mississippi clearly vulnerable to change, other groups kept pouring into the state—not necessarily to work with the NAACP.

This problem began developing in May 1961, when the first group of CORE freedom riders finally reached Jackson. Evers had to contend with these and other young zealots from organizations like SNCC and SCLC demanding and expecting NAACP support for their programs—even the NAACP's membership lists—without in turn contributing to the added financial and operational burdens. He was thus confronted with problems for which Mitchell had tried to provide some procedural guidelines the previous year. Unlike Mitchell, who was spared direct involvement in intergroup politics, Evers was caught in the middle, as an impatient Wilkins worried about finding funds for bail and other forms of assistance as well as protecting his organization's integrity. At one point, when Aaron Henry called attention to the serious dislocation of black workers and families in the delta as a result of automation, Wilkins responded that one of the difficulties in associating "with ancillary organizations" was that "we become involved with some tangential enterprise which ultimately leaves the NAACP's leadership more deeply committed than was first assumed."

Desperate for help, Evers at times betrayed a willingness to cooperate with Martin Luther King and CORE's James Farmer. That only got him into more hot water with his superiors, especially Ruby Hurley, who was feeling the direct pressure from King in her Atlanta regional office.

The relationship between the national and state offices was fraught with political traps and other conflicts. The NAACP was a national institution with a long-established bureaucratic apparatus, rather than a regional organization like SCLC, CORE, and SNCC. Thus it was much easier for the newly created groups with their zealous adherents to focus on single issues or shift from one location to another. Indeed, one of the most persistent criticisms of King, which more than often came from people outside the NAACP, was that he would come into a city, start a demonstration, and fly out within a few days, leaving the local activists to suffer the consequences of challenging discrimination. Local NAACP leaders could not do that; they were permanent residents of their communities. These same local leaders were the main source of the NAACP's strength; its branches were its backbone. Henry, who succeeded McCoy in 1960 as president of the Mississippi State Conference of NAACP Branches, was one such leader. He regarded Mitchell, Wilkins, and Current as a triumvirate who "gave our state a tremendous amount of time and concern in helping us devise a strategy by which" blacks in Mississippi could free themselves from the caste system. But having a larger, national organizational agenda, Wilkins, especially, could not devote as much time to one state as Mitchell. Henry was "not too sure that the glamor of bringing Roy Wilkins in as opposed to the effectiveness of bringing in Clarence Mitchell was ever really understood by the branch leadership throughout the country." Everybody "was ga, ga, ga, here's Roy," when the national leader appeared. "But I considered Clarence the major strategist of the organization, at least during the period from 1960 to 1978," when he retired.

The personal relationships and sympathetic displays of understanding were what mattered most to Medgar and Myrlie. By 1963 Evers's premonition of death was as ever present as King's would be five years later. Medgar and Myrlie were closer to Mitchell than to anyone else on the national office staff. Following the creation of the Mississippi field office in 1955, Mitchell visited the state at least twice a year and was always on call. If he was a big brother to Medgar, he was a father figure to Myrlie. She could never forget how he had brought her back together with Medgar during one particularly difficult period, when Mitchell was in Jackson for a speaking engagement.

Blacks during that period were not welcome in hotels, so in Jackson the Masonic Temple on John R. Lynch Street, where the NAACP office was also located after having been moved from Farish Street, served for all functions. Medgar found wry amusement in the new address because of the NAACP's historic association with "lynching." But, more than anything else, the location inspired pride, because John R. Lynch was a famous black politician who became speaker of the Mississippi House in 1872 and later served three terms in Congress. Myrlie and two other women were responsible for getting the banquet and meeting halls ready. They cleaned the place, did the cooking and brought in the food, picked up people at the airport, and chauffeured visitors around. On Sundays, she played the organ at church. Loneliness was another problem. Their men were so busy with NAACP work that Myrlie and a group of her friends called themselves "NAACP widows."

At home, during the rainy season, water seeped into the gas heater, which was under the floor of the house. Medgar and Myrlie had no money for repairs, a situation that stretched their nerves to the limit. The breaking point finally came when, triggered by a some small disagreement, they had a heated argument and Myrlie caught a midnight bus for Vicksburg, her parents' home, about forty miles from Jackson. The children were already there to escape the heatless house. She "was not leaving for good. But it was the first and only time that I ever left in anger." Her parents knew something was wrong as soon as they saw her, but she told them nothing.

After a quick trip to Atlanta, Evers and Mitchell returned to find that Myrlie was still away. So Evers asked, "Clarence, what do I do? Do I let this go, and go on to be a single man to pursue all these things I am involved in? Should I let her stay there and just sweat it out?" Mitchell asked him, "Do you love her?" Evers replied yes. "Then go get her," Mitchell said.

Arriving in Vicksburg, Mitchell responded to a "What's wrong?" query from Myrlie's parents with a smile and maneuvered the couple into a quiet corner of the house, away from her aunt and grandmother, who were living there. Myrlie thought "that was a miracle." He helped them resolve their differences and remained in close touch after that. "He counseled us," explained Myrlie, "not only in the sense of our love for each other, but also about staying together." Afterward, "Clarence continued that type of fatherly advice to us. He would sometimes just pick up the phone and call for no reason at all just to see how we were doing, how we were handling the stress. I am sure—I can't speak for Medgar, but I know for myself—I never considered breaking up after that." She found that Mitchell "had such a marvelous way of instilling family, of tying the Association, your family and your personal lives together." Mitchell taught her the importance of giving "our young men in the Association" the support they needed to do the job. He "had a very soft yet very strong and forceful manner." So much so that "I felt like Clarence was the one person that I could talk to about my frustrations with the Association." She was very peeved about the lack of appreciation for her husband's work.

Dealing with the death threats was impossible. Evers tried to make light of the fear and attempted to be reassuring by telling everyone, "I think everything is going to be all right. . . . We'll have things straightened out soon." He also said, "Don't worry. If I die, I know it will do some good." But Myrlie could not be so sanguine. She was particularly upset by what she felt was a lack of understanding from Evers's superiors. She felt "that the only time the national office warned Medgar to be careful was when a member of the New York staff was with him. They would come in, do their work and get out, sometimes within a few hours. I wondered, resentfully, if they really cared about Medgar's life as much as they obviously cared about his work. Medgar, I guess, understood it, because he never complained." But the threats and the taunts became more frequent. For Myrlie, "the danger was so real, and it had escalated to a point where anybody who was involved knew that something was going to happen very soon."

Evers was among nine black leaders who had been attacked by name in a Delta newspaper ad. When the Reverend George Lee, whose name was also mentioned in the ad, was killed shortly afterward in 1955, everyone began taking the "death list" more seriously. Five fled the state, leaving three. Evers's name topped the list by 1963. Dr. Gilbert Mason of Biloxi had been arrested in 1960 for participating in the Gulfport NAACP branch's wade-in at the beach and would be leading another one in the coming summer. Mason had received a revised "hit list" of other NAACP activists that also included himself, Evers, Aaron Henry, Dr. Felix H. Dunn of Gulfport, and, from Jackson, R.O.T. Smith, Sr., Sam Baily, and Meredith. Mason, assured the list was reliable, warned Evers and the others so that they could take precautions.

Members of Mason's family and friends with firearms accompanied him on his rounds to the hospital and on house calls. "I recognized the danger and the viciousness of white southerners—Ku Klux Klanners, the Citizens' Council, individual ruffians and rabble rousers," explained Mason in an interview. His clinic was bombed on October 1, 1962. They were like a "rabid, mad dog—rabid, and mad. . . . Whatever a rabid dog does, you can expect it. So is anything the Kluxers do." Any Ku Kluxer who came within a block of his house between the "hot period" of 1960 and 1963— "they knew this—took his life in his hands."

In February, shortly after the NAACP had begun intermittent picketing and other demonstrations in downtown Jackson, Mitchell had arranged for the national office to pay for a speaking tour for Medgar and Myrlie so they could escape the tension. Their first engagement was an NAACP branch meeting in Baltimore. Juanita Mitchell remembered, "We just opened up the Belvedere Hotel—got a suite for them so they could be away from Mississippi." They came up on a Friday night, and Evers spoke that Sunday.

Subsequently, while addressing a rally at the Reverend E. Franklin Jackson's AME Zion Church in Washington, Evers said that he feared for his life when he returned home because of the rising number of threats that were being made against him. Joseph Rauh, who attended the rally, called Arthur M. Schlesinger, Jr., special assistant to the President, and informed him of Evers's fears. According to Rauh, "Arthur soon called me back and said he had spoken with Bobby Kennedy." Rauh supported the common view that the FBI's policy was to provide no protection in such cases for whites or blacks. Not even Walter Reuther, who once asked the Justice Department to provide him with protection on a trip to the South, received it. Rauh believed the FBI might have been quietly watching Evers. But it did not acknowledge such activity, to avoid the charge that it had failed if that turned out to be the case.

The following month, Mitchell welcomed the news that "at last Mississippi has been called upon to face the question of desegregation of the public schools." In a lawsuit filed on March 4, the NAACP Inc. Fund asked the U.S. district court to order the Jackson school board to develop a reorganization plan for a "unitary nonracial system" to eliminate discrimination among principals, teachers, and students. Among the six plaintiffs were Medgar and Myrlie Evers in behalf of two of their three children. They made a pact: Myrlie promised Medgar that if he was killed she would continue to press the suit.

A month to the day before Evers was assassinated, Mitchell returned to Mississippi to address a mass rally—a point in time that Myrlie used to mark the final buildup in events leading to that fateful moment. After Mitchell had spoken, Medgar announced an NAACP plan to boycott

Barq's soft drinks, Hart's bread, and McRae's Department Store in Jackson. All three depended heavily on black patronage, but were large contributors to the White Citizens' Council. Evers explained to Mitchell that the Jackson police had a program for speedily arresting demonstrators— and boosting the local treasury as well as the population at Parchmant Penitentiary. Mitchell was very impressed with the protest plan Evers had mapped out.

That night, Evers drove him around the city. Passing Jackson's now-infamous Memorial Stadium, Mitchell was chilled by the haunting atmosphere. There the previous September, as the conflagration over Meredith's attempt to enroll at Ole Miss approached its bloody denouement, Governor Ross Barnett had lifted the packed stadium to new heights of racist ecstasy. No setting could have been more appropriate for the historical catharsis than the American rite of passage of a bone-crushing football game. At half time, just after Ole Miss students had raised to a deafening roar what some thought was the largest Confederate flag in the world, inspiring their team, the Rebels, to move ahead of Kentucky 7 to 0, bedlam broke out with the growing chant, "We want Ross! We want Ross!" The mighty thunder from forty-six thousand throats was the signal for the governor to step forward to the microphone. A normally reserved man, Barnett responded symbolically. "I love Mississippi," he shouted, rocking the stadium. "I love her people. I love our customs." A Nazi leader could not have done better. "Yes, it was just the way Nuremberg must have been," remarked a student happily.

Now, "it was so quiet," Mitchell thought. "Here we were, after midnight, visiting all these scenes where there had been these terrible outbursts." He let his "imagination fill in the gaps created by the absence of people from the stadium plus the late hour. You would think of what it must have been like when the meeting was taking place."

When they reached Evers's house, "a large dog that was supposed to be a watchdog," but that did not seem to be a good one, came out and the porch lights were turned on. Immediately it struck Mitchell that Evers was silhouetted against the light. "If anybody wanted him for a target, that was an ideal position for him to be shot." Because Evers continued to enter his house in that manner, Mitchell was later not sure whether he warned Evers about the danger of what he was convinced "was the wrong way to come in." Even if he did so, there is the possibility that the fatalistic Medgar decided there was nothing much he could do to protect himself if someone was going to kill him; or, exhausted as usual, perhaps he forgot to heed the warning. Myrlie, as was her custom, was waiting to greet them. The children were up, and Mitchell was struck by Myrlie's cheerfulness.

"Myrlie fixed a little repast for us. We sat there eating it. Then there was the sound of a car coming by. Immediately there was tension," but nothing happened. "Whatever it was, they obviously had good reason to be concerned." Mitchell, like Rauh, had informed the White House, the Department of Justice, and lawmakers in Congress of the dangerous climate in Jackson, but apparently no appropriate action had been taken.

The NAACP boycott of stores in downtown Jackson was quickly widened to include virtually all the stores on Capitol Street, the main shopping area, and it was a resounding success. Sweeping aside Evers's early reservations, college students further electrified the atmosphere by announcing plans to hold sit-ins at the Woolworth, Walgreen, and H. L. Green stores, as high-school students launched large-scale demonstrations. The national NAACP office sent in Willie Ludden, its youth field secretary, to help organize the demonstrations and give them a sense of purpose. As the students flooded Capitol Street in NAACP sweatshirts with single letters on them, they would, at a signal, arrange themselves to spell DON'T BUY ON CAPITOL STREET. The police were not to be outdone. Arresting the youths, they packed them into paddy wagons and garbage trucks and sent them to the state fairgrounds, which had been converted into an ill-equipped emergency jail surrounded by a chain-link fence. They remained there for more than a week, until the NAACP national office was able to provide $200,000 in bail money, but the funds soon ran out.

With Jackson having become an unvented pressure cooker, Mayor Allen Thompson sought negotiations. It soon became clear that he had no intention of reaching a fair settlement when he rejected ten of the fourteen people on the list the NAACP had given him as possible representatives of the black community on the biracial committee. Of the ten blacks he substituted for those he had removed from the NAACP list, four of them were well-known collaborators—two were Percy Greene, the *Jackson Advocate* editor, and Joseph Allbright, a public relations man who worked with the segregationist State Sovereignty Commission. Finally, on May 28, Thompson negotiated directly with the NAACP, and before the meeting was over, he agreed to several desegregation demands, such as to accept applications from blacks for jobs as policemen and school crossing guards, to declare that all public facilities were open to all citizens on an equal basis, and to remove all Jim Crow signs from public buildings. Blacks regarded Thompson's concessions as a major victory. But within minutes after the agreement was announced, Thompson repudiated it. That day, the sit-in demonstrations began, intensifying the protests. News photos showing a white man kicking one of the demonstrators on the floor of the Woolworth store in the face attested to the climate of violence.

The splintering glass and muffled explosion that Myrlie heard around midnight a day later outside her ranch house as a car passed on the street were an ominous warning. It was scary, but only potentially dangerous. Investigating, she saw flames from the fire bomb that had been thrown licking the air near the full gas tank of the family station wagon. She braved the lonely night to put it out quickly with a garden hose, as the children slept inside the house.

That Saturday, June 1, as Governor George Wallace continued to defy a federal court injunction by blocking the enrollment of two black students at the University of Alabama, the news flashed across the nation that Roy Wilkins, gaunt, smartly dressed with sunglasses and a sporty straw hat, was arrested in downtown Jackson along with Evers for picketing the Woolworth store. They were booked on a felony charge and released on a cash bond of $1,000 each, as the police arrested another one hundred protesting black children and carted them off in the usual manner to the fairgrounds as they chanted, "We want freedom, yeah."

"Only the ovens were missing," Wilkins said in describing what he called the "Nazi-like concentration camp" to which they were being taken. The appearance of Dick Gregory, the acerbic comedian, and Lena Horne, the celebrated singer, in Jackson to support the protests helped create a holiday mood of excitement for the children. With the police arresting all the black people within range of the demonstrations, whether they were participating or not, some 664 of them had been booked by the end of the first week in June, as the NAACP defied a state court injunction against the protests that Mayor Thompson had obtained.

Evers assumed greater prominence by winning an unprecedented opportunity on a local television station to refute charges that the NAACP was an outside group inciting the uprising. The mass meetings that the NAACP began holding every night were also helping to make Evers become for Jackson what Martin Luther King had been for Birmingham—a moral symbol and catalyst. In a prophetic gesture at one of these meetings, Myrlie listened in shock as Medgar quietly told his hushed audience, "I love my children, and I love my wife with all my heart. And I would die, and die gladly, if that would make a better life for them."

Myrlie saw him "age ten to fifteen years in the past two months. You can't live with a man, love him, have his children," and not see what was "happening to him without being awfully worried, and without getting very angry with anybody who didn't seem to care, or who didn't appreciate his service," she recalled.

Adding to the strain and the increasing sense of doom was Evers's awareness that he was being followed. Two or three policemen whom Myrlie would later recognize had been shadowing his every step for two or three months. Their vigilance did not deter him, even after they once tried to run him over with their car. They had made a pretense of investigating the fire bombing of his home with no result, so he and Myrlie knew them well. Medgar did not immediately mention to Myrlie that he found it strange when he saw three white strangers sitting in the NAACP office that night, after the mass meeting at which he had prophesied his death. He simply reminded one of them, who was smoking, of the fire code, and the man put out his cigarette. They left after a secretary asked if she could help them. Gloster Current, who was sitting right across the room from them, would later recognize one of them as Byron de la Beckwith, Evers's accused assassin.

Newspapers on Wednesday, June 12, were emblazoned with the headlines saying that the University of Alabama had finally admitted the two black students, Vivian Malone and James A. Hood, the first since Autherine Lucy had been driven off the campus. Governor Wallace, standing face to face with the federal might represented by Deputy Attorney General Nicholas deB. Katzenbach, had done more than blink. He had bowed to a higher authority. By keeping his campaign pledge to "stand in the schoolhouse door" in an attempt to bar desegregation of the institution, however, he had made his point of challenging the "intrusion" of the central government. He had now become a national figure and would most certainly be heard from again. Sitting in her living room Tuesday night, awaiting Medgar's arrival from another of the series of rallies, Myrlie found hope in the Wallace facedown and the deep moral tone that President Kennedy set in his celebrated outline of the civil rights bill he planned to submit to Congress. Kennedy had at last begun to provide the type of forthright leadership the NAACP was seeking from him.

That night, however, which was actually the first hour of Wednesday morning, events in Jackson also came to a head—literally with the sound of a .30-06 caliber rifle. Fifteen minutes earlier, Evers had dropped Current off at the home of NAACP attorney Jack Young after a mass meeting at the New Jerusalem Baptist Church. "I'm tired," Evers said. "I want to get home to my family." Current could never forget how "he just held my hand, and held it, and held it," as he said good night. Not long afterward, Current called Mitchell at his home in Baltimore to inform him that Evers had been shot in the back at 12:30 A.M. and killed by an assassin hiding behind a honeysuckle thicket in a ditch across the street, as Evers got out of his light blue 1962 Oldsmobile sedan, which was parked in the carport behind Myrlie's station wagon. He died forty-five minutes later at University Hospital.

It was Myrlie who, screaming, had told Current at Young's home in Jackson that "they've killed my husband. They've killed my husband."

Upon hearing the shot, she and the children, who were still up awaiting their father's arrival, had thrown themselves onto the floor as Medgar had taught them to do in the days just past. They had been watching a late movie in the living room. "Oh, my God, my God," Myrlie screamed upon opening the door. She saw Medgar lying face down at the doorway in a pool of blood. The children screamed, "Daddy, Daddy." Behind him on the carport were the papers and some sweatshirts he had dropped. Across the front of one, she read the slogan JIM CROW MUST GO. Neighbors placed the nearly lifeless Medgar on a sheet and then on a mattress, and drove him off to the hospital as Myrlie ran into the house and prayed. Medgar's last words to those with him in the car were "Sit me up. Turn me loose." About that same time the local television station had interrupted its regular program with a bulletin that "Jackson NAACP leader Medgar Evers has just been shot." Jackson had replaced Birmingham as the national symbol of shame.

Evers had got out his car silhouetted against the light, a perfect target for a marksman, just what Mitchell thought he should not have been doing. The bullet from the World War I Enfield with a six-power Goldenhawk telescopic sight entered right below the shoulderblade, tore open his chest, went through the living room window and a dining room wall, ricocheted off the refrigerator, damaged a coffeepot on a counter, and came to rest on the opposite counter beside a watermelon. Strangely, the policemen who usually followed Evers home had not done so that night. Ten hours later, police found the rifle in a clump of vines near where it had been fired.

Cold fury swept Jackson's blacks that Wednesday morning. The daily demonstrations took on a new fervor as thirteen black ministers and businessmen filed slowly out of church for a mourning march downtown. The police, who were awaiting them with rifles and blue steel helmets, stopped them two blocks away, ordered them to disperse, then piled them into a paddy wagon when they refused. Within minutes, youths who had set out from the NAACP office arrived singing such freedom songs as "Woke Up This Morning with My Mind on Freedom" and "Ain't Gonna Let Nobody Turn Me 'Round." The demonstrations now had a real purpose. The police arrested the youths, too. The stream of paddy wagons and garbage trucks filled with their human cargo continued in a different parade to the fairgrounds. The NAACP announced it had posted a $10,000 reward for information leading to the killer, which was quickly raised to $21,000 by the city and other sources.

Mitchell did not remember too much about what happened next that night, but Simeon Booker, an editor for *Jet* magazine and a close friend, did. Distraught to the point of madness, Mitchell got dressed and drove to his office in Washington. A frantic Juanita called Booker, urging him to check on her husband because she did not know what he would do. Mitchell admitted his "mind was torn up." Hot tears burned his face as he sat at his desk in his office "trying to do something" at four o'clock in the morning. But "at that time of the night it was hard to get anybody" by telephone. Mitchell, who then was often dubbed the "lost senator," was particularly bitter because everyone "knows that such a penalty was awaiting any civil rights leader in the South. The government knows this. Justice Department knows this. The White House knows this. But what do they do?" Nothing. He correctly predicted that within a few hours "you'll see the goddamnest biggest groundswell of testimony of reactions you've ever seen, but most of it will be empty, political. The statements are just words."

Wilkins, blaming white southern politicians, was equally caustic. They were "not content with mere disenfranchisement," he said, but "have used unbridled political power to fabricate a maze of laws, customs and economic practices which has imprisoned the Negro." Furthermore, the southern states had "its outpost in the Congress of the United States." There, "by their deals and maneuvers," its representatives "have helped to put the man behind that deadly rifle on Guynes Street," where Evers had lived. He said, "The killer must have felt that he had, if not an immunity, then certainly a protection for what he chose to do." While the assassin represented "the spiritual suicide" being committed by whites "here in the land fashioned as the home of free men," Medgar Evers symbolized a constant threat to "the system that murdered him." So, "in the manner of his death he was the victor over that system."

Afterward, little things, like the emotional endings of state and branch meetings on Sunday afternoons, took on an enhanced meaning for Mitchell. "We would form a big circle and sing, 'God be with you 'til we meet again.' There would be tears in people's eyes." On one occasion when Mitchell came down from the platform to join the circle, he stood beside an old man. "He was almost in a state of collapse because it was such a deep emotional experience for him. As well might have been the case, because none of us could know whether by the next meeting some of those present would be dead. Indeed, that happened. Medgar, after all, was in one of those meetings before he died."

Traveling from Washington for the funeral that Saturday morning, it struck Mitchell as "so odd" to see Dr. Ralph Bunche, United Nations undersecretary for special political affairs, fast asleep on a curved, wooden bench in the deserted New Orleans airport, where they both were waiting for a connecting flight to Jackson. Bunche, known for his post–World War II role in the Palestine settlement and creation of Israel, and as a civil rights activist, could have been another assassin's target. But nobody was thinking of danger then.

Developments following the funeral in the steamy auditorium of the Masonic Temple, while outside the temperature had been above 100 degrees for the past three days, engendered some unintended slights and much violence. Mitchell and other NAACP leaders were annoyed that John Doar, a white Department of Justice official, was given all the credit for quelling a near riot that erupted in Jackson when the mourners set off three abreast, behind an eight-man police motorcycle escort, from the Temple over the mile-and-a-half route to the Collins Funeral Home on North Farish Street. Mayor Thompson had lifted the city ban on parades to permit the funeral march. Some two hundred blue-helmeted police had sealed off the carefully arranged route through the city's black section. Most businesses were well shuttered. Trouble was imminent. The previous night, the younger members of the Jackson Movement's executive committee had urged that the funeral march pass along Capitol Street, in the white business district. They were defeated 8 to 4, but few expected them to accept the decision. As the group of younger blacks and whites crossed the intersection with West Capitol Street, they began violating a condition of the permit requiring the parade to be quiet.

At the end of the march, as Mitchell sat with a group enjoying a cold drink, someone rushed in to warn that those two hundred boys and girls at the end of the column, singing "We Shall Overcome," were indeed attempting to veer onto Capitol Street. Surging down the street, they had begun shouting, "We want the killer! We want the killer! We want the killer!" and "Freedom! Freedom! Freedom!" Mitchell rushed outside and saw John Salter, a white sociology professor, bleeding from a beating he had received from the police. He was one of those who had started leading the youths into what Mitchell feared was a police trap. The police were chasing people onto porches and elsewhere, while rocks and bottles rained down from buildings. At the end of the street, Mitchell saw the police with shotguns, rifles, and pistols drawn, waiting in a military-style wedge formation. He feared "a lot of them would be killed" if the marchers tried to get through.

Mitchell joined Current, NAACP general counsel Robert Carter, and Frank Reeves, once a special attorney to the Washington Bureau and later a member of the Kennedy administration, in heading off the confrontation with the police. Current, Carter, and Reeves, dodging flying rocks and bottles, managed to avoid further bloodshed by holding back the marchers, while a local black minister with a megaphone marched down the street urging the crowd to turn back. Mitchell was thankful they did. It was then that Doar, standing before the police in shirt sleeves in a dramatic photo opportunity, also urged them to turn back and stop throw-ing bottles.

Myrlie at first had rejected a suggestion from the American Veterans Committee that Medgar be buried at the Arlington National Cemetery. She wanted him to be buried at the family plot they both had bought at the black cemetery in Jackson. At Ruby Hurley's suggestion, she recon-sidered, after she was convinced that Arlington would be more appropriate because more people could visit the site there. Mitchell made the arrange-ments for the burial in Washington, as well as for the President and repre-sentatives of the national government to pay their last respects to the murdered World War II veteran and to express their condolences to Myrlie and his children. Joining the Washington NAACP branch in meeting the flag-draped casket at the Union Railway Station that Monday, he accom-panied the mile-long march of one thousand mourners to the John Wesley AME Church, as an old man in a World War I uniform behind the hearse and a police escort led the crowd. More than twenty-five thousand people streamed past the casket in the church that day.

Inspecting the grassy gravesite beside Custis Walk near Sheridan Gate, with tall oak trees in the background, Mitchell was struck by the serene beauty of the area. He thought that the grave was unlike others he had seen, which were muddy and gloomy. "It looked cheerful. Something brown had been placed at the bottom that made it almost look inviting." Turning to someone beside him, he said, "Gee, you almost feel you could get in there and lie down." The person "looked at me sort of funny, as if I was off my rocker. But I really felt that way."

Evers was buried there with full military honors exactly a week after he was killed. "He is not dead, the soldier fallen here," intoned Bishop Ste-phen Gil Spottswood of the African Methodist Episcopal Church, chairman of the NAACP, in Arlington's tiny Fort Myer Chapel, shortly before the body was interred. "His spirit walks through the world today." As the smoke from a rifle volley hung over the plain gray casket, Wilkins gave the final tribute: "Medgar Evers believed in his country; it now remains to be seen whether his country believes in him." Mitchell then led the two thou-sand mourners in singing, "We shall overcome."[2]

Evers's death was not in vain. Early in October 1962, Washington Bureau counsel Pohlhaus, in attempting to enlist the FBI's assistance, of-fered to provide the agency with a list of NAACP officers in Mississippi. The official with whom he spoke replied that it was not FBI policy to provide protection to threatened individuals. Furthermore, FBI agents in the area already had been assigned to Oxford for surveillance on the Mer-edith case. He said that the FBI had been in contact with Evers and would continue to be in touch. Sensing that the official would not protect the identity of NAACP officers on the list, Pohlhaus decided against submitting it to the FBI. Pohlhaus and Mitchell knew that the problem resulted from the FBI's unwillingness to endanger its close working relationship with local police on ordinary crime by becoming involved in civil rights violence. Given the public knowledge of the widely circulated "death list" of NAACP leaders in Mississippi, FBI agents in the region must have been fully aware of the identities of at least some of those people. What Pohlhaus really wanted, therefore, was an expression of concern from the FBI and a promise for active cooperation.

Pohlhaus's original willingness to supply the FBI with a list of NAACP officers was counter to the NAACP's policy of not revealing its membership, and thus underscored the association's anxieties over the crisis in the state. The NAACP was then on the verge of winning its battle against attempts by several southern states to force it to turn over its membership lists to them. Evers's assassination, the difficulty of getting cooperation from the FBI and the Justice Department, and, later, the failure to win conviction of Byron de la Beckwith because his two trials ended in hung juries strengthened Mitchell's demands for legislation to protect citizens from racial violence. Rigidly courteous, with antebellum manners and antebellum airs, Beckwith was a family man and regular churchgoer. He lived in the Delta town of Greenwood, where the names of his kin were everywhere—on street signs, storefronts, and courthouse office doors. He was a Mississippi metaphor.[3]

Following the White House reception that President Kennedy held for Myrlie Evers after her husband was buried, Aaron Henry joined Mitchell in asking the House Civil Rights Subcommittee for a law that would permit the Justice Department to act at the earliest sign of danger rather than after violence had occurred against civil rights workers. "Any fool could see what was going to happen" to Evers, Mitchell said. "But while they fiddled around someone got in the bushes and shot him" from across his driveway as he came out of his car. Mitchell, denying that such federal protection would represent creation of a "national police force," as one critic charged, stressed that the main obstacle to the needed law was the nature of the FBI's relationship with local police.

Mitchell discovered that Medgar Evers's assassination had "a cannonball effect on the nation." It set off new demands for civil rights legislation, with Mitchell proclaiming there should be "no filibuster nonsense" in Congress. Despite the absence of the Part III provision for protecting a citizen's rights against racial violence, which had been deleted from the 1957 civil rights bill, the tragedy more than likely could have been avoided had FBI Director Hoover been devoting his agency's resources to protecting rather than to the surveillance of civil rights leaders, especially Martin Luther King.

Even segregationists like Sam Ervin expressed alarm over Evers's murder—a development that led Mitchell to call for "a little less deploring and a little more protection." Mitchell had earlier welcomed expressions of concern from Senate Majority Leader Mike Mansfield and Minority Leader Everett Dirksen. They agreed that President Kennedy had no alternative but to send federal marshals into Alabama in the wake of the freedom rides, and that the May 1963 Birmingham riots would increase demand for civil rights legislation. Ervin concurred that Kennedy's action regarding Birmingham was in accordance with the law. Humphrey said the civil rights struggle in the South would embarrass the country in terms of the cold war, causing some nations to regard the United States as "crude and immoral."[4]

The most obvious obstacle to civil rights legislation remained the filibuster. Another was that Senate Majority Leader Mansfield was as unwilling as his predecessor, Lyndon Johnson, to use the real and implied powers of his office to buck historical racist forces. In fact, Mansfield's greatest accomplishment in 1961 was considered to be his cooling off of the fights over the cloture rule, by shunting aside the Democratic party's commitment to reform at the beginning of the Eighty-seventh Congress. He did that by promising to use his powers as chairman of the Senate Rules Committee to champion a change to a three-fifths cloture rule.

The only recognized prerogative that the majority leader had was the traditional right to be recognized by the president of the Senate over his colleagues; the advantage enabled him to seize the initiative whenever he desired. He had no constitutional authority at all, but his unwritten charter gave him nearly absolute power over the scheduling of bills in the Senate, the scheduling of all its business, and leadership of the Steering Committee. The other recognized instruments of influence for a Democratic majority leader were the Democratic Party Conference and Policy Committee. With those rights and instruments, he could obstruct the wishes and needs of all senators, influence committee appointments, and dominate policy. He had great influence at the White House, especially when the occupant was a member of his party; in those instances, some students of government regarded the power of the majority leader as being third to that of the President and the speaker of the House, and equal with the secretaries of state, defense, and the treasury.

The Democratic Party Conference was composed of every senator who was a member of the party. The conference chose the party's leaders and provided a forum. Johnson considered the conference as too unwieldy, and unsuitable for his highly personalized leadership style. He therefore used it primarily to ratify his selection of party officers during the few times he convened it. The Policy Committee traditionally was responsible for preparing the schedule of legislation and formulating strategies for action in the Senate. It served as a sounding board that enabled Johnson to know, before going onto the Senate floor, about the concerns and interests of members of the committee on legislation being considered. Johnson appointed power brokers like Richard Russell of Georgia, Lister Hill of Alabama, and Robert Kerr of Oklahoma to this committee, and thus considerably enhanced his influence. Another function of the Policy Committee for Johnson was to obtain a geographical and ideological balance for parliamentary maneuvering on the Senate floor. Through the fifteen-member Steering Committee, Johnson assigned party members to standing Senate committees, which held hearings and marked up bills for consideration by the full Senate. The standing committees determined substantive legislative policy and the workload by the timing and the type of legislation they reported out.

Students of the Senate characterized the personality differences between Johnson and Mansfield as those between an extrovert and an introvert. "Johnson ran and Mike walks," said an observer, "but they both come out at about the same place." In terms of geographic circumstances, Johnson's "were different; as a Texas southerner he had to walk on more eggshells." Johnson was folksy and power-conscious; the colorless fifty-eight-year-old Mansfield was a haughty, very distant Montanan who shied away from wielding power. The personality and style differences aside, the succession from Johnson to Mansfield accomplished no more than a modification in goals—from an overriding concern for moderation in differences between the North and the South to accommodation to the prerogatives of fellow senators.

Frederick W. Collins, a veteran reporter in Washington, observed: "That a leader can lead without constant brilliance in generalship, mastery, intrigue, pressures, threats, coaxings, parliamentary acrobatics or tireless use of some mysterious 'technique' is a truth hard for most observers of the Senate to grasp. In some circumstances, it would be impossible. In Mansfield's case, it is not only possible, but what actually happens."

Mansfield had served as whip, or assistant floor leader, during Johnson's first four years as majority leader and was the undisputed choice to take over in 1961. He was not eager to assume the post, but bowed to a draft by his party colleagues and President Kennedy. One reason why he did not want the job was that, as a Catholic, he believed some people might consider it too much to have a majority leader and a president who were both Catholics. Kennedy dispelled that concern. Many Democrats actually welcomed him as a relief after eight years of Johnson's overbearing, hard-driving style. Johnson had to have his finger in every pot; Mansfield used other people's fingers as well as his own. "My job," he explained, "is to represent the Senate to the President, and the President to the Senate. I'm the Senate's agent, primarily. It's kind of a spot and one of the reasons I didn't want the job." The "spot" to which Mansfield referred was the Senate's extreme jealousy over its independence. Senators were inclined to charge their leader with being too solicitous of the President's position at the expense of the Senate's. On the other hand, the President had his own jealousies about the power of the majority leader. It was Mansfield's job to balance the division of loyalties between the two institutions that came with his office.

While Johnson had wrapped up himself in all the powers and functions of leadership, Mansfield rejected the use of some traditional sources of influence that came with his office, such as manipulating committee assignments as Johnson had done in order to enhance his position. Mansfield felt that that responsibility was better exercised by the Steering Committee through the secret ballot. Johnson had modified the tradition of assigning his colleagues to committees according to seniority by using the Steering Committee to place every Democrat on a major committee, thus amassing credits. In his book, some senators were more equal than others, according to how they served his purposes. Mansfield, by contrast, saw himself as "one among peers." He encouraged a greater expression of individualism than Johnson had done, and a broader participation of his Democratic colleagues in important aspects of their party's affairs. There was no difference, though, in the extent to which both men respected the Senate as an institution.

Johnson's legendary rule as majority leader was a paradox in terms of civil rights. His reputation grew from his accomplishments in areas other than that of helping the struggle for racial equality to advance in a meaningful way. Like Johnson, Mansfield as majority leader would not demonstrate the type of commitment that Mitchell believed was needed to win passage of the legislation he was seeking.

Mansfield's attitude toward reforming Rule XXII was as conservative as Johnson's, so there was no more likelihood of liberalizing the rule now than there had been in the past. Johnson's defense of the Senate's rights of unlimited debate had been more brutal in 1959 than in 1957, and revealed the extent of his strength by the way he exercised his power. He was also driven by a fear of being outmaneuvered by the Republicans. That threat was evident from what was clearly a liberalization of William Knowland's views on the filibuster. Knowland did not make any specific commitment to Mitchell and his allies in their meeting in May 1958, and he subsequently found that there was diminishing interest in his own proposal to impose cloture by two thirds of those present and voting. Knowland was now favorable to carrying over the rules from one Congress to the next, but Vice President Nixon had beaten him in adopting that position when he expressed support in 1957 for this approach, with his ruling that under the Constitution the Senate was a continuing body and thus could adopt new rules at the beginning of each new session. Knowland agreed with Mitchell that the lobbyist's approach, which was the same as Nixon's, would have political and parliamentary force. He indicated he would not fight for this point if there was general agreement on the cloture voting procedures. Attempting to get Knowland to back Johnson into a corner, Mitchell suggested that if the minority leader's purpose behind the two-thirds vote was to ensure adequate debate, then perhaps he might support a provision offered by Paul Douglas of Illinois for majority cloture after three weeks of debate instead of two. Although Knowland indicated this position might be considered, he showed little enthusiasm for it.

Mitchell had no doubt that Knowland would have supported the reformers more fully had he seen an opportunity to upstage the majority leader. Johnson was as much an embodiment of the Senate's institutional character as Mitchell was a symbol of the struggle for constitutional justice. Pitted against Johnson even after he had left the Senate, Clinton Anderson of New Mexico and his liberal cohorts continued to press for reform in the cloture rule in response to Mitchell's messianic zeal. The futile struggle would serve more to sensitize the Senate on the need for passage of civil rights legislation than as a meaningful strategy for making it easier to cut off filibusters.

The filibuster reformers had been considerably encouraged by the 1958 landslide that gave the Democrats a 64 to 34 majority in the Senate, and promised to wage their battle in the coming session of Congress "no matter how long it took." Johnson had seen the picture differently, as a test of his ability to avoid an open split between the northern and southern wings of his party. Events at the beginning of the Eighty-sixth Congress went poorly for the reformers.

In January 1959, after a series of maneuvers by Paul Douglas and other liberals, Johnson led the way in tabling, by 60 to 36, the familiar motion from Anderson to recognize the Senate's right to adopt new rules at the beginning of each new Congress. That left in place the 1949 Rule XXII, which barred the use of cloture to end debate on the procedural question. Confident it would be defeated, Johnson next permitted the Senate for the first time to vote directly on the question of majority cloture. The resolution was handily defeated, 28 to 67. He then completed his 1957 strategy by winning 72 to 22 approval for a provision that would cut off debate with the consent of two thirds of the senators present and voting, rather than two thirds of the entire membership. The change was more cosmetic than real, since the entire membership was usually present for cloture votes, but it precluded any follow-up attempt by the reformers to try to win support for their goal of cutting off a filibuster by a simple majority vote. Johnson also got the Senate to vote that "the rules . . . shall continue from one Congress to the next." The question of whether the Senate was a continuing body was now not paramount for Mitchell; the reality of the defeat was. Mitchell knew that the largest vote on a civil rights issue (the FEPC bill in 1946) was 55—11 fewer than what was needed for cloture from a total of 98, including Alaska's newly added votes.

The other painful reality for Mitchell in 1959 was that 21 Republicans and 18 northern Democrats had joined forces with the southerners in order to maintain the stringent filibuster rule. He said the vote showed that the senators believed it was "more important to preserve endless, pointless frustrating talk" than to stop Faubus from wrecking the public schools or to halt mobs in Mississippi. The action on the 1960 Civil Rights Act showed even more the extent to which the Senate's leaders under Johnson had increased their strength.[5]

In 1961 Mitchell could only complain that leaders of both parties "showed how they could throw things into reverse" when they wanted to, as much as how they could achieve positive results as they had done by pushing through the appointment of Robert Weaver as administrator of the Housing and Home Finance Agency. That futile struggle to reform Rule XXII more than ever was a tip-off to the difficulties that lay ahead in getting President Kennedy to implement his civil rights promises. Like Eisenhower, Kennedy remained a disinterested observer, as Mansfield killed the effort in the Eighty-seventh Congress by referring a resolution from the persistent Anderson that would require three-fifths rather than two-thirds cloture to the Senate Rules Committee. Mansfield had promised to get the committee to report out a rules change "at a later date." But that effort also failed—with the majority leader's help.

Senator Keating, expressing the liberals' frustrations, reminded his colleagues that "a hands-off attitude on the part of the President in regard to congressional reforms can no more be justified than a hands-off attitude on the part of Congress in regard to the operations of the Executive establishment." This frustration was accented by another difference in styles between Mansfield and Johnson: The Texan always worked hard for an item once he had committed himself to it. So even though Mansfield had expressed an interest in Anderson's three-fifths resolution, he was now more eager to skip the issue than to press for the measure's success. Johnson would not have made that promise unless he meant to keep it—one reason why Mitchell did not get along as well with Mansfield.[6]

The 1963 struggle to modify Rule XXII, reflecting the prevailing climate, was the most intense ever waged. It centered again on a motion by Anderson to adopt a three-fifths cloture rule. The question of whether the Senate was a continuing body operating under existing rules, or whether it could change its standing rules and adopt new ones by regular parliamentary procedure—a majority vote—at the beginning of a session, was still the dividing line between those who wanted to modify Rule XXII and those who did not.

The 1963 attempt involved politically active local NAACP leaders and Leadership Conference for Civil Rights activists who were all brought into Washington to participate in the lobbying blitz. Mitchell, having been involved in the 1949 battle, made an uncharacteristic mistake by holding to the belief that the struggle would "be won or lost in the White House" and urging President Kennedy to express his strong support for the reforms. He stuck to this position because there was no realistic alternative political leverage. He felt that Kennedy's leadership was needed, first, to make Vice President Johnson cooperate fully while presiding over the Senate; and, second, to ensure that Mansfield and Dirksen mobilized the required votes among nonsouthern Democrats and Republicans. No one was more aware of the limitations of his office than Kennedy. He remained silent on events in the Senate, revealing his firsthand knowledge of underlying sensibilities and political consequences. But he openly participated in the struggle to expand the House Rules Committee—a contradiction that bothered Mitchell. Kennedy warned that if the twelve-member committee was not expanded, "our whole program . . . would be emasculated." That specious admonition only further increased Mitchell's frustrations because he knew the struggle was more symbolic than substantive.

In a January 24, 1963, meeting that lasted nearly two hours with Mitchell, Wilkins, Herman Edelsberg of the Anti-Defamation League, Arnold Aaronson of the Leadership Conference on Civil Rights, and Jacob Clayman, a top official of the Industrial Union Department of the AFL-CIO, Johnson attempted to deflect attention on to other issues. But the civil rights representatives kept the focus on the filibuster. Seeking to get at least an indirect expression of support from the White House while also drawing on Johnson's influence with the Democrats, the delegation stressed that the Vice President had the authority to ensure that the rules issue was brought to a vote. Clayman observed that many people regarded the Vice President as one of the leaders of the Democratic party and did not feel he was a "neuter gender" in the fight to implement his party's platform. Aware senators like Mansfield regarded him as "an agent of the executive branch"; Johnson insisted that that was the majority leader's responsibility. Most certainly, he also was not about to contradict his own established position. He argued instead that the sessions were too short and the liberals were not using all available parliamentary advantages. He certainly knew better, that even an all-out effort by the reformers would fail. Nevertheless, he offered to advise some of the senators on parliamentary tactics, but only if they sought his help.

Still attempting—unsuccessfully—to back Johnson into a corner, the civil rights delegation told him that many observers assumed that he would use his vice presidential office to rule in favor of the South. The current struggle was "a test in the eyes of many people." They were watching to see whether he would follow Richard Nixon's precedent and rule that under the Constitution each Congress could adopt its own rules, and thus give the Senate a chance to vote on the proposed changes, or whether he would adhere to his standard position and deny this opportunity. Unfazed, Johnson insisted he would be fair but said he could not reveal how he would rule on procedure. Contradictorily, he remained very critical of senators seeking to change the rules, maintaining that if they were more resourceful, more energetic, and more familiar with parliamentary procedures, they could win. Johnson insisted that rules change opponents were not as strong as they had been in the past when, as majority leader, he was able to block reforms.

As expected, Johnson refused to take a stand on the issue while presiding. When Anderson pressed him, he ruled that under precedents the Senate and not the presiding officer had to decide the question. In vain Keating urged Johnson to put the question to a vote immediately and avoid a filibuster. Johnson said he had no authority to do that, so he let the Senate debate it. On January 31, a majority (53 to 42) of senators, with Johnson's help, then tabled the Anderson motion to adopt a three-fourths cloture rule. Now a two-thirds majority was needed to end the continuing debate over whether to change the rule. But the vote on February 7 for cloture was 54 to 42—10 short of the required margin—and the attempt failed.

A disappointed Mitchell nevertheless now regarded the cloture vote as only a technical defeat because for the first time a majority of senators revealed a willingness to change the rules. More confident than ever, he turned his attention to the legislative battle. The 1961 and 1963 debates had left in effect the modest revision that Johnson had engineered in 1959 requiring two thirds of the senators present and voting to impose cloture. Experience spared him illusions about the difficulties ahead.[7]

Acknowledging this reality as he joined Mitchell in the gallery on the day the Senate tabled the Anderson motion, Rauh told his friend, "I know that we do not have the votes, but I have come today because I want to be on the deck with you when the ship goes down." Mitchell was upset when

The Washington Post, strongly defending Johnson for his hands-off stance, aimed an editorial torpedo at Rauh for charging that the Vice President's "first loyalty is to the Southern racists." In the manner that characterized their sense of mutual protectiveness, Mitchell told the *Post* that its contention that Rauh's charge was an "intemperate abuse" should also have been aimed at him because they both shared the same feelings about Johnson. He said it was fortunate that the civil rights cause had been advanced by "men like Mr. Rauh who are not discouraged by criticism." Optimistically, he said that there were many similarly courageous people who were getting elected to the House and Senate. "However, I have noted that filibuster corpsmen and the gentlemanly advocates of racial segregation always seem to fare better in the news and editorial columns of the Washington daily papers than men like Senators Douglas, Javits, Case and Humphrey who do not compromise on civil rights."

Anyone following the filibuster debates, he admonished the *Post,* knew "it was a sham battle from the beginning to end. There was no possible way for the stalling to be effective without tolerance and cooperation by the Senate leadership and the Vice President." He said that the Vice President provided an example of his influence on February 7 right after the cloture vote when, as presiding officer, he ignored Javits, who was strenuously raising a point of order, and gaveled him down. Continued Mitchell:

> I defy anyone to show an instance of similar treatment given the filibuster bloc. I insist that if the presiding officer had been about one hundredth as firm with the filibuster team as he was with Senator Javits the outcome would have been different. I also insist that the firmness need not have been the crushing kind of silencing that was used on the Senator from New York.[8]

Mitchell was further upset by what he felt was the deliberate omission of the proceedings involving Javits from the February 7 *Congressional Record.* He explained in his *Baltimore Afro-American* column, "From the Work Bench," that the proceedings were only reported in the February 11 *Record* because Javits had insisted. That omission increased his fear that the steamroller had begun to move in the Senate—an unfortunate omen for civil rights legislation. These tactics, he said, "may be tolerable in secret organizations or some private clubs, but they are not to be sanctioned in the U.S. Senate or in any other body" composed of elected officials in a democracy. He maintained that Americans wanted their government to be "a model of dignity and fair play" and did not want to see "great issues swept under the rug with the filibuster broom." To ensure fair play, he said, Americans should demand an end to "dilatory and obfuscating tactics" that were preventing the Senate from performing it constitutional function.

The basic problem, Mitchell felt, was that there were "just not enough people [in Congress] who believe that colored citizens are entitled to equal treatment under law." He emphasized this attitude by noting that in 1961, 32 Democrats, many of whom were from outside the South, had joined 18 Republicans in killing the Anderson resolution. He felt that Anderson's three-fifths proposal, which had had a much better chance of passage than had the alternative majority-vote resolution, "would have been a slight improvement over the present" two-thirds rule. The modification would have made it easier to pass civil rights legislation. Now in 1963, Mitchell bitterly charged, the only effect of Johnson's ostensible neutrality as presiding officer was to strengthen opponents far more than their numbers warranted. At the same time, the "use of gentle tactics" by Mansfield and Dirksen against opponents enabled them to frustrate those who wanted change.

Ruefully observing that Kennedy had not hesitated to participate in the 1963 struggle to enlarge the House Rules Committee from twelve to fifteen members, Mitchell declared that it was "pure fiction" to assume "that it is proper for a President to seek changes in the procedures of the House, but improper for him to seek changes in the Senate." Particularly frustrating was that the Senate rules struggle was far more important than that in the House. Furthermore, given its very limited scope, Mitchell saw "no reason for dancing in the streets because of the so-called liberalization of the House Committee on Rules."

The House Rules Committee fight, which had begun full-blown in 1961, was the climax of a long struggle by liberals to remove a roadblock caused by Chairman Howard Smith's conservative control over bills that were on their way from standing committees to the House floor. It had erupted as a dramatic showdown between House Speaker Rayburn, who was backed by the incoming Kennedy administration and the liberals led by the Democratic Study Group,* and conservatives led by Howard Smith with the support of "loyalist" southerners headed by Georgian Carl Vinson. Rayburn said that expansion was the most "painless" way to weaken the conservative grip on the committee. Rayburn reached that conclusion after other attempts, such as reinstituting the "twenty-one-day rule" under which a committee chairman could petition the House speaker to bring up a bill if the Rules Committee had not granted it a rule within twenty-one calendar days, had failed. After an intense debate, the House adopted the plan in 1961 to expand the Rules Committee from twelve to fifteen mem-

*The Democratic Study Group was composed of one hundred liberals in the House who were mainly from the North.

bers by 217 to 212 roll-call votes, for the duration of the Eighty-seventh Congress only.

One Sunday in December, in preparation for the 1963 battle to liberalize the House Rules Committee again for the new Congress, the Leadership Conference announced its intention to back the effort to retain the fifteen-member committee. The LCCR noted that, in addition to rejecting the education and urban affairs bills, the committee had pigeonholed twenty-two others. At the December meeting on the issue, Biemiller reported that the House leaders knew they did not have more than 210 votes to get a fifteen-member committee. On the eve of the vote in the House on the issue, the Leadership Conference was surprised to learn that, based on a survey of about two hundred congressmen, there was substantial support for the fifteen-member committee as well as for the twenty-one-day rule. The fact, however, that the House leaders who were pushing for a change decided to make the fifteen-member committee permanent, rather than trying to have the twenty-one-day rule readopted, showed that there was considerable doubt about the success of the latter alternative.

On Wednesday, January 9, the House approved the proposal for a fifteen-member Rules Committee by 235 to 196. The Leadership Conference regretted that the House leadership and the White House did not try to get the twenty-one-day rule procedure adopted; neither did they attempt to see whether the House would have accepted a change to another alternative, a seven-day rule. "They did not even take a nose-count on those two proposals," the Leadership Conference noted. "They fought merely to stand still." The Leadership Conference noted that *The Washington Post* similarly said in an editorial:

> Unfortunately, there was no fight to make the Rules Committee a responsible tool of the central House leadership or give the speaker and his aides power to circumvent the committee when necessary. At the very least the House should have added the 21-day rule to the equipment of its hard-pressed Speaker, Mr. McCormack, and the substantial vote for the larger Rules Committee suggests that it could have done so, with vigorous and skillful leadership.

Mitchell concluded that simple arithmetic showed that previously "we faced a four to four roadblock"—four Democrats joining with four conservative Republicans to block civil rights. He now felt, based on the committee's ideological alignment, that the expansion meant only that five Democrats and five Republicans would comprise the new roadblock.

Mitchell thought that GOP conservatives might join liberal Democrats to grant a rule on some civil rights measures, as had been done in the past.

The new members might also give "the kind of token and surface support for some aspects of civil rights" that had previously been given. But the membership change had "neither increased nor lessened" chances for success. He believed that one southern addition might vote for liberal but not civil rights legislation. That meant that the South would "pose a new and stronger threat to any anti-segregation amendments that may be included in such legislation." His main concern was the intentions of the administration, which saw what it erroneously regarded as a narrow victory in the Rules Committee as another indication of difficulties ahead for its legislative program. But while the administration was profoundly relieved that it had done so well in this test of strength, Mitchell was painfully aware that Chairman Smith still retained undiluted power to schedule committee meetings.

Still ringing in Mitchell's ears was Kennedy's declaration, made during the 1960 campaign, that "as a legislative leader the President must give us the legal weapons needed to enforce the constitutional rights of every American. He cannot wait for others to act. He himself must draft the programs—transmit them to Congress and fight for their enactment." In early 1961, Mitchell said: "That statement was made at promise-making time," during the campaign. "This is now promise-fulfillment time."

Mitchell told an NAACP audience in Houston in September that the President had many assets if he decided to fight: "He is blessed with great personal charm and broad practical knowledge of what must be done to get a bill through. He has the most capable and shrewdest legislative advisers in the world—Mr. Sam [Rayburn] from Texas and Vice President Lyndon Johnson. In addition, many of the bright young men who served with the President when he was a member of the House and Senate are now seasoned and mature leaders in Congress. Senator Hubert Humphrey is the assistant majority leader. Senator Thomas Kuchel is the assistant minority leader. Representative Adam Clayton Powell is chairman of the powerful House Labor Committee, and that old fighter from Brooklyn, Representative Emanuel Celler, is still chairman of the House Judiciary Committee. If the President sounds the call to arms for a civil rights fight it will be possible to get a far stronger bipartisan alliance to support him than the opponents can muster in the form of a coalition between southern Democrats and ultra-conservative Republicans."

Mitchell skipped what Simeon Booker had labeled "the White House anti-slavery reception" that President Kennedy gave as part of the Emancipation Centennial celebrations. Mitchell did not believe the administration's sorry record on civil rights legislation merited his presence. More appropriately billed as a Lincoln's Birthday buffet—one of several observances throughout the country—the gala was a marked social advance over Eisenhower's black stag parties. Kennedy, nonetheless, was very careful about sending the wrong message to the South with too much publicity about the event. Among the eight hundred or so guests who attended the evening in Camelot were Juanita Mitchell and her mother. Juanita could not pass up the opportunity to get a glimpse of Jacqueline Kennedy's legendary glamour. The White House tactfully reminded its guests of the political significance of the buffet with a beautiful souvenir pamphlet showing how much civil rights progress had been made under Kennedy. Earlier that day, the Civil Rights Commission had also provided a somber birthday present by releasing its report *Freedom to the Free,* which traced civil rights progress over the past one hundred years.[9]

John Kennedy had disowned the package of six bills that Senator Joseph Clark of Pennsylvania and Congressman Celler had drafted and introduced at his request on May 8, 1961. The Clark-Celler bills called for elimination of the poll tax and literacy tests in elections, the beginning of school desegregation in all districts by 1963, technical and financial assistance to expedite school desegregation, authority for the attorney general to initiate civil rights cases, a federal FEPC law, and establishment of the Civil Rights Commission as a permanent agency. White House Press Secretary Pierre Salinger, scuttling this effort, told reporters that the elements of the Clark-Celler package "are not administration bills. The President does not consider it necessary at this time to enact civil rights legislation." The day of Salinger's announcement, Mansfield, after meeting with the President, said, "We want to get a program outlined by the President through and after that we will consider civil rights if necessary." The withdrawal confirmed Mitchell's fears that a political decision had been made to sidetrack the civil rights legislative program and concentrate instead on executive action.

The only civil rights legislation that emerged from Congress in 1961 was approval of a two-year extension for the Civil Rights Commission, which was scheduled to expire on November 9. Liberals were thwarted in their attempts to attach amendments to other bills to (1) extend the commission for life, (2) or, as an alternative, for four years, (3) to authorize civil suits for injunctive relief (in another attempt to revive the defeated Part III of the 1957 Civil Rights Act), and (4) to authorize federal aid to school districts seeking to desegregate.[10]

Very early in 1962, in a bipartisan strategy session on civil rights, liberal senators selected bills each would introduce or cosponsor. Javits announced on January 17 that he and several other senators were offering an amendment "to make the right to vote available to all citizens who have a sixth grade education" and that he would introduce his measure as an amendment to an appropriate bill.

Eight days later, in response to President Kennedy's call in his State of the Union Message for an end to voter discrimination through literacy tests* and poll taxes, Mansfield offered a bill, cosponsored by Minority Leader Dirksen, for the administration that included only federal elections. The Javits amendment covered local and federal elections. Mansfield used his authority as majority leader to ensure that the Senate would consider his bill before the Javits amendment, while at the same time blocking an attempt to bring the Javits measure onto the floor. Also, instead of the administration bill being introduced simultaneously in the House as was customary, it was not done in the lower chamber until February 1, further arousing suspicion of subterfuge.

Instead of sending the Javits amendment to the Senate Rules Committee headed by the majority leader, Vice President Johnson ruled that it should go to the Judiciary Committee graveyard under James Eastland. Javits appealed the ruling to send his amendment to the Judiciary Committee, while Mitchell urged the Senate to overrule Johnson and send it to the Senate Rules Committee where it would have a better chance of surviving. Finally, Mansfield and Dirksen pledged they would ensure that the Senate considered the literacy test issue within ninety days. The Senate then approved 61 to 25 a Mansfield motion to table the Javits appeal.

On April 24, 1962, Mansfield called up his bill as an amendment to another bill already on the calendar, thus bypassing the Senate Judiciary Committee. The Mansfield-Dirksen bill provided that the government's existing powers to sue to protect the right to vote would be applied where local authorities defied the new law. The proposal's basic benefit was that it would have made having a sixth-grade education conclusive proof of literacy and shifted the burden of proof from the government to local registrars, who administered voter requirements. The bill extended to Puerto Rico, and thus covered Puerto Ricans in New York, but civil rights forces thought it was severely flawed by being limited to federal elections.

No matter how sincere the administration's intentions were, any literacy test requirements would still be open to subjective standards set by southern voter registrars. A proof of greater sincerity would have been a willingness to permit the bill to be broadened with strengthening amendments. That was the purpose of the Javits amendment. For their part, the NAACP and its allies had hoped to offer at an appropriate time carefully drawn amendments giving the attorney general authority to seek injunctions to protect Fourteenth Amendment rights, providing federal assistance

* According to the Justice Department, twenty states required literacy tests: Alabama, Alaska, Arizona, California, Connecticut, Delaware, Georgia, Hawaii, Louisiana, Maine, Massachusetts, Mississippi, New Hampshire, New York, North Carolina, Oregon, South Carolina, Virginia, Washington, and Wyoming.

to accelerate school desegregation and requiring good faith compliance, and extending the statute to cover state elections.

From the manner in which the Javits amendment was sidetracked, it was clear that the administration disapproved of it. It was not possible for it to pass without administration backing. Mitchell observed that once more the anti-civil-rights coalition was not simply a Republican-southern Democratic bloc but was widespread.

The fact that two years after passage of the 1960 Civil Rights Act—which was meant to strengthen the 1957 act—the administration was proposing further remedial legislation against voting discrimination showed how ineffective those laws were in ending Fifteenth Amendment rights violations in some states. One clear advantage the NAACP was enjoying over earlier periods was the Civil Rights Commission's independent documentation of violations that supported the organization's complaints. Another was that under Robert Kennedy, the Justice Department by April 1962 had filed no less than twenty-four separate actions in Alabama, Georgia, Louisiana, Mississippi, and Tennessee, and was preparing more lawsuits. By proposing to correct discrimination in literacy tests, President Kennedy showed that he recognized that lawsuits alone could not remedy the problem. The NAACP felt the administration's approach was piecemeal and inadequate.

Senator Ervin sounded another somber note by announcing that his Subcommittee on Constitutional Rights would soon begin hearings on the Mansfield-Dirksen bill. As Ervin opened hearings, he promised to provide the Senate with "a thorough source of information on all" relevant questions.

Roy Wilkins ignored the posturing and sharply criticized the administration bill and similar measures, "regardless of their merits as voting bills," as inadequate. "While we recognize the long range effect of any effort to extend and protect the voting franchise, we remain keenly aware of other immediate and critical needs in the area of civil rights." Wilkins expressed strong support for the Javits amendment and said that even more was needed "to cleanse federal elections of racial discrimination." He noted that the Supreme Court had stated clearly in 1879 in Ex parte *Siebold* that Congress had the power to take over federal voter registration and management of those "elections machinery, lock, stock and barrel."*

---

*The Supreme Court held:

Congress may, if it sees fit, assume the entire control and regulation of the election of Representatives. This would necessarily involve the appointment of the places for holding the polls, the times of voting, and the officers for holding the elections: it would require the regulation of the duties to be performed, the custody of the ballots, the mode of ascertaining the result, and every other matter relating to the subject.

Reaffirming this authority over federal elections in Ex parte *Yarborough,* the Court ruled that Congress could "provide, if necessary, the officers who shall conduct them and make return of the results."

Wilkins thought it surprising, in light of the Supreme Court's decisions supporting the NAACP's position, that so much outrage was expressed in Congress over the Javits proposal for federal referees. "From the clamor, one would have thought the proposal was completely foreign to American democracy and had never been broached before." But, he noted, the Civil Rights Commission had endorsed the referee proposal. He therefore urged support for a broader voting rights bill that had been offered by Michigan's Philip Hart, but that support was not given.[11]

Attorney General Kennedy told the House Judiciary Committee that the literacy problem was particularly acute in states with large black populations. In 1959, not one voting age black was registered to vote in sixteen southern counties where blacks were the majority. Fewer than 5 percent of eligible blacks were registered in forty-nine other such counties. Kennedy said that the main reason for this problem was the "literacy interpretation or similar performance tests"—a reality that had been documented by the Southern Regional Council. The Civil Rights Commission reaffirmed those findings in its 1961 report and recommended enactment of a federal law to make a sixth-grade education sufficient for any state literacy test.

Because of the wide discretion currently held by persons administering literacy tests, the attorney general said, opportunities for discrimination were endless. He explained that particular cases could in time be corrected through litigation, but that that would not curtail future abuses of discretion. He proposed "the substitution of an objective standard" based on a sixth-grade education "for the present subjective color bar to federal voting."

Southerners attacked the bill on two main fronts. They first charged that it was unconstitutional because it attempted to impose federal qualifications for voters when the Constitution (Article I, Section 2) clearly provided that requirements were the province of the states. They also charged that the government had not used the 1960 Civil Rights Act to get federal courts to end alleged literacy test abuses. They were up against Javits, though, who demanded: "If federal courts have the power to correct these abuses on an individual and piecemeal basis, why doesn't the Congress have the power to do it on a comprehensive basis, particularly since the 15th Amendment specifically authorized Congress by appropriate legislation to enforce the voting rights of Negroes?"

The attorney general noted that legislation to eliminate poll taxes either by statute or by constitutional amendment had been introduced in every session of Congress since 1939. Five times between 1942 and 1949, the House had passed such a statute; three times the Senate killed such a statute by filibuster. The attorney general further stated that in recent years Florida, Tennessee, South Carolina, and Georgia, among other states, had repealed their poll tax, leaving only Alabama, Arkansas, Mississippi, Texas, and Virginia with the discriminatory requirement. While stressing that poll taxes were not only antiquated but also "arbitrary and meaningless," he left it up to Congress to determine how to eliminate them. He told the committee that he felt legislation abolishing the poll tax for federal elections was constitutional.[12]

Mitchell welcomed the attorney general's outline of the problem, but was adamant that Congress also had power under the Constitution to abolish poll taxes for state elections. He told a subcommittee of the House Judiciary Committee that the Reverend Theodore Hesburgh, president of the University of Notre Dame and a member of the Civil Rights Commission, expressed the "shame that all Americans should" have felt "at the spectacle of college graduates being subjected to reading and writing tests by registrars as though they were primary grade children and then being denied the right to vote without reason or explanation." That shame, Mitchell said, "should be intensified" by recent elections in India, where there was "an overwhelming problem of mass illiteracy." Nevertheless, those elections made India the world's largest democracy and gave citizens of that country a much better opportunity to vote on their government's policies than Americans had in some states.

Mitchell urged the committee to follow the Republican party's recommendation to ban literacy tests by a simple statute rather than by a constitutional amendment, as some were suggesting. He noted that the Kennedy administration had also indicated its willingness to support the NAACP's position.

Mitchell regarded the May 9, 1962, vote of 53 to 43 against a motion to invoke cloture on debate of the Mansfield-Dirksen literacy bill as another "test of whether senators really want action on civil rights." Mansfield next moved, as he had previously announced he would, to table the literacy test bill, then turned around and voted against his motion. He said his plan was to see whether the Senate voted "preponderantly" against tabling and, if it did, to try for another cloture vote.

His colleagues opposed tabling by a 64 to 33 vote, in a curious display of esprit de corps. On the second cloture attempt, without a single senator switching his previous position, they voted 52 to 42 to continue debate. (The difference in the vote counts was due to absences.) The next day the Senate gave the bill the coup de grâce by voting 49 to 34 to lay it aside. In the subsequent recriminations, Mansfield defended the administration, saying that it had not been lethargic in its support as some had charged. He complained that civil rights forces had lacked enthusiasm for an all-out fight during what the majority leader called a "desultory" filibuster. That assertion went unchallenged because the civil rights bloc had set its heart on the much stronger Clark-Celler package of bills. The reason Mitchell and the NAACP's allies did not fight for the cloture bill was that they felt a quarter loaf was not worth the effort. They nevertheless learned some important lessons. (During a strategy session with Paul Douglas in April, Mitchell and Rauh had agreed that Rauh would lobby liberal Democrats to win support for the bills and Mitchell would do the same with Republicans. That arrangement showed why many people in Washington always believed that Mitchell was a Republican rather than a registered Independent.) The White House claimed the defeat proved that "we can't get a civil rights bill through Congress."[13]

Given the resounding failure of the Eighty-eighth Congress (1963–64) to modify the cloture rule, this struggle, as well as another over a communications satellite bill, served as reminders of how much lawmakers voted their interests. Liberals opposed the satellite bill, arguing that it was a giveaway to AT&T, and tried during their five-day filibuster in August 1962 to educate the public on the brand-new issues involved. They lost the intensely fought battle because those who previously had refused to vote for cloture to pass civil rights did so to pass a measure in which commercial interests and advancing technology were of paramount importance for them.

For Mitchell, the switch unmasked the hypocrisy of the filibuster supporters, who heralded the success—the first in thirty-five years—of invoking cloture on a bill as proof that the two-thirds rule was not an insurmountable obstacle. Mitchell agreed because he had reached that conclusion a long time ago. He reminded the senators that the 63 to 27 vote "was merely a formalized record of arrangements of the kind that Vice President Johnson made informally when he was majority leader in the Senate." He had in mind "the formula" Johnson had used in 1957 and 1960 to win approval of the civil rights bills. Debate then was limited and firm commitments had been obtained to table amendments that were not included in the package supported by the majority of senators.

Mitchell believed that the satellite bill lesson could be applied to civil rights. Conservatives could not impose cloture without (1) a substantial number of liberals voting with them, (2) a "generous sprinkling of cloture foes who switch positions and vote" to cut off debate, and (3) the absence of a large number of "unreconstructed filibuster" supporters. He maintained that the key ingredient was leadership. Both the administration and Senate leaders fully supported the communications satellite bill, so they won.

The fight over the poll-tax constitutional amendment bill revealed an ironic conflict. Much of the South, as expected, opposed it. But the administration and its supporters in Congress pulled out all the stops for its passage, while the NAACP and its allies avoided a strong fight against it.

The NAACP was opposed to removing the poll tax by a constitutional amendment because it believed that, owing to the long and cumbersome process that it would have to undergo before it could be adopted, there was "no great reason to expect success." Mitchell feared that accepting such an amendment "would appear to be conceding that a law passed by Congress would be unconstitutional." He said that that would be a bad precedent, since the constitutional issue was raised whenever civil rights legislation was considered.

Another reason for the NAACP's opposition, Mitchell explained, was that the constitutional amendment method would get lukewarm civil rights supporters in Congress off the hook. That method would give them an opportunity to avoid a vigorous battle in which they would have to indicate for the record whether or not they supported the right of blacks to vote, because they knew that opponents in the states would ultimately block its ratification. Mitchell expressed confidence that, because of the increased interest in the franchise that Congress had shown, an anti-poll-tax bill could be passed, but he feared that Congress would not consider such legislation during the seven years the law allowed for the amendment to be ratified by three quarters of the states. Noting that both the Republicans and the administration had endorsed a sixth-grade literacy voting-qualification level, he urged lawmakers to support their party platforms by combining the literacy and poll tax provisions in one bill. Congress chose the two alternatives less favored by the NAACP.[14]

The amendment was sponsored in the Senate by Florida Democrat Spessard Holland, who had introduced one in every Congress since 1949. He urged southerners to support the measure in order to show the country that the South was reasonable on civil rights. Mitchell was quick to detect in Holland's proposal a provision that "nothing in this article shall be construed to invalidate any provision of law denying the right to vote to paupers or persons supported at public expense or by charitable institutions." Before Senator Douglas and other civil rights supporters could take steps to remove the provision, which they knew would be used to continue discrimination against blacks, Holland withdrew it. The Senate then approved the poll tax amendment 77 to 16 after ten days of debate. Despite NAACP and ADA pleas, all Senate liberals voted for it. Only the southerners, Holland's optimism notwithstanding, voted against it, underscoring once more the region's intransigence.

In the House, the constitutional amendment bill had to be forced out of Howard Smith's Rules Committee on August 27 under a suspension of the rules. This procedure required a two-thirds vote to bring the measure onto the House floor, but it had to be voted up or down without any amendments being attached to it. The NAACP's allies did not have an opportunity to vote on a proposal to outlaw the poll tax by statute because of a lack of time. Conceding to what was more a setback than defeat after the House passed the constitutional amendment bill 294 to 86, Mitchell urged NAACP branches to "make a good faith effort to help get" it ratified as he turned to the larger political struggle.

The above skirmishes showed how far Congress was from passing meaningful civil rights laws at the time when demonstrations in the South were gathering force, and exposed clearly the gap in the NAACP's program that King and the student demonstrators were filling. A moral awakening was needed in the nation to boost the NAACP's struggle for civil rights legislation in Congress.

Mitchell's earlier conclusion that enough senators did not care about civil rights held true for the rest of 1962. He was also convinced that virtually no lawmaker without strong black constituencies who normally voted against cloture saw the need to incur the wrath of southern committee chairmen who controlled ten of the fifteen Senate committees.[15]

Dirksen was a perfect example. On January 8, 1963, the day before the new Senate convened and the filibuster rule fight was resumed, Mitchell asked the minority leader to cooperate with Senate liberals and not make a motion that would have undercut them and forced the adoption of the old two-thirds cloture rule. Angrily, Dirksen complained that during the 1962 reelection campaign, blacks in Chicago, particularly those writing for the *Defender,* had ridiculed him as being an enemy of civil rights. A surprised Mitchell reported, "Senator Dirksen spoke rather frankly to me and he seemed to be speaking from his heart. He said he really meant it. He said he did not feel like he had any obligation to go out of his way for the Negro." Dirksen, himself, while maintaining that he had "a great regard for" blacks, "and they have been very kind to me," explained that he had no objection to Mitchell but to "the organization he represents." He recalled, "I carried the flag in the Eisenhower administration for all civil rights legislation and got a good deal of it through." But the NAACP, based on reports in the Chicago newspapers, had not "demonstrated any real appreciation." Not only did he support the 1957 and 1960 Civil Rights acts, but he also voted for the filibuster rule change in 1959 and strongly supported President Kennedy's appointment of Thurgood Marshall to the U.S. Court of Appeals for the Second Circuit.

Dirksen told Mitchell that he would withhold his motion to table the rules change only if convinced that liberals had "a serious chance to win." If the maneuver would simply bog down the Senate in prolonged, useless debate, he would not tolerate it. Returning subsequently to Dirksen's office for another meeting after the senator had announced that he would offer his motion to kill the rules change effort, Mitchell found him "very agreeable" to postponing his action. Republican senators like Pennsylvania's Hugh Scott, meanwhile, who depended on the black vote for election, at a Policy Committee meeting won an agreement from the minority leader that Mansfield, as majority leader, had a greater responsibility for the conduct of the Senate. Dirksen agreed that he would not make the tabling motion unless the Democrat joined him in doing so. The fact that the cloture rule modification struggle was killed by this bipartisan agreement was no consolation to Mitchell. Dirksen, he was reminded, had to be courted with special care.[16]

Despite the common purpose of the celebrated "Big Six," Mitchell had little contact with most of the leaders of the other civil rights organizations, with the exception of Whitney Young, executive director of the National Urban League. The other groups were CORE, which, like the NAACP was a membership organization, the National Council of Negro Women, SCLC, and SNCC. The latter three, and the NUL, which was founded a year after the NAACP, were service organizations. The NCNW, while not on the firing line, was influential. The SCLC was the embodiment of Martin Luther King's personality and philosophy; SNCC was characterized by the zeal of its activists. Philip Randolph was not considered a member of the Big Six because the Brotherhood of Sleeping Car Porters was a labor union; highly respected as the pillar of black leadership, he added a radical edge to the group.

As an indication of their mutual affection and esteem, Randolph called Mitchell the "quarterback of the movement." The Brotherhood, the NUL, and the NCNW had working bases in Washington, while the others were primarily engaged in nonviolent direct action demonstrations in the South. Mitchell's chief lobbying allies were labor, religious, and liberal groups like the American Jewish Congress, the American Jewish Committee, the Anti-Defamation League of B'nai B'rith, the Americans for Democratic Action—all of whom were now the backbone of the Leadership Conference on Civil Rights—and local NAACP branch leaders like Aaron Henry, the Reverend I. DeQuincey Newman, NAACP field secretary in South Carolina, and Kelly Alexander, Sr., of North Carolina. The direct access that these and other local NAACP leaders had to Mitchell considerably increased his political arsenal as well as his contributions to the struggle outside Washington.

Delbert Woods, chairman of the Labor and Industrial Committee of the South Carolina State Conference of NAACP Branches, provided an example of this relationship. A painter at the Charleston Navy Yard, Woods in 1963 was the equivalent of his employer's equal employment opportunity officer and spent most of his time on the job handling hundreds of racial discrimination complaints from fellow black workers. Woods got into a furious dispute with his superiors after they read a newspaper report claiming that he had attended a civil rights rally in a nearby city when he was supposed to be home on sick leave. Seeing an opportunity to intimidate or to get rid of him, his superiors threatened to report him to the shipyard's admiral. Woods replied, "Well, the big boys, they outrank me. I tell you what. I'll get you a reply from people who outrank them." He called Mitchell just as he was rushing off to a meeting on the Hill.

"You know," recalled Woods, "when Clarence gets excited he stutters." Woods knew him well because he normally called him once a week. Mitchell asked, "Delbert, what's the man's name?" Woods told him. Right away, Mitchell fired off a telegram to the shipyard warning that its inquiry into Woods's civil rights activities was improper. Then he appealed in Washington to those who influence admirals. At seven o'clock the following morning, Woods's supervisor told him that "all hell had broken loose." He had been ordered "to drop this matter right now and not to bother with it any more and to extend their apologies for any inconvenience they may have caused you." When his supervisor repeated in bewilderment, "I don't know what happened," Woods replied, "I know." He reminded his boss that he knew people who outranked the "big boys." He had no further problems after that.

Alexander, another close friend, explained, "The average branch person always knew him." Mitchell "never lost touch with the common people." His friendship was especially valued because "he always had something good to say about local people." He never said "anything derogatory about anyone." He praised branch people as much as he did supportive lawmakers and studiously educated them on the many important issues with which he was grappling in Washington. Alexander found that "once he appeared anywhere, everybody always wanted him to come back." This was particularly true in the South, especially in Mississippi. As he had begun doing years earlier, Mitchell continued working with Alexander implementing various civil rights programs, such as building a black political base in North Carolina and the rest of the NAACP's dangerous southeast region.[17]

With whites becoming much more active in the ranks of top leadership as well as on the front lines in the South, the benefit of a broader-based mass movement was more obvious than ever. Wilkins through the LCCR was enjoying the scholarly input of such activist lawyers as William Taylor, who, among other things, urged in 1960 that the next President "should bring together at one or more White House conference white and black leaders from throughout the nation" for the purpose of creating trust and "finding the means for orderly transition to a desegregated society." Taylor said that the President "should establish within the executive office an officer who will maintain continuing liaison with representatives of national organizations which advocate civil rights." Taylor may not have directly contributed to Kennedy's subsequent appointment of a White House civil rights specialist, but his articulation of the idea certainly helped convince others of the need. (Kennedy at first regarded the issue of a specialist as strictly political and only wanted to "get rid of this civil rights mess.")

The mass movement's full development by mid-1963 brought other expressions of welcome from Wilkins. "I can't stress too much this struggle for civil rights ought not to be a struggle between Negroes and Whites," he said. "It should be a joint effort by whites and Negroes who want the best for the country." The reality of an entrenched and unstoppable social revolution involved not only blacks who were determined to cast off the stigma of second-class citizenship, but also sympathetic whites who were driven by a moral awakening.

Mitchell's close ties with labor were almost an anomaly, given the very acerbic relationship now existing between the unions and the NAACP national office as a result of attacks by Herbert Hill, the association's labor director, on endemic union discrimination. As the NAACP's head, Wilkins played a major role in containing tensions and maintaining a balance between the required aggressive attacks on discrimination by Hill and Mitchell's continuing courtship of the labor movement's support for his lobbying Congress. Joseph Rauh explains, "Clarence didn't cooperate with people who were discriminating. He cooperated with people who wanted the same results as he even though in every union there may have been some discrimination." At one point, George Meany blasted the NAACP in an extremely bitter speech in New York for urging decertification of unions that practiced discrimination. Nevertheless, Mitchell was especially helped by the AFL-CIO president's private feelings that racial discrimination within unions was undermining the labor movement, and Andrew Biemiller, the organization's legislative director. A Socialist who was once a Democratic congressman from Wisconsin, Biemiller threw the AFL-CIO's total support behind Mitchell and the Leadership Conference on Civil Rights. That commitment made available not only the labor movement's powerful financial backing but also its whopping political clout that reached into most states, except the South.

Given their universal grass-roots outreach, the Christian churches were another major source of mass political strength for the expanding civil rights coalition. Mitchell felt that the churches' deep involvement was required in states where there was not a sufficiently large combination of blacks, liberal whites, and labor groups to provide the type of political leverage needed to win votes in Congress to pass civil rights legislation.

Though he acknowledged they were a major force, he did not regard them
as the "decisive" factor, as some would later claim, in the struggle. Everybody was needed, he explained. For example, had there been just the
churches and not Walter Reuther, "I think we would have been in considerable difficulty." The labor groups "had a great deal of know-how" in
approaching individual lawmakers. Biemiller, with his political and liberal
background, was "just indispensable." Mitchell did not think that "we
could have won" the struggle for legislation with only the head of the
National Council of Churches and not Biemiller. "By the same token, I
think if we'd had Andy without them, we couldn't have won. So they were
all important in my judgment."[18]

Although the foundations for the dramatic entry of the churches into
the struggle were well established, Mitchell still perceived major gaps between promise and fulfillment.

In response to a request from Burke Marshall, assistant attorney general
for civil rights, for his observations on racial practices among the churches,
Mitchell in September 1962 summarized his views:

Methodists Following the merger of the Methodist Episcopal Church,
the Methodist Church South, and the Methodist Protestant Church in the
late 1930s, the Methodists had divided the country into geographical jurisdictions and established a central one that included nearly all black members. The absurdity of this arrangement was illustrated by the Washington
and Baltimore conferences (annual business and pastoral meetings). White
Methodist ministers were members of the Baltimore Conference, while
black ministers in Baltimore were members of the similarly segregated
Washington Conference. There was a plan to permit black churches to
transfer into the white conference, but it was more complicated than the
public school desegregation plans that southern legislatures dreamed up to
frustrate implementation of the *Brown* v. *Board of Education* decision. Despite the Methodists' many pronouncements against racial discrimination,
their true attitude was best revealed by the firm segregation policies for
their members.

Baptists This was the most segregated denomination. A few Baptist
leaders and southern educational institutions had attempted desegregation.
But white Baptists in the South were the most numerous and militant
segregationists. White Baptist ministers were usually silent or prosegregation, often quoting biblical justification for their racial biases. The controlling boards of deacons silenced the few pro-civil-rights white Baptist
ministers by summarily dismissing them.

Episcopalians Once having a few blacks in strictly segregated
churches supported by white institutions, the Episcopal Church more
recently was attracting middle-income Baptists and Methodists by its

sincerity in promoting goodwill. But most congregations were still segregated.

Roman Catholics   Church doctrine required that all services be open to everyone without racial distinction. Although there was some breach in policy, the 1958 statement of the bishops of the United States that declared segregation could not be "reconciled with the Christian view of our fellow man" reflected the prevailing attitude. Most seminaries and religious orders therefore openly accepted all races. Figures provided by the National Catholic Welfare Council showed that there were 131 black priests in 19 dioceses and 19 religious orders, and 983 black nuns in 109 orders. Additionally, there were 65 black Americans enrolled in seminaries. Worldwide, there were 30 black bishops, 5 archbishops, and 1 cardinal.

The Roman Catholic dioceses in such cities as St. Louis, Washington, Richmond, Raleigh, Nashville, and Fort Smith, Arkansas, led many communities in school desegregation before the Supreme Court's May 17, 1954, decision. The only educational institutions in Mississippi, Alabama, and South Carolina that were fully desegregated were Catholic. Forty-five Catholic interracial councils plus the Third Order of St. Francis contributed to this remarkable progress by adopting major social-action programs.

Presbyterians   There was a systematic and sincere desegregation program within the northern church. Black membership was nevertheless small and unimportant compared to the national racial problem.

Unitarians   Although black membership was small, there had been an effective and extensive effort to welcome minorities in all parts of the country. Segregation seemed to be nonexistent.

Seventh Day Adventists   Black membership was small among mostly segregated churches, although there was some effort to integrate their membership. But the size of the black membership minimized the national impact.

Jehovah's Witnesses   Black membership appeared to be increasing. Racial isolation was based on neighborhood patterns rather than imposed from above. Mixed teams often canvassed for new members. National meetings were also desegregated.

Mitchell summarized his impressions with a story of a black janitor who one day told the pastor of the white church for which he worked that he would like to become a member. Frightened by the possible uproar that would result in his congregation if he admitted the black man, the minister told him he would have to wait while the minister talked to the Lord. After months passed and the janitor said nothing more about his request, the minister asked him why he had made no further effort to join. The janitor said, "Well, Reverend, I talked with the Lord and he told me not to bother because he had been trying to get in this church ever since it was founded, but he had not been able to make it himself." Mitchell said he felt that if "the Good Lord" ever got into most churches, blacks would be able to follow him. So far, He was still "standing outside the fast closed door" in most Protestant churches.

Despite his disappointment, Mitchell, a staunch Methodist, never rejected the Church, as many blacks had done. He lamented the superficiality of the Christian churches, but his faith was buttressed by increasing signs of change and his inspiring relationship with his bureau counsel.

A devout Catholic and lay missionary, Pohlhaus was actively seeking racial justice not only through his work with the NAACP but also through the Catholic interracial councils. In January 1963, he urged the National Catholic Conference on Interracial Justice to step further out front by organizing the community in the struggle against segregation. Noting that the NAACP branches were holding a series of legislative rallies throughout the country, he recommended that local affiliates of the conference do likewise.[19]

The seismic reverberations of the civil rights demonstrations that were shaking the nation were also having a historic impact on the religious institutions, which would manifest itself very visibly in the National Conference on Religion and Race that was held on January 14–17, 1963, at the Bridgewater Hotel in Chicago—the first such ecumenical conclave. The conference was the brainchild of Matthew Ahmann, a young Catholic layman, with the cooperation of Rabbi Marc H. Tanenbaum of the American Jewish Committee, and J. Oscar Lee, executive director of the Department of Racial and Cultural Relations of the National Council of Churches. It was convened by the NCC, the Social Action Department of the National Catholic Welfare Conference, and the Social Action Commission of the Synagogue Council of America. Although the conference drew some criticism for "being out of touch with the realities of the racial revolt in America," it served as a landmark ecumenical catalyst for active broad-based religious involvement in the civil rights struggle.

Among the many follow-up activities were the formation in Washington six months later of an interreligious committee on race relations headed by Archbishop Patrick A. O'Boyle, a Catholic; Bishop John Wesley Lord, a Methodist; Bishop William F. Freighton, an Episcopalian; Rabbi Lewis A. Weintraub, president of the Washington Board of Rabbis; and Bishop Smallwood Williams, a black leader of Bible Way Church Worldwide. In its most forceful statement on race, the NCC, speaking for its thirty-one denominations, left no doubt that the issue was no longer peripheral but "front and center." In a statement adopted on June 7, the NCC's General

Board declared, "Words and declarations are no longer useful in this struggle unless accompanied by sacrifice and commitment." The Union of
American Hebrew Congregations and the Central Conference of American
Rabbis, through the Commission on Social Action of Reform Judaism, also
adopted a comprehensive policy in 1963 in support of "the Negro revolt."[20]

The civil rights demonstrations quickly assumed a life of their own, so
much so that they moved beyond the direct control of sponsoring organizations. Except in Congress, where Mitchell was the guiding force, the students were setting the pace of the movement. The NAACP nevertheless
maintained its commanding presence in the movement in the South as well
as in the North through its network of branches and the Leadership Conference on Civil Rights, which was formally organized in 1963 with an administrative structure.

Previously, there had been little organized coordination on lobbying
between Mitchell and the conference. While Mitchell focused on Congress,
Wilkins, with the help of Arnold Aaronson, the LCCR's secretary, concentrated on mobilizing support from other organizations. Mitchell at the time
spoke only for the NAACP. When necessary, with Wilkins's approval he
would enlist Joseph Rauh's assistance in testifying on some bill in behalf of
the coalition. Most times, though, while following the general NAACP
position, Rauh testified as an ADA representative. For example, on one
occasion in 1959, upon being asked by Mitchell to testify on a civil rights
bill, Rauh asked him to obtain clearance from Wilkins for him to do so.
They next established a schedule of appearances: first, for Wilkins to testify
in general terms in behalf of the LCCR and the NAACP; second, for Rauh
to speak in more specific terms for the LCCR and the ADA; and third, for
supporters from other groups to present their views. This process was cumbersome. After Rauh had carefully edited the testimony that the ADA office had prepared for him, he submitted it to Mitchell for clearance and to
an LCCR representative to ensure that it was in order.

The LCCR's well-coordinated lobbying blitz in early January 1963 for
changing Rule XXII, though unsuccessful, underscored the benefits of such
an operation, as well as the need for a Washington office (the LCCR's address was still the NAACP's New York headquarters). The Kennedy administration's foot-dragging on civil rights legislation plus the turmoil in
the South showed the need for a powerful and well-coordinated lobbying
operation.

Three weeks after more than sixty national organizations agreed on July
2, 1963, in New York to establish a formal lobby, the LCCR's Washington
office was opened in the Mills Building, owned by the Industrial Union
Department of the AFL-CIO. Also helping with funding, equipment, and

personnel were George Meany (indirectly through affiliated AFL unions), the NAACP, several Jewish groups, the American Veterans Committee, the International Union of Electrical Workers, the United Auto Workers, and ADA. In announcing the creation of the office, Wilkins, the LCCR's chairman, said that its "sole purpose will be to persuade this Congress to pass the strongest possible civil rights bill." Mitchell was now named the conference's legislative chairman, Rauh its legal counsel, and Aaronson its secretary.

Somewhat ironically, the opening of the LCCR's Washington office was sparked by internal rivalries. Walter Reuther, renowned for his ability to take charge, saw an opportunity to increase his power by initiating the LCCR's move to Washington. He planned a fancy filet mignon luncheon at the Statler-Hilton to follow a celebrated White House conference on June 22, 1963, with President Kennedy and top civil rights leaders, including himself, when he would announce his plans for the LCCR.

Aware of his intentions, Rauh and Aaronson alerted Wilkins. As Kennedy finished giving the leaders their marching orders, saying, "This is what I intend to do. I am looking to you people to really get behind me and push [the administration's civil rights bill]," Wilkins jumped up and announced that the Leadership Conference was prepared to open a Washington office and would take up the challenge. An undercut Reuther could only go along with Wilkins.

Three and one-half years later, distancing itself from anarchist Stokeley Carmichael, the new leader of SNCC, and his black power movement, the LCCR would further formalize its operation by adopting a statement of purpose and bylaws that firmly embraced the goal of integration. Because this philosophy was anathema to Carmichael, who, particularly, was feuding with King, the student leader declined an invitation for SNCC to sign the LCCR statement and thus spared the coalition further headache by withdrawing.

The consolidation of the civil rights coalition's operations was another confirmation of black political maturity that would further enhance the position of minorities with the political parties. The LCCR's initiative was also significant in that for the first time in the civil rights struggle, there was another apparatus working alongside the NAACP Washington Bureau solely in quest of civil rights legislation.[21]

Mitchell himself had now assumed a new personal distinction, having completed in 1962 a four-year night course at the University of Maryland Law School. Like Juanita, who had followed Charles Houston's advice and earlier earned her law degree at the University of Maryland, he was now a lawyer. During study, he found his extensive knowledge of the court system very helpful and felt that his professors "knew what they were talking about." He enjoyed the experience of going back to school even though, dog tired, he had to do such unusual things as puffing on cigars in the hallway during breaks to stay awake. Specializing in constitutional law, he gained a broader appreciation for the political process. Three years later, he would be admitted to the State Bar of Maryland.[22]

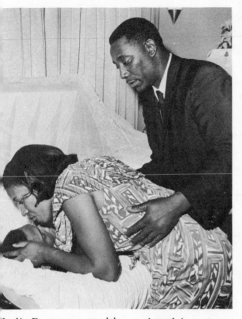

Myrlie Evers says good-bye to her slain
husband, Medgar, as Charles Evers
accompanies her. AP/WIDE WORLD PHOTOS

Senators Everett Dirksen and Mike Mansfield
confer after filing a petition to limit debate on
the literacy test bill.
AP/WIDE WORLD PHOTOS

Mitchell (*fourth from left*) at Medgar Evers's funeral, 1963 AP/WIDE WORLD PHOTOS

Juanita Mitchell, leading a Maryland NAACP delegation, helps lobby for the civil rights bill, 1963. AP/WIDE WORLD PHOTOS

Joseph Rauh, Mitchell, and Roy Wilkins confer at an NAACP legislative conference, 1963. UPI/BETTMANN NEWSPHOTOS

Mitchell meets with the Committee of Hall Monitors during the fight for the Civil Rights Act of 1964. FRED HARRIS

Mitchell celebrates passage of the 1964 Civil
Rights Act with Representative Emanuel
Celler, Hubert Humphrey, and
Representative William McCulloch.

Mitchell and Joseph Rauh discuss strategy
with President Johnson at the White House,
1964. COURTESY THE LYNDON BAINES
JOHNSON LIBRARY

President Johnson signs the 1964 Civil Rights Act.

Mitchell and the President confer on the fair
housing bill, 1967.
WASHINGTON BUREAU, NAACP

President Johnson hands Mitchell a pen used
to sign the fair housing bill, 1968.
WASHINGTON BUREAU, NAACP

Johnson meets with black leaders on April 5, 1968, the day following the assassination of the
Reverend Martin Luther King, Jr. WASHINGTON BUREAU, NAACP

Thurgood Marshall before a Senate Judiciary Subcommittee hearing on his nomination for a U.S. judgeship, 1962

Mitchell meeting with Representative Margaret Chase Smith

President Johnson congratulates Robert C. Weaver, the nation's first black cabinet member, 1966.

Mitchell receives the NAACP's Spingarn
Medal, 1969.

Mitchell, upon being awarded the Spingarn
Medal in 1969, shares the dais with newly
elected public officials of Mississippi as he
delivers his speech.

Mitchell casts a vote as a member of the U.S.
delegation to the United Nations, 1975.
THE BALTIMORE SUN

Mitchell *(second from left)* and other civil rights
leaders meeting with President Ford, 1975
COURTESY OF THE GERALD R. FORD LIBRARY

Arnold Aaronson, Walter Mondale, and
Clarence Mitchell at a Leadership Conference
reception, 1978

President Carter presents the Hubert Humphrey Appreciation Award to Mitchell at a Leadership
Conference on Civil Rights banquet, 1979.

Monsignor Higgins, George Meany, Muriel
Humphrey (widow of Hubert Humphrey),
Mitchell, and Andrew Biemiller at a
Leadership Conference awards ceremony

President Carter presents the Medal of
Freedom to Mitchell, 1980. COURTESY OF
THE JIMMY CARTER LIBRARY

Clarence and Juanita Mitchell with Chief
Justice Warren Berger at a reception for
newly elected federal judges

Mitchell with Joseph Rauh

CHAPTER SEVENTEEN

Guiding the Forces
Through the Turbulence

Mitchell's hand was further strengthened by the Civil Rights Commission's report *Freedom to the Free,* assessing conditions for blacks one hundred years after the Emancipation Proclamation. Despite the abysmal discrimination still prevalent, much racial progress had been made during the past two decades in voting, employment, transportation, and education, and in desegregating the armed services and the District of Columbia. The commission concluded that "more forces were working for the realization of civil rights for all Americans than ever before in history." The NAACP's ten-year goal of "Free by '63" was not yet fully a reality, but African Americans were on the threshold of fulfilling that mission.

Because Mitchell knew that Congress was poised for action, he regarded the Kennedy administration's pessimism over legislative prospects for 1963 as inexcusable. The Democrats controlled the House by 258 to 176 and the Senate by 67 to 33. John Kennedy, however, believed the Eighty-eighth Congress would be "slightly against us more than it was," but "we are about where we were the last two years. . . . Every vote will be three or four votes either way, winning or losing."

The filibuster rules change debacle that January was the first critical development in this phase of the legislative struggle. Mitchell believed that had the fight been abandoned at that point, it was "unlikely that the focus could have been redirected to legislation." In addition to the NAACP, the NAACP Legal Defense and Educational Fund was conducting an onslaught in the courts against state-imposed school segregation, and the association, with the support of its allies, had intensified its pressure on the White House for executive action. The civil rights demonstrations in the South were also commanding significant amounts of national attention.

Yielding to the NAACP's demands for action, the Department of Justice on January 18 filed suits aimed at desegregating public schools in Alabama, Louisiana, and Mississippi, as well as those serving children of military personnel in Prince Georges County, Maryland. Mitchell was particularly concerned that Justice's arguments should show that the federal government had spent more than $36 million to help build and operate those schools, which remained segregated. That was a considerable increase in funding from more than ten years earlier when he had begun seeking federal leadership to end such abuse. [1]

Contributing to Mitchell's concern that national attention could also be diverted from legislation was the fact that the bipartisan civil rights coalition that he had developed in the Congress was showing signs of strain. Republicans were more individualistic and welcomed opportunities to take the initiative. John Lindsay, the congressman from New York's "silk stocking district"—a wealthy "suburb" within the city's compacted urban mass—was demonstrating concern long before the first session of the Eighty-eighth Congress began by calling the Washington Bureau for legislative suggestions. He was a charter member of the Wednesday Club, a small group of liberal Republicans who were determined to push the Democratic leadership in Congress as well as the Kennedy administration on civil rights. Deeply admiring Mitchell for his integrity—he always gave "a straight answer," and "a handshake was good"—Lindsay, at the beginning of his third term in Congress, had established a solid relationship with him.

Lindsay's goal was to find a common denominator around which fellow Republicans in the House could rally. Joined by William McCulloch and Maryland's Charles McC. Mathias, these lawmakers introduced on January 31 a five-part proposal whose goals were (1) to make the Civil Rights Commission permanent; (2) to create a strong "Commission for Equality of Opportunity in Employment," with statutory powers enabling it to enforce directives against job discrimination; (3) to give the attorney general civil injunction authority to desegregate public schools (a revival of the 1957 Civil Rights Act's deleted Part III); (4) to provide federal technical assistance for states desegregating their school systems; and (5) to establish a sixth-grade education as the standard literacy requirement for voter registration. They declared that the administration's failure to press for comprehensive civil rights legislation was "one of the most serious shortcomings of the last Congress."

In the Senate, Mitchell also helped impatient members draft "a very good package." The Democrats were reluctant to give it bipartisan support until they had seen what President Kennedy would offer. Nevertheless, eleven days after the House Republicans had acted, Senator Joseph Clark of Pennsylvania broke away from the other Democrats and, with Republican backing, introduced two civil rights measures, supported by enforcement powers. The first would require every school board operating racially segregated public schools to adopt a desegregation plan and to provide technical and financial resources to help desegregate those schools (the 1958 Paul Douglas bill). The second measure, concerning equal employment rights, would make available administrative court remedies in cases involving labor unions and firms with more than fifty employees.[2]

Rather than taking this hint that the time was overdue for his leadership, Kennedy merely sought to deflect the increasing pressure by submitting to Congress on February 28 what was essentially another voting rights bill. The administration's initiatives were obviously very late and inadequate. Evidently deciding to run in 1964 on his record of unprecedented black appointments and aggressive executive action, he failed to use this opportunity to implement the exemplary 1960 Democratic platform, as civil rights forces were urging. Instead, he limited himself to recommending to Congress minimal additions to the 1957 and 1960 Civil Rights acts plus a program of federal technical and financial assistance to aid school districts undergoing desegregation and to eliminate the "separate but equal" concept from the Morrill Land Grant College Act.

The Kennedy administration bill's five basic voting provisions were (1) prohibition of different standards, practices, or procedures for all persons seeking to vote in federal elections; (2) a requirement that literacy tests for voting in federal elections be in writing or be transcribed; (3) creation of a presumption of literacy based on a sixth-grade education in federal elections; (4) expeditious handling of voting discrimination cases; and (5) appointment of temporary voting referees where less than 15 percent of eligible voters of any race were registered.

Kennedy gave his administration a pat on the back for ending discrimination and segregation, as a result of voluntary agreements, in employment; in certain areas of federal activity like the Army and Air Force reserves and the Coast Guard Academy; at interstate bus and railway terminals, and at fifteen airports. In such areas as public accommodations he promised that his administration would "continue to encourage and support action by state and local communities, and private entrepreneurs, to assure" further progress.

Among his detailed criticisms, Mitchell maintained, as he had in 1962, that the administration's limitation of its voting proposals to federal elections was "unfortunate." That meant, he said, that the administration had bought "the erroneous constitutional arguments of the filibuster bloc." That sentiment applied to the bill's other features as well.

Furthermore, in a more expansive "Evaluation of Administration Program" memorandum prepared by Frank Pohlhaus, the NAACP concluded that the administration's program for ending discrimination and segregation through executive action fell "woefully short" of the comprehensive recommendations that Wilkins had presented to the White House in 1961. The NAACP charged that the administration's failure "to adopt a *total* program" based on an enforceable civil rights code, as it had recommended, was "one of the reasons that the colored community and the majority of civil rights organizations lack full confidence in the Administration's ability to constructively channel the increasing demands for civil rights." By delays and its piecemeal approach to the extension of equal opportunity, the NAACP said, the administration had been "forced into a position of reacting to a series of crises that could possibly have been avoided by a more forthright approach and more constructive leadership." Regarding the President's legislative proposal, the NAACP felt that he had yielded before the fight began. LCCR representatives, in a hastily called meeting, similarly found little solace in the sheaf of civil rights bills that Mitchell brought into the meeting, and they could only hope that the second Kennedy administration would be an improvement over the first.[3]

Seeking an appropriate response to the Republican initiatives, Humphrey, Douglas, Clark, and Philip Hart, in a meeting, favored a more vigorous posture by the administration. They agreed to support Kennedy's February 28 proposals to build a broader base of support among Democrats, to push for this support at the White House, and not to take any public steps that could be implied as criticism.

The Democrats' dilemma only encouraged the Republicans. On March 28, the jockeying in Congress became more overtly partisan when eight GOP senators with solid civil rights records introduced a comprehensive seven-point program. They were Clifford Case, Jacob Javits, Kenneth Keating, Thomas Kuchel, Hugh Scott, and J. Glenn Beall, Jr., of Maryland. Mitchell observed that Hawaii's Hiram L. Fong, who had faithfully backed the filibuster reform struggle in January, again supported them. But he seemed disappointed that his friend Leverett Saltonstall, who had not been as supportive in the filibuster fight, had joined in sponsoring just one of the bills—and that was only to make the Civil Rights Commission permanent.

Not surprisingly, the Democrats declined an invitation by the Republicans to make this a bipartisan effort. Mitchell felt that "most of the liberal Democratic senators" wanted to support the Republican program but refrained from doing so because they did not want to embarrass Kennedy. According to Mitchell, the President had made a "very tragic error" not to approve "this kind of package." Trying to be optimistic, he gave Kennedy the benefit of doubt and said that the administration's civil rights message "exposed a willingness to take more if Congress would give it to him."[4]

The Republican maneuver placed the President's proposals in an even more unfavorable light and would probably have resulted in a damaging partisan contest had Mitchell not been able to keep the bipartisan coalition from breaking apart. The present contest was a sharp departure from earlier years when he began shaping a bipartisan working group on legislation. Warning of the danger of partisan bickering, he noted that in 1955 and 1956 the positions had been reversed. Although the Republicans submitted to Congress a four-part civil rights program then, there was much speculation about whether Eisenhower really wanted the whole package. Nevertheless, Beall, Case, Javits, Keating, Kuchel, and Scott joined the Democrats in fighting for the complete program. Mitchell felt that it would "be most unfortunate" for civil rights if any partisan attempt was made to "dismiss the action of these Republicans on political grounds." Instead, he said, their initiative should be regarded as an opportunity "for the President and all forward looking Democrats to shift from the weak proposals to the stronger offerings." He was concerned that neither Democratic nor Republican Senate leaders favored the strong package. That was because Mansfield was taking his cue from Kennedy, and Dirksen was simply conservative. He warned that that meant senators who came from key states that would determine the outcome of the 1964 presidential election had to hammer away to get something more than what Senator Douglas called "soup made from the shadow of a crow that had starved to death."

Maintaining a bead on the Democrats' failings, Mitchell said that most people who supported the party thought of it as being composed of lawmakers like Douglas. "They do not think of it as the party of Senator Eastland. Yet the President's program is more in the nature of a plan to conciliate Eastland than it is a plan to carry out the Douglas program." The GOP program, he said, gave the Democrats an opportunity to "make amends for their past mistakes." He hoped they would accept the opportunity "in a statesmanlike manner."[5]

The Republicans sought to benefit from their advantage by regretting in their news release that the President had not seen fit to implement the Civil Rights Commission's 1961 recommendation for comprehensive legislation in voting, education, employment, housing, and the administration of justice. That recommendation was the basis of their seven-point program. But there was a backlash to their assertiveness; a Senate Republican caucus of all thirty-three members rejected a call from Javits to adopt a strong resolution committing them to civil rights and reforming the cloture rule, because Republicans like Minority Leader Dirksen were wary of allowing the Democrats, who still had overwhelming black support, to get credit for any civil rights legislation that was passed. They adopted a compromise position drafted primarily by Dirksen that omitted any mention of cloture.

Despite widespread pessimism among civil rights allies, Mitchell assumed that the logjam was breaking. He effusively thanked the Republicans for their support. He told Case, Keating, and Beall that at a time when Mississippi citizens were trying to exercise their right to vote, they had "proclaimed a set of objectives that should be the goal of all Americans who believe in fair play." He noted their "gallant and persistent effort" in the recent filibuster fight and said their support was a challenge that commanded "those of good will" to unite behind the civil rights banner. "May the Divine power that directs men to do right guide all of us to a course of action that will lead to complete victory."[6]

Mitchell was well positioned to benefit from Martin Luther King's epic confrontation with Public Safety Commissioner Bull Connor in Birmingham, where the city's onslaught on the demonstrators with police dogs, fire hoses, and mass jailings aroused the nation as never before to the moral abomination of Jim Crow. Birmingham exemplified the radical expansion of protests in the South, from single-issue grass-roots demonstrations at lunch counters and other public facilities, to the all-inclusive mass gatherings that called for improvements in employment, housing, school integration, and police protection—the basic NAACP program.

With the demonstrations overshadowing much of the other civil rights activities, Mitchell acknowledged that they revealed the need for legislation in the area of public accommodations. He never could find much evidence that they "had any effect on the votes that were needed" in Congress. He did not mean that the demonstrations never changed anyone's mind; rather, he did not think the demonstrations "changed enough minds to do the whole job." Furthermore, the demonstrations "didn't have the slightest effect on chairman Judge Smith. The only way we got it was because we had enough votes to out-vote him, and the votes we got were the votes we would have gotten, demonstrations or no demonstrations, because they were the people who wanted to do something." Mitchell was as much a catalyst in Washington as Martin Luther King was in the South.

He regarded President Kennedy's determination to more or less soft pedal civil rights despite his obvious alarm over the crisis as one confirmation of his assessment. Kennedy, responding to the Birmingham crisis, seemed almost to invite ridicule when he declared during his May 8 news conference that the federal government lacked authority to intervene and protect the rights of the demonstrators against Bull Connor's atrocities. Mitchell welcomed the challenge from Senators Javits and Keating, and

Congressmen Celler, Lindsay, McCulloch, and Mathias that Kennedy could use existing laws to protect the demonstrators. More important for Mitchell, the federal government's impotence underscored the need for new protective laws in this area.

Kennedy, nevertheless, was pushed by Birmingham and similar events to give leadership. Among other things, he began holding White House conferences with business leaders, women's groups, and others to enlist their support for his civil rights and social initiatives. Mitchell found that those efforts had no effect on the Rules Committee, whose members continued to throw roadblocks in the way of civil rights legislation.

Reinforced by the benefits of the moral upheaval below the Mason-Dixon Line, Mitchell and his allies in the Leadership Conference on Civil Rights transformed the drawn-out hearings on Capitol Hill between the spring and fall into a new kind of passion play. Mitchell's close relationship with a bipartisan group of House members as he continued pressing the administration for stronger legislation and very carefully monitored the content of bills submitted by his friends further strengthened this drive. Frank Pohlhaus expressed concern to Lindsay over one provision of the January 31 House Republican bill stating that the authority granted to the attorney general in school segregation suits could not be exercised until state remedies had been exhausted. Pohlhaus explained that although the bill required a "plain, speedy, and efficient remedy," the NAACP's experience in seeking application of the Supreme Court's 1955 "with all deliberate speed" mandate in school desegregation cases was that this directive on how the *Brown* v. *Board of Education* decision was to be implemented was not substantial. "If adopted in its present form, we look forward to prolonged and complicated litigation to secure an interpretation of this language" while delays in compliance continued. He recalled that during the debate on the 1957 Civil Rights Act, supporters, with Attorney General Brownell's help, were able to delete a "crippling" amendment that would have limited the Justice Department's authority to act in school desegregation cases if a "plain, speedy, and efficient remedy" was available under state law. The Washington Bureau asked Lindsay to delete this provision from the bill, and he agreed.

The labor movement helped considerably by reacting with alarm over rumors that the administration would not include an FEPC provision in a second bill now being prepared. Led by the AFL-CIO's Biemiller, a labor-civil rights delegation that included Mitchell told Humphrey, the Senate whip, in a June 5 meeting that the proposed administration bill would be "a patent compromise in a no-compromise situation." The group said all-out fights were made only on all-out measures. Humphrey assured the group that he agreed with the demand and had communicated these views to the President.

George Meany reaffirmed Biemiller's demand for the inclusion of an FEPC provision in the bill. He told Congress that the unions needed the support of the federal government in order to eradicate racial discrimination within their ranks. Despite the executive orders that Truman, Eisenhower, and Kennedy had issued barring job discrimination in government contracts, such discrimination was widespread in that area as well as in the area of private employment. He said it would be useless to try to discipline with expulsions unions that discriminated. He asked for strong and enforceable fair employment legislation because "we have a civil rights problem within our midst." He said the AFL-CIO was working "diligently to eliminate segregation, not only in our unions but in all American life." Without federal help, he said, he did not think that was possible, because the AFL-CIO was only a confederation of independent unions and had no authority over how its members were operated.

The AFL-CIO expressed similar views to Kennedy through Hubert Humphrey. On June 7, Biemiller sent Humphrey a memorandum stating the AFL-CIO's position on the administration's civil rights package that had been submitted to Congress, and asked him to forward them to the President. "There is no FEPC in the package," the memorandum said. "Probably the one piece of legislation most required in America today is an FEPC." The most urgent need of blacks, it said, was for job opportunities, and that need was "directly related to slums, juvenile delinquency, crime and disease. FEPC will have a tremendous impact on the cultural level of the poor Negro." The memorandum noted that there was a "grave danger of violence in the North flowing principally from want of jobs for Negroes. Chicago, Detroit, New York, Los Angeles and Washington" were "tinder boxes." It said that the situation was "undoubtedly worse in" those cities than in Philadelphia, where there had been recent trouble. Biemiller reminded Humphrey that Meany had spoken with him about Kennedy's civil rights package from Geneva, "and I can affirm that his personal support for these views is quite emphatic." The memorandum, he said, represented the position of the labor movement. It concluded that "the labor movement cannot itself afford to settle for less than strong, forthright legislation. Any bill which does not include the provisions" outlined, especially the FEPC provision, "will have to be termed inadequate by the AFL-CIO."[7]

Helping to highlight the need for a national FEPC law were such activities as NAACP pickets in downtown Lawrence, Kansas, carrying signs that read, WE WANT TO WORK WHERE WE SHOP, and violent demonstrations at construction sites in New York City and Newark, New Jersey, that were resulting in scores of arrests. Demonstrations were also occurring at construction sites in Philadelphia. The paradox of these protests against discrimination by AFL-CIO affiliates underscored Mitchell's influence with Meany.

Additionally, Mitchell welcomed testimony from other groups like SNCC on civil rights problems in the South. He substantiated SNCC charges of extensive delays by the federal courts in handling complaints by noting, as an illustration, that the 1960 Justice Department suit filed in the Southern District of Mississippi against Biloxi and Harrison County to desegregate the beaches still had not been decided. *

There are many additional positive factors, Mitchell felt, that helped the fight in Congress. One was the determination of Congressman Celler, chairman of the House Judiciary Committee, supported by William Mc-Culloch of Ohio, to hold hearings and to insist on a strong bill. McCulloch had played a major role in the passage of the 1957 act. Several congressmen, including a member of the House Judiciary Committee, had also learned firsthand about the South's extensive segregation system from touring the region. The outrage that Congressman Charles Diggs expressed over the fire bombing of the home of Dr. Aaron Henry in Clarksdale on April 11 aroused considerable concern in Congress. Appearing on a local New York television program with Congressman Celler, Diggs said that the incident reminded him of his experience when a Molotov cocktail was thrown through a window of the home where earlier he had been staying in Greenwood, Mississippi, setting it afire. Diggs had also been staying at Henry's home, but he was not there when it was fire-bombed. Diggs told his television audience that his experience in Greenwood was "a typical reflection of the sentiment" in the Mississippi Delta area. He recalled that William L. Moore, a white mailman from Baltimore who had been walking along a highway to demonstrate against the denial of the civil rights of blacks in the South, had been murdered in Greenwood.

Mitchell sent telegrams to Senate leaders and several powerful members of the House noting that this was not the first time that the property of civil rights leaders in Mississippi had been targets of "cowardly attacks under the cover of darkness." He said that providence had saved Diggs's life this time. But strong measures to "prevent other and more deadly incidents of this kind" were needed. The shock waves from the murder of Medgar Evers on June 12 in Jackson, Mississippi, indicated that the na-

---

* Despite the *Briggs* case, which was included in the May 17, 1954, *Brown* v. *Board of Education* school desegregation decision, and the subsequent *Brunson* v. *Board of Trustees of School District No. 1 of Clarendon County, South Carolina*, there had been no final court order to open the state's public schools to blacks. Other examples of frustration included *Davis* v. *East Baton Rouge School Board*, where, despite a decision in May 1960 the school board was given until July 1963 to implement the order; and *Koen* v. *Knight*, filed in the Southern District of Alabama in August 1960 to enjoin segregation at the state Vocational Technical School at Mobile, was still in the pretrial stage.

tion's patience with racial conditions in the South had reached its limit. President Kennedy's forcing Governor George Wallace to back down and permit two black students to enter the University of Alabama at Tuscaloosa was another indication of the national resolve.

Mitchell felt "considerably fortified" by a luncheon meeting he had with several conservative Republicans such as Donald Bruce of Indiana and Alphonzo Bell of California, arranged by Congressman Charles Goodell of New York. Mitchell found their economic views much different from those of liberal members of Congress, but on civil rights they pledged their full support, particularly on legislation to provide safeguards against discrimination. That pledge was one important reason, Mitchell later said, "why at a very early stage it was possible to foresee victory for the civil rights bill." He found that many other civil rights supporters, without the advantage of having open lines of communication with unlikely contacts like these, "kept looking over their shoulders for an emergence of the coalition between northern Republicans and southern Democrats against the bill." But, based. on the changing political tides, he knew better. He was confident that on straight civil rights questions, "the great majority of Republican members of Congress voted with the northern liberal Democrats."[8]

On June 19, the day Medgar Evers was buried in Arlington National Cemetery, Kennedy sent Congress his revised civil rights program, fervently declaring: "In this year of the Emancipation Centennial, justice requires us to insure the blessings of equality for all Americans and their posterity—not merely for reasons of economic efficiency, world diplomacy and domestic tranquility—but, above all, because it is right." Determined to go only so far, Kennedy still had his foot firmly on the brake. His message was based on the administration's best estimate of what Congress would pass rather than on what was needed. His omnibus civil rights bill was an improvement over the first, but it was much weaker than the Senate Republican package. Fearing this thrust, Mitchell had earlier told Celler's Judiciary Subcommittee No. 5 that "I have been around here long enough to know that if you start off with a program that emphasizes voter registration and legislation to protect the right to vote you will wind up not only with that but also it will be a watered down version of what you started out with." He remained convinced that "the main thing that is needed is something like Part III." Nevertheless, Kennedy's civil rights proposals were the most comprehensive a President had ever sent to Congress.

Once more, Kennedy undermined this historical step by being too political. His earlier civil rights proposal had not been intended for final action until the next session; now his second was aimed at getting off the streets blacks who were targeting not only the *public policy* of segregation in the South but also the *private practice* of discrimination in the North.

The battle lines were now sharply drawn. There were three sides: Mitchell and the civil rights forces who felt the best strategy was to start with the strongest bill possible and fight for it every inch of the way; the administration, which was determined to seek only what it believed it could hold on to in the difficult legislative process ahead; and the southerners, recognizing the irrevocable handwriting on the wall and thus trying to weaken any bill that passed by them.

Said the irascible southern constitutional expert Sam Ervin: "This civil rights bill is the most sharp and divisive measure in this area since the Reconstruction Acts of 1867. It is a drastic assault on the principles of constitutional government and the rights of individuals."[9]

With the 1957 and 1960 struggles serving as dress rehearsals for the real battle, the strategies more than ever were determined by two fixed positions. One was held by lawmakers representing principle and substance; the other was held by the southerners, who were determined to hold the ground and at least slow the changing social tide if they could not stop it. The southerners knew that they would be pushed back; their only concern was, how far? Mitchell and the civil rights forces wanted it to be as far as the Constitution permitted; the southerners were determined it would be no further than the outside limits of their hallowed customs. The troubling reality for Mitchell was that rather than throwing the full weight of the federal government behind the civil rights forces, whose cause it verbally espoused, the Kennedy administration made a political decision to steer a middle course.

The President's program was introduced in three separate forms in the Senate. The omnibus package, S. 1731, offered by Mike Mansfield with forty-five sponsors, was referred to Eastland's Judiciary Committee (its eight titles related to voting rights, public accommodations, school desegregation, the Community Relations Service, the Civil Rights Commission, nondiscrimination in federal programs, the Commission on Equal Employment Opportunity, and miscellaneous provisions). A Mansfield-Dirksen version (S. 1750), without the public accommodations Title II proposal, was also referred to Judiciary. The Title II provision was separately introduced with forty-six sponsors as S. 1733 and was referred to the Commerce Committee. In the House, the President's program (H.R. 7152) was referred to Judiciary Subcommittee No. 5, also headed by Celler, which was holding hearings.

Title I of the omnibus bill repeated without substantial change the President's earlier voting bill. Although the provision improved the 1957 and 1960 Civil Rights acts, the Leadership Conference joined Mitchell in regarding it as too moderate. The LCCR preferred stronger voting bills that were pending, which included, among other things, the type of registrar system proposed by the Civil Rights Commission in 1959 and rejected in the 1960 legislative battle. The conference felt that this type of provision for administrative enforcement of the law through a system of registrars could provide mass enfranchisement, which court-mandated programs had not been accomplishing.

Title II was regarded as the most important feature of the administration's bill and was expected to spark the sharpest fight in Congress. It would establish the right to receive service free from discrimination in places of public accommodation and in business establishments. Discrimination victims would have the right to sue for preventive relief. The attorney general could also enter a lawsuit or initiate court action, though before filing a suit, he would be required to refer the complaint to a Community Relations Service provided under Title IV of the bill and to any appropriate state agency authorized to bar discrimination.

This section immediately became embroiled in a dispute over whether protection should be conditioned on the Fourteenth Amendment or on the commerce clause of the Constitution (Article I, Section 8). The bill relied on both foundations, but the attorney general in subsequent testimony before the House Judiciary Committee stressed exclusively its reliance on the interstate commerce power provided under the Constitution.

Title III would provide technical assistance, grants, and loans to school boards implementing school desegregation. More important, it authorized the attorney general to institute civil action to enforce school desegregation. Attorney General Kennedy explained that this title "would thus combine a program of aid to segregated school systems, which are attempting in good faith to meet the demands of the Constitution, with a program of effective legal action by the federal government." He felt that these programs would "smooth the path upon which the nation was set by the *Brown* decision" and were "second only to the public accommodations title in furthering civil rights in America."[10]

The Leadership Conference, considered this proposal too moderate. Title III contained no requirement that school districts begin compliance with the Supreme Court's decision in 1963 as the Democratic platform had promised or as the pending Clark and Celler bills (S. 772 and H.R. 1766) required. Furthermore, the administration's bill limited the attorney general to bringing suits only where complainants had been unable to institute legal proceedings. This restriction was not included in the authority to act that was granted in 1957 in voting cases. The LCCR noted that there was no provision in the bill for a comprehensive Part III authorizing the attorney general to bring suit, not only in school cases, but also in all situations where persons were denied their constitutional rights because of race, color, religion, or national origin. The LCCR felt that such a provision would reach all public facilities not covered by the administration's bill as well as give the attorney general power to enjoin state interference with peaceful protests in such places as Birmingham.

Title IV would create a Community Relations Service to help resolve segregation problems. The LCCR felt this agency would be useful if the bill enacted provided strong protection for the constitutional rights of minorities. It would be truly valuable if it were a complement to enforcement authority, but it could not be considered a substitute for such powers.

Title V provided for a four-year extension of the Civil Rights Commission. The Leadership Conference thought that a proposal to make it permanent would have been better.

Title VI authorized the withholding of federal funds from any program or activity receiving federal assistance. The Leadership Conference thought that this provision was too moderate since it was believed that the President already had this authority. It would nevertheless provide congressional support for his executive authority, so the LCCR supported it.

Title VII would give the President's Committee on Equal Employment Opportunity statutory authority. The administration bill omitted the FEPC provision that the President had recommended in his message. Nicholas deB. Katzenbach, then deputy attorney general, was fighting Rauh tooth and nail defending that omission, because he had promised William McCulloch the bill would be as they both had agreed, and he feared it would get taken out in the Senate. The LCCR felt that the requested authority would strengthen the agency, but it was not a substitute for a national FEPC. The conference maintained that such a law was urgently needed and it recommended adoption of one of the pending FEPC bills in Congress.

Kennedy's omnibus bill was one of about 150 different civil rights bills that had been introduced in the House since January alone. The most important were two bills that had been sponsored by Lindsay, a broad one (H.R. 3139)* on January 31, and another (H.R. 6720), a public accommodations bill based on the Fourteenth Amendment, on June 3. There was little likelihood that most of the bills in the House or Senate would be reported, but they were a good source of ideas and inspiration.[11]

The day after Kennedy unveiled his second civil rights proposals, leaders of the NAACP, SCLC, SNCC, and CORE rejected the President's call for a moratorium on demonstrations across the nation, saying they would be continued and would be peaceful. In his June 19 message, Kennedy,

_____

* H.R. 3139 would (1) make permanent the Civil Rights Commission, (2) establish a federal Commission for Equal Employment Opportunity, replacing the one established by executive order, (3) authorize the attorney general to initiate suits on behalf of citizens denied admission to segregated schools, (4) offer federal technical assistance to help states desegregate their public schools, and (5) provide a legal assumption of a person's literacy for voting purposes if he had completed six grades of school.

calling for a moratorium on the demonstrations, said unruly tactics or pressures would not help and might hinder the effective consideration of these measures. The civil rights leaders praised the new proposals but said they did not go far enough. King stated that whenever violence followed demonstrations, it was due to the repressive action by city officials or the police bent on denying blacks their constitutional right of peaceful protest. King said that "while we abhor violence and will do all within our power to prevent any Negro in the struggle from engaging in aggressive or retaliatory violence, we cannot in all good conscience bring an end to the demonstrations until the conditions causing them are removed."

Mitchell said if the President wanted to call on individuals to cease their actions, he should call on those who "thwart our campaigns which are based on lawful practices." Then, in a speech to a seminar for foreign correspondents at the University of Pittsburgh, Mitchell declared: "It is my personal belief that the most precious gift that our country offers is our ideal that men are created equal and entitled to equal treatment under just law. I believe that we shall perfect and strengthen this view and that it will be an inspiration to all men wherever they strive for liberty."[12]

The climate of militancy was further heightened by the revival of Philip Randolph's twenty-two-year-old dream for a march of one hundred thousand African Americans on Washington for "jobs and freedom." The march idea was revived a few days before January 1—exactly a century after the Emancipation Proclamation—by Bayard Rustin; his friend Tom Kahn, a lanky white student at Howard University; and Norman Hill, a slightly built program director for CORE. They prepared a memo for Randolph that urged it was time to dramatize the need for jobs for blacks with a mass march on Washington. A problem with Randolph's first announcement of the march shortly afterward was that he had consulted no other civil rights leader before going public. He simply told a reporter offhandedly that "we're going to march." Now Randolph invited several other organizations to participate—but not the SCLC, apparently because King had tried to co-opt the march idea. Wilkins confirmed this when, in dismissing a call by King for a march, he said, "Somebody just made a premature announcement. I had discussed the plans with A. Philip Randolph six months ago. It was his idea." On June 22, a few weeks after Randolph's second call following a White House meeting between Kennedy and a group of civil rights and labor leaders, Walter Reuther suggested to Randolph that he broaden the march to include all the major black protest groups, and he agreed. On July 3, about thirty civil rights, religious, and labor leaders held their first follow-up meeting—a "summit conference," as the press billed it—at the Roosevelt Hotel in New York to begin implementing a March on Washington (MOW) program that the NAACP had presented.

While those plans were developing, Mitchell concentrated on implementing an NAACP convention resolution he had gotten adopted for a national "Legislative Strategy Conference on Civil Rights."

The NAACP legislative conference, held on August 6–8 at the Washington Statler-Hilton Hotel, was distinct in its scope and purpose from Randolph's proposed August 28 MOW. It provided local NAACP leaders with a thorough briefing on pending civil rights legislation, enabled them to meet with their representatives in the House and Senate from whom they sought commitments of support, and developed plans for consistent and continual grass-roots activity back home. The NAACP Washington Bureau summarized for its troops the obstacles to passing legislation in Congress and the NAACP's basic strategy for maneuvering through the parliamentary minefield in the House and Senate.

The approximately 645 delegates from NAACP branches and other organizations representing thirty-six states focused on Subcommittee No. 5, which had a majority of staunch civil rights friends, to ensure that it recommended to the full Judiciary Committee a much stronger bill than Kennedy had proposed. The NAACP stressed that failure to include its amendments in the final Judiciary Committee product would "make it extremely difficult to strengthen the civil rights bill on the House floor," since it was much easier to include those features in committee. The delegates secured pledges for those amendments and for the signing of a discharge petition to get the bill out of Howard Smith's Rules Committee. The legislative conference was crucial to the NAACP's strategy to bypass Senator Eastland's Judiciary Committee, which was not expected to report out a civil rights bill. The House-adopted bill had to be placed directly on the Senate calendar for prompt debate.

One crucial commitment that was won was House Speaker John W. McCormack's promise that Congress would remain in session until it acted on the President's civil rights program. Another was Congressman Celler's assurance that the Judiciary Committee would strengthen the Kennedy bill by adding the desired FEPC and Part III provisions. Michigan's Senator Philip Hart, another staunch NAACP ally, assured the conference that the Senate was within 7 or 8 votes of the 67 needed for the likely filibuster. Among the 62 senators and 166 congressmen they visited, the delegates, as expected, found more resistance in Congress to the public accommodations amendment than to the FEPC and Part III amendments.

An overriding consideration was Dirksen's attitude on public accommodations. Mansfield's courtship of his GOP counterpart contrasted sharply with Mitchell's forceful advocacy. As a whole, despite the marked slowdown in legislative activity in 1963, the Senate responded well to Mansfield's loosening of the reins. Much of his prior three years had been devoted to mopping up proposals left unfinished from previous Congresses. He kept the machinery well oiled and running smoothly by avoiding any attempt to push through controversial proposals. His nurturing of a congenial atmosphere on both sides of the aisle was crucial to the prospect of passing the civil rights bill. He worked to avoid a flat condemnation by Dirksen of the public accommodations provisions in order to avoid needless complexities in later negotiations. Preliminary negotiations had begun on June 3 between the two leaders and their staffs and were continuing. Previously, not only had Dirksen been kept informed by Mansfield, but the minority leader also had conferred regularly with the President and attorney general. The result was that on June 13 Dirksen had informed Mansfield that he supported all the administration's omnibus provisions except public accommodations.

Dirksen personally expressed this opposition to the public accommodations amendment when he addressed the NAACP delegates at one session of the conference. Having cosponsored every other section of the Kennedy proposals, he promised that Congress would pass a "reasonable civil rights bill," but he refused to discuss the public accommodations section with delegates. Standing beside the minority leader at the microphone, Mitchell chided him for his opposition and declared that his position was unfortunate. "It is not a question of whether you are for this title," Mitchell said, "but whether you are going to do something about these people," who were being beaten, shot at, or even killed when they went into a restaurant. Dirksen nevertheless maintained that although the NAACP might not like his stand, "I don't go around particularly trying to please everyone." He assured his audience that he would adhere to his conviction "and pursue it according to my lights."

Mitchell afterward concluded that "we are running" at the expected pace. There were "by no means any reports of conversion to civil rights of diehard states' righters and other hostile legislators." But, placing considerable hope in getting support from the Midwest and the West, he was confident of success. Juanita, who had succeeded her mother as president of the Maryland State Conference of NAACP Branches and was a delegate, gave assurances that she would work on a shaky Eastern Shore congressman who said he would "search his soul and decide according to my ability, for or against" the bill when it came to the House floor. Mitchell urged the delegates to conduct follow-up meetings with other hesitant or opposing lawmakers.

Encouraged, he predicted that the bill would clear the House Rules Committee and that it would reach the Senate floor for a vote. That confidence was based on the consensus that there was enough bipartisan support in Congress to pass the provisions the NAACP wanted. Mitchell then announced the creation of a follow-up strategy committee that was composed of representatives from the NAACP, the UAW, and other cooperating organizations of the Leadership Conference on Civil Rights. He was also able to draw on the resources of other organizations or persons who were not closely tied to the LCCR or closely involved in the coalition's strategy sessions.

For those like Pohlhaus who were in the heart of the struggle, the importance of the legislative conference could not be overstated. The delegates, as a result of their visits with lawmakers, confirmed the NAACP's stand that there was enough bipartisan support in Congress to pass the provisions that were being sought to strengthen the Kennedy civil rights bill. [13]

Mitchell assumed a similarly commanding role in planning the March on Washington, which was intended to reinforce the legislative conference by bringing public pressure, in addition to private, to bear on Congress and the White House. First, with the help of Wilkins, whose blessings were necessary for success, he moved to ensure that the stated purpose of the march, "jobs and freedom," was supported with the specific demand for passage of civil rights legislation by Congress. The MOW, among other things, listed ten civil rights demands, the first of which was comprehensive and effective legislation to guarantee all Americans access to public accommodations, decent housing, adequate and integrated education, and the right to vote. It requested the withholding of federal funds from all programs that discriminated, desegregation of all school districts in 1963, enforcement of the Fourteenth Amendment and a reduction of congressional representation in states where citizens were disfranchised.

The purpose of the MOW was also to focus national attention on the need for an executive order banning discrimination in all housing supported by federal funds, authority for the attorney general to institute injunctive suits when any constitutional right was violated, and a massive federal program to train and place all unemployed workers on meaningful and dignified jobs at decent wages. The MOW called for a national minimum wage act that would give all Americans a decent standard of living, a broadened Fair Labor Standards Act to include all areas of employment that were excluded, and a fair employment practices act barring discrimination by federal, state, and municipal governments, and by employers, contractors, employment agencies, and trade unions.

Bayard Rustin, as the MOW's field marshal, was responsible for keeping the several rival organizations involved working together and for issuing rapid-fire volleys of bulletins, press releases, handbooks, charts, schedules, and all the other necessary minutiae of planning. Four other officially designated leaders representing the AFL-CIO and Protestant,

Catholic, and Jewish organizations, the white participants, were included. The march would go only eight tenths of a mile from the Washington Monument to the Lincoln Memorial, but the logistics were a nightmare. Rustin enlisted Mitchell's help on the MOW because he needed someone with clout to pull together people from the various agencies, particularly since the President opposed the march.

With Wilkins's approval, Rustin got him to direct the planning of such details as obtaining 3,000 to 4,000 Army blankets for early arrivals on the Washington Mall, persuading the U.S. Health, Education and Welfare Department to develop menus; coordinating the work of the FBI and local police; arranging with the city for liquor stores to be closed the day of the march; and providing toilets, portable water fountains, first-aid stations, manned by forty doctors and eighty nurses, and ambulances to be scattered under the Washington Monument and along the march route. Planners urged marchers to bring plenty of water but no "alcoholic refreshments." Peanut butter and jelly sandwiches were appropriate but nothing with mayonnaise, "as it deteriorates, and may cause serious diarrhea." They reminded everyone to wear low-heeled shoes, to bring a raincoat, to wear a hat and sunglasses. Children were to be left at home. Much of the logistical planning was done by a committee headed by Mitchell and Rustin that held weekly meetings at which representatives of the various federal and city agencies were present. "People don't know, but Clarence played a very major role," said Rustin.

At Randolph's request, Mitchell also arranged for a meeting at which the labor leader could brief key senators. He countered demands from lawmakers like Celler to cancel the march for fear it would "prejudice the cause of the Negro" in Congress by declaring that the demonstration was "no more irresponsible than members of Congress saying they will talk to death the President's plea for human rights." Not even those briefing sessions or lectures could calm the panic in the Congress and the White House.

The August 28 march itself came at the middle of the House hearings on the civil rights bill, when Mitchell was engaged in what he called "the tricky business of explaining objectives and agreeing upon language that would be acceptable to the proponents of the bill in and out of Congress." The air of apprehension was heavy. Many feared that belligerent blacks would invade offices, intimidate secretaries, and possibly stage sit-ins. Although no business was supposed to have been conducted that day, the House remained in session, debating the railroad strike bill. The District of Columbia mobilized a force of fifty-nine hundred men, including the National Guard, while at nearby bases, four thousand soldiers and marines remained on standby alert, as access of visitors to the House and Senate office buildings was limited.

Mitchell kept his office open all night on the eve of the march in order to greet and assist visitors. His "good friend" and third son, Michael Bowen, stayed with him. They were supposed to take turns sleeping on the small folding bed Mitchell had bought for the occasion, but Michael was the primary beneficiary. While nodding in the folding chair he had brought from home, Mitchell, startled by the ringing telephone, "made the wrong move" as he reached to answer it and crashed to the floor. It was a light moment he enjoyed recalling.

On the morning of the march, he thought the NAACP's John Morsell made an "unforgettable picture" as he watched over the hundreds of placards being stacked on the grass while ominous thunderclouds gathered. Fortunately, the day turned out beautiful, because the protective tarpaulin they were trying to spread was not big enough to cover all the placards. Mitchell's belief that Divine Providence had spared the marchers was confirmed the next way when, as he and Michael were walking through the streets, a slight drizzle turned to a downpour just as he had said to his son, "Those preachers sure held back the rain yesterday."

The day of the event, as the ten MOW cochairmen made their rounds with congressional leaders, Mitchell thought "the Senate and House looked like a neighborhood market for urban renewal or general demolition." Some civil rights leaders, convinced the effort would be futile, did not see the need for working with Congress. They felt that the pressure should be on Kennedy to issue an executive order. Finally, the MOW leaders accepted Mitchell's position, that it would be unthinkable to have such an event without involving the leaders of Congress. Mitchell set up meetings with McCormack, Halleck, Mansfield, and Dirksen. He wanted to have the bipartisan leadership of the House and Senate together at one meeting, but because of politics, thirteen leaders from the demonstration had to pay three separate visits on Capitol Hill. First, they saw Mansfield in the Old Senate Office Building; they next met with Dirksen and Halleck in the senator's office; finally they spent nearly an hour with McCormack and Representative Carl Albert of Oklahoma, the House Democratic leader, in the speaker's office. A few demonstrators violated the plans and visited other legislators in their offices, but that caused no problems. In fact, some senators welcomed trainloads and busloads of constituents.

The meetings consumed more time than had been anticipated. Consequently, "right in the middle of a meeting" with McCormack, Mitchell recalled, someone rushed in and announced, "The troops are getting awful restless out there" and were about to step off from the Washington Monument. As the others rushed off to join the tens of thousands of shuffling feet and oceans of bobbing placards proceeding along Constitution and Independence avenues, Mitchell chose to miss marching in the front ranks, because he felt that a few extra minutes with McCormack would provide more lasting benefits than basking in the evanescent light of glory. McCormack, who always treated him with kindness and good humor, remarked that this was not the first time leaders had had "to run to get ahead of their followers."

Mitchell also had to "perform a few chores" such as ensuring that the seventy-five lawmakers attending the march had transportation to the Lincoln Memorial. He thought it amusing that after he had made all the arrangements with the Capital Transit Company for a bus to carry the lawmakers, Adam Clayton Powell tried to take control of what had at first been viewed as a dirty job. Actually, Powell's maneuver was not surprising since it was he who had proposed that lawmakers participate in the march. Mitchell himself had had reservations about the idea, because Congress's esteem among the marchers was so low. But the invitations had been issued. After Mitchell had seen that everything went smoothly and the lawmakers were on the bus, there was no room for him. He had to enlist the help of the police to get to the Lincoln Memorial. His only regret about not marching in the vanguard, he told Paul Douglas, was "that I did not catch up with you to walk in the Douglas regiment of the Army of the Free."

In their meetings with leaders of Congress and subsequently with the President, the MOW delegation at times had the frustrating sense of going in circles. The meetings were cordial and beneficial, but MOW leaders found that many lawmakers were still sitting on the fence. The patrician Mansfield said he supported the bill in any form, but he showed no inclination to exert a special effort to gain its passage. Overall, Mitchell thought, "All this probably hasn't changed any votes on the civil rights bill, but it's a good thing for Washington and the nation and the world." The similarly haughty Dirksen said he did not believe the demonstration would be an advantage or disadvantage. "I go on feeling that the members of the national legislature have a responsibility to render an independent judgment on these matters, to get all the facts and, mindful always of their constitutional responsibilities, proceed from that broad base," he said.

McCormack was the only leader who expressed a belief that "an orderly march might be helpful" in winning support for the civil rights bill. He said that FEPC and "across the board Part III," to authorize the attorney general to protect Fourteenth Amendment rights, would pass if—and it was a big if—the Judiciary Committee added the provisions to the bill. But he did not promise to help. Celler, too, said he would agree to the two provisions—but that depended on his subcommittee's acceptance.

The President acknowledged the need for FEPC legislation and Part III–type protections to prevent future Birmingham atrocities, and gave the impression that he would accept those amendments to his bill, but he hesitated to urge those additions, preferring to leave the decision to Congress. So the Leadership Conference concluded that if the circle was to be broken, "it is up to us." The appearance of the lawmakers at the march also helped. When they arrived that afternoon at the mall, someone began chanting, "pass the bill, pass the bill," a message that sank in.

The day after the march, President Kennedy himself marveled that there had not been a single arrest during the event and congratulated Mitchell: "Well, Clarence, you did it." A similarly impressed George Meany extended his compliments by sending the Leadership Conference a check for $10,000—the first direct contribution from the AFL-CIO. Meany had been invited to be one of the MOW's ten leaders, but he declined to participate, enabling Walter Reuther to become a part of that historical event. Meany did so because he had no stomach for demonstrations. He was also leary of King's alleged Communist ties and afraid the event would end in conflagration.

A generation later, many Americans would elevate King to mythical heights. He would become the symbol who kept the dream alive. *Time* magazine, however, in the wake of the march, observed: "Obviously, no Negro can speak for all. No organization can represent all Negro aspirations. But in the late summer of 1963, as the revolution intensifies, if there is one Negro who can lay claim to the position of spokesman and worker for a Negro consensus, it is a slender, stoop-shouldered, sickly, dedicated man named Roy Wilkins."

Because many blacks saw the march as an end in itself, a massive demonstration that would somehow end all their troubles, Mitchell found it "difficult to get the country to understand that a tremendous amount of work had to be done" to reap permanent benefits from it. Several times "otherwise knowledgeable people" questioned whether the civil rights bill would be passed before Christmas. When he told them that that was not likely, those persons "threw up their hands in disgust, saying it was obvious that Congress would not act and other means," such as executive action, "must be used to secure redress of grievances." He was assured of support from the NAACP branch structure and the LCCR as he turned his full attention to shaping the bill.[14]

Perhaps because of those doubts, Rustin and others initially proposed that the movement, in addition to seeking passage of civil rights legislation, should establish economic goals. King, meanwhile, turning his attention back to the South, began working on a Montgomery Mass Action Plan, to break the back of segregation in Alabama, that quickly mushroomed to include a proposal for a national economic boycott. Roy Wilkins, knowing that this would have doomed any chance of passing civil rights legislation, pressured King to abandon the boycott plans. At the same time, King's difficulties in getting Birmingham and other southern cities to live up to desegregation agreements with SCLC underscored the reality that the benefits of demonstrations and economic boycotts were oftentimes only short-term.

Assisting Mitchell (in addition to the LCCR steering committee) was a closely knit LCCR staff team that included Marvin Caplan, a former newspaper reporter with wide experience in neighborhood race relations work who was assigned to the coalition organization by the Industrial Union Department of the AFL-CIO; Violet Gunther, former national director of the ADA; Bernard Bailey, of the United Auto Workers; and Geraldine Boykan of the LCCR. Helping Mitchell lead the weekly strategy meetings that were often attended by more than fifty organizational representatives were regulars Joseph Rauh, Andrew Biemiller of the AFL-CIO, Jack Conway of the AFL-CIO's IUD, and James Hamilton, executive director of the Washington office of the National Council of Churches.

The LCCR Washington representatives assumed much of the responsibility for explaining day-to-day developments on legislation to their organizations, which soon numbered more than eighty. Their most important function, however, was their direct involvement in the effort to win passage of the bill; they attended periodic meetings with lawmakers in order to determine where they stood on the civil rights measure, lobbied for commitments for strengthening amendments, and worked out new strategies for improving the bill's chances.

The LCCR staff performed other important duties as well, such as assembling information on lawmakers that included their religious and organizational affiliations and their political supporters and campaign contributors. Using this data, campaigns were conducted in the lawmakers' home districts in order to influence them, with the help of constituents who were not normally involved in civil rights activities. One noteworthy problem encountered involved lawmakers who gave firm commitments of support but, to avoid flak at home, responded evasively or in general terms to constituents inquiring about their civil rights positions. This situation required finesse, diplomacy, and a sophisticated communications operation on the part of Mitchell's staff in order not to destroy those lawmakers' delicate balancing acts. Mitchell's access to the NAACP branch network was crucial in aiding such lawmakers by getting local leaders to discreetly extend support to them on their home turf without being specific where there was no need to do so.

The churches eagerly answered the call to develop grass-roots support for the bill. Mitchell and Rauh designated one occasion as the real turning point in the national attitude of the churches about civil rights. Normally, whenever a committee was about to mark up a bill, both men would stand outside the room and urge the members as they went in not to delete certain provisions, or to add in others. One day in 1963 when Subcommittee No. 5 was about to mark up the civil rights bill, they arrived to find "two dozen of the most beautiful young Episcopal ministers in a row there" performing the lobbyists' task.

The LCCR recognized the churches' importance by urging them "to take the lead in approaches to congressmen on the Judiciary Committee." The request was hardly necessary since the churches already had begun transforming words into deeds. Earlier in 1963, the Reverend Eugene Carson Blake, representing the National Council of Churches, Father John Cronin of the National Catholic Welfare Conference, and Rabbi Irwin Blank of the Synagogue Council of America, all members of the Leadership Conference, took what was termed an "unprecedented" and "historic" step when they presented joint testimony on civil rights in the spirit of ecumenism before congressional committees. A steady stream of representatives of the three major faiths also joined the trek to Washington. These visits were boosted by delegates attending the annual convention of the National Council of Churches in Philadelphia, who were asked to return home via Washington after meeting with lawmakers.

Outside the nation's capital, religious "grass-roots" mobilization was exemplified by activities in the crucial Midwest, where a special effort was made to whip up sentiment in sixteen states, from Ohio to the Rockies. The area included the fundamentalist Bible Belt. The Council for Christian Social Action of the United Church of Christ organized a series of interfaith workshops in the region, the first of which was held in Columbus, Ohio. The newly created Commission on Race and Religion, an arm of the National Council of Churches, held a meeting of members from thirteen states at the University of Nebraska in Lincoln in September. The religious community's organized support was particularly important in reaching those lawmakers who had few or no black constituents. Sunday sermons provided another sharp boost in pro-civil-rights mail to Washington.[15]

Kennedy's second civil rights message on June 19 gave new vigor and focus to the hearings in Congress. Anticipating the battle ahead, Mitchell's advisory that today's cloud, "no bigger than a man's hand," might be tomorrow's hurricane, applied not only to efforts to clarify the President's power to withhold federal funds but also to planned strengthening amendments. Mitchell and his allies held frequent meetings with members of the Judiciary Committee, where action was progressing well with Celler's full cooperation, and with other members of the House, in order to stress the importance of supporting an FEPC bill with enforcement powers and the need for giving the attorney general powers to protect Fourteenth Amendment rights under Part III. Because civil rights supporters on the committee controlled these early proceedings, Mitchell's main problems were not with opponents in Congress but with Attorney General Kennedy, whose goal was nothing more than a moderate bill.

Roy Wilkins tackled the public accommodations opposition head-on. The southerners bitterly opposed this section, maintaining it was an assault on the "most precious of their rights"—the right to manage private property. In his appearance before the Senate Commerce Committee, he delivered a statement on human dignity ("Humiliation Stalks Them") that matched the intensity of Martin Luther King's April 16, 1963, letter from a Birmingham jail that appealed to the moral conscience of "My dear Fellow Clergymen" and the world. As citizens of the United States, Wilkins declared, Americans were entitled to protection by Congress from infringement of their rights based on color discrimination. The "affronts and denials" that Title II would correct, he said, were not abstract problems, as some tended to regard them, but were "intensely human and personal." Very often those denials "harm the physical body, but always they strike at the root of the human spirit, and at the very core of human dignity." He noted that black Americans suffered indignities "in nearly every waking hour" caused by "differential treatment in, or exclusion from, public accommodations of every description."

He related the travail of a black family in trying to find accommodations to rest while driving from one part of the country to another. Owing to the ever present uncertainty whether they would be accommodated, blacks very carefully had to plan their stops along the way, with friends or at an isolated black lodging place, or endure the hardships of exclusion. "The players in this drama of frustration and indignity," he maintained, "are not commas, or semi-colons in a legislative thesis; they are *people*, human beings, citizens of the United States of America" (emphasis Wilkins's). Blacks, he said, recalling the launching of the second phase of the civil rights movement on February 1 in Greensboro with the sit-in demonstrations, were no longer in a mood to wait. He said indifference such as that suffered by the Greensboro students, one of whom was an Air Force veteran and an officer of his North Carolina A and T NAACP chapter, "will serve to prolong and intensify the eruptions of protest now underway throughout the country." Wilkins urged that all establishments serving the public, from gasoline filling stations and the proverbial "Miss Murphy's boarding house" to "huge emporiums or hostelries" be covered by any public accommodations law Congress enacted.

Wilkins challenged contentions that public accommodations provisions were an invasion of "property rights." He maintained that this was a strange argument reminiscent of slavery times. Then opponents of emancipation had argued that freeing human slaves was an invasion of property rights. With a direct shot at Everett Dirksen, he declared, "Today, one hundred years later, if the United States legislates to secure non-discriminatory treatment for the descendants of the slaves, it will be invading property rights. It is ironical that a proponent of this argument should be a representative of the State of Abraham Lincoln."[16]

The Kennedy administration remained opposed to strengthening its original bill and sought to restrict coverage of Title II by basing it on the commerce clause of the Constitution. There were strong doubts about whether the administration really wanted a public accommodations title. Attorney General Kennedy stressed the economic costs of discrimination in public accommodations and the disruption such injustice caused to interstate commerce. He would later mention the moral need for protection against discrimination in the area of public accommodations. But in his first statement to the House Judiciary Committee on June 26, he said nothing about its being a moral wrong or a violation of the equal protection clause of the Fourteenth Amendment.

Robert Kennedy granted that the public accommodations concept was not new; thirty-two states already had similar laws, most of which were "far more encompassing and far more stringent than the legislation we have suggested." He added that federal public accommodations action based primarily on the commerce clause of the Constitution would be similar to that taken under the National Labor Relations, the Taft-Hartley, the Fair Labor Standards, and the Agricultural Adjustment acts. He said the provision was needed immediately for easing racial strife and he proposed initially that the statute cover "hotels, motels, restaurants, theaters, and other places of amusement, department stores, drug stores, gasoline stations and the like." He later expressed a willingness to exempt barber shops, beauty parlors, and swimming pools, which he maintained did not cater to travelers. Kennedy caused laughter when Celler asked him what he meant when he said that Title II would apply only to accommodations involved to a "substantial" degree in interstate commerce. His answer: "More than minimal." A sharper exchange occurred when Lindsay asked him about the rumors in the Capitol Hill cloakrooms that the administration did not want Title II. Kennedy responded, "I don't think the President or I have to defend our good faith to you or anyone else."[17]

The NAACP and its allies remained opposed to restricting the basis for Title II to the commerce clause. Robert Kennedy readily acknowledged to the Senate Commerce Committee that there were two main costs involved in segregation in public accommodations: that of human dignity, which was "quite apart from the moral damage" that such discrimination inflicted, and that of placing artificial restrictions on the market concerning goods obtained through interstate commerce, which interfered with the natural flow of merchandise. White people, whether they were prostitutes, narcotics pushers, Communists, or bank robbers, he noted, were welcome at establishments that did not admit certain federal judges, ambassadors, and members of the armed services because of their skin color. There was no question, he said, that Congress had the power to regulate commerce that involved the flow of goods between the states. That was done under the thirty-eight laws that he listed. "If Congress can, and does, control the service of oleomargarine in every restaurant in the nation, surely it can insure our non-white citizens access to those restaurants." The real issue, he said, was whether Congress should or should not ban racial discrimination in places that were open to the public. In determining that question, he said, "we must give weight to a consideration of the right that will be lost."

The attorney general stressed that he believed that the federal government had "a clear responsibility to help put a stop to discrimination." He maintained that the constitutional authority of Congress to enact the administration's proposed public accommodations title was derived from both the commerce clause and the Fourteenth Amendment, "but our primary reliance is on the commerce clause." Each of the facilities covered under Title II, he said, had a "direct and intimate relation to the movement" of people across state lines. So it was beyond question that the administration's bill was within the area of a legitimate exercise of Congress's authority over interstate commerce. Similarly, he said, the bill relied on the power under the Fourteenth Amendment to prohibit the denial of equal protection of the laws to any person. However, Kennedy said, the administration recognized that in 1883 the Supreme Court had held in the *Civil Rights Cases* decision that Congress did not have power under the Fourteenth Amendment to prohibit discrimination in privately owned places of public accommodation, as it had done under the 1875 public accommodations law, which it then overturned; furthermore, the power of Congress under the amendment was "only over discrimination accomplished by state action." In the ensuing eighty years, he said, much of the force of that decision had disappeared. State relationships with business had become more varied and complex, and views of what action might be attributed to the state had changed. He acknowledged that, based on the number of recent cases in which the federal courts had held that private decisions to discriminate could be attributed to state action under the Fourteenth Amendment, the Supreme Court might well uphold the constitutionality of a public accommodations law based on that protection. "However, the 1883 Decision has not been overruled and remains the law of the land." He said that was the reason why the administration was relying on the commerce clause.

Joseph Rauh, as the Americans for Democratic Action representative before the Senate Commerce Committee, took a view sharply different from the administration's. He granted that as recently as in 1960, in *Boynton* v. *Virginia*, the Supreme Court had held that the Interstate Commerce Act, which forbade discrimination in motor vehicles serving as interstate common carriers, granted to all persons, regardless of race, a federal right to be served in a restaurant operated as a part of a carrier's terminal facilities, although the restaurant was not operated specifically by the carrier. Based on that reasoning, he suggested, the commerce clause clearly gave Congress the right to forbid discrimination in places of public accommodation that utilized supplies or personnel from outside the state. Thus, he said, it was impossible to argue otherwise.

Furthermore, Rauh said, the National Labor Relations Act had an even broader scope, since it regulated activities "affecting commerce." Congress could regulate those intrastate activities that affected interstate commerce. He explained that the Supreme Court had held that the National Labor Relations Act applied to retailers whose sales were wholly intrastate and only one ninth of whose purchases were outside of the state. Congress, he said, even had the authority to regulate the wheat that a farmer grew on his own farm, solely for his own consumption, even though the amount he grew was trivial.

There was also another appropriate constitutional base for ending discrimination in all public facilities, he stressed, and that was provided under the Fourteenth Amendment. He dismissed the argument that the Supreme Court's decision in the *Civil Rights Cases* foreclosed any action under the Fourteenth Amendment to prohibit discrimination in public accommodations, because since 1883 there had been "a steady broadening of the concept of state action." The Court's arguments in *Shelly* v. *Kraemer* that barred lower courts from enforcing restrictive covenants in the sale of private housing, he said, as well as those in *Burnton* v. *Wilmington Parking Authority* that prohibited discrimination in a restaurant that was leased from a Delaware governmental agency, were applicable to discrimination in privately owned restaurant, hotel, retail, and entertainment facilities.

The other argument against basing Title II on the Fourteenth Amendment, Rauh noted, was that such a law would involve the regulation of private property by Congress, and that would be unconstitutional. That argument was as outmoded as it was extreme, he said, for it blindly attempted to "relegate to the ash heap the ever-ascending precedents" that permitted regulation of property rights in the public interest. He added:

Just as *Plessy* v. *Ferguson* did not stand the test of time, the reasonable probabilities are that the 1883 decision will one day be overruled or distinguished into oblivion. The 1883 case is a shell that is only waiting for its obituary notice. It is a shell, because on the one side the Court has moved away from the narrow concept of state action, and on the other side the Court has moved away from the idea that property may not be regulated in the public interest.

Jacob Javits, who supported the basic LCCR position, told the Senate Commerce Committee that the basis for action under the commerce clause was firmly established in dozens of congressional enactments under that clause that included the National Labor Relations Act, the Fair Labor Standards Act, the Agricultural Adjustment Act, and the Pure Food and Drug Act. He said the bill that was being considered was validly within Congress's interstate commerce power because the practices that it was seeking to regulate were "a burden upon interstate commerce." Denial of services and accommodations on the basis of race or color, Javits said, interfered with the "freedom of interstate travel of Negroes." The Fourteenth Amendment would support legislation along those lines, he said, although it would "probably be best to spell out the reliance on the amendment by expanding the definition of establishments covered by the bill in order to make it clear that it proscribes discrimination on grounds of race or color by any business in which such discrimination" was enforced by the state.

The underlying reality for those who supported the public accommodations bill was that social and economic legislation that served as the framework for extending the benefits of a highly industrialized society to the masses was based on the plenary powers of the commerce clause. The battle was joined on the Senate floor by Kenneth Keating, who introduced an amendment to base the public accommodations title on the Fourteenth Amendment as well as on the commerce clause.

John Lindsay and Missouri's Richard Bolling, as a bipartisan team, with the help of Rauh and other LCCR lawyers, had the Solomonic assignment of working out public accommodations language that would satisfy the Republicans and Democrats as well as the civil rights forces. Noting that the controversy had "deep political and substantive roots," they based their proposal, which was accepted by the LCCR, on a combination of the commerce clause and the Fourteenth Amendment. The reasoning was that the Republicans "quite naturally" felt a proprietary interest in the post–Civil War Thirteenth and Fourteenth amendments, which had been enacted under their leadership, while the Democrats had been the primary force that instilled life into the commerce clause beginning during the New Deal with a series of regulatory measures.

Reaffirming the views of its drafters, the LCCR statement concluded that it was "almost ludicrous to suggest that the Supreme Court, which has long protected the rights of Negroes while Congress stood idly by, should now, when Congress at long last does begin to move, find constitutional deficiencies in its action."

Noting that, after some later modification, the operating section of the administration bill was still predicated on the commerce clause alone, the LCCR recommended that, to avoid technical confusion resulting from apparently limiting prohibitions against discrimination to interstate travel, it would be preferable to rely on a dual foundation that included the Fourteenth Amendment. It felt that the operating section of the bill should be rewritten to eliminate commerce clause limitations and that it *simply forbid discrimination in all facilities open to the public except those which Congress deems it necessary to exempt*" (italics LCCR's). This way reliance would be on both constitutional bases, "but neither would serve as a limitation on public facilities covered by the bill."[18]

The Leadership Conference had the impression that the administration's strategy was to expedite the passage of a civil rights bill with minimal political cost in the South. That meant that it did not have to be fully effective, just strong enough to alleviate pressure from blacks and their supporters for protection of their rights. Nicholas Katzenbach, rejecting that cynical viewpoint, sincerely believed the administration's strategy would best ensure passage of a good bill. This approach, which was worked out with Lawrence F. O'Brien, special assistant to the President for congressional affairs, and his staff, was to get the Republican leadership, namely McCulloch, to agree on the language of a bill and thus avoid GOP opposition on the House floor. The first thing McCulloch insisted on was that there should be no march up the hill in the House and down again in the Senate, as had occurred with the 1957 and 1960 civil rights acts. The LCCR strategy, then as now, was to get the strongest bill possible through the House and be prepared for compromise in the Senate. This strategy had worked well with Majority Leader Lyndon Johnson. But McCulloch now said he would not tolerate that, because he had been badly hurt by supporting that weakened bill. He demanded and won a commitment from Robert Kennedy and Katzenbach that they would oppose any weakening of the House-passed bill in the Senate. As was evident from the battle over FEPC, however, the Leadership Conference, in particular Mitchell and Rauh, opposed this tactic, preferring to stick with the one that had worked, at least in part, twice before.

So the Leadership Conference and the administration remained at loggerheads on several aspects of the civil rights bill. Katzenbach explained that Robert Kennedy hated to have to take anything out of the bill. "But, based on the tactics we had laid out, that was the price he felt he had to pay for getting a bill" through Congress. Katzenbach found that this strategy served the interests of civil rights very well, because the administration did not appear to be the Leadership Conference's mouthpiece. Such a strategy, applied to any special-interest group, left the Justice Department to work more freely with moderate and conservative Republicans, whose votes, everyone acknowledged, were crucial for success.

Regarding the Title I voting provisions, to which this strategy also applied, Robert Kennedy explained that the new literacy proposal provided "for a rebuttable rather than a conclusive presumption of literacy upon a showing that the applicant has completed six grades of schooling." He said that this change from the administration's 1962 position was made owing to "feelings expressed by some that in all fairness a registrar should have the opportunity to show that a particular person with a sixth grade education is not actually literate." Astonishingly, he expressed belief that the "practical result" would be the same.[19]

Mitchell's open confrontation with the Kennedy administration came not on public accommodations, although differences there remained intense, but over Part III, addition of an FEPC provision, and broadening of the voting section to cover state elections. He had gotten the NAACP annual convention during its meeting in Chicago to adopt a resolution declaring that the Kennedy civil rights program was "inadequate to meet the minimum needs of the existing situation." The resolution commended the President's bill "as a step toward discharging the moral obligation of the Federal government to its Negro citizens" and reiterated the NAACP's demand for a fair employment practices committee "with adequate authority to compel the attendance of witnesses and production of evidence and enforcement of its decrees."

The problem with the administration's apparent reassurance on the FEPC and Part III provisions was that it had been given by Vice President Johnson in a famous June 22 meeting with civil rights leaders, after the President had left the room. As usually happened when Wilkins visited Washington, Mitchell did not attend the meeting because of the problem of protocol. As the NAACP's legislative expert, he did not like being placed in a position where, whenever differences occurred, he would have to disagree with his boss in meetings outside the association. Rauh, however, expressed Mitchell's views. That meeting was the one at which Kennedy had said he might lose the election on the civil rights issue, but since it was a moral one he had no choice. For some reason that he could not recall, Rauh addressed Johnson instead of Robert Kennedy. He asked, "Mr. Vice President, would the administration object if we tried to get a broader bill, including FEPC and Title Three?" Johnson replied, "No, there would be no objection." Johnson assured the group that the administration would regard those sections with "flexibility." It was the attorney general who was directing the administration's civil rights policy, but he had remained silent. The civil rights leaders had felt they had a right to assume that this was administration policy.

In truth, the administration was opposed to the FEPC and Part III provisions, which were included in the bill Subcommittee No. 5 reported to the full House Judiciary Committee on October 2. With Celler's support, New Jersey Democrat Peter Rodino had agreed to introduce in the subcommittee an FEPC amendment. The administration feared that such an amendment would burden the bill and jeopardize its passage, while some Republicans warned that the provision would either sink the bill or result in emasculation of other sections.

At one point during the maneuvering near the end of July, "just as we were feeling happy about the progress of the legislation," Mitchell recalled, the civil rights forces were confronted with a problem in the House Education and Labor Committee when Adam Clayton Powell, its chairman, threatened to force floor action on an FEPC bill before him if Celler refused to add such a provision to the administration measure. Mitchell was thankful that Powell and not North Carolina's Graham Barden now headed this committee. Supporting FEPC, Powell appointed California's James Roosevelt to head a subcommittee on the bill composed of Goodell and other friendly congressmen. Upon reporting out the FEPC bill (H.R. 405), Powell and other committee members announced that they were about to initiate a discharge petition to get the bill promptly out of the Rules Committee.

Fears immediately arose that southern Democrats and Republicans on the committee would quickly approve the bill and send it to the House floor, where it would have been defeated and thus embarrassed the Kennedy administration. After meeting with Mitchell and six other Leadership Conference representatives,[*] Celler, in consultation with Rodino and House Speaker McCormack, agreed it would be better to merge the FEPC bill with the civil rights bill in the Judiciary Committee. This decision mistakenly sparked a charge of foot-dragging. Mitchell, welcoming the agreement, thought it was fortunate that Roosevelt, who had sponsored the FEPC bill, and other Labor Committee members agreed to let the Judiciary Committee handle the issue.

On the eve of the subcommittee's approval of the NAACP-favored bill, as he launched a speaking campaign for its approval, Mitchell referred to

[*] The other LCCR representatives were Biemiller (AFL-CIO), the Reverend Walter E. Fauntroy (SCLC), Rauh (ADA), Dr. Deborah Wolfe (National Council of Negro Women), Jack Conway (IUD), and Aaronson (secretary of the LCCR).

the four black girls who had been killed on September 15 by the Ku Klux Klan bombing of the Sixteenth Street Baptist Church in Birmingham; he said they were among the "countless number" of children who grew physically but died spiritually when their aspirations and hopes were crushed and broken in a ruthless system that assigned them to second class status solely because they were black." Mitchell declared that all who had been "neutral or indifferent in the struggle for human freedom" had now been given a chance to see the "tragedy that we in the NAACP have witnessed and fought" against since 1909. He warned that not all the wrongs that had "stunted or blotted out the lives and dreams of our children" would be corrected by passage of the civil rights legislation, "but a strong and meaningful bill will give the nation much needed machinery to begin correction."

Mitchell was confident that as a result of the NAACP legislative strategy session in August and the daily LCCR working sessions, "we have comfortable majorities" in the full Judiciary Committee to pass the features he favored. Despite "these clear signs of strength and in spite of the urgency of the times," he charged, the attorney general, representing the President in secret strategy sessions, was "trying to deny the full civil rights bill a fair chance for floor consideration." Additionally, Mitchell held frequent negotiations with White House and Justice Department representatives as attempts were made to shape a compromise. Mitchell thought that despite sharp disagreements, "our relationships were refreshingly friendly and informal."

That description especially applied to his relations with Robert Kennedy. "The attorney general was always very cordial, always happy to see me or anybody else who came in" to visit him. "But, almost invariably, we got into some kind of very heated disagreement before I left because he would not be willing to veer away from the standard procedures" in dealing with civil rights violations. One example was Justice's refusal to seek indictments when it did not believe it could get any. Another was the administration's insistence on an earlier voting bill. Mitchell felt that if the voting bill became the first priority, as was shown in 1957 and 1960, those looking for the easiest political escape route would jump onto that measure, pass it, claim a victory, and throw the rest "on the junk pile." Mitchell believed that from a tactical standpoint, it was best not to get caught in that trap. Now they sharply disagreed over the scope of the civil rights bill. Even though the national civil rights crisis was confirming Mitchell's conviction that the administration was wrong on the FEPC question and other provisions of the bill, John and Robert Kennedy refused to shift their position.[20]

Had Robert Kennedy been the usual civil rights opponent, Mitchell's task would have been relatively easy. For one thing, he would have been emotionally prepared for the confrontation. His antagonist, however, was not a segregationist but only someone who was determined to set his own pace on the Hill. As the administration's point man on civil rights, he maintained that "the debate should not be about the relative strength of the proposals but about their relative chances for passage." Furthermore, intensely competitive, he welcomed almost any challenge, whether he was scrapping to make the 1948 Harvard football team, stepping on toes at the 1960 Democratic Convention, or champing at the bit to take on Teamsters boss Jimmy Hoffa in a relentless pursuit of organized crime. Robert Kennedy played to win. The problem was that Mitchell did not regard the struggle for his constitutional rights as a game; for him it was life, the essence of his being.

Impatient with the administration's shenanigans, Celler, with Mitchell and Rauh at his side, on September 25 announced that Subcommittee No. 5 had approved the bill with everything the civil rights forces wanted. Celler had been caught between a genuine desire to follow his President's leadership and the strongly liberal nature of his own philosophy and political base. Now he chose to follow his conscience. Rauh recalled, "Misty eyes made it difficult for us to read the text of the dream bill." The two lobbyists then called for full Judiciary Committee approval "without dilution or delay."

Seven days later the subcommittee formally reported out the bill and sent it to the full Judiciary Committee, which planned to begin hearings on October 8. Led by President Kennedy, the administration now pulled out all stops to water down the bill. Many administration-inspired newspaper stories and columns called the civil rights forces "impractical" and "extreme," in an attempt to weaken the bill in the full Judiciary Committee.[21]

Mitchell was fit to be tied when Robert Kennedy was granted his request to testify on the subcommittee bill in an executive session of the Judiciary Committee from which he and NAACP allies were barred. Standing outside the closed hearing-room door, Mitchell talked to everybody available, including Katzenbach and many reporters. Katzenbach was an important member of the group that served as a liaison between the Justice Department, led by Robert Kennedy, and the Judiciary Committee, particularly McCulloch, who had strong objections to some provisions, like the public accommodations section, of the subcommittee bill. Mitchell called the expected cutback "a shame" and said there was "no reason for this kind of sell-out." He was especially upset that "everybody in there is a white man, and what they are doing affects 10 percent of the population that is black. I don't know if the Negroes are being protected." That was the same complaint that NAACP and other demonstrators had made to Robert Kennedy on June 14, when three thousand of them massed outside the Justice Department.

Mitchell told reporters outside the committee room that the administration should have been in there fighting for the subcommittee bill. Instead, the attorney general was trying to get people who were committed to it to change their position. He correctly charged that the administration's basic strategy was to write a bill in the House Judiciary Committee that "will be so restricted that it will sail through the full committee, through the Rules Committee and gain floor approval in the Senate and House with only token opposition." But, because the strategy was seriously flawed, he was sure it "would not work even on a bill to reaffirm our belief in the Ten Commandments or the Bill of Rights." The first priority for passing civil rights legislation, he felt, was unequivocal administration support for a strong bill. Second was the execution of a carefully developed lobbying strategy to win its passage. He was certain 214 House votes were available for the subcommittee bill and felt that 117 more were possible, but the only guarantee for getting these was hard work.[22]

On October 16 the Leadership Conference sent Celler a three-page letter urging him not to back down from the subcommittee bill. The civil rights forces also won support from Case, who criticized the Justice Department for demanding the removal of Part III. Case demanded to know whether anything had been learned from the demonstrations. He noted that the Justice Department had told him, too, it had no power to intervene in matters "crying out for intercession."

Robert Kennedy maintained, "What I want is a bill, not an issue." He played on the reluctance of the Republicans to support a bill with an exclusive Democratic trademark to win concessions in the Judiciary Committee executive session. He accepted the change that made the voting title apply to state as well as federal elections, but criticized another change that would allow the impounding of ballots cast by persons found qualified to vote by temporary referees. Robert Kennedy continued his attack on the subcommittee amendments to Title II, maintaining they were too broad and not clear. Taking issue with the attorney general, Pohlhaus, in a memorandum for Mitchell, maintained that reliance should be only on a bill that was all-inclusive, except for specified exclusions, rather than on a measure providing limited coverage.

As was well known, the strongest disagreement between the NAACP and the administration involved legal and policy questions as well as the basic philosophy underlying the bestowing of authority by Title III to the attorney general to file injunction suits to protect Fourteenth Amendment rights. Robert Kennedy, overlooking the long struggle for antilynching laws and for other protections against violence in the South, erroneously argued that the initial proposal for Part III–type provisions had been intended for the protection of substantive constitutional rights in the enforcement of the 1954 school desegregation decision. Since 1957, Kennedy said, the concept had been broadened to include authority for the attorney general to enforce individual rights and had "become a symbol for those favoring faster federal action to end racial discrimination." Maintaining that Part III authority for the attorney general would, in effect, constitute creation of a national police force, he strongly opposed the subcommittee's addition. He felt that the administration bill was intended to serve the purpose of the subcommittee's Title III.

Pohlhaus insisted that the attorney general's arguments were insubstantial. He said the NAACP could not share Kennedy's reluctance to keep federal courts from ruling on fundamental civil rights questions. According to Kennedy, determinations had "historically [been] made by local police officers, as to how many people should be allowed to protest, in what manner, and at what time of day." Pohlhaus interpreted that position as an appeal for adhering to the status quo. He maintained that regardless of the shortcomings of federal judges described by Robert Kennedy, it was they who had broken the historical pattern of segregation supported by law. Their decisions, appealable to higher courts, were much more likely to provide justice than relying on the "historically" enforced police authority of the Bull Connors. Pohlhaus said in his memorandum that:

> I considered the attorney general's speculations on the establishment of a police state and the creation of anarchy by the withdrawal of local police protection to be myths created to frighten Congress into going along with his attempt to water down the present bill.
>
> His speculations on the wide scope of the bill also appear to me to be made in an attempt to undermine the bill. The authority granted will be discretionary. I cannot visualize any attorney general in the foreseeable future using it in the manner he suggests. If, however, this is a real problem, the solution is to limit the bill to the remedy necessary, not to kill Title III.
>
> All in all, I feel his testimony on Title III shows a callous disregard of the real human suffering to which thousands of southern Negroes are being daily subjected.

That perception was in sharp contrast to the later humanistic image of Robert Kennedy.[23]

Given the administration's opposition, Mitchell told the annual ADA conference in Washington that the current danger to civil rights was not the Barnetts of Mississippi, diehard segregationists like Governor Wallace of Alabama, or trigger-happy sheriffs in backwoods Dixie. "Each time they stage their sorry little charades of standing in doorways or debasing the reputations of police dogs," he said, "they set off a wave of revulsion that wins hundreds of friends for equal treatment under law." Instead, the danger came from those who thought "Papa knows best." They were the people who wanted "to give colored Americans what they think we ought to have and not what we know we need." He recalled that the "ink was hardly dry on the subcommittee bill before a whole regiment of commentators, administration operators and sophisticates in the liberal camp were trying to show that it went too far." Far in the forefront of this group, he repeatedly charged, was the Justice Department, which was spreading word that Republicans would not support the strengthened bill.

It especially galled Mitchell that Justice was "singularly free from knowledgeable" black lawyers "in top policy levels," and therefore there was no input from blacks on civil rights in the department. "Although the burden and victories" in the civil rights struggle had been carried by brilliant black lawyers, not one was on Justice's top staff. He declared that "when the day to day Justice Department operations on civil rights are determined by an all white board of strategy, something is missing." He was similarly bothered that the Judiciary Committee executive session that he was not permitted to attend was all white and had no input from black experts. The time had long passed for desegregating the Justice Department's policy-making level, and he prayed that soon there would be more blacks in Congress and on committees like the Judiciary.

He declared that there were no civil rights leaders or groups who would approve any plan of action that began by giving away 50 percent of the civil rights package even before debate in Congress began. Based on his head count, Mitchell was confident that if enough Democrats from outside the South stood firm, Republicans would help get the bill passed in its present form. He called on his NAACP field troops to "take off the lambskin gloves" and wage an all-out fight for a strong bill.[24]

While welcoming the news that the full House Judiciary Committee would begin voting on the civil rights bill on October 22, Mitchell remained bitter. He complained to Charles Mathias and John Lindsay that some of the attorney general's suggestions had done "incalculable harm to civil rights." After making them in "secret," according to Mitchell, Robert Kennedy publicly described his suggestions as an effort to get a "more reasonable" bill than the subcommittee version. Mitchell felt that it was "a grave injustice" to so depict the subcommittee bill.

Mitchell's complaints were a last-ditch attempt to get Lindsay and Mathias to help stop erosion of the bill. He recalled that back in March after Senate Republicans had introduced a public accommodations provision utilizing the commerce clause, two senators introduced a bipartisan measure that relied on the Fourteenth Amendment. Lindsay himself led a group of congressmen in introducing a public accommodations provision based on the Fourteenth Amendment. Lindsay himself led a group of congressmen in introducing a public accomodations provision based on the Fourteenth Amendment. Mitchell said that civil rights forces believed that the Judiciary Committee had worked out a compromise that was acceptable to Republicans and Democrats. Though the attorney general maintained that it was necessary to strike out the Fourteenth Amendment provision to win bipartisan support for the public accommodations title, Mitchell remained worried because details of the compromise were "shrouded in secrecy."

Regarding Robert Kennedy's objections to Title III, Mitchell noted that when Attorney General Brownell first offered it (as Part III) for the Eisenhower administration, President Kennedy, as a senator had voted for the Republican initiative. "Surely a proposal which had such distinguished bipartisan support in 1957," he said, could not "fairly be described as one" that gave excessive power to the executive branch. Mitchell "earnestly hoped" that the full committee would support the subcommittee's recommendations.

Mitchell refuted the contention that the Republicans would not support a strong bill. He said that, based on his count, he had told administration officials in private and in public that such an assumption by them was erroneous. He maintained that there were 18 votes in the full committee plus possibly another 6 for a strong bill. Six Republicans, he said, had assured him they would firmly support a strong bill. He felt that other Republicans who had not given similar commitments would probably support such a bill. He urged the Republicans on the Judiciary Committee to issue a joint statement in order to halt the increasing drift toward a weakened bill.

Directly intervening, President Kennedy held a secret strategy conference with Celler, McCulloch, McCormack, Minority Leader Charles Halleck of Indiana, and other key legislative leaders on October 23 in order to explore possibilities for a compromise bill that the Judiciary Committee would approve. The following day, just before a series of intensive negotiations between Republican and Democratic leaders and the administration, Halleck indicated he would help the Judiciary Committee block approval of the strong subcommittee bill. After the compromise was worked out, the Judiciary Committee approved a toned-down bill, H.R. 7152, on October 29.[25]

Although grieving, Mitchell and the LCCR felt that the compromise,

approved by a 19 to 15 vote, was a significant improvement over the administration bill thanks to Celler's considerable help. In addition to a
strong public accommodations section, it included a national FEPC law
enforceable in the courts, and authority for the attorney general to intervene in civil rights suits involving a denial of equal protection of the law.
It also added two titles to the bill providing for a voting census and for
court appeals in certain civil rights cases where they were not then allowed.

The political factors that contributed in 1963 to the bill's to success,
included: the pressure resulting from the introduction of bills by the Republicans early in the year; the brutal treatment of civil rights demonstrators in the South, which underscored the need for Part III powers for the
Justice Department to preserve Fourteenth Amendment equal protection
rights, as well as for broad federal criminal penalties; demonstrations in the
North that called for a national FEPC law; the NAACP annual convention's
reaffirmation of its call for comprehensive civil rights legislation; the
NAACP civil rights legislative conference in Washington, which focused
specifically on lobbying through personal contacts with lawmakers; and the
March on Washington, which galvanized mass support behind the struggle.[26]

Having crossed the first major hurdle, Mitchell turned his attention to
the recent political infighting in order to glean lessons for the remainder of
the struggle. He observed in a monthly report, as a basic postulate, that
both Republicans and Democrats wanted to win elections and support for
presidential candidates in the North and South. A considerable number of
Democrats believed that there should be no civil rights legislation because
it tended to split party ranks on other important issues. Several Republicans asserted it was useless to try for the black vote, arguing that instead
there was a good chance of winning more congressional seats and greater
support North and South by taking an anti-civil-rights stand.

These negative forces were all at work while the House Judiciary Committee was considering the civil rights bill. Although Mitchell was convinced there was enough bipartisan support on the committee to gain
approval for the broadened bill the NAACP wanted, much of the news
media and Robert Kennedy not only opposed but also exaggerated the
strengthening provisions. Some Republicans therefore decided that the administration was in an "embarrassing position" and could not escape without hurting itself either among northern blacks or southern whites.
Mitchell felt that at this point the administration should have pushed to
get the bill onto the floor "where all could see who supported its provisions." Instead, the administration twisted the arms of liberals who were
for the subcommittee bill. The President urged the Democrats to remain

flexible in order to support a revised subcommittee bill, while he called on House Republican leaders to get their liberal members to abandon the measure. The liberals at first refused to back down because the White House had not provided a written version of its proposed revisions, but several later relented.

Mitchell believed that perhaps the most important reason for this surrender was a widely circulated report that southern Judiciary Committee members would vote for the subcommittee bill because they believed it was too strong to pass the House. He was appalled by such "incredible behind the scene moves" calculated to scare off the Republicans. Several liberal Republicans from strongly black districts consequently said they did not want to appear to be cooperating with the southerners in killing the bill. Although the Republicans did not finally decide to abandon the subcommittee bill until they had met early on the morning of October 28, the administration, hoping others would follow, had already spread word that three liberal Democrats had shifted their support. Mitchell was unable to persuade these three lawmakers to reverse their positions.

After the vote, a new problem arose involving Republicans opposed to Halleck's leadership, who split into two groups. One, composed of conservatives, opposed any cooperation with the administration that would boost its accomplishments. The other group, composed of liberals and conservatives, insisted the Republican party should develop a constructive record on issues like civil rights, and that this required avoiding cooperation with southern Democrats. The purely conservative group charged that Halleck had helped get the civil rights bill out of the committee and that it would cost them four or five possible seats in the South. The others charged that the administration had "sold a bill of goods" to Halleck by maintaining the measure approved by the full committee contained Republican recommendations, and the minority leader had gone along without obtaining real proof. Mitchell said that the so-called proof offered appeared in "an amazing document circulated among Republicans." It asserted that "upon Republican demand," the public accommodations title was narrowed and the voting rights section was restricted to federal elections, while a jury trial amendment, a totally new feature, was added. Mitchell found that although no one would reveal any names, some Republicans were insisting that the document would help win final passage of the bill.[27]

Mitchell joined other African Americans in mourning the assassination of John F. Kennedy on November 22, 1963. The shock of the young President's death cast the civil rights struggle in a totally new light. Not only had an increasing number of Americans been aroused to the extent of moral wrongs that were being inflicted on a segment of the population, but they were now struck by a deep sense of guilt that sharply questioned the national character. Consequently, there was overpowering sentiment for passing "the Kennedy civil rights bill" as House Democrats began the second phase of their struggle—getting it through the Rules Committee— during the period of national mourning. Howard Smith, as expected, intended to bottle up the bill, but the tide was clearly against him. Led by Richard Bolling and Clarence Brown, Sr., the bipartisan Rules Committee veterans of the 1957 civil rights fight, civil rights forces began plotting to free the bill from the chairman's grip.

On December 3, determined to force Smith's hand, Brown found that while his colleagues supported him, they all wanted Smith to have a fair chance to do his own maneuvering. They felt it was necessary to live with Smith, but they also agreed that Bolling was free to act. Brown therefore began seeking an immediate meeting with Smith in order to discuss the possibility of an agreement that would permit hearings for ten days before Christmas and for another week early in 1964. Bolling and Brown reasoned that the bill could not be called up until late January anyway. The proposed schedule would enable the bill to be reported out and passed by the House before the end of January.

Brown knew that the bill's supporters were not going to punish Smith for sitting on the bill, but that they would insist on action. Brown planned to tell Smith he ought to be smart and avoid being embarrassed by Bolling in the committee. Smith could do that by announcing hearings and not permitting the opposition to waste a lot of time. Brown conceded that Smith might "tell me to go to hell," but he was prepared to take the chance and promised to let Mitchell know what happened.

Brown declined Mitchell's invitation to attend an upcoming Leadership Conference on Civil Rights meeting because, as a rule, he tried to avoid any appearance of conflict of interest involving matters before the Rules Committee. He asked Mitchell to inform the LCCR that he was cooperating with Bolling to get the bill out, but not by the discharge petition method.

Meanwhile, Bolling initiated a resolution for the discharge petition even though Brown would not sign it. Brown's intentions did not bother Mitchell. He was fully aware of Brown's views and that his objection to the petition was the Ohio Republican conservative's standard position.

In response to the petition drive, the Leadership Conference held an emergency meeting on December 4 and announced that it would begin a national mobilization to arouse support for freeing the bill from Smith's committee. Washington representatives were given lobbying assignments, and others were called in to assist the effort. The United Steelworkers of America, for one, called in nearly 200 of its local leaders to spend a week in the nation's capital contacting House members. Civil rights forces estimated that about 172 congressmen had pledged to sign the discharge petition and that it was possible to win over the remaining number that was required.

On the morning of December 5, Brown called Mitchell to inform him that he had met with Smith the previous night. Brown told Smith that the heat was getting so great regarding the bill that he would have to get rough if the committee chairman did not agree to take prompt action. Appealing to their friendship, Brown said he did not want to have to push him, but something had to be done. Brown urged Smith to announce that he was going to hold hearings on the bill the coming week. Smith balked at that demand but agreed to issue a statement saying that hearings would be held when Congress returned in January. Furthermore, even though he was greatly opposed to the bill, he said he would not permit any undue delay. Brown therefore estimated that the bill would be disposed of by the end of January. He told Mitchell he too was issuing a statement, whose basic thrust was that he was agreeing with Smith on the January date for the hearings because the Rules Committee did not receive the bill until November and had only received the Judiciary Committee's report the previous day. Smith, of course, used this development to emphasize that the Rules Committee, in reality, could not hold hearings until January.

That same day, as agreed, Smith announced he would begin hearings on January 9. He conceded on the House floor that the members of the Rules Committee could take the bill "away from me, and they can do it any minute they want to." His reference was to a parliamentary procedure whereby a majority of the committee could vote out the bill over his objections. It was apparent that at least five Democrats and all five Republicans on the committee were inclined to do so. Putting up a show of strength he said he would not "encourage dilatory tactics."

Despite Smith's announcement, there was no assurance that he would not later employ delaying maneuvers. On December 9, Celler went ahead and filed the discharge petition and became one of the first to sign it. Mitchell was certain that strong support from civil rights forces had strengthened Brown's hand in negotiations with Smith.

Eager to get home for the holidays, several congressmen delayed signing until their return in January. Even civil rights supporters did not want to get caught in a struggle on the House floor just before the Christmas recess. Mitchell was confident that as the signatures approached the magic number of 218, hesitant House members would sign.

Mitchell advised the civil rights leadership that strong pressure would have to be maintained on Congress during the remaining struggle and the delegates who had attended the August legislative strategy session should be prepared to return on short notice to Washington when the bill reached the floor, and subsequently at "strategic times" during the Senate debate. He promised to give at least a week's notice when the forces were needed, but it was clear that that might not always be possible.[28]

The question of executive leadership remained paramount in Mitchell's mind as he continued developing strategy for the next stage of the battle. Mitchell felt that the basic problem with the Kennedy administration had been its slowness in recognizing the gravity of the civil rights problem. Once it did, to the credit of the President and his advisers, they moved and "harnessed" the major energies of the country to try to resolve the conflict.

Despite his appreciation for the strong emphasis John Kennedy placed on morality in the civil rights struggle, Mitchell was disillusioned by the administration's habitual concession to political expediency. That weakness placed the administration in the embarrassing position of pulling out all the stops to prevent the full Judiciary Committee from approving the bill it had said the subcommittee would never report. It canceled meetings, called in backers of a strong bill for conferences with the President and mustered the power of the House leadership in the quest for a "moderate" bill. That was exactly the opposite of the role Mitchell thought the executive branch should play in this critical struggle. Little wonder, therefore, that while sharing the popular affection for John Kennedy and being careful that his criticisms were absolutely fair in order not to offend anyone, Mitchell, as he let slip in a moment of anger, thought the "Kennedy administration's conduct on civil rights was reprehensible." Inherent in his lament was the regret that Kennedy's implementation of his moral commitment to ending racial inequality paled in comparison to his pursuit of his vision to conquer the vastness of space. The public's perception of John Kennedy's contributions to civil rights was sharply different, however, because few knew the difficulties Mitchell had experienced in obtaining the required leadership for forthright action.[29]

CHAPTER EIGHTEEN

The 1964 Act:
A Dream Realized

C larence Mitchell hailed the November 27, 1963, message to Congress from the newly sworn in President Johnson declaring that passage of the Kennedy civil rights bill was his first priority. He felt that "it was a great day for our country when a President who was born in the South" called upon Congress "to move forward to eliminate from this nation every trace of discrimination based upon race or color."

Mitchell had mixed feelings about Johnson. He expected to have "a hard time" with the Texan in the White House. More than ever, he wanted a supportive President because such backing would automatically commit the leadership of the Democratic majority in Congress to the struggle. Johnson's special message dispelled his fear.

Deeply moved by the tragedy, propelled by a moral obligation to fulfill Kennedy's civil rights program, and wishing to reassure the nation with a sense of continuity, Johnson declared: "We have talked long enough in this country about equal rights. . . . It is time now to write the next chapter—and to write it in the book of law." Those words were etched in Mitchell's mind, if in no one else's, and elevated the new President's standing with the lobbyist.

Seeing Johnson, whom he had first met in 1953, in a human rather than a political light, Mitchell understood him much better. Mitchell never had any doubt that Johnson was opposed to discrimination and all other "indicia of servitude among Negroes." Their sharp differences had resulted from approach. Mitchell the lobbyist had overlooked the reality that, as a member of the Senate, Johnson kept foremost in mind the limitations of his political base at home and of the majority leader's office. Mitchell nevertheless had welcomed Johnson's belief that social conditions were improving in the country, "so that at some point the civil rights problem would be behind us." While he was in the Senate, Johnson also wanted to see more progress made on civil rights, but, as always, he believed that such legislation would divide the Congress when progress was needed on economic matters. He felt that most Democrats were poor and therefore interested in social legislation. So, if they could be working together for those benefits, "they wouldn't get into these bruising fights in Congress." Furthermore, Johnson believed that if blacks gained proper economic and voting rights, much of the civil rights problem would disappear. Mitchell remembered Johnson's saying "again and again that people should have the right to vote." But Johnson felt that to achieve that goal it was best to concentrate on court and executive actions in order to avoid splitting the Democratic party in Congress.

Mitchell had always found Johnson honest and open. His respect for him was further enhanced by Johnson's being a refreshing change from other southerners in Congress, who were always hostile to civil rights. Recognizing Johnson's philosophy, Mitchell refrained from pressing disagreements to the point of animosity, because he realized that Democrats had attitudes on social and civil rights legislation that were similar to Johnson's. "Many of the colored Democrats thought that way too."[1]

Despite his six votes earlier in the House and Senate against civil rights, Johnson had voted for the 1957 Civil Rights Act and its 1960 amendments, which he had shaped to his liking as moderate voting rights bills. Johnson also enthusiastically supported what Mitchell called the anti-dynamiting provision in the 1960 act and worked hard to gain backing from the Texas delegation for the bills.

As further demonstration of his limited flexibility and his favoring executive action, Johnson in 1960 supported a motion to table a measure that would have given legislative backing, sought by Mitchell, to the Committee on Government Contracts. Mitchell was aware, based on his conversations with the majority leader, that Johnson knew the committee would nevertheless continue to exist as a result of the next Eisenhower executive order. While winning favor with the southerners, Johnson did not destroy the program. Then when President Kennedy incorporated both of Eisenhower's fair employment committees into one Committee on Equal Employment Opportunity, as Vice President, Johnson enthusiastically agreed to become its chairman. Here again, though, Mitchell sharply differed with Johnson by continuing to feel that this committee was only a holding action to keep the FEPC idea alive until Congress gave the agency legislative authority and strengthened it. To the extent that he could, Mitchell welcomed Johnson's forthright leadership of the committee even though he never believed that its accomplishments were as great as many people had claimed. Seeing Johnson in a different light now, Mitchell realized that it was he, as majority leader, who had found an "ingenious" way to get Congress to extend the life of the Civil Rights Commission in 1960, as much as he had engineered the defeat in 1958 of attempts to pass legislation to undermine the Supreme Court because of decisions upholding First Amendment rights in internal security cases and the Fourteenth Amendment in civil rights cases.

Johnson's moderate image was buttressed by his close association with Humphrey, who had served as the majority leader's line to the liberal camp. Mitchell recalled one meeting prior to the establishment of the alliance at which Johnson had told him, "You know, what I wish the liberals would do is have somebody who is their spokesman that I can deal with." He named several persons, some of whom he said could not work with him (no doubt, men like Wayne Morse and Paul Douglas); others he felt would be unable to make agreements stick. He told Mitchell that Humphrey would be an ideal person "and said a couple of things which made it clear to me that he had checked with" Humphrey on possible revisions to the 1957 Civil Rights Act. Although Johnson never confirmed that Humphrey had agreed to be his liberal liaison, Mitchell welcomed that insight into the majority leader's thinking because he had always been very close to the Minnesotan.

More important, in considering the significance of Johnson's November 27 message to Congress, Mitchell recalled that he never easily gave a commitment of support, but once he did, "he would work tirelessly to see" that his commitment was fulfilled. Mitchell could confidently state in his December 6, 1963, report: "It is the Director's opinion that the statements made by the President in his speech to Congress were unequivocal commitments. It is also the Director's opinion that the President will work with tremendous energy and effectiveness to get legislation passed."

Mitchell now assumed much of the blame for strains in his relations with Johnson. The lobbyist always tried "to deal with people on the basis of one human relating to another," and he assumed that others were being guided by their convictions. He tried to maintain cordial relations even with southern senators (except those like Eastland) who he knew would not vote for civil rights. In Johnson's case, apart from the political rules under which the Texan operated, Mitchell was well aware of the principal stages in which he had matured as a humanist. He concluded that their differences had arisen primarily because he had not yet learned the lesson that

Johnson was teaching him: "Clarence, you can get anything you want if you've got the votes. How many votes have you got?"

At first when Johnson began saying that to Mitchell, the "hackles" would rise. As he continued reflecting on the refrain, "the more I realized that this was the best advice that anybody could give."[2]

Mitchell then became aware of a common problem. Many people pressing for legislation would estimate rather than actually count the votes they had, or they would accept the word of the House speaker, the party whip, or a committee chairman. But the only certain determination was to find out what each lawmaker would do. By following that careful procedure, Mitchell often found votes in surprising places. That had been the case with Clarence Brown, Sr., when the battle for the 1957 Civil Rights Act began. To Mitchell the Ohio Republican was a good example of why it was inappropriate to "cram people into tight molds" marked "liberal and conservative." Not only was Brown eager to help in outvoting Howard Smith on the House Rules Committee, but they also developed a long-standing friendship. Through Brown, Mitchell "learned to see many members of Congress in a new light," and it always "was worthwhile to follow his advice in seeking the support of members who seemed hopeless." Brown was right so often that Mitchell could not "remember any time when he was wrong."

A good example of Brown's philosophy, and thus the extent of his flexibility in working with Mitchell, was the resolution he sponsored in June 1963, with the backing of a similarly conservative House coalition that prohibited the President from creating any new executive departments through powers granted him under the 1949 Reorganization Act. Eisenhower had used those powers to create the Department of Health, Education and Welfare; now Brown wanted to prevent John Kennedy from enlarging the federal bureaucracy by establishing the Department of Urban Affairs. Southerners supported him because Kennedy had planned to appoint Robert Weaver secretary of the new department. Mitchell understood that Brown's stand was in keeping with his conservative views and was not racially motivated, so though they strongly differed, Brown's actions caused no enmity. That, too, was one reason that Mitchell was not afraid of a resurgence of the Republican–southern Democratic coalition. He had learned that lawmakers' key motivation was rounding up votes.

Another problem with counting votes, Mitchell found, was that many Democrats did so only among themselves while estimating their strength across the aisle. That failure contributed to his sharp differences regarding vote counts with the Kennedy administration. Mathias joked that the way Mitchell and Rauh counted votes was that if they were not kicked out of a senator's office they assumed they had his support. Lawrence O'Brien, special assistant to the President for congressional affairs, replied, "This is ridiculous," when Mitchell told him there were enough votes to include an FEPC provision in the civil rights bill. O'Brien, who formalized the liaison office under President Kennedy, was admittedly a lobbying novice. Initially, Mitchell said, "we moved cautiously and carefully." Once O'Brien had gotten over the notion "that I didn't know what I was talking about," Mitchell found him helpful.

Others similarly contested Mitchell's count as overly optimistic when he was certain that there were 214 votes and possibly another 117 in the House for the strong subcommittee bill, but time would prove him right. He had determined that count with the help of delegates attending the NAACP legislative strategy session in August. On that occasion, Mitchell welcomed his "very good fortune of getting in people who were really top notch operators in the Republican Party," like Samuel C. Jackson, a young black lawyer from Topeka, Kansas. Jackson and others like Harry Kingman of the People's Lobby from California were dedicated individuals who served as his "informal lobby." Mitchell found that those who counted only Democrats usually came up with figures that were too low. Like Johnson, he counted both Democrats and Republicans.

There were other noteworthy confirmations of the value of Mitchell's vote counting, as in 1958 when he found the one vote that helped Johnson kill Howard Smith's bill to render future federal laws invalid where they conflicted with state laws (unless they were specifically preempted by Congress). He no longer had any doubt that that was the way to get things done. Of course, it was equally important to have "a strong President" advocating similar views. Though Mitchell treasured and benefited considerably from this lesson, there remained an important difference between Johnson and him. For Johnson, the vote was everything; for Mitchell, principle came first.

Mitchell was equally impressed by Johnson's intimate knowledge of fellow senators. He recalled that once Johnson, as Vice President, attempted to preside over a meeting of liberal senators and LCCR representatives so that he could maintain ties with his former colleagues. Joseph Clark of Pennsylvania, who never cared for him, said, "What's he doing in here? This is a meeting of senators." Johnson, he said, had "no business being in here." Smarting from the rebuff, Johnson showed his superior knowledge of the Senate by dismissing as "a joke" a suggestion that Rule XXII remained an insurmountable barrier to passing needed legislation. Mitchell recalled that at the meeting "he went down the line, man by man, of the senators indicating why physically they could not carry on a filibuster" for an extended period. For example, he explained that the old Georgia war-horse Richard Russell had emphysema and could not talk long, and archfoe James Eastland had a drinking problem, so he was not as "formidable as other people thought he was." For Mitchell, "it was the most amazing analysis of his former colleagues." It was also "very valuable information, because I had always felt that the filibuster crowd could get away only with what the Senate" wanted to allow. Mitchell was encouraged that Johnson's assessment "was such a wonderful vindication of my point of view."

Mitchell knew that a filibustering senator was helped by his right to retain the floor by unanimous consent if another senator wanted to speak on an unrelated matter. By yielding under those terms, the filibusterer was able to get needed rest. It bothered Mitchell that members knew the practice should be stopped, but the unwritten rules of courtesy prevented anyone from objecting.

Mitchell felt Johnson's close identification with southerners like Russell was a personal handicap. Had Johnson developed a progressive image like Roosevelt's independent of the South, even though he was not one hundred percent for civil rights, Mitchell believed, his stand on social issues would have won him considerable support from blacks. But Johnson was too shrewd a politician to eschew an alliance with Russell. Johnson and Russell respected each other highly and treasured their friendship. Mitchell recognized that Russell's friendship assured Johnson overwhelming support from southerners and conservatives outside the region, but that was not sufficient to assure Johnson success in a quest for national office; or, if it was, Mitchell believed, it would not have been for the good of the country. In the White House, Johnson assumed leadership of the struggle that Mitchell had led in 1957 and, as Russell acknowledged, threw "the full weight of his powerful office and the full force of his personality—both of which are considerable" against the Georgian to secure passage of the civil rights program.

Mitchell believed that it was President Kennedy who had been handicapping Johnson when he was Vice President, rather than vice versa. Kennedy always felt that his Vice President wanted to get involved in civil rights more than was necessary. Free of regional restraints, Johnson eagerly sought to shed his provincial image by speaking frequently on the subject between 1960 and 1963. Kennedy, who believed that it was only necessary to speak out on civil rights when it would help him, resented Johnson's intrusion, especially during the height of the civil rights turbulence in 1963. Mitchell concluded that Johnson "was in a kind of a neutral role on legislative matters." He was not sure whether Johnson "was disposed to do much or was in a position to do much."[3]

Mitchell realized that Johnson was changing when he heard him at the National Press Club in Washington on May 26, 1961, following his trip to

Southeast Asia, declare himself "a man with a missionary zeal." Johnson
had witnessed poverty and hunger, conditions that he knew also afflicted
America and which he felt were threats to peace and freedom. He expressed
his agreement with an Indian government official that danger was near in
the region: "No one can go there and talk there and look there without
being aware of how great the danger is." He also saw "compelling evidence" that salvation was near. "Throughout those lands, men are moving—moving toward the goals which fulfill freedom." Those were "not
sleepy and slumbering lands," he said. Those were "not indifferent and
unconcerned peoples." He concluded that danger was "near—but with this
thrust, with this energy, with this drive, there is strong reason to believe
that salvation is nearer than the illusions of distance permit us to see."
Johnson was in Asia when Birmingham was exploding over the freedom
riders and the Senate was on the verge of defeating the antisegregation
amendment to the school aid bill.

Mitchell concluded that "something had happened on that trip that was
useful to the country, and I told him so." He thought the trip had given
Johnson a global perspective on human suffering and yearnings. Johnson
thus realized the urgency of civil rights at home after he had seen the
damage that was being suffered abroad by his country as a result of its poor
race relations. His new perspective was reinforced by the sizable increase in
Mexican and black voters in Texas that was freeing Johnson from the southern influence.[4]

Though he had viewed Johnson's assumption of office following Kennedy's assassination with much reservation, the November 27 message to
the joint session of Congress removed all doubt from Mitchell's mind about
the new President's sincerity. He knew that the civil rights forces had a
leader in Johnson who was not only as committed as they were to passage of
a strong bill but who also was ideally positioned to exercise his immense
influence with his colleagues in a manner that Kennedy could not. Mitchell
did not think that Kennedy enjoyed Johnson's rapport with people in Congress on whom arm-twisting was required. Despite his fourteen years in
Congress, eight of which had been in the Senate, Kennedy was considered a
junior member and was not positioned to reason with people who needed
such persuasion. For a group that revered longevity of service and dispensed
rewards on the basis of seniority, Kennedy was regarded as an intellectual
upstart. Consequently, Mitchell often heard grumbling among the upper
ranks in Congress concerning Kennedy about "that young fellow sending
over suggestions."

Equally important was Mitchell's understanding of the fundamental
differences in the attitudes of Democrats and Republicans toward civil
rights. His experience was that the Democratic party's record on this issue

"was always beyond reproach" (aside from the southerners, who were regarded as separate). The President said "the right thing, and liberal Democrats would always vote the right way." In contrast, "the Republicans would vote the right way in the House," but in the Senate they would split and "be clearly identified with the southern Democrats." Underlying this assessment was the political anomaly of the southern Democrats' separate identity. Mitchell always found it amusing—and amazing—to hear northern Democrats campaigning for office declare, "We're for civil rights as a party. We've got to break that coalition of Republican and southern Democrats." The intention, which somehow succeeded, was to give the impression that southern Democrats were a different party.

Mitchell thought that was very clever—"because once the election was over, the Democrats, North and South, usually merged and worked together" again. While "the fraternity between the southern and northern Democrats was always there after the election," it was the coalition of northern Republicans and southern Democrats, working in a de facto alignment along parallel ideological lines, that usually spelled doom for civil rights. As in 1957, Mitchell now had to isolate the South by ensuring that this coalition did not regroup to again defeat meaningful civil rights legislation. His most important step in executing that strategy would be to have Johnson exercise his immense influence on the Republicans, especially the difficult Everett Dirksen.

Dirksen's role was pivotal both because of his position as minority leader and as a moderate conservative. He had given Johnson critical help in the 1960 civil rights battle. Now Dirksen owed a demonstration of support to House Republicans like William McCulloch and the entire Illinois congressional delegation, who together had voted for the 1960 bill 138 to 34. Dirksen's obligation to McCulloch and company would benefit Mitchell because the House Republicans were also supporting the current battle for civil rights legislation.

This was another example of how Mitchell courted the Republicans faithfully and why even Rauh at times believed he was a Republican. Mitchell was aware of that widespread belief, but he did little to discourage it because he enjoyed its obvious advantage.[5]

As the undisputed leader of the legislative battle to pass H.R. 7152, Johnson reached out for Rauh, his onetime political nemesis. Rauh wielded considerable political clout as national vice chairman of the ADA and acting chairman of the Democratic Central Committee of the District of Columbia. Furthermore, as a District delegate to the 1964 Democratic National Convention, he would have considerable influence at that crucial summer event.

Johnson used the funeral of former Senator Herbert Lehman, a New Deal liberal who died on December 5, to begin a rapprochement that would include wining and dining Rauh and his wife at the White House until the Vietnam War caused a bitter split. He stunned Rauh with an invitation to accompany him and a planeload of guests to Lehman's funeral in New York. Upon receiving the call, "I didn't want to make a fool of myself" by showing up at the White House 7:00 A.M. the following morning as instructed only to discover he had been duped. So Rauh asked the caller for his phone number. "And, by Christ, it was the same guy" who answered when he called back.

On the trip, Johnson was very courteous and invited Rauh to meet with him at the White House. They talked about the civil rights bill. Rauh told him it would be best if Mitchell were invited to join them in their next meeting, setting the stage for a crucial session on January 21, 1964.[6]

Johnson, meanwhile, stepped up his drive to get the bill out of the House Rules Committee and through the House. Soon after taking office, he began a series of meetings with individual civil rights leaders. Internally, he set up a subcabinet group on civil rights to review and accelerate action and maintained considerable interest in this area.

Andrew Biemiller recalled meeting with the President in his office as a telephone call came through on the open squawk box. When Biemiller told Johnson that Congressman J. J. Pickle of Texas wanted to talk with him, the President instructed his visitor to inform the caller that he would do so only after he had signed the discharge petition to get the bill out of the Rules Committee. Biemiller thought that was really "laying it on the line." His treatment of Pickle was also the beginning of the President's drive to get the rest of the Texas congressional delegation behind the bill. Biemiller thought that "Lyndon was a very peculiar guy." Once he had made up his mind to do something, he was going to do it. He felt that that was the reason Johnson and George Meany got along so well. It was also the reason Mitchell found them both so valuable.

Also laying it on the line during their appearances before the Rules Committee were Celler and McCulloch. Celler warned Judge Smith, "You can no more stop [the civil rights movement] than you can stop a tide." He explained that black Americans still wore some of the badges of slavery: It was "small wonder that Negro patience is at an end." McCulloch, whose head was "still bloody from 1957," repeated his warning that he would never be a party to a strategy whereby House members voted for a strong version of H.R. 7152 with the expectation that the Senate would water it down. McCulloch represented urban Republicans on the Judiciary Committee such as John Lindsay and Charles Mathias, who had joined with urban Democrats in supporting Celler.

Presaging success, Rauh called Johnson on January 21 to let him know that he and Mitchell had met with House Speaker McCormack and obtained his commitment that the bill would be out of the Rules Committee by the Lincoln holiday recess. McCormack had given the two men permission to quote him. Rauh also informed the President that he and Mitchell would launch an all-out lobbying effort with "their congressmen friends."

So, as scheduled, after holding nine days of intermittent hearings, the Rules Committee on January 30 reported out H.R. 7152 by a vote of 11 to 4. As a good omen, South Dakota seven days earlier had become the thirty-eighth state to ratify and thus help pass the Twenty-fourth Amendment to the Constitution, outlawing the poll tax as a prerequisite for voting in federal elections. One Rules Committee member who voted for the bill observed that it was the first major legislation he had seen that was shaped "almost identical with the platforms of the two major parties in the immediately preceding presidential election." Clarence Brown, who with Richard Bolling was responsible for forcing Howard Smith's hand, was not satisfied with this accomplishment. He appealed to House members to conduct the pending debate "on so high a plain that we can at least say to our children and grandchildren we participated in one of the great debates of modern American history and we did it as statesmen and not as quarreling individuals."[7]

The previous day, anticipating approval, Roy Wilkins wired key NAACP branches advising them that the House was about to begin action on the civil rights bill on February 3 and urging the more influential leaders to come to Washington to lobby. He stressed that he preferred visits by branch leaders who knew their congressmen. NAACP delegates came from ten states to supplement the Leadership Conference's forces under Mitchell's direction.

An army of LCCR and NAACP lobbyists with carefully crafted instructions greeted the lawmakers upon their return from the Christmas recess and maintained direct contact with them to ensure that they "voted the right way."

The main difference between the civil rights demonstrators and the coalition was in their manner of expression. Both were political forces, with the same goals. The demonstrations, though, were mass outpourings of general discontent, local means of attracting public attention to racial injustices. The coalition, on the other hand, used carefully focused organizational and other forces of pressure to target lawmakers in order to achieve well-defined objectives.

Mitchell welcomed the help that King and the student activists were providing in the South. Perhaps their most dramatic impact was on the churches, especially the conservative denominations, which were translating to their congregations from their pulpits the meanings of the social revolution whose goal was to accord their black countrymen equality. Although Mitchell did not find much evidence that they "had any effect on the votes that were needed," he knew that by keeping the discrimination problem in the news, SCLC, SNCC, and CORE were keeping liberals in Congress alert. King's impact on Congress was limited because his movement was episodic. He was much more effective with the executive branch, where it was much easier to exert political pressure. King lacked the types of well-structured programs and overall strategy that were so essential to the NAACP's success. His goal was freedom and an end to injustice, but his strategy was based on appeals to the moral conscience and on a series of tactical strikes around demands to local governments.[8]

The effect of the demonstrations on the next stage of the battle in the Committee of the Whole could have been no more than minuscule. Because there were no recorded votes at this stage, only teller votes in which members paraded down the aisle to be counted, House members could escape accountability by leaving the floor or by voting any way they wanted. More than 220 representatives were committed to vote for an undiluted civil rights bill, but unless they were on the House floor, those commitments would have been for naught.

Based on earlier experience, Mitchell organized the Leadership Conference forces into gallery watchers who were assigned where possible to congressmen they knew. Each LCCR representative was assigned to watch four or five members who were reasonably expected to back the bill to monitor their actions. This tactic worked because a full gallery served to let lawmakers know they were being watched, whether or not that was actually so. Opponents derisively called the watchers "gallery vultures." They worked in concert with the O'Grady Raiders stationed in the House office buildings—a tribute to the zestful leadership of Jane O'Grady of the Amalgamated Clothing and Textile Workers Union.

The nerve center of this operation, where strategy was discussed with lawmakers and White House liaisons, was the office of Congressman Frank J. Thompson, a New Jersey Democrat. He was in charge of an informal "whip system" to keep pro-civil-rights members on the floor. Each morning he met for a half hour with LCCR leaders to assess progress.

During the nine days the House considered H.R. 7152, title by title, debate was, overall, moderate. Celler and McCulloch, assisted by Democrats Rodino, Byron G. Rogers of Colorado, Robert W. Kastenmeier of Wisconsin, Don Edwards of California, and Republicans Lindsay, Mathias, and J. Harry McGregor of Ohio, steadfastly blocked weakening amendments.

At another point, when Democratic Whip Hale Boggs of Louisiana was about to support a move to weaken Title VI, which would outlaw discrimination in federally financed programs, Lindsay challenged the proposed amendment as "the biggest mouse trap that has been offered since the debate on this bill began." He said he was "appalled" that the majority whip was supporting the move to gut the bill. "Does this mean there is a cave-in on this important title?" he demanded. The House rejected the amendment 80 to 206.[9]

The only anxious moment came on February 8 over consideration of the FEPC title when Judge Smith, cagily waiting in the wings, pounced on Title VII by introducing an amendment to include sex among the types of discrimination that would be barred. Fearing that the sex issue would put the bill at risk with the Republicans, Democratic sponsors launched an all-out attack on the amendment. Among those opposed was Oregon Democrat Edith Green, an implacable foe of sex discrimination who had devoted her whole career to this issue. She declared that women had suffered from discrimination, but nothing near what blacks had experienced. She therefore broke ranks with her female colleagues to urge that the House "not add any amendment that would place in jeopardy in any way our primary objective of ending that discrimination that is most serious, most urgent, most tragic, and most widespread against the Negroes of our country." The House, nevertheless, adopted the amendment. Katzenbach later explained that he was among those who were "scared to death it would kill it." The Justice Department, too, was very much opposed to the sex amendment. Mitchell, however, offended by discrimination in any form, did not believe that it would hurt the bill and said so. How much he influenced the result was not certain, but he was happy with it.

Clarence Brown, among others, continued providing valuable assistance. By a nod or a wink, he assured Mitchell that their plans were working. He was then suffering considerably from arthritis, but Mitchell was grateful that "he was always present on the floor to vote against crippling amendments" and consistently favored strengthening provisions. Mitchell sometimes thought "he was waging a terrific battle just to stand erect, but his voice always rang out strong and clear."[10]

On February 10, two days before Lincoln's birthday, the House approved by a 290 to 130 margin the most sweeping civil rights measure ever to clear either house of Congress in the twentieth century. Thanks to the bipartisan group of congressmen in the House Judiciary Committee who had negotiated the compromise, no crippling amendments were added. As the bill was sent to the Senate, McCulloch and other influential Republicans again warned they would withdraw their support if the Senate deleted the measure's controversial provisions. Mitchell recalled:

> After we left the House that night, Roy and I were waiting for a television crew. They thought it would be best to do the show on the steps of the Capitol. It did not seem like such a good location to me because it was bitter cold and snow was falling. Most of the people had left and there was a kind of eerie feeling as Roy stood there waiting for the equipment men to get set for the shots. Soon, however, it became more meaningful as he talked and the camera began filming. I knew that we had just won an important part of the fight, but hearing it as a news comment helped to give it perspective and historical depth. I have always loved the Capitol and now there was another reason for a faster pulse beat when I looked at it.
>
> Over at the Congressional Hotel, the civil rights team was meeting in gay victory spirits. Someone put a champagne glass in my hand but, remembering I did not drink, quickly exchanged it for a glass of tomato juice. We were all happy. I doubt very much that any group of persons lobbying for a bill really liked each other as much as we. We had not been there very long before Joe Rauh, Vi Gunther, Andy Biemiller, Marvin Caplan and Jack Conway had started making plans for the Senate. This was another quality of our team. They were never so impressed with a victory that they forgot to plan for the next fight.[11]

Reporting on this progress to the NAACP executive committee, Wilkins could hardly find words to praise Mitchell. He said he was "doing a simply magnificent job" of heading up the whole lobbying operation: "As fine a job as he has done on previous occasions. His work on this has been superlative. His coordination with the White House, labor, the attorney general, House members, lobbyists and others is the talk of everyone with whom the secretary came in contact." By then, Mitchell told Wilkins in one of his regular reports, "Joe [Rauh] and I have gotten to the place where we think something is wrong with the telephone if we do not exchange at least one call a day." Mitchell and Rauh had a well-defined relationship in which the ADA representative contributed his extensive technical skills in crafting legislation and the NAACP lobbyist established the basic policy issues. In meetings together, Rauh always let Mitchell lead in discussions.

Johnson extended his compliments to both men in a different manner. As Mitchell and Rauh were in a "foot race" over to the Senate to begin work there, a messenger informed Rauh that Johnson wanted to speak with them on the phone in the Congressional Hotel. Mitchell was thrilled that there was Johnson barking out orders: "All right, you fellows, get on over there to the Senate and get busy because we've got it through the House. Now we've got the big job of getting it through the Senate." Mitchell could have had no better reward for his efforts. He thought it was "really a fascinating thing" that the Chief Executive could have been following the struggle so closely that he knew how to reach his field generals so quickly.[12]

Indeed, the Senate was the real problem. Given the House's past support for civil rights, it was no surprise that the battle there was just a warm-up skirmish. In the House, explained Mitchell, with sufficient work and vigilance "you could be reasonably certain of getting what you wanted." At the same time, the House struggle was in fact much more difficult than some thought. The crucial moment in the House always came when the bill was in the Committee of the Whole. In the Senate, success depended on not only how hard you worked, but also how skillfully you performed. Mitchell had to have not only a good working force, but also one the Senate would respect: "The President supplied that force," Mitchell said. Nevertheless, although the Senate would be more difficult, he was optimistic. He expected that Humphrey and Kuchel, with whom he enjoyed working, would carry most of the load.

Kuchel's talent for winning elections had made him the number one Republican of the nation's most populous state. Nine times he had run for office in California—assemblyman, state senator, state controller, and U.S. senator—and had won every time. In the Senate he had aligned himself with middle-of-the-road Republicans led by Vermont's George D. Aiken. As his party's whip, Kuchel now sat on the GOP's top councils. He was as much a favorite of Democrats as of Republicans because he was open and honest. Whenever he could, he helped his colleagues, regardless of party. He was not everyone's favorite, however. The ultraright had marked him for defeat in the next election owing to his moderation. But the civil rights forces loved him.

Mitchell found that the White House expected Dirksen to help, but it was also "thought that we must be very careful not to get his dander up. Oddly enough, I believe that Dirksen really will cooperate as a favor to the President." According to Mitchell:

> Getting ready for the Senate fight was interesting because I was suddenly reminded of the years that had passed since we started in the fight for civil rights legislation. One Saturday afternoon, Joe and I met with John Gilman Stewart of Senator Humphrey's staff.

We were waiting for Kenneth Teasdale, one of the Senate experts on rules. He came in with an armful of books and with a businesslike air of a man who knew what he was talking about. Afterward Joe and I said, almost simultaneously, "He was probably in high school when we first tried to get FEPC through Congress." Like the Justice Department group, Ken and Charles Ferris were easy to work with. They had the essential qualities needed in the Senate, which were an even temper, a good mind, and the ability to be alert after midnight when there was a Senate session. [13]

At the January 21 meeting with Mitchell and Rauh, Johnson had made it clear that he opposed any changes in the bill in either the House or the Senate. He also informed the Senate leadership of that determination. Recognizing the likelihood of not getting strengthening amendments and the danger of adopting a strategy that differed from the President's, Mitchell recommended that the Leadership Conference heed the President's advice. While opposing all weakening amendments, the LCCR left the door open for strengthening provisions.

The most dramatic development at the meeting was Johnson's saying he did not care if the Senate worked on anything else until the certain filibuster was defeated and the bill enacted, even if that took three months. That meant that Johnson, like Mitchell and Rauh, believed Congress could be made to pass civil rights laws, filibuster or no filibuster. No one knew better than the lobbyists and Johnson the importance of presidential leadership. His strongest weapons were the prestige of his office, his constitutional status as independent of and coequal with the other two branches of government, and his personal embodiment of the dignity and might of the nation.

As he gave out instructions, Mitchell presented him with a list of eight senators whom he suggested the President contact. Topping the list was Dirksen. [14]

Mitchell did not believe that "there was anything I could do with Senator Dirksen because he had boasted about throwing me out of his office." Actually, Mitchell explained, he had not thrown him out. They had only gotten into a heated argument when Mitchell had met with him and asked for his help in the January 1963 battle to curb the filibuster and Dirksen complained that blacks did not help him in his reelection campaign. The manner in which both men now treated the incident showed how tense the situation had become. Explaining the reason for Dirksen's pique, Mitchell recalled the senator saying, "Clarence, you are through. I don't want to have anything to do with you at all because you haven't done your homework. None of the Negroes voted for me up there in Illinois, and I'm

598 DENTON L. WATSON

through with them." Furthermore, Dirksen complained, although he had given John Sengstacke, publisher of the *Chicago Defender*, tickets to a football game, he did not support him in his newspaper as much as the senator felt he should have.

Finally, Mitchell told Dirksen that "you don't need me standing here arguing with you." To "mollify him a little bit," he introduced the companion who had accompanied him to the meeting as a black Republican who had voted for the senator. Upon leaving, though, Mitchell's companion gave the lobbyist a chuckle by saying: "That Senator Dirksten is a very difficult man. I'm sure glad I voted for [his opponent]."[15]

Given Dirksen's difficult personality, Mitchell felt that, because of their friendship, Johnson was the best person to win his support. Others on the list Mitchell had given Johnson included Old Guard Republicans like Carl T. Curtis of Nebraska and Frank Carlson of Kansas, and Democrats Alan Bible and Howard W. Cannon, both of Nevada. Mitchell felt that Cannon and Bible came from a state "where they had all kinds of reasons for voting for cloture." Though Mansfield had played a crucial role in the bill's early progress, Mitchell regarded him as another major problem because he did not believe outsiders should meddle in Senate business. It would have been impossible for Mitchell and Rauh to work with him, so they asked Johnson to appoint Humphrey floor manager of the bill.

An indication of the communication barrier was that Mitchell never found out how Johnson managed to get Mansfield to name Humphrey floor manager in charge of day-to-day strategy. The key, however, was Mansfield himself and not Johnson.

As the House neared completion of its work on the civil rights bill, the majority leader had asked Humphrey to become floor manager when it reached the Senate. In addition to the obvious reason of Humphrey's impeccable civil rights credentials, Mansfield's initiative made sense. The majority leader had a natural aversion to assignments that involved sustained public attention. He also believed that his most effective contribution to the battle would be to maintain a somewhat disinterested position so that he could continue his frequent off-the-record visits with Dirksen in the hope of winning him over. To do that, he could not be identified as the principal defender of the bill's most controversial features. Mansfield also wanted to avoid damaging confrontations with the eighteen southern Democrats, many of whom were chairmen of standing committees whose cooperation he needed on countless other items. As leader of the Senate Democrats, he also wanted to preserve stability within his party.

Humphrey was an excellent choice for other important reasons. one being that he wanted the job. He regarded the assignment as the ultimate reward for his fifteen-year struggle to pass civil rights legislation in the

Senate. As he himself acknowledged, "This assignment was one I appreciated, yet one that I realized would test me in every way."[16]

Dirksen no doubt named Kuchel as his surrogate for similar reasons. Mitchell regarded the Humphrey-Kuchel team as a wonderful arrangement, "because we always had direct access to them and got along very well." Giving the whips those jobs was a departure from the custom whereby chairmen of relevant committees or subcommittees became floor leaders of bills they reported out. In this case, though, that would have been James Eastland, chairman of the Judiciary Committee, a totally inappropriate prospect.

There was not much that could be done with the diehard segregationists. Nevertheless, Mitchell and Rauh discussed with the President the importance of trying to soften this opposition. Another agreement that fitted Mansfield's overall strategy neatly was that, as Johnson stressed, there was to be no attempt to invoke cloture until all the bitter-enders had worn themselves out talking. Many senators, wanting to give opponents every opportunity to state their case, would not vote to invoke cloture in the early stages, only after considerable debate. And, if the bid for cloture was lost, opponents would have the upper hand to force compromise. They also discussed the growing strength of the black vote as a possibly helpful factor.

Mitchell was impressed by Humphrey's definition of the problem of getting cloture in a January 17 speech at Johns Hopkins University. The senator said that the only way to get "a truly meaningful bill—filibuster or no filibuster" was if the Senate displayed the type of bipartisan spirit of statesmanship that had been shown by Charles Halleck, House minority leader, and William McCulloch, ranking minority member on the House Judiciary Committee. Humphrey observed that there were many people who believed the Kennedy compromise bill was not strong enough. Despite his sympathy with such opinions and his own desire to strengthen it, he said, the salient point was that a bipartisan agreement had been reached on an effective bill. As Johnson had said in his State of the Union Message, Humphrey reiterated, bipartisanship on civil rights was now a moral issue. Humphrey urged the Senate to call on Dirksen to help provide a minimum of 25 Republican votes to end the filibuster.

From the beginning of the final push, Humphrey, like Mansfield, maintained close contact with Dirksen, visiting with him regularly in order to encourage him to assume a more prominent role, seeking to find out what changes he wanted to propose, and urging him to call meetings to discuss the bill. Humphrey appealed to his sense of patriotism and duty. In addition to knowing that Dirksen was aligned with business interests who would be opposed to the bill, Humphrey was also aware that the minority leader had a flair for drama and was tickled by the sound of his mellifluous voice ringing through the Senate chamber. He loved commanding center stage in the legislative game, and the Democrats were making sure he got it.

Humphrey expanded on Johnson's honeyed courtship of Dirksen in other forums, such as a March 8 appearance on *Meet the Press*. Earlier that week, after having been chosen the bill's floor manager, Humphrey ebulliently declared his sincere belief that "when Senator Dirksen has to face that moment of decision where his influence and where his leadership will be required in order to give us the votes that are necessary to pass the bill, he will not be found wanting." When asked how he was going to get Dirksen's agreement "on the compulsory aspect" of the public accommodations section, Humphrey replied, "I have watched Senator Dirksen in the Senate for some time, and by the way, I didn't say what I said [in warm compliment] about him to get his vote." He expressed confidence that once the senator had given "his full thought and time to the public accommodations section, without materially changing that section, he will be able to support the bill and help us in its passage."[17]

Helping Humphrey, Mansfield, and Kuchel to organize the pro-civil-rights Senate forces were Philip Hart of Michigan, Warren Magnuson of Washington, and Joseph Clark. With the added assistance of Katzenbach and Burke Marshall, they developed a system of bipartisan floor managers, or "captains," who were responsible for sections of the bill.

Humphrey was Mitchell's liaison with the President, but Johnson still maintained regular contact with Mitchell by calling him at his home in Baltimore at night or early in the morning to discuss developments and to issue marching orders. Top staff members of pro-civil-rights senators worked together as a team. A registration system and a "duty list" were developed to ensure that senators were available at all times for quorum calls and to assist them with their schedules. That procedure was especially necessary for senators facing reelection, who had to slip away periodically to make speeches. Mitchell felt that the system gave senators all the time they needed "to be out of the city without adversely affecting" debate on the bill. Humphrey and Kuchel published a regular "Bipartisan Newsletter" to help senators keep abreast of pertinent developments. They took special pleasure in highlighting the baselessness and hypocrisy of southern opposition. A "Quorum Scoreboard," or record of senators who answered quorum calls, was maintained and kept members on their toes by showing who was available when needed. "For the first time in the history of civil rights legislation," Mitchell concluded triumphantly, supporters "were as well-organized and as well-prepared as the opponents had been in the past."

Mitchell and Rauh, who were especially fearful of an early attempt to apply cloture, had so informed Mansfield during the closing days of the House debate. Their often heard slogan was "Cloture means compromise." Despite pledges by Humphrey and Kuchel that cloture would not be attempted unless the votes were certain, their fear of a secret deal between Mansfield and Dirksen remained paramount in the early weeks of the battle.[18]

Off the Hill, preparation was just as systematic. Representatives of the Catholic, Protestant, and Jewish faiths, with the assistance of Humphrey's staff, scheduled a National Interreligious Convocation at Georgetown University for April 28 in order to reach out to lukewarm senators and as a display of religious unity on civil rights. This was to be the first largely white "demonstration" in support of civil rights.

At the same time, the Leadership Conference agreed to continue the weekly meetings that had been held during the House fight. Mitchell explained that at the critical stage in the Senate fight, the LCCR would again set up an office in the Congressional Hotel. As usual, he served as chairman of those meetings, which initially were held on Mondays and Thursdays but eventually became daily sessions.

Anticipating public demonstrations, Mitchell laid out three criteria for cooperating with them. They must have "maximum constructive effect on the Senate"; be staged when most needed, and not to duplicate other programs; and help assure continual activity over the expected prolonged period of debate. In effect, Mitchell was ensuring that the other organizations respected his operating domain as much as they respected one another's in the South. Here much more than egos were involved; Mitchell knew that many senators would have been only too happy to find any excuse to help kill the bill. Nevertheless, he had to live with the potential danger of unintended sabotage when King, on March 26, announced on the Capitol steps that if the filibuster lasted beyond May 1, his SCLC would "engage in a direct action program here in Washington and around the country." The demonstrations did not occur, but Mitchell felt that they hung "like a Damoclean sword" overhead.[19]

H.R. 7152 reached the Senate on February 17. Having stopped the bill at the desk, Mansfield had to decide whether to follow the 1957 strategy of using Rule XIV to place the bill directly on the calendar as the civil rights advocates wanted or to follow the normal parliamentary route of referring it to Eastland's Judiciary Committee, where it was certain to die. (See Appendix 1 for Pohlhaus's explanation of the procedure.) Although Humphrey and Kuchel were the bill's floor managers, Mansfield retained responsibility for the early direction and conduct of the civil rights debate and made it clear he intended to remain visibly in charge until H.R. 7152 was on the calendar and the pending business of the Senate. At that stage, one fact was foremost in his mind—that the best way to adhere to Johnson's no-amendments policy was to place the House bill unchanged before the Senate. And Rule XIV was the surest route. That consideration outweighed Mansfield's inclination to avoid offending the procedural sensibilities of uncommitted senators.

Mitchell, meanwhile, regarded a move to take up a farm bill before H.R. 7152 as the first potential hitch in the battle plan. He discussed at length his fears of undue delay with Humphrey and Kuchel on February 25 in one of a series of meetings and won assurances that the civil rights bill would get prompt consideration. In another session three days later, Humphrey and Kuchel warned of the importance of keeping emotions and acrimony at a minimum and therefore rejected as counterproductive the lobbyists' suggestion to arrest absent senators for not carrying out their constitutional duties during the upcoming debate in order to maintain quorums. The manner in which the procedural debate was conducted showed the importance of these concerns to the leadership.

On February 26, Mansfield easily won the first stage of the battle when he moved to bypass the Judiciary Committee and place the bill on the calendar. Staging a rerun of the 1957 battle over the use of Rule XIV, Richard Russell, generalissimo of the southern opposition, again raised unsuccessfully a point of order against the use of the procedure. This time, Lee Metcalf, Mansfield's junior partner from Montana, as presiding officer, simply overrode Russell by citing the 1957 precedent rather than deferring to the full Senate for a decision. Russell put up a vigorous fight that lasted several hours, but Mansfield won 54 to 37.

Mansfield, wavering between his desires to be fair and to expedite the procedural process, offered to refer the bill to the Judiciary Committee with instructions to report it back to the Senate "without recommendation or amendment" within six days. Eastland rejected the Mansfield offer because, he said, "the net result would be that we would be handcuffed."

Mansfield's indecision became more pronounced on March 9, when the southerners grabbed the opportunity he had left open for them to begin a filibuster on his motion to consider H.R. 7152. From that point on during the entire three-month struggle over the civil rights bill, Mitchell seldom left the Capitol. The southerners had suggested that the filibuster would not last very long, probably five days or less. But the wrangling lasted seventeen days as Mansfield, now like an experienced angler, patiently played the line as he waited for an appropriate time to bring events to a conclusion. He avoided opportunities for minor advantage that would have embarrassed the southerners but that might also have incurred lasting ill-feelings that this foes could exploit.[20]

As a study of gentlemanly collegiality, with opposing sides being strenuously cordial to each other, debate in the Senate hardly has its match. The prevailing convention was that although disagreements were obviously a normal ingredient of all debates, invective and personal attack were clearly exceptions to decorum. The civil rights forces had decided to withhold their rebuttals of the southerners' criticisms of the bill. But seeing an opportunity to exploit their weaknesses, Humphrey and Kuchel agreed to take them on and to answer some of the southerners' contentions on the floor rather than letting them fill the record with trivia and plainly wrong information during their filibuster. Humphrey thus won a concession from Allen J. Ellender when the Louisiana Democrat, admitting that blacks were disfranchised in his state, said that "in many instances the reason why the voting rights were not encouraged is that the white people are afraid they would be outvoted. Let us be frank about it." Mitchell regarded the Humphrey-Kuchel strategy "as a highly important decision." Opponents were unable to counter factually that strategy because the civil rights proponents had a mass of information documenting racial injustices.

The supreme display of fraternity was provided by Willis Robertson of Virginia, who, after he had finished denouncing every title of the bill, walked over to Humphrey and offered him a Confederate flag for his lapel. Humphrey graciously accepted the gift and praised Robertson for his "eloquence and his great knowledge of history and law, but also for his wonderful . . . gentlemanly qualities and his consideration of us at all times." Robertson was equally effusive in his praise as he demonstrated the extent to which the bitterness of the Civil War was now being replaced by colorful legend that exemplified national unity—"I told the senator that if it had not been for the men from Wisconsin and Minnesota, when Grant finally came down into Virginia, we would have won, but they formerly belonged to Virginia. We could have whipped them." Then, arm in arm, Humphrey and Robertson walked to the majority whip's Capitol office for early evening refreshments.

In such an atmosphere of gentility, without any obvious signal, the southerners stopped talking on March 26, the eve of the Easter recess. The Senate approved Mansfield's motion to consider the bill by 67 to 17, with only the southerners objecting, revealing the overwhelming desire to move on to the substantive debate. A primary consideration for Russell in avoiding a cloture vote was the danger of offending those whose support he might need in the crucial battle ahead.[21]

Shortly after that vote, Wayne Morse staged another 1957 rerun by moving to refer the bill to the Judiciary Committee until April 8 even though the similar effort by Mansfield had earlier failed. Mansfield had no trouble tabling his motion. "How many days would we have to repeat the ordeal of the last two-and-a-half weeks?" he demanded.

On March 19, aware of Morse's intentions, Mitchell had wired the Oregonian that "if there is any one thing that strains the faith of citizens, it is a persistent effort to give an aura of respectability to committee hearings on civil rights [run by Eastland]." He said, "To the man in the streets, this is the equivalent of the stacked deck, the hanging judge and the executioner who enjoys his work." Mitchell added that most questions in the committee "are really one thousand word speeches." Furthermore, much of the time was spent by Sam Ervin "telling jokes about Uncle Remus, Brer Rabbit or some other kind of folklore." Mitchell concluded, "Our country should not ask its colored citizens to stand aside for international coffee problems when they are being arrested, beaten and bitten by dogs simply because they seek to purchase this beverage at public lunch counters."

Morse inserted the telegram into the *Congressional Record*. The senator told his colleagues, "You've got to expect this kind of attack and emotionalism in this debate." He still disagreed that this was "the best way to advance the interests of the Negroes in America." He added that he was "not going to yield to duress, abuse or threats that seem to me to be implied in this telegram." Javits told Morse he had attended a meeting the previous day at the Civil Liberties Clearing House, where Mitchell read the telegram. Javits disagreed that there was any element of coercion in the wire. Later, when Humphrey, with Kuchel's acquiescence, in one of the Monday-Thursday strategy sessions again suggested trying what would have been a premature cloture vote, he ran into a Mitchell buzzsaw. Nevertheless, Mitchell had less to fear from premature cloture suggestions than from quorum calls and damaging amendments.

Mitchell believed that Morse was honestly concerned about adhering to technical procedures. To accommodate him after the 1957 confrontation, the civil rights forces in 1960 permitted the bill to go to the Judiciary Committee with instructions that it be reported out within a specific time. Now, once more, they preferred to use the speedier bypass parliamentary technique.[22]

The pressure to weaken the House bill was constant. Young Edward M. Kennedy of Massachusetts urged its passage as tribute to his brother. With his voice breaking, he said that he was interested in the bill because he wanted "to see an America where everyone can make his contribution, where a man will be measured not by the color of his skin, but by the content of his character."

Mitchell "branded as false" the many reports that a compromise had been reached. He explained that those rumors were "based on speculation" by persons ignorant of what was happening or were being proposed by opponents "as a trial balloon" in order to determine a bargaining area. In response to an inquiry from Wilkins about parts of the bill that were most vulnerable to attack or deletion, he confidently stated that "it seems certain that we have the votes to hold all titles of the bill," despite statements by conservative columnist David Lawrence and others about possible compromises. It had also been rumored that Johnson had struck a deal with the southerners in order to win their support for his tax bill. But Mitchell said the White House, the Justice Department, and other agencies were giving "excellent liaison at the top level." He expressed full confidence in Johnson's sincerity and emphasized that there was "no reason to believe that his present position will change."

Mitchell was also closely in tune with the Justice Department on the substance of the bill. In a session with Katzenbach and Burke Marshall, he and Rauh, despite Johnson's warning against seeking strengthening provisions, could not resist the temptation to examine parts of the bill that "might be subject to constructive amendments." They wanted, for example, to put back in Title I a section on the appointment of voting referees that had been lost in the House. Title III contained a restricted version of the Part III proposed for the 1957 Civil Rights Act. Mitchell and Rauh wanted to strike the requirement that private action had to be started before the attorney general could intervene. Mitchell felt that because this title was particularly important and enjoyed considerable Republican support in the House, it did "not seem particularly hazardous to try to perfect it." He felt that the "one formidable impediment" was continuing Justice Department opposition.

Mitchell also believed that Title VI presented a real problem because of the considerable dissatisfaction in the Senate over review requirements that must be met before funds were cut off. He feared "a real clash" between Republican Norris Cotton and John O. Pastore of Rhode Island, who was subsequently assigned as manager of the title, because Pastore might "advocate stronger and more desirable language." In the House, to avoid losing southern votes in exchange for Federal Housing Authority, antipoverty, and other social welfare legislation, the Democrats had included the requirement for presidential review and notice to Congress before funds could be cut off. Mitchell feared that this title would "cause considerable strain on our bipartisan alliance" in the Senate as more liberal Democrats pushed to strengthen the concept that where federal dollars were spent there should be no discrimination.

There was much less possibility of bipartisan conflict between liberals Clark and Case, who were managers of Title VII (equal employment). But, given the politics involved, Mitchell did not believe that efforts by Senate Democrats and Republicans who wanted broader coverage would be very productive. For example, some senators wanted to scrap the House provision that relied on the courts instead of on administrative orders for enforcement, which they preferred. Mitchell believed that House Democrats would accept changes on enforcement but they would be unwilling to agree to broader coverage because of commitments that had been made to one southerner in exchange for his help in winning approval for the title.

Despite his great urge to continue pressing for a stronger bill, Mitchell accepted the fact that Justice did "not want any amendments—pro or con." The Washington Bureau's detailed title-by-title review of the bill, which Mitchell sent to Wilkins and to administration officials, in which concerns of other advocates were also examined, served to remove possible conflict with the Justice Department and thus enabled the civil rights forces and the administration to avoid destructive disputes during the Senate battle.

After Mitchell and Rauh met with Humphrey, Kuchel, and the captains every morning, Mitchell remained in touch during the day with the Senate strategists on tactical matters, sometimes conferring with them until past midnight. Humphrey was available at all times. That meant he was seeing Mitchell and Rauh two, three, or four times a day. Sometimes their conferences were hurried exchanges in the hallway. The lobbyists often had to interrupt Humphrey's lunch or dinner. Just as frequently, the main Senate entrances were closed, the main lights out, and the elevator service curtailed when they parted company with Humphrey at night. Mitchell felt that he and Rauh might well have worn out their welcome with Humphrey, "but he never showed it." At times when Humphrey had endured a particularly trying day, Mitchell would remember an anecdote about Abraham Lincoln that had Lincoln saying something like "Here comes those same damn three fellows again." Humphrey would enter his office with a throng of admirers or newsmen a couple of steps behind. The door would close mercifully. There waiting for him inside were Mitchell, Rauh, and Biemiller, who sometimes joined them.

As with the House debates, the LCCR's eighty-six members provided representatives who were again paired with senators in teams. Owing to the need for immediate contact during quorum calls and at other crucial moments, no coalition representative was assigned more than two senators. Mitchell met with them every Wednesday at 2:00 P.M. to exchange information and parcel out assignments. Those meetings became more frequent as activity intensified, until finally Mitchell and Rauh were meeting with teams of staffers, primarily from Humphrey's office and the Justice Department, every day from morning until midnight. Mitchell and Rauh also met regularly with Senate staff members.

To relieve demands on senators and their staffs in the later stages of the debate on the hill, Mitchell began concentrating on meeting with Humphrey, to discuss developments, in the corridor, cloakroom, or whip office.

He would then pass on information to cooperating organizations. Rauh, meanwhile, representing the ADA and the UAW, and Thomas Harris, representing the AFL-CIO, assisted by Frank Pohlhaus and lawyers from other organizations, concentrated on working with Senate staffers in studying the numerous amendments.

The civil rights forces had many things in their favor. The first continued to be Johnson's intimate leadership style. The second was Humphrey's deep moral commitment, amenable personality, and extensive experience. Third was Mansfield's ability to manipulate Dirksen by letting him have the spotlight as the decisive moment approached. It was clear that a substantial Senate majority favored the bill without dilution—but that still was not enough for cloture. After the danger of premature cloture passed, the next major threat would be crippling amendments.[23]

Debates began in earnest on March 30, and, until April 10, civil rights forces presented their case with a few southern speeches intermixed. Humphrey's reassurance to his colleagues that the bill would not be rammed through the Senate undergirded the businesslike amiability that Mansfield had established. There would be "full and extensive debate," he promised. He served notice that supporters would analyze the bill title by title in their presentation speeches and issued "this friendly challenge: we will join with you in debating this bill; will you join with us in voting on H.R. 7152 after the debate has been concluded? Will you permit the Senate, and, in a sense, the nation, to come to grips with these issues and decide them, one way or the other?" He "devoutly" hoped his challenge would be accepted. And, indeed, it was.

Mansfield, fearing the toll on the senators' health, avoided round-the-clock sessions as he had done during the procedural debate. He was very unlike Johnson, who in 1960 had forced the Senate to remain in continuous session for nine days with only a Sunday respite. Johnson wanted Mansfield to follow his example, but the majority leader refused. He did, however, make the current sessions long enough to demonstrate he meant business. This attitude conformed with his belief in the independence of the Senate as an institution. Unlike Johnson's personalized style of amassing power around the prerogatives of the majority leader's office, Mansfield preferred a decentralization of responsibilities and relied on senators to fulfill obligations of their office.

The southerners, despite their handicaps, began performing well under Russell's experienced leadership, but they still were no match for the well-prepared liberals. Russell deployed his eighteen southern debaters in three six-man platoons in an unsuccessful attempt to break apart the normally fragile liberal coalition. He had succeeded in the past because the pressure to give up the fight usually was on the nonfilibustering senators. The southerners also hoped Dirksen would rebel against the badgering from civil rights forces and side with them.

Now, though, the tables were turned. Mitchell realized that the key factor was that Johnson was on the other side—and as leader. Johnson had great respect for the southern opposition and knew that Russell was an expert on *all* the Senate rules. In contrast, as he told Humphrey, he feared the liberals would go down to defeat because they never took time to be as expert on the rules. That belittling assessment helped Humphrey to strengthen his guard and made him determined to succeed.[24]

All of these "time-consuming" activities, Mitchell soon found, were taking a toll on everyone's patience. Humphrey early had foreseen that the ordeal would be long, so he had steeled himself for the difficult weeks ahead and vowed to remain patient and maintain good working relationships with his southern colleagues. For Mitchell, who had a more direct interest in this struggle, personal anxieties increased the strain. Without admitting the battle's effects on himself, he made a special effort to express his "deep and sincere appreciation" for the "persistence, general good humor, hard work and spirit of good sportsmanship" that characterized relationships among civil rights proponents "both in and out of the Senate." He especially appreciated the "enormous burden" that Humphrey and Kuchel were carrying during the filibuster. Additionally, Kuchel was fighting a strong political challenge at home in California and was also concerned with Arizona's attempt to divert a substantial part of his state's water supply.

Quorum calls continued to be a problem. By simply stating, "I suggest the absence of a quorum," an opponent could send pro-civil-rights forces scrambling to round up the fifty-one senators needed to keep the Senate in session. Failure to find the minimum number would force a recess or an adjournment. On one occasion, had the civil rights forces been able to produce a quorum promptly, Humphrey felt, it would have been possible to call for a vote on various parts of the bill since the southerners had exhausted their speakers and topics. The bipartisan leadership was particularly embarrassed on April 4 when Mansfield had to recess the session for lack of a quorum. Earlier, it had taken up to an hour to produce the fifty-one senators.

Mitchell and the Leadership Conference redoubled their own vigilance in order to avoid such problems. The system was so improved that a week after the embarrassment, the Senate leadership rounded up a quorum in ten minutes. Again demonstrating its effectiveness two days later, the LCCR brought a group of senators by police escort from the President's box at a baseball game to the Senate floor in twenty minutes. Reported the "Bipartisan Newsletter": "Kept in good shape by their sprint back to the Senate

Chamber from the ball park and the theater on Monday, civil rights senators averaged 19 minutes in two quorum calls."[25]

By mid-April the focus was more than ever on Dirksen. Despite the Leadership Conference's slogan, "We are opposed to all weakening amendments," Mitchell early conceded that it was "inconceivable" the Senate would not make some changes in the House bill. He acknowledged that the most vulnerable areas were the FEPC and public accommodations sections. In addition to opposing public accommodations on principle, Dirksen regarded the FEPC proposal as a red flag for the simple reason that it would apply to Illinois. He therefore was totally opposed to Title VII. To help avoid any serious damage to these and other sections, the Leadership Conference now agreed it would help if "no constructive amendment" was considered without prior discussion with supporters in the House. Mitchell began finding that the real problem was the "panic" that occurred almost daily when senators met to discuss amendments offered by Dirksen.

"A great many senators," Mitchell found, assumed that if Dirksen could be persuaded to support the bill with enforceable FEPC and other titles intact, most Republicans would vote for cloture. But Dirksen for many days was unwilling to discuss his proposals with pro-civil-rights senators, heightening the tension.

The Justice Department and the civil rights forces, foreseeing this opposition, had moved to head it off in the House Labor Committee by getting the Democrats to accept verbatim the convoluted, poorly worded, FEPC bill that had been offered by Michigan Republican Robert P. Griffin. Now Justice was able to argue, "That's your Republican bill. What the hell are you complaining about?"[26]

Then came the break. Dirksen offered a series of amendments on the FEPC title to the GOP Policy Committee and subsequently to a Senate Republican caucus. But these were only a small segment of the more than seventy amendments touching on every section of the bill that his staff had developed. Liberal senators bitterly attacked two of the amendments they felt would cripple the proposed Equal Employment Opportunity Commission. One of these provisions would bar the commission from seeking court orders to enjoin discriminatory employment practices; the other would permit state fair employment agencies, upon request, to assume control of discrimination complaints. Critics feared that southern states would set up "paper" FEPC agencies to frustrate this procedure.

After deciding to withhold most of his proposals, ostensibly to gain a consensus, Dirksen on April 16 offered another ten amendments that still were generally crippling. Mitchell thought that the worst was one that would place the entire court enforcement burden on the aggrieved individual by requiring that all persons discriminated against file complaints; interested organizations would be forbidden to bring charges of unlawful employment practices. Another proposal would exempt from coverage all employers in states with fair employment laws and all government contractors subject to the 1961 equal employment executive order. This provision, Mitchell feared, was an "open invitation" to states to set up "sham agencies to avoid federal jurisdiction."

Mitchell found that media coverage was one of the most trying parts of the fight. The press made it difficult for him to engage in discussions on Dirksen's amendments, because he feared that reporters would distort "the slightest hint of endorsement." The "one thing that we did not need was a fight among" the pro-civil-rights lawmakers. One evening when Mitchell turned on his car radio he heard on a newscast that the President had made a secret deal with Russell to kill Title VII. Mitchell's confidence in Johnson's intentions was such that he immediately issued a statement challenging the report as incorrect. Still feeling that "this is outrageous," he next called the White House and was assured the story was false. He remained disturbed that although the leadership of Humphrey and Kuchel "continues to be of excellent quality," some journalists were attempting to "take advantage of every flaw," not just attempts at a compromise, but also difficulties in producing quorums, to make it appear the pro-civil-rights senators were ineffective. Mitchell observed that senators emerging from closed-door sessions on proposals compounded the problem by leaking information that was often overplayed. Dirksen's frequent news conferences especially gave undue attention to his amendments.

Mitchell did not believe that some of Dirksen's FEPC amendments would hurt the bill, and he felt that if those were accepted, the minority leader would be more inclined to extend support on other sections. One such proposal would remove a provision from Title VII barring atheists from protection against discrimination. Another provision would have treated union hiring halls as employment agencies and thus subjected them to the title's coverage. While Mitchell and some coalition members approved this hiring hall provision, labor opposed it, fearing that it would expose unions to some harmful state regulations without ending discrimination.

Labor therefore began working out a compromise with a group of senators and Justice Department officials that shifted part of the amendment to another section of the bill and thus retained the constructive aspect of Dirksen's proposal. Mitchell thought that that effort showed that "all parties" were making "an honorable effort to recognize and accept any clarifying or perfecting amendment that Senator Dirksen may have." At the same time the civil rights forces were steadfastly opposing weakening amendments, some of which were also offered by the AFL-CIO to Title VII. Mitchell welcomed assurances Humphrey and Kuchel gave "again and again" that they too remained opposed to such amendments.

Their assurances, however, did not remove the threat, which was seriously aggravated by the quicksilver change of events. Often, Mitchell found, a development in the morning would be completely changed by the afternoon. That was the situation on May 6 while he was in Nebraska drumming up support throughout ten western states for cloture. He was expecting the Senate to vote on an amendment offered by Herman E. Talmadge of Georgia to require a jury trial in any criminal contempt proceedings arising under the bill. Though Mitchell was in telephone contact with associates in Washington, the time of the vote was changed before he could receive word. The amendment was next withdrawn in preference for one offered by Thruston B. Morton, Republican of Kentucky, to require, under the criminal code, jury trials in all criminal proceedings.

The jury trial amendment remained a tricky problem. Ever since the 1957 jury trial fight, Mitchell found, there had remained a strong sentiment for granting jury trials in criminal contempt cases. Those feelings were reinforced by the demands of Governor Ross Barnett of Mississippi and his then Lieutenant Governor Paul B. Johnson for a jury trial upon being charged with criminal contempt for violating a Fifth Circuit Court of Appeals order directing the admission of James Meredith to the University of Mississippi in 1962. The case went to the Supreme Court after the court of appeals divided 4 to 4 over whether they were entitled under the Constitution to a jury trial. Although the Supreme Court ruled on April 6 that they were not necessarily entitled to a jury trial, the vote was a narrow 5 to 4. Mitchell felt that because the liberals on the court had contributed to the close vote, Talmadge was encouraged to offer his amendment on April 21.

That same day, Dirksen told Humphrey he was joining Talmadge in the fight. Mansfield and Dirksen then agreed on a substitute amendment, and plans were readied for a vote two weeks later after Russell had given assurances the southerners would permit it. That was still on May 6, when Mitchell was in Nebraska. Rather than voting on the Mansfield-Dirksen jury trial amendment, the Senate acted on the other one that Morton had offered and rejected it 46 to 45. That development led Dirksen to complain that he had been misled because he had thought the Mansfield measure was being offered instead.

Mitchell felt the Mansfield-Dirksen jury trial amendment was particularly troublesome because of the attention it was attracting. According to the Justice Department, its inclusion would not have hurt the civil rights bill since the same language was already in the 1957 and 1960 laws. The only difference was that this amendment would have reduced sentencing from up to forty-five days with a maximum $300 fine to only thirty days with the same fine. Some liberal senators who voted against it in 1957 did not want to turn around and support it now. Others from strongly pro-civil-rights states who were up for reelection feared that voting for it would hurt them. At the same time, civil rights opponents and the news media were exploiting the issue by saying that failure of the Mansfield-Dirksen jury trial compromise to get a big vote would be a sign of weakness. The fact that such a claim was far off the mark mattered little, Mitchell felt. The haggling was damaging to the effort to pass the bill. Above all, it was increasing pressure for a premature cloture vote.

Mitchell felt that it was also clear from the Senate's 74 to 19 defeat of another jury trial amendment that was offered by Kentucky Republican John Sherman Cooper that there was no consensus on the issue. The Cooper amendment would have denied jury trials only in cases involving public officials charged with contempt.

Colorado's Gordon Allott, a pro-civil-rights senator, then made the point that activity on the jury trial amendments was giving a false sense of progress. He warned against consuming more time on another package of amendments, because, each time that happened, "the chance of cloture becomes more remote or is pushed back."

During the time that the battle was raging for passage of the 1964 Civil Rights Act, James Farmer spent two days in jail for leading a hapless stall-in to tie up traffic at the New York World's Fair on April 22, "to bring the spotlight of public attention" onto injustices in the city. For much of the time afterward, he would be battling "cannibalizing" attempts within CORE to take over the leadership; thus his organization's contribution to the passage of the civil rights law was minimal. More ominously, some political observers, especially civil rights opponents, began speculating that the candidacy of Governor Wallace of Alabama in the Wisconsin, Indiana, and Maryland presidential primaries would have an important impact on the Senate debate. Wallace's goal was to defeat the civil rights bill by scoring a progressively higher vote in each state, capped with an actual victory in Maryland. By increasing opposition to civil rights in the North through the spread of the states' rights gospel, he also hoped to "conservatize" both parties. That development, he felt, would make Democratic and Republican liberals in Washington change their thinking about what he called the "alarming trend." The Wallace phenomenon gave rise to claims of an increasing "white backlash" in the North.

Though Mitchell would later express relief that Wallace, his impressive showings notwithstanding, had no actual effect on the eventual cloture vote, the Alabamian did encourage stalling in the latter part of April and subsequently, when the outcome of the primaries in Indiana on May 5 and in Maryland on May 19 were awaited. The "white backlash" he unleashed took the shape of a reactionary force that began eroding the pro-civil-rights public opinion that had been building between the March on Washington and the April 28 Interreligious Convocation. However, Mitchell found that President Johnson was a most powerful counterforce to Wallace; from his White House pulpit he stood by his declaration that "this bill is going to pass if it takes us all summer."[27]

No one, not even the normally agreeable Humphrey, was immune to the frustrations of the filibuster. Despite his earlier pledge to be even-handed, at one point he said that some senators were acting like "adult delinquents" and he condemned the southerners' "talk" tactics. Mitchell welcomed his observation that those really responsible for blocking a successful cloture vote to end the filibuster were the nonsoutherners. In addition to Dirksen, Mitchell also noticed, even senators who were not directly involved in the fight began showing signs of weariness.

While maneuvers continued on the floor, behind-the-scenes negotiations on a compromise, which had begun on May 5, intensified among Dirksen, Humphrey, and the Justice Department. As a sop to Dirksen's ego, those negotiations were held in the minority leader's rather than Humphrey's office. (Normally they would have been held in the majority leader's office.) Other Democratic and Republican senators frequently joined in. Senate staffers handling the details at the same time decided it was best to keep Mitchell and Rauh out of it, "so they wouldn't blow everything out of the water." They were aware that "Dirksen was not that secure," John Stewart, Humphrey's staffer, explained, so they themselves began hammering out the substitute bill. That mode of operation only increased anxieties within the Leadership Conference. Unknown to those staffers was that Mitchell had accepted the inevitability of compromise, but it had to be one that he could swallow with good conscience.

Humphrey earlier had refused to negotiate with Dirksen until he had received the full complement of Dirksen's demands, not only on the FEPC, but also on the public accommodations and other titles. Later he relented in order to get things moving. Although Mitchell and Rauh were comfortable with Humphrey as floor manager, Katzenbach did not believe that that was the best idea because the Minnesotan was too closely identified with civil rights. Mansfield had withdrawn from the leadership because he wanted to avoid a similar predicament. Humphrey's alignment made it impossible for him and Kuchel, who was also closely identified with civil rights, to work effectively with conservative Republicans like Roman L. Hruska of Nebraska and Bourke B. Hickenlooper of Iowa. Katzenbach, as Johnson used to say, was more influential with Dirksen than anybody else because the deputy attorney general was a moderate and the Justice Department was at strong odds with the Leadership Conference. In fact, Katzenbach, trying to maintain the bill's substance, almost became an alcoholic during the endless sessions in Dirksen's office along with Hruska and the minority leader's aides, redrafting and redrafting and redrafting it, while drinking heavily.

At a meeting with Humphrey on May 11, Mitchell, Biemiller, Marvin Caplan, Walter Fauntroy, and other LCCR representatives insisted on seeing the full text of the Dirksen amendments. The LCCR representatives pointed out that while they had confidence in those conducting the negotiations, it was impossible to convince anyone that the heart of the legislation was not being traded away. They demanded assurances that the bill was not being gutted and the inclusion of LCCR lawyers in the negotiations. Other senators at the meeting increased their fears by saying that they had not seen the Dirksen amendment language, either. A Justice Department spokesman compounded the difficulty by saying that much of what was being discussed was not in writing. Finally, Humphrey promised he would try to solve the problem, but he was never really able to until what became known as the Dirksen-Humphrey compromise was hammered out. Then everyone was presented with what was a fait accompli.[28]

The resulting tension caused an explosion at one of the regular Monday-Thursday strategy sessions when Humphrey innocently relayed to the meeting the complaints of some senators that "we ought to get the hell off civil rights and onto something else." Suggesting a compromise, he asked, "Clarence, don't you think maybe we ought to have [a cloture vote]?" Rauh was not sure whether Mitchell was sitting or standing as, eyes flashing, he launched into one of the most eloquent speeches the ADA leader had ever heard. "Senator, blacks in this country have been patient for years, for decades, for centuries," Mitchell declared. "We have had atrocities committed on us. I think the Senate and its leadership can be patient just long enough until we can get the two-thirds vote we need."

He said that southern senators were using the rules to wear out the civil rights forces with quorum calls; the time had come to use the rules to have the sergeant-at-arms arrest the southerners and bring them to the floor to help make quorums.

As Rauh was thinking "This is marvelous, you will never get the cloture vote now," Humphrey himself broke the tension by declaring, "Clarence, you are three feet off your chair." To avoid scuttling the whole effort, Rauh suggested using instead the rule that no senator could make more than two speeches on any given subject. This was another suggestion that Rauh and Mitchell had made earlier to Humphrey and Kuchel, but both were again rejected.

Negotiations continued. Messages, telephone calls, and personal visits poured in as both Humphrey and Dirksen urged a strong bill. Mitchell kept abreast of developments with the help of intermediaries like Republicans Aiken and Saltonstall, who served as his conduit to Dirksen. At the May 11 meeting, the LCCR representatives had also complained about the Senate's agonizingly slow pace. It was agreed that the real problem was not the southern senators but senators from the western, northern, eastern, and central states. The time had come, it was felt, to "put the finger" on those senators who had not committed themselves to vote for cloture.[29]

Then on May 13, with a Dirksenian flair, the gravel-voiced leader announced in the Senate, "There comes a moment when there's a feeling in the air that the time has come for action, and we're about there." The second stage of negotiations could now get under way. Despite earlier fears, Mitchell and his Leadership Conference allies breathed easier after they received a copy of the Dirksen-Humphrey compromise (generally called the Mansfield-Dirksen substitute civil rights bill). They then realized that Humphrey's good humor, patience, and courage had won the day.

The language of the compromise differed considerably from that of H.R. 7152, but the bill's provisions were not substantially altered. The changes emphasized giving state and local authorities a first chance to resolve complaints and concentrated in the attorney general's office governmental authority to file suits to end specific instances as well as patterns and practices of discrimination. Persons suffering discrimination in public accommodations and places of employment had to seek remedy through an appropriate state agency before appealing to Washington. Since there were no such agencies in the South, Russell was close to the mark when he suggested that Dirksen had aimed the bill more directly at his region. Although the compromise barred the attorney general from suing on behalf of aggrieved individuals, he could intervene in such cases. Mitchell therefore concluded that these and other changes were designed to soothe Dirksen's ego and so were more cosmetic than substantial.

In its carefully crafted statement that was designed to arouse neither liberals sensitive to changes in the House bill nor conservatives chafing at the irrevocable flow of history, the Leadership Conference said it had to make a "line-by-line analysis" before determining to what extent some provisions had been weakened and would affect enforcement.

On May 26, the eve of Humphrey's fifty-third birthday, the Dirksen-Humphrey compromise was introduced as a substitute for the language of H.R. 7152. Six days later Mansfield announced that the leadership would file the cloture petition on June 6, and the Senate would vote upon it on June 9. The all-out drive for cloture was on.

In these delicate moments, it was hardly surprising that a hitch would

develop. Jealous of Dirksen's leadership, Hickenlooper had been sniping at
the compromise. He had walked out of the negotiation sessions, so he was
not bound by the results. Fellow Republicans Thruston Morton and Norris
Cotton joined him in expressing dissatisfaction with the Mansfield-Dirksen
substitute and the manner in which it had been negotiated. They next
asked for unanimous consent that three amendments they wanted to offer
be acted on before cloture. Hickenlooper said he had the support of seventeen to twenty Republicans. Neither side dared offend him. The alternative
was clear, as Dirksen advised. Whichever side offended them would surely
lose the mathematical cloture game. South Dakota's Karl Mundt explained,
"We went to the leaders and told them we had the controlling votes for
cloture and that we were insisting on these votes before we would consider
cloture." He added, "We represent the mainstream of thinking in the party
and we are getting tired of deals made by our leaders with Bobby Kennedy."

Russell too was caught off guard and in a damned-if-you-do, damned-
if-you-don't bind. If he permitted the Hickenlooper request, cloture was
assured; if he blocked it, the Iowan's wrath would be turned on him, and
he would still lose. Russell asked for an overnight delay to think things
over. During debate on the request, Humphrey, in a statesmanlike flourish, promised Hickenlooper and the other senators that any amendments
adopted before cloture was invoked would be included in the bill. Under
parliamentary rules, his pledge was not required. But, said Humphrey,
"there is such a thing as honor in the Senate." The following day, Russell
agreed to the unanimous consent request, and the Senate began discussing
the amendments on June 8. So the cloture vote was delayed for a day.

Mitchell kept Johnson abreast of developments, and the Senate leaders
assured the President they would not attempt cloture until they were certain they had the votes. Mitchell disputed the "many reports" that Johnson
had been asked to put pressure on the senators as the Leadership Conference
waged an all-out effort to line up votes. He was aware that Johnson did not
have to be asked, but was working on his own initiative.

On June 9, the Senate passed the Morton jury trial amendment, 51 to
48, but it rejected by 40 to 56 the Hickenlooper amendment to eliminate
funds for training school personnel to deal with desegregation problems. It
also rejected by 33 to 64 an amendment offered by Ervin to kill the FEPC
title. The Ervin amendment had been offered as a substitute for the Cotton
amendment, which would have limited FEPC coverage to employers and
unions with 100 workers, rather than 25. The Cotton amendment was also
rejected, 34 to 63.

That night, Johnson called Humphrey to get a count on cloture, which
was to be tried the following day. Humphrey was confident he had 2 or 3

more than the necessary 67. His count included the ailing California Democrat Clair Engle. Later that night, Humphrey learned that Hickenlooper and John R. Williams, a Delaware Republican, both of whom previously had been uncommitted, would also vote for cloture. A happy Humphrey called the President to report the good news.

The following morning, Humphrey learned that another Republican, Carl T. Curtis of Nebraska, wanted to be on the right side of history. Then, just before going into the Senate, his calls to fellow Democrats Ralph W. Yarborough of Texas, J. Howard Edmonson of Oklahoma, and Howard W. Cannon of Nevada assured Humphrey he had the votes to win.[30]

June 10, 1964, saw the climax of the struggle. Mitchell had sat through the only all-night filibuster* for 1964 that had been staged by West Virginia's Robert C. Byrd. As he watched, Byrd read from an endless stack of papers, "writhed in agony," and "swayed from side to side like a metronome"; Mitchell thought it hard to believe "that a man can manage to look ridiculous" for such an extended period.

Then, before packed galleries that began filling at 7:00 A.M., senators' wives who were standing, and high Justice Department officials seated on stone steps, the Senate four hours later voted 71 to 29 to cut off debate—the first time that cloture had ever been invoked in a civil rights debate since Rule XXII was adopted in 1917. King then was leading demonstrations in St. Augustine, Florida, which even he complained were eating up so much of his time that he could not give sufficient attention to the broadscale activities planned under SCLC's "Alabama Project." Forty-four Democrats and 27 Republicans voted for cloture, while 23 Democrats and 6 Republicans were opposed. Another measure of the event's historical importance was that all 100 senators voted. Engle, recuperating from brain surgery, had to be wheeled into the chamber. With a steel collar around his neck and his left arm in a black silk sling, he motioned "aye" by pointing to his eye and nodding his head affirmatively. The odd man out was Arizona's Carl Hayden. Having promised Johnson he would support cloture if his vote was needed, he stayed off the floor during the crucial moments. Afterward he walked in to cast a symbolic "no."[31]

Mitchell's determination to keep Title VI, barring discrimination under any program receiving financial assistance, as well as Title VII, had paid off. He was amazed at the amount of pressure that had been exerted upon him to have the NAACP not insist on keeping Title VII in the bill. Even a former top official of the Roosevelt administration who knew him well

---

* The filibuster staged by Robert Byrd lasted fourteen hours, thirteen minutes. It was surpassed only by South Carolina's Strom Thurmond, who spoke for twenty-four hours, eighteen minutes against the 1957 Civil Rights Act.

appealed to him from Europe to abandon that fight. Furthermore, he recalled, "this harassment did not stop with us," the civil rights leadership,
indicating that lawmakers were under intense pressure too.

Another opposition strategy was to claim that "if we pushed hard for
those titles, we would lose public accommodations." But Mitchell knew he
had the votes to get Titles VI and VII. Those titles contained the essence of
Mitchell's long struggle for an FEPC law and the "Powell Amendment."
Mitchell thought it fortunate that the attempt to sink Title VII with the
sex amendment backfired. Not only did the civil rights groups accept it,
but this wholly new feature strengthened the equal employment title by
expanding its coverage to include women, in addition to barring discrimination on the basis of race, color, religion, or national origin. Mitchell
thought it historically significant that the equal employment as well as the
public accommodation titles were introduced by Republicans—Javits and
Case, respectively.

He deeply appreciated the help of House Speaker McCormack, Celler,
and McCulloch to include Titles II, VI, and VII in the bill in the Judiciary
Committee. Title VII opponents were particularly surprised by the determination of Meany, Biemiller, and Johnson to keep it in the bill. "Without their efforts," he felt, "Title VII might well have been lost" in the
House. Humphrey and Kuchel similarly were determined to keep those
titles. So were others like Hart, Morse, Douglas, Keating, Scott, and, of
course, Javits. Even some conservatives supported Title VI because they
agreed that federal nondiscrimination standards should apply where federal
funds were spent.

Title IX was an evolution of the 1957 Part III concept. Although it
still did not go as far as Mitchell wanted, it authorized the attorney general
to intervene in suits charging a violation of the Fourteenth Amendment
owing to a denial of equal protection of the law. Another section clarified
existing law regarding the right of a defendant to have his case tried in
federal court. The NAACP could enter into such cases.

Title III of the bill, which was designed to ensure compliance with
Supreme Court decisions barring discrimination in facilities like libraries
and hospitals, covered another area that had long been a burr under Mitchell's skin. Now if he was arrested, as he had been in 1956 in the Florence,
South Carolina, railroad station for entering the "white" waiting room, the
Justice Department would have no excuse for not intervening in his behalf.
While the voting (Title I) and Civil Rights Commission (Title V) titles
were also influenced by his earlier struggles, the public accommodations
section (Title II) was an outgrowth of the sit-ins and other demonstrations.[32]

During the remaining days of debate, there followed a last-ditch, desperate assault on the bill. Senators offered over 500 amendments. After cloture, a Senate majority beat back the worst of the 118 amendments that were considered. It accepted only 12 to clarify the compromise bill. With all hope gone, the southerners could only vent their bitterness. Their wails on the final day before the vote sounded like death scene arias of an endless opera.

Humphrey went through the last two days of the debate in a daze. On June 17, just after the civil rights forces had scored a triumph on the floor, Mitchell and Rauh jubilantly rushed into his whip office only to find their friend in tears. He had just learned from his wife Muriel that their son had a cancerous growth in his throat that would require extensive surgery. Humphrey desperately wanted to be by his son's side, but he felt he had to stay in the Senate until the debate ended and the bill was passed. His two friends could only try to console him. Fortunately, the operation turned out as well as the Senate fight and his son recovered.

On June 19, one year to the day after John Kennedy had sent the bill to Congress, the Senate passed what was now the Dirksen-Mansfield substitute (Humphrey-Dirksen compromise) bill 73 to 27. The House followed suit on July 2, approving it by a 290 to 130 vote after Clarence Brown had again helped overcome angry resistance from Howard Smith on the Rules Committee.[33]

Moments following the cloture vote, a very happy Mitchell was standing on the Capitol steps in the 105-degree heat basking in historic glory as he waited once more for a television network camera crew to set up for an interview. Beads of perspiration ran down his unshaven face. During the long night before, he had had only "some coffee, danish pastry and tomato juice. But this bill was my meal." Nearby, Roy Wilkins told reporters, "Clarence Mitchell was the man in charge of this operation. He perfected and directed flawlessly a wonderful group of representatives of church, labor and all facets of the community to make this possible."

Mitchell credited "team work and keeping our tempers" for the success. "What this has done is to remove from the Presidential campaign the issue of racial relations in this present Congress." For a while, that had been a danger as some lawmakers had tried to drag the final vote past the upcoming political conventions. "Now that cloture has been invoked," Mitchell said, "this will mean in the coming election everyone will have to run on merits of the issues." They could not hide behind civil rights anymore.

Spotting a group of Justice Department staffers leaving inconspicuously, Mitchell sprinted over to their car and shook their hands. He found he could not say much more than "Thank you," but he believed "they knew I meant much more than that." Across the street, he wrung the hands of Katzenbach, Marshall, and other Justice Department staffers. "For one moment we were all school boys on graduation day," he recalled.

Those thoughts took him back to the previous year, when the countless meetings had begun with other Justice Department and White House aides. Although there were sometimes sharp disagreements, he again recalled, "our relationships were refreshingly friendly and informal." Without exaggerating, he felt that his sessions with Katzenbach, Marshall, Lawrence O'Brien, Charles Daly, and Mike Manatos were "in good fellowship, and there was genuine warmth about them."[34]

Mitchell always had difficulty extending credit to the lawmakers who he felt most deserved it for passage of the 1964 Civil Rights Act because of his appreciation for everyone's efforts. Nevertheless, the first names that usually came to the fore were those of Celler, for getting a strong bill out of the House Judiciary Committee; McCormack, for his overall support; and Humphrey, who had carried the ball through the Senate. Russell similarly praised Humphrey's leadership. Russell was one of the steadfast opponents of civil rights with whom Mitchell had long established cordial, if formal relations. Even Humphrey considered Mitchell's ability to get along with the southerners uncanny. Once, Russell, like Lyndon Johnson and Olin Johnston, might have displayed nervousness about being seen with Mitchell. But not anymore. The day the Senate passed the bill, while riding with Russell on a conveyor to the Senate wing, the implacable foe of civil rights told Mitchell that, "if it had not been for Senator Humphrey's fairness in giving a full opportunity to the opposition to present its views," it would not have been possible to pass the bill. After that Mitchell regularly rode the conveyor with southerners as well as civil rights allies.

Johnson, of course, was the other major factor. Russell said that the President "put so much pressure on everybody that there wasn't any doubt about this bill getting through." Mitchell felt that Russell "seemed almost to be feeling the pain of the pressure" as he talked. He could never forget the expression on the Georgian's face. As a result, while Russell "could have hurt us in a lot of ways," he never did. "I think he really was convinced on the basis of whatever the President had told him" that it was important to pass the bill. He was equally sure that, as a former senator, Johnson did not use threats or "crude tactics." Rather, he turned the trick by employing "constant persuasion and arguments, and stayed in touch." Mitchell also saluted Johnson's fellow Texans Ralph Yarborough, who had supported the 1957 act, and Congressmen Jack Brooks, Albert Thomas, Pickle, and Henry B. Gonzales for their favorable votes.

Martin Luther King flew in from St. Augustine to attend the ceremony when President Johnson signed the Civil Rights Act of 1964. That evening, as Mitchell joined the crowd in the East Room, he thought:

In the muted majesty of the White House, one could not hear the chant of street demonstrations nor the precise English of Roy Wilkins testifying at the witness table. It was not possible to see the tears in the eyes of Mrs. Medgar Evers—widowed all too young. There was no hint of the cheerful bustle of a two-hundred-member Maryland NAACP delegation headed by Lillie Carroll Jackson and Juanita Jackson Mitchell, en route to Washington for a day of lobbying. These and countless other actions had made this day possible.

Everyone rose to applaud the President as he entered. Mitchell watched him, smiling, moving with his customary quick step as he paused to shake a hand here and there. When he reached Mitchell, the lobbyist did not say anything that he felt "would sound magnificent in a history book." His words simply were "Thank you, Mr. President, for your leadership." For him, that expression of gratitude "covered a series of events that turned the country right side up." Mitchell was all too well aware that even though he had not been involved in detailed planning and negotiations, the President was the most important element in the development and execution of the political strategy. He had provided the national leadership required to wage the all-out battle. His support was vital to maintaining morale during the trying period of the filibuster, when it was easy for the pro-civil-rights forces to fall victim to concession and compromise.

After the signing ceremony, as Mitchell was walking with Wilkins and Randolph on the White House lawn,

> "it just seemed such a marvelous culmination of those men's activities through the long, long years, that I was truly pleased, not only because of the realization that the bill had been passed and signed, but that I was in the company of men who had had a longtime interest in the struggle. Of course, Dr. King was interested in that, too. But I was not as close to him and his interest in legislation had not been as long because of his youth."[35]

The 1964 Civil Rights Act, the most comprehensive in the nation's history, was a mighty symbol of the revolutionary social change that the nation was undergoing. The NAACP regarded it as a "Magna Carta of Human Rights." It was "both an end and a beginning; an end to the federal government's hands off policy; a beginning of an era of federally protected rights for all citizens." In terms of importance, it ranked next to the Declaration of Independence and the Emancipation Proclamation. Like the Constitution, it would have to be strengthened and amended by more legislation. But its passage represented a monumental social transition that was more remarkable for its absence of staged conflict. Mitchell's expression of gratitude was thus a historical understatement.

Mitchell was forever grateful that he had witnessed the "great turning point in American race relations," first, in 1947 when Truman officially supported the principle that racial segregation must be ended. Now Kennedy and Johnson had "helped to bring Congress in step with other branches of our government" by supporting the 1964 Civil Rights Act. It was always his hope that the rights of individuals would "be protected no matter whether those who need such protection be humble unknowns or famous leaders of thought and action." He was "also seeking to build a society in which all citizens will accept their personal responsibilities to build wholesome communities throughout the land." He believed the 1964 act would help make that hope a reality.[36]

One historical footnote Mitchell thought pertinent to the passage of the 1964 Civil Rights Act was that, as governor of California, Earl Warren had appointed Richard Nixon, William Knowland, and Thomas Kuchel to the Senate before they won election on their own. All four Republicans, to varying extents, upheld their party's Lincolnian tradition by contributing to the passage of the most comprehensive civil rights law since 1875. Nixon, as Vice President and president of the Senate, made crucial parliamentary rulings that helped the 1957 Civil Rights Act become a reality. Knowland, a conservative Senate leader, played a role in 1957 that was similar to that of Kuchel, a liberal, in 1964.

The most crucial role, of course, was played by Warren as Chief Justice of the U.S. Supreme Court in handing down the landmark *Brown* v. *Board of Education* decision in 1954. That ruling struck a mighty blow against segregation by reaffirming the Fourteenth Amendment's principle of equal protection under the law. Because the Supreme Court, in a series of decisions following adoption of the Fourteenth Amendment that was capped by *Plessy* v. *Ferguson,* had struck down legislative guidelines enacted to implement the promises of the post–Civil War amendments (the Thirteenth, Fourteenth, and Fifteenth), black citizens were deprived of protections for their constitutional rights. Now, once more, the Congress had followed the Supreme Court in reinvesting the original spirit of equality in those amendments. Mitchell felt that Johnson's determination to press the civil rights struggle in Congress was buttressed by the Warren Court's record of upholding the Fourteenth Amendment. Without that combination of leadership from the executive branch and the Supreme Court, Mitchell did not believe Congress would have enacted such a comprehensive measure that translated the substance of *Brown* into law.

One of the clearest indications of this action was the public accommodations section of the 1964 Civil Rights Act. Explaining this relationship in a *Nebraska Law Review* article entitled "The Warren Court and Congress: A Civil Rights Partnership," Mitchell noted that back in 1949 William R. Ming, a close friend who was a well-known civil rights lawyer and NAACP activist, had suggested a possible legal attack on public accommodations segregation by applying the Supreme Court's reasoning in the restrictive covenant cases in which that form of residential discrimination had been barred. Ming argued, in a *University of Chicago Law Review* article:

Judicial remedies appear available for the victims of racial segregation even in the absence of state statutes. For example, if a Negro presents himself for admission to a privately owned place of public accommodation, such as a hotel, and is denied admission solely on account of his color, it has generally been held by state courts that, in the absence of a statute to the contrary, he is without remedy. But the *Restrictive Covenant Cases* require such a decision to meet the test of the Fourteenth Amendment, and the Supreme Court's analysis of that amendment should compel reversal. The decision of the state court would be "state action" as now defined. Moreover, it is this "state action" which denies the plaintiff damages and the basis of the court's denial of damages is the race and color of the plaintiff. It thus follows that he has been denied equal protection of the laws in violation of the constitutional prohibition.

A decade later, Mitchell explained, Jack Greenberg, then an attorney with the NAACP Legal Defense and Educational Fund, in his book *Race Relations and American Law* discussed "the possible form that such statutes should take. He also noted that there was respectable historical precedent in the English Common Law which bound innkeepers 'to receive and lodge all travelers and to entertain them at reasonable prices without any specific or previous contract, in the absence of reasonable grounds for refusal.'"

Prompted by Greenberg's research, Mitchell studied two earlier cases that were related to the duties of innkeepers under common law. He found that in one, a 1913 Tennessee case, the court ruled that an innkeeper "has no right to say to one, 'you shall come into my inn,' and to another, 'you shall not,' as everyone conducting himself in a proper manner has a right to be received; innkeeper being a kind of public servant, having the privilege of entertaining travelers and supplying them with what they want." A

Rhode Island court in 1936 handed down a similar decision. Mitchell concluded that although those cases did not involve the question of serving blacks, "their statement of the law shows that the argument of segregation advocates about public accommodation laws invading rights or privacy of the owners of establishments open to the public was not sanctioned in the early decisions of the British Courts when dealing with innkeepers." Greenberg pointed out that Delaware, Mississippi, Florida, and Tennessee rejected the common law on innkeepers by statute. Other jurisdictions practiced similar forms of discrimination against blacks. Greenberg therefore concluded that the best way to correct private action related to innkeeper laws was to pass an appropriate civil rights law.

Mitchell's own conclusion was that state statutes to nullify the common law in this area showed that

> supporters of segregation did not intend to take any chances on giving Negroes a legal right of entry to places of public accommodation by failure to close all loopholes in the statutory or common law. This kind of ingenuity would seem to indicate that results were obtained with sufficient state involvement to warrant an attack under the Fourteenth Amendment. Unfortunately, it is also my opinion that without the Warren Court that attack would not have succeeded.

He was grateful that there was sufficient sympathy in Congress for the rights of blacks in light of this problem.

One strong advocate for basing the public accommodations section on the Fourteenth Amendment had been Senator Cooper of Kentucky, highly respected among his colleagues for his views on constitutional law. Cooper expressed the confidence of fellow lawmakers who believed the Warren Court would uphold a carefully drawn statute along those lines.

By the same token, there were many who remained fearful of violating the rights of "Mrs. Murphy" (of the proverbial "Mrs. Murphy's boarding house"). So a "Mrs. Murphy" provision exempting owner-occupied guest houses with five of fewer rooms for rent was kept in the bill. Mitchell concluded: "Fortunately for all concerned, the long standing friendship between Chairman Emanuel Celler of the House Judiciary Committee and the ranking Republican Representative William McCulloch, enabled the House to resolve the problem by basing the bill on both the Fourteenth Amendment and the Commerce Clause." A similar good fellowship between Humphrey and Kuchel provided the support for the dual reliance on the commerce clause and the amendment.

The strength of the Fourteenth Amendment foundation was similarly spread throughout the other sections, assuring equal protection in employment, in public facilities, in education, in the spending of federal funds, and in suits charging denials of the law. Mitchell felt that Title IV, giving the U.S. Office of Education and the attorney general authority to assist in school desegregation, was further evidence that a majority of Congress wanted to keep in step with the Supreme Court on civil rights.[37]

CHAPTER NINETEEN

The Man on the Totem Pole

The ink was not dry when, after he had signed the 1964 Civil Rights Act, President Johnson held an informal, off-the-record meeting with civil rights leaders and Cabinet officials to stress that everyone had a responsibility for letting blacks know that their rights were now secured by law, so demonstrations were unnecessary and possibly self-defeating. He issued instructions that care should be taken in selecting cases to test the law before the Supreme Court to guard against any initial decision that might cast doubt on it, even though he was confident about its constitutionality. Immediately afterward, the civil rights groups moved to test compliance with the new law in the South.

A task force of NAACP national board members, on an investigative tour of several towns in Mississippi, managed to meet with some police officials and to desegregate hotels and other facilities in Jackson, but the level of violent resistance still existing that July was all too evident. The delegation therefore recommended that the federal government assume administrative responsibility for Mississippi and that the Civil Rights Commission hold hearings in the state on the breakdown of law and order and the deprivation of basic civil rights. The task force also initiated other steps that would lead to a struggle for more laws to protect individual safety.

The NAACP and the Leadership Conference on Civil Rights further embarked on a second course to gain enforcement of the new law in other areas as well as barring discrimination in federal activities. As that program was unfolding, Selma, Alabama, erupted as a national symbol of the denial

of voting rights for blacks in the South. A third civil rights battlefront thus
was opened in early 1965.

Considerably influencing these developments were the swirling forces of
white backlash that roiled the political waters in the summer of 1964.
Mitchell, in addition to being called the "lost senator," was now declared
to be "the man on the totem pole" as he gained increased public attention
and unparalleled respect due to his effectiveness on the Hill. He observed:

> It will not always be popular to insist upon a planned and or-
> derly course of action. In the face of the great wrongs that have
> been used to deprive us of our rights, the voice of emotion is often
> more persuasive than the voice of reason. Yet, throughout its long
> and successful history, the NAACP has always put reason above
> emotion.
>
> Emotion has caused us to burn with anger at the murders of
> civil rights workers and the second-class schools set aside for our
> children. But even as our hearts urged us to act with speed and
> with strength, our heads dictated action according to plan. We
> have used the picket line, the mass march, the courtrooms, the
> legislatures and the Congress to wage our fight. History has vindi-
> cated our program.

Because of the tensions created by the competing forces of emotion and
reason, political paradoxes always presented Mitchell with severe personal
tests.[1]

Barry Goldwater wore George Wallace's mantle of bigotry into the Cow
Palace of San Francisco and was crowned his party's presidential candidate
at the Republican National Convention. The GOP, sixteen years after the
Democrats had resoundingly rejected any such threat on the national level,
was now undeniably a captive of the Dixiecrat ideology as well as of a
nihilistic conservatism that would control its philosophical direction in
coming years. In Mitchell's words: "In one breath they talked about preserving states' rights. In the next breath they were advocating Federal intervention to 'make the city streets safe.'" He heard them declare their
support for civil rights, but they also favored policies that would protect
only whites. "In short, they were for or against whatever would deceive the
gullible and catch the unwary in a booby trap." He had no doubt that
many who had supported Goldwater "wanted to capitalize on sensational
and lurid fears or prejudices to win" in November.

That development, especially during the period of national worry over
the disappearance of three civil rights workers near Philadelphia, Mis-

sissippi, seemed a crass abandonment of the principles of common decency for which the Grand Old Party had stood since the Civil War. The Arizonan became the standard-bearer of white backlash and reactionary politics after Wallace abandoned his quixotic quest for high office. The NAACP's deviation from its traditional nonpartisan policy to call for Goldwater's defeat revealed black Americans' shock and anxiety.

For Mitchell, the choice for the presidency was simple. Goldwater's votes against the civil rights bill had made him "totally unfit to be President." The senator, he maintained, "could not have been unaware that his position would be used as a rallying point" for all who wanted to defy the law. He presumed Goldwater knew that his suggestion that extremism was sometimes acceptable would be well received by "would-be vigilantes bashing colored customers in the head in Alabama and Florida."

Despite his unhappiness, he advised blacks against bolting the Republican party. "It is precisely because the club swingers and the scofflaws would like to see one of the major parties become a roosting place for intolerance that men of goodwill must stay in the GOP and work to make it a rational organization." He cited the Democratic party as an example of what could be accomplished by "staying and even fighting to get in." But the Democrats, too, were experiencing their trials.[2]

The 1964 Democratic National Convention convened in Atlantic City that summer with the depth of the party split over civil rights providing the only real suspense, overshadowing questions about Lyndon Johnson's running mate and every other issue. No setting could have been more appropriate for this wrenching drama of politics versus morality. Atlantic City, with sixteen and a half miles of boardwalk and one of the most prized stretches of beachfront in the country, had once been the most fashionable resort on the east coast. The convention was supposed to help the city recapture some of its past glory, but it would have required much more than the intraparty fireworks to breathe new life into what some considered was an aging, stretched-out Angkor Wat. For the Democratic party to avoid a fate similar to the city's decay, Johnson had to orchestrate events in the tightly controlled manner of which he was a legendary master.

Both Alabama and Mississippi were openly rebellious over the Civil Rights Act, so much so that George Wallace had pushed a law through his state legislature stating that its electors would be "independent Democrats." The law made it impossible for President Johnson's name to be on the ballot in Alabama under the Democratic label, so Alabama would take a walk in less dramatic fashion. It was the sixty-eight-member Mississippi Freedom Democratic party (with four whites), formed earlier in April, that captured the national spotlight by the intensely emotional moral drama it presented.

The MFDP's fervent demands to be seated at the convention in place of the regular lily-white, segregationist delegation, and its subsequent call for expulsion of the Magnolia State's representatives in Congress, symbolized how much the civil rights movement had progressed and how much more was yet to be accomplished. An era that had begun in 1948 was about to close and another to open. The Democratic party, once dominated by the segregationist South, would never be the same racially. The regular Democrats made no bones about their determination to maintain the racial status quo, while the MFDP, composed of some of the state's most radical blacks, was waging an all-out battle to register one hundred thousand or more of the state's disfranchised minority group members and others who supported them. Both the regulars and the MFDP that summer followed the required procedures for selecting convention delegations. The difference, according to the MFDP, was that the challengers' meetings in Jackson on August 6 were "open to all Democrats," while the regulars' meetings, held the same day in the same city, effectively barred blacks.

Sympathy and morality were overwhelmingly in favor of the MFDP, but not politics. The regulars were legally and politically in control, but they were Democrats in name only outside Mississippi. History had rendered them absurd. They had given every indication that they would not support the party's national ticket in November, even though they said a slate of electors pledged to the official candidates would be on the 1964 ballot. They had abandoned the party in 1960 over John Kennedy's nomination to support an unpledged slate of electors, and were about to do so again in 1964. With favorite son Wallace having taken himself out of the race, they were committed to Goldwater, whose goal was to capture the white ethnic industrial vote. This blue-collar vote had been the backbone of the Democratic party since the New Deal and had been the basis of Wallace's strength in the North and South. Haunting the national leadership was the 1948 scenario, in which half of the Alabama delegates and all of the Mississippi delegation had walked out to protest the civil rights plank. Next, Alabama, Louisiana, Mississippi, and South Carolina kept Truman off the ballot, and Dixiecrat candidate Strom Thurmond, now a Democratic senator, carried those self-declared outcast states. The aftermath was the so-called 1952 loyalty pledge, which committed any delegation seated at that and subsequent conventions to use every "honorable means" to have pledged Democratic candidates or electors on its state's ballot under the party name.

The MFDP was not only pitted against the segregationists and Johnson, but also against his expected running mate, Hubert Humphrey, who was responsible for working out a compromise. Joseph Rauh, the Mississippi challengers' lawyer, was caught in the middle. Liberalism was at

war with itself, and Rauh was a study of conflicting loyalties. His honeymoon with Johnson over the past year was the talk of Washington. Many
had pilloried him earlier in the year for running on a "United Democrats
for Johnson" ticket for reelection as Democratic chairman of the District of
Columbia, but his unanimous victory in May showed the extent of respect
and attraction he commanded. Controversial, he had become a favorite of
The Washington Post's news columns; colorful and smart, he was a regular at
Washington's political conclaves and soirees. His fearless defense of victims
of the Red scare had made him somewhat of a celebrity around Washington. Tall, now fifty-five, with unruly gray hairs straggling in all directions,
he was a study in professorial respectability with his floppy bow ties and
ever present broad smile. The previous year, Rauh had been appointed
general counsel of the UAW, after having served as its Washington attorney
since 1951. That promotion only intensified his controversial role now. He
was also the district's delegate to the convention and a member of the
convention credentials committee.

As delegates gathered in the city of sea and sunshine late that August,
there was, top administration officials complained, no sign of compromise,
especially from Rauh, from whom they apparently expected some help.
Emotions ran high during the three days that the credentials committee
wrestled with the issue, with big-state delegations being swept by moral
fervor on one side and the southerners standing their legal ground on the
other. Rauh, a modern-day Joan of Arc for whom principle was life, was
reveling in his mission. In a choked voice, he declared with devastating
truth that the Freedom party delegates were "willing to die" for Lyndon
Johnson and the party. They were also willing to die for freedom. Among
the witnesses he produced were the Reverend Edwin King, the calm white
chaplain of Tougaloo College, and Rita Schwerner, widow of one of the
three civil rights volunteers who had been slain in Mississippi that summer. Additionally, Roy Wilkins, Martin Luther King, Jr., and James
Farmer testified in support of the "rump group," as the regulars called the
challengers. As intense as were the testimonies in depicting the moral and
physical horrors of Mississippi, none that Saturday afternoon in the hot,
muggy credentials committee meeting room was more gripping than that
from Fannie Lou Hamer, the Ruleville sharecropper of mythical fame:

> I was carried to the county jail and put in the booking room.
> They left some of the people in the booking room and began to
> place us in cells. I was placed in a cell with . . . Miss Ivesta Simp-
> son. After I was placed in the cell I began to hear sounds of licks
> and screams. I could hear the sounds of licks and horrible screams,

and I could hear somebody say, "Can you say 'Yes sir,' nigger? Can you say 'Yes sir'?"

And they would say other horrible names.

She would say, "Yes, I can say 'Yes sir.'"

"So say it."

She says, "I don't know you well enough."

They beat her, I don't know how long, and after a while she began to pray and ask God to have mercy on these people.

And it wasn't too long before three white men came to my cell. . . .

I was carried out to the cell into another cell where they had two Negro prisoners. The State Highway Patrolman ordered the first Negro to take the blackjack.

The first Negro prisoner ordered me, by orders from the State Highway Patrolman, for me to lay down on a bunk bed on my face, and I laid on my face.

The first Negro began to beat, and I was beat until he was exhausted. . . . After the first Negro . . . was exhausted, the State Highway Patrolman ordered the second Negro to take the blackjack. The second Negro began to beat and I began to work my feet, and the State Highway Patrolman ordered the first Negro who had beat to set on my feet and keep me from working my feet. I began to scream, and one white man got up and began to beat me on my head and tell me to "hush."

One white man—my dress had worked up high—he walked over and pulled my dress down and he pulled my dress back, back up. I was in jail when Medgar Evers was murdered. All of this is on account we want to register to vote, to become first-class citizens, and if the Freedom Democratic Party is not seated now, I question America. . . .

Mitchell had heard a similar tale of horror nine years earlier from Beatrice Young of Jackson. Now, Hamer had suffered a bestial pummeling in James Eastland's Sunflower County simply because she had led twenty-eight blacks in registering to vote. Rauh, in effect, repeated his 1948 strategy of putting the moral monkey on the Democratic party's back, and this time television was there to capture the event. Despite his idealism, Rauh was a realist and knew that it was only by such public exposure that he could hope to avoid total defeat from "our great President," whom he would still have to support in the end.

Mitchell's agony during this battle was compounded because he could only stay in the background. Further complicating his conflicting loyalties to Johnson, Humphrey, and Rauh, he welcomed the MFDP challenge as long overdue. Had it come four years earlier when Mitchell himself was accused of wanting an issue because of his demands for an even stronger civil rights plank, rather than a good platform on which the Democrats could run, he would have had no problem. But the last thing he wanted to do now was to appear to be ungrateful to Johnson or to endanger his election chances, especially when he regarded the passage of the 1964 Civil Rights Act as a promise of benefits to come. Many black militants, however, were openly against Johnson. Other paradoxes abounded. A memorable example of Mitchell's dilemma was the NAACP Washington Bureau's demand in 1956 that Congress expel the Mississippi delegation because of the state's unbridled racial violence. Mitchell desperately wanted the MFDP—led by his good NAACP friend Aaron Henry, who had staged a symbolic but unsuccessful run for governor on the Freedom Ballot the previous October, Fannie Lou Hamer, and Robert Moses, a transplanted Harvard graduate and SNCC activist—to win.

In Mitchell's mind also was the reactionary danger Barry Goldwater posed in November. Like many others, he did not want a rerun of the 1948 Dixiecrat bolt, because Johnson dared not risk losing more of the South by letting the MFDP score a runaway victory. As in other situations involving intense personal conflicts, Mitchell hardly spoke about his dilemma afterward, except to say that he had supported the MFDP. Part of the problem, he acknowledged, was that "it used to be we'd come here and urge enactment of laws. Now we've got the laws." Mitchell was equally aware that at long last the curtain had been drawn on the lily-white Democratic party of the South. He had helped to end the southerners' dominance in Congress, and ever since he landed in Washington he had been banging on the Democrats' heads about the Dixiecrat cancer in their midst. Now he saw the profound ripple effects of change in Congress on the party structure. No longer would the Democratic party of the South have absolute veto power over its convention nominees. The chant of integration demonstrators outside the hall for "freedom now" was almost a gratuitous recognition of the history unfolding inside, where salt-and-pepper delegations from California, Illinois, Ohio, Michigan, Pennsylvania, and New York sat with no visible awareness that their old-shoe companionship once had not been so. Even Tennessee, North Carolina, and Georgia had brought black delegates on their own, and none of the other southern states followed Alabama and Mississippi out the door.

Mitchell wholeheartedly favored the compromise that was engineered by Johnson's surrogates Hubert Humphrey and Walter Reuther, who had been flown in to help settle the conflict. Reuther had joined Rauh in 1960 in opposing Kennedy's selection of Johnson as the vice presidential candidate. Neither the regulars nor the challengers were happy with the proposed solution. The compromise offered to seat those regulars who pledged to support the national ticket in November and, in an unprecedented move, gave the MFDP two at-large seats. It also pledged that no state delegation that had been selected with regard to race would be seated in 1968, and set up a special committee to ensure this result. The compromise was a victory for Johnson and a triumph for the MFDP. But the moral visionaries were not interested in pragmatism, only unrelenting principle; and their opponents could never accept defeat gracefully, even if judgment day had been postponed for four years.

Rauh declared, "They shouldn't have offered seats to the racists and they should have offered us their seats." But he conceded that "it was as much as we could get." He voted against the compromise in the credentials committee, but counseled the MFDP to accept it as a historic step forward. The regulars, offered a solution they could not accept, announced as they walked out that "we did not leave the national Democratic Party, it left us."

Aaron Henry was inclined to accept the compromise, but he publicly supported his more radical MFDP associates, Hamer and Moses, despite Humphrey's unprecedented assurance. Theirs was a quest of moral absolutes.

Ironically, this struggle, like the demonstrations in the South, cast Mitchell as a moderate in contrast to Hamer and Moses and other leaders like Martin Luther King, James Farmer, and James Forman, head of SNCC. The true difference, though, was that Mitchell's goal was more carefully defined and demonstrably attainable within certain limitations—especially since Congress was implementing the NAACP's program.

But Rauh's decision, despite its long-range benefits, aroused considerable bitterness within the MFDP and sparked an irreparable break. After rejecting the compromise, the MFDP staged a demonstration by symbolically taking over the places that the Mississippi regulars had vacated. Mitchell's "From the Work Bench" observation on the struggle revealed how he felt.

> Mr. Rauh is one of the most dedicated people that I have known. He took the lofty path of principle in the dispute about whether the Mississippi Freedom Party should be seated at the convention. At great personal sacrifice and in the face of monumental pressures, he took on the task of being counsel for the Freedom Party. His brief, his handling of witnesses and his argument before the Credentials Committee should be required reading in political science courses.

The Mississippi Freedom Party had an eloquent story and a debatable legal case. Mr. Rauh's handling gave the story a breath of life and a quality of suffering reality that moved even the most experienced politicians to a state of tears. Most lawyers agreed that he also established the legality of the Freedom Party's claim in a court that traditionally seeks to lean heavily on the equities—the national convention.

After his truly magnificent performance that won place, status and a long range plan for preventing future discrimination, Mr. Rauh found himself in the unhappy position of a lawyer whose clients announced that they would not accept the decision even before he could explain it to them. A man of lesser status would have exploded. He declined to be bitter.

Dr. Henry's words and conduct showed that the country must understand that leadership among colored people is not monolithic. The NAACP understands this because it has always had capable and effective leaders who could be articulate spokesmen in state and local communities. Indeed, Dr. Henry is one of these. However, very few of the non-NAACP leaders understand this and almost none of the television, radio and national political leaders realize it.

It is no longer possible to get solutions to problems by having sessions with just the top echelon of colored leaders. That is why no one leader, and perhaps no combination of colored leaders, could persuade the Mississippi group to accept the compromise that would have permitted the seating of two delegates at large and others as observers.

It is safe to say that this solution was a victory. It could have been accepted with honor. However, Dr. Henry and his followers chose to turn it down. His public statement said it was rejected because it did not give redress to all the members of the delegation. Unlike Bull Connor of Alabama and the majority of the so-called Mississippi regulars, Dr. Henry made it clear that he and his followers would stand in the Mississippi place, but would not defy convention authorities if asked to move from in front of other delegates.

Some television commentators tried to make it appear that by standing on the floor, Dr. Henry was being discourteous to the President. The ridiculous nature of this innuendo was apparent each time one looked at the churning masses of delegates, visitors and hangers-on who would not be seated even though the chairman constantly implored them to do so.

It is fair to say that there seemed to be strong sentiment in the

convention in favor of acceptance of the Credentials Committee solution of the Mississippi dispute. Yet, it was equally apparent that
the witnesses for the Freedom Party had won the hearts of the vast
majority. Perhaps the most eloquent testimony on this was the delegate from one of the Dakotas who made seats available "especially
for the ladies" after the Freedom Party members had been standing
for almost an hour.

His gesture of good will came in spite of his spoken approval
of the Credentials Committee solution. It is my opinion that
there are more people like him in our country than there are so-
called backlashers. The victims of discrimination have a heavy obligation to spurn lawlessness and to act with fairness and dignity
themselves, but it is also clear that free men respect their rights
to hold out for what they believe to be proper redress of their
grievances.[3]

The next paradox resulted from the MFDP's subsequent attempt in
1965 to unseat the Mississippi congressional delegation. When the
NAACP staged its well-documented challenge in 1956, blacks were still on
the sidelines hammering for a crack in the system. Symbolism appeared an
appropriate substitute for achievement in the face of vigilante terrorism in
the South. Seeking to build political pressure, the NAACP declared that
the "tempo of warfare" had brought the nation to "the state where the
Federal Government must assert the Constitution as the supreme law of the
land or surrender to the forces of anarchy in Mississippi." Now, while
expressing sympathy for the MFDP's complaint, the NAACP declared that
it did not endorse the group's methods.

In presenting the reasons for opposition, Frank Pohlhaus, who had prepared the NAACP's elaborate 1956 brief, noted that the principal legal
issue was whether the Mississippi elections in November 1964 were being
contested within the meaning of the relevant federal statute (2 U.S.C.
201–226) governing such challenges. The NAACP noted that precedents
existed on both sides, but the most recent challenge showed that Congress
overwhelmingly did not feel a noncandidate could contest an election. This
view was supported by most of the Leadership Conference lawyers, who felt
that the three MFDP contestants did not "qualify as *bona fide* candidates."
Furthermore, the NAACP noted, Congress, by 276 to 149, had seated the
Mississippi delegation in January 1965 without qualification. That meant
the members could be unseated only by expulsion, which required a two-
thirds vote of the House—a hopeless prospect given the earlier lopsided
loss.

The NAACP felt that better alternatives were offered by an NAACP

Legal Defense and Educational Fund lawsuit to reduce or unseat the state's representation in Congress, hearings by the Civil Rights Commission in Mississippi, and a voting census that was to be conducted under Title VIII of the 1964 Civil Rights Act. The MFDP rejected that advice as well as pleas from the ADA to postpone the challenge until January 1966, when new developments might offer a better chance for success. Not surprisingly, Mitchell, Rauh, and Andrew Biemiller were pointedly absent in September when the Leadership Conference reluctantly endorsed the MFDP challenge. Four days later on September 17, the House, by 228 to 143, dismissed the challenge. Once more, principle had fallen victim to myopia. But the underlying problem remained unresolved, as the MFDP would continue to show with unrelenting zeal. A century after the promise of freedom to the slaves had been kept, the promises of equal protection and the right to vote without racial discrimination were still unfulfilled.[4]

Mitchell felt that the appropriate response to white backlash was a much deeper dedication to the eradication of all forms of racism in society and to upholding duly constituted law. Despite the trouncing that Barry Goldwater received at the polls in November, Mitchell did not believe the Arizonan had been defeated because the overwhelming number of Americans rejected his brand of racial politics during the campaign. He felt there were other factors behind Goldwater's defeat, such as his inept campaign. Mitchell regarded the backlash phenomenon as "a creation of the gimmick minded." What Americans were now calling white backlash was the same prejudice he had experienced during his college days, when his debating team had been guests at Bates College and the headwaiter at one of the best restaurants in Lewiston, Maine, put a screen around him and other members of the Lincoln University team. "Today those prejudices have been stifled to some extent by better enforcement of civil rights laws. Yet their existence crops up from time to time."

More than ever, he saw a need for stronger leadership from the federal government in enforcing civil rights laws and upholding the Constitution, and for the President to set a strong moral tone for the nation. He shared the view of someone he once heard say, "President Johnson was born for the times in which we live" because of his support for civil rights and advocacy of social legislation. He was grateful, he told Johnson, "that the hand of Providence rests on your shoulder as you steer the nation toward just peace abroad and domestic tranquility at home." No sycophant, Mitchell intended to let Johnson know that in addition to supporting civil rights legislation, he was expected to fulfill his Great Society promises in all other areas, especially the goal of equal education and economic rights for blacks. He urged Johnson to name Humphrey as his running mate. By so repaying

Humphrey for his faithful support and dedicated leadership of the recent civil rights battle in Congress, Johnson would demonstrate his continuing commitment to racial justice. Johnson's granting of that wish enabled Mitchell to turn his attention to other urgencies that fall.

It was most important that there be no election defeats of civil rights supporters that could be taken by those who were not fully committed to the goal of equality for blacks as a rejection because they had voted for the omnibus 1964 bill. When Mitchell received a desperate plea for help from Congressman McCulloch, he therefore became alarmed. "He seemed very distraught when I talked to him," he told Wilkins. Among other things, McCulloch was very concerned that blacks in his district were unaware of his strong support for civil rights. Wilkins promptly responded with appropriate letters to NAACP branch leaders informing them that the association had "promised to vote for any congressman who supported and voted for civil rights legislation." Such cooperation, Mitchell felt, constituted a moral obligation, as deeds that matched "our statements about political action," and that were richly repaid.

According to Mitchell:

> Perhaps the most significant sign of change in our country occurred in November, 1964. At that time the overwhelming majority of colored voters cast their ballots for a presidential candidate who was born and raised in the South. It is equally important to remember that President Lyndon B. Johnson is one of those rare public officials who promised to work for the end of second-class citizenship before he was elected, who continues to assert that intention after the election and who matches his words of hope with deeds of accomplishment.[5]

Just as important, he felt, the sweeping Johnson-Humphrey victory reflected an unprecedented national sentiment for human justice and had produced a Congress that was more sensitive to its responsibilities. Not only were McCulloch and other lawmakers openly supported by the NAACP reelected, but losses among stalwart civil rights supporters were small. As a bonus to McCulloch's coming "through with flying colors," two Republican opponents in the House were defeated. Furthermore, all southerners who voted for the 1964 Civil Rights Act were returned to Congress. They included congressmen like Claude Pepper of Florida, who in the past had been punished for supporting civil rights, and others from Tennessee, Georgia, and Texas.

Pepper was a particularly important symbol. Mitchell was so impressed with him that he seldom missed a chance to hear him speak in the Senate.

Pepper was from a similarly humble background and articulated social issues very well. He was defeated in 1957 by tactics his opponents used to brand him as too liberal, especially on race issues. During meetings in Florida where racial prejudice was rampant, for example, they would arrange for a black man to rush to the front of the audience and shake Pepper's hand. Mitchell often spoke with Pepper about those incidents, but the senator never betrayed any regret about not "going against the tide on racial matters" even though that stand had contributed to his loss.

Mitchell was equally pleased that Ralph Yarborough of Texas, despite widespread fears he would be defeated for consistently supporting civil rights, was returned to the Senate. There were, however, two regrettable losses in the Senate—New York's Kenneth Keating and Maryland's J. Glenn Beall, both Republicans. But they were replaced by Robert Kennedy in New York and Joseph Tydings in Maryland, who were also civil rights supporters. The Keating defeat left a Republican vacancy on the Judiciary Committee, while Beall's left one on the Labor Committee. Both committees dealt with civil rights legislation. Given other gains, Mitchell was not overly concerned about their replacements. For example, Barry Goldwater's retirement made Jacob Javits the ranking Republican on the Labor Committee, which considered FEPC proposals and similar civil rights measures. Additionally, Mitchell regarded the election of Joseph M. Montoya of New Mexico, Ross Bass of Tennessee, and Fred R. Harris of Oklahoma to the Senate as good civil rights news.

In Minnesota, Walter F. Mondale, another civil rights stalwart, was appointed to complete Humphrey's unexpired term. The white backlash undercurrent notwithstanding, Mitchell considered these successes much more than an indication of a national rejection of the Wallace-Goldwater philosophy and the strength of Johnson's coattails. The strong prevailing civil rights climate, if properly used, could lead to still more impressive advances in Congress.

Another expression of support was the Supreme Court's sweeping and expansive reading of the commerce clause in rendering its judgment upholding the constitutionality of Title II against a challenge by the Heart of Atlanta Motel. The Court declared that its reading of the legislative history of the title made it conclude that Congress had the power to regulate activities of the motel that had a bearing on the national interest and that it was not necessary to go beyond the commerce clause in rendering its decision. The Court left the way clear for Congress to create additional legislation within the federal antidiscrimination requirements when there was a need to do so.

Further proof for Mitchell that progress was being made in fulfilling the promise of democracy included the election in 1961 of Clarence III to the Maryland House of Delegates. His third son, Michael, meanwhile, had joined the NAACP youth movement his mother had started a generation earlier. The NAACP Youth and College Division had grown to 307 youth councils and 91 college chapters. As chairman of the NAACP National Youth Work Committee, Michael was pushing the association to meet aggressively the challenge from other organizations by significantly expanding its youth program. But it was well understood that opening the gates to the promised land of equality was not enough. Much more had to be done before blacks could freely pass through, and a new generation of Mitchells—if they adhered to their parents' principles—would be an important part of the future movement.[6]

Mitchell's conclusion that white backlash was not a new phenomenon but only the flaring up of underlying racial attitudes was best symbolized by Selma, Alabama, just as that small southern city demonstrated the region's intransigence in denying blacks the right to vote.

Selma's blacks were supposed to be invisible at the polls. On Sunday, March 7, 1965, however, they became very visible when television evening news broadcasts portrayed, for millions of viewers across the nation, the bloody attacks by Alabama state troopers and the possemen of Sheriff James Clark, Jr., on unarmed SNCC and SCLC demonstrators on U.S. Highway 80 as they attempted to cross the Edmund Pettus Bridge on their way to Montgomery, the state capital, to protest their disfranchisement in Dallas County. Television viewers saw fleeing marchers reeling from tear gas as blue-helmeted troopers and possemen on horseback chased them with nightsticks cracking on their heads. Outraged, members of Congress denounced the attacks as "an exercise in terror against citizens who were demonstrating peacefully for the right to vote." President Johnson met with Attorney General Katzenbach about Selma; even Governor George Wallace summoned Sheriff Clark to his office in Montgomery and denounced him for the violence. "The Governor was real upset and mad at Clark," Mayor Smitherman said.

Selma was a state of mind. A guidebook described it as "an old-fashioned gentlewoman, proud and patrician, but never unfriendly"—that is, except to blacks. In surrounding Dallas County, the voting age population in 1961 was 29,515, of whom 14,400 were white and 15,115 were black. Only 1 percent of those blacks were registered compared to 64 percent of whites. Attorney General Nicholas Katzenbach explained, "Between 1954 and 1961 the number of Negroes registered had mushroomed: exactly 18 were registered in those seven years." That brought the total number of registered voters in Dallas County—after a four-year struggle in the federal courts—to 383.

Statistics dramatized the problem elsewhere as well. Throughout Alabama, the number of blacks registered to vote between 1958 and 1964 had increased by 5.2 percent to 19.4 percent of those eligible. That compared with 69.2 percent of eligible whites who were registered. In Mississippi, registered black voters had increased from 4.4 percent of eligibles in 1954 to an estimated 6.4 percent in 1965. Meanwhile, available figures showed that 80.5 percent of eligible whites were registered. In Louisiana, blacks had stood still between 1956 and 1965, with registration rising from 31.7 to 31.8 percent, while 80.2 percent of whites were eligible to vote. The Justice Department's own conclusion was that "the three present statutes have had only minimal effect. They have been too slow."[7]

Mitchell did not see the problem as being with the 1957, 1960, and 1964 civil rights acts but with their enforcement. The 1957 Civil Rights Act authorized the attorney general to institute suits to correct abuses of voting rights in state and federal elections and to end intimidation of voters. The 1960 amendment sought to strengthen the 1957 act by permitting the attorney general to inspect voting records, which were to be preserved, and giving federal courts power to appoint voting referees. The ratification of the Twenty-fourth Amendment to the Constitution outlawing the poll tax in federal elections was another benefit. Title I of the 1964 Civil Rights Act was further meant to expedite voting complaints by providing for direct appeals before three-judge federal courts, which in turn would speed hearings before the Supreme Court. This law covering federal elections prohibited the use of discriminatory voting qualifications, standards, and practices; the rejection of applicants for immaterial errors or omissions in completing registration forms; and the use of literacy tests that were not administered in writing. The law also established a sixth-grade education as a presumption of literacy.

Convinced that the problem was not with the laws but with the people administering them, Mitchell reacted with consternation to criticism that the 1957 and 1960 statutes were "no good and should be junked." He felt that such attitudes were unfair because those laws had enabled hundreds of new voters to register in Tennessee and had ended economic reprisals there, and had enabled minorities in Macon County, Georgia, to vote in sufficient numbers to elect blacks to public office. With enforcement, there could also be a significant increase in black voter registration in other areas of the South, such as Tuskegee, Alabama, and even in Selma, thus setting the pace for the rest of the region.

The problem, he maintained, was the difficulty in getting some southern judges to enforce the laws, the refusal of voting registrars in Selma and other pockets of resistance to enroll blacks in sufficient numbers, and the continuing use of the poll tax in state and local elections.

Mitchell felt that the government's "painfully slow pace" in enforcing the law was demonstrated by a pending federal attack on Mississippi voting laws that could have been decided at least four years earlier had the Justice Department heeded the advice of Harold Tyler, now a federal district judge in New York. As head of the Civil Rights Division, Tyler had urged a broad attack on those laws. Mitchell believed that Tyler was right on legal grounds, but he was overruled as a matter of policy. "The result was that at least two national congressional elections and one presidential election were virtually for whites only in many counties in Alabama, Mississippi and Louisiana."

Similarly, the weak provision for appointing federal referees had been incorporated in the 1960 act in the belief that federal judges could "rise above the environment" from which they came and uphold the law. The theory was that once a judge found a pattern of discrimination in voting he would correct the problem by appointing a referee to supplant the local registrar who was causing the problem. This proved to be a slow process, and was the primary factor provoking the impatience of black residents of Selma demanding to be registered and the resulting bloody violence that erupted to haunt the nation. Mitchell was painfully aware that had Congress adopted the NAACP proposal for registrars, or examiners, instead of referees, thousands, rather than hundreds, of new black voters would have been registered.

The Eisenhower Justice Department shared much of the blame for lack of enforcement because it had wanted the courts, through referees, and not the executive branch through registrars, to have primary responsibility for enforcement. But now the Justice Department, too, was complaining strenuously about the snaillike progress in the courts and unrelenting opposition from local officials in blocking enforcement.[8]

Katzenbach was very embarrassed by the inability of his agency to deal with the problem. He forcefully maintained that it was not due to a lack of energy or dedication by Justice but to "the inadequacy of the judicial process to deal effectively and expeditiously with a problem so deep-seated and so complex." For example, he said, it now required as much as six thousand man-hours to analyze voting records in a single county—"to say nothing of preparation for trial and the almost inevitable appeal." Furthermore, he explained: "The story of Selma illustrates a good deal more than voting discrimination and litigating delay. It also illustrates another obstacle, sometimes more subtle, certainly more damaging. I am talking about fear."

Consequently, four Justice Department intimidation suits against Sheriff Clark and local officials had brought only continuing delay and defiance. Those were in addition to the Kennedy-Johnson administration's first vot-

ing rights suit, which was filed on April 13, 1961. Katzenbach complained
that the case had taken thirteen months to come to trial, and after another
six months, the U.S. district court handed down a decision in which it
ruled that the previous voter registrars had indeed discriminated against
blacks; but it concluded that the current board of registrars was not responsible, so the judge refused to issue an injunction against discrimination.
The Justice Department appealed, and two and a half years after the suit
had originally been filed, the Court of Appeals for the Fifth Circuit reversed
the district court and ordered it to enter an injunction against discrimination. Katzenbach said the Justice Department urged the court of appeals to
direct the registrars to judge black voter applicants by the same standards
that had been applied to whites until the effects of past discrimination had
been removed. Though the court of appeals recognized that the requested
relief might be needed in some cases, Katzenbach said, it did not issue the
order.

Several months after this failure, the Justice Department reopened this
case based on more evidence of discrimination and won a decision on February 4, 1965, from the district court that enjoined the use of the county's
complicated literacy and knowledge-of-government tests and entered orders
intended to correct the delays. The four other cases were in various stages of
litigation and Katzenbach was not very hopeful about their results. There
was only "one conclusion that could be drawn" from the story of Selma, he
said: "The 15th Amendment expressly commanded that the right to vote
should not be denied or abridged because of race. It was ratified 95 years
ago. Yet, we are still forced to vindicate that right anew, in suit after suit,
in county after county."

Since there was very little disagreement on the severity of the problem
and the need for better enforcement of the laws, the debate again turned to
the question of referees versus registrars. Mitchell felt Little Rock, Oxford,
and Selma all showed that no matter who was in the White House, the
President had to uphold the law, even if he had to do so with the armed
forces. He remained committed to the idea of federal registrars with more
authority as an administrative means of obtaining compliance with the law.
Their advantage was that, being responsible to the President (rather than to
the courts, as was the case with referees), the registrars would reflect his
attitude and thus be more responsive to complaints.

Another benefit of registrars, Mitchell argued, was that, fearing the
sudden increase of a large number of voters, local politicians would try to
avoid arousing their enmity by moving first to get them on the books. "Yet
even with registrars, there remains the mystery of what will the resourceful
voter discrimination cohorts think up next to keep things tied up in the
courts?" To avoid the noncompliance problem, he said, any new legislation

had "to be subjected to every acid test" before it was sent to the President's desk for his signature.[9]

With activity increasing in Congress on voting proposals during the first two months of 1965, Mitchell and Rauh on February 4 led a meeting with Senators Paul Douglas of Illinois and Russell Long of Louisiana, the new majority whip, in considering responses to the brutal repression of blacks in Selma and elsewhere. In January, Mitchell had strenuously opposed Long's succeeding Humphrey as majority whip. That was political irony since Douglas supported Long and helped him get elected to that position.

Mitchell was to discover, as Douglas had predicted, that Long would become a valuable civil rights supporter. That evolution was already evident as Long was among a group of southern Democrats like fellow Louisianian Allen Ellender and Richard Russell who had adopted a pragmatic view toward civil rights and were calling for compliance with the 1964 act. Mitchell felt that Long, whom he found "affable and able," was like many young southern politicians who could see that by the time they reached middle age blacks would be a decisive factor in all aspects of the region's life. Those who controlled the political system wanted to minimize racial friction. Long was a populist whose views jibed perfectly with the goals of the Great Society and the basic economic philosophies of mainstream blacks. His strong advocacy of voting rights for blacks made him an even more crucial factor in this phase of the legislative struggle.

Long told the group that he could get voting referees appointed immediately in Louisiana if a suit was filed in the federal district court where a friendly judge was serving. He said that the judge in what he termed "my district" was his former law partner and that his request to the court had delayed a test of the civil rights law until after the election. He assured the group that this judge as well as another in a different part of the state would now respond favorably to a lawsuit. However, he was not sure whether the judge who sat in northern Louisiana would be as sympathetic.

The mention of an unsympathetic judge immediately shifted discussion to the question of voter registrars. Douglas and the others in the meeting were surprised that Long supported this idea, which previously all southerners had opposed. Under the plan Long outlined, the President would assign registrars to any county where 40 percent of black voters were not registered. Long said that that criterion would be especially helpful in counties where blacks outnumbered whites. He added that local sheriffs feared having blacks vote in such areas, but that they could be persuaded to let 40 percent register to keep out the federal government. He also felt that with such a large portion of blacks registered, local officials would be so eager to get their votes that the racial issue would be removed effectively from southern state politics.

Long explained that it was important to include state elections in any bill proposed. "In my state," he said, "it is important to have the sheriff behind you." If states were covered, the sheriff would have to appeal to the same voters on whom Long depended, and they included blacks. Otherwise, he said, the sheriff would feel he could get elected with the Ku Klux Klan vote. He would thus continue opposing registration of blacks and any candidate for federal office who advocated an end to voter discrimination. The group welcomed Long's observations and looked forward to his help in the coming battle.

The Selma-to-Montgomery march aroused national sympathy with rare fury. As Bull Connor had done in Birmingham for the 1964 Civil Rights Act, so did Jim Clark in Selma do for voting rights. Impelled by the outrage, Johnson recommended to Congress new legislation to enforce the Fifteenth Amendment. [10]

From his seat in the House gallery, Mitchell watched with immense pride as Johnson delivered his extraordinary voting rights message to a joint session of Congress on the constitutional rights guaranteed by the First, Fourteenth, and Fifteenth amendments. Johnson declared that there could be no argument over whether every American must have an equal right to vote. There was no duty that weighed more "heavily on us than the duty to ensure that right." There were no constitutional or moral issues involved here, he said. It was "wrong—deadly wrong—to deny any of your fellow Americans the right to vote in this country." He called on Congress to pass the bill he was offering. Even then, he said, the battle would not be over. Selma was part of a far larger movement that reached into every section and state of the country. The struggle by blacks for the vote best symbolized their struggle for the full blessings of American life. "Their cause must be our cause too, because it is not just Negroes but really it is all of us, who must overcome the crippling legacy of bigotry and injustice." His ringing conclusion—"And we shall overcome"—was a triumphant embrace of the civil rights cause. Few missed the historical significance.

Mitchell was never subject to hero worship, but following Johnson's speech he came close to it. He was filled with immense pride as Johnson faced the justices of the Supreme Court, the members of the Cabinet, the entire Senate and House. To his left "sat the ambassadors and representatives of most of the civilized people on the face of the earth." To an NAACP audience in Longview, Texas, Mitchell explained: "To me, this was a moment of enormous significance. President Lyndon Johnson, a product of the South, as the Chief Executive of the richest and most powerful nation in the world, was delivering a speech which, in addition to lighting the flame of hope at home, could also inspire the white, black, yellow and the brown men from distant lands—some of whom only recently have thrown off the yoke of colonial oppression. Yet it would not have been possible for President Johnson to hold this high office or receive such enthusiastic backing from the Congress of the United States if it had not been for men and women like you. As the frontline workers for freedom, you have labored successfully to build a moral, social and political climate which makes it possible to elect a President and a Congress dedicated to protect the rights of all Americans." Mitchell suggested that Johnson's journey to the White House had begun on the day that blacks were permitted to participate in the electoral process. (Johnson was first elected to the Congress in 1937, when an increasing number of black and Spanish-speaking voters were changing the racial and ethnic composition of his district. This change was accelerated in 1944 when the NAACP won its lawsuit [*Smith* v. *Allwright*] striking down the Texas white primary.)[11]

As the struggle over legislation picked up speed, Mitchell predicted before a National Workshop for Religious Liberals in Washington quick passage of the 1965 Voting Rights Act. He saw no problem in the House and figured there would probably be a filibuster in the Senate, "but I expect it will fizzle." A good reason was that several southern senators had indicated to him that they wanted the bill to pass. He refused to reveal the senators' names "for fear of getting them in trouble with their constituents."

Not surprisingly, there were still several hurdles ahead even before the battle in Congress was fully under way. A serious one for Mitchell was "the desire of some organizations and persons to make a record of producing the bill." One obvious complicating factor was criteria for voting rights legislation outlined by the southern contingent composed of Farmer, Forman, King, and Lawrence Guyot of the MFDP. With the 1957, 1960, and 1964 voting rights provisions in mind, they declared that it was their duty and responsibility "to militate against any manoever [*sic*] that would dissipate our energies by tokenism of still another fraudulently ineffectual piece of legislation."

Adding salt to Mitchell's wounds, they declared that it was "the Civil Rights Movement"—composed of SNCC and CORE and guided by King—that had produced the current "groundswell of opinion" that could be channeled to action that would "lay to rest the national disgrace of citizens without votes." Their major objection was to getting new legislation that would cover only so-called hard-core areas arbitrarily "based on quotas." They were particularly concerned about rumors that the administration's legislation would apply only where registration of blacks was less than 15 percent of blacks eligible to vote. (See Appendix 2 for an explanation by Lee C. White, White House counsel, of the history of this idea.)

The Justice Department maintained that this belief was erroneous. Under the criteria it was considering, enforcement of the law would be triggered by a specified percentage of abuse in states or counties having literacy tests. Where abuse was found, literacy tests would be suspended and federal examiners would be authorized to act for as long as ten years.

Justice's position was that SCLC, SNCC, and CORE particularly favored voting rights bills that had been introduced in the House by Republican John Lindsay and Democrat Joseph Resnick, both of New York. The Lindsay bill would revise extant voting rights laws that gave federal district court judges responsibility for enforcing the law and provide a forty-day limit on the time required for the finding of a pattern of discrimination. If the court failed to meet that deadline, it would be required to appoint federal registrars. The Resnick bill provided for a six-man commission appointed by the President to determine the existence of a pattern of discrimination and to use the full power of the Fifteenth Amendment, facilitated by various procedures, to end such abuses. The Justice Department, however, felt that its contemplated proposal was stronger than the Lindsay bill, and that the Resnick measure raised serious constitutional problems.

The administration bill was sweeping, even though it did not contain an outright ban on the poll tax. It applied to every kind of election, federal, state, and local, including primaries. Its main focus was dealing with the two principal means of frustrating the Fifteenth Amendment: the use of offensive, vague, unfair tests and devices that were designed to disfranchise blacks, and the discriminatory use of the various registration requirements. The bill outlawed these tests under certain circumstances and ensured the fair administration of the registration system by giving federal examiners control of the process where necessary. The bill covered the six southern states and several counties and electoral subdivisions of other states where voting discrimination was most blatant. It barred all restrictions on voting other than age, residence, conviction of a felony without subsequent pardon, or mental incompetence. Most important, the bill invested the executive branch with primary responsibility for enforcing the law and provided civil and stiff criminal penalties for violations.[12]

This was merely a preliminary skirmish that served to alert the various sides to representative views and anxieties and excited discussion of the most effective approaches to the problem. Unfortunately, the views of SNCC, CORE, and SCLC were based on inaccurate rumors or faulty intelligence. Lacking a comprehensive perspective of the potential obstacles in Congress and of the viewpoints that were influencing the structuring of the administration bill, the expressed concerns of SNCC, CORE, and SCLC were more emotional than reasoned. Furthermore, as Mitchell knew so well, "you only get what you have the votes to get." The tricky terrain on which everyone was moving was revealed when Congressman Emanuel Celler "inadvertently" dropped on the House floor, thus making it public, a letter from King urging him not to oppose the poll tax.

Looking back, Mitchell explained, "These were people who had good intentions but were difficult to work with." History vindicated his instincts "not to get into picayune fights." The problem at the time was how to establish a "trigger" to get examiners appointed in areas with low or nonexistent black voter registration, and to determine the length of their terms. Could the terms be in perpetuity or should they be limited to off periods in the years? [13]

Despite their irritation with the southern contingent's attitude, Mitchell told one audience, there was agreement "in the civil rights councils" on certain ideas that kept everyone moving in the same direction. The first was that first-class citizenship was nonnegotiable. He felt that the objectives of the "Freedom Now" goal proclaimed by the demonstrators in the South were so dear to the hearts of civil rights supporters that it was "no exaggeration to say that our nation faces a choice of achieving results in a rapid and orderly manner or by a massive test of strength in the streets of the cities or the swamps and roadways of rural areas." He believed most people wanted the former and that the results could be obtained by the lawful use of the Constitution and federal statutes.

The second wide area of agreement concerned the implementation and eventual strengthening of the 1964 Civil Rights Act on the basis of experience. The third involved the right to vote. That meant getting a strong bill passed in the first session of the Eighty-ninth Congress. But, he stressed in establishing his basic fighting position, no bill could do the job unless it outlawed poll taxes in state and local elections and gave full protection against violence in areas where discrimination was most acute. [14]

During a February 24 meeting of the Vice President and the attorney general with members of the House's liberal Democratic Study Group, who had visited Selma, the consensus was that no specific bill would be endorsed. Instead, emphasis would be placed on the registrar proposal and the elimination of literacy tests. Pohlhaus, who represented Mitchell at the meeting, thought the highlight was the appearance of the chairman of the House Judiciary Committee. Celler said he expected the President to deliver his message to Congress soon. Celler leaned heavily toward President Kennedy's earlier 15 percent registration proposal plus the elimination of the poll tax in state elections by statute and "some beginning" on enforcing the equal protection clause of the Fourteenth Amendment. He assured the group that he would be willing to fight for complete elimination of the literacy test. Wilkins, in a subsequent meeting with the President, urged him to include in his recommendation provisions for federal voting registrars as well as abolition of literacy tests in both local and federal elections.

During a subsequent March 11 meeting at the Justice Department, Mitchell learned that the administration was incorporating the "trigger" idea in its proposal. This would enable the attorney general to certify, based on census data, that there had been a denial of the right to vote. Registrars could then be appointed, but local governments or states could appeal to the Civil Rights Commission and ultimately to the courts. Differing with the civil rights forces, Justice would continue poll taxes but authorize voting registrars to collect them for the state. Justice would also continue literacy tests in areas not affected by voting discrimination. Literacy criteria, however, would be established for areas where a pattern of discrimination was evident. Finally, Justice planned to propose a ten-year cutoff date for the law of 1975.[15]

These proposals were encouraging but not all satisfactory to the LCCR. To ensure that the administration bill was suitable, Mitchell, Rauh, and Pohlhaus joined a bipartisan Senate group in developing a model bill. The group worked in informal sessions after long committee meetings, at night and sometimes on Sundays. Then, on March 15, Senators Douglas and Clifford Case, the principal sponsors, * introduced S. 1517.

The Justice Department, which had been working with the bipartisan Senate leadership on the administration bill, agreed to incorporate many features of the Douglas-Case bill in its proposal, but Mitchell was unable to get the administration to include a ban against the poll tax in its bill (S. 1564). Eager to appear cooperative with the Johnson administration, Mitchell told Wilkins that his report on these differences was not provided "in a spirit of criticism but only to indicate that there were honest differences of opinion in regard to coverage." One good reason for his calm was his confidence that a substantial majority of the House and Senate favored expansion of the administration bills rather than restricting it. Still, to be certain, he felt he had to poll all possible supporters in the House and Senate before determining how solid that backing was.

His confidence was also based on the knowledge that he had available "the same fine all-out support" that had been marshaled in 1964 from among NAACP members and LCCR allies. He was confident "that in all of the great events that are helping to erase the stain of racial bigotry, the forces of freedom are drawn from all races, all religious faiths and all economic groups that compose the population of the United States." Owing to

---

*The other sponsors were Joseph Clark, John Sherman Cooper, Hiram L. Fong (R-Hawaii), Philip Hart, Jacob Javits, Pat McNamara (D-Mich.), William Proxmire (D-Wisc.), and Hugh Scott.

the intensity of public opinion demanding action, the legislation was moving through Congress on its own momentum.

Mitchell believed that the administration bill would give federal officials essentially the same powers and impose on them the same obligations that state officials had when the Fifteenth Amendment was adopted in 1870. But, as Wilkins told the House Judiciary Subcommittee No. 5, although it went "further than any other bill ever introduced on this subject," it still was "not enough."

On behalf of the Leadership Conference, Mitchell offered strengthening additions in order to eliminate the poll tax in state and local elections; remove a requirement in the bill that a person wanting to register must first be considered by a state official before enlisting the help of a federal registrar or examiner; extend coverage of the registrar or or examiner provisions of the bill so that persons who had been wrongfully denied the right to vote, regardless of their location, would be covered by the bill; and extend to the maximum protection of voters from all economic and physical abuse.

Predictably, the subcommittee quickly approved the NAACP strengthening amendments. Although he would later change positions and offer a much weaker measure, McCulloch, ranking Republican on the Judiciary Committee, joined Celler in strongly supporting the bill. It had also been endorsed by two southerners Mitchell admired, Congressman Brooks Hays and Pepper. Hays explained that "it's because I love the South" that he wanted to see the voting doors opened. He said he believed that the South would be happier if they were. Several other provisions were added to the House bill (H.R. 6400), most of which Mitchell felt were improvements. He was confident the harmful ones would be removed on the House floor. Soon, however, the poll tax provision would flare as the big bone of contention with the Justice Department.[16]

The bill's seemingly pro forma progress was marked by other differences from previous congressional battles. Unlike the past three times that Congress passed a civil rights bill based on stronger House versions, the voting rights bill now was being pushed simultaneously in both houses. This procedure indicated the extent of confidence about its success.

In the Senate, Eastland was playing his usual games with the administration bill. It had been sent to the Judiciary Committee on March 18 by 25 Republicans and 42 Democrats, with instructions to report it no later than April 9. Opposing that move were 11 southern Democrats and 2 Republicans. Five southern Democrats and 2 southern Republicans voted

for the motion, which was similar to that which had been used in 1960.*
To no one's surprise, Wayne Morse raised no objections. (In addition to
1957 and 1960, the Senate also used the bypass procedure in 1962 for the
poll tax amendment.)

Outflanked, Eastland gave most of the hearing time on the bill to hostile witnesses, emphasizing his resourcefulness in obstructing civil rights
legislation. As the Leadership Conference had done in the House, Mitchell
requested that the Senate Judiciary Committee permit the civil rights
forces to consolidate their testimony. The response was that the committee
would have had to ask for more time to consider the bill. Not wanting to
be accused of causing this delay, Mitchell submitted the testimony that
Wilkins and Rauh had presented to the House committee.

Mitchell was very grateful that a group of nine liberal members† on the
Senate Judiciary Committee defeated five opponents in voting to include in
the bill the poll tax and other strengthening features that had been included in the House committee. This victory as well as that in the House
Judiciary Subcommittee No. 5, which similarly approved bills that were
substantially stronger than the administration bill, ended Mitchell's honeymoon with the Katzenbach Justice Department. Both committee versions
had features that abolished poll taxes in state and local as well as federal
elections, authorized poll watchers to ensure that voters were allowed to
vote and that their ballots were counted, and made private citizens as well
as state and local officials criminally liable for interfering with voting rights
guaranteed by the bill. The bills suspended literacy tests or similar
qualification practices in all eighteen states where they were being used.
The Senate then voted to take up the bill on April 21 following the Easter
recess. Unlike 1964, the southerners did not debate the motion to bring up
the bill—an indication of the invincibility of the voting principle.[17]

It bothered Mitchell very much that while the poll tax was no longer
required to vote against Eastland in a senatorial election, it was still a
prerequisite for voters who opposed Sheriff Jim Clark. He believed that the
constitutional amendment banning the poll tax had played an important
role in 1964 in removing that barrier to blacks in federal elections and
wanted to see similar progress in state and local contests. That the issue
was still a burning one could be seen in the history of the anti-poll-tax
struggle. Prior to adoption of the poll tax amendment, federal legislation

---

* The two Republicans who opposed the motion were Margaret Chase Smith of Maine and Strom
Thurmond of South Carolina. The southern Democrats supporting the move were J. William Fulbright
of Arkansas, Fred R. Harris of Oklahoma, Ross Bass and Albert Gore of Tennessee, and Yarborough;
the Republicans were John Cooper and Thruston Morton, both of Kentucky.
† The senators were Democrats Birch Bayh of Indiana, Quentin N. Burdick of North Dakota, Philip
Hart of Michigan, Edward M. Kennedy of Massachusetts, Edward V. Long of Missouri, and Joseph
Tydings of Maryland, and Republicans Fong, Javits, and Scott.

to eliminate it, either by constitutional amendment or statute, had been introduced in every Congress since 1939. The House of Representatives passed anti-poll-tax bills on five occasions and the Senate twice proposed constitutional amendments. The problem was that elections in the South were numerous. Someone was always running for sheriff, judge, tax collector, dog catcher, and other minor offices. Those positions were not important in places like New York, but they were in the South.

As Russell Long had explained, the sheriff was more powerful than the governor or the President in some rural southern counties because he could amass a modest personal fortune in fees in addition to his salary. Many sheriffs would protect their jobs by any means to keep the voter rolls small. Unlike someone like Eastland, the sheriff was an ever present factor in the life of local residents, so the poll tax was often a life-and-death matter for blacks. This was the realization driving Mitchell.

He believed that although many people, including President Johnson, regarded the poll tax as a nuisance, they wanted to avoid settling the issue by statute because of their previous insistence that the problem could be solved by the constitutional amendment. Johnson was not openly or actively opposing the statute, but Mitchell suspected that the Justice Department was sensitive to his previous positions. Mitchell realized that had Johnson departed from his earlier position and supported abolition of the poll tax by statute, he would have embarrassed his moderate southern friends. And they were very helpful in achieving cloture. So Johnson's strategy worked.

Mitchell maintained that many "high sounding constitutional arguments" were being offered against a statute covering state and local elections, "but most realists will admit that the main argument against including a poll tax repealer in the new bill is political rather than legal."

Mitchell was encouraged that Katzenbach had been "willing to listen and counsel with us on the bill" despite his vigorous opposition to the poll tax statute. As Celler seemed about to give in to Katzenbach's objections to include the poll tax ban in the bill, Mitchell appealed to him and won his agreement to let the subcommittee decide the issue. That decision, for which he was very grateful, "enabled us to get sufficient support to have the amendment approved."[18]

The day after the Senate reconvened, Mitchell wrote Johnson urging him to intervene because there was a grave danger that the voting rights bill would be seriously defective in the four states (Alabama, Mississippi, Texas, and Virginia) that still had poll tax requirements for voting. He was clearly alarmed that supporters of the legislation who began meeting behind the scenes in the Senate to resolve controversial issues would buy the Justice Department's arguments. He told Johnson that the attorney general was insisting that there was a risk the Supreme Court would declare an anti-poll-tax provision unconstitutional. Mitchell, of course, felt otherwise. Johnson remained publicly noncommittal on his approach to the poll tax.

Mitchell did not mention it then, but on another occasion he noted as an example of the provision's constitutionality that the Supreme Court held in *Harman* v. *Forssenius* that Virginia's "poll tax was born of a desire to disenfranchise the Negro"—a clear violation of the Fifteenth Amendment. During the 1902 Virginia constitutional convention, the Court explained, the sponsor of the suffrage plan containing the poll tax as a central feature expressly stated its intention:

> Discrimination! Why, that is precisely what we propose; that, exactly, is what this convention was elected for—to discriminate to the very extremity of permissible action under the limitations of the Federal Constitution, with a view to the elimination of every Negro voter who can be gotten rid of, legally, without impairing the numerical strength of the white electorate.

Mitchell was aware that four other southern states that enacted the poll tax in this period did so to bar blacks as well as poor whites from the franchise. He felt that he was on solid ground when he told Johnson that many "outstanding lawyers in and out of Congress" did not agree with the attorney general. He noted that the Senate Judiciary Committee and House Subcommittee No. 5 had included the anti-poll-tax provision in pending bills. "Only this morning I talked with a highly respected senior member of the House who comes from the so-called Deep South." He said the anti-poll-tax provision was "absolutely essential" if "the necessary" job was to be done. He further explained that "although I admire and respect the Attorney General for his many good works and great contributions to human rights, I must say that he and other administration representatives seem to be working overtime to extirpate the anti-poll-tax provision from the [committee bills]." He therefore asked Johnson to take whatever action he deemed appropriate to ensure that the provision was retained. Expressing regret for adding to Johnson's "numerous other problems," Mitchell explained that, unlike the 1964 battle, "I have not been given an opportunity to make an informal presentation to you in person."

Mitchell issued a press release announcing that he had asked the President to intervene in the dispute. While not releasing the text of his letter before it had reached the President's desk, he explained, his public announcement was meant to ensure that the letter would not "be buried under other mail" and thus would reach its destination. He said that the letter had been "prompted by a startling accumulation of evidence that some individuals in and outside of government are working overtime to raise a dubious constitutional question against outlawing the poll tax by statute."

Noting, among other things, editorials in *The Washington Post* and an article in *The New Republic,* Mitchell said he was "especially disgusted" that opposition was coming from some intellectuals who were "always for the rights of Negroes in theory, but somehow seem to desert the ranks on implementation." That had happened in 1957, 1960, and 1964, he said, "and I am completely fed up with those who march under the civil rights banner at parade time, but give help to the opposition by making obfuscating comments when the real fight begins." Throughout this battle, he continued to feel that "some of the worst troubles were coming from those who were supposed to be on our side," and wished that "these liberals would shut up for a while."

Mitchell also had in mind the attempt by friends outside Congress to get the NAACP to abandon demands for keeping Title VI in the 1964 civil rights bill. Charges that the NAACP was rocking the boat notwithstanding, he was adamant "that we have set our course in this and we shall have a bill that ends the shameful practice of charging the people of Virginia, Texas, Mississippi and Alabama hard cash for the right to vote."

While not responding as directly to Mitchell's personal appeal as he did to a reporter's question on this issue in a subsequent news conference, Johnson made clear that he remained strongly opposed to the poll tax. As to whether it should be banned by statute or by a constitutional amendment, he felt that that was a decision for Congress to make. He instructed Katzenbach to meet with lawmakers interested in this subject in order to make sure that the poll tax was eliminated by constitutional means.

Despite the standoff, the administration believed that the "Leadership Conference people" were "at least partially persuaded to consider revised language in the legislation." The clear implication in a memorandum from Lawrence O'Brien to the President in preparation for a meeting with Martin Luther King was that it was easier to work with the Leadership Conference. Unlike written protests from Mitchell and Wilkins, who also appealed for the President's help, King now threatened to demonstrate in support of the poll tax provision. How much revision the Leadership Conference would accept was the big question.[19]

As debate in the Senate entered its third week, focus centered on a substitute bill introduced jointly by Mike Mansfield and Everett Dirksen that omitted the poll tax and other provisions that had been added to the administration measure in the Judiciary Committee. Dirksen, who no doubt had felt a pride of authorship in the administration bill, seemed to have been angered by the liberals' amendments and was determined to block those features. Liberals, at the same time, were pinning their hopes on an anti-poll-tax amendment that had been offered by Massachusetts Democrat Edward Kennedy. This effort failed on May 11 when the Senate by 45 to 49 rejected the Kennedy amendment. Mitchell found Ted Kennedy to be more supportive than his brothers of civil rights legislation and welcomed his participation. Helping to tip the vote was a letter opposing the amendment from Katzenbach, which Mansfield read to the Senate. Katzenbach said the amendment would only present "constitutional risks" to the voting rights bill because it was not clear whether Congress had the power to legislate such a ban.

Mitchell and others favoring the stronger bill were given some hope for possible success the following day when the House Judiciary Committee reported out its comprehensive amended version. House Speaker McCormack provided further encouragement by promising that the lower chamber would adopt an outright poll tax ban. Mitchell knew that the final outcome would depend on the product from the Senate, so he angrily criticized developments there.

Anyone who knew the facts he said, also realized that the "Kennedy amendment was defeated by small-minded considerations on the part of northern and western senators rather than by noble constitutional arguments from the South." Perhaps, he said, the most statesmanlike statement on the day of the vote was made by Russell Long, identified with the segregation wing of the Democratic party for all of his political life in Washington. Long urged passage of the Kennedy amendment because the poll tax was used to discriminate against all poor people who wanted to vote regardless of race. Mitchell thought it ironic that as Long was voting for the amendment, senators from Indiana, Kentucky, Minnesota, and Vermont were helping to defeat it.

He explained:

> Senator Long's action is the kind of realism that all of us must use. I presume he has not changed his views of racial segregation, but he knew that the poll tax promotes corruption. He knew that those who introduced it in the South intended to use it to suppress poor whites as well as colored people. He had the courage to vote for the interests of the poor people, even though some of his political enemies might accuse him of being soft on civil rights.

Mitchell rejected the Mansfield-Dirksen substitute bill as an "emasculated and makeshift version" of the voting rights measure. Its introduction, he said, meant that the President's noble objective was beginning "to take the shoddy form of a makeshift bill. The process of legislating by compromise has set in." He regarded the substitute as "combining the accelerator and the brake so that each time you step on the pedal to speed things up you automatically come to a halt."

He conceded that the compromise would permit the use of federal registrars in enrolling African Americans in Alabama, but charged that it would also permit the state to escape coverage almost immediately by pretending that it had stopped discriminating. He told the black citizens of Mississippi that Congress thought it was terrible they had to pay a poll tax to vote and yet neatly passed the buck on who should correct the injustice, ultimately to the Supreme Court (which Dirksen was attacking because its recent reapportionment decisions improved democracy by correcting population imbalances in congressional representation). And he was revealingly silent on protection for civil rights workers in the South.

It bothered Mitchell that Dirksen, with Mansfield's cooperation, more than in 1964 was dictating the scope of the legislation as the southerners helped with a filibuster. Mitchell demanded to know who won the election in November. "Apparently there are officials in the executive branch of Government who believe that in spite of what the record may show, it was Senator Dirksen who became the chief executive—at least in the area of civil rights legislation," he declared. That group, he said, which included tacticians planning passage of the voting rights legislation, insisted that notwithstanding the pledges of the President, Dirksen had to have the final word on the bill. "They do not bother to count how many votes are available for a position on its merits. All they ask is, will Senator Dirksen give it his approval." Owing to this attitude, he said, much time was spent "in a fratricidal struggle between those who have the same objective" of relieving the untenable situation in the South.

He charged that those insisting the bill must be drawn to Dirksen's specifications believed that the southerners still had the power to stage a successful filibuster. The first fallacy of that view, he explained, could be seen in the health charts. While he did not take "pleasure from the illness or indisposition of senators," he said, more than in 1964 "most of the filibuster generals are too old, too sick and too tired to talk for more than three or four weeks at the most." That reality especially included Russell, who was too sick to lead the filibuster. He felt that without their leader, southern Democrats were "not really very formidable."

The "second factor overlooked by the Dirksen civil rights wing," he said, was that the national political climate was very different from that of 1964. Then, it had only been possible to guess about the voters' feelings on civil rights. Now it was clear the nation favored an enlightened approach. "All of this should mean that the views of Senators Jacob Javits, Philip Hart, Paul Douglas, Clifford Case, Hugh Scott and others like them should be decisive in determining the contents of the 1965 Voting Rights bill. Advice, cooperation and leadership from Senator Dirksen are of great value, but they should not outweigh these same factors on the liberal side of the Senate scale."[20]

Mitchell's complaints were to no avail. The Senate merely accepted an amendment, sponsored by the bipartisan leadership, to the Mansfield-Dirksen bill that was a congressional declaration that poll taxes infringed on the constitutional rights to vote. Other changes brought the substitute bill closer to the Kennedy amendment, but the Senate still avoided an outright ban on the poll tax. Another significant amendment provided for the assignment of poll watchers in areas covered by the bill.

Even though supporters of a stronger bill were confident they would win because they had been so successful in the House, they were unable to get their wish. The final stage of the Senate debate lacked the high drama of 1964. There were no impassioned speeches or determined shows of resistance from the southerners, only subdued protests. Once more it was evident the right to vote was too powerful an issue for even the southerners to resist. For the second time in history in successive years, the Senate on May 25 voted 70 to 30 to end a filibuster on a civil rights bill. Democrats from five southern states voted for cloture. The following day the Senate passed the voting rights bill 77 to 19 and sent it to the House.

There, Republicans backed away from a very weak substitute bill that was being pushed by McCulloch and Gerald R. Ford of Michigan, the new minority leader—with Dirksen's support—because they did not want to appear to be supporting the southerners in defeating the stronger bill. With Howard Smith's wings clipped by a new rule that had been adopted in January for the House Rules Committee giving it twenty-one days to report out bills, the conservative Virginian was no longer a significant problem. The House passed its bill on July 9 without too much difficulty. During the four days H.R. 6400 was debated in the House, the LCCR marshaled its forces of regular Washington representatives supplemented by out-of-towners to keep pressure on lawmakers. They employed their practiced vigilance from the gallery once more when the House was in the Committee of the Whole. The Congressional Hotel was again the operational nerve center.[21]

Because the bipartisan Senate leadership had the votes, Mitchell accepted the inevitable success of the Mansfield-Dirksen substitute as the House-Senate Conference Committee met to work out differences. To avoid much longer delays, the civil rights forces finally urged the House members to give up the demand for the stronger anti-poll-tax provision. Mitchell was satisfied that the Mansfield-Dirksen substitute had been strengthened enough to make it workable. Now he concentrated on getting the bill to apply to state as well as federal elections. He contended that that was a sound course because the 1957 act applied to both. It was a tribute to Brownell's legislative drafting skills, he recalled, that "many people were surprised to learn that they had passed a piece of legislation which applied to state as well as federal elections." Brownell scored that coup by making the legislation require the renumbering of existing codes of law so that the states would be automatically covered. Southern opponents, after discovering the law's comprehensive scope, refused to implement it fully. Mitchell knew that that weakness had to be remedied, and he felt the 1965 law achieved that goal.

As finally approved by Congress, S. 1564—the Voting Rights Act of 1965—based on a trigger to activate the law, suspended the use of literacy tests or similar voter qualification devices in Alabama, Georgia, Louisiana, Mississippi, South Carolina, Virginia, and thirty-nine counties of North Carolina, and authorized the appointment of federal voting examiners (or registrars) in those areas. It required that all laws affecting voting passed by those states or counties be approved by the U.S. attorney general or the U.S. District Court for the District of Columbia before they could become effective. The act contained the declaration that state poll taxes discriminated against the right to vote and directed the attorney general "forthwith" to begin court proceedings against those requirements. So, concluded Mitchell, "after five years of shameful events that increased tensions at home and caused embarrassment abroad, Congress finally gave a remedy it could have given in 1960." In effect, Mitchell never got all he wanted, but he had considerably influenced the results. The legislative process in civil rights was incremental and he had helped the nation to move that much closer to fulfilling its constitutional ideals.

Two days before signing the bill into law on August 6, Johnson paid a surprise visit to the Capitol, where he praised Mansfield and Dirksen for their "patriotic cooperation" in getting the bill passed. Mitchell, as he had been with Humphrey in the crucial biennial fight in January to modify the filibuster, was much more sympathetic toward the President for his noncommittal stance on the poll tax. Johnson warmly praised both the Senate and the House when each passed its bill.[22]

Subsequently, Katzenbach explained that his opposition to the poll tax was based on legal, not political, grounds. "I was absolutely persuaded that we would get rid of the poll tax faster by a decision of the Supreme Court than we would have if we included the provision." He was aware that a case involving the poll tax was up before the Supreme Court at that time, and, "so far as you could read tea leaves, I was persuaded that the court would hold it unconstitutional." He also believed that if Congress enacted the anti-poll-tax bill, the Court would not have abolished it, but instead waited for the statute to become effective. "I never had any doubt at all that Congress had a right to do this. But I didn't want to put that poll tax off for a year." He told Ted Kennedy, "Go ahead" and introduce the poll tax bill. "If it does you some good in Massachusetts, go ahead. I have the votes to beat you." Whether or not Kennedy's action won points at home is a question, but he certainly won Mitchell's admiration.

Afterward, Mitchell was especially conciliatory toward Katzenbach, believing that the attorney general's intentions had been honorable. The Supreme Court's subsequent rulings on the poll tax confirmed his belief in Katzenbach's sincerity. In the inevitable case testing the constitutionality of the Voting Rights Act, Katzenbach explained that "South Carolina helped me out considerably by asking the Supreme Court to take original jurisdiction." He "couldn't have been more ecstatic since we got the constitutionality of the act settled in very near record time."[23]

Toward the end of 1965 when the Justice Department scored a historic breakthrough by getting an all-white Alabama jury to convict three Ku Klux Klan members for the murder of Viola Gregg Liuzzo, Mitchell was beside himself in praise of Katzenbach and John Doar, assistant attorney general, for their diligent prosecution of the case. The convictions were under the 1870 law prohibiting conspiracy to deprive citizens of their civil rights. Mrs. Liuzzo, a white member of the Detroit NAACP branch participating in the Selma-to-Montgomery march, was shot to death March 25. Two state juries in Lowndes County, where Mrs. Liuzzo was killed, had failed to convict one of the men for murder. The first trial ended in a hung jury and the second in acquittal. In a despicable crime such as that involving Mrs. Liuzzo, Mitchell said, it was difficult to express appropriate outrage. He could only say it was reassuring to see the United States working to enforce the laws and jurors courageously carrying out their duties.

Typical of his new statesmanship was his approach toward Katzenbach and Doar. "Like many other persons in the civil rights field, I have been unsparing in my criticism of them and there is a continuing possibility that I shall have more sharp words to say about them in the days ahead." He hoped, nevertheless, that he had not lost sight of "their personal qualities that make them dedicated public servants and men of genuine good will."[24]

A truly poignant moment in the struggle for the Voting Rights Act involved Mitchell's friend Clarence Brown. Early on the day the House Rules Committee voted to send the bill to the full House, Brown called Mitchell to let him know that he had left the hospital where he had almost died, in order to participate in that crucial step.

One bright morning, while visiting him in his small office in the Capitol, Mitchell was struck by the pleasant aroma of the old leather couch, the squeaky swivel chair, and Brown's businesslike friendliness. Upon conclusion of the conversation, Mitchell realized that that might well have been his way of saying good-bye. Since 1956, Brown had been an especially valuable ally to Mitchell because he was a midwestern conservative. Mitchell had won his friendship by appealing to his sense of decency and his desire to uphold the Constitution. Brown had to return to the hospital and Mitchell suspected he knew it would be for the last time. "We parted with a handshake and a chuckle from him as he gave the usual warning to 'look out for tricks.' It was my last picture of him. I shall always think of him with warmth and appreciation."[25]

CHAPTER TWENTY

Acclaimed the 101st Senator

August 6, 1965, was another high point for President Johnson as he signed the 1965 Voting Rights Act in the small, ornate President's Room of the Capitol, just off the Senate chamber. "Today is a triumph for freedom as huge as any victory won on any battlefield," he declared. There, 104 years earlier, President Lincoln had signed a bill freeing slaves who had been impressed into service by the Confederate Army.

Less obvious was that this was also the twentieth anniversary of Hiroshima. Unlike the atomic holocaust that ended the world's most destructive war in defense of Western democracy, the Voting Rights Act was a unique, peaceful step in fulfilling the promise of American citizenship. America, nevertheless, was still far from being at peace with itself even though, as Johnson noted, the new law removed the "last major shackle of those fierce and ancient bonds" from more than two million descendants of African slaves. "Today the Negro story and the American story fuse and blend."

Six days later the ferocity of the racial riots in the Watts section of Los Angeles—the worst since the bloody racial outburst in Detroit in 1943—stunned the nation with a warning that many more fundamental problems of citizenship were yet to be resolved. Johnson opened the gates for African Americans to enter the mainstream of citizenship, but many of the victims of oppression, more than ever, were impatient with the slow pace of progress and vented their emotions in an orgy of destruction. Devoid of the moral aura of the nonviolent demonstrators in the South, the riots fed volcanic hatreds and a white backlash that was at once ominous and destructive.

Watts was the Birmingham of the North; the pressure of urban poverty in that Los Angeles community was the catalyst, rather than any single personality. The resulting white backlash was much more intense and ominous than the reaction to the civil rights demonstrations. In those protests, despite strong opposition from the South, demands for constitutional rights couched in moral appeals awakened the conscience of much of the nation.

The burning and looting of property in the North was a different use of language that made blacks appear to be speaking out of turn, to be uppity and needlessly confrontational. The fact that the riots were another form of protest, though unorganized and deliberately destructive, recalled for many whites wild fears of slave revolts. These fears were reinforced by the strident rhetoric of the "black power" movement and the flourishing black nationalism. Additionally, as George Wallace was demonstrating, whites were beginning to feel that blacks had gotten too much from civil rights legislation, New Frontier, and Great Society social programs. The resulting massive intensification of white backlash would manifest itself in the 1966 elections in California, where Governor Edmund G. "Pat" Brown was expected to be reelected easily, but, joining Wallace in riding the backlash, with a political machine that was much slicker than Barry Goldwater's, onetime movie actor Ronald Reagan would capture the governor's mansion and begin nourishing presidential ambitions with far-right support. This victory of the Birchite posing as a moderate, the foe of the Tennessee Valley Authority, the progressive income tax, and the 1964 Civil Rights Act, would in time have enormous consequences for civil rights.

Americans in 1965 should not have been surprised by the intensity of black unrest, given earlier warnings in places like Cambridge, Maryland; Cleveland; and Harlem. But much of the nation was still asleep concerning the less obvious racism in the North—systemic patterns of inequality were evidenced by the de facto segregation of housing confined within urban ghettos, of stultifying school systems, and job discrimination, all of which sapped the human spirit. These problems were as deeply rooted, and often much more so, as the South's Jim Crow system.

The Watts riots dramatized the hopelessness of American urban life. Many people, however, felt that the end of the line had been reached on possible federal laws against discrimination. Mitchell believed there was much unfinished business remaining. The right of blacks to serve on state and federal juries was one such outstanding issue. Protecting blacks and civil rights workers against violence was another. Additionally, discrimination in housing remained a national sore.

But, Mitchell found, while most civil rights advocates agreed on legislation to protect the right to serve on juries and to protect individual safety, they did not believe it was possible to get an antidiscrimination housing law through Congress; this was the toughest, and the most sensitive, legislative issue. In contrast, voting was the easiest. It was the heart of the democratic concept and it cost the general citizenry nothing. Housing involved a significant economic factor. For most families, it was the largest investment, and the prospect of forced integration brought on the fear of plummeting real estate values. Housing also had immense social implications in that it was the foundation of a community. Proposed housing legislation was intrusive and to many people seemed to violate the sanctity of their home. It said that the government was going to force people of different races and backgrounds to live together. For those reasons, many proponents of a housing law believed it would be impossible to get past the enormous power of the real estate industry, as well as the local resistance (another form of white backlash) that would arise.

Many civil rights leaders felt that Johnson should issue an executive order that was more comprehensive than the one President Kennedy had issued on November 20, 1962, barring after that date discrimination in government-sponsored housing programs and federally insured mortgages. Mitchell, however, was strongly opposed. He felt that Congress should and could be made to pass legislation barring discrimination in housing. He thought Joseph Rauh was with him personally on that question, but, officially, the ADA was not. Along with the National Committee Against Discrimination in Housing, it preferred an executive order over legislation.[1]

To develop a consensus on the issue, Johnson convened a meeting in the White House Cabinet Room on March 18, 1966, with civil rights leaders and their activist allies.* Among other things, he reported that an effort was being made to increase considerably the national housing supply in order to meet current and future needs. The big question was whether the nation was going to continue building segregated dwellings. Could every American, he asked, live where he wanted provided he or she could afford the desired property?

Mitchell remained the lonely exception among the black leaders in believing that Congress could be made to pass fair housing legislation. Other black leaders demanded an executive order, but Johnson did not want to deal with the problem piecemeal. Like Mitchell, he preferred a national commitment rooted in law. A good client, he listened attentively as At-

*Martin Luther King, Jr., Whitney Young, John Lewis, A. Philip Randolph, Roy Wilkins, Floyd McKissick, Dorothy Height, Clarence Mitchell, Andrew Biemiller, David Brody, Joseph Rauh, and Senator Clinton Anderson.

torney General Nicholas Katzenbach counseled that the President did not have the authority to issue the broad order suggested. That advice raised the hackles among those who feared that the President was trying to trick them by taking the easy way out and avoiding responsibility for an executive order. That was not so at all. The times were certainly wrong for such sensitive civil rights legislation. Mitchell realized, however, that the black leaders failed to understand that Johnson prided himself in his working knowledge of the Congress and would not have proposed legislation unless there was a remote possibility he could win. Their distrust of a President who had done so much for civil rights caused a normally mild-mannered Vice President Humphrey to declare, "Well, there isn't going to be any executive order. You might as well make up your minds on that."

Mitchell got the impression that some of the civil rights leaders had closed their minds to congressional action. His concern was heightened by King's groping for a national program, which led him to embark on his war on slums and segregated housing in Chicago and to begin his denunciations of the Vietnam War, efforts that were undermining the NAACP's legislative struggle in Washington. Apart from staging the Selma march, King had done little to help get the Voting Rights Act through Congress. Mitchell did not mind that King was playing such a limited role in Washington, but he was bothered by the SCLC leader's disregard for the sensitivity of the lobbying process, as was evident from his call for "a massive economic withdrawal program" across the nation and "an economic boycott of Alabama products."

Mitchell thought the benefits of legislation over an executive order were so obvious that the question was not even debatable. He welcomed the prospect of the battle even though housing legislation might bog down in Congress. After defending Johnson at the meeting, he declared that as far as he was concerned, "when the President of the United States feels that we can go the route of legislation, I'm with the President." Subsequently, Johnson explained that he was not so sure he could win the struggle in Congress. But "he was wrong there. I felt we could win," said Mitchell. While discussing Dirksen's role, Johnson told Mitchell, "I was able to get the old man to support the Civil Rights bill in 1964, but I don't know what I can do with him this time." Johnson, nevertheless, threw all his energies into the battle and won over the minority leader.

After the group agreed that the administration would seek housing legislation, Johnson said, "Well, I'm going to whip the teacher on this one, and I don't want you fellows running off on me." Mitchell asked him what he meant. Johnson explained that, as a boy in Texas, he and some schoolmates decided they were going to whip a teacher whom they did not like. When Johnson grabbed the teacher, he turned only to discover all his friends running off over the hill, and the teacher was able to "whip the daylights" out of him instead. Mitchell promised Johnson he would not run off and leave him stranded with the housing bill.[2]

As the Civil Rights Commission had concluded in 1963, there was another problem still facing African Americans. The continuing failure to win indictments or convictions in the long series of civil-rights-related murders plus the common practice of southerners of excluding blacks from juries made the travesty of state and local criminal justice systems in the South all the more glaring. Unpunished murders included those of Medgar Evers, William Moore, the four girls in the Birmingham church, Jimmie Lee Jackson (a black Alabamian who was earlier killed in Marion, Alabama, by a trooper during another demonstration), and Vernon Dahmer. The murder of Army Colonel Lemuel A. Penn on a Georgia highway in July 1964 as he was returning home to Detroit further emphasized the need for the type of antilynching legislation the NAACP had been seeking since the 1920s and reinforced the association's campaign against the newer forms of clandestine civil rights violence such as bombings and assassinations. Even though the Justice Department won convictions for the Viola Gregg Liuzzo murder, a week later another all-white state jury acquitted three Selma businessmen of killing the Reverend James Reeb of Boston, also during the Selma voting rights demonstrations. Wilkins maintained, "So long as such crimes go unpunished, none of us, white or colored, can be assured of the rights guaranteed by the Constitution and by the great congressional enactments of recent years. Rights exercised in fear are not rights at all. To us it is both fitting and logical that Federal rights should as far as possible be protected in Federal courts."[3]

Thus for the NAACP, the period was one of accomplishment as well as challenge. While pressing to enforce the new laws, the NAACP began mobilizing its resources to reverse the cumulative effect of nearly a century of neglect of Section 5 of the Fourteenth and Section 2 of the Fifteenth amendments, which authorized Congress to enact appropriate legislation to enforce those protections. Mitchell called for an even stronger NAACP as he rallied support to close loopholes in existing civil rights laws, to strengthen others, and to ensure that they were enforced. He invited NAACP audiences to "keep in mind the fact that our organization does not bend the knee to any power or combination of powers except to the people who are its members. We stand before the committees of Congress, we enter the courts, we walk the picket lines and we mobilize for justice without any thought of restraint by big contributors or secret behind-the-scenes financial interests." He proclaimed that the NAACP was an instrument of the people and that its policies were shaped by the people. From a humble beginning, the association had grown into an operation with an annual budget of $1 million that soon must be increased to $5 million or $10 million to continue the fight against racial injustice.

He maintained that the job of building the "temple of freedom in the United States" was moving on schedule, but it was not complete. "In the area of legislation, we can and we must pass a federal law that will hit the pocketbooks of local segregationists who run such places as Lowndes County, Alabama, and Bogalusa, Louisiana. We have numerous federal laws that contain criminal penalties for dynamiting, intimidation and other forms of assault on those who seek their civil rights. The 1960 Civil Rights Act, for example, in dynamiting cases provides a penalty of up to ten years imprisonment and a ten thousand dollar fine. If death results from such violence, the penalty can be life imprisonment or even the death penalty if that is the recommendation of a jury."

Despite those and other laws, he noted, the bombings, the murders, and the mayhem continued. Juries in the South were "usually the escape hatch for civil rights violators." That weakness could be corrected, he said, if jurors knew it would cost them personally under an indemnification law when such crimes went unpunished. Compounding this problem were state and local law enforcement officers who refused to conduct investigations, prosecutors who failed to indict, and hostile judges.

He urged strengthening Title VII of the 1964 Civil Rights Act, the equal employment provision, and called for passage of the strong amendment to do so that was sponsored in the House by California Democrat Augustus F. Hawkins. He reiterated the need for the type of effective national legislation against discrimination in housing that Johnson was considering. "We must move," he said, "we must probe, we must win on a thousand fronts in a thousand communities. Almost all that we have done, almost all that we do now, and almost all that we or any other freedom seekers will do in the future rests on law."[4]

Those concerns were reinforced as Rauh and Frank Pohlhaus stepped up their research on remedies for civil rights violence. They realized that law enforcement was one of the most sensitive areas of federal and state relationships and that effective legislation there was much more difficult to perfect and enact than the 1964 and 1965 acts. The need for further federal action was therefore great and immediate, and the risks of failure too dangerous for the present situation to be left unaltered.

One of the most intractable problems was with some federal courts and juries in the South. However, most federal investigators, prosecutors, jurors, and judges, even in the South, were less subject to local racist influences and economic and social pressures than were their state counterparts. For example, had the federal court assumed jurisdiction, the jurors in the Emmett Till case would have been drawn from eight counties rather than only from Tallahatchie; and the murderers of Viola Gregg Liuzzo, from the beginning, would have faced jurors selected from twelve counties in Alabama rather than merely from Hayneville. There was also a strong belief within the Leadership Conference on Civil Rights that the assertion of Washington's authority in the area of personal security would enhance the administering of justice.

The Leadership Conference argued that the conditions demanding jury reform had been created by national neglect. Despite adoption of the Fourteenth Amendment and the Supreme Court's upholding, in Ex parte, *Virginia* in 1789, the statute making jury discrimination a criminal act, such exclusionary practices still were widespread and systemic in southern states.

Closing the law enforcement gap also had to include correcting weaknesses in the laws for prosecuting civil rights violations, mainly two post–Civil War statutes* that provided criminal penalties for racial violence by private persons and public officials. Truman's Committee on Civil Rights, in *To Secure These Rights,* and, more recently, the Civil Rights Commission's report on the administration of justice, called attention to those weaknesses. Unamended in any major form since their passage, those statutes were outdated and difficult to enforce.

Furthermore, as a result of Supreme Court decisions, notably in the *Screws* v. *United States* case where the convictions of a sheriff and two deputies for the brutal beating and murder of a man were reversed by the Court because their intent to violate their victims' constitutional rights of due process had not been shown, enforcement of the post–Civil War statutes was sporadic. Even had the convictions been upheld, the sheriff could not have been sentenced to more than one year in prison because violation by a law enforcement officer was a misdemeanor. The failure of the existing federal criminal civil rights laws, notably the post–Civil War statutes, where the Justice Department did use them, was best demonstrated by a report from the attorney general showing that for 1964, of 2,656 complaints, 27 grand jury presentations and 20 indictments, there was 1 conviction.

Provisions for a more aggressive use of the laws by the Justice Department were included in the criminal violations sections of the 1960 and 1965 acts. However, FBI Director J. Edgar Hoover remained reluctant to involve his agency in such cases.

In preparing their review, Rauh and Pohlhaus found considerable support for the following principles: the federal government's full constitutional authority should be mobilized to protect personal security of blacks and other civil rights workers; racial assaults should be made federal crimes; proposed federal legislation should be comprehensive and include both criminal and

* 18 U.S.C. 241 and 242, but also 243.

civil (injunctive and indemnification) relief; every device to ensure fairer jury panels that included blacks should be utilized; wherever possible, administrative processes should be used; a "Personal Security Act of 1966" proposed by the Leadership Conference should be strong enough to meet the need; and efforts should be redoubled to obtain full utilization of existing federal authority, including a greater presence in areas of racial unrest.[5]

Toward the end of 1965, as Mitchell hoped when he, Rauh, and Pohlhaus met with congressional staff members and executive branch lawyers to translate their consensus into legislation, Johnson adopted the Leadership Conference's goals as part of his administration's 1966 civil rights package. In his State of the Union Message, he proposed establishing firm requirements for nondiscriminatory selection of juries in federal and state courts and giving the attorney general the power necessary to enforce this law. He also proposed strengthening the authority of federal courts in trying cases involving criminal violations of civil rights.

The Justice Department had the main responsibility for developing the administration civil rights bill. Meanwhile, the Leadership Conference bill was introduced under the bipartisan sponsorship of Senators Douglas and Case. Mitchell expressed the belief of most civil rights groups that the Douglas-Case bill contained basically what was needed. Regarding the bill introduced by Maryland's Charles Mathias and eighteen House Republicans, he said that while it was not as comprehensive as the bipartisan measure, "it was a good faith effort to show support for civil rights legislation" and would help in rallying votes later on.

Mitchell welcomed the Leadership Conference's "frank and constructive" working relationship with the Justice Department. He did not mind that the administration waited until after the Easter recess to introduce its bill. That delay was prompted by the Justice Department's review of two decisions by the Supreme Court on March 28 in *United States* v. *Price* and *United States* v. *Guest,* both of which broadened previous interpretations of the post–Civil War statutes. The Court unanimously held that the federal government could try, on charges other than murder, persons it believed had participated in the slayings in Mississippi on June 21, 1964, of civil rights workers Andrew Goodman and Michael Henry Schwerner, both from New York, and James E. Chaney, from Mississippi, and also the killing of Lemuel Penn in Georgia as he was returning home to Washington after having completed special military training. Commenting on the actions of Cecil Ray Price, the deputy sheriff of Neshoba County in whose jail the three civil rights workers had been detained, the Court noted that after the three men were released at night, Price and seventeen other defendants allegedly intercepted them by car on Highway 19 near Philadelphia and soon afterward beat, shot, and killed them. Their bodies were discovered that August, buried under an earthen dam near Philadelphia, after a massive search by the FBI and U.S. sailors. The Court in *Price* declared for the first time that the federal government could punish individuals for interfering with the constitutional rights of citizens to travel from one state to another. Six justices further said in concurring opinions that Congress had the constitutional authority to pass broader laws against racial violence.[6]

During a meeting of black leaders at the White House, Mitchell explained the intricacies of the administration's legislative package and summarized their chances of passage. "He's our quarterback," Randolph said to Johnson. "We rely on Mr. Mitchell's judgment." Mitchell's abstinence from drink and smoke added to his growing legend. Calling him now "Clarence (Rock) Mitchell"—*Rock* standing for Rock of Gibraltar—*Jet* noted his fondness for growing roses at his Chesapeake Bay cottage for relaxation. Mitchell would later be acclaimed the "101st Senator," a tribute that only the crassly presumptuous could dream to inherit.

Johnson's housing legislation was more comprehensive than that proposed by those who favored an executive order. In his civil rights message on April 28, the President asked Congress to provide blacks and civil rights workers with the protection of more effective criminal statutes; to prohibit racial discrimination in the selection of federal juries and empower the attorney general to sue to end similar bias in state courts; to broaden the attorney general's authority to sue to end discrimination in public schools;* and to declare a national policy and create effective remedies against racial discrimination in the sale or rental of housing.

The request for broader authority for the attorney general in school desegregation cases was influenced by the intense battle over enforcement of Title VI of the 1964 Civil Rights Act. Under that law, the attorney general was authorized to file desegregation suits where local pressure or the poverty of individual complainants made private suits impossible. Yet the attorney general was still required to receive complaints from private citizens before he could act. Johnson proposed amending the 1964 Civil Rights Act to permit the attorney general to file suits on his own initiative. His second amendment would empower the attorney general to deal with interference against voluntary school desegregation in areas where the Office of Education was proceeding to implement the law without compulsion of court orders.

As expected, Johnson tied his housing discrimination proposal to his

*This provision had originally been proposed in 1959 by Emanuel Celler when the House Judiciary Committee considered the Civil Rights Act of 1960, but it was knocked out in final passage. A modified version was included in Title III of the 1964 Civil Rights Act, requiring the attorney general to receive a complaint from aggrieved individuals before filing suit and imposing other limitations.

broader Great Society program, which contained elements for ensuring equality of all citizens that were not technically within the civil rights area. It was self-evident, he said, that the problems with which the nation was struggling

> form a complicated chain of discrimination and lost opportunities. Employment is often dependent on education, education on neighborhood schools and housing, housing on income, and income on employment. We have learned by now the folly of looking for any single crucial link in the chain that binds the ghetto.
>
> All the links—poverty, lack of education, underemployment and now discrimination in housing—must be attacked together. If we are to include the Negro in our society, we must do more than give him the education he needs to obtain a job and a fair chance for useful work.

He noted that, acting under the Civil Rights Act of 1866 and the Fourteenth Amendment, the Supreme Court had invalidated state and local laws that were designed to discriminate against blacks. Various public housing acts and Kennedy's executive order were meant to increase opportunities in dwellings for more Americans, but those initiatives were inadequate. Executive Order 11063, for example, covered only FHA and VA mortgages issued after November 20, 1962, and federal housing programs. Johnson proposed that the federal antidiscrimination ban be extended to include all privately insured housing.[7]

Mitchell was oblivious to the strong national tide now rising against further civil rights legislation. He was certain that the Civil Rights Act of 1966 would pass if all who wanted to end housing discrimination got behind the President, "one of the most remarkable men of our times." He was often irritated with some liberals who remained distrustful of Johnson. Some people, he found, "were always going to be suspicious of everything, and we had some of them present" among the civil rights allies. He feared they were not reacting from the head but viscerally. He admitted to possessing a similar trait, but it worked in the other direction. "I think you certainly have a right to assume that a person is going to be fair if you know, in the long experience of relationships with him," that when he departs from his usual course he is sincere in his judgment.

Johnson, he said, worked for the cause of human rights and to translate his promises into concrete action. Based upon reaffirmations of this commitment he had received in the recent meeting with the President, Mitchell was confident that Johnson would "do his part to get the bill passed." Mitchell told an NAACP membership meeting that "in a democracy, no man, not even the President of the United States, can do the whole job by himself. The success of the President's program for full civil rights and the realization of our dreams for equal justice under constitutional law depend on all of us working in our areas of influence to accomplish these results." It was not enough, he said, for the President to be for strong civil rights legislation. "We cannot predict how long this fight will last, but whether it takes what is left of spring, the whole summer or the period right up to election day, we must insist that the Congress stay in session until this legislation is passed."8

In addition to passage of the administration bill, the NAACP sought inclusion of strengthening amendments to provide the following: an "automatic trigger" similar to the literacy test feature in the Voting Rights Act providing for federal examiners who, based on statistical information, would suspend discriminatory state jury qualification requirements when it was clear that blacks were not participating; amending Title VII of the 1964 Civil Rights Act to correct discrimination in state and local public employment practices that, among other things, resulted in all-white administration personnel in many criminal justice systems; an indemnification program for civil rights victims or their survivors; and a program supporting the administrative enforcement of civil rights laws to relieve private persons of the burden of filing complaints.

As he joined Mitchell in urging Congress to grant the attorney general the requested authority to combat discrimination in education, Wilkins told Subcommittee No. 5 of the House Judiciary Committee that it did little good to claim that complaints from individuals were confidential. Black leaders and parents were well known to racial terrorists, he said. A new approach was needed that would place initiative for filing desegregation suits with the Justice Department. Another reason, he said, for urging this provision was that Title VI of the 1964 act reached only programs and communities that accepted federal funds, while the Fourteenth Amendment covered all public schools and facilities. He stressed the importance of legislation by explaining that it was not until Congress passed a law that the nation had "an increase in voluntary compliance and rather noticeable change in the attitude of the people themselves." That progress contrasted with the previous defiance of Supreme Court orders, when people felt "they were not committing such a crime."

Wilkins said that housing discrimination was blatant, and that the best evidence was the residential pattern in growing inner-city ghettos, which were surrounded by rigidly segregated suburbs. Housing bias nullified gains made elsewhere in the fight against inequality. "Residential segregation means segregation in schools, playgrounds, health facilities, and all other aspects of our daily lives," he said. It had impaired opportunities opened by the fair employment laws. Moreover, it was "the most potent source of intergroup tension," which too often exploded in violence in communities like Cicero, Illinois; Levittown, Pennsylvania; and Watts. Wilkins strongly agreed with the McCone Commission Report on the Watts riot, which concluded that there was no alternative solution to implementing revolutionary attitudes "that will disturb some of our institutions."

Wilkins challenged proposals like the one to which the attorney general had agreed excluding the mythical "Mrs. Murphy's boarding house" from coverage because that would be an unnecessary compromise with principle. He said, "Once Congress recognizes that housing bias worked a harm to the national interest that it has power to prevent, it should do the job that needs to be done. It should not leave pockets of bias in the housing market." He stressed that breaking the vicious cycle confining blacks to second-class housing status could only be done by a total program, legislative and executive.

Wilkins stressed that the rights with which the NAACP was concerned were federal and rooted in the Constitution. That was one reason why the NAACP sought creation of a program to indemnify survivors of the victims racial violence like Vernon Dahmer of Hattiesburg, Mississippi. He died of burns and his wife and daughter were hospitalized with similar injuries received when night riders firebombed his home and grocery store on January 10, 1966, after he had placed a sign on his lawn announcing that he would collect and pay the poll taxes of local blacks. Because Mitchell felt that denial or abridgment of those rights by violence was a matter of federal concern, he opposed suggestions that all crime victims should be covered under the indemnification program. Usual crimes, unlike civil rights violations, he maintained, were primarily within the jurisdictions of local government. In sum, he said, the proposed legislation merely sought to achieve a brand of American justice to which Johnson had referred in his June 5, 1965, speech to the graduating class of Howard University. The President had asked, "For what is justice?"—and responded—"It is to fulfill the fair expectations of man. American justice is a very special thing. We have pursued it faithfully to the edge of our imperfections and we have failed to find it for the American Negro."[9]

Opponents were well prepared for attack when the administration introduced the sensitive housing bill in Congress. The first hint of trouble ahead came just before Johnson unveiled his legislative package. Following what Mitchell regarded as a "good faith," confidential meeting of several civil rights representatives with Ramsey Clark, deputy attorney general, Drew Pearson and Jack Anderson reported in their syndicated column details of the pending proposals that had been discussed. Mitchell charged that the Pearson-Anderson account deliberately distorted the jury reform and housing sections.

Now Senate Minority Leader Dirksen called the civil rights bill "absolutely unconstitutional," and said it bore no relation to interstate commerce as Katzenbach was arguing. North Carolina's Sam Ervin could not help but observe, "For the first time, we have a bill which proposed that other than southern oxen are to be gored." Even civil rights stalwart Jacob Javits was nervous, claiming that the provision "invited a bitter civil rights battle" that was unnecessary. He thought it would have been better had Johnson extended the executive order on housing.

Without any doubt, the housing title was a red flag. Unlike the 1964 and 1965 acts, which had a strong regional focus, housing was national legislation and something akin to *Guess Who's Coming to Dinner,* the movie about interracial love starring Sidney Poitier and Katharine Hepburn. Defending it, Attorney General Katzenbach said it was tied closely to interstate commerce because "the construction of homes and apartment buildings, the production and sale of building materials and home furnishings, the financing of construction and purchases all take place in or through channels of interstate commerce." He maintained that interstate commerce was "significantly affected by the sale of even single dwellings, multiplied many times in each community." Citing a 1942 case, he said the Supreme Court held that the Agricultural Adjustment Act, even as applied to a farmer with twenty-three acres of wheat, all of which was consumed on his farm, was a valid exercise of the interstate commerce power. He said the administration had decided to seek a housing discrimination law rather than extend the prohibition on discrimination in some federally financed dwellings because a legislative provision would place responsibility for enforcement on private lending institutions rather than on the courts.[10]

The political thicket posed a formidable barrier even though federal housing experts and others sympathetic to the President's goals felt the "fair housing" title would not affect residential patterns any time soon. *The Wall Street Journal* reported that the basic problem was economic. The Census Bureau figured the median black family income in 1964 at $3,724 a year, about half that of white families. Mitchell himself told the *Journal,* "The ordinary colored fellow just doesn't have the money to buy into the suburbs." The irascible Ervin too observed, "The largest slums and ghettos of which we hear so much are in states with fair housing laws, and no appreciable change in housing patterns ever followed this enactment." Yet cracking the housing barrier was more than a symbolic goal; the fair housing law was an essential complement to the other measures that were needed to end the national scourge of racism and assure full equality for all citizens.

In an attempt to lessen opposition, the administration agreed to the weakening of the housing title. This was done by an amendment that was offered in the House Judiciary Committee by Maryland Republican Charles Mathias that substantially reduced the provision's scope. Given the Senate's opposition, Mathias regarded it as somewhat impudent for the House to press ahead with the bill. Even so, the issue was an absolute stalemate in the lower chamber. Trying to figure a way out of the impasse, one morning as he was driving down Connecticut Avenue to work, it occurred to him that "some little adjustments"—compromises—could be made in the bill to get it moving. "You had to step back a little bit," recalled Mathias. "But it was the key to going forward." On the Hill, he immediately went to see William McCulloch, and then Celler. They thought the idea might work. "But we couldn't go forward unless we had Clarence's blessings." Mathias knew the proposition was tough for Mitchell to accept because, after a long, dry century, the civil rights forces had experienced repeated victories. No one was in the mood to compromise much. To Mathias's relief, "Clarence looked at this proposal and realized, with his experience— a long familiarity with the way the Hill worked—that by adopting it we could get the bill passed and move it from the House to the Senate. That is exactly what we did."[11]

The original administration provision would have prohibited racial, religious, or ethnic discrimination by owners, real estate brokers, developers, or their agents in the sale or rental of all housing. The Mathias amendment basically exempted one- to four-family owner-occupied houses offered for sale or rental by the owner (a "Mrs. Murphy's" provision). A person living in such a dwelling was free to reject, on racial grounds, an attempt by a black to purchase the property or to rent any of its units. The Mathias amendment would deprive blacks access to a substantial portion of the housing market.

Nevertheless, when the House Judiciary Committee reported out H.R. 14765 on June 30, Chairman Celler could only feel relief that "at long last, we will have a fair housing provision. Without it, the civil rights bill would have been like a wine cellar without a corkscrew." In addition to the Mathias amendment, the other significant modification approved by the full committee was a provision giving the attorney general power to bring civil injunctive suit against persons interfering with or seeking to interfere with rights protected by federal law. The rest of the bill barred descrimination in the selection of federal or state juries and authorized the attorney general to sue to desegregate schools and places of public accommodation.

Conservative Republicans and southern Democrats still were opposed to the housing title. With the backing of the National Association of Real Estate Boards (NAREB), the only major national organization conducting an active lobbying campaign against the open housing provision, they took their fight to the House floor. The major challenge for supporters still was how to save the housing title.[12]

While the Senate Subcommittee on Constitutional Rights under Ervin conducted its own hearings, the Leadership Conference followed its usual procedures in preparing for battle out of the Congressional Hotel. Wilkins, in a news conference held during a rally on July 26, announced that the LCCR was opposed to any amendments, including a second "clarifying" provision offered on the House floor by Mathias to severely limit the title's coverage by permitting real estate brokers to discriminate when selling or renting a house if the owner instructed the broker in writing to do so. The amendment exempted from coverage nearly 40 percent of existing white-owned housing in the nation—just about all single-family, owner-occupied dwellings in the suburbs. (The usual percentage used was 60 percent of all dwellings, including those owned by blacks.)

Wilkins maintained that the title had already been weakened in committee. Two days later he and Mitchell met with House Minority Leader Gerald R. Ford of Michigan for an hour in a vain attempt to win his support for the housing title. The GOP Policy Committee on August 1 formally opposed it in a blistering statement. It said the housing title "was politically motivated and unrealistic." The die was cast.

The following day, in a very studied, low-key response to "Republican Congressmen" that was nevertheless directed at Everett Dirksen, the leading opponent, Mitchell observed that without bipartisan support none of the recent civil rights laws would have been passed. He therefore hoped the Republicans would support the housing title in the spirit of national interest.

Citing "examples of how those who opposed any kind of civil rights legislation" in the past attempted to block such measures, Mitchell recalled that when the Eisenhower administration first proposed the 1957 act, southern Democrats and some Republicans in the House immediately attacked it. New York Congressman William E. Miller, a leading opponent, expressing some of the arguments that were now being used against the housing title, in 1956 joined a floor fight to return the bill to the Judiciary Committee. Mitchell was thankful that a courageous Minority Leader Joseph Martin of Massachusetts, with the help of "able civil rights supporters in the Republican Party," blocked Miller's attempt. Although the 1957 act was mild, he noted, it was attacked with the same ferocity as those who were now calling the housing title a "maze of federal procedures."

Next in 1964, he noted, some of the housing title opponents tried to kill the public accommodations provision by spurious legal arguments. Once more, McCulloch and most of the men who had supported Martin in 1956 joined in a bipartisan show of strength to save the title. In 1965, the same opponents of the housing title attempted to have the Republican party abandon its traditional opposition to the poll tax. The late Clarence Brown of Ohio helped save the poll tax ban.

The nation, Mitchell said, was now in a crisis. He pointed to NAREB's relentless campaign to defeat the housing title as an example of continuing efforts to divide Americans on the basis of race and class. Although the housing title could not accomplish any miracles, he said, it could "be a great help in setting patterns for racial harmony throughout the land." He maintained that its defeat would benefit only those who had contempt for law and order. [13]

That this pointed political response came from Mitchell and not the Leadership Conference showed how divisive the issue was. Staunch allies like the United Auto Workers and the United Steelworkers of America stayed with Mitchell and publicly opposed the weakening amendment. The more conservative AFL-CIO and several unions favored it.

Opposition in the House, too, followed no set pattern. It was strongly bipartisan and crossed ideological lines. Unlike the Republicans, the Democratic leadership supported the title. Even as Mitchell frantically worked to change the GOP's stand, the House on August 3 approved by a one-vote margin the Mathias amendment after first soundly rejecting it—when the vote was not recorded. Richard Bolling demonstrated the split among liberals and how much lawmakers were fearful of their constituents' wrath by casting the tiebreaker in favor of the amendment. Blacks, too—all Democrats—were split. Robert N. C. Nix of Philadelphia, slightly less conservative William Dawson of Chicago, and Charles Diggs, a moderate, voted for the amendment. John Conyers, Jr., of Michigan and Augustus Hawkins opposed it. Adam Clayton Powell, who had contentiously ruptured his once close relations with Mitchell in 1963, was absent. Mitchell's good friend Celler was also absent owing to illness. His strongly liberal colleague, Peter Rodino of New Jersey, read his statement: "I have learned that the all-or-nothing attitude produces nothing except a slogan. We have always the vision of human perfectibility before us, and mankind has taken faltering step after faltering step toward it." [14]

The night before the first vote on the Mathias clarifying amendment, Mitchell told Johnson, they had "what seemed to be a firm count of about 170 votes for the title" in its stronger form. But the bill's managers felt they could not take a chance on trying to pass the bill without further weakening it. Since they were all friends of civil rights, he was certain they exercised their best judgment.

That signal for significant compromise set the stage for the House to pass the bill with what was left of the housing title on August 9. Mitchell told Rodino he deserved "great credit for the way" he used his abundant patience and skill. Similarly thanking New York Republican Frank J. Horton for his help, he agreed that, in some ways, the 1966 Civil Rights Act "was one of the most difficult we have faced because of the legal technicalities involved and also because of the housing feature." On the whole, he said, this first round in the fight was good, even if the housing title was not what the times demanded. It would be useful if it was not further weakened in the Senate.

Mitchell subsequently explained "that without the so-called Mathias clarifying amendment, there were approximately 18" more members who would have supported a motion by West Virginia Republican Arch Moore to strike the housing title. That motion lost by a 222 to 190 vote. Mitchell found it significant that the 18 votes were from California, Illinois, Maryland, Massachusetts, New Jersey, New York, Ohio, South Dakota, Texas, and Wisconsin—all states outside the old South. Sixteen of these members were Republicans from districts where the civil rights forces were weak or lacked any base. The urban riots, he found, had helped to produce a crisis of conscience, epitomized by one Republican who wrote him: "Dear Clarence: Thanks for your kind letter of August 15. Please call me at your convenience—I am catching hell at home!" He was also confronted with a general anti-civil-rights attitude that was revealed by expressions like "rights required responsibility." Not surprisingly, the House added a provision to the bill it passed making it a crime to travel in interstate commerce with intent to incite a riot or support such disturbances.[15]

In August and September 1966 continuing racial violence in several northern and southern cities, combined with the heated rhetoric of black anarchists and black nationalists, Martin Luther King's promise to "dislocate" life in America's major cities, and his stepped-up attacks on the Vietnam War, transformed the civil rights struggle into a Tower of Babel. Robert Kennedy encouraged King to organize protests in the Chicago area against residential segregation, but they eventually had to be abandoned owing to violent opposition. Walter White could have told King what to expect in Cicero, the Jackson of the North. Back in 1951, local residents had gone berserk when a black World War II veteran tried to move his family out of the South Side Chicago vermin-infested prison to which they had been confined because of housing discrimination and into a twenty-family apartment house that a group of blacks had bought in Cicero. Al

Capone could maintain his headquarters amid the neat brick houses occupied by Polish-, Dutch-, Italian-, German-, and Greek-Americans, but
not the college-trained couple and their eight- and six-year-old children.
Two days after the riot, White found that "the atmosphere of bitterness
and potential renewal of almost insane determination to bomb and destroy
brick by brick the attractive" building "was almost tangible." Almost as
bad, Dr. Percy Julian, the world-famous black scientist who discovered
cortisone, extracted synthetic hormones from soybeans, and invented the
foam method of extinguishing fire, had hired guards the previous year to
protect his family and home in adjoining Oak Park. Bombings of homes
bought by blacks were so numerous that the local sheriff had lost count.

Mitchell was not surprised by King's fiasco. First, he believed, Chicago's blacks, immersed as they were in their city's violent mores, had no
respect for King's nonviolent tactics. Second, Mayor Richard Daley's political machine was hostile to any disturbance of the status quo. No worse
backdrop for the unfolding struggle in the Senate could have been imag-
ined.

Furthermore, on September 3, at Adam Clayton Powell's invitation,
169 black activists from thirty-seven cities in eighteen states and the District of Columbia met in closed session in Washington to discuss "black
power." Powell defined the concept as a "means for black people to make
changes in society to achieve self-determination, self-respect and self-defense, in other words, mobilizing black strength to serve the needs of black
people." He declared the civil rights revolution dead and said that existing
civil rights laws were useless to blacks facing de facto segregation that was
beyond the reach of those statutes. He said that "it doesn't matter to me at
all" whether the 1966 bill passed.

On the other side of the picture, George Wallace remained a powerful
national symbol outside the South in stark contrast to Paul Douglas, who
was defeated in Illinois by Charles Percy. Douglas told Mitchell that King's
Chicago demonstrations contributed to his loss, a development that Percy
himself had predicted. King, though serving as a moral standard-bearer,
remained unconcerned about the political consequences of his activities. He
expressed support for Johnson's fair housing legislation, but maintained
that that was not enough. He wanted the movement to tackle "basic class
issues, between the privileged and underprivileged."

Polls showed that the racial question was the top domestic issue in
1966 and underscored the extent to which white backlash had become an
election issue. While in 1964, 34 percent of Americans had believed that
blacks were moving too fast; in 1966, 85 percent thought so. In the
North, white resentment was caused primarily by the prospect of open
housing legislation, proposals to transport inner-city children to suburban

schools, fear of crime largely associated with urban ghettos, and a break-down of "law and order"—all of which spelled *riots*. In the South, consid-erable opposition was engendered by HEW's school desegregation guidelines, enforcement of the 1965 Voting Rights Act, and general resent-ment over Johnson's "socialistic policies" (which were benefiting more whites than blacks) and his "softness" on race.

Meanwhile, Majority Leader Mike Mansfield announced that the Senate would begin debate on September 6. He said the bill would not be sent to the Judiciary Committee, James Eastland's civil rights graveyard, but would be placed directly on the calendar. Certain of a filibuster, he ob-served that it could only be broken by Dirksen, who was adamantly op-posed to the housing title. "Without him we can't get cloture."

Mitchell, as in the past, felt that cloture was a difficult but not insur-mountable challenge. In an oblique criticism of Mansfield, he complained that since southern civil rights opponents, afflicted by age and ill health, were unable to wage an old-style filibuster, the only way they could now do so would be through dawdling debates, absence of quorums, and short working hours. In order to succeed, he felt, this "new filibuster" required the help of either one or both Senate leaders. Mitchell expressed strong concern to Mansfield in a telegram about a suggestion from the bipartisan Senate leadership "that the 1966 Civil Rights bill could go over to next year." That would have avoided the elections. He said postponement "until the 90th Congress would be a disaster of proportions that it is now hard to describe." Noting that Johnson had "shown great courage in taking a stand for human dignity," he expressed hope that there would be no change in plans to act on the bill in 1966.

At the same time, he told Wilkins there was "an excellent chance" the civil rights forces could win passage of the bill, including the housing title. To succeed, he felt that it was necessary to have a Senate quorum available during debate. He asked Wilkins to write the senators a strong letter urg-ing them to help. The second important advantage, he told Wilkins, was "a commitment from your senators" that they would be present and vote for cloture to limit debate as well as insist upon retaining the housing title. "I hope you will do everything that you can to see that there is a strong outpouring of sentiment for the bill," he urged his boss. He attached a copy of an NAREB letter to emphasize "what we are up against," underlin-ing the group's call to its members to "help generate an immediate wave of indignation by all citizens" against the housing title.[16]

Michigan's Philip Hart was the floor manager of the bill. Unlike past struggles when bipartisan teams of captains were assigned to each title of a measure during debate, now, following a meeting with Mitchell, only reg-ular Republican supporters were given that responsibility. The strategy evolved as a result of Mitchell's earlier meetings with various people, including key representatives of the administration. It was designed to out-maneuver Dirksen, the main roadblock. The title captains were Javits, Case, Hugh Scott, Thomas Kuchel, John Sherman Cooper, and Hiram Fong. Active support was also obtained from Robert P. Griffin of Michigan and Leverett Saltonstall. Even so, Saltonstall and several other regular Republican allies could only be counted among the "possibles" on the housing title.

Mitchell's fears about the difficulty of maintaining a quorum were soon borne out. On September 14, by a vote of 54 to 42, and five days later, by 52 to 41, the Senate failed to invoke cloture to end a filibuster of the procedural motion to take up the bill. These developments, while indicating that a majority existed in both chambers for the housing bill, further worsened Mitchell's relations with Mansfield—a breach that was made more obvious by Humphrey's absence from the Senate. Mitchell sharply criticized the majority leader's prompt move for a second cloture vote following the first debate. He urged Mansfield to delay action in order to give the civil rights forces more time to round up votes. Mitchell and Rauh issued a statement saying that not only was Mansfield making a "tragic mistake" in calling for a second vote so soon, but that he also had to share blame with Dirksen for what was happening to the civil rights bill. Mitchell charged that the defeat meant a return to rule by the minority in the Senate.

Mansfield said that he had anticipated that reaction and insisted his move was designed to "give us a chance to show our maximum strength." Hart joined in criticizing his friends, maintaining that "those who ask more time should come in and show us where they could get ten more votes. I don't believe they could do it." Mitchell said his own tally indicated that, given time, 64 senators might be persuaded to vote for cloture. He was troubled that the failure of the first vote "gives the green light to those irresponsible groups who say you must not have faith in the legislative process, and the only way is force." Dirksen had the last word in more ways than one. He correctly described the second cloture attempt as "evidence of last-minute hope and I think that hope will be dashed."

Immediately after the second vote, Mansfield moved to end further consideration of the bill by calling for the Senate to adjourn. That maneuver killed a pending motion by Philip Hart to consider the bill. Mansfield said that, in the present atmosphere, attitudes were clear that it would have been futile to take up the bill again. The cloture vote could "only be interpreted as a vote against civil rights legislation in this session." Although the bill remained on the calendar and could be called up subsequently, for all practical purposes it was dead for the Eighty-ninth

Congress. That was the first defeat of a civil rights bill since passage of the 1957 act, and it was a sharp setback for the administration.[17]

Taking the fight to the public in the name of the Leadership Conference, Mitchell said that despite the "numerous pall bearers and epitaph writers" who were proclaiming that the 1966 civil rights bill was dead, it could still be revived if there was a will to do so. "Those of us who have been working for its passage believe that the fight should go on even after the election and in the new Congress, if necessary."

The main stumbling block, the Leadership Conference charged, was Dirksen's "intransigence and subtle appeals to race prejudice." The LCCR urged Johnson to exercise his full powers to keep the measure alive and to call a special session after the November elections, if necessary, to gain passage in 1966. At the same time, the LCCR promised that the first order of business in January would be an attempt to change the cloture rule.

Mitchell explained that the filibuster showed the power of the "establishment" senators—Richard Russell and Dirksen—in "causing inconvenience for those who are on the fringes of the inner circles." When Russell and Dirksen were absent for personal or business matters, he said, no important votes were scheduled; neither were any important quorum calls made because the revelation of their absence would have embarrassed them. But those "little unwritten rules" did not apply to liberals who supported civil rights. When they had to be absent, their opponents insisted on calling for quorums and then turned around and said the liberals were not interested in civil rights. "To add insult to injury," Mitchell said, "Senator Dirksen was busily recruiting Republicans to help in giving the appearance of a filibuster while at the same time pretending that he was conducting a fair fight against the bill."

Mitchell rejected suggestions that the fight was lost because of a cooling off of interest in civil rights, the rise of the "black power" movement, or adverse reaction to the riots in Watts. The most obvious reason was that "we did not get those votes in the same measure that we have had them in the past." Why? Blacks and civil rights supporters themselves were not working hard enough to hold their representatives accountable. He noted that delegations like those from Kansas, which previously had supported civil rights, were opposed in both the House and the Senate. He thought it regrettable that some people were trying to penalize all black citizens for the actions of a minority of lawbreakers, "but no amount of hand wringing or exhortation and appeals to reason will change that picture unless" civil rights supporters registered their concern at the polls in November. He was very concerned that he could not name any city or state where the people who wanted civil rights progress exercised their maximum strength at the polls. "They don't do it because getting out the vote requires organization, hard work and personal sacrifice. It also requires a willingness to work without hope of being mentioned in the newspapers or photographed by television cameramen."

Additionally, he said, "we must ask ourselves whether we are keeping the true perspective so that one sees civil rights as something broader than any single racial group or bigger than any single class of our American residents." He stressed "residents," because he felt "that as a people we must care about the welfare and rights of all our fellow human beings within our borders—whether they be citizens or migrant workers from Mexico or the West Indies."[18]

Mitchell regarded the November midterm elections as a setback owing to the defeat or withdrawal from politics of several friends like Douglas. Nevertheless, he still saw much hope in the returns. Many of those who had been under the heaviest attack for supporting civil rights survived even though some had few blacks in their districts. Examples were Congressmen McCulloch, Mathias, and James Corman of California. He was also encouraged because several Democrats who were defeated were replaced by civil rights supporters.

Others like Katzenbach were similarly encouraged—and, no doubt, surprised. Mitchell found a general resentment among supporters because the administration had pushed the bill before the election even though they personally believed in open housing. No one lost his seat on the issue, but housing remained sub rosa—no one came out against it, and very few came out for it. For Katzenbach, the lesson was that open housing was not as important as it had been feared, and it was regarded as very important for the Senate. The administration pressed ahead as Ramsey Clark, upon succeeding Katzenbach as acting attorney general, assumed command of the struggle.

Mitchell regarded Clark as a natural ally. A quiet, tall native Texan, the son of a Supreme Court justice, and a Marine Corps veteran, Clark possessed a sharp mind. He endeared himself to Mitchell through his affinity for unpopular causes, especially civil rights, which he vigorously pursued despite opposition from the most formidable foes in the South. He was somewhat of an enigma in Washington, blending unobtrusively into the background at those ubiquitous Washington parties he felt duty-bound to attend. He struck some as the most interesting and difficult to understand member of the Johnson Cabinet.

Mitchell found additional hope in the Supreme Court's mention in *United States* v. *Price* of a speech by Senator John Pool of North Carolina in the second session of the Forty-first Congress, when he introduced an amendment to the Enforcement Act of 1870 that became Sections 241, 242, and 243 of Title 18 of the U.S. Code. Pool said:

> The liberty of a citizen of the United States, the prerogatives, the rights, and the immunities of American citizenship should not and cannot be safely left to the mere caprice of states either in the passage of laws or in the withholding of that protection which any emergency may require. If a state by omission neglects to give to every citizen within its borders a free, fair, and full enjoyment of his rights it is the duty of the United States Government to go into the State, and by its strong arm to see that he does have the full and free enjoyment of those rights. [19]

In a meeting with Mitchell, Wilkins, and Rauh representing the Leadership Conference, Clark and John Doar outlined the administration's civil rights package. It included provisions for state and federal jury selections, new cease and desist powers for the Equal Employment Opportunity Commission, the protection of individuals in civil rights activities, and open housing. Clark said the Justice Department was omitting the proposal offered in 1966 to give the attorney general the right to initiate suits to desegregate schools and public facilities because it was not as important as previously as a result of progress in those areas.

The Leadership Conference recommended that in addition to giving the Equal Employment Opportunity Commission authority to issue cease and desist orders, its coverage be broadened to include state and municipal governments; and the housing antidiscrimination title provide for gradual implementation but cover servicemen and Vietnam veterans immediately and, as in 1966, also for a Fair Housing Board. Justice Department officials were cool to the renewed suggestion to include an indemnification provision in the bill and rejected another for a jury selection "trigger." But they agreed to include a broad prohibition against sex discrimination.

On strategy, the Leadership Conference suggested introducing a single bill as well as individual measures covering the various titles so that in the Senate they could be parceled out to several committees like Commerce, Education, and Labor, and not be bottled up in Eastland's Judiciary Committee. On other issues, the Justice Department expected that an effort would be made to pass an antiriot bill. The consensus was that such a bill was unnecessary; it was agreed an attempt would be made to head off such a measure. [20]

As Clark had indicated, the President soon sent Congress his civil rights message, in which he made adopting a national policy against discrimination in housing a first priority. The administration's 1967 civil rights bill followed the general line of agreement with the Leadership Conference. It even included a modified indemnification provision to allow victims of violence to file civil suits for damages and injunctive relief.

Hart was again floor manager. Walter Mondale, in the footsteps of his mentor Hubert Humphrey, whom he succeeded, assumed responsibility for the most difficult housing section, sponsoring it with a bipartisan group of twenty-one other senators. Joseph Clark and Jacob Javits introduced the equal employment opportunity provision. Joseph Tydings, as chairman of the Subcommittee on Improvement in Judicial Machinery of the Senate Judiciary Committee, initiated hearings on the several bills that had already been introduced on federal jury selection reforms.

The separate-bill strategy was not without pitfalls. Opponents said it was adopted to enable the civil rights forces to jettison the housing title if it again became too hot. Forewarned by Hart, Marvin Caplan of the Leadership Conference alerted Mitchell that the housing title faced serious problems in the Banking and Currency Committee. Alabama's John Sparkman was chairman of the full committee as well as of the housing subcommittee. Because he opposed the housing bill, it was feared he would vent his full hostility against it in his subcommittee. The bill would fare much better in the Subcommittee on Financial Institutions, headed by William Proxmire. The trick was getting Sparkman to refer it there. A better alternative for handling it was the Senate Interstate Committee, headed by Warren G. Magnuson of Washington, but he faced reelection in 1968 and was not eager to touch it. A similar problem was posed by sending the EEO bill to the Senate Labor Committee, headed by Alabama's Lister Hill, who opposed it. The strategists finally decided that Mondale and Edward Brooke, both of whom were experienced former attorneys general of their states, would be able to overcome whatever obstacles they encountered and move the bill through the Banking and Currency Committee. Regarding Sparkman, Mitchell explained that "we knew he wouldn't support it. But due to his fairness, he wouldn't throw any artificial roadblocks in our way," such as not holding hearings. Additionally, Hart got the White House to use its influence to obtain a gentleman's understanding from the southern chairmen that they would not obstruct the bills and would report them out.

Other early difficulties included drumming up popular support behind the bills as hearings began. Mitchell told Ramsey Clark that publicity could probably be generated around the work of Proxmire's subcommittee and through Leadership Conference meetings planned for Washington in May as well as other activities around the country. But, Mitchell feared, while there was no lack of civil rights activity, much of it, like the riots and black power rhetoric, was negative because so many people doubted the sincerity of Congress. He felt that Congress had to assume responsibility for changing the atmosphere. Although the Senate posed filibuster problems and moved more slowly than the House, Mitchell believed there was an advantage with starting the process there—rather than in the House, as was usually done with civil rights measures because they stood a better chance of success there. No matter which of the bills was first reported, it could be amended with the others to create a total package that would be sent to the House.[21]

The legislation's fate in the House, however, set the pattern for how it would be handled by the Senate Judiciary Committee. Opting for the easier course, the normally sympathetic House Judiciary Committee early approved a bill (H.R. 2516) designed to protect civil rights workers. This was the least controversial of the administration's proposals.

Then, in an atmosphere of inner-city violence capped by the bloodiest conflagrations of all in Newark, New Jersey, and Detroit, the full House in August adopted, in addition to an earlier antiriot bill, an amendment to the civil rights workers protection bill to extend its coverage to policemen attempting to stop a riot or to firemen fighting fires. The quarrelsome debate in the House revealed deepening divisions and doubts over the course of race relations in the nation. The House passed H.R. 2516 by a vote of 326 to 93. Members left no doubt the bill was intended to protect blacks against white supremacists as well as to punish black power advocates like H. Rap Brown, director of SNCC, and Stokely Carmichael, the group's former leader.[22]

Despite Congress's negative tone, Mitchell welcomed the promise of the basic bill. It would protect persons registering or voting, enrolling in public schools, participating in federal or state services, involved in union or employment activities, serving as jurors, using public accommodations or any common carrier, and anyone participating in federally assisted programs. The rights of most of those classes had been established in the 1964 and 1965 acts but they needed to be strengthened. The bill also significantly increased penalties for violating existing civil rights laws.

Working under a deadline for reporting out H.R. 2516, Ervin got his Subcommittee on Constitutional Rights to substitute by a 5 to 1 vote more restrictive provisions for the House-passed text. That forced the administration to make an extraordinary effort to save face. It was done by flying Hugh Scott back from Great Britain, where he was about to begin a series of lectures at Oxford University, in order to provide the deciding vote in an 8 to 7 decision for an amendment to substitute for Ervin's bill the basic administration civil rights protection text offered by Hart. The committee then rejected, by a vote of 7 to 8, a series of amendments Ervin offered. Eastland also tried to add an open housing provision to the bill, but this was defeated 0 to 11. Eastland had earlier predicted that the housing provision would kill H.R. 2516 because "Northern people will not have anything to do with so-called civil rights laws which incorporate opening housing that applies to them."[23]

Mitchell praised Hart's persistence in steering the bill through the tricky parliamentary process. His support enabled Mitchell to anticipate that the bill would be the pending business in January when the new session began. Despite earlier predictions that the rest of the administration package was dead, Tydings, insisting that jury reform was not a civil rights matter, managed to get the Senate to pass the federal Jury Selection and Service Act of 1967 barring discrimination on the basis of race, color, religion, sex, national origin, or economic status. Apart from approval by the Senate Banking and Currency Committee, no action was taken on the housing bill in either the House or Senate. The EEO title remained stalled in committee.

In a telegram to Johnson, Mitchell complained that the civil rights forces were working against "great odds and counter pressures generated by the real estate lobby, unscrupulous office seekers, and fair weather friends who have stirred up old fires of race prejudice to block" the housing proposal. However, he said, the strong votes in the House for the bill and in the Senate for cloture "show that we have the strength to win on the merits." He said he remained on the alert for further action because he was confident Johnson would "find a way to continue the battle for fair play in the housing market place." He said it was impossible to believe the majority of Americans would continue to tolerate the current national disgrace of discrimination in the housing market.

Mitchell's appeal to Johnson underscored the shifting civil rights picture. The ranks of civil rights allies had thinned out considerably, so that Mitchell was left with only regular standbys. Furthermore, King and the SCLC were not helping by pressing plans for their Washington project— the Poor People's Campaign—which was designed to disrupt life in the nation's capital with massive civil disobedience. That meant the President had to do much more than in 1964. As Vice President, Humphrey could not help as much as he had when he was in the Senate, but he was still very supportive. Mitchell regarded Barefoot Sanders, who had succeeded Lawrence O'Brien as the White House legislative liaison, as "the most pleasant kind of person to work with. He never got visibly angry" at any of their meetings. He seemed to be around whenever he was needed and was always "working at a steady, pressurized pace."

Mitchell also enjoyed working with Ramsey Clark, for whom he had early developed a deep respect and affection. Based on what he knew about Clark dating back to when he had headed the Lands Division of the Justice

Department, as well as what he had learned through his intelligence sources, he "felt very good about" Clark's stand on civil rights. During the riots in the summer of 1967, Johnson called Mitchell at home early one morning and, after discussing a number of things, said, "What about my boy? I'm thinking of making him attorney general." Mitchell was certain he was going to appoint Clark, the son of Associate Justice Tom Clark, to the position, regardless of what he said, but he welcomed the opportunity to give Clark high marks. Johnson told Mitchell he was looking to the attorney general to coordinate and guide the administration's civil rights program and instructed Mitchell on how he could help in implementing it. He remained as committed as Mitchell to the goal of an open housing law.[24]

The problem remained Dirksen. Mitchell was bitter about his opposition to civil rights legislation, noting that he voted in the Judiciary Committee to support Ervin's version of the bill over Hart's, and frequently said he opposed the administration's measure because it would protect blacks but not whites. Dirksen's insistence he would do nothing to stop a filibuster doomed further action in the Eighty-ninth Congress.

Unleashing a blistering attack during a United Steelworkers of America civil rights conference in Columbus, Ohio, Mitchell said the minority leader was a great law and order advocate, but he did "not favor giving the government adequate power to punish Klansmen, vigilantes and the mobsters who dynamite, shoot, burn and murder for the sole purpose of preventing American citizens from exercising their constitutional rights."

Mitchell vowed: "We in the civil rights organizations are determined to keep the fight for human dignity within the framework of the U.S. Constitution. We are going to continue to work with constitutional weapons, no matter what may be done to stop us.

"Yet we are neither deaf nor blind. We hear the voices of those who insist that violence and destruction must be used. We see the awful results that come from government indifference to the pleas of justice and for remedies against wrongdoing. Senator Dirksen has, perhaps unwittingly, become an ally of those who advocate lawlessness as a solution to problems.

"He is saying, in effect, that the government of the United States has no obligation to protect our citizens from modernized lynching by law enforcement officers. He would have the government continue to give a mere slap on the wrist to the criminals who spread terror among the inhabitants of the entire South.

"Of course, Senator Dirksen is against crime in the streets and he is against riots in the North. The big difference between his position and that of civil rights advocates is that he does not go the whole way. We are against crime in the streets, we are against riots in the North, but we are also against crime on the plantations and in the swamps of Mississippi. We are against mob rule anywhere by anybody."

Until 1957, Mitchell said, "James O. Eastland was the greatest single roadblock to civil rights legislation. That dubious honor has now passed to Senator Dirksen. It is indeed ironic that the senior senator from the state of Abraham Lincoln has become the flag bearer in the army of the segregationists."[25]

The great fear propelling Mitchell in the beginning of 1968 was that should Congress fail to enact a fair housing law its action would be interpreted as a sanction for residential segregation. The civil rights family still was not united on strategy. King, unconcerned about the intricacies of legislative strategy, had announced he would go "all out" to defeat Johnson in 1968. On December 15, Mitchell had scored a major breakthrough when the Senate leadership made H.R. 2516 the first order of business for 1968. With Rauh, he began working to make the bill a vehicle for the open housing and equal employment opportunity amendments. For liberal senators like Hart, sitting down to Christmas dinner amid the turbulence of the times, the prospect of getting the bill through Congress loomed as no easy task.

On January 4, 1968, Mitchell expressed his concern to Wilkins that there was some thought of separating the housing title and not voting on it until later in the year. Two weeks later in another meeting with Hart, Mondale, and Tydings, Mitchell opposed the suggestion to let the housing provision wait. He reasoned that although it was possible to have two civil rights battles in the Senate in 1968, it was very improbable that the leadership would permit two party-splitting confrontations in the same election year. Tydings felt that getting other Great Society job creation legislation through Congress might be more important than the pending riot control bill. Mitchell agreed, but insisted that creating more jobs and ending housing segregation were equally important. Mondale was enthusiastic at the outlook and agreed to cosponsor the housing amendment with Brooke, who was absent but telephoned his support to the meeting. The group parted with the understanding that a genuine fight would be made for the EEO and housing amendments. But Mitchell told Wilkins that, "this being Washington, I am sure that various forces are at work and will continue to restrict the consideration to H.R. 2516."

Mitchell urged Wilkins, in his report to the NAACP annual meeting, to call for the Senate to amend the pending worker protection bill (H.R. 2516) with two other provisions to give the Equal Employment Opportunity Commission cease and desist authority (S. 1308) and with the fair housing measure (S. 1358). That gave the NAACP's stamp of approval to

688   DENTON L. WATSON

the strategy. Mitchell favored those moves for the Senate because, in the House, amending H.R. 2516 in that manner with two unrelated bills would leave it open to challenge under the germaneness rule. He felt that Wilkins's expressed support was important for changing the minds of some senators who did not want to add anything to the worker protection measure. He informed Wilkins that the President said he had "told those boys" in Justice that he wanted all he could get, including housing. Mitchell believed that was the best way to achieve that goal. He felt, furthermore, that initiating action in the Senate would help spare supporters in the House from a recurrence of attacks in the 1968 elections that they had suffered two years earlier.

The question then arose how to get the Banking and Currency Committee's views on fair housing on record. Because there had been no committee report, no guidance regarding legislative intent was provided. Mondale and Brooke therefore compiled an impressive document based on the hearings that served as the committee report, and this became the basis for debate on the Senate floor. [26]

Three days after the Senate began debating H.R. 2516, Mitchell intensified his drive for bipartisan support for this strategy in another meeting with Hart, Ted Kennedy, Javits, Percy, and Scott as well as legislative assistants of several liberal senators.* Mitchell pointed out that the Leadership Conference on Civil Rights and the Urban Coalition, a recently formed nonpartisan pressure group, favored adding the two amendments to the worker protection bill. Edward Kennedy, like Tydings, felt that perhaps the civil rights bill was not as important as the creation of additional jobs. Mitchell and other Leadership Conference representatives with him at the meeting, maintained that both were important. The senators did not commit themselves to offering the amendments, although Mitchell thought Javits and Scott favored this approach. Later, Scott confirmed Mitchell's impression by explaining on the Senate floor that the lobbyist had chided him for his hesitancy. Percy, and Kennedy after his objections had been disposed of, seemed inclined to support this move, but Hart was not eager for such a fight. Nevertheless, he subsequently tried the strategy and once more became floor leader after Mitchell had persuaded him that "it was now or never for civil rights." Hart then decided "we might as well go for broke." [27]

Johnson's "calm, strong and statesmanlike" delivery of his State of the Union Message reassured Mitchell of his sincerity in leading the struggle

*The legislative assistants represented Joseph Clark, Case, Tydings, Daniel B. Brewster (D-Md.), Birch E. Bayh (D-Ind.), Daniel K. Inouye (D-Hawaii), Eugene J. McCarthy (D-Minn.), Abraham A. Ribicoff (D-Conn.), Harrison A. Williams, Jr. (D-N.J.), Claiborne Pell (D-R.I.), Edward V. Long (D-Mo.), Vance Hartke (D-Ind.), Mondale, Brooke, Gaylord A. Nelson (D-Wisc.), Robert P. Griffin (R-Mich.), Mark O. Hatfield (R-Ore.), Robert Kennedy, Proxmire, and Kuchel.

for a just nation characterized by "compassion for the sick, the poor, the helpless and the forgotten." He told Johnson that those who believed in fair play owed the President "a word of historic appreciation" for his commitment to those goals. As an expression of his own appreciation, Mitchell said, he was working to get support for pending civil rights legislation in which the President believed. He also told Johnson there was no expression of his commitment to racial justice more eloquent than the presence of two distinguished blacks in the front rows of the House chamber during delivery of his message. They were Associate Justice Thurgood Marshall and Dr. Robert Weaver, secretary of housing and urban development. "Wherever men and women of reason watched the television screen they could gain inspiration from this evidence of a high fulfillment of America's promise," Mitchell said. Johnson's message signaled an all-out battle in Congress.

Mitchell that same day called on the NAACP's state conference presidents and regional and field directors to write their senators to complain about "the sham battle" that was being waged by opponents of the three key civil rights bills, two of which—the housing and fair employment proposals—were still "on ice" in committees.[28]

As in the past, the first real danger came from attempts to water down the bill. Faced with this possibility, Senate liberals began looking for a compromise. One important issue involved was whether the bill should be based on the broad provisions of the equal protection clause of the Fourteenth Amendment, as civil rights proponents wanted, or on the interstate commerce clause, which opponents favored because it would limit the bill's coverage of state and local activities.

Ervin, playing his usual role, continued to argue that bills based on the Fourteenth Amendment were unconstitutional even though the Supreme Court, since *Brown* v. *Board of Education,* had consistently ruled otherwise. The Justice Department joined the Leadership Conference in regarding the attempted "flight from the Fourteenth Amendment" as possibly the worst element in this struggle. Justice regarded this retreat as having practical as well as political ramifications because much civil rights legislation in the future would be predicated on this constitutional provision. In addition to the housing bill, which was in part based on the Fourteenth Amendment, other Justice Department proposals to improve the administration of justice in state courts in the South and a host of civil rights programs drew heavily on this provision and would continue to do so in the future. The department concluded that a retreat now from the Fourteenth Amendment would never be retrieved.[29]

On February 6, the Senate approved by a 54 to 29 roll call vote a motion offered by Hart to reject such a limiting amendment from Ervin as well as a proposal by Dirksen to eliminate a provision in the bill targeting it to racially or religiously motivated crimes.

That development prompted Mondale and Brooke to cosponsor a fair housing amendment that was almost identical to the administration bill. The southerners clearly had miscalculated and their blindness strengthened the position of the open housing advocates. Without their filibuster of a bill to protect lives, that would not have happened; instead, their intransigence aroused sympathy for civil rights. Like Johnson, Mitchell, and others committed to civil rights, Mondale used this opportunity and the urban unrest to good advantage by arguing that the housing provision's fate was important to the outcome of the struggle for leadership in the black community. Mansfield opposed the amendment on grounds it would defeat the entire bill.

Two weeks later, the Senate showed unexpected support for both provisions when a solid majority, 55 to 37, voted to end debate. Even though that was short of the two thirds required for cloture, the message was clear. A majority supported the worker protection bill and the open housing amendment, and the vote of approval was larger than the one on September 19, 1966, when the Senate last took a stand on the issue. More Republicans voted for cloture even though Dirksen, still opposed, said he wanted to find a "moderate, equitable and enforceable" alternative. Mondale noted that the 1966 provision covered only 40 percent of housing compared to 96 percent under his amendment.

A further demonstration that the tide had turned was the 34 to 58 roll-call-vote defeat the following day (February 21) of a motion from Mansfield to table the open housing amendment. Mondale and Brooke intensified their efforts to come up with a "reduced" substitute before a second cloture vote.[30] Mitchell was confident that, assuming the civil rights forces got all 58 sure supporters that Monday, he could round up 3 more Democrats and possibly 5 Republicans for February 26, the next scheduled date for action. That would provide 66 votes—one short of the required 67 if all 100 senators voted. Mitchell wired the President that although the February 26 vote did not look encouraging, he had learned that Dirksen was reconsidering his position. He reported that he could use more time to find the necessary votes and would continue exploring all possibilities over the weekend. He urged Johnson to do whatever he deemed appropriate to assure success of the cloture vote on Monday.

While attempts were being made to win over the three Democrats, the Republicans posed a different problem. They wanted substantive changes in the bill. Negotiations with them began on February 22 and continued over the weekend. Mitchell, in a two-hour meeting that Rauh also attended, learned from Senator Jack Miller of Iowa that one Republican demand was to gain coverage of all housing that had some government connection. He wanted to abolish the November 20, 1962, starting date imposed by Executive Order 11063 and base the provision on whether the existing relationship between the government and the parties involved was still in effect. FHA mortgages, Mitchell learned from Robert Weaver, lasted for twelve to thirteen years. So, he concluded, the Miller idea would indeed provide broader coverage than the Kennedy executive order.

Miller's proposal would also cover transactions of brokers, agents, lenders, and other persons licensed by the state. However, he did not believe coverage of privately owned, nongovernment-assistant housing was constitutional. And there was the rub. Saying he was available Friday, Saturday morning, and Sunday to work on a compromise, Miller offered to meet with Hart and other supporters. Mitchell agreed to arrange the meeting. If no agreement was reached by Monday, Miller said, he would vote against cloture but would continue working until an agreement was reached. Miller also proposed technical changes to other sections of the bill that Mitchell and Rauh felt they could live with, so the real problem remained housing. At the same time, Brooke, Mondale, and Hart had prepared a confidential compromise that they submitted to Dirksen. Early in February, Dirksen, in conjunction with Javits, had begun considering a compromise. The final results depended on extensive negotiations.

The extent to which lawmakers like Miller kept their hands close to their chests, making it possible for only a few people like Mitchell to know which way they were leaning, was shown by a report from presidential aide Mike Manitos to Johnson. Manitos acknowledged that it was only after the Iowan had voted for cloture on the third attempt, that the White House knew they had won him over.[31]

The failure of the second cloture attempt on February 26 was therefore merely procedural. Because one GOP senator switched his vote, a majority of Republicans (19 to 17) now favored cloture. That meant Dirksen was in the minority. The vote contrasted sharply with that of 1966, when a minority of Republicans had favored the weaker housing bill 10 to 20.

Mondale's announcement two days later that he and Brooke were tabling their amendment and that "the distinguished senior Senator from Illinois" would offer an alternative fair housing provision was a classic understatement. "I state simply that I believe his proposal constitutes a very important step forward in the cause of human brotherhood," Mondale declared on the Senate floor. Outside the chamber, he termed the compromise "a miracle" and much more than had been anticipated "just a week ago." The substitute amendment covered 80 percent of all housing.

Dirksen's melodramatic explanation of his reasons for accepting the compromise was historically appropriate. He recalled that in September

1966 he had taken "the firm, steadfast position" that fair housing was the domain of the state because it was essentially an enforcement problem. But, he said, there were "only two categories of people who do not change their minds in the face of reality." The first was "embalmed in the last resting places" and could not do otherwise; the second was confined to mental institutions.

He changed his mind, he said, because he did not want to worsen the restive condition of the country; "I do not want to have this condition erupt and have a situation develop for which we do not have a cure and probably have more violence and more damage done." Another reason he gave was his concern for Vietnam War veterans. To appreciate that tragedy, he said, anyone could visit some of the veterans at Walter Reed Hospital. On many of his visits there, he had given floral bouquets received from friends to those troubled souls. "Unless there is fair housing as this title connotes—and I ask that the title be changed and simply made 'fair housing'—I do not know what the measure of their unappreciation would be for the ingratitude of their fellow citizens, after they were willing to lay their lives on the altar and in so many instances left arms and legs 12,000 miles behind." He said, "I am not going to charge my conscience with that sort of thing, believe me." In other words, his actions were taken in the national interest, and out of "my own concept of duty."

Dirksen dismissed other reasons that were suggested for his action. It was impossible, though, to overlook his egocentrism, his sense of personal grandeur and historic importance. For Dirksen to abandon the NAREB position he had adopted so unequivocally in 1966 required not only the pressure of national events but also intense and persistent courtship from his colleagues. Only that morning at ten o'clock, he informed them, he had held the last conference in his office with Messrs. Roman Hruska of Nebraska, Howard Baker, Jr., Hart, Brooke, Javits, and the attorney general. He acknowledged that Ramsey Clark had "probably spent more time in my office" than in any other senator's office since assuming the post. Clark's three top staff members were also regular visitors there. Furthermore, that conference was the tenth or eleventh on housing that had been held in his office; they had included not only Clark but other people like Mansfield. The question of Dirksen's pride of authorship was an additional ingredient that had to be considered. As in 1964, the civil rights forces accorded him the opportunity to place his personal stamp on the legislation.[32]

Simple, pragmatic politics was crucial even though Dirksen eloquently tried to dismiss such considerations. Several GOP senators, including his son-in-law Howard Baker, a freshman from Tennessee, urged him to take the initiative in preparing a compromise in order to give members of their party a stronger civil rights record on which to run in November. The

February 26 vote showed he was "losing his grip" on his party, so he opted to be on the winning side.

Another factor was that the White House had organized pressure on the GOP following the second cloture vote and had urged the Leadership Conference to "put Nixon and Rockefeller on the spot" so they would get fellow Republicans to support the bill. Richard Nixon and Nelson A. Rockefeller were presidential candidates. Philip Randolph and Bayard Rustin, executive director of the A. Philip Randolph Institute, promptly issued a public call for them to express their support. Wilkins also sent a telegram to the Republican senators urging them to vote on March 1, the third scheduled cloture attempt, for the minority leader's substitute.

In the end, Mitchell's role in mobilizing and focusing political pressure on the Republicans was the most obvious factor in changing Dirksen's mind. This strategy, directed with laser intensity, would be equally effective on House Minority Leader Ford.

Based on his own intelligence, Mitchell was able to assure the White House that efforts to win GOP votes were working. Once a majority of Republicans had been won over, Dirksen was sure to follow. Mitchell also credited Johnson's magic touch with Dirksen, through their secret alliance, with helping to bring about this miracle. He explained that Johnson had helped the minority leader's 1962 campaign by ensuring that the Democratic opposition was weak. Mitchell insisted, "It's my belief that he might have had trouble getting reelected in Illinois if there had been a strong Democratic fight against him. I don't think it was strong. Of course, there could be many challenges to that assessment. But that is my belief, and it was based on conversations with the President and my assessment of the Illinois situation."

Rauh provides a somewhat different picture of that campaign, which might explain why Mitchell insisted he was holding to his view. He credits President Kennedy with ensuring Dirksen's reelection by undercutting his Democratic opponent, Congressman Sidney Yates, who was doing well in the campaign. Wishing to help Dirksen so that he would continue as minority leader, Kennedy sent a plane for him in October during the Cuban missile crisis, ostensibly to get his advice. That gesture, which boosted Dirksen's prestige, ensured his victory. Yates, who subsequently was returned to the House, never forgave the Kennedys for that action. Rauh concedes it is possible that Johnson had advised Kennedy on how to help Dirksen.[33]

The February 29 preliminary report of the President's National Advisory Commission on Civil Disorders provided a somber backdrop to the struggle over the fair housing legislation. The commission declared, "Our nation is moving toward two societies, one black, one white—separate and unequal." The report might not have had a direct impact on the legislative struggle, but, given the frequent references to the urban disturbances and expressed anxieties over the national well-being, its influence was considerable. That same day, Dirksen, without prior approval of the bipartisan, liberal supporters of the Mondale amendment, obtained unanimous consent for modifications to the compromise that weakened it. Even though his action almost tore apart the bipartisan coalition, the measure remained strong enough to retain support.

Dirksen's imprimatur was not sufficient to avoid a third cloture defeat on March 1. In the kind of speech that always enthralled Mitchell, he explained how he virtually got down on his knees to plead for help from a senator in his party, to no avail. Hruska completed the drama by admitting that it was he who had rejected Dirksen's pleas.

Three days later the Senate invoked cloture and ended debate by a 65 to 32 vote on the minority leader's amendment to H.R. 2516. That same day, King announced that his Poor People's Campaign would kick off on April 22 in Washington. On March 11, the Senate passed the worker protection bill with the fair housing amendment by a 70 to 20 roll call vote and sent it to the House. Included in the bill were antiriot and Indian constitutional rights provisions that the Senate had attached. Three Republicans opposed passage, while three southern Democrats voted for the bill.

Pointing to the type of overall commitment that had been required for passage of the bill, Mitchell wrote to Missouri NAACP state conference president Harold Holiday that Senator Edward V. Long of Missouri, an unheralded champion of civil rights, had postponed various engagements, one in South America, to be present for the March 4 cloture vote. In the previous attempts, the Missouri Democrat had voted consistently for cloture and against the effort to table the bill. His was one of the crucial 8 to 7 votes on October 25 in the Judiciary Committee. Noting that Senator Long had also voted for Thurgood Marshall's confirmation, Mitchell explained, "This kind of effective and consistent support is what makes civil rights victories in the Congress." The remaining House struggle provided another aspect of this lesson.[34]

Whereas Mitchell's friends had carried the political ball in the Senate battle, the delicate nature and complexity of the struggle in the lower chamber required him to play a more direct role in orchestrating developments there. The priority in the Senate had been to fashion and win support for a strong compromise; now the goal was to preserve that measure intact.

On March 14, the Senate gave final approval to a federal jury reform bill and sent it to the President. The bill provided for random selection of juror names from voter lists and barred discrimination on grounds of race,

color, religion, sex, national origin, or economic status. That same day
Ford, for the first time, publicly expressed support for open housing legislation. However, he said there should be a conference on the bill and that
he would oppose the Senate version. Ford wanted the bill modified to conform with the 1966 measure, which he had opposed. That bill permitted
real estate brokers to discriminate in the sale or rental of single-family
homes when the owners asked them to do so. The 1968 Senate bill exempted only single-family housing that was sold by the owners without
help from a real estate broker and rooms in dwelling units occupied by no
more than four families and in which the owner lived in one of them (a
Mrs. Murphy's provision).

To avoid the changes Ford and other opponents of H.R. 2516 wanted,
it was necessary to stave off modifications on the House floor that would
require the bill to be sent to conference, where it would have been butch-
ered in the behind-the-scenes politicking. Once more, House Speaker
McCormack's support was crucial. He immediately dismissed the thought
of sending the bill to the Judiciary Committee for consideration of the
Senate amendments and supported the move to obtain concurrence. But
the House denied Majority Leader Celler's request for unanimous consent
to concur with the Senate amendments, sending the bill to the House
Rules Committee.

There, for the first time since 1957, when they had voted solidly
against civil rights, the Republicans lined up with the southern Democrats
to reject a move to send the bill to the House floor. As Mitchell complained to Nixon, not one Republican on the Rules Committee supported
the Senate's fair housing title and, so far, not one was willing to follow the
1960 and 1964 precedents by giving other House Republicans a fair chance
to vote on the bill. He charged that the majority of the House Republican
leadership and all the Republicans on the Rules Committee wanted to send
the bill to a conference, where it most likely would have adopted the GOP
provision giving real estate brokers and agents power to discriminate. In
those earlier contests, Mitchell had isolated the diehard southerners by winning over enough Republican votes with Clarence Brown's help. Now he
intensified political pressure on the Republicans.

The civil rights forces began planning around the Rules Committee's
schedule to report out the bill on April 9. Their strategy called for two
important votes the following day when the bill reached the House floor.
The first would be on a motion to call for the previous question, which was
the procedure to take up the bill itself. If that motion carried, the House
would consider a resolution calling for acceptance of the Senate bill. Approval would enable the bill to go directly to the President.[35]

Blacks were demonstrating in Memphis in support of the striking garbage collectors when Mitchell began meeting with several moderate and conservative Republicans who were not on the Rules Committee and winning valuable support for the Senate bill. He learned that although Ford's public stance had not changed, the minority leader would remain neutral so that additional GOP support could be gathered. Mitchell realized that all the Republicans who were insisting that the Indian rights and antiriot, or "Molotov bomb," amendments were roadblocks had voted against the housing bill in 1966.

He distributed a review he had prepared of the recent struggle in the upper chamber as well as the highlights of the GOP's past support for civil rights legislation. He expressed special appreciation for Brooke's skilled leadership as Republican floor captain of the bill during the Senate battle. Owing to the cooperation Brooke and his close associates engendered, all but six Republican senators supported Brooke's move to table his bill and accept the Dirksen compromise. These naysayers were led by Strom Thurmond, who had deserted the Democratic party in the name of states' rights. Obviously, said Mitchell, "Thurmond does not represent the views of the Republican Senate leadership nor the majority of his party." But, among blacks, he was the best-known Republican who voted against the bill. Many blacks, he said, believed Thurmond was the Republican party's Eastland. Blacks would therefore be watching to see whether Republicans in the House supported Brooke's cooperation with his Democratic colleagues or followed Thurmond's obstructionist tactics.

Acceptance of the bill, Mitchell said, would deprive both black and white racists of an issue that was creating extreme tension in the country. Black extremists, he said, were trying to destroy faith in constitutional methods of seeking progress by claiming that Congress was too prejudiced to pass a meaningful bill; white racists, in contrast, were busy blocking federal legislation while also trying to destroy state and local fair housing laws.

For example, he explained, Spiro T. Agnew, the Republican governor of Maryland, had gotten the state legislature to pass a fair housing law in 1967. Because of opposition from segregationists, the question was being put to a referendum in November 1968. Maryland segregationists had also blocked operation of a fair housing ordinance passed by Montgomery County, outside Washington, D.C. He anticipated that when the Senate bill became law most efforts to nullify such state statutes by appealing to bigotry would end. Indeed, he said, the provisions of the Senate bill that gave bona fide state fair housing laws a chance to work might well increase the number of state and local laws. That was what happened when the 1964 public accommodations title became law.

Mitchell noted that in 1966, Mathias, in the best tradition of the Republican party, had reminded his colleagues in the House that that year was the one-hundredth anniversary of the 1866 Civil Rights Act that, among other things, had given blacks the right to own real property. The *Congressional Globe* revealed that opponents had considered the idea revolutionary and unconstitutional. Now those claims were absurd.

That contest reminded Mitchell of a similarly intense one in 1956 that had been led by Joseph Martin of Massachusetts and William Miller of New York, when Martin, as minority leader, declared: "I want to tell the Republicans in this House if they follow the southern democracy in the defeat of this bill, they will seriously regret it. . . . [T]his bill has been jockeyed into the position where the one group who will be blamed for [its] defeat, if it is defeated, particularly upon this motion, is the Republican Party. I just want to point out to the Republicans not to fall into this trap." House Republicans heeded Martin's warning and the bill became the Civil Rights Act of 1957. Mitchell also recalled the overwhelming support the bill had from Republican leaders in both the House and Senate.

He explained that the Indian rights amendment was a trap. As in 1964 when opponents had included sex among the forms of discrimination prohibited in the hope it would sink the bill, Mitchell had watched from the Senate gallery as Ervin moved to amend H.R. 2516 with the provision guaranteeing constitutional rights for Indians. The Senate passed the Indian rights bill on December 7, 1967. Ervin's action reminded Mitchell of the many times he and his supporters in Congress had struggled to attach antidiscrimination provisions to broad legislation such as federal aid to education, housing, and health. He thought about objections from "many valued friends" who felt it was a mistake to burden popular bills with nondiscrimination amendments. It seemed the Indian rights amendment might cause considerable trouble in the House. Nevertheless, he "recommended to all of my associates that we insist on keeping it as part of the bill." Although the presiding officer now ruled the Ervin amendment was not germane to the civil rights bill, the Senate, on March 8, 1968, unanimously voted to attach it anyway.[36]

In the House, opponents attacked the bill by charging that the amendment would jeopardize the rights of American Indians. Two congressmen, one from each side of the aisle, even denounced blacks for being willing to sacrifice selfishly the interests of another deprived minority. Mitchell happily noted that Ben Reifel, a full-blooded Sioux Indian who was a Republican congressman from South Dakota, denied those charges in his successful defense of the bill.

Mitchell argued that, aside from the Indian rights provision being "a gesture of fairness to a long deprived part of population," it would most certainly be retained in conference owing to wide support. Similarly, the

House and Senate had overwhelmingly voted for the antiriot amendments. The opponents' desire to send the bills to a House-Senate conference obviously had nothing to do with the nature of those provisions.

Knowing that the Senate-passed bill was a bipartisan product, with the obvious support of many eminent constitutional lawyers, were there any serious discrepancies in the proposal that would make it unworthy of approval in its present form? A careful review of Senate opponents' arguments, Mitchell said, showed that they were all adequately answered, and many had been without merit at all. The primary objective of those pressing hardest to send the bill to conference was to have included a provision to permit real estate agents to be parties in racial discrimination. He warned that that would be a tragedy. Blacks would know that Congress had refused to give a needed remedy, through the orderly process of legislation for the protection of constitutional rights.[37]

The final push for passage of the bill was overshadowed, first, by Johnson's March 31 announcement that he would not seek reelection and, second, by King's assassination on April 4 in Memphis, where he was supporting the striking garbage collectors. During a meeting of civil rights leaders with the President the day after King's murder, Mitchell agreed with Whitney Young, executive director of the National Urban League, that an appropriate gesture was to call on Congress to pass the housing bill as a memorial to the slain leader. As riots raged within sight of the Congress in reaction to the murder, Mitchell had to work frantically to avoid further delays before the start of SCLC's Poor People's Campaign, which would have killed all chances for passage of the bill in 1968.[38]

Meeting with Ford on April 8, Mitchell found him surprisingly pleasant in view of a letter critical of him that he had earlier written to Nixon. Ford told Mitchell he had misunderstood his position because at no time had he ever said he would vote against the housing bill. He maintained that his concern was procedural. Mitchell reminded him of the numerous statements he had made to the press and showed him copies of real estate publications that mentioned he would probably help in weakening the housing bill. Ford answered the reports Mitchell had heard by saying he would not attempt to persuade any member to vote with him but would leave each member free to decide for himself. "You know this will be important, Clarence," he asserted, to which Mitchell responded, "Well, Gerry, I know that you have been trying to take a lot of votes away from us and it will be helpful if you do not insist upon having persons vote against the previous question as a matter of party policy."

Again, Ford gave assurances he would not do that. He said, "I intend to vote against the previous question, but if that effort to send it to conference fails, I intend to vote for the Senate bill."

Following their discussion of Mitchell's historical review of Republican support for civil rights legislation, Ford told the lobbyist he could show him letters to his constituents in which he said he would support the housing bill on final passage. Mitchell assured him that had he had the minority leader's forum in the House, it would not have been necessary for him to launch a public attack. They ended their meeting in laughter.

Mitchell portrayed the struggle as one "between a Goliath of prejudice and selfishness and a David of hope and justice." John B. Anderson of Illinois, acting in the Lincolnian tradition, served as Mitchell's Republican ace and foil on the Rules Committee. Tennessee's James H. Quillen, the GOP point man on the committee, used the Memphis garbage workers strike to launch a bitter attack on the bill. On April 9, Anderson provided the crucial vote to defeat, 7 to 8, a motion to send the bill to conference. The committee then voted to send the bill to the full House. McCulloch, ranking Republican on the Judiciary Committee, and Charles E. Goodell of New York, chairman of the Republican Committee on Planning and Research, urged acceptance of the Senate amendments.

Ford remained a man of his word. The next day he moved to send the bill to conference. But Ray J. Madden, Democrat of Indiana, successfully countered with a motion for the House to adopt Resolution 1100, thereby agreeing to the Senate amendments. That was the crucial test. Those voting for Madden's motion wanted to keep the bill alive. During the debate, Anderson, who had acknowledged he had once wanted to send the bill to conference, made an eloquent plea for passage that Mitchell thought rivaled King's "I have a dream" Lincoln Memorial speech in 1963. Mitchell watched as the House, "in a remarkable display of principle," voted 229 to 195 to approve Madden's motion, thereby accepting the Senate bill without change or amendments. Ford now joined the House in approving the bill and sending it to the President, who signed it the following day. The new law covered 80 percent of all housing sold or rented after 1969. King's assassination was a major theme during the House debates. How much of an effect his murder had on the majority vote, however, was a question because the riots were costly.[39]

Mitchell thought it fortunate that opponents of the Indian rights amendment so overstated their case in the House that they lost support. He believed that the amendment gave "us an opportunity to remind the country that there are some problems in common among all racial, religious, economic and political groups." If everyone worked together unselfishly, he told a friend, "it will be possible to raise the standards of all of our people to the level that the President, you, and the vast majority of Americans desire."

Once more, Mitchell thanked Bolling for his "good judgment and skillful planning" in helping to get the bill out of the Rules Committee. Because an earlier attempt to have the bill reported out and brought to the floor on March 27 had failed, events on April 9 were vitally important. That was the day of Martin Luther King's funeral in Atlanta, but it was essential for some to remain in Washington. Mitchell declined an offer from Vice President Humphrey to join his party on the flight to Atlanta. It was fortunate, he told Bolling, that he too had remained in Washington. "If you had not been present, we would not have been able to win the Rules Committee vote that made final floor action possible on April 10."[40]

Mitchell regarded Johnson's leadership as priceless. "He had assets that nobody else had, and he used all of them in our favor." He hesitated to state for the record many of the things Johnson had done to help in the struggle. They were not illegal, but he feared embarrassing anyone. Nevertheless, he cited Johnson's help in Dirksen's 1962 reelection campaign as one example.

Mitchell's praise for Johnson contrasted sharply with his criticisms of some black leaders, especially Charles Evers of Mississippi and Floyd McKissick, head of CORE, for saying that the Fair Housing Act was no good or insignificant. "'Floyd,' I asked, 'did you read the bill?' Floyd told me he hadn't had time. . . . Now I can understand that, but what makes me so mad is if these leaders say these bills are nothing, then the poor Negro asks, 'If this is nothing, what is there?'" Such "mealy mouthed and deprecatory assessments" of significant civil rights victories in the courts and in Congress, he believed, were responsible for the prevailing confusion among youths. Actually, he explained, until passage of the law, "many people thought that we had been had, that the President had wriggled out of an executive order." But he never felt that way because in late 1965 Johnson had told him in a private session what he was prepared to do.

In a speech prepared for the President's signing of the Fair Housing Act of 1968, but which he was unable to deliver at that time because he did not feel that it would have been appropriate for him to disrupt the program, Mitchell told Johnson that the occasion was eloquent testimony of his determination to make democracy a living reality for all citizens. He recalled the early days, when Celler and McCulloch had fashioned the original bill in 1966. Then in 1968, he said, Dirksen, rising to substitute his proposal for the pending bill, had reminded the nation and the world that this legislation was designed to vindicate the sacrifices of young war veterans. Continuing, he said:

> His desire to support the fair housing legislation was immediately backed by the former lieutenant governor of Michigan, Phi-

lip Hart, who was also a Catholic, and three former state attorneys
general. It is significant to note that one of them, Walter Mondale
of Minnesota, is a Protestant; another, Edward Brooke of Massachusetts, is an American of African ancestry; and the third is Jacob
Javits of New York, a member of the Jewish faith.

In the House, this bill had unqualified backing from John Mc-
Cormack, Majority Leader Carl Albert, and many other members
on both sides of the aisle. Representative Ben Reifel, a fully enrolled member of the Rosebud Sioux tribe of South Dakota, helped
save the important amendment on the rights of American Indians.
From all sections of our country, from our religious faiths and both
political parties, this bill emerged as the will of the people of this
nation. This could not have happened if you had not had the abiding faith, the great determination and the unflagging diligence to
urge this country to act in meeting a great problem.

Three of my four sons have placed me in a category with you.
They have made me a grandfather. It is my belief that what you are
doing and you have done will make it possible for the children of
their generation to grow up in a country and a world where there
will be peace, where there will be democracy and where there will
be continued progress towards the goal of universal brotherhood.

Mitchell had similar appreciation for Hart's help. He had first known
him when he was attorney general of Michigan. He found him unique in
that he had no enemies in the Senate and could work with any member,
whether he was for or against him. As an example of this universal rapport,
Mitchell noted that no one gave a second thought to such things as status
when it was suggested that Hart's office be used for strategy sessions. With
others these prerogatives were always a problem. Furthermore, Hart "was
so sensitive on the problems of people that you almost felt he literally
suffered as he thought about such problems."

Hart was therefore an ideal successor for Humphrey as floor manager
and shared a similar level of esteem as Mitchell. The bond that he had
developed with Humphrey, was so solid that "we got to the place where we
could just sit as you and I are now talking and be completely frank with
each other about our hopes, fears and views on various things, many of
them very confidential." Across the aisle, his friendship with Scott was just
as close. Other good friends included Case and Kuchel, and, of course,
Javits.

In contrast, Mitchell found Dirksen an intriguing challenge. When the
Illinoisan first came to the Senate, their relationship was friendly to the
point where Dirksen, in preparation for a campaign, included Mitchell in a

promotional film that he shot on Capitol Hill, in one scene of which the senator appeared out of the background in a brilliant sunset to shake Mitchell's hand. Dirksen's conservative Midwest background sparked sharp, personal differences between them. Once Dirksen was assured that the spotlight would be turned on him during a debate, however, he could be extremely helpful.

But "with all of his faults," Mitchell found it much easier to work with Dirksen than with Mansfield. The Montanan was aloof and never failed to believe that "Senate business should be handled by senators, and we poor mortals on the outside ought not to get involved too much." One day, attempting to break through this wall, Mitchell stopped by Mansfield's office to thank him for some commendable action he had taken. "But, really, I got such a cool reception—about a minute of his time as he was virtually walking out the door—in a manner that I so considered utterly lacking in courtesy that I regretted very much that I had gone to thank him."[41]

The widespread recognition Mitchell got for his role in the passage of the 1968 Fair Housing Act was rich compensation for his many trying years as a lobbyist. In an editorial, *The Washington Post* commented that the real heroes of legislative battles were often unsung while others who were most visible got the hurrahs. So a "special salute" was in order for Mitchell "for the part he played in bringing the latest civil rights bill to enact-ment—and for the part he played in the adoption of every civil rights measure for more than a decade past." His faith in the Congress and the American people, the *Post* said, "steadfastly thwarted and denied failure" in the long struggle for such legislation. "All Americans are in debt to him." Similarly, in a follow-up article, the newspaper noted *Congressional Quar-terly*'s extensive documentation of the lobbyist's key role in passing the law.

Ramsey Clark, who had enjoyed a long affinity with Mitchell ever since confrontation over the Justice Department's effort to give states jurisdiction in the 5,050 federal enclaves in the United States had a unique understand-ing of Mitchell's contributions to making his legislation a reality. When Clark became head of the Lands Division of the Justice Department in 1961, the problem of extending Fourteenth Amendment rights to Indians and others like civilian employees stationed at the Perry Point (Maryland) Veterans Hospital, which was on land under exclusive federal control, was still tugging at the Congress. Perry Point employees, for example, could not vote in state elections and, like Indians, were not protected by state laws. By the same token, state segregation laws could not apply to resi-dents in federal enclaves.

Clark, like Humphrey, wanting to extend Fourteenth Amendment pro-tections to those citizens, began pushing a bill to authorize surrender of federal jurisdiction of those enclaves to the states. Like Humphrey, he did not see the civil rights implications of the issue—that states would be able to extend segregation into the enclaves—until Mitchell made him aware of them. For a while, consideration was given to including an antisegregation amendment in the bill. But Pohlhaus pointed out that even with such a provision, blacks in federal enclaves would be worse off. Javits helped resolve this problem by holding up the bill while the civil rights implications were studied. When Clark did understand the problem, Mitchell recalled, "Clark, who always was a very sensitive person, seemed deeply ashamed that he had been any party to this, and he never gave it any real importance after that."

Clark respected Mitchell's vigilance and his ability to detect civil rights implications in areas that others would have overlooked. His appreciation of Mitchell's concerns enabled him to understand the frustrations the lobbyist had felt with the Kennedy administration and the feelings of oneness he shared with Johnson on civil rights. Like Mitchell, Clark was convinced that the Kennedys—John and Robert—were deeply committed to the *idea* of civil rights. Clark, though, understood the Kennedys' commitment as akin to their sympathy for the problems of poor Irish Americans. Thus, Robert would be very passionate about civil rights, but he worried about what he sarcastically called the many "friends" he had created in the South as a result of the administration's support for civil rights. Despite this worry about losing the South by creating enemies there, John and Robert never wavered in their commitment to the idea. On legislation, though, they fell flat—that is, until the Birmingham demonstrations and assassination of Medgar Evers forced them to take a radically different position.

In contrast, Johnson had civil rights in his bones. In part, Johnson's understanding was cultural; he had come from a background of poverty similar to Mitchell's, and Texas was part of the old South. Johnson's attitude was different from that of most southerners. Had he come from east Texas, very probably he would have been a racist, but he came from the hill country, where there had been no slaves of any number, because cotton could not be grown there. A different form of settler lived in that region—not the early English, but the new Germans and other new groups. To the west of Johnson there were the Chicanos from Mexico; the blacks were to the east. His early experience teaching Chicanos reinforced his own personal experiences with poverty—an understanding that was enhanced by Johnson's earthiness. There was nothing elitist or aristocratic about him.

Those qualities plus Johnson's sense of history, his sincere desire to guide the nation through a period of grief following John Kennedy's murder, and to help the American people do something decent to atone for it, made him not only embrace fervently his predecessor's commitment to racial equality and social justice, but also use his singular knowledge of the Congress to steer the Kennedy bill to passage. There was no more noble human ideal than that of abolishing poverty and racial injustice, and Johnson truly believed this, as he made eloquently clear in his Howard University speech. His use of the phrase "We shall overcome," against the almost unanimous advice of his advisers, emphasized Johnson's inherent, natural, regional, cultural, and personal commitment to ending racism and human injustice—as well as his political instincts.

Johnson knew there had to be an appropriate climate for legislation to be passed. There had to be popular demand. That was why, with "law and order" on the ascendancy in late 1965, he did not push for the passage of the 1966 civil rights bill as hard as Wilkins thought he should have done. Johnson had gone against the tide in proposing legislation barring discrimination in housing rather than issuing an executive order. There had to be an expression of national will to make the provision work. But he bided his time in waging an all-out fight for it until he knew the time was right.

Clark felt that "if we had paddled harder we could have gotten more out" of Congress in 1964 and 1965. Regarding the 1964 Civil Rights Act, he thought Title VI could have been more comprehensive, and Title VII could have had enforcement language. The problem of the literacy requirement extension in the 1965 Voting Rights Act could have been avoided. But much more than was necessary was conceded to Dirksen. Clark said, "I think we could have rolled over him. I think we conceded him too much power. I think he found himself, and he certainly was, in a key strategic legislative position in the Senate. If we had put more heat and less entreaty we could have succeeded. We almost went up there hat in hand and said, please. So he just had more fun toying with the legislation." Clark did not mean to denigrate the importance of the 1964 and 1965 acts but to empathize with Mitchell's continuing struggles over enforcement of Title VI, strengthening Title VII, and the approaching battle over extending the Voting Rights Act.[42]

There was no doubt that during the actual struggle for the legislation Mitchell shared Clark's views. Subsequently, though, given his broader knowledge of other aspects of the struggle outside Clark's range, it was more probable that Mitchell would have sided with Katzenbach, who almost violently disagreed with his former subordinate and successor over whether the 1964 Civil Rights Act and the 1965 Voting Rights Act could have been stronger. Katzenbach believed that the administration had gotten as much as it could out of Congress in those years. The differences between Clark and Katzenbach revealed the dynamic tensions that existed within the Kennedy and Johnson administrations over civil rights and showed why Mitchell, the principled political realist, found the support of both attorneys general so valuable.

In 1968, there was no doubt that Dirksen had much more power than in 1964 because the groundswell of public opinion was against civil rights. It was therefore also highly unlikely the civil rights forces could have gotten any more out of Congress that year. Many liberals, too, had lost interest in the struggle. The momentum was gone and the immediate future was very ambiguous. Furthermore, while Wilkins had been distracted by attacks within the NAACP on his leadership and his participation on the National Advisory Commission on Civil Disorders, Johnson's attention was consumed by the Vietnam War, requiring him to delegate to others much of the responsibility for this struggle. In this climate, Mitchell's contributions, with Rauh's faithful support, were indisputable. "I don't know how many people can get senators to sleep on cots for something that's going to cost them votes," said Clark. But Mitchell did during the crucial Senate votes.[43]

CHAPTER TWENTY-ONE

Confronting the Politics of Reaction

I n the days of the Great Depression, we were afflicted with a plague of prophets and self proclaimed divinities. Most of them had ordinary names like John Smith or Sam Brown. They knew that if John Smith or Sam Brown had something to sell the public there was a need to do the selling under bright lights and with full opportunity for the prospective buyers to make a close inspection.

Interestingly, when the Smiths and Browns changed their names to something exotic like Prophet Zingunga or the True God Schmoggles, business would pick up. Meetings could be held in dimly lighted rooms, magic powders could be sold in sealed envelopes and the gullible fought for a chance to pay a dime for a "lucky number" or a special enemy destroying rag doll.

Now the Smiths and Browns are adopting what they say are African names. They shave their heads in contrast to their prototype who wore turbans and clothing roughly similar to the garb of the people of India. Where depression-type prophets and godlings enjoyed using the poetic and sonorous phrases of the Old Testament or the Koran, their modern descendants like to use dirty four letter words, bits of philosophy and a special jargon which they say is the language of the man in the street.

Perhaps the wearers of the so-called Afro hair styles are really sincere, but I know some of them who were steady customers in the "process" shops only a few years ago. Somehow, it is hard to see much difference between the type of person who wants to attract attention by letting his hair grow long and wooly and the person who wants to gain notice by getting the slickest treatment possible for carefully cultivated long hair.

I would like to make a suggestion to this new cult. First, give your real names. Next, discard the dark glasses so your eyes may be seen. Then get normal hair cuts. Get rid of the robes, the odd head gear and the dirty words. Drop the racial epithets and the advocacy of mayhem and murder. When these things are done, state your ideas in simple language. Only then will it be possible to know whether we are hearing a message from the heart or the usual claptrap of charlatans.[1]

Inevitably, once basic civil rights goals had been achieved, the movement would lose steam. The difficulties in charting a new course for the remainder of the twentieth century were obvious to those sincere in working for change. Rationality, experience, and vision could provide a second wind for some of the exhausted and guidance for the younger generation who most recently had entered the movement. Mitchell believed that one of the best indicators of progress was that all four senators from Tennessee and Kentucky and one from Texas voted for the 1968 Fair Housing Act. In the House twelve members from Florida, Kentucky, Louisiana, Tennessee, and Texas also voted for it. Those states were once totally opposed to any civil rights laws. So, he declared, at this stage in history, Americans had three choices: "We can retreat to a segregated society, where we will have all-black or all-white communities living in fear, exploitation and frustration. We can have token relationships with each other across racial lines and, thereby, deprive thousands of Americans opportunities; or we can step boldly into the future where we will all be emancipated from the shackles of racism and discrimination."

In effect, African Americans were well positioned to launch the third phase of the movement for political and economic development. Instead, as Mitchell lamented in his "From the Work Bench" column, the Babel created by the opportunists and the black revolutionaries, or anarchists, posed an ominous distraction and diversion and an excuse for those who believed blacks had achieved too much to start pushing for a rollback of civil rights progress. The confusion amid the raging violence in the cities was a balm to southern racists, a boon to northern white backlash merchants, and a drain on the energies of sincere white supporters and activists devoted to the struggle against racial injustice.

Mitchell was most angered by the recurring question, "Who is the leader of colored people in the United States?" He responded by stressing,

"There is no one person who can speak for all of us." Even Martin Luther King did not pretend to do so. Throughout King's southern base, there were hundreds of local NAACP leaders to whom the nation had to look for direction in solving racial problems. *We do not move because someone presses a button in New York or Washington. We act because we have a common determination to keep the nation great and also to assure that its wealth and its opportunities are shared by all of its people without regard to color of skin"* (italics Mitchell's).

The counterpoint to the established civil rights leaders like Mitchell, now labeled "moderates," were "black power" anarchists like Stokely Carmichael, who had supplanted John L. Lewis as head of SNCC, militants like Floyd McKissick, a former NAACP leader in North Carolina, who had succeeded the more mainstream James Farmer as head of CORE, and Black Panther party founders Huey P. Newton and Bobby Seale.

These black radicals had flashy ideas but no bankroll and no meaningful political support. Nevertheless, their angry appeals sparked roaring flames of pride among young blacks on college campuses and throughout inner-city ghettos. The Black Muslims at least had a program based on self-help. Nevertheless, they, along with the other radicals, were romantics reflecting a millenarian strain who maintained it was possible for blacks to make it the rest of the way without the help, and outside, of the system.

Their separatist and generally antiwhite gospel was sacrilege to veteran ("moderate") leaders like Wilkins, Mitchell, and Whitney Young of the National Urban League, who were attempting to hold to the traditional course, which meant working within the system and using the Constitution and the new laws to achieve full equality for blacks. In between was King, a pariah to the anarchists and an enigma to both the militants and the moderates, seeking a new agenda in the North and extending his voice to the peace movement out of conviction.

For Mitchell, whose role in Washington remained well-defined throughout this shake-out period when new agendas were being sought, "black nationalism," the all-encompassing rubric for the mélange of racial philosophies, represented the death of the civil rights movement. Mitchell, of course, was well aware of the differing strains of philosophies, both constructive and destructive, being labeled black nationalism. He was bitterly opposed to nihilistic expressions of racial pride from black power advocates and the Black Panthers that matched the abhorrent white supremacist doctrine—a form of self-hatred that was breeding violence and destruction in the urban centers—more so than to the original philosophy of Marcus Garvey, whose colorful uniforms and regalia of the 1920s had been anathema to him. As he said of Garvey, "In later years, I realized that he was a man motivated by many things, some of which were high purposes." But, in his youth, Garvey did not appeal to him.

Ironically, none of those now preaching black power and black pride and armed self-defense by blacks was prouder of his racial heritage or had a better understanding of his historical roots than Mitchell. The difference was in his sound sense of history, his commitment to a cause, his realistic and meaningful program, and his manner of expression, as was demonstrated by the enormous drive that had been propelling him since the early 1930s in the struggle for human dignity. Without a vision, the black power merchants could not establish goals and a program.

Mitchell was somewhat handicapped in counteracting the "moderate" image because, with the notable exceptions of Adam Clayton Powell and Edward Brooke, his principal allies throughout his struggle for the passage of civil rights laws up through 1968 were white. (Samuel Jackson during the Nixon administration would become his quiet counterpart to Joseph Rauh within the government.) Yet none of those whites with whom he worked so closely could ever state that Mitchell at any time was not conscious of his racial mission. His belief in the humanity of all people was the bridge that transcended the badge of skin color and drove him to seek equality for all persons under the law. He explained:

> It seemed to me we needed to hold to course because that was the only sensible thing to do. A lot of those attacks on whites were very divisive and counterproductive. Attacking all whites was extremely dumb because that ruled out a whole lot of people who, in some instances though white, had more of a commitment to civil rights than a whole lot of blacks.
>
> I knew firsthand those who had worked with us and were really carrying the laboring responsibilities from day to day over the years. I am sorry to say there were a whole lot of blacks who weren't involved and weren't as determined to get these results as were some of the whites with whom I worked. So to me it was just the worst kind of betrayal of friends to talk about ruling out every white person, no matter what their background and commitment might have been. I was very exasperated with some of the rhetoric that emerged in that period and never failed to say so.[2]

High on the list of such dedicated whites were Harry and Ruth Kingman of the Citizens' Lobby for Freedom and Fair Play. They were unique in their effectiveness in rounding up votes in Congress. As Californians, they normally concentrated on the West Coast, but they were equally adept at working their New England and Southwest contact lists. Mitchell figured that their record through 1968 was "about 95 percent effective." For example, he explained, the senators whom the Kingmans persuaded to vote for cloture on limiting debate on the housing bill were "the most difficult to convince" even though they favored civil rights as a matter of principle. Mitchell was particularly impressed that the votes they garnered came "because of their salesmanship and tireless effort in personally seeing congressmen and senators."

Mitchell lashed out at the purveyors of "irresponsible talk about going it alone"—the black separatists—and at the "so-called black nationalism" ideology. For more than a century, he told one audience, blacks had been working to enter the mainstream of American life. "We have been trying to build a desegregated society and a code of fair treatment that does not consider the color of a man's skin, the texture of his hair or where his ancestors came from." Yet, as that goal was in sight, demagogues arose who were seeking to "replace the physical prisons of racial segregation with the mental chains of segregated thinking." He urged blacks not to be led by such opportunists. Separation had "not worked for white hate merchants in the South" and neither would it for "the apostles of racism in Chicago, New York, Philadelphia or Baltimore." He urged blacks to turn their "backs on Ku Klux types, whether they be white men covered with bed sheets or colored men covering their race prejudice with silver-tongued phrases and slick slogans."

Mitchell's view of the black power phenomenon was less doctrinaire than Wilkins's. Mitchell himself was the product of a radical youth movement in Maryland. He was not exposed during childhood to the brutality of Jim Crow, but his "up-South Baltimore" was considerably worse for blacks than Wilkins's urbane St. Paul, where racism was more subterranean.

Furthermore, although Lillie Carroll Jackson, Juanita, and the children did not serve daily with Mitchell in Washington, they were inestimable complements and influences. Juanita and her mother were an immovable force in the quest for black equality—not for Du Bois's "talented tenth" but for the masses. They invited militancy, rejecting only suicidal revolutionary ideologies like black separatism and anarchism. "Little Clarence," as Mitchell's oldest son was called during his father's lifetime, epitomized this radicalism, serving as a burr under the skin of Maryland's white power structure and later the Reagan administration—a role that made him a prime target for devastating political counteroffensives. Wilkins did not benefit from such intimate influences. Unlike Wilkins, who was ideologically opposed to all strains of black nationalism, Mitchell separated the genuine believers in racial pride like Garvey and Malcolm X from the opportunists.

While noting that it was Stokely Carmichael who had popularized the "black power" slogan in 1966, Mitchell recognized that it had no standard definition. It was "a mirror of people's views." Carmichael's initial concept as a rallying cry was "We must come together around the issue that oppressed us—which is our blackness." He defended black power as neither black supremacist nor antiwhite. McKissick said black power meant "total control of the economic, political, educational and social wealth of our community, from top to bottom." Wilkins said it was simply "anti-white power," another term for "going it alone." Similarly, King said, "It gives the impression that we are calling for exclusive power and a kind of black nationalism that does not involve a coalition with whites." Young called for the National Urban League to repudiate any group "that has formally adopted black power as a program, or which ties in domestic civil rights with the Viet Nam conflict."[3]

Not all whites were frightened by the term. Mitchell was surprised to hear William McCulloch, from a highly conservative all-white area of Ohio, give his own constructive definition of black power in a House hearing and declare, "If that's what black power means, I'm for it."

Mitchell's attempt to understand human motivations gave him mixed feelings about Malcolm X; he concluded that the Black Muslim leader's image had been grossly distorted by the news media. Even though "he was the kind of person who would make terrible speeches about white people," Mitchell felt that Malcolm X was not as disrespectful of the law as his early rhetoric might have indicated. He recalled the time that Malcolm X had visited the Senate during a crucial civil rights battle. The entire security detail had rushed over to Mitchell in the gallery for advice on how to treat him. "My answer was, just like any other citizen. I don't think he is going to create any trouble." So Malcolm X and his coterie of bodyguards were permitted to take their seats in the Senate gallery. Because it was crowded, he, like other visitors without special approval, was only allowed to remain for a few minutes, after which they had to leave to make way for other visitors.

Mitchell saw Malcolm X and his group quietly leave at least twice as the rules required and return when they were permitted to do so. Then, upon being advised on the Senate floor about what was happening, Jacob Javits arranged for the black leader to be seated in an area from which he and his associates did not have to move.

Afterward, Mitchell was amused as the news media tried to stage a confrontation between Malcolm X and Martin Luther King. "To their great disappointment," instead of being hostile, both leaders "greeted each other as long lost friends with happy handshakes and virtually embracing." As he blamed the press in the shaping of Malcolm X's image, Mitchell also blamed them for giving national and international stature to blacks preaching lawlessness and violence.

Mitchell's belief in the universality of humanity did not save him from the contradictions between America's democratic principles and its racial mores. He recognized and accepted the need for constructive philosophies on race that differed considerably from his and identified strongly as a black with some of the most radical ideologues. The big difference, of course, was that Mitchell's philosophy was inclusive of other groups. He was violently opposed to excluding anyone from the enjoyment of his human and constitutional rights. His philosophy of political humanism was rooted in the belief that "the forces of freedom are drawn from all races, all religious faiths and all economic groups [who] comprise the population of the United States."[4]

Ramsey Clark could never forget a "touching experience" that revealed the extent of Mitchell's immense drive as well as his racial pride. On a flight to North Carolina for an NAACP banquet, Mitchell "talked about looking forward to the day he—he meant himself as well as his people—could move back to North Carolina—meaning North Carolina, Mississippi and those other states in the South—and live where he and they wanted to live with dignity and equality in places that their forebears had suffered so much.

"You could tell he wanted that very much," according to Clark. "It was like he wanted to go back home and just relax. But he knew he couldn't because he had miles to go before he slept, and he had to keep the struggle and keep the faith. It was a sentimental journey for him in a way."[5]

Mitchell, like many other blacks, was uncomfortable not only with Martin Luther King's philosophy of nonviolence, but also with the SCLC's ability to grab center stage, and, most important, with his opposition to the Vietnam War. He believed that King was as close to being a saint as any person in the twentieth century. But, for Mitchell, King's elevation of moral law over the Constitution in a struggle for constitutional rights within the sociopolitical sphere was causing contradictions that were not necessarily helpful to African Americans. Mitchell, too, believed firmly in the preeminence of moral law. He also believed that a pragmatic balance had to be maintained. For example, he concluded that some of the violent expressions among black youths were a reaction to the humiliations they had suffered in the South under the strategy of turning the other cheek and "loving" those who physically persecuted them.

Furthermore, as he had done in 1956 when he was arrested in South

Carolina for using the "white" waiting room at the Florence railroad station, Mitchell believed a citizen had the right to challenge an unfair law. He did not believe the strategy of staying in jail could work in the long run in a democracy. He noted that opponents of the 1954 school desegregation decision had adopted similar tactics, and in many instances the resulting violence blocked implementation of court orders. It was hard for him "to see how you can be against civil disobedience when white people practice it and not be against it when colored people practice it." King would have responded that the difference was between a just and an unjust law. But Mitchell believed the better alternative was to change the unjust law. And, indeed, it was the NAACP's approach, in the courts and Congress, that vindicated King's nonviolent tactics. Both tactics were essential to progress.

In addition to finding King a very interesting person, Mitchell "always felt that underneath his idealism there was a very strong practical sense so that he was thinking ahead each time he made a move." He acknowledged that if African Americans had not adopted nonviolence, there would have been a bloodbath. "To the extent that it was a matter of saving lives, I could see that it made sense. But, as a philosophy, I just could never accept it as one that I would live by." Mitchell was an advocate of self-defense—a right protected by the Constitution. "I could never accept the philosophy of letting your enemies kick you around, spit on you, and do all the other things they were doing." He knew that "there was greater sympathy for blacks when someone was shown on television being dragged down the courthouse steps, with his head bumping on every step, or being routed with fire hoses, or being bitten by police dogs" than there would have been had demonstrators been fighting back, as some black radicals were now advocating.

His alternative for combatting such an injustice was to fight harder for civil rights laws and in the courts. "I believe," he explained, "as the NAACP does, that you must use all your constitutional rights and constitutional tools to challenge the law, that if you land in jail you get out on bail and continue the fight in the courts." Despite his great humility and sensitivity, he could only hope that he too could forgive his enemies, but "it was not easy."

One form of behavior he never really forgave, as an example of "when people would do things which were very unfair," was that of King and Walter Fauntroy, the SCLC's Washington representative, during the signing of the 1965 Voting Rights Act. Even though the President's Room in the Capitol was unusually small, Johnson held the signing ceremony there to underscore the historical significance. Mitchell was most unhappy that many of the people who had been invited had not been directly involved in the legislative battle but they were all given prominent seats in the Rotunda, where the preliminary ceremony was held, while "we who had really been working to get the bill through" were placed in the back. "Joe Rauh saw something on my face which reflected how I felt."

Just as Mitchell was about to walk out in disgust, Rauh told a Johnson aide, "You can't do this. You've got to have Clarence up in these seats where they actually go in to the signing." The rest of the guests had to remain in the Rotunda. Mitchell was then given a chair of prominence.

Adding insult to injury, as the group moved into the President's Room, King and Fauntroy tried to jump ahead of Mitchell and to knock him out of the line. "Unfortunately for them, I was in a stance where, instead of knocking me out, they knocked themselves up against the wall." Enjoying the incident, an observer said, "Gee, Clarence, I didn't know you were such a good football blocker"—a point that, even if humorous, underscored the interplay of moral law and human behavior.

In a more serious vein, Mitchell regretted that all too frequently events like those were organized from a public relations point of view. The goal was to get the more popular leaders in a picture rather than the people who had worked in the trenches. Mitchell felt that people like Rauh and Arnold Aaronson, who had worked day and night to get the bill passed, got little or no recognition.[6]

Like Wilkins and Whitney Young, Mitchell was opposed to King's joining the peace movement in opposition to the Vietnam War. This split in the civil rights ranks crossed racial lines and also involved Mitchell's most faithful ally, Rauh, and other liberals. Because he was a Nobel Peace Prize laureate of international standing, King's role was particularly important; this was due also to his immense influence within the civil rights movement and on social and political events in the nation.

As King's foray into Chicago in 1966 had shown, however, his leadership had lost focus. King did not even support Paul Douglas in the midterm senatorial race. An elder moderate black leader lamented:

> The tragedy is not that King is going to the peace issue but that he is leaving civil rights. Instead of providing the inspirational leadership, the magnetism, he's diverting energy and attention from the basic problems of poverty and discrimination. And how are you going to denounce Lyndon Johnson one day and ask him the next for money for poverty, schools and housing.

Despite qualified disclaimers, King was locked into this new course.

Mitchell saw no conflict in denouncing Johnson or any other political leader for policies he thought were bad for African Americans. Had he believed, like King, that the peace cause would directly benefit African Americans, he would have said so. In addition to basing his stand on moral grounds, one of King's most convincing reasons for opposing the Vietnam War was that it was draining funds from Great Society and other programs beneficial to minorities. Mitchell, however, had ample support for his contrary views. Had Humphrey won the 1968 election, King's argument might have held up; but it could not with Nixon in the White House. Richard Nixon's hostility toward the Great Society was not due directly to budgetary questions but to a fundamental philosophical difference with its underlying premise. The Nixon administration's fight against inflation through austerity spending would hurt social programs more than the Vietnam War.

Mitchell was all too well aware that the $4.4 billion the Bureau of Budget estimated was needed to feed the poor annually was less than two months' funding for the Vietnam War. He did not believe that if the war ended overnight those funds would be diverted immediately to domestic needs. "No, my friends. Whenever and, however, the war ends, there will be a great political drive to divert those funds into channels that will benefit a few people and not the poor and the deprived."

Like many other Americans, Mitchell initially was unsure about the issues involved in the war and thus accepted the administration's propaganda that the capture of Vietnam by the Communists would severely damage U.S. interests in the region. In addition to his personal and political loyalty to Johnson, he held a view traditional among African Americans that it was in their interest to support their country in foreign excursions. "I can't remember any period in this country's history, and certainly not in the period of my lifetime, when blacks didn't want to be in the Army or the Navy," he maintained.

Blacks saw such wars as opportunities to win acceptance as full-fledged citizens. For Mitchell, Vietnam was no different. As long as they were not relegated to mess boys or engineers digging ditches, he felt that blacks wanted to be in there right along with everyone else. "You may remember in World War Two we had this double victory campaign, which was victory at home on employment opportunities, and programs like that, and victory abroad by having people in all the units of the armed services, not just in segregated stevedore battalions." (Mitchell did not serve in World War II because he was married and had two children.) His prime reason for differing with King was not fear of antagonizing Johnson, but his belief that when the country was at war blacks had a duty to serve and would benefit from the opportunities opened up to them.

Mitchell, though, drew a very fine line between those who opposed the Vietnam War and those who were using the Vietnam War to attack

Johnson. Rauh's joining the anti–Vietnam War movement did not affect their relationship at all, but Mitchell was very upset with liberals who used the war to attack Johnson and denounced them at a Leadership Conference banquet. "I felt that by attacking Johnson they were playing into the hands of the anti-civil-rights forces in the country," he explained.

In subsequent years he was even more embittered by those attacks. He charged that Johnson's detractors were racists because they were merely using the war as a palpable excuse to condemn him for his strong advocacy of civil rights and support for African Americans.

Taking a similar stand was Associate Justice Thurgood Marshall. He felt that Johnson "wasn't thrown out because of Vietnam; they just used that as an excuse to get rid of him" because "he was too far out for Negroes and civil rights." These views were sustained by the fact that although Nixon intensified the Vietnam War and expanded it into neighboring Cambodia, destroying that once beautiful country, he never suffered the opprobrium that was heaped on Johnson even though Nixon's Indochina policies were based on the same imperialistic motivations and were just as disastrous as his predecessor's.[7]

Unlike King, therefore, whose civil rights program was shaped by a philosophy of moral humanism and forbearance that appealed to the conscience; and unlike the positions of King's liberal supporters, which were shaped more by an opposition to human injustice than by the African American experience, Mitchell's political humanism was geared to practical accomplishments and progressive achievements. It was founded on a blend of his strong belief in Christianity and the Constitution and the practical imperatives of the legislative process. King, despite being practical, as a spiritual leader generally overlooked the logistics of the struggle, acting instead on the basis of his moral ideals. That was especially so in the later stages of his work. Mitchell was the opposite, using forbearance of a person's views in establishing strategy to protect the constitutional rights of blacks.

He explained: "I think that in the world of political action there were many people who had high, moral principles. But those principles were never activated if it was to a political disadvantage to follow them. I know this to be a fact because I had talked with so many of our opponents from the South and other parts of the country who were sympathetic to what we were seeking but who felt they just couldn't get reelected if they did what their moral convictions dictated. So I would say that, certainly the moral compulsions are there. They are very important in trying to win public support. But I am afraid that if there is a moral conviction to act but not enough votes to assure that the actor can get reelected, moral conviction does not prevail."

By the same token, he found that moral persuasion was effective in cases where blacks had minimal political power but constituents did not care what their congressmen did on civil rights. One good example was Arthur V. Watkins, a conservative Republican senator from Utah in the 1950s. Mitchell did not believe that the average citizen of Watkins's state cared one way or the other how he voted on issues affecting African Americans, so Watkins was able to follow his moral beliefs freely. In New York, Javits, who had an impeccable civil rights record, could never win support from African Americans in New York City because of their strong allegiance to the Democratic party. In other areas of the state, however, minorities supported him, but that support was never crucial to his political fate. "Yet, in spite of that," Mitchell said, "he was always absolutely perfect in his support for us on civil rights. He, in addition to being very important in the Senate, was most tenacious and persuasive. So that we had wonderful help from him, not only in the Senate but also when he was a member of the House."

The political imperatives that were Mitchell's rudder mattered less to King and other black activists, who in their philosophical or personal zeal failed to recognize the critical importance of Johnson's leadership in the struggle for civil rights legislation.

Louis Martin recalled how King, having grown accustomed to White House entreaties, and a Nobel Peace Prize winner to boot, caused protocol problems by insisting on private meetings with Johnson and then actually canceling two appointments. The President was made most unhappy by the snubs. Mitchell, having worked so hard to open the White House door for blacks, knew only too well the value of such meetings and would never have treated any President, not even Woodrow Wilson, then the archetypal racist, that way.

That ability to find a common ground on which to establish alliances also enabled Mitchell to work so well with labor unions. He knew that almost all the major unions had some form of institutionalized segregation in their rituals, constitutions, or membership practices. Yet he shared Philip Randolph's view that it "would be a fatal mistake" for black workers to regard unions, per se, "as our enemies." Therefore Randolph focused "on cleaning up discrimination in the labor unions, and that, in my judgment, was a tremendously valuable contribution to this country."[8]

Mitchell maintained that, following the murders of King and Robert Kennedy in 1968, rather than "the lamentations about lawlessness" on radio, television, public platforms, and in the press and other expressions of remorse, Americans should have dedicated themselves to constructive behavior. Instead, he observed, experience had shown that this kind of grief did not always inspire people to seek to build a better world.

While recognizing that the need was greater than ever to hold to course, Mitchell would adjust to compensate for the pressures that had thrown the civil rights movement into confusion and made it formless, fractured, and ill-focused. For black militants and revolutionaries the "system" and all whites had replaced the bigoted southerner as the enemy. Mitchell, as he made clear in a statement supporting the Office of Economic Opportunity, felt:

> No one can provide a simple formula for preventing riots. All will agree that demagogues who fan the flames of hate or participate in acts of violence should be dealt with sternly and swiftly in a manner approved by the United States Constitution. But we also have a duty to try with might and main to use our wealth, our brain power and our resources to correct the causes of want and despair. We must find ways to build confidence, to provide opportunities for self betterment to lift the level of those lowest down in our country.

President Johnson's Great Society programs, he felt, were one way of accomplishing that goal. The other way was through the type of political leadership Johnson was displaying.[9]

Earlier, Mitchell had found much to cheer about when Johnson appointed Robert Weaver as secretary of the newly created Department of Housing and Urban Development, Thurgood Marshall to the Supreme Court, and Andrew F. Brimmer as a member of the Federal Reserve Board. These appointments were all historic firsts for blacks, leading Mitchell to declare that Johnson had "set the pace for building an America in which all men have true opportunity to overcome racial, religious and other artificial barriers."

Unlike the appointments of Marshall and Brimmer, which seemed to have caused Johnson no difficulty, the naming of Weaver to the Department of Housing and Urban Affairs was a trying one for both the President and the potential nominee. Johnson kept the position dangling before Weaver—whom friends called "the brains"—for four months while he ostensibly weighed the suitability of some three hundred candidates for the job. Actually, Weaver's appointment was delayed because of intense debate and maneuvering over how HUD should be structured. Weaver had seen Congress kill John Kennedy's attempts to create the landmark agency twice, because the President had made it clear he intended to elevate the housing expert from administrator of the Housing and Home Finance Agency to HUD secretary. Weaver knew that the proposed department did not rank high on Kennedy's legislative agenda; furthermore, he knew that the type of reluctance to expand federal power that had characterized President Eisenhower's attitude toward the administration of urban programs was still widespread in Washington. At the same time, as the Johnson administration wrestled with launching the Great Society, some influential White House officials like Joseph Califano were suggesting that the best way to sell the War on Poverty to the country was for the President to name Sargent Shriver, director of the Office of Economic Opportunity, as HUD secretary, and Weaver or another black as undersecretary. Those and other factors increased Weaver's frustrations to the point where he informed the White House that he intended to resign from the HHFA. Angrily, he let it be known that his "feelings toward Johnson were less than warm." Johnson's treatment of Weaver, however, was no different from the manner in which he had kept Katzenbach dangling for months while he served as acting attorney general. The last thing Weaver intended to do was to serve as acting secretary of HUD.

To avoid precipitous action by Weaver, Johnson had Mitchell relay a message through Wilkins to him that he should not resign. Johnson made sure that Louis Martin delivered similar encouragement, while he kept everyone in suspense over his intended action until he made the surprise announcement at a news conference in the Fish Room of the White House, to which he had invited his entire cabinet for what he called "a proud moment for America." Subsequently, Johnson told Weaver's wife, Ella, that he had intended all along to appoint her husband secretary.

Mitchell said Johnson provided a "magnificent example of how the fight for decency and progress" was being won when, on October 2, 1967, he walked unannounced into the chamber where the new Associate Justice Marshall was taking his oath of office. The process had begun when John Kennedy first moved in 1961 to appoint Marshall, who was then director-counsel of the NAACP Legal Defense and Educational Fund, to the U.S. Court of Appeals for the Second Circuit. Almost immediately, some New York political figures began trying to block this appointment by attempting to get an African American appointed to the lower district court in their state, in order to save the seat on the preferable appellate court for a white person. Mitchell worked with Jacob Javits, Kenneth Keating, and Roman Hruska in freeing the appointment from the Senate Judiciary Committee, where James Eastland and other southerners had frozen it for almost a year.

Mitchell believed that in subsequently appointing Marshall as solicitor general, Johnson revealed his intention to place him on the Supreme Court as a significant symbol of change. Johnson, he said, did not want "a black who was out of touch with people," but one like Marshall who "had an earthy quality" and had broad experience with everyday problems and with

humanity. When he decided to do so, Johnson "knew that neither Senator
Eastland nor anybody else nor any combination could stop him because he
knew how to get things done." Although there were rumors of a political
trade-off, Mitchell was certain of success. It could have been, said Mitchell,
"that Eastland realized that he'd better not offer any real resistance because
it might hurt him in other ways, which the President was capable of
doing" and would have done if necessary. Johnson made sure that Mitchell
understood that he had appointed Marshall and Brimmer on his own voli-
tion and not because the lobbyist or Roy Wilkins had asked him to do so—
and he gave Mitchell permission to state that fact.

Mitchell recalled that in discussing especially the Brimmer appointment with him, Johnson said he was doing so because he wanted to let
white people know that blacks ("I don't know whether he said 'blacks' or
'niggers,' because he was still wrestling with that, the pronunciation of
Negro") could be "something other than judges, lawyers, and doctors. They
could make their way in the business field, and Brimmer in his judgment
was a superior person." [10]

Mitchell was very upset over the opposition—which eventually succeeded—to Johnson's 1968 nomination of Associate Justice Abe Fortas for
Chief Justice of the United States. He felt that though the ostensible reasons for much of the criticism leveled at Fortas concerned his alleged "participation in policy-making" and conflicts of interest, the true reasons for
the attacks were the associate justice's decisions to "protect the constitutional rights of the humble and the deprived," including black citizens. It
was well known in Washington that conservative Republicans and southern
Democrats regarded Fortas as too progressive and were horrified at the
thought that he would be continuing the policies of the Warren Court.
Fortas was forced to resign from the Supreme Court in 1969 after he conceded that he had arranged in 1965 to receive a fee of twenty thousand
dollars a year for life from the family foundation of Louis E. Wolfson, who
was serving a one-year prison term for selling unregistered securities.
Mitchell blamed the type of "harsh words and the unfair attacks" that
characterized the Fortas case, "the thinly covered appeals to racial and religious prejudice" that were often used to destroy the reputations of good
men and institutions, for contributing to the racial violence in the country.

Little wonder that Mitchell was almost moved to tears when he expressed his gratitude to Johnson for his leadership, during a farewell ceremony that black government workers held for the President in December
1968. Expressing his profound regret, which "weighs heavily on my
heart," about Johnson's decision not to seek reelection, Mitchell prayed
that the President would name Humphrey as his successor. "Among all of
the men being mentioned," Mitchell wrote to Johnson, Humphrey "alone

has the long and dedicated personal record of commitment to the millions in our Country who are not always articulate, who seldom appear on our television screens, who do not resort to violence and destruction but who, nevertheless, share your devotion to the building of the future."[11]

Social and political schisms had other repercussions within the civil rights coalition. Many allies like the ADA, seeing the war as a more important issue, had not only turned against Johnson but also against Humphrey, of all people, in favor of Senator Eugene J. McCarthy of Minnesota. Humphrey had been a founder of the ADA. Although Mitchell and McCarthy had been friends for many years, Mitchell was concerned that, unlike Humphrey, McCarthy had never given civil rights the same priority that he gave other legislative issues. That meant he was not a member of the team. For example, during the fight for the 1968 Fair Housing Act, McCarthy "had to make a choice on whether he would be present during the floor fight or spend the major part of his time campaigning. He chose to spend most of his time on the campaign trail." Consequently, of the seven crucial votes on the 1968 civil rights bill, he missed five, including the March 4 cloture vote.

Mitchell was therefore "very irritated with those who, for want of a better word," were called liberals. He thought that by supporting McCarthy "they were running out on Humphrey." He believed it was the worst kind of betrayal: "That was exasperating to me because Humphrey had been so faithful in his whole approach on things. It just seemed to me that all of us were duty-bound to support him consistently."

Rauh was among those who went for McCarthy on the war issue, although he campaigned for Humphrey after the convention. Mitchell forgave Rauh, preferring to see his friend's action as "a little bit different in that he was fond of Humphrey personally." Many liberals, however, along with millions of blacks who sat out the 1968 election claiming that there was no difference between the two candidates, made a political decision that helped to doom Humphrey's chances and ensure that Richard Nixon, riding the crest of white backlash and guided by his Southern Strategy, would squeak through to victory in November.[12]

Despite those gloomy happenings, Mitchell found much hope in the course of political history. He was very troubled, therefore, by the "biased and vindictive" coverage of the 1968 Democratic convention by the CBS and NBC television networks, which focused on attacks on Humphrey rather than on positive developments. Mitchell thought it was historic that there were 218 black Democratic delegates and 180 alternates in Chicago. Furthermore, all states of the old Confederacy were represented by interracial delegations. While in the past organized labor delegates were the largest pro-civil-rights bloc, in 1968 blacks outnumbered labor. Blacks also served on key convention committees.

Mitchell found the racial politics of the delegations from Mississippi, Alabama, and Georgia particularly enlightening. Both Humphrey and McCarthy supported the Mississippi Loyal National Democrats, the racially mixed group who scored a resounding victory by defeating the state's regulars. Mitchell hailed the political wisdom of Aaron Henry, who practiced his own middle-of-the-road political philosophy, as well as that of his partner Charles Evers, brother of Medgar, by ironing out differences among civil rights groups at home before coming to the convention and repeating the 1964 compromise.

The contending Alabama and Georgia delegations epitomized the period's political turmoil. Challengers in these states were more interested in replacing Humphrey with McCarthy than with racial or social progress. Mitchell determined these intentions by conducting his own poll. He asked one challenger who wanted to oust the official Alabama delegation, ostensibly because it was pro-Wallace, whether she would support Humphrey if she were seated. "She angrily replied that she would not. In contrast, one of the so-called pro-Wallace delegates voluntarily announced that he would support the convention nominee." Another challenger wanted to unseat the notable civil rights attorney Arthur Shores, whom a fellow Alabaman described as "the man whose home had been bombed times without number." But, as Shores predicted to Mitchell, diehard segregationists who refused to pledge their loyalty to the party's ticket dropped out, permitting blacks, loyal alternates, and members of the Alabama Independent party to replace them.

In Georgia, the complete displacement of the official state delegation would have resulted in the ouster of prominent black delegates. Mitchell regarded the decision to seat both the official delegation and the challengers and to divide their votes a wise decision.

Although Mitchell was not as encouraged by the less than fifty black delegates at the Republican convention at Miami Beach, he was inspired by the presence of Brooke. He found much hope in the promise by the nation's lonely black senator to work for a more liberal GOP. Given the Republican party's precipitous tilt rightward, Brooke was a historical paradox. That was most evident by Governor Ronald Reagan's response to the question if he were President, would he help to eliminate the filibuster and committee obstruction to civil rights in Congress? Reagan responded, "Well, that's a hypothetical question"—a stance Mitchell thought curious.

Mitchell readily understood the grim significance of the November election results. More than nine million people showed they "wanted to return to stone age civil rights by voting for George Wallace." And although Wallace did not win, Mitchell thought President-elect Nixon was severely handicapped in race relations because much of his campaign appeal had been based on spreading fear and prejudice. Mitchell concluded that "without these two elements he could not have won."

Confirming that view, Strom Thurmond, the prosegregation Democrat-turned-Republican, had declared that Nixon's position on some aspects of school desegregation was similar to that of the South Carolinian. Mitchell therefore anticipated rough sledding in the Ninety-first Congress. "We can expect that counterfeit suggestions, based on so-called self-help and private enterprise financing, will be pushed by those who want to get rid of the anti-poverty program, the Model Cities program and advances that we have made in education, health and other areas," he correctly predicted.[13]

Mitchell's balm during this period of uncertainty remained Johnson, to whom he related the story of a young black doctor:

A wealthy new hospital serving a large and somewhat preju-diced community considered putting the doctor on its staff. Some of those who control the institution were reluctant. They gave in when they were reminded that the hospital had to be in compliance with Title VI of the 1964 Civil Rights Act in order to receive Federal funds. The doctor became a staff member. Not long after he joined the staff his wife gave birth to their first child at the hospital. The doctor's mother and father gave the name of the in-fant to a nurse inside the viewing room. A white lady who was admiring her new grandchild in the room heard the name and said, "I know your son; he saved my husband's life." She then told how her husband, a truck driver, had been taken from his cab with few life signs and rushed to the hospital. The doctor quickly assembled the team that handles such emergencies and the driver recovered.

Shortly after that, the doctor's parents were introduced at a political rally in a large hall. A very dignified, well dressed white couple came to the platform to say that they were grateful for the doctor's work in the recovery of their son. Their son had been brought to the hospital from his college in Boston. He was para-lyzed and in a coma. The doctor made a diagnosis and prescribed a course of treatment that brought the young man out of the coma. There followed a long period of treatment that overcame the paral-ysis. The young man recovered and is now a practicing lawyer.

The doctor in this story is Keiffer J. Mitchell, my second son, who is now on a fellowship at Johns Hopkins Hospital and an instructor on the medical school faculty.

Title VI, which you made possible, gave a young doctor a

chance to prove his worth. He made the most of that chance, and, while doing so, earned the gratitude of the wife and children of a truck driver who probably had never heard of that statute. That doctor also won a place in the hearts of two parents who feared that their son would either come to an untimely end or be an invalid for life. No doubt, they, too, were unaware of how Title VI made it possible for the doctor to be in the place where he could help when his skill and determination were needed.

As I move about the country and see young men and women at airline ticket counters, working in banks and moving into the main job stream of American life I think of the Equal Employment Opportunity law. As I see integrated housing and apartment developments even in the most resistant suburbs, I think of the Fair Housing Act. The reassurances of the worth of your efforts are endless.

We can all be thankful that the Divine plan put you in the White House and you seized the opportunity to build a virtual temple of freedom and respect for human dignity upon the solid rock of law. You have left Washington, but I want you to know that many of us who remain behind will always defend that temple. We are not fearful when adverse winds blow or storms rage. We believe that the temple that you built will endure as long as the Nation endures.[14]

Epilogue

"As long as we base the concept of civil rights on the Constitution of the United States, if there should ever come a time when civil rights would die, the Republic would die. Therefore, we have to keep in mind that when we talk about civil rights, we are talking about those fundamental liberties that the Constitution guarantees." [1]

Guided by that belief, Mitchell reacted with consternation to suggestions that the civil rights struggle was over following passage of the 1968 Fair Housing Act and that the movement's focus had shifted to "human rights," that is, social concerns as opposed to the denial of constitutional liberties for African Americans. No one was more aware than he of weaknesses in the newly passed laws. Compromise was an axiom of the legislative struggle. Progress could only have been made step by step. As long as this struggle was moving forward, even though he never got all he had sought in each legislative breakthrough, he was satisfied that one day he would achieve his goal. Each law was a building block reinforcing the foundation of constitutional liberties. The NAACP had been his primary vehicle for achieving this bloodless revolution and he pinned all hope for future civil rights progress on its ability to survive. "The NAACP is all we have left," he repeatedly told Juanita, noting that the young competitors had become debilitated or had died. "We must never do anything that would divide it."

The award to Mitchell in 1969 of the Spingarn Medal, the NAACP's highest tribute for exemplary achievement to a person of African descent, was an appropriate recognition of his contribution to this long struggle and his love for the organization. The Spingarn Medal was a capstone to his lobbying career, a signal that the quest for equal justice and human dignity, in which he had played such a crucial role, had indeed brought progress not only for the historical victims of racial discrimination but also for the nation.

Sharing the award with his family, he paid special tribute to Lillie Carroll Jackson, who had helped guide him over the years. Of Juanita's selfless devotion and lifelong sacrifices, he noted that "it is a vindication of Dr. Jackson's intentions that Mrs. Mitchell used her legal talents to desegregate every institution in the whole state of Maryland."

Clarence III and Michael,* who during his father's lifetime served on the Baltimore City Council, were his shining examples of political progress. Another indication of the political advancement of African Americans in his state would be the election of his brother Parren to Congress from Baltimore in 1970.

Mitchell used the occasion of the Spingarn award on July 1, 1969, in Jackson, Mississippi, to address the nation in a broad, expansive style befitting his role as a member of the team that had helped instill new life into the Constitution by expanding the concept of individual liberties and justice. The Spingarn Medal, he noted, bound him to other distinguished recipients like Walter White; Thurgood Marshall; Roy Wilkins; Dr. Channing Tobias, the late chairman of the NAACP national board of directors; William Hastie; Dr. Carl Murphy; Dr. Robert Weaver; Daisy Bates, the powerful NAACP spirit who made desegregation of the Little Rock Central High School a reality; and Medgar Evers. There could have been no better location than the Magnolia State—the soul of the civil rights struggle—for this tribute to Mitchell.

"From the streets and plantations of Mississippi, where Medgar labored ceaselessly and without fear," he declared, "to the majestic chamber of our highest tribunal where Mr. Justice Marshall protects the constitutional rights of all who come before that court, these persons have blazed a trail that leads from the jungle of bigotry and selfishness to the mountain tops of free society." He advised that anyone truly interested in black history had only to study the lives of the Spingarn Medal winners.

As an American whose forebears had contributed to building the nation and as a spiritual kinsman of the founders of this country, he declared, he had a right to all the blessings bestowed by the Constitution and had spent his life working to ensure that all citizens shared in them. With Nixon in mind, "I, too, am a law and order man," he said. "But I am a man who seeks just law, and I am a man who seeks the kind of order that makes freedom grow instead of stifling it."

Nothing made Mitchell prouder or inspired him more than the awareness that all three branches of the national government were now equal partners in the civil rights struggle. Having won the fight for their passage, he said, "we shall see that these statutes work. We must not let

---

*In a case involving the Wedtech Corporation, a Bronx, New York, military contractor, Michael and Clarence III were convicted of wire fraud and attempting to obstruct a congressional investigation, as well as of other criminal charges, subsequent to their father's death, and sentenced to the Lewisburg Federal Prison Camp. Although their appeals of the Wedtech convictions were pending, both men were ordered to serve their sentences and did so. Mitchell was spared the pain of this family tragedy.

them be tampered with. We must improve them whenever and however it is necessary to do so. We must also be on guard against and repudiate those forces that would destroy us and our country by causing us to lose faith in the power of just law. Whether it comes from a Ku Klux Klan meeting in a cow pasture, or a street corner meeting in Harlem, the voice that ridicules our Constitution, that demeans the United States Supreme Court, and distorts our civil rights laws is the sound of man's ancient enemy, namely ignorance." The greatest irony, he said, was that both white and black racists were always clamoring to get their cases to the Supreme Court for a fair opinion when they got into trouble.

He had hoped to avoid an early fight with the Nixon administration, but its attack on the 1965 Voting Rights Act and threats to undermine Title VI of the 1964 Civil Rights Act left him no choice but to launch a new stage in the legislative struggle for enforcement of the laws. "We are challenged to fight for what we have won and we accept that challenge," he declared.

He was determined as much to save the Republic from any threats that would undermine its foundations of liberty as to fight to rescue "the Republican Party from its new-found allies like Senator Strom Thurmond," who were militant enemies of civil rights. He did "not object to putting the spirit of Abraham Lincoln into Mr. Thurmond, but we do object to putting the spirit of Mr. Thurmond into the party of Lincoln."

Based on the 1968 election returns, Mitchell had concluded that the Republicans did not capture the White House because they were the overwhelming favorite of the American people. Nixon won with only 43 percent of the popular vote. Mitchell did not consider that a mandate for him to pursue his conservative agenda.

Mitchell's admonitions turned out to be more a prayer than a warning that reality would slow the new administration in expanding its Southern Strategy—consolidation of the GOP's newfound strength in the South with the more than 13 percent of the votes Wallace had received in 1968 as a third-party candidate.

Nixon was bitter toward blacks, in large part because he believed they deserted him for Kennedy in the 1960 election owing to a sympathetic phone call his opponent had made to Martin Luther King while he was languishing in an Alabama county jail during the civil rights demonstrations. "This one unfortunate incident in the heat of a campaign served to dissipate much of the support I had among Negro voters because of my record," Nixon complained. But a *Wall Street Journal* article, well before King's arrest, showed that Nixon would not have benefited from the Eisenhower administration's gains among black voters in 1956. Nixon was

not being influenced by facts but by his belief that blacks did not appreciate his civil rights support.

Mitchell was very concerned that reactionary forces in the Republican
party wanted a Supreme Court that would turn back the clock on civil
rights and related decisions. Guided by his optimism, he did "not believe
that Americans as a whole want that kind of Supreme Court." Neither did
he believe that the majority of Americans shared the opposition of the
Dixiecrat wing of the Republican party to the spending of tax dollars to
build schools, to providing decent homes for low-income families, and to
feeding the hungry. So he did not "hesitate to predict that if the new
administration follows the counsel of the senior senator from South Carolina, Mr. Thurmond, it may carry that state in 1972 but it will not carry
the United States in that election." Nixon, of course, did exactly that,
causing the NAACP to depart from its normally nonpartisan stand and
accuse his administration of being the most antiblack since Woodrow
Wilson. The NAACP would later conclude that the Nixon administration
was a mixed blessing; it was helpful in some areas and a disaster in others.

Mitchell was proud that until Nixon's election to the White House
there had been considerable civil rights progress, which was due to: the
time, money, and legal talent that blacks had devoted to an unending
series of attacks in the courts against racial segregation and discrimination
that had produced a massive body of law outlawing the "separate but
equal" doctrine; the NAACP's expanding program to hold members of the
House and Senate accountable for their actions in Congress and to increase
black political power at the polls; and leadership from the White House in
the struggle against racial injustice, poverty, and social want.[2]

Now, in 1969, revealing his alarm over the turn of events, Mitchell
complained to Congressman William Clay, a Democrat from Missouri,
"Our people do not trust the Nixon Administration." He noted that this
distrust was spawned during the 1968 presidential campaign by Nixon's
appearances and the tone of his speeches, which were laced with such
phrases as "crime in the streets," "not letting the Supreme Court be a
school board," and "too much permissiveness" that were read as appeals to
racism. Sure enough, not only did Nixon appoint an all-white Cabinet that
made it appear that the executive branch was being resegregated, but very
soon afterward he began intensifying distrust among the races by pushing a
civil rights program designed to slow enforcement of the civil rights laws,
especially Title VI, and decisions of the courts involving public school
desegregation.

Mitchell found support for his judgment of Nixon and other Presidents
dating back to Roosevelt in George Sinkler's scholarly assessment, *The Racial Attitudes of American Presidents—From Abraham Lincoln to Theodore Roose-*

velt. The Sinkler study took its thesis from an eminent intellectual's observation that "the assumption that 'human thought arises and operates in a definite social milieu' becomes crucial in any investigation of the ideas of men."

Initially, Mitchell's difficulties with Nixon as President were tempered by the earlier good working relationship they both had enjoyed. Mitchell felt that the major problem with him was that at the time he entered the White House civil rights was rated low among national priorities. Without Nixon's support, there would have been no 1957 Civil Rights Act. "From my personal experiences with him as Vice President under Eisenhower and during the time between his defeat in 1960 and his victory in 1968, I would say that if the nation had continued its high commitment to civil rights that had characterized the Kennedy-Johnson period, President Nixon might well have been one of the great civil rights advocates of our times."

As Vice President, Nixon had sought support from blacks and helped them considerably on civil rights. Mitchell recalled Nixon's once saying to him, "You know, Clarence, the Vice President of the United States is not very important. But people don't know that." He told Mitchell whenever he had visitors to Washington who wanted "to see somebody important, I will be available." He kept that promise.

Like Henry Cabot Lodge, Nixon was a valued conduit to conservative Republicans. During the struggle for the 1968 Fair Housing Act, Mitchell asked him to help round up support. From the campaign trail in Wisconsin, Nixon informed Mitchell that "I talked to Congressman Gerry Ford on the telephone and told him I was sending a copy of your letter to him. He assured me that he and other members of the House leadership would be in touch with you." The legislation passed as a result of this conservative support.

Nixon always impressed Mitchell "as the kind of person who could go either way, depending on how much of a game it was in a given direction. That was remarkable." Blacks, as a whole, also strongly suspected Nixon's sincerity and, as his gyrations on civil rights showed once he was in the White House, they had good reasons for not embracing him. The most damaging effect of Nixon's racial policies was that they ended the period of forthright presidential leadership in the protection of civil rights and, with the help of some black militants, brought the movement to a standstill. Diehard white segregationists and northern whites opposed to programs like school desegregation regarded Nixon as a friend.

Mitchell felt that these harmful attitudes were also encouraged by Nixon's attempts to pack the Supreme Court with "strict constructionists." They were constitutional fundamentalists who believed the Constitution was meant to be read literally rather than as a living document capable of

being adapted to changing historical and social currents. Mitchell led the
successful struggle to block Nixon's appointments of Clement Haynsworth
and G. Harrold Carswell to the Supreme Court. But he failed in his third
attempt to prevent confirmation of William H. Rehnquist and the creation
of an identifiable Nixon Court that was not as socially aggressive as was the
Warren Court. Those developments set the stage for the more ideologically
conservative Ronald Reagan to tilt the balance on the Court sharply rightward.

On the positive side, Mitchell welcomed Nixon's support, though
sometimes reluctant, for such efforts as extension of the 1965 Voting
Rights Act, the strengthening of the Equal Employment Opportunity
Commission, the creation of a Minority Business Enterprise program, and
increases in civil rights enforcement budgets. Initially, caught between his
labor allies and his liberal friends, Mitchell remained neutral during the
bitter battle in Congress to establish the Philadelphia Plan with its trend-
setting goals and timetable affirmative action principles. George Meany,
supporting the building trade unions, opposed the plan. After the plan was
adopted, Mitchell became one of its staunchest supporters. Mitchell regarded Nixon's support for the Voting Rights Act particularly interesting
given his earlier opposition. Mitchell blamed Attorney General John
Mitchell's lack of understanding of the underlying issues for that problem.
He felt that had Nixon really wanted to hurt the civil rights forces he could
easily have done so.

Nixon's support for some civil rights issues and opposition to others led
some students of history to conclude that his attitude toward civil rights
was confused. Mitchell thought otherwise. He was convinced that Nixon
had a deliberate strategy for dealing with civil rights tailored to the national climate. As John Ehrlichman clearly documents in *Witness to Power*,
Nixon's aim was to engineer a "centrist strategy" that was neither conservative nor liberal. According to Ehrlichman, he established a stance on
civil rights and social policy that was within a *conservative center* as compared
to the *liberal center* of the Kennedy-Johnson period. This seismic shift in the
national mood was accentuated by the Vietnam War's replacement of civil
rights as the preeminent issue.

Consequently, Mitchell lost several crucial battles with the Nixon administration because the NAACP often was unable to come up with an
antidote to the Southern Strategy. An important reason was that this racial
policy was presented with a "new populism" patina even though it was
nothing more than "separate but equal" in a new package.

Less antiblack than prowhite, Nixon presented the NAACP with an
unaccustomed slick stage on which to perform. Had his policies been as
blatantly racist as some charged, it would have been relatively easy for the

NAACP to counter them. The national sense of moral concern and desire to protect newly established constitutional principles were still strong, despite the white backlash. Rather than launching a frontal attack on civil rights, Nixon inaugurated a new era of racial politics. The difference was crucial. He exploited the emotional school busing issue with a vengeance. He assid-uously created hysteria among white parents in northern urban schools over the prospects of public school integration and led Congress in rendering ineffective the guidelines for implementing Title VI of the 1964 Civil Rights Act and in barring the use of federal funds for school busing. Mitchell recognized the virulence of Nixon's Southern Strategy and, where possible, would have welcomed a chance to delay some aspects of the school integration program to deprive Nixon of opportunities to exploit racial fears until a more sympathetic occupant was in the White House. But any tactical retreat like that would have opened him and the NAACP to charges of surrender and retreat, so Nixon was also victorious in backing the NAACP into a corner by denying it any room to maneuver in pursuit of its unbending course.[3]

Mitchell found President Ford to be a relief, but not by much. He knew Ford's strengths and weaknesses well from having worked with him since 1949. As a congressman, Ford established what Mitchell called a "narrow gauge approach to civil rights." He opposed such legislation in its early stage and only voted for it when passage was inevitable. Mitchell's manner of assessing Ford was consistent with the way in which he judged all lawmakers and administration officials; his ultimate determination was based more on their final actions on civil rights than on their personal attitudes or early opposition.

One example concerning Ford was his support in 1970 for the Nixon administration's effort to restrict the effectiveness of the voting rights law and his offering the substitute favored by the White House that passed the House but not the Senate. Another was Ford's support of attempts by those wanting to weaken the fair housing bill the Senate passed by sending it to a conference. After the NAACP mobilized bipartisan support to block both attempts, Ford voted for the strong bills on final passage.

Mitchell's assessment of Ford was also conditioned by the circumstances under which he became President. Nixon's premature departure from the White House owing to the Watergate scandal had had a traumatic impact on the nation, and there was a need for a period of quiet and caution in addressing sensitive issues. Ford reflected this "mood of the nation in his low-key approach to many problems, including civil rights." Mitchell was afraid that, in this atmosphere, it was possible for those advocating the status quo to gain the advantage and push things backward to the status quo ante. The result was a further strengthening of the conservative mood throughout the country.

Because of his short tenure in office, Ford did not have much opportunity to establish a substantial civil rights record. He continued Nixon's forceful opposition to busing and encouraged those in Congress pushing amendments to block court-ordered school desegregation programs. But Mitchell felt that he strengthened equal employment concepts and the principle that the nation should move forward in protecting the rights of all its citizens. He bucked considerable opposition within his administration and gave full support to the 1975 extension of key provisions of the voting rights law. He also supported the Equal Employment Opportunity Commission when it was embroiled in turmoil.

Jimmy Carter confirmed Mitchell's belief that there had been a 180-degree change in the racial attitudes of Presidents. He first met the former Georgia governor when they both served on a discussion panel sponsored by the Brookings Institution in Washington. Mitchell found him disarming and informal as they chatted during a simple lunch in the Brookings cafeteria.

Because he was a southerner, Carter's commitment to racial equality was as much a paradox as was Johnson's. Mitchell's biggest fight with Carter was over the appointment of Griffin Bell as attorney general. Mitchell called Bell's appointment a betrayal and said that if Carter had indicated during the campaign that he would select this southern conservative for such a sensitive post in his administration, sizable numbers of blacks would not have voted for him.

Mitchell scoffed at Bell's assertion that he had worked behind the scenes in Georgia to keep the schools open during the desegregation struggles. Mitchell failed to block Bell's appointment, but he was pleased that even before the hearings had finished, Bell came to him and said, "I want you to know that the doors of the Justice Department are always open to you." The fact that Bell kept that promise and they worked closely afterward confirmed Mitchell's experience that even when the NAACP failed to block appointments of people it opposed, criticisms usually helped to sensitize them on civil rights issues.[4]

In a get-acquainted meeting with Bell in April 1977, for example, Mitchell presented the attorney general with a review of the current status of civil rights enforcement by the Justice Department, which was his yardstick for measuring progress.

• Mitchell noted that since the middle years of the Johnson administration, the Justice Department had been responsible for enforcing Title VI of the 1964 Civil Rights Act prohibiting discrimination by anyone receiving federal funds. These requirements were strengthened by Nixon's Executive Order 11764.

Furthermore, in August 1976, after several years of inaction, the Justice Department ordered each federal agency with Title VI responsibilities to adopt regulations that stated their compliance standards and timetables. The regulations were meant to correct the long delays people were experiencing when they complained that discrimination was continuing where federal funds were being used. Mitchell regarded the regulations as a step forward, but he had found that not much happened unless Justice prodded those agencies. Proper enforcement, he felt, also required adequate staffing of the federal programs section of the Civil Rights Division and strong leadership.

• The Justice Department had "one of the worst records" regarding activities of the Law Enforcement Administration Agency. Justice had failed to end employment discrimination by police departments, correctional agencies, and courts that received LEAA funds. Consequently, to mandate stronger civil rights enforcement, Congress twice (as recently as 1976) amended the law. The NAACP urged and won appointment of a new LEAA administrator who was committed to proper enforcement.

• The need for a more aggressive Justice Department anti-discrimination program in state and local employment was increased by expansion of the EEOC's coverage to include public sector jobs. In 1976, however, Mitchell was concerned that "only a couple dozen suits" were filed, and those were focused almost entirely on discrimination in police and fire departments.

• There was a need to change Justice's policy in defending civil rights suits against the federal government. Several cases, including Rauh's *Adams* v. *Richardson,* had been brought as a result of the government's failure to enforce civil rights laws. Justice customarily had been referring such cases to its Civil Division, which used every technical maneuver it could in defending them without regard to their merits. In 1976, Stanley J. Pottinger, assistant attorney general, told civil rights groups that a new policy had been instituted under which such cases would be sent to the Civil Rights Division for assessment of their merits. Upon determining that those lawsuits were valid, the division would press agencies to settle or to get their own lawyers to defend themselves if they refused.

• The NAACP asked the Justice Department to increase the appointment of black lawyers in Washington and in U.S. attorney's offices and to provide leadership in their appointments to the federal bench.

• The NAACP further asked Justice to rescind its guidelines on employment testing, which had been approved over NAACP protests in the closing days of the Ford administration. They were different from the EEOC guidelines approved and were causing confusion. (Justice complied with the request.)[5]

Mitchell believed that the radically changed social milieu in which Carter served robbed him of an opportunity to make as great a contribution to the civil rights struggle as Johnson. But, as the Justice Department's positive response to those items Mitchell had submitted showed, the Carter administration's contributions were considerable even if they were not appreciated by many blacks themselves. Mitchell thus regarded Carter as an especially welcome improvement over the opportunistic Nixon.

Mitchell found Carter's commitment to civil rights at home as firm and sincere as to human rights abroad. As the new chairman of the Leadership Conference (Mitchell succeeded Wilkins upon his retirement in 1976), he told the Democratic National Convention in 1980 that on the employment and business fronts, Carter "has battled for improvements ever since he took the oath of office." With Carter's support, Mitchell engineered a massive overhaul of the EEOC. The agency was never given the cease and desist powers the NAACP wanted, but it was strengthened in many other ways.

Next to the Civil Rights Division of the Justice Department and the Civil Rights Commission, Mitchell regarded the EEOC as the third foundation of the federal government's enforcement program and gave the agency unstinting support. Since December 1977, it had won $30 million in back pay and benefits for women, blacks, and other minorities who were victims of discrimination in employment.

One of the first pieces of legislation the Carter administration got through Congress was the Youth Unemployment and Demonstration Projects Act that gave training and employment to 750,000 youths, 300,000 of whom were black. Carter further supported establishment of a watchdog function in the Office of Management and Budget to ensure that federal agencies themselves implemented fair employment policies.

He similarly gave total support to Congressman Parren Mitchell's 10-percent-set-aside amendment to the Public Works Act of 1977. Consequently, minority-owned companies received $600 million, or 14 percent of the $4 billion spent under the act.

On August 16, 1978, Carter issued four executive orders dealing with urban problems. They required the construction of federal buildings in the cities where that was possible, in order to provide jobs and other tangible benefits to abandoned areas; the careful consideration of the impact of urban renewal programs on population centers; the purchase of goods and services from areas with high jobless rates; and the creation of an Interagency Coordinating Council to provide close consultation among major government agencies responsible for urban programs.

Carter made an unprecedented number of appointments of women and minorities to high positions in government, but it was within the judicial branch, Mitchell felt, that he demonstrated his courage and spirit of fairness to "accomplish something that no other President ever tried before." The NAACP and the Carter administration had collided over a bill to provide more federal judges because it contained an amendment offered by Senator Eastland that would divide the U.S. Court of Appeals for the Fifth Circuit in the volatile Southeast. Both the NAACP and the NAACP Legal Defense and Educational Fund were convinced that the proposed splitting off of moderate Texas and Louisiana from the negative Mississippi and the rest of the South would harm civil rights cases before that circuit. With the help of Peter Rodino, chairman of the House Judiciary Committee, the NAACP delayed the bill's passage until the amendment was removed. Instead, a compromise provision was included that created four administrative units within the Fifth Circuit.

By opening wide the door of the federal judiciary, Carter, in Mitchell's words, became the first President "to change the federal bench from a predominantly white male institution of government to a body of jurists that, North and South, East and West is a cross section of America." That contribution would "have untold constructive influence on the lives of our children and their children in the years ahead." No appointment better symbolized Mitchell's own contributions to those changes than that of Nathaniel Jones, his friend and then NAACP general counsel, to the U.S. Court of Appeals for the Sixth Circuit in Cincinnati. Working with Samuel Jackson and other influential civil rights activists, Mitchell pushed Jones's appointment through a minefield of opposition.

Another appointment Mitchell welcomed was that of Matthew Perry to the U.S. district court in South Carolina. A longtime NAACP leader in his home state as well as a combative Mitchell ally on the NAACP national board of directors, Perry had more recently been a judge on the U.S. Military Court of Appeals. His political acumen, enhanced by Mitchell's support in Washington, was demonstrated by the bipartisan support he won from Dixiecrat-Republican Strom Thurmond and Democrat Ernest F. Hollings, both of South Carolina.[6]

This evolution of attitudes from Roosevelt to Carter could not have occurred without a confluence of forces as profound in their impact on the course of the nation's history as were the Civil War and Reconstruction. In addition to their increased political awareness, blacks benefited from the new revolutionary concepts of constitutional justice that were resulting from the NAACP's campaign for full citizenship rights in the wake of the *Brown* v. *Board of Education* judgment.

In judging the civil rights records of Presidents and other public officials, it was always uppermost in Mitchell's mind that they were human. Mitchell was therefore very upset when the Congressional Black Caucus one year pointedly announced that Carter was not invited to the group's annual awards banquet in Washington because he had let down blacks. In the packed banquet hall in the Washington Hilton Hotel, Mitchell reminded the caucus that whatever some of its members might have felt about Carter, they had made a very serious mistake by not respecting the office of the presidency. He recalled that for many years blacks had struggled to get presidential recognition. Now that this was offered voluntarily, common courtesy decreed that it be reciprocated, regardless of personalities or politics.

Mitchell used his position as elder statesman to issue his rebuke. Younger blacks in the audience, attired in designer labels and enjoying their $125-a-plate dinner in the Hilton's resplendent setting but apparently unaware of the sacrifices that had been made to allow them to enjoy the trappings of first-class citizenship, or that the Old Warrior, as Mitchell was also affectionately called, never backed away from a good fight, began hissing and booing him.

Welcoming the challenge, Mitchell responded, "I once saw a lynching in the South. I consider this booing and hissing—this denying someone's right to speak—a lynching."

After a brief pause, he added, "And if any of the booers cares to repeat this sort of conduct outside in the alley, I'll meet you there." No one accepted the challenge.

Mitchell regarded as an example of the humanness of Presidents a White House ceremony at which he had exercised his thirty-year seniority in a different manner in order to praise Carter for having issued an executive order. A grateful Carter then responded that quite often public officials "don't get an adequate recognition when they do make progress." He promised that his wife would also be working to stimulate private input for the redevelopment of urban centers. Mitchell said he was distressed that the news media as a rule not only did not grant Carter deserved recognition, but went out of their way to distort his civil rights contributions.

Mitchell felt that it was very important to set the record straight because his praise was not meant to boost Carter's ego as much as to reinforce respect for the institution of the presidency and emphasize the importance of leadership. Because negative assessments in the media and elsewhere were commonplace, he feared that the unrelenting criticisms and attacks on institutions of government might cause a loss of faith among the people and undermine the systems under which they lived. Finally, Mitchell declared: "I believe the system is a good one. I believe it can be made better. I believe it has the potential to be made better. To the extent that it is made better depends on us and what we do at the ballot box."[7]

Mitchell was particularly concerned about the Civil Rights Division of the Justice Department because, along with the Civil Rights Commission, it was essential to the federal government's leadership in protecting hard-won constitutional rights for black citizens. Each agency complemented the other, and together they were the first line of defense. From its inception, the commission served as the nation's well-informed conscience, supplying statistics, examples of discrimination, and other data to support its reports, which were crucial to the passage of all subsequent civil rights laws and the development of an increasing awareness of the problem of racial injustice. Every debate on legislation since 1960 was studded with references to the commission's reports and recommendations.

Mitchell found the commission especially valuable because it served as an official voice, which neither the NAACP nor the Leadership Conference on Civil Rights could provide, in authenticating the existence of discrimination and other forms of racial abuse. He likened the commission's reports to the stamp of approval that the Department of Agriculture placed on meat. The stamp did not change the product's quality; it only assured the public that it had been evaluated by a disinterested government agency. Two examples that Mitchell used to demonstrate the commission's importance dealt with voting. The commission's reports were crucial to Congress's changing from the court-appointed voting referees provided by the Civil Rights Act of 1960 to the examiners appointed by the Civil Service Commission under the Voting Rights Act of 1965. The commission's reports were also important in broadening the law's coverage under the 1975 extension to include American Indians, Asian Americans, Alaskan natives, and Hispanics.

Since the effectiveness of the Justice Department's Civil Rights Division in protecting the rights of minorities depended upon a strong Civil Rights Commission, any diminution of the authority of the commission drastically weakened the executive branch's leadership in the struggle against discrimination. Thus, during the 1980s Mitchell viewed with utter dismay calls to end funding for the commission because the Reagan administration had all but destroyed its ability to expose civil rights violations within the federal government and throughout society. (Mitchell knew, however, that the commission's propensity under Reagan to act like a dog trying to bite its own tail was due to the inability of civil rights supporters to marshal the proper political counterforce.)

Some thought President Reagan's popularity made opposition impossible. Mitchell, however, thought that it would have been an easy task to counter Justice's disastrous attacks on established civil rights policies. (But, despite his vast lobbying experience, no one asked for his help.) His first step in attempting to persuade the Reagan administration's Justice Department to halt its onslaught on civil rights would have been to make it aware of the civil rights community's priorities. But the likely response to that strategy would have been that the new and complex civil rights terrain and Reagan's popularity made it difficult to counter his actions.[8]

The leadership demonstrated by the Roosevelt, Truman, Eisenhower, Kennedy, and Johnson administrations in desegregating the armed services and winning acceptance of the principle of equal opportunity reflected developments in the broader civil rights struggle. Although racial problems were hydra-headed, the military was one area where progress was readily measurable.

With World War II serving as an even greater catalyst for social change than the New Deal, the armed services were forced by manpower needs to begin reevaluating their regard for blacks as fighting men. The Selective Training and Service Act, which Congress passed in 1940, establishing the first compulsory draft in peacetime, made a cautionary step forward by providing for enlistments of volunteers and draftees without regard to race or color. That provision was in part the result of the NAACP's six-year campaign to increase the numbers of blacks in the services. However, as was clear in 1948 from Philip Randolph's threats to lead a black boycott of the armed services if Truman and Congress did not take steps to end discrimination in the military, segregation in that area remained the rule.

Forced by manpower needs, the Navy in 1946 had moved from a policy of partial to full integration of its personnel, but its all-white Marine Corps and nonwhite Stewards' Branch were glaring exceptions to this policy. The racial reforms that were occurring in the Army were also promising signs of progress. The challenge was to translate the Navy's postwar racial policy into widespread equal treatment and opportunity for blacks throughout all the services.

As Truman's Executive Orders 9980 and 9981 showed, race relations in the armed services were influenced by the many forces shaping the civilian society. The most notable of those were the New Deal, which fostered the sense of government responsibility for the welfare of all citizens; the exposure during World War II of Americans to numerous international influences; the defense of America's democratic ideals; the NAACP's determination to obtain constitutional protections for the rights of black citizens under the equal protection clause of the Fourteenth Amendment; the emergence of the black vote as the balance of political power; and the realization throughout the military that segregation and discrimination were counterproductive to the efficient utilization of manpower.

Mitchell's contribution to that struggle was to push the military and the executive branch to speed the process of change. As the earlier contributions of Walter White and Randolph showed, he was not alone in the struggle. Lester Granger, head of the National Urban League, similarly played a key role as adviser to the Navy and the Defense Department on racial matters. Thurgood Marshall and Roy Wilkins also made important contributions. But Mitchell's relations with the executive branch and the Congress gave him a special advantage in this mission.

Mitchell was always aware that despite the NAACP's consistent leadership, the progressive lowering of racial barriers in the armed services, with few exceptions, followed very closely and was dependent upon the increasing political strength and activism of blacks, the positive responses of the federal government and the general society to civil rights demands, the passage of civil rights laws, and a strong appreciation within the military itself of the need for change. When he came up against immovable walls of segregation, such as in the National Guard, his alternative to leadership from the executive branch and military commanders was the passage of effective civil rights laws that would cover the services as well as civilian society. Laws, of course, to be worthwhile had to be enforced, but without them, there was no demonstration of the national will that could spur commanders to ensure full equality of treatment for servicemen.

By 1960, integration of the armed services was a resounding success. Nevertheless, even after the NAACP had obtained the integration of schools on military posts and federal lands that were operated by the national government as well as by local school boards, it remained for the proper enforcement of Title VI of the 1964 Civil Rights Act to end off-base segregation that affected military personnel and dependents. Racial problems in other areas such as overseas bases, the organized reserves, state-controlled National Guard units, off-base housing for servicemen, recreation facilities and other forms of public accommodations, as well as unequal justice, required the type of strong leadership that Mitchell had long demanded from commanders. And the laws made that possible.

The biggest problem was institutional racism, a complex mixture of sociological forces and military traditions. Throughout the remaining phases of the struggle, Mitchell was forced to battle the underlying inertia within the military. That resistance was strengthened by the threats from powerful southern members of the Armed Service Committees to cut off funding for needed administration defense programs if the military obeyed the law.

After a futile period in the early 1960s of seeking voluntary compliance with Defense Department directives and civil rights laws, Robert S. McNamara played a crucial role by demonstrating his commitment to equal opportunity. Among other steps, coupled with the use of Defense's vast economic powers, he established an aggressive new policy to fulfill the promise of Truman's executive order covering the armed services. As McNamara, a progressive secretary of defense, told Morris J. McGregor, Jr., author of *Integration of the Armed Forces, 1940–1965*, "I was naive enough in those days to think that all I had to do was show my people that a problem existed, tell them to work on it, and that they would then attack the problem. It turned out of course that not a goddamn thing happened." So he issued a directive outlining the department's obligations under Title VI of the 1964 act. The law gave Defense the courage summarily to bar attendance of all military personnel at segregated institutions. The role of local commanders was paramount in the implementation of the directive.

On February 15, 1965, McNamara also ordered an end to all segregation within the National Guard and adoption of programs "to ensure that the policy of equal opportunity and treatment is clearly stated." Owing to his leadership, Defense that year could confidently state that all National Guard units were integrated. Two years later another McNamara order placed landlords who refused to rent to blacks off-limits. The order was directed at areas around Andrews Air Force Base in Maryland and on the Washington outskirts. Mitchell noted that McNamara made it clear that it was only the first step forward ending such discrimination.

Expressing his profound appreciation to McNamara for his leadership, Wilkins told him on his last day in office that he had been perceptive as well as sympathetic and innovative in his approach to racial problems. Although not all problems were solved, Wilkins observed, his policies significantly advanced the cause of equality in the military services. The effort in the Senate to pass the fair housing legislation, he said, vindicated McNamara's foresight. By the same token, the Fair Housing Act of 1968 undergirded the McNamara order by strengthening the national consensus for the elimination of residential segregation.[9]

One paradox of the struggle in Congress was the extent to which the Senate filibuster lost its importance to Mitchell in the most crucial phases of his quest for civil rights laws. Experience had taught him that the filibuster was "just a kind of convenient escape hatch for a lot of people" who did not want to act on civil rights legislation. They excused themselves from voting for it by arguing that the rules needed to be changed. But he had found that a great many lawmakers who avowedly supported the right to unlimited talk did not themselves apply that rule "as a practical matter to how" the Senate functioned day by day.

The biennial struggle in 1965 to modify Rule XXII was therefore instructional. Unlike the past, Mitchell was not eager for a fight over the rules even though he still wanted to remove the "escape hatch."

A more important consideration for Mitchell was that any attempt that year to change the rules would have placed Vice President Humphrey in an extremely difficult position. That was an indication of how much the political terrain had changed with Johnson in the White House. Humphrey would have been faced with the question because the Senate postponed action for two months, during which time he had been sworn in as Vice President. That meant that as presiding officer of the Senate, Humphrey would have had to decide whether to rule in favor of the liberals, who maintained that under the Constitution each new Congress was entitled to adopt its own rules by a simple majority, or adhere to the position Johnson had traditionally taken—that because two thirds of senators carried over each election year, the Senate was a continuing body. By upholding Johnson's position, Humphrey would have alienated his liberal friends in the Senate; taking a contrary stand would have embarrassed the President. Owing to that "complication," as Mitchell put it, the Leadership Conference instead opted to face the southern filibuster on civil rights legislation.

Wilkins further emphasized the dilemma by his response to Mitchell's report on a meeting in which it was decided not to back Humphrey into a corner. Wilkins agreed that after Humphrey's extended "devotion to the civil rights cause," to demand now that he "take what may be a collision course with the White House is asking a bit much." He was more concerned that "no one can tell what kind of effect the MLK-Selma push"—for stronger federal voting rights laws—would have on Congress.

> We shall see what we shall see. I suppose the Southern Negroes, having received practically no dividends from political moves in the Congress, due to their disfranchisement are not disposed to consider political pros and cons and what we call strategy. They are unaccustomed to such estimates and are dedicated to the weapon of unrelenting pressure relieved by no political niceties.

As expected, filibuster reform opponents spared the civil rights forces any further conflicts of conscience. The matter quietly died in 1965 after the Rules and Administration Committee, to which it had been referred, reported back unfavorably on two resolutions. One would have permitted cloture by three fifths of senators present and voting, the other by a simple majority. Neither resolution was called up.

But even with what Mitchell considered an ideal combination of a majority of members and a presiding officer (Vice President Humphrey) who favored the principle that the Senate had the right to change its rules at the beginning of a new Congress, the effort again failed in 1967—badly, with Dirksen's help. On January 18, Humphrey followed precedent and avoided ruling directly on the issue. Nixon, in 1957, 1959, and 1961, had referred the question to the Senate, but the Senate never voted on the question. Now, attempting to help the liberal cause, Humphrey referred the question to the Senate for a vote rather than for a debate as Johnson had done in 1963. The Senate, however, still voted 37 to 61 against a point of order raised by Dirksen. Essentially, the vote was against the right of a majority to change Rule XXII. Dirksen's stand meant he had reneged on his promise to help achieve change under the existing rules. The minority leader's switch was not surprising since he had no intention of facilitating the battle for a fair housing law. Next, the Senate sustained the Dirksen point of order by a 53 to 46 vote, thus blocking any change in Rule XXII by a majority vote.

Following that disappointment, the antifilibuster forces sought to change the rules by invoking cloture under the 1959 rules. If that first step had succeeded, they would have attempted to change Rule XXII from the two-thirds cloture requirement to three fifths of senators present and voting.

Dirksen remained the roadblock. Mitchell watched as he "performed the usual feat of going in two different directions at the same time." After joining Mansfield in filing a cloture petition to end the filibuster against the attempt to change the rules, he announced he would vote against cloture. On January 24, the Senate again voted 53 to 46 against cloture, and Mansfield killed any further hope for the civil rights forces by adjourning the Senate. That left the matter in a parliamentary limbo by keeping it on the calendar with no chance for consideration.

After two more abortive attempts in 1969 and 1971, a break finally came in 1975 when the Senate modified Rule XXII to make it possible for three fifths of the entire Senate (sixty members) to invoke cloture. The heading on the Leadership Conference's report summarized the ambivalence about this anticlimax: "The New Filibuster Rule: Is It a Victory?"

Mitchell's conclusion was that only time would tell whether the change was valuable. Hanging in the back of his mind was the warning by his old southern opponents that the civil rights forces would rue the day when they won this battle. Given the historic shift in the legislative pendulum, civil rights foes now had become the principal advocates of change as they battled against enforcement of the laws or to weaken them. The question whether it would have been better to stick to the old rule continued to bother Mitchell even though in principle he was committed to change.

Mitchell praised Rauh for having "set an all-time record for determined, effective and constructive effort in the long struggle to get a more liberal rule on limitation of debate in the Senate." He recalled that in the crucial but unsuccessful 1963 fight, Clinton Anderson had noted that his lobbying partner "had done the most in research and development of the legal arguments supporting the struggle for the Senate's right to change its rules by a majority vote at the beginning of each new Congress." The Leadership Conference never shifted from that position.

Mitchell was consoled that Vice President Nelson Rockefeller had joined Nixon and Humphrey in believing that the Senate had the right to change its rules by majority vote at the beginning of a new Congress. Mitchell hailed Rockefeller's ruling as "a bright spot in the nation's history." He warmly thanked him for that stand as well as Walter Mondale and James B. Pearson, Republican of Kansas, for "their very diligent effort to change the Senate rules." By then not only had Congress passed the basic civil rights laws, but it had also extended the 1965 Voting Rights Act and taken the first step toward strengthening the Equal Employment Opportunity Commission.

Ultimately, Mitchell regarded as "a kind of burlesque" situations where "people from Mississippi and other states who have always said the filibuster was so sacred voting to cut off debate" when liberals were using it against antibusing amendments. Other reasons for complaint included southerners' using cloture to speed action on a tax cut bill in 1978 and to block attempts by liberals to force the Senate to accept a Humphrey-Hawkins full employment bill. Herein lay his lesson for future lobbyists. The national will to uphold principles of equality had to be stronger than the rules Congress imposed on itself if the rights of minorities were to be protected.[10]

Indeed, as Goethe sang, *"Entbehren sollst du, sollst entbehren"*—"Thou shalt forgo, shalt do without"—so did Mitchell, like Du Bois, admonish by his deeds:

> And I care not to garner while others
> Know only to harvest and reap
> For mine is the reaping of sowing
> Till the spirit of rest gives me sleep."

Appendix 1

MEMORANDUM
TO: Messrs. Clarence Mitchell and Joseph Rauh
FROM: J. Francis Pohlhaus
RE: Civil Rights Bills: Parliamentary Procedures
DATE: (Written in 1964)

In view of the forthcoming Congressional debate on the civil rights bill, a review of the parliamentary procedures used in 1957 and 1960 to secure Senate consideration of civil rights bills is appropriate.

In 1957, the bill was brought to the Senate floor without reference to the Judiciary Committee. This was done under Rule XIV of the Senate. A point of order was raised against this procedure, on the ground that it violated Rule XXV of the Senate, enacted by the Reorganization Act of 1946. In order to clarify the issue, the pertinent provisions of the rules and law are set out.

RULE XIV

1. Whenever a bill or joint resolution shall be offered, its introduction shall, if objected to, be postponed for one day.

2. Every bill and joint resolution shall receive three readings previous to its passage, which readings shall be on three different days, unless the Senate unanimously direct otherwise; and the Presiding Officer shall give notice at each reading whether it be the first, second, or third: *Provided,* That the first or second reading of each bill be by title only, unless the Senate in any case shall otherwise order.

3. No bill or joint resolution shall be committed or amended until it shall have been twice read, after which it may be referred to a committee; bills and joint resolutions introduced on leave, and bills and joint resolutions from the House of Representatives, shall be read once, and may be read twice, on the same day, if not objected to, for reference, but shall not be considered on that day nor debated, except for reference, unless by unanimous consent.

4. Every bill and joint resolution . . . of the House of Representatives which shall have received a first and second reading without being referred to a commit-

tee, shall, if objection be made to further proceedings thereon, be placed on the Calendar.

   5. . . .

   6. . . .

RULE XXV

1. The following standing committees shall be appointed at the commencement of each Congress, with leave to report by bill or otherwise:

• • • • •

(k) Committee on the Judiciary to consist of fifteen Senators, to which committee shall be referred all proposed legislation, messages, petitions, memorials and other matters relating to the following subjects:

• • • • •

   1) Judicial proceedings, civil and
      criminal, generally.

• • • • •

  12) Civil liberties

• • • • •

SECTION 101, REORGANIZATION ACT OF 1946

The following sections of this title are enacted by the Congress:

a) As an exercise of the rule-making power of the Senate and House of Representatives respectively, and as such they shall be considered as part of the rules of each House, respectively, or of that House to which they shall specifically apply; and such rules shall supersede other rules only to the extent that they are inconsistent therewith.

• • • • •

On June 19, 1957, the Vice-President laid before the Senate H.R. 6127, which had passed the House the previous day.

He stated that without objection the bill would be read the first time by title, which was done.

At this point the minority leader, Mr. Knowland, obtained the floor and proposed a parliamentary inquiry:

"Am I correct in stating that the second reading cannot be held on this legislative day, except by unanimous consent?"

On receiving an affirmative answer, he gave notice he would object if a request for second reading were made, and when Senator Russell made such a request, he and Senator Douglas objected.

The following day, the Vice-President again placed the bill before the Senate for a second reading.

Senator Knowland announced that after the second reading it was his intention to object to further proceedings on the bill at that time, and after the second reading, he did so object, pursuant to Rule XIV, Subsection 4, of the Rules of the Senate.

Senator Russell made a point of order that this subsection was superseded by the Reorganization Act of 1946, which rewrote Rule XXV of the Senate.

It was his argument that the language of Subsection 1(k) and other subsections establishing committees to which "shall be referred all proposed legislation" of a given nature made the reference of all bills to committee mandatory.

Senators Knowland, Douglas, and others argued that there was in fact no conflict in the two rules, that the Reorganization Act provided for the superseding of existing rules "only to the extent that they are inconsistent therewith" and that the referral under Rule XXV applied only after the Senate decided that a bill would be referred.

After expressing his opinion (but not formal ruling) that the point of order was not well taken, the Vice-President submitted it to the Senate for a vote on June 20, 1957.

Proponents of the bill held that an objection to consideration automatically placed it on the calendar. Opponents held that reference to committee was mandatory, regardless of the objection. The Vice-President's opinion, while favoring the proponents of civil rights, did not entirely support their position.

Mr. Nixon stated his opinion that a single objection would place the bill on the calendar only if not challenged, but could not defeat the Senate's will to refer a bill to committee by majority vote. The way to challenge the objection, he stated, was to raise a point of order, as Senator Russell had done. Then the Senate by voting on the point of order could determine the matter of referral.

On a vote, the Senate overruled the Russell point of order by a vote of 45 to 39. Thereupon, the bill went on the Senate calendar.

On July 8, 1957, Senator Knowland moved to proceed to consideration of the bill. This motion was adopted on July 16, 1957, on which date debate on the bill began. The bill passed the Senate on August 7, 1957. On August 27, the Senate took up the House amendments to the Senate-passed bill, and agreed to them on August 29.

In 1960, a different procedure was used. A civil rights bill in the form of an amendment was offered to a minor House-passed bill (H.R. 8315) on February 15. The amendment was sponsored by Senator Dirksen. On February 23, Senator Dirksen withdrew his amendment and resubmitted the bill in the form of a substitute.

While debate on the Dirksen bill was in progress, the House took up, on March 10, H.R. 8601, a similar bill.

On March 24, the House passed H.R. 8601. Senator Johnson moved that it be referred to the Judiciary Committee with instructions to report it not later than March 29. H.R. 8315 and amendments were then set aside.

On March 30, Senator Johnson moved to take up H.R. 8601. His motion was adopted 71 to 17. On April 8, the bill as amended passed the Senate 71 to 18.

The House concurred in Senate amendments, so no further Senate consideration was necessary.

Since it appears that the method used in 1957 to bring up the bill will be utilized this year, some further consideration should be given to the debate, the opinion of the Vice President, and the vote.

The Senate vote overruling the Russell point of order appears to establish as a precedent an interpretation of Rule XXV to the effect that this rule does not make mandatory referral of bills to committees.

Unfortunately, in the light of the Vice-President's opinion, the interpretation of Rule XIV is not as clear.

The Vice-President, in putting to the Senate the vote on the Russell point of order, did so in such a way that the Senate was voting on whether or not it wanted to send that particular bill to committee. The vote was, as he put it, not on a procedural issue, but the "substantive" issue of whether or not the majority of the Senate preferred that the civil rights bill be referred.

In his opinion he made it clear that he did not think that a single objection sent the bill to the calendar.

Thus the Senate could, without upsetting the precedent of June 20, 1957, and consistent with the Vice-President's opinion, in a different case, send a bill to committee by majority vote, notwithstanding an objection made under Rule XIV, Section IV.

It is incumbent, therefore, on the supporters of civil rights in the Senate to have a majority opposing referral to committee in the event the chair puts the question to the Senate.

Another important consideration is who secures the floor when the bill is at the presiding officer's desk. There appears to be a precedent that if the party obtaining the floor requests referral to committee, objection will not then lie under Rule XIV to prevent further proceedings. This observation is based on the extended discussion of the handling by Senator Vandenberg in 1948 of a dispute between Senators Wherry and Fulbright on the oleomargarine bill. In that instance, Senator Wherry obtained the floor to raise the jurisdictional question of what committee the bill would be referred to. Senator Fulbright subsequently objected to referral to committee under Section IV of Rule XIV. Senator Vandenberg, president pro tempore of the Senate, expressed his opinion that Senator Wherry's questioning of committee jurisdiction took precedence, since he had the floor before Senator Fulbright. The Senate, when the question was submitted to it, so voted, and the bill was referred to committee.

It is assumed that the leadership will be aware of these possible problems and will be in control of them. They are raised in the exercise of caution since the now presiding officer voted in support of the Russell point of order in 1957.

In order to preclude an unfavorable ruling by the chair, it might be advisable to table a point of order if it is raised as it was in 1957. The discussion between Senator Douglas and Vice-President Nixon on the Russell point of order indicates a tabling motion would be in order.

The discussion in 1957 showed that once a bill is on the calendar it can only be referred to committee by the adoption of a motion to take up, followed by the adoption of a motion to refer to committee. It cannot be referred directly from calendar to committee.

Reference to committee should be avoided at all cost. As was pointed out in the discussion between Senator Douglas and Vice-President Nixon, this could lead to four filibusters on:

1. motion to take up the resolution to discharge the committee,
2. adoption of the resolution,
3. motion to take up the bill,
4. adoption of the bill.

If, however, the bill is referred to committee to be reported out at a time definite, as was done in 1960, only the two filibusters could ensue, as the bill goes on the calendar when reported by the committee. I am not aware of what would happen if the committee refused to follow the Senate's instructions to report the bill.

House-passed bills are laid before the Senate in the morning hour only, except by unanimous consent. In the meantime they stay at the presiding officer's desk. In this connection it is interesting to note the procedure followed in 1960.

When the bill came to the Senate the Senate was in a prior legislative day. It had a morning hour, however, by unanimous consent. During this morning hour, the bill was read for the first time. Senator Johnson requested unanimous consent for a second reading, but objection was lodged. He then moved to adjourn the Senate for three minutes, which was done. When the Senate reconvened, he had a second reading of the bill, then moved its referral to committee.

This would indicate that pending business before the Senate would not necessarily be an obstacle to action on the civil rights bill when it reaches the Senate.

Appendix 2

DIFFERENCES BETWEEN ADMINISTRATION'S
FEBRUARY AND JUNE 1963 VOTING PROPOSALS
AND TITLE I OF THE CIVIL RIGHTS ACT OF 1964*

The voting legislation proposed by President Kennedy in June 1963 was substantially identical to that which he had proposed the previous February.

The most significant change made in President Kennedy's proposals, as enacted as Title I of the 1964 Act, was the omission of the temporary voting referee provisions. The February and June proposals would have granted temporary interim relief while voting suits were proceeding through the courts. It would have authorized the court to appoint temporary voting referees in cases where the complaint requested a finding that a pattern or practice of discrimination existed and the Attorney General stated that fewer than 15% of the eligible Negroes in the particular area were registered to vote. In such cases, upon evidence taken either by the court or its voting referee establishing that an individual has been refused registration since the institution of the suit despite his eligibility to vote under State law, the court could issue an order declaring him qualified to vote. Failure of an election official to permit him to vote, after receiving notice of the order from the Attorney General, would constitute contempt of court. If it were ultimately determined in the suit that no pattern or practice of discrimination existed in the particular area, an order qualifying an applicant to vote would be of no effect in a subsequent election.

The temporary referee concept was dropped during consideration by the House Judiciary Committee and, in its place, a provision for impaneling of a three judge court to hear voting suits was added to meet the problem of delay in litigation. (A provision for expeditious proceedings in all voting cases was retained.) It should be noted that the 1963 referee proposals were for appointment of referees during the pendency of litigation and thus raise issues somewhat different from those involved in consideration of other registrar proposals now pending. Major objection to the 1963 referee proposals came from Congressman McCulloch and others, who voiced great concern over the possibility of allowing persons, registered by the interim registrar, to vote before a final judgment had been entered in the discrimination

*From the files of Lee C. White, L.B.J. Library, 1964

suit. The possibility of holding the ballots of such registrants in abeyance, to be counted only after final judgment, and only then if sufficient in number to change the outcome of the election, was attacked as having potentially too unsettling an effect on elections. Though there is no way to actually know whether this was the case, it may be that part of the concern about the temporary referee provisions as originally proposed was a reflection of a fear that the authority granted would be used to register a substantial number of Negroes prior to the 1964 election.

(Though not proposed by the Administration, there was substantial pressure to make Title I of the 1964 Act applicable to state as well as federal elections, and, in fact, the bill proposed by the House Judiciary Subcommittee would have done this. It was changed in the full Committee, however.)

Appendix

WHAT'S IN THE CIVIL RIGHTS ACT?

(A quick look at the major provisions
of the law President Johnson signed July 2, 1964)

I. VOTING—This section does not establish any new rights. It seeks only to protect the right to vote guaranteed 100 years ago by the 15th Amendment to the Constitution. It bars registrars from giving would-be Negro voters tougher literacy tests than whites or disqualifying them for minor errors. It would apply primarily to Federal elections, but it would affect state and local elections held at the same time, unless a separate voting procedure were established for these contests.

To speed up voting suits (suits brought under the 1957 and 1960 Civil Rights Acts have often dragged on 2 to 4 years) the U.S. Attorney General or a defendant could ask for a trial by a three-judge court. This would permit a direct appeal to the U.S. Supreme Court. In all such suits it would be presumed by the court that anyone who finished the sixth grade was literate enough to vote and the state would have to try and prove the opposite.

II. PUBLIC ACCOMMODATIONS—This section is designed to extend into all states the kind of public accommodations laws now in effect in 30 states and the District of Columbia. It would prohibit discrimination in hotels and motels and other places of lodging; restaurants and other eating places; theaters, sports arenas and concert halls; gas stations. It would also apply to any business that segregates under state or local law. If a business is located in a place covered by the law (a barbershop in a hotel, for instance) or if it contains a covered establishment (a department store with a restaurant) it, too, must serve everyone.

The section exempts private clubs and small boarding houses, with five rooms or less, in which the owner lives.

Enforcement—A person denied service can sue to obtain his rights and the Attorney General can intervene, at the court's discretion. Where he has reason to believe there is "a pattern or practice" of discrimination, the Attorney General can bring his own suit and ask for a three-judge court to speed things up.

In a state with its own public accommodations law, the individual would have to notify the local enforcement agency 30 days before filing suit. In states without such laws, the court can refer the complaint to the Federal Community Relations Service, established by Title X of the law, for 60 days and extend that to 120.

In suits brought by the Attorney General there would be no referrals to the Service and no 30-day notices.

VII. PUBLIC FACILITIES—This section is meant to obtain compliance with Supreme Court decisions outlawing discrimination in such publicly supported facilities as libraries, hospitals, museums and playgrounds. The government could sue to obtain compliance if it were too costly or too risky for the injured party to do so.

If the problem still remains, the aggrieved party can file a civil suit. The court can appoint an attorney for the complainant, waive fees and permit the Attorney General to intervene. It can also give the state agency or the EEOC another 60 days to try to settle differences.

As in the section dealing with public accommodations (Title II), the Attorney General can bring suit to end "a pattern or practice" of discrimination. He doesn't have to wait; he can ask for a three-judge court; and cases he files are to be handled as quickly as possible.

In cases brought by individuals, the court, besides issuing an injunction against a discriminating employer or union, can also require hiring or reinstatement with or without back pay.

VIII. VOTING STATISTICS—As a guide for future action by the Justice Department, the Civil Rights Commission and Congress, the Commerce Department is directed to conduct a voting census by race in sections of the country selected by the Commission.

IX. COURT PROCEDURE—This section is designed to clear up a cloudy area in existing law covering civil rights cases where a defendant tries to get his trial switched from a state to a Federal court on the grounds his rights may be denied in a state hearing. The new law specifically grants the defendant the right of appeal if a Federal court sends the case back to the state court.

Under another provision, the Attorney General is authorized to intervene in suits charging violation of the 14th Amendment because of a denial of equal protection of the law. This could permit intervention in many test cases brought by civil rights groups and may give peaceful demonstrators a legal weapon against police who use dogs and hoses on them.

X. COMMUNITY RELATIONS SERVICE—This establishes, in the Commerce Department, a Community Relations Service with authority to help local communities and individuals reach voluntary settlement of differences arising from problems of discrimination. The service is strictly diplomatic. It has no enforcement power and it is under legal requirement to keep its files secret.

XI. JURY TRIAL, MISCELLANEOUS—This provides for a jury trial in all criminal contempt cases arising under sections of the Act dealing with public accommodations, public facilities, education, Civil Rights Commission, Federally assisted programs and employment (Titles II through VII). In voting cases, a judge may still try a person for criminal contempt without a jury. However, if he imposes a fine of more than $300 or a sentence of more than 45 days, the defendant would be eligible for a new trial with a jury. Judges could still use civil contempt powers, without trials, to enforce any title of the bill.

Other provisions in this section protect existing rights under Federal and state law and authorize appropriations to carry out the Act.

Prepared and Distributed by   The Leadership Conference on Civil Rights
                               132 Third Street, S.E.
                               Washington, D.C.

7/27/64

Notes

INTRODUCTION

1. Baker, *CR,* 98th Cong., 2nd sess., 3/19/84, p. S. 2839; "The President's Remarks at a Reception Given in His Honor by Negro Presidential Appointees," 12/17/68, *PPP,* Vol. II, p. 1201; Denton L. Watson and Joseph R. L. Sterne, "A Magnificent Lion in the Lobby," *Sun Magazine* (3/10/85).

2. CM speech, 6/5/56, MP; CM letter to RW, 4/27/55, NAACP WB-45, LC; Pohlhaus letter to Charlie L. Ayres, 12/8/58, MP.

3. DW interview with Davis and Weaver; Davis was director of the FEPC's division of Review and Analysis while Trimble was a senior field representative in the division of Field Operations, Zaid, *Preliminary Inventory;* CM speech, 3/24/62, MP; CM speech draft for Lincoln Alumni Dinner, 1966, MP.

4. Bolling, *House Out of Order,* pp. 133, 174; CM interview, CRDP, pp. 59, 64; *Danville* (Va.) *Register,* 10/17/65, p. 8-A; Ehrlichman, *Witness to Power,* p. 240; interview with Mitchell.

5. *Register,* op. cit.; *The Crisis* (3/15), p. 246; *Legislators,* pp. 6–7.

6. Bruce C. Bereano, "The Face of Lobbying Is Changing," guest editorial, *Skirmisher* (Md) (12/83), p. 10; Crawford, *Pressure Boys,* pp. 2, 3, 5–7; Hamby, *Beyond the New Deal,* p. 323.

7. *Register,* op. cit.; interview with Rauh; Rauh remarks, NAACP retirement tribute to CM, 3/14/79, Washington Hilton Hotel.

8. DW interviews with Earlene Bollin and Jane O'Grady.

9. DW interviews with Kivie Kaplan and Rauh; *WP,* 7/20/55; "Man in the News," *NYT,* 3/7/58; Drew Pearson, "The Washington Merry-Go-Round," *WP,* 12/15/56; WB report, 12/2/53, NAACP II A-656, LC.

10. Rauh, "The Truth About Congress and the Court," *The Progressive* (12/58).

11. DW interviews with Mitchell family; *ES,* 5/3, 10/1/74; *BAF,* 5/7/74; *NYT,* 10/7/75, editorial, 11/26/75; *WP,* 10/8/75, 6/10/80; CM letter to RW, 8/12/75, MP; *The Sun,* 3/27/84; DW interview with JM; *BS,* 6/10/80.

CHAPTER ONE

The following works, not all mentioned below, were essential for this chapter: Clark, *The Eastern Shore;* Dixon, *The Leopard's Spots;* ———, *Clansman;* Kellogg, *NAACP;* Ottley, *Black Odyssey;* Raper, *The Tragedy of Lynching;* Walsh and Fox, *Maryland, a History;* White, *A Man Called White;* Zangrando, *The NAACP Crusade.*

1. CM article, *BAF,* 10/21/33.

2. DW interview with CM; *Outlook,* Vol. 159 (12/31), p. 521; Alfred Dashiell, "Commentary," *The New Republic* (2/17/32), p. 20; *BAF,* 10/21,

10/28/33; Michael S. Holmes, "The Blue Eagle as 'Jim Crow Bird,' the NRA and Georgia's Black Workers," *Journal of Negro History,* 1962, p. 279; *BS,* 10/17, 10/18, 10/19, 10/20, 10/21, 10/22, 10/23, 10/24/33; *ES,* 10/19, 10/20, 10/21/33; *The New Republic* (2/17/32), p. 20, (12/20/33), pp. 159–161; Walsh and Fox, *Maryland, a History,* pp. 672–768; RW, "Mississippi Slavery," *The Crisis* (4/33), p. 81; Robert C. Weaver, "A Wage Differential Based on Race," *The Crisis* (8/34), p. 236; Gustav Peck, "Negro Workers and the NRA," *The Crisis* (10/34), pp. 298–299, 304; James Weldon Johnson, *Current History,* Vol. 19 (1/24), pp. 596–601; *Thirty Years of Lynching in the United States, 1889–1918,* National Association for the Advancement of Colored People (April 1919); Ottley, *Black Odyssey,* pp. 85–128; Clark, *The Eastern Shore.*

3. DW interview with CM; CM testimony submitted to the Senate Subcommittee on the "Punishment for the Crime of Lynching," Frederick Van Nuys, chairman, Senate Committee on the Judiciary, 2/20/34, 73rd Cong., 2nd. sess., pp. 168–169. Others testifying notably were Sen. Edward P. Costigan of Colorado, Walter White, Arthur B. Spingarn, chairman of the NAACP National Legal Committee, Charles H. Houston, Dean of Howard University Law School, Herbert K. Stockton for the NAACP, Juanita E. Jackson, City-Wide Young People's Forum of Baltimore, pp. 1–162; ———, *Hearings,* Vol. 5, p. 168, 2/21/34; *BAF,* 12/2/33; *BS,* 12/19, 12/21/33; James Weldon Johnson to White, NAACP Papers, Reel 3, 9/26/27, LC; Mary White Ovington, "The Year of Jubilee," *The Crisis* (1/34), p. 7; Houston speech to the National Conference of the International Labor Defense at the Hamilton Hotel, Washington, 7/8/39, Reel 2, NAACP, LC; White, "I Investigate Lynchings," *The American Mercury* (1/29), pp. 77–84; Moorfield Storey letter to James Weldon Johnson, 2/12/26, Reel 10, NAACP LC; "Is the Mob to Rule?" *The Christian Century,* Vol. 50 (12/13/33), pp. 1568–1569; "Lynchings Must Be Stopped," *The Christian Century,* Vol. 54 (4/28/37), pp. 544–545; *The Nation,* Vol. 137 (11/1/33), p. 497, (12/6/33), pp. 635–636, (12/13/33), pp. 666, 672; *Literary Digest,* Vol. 116 (12/9/33), pp. 5, 6; "Aftermath: Rolph's Lynching Stand Causes National Storm," *Newsweek,* Vol. 2 (12/16/33), pp. 9–10.

4. *BS,* 10/19, 11/18, 11/21, 11/25, 11/28, 11/29, 11/30/33; 1/17, 1/22, 1/23, 1/24, 1/26, 2/24, 3/14/34; *ES,* 10/20, 10/23, 11/2, 11/20, 11/22, 11/27, 11/28/33, 1/23/34; *NYT,* 10/29/33; *BAF,* 12/2, 12/21/33; Walsh and Fox, op. cit., DW interview with CM; editorial and Ritchie Letter to *The Catholic World,* Vol. 138 (2/34), p. 522.

5. White, *A Man Called White;* 1/19/27, letter from L. C. Dyer to George W. Norris, chairman of the Senate Judiciary Committee, Reel 2, NAACP, LC; *Hearings,* op. cit., n. 3.; *BS,* 2/20/34; *BAF,* 10/28/33, 2/3/34; *The Commonweal,* Vol. 19, 12/15/33, p. 175; *Literary Digest,* op. cit.

6. Raper, *The Tragedy of Lynching; BS,* 10/23/33.

7. *BAF,* 10/28/33, 11/4/33.

8. CM recollections (n.d.), MP.

9. Wilkins, *Standing Fast,* p. 129.

CHAPTER TWO

1. DW interview with CM; Carter, *Scottsboro;* NAACP 1976 *Annual Report,* p. 6; *NYT,* 3/8/33, 10/29/33.

2. Du Bois, "Three Centuries of Lynching," *The Crisis* (12/47), p. 363. This article was an adaptation of Du Bois's introduction to "A Statement on the Denial of Human Rights to Minorities in the Case of Citizens of Negro Descent in the United States of America and an Appeal to the United Nations for Redress." The basic theme of this article, the continuing subjugation of blacks by pitting poor whites against them through political and industrial tyranny, is central to Du Bois's thought. See also, for example, p. 224 and other *Crisis* selections in Moon, *The Emerging Thought of Du Bois.*

3. Raper, *The Tragedy of Lynching.* Fright was a potent weapon in the Scottsboro Boys' first trial—Carter, op. cit., p. 74.

4. DW interview with CM, Norris, and NAACP attorney James Meyerson; Legal Files, NAACP headquarters.

5. Carter, op. cit., p. 48.

6. Carter, op. cit., pp. 1–50; interview with CM.

7. *NYT,* 5/8, 10/29/33; Carter, op. cit., pp. 116, 250.

8. Carter, op. cit., p. 189; *NYT,* 3/8/33.

9. DW interview with CM; Carter, op. cit., p. 276.

10. DW interview with CM; CM interview in *BAF,* 10/10/76; Carter, op. cit., pp. 174–192, 278; *NYT,* 3/18, 4/16/33. *NY Post,* 1/28/36; CM's opinion of the people around the courthouse did not jibe with that of Samuel S. Liebowitz, the chief defense lawyer—see Carter, op. cit., p. 192.

11. CM in *BAF,* 10/30/76; also Carter, op. cit., p. 296.

12. Carter, op. cit., p. 184; Du Bois in *The Crisis* (9/31), pp. 313–315; Clarence Darrow, "Scottsboro," *The Crisis* (3/32), p. 81; "A Statement by the N.A.A.C.P. on the Scottsboro Cases," *The Crisis* (3/32), p. 82; Du Bois, "Postscript," *The Crisis* (1/34), p. 21; Du Bois, *Dusk of Dawn,* pp. 298–299; *NYT,* 3/11, 3/18, 3/28, 3/29, 3/31, 4/1, 4/16/33; CM, interview CUOH, p. 21.

13. Carter, op. cit., p. 199; *NYT,* 3/31, 4/1/33.

14. *NYT,* 3/11/33; White to Daisy Lampkin, 4/28/33, Reel 3, NAACP, LC; Houston letter, 5/19/34, to Richard W. Hale, re: *Commonwealth of Virginia* v. *George Crawford,* in the Circuit Court of Loudon County, Virginia, October Term, 1933, NAACP petition in Reel 2, NAACP, LC; see also *Crawford* v. *Hale,* 290 U.S. 674 (1933), 65 F.2nd 739 (1933); Leon A. Ransom and Houston, "Suggested Outline of Procedure for Attack upon an Indictment by Reason of the Unconstitutional Exclusion of Negroes from the Grand Jury," *Crawford,* Reel 2, NAACP, LC; *NAACP Annual Report,* 1933, pp. 12, 13; "Judge Upholds Virginia Lily-White Jury System" and "Crawford Case Parallel to Euell Lee's," *BAF,* 11/11, 12/16/33; White, "George Crawford—Symbol," *The Crisis* (1/34), p. 15; "The Crawford Case," statement by NAACP, Parts I and II, *The Crisis* (4/35), pp.

104–105, 116–125, (5/35), pp. 143, 150; Richard W. Hale, "Justice and Law," *The Crisis* (5/34), pp. 142–144; editorial, "The Crawford Case," *The Crisis* (5/34), p. 149; "Crawford Defends Dr. Chas. Houston in an Interview" and "NAACP Critics Not Satisfied with Crawford Story," *BAF,* 3/9/35; *BAF* editorial quoted in Carter, op. cit., p. 97; *NYT,* 3/21, 3/31/33; Houston and Ransom, "The Crawford Case: An Experiment in Social Statesmanship," *The Nation,* Vol. 139 (7/4/34), pp. 17–19. One of the points Houston made in this article was that as early as 1879, in Ex parte *Virginia,* the U.S. Supreme Court had proscribed the action of Virginia in excluding blacks from state juries, but Virginia, like Alabama, had ignored the decision and continued the practice.

15. White to Lampkin, op. cit., note 14; Houston, op. cit., *The Crisis,* note 14; White, op. cit., *The Crisis,* note 14; Carter, op. cit., pp. 198–199.

16. CM, "Observations and Reflections" column, *BAF,* 1/20/34.

17. Carter, op. cit., pp. 319–322; *Norris* v. *Alabama,* 294 U.S. 589-90 (1935).

18. Carter, op. cit., pp. 300, 302, 322, 329, 369–413; Scottsboro files, NAACP Legal Department; Guy Johnson, "Negro Racial Movements and Leadership in the United States," *American Journal of Sociology,* Vol. XLIII (1937), p. 71.

19. Chadbourn, *Lynching.*

20. Raper, op. cit., p. 46.

21. Carter, op. cit., pp. 296, 286.

22. CM, interview CUOH, pp. 7, 22.

CHAPTER THREE

1. DW interview with CM, JM, George, and Parren Mitchell, Anna Mae Gittings; Charles Wagandt interview with CM for MHSOH 8209; *BAF,* 10/27/34.

2. DW interviews with Gittings and JM.

3. DW interviews with Gittings, CM, George, and Parren.

4. DW interviews with Vivian Young and Llewelyn Walker, two of CM's high school classmates.

5. DW interviews with Gittings, Parren, and George.

6. W. Ashbie Hawkins, "A Year of Segregation in Baltimore," *The Crisis* (11/11), pp. 27–30; Lynch, *The Black Urban Condition,* pp. 35–36, 230–232; CM, "Baltimore, Our Baltimore," a typewritten article, MP; Parris, *Blacks in the City,* p. 215.

7. DW interviews with CM, JM, and Gittings; *BAF,* 12/1/59.

8. DW interview with CM; Lincoln University promotional newspaper in MP; *The Crisis* (8/40), pp. 245, 250; Bland, *Private Pressure;* Kluger, *Simple Justice.*

9. DW interview with CM and Raymond Hatcher, his Lincoln University classmate living in Minneapolis; DW interview with CM; Wagandt, MHSOH 8209; poem and class song in MP; *BAF,* 6/11/32; CM's comments at New Deal symposium, LBJL, 3/3/83.

10. DW interview with JM; *Baltimore Magazine* (4/73); Lillie Carroll Jackson Museum flyer, MP; reprint from *Sun Magazine* (7/15/79); "Lillie Carroll Jackson Museum News."

11. DW interview with JM.

CHAPTER FOUR

1. DW interviews with CM and JM; W. Ashbie Hawkins, *The Crisis* (11/11), pp. 27–30.

2. DW interview with CM; Du Bois, "Of the Dawn of Freedom," *The Souls of Black Folk,* p. 23.

3. DW interviews with CM and JM; Lynch, *The Black Urban Condition,* p. 231.

4. DW interviews with CM and JM; CM, CUOH, pp. 11, 12; CM paper, "Baltimore, Our Baltimore," MP; see also Konvitz, *The Constitution.*

5. DW interviews with JM; *FAS Reports,* University of Pennsylvania newsletter, 11/81.

6. DW interviews with CM and JM.

7. Ibid.; City-Wide Young People's Forum programs in MP.

8. *BAF,* 1/9/32.

9. DW interviews with CM and JM; Forum Records, MP.

10. Ibid.; CM letters to JM, MP.

11. CM columns, "Observations and Reflections," *BAF,* 12/16, 12/30/33, and 6/2/4; Ottley, *Black Odyssey,* pp. 261, 263.

12. DW interviews with CM and JM; Lynch, op. cit., p. 231; Henry Lee Moon, "The Black Boycott," *The Crisis* (5/66), pp. 249–254, 278.

13. CM, *BAF,* 5/12/34.

14. *BAF,* 6/2/34.

15. CM column, *BAF,* 6/2/34.

16. CM, "National Impact of Maryland's Civil Rights Activity," 11/23/76, MP; *New Negro Alliance* v. *Sanitary Grocery Company,* 303 U.S. 552 (1938).

17. Ibid.; DW interview with CM.

18. Du Bois, "Postscript," *The Crisis* (12/31), p. 431.

19. Houston, *The Crisis* (10/35), p. 300, (12/35), pp. 364, 370; CM, "National Impact" op. cit., n. 16; Houston letter to K. Norman Diamond of *Yale Law Journal,* 4/14/36, NAACP I C-198, LC; *NAACP Annual Report,* 1935, pp. 16, 17; NAACP Report in NAACP I D-89, LC.

20. DW interviews with CM and JM; McNeil, *Groundwork,* pp. 138–139; Kluger, *Simple Justice,* pp. 191–192; *Murray* v. *Maryland,* 169 Md. 478; 182 A. 590 (1936): 169 Md. 478 (1937); *Piper* v. *Big Pine School District.*

21. Editorial, "Like the Five Foolish Virgins," *BAF,* 6/35.

22. DW interviews with CM and JM; CM in *BAF,* 6/22/35; *Gong Lum* v. *Rice,* 275 U.S. 78 (1927).

CHAPTER FIVE

Additional insights into the politics of the period were provided by Du Bois, *Dusk of Dawn;* Morrow, *Way Down South;* Weiss, *Farewell;* Moon, *Balance of Power.*

1. DW interviews with CM and JM. For articles on Elisabeth Coit Gilman, see *BS,* 7/27/30; Paul W. Ward article, *ES,* 5/18/30, "Home News" sect., 12/22/38, 12/14/50; *Maryland Leader,* 1/23, 1/18, 2/15, 9/20, 10/25/20; 11/1/30; 11/10, 11/17/34; Walsh and Fox, *Maryland, a History,* 688, 710; *BAF,* editorial, 6/2/34. For material regarding black interest in socialism, see *BS,* 4/17/28, 10/1/34; *ES,* 3/11/31, 5/29/34; editorial, *BAF,* 6/11/32; Norman Thomas, "Socialism's Appeal to Negroes," *The Crisis* (10/36), pp. 294–295, 325. For a much different perspective on the Socialists and African Americans, see Du Bois, "Postscript," *The Crisis* (9/31), p. 315; "Declaration of Principles," *The American Socialist Quarterly* (Summer 1934), pp. 3–59; *Maryland Manual,* 1933, pp. 283–90; Foner, *American Socialism,* pp. 51, 53, 72. For other information on the political ferment, see *BAF,* editorials, 7/21, 8/13, 9/15, 11/3/34, and news stories 10/6 and 11/10/34.

2. DW interview with CM and JM; *BAF,* 10/27/34, p. 13, 11/3/34, p. 4; Stanley High, "Black Omens," *The Saturday Evening Post* (6/4/38), pp. 14 ff.

3. CM columns, *BAF,* 1/12, 5/19, 9/23/34; *BS,* 11/7/34; *ES,* 11/8/34, 12/21/35; Walsh and Fox, op. cit., p. 687.

4. CM typewritten campaign flyer, MP; *BAF,* 10/27/34.

5. CM columns, *BAF,* 5/19, 11/10/34, editorial, 12/22/34, 1/12/35.

6. CM comments at "The New Deal Fifty Years After: An Historic Assessment," LBJL, Austin, Texas, 3/3/83; Norman Thomas, "Can America Go Fascist," *The Crisis* (1/34), pp. 10–11; Harold Preece, "Fascism and the Negro," *The Crisis* (12/34), pp. 355, 366; David H. Pierce, "Fascism and the Negro," *The Crisis* (4/35), pp. 107, 114; editorial of the month, "Father Coughlin and Huey Long," reprinted from *Pittsburgh Courier* in *The Crisis* (6/35); *NYT,* 4/14/35, p. E-7; *Village Voice* (New York), 5/21/85, p. 24; *Philadelphia Tribune,* 9/12/35, p. 1; Ira A. Reid, *The Negro Community of Baltimore* (Baltimore: Baltimore Urban League, 1935), pp. 39–40; Fairbanks, *A Statistical Analysis,* pp. 55–80; Maryland Report of the Governor's Commission on Problems Affecting the Negro Population," Joseph P. Healy, chairman, 3/43, pp. 13–16; Schlesinger, *The Politics of Upheaval,* pp. 27, 104; Walsh and Fox, op. cit., p. 678; Graham, *Huey Long,* pp. 54–56.

7. *BAF,* 1932; CM columns, *BAF,* 1/12, 1/19, 1/26, 2/2, 8/3, 8/10/35. *The New Republic* (6/35), p. 10.

8. CM column, *BAF,* 1/26/35; Parris and Brooks, *Blacks in the City,* pp. 26–29.

9. DW interviews with JM; "Methodist Evanston Conference," *The Christian Century* (9/19/34), p. 164; "Methodists from New York Body," *The Christian World* (9/19/34); *Newsweek,* Vol. 6 (8/24/35), pp. 17–18; "Methodist Reunion," *The Christian Century* (8/28/35), pp. 1078–80; "Decision Confronting Methodists," *The Christian Century* (1/1/36), pp. 6–7, (1/22/36), pp. 147–149,

(3/11/36), p. 403; *Literary Digest,* Vol. 121 (5/16/36), p. 33; *The Christian Century* (5/20/36), p. 745; "Methodists Vote for Unification," *The Christian World* (5/20/36), pp. 741–742; "Methodist Youth Attack Bishop" at Berea, Ky., *The Christian Century* (9/16/36); "Methodist Youth Oppose Plan of Church Unification," ANP news service, Berea, Ky., 9/17/36; *The Christian Century* (10/21/36), pp. 1383–1385; *Newsweek,* Vol. 9 (2/13/37), p. 21; *The Christian Century* (2/17/37), p. 204; Frazier, *Black Bourgeoisie,* p. 20; Hutchinson, *The Story of Methodism,* pp. 159–160; Wolseley, *The Black Press;* for report on NAACP youth, see *The Crisis* (8/33), pp. 246, 248; JM hired by Walter White, minutes of the committee on administration, and memorandum from secretary, 4/1/35, NAACP National Office; "Negro Students Challenge Social Forces," *The Crisis* (8/35), pp. 232–233, 251; "Youth Let Us Awake," a program for the first youth participation in the 27th Annual NAACP Conference in Baltimore in 1936, and other similar documents in MP; "NAACP National Youth Program Importance to NAACP," *The Crisis* (9/36); *Atlanta Daily World,* 11/20/36; JM's handwritten letter report to White, 11/26/36, from 1216 Druid Hill Avenue, Baltimore, Reel 3, C-65-66, NAACP, LC; "We Build Together a World of Justice, Freedom, and Equality," *The Crisis* (7/37), p. 217; "Largest Youth Conference," *The Crisis* (8/37), p. 249; JM did not limit her activities to youths, but also helped to strengthen the NAACP branches, *NY Post,* 10/30/37; White responds 11/30/37, to JM's request for her to represent the NAACP at American Youth Congress conference in Washington 12/6/37, by cautioning her that, in addition to his needing her full services for the NAACP youth program, the Congress, the American League Against War and Fascism, and the National Negro Congress were controlled by the Communists, Reel 3, NAACP Papers, LC; White, "The Youth Council of the NAACP," *The Crisis* (7/37), p. 215; JM leads NAACP antilynching campaign, 2/1, 2/10/38, letters to White, MP; articles on student radicals, *NYT,* 12/29/35, p. 22, 12/30/35, p. 7; several of the black press, such as *Savannah Tribune,* 12/10/36, reported on JM's visit to the Scottsboro Boys; "Youth Demonstrate Against Lynching," *The Crisis* (12/36), p. 378; Meir and Rudwick, *CORE,* pp. 3–71; Peck, *Freedom Ride,* pp. 14–72; NAACP Annual Report 1938.

10. DW interviews with CM and JM; CM letters to JM, MP; Walter White's letter to CM, 4/28/37, CM letter to Mary McLeod Bethune, 12/10/37, CM letter to Arnold T. Hill, 12/10/37, CM letter to JM, 12/10/37, all in MP; *BAF,* 5/22/37; "The Legacy of Forrester B. Washington, Black Social Work Editor and Nation Builder," booklet composed of excerpts from the Proceedings of the 50th Anniversary of the Atlanta School of Social Work, 11/12–14/70, Atlanta; "The Reflections of Florence Victoria Adams," published in cooperation with the Atlanta University School of Social Work, 1981, by Shannon Press, Ltd.

11. DW interviews with JM and Louise Smith Woodward at her home in Austin, Texas; CM's extensive collection of love letters to Juanita, MP; *BAF,* 9/4/37, 11/27/37, 9/10/38; *Pittsburgh Courier,* 8/20/38.

CHAPTER SIX

The following works, not all mentioned below, were essential for shaping this chapter: Davis, *Journal of Negro Education,* 1944, pp. 340–348; *First Report* and

Final Report, of the FEPC; Frazier, *The American Journal of Sociology,* 11/42; Garfinkel, *When Negroes March;* Hardin, "The Role of Presidential Advisors"; Hill, *Black Labor;* Israel, *State of the Union Message;* Kesselman, *The Social Politics;* Logan, *What the Negro Wants;* Northrup, *Organized Labor;* Zaid, *Preliminary Inventory; Inventory of the Records* (NA); Ransom, *Journal of Negro Education,* 1943, pp. 405–416; Ross, *All Manner of Men;* Ruchames, *Race, Jobs;* and Weaver, *Negro Labor.* Other important sources were the Robert Martin CRDP interview and an 11/30/73 interview by Hardin with Weaver, a copy of which was obtained from the New York State School of Industrial Relations, Cornell University; a Du Bois editorial on Herbert Hoover, *The Crisis* (11/32), p. 362; and White, *A Man Called White* and *How Far the Promised Land?*

1. DW interview with CM; CM, 4/28/38, to Ivy Boone, secretary to the president of *BAF,* MP; *Minneapolis Spokesman,* 4/18/41; letter, 4/28/41, from Paul Amadan, superintendent of schools, St. Paul, to CM, MP; Franklin, *From Slavery to Freedom,* pp. 265–268; Spangler, *The Negro in Minnesota.*

2. DW interviews with CM and JM; Israel, *State of the Union Message;* Weaver, *Opportunity* (7/35), p. 202; Weaver, *Atlantic Monthly* (9/43), pp. 54–56; Weaver, *Journal of Political Economy* (9/44), pp. 234–249; Weaver, *Negro Labor,* p. 83; *NAACP Annual Report,* 1933, pp. 6–8; Weaver, *Journal of Negro History* (1/50); "National Conference on the Economic Crisis and the Negro," *Journal of Negro Education* (1/36); White, *The Saturday Evening Post* (10–12/40), pp. 58 ff.

3. DW interviews with CM and Weaver; CM, "Baltimore, Our Baltimore," MP; for outline of OPM's objectives, see Record Group 179, Records of the War Production Board, Negro Employment and Training Branch, NA; "National Defense Labor Problems," *The Crisis* (10/40); Weaver, *Negro Labor,* p. 16; *BS,* 3/13/42; "Two Years with the Joint Committee," booklet, RG 183, USES, Box 1396—files of Lawrence A. Oxley, NA; *NAACP Annual Report,* 1933.

4. Weaver, *Negro Labor,* pp. 10–13; Weaver, *Opportunity* (10/36), pp. 295–298; Weaver, *The Crisis* (8/34), p. 236; *NAACP Annual Report,* 1933, pp. 6–8; Roosevelt's letter to Hillman, 9/12/40, Sidney Hillman's letter to John P. Davis, 9/27/40, and National Defense Advisory Commission's release, 8/31/40, RG-228, Committee on FEP, Entry 8 PI 147, Office Files of Malcolm Ross, Folder "Negro File," Box 69, NA; the "Survey" is mentioned in "The Crusading Spirit of Robert C. Weaver," Robert L. Gill, Morgan State College, Schomburg; re the Homestead Subsistence Bureau, White to Weaver 11/24/33, Schomburg.

5. DW interview with CM; Weaver to Walter White 8/23/40, and 8/7/40, Schomburg; Weaver, *Negro Labor.*

6. *The Crisis* (10/40), pp. 319–320; *Current Biography,* 1961, p. 474; Weaver, *Negro Labor;* Weaver, *Journal of Negro Education* (10/58).

7. DW interview with CM; CM on Weaver for Alma Rene Williams, 5/30/73, dissertation in MP.

8. DW interview with CM; Weiss, *Farewell,* pp. 136–156.

9. DW interviews with Weaver, Davis, and CM; most of these recollections are from CM, CRDP, pp. 21–31, 25–32; see also Weiss, op. cit., pp. 136–156; William A.H. Birnie, *The American Magazine* (1/43); Ross, *Journal of Negro History* (1/75), pp. 1–29.

10. DW interviews with Weaver, Davis, and CM; memo from Dorothea De Schweinits to Philip L. German, 6/28/43, re: "The Shootings at Sun Shipbuilding and Drydock Company on June 16," MP; Negro Employment and Training Branch, OPM Organization, WPB 016-467, NA; "Minorities in Defense" booklet with outline on the FEPC, WPB 015-737, NA.

11. DW interviews with CM and Rauh; Garfinkel, *When Negroes March;* Logan, *What Negroes Want,* p. 130; Weaver, *Negro Labor;* Hardin, "Presidential Advisors"; "Minorities in Defense," WPB, 015-737, FEPC Organization, RG 179, NA; Bailey, *Congress;* Hamby, *Beyond the New Deal.*

12. DW interview with Davis; "Our Stake in a Permanent FEPC," *The Crisis* (1/45), pp. 14–15, 29; White's 2/15 statement to the FEPC during the committee's hearings in New York, 2/16–17/42, copy in RG 228, Box 462, Office files of Eugene Davidson, NA; Zaid, *Preliminary Inventory;* Weaver, *Negro Labor,* pp. 136–140; NAACP 2/15/42 statement, by White, to FEPC hearings in New York 2/17/42; Garfinkel, op. cit.; Frazier, *American Journal of Sociology* (11/42), pp. 369–377; Hardin, op. cit., p. 60; participating in conference with FDR (and administrative reps., Frank Knox, sec. of navy, Henry L. Stimson, sec. of war, Lt. Gen. William S. Knudsen, dir. gen. of OPM, Sidney Hillman, assoc. dir. gen. of OPM, Aubrey Williams, dir. of the NYA, and New York Mayor F.H. La Guardia) and Randolph were White, Frank R. Crosswaith, sec. of Harlem Labor Union, Mrs. Layle Love, a Harlem teacher rep. the March on Washington Movement, *NY Herald Tribune,* 1/31/46.

13. *NAACP Annual Report,* 1943, pp. 19–21; FEPC, *First Report;* Ruchames, *Race, Jobs,* pp. 15, 28; *The Crisis* (1/45), pp. 14–15; see materials in NAACP II A-472, LC.

14. FEPC, *First Report;* DW interview with CM.

15. Malcolm McLean letter, 9/25/42, to Gen. Frank Sherry, Hardin, op. cit., pp. 78–83; *NAACP Annual Report,* 1943; memo from Lawrence A. Appley, dep. chairman and exec. dir., WMC, to regional, state, and area manpower directors, RG 211, WMC, Records of the Office of the Vice Chairman (Labor Relations), Entry 12, Inventory 6, RF 1943–45 Folder: FEPC, NA; *Final Report,* pp. 12–17; transcripts of "Hearings and Complaints of Discrimination Against Railroads," September 15, 1943, RG 228 Box 305 Entry 19, NA; DW interview with Weaver.

16. DW interview with Davis; White's 2/15/42 statement, op. cit., n. 12; the NAACP's complaints had been documented in a detailed report five months earlier by the Federal Security Agency of the Bureau of Employment Security, which found that despite "the increasing difficulty of finding experienced skilled and semi-skilled workers, many employers continue to refuse to hire available Negroes for production work." This discrimination, the government reported, was harmful to production—MP.

17. CM memo, 12/17/42, to George M. Johnson, WMC assistant executive secretary, MP.

18. CM love letters to JM, MP.

19. DW interviews with Weaver and Davis; Zaid, op. cit.

20. Weaver, *Negro Labor; First Report* and *Final Report*.

21. Office of War Information, NAACP II A-269, LC.

22. *Steele* v. *Louisville and Nashville Railroad Company*, 323 U.S. 192 (1944); *Tunstall* v. *Brotherhood of Locomotive Firemen and Enginemen* 323 U.S. 192 (1944); the *Steele* and *Tunstall* decisions, as well as *Wallace Corporation* v. *The National Labor Relations Board*, 323 U.S. 248 (1944), were expected to have an important impact on the FEPC's work—see *First Report*, p. 62; Houston, "Foul Employment Practice on the Rails," *The Crisis* (10/49), pp. 269–271, 284–285; see NAACP II B-101, LC, for complaints and discussion.

23. Malcolm Ross, before the Select Committee to Investigate Executive Agencies (H. Res. 102), "The Railroad Cases," 3/13/44, Washington, and FEPC Summary of Findings and Directives in the 9/15–18/43, hearings re Chesapeake and Ohio Railroad Company, issued 11/18/43; Northrup, *Organized Labor; James* v. *Marinship Corp.*, 25 Cal. 2d 721 (1945), and *Williams* v. *International Brotherhood of Boilermakers*, 27 Cal. 2d 586 (1946); Hill, *Black Labor*, p. 403.

24. See memos and other documents in RG 228, Records of the Committee on FEP, Division of Field Operations, IE 2-48-25-2, Office Files of Clarence Mitchell, Box 459, and Ross Files, Box 69, NA.

25. Confidential report of the National Resources Planning Board, Field Office, Atlanta Office, 1/12/42, RG 228 IE-2-18-25-3, Ernest G. Trimble, NA; editorial, *Anniston* (Ala.) *Times*, 2/17/42—a copy can be found in IE-2-48-25-3, RG 228, Box 469, Trimble Files, NA; CM memo to Lawrence W. Cramer and George M. Johnson, 6/1/43, and *The Mobile Press*, 5/31/43, p. 1, story on strike, in MP; see CM memos to Malcolm Ross and others RG 228, 2-48-25-2, Mitchell Files, Box 461, NA; interview with Davis and his 5/25/44 memo to Ross in RG 228, Mitchell Files, Box 458, NA; interview with CM.

26. DW interviews with CM and Davis; *NAACP Annual Report*, 1943, pp. 23, 27–28; RG 228, Mitchell office files, Boxes 458 and 461, NA; RG 228, Office Files of Malcolm Ross, Box 64, and in Entry 8, PI-147, Box 71, NA; Office Files of Trimble, Box 469, NA; RG 228, Entry 29, PI-147, Office Files of Cornelius Golightly, Box 398, NA; CM memo 6/1/43 to Cramer and Johnson, RG 228, Box 458, NA; *NAACP Annual Report*, 1942 and 1943.

27. The report on CM's meeting with Daniels is from CM memo to Files, 8/4/44, MP; interview with CM; CM, CRDP, pp. 23–25, 36; Weaver, *Negro Labor*, p. 167.

28. DW interview with CM; CM, CRDP, pp. 59, 60–61; CM column, *BS*, 9/2/79.

29. DW interview with CM; Weaver, *Negro Labor*, pp. 153–191.

30. CM memo, 11/27/44, to Will Maslow, and Bi-Weekly Reports (this set of 44 reports covering 8/43 to 6/45 provides an excellent overview of the FEPC's progress in its most productive period), RG 228, FEPC Entry 40 PI-147, Mitchell Office Files, NA.

31. Lawrence A. Oxley, Bureau of Employment Security, "Employment Security and the Negro," *Security Review*, Vol. 7, No. 7 (7/40), pp. 12–15, RG 228, Box 5, 64-A249, "History of USES," NA; Weaver, *Negro Labor;* see Ross on

reconversion, RG 228, Entry 8, PI-147, Office Files of Malcolm Ross, Folder—"Extra Copies," Box 64, and Folder—"Speeches" Box 69; also, Ross, "Racial Tensions in Industry," paper at the Fifth Conference on Science, Philosophy and Religion, 9/10/44, RG 179 WPB 241.13, Labor-Negroes, both in NA; *Smith* v. *Allwright,* 321 U.S. 649 (1944).

32. *Pittsburgh Press,* 6/29, 6/30/45, and Thomas L. Stokes column, 7/14/45; *Pittsburgh Post Gazette,* 7/12, 7/17/45; see Trimble files, RG 228, Box 464; Randolph to White, 9/28/43, recapping events that led to creation of a National Committee for a permanent FEPC, NAACP II-266, LC; Zaid, op. cit.; Ruchames, op. cit.

33. CM column, *BS,* 7/10/83; CM article in *NAACP Bulletin,* DW Files; Bailey, *Congress Makes a Law;* CM lecture on Presidents, Morgan State Univ.

CHAPTER SEVEN

1. CM speech 1/30/49, NAACP Group II A-526, LC.

2. DW interviews with CM and JM; on creation of the NAACP WB, see "Legislation," *NAACP Annual Report,* 1916; "NAACP's Legislative Watch," *The Crisis* (2/17), p. 166; George S. Schuyler, "Something About Lobbyists," Observations Column, *Chicago Defender,* 12/27/19, a copy can be found in NAACP Reel 9, LC; see also materials in NAACP II A-33, NAACP II A-662, LC; James Weldon Johnson to Municipal Court Judge James A. Cobb, 2/18/30, NAACP, Reel 11, LC; Walter White memo to NAACP Committee on Administration, minutes, 2/26/42 meeting; report of sec., NAACP Bd. minutes, 6/42; report of sec., NAACP Bd. minutes, 9/42; report of sec., NAACP Bd. minutes, 10/13/42; CM CRDP, pp. 33, 38; for climate and problems of reconversion, see 11/21/45, letter to CM from Theodore E. Brown stating, "The closing of offices and further curtailment of personnel mean that the fight to carry on will be infinitely harder than it has been in the past. At a time when we most need services such as you have offered, circumstances are depriving us of them," MP; "Letter of Transmittal and Resignation," *Final Report;* CM annual report, 1950; Ernest E. Johnson, "Reconversion: America's No. One Problem," *The Crisis* (10/45), pp. 282–283, 301; Hill, *New Politics,* pp. 1077–1078, pp. 37–39; Wilkins, *Standing Fast,* pp. 128–30; Berman, *The Politics of Civil Rights,* pp. 36, 183; Ransom, *Journal of Negro Education,* pp. 405–416; Hill, *Black Labor,* p. 39; Ruchames, *Race, Jobs,* pp. 31, 35.

3. For CM labor committee activities, see his confidential 11/2/46 report to Walter White on CIO Convention in Atlantic City, "Personal and Outgoing" folder, MP; "first monthly report of the labor secretary," plus CM 8/31, 9/30, 10/31, 11/30/46, and 1946 annual report, 4/3, 5/24, 6/2, 7/3, 12/2/47 reports, MP; see NAACP labor sec. materials at LC, NAACP II A-520, II A-525, II A-526, II A-654, II A-655, II A-656, NAACP WB-124, LC; NAACP Bd. minutes 6/49; CM testimony on occupational changes before the House Subcommittee on Fair Employment Practice Legislation, 5/19/49, NAACP WB-69, and WB-194, LC; memo, 9/16/49, "Employment of Construction Workers," from

Wilkins to NAACP branches, NAACP II A-520, LC; Houston 11/25/45, to Truman and 12/7/45, response in Office Files, HSTL; CM recommendation on quotas and NAACP Bd. response, minutes, 9/12/49; for additional materials on NAACP attitude on quotas, see NAACP II A-486, II A-525, and II B-101, LC; requirement of racial information by industries, Ruchames, *Race, Jobs,* p. 31; 24th Infantry riots, see *NAACP Annual Report,* 1918. p. 37, *The Crisis* (1/18), pp. 130–131, and Kellogg, *NAACP,* p. 260–262, and for the East St. Louis riots, see Kellogg, pp. 221–227; Walter White provides a firsthand report on 1943 Detroit race riot in memo to the President, 6/29/43, and White and Thurgood Marshall, "What Caused The Detroit Riot, An Analysis," NAACP booklet, DW Files; "Report of the Special Counsel on the Detroit Riot," NAACP Bd. minutes, 7/14/43; Weaver, *The Journal of Negro History* (1/50); 1/7/48 memo on Executive Order 9346 by an administration official, and a copy of which CM sent White the same day provides an excellent summary of its inadequacies, "Personal and Outgoing" folder, MP; DW interview with John A. Davis; CM 5/19/49 statement, op. cit., n. 3; on the struggle against racial records, see McGregor, *Integration of the Armed Forces,* pp. 224, 380–385, 574–577.

4. "Brief Sketch of the History and Functions of the Public Employment Service," Washington National Records Center, Accession No. 64A.249, Box 6, NA; fight against job discrimination in federal agencies, labor sec.'s monthly report 6/3/60, in NAACP Bd. reports; CM reports on meetings with Labor Sec. Schwellenbach and other background action in MP; monthly reports of NAACP labor sec. 1946–1949, all in MP; 8/31/46 paper on reconversion problems involving USES, 10/31/46 paper for response from governors, 2/1, 4/3/47 paper on state FEPCs, 5/2/47 paper on reconversion problems with USES, 9/3/47 paper on meeting with Schwellenbach on apprenticeship training, 11/1/47 paper on problems of migratory agricultural workers, and state FEPC, 12/2/47 paper on discrimination in labor unions and throughout Washington and on USES reconversion problems, 12/23/47 annual summary of discrimination problems, MP; CM 1/27/47 letter to Gloster Current, in "Mitchell Action Re FEPC—1947" folder, NAACP II A-525, LC, and other related materials in NAACP II B-114, LC; article in *BAF,* 4/26/47, based on CM testimony before a Senate Appropriations Subcommittee on the USES; CM 11/21/47 memo to the files, re problems with the Atomic Energy Commission, MP; CM testimony before Senate Committee on Appropriations, *Hearings,* 80th Cong., 1st sess., 4/7/48.

5. DW interview with CM; *Final Report,* pp. 12, 28, 31; NAACP WB-154, and WB-155, LC; CM 12/9/47, statement before the Senate Civil Service Committee, folder NAACP/No. 103, MSRC-HU; labor sec. 6/2/47, 11/1/47 and 1948 annual reports, MP; *Washington Times Herald,* 2/3/48; *Washington News,* 2/3/48.

6. See materials in NAACP WB-154, WB-155, LC; CM 3/24/48 testimony before the Civil Service Commission, and 3/27/48 statement by reps. of leading black organizations who met in NAACP's office, MP; CM 3/1, 3/31/48 reports, MP.

7. White, *A Man Called White,* pp. 330–331; CM 12/11/46, confidential

memo in "Personal and Outgoing" folder, MP; CM on Schwellenbach, "Notes on the Taft-Hartley Act," *The Crisis* (10/48), p. 301; CM testimony before the House Subcommittee on Fair Employment Practices Legislation, 5/19/49, NAACP WB-69, LC.

8. Truman, State of the Union Message, 1/5/49, *PPP,* p. 1; text of Truman Civil Rights Message to Congress, *NYT,* 2/3/48, p. 22; reports of labor sec. for 3/1/47, 2/5/48; Peter Kellogg, *The Historian* (11/79); *To Secure These Rights;* Morgan, *The President and Civil Rights.*

9. DW interview with John A. Davis; *Shelly* v. *Kramer,* 334 U.S. 1 (1948); Berman, op. cit., pp. 74–77, 96, 192; 4/7/47 telegram from Matthew J. Connelly, sec. to HST, responding to 4/1/47 letter from Walter White, informing NAACP leader that HST would see him, Office Files, HSTL; following 4/11/47 meeting with HST, White expressed delight that HST had agreed to speak at the closing session of the NAACP Annual Conference at Lincoln Memorial on Sunday, 6/29/47, Office Files, HSTL; report of labor sec., 4/49, MP.

10. Labor sec. 9/20, 11/46, and 1946 annual reports, 4/47, 5/47 reports, MP; President's Committee on Civil Rights Folder, NAACP II A-468, LC; Maslow, *The Nation* (4/14/45); RW speech, 1/15/50, NAACP WB-26, LC.

11. McGregor, op. cit., pp. 311–312; CM in 10/30/47 letter to the editor of *BS,* challenged the contention that the drive for civil rights legislation represented social meddling; White re political prospects, *Collier's* (11/22/47); CM memo to the files on placing FEB in Bureau of the Budget, 11/14/47, plus an extensive series of letters and memos, MP; CM suggestions to RW for meeting with HST, NAACP II A-203, LC; reports of labor secretary for 11/1/47, 2/5, 4/1, 4/30, 8/31/48, MP; in a 1/17/48 letter to White, CM suggested EO 9980 could serve two purposes: spur the Republicans into some positive action on FEPC legislation, and keep the idea alive if Congress failed to act, "Personal and Outgoing" folder, MP; Morgan, op. cit. (during World War II, White led the NAACP in a vigorous "Negro and National Defense" campaign against racial discrimination and segregation in the armed services) NAACP Bd. minutes, 6/40; re Randolph's background and Grant Reynolds, see *Jet* (8/5/65), p. 8; CM 5/19/54, testimony, op. cit., n. 2; re White's disillusionment with the National Council for a Permanent FEPC see 10/14/46, NAACP Bd. minutes, White's letter to Leslie Perry NAACP II A-269, LC, Kesselman, *The Social Politics of FEPC,* pp. 9, 148–153; Berman, op. cit., provides an excellent study on HST's civil rights politics, for example, see pp. 30, 31, 34, 97, 126, 183–196, 204; *Pittsburgh Courier,* 9/22/45, p. 6, as quoted by Berman, op. cit., p. 26; Walter White and the Negro Press opposed Randolph's call for civil disobedience, Berman quoting *Pittsburgh Courier,* 4/10/48; Ruchames, op. cit., p. 86; CM's "Chronological Account," attached to 8/25/48, memo to NAACP branches from Dr. Louis T. Wright, chairman of the NAACP Bd., NAACP WB-69, LC; re the Russell amendment, CM on getting around the provision and keeping FEPC idea alive, see DW interview with CM, CRDP, p. 34, Berman, op. cit., p. 185, and National Council for a Permanent FEPC's assessment of the amendment, 11/7/50, NAACP WB-69, LC; re use of FBI, see Mitchell column, *BS,* 11/22/81, op-ed page.

12. CM letter to C. Girard Davidson, "Personal and Outgoing" folder, and related materials, MP; report of labor sec. for 12/1/48, MP.

13. CM 5/28, 9/30/48, 1948 annual report, MP; White's 6/26/48, "Memo to Branches" on battle for FEPC legislation, NAACP II A-390, LC; CM letters, 8/10/49 to Frank Fairley, New Orleans postmaster, 8/19/49 to J.J. Martin of Savannah, Ga., exchange of correspondence with Arthur J. Chapital, Jr., president of the National Alliance of Postal Employees, and other materials, NAACP WB-154, LC.

14. Reports of labor sec. for 9/30, 11/1, 12/3/48, MP; Hamby, *Beyond the New Deal,* pp. 170–173; NAACP Bd. minutes, 4/11/49; see also Berman, op. cit., p. 134, note 181, re White's complaint to Truman.

15. CM 5/19/49, testimony before the House Subcommittee on FEP, NAACP WB-69, LC; CM 6/30/49, speech, op cit., n. 1.

16. For even earlier political mobilization activities, where James Weldon Johnson discusses strategy on the Dyer antilynching bill, see Johnson to Moorfield Storey, 11/15/22, "Lynching/Blacks on Juries" files, NAACP Reel 3, LC; Houston, in a speech to the National Conference on the International Labor Defense, 7/8/39, said: "One of the things you should realize—at least one of the things I believe—is that the Negro people represent the balance of power, the ultimate balance of power in any liberal movement in the United States. We are now the balance of power so far as national politics is concerned, and even back so far as the Civil War, it was the 200,000 Negro troops in the National Army, representing also a loss of 200,000 workers in the Confederacy, which was the balance of manpower which turned the tide of the Civil War"—NAACP Reel 2, LC; Washington Conference on Negro Needs, and draft memo of blacks in the 1940 election, NAACP II A-212, and II A-236, LC; CM, CRDP, pp. 43, 61; at a special 7/31/43 call meeting, the NAACP Bd. voted to send to each member a copy of a "Tentative Draft of Position of the N.A.A.C.P. to Be Taken in Proposed Conference of Twenty-five National Negro Organizations" that White wanted to present to the Republican and Democratic National conventions; Oct.–Dec. 1943 activities leading up to political statement, "Declaration of Negro Voters," NAACP II A-234, LC; report of sec. on "The Political Conference," NAACP Bd. minutes, 12/43; White to Weaver: "At the March [1944] meeting of the Board, the Committee on Restatement of NAACP Policy on Partisan Political Activity was instructed to prepare a statement "embodying the objectives of Negro citizens which could be presented to the platform drafting committees of both political parties," NAACP II A-666, LC; report of the sec. for 6/44, NAACP Bd. reports, p. 5; on conference of 25 national Negro organizations, White's memo to the board with tentative statement, NAACP Bd. minutes 8/1/44; Berman, op. cit., pp. 107, 108.

17. 3/23/48, News Release on "Declaration of Negro Voters," NAACP II A-234, LC; 7/30/48, Statement by Cooperating Organizations Seeking Enactment of Civil Rights Legislation, folder, "Civil Rights Legislation," NAACP II A-390, LC; report of labor sec. for 12/1/48, MP.

18. NAACP II A-187, II A-234, II A-399, and II A-666, LC; sec.'s report,

2/49, NAACP Bd. reports; White's 6/27/48 speech to the NAACP Convention in Kansas City, Mo., DW Files; NAACP Bd. minutes 4/11/49; Berman, op. cit., pp. 161–162 for extent of southern control of the 81st Congress.

19. "Civil Rights Legislation, 81st Congress" folder, NAACP II A-203, LC; Truman's State of the Union Message, 1/49; Stewart, "Independence and Control"; Berman, op. cit., pp. 142, 148, 161–162; NAACP Bd. reports, 1/3/49; resolution for Annual NAACP Meeting, 1/3/49, in Bd. minutes; for issues involved in the Senate rules battle and White's determination to seek defeat of those senators who voted against change, see "No Time to Go Fishing," *New Republic* (3/21/49); when White suggested an article on the administration's handling of civil rights, Mitchell cautioned him against attacking Truman directly: "At this time we have direct relationship with the President through you. Others in the Association may publicly express opinions about what he might have done, but in your case any criticism should be based on very carefully documented facts. We do not have this on the civil rights program because we have no way of knowing from first-hand knowledge what transpired between the President and Senator Lucas during White House conferences on the handling of civil rights legislation," CM memo 3/18/49, to White, NAACP II A-203.

20. Column by Virginia Gardner, *Denver Challenge,* 3/3/47; reports of labor sec., 6/2, 9/3/47, 12/3/48, 1948 annual report, MP; CM, *The Crisis* (10/48), p. 300.

21. Report of the labor sec., 3/1/47; Berman, op. cit., pp. 144–145; Lee, *Truman and Taft-Hartley; The Black Dispatch,* 4/26/47; *WP,* 1/4, 3/7/49; *BS,* 2/24, 3/7/49.

22. Report of the labor sec., 9/3/47, MP; CM, *The Crisis* (10/48), pp. 300–301.

23. Berman, op. cit., p. 156; CM, "Education UAW Style," *The Crisis* (3/49), p. 73.

24. DW interview with CM; "National Labor Relations Act of 1949," CM testimony, 3/15/49, before the Special Subcommittee on Education and Labor, House of Reps., 81st Cong. 1st sess., on H.R. 2032, *Hearings,* pp. 799–812; Larus and Brother Company (62 NLRB, 1075); Atlanta Oak Floor Company (62 NLRB, 973); defeat of Parker, *NAACP Annual Report,* 1930, and White, *How Far the Promised Land?* pp. 78–79.

25. Report of the labor sec., 3/1/47, MP; Gardner, *Denver Challenge,* 3/3/47; CM testimony, 2/47, before the Senate Subcommittee on Labor.

26. Berman, op. cit., pp. 159–160.

27. Assistant sec. report to the board, 6/49, NAACP Bd. reports; DW interview with Rauh; *WP,* 8/21, 8/24/46.

28. CM memo to Wilkins, 12/1/48, NAACP II A-203, LC; members of the Joint Committee on Civil Rights to whom Dr. Channing Tobias, NAACP Bd. chairman, sent a telegram on 2/11/49, were the National Catholic Welfare Conference, American Jewish Congress, Social Action Committee of CME Church, CIO, AFL, National Medical Association, ADA, National Council of Negro Women, American Council of Human Rights, American Jewish Committee, Negro News-

papers Publishers Association, National Council for a Permanent FEPC, American Civil Liberties Union, National Baptist Convention, AME Church, AME Zion Church, and the American Veterans Committee, NAACP II A-203, LC; interview with CM.

29. Report of 11/10/49 meeting of steering committee and the 11/28/49 meeting of organizations, NAACP Bd. minutes, 12/49; report of the acting sec., 2/5/50, NAACP Bd. reports; NAACP Bd. minutes, 5/9/49, and 2/14/50; see materials in NAACP II A-66, II A-187, II A-188, II A-192, II A-193, II A-194, II A-234, II A-390, and II B-117, LC; *NAACP Annual Report,* 1949.

CHAPTER EIGHT

1. DW interview with CM; NAACP Bd. minutes, 5/10/49 and 5/8/50; NAACP news release, 5/10/50, that White's resignation was not accepted and other pertinent materials in NAACP II A-600, LC; for other materials from the black press on White's divorce and remarriage, see NAACP II A-601, LC; White, *Negro Digest* (12/49); White, *Saturday Review,* (10/11/47).

2. Interviews with JM and Weaver; White memo to the NAACP Bd. 5/24/49, NAACP II A-600, LC; the conclusion that CM was moving into Perry's area is drawn from materials on the two men's programs in NAACP WB-69, WB-70, LC, also, see WB report, 5/4/49, and report of acting sec., NAACP Bd. minutes, 3/15/50.

3. White to Ewing, 5/21/48, Papers of Oscar R. Ewing, HSTL.

4. CM memo to White, and clippings from the black press such as *BAF* and *Pittsburgh Courier,* both of 1/14/50, NAACP II A-655, LC; Perry's resignation and Mitchell's appointment, NAACP II A-655, LC, and NAACP Bd. minutes 8/3/50.

5. Brief for appellants in *Oliver Brown* v. *Board of Education of Topeka* on reargument, in appeals submitted to the Supreme Court, October Term, 1953; Meyer, *The Amendment That Refused to Die;* Hofstadter, *The Age of Reform;* Maslow, *University of Chicago Law Review* (Spring 1953), pp. 363–392.

6. Ruchames, *Race, Jobs,* pp. 199–202; Ernest E. Johnson, "Legislation in the 79th Congress," *The Crisis* (1/45), pp. 9, 30; brief for appellants, op. cit.; Meyer, op. cit.

7. NAACP Bd. minutes 11/25/46; *The Crisis* (3/47), pp. 51, 80, 94.

8. "Congress at the Halfway Mark: Speaker Sam Rayburn Will Need All His Persuasive Powers to Steer 'Fair Deal' Toward Enactment," *U.S. News & World Report* (4/7/50); *U.S. News & World Report* (4/28/50); Arthur Krock, "Fog Over the Political Landscape," *NYT Magazine* (11/4/50), pp. 3 ff; on 1950 election results, see *NYT,* 11/8/50 and 11/9/50; "Senator Harry Byrd," *WP,* 12/26/82; "John Sparkman, 85, Ex-Senator Dies," *NYT* (11/17/85), p. 44; *NYT Magazine* (7/10/53), pp. 10, 11; *NYT Magazine* (1/14/51), pp. 10 ff; on Javits, see "Profiles, The Gentleman from New York—II," *The New Yorker* (1/28/50); "A Sturdy Foe of Cant," a review of the autobiography of Emanual Celler by William S. White, *NYT Book Review* (3/15/53); on Ives, see *NYT,* 11/8/50, pp. 4, 8,

8/27/52, editorial on 8/30/52, p. 12, and 11/6/52, p. 1; "Adam Powell Dies in Miami," *NYT*, 4/6/72, p. 47.

9. Labor sec. report, 1/31/50, WB report 1/50, NAACP II A-656, LC; Ruchames, op. cit., pp. 200–202.

10. *The Crisis* (10/50), pp. 549–550; Ruchames, op. cit., pp. 206–209; Berman, *The Politics of Civil Rights*, pp. 169–171; CM memo to RW, 2/10/50, NAACP II A-656, LC; CM explains delaying tactics, speech, 2/18/50, NAACP II A-526, LC; monthly report of NAACP labor sec., 3/3/50, NAACP II A-656.

11. CM memo, 4/6/50, to RW on his meeting with Scott Lucas and Francis Myers on FEPC, NAACP II A-266, LC; labor sec. reports, 3/3/50, and 4/3, 5/1, 5/31/55, NAACP A-656, LC; report of acting sec., NAACP Bd. minutes, 5/50; Ruchames, op. cit., pp. 209–213; Berman, op. cit., p. 173; "Democrats Fail on FEPC," editorial, *The Crisis* (6/50), pp. 374–375.

12. I.F. Stone, "Where There Is Vision," *The Nation* (2/2/46), pp. 118–119; DW interview with Rauh; CM speech, 12/6/51, MP.

13. On the 7/14/50 Howard U. strategy session, see CM 7/17/50 memo to RW, NAACP II A-266, LC; on CM's 8/10/50 meeting with Stuart Symington, see 9/11/50 report of the sec., NAACP Bd. minutes.

14. Howard U. strategy session, op. cit.; *NYT*, 11/8/50, p. 4, 11/9/50, p. 11, and Arthur Krock column, p. 32; see *CQ*, 8/24/56, p. 1052, and *The New Republic* (8/20/56), p. 10, for background on Nixon.

15. Berman, op. cit., p. 301; CM 11/9/50 memo to White NAACP WB-111, LC.

16. CM memo, 2/21/51, to White, NAACP WB-111, LC; Berman, op. cit., pp. 183–184; Evans and Novak, *Lyndon B. Johnson*, pp. 39–40.

17. CM 12/8/50 memo to White, NAACP WB-111, LC.

18. Humphrey news release, 1/15/51, NAACP WB-272, LC; CM letter to Ives in 1/51, NAACP II A-266, LC; Berman, op. cit., p. 184.

19. In his 1/12/51 newsletter, CM reported that White and he met with Charles E. Wilson, director of Defense Mobilization, on 1/4/51. Wilson promised cooperation on a proposed executive order creating an FEPC with enforcement powers; appointment of qualified persons on the nonsalaried policy-making boards and committees established under Wilson's direction, particularly boards and committees dealing with manpower and training problems; and effective liaison through a top staffer who would have direct access to Wilson, MP; on 1/23/51, CM submitted a proposed executive order to Wilson, NAACP WB-272, LC, and NAACP Bd. minutes, 2/13/51; for 2/28/51 meeting that Truman held with black leaders, see report of sec. to board for March and 3/12/51, NAACP Bd. minutes, also Berman, op. cit., pp. 186, 187; CM memo, 4/26/51, on meeting he held with Wilson, NAACP II A-266, LC; CM draft news release to Henry Lee Moon, 4/17/51, that "Wilson Pledges Support for FEPC Executive Order," NAACP WB-272, LC; *The Crisis* (4/51), p. 258; in a 2/15/51 letter to White, CM lists as Truman's "major failures" on racial matters the appointments of Jesse M. Donaldson as postmaster general, Carl R. Gray, Jr., as administrator of the Veterans Administration, and the failure to name blacks to such agencies as the

Loyalty Board and as district commissioner in Washington, and the apparent lack of effort to get a satisfactory majority leader in the Senate; NAACP news release, 5/3/51, NAACP II A-269, LC.

20. *The Crisis* (4/51), p. 258; NAACP memo to state conference officers, 4/25/51, and other materials, NAACP II A-188, LC; "NAACP Cites Record of FEPC Stalling," news release, 5/3/51, NAACP II A-269, LC.

21. NAACP news release, 5/10/51, and text of Humphrey's 2/25/51 telegram to White, NAACP II A-188, LC; CM memo to White, "Status of Civil Rights Legislation in the 82nd Congress," revised 6/21/51, NAACP II A-525, LC; Current's letter to CM, 4/17/51, NAACP II A-655, LC.

22. Text of HST order, NAACP WB-272, LC; early copy of order, which CM never told White he had seen, "To Improve Non-Discrimination Provisions of Federal Contracts," 11/27/51, NAACP WB-69, LC; CM advised White of order's contents, letter, 11/29/51, NAACP WB-272, LC; telegram from White and Randolph to Truman, 11/30/51, quoted by Berman, op. cit., p. 192; CM explains weaknesses in 12/6/51 speech, NAACP II A-655, LC; CM, "President Truman's 'FEPC,'" *The Crisis* (1/52), p. 5—in this article, CM argues that segregation equals discrimination; White's memo to the NAACP Bd. prepared by CM and submitted as per CM's request in 12/13/51, letter, NAACP WB-272, LC; CM explained to board at 12/10/51, meeting (see minutes and other background materials in NAACP II A-208, LC) that a plan had been worked out some time previously through which the Department of Justice could secure enforcement of nondiscrimination clauses in government contracts by getting an injunction. This plan was submitted to Justice with the request that it be acted upon but that was not done. CM said it would have been possible for contracting agencies to use this technique through Justice to get actual enforcement of the nondiscrimination requirement. Much would depend on the kind of committee appointed. In response to a complaint from one board member that nowhere in the order could he find any implication that a contracting agency had the right to seek an injunction through Justice to enforce the order, Mitchell said that if the right kind of committee was appointed it would get a contracting agency to use that technique. The board, nevertheless, stated clearly that in no way was the committee to be considered an answer to the NAACP's demand for an FEPC because its most obvious weakness was that it lacked some enforcement machinery. "The order issued by the President is a makeshift order at a late hour," the board said. Mitchell said that when he received the text of the order a few days before it was issued, he sent a communication saying that he hoped it would not be issued because it was not effective.

23. Sec. report, NAACP Bd. minutes, 12/51, 1/52, 3/52; CM report to the board, 6/9/52; CM statement to the Committee on Government Contract Compliance, 6/9/52, NAACP II A-208, LC.

24. Sec. reports, 4/52, 5/12, 9/28/52, NAACP Bd. reports; CM, "Important Civil Rights Legislation in the 83rd Congress," NAACP II A-187, LC; WB report, 2/6 and 5/8/52, and 1952 WB annual reports, NAACP II A-656, LC; CM memo, 1/17/52, on conferences with McFarland and Douglas, NAACP II A-187,

LC; CM, "These Are the Issues," *The Crisis* (10/52), pp. 483–486; Humphrey outlines the Federal Equality of Opportunity in Employment Act, *The New Republic* (7/21/52).

25. Report of sec., 5/14/51, NAACP Bd. reports, and WB Newsletter, NAACP II A-655, LC; CM, "The People v. Winstead of Mississippi," *The Crisis* (5/51), pp. 307–311; WB annual report, 12/28/51, DW Files; *CQ,* 3/16/51, pp. 411–412, 4/13/51, p. 561.

26. WB news release, 1/25/51, and CM memo, 5/17/51, to White, and other materials, NAACP II A-655, LC; WB report, 3/5/52, DW Files.

27. *Time* (8/30/63), p. 11; good sources on school desegregation battle are Kluger, *Simple Justice,* McNeil, *Groundwork,* and "Along the N.A.A.C.P. Battlefront," *The Crisis* (6–7/51), pp. 396 ff; *Sweatt* v. *Painter,* 339 U.S. 629 (1947); *McLaurin* v. *Oklahoma State Regents,* 339 U.S. 637 (1950); for early efforts on federal aid to education bills, see assistant sec. report, 6/49, NAACP Bd. reports; CM statement to national conference on federal aid to education, 11/13/50, NAACP II A-526, LC; WB report, 11/5/51, NAACP II A-656, LC.

28. Sec. report, 12/51, in 1/52 NAACP Bd. reports; *NAACP Annual Report,* 1951, p. 5; Current, "Martyr for a Cause," *The Crisis* (2/52), p. 73; "NAACP Letter to President Truman Asking Presidential Action in Christmas Slaying of Harry Moore," *The Crisis* (2/52), p. 105; Mitchell, *The Nation* (9/27/52), pp. 268–271; CM memo, "Voting Records of North Carolina Congressmen and Senators," 3/22/59, NAACP II A-188, LC; CM letter to Sarah McClendon, and McClendon column in *El Paso Times,* 12/24/52, NAACP WB-171, LC.

29. White's plans for voter mobilization, NAACP Bd. minutes, 1/7/52; "Declaration of Negro Voters," sec. report, and board recommendation that he proceed with plans, 3/10/52 NAACP Bd. minutes; 5/12, 6/9/52 NAACP Bd. minutes.

30. CM speech (n.d.) before the Detroit NAACP branch at St. Stephen's AME Church, NAACP II A-526, LC.

31. Berman, op. cit., p. 197, from NAACP press release, 4/3/52.

32. RW memo, 7/31/52, on press conference held by Stevenson in Springfield, Ill. 7/20/52, based on those portions of the Democratic national platform dealing with FEPC and Senate Rule XXII, as quoted in *NYT,* 7/31/52, NAACP WB-151, LC; DW interview with Rauh, and *Congress and the Nation,* pp. 12–13; White's nine-point presentation to both campaigns and his subsequent statement on Sen. Sparkman, report of the sec. and other action, NAACP Bd. minutes, 9/8/52; CM's oral report to board on conversations he had had with Sparkman following the Democratic National Convention, NAACP Bd. minutes, 9/9/52; for more on White's efforts to get the political parties to adopt strong civil rights positions, see also Berman, op. cit., pp. 201–234.

33. CM 8/1/52 memo to White on his postconvention meeting with Sparkman, NAACP WB-111, LC, and Berman, op. cit., p. 218.

34. For Drew Pearson's report on Eisenhower's reversal, see NAACP Bd. minutes, 10/13/52; White, *How Far the Promised Land?,* p. 82; for assessment of the election, see *NYT,* 11/2/52, IV, p. E-1, and 11/6/52, pp. 1 ff; CM letter to

Henry Cabot Lodge, Jr., 12/4/52, NAACP II A-187, LC; NAACP Bd. minutes, 11/10/52.

35. NAACP news release 12/18/52, NAACP II A-269, LC; William S. White story in *NYT*, 1/11/53, p. E-5; CM speech before Alabama State Conference of NAACP Branches in Birmingham, 11/9/51, NAACP II A-526, LC.

36. Humphrey quote in National Council for a Permanent FEPC 10/21/47 news release in Hubert Humphrey Papers, Minnesota Historical Society, used by Peter Kellogg, *The Historian*, 11/79; Hamby, *Beyond the New Deal*, pp. 481–484, 496.

CHAPTER NINE

1. CM, Lee Nichols Collection Center of Military History, quoted in McGregor, *Integration*, p. 474; *Brown* v. *Board of Education; To Secure These Rights*.

2. CM, *The Journal of Negro Education* (Summer 1954), p. 203; Kellogg, *The Historian* (11/79); Marshall, *The Annals* (5/51), p. 102; DDE speech in Harlem, *WP*, 10/26/52; DDE State of the Union Message, 2/2/53, *PPP*, p. 12.

3. DDE, op. cit.; *NYT*, 2/10/53; *Times-Herald*, 6/16/53; report by May Childs Nerney on "Segregation in the Government at Washington," 9/30/13, NAACP, Reel 6, LC; "Report of Segregation in the Nation's Capital," in NAACP II A-363; for other documents and reports on D.C. segregation, see NAACP II A-350, A-363, and NAACP WB-59, LC; Victor R. Daley, "Washington's Minority Problem," *The Crisis* (6/39), pp. 170–171; *To Secure These Rights*, pp. 99–100; Brownell assured Mitchell in their first meeting that he had assigned members of his staff to explore how far the President could go in eliminating segregation in Washington—WB report, 5/4/55, NAACP II A-656, LC; NAACP WB press release, 6/10/53, NAACP WB-157, LC.

4. Article by CM in *Chicago Defender*, 50th anniversary edition, 1955, p. 18-b; "Washington, Jim Crow Capital of the United States," *BAF*, 5/18/35, p. 18.

5. WB report, 3/26/47, CM 3/26/47 letter to James C. Evans, and other materials in NAACP WB-176, LC; *WP*, 6/15/49; WB reports, 3/3, 5/31, 7/17, 7–8/50, 10/2/50, 1950 annual report, WB reports 8/31, 11/5/51, all in NAACP II A-656, LC; *Baltimore News-American*, 9/17/78; *Washington Star*, 2/7/79; see NAACP WB-59, LC, for other materials on NAACP efforts to desegregate the nation's capital.

6. *WP*, 5/25, 6/16, 11/20/51; CM 4/20/53, memo to RW, "Meeting of Subcommittee of Leadership Conference, 4/17/53, along with Arnold Aaronson's 5/12/53 "Report of Conference with Attorney General Brownell, NAACP II A-350, LC; *District of Columbia* v. *the John R. Thompson Company, Inc.*, 346 U.S. 100 (1953); Phineas Indritz, "Racism in the Nation's Capital," *The Nation* (10/18/52), pp. 355–357; *NYT*, 3/11/53, p. 26; *WP*, 4/29 and 6/9/53; WB *Newsletter*, 8/10/53, MP; Ethel Payne's article in *Chicago Defender*, 4/3/54.

7. *NYT*, 11/26/53, pp. 27, 28; "Proposed Order of the Board of Commissioners, District of Commissioner," drafted by the NAACP D.C. branch, NAACP II A-350, LC; WB report, 12/7/53, NAACP II A-656, LC; CM, "Civil Rights

Under the Eisenhower Administration, 1953–1954," NAACP II A-577, LC; White, *The Saturday Evening Post* (4/54), pp. 32–33.

8. *NAACP Annual Report*, 1953, pp. 5–6; CM, "10-Year Program," 10/1/53, NAACP WB-26, LC; "Civil Rights Under the Eisenhower Administration," op. cit., n. 7; CM letter to Henry Cabot Lodge, Jr., 12/4/52, II A-208, LC; CM to Dwight Palmer, 12/4/52, NAACP II A-208, LC.

9. WB report, 4/3, 5/4/53, II A-656, LC; *NYT*, 4/24/53, p. 16; White's letter to Dwight Palmer, 4/15/53, NAACP II A-208, LC.

10. CM on 8/18/53 sent White a copy of *Evening Star* 8/17 editorial praising the choice of Nixon, NAACP II A-202, LC; statement by White and CM, WB press release, 8/13/53, NAACP WB-157, LC; CM, "Background on NAACP's Successful Drive for Action Against Discrimination by Government Contractors," 8/21/53, and other materials such as WB report, 9/9/53, in NAACP II A-208, LC; *Chicago Defender*, 8/22/53.

11. DDE "Dear Jimmy" letter to Byrnes, 8/14/53, DDE Diary Series, DDEL; NAACP Bd. minutes, 7/53, 8/53; DDE to Nixon, 9/4/53, DDE Series, Box 3, DDEL.

12. NAACP WB press release, 9/10/53, and other materials, NAACP II A-208, LC; NAACP WB press release, 9/11/53, NAACP WB-157, LC; editorial, *Evening Star*, 8/18/53.

13. List of persons attending 11/30/53 meeting is attached to White's 11/5/53 memo on CM suggestions—this and other materials are in NAACP II A-208, LC.

14. "Analysis of Recommendations Made by Private Agencies to Committee at November 1953 Meeting and Committee Action Thereon," 6/16/54, sent to White by Jacob Seidenberg, executive director of the Committee on Government Contracts, on 6/30/54, NAACP II A-208, LC; White House press release, 9/7/54, NAACP WB-83, LC; WB 1955 annual report, DW Files; "Suggestions for Improving Work of Committee on Government Contracts," 1/13/55, NAACP WB-83, LC; 1/19/55, Mitchell's letter to Seidenberg on complaints, NAACP II A-208, LC.

15. White House press release, 1/18/55, on Executive Order 10590, NAACP WB-69, LC; CM memo, "Statement of the National Association for the Advancement of Colored People Presented to the President's Committee on Government Employment," 4/19/55, copy sent to Wilkins on 4/20/55, NAACP II A-208, LC; WB report, 5/2/55, NAACP II A-656, LC; McGregor, *Integration*, p. 162.

16. James Mitchell's speech at Conference on Equal Job Opportunity, 10/25/55, NAACP II A-208, LC.

17. WB reports, 10/2/50, WB 1950 annual report, 2/2, 3/3, 6/4/51, NAACP II A-656, LC; exchange of correspondence between CM and White and military officials and other materials in NAACP WB-141, LC; WB report, 8/31/51, NAACP II A-656, LC; McGregor, op. cit., pp. 149–151, 168–196, 380–385, 398–445, 614–616; on defeat of the Russell armed services amendment, which was one attempt to reintroduce segregation into the military, see CM, *Journal of Negro Education* (Summer 1954), pp. 204–211; Dalfiume,

Desegregation, pp. 210–212; *McLaurin* v. *Oklahoma State for Higher Education,* 339 U.S. 629 (1950); CM testimony before the Preparedness Subcommittee of the Senate Committee on Armed Services, 1/24/51, NAACP II A-655, LC; Matthew's response to Dr. Cobb's complaint, and Cobb's letter explaining the U.S.S. *Missouri* incident to Eisenhower, both in NAACP WB-142, LC; letter from W. McL. Hague, rear admiral, USN, chief of industrial relations, 2/4/52, and other materials in NAACP WB-142, LC; Virginia *Pilot,* 4/19/52; re Air Force, WB press release, 1/23/53, NAACP WB-157, LC.

18. McGregor, op. cit. (re Rosenburg, pp. 392, 393; re the end of segregation in the Army and throughout the armed services, pp. 452–455, 473–479; re Anderson's actions, pp. 483–486); also WB report, 2/4/53, NAACP II A-656, LC; memo for the sec. of defense, 5/25/53, DDE OF142, A4(1), DDEL; WB press release, 2/2/54, MP; press release from James C. Hagerty, 3/25/53, and other materials, NAACP WB-141, 142, LC; Mitchell to Rabb, DDE GF 124-A-1, Box 910, DDEL; WB monthly report, 4/3/53, and other similar materials, NAACP II A-656, LC; story by Alice Dunnigan in *Cleveland Plain Dealer,* 6/19/53; CM, *Journal of Negro Education,* op. cit.; *NYT,* 8/21, 8/22/53; *Carolina Times,* 9/5/53; *News and Courier,* 10/24/53; CM, "Negroes Now Eat Upstairs," *The Crisis* (12/53), pp. 585–588; report on CM in *Atlanta Constitution,* 2/27/54; WB annual report, 1954, NAACP II A-656, LC.

19. CM to Charles S. Thomas, sec. of navy, 1/14/55, and other materials in NAACP WB-142, LC; CM to Scott McLeod, administrator, Bureau of Security and Consular Affairs, 1/21/55, and other materials, NAACP WB-44, LC; McGregor, op. cit., p. 481; CM speech, 11/7/54, NAACP II A-526, LC.

20. WB report, 4/6/55, NAACP II A-656, LC; WB report, 10/10/57, NAACP III B-241, LC; CM article, 11/5/56, sent to Arnold Aaronson 11/6/56, NAACP WB-71, LC.

21. McGregor, op. cit., pp. 487–488, 489, 491, 493; WB monthly reports, 10/13, 11/5/52, 2/4, 4/3, 5/4, 10/6, 12/3/53, NAACP II A-656, LC; CM series of correspondence in NAACP WB-171, LC; news release, 10/4/52, with copy of CM 10/2/52, letter to Robert A. Lovett, sec. of defense, attached, NAACP III B-249, LC; *NYT,* 3/20/53; Roger W. James memo to Shanley, 3/20/53, and other materials in IF 142 A-4(1) DDEL; CM, "Recent Highlights in the NAACP Campaign Against Segregation in Schools on Military Posts," 3/25–6/11/53, plus "Additional Steps," through 1/12/54, MP.

22. WB reports, 12/7/53, 5/5, 11/4/54, NAACP II A-656, LC; WB news release, 2/2/54, and other materials, NAACP WB-171, LC; CM, *Journal of Negro Education,* op. cit.

23. McGregor, op. cit., p. 162; WB annual report, 1954, plus monthly reports 4/6, 10/6, 11/9, 12/7/55, NAACP II A-656, LC; WB annual report, 1956, NAACP III B-241, LC; Mitchell-Pohlhaus statement, 9/28/54, plus a lengthy protest to Charles E. Wilson, 10/19/54, and other materials in NAACP WB 171, LC; Mitchell's 11/5/56 article submitted to Arnold Aaronson 11/6/56, NAACP-WB 71, LC.

24. For initiation of CM involvement and explicit policy of Army on the

treatment of blacks in the National Guard, see WB report, 2/2/51; *CQ,* 11/26/54, p. 1139; CM background memo, 7/15/55, on reserve training bill, NAACP WB-124, LC; WB reports, 2/8, 3/8, 4/6, 5/2, 6/6, 9/8, 10/6/55, and 1955 annual report, NAACP II A-656, LC; CM testimony on H.R. 2967, "A Bill to Provide for Strengthening of the Reserve Forces," 3/3/55, before Subcommittee No. 1 of the House Armed Services Committee; Mitchell's series of telegrams, 5/18/55, to congressmen re their votes on the National Reserve Training Plan, MP; Powell rejects Eisenhower's complaint on "extraneous" matters, *WP,* 6/10/55, and *CR,* 6/19/55, p. 6774, also RW's response, 6/9/55, NAACP II A-274, LC; *NYT,* 6/24, 6/28/55; *Nashville Tennesseean,* 6/28/55; *Evening Star,* 6/27/55; WB press release on segregation of National Guard units, 1/6/55, NAACP WB-44, LC; WB press release, 12/1/55, on a CM debate on the anti-segregation amendment, MP; CM, *Journal of Negro Education,* op. cit., p. 213.

25. *Shelly* v. *Kraemer,* 334 U.S. 1 (1948) and *McGhee* v. *Sipes,* 334 U.S. 1 (1948); WB reports, 4/4, 12/5, 12/28/51, NAACP II A-656, LC; WB Newsletter, 2/27/52, DW Files; DW interview with Weaver; reprint of Weaver speech in *The Crisis* (6–7/52), pp. 347–348; memo, "Authority and Power of the Administrator of the HHFA," prepared by the NAACP, 1/11/52, DW Files.

26. *Shelly* v. *Kraemer;* WB report, 12/7/53, NAACP II A-656, LC; White's letter, 2/1/49, to the President, with a memo on "Discrimination by the FHA"; see, for example, CM letter to Cole, 2/5/54, NAACP WB-157, LC; Mitchell's statement before Senate Banking and Currency Committee, 3/24/54, NAACP III B-249, LC.

27. CM 3/2/53 statement opposing Cole's appointment, WB reports, 2/4, 3/3, 4/3, 6/1, 9/9/53, and other related materials in NAACP II A-656, LC; hearing on nomination of Cole before the Committee on Senate Banking and Currency, 83rd Cong., 1st sess., 3/2/52, pp. 27–34.

28. CM 5/7/54 memo to White complaining about defeat of antidiscrimination amendment, and related materials in NAACP WB-91, LC.

29. WB 2/8/54 news release with Cole's 2/5/54 attached, Cole's 4/6 letter to Homer Capehart, chairman, Senate Banking Currency Committee, with CM's 4/8/54 letter to Capehart—all in NAACP WB-91, LC; WB report, 6/6/55, on CM's appearance before the Senate Banking and Currency Committee on 5/19/55, to push for the antisegregation safeguard, NAACP II A-656, LC; the House defeated the antisegregation amendment 158-112—WB report, 9/8/55, NAACP II A-656, LC; CM's 12/3/54 letter to William R. Hudgins, president of the American Savings and Loan League, with NAACP recommendations at the Conference on Minority Housing Problems in Washington attached, and other materials in NAACP WB-91, LC; re quota and broad background on housing discrimination, see, for example, WB press release on Cole's quota proposal, 1/18/55, NAACP WB-44, LC, WB report, 2/8/55, NAACP II A-656, LC; CM testimony before the House Banking and Currency Committee, *Hearings,* 84th Cong., 1st sess., 6/9/55, on "Housing Amendments of 1955" (H.R. 5827).

30. CM article for *BAF,* submitted 11/1/74, to Elizabeth Murphy Moss, MP; "The Facts in the Case of Dr. Frank S. Horne," prepared by the National Commit-

tee Against Discrimination in Housing," and "Report on the Horne-Morrow Case," 3/19/65, by Frances Levenson, director NCDH, both in NAACP WB-91, LC.

31. Ruby Hurley's memo, 4/22/54, to CM, attached to CM's 5/5/54 response, and other materials in NAACP WB-92, LC; WB press release, 4/24/53, NAACP WB-157, LC; CM memo to White, "Suggested Statement for Ten Year Program," NAACP WB-26, LC; WB report, 9/9/53, NAACP II A-656, LC; WB report, 3/9/54, NAACP WB-86, LC; "Civil Rights Under the Eisenhower Administration, 1953–1954," n. 7; CM's commencement speech, Lincoln University, Penn., 6/5/56, DW Files.

CHAPTER TEN

1. *The Crisis* (6–7/54), p. 347; CM speech, 5/18/54, NAACP II A-526, LC.

2. *NAACP Annual Report,* 1955, pp. 9–10; editorial on the White Citizens' Councils, *Montgomery Advertiser,* 11/30/54, and article attacking NAACP for "conspiracy to destroy our Southern way of life," 5/10/57; Stan Opotowsky, "White Citizens Councils, Dixie Dynamite, The Inside Story," *NY Post,* 1/7–20/57; J. Claude Evans, "A Key to Understanding the South," *The Messenger* (10/9/56), pp. 14–17; Herbert Hoover, "Racial Tensions and Civil Rights," 3/1/56, DDE Diary Series, Box 33, DDEL; Henry Lesesne, "Lynching by Law," *Negro Digest* (9/56), pp. 94–96.

3. DW interviews with Clarence III and JM; WB report, 10/7/54, NAACP WB-164, LC; *BAF,* 10/9/54.

4. CM telegram, 4/15/55, to *Chicago Defender,* MP.

5. White's letter to CM, 3/21/55, NAACP II A-577, LC; *BS,* 3/22, 3/25/55; Alfred Duckett, *Chicago Defender,* 50th anniversary issue, 1955; editorial, ———, 4/2/55; *NYT,* 4/2/55; editorial, *WP,* 3/24/55; *BAF,* 3/29/55; to *BS,* 3/24/55, MP; see steady exchange of letters between White and Hoover in NAACP II A-274, LC; RW letter to CM, 1/27/55, NAACP II A-577, LC.

6. DW interviews with CM and JM, Weaver, and Rauh; RW letter to CM, 7/18/55, NAACP II A-188, LC.

7. CM memo, 2/5/54, to White, NAACP II A-656, LC; CM letter to White recommending Pohlhaus's appointment, 6/3/54, Pohlhaus letter to CM, 5/31/54, and statement on Pohlhaus background, all in NAACP WB-151, LC.

8. *NAACP Annual Report,* 1951; RW memo, "Reign of Terror in Mississippi," to DOJ, 9/7/55, DW Files; DW interview with Henry and CM on Till; statement of Courts, 2/16/57, before Senate Subcommittee on Constitutional Rights, NAACP WB-142, LC; Evers, *For Us the Living,* pp. 169–170; CM speeches 10/5, 12/15/55, both in NAACP II A-526, LC; report of sec., 10/55, NAACP Bd. reports; NAACP pamphlet, "M Is for Mississippi and Murder," DW Files; Evers, op. cit., pp. 174–175.

9. CM 11/54 report on Mississippi to NAACP Bd., NAACP II A-526, LC; RW letter to Rev. J.L. Tolbert, 6/21/56, NAACP WB-154, LC.

10. Courts's 2/16/57 statement, op. cit., n. 8; CM speech, 11/25/55,

NAACP II A-525, LC; CM 11/54 Mississippi report, op. cit.; NAACP Bd. minutes, 12/13/54; CM report on meeting with Farmers Home Administration official, 3/8/55, NAACP II A-656, LC; WB reports, 3/8, 4/6/55, NAACP II A-656, LC; NAACP Bd. minutes, 11/8, 12/8/54; CM statement for Fraternal Council of Negro Churches, NAACP WB-45, LC; CM letter to Olney, 10/27/56, WB-97, LC.

11. Evers, op. cit., p. 171; NAACP press release, 1/12/56, NAACP III B-152, LC; "The Lynching of Emmett Till: Chronology of a Tragedy," 8/24–9/10/55, DW Files; *Sweatt* v. *Allwright, Terry* v. *Adams,* 345 U.S. 461 (1953); RW memo to DOJ, 9/7/55, CM letter, 9/7/55, with draft press release, Mitchell to Olney, 10/27/55, and CM letter to Clifford Case, 11/20/55, all in NAACP WB-97, LC; Marshall to Olney, 3/21/56, NAACP III C-3, LC; White memo to Robert Carter, 8/21/46, and Marshall to Tom C. Clark, 12/27/46, NAACP II A-274, LC; NAACP press release, "National Organizations Meet to Plan Joint Action on Wave of Terror in South," 8/8/46, NAACP II A-274, LC; White, "U.S. Department of (White) Justice," *The Crisis* (10/35), p. 309.

12. CM 12/2/55 memo to Brownell, Pohlhaus memo on "Possibility of Unseating the Mississippi Delegation," both in MP; in a memo to CM, "Department of Justice and the Mississippi Situation," 9/13/55, Pohlhaus said "the greatest obstacle to federal action in Mississippi is the Department of Justice's rigid adherence to certain policy decisions on civil rights cases that were made in the past which are not necessarily valid at the present time": (1) Justice's deferring to state action if there is concurrent jurisdiction, and (2) Justice's reluctance to institute a civil rights case unless there is a reasonable assurance of a successful action, WB-97, LC; CM confidential memo on his meeting with Brownell, NAACP III B-62, LC; CM draft letter for RW and DDE, NAACP WB-45, LC.

13. CM informed Marshall, 10/20/55, that the WB was beginning the study, NAACP III B-435, LC; Pohlhaus, "Possibility of Unseating," op. cit., n. 12.

14. WB legislative memo, "Mississippi and the Pending Civil Rights Bills," 11/55, NAACP WB-97, LC; *Screws* v. *United States,* 325 U.S. 91 (1945); WB report, 10/6/55, DW Files; CM 11/25/55 speech, op. cit., n. 10; Branch, *Parting the Waters,* p. 128.

15. *WP,* 2/29/56, p. 10; *NYT,* 2/29, 3/11/56; *Washington Evening Star,* 2/29/56; *Sumter Daily,* 2/29/56; Associated Press, 2/29, 4/10/56; *Florence News,* 3/1/56; *Pittsburgh Courier,* 3/3, 3/10/56; *BAF,* 3/3/56; interview with JM; on Jim Crow interstate travel, see WB reports 2/4, 3/3/54, 2/8/55, NAACP II A-656, LC; DDE response to Ethel Payne for *Defender* publications, 7/7/54, news conference, *PPP; NAACP Annual Report,* 1955, p. 7; CM letter to John W. Heselton, 3/25/55, NAACP WB-45, LC; Diggs telegram, 2/28/56, to DDE, DDE G.F. 124-A-1, DDEL; CM column in *BS,* 3/9/80; CM letter, 10/4/56, to Olney and related correspondence, NAACP WB-97, LC.

16. DW interview with CM; DW, "Reagan's Attacks on Rights," *NYT,* 11/3/83, p. 31A; CM speech, 3/1/57, NAACP III B-207, LC.

17. Courts's 2/17/57 statement, op. cit., note 8; Evers, op. cit., p. 179; DDE's news conference on Little Rock, *NYT,* 9/6/56.

18. Fred Rodell in *Look* (4/3/56); Waring, *Harper's Magazine* (6/3/56); *The Saturday Evening Post* (6/6/59), p. 122; "Report of Conference Between Little Rock School Superintendent and NAACP Representatives," 5/29/57, NAACP WB-196, LC; speech by Daisy Bates before Tenth Annual Civil Liberties Conference, DW Files; "Little Rock: The Chronology of a Contrived Crisis," NAACP III B-200, LC; "Violence at Little Rock," *NAACP Annual Report,* 1957, p. 9.

19. CM telegram to DDE, 9/26/57, DDE 124-A-1, DDEL.

CHAPTER ELEVEN

1. CM speech, 6/5/56, MP; WB annual report, 1955, MP; CM statement, 2/10/49, submitted to the Senate Committee on Labor and Public Welfare and his testimony in 3/49 before the House Committee on Education and Labor, both on repeal of Taft-Hartley, DW Files; CM testimony with Waddy on S. 3295, the bill to amend the Railway Labor Act, *Hearings,* Subcommittee of the Senate Committee on Labor and Public Welfare, 81st Cong., 1st sess., 5/50, pp. 242–252; for text of amendment, see CM testimony on S. 3295, *Hearings,* Senate Labor Committee, 2nd sess., 5/18/51, p. 302; reports of NAACP labor sec., 5/31, 6/7, 10/2/50, and WB 1950 annual report, MP.

2. WB report, 1/51, NAACP Bd. reports; CM letters, 1/8/51, to J.H. Calhoun, and 1/12/51, to John Thodd Scott, chairman, National Mediation Board, NAACP WB-60, LC; *NYT,* 12/12/50, p. 42, and 1/1/51, p. 1.

3. CM testimony on H.R. 115, *Hearings,* House Committee on Education, 83rd Cong., 1st sess., 3/31/53, pp. 2069–2073; WB reports, 10/13/52, 2/4, 3/3, 4/3/53, 5/5/54, NAACP II A-656, LC; WB press release, 1/29/53, NAACP WB-157, LC.

4. DDE, *Mandate for Change,* pp. 291–292, 483; *Hearings,* 3/31/53, pp. 2059 ff.

5. WB 1953 highlights, NAACP II A-656, LC; CM letter to Ives, 5/5/53, and other materials in NAACP WB-176, LC; WB report, 5/4/53, NAACP II A-656, LC; CM, "A Report from Washington," DW Files; NAACP Bd. minutes, 5/11/53; *WP,* 5/6/53; CM letter to DDE, 8/3/53, GF Box 169, File No. 126-K, DDEL; WB report, 6/1/53, NAACP II A-656, LC; CM memo to Aaronson, 4/25/55, NAACP WB-26, LC.

6. CM suggested paragraph to Thurgood Marshall for speech, 6/19/56, MP; for background on federal aid to education battles, see *CQ,* 2/18/55, pp. 159 ff; CM speech before the Ohio State Conference of NAACP Branches, 9/22/56, and other materials in NAACP WB-70, LC; Houston memo, "Protection of Negro Interests in Program for Federal Aid to Education," NAACP, Reel 2, LC; CM letter, 3/1/50, to George Guernsey, assistant director of education, CIO, and other materials in NAACP WB-70, LC; NAACP press release, 11/16/50, NAACP II A-274, LC; report of labor sec., 4/3/50, MP.

7. NEA memo supplementing testimony on S. 968, 2/28/55, MP; Pohlhaus memo on federal aid to education, 12/14/54, NAACP WB-70, LC; WB news release, 2/2/55, on opposition from Council of State School Officials, and

Marshall's explanation in NAACP press release, 2/3/55, NAACP II A-274, LC; WB review of state legislation to preserve segregated schools, 2/28/55, NAACP WB-122, LC; letter from Constance Baker Motley to Alexander Viggiani, 1/12/51, Public School No. 16, Bronx, NY, NAACP II A-274, LC; CM letter to Joseph Campbell, 12/5/55, NAACP WB-71, LC; CM testimony on Federal Assistance to Increase School Construction Bill (S. 968), and on Agnes Meyers's threat, *Hearings,* Senate Committee on Labor and Public Welfare, 84th Cong., 1st sess., 2/21/55, p. 368; for text of cited version of amendment, see WB report, 2/8/55, NAACP II A-656, LC; CM statement before the House Subcommittee on Education, 4/11/56, referring to the *CR,* 1/24/56, p. 1033, for another variation of amendment: "[State plans shall] provide that school facilities of the state are open to all children without regard to race, in conformity with the requirements of the United States Supreme Court decisions; except that if a state plan does not so provide, it shall not prevent payment of funds authorized under this act to such state for use in counties or other political subdivisions within the state that are operating their schools in conformity with said Supreme Court decisions"; re Lodge's support, WB reports, 5/4/49, 4/20/50, MP; *WP,* 2/1/55; DDE educational message, *CQ,* 2/11/55, pp. 142 ff; CM letters to several congressmen in June and on 12/5/56, noting extent of state defiance, NAACP WB-71, LC; CM testimony on "Emergency Federal Aid for School Construction," *Hearings,* Senate Committee on Labor and Public Welfare, 84th Cong., 1st sess., 1/55; WB report, 3/8/55, NAACP II A-656, LC.

8. WB report, 6/6/55, NAACP II A-656, LC; CM "draft" on meeting with Allott, 4/14/55, NAACP WB-70, LC; WB reports, 4/6, 5/2/55, NAACP II A-656, LC.

9. RW to Lehman, 4/20/55, CM exchange of letters with Udall, and other materials, NAACP II A-274, LC; for Barden's strategy re the antisegregation amendment to the Davis-Bacon Act, see CM draft statement, 1/24/56, WB-71, LC.

10. RW to Powell, 7/7/55, NAACP II A-274, LC; CM memo to NAACP branch presidents, 6/13/55, NAACP WB-111, LC; CM to Powell, 7/29/55, NAACP WB-91, LC; *WP,* 6/10/55.

11. CM letter to RW, 7/22/55, NAACP II A-274, LC; CM telegram to Powell, 7/20/55, and other materials, NAACP WB-71, LC; WB report, 4/6/55, NAACP II A-656, LC; WB annual report, 1955, DW Files; report of the Committee on Education and Labor on H.R. 7535, 7/28/55, Washington: Government Printing Office.

12. CM to Joseph Campbell, 12/5/55, and other materials, NAACP WB-71, LC; *ES,* 11/29/55; *Chicago Sun-Times,* 11/30/55.

13. UAW press release, 1/26/56, and NEA press release, 1/25/56, NAACP WB-71, LC; United Electrical Workers press release, circa 4/18/56, NAACP III B-96, LC; Goldberg letter to Meany, 1/16/56, WB-41. LC; *Bolling* v. *Sharpe,* 347 U.S. 497 (1954).

14. WB report, 2/9/56, III B-241, LC; CM to Udall, 2/21/56, WB-71, LC; Truman's "Memorandum of Disapproval," 11/2/51, WB-70, LC; WB report,

2/9/56, NAACP III B-241, LC; CM to Udall, 2/21/56, NAACP WB-71, LC; Eisenhower's views on the Supreme Court's 1954 decision, *NYT,* 1/25/56, p. 12, 3/15/56, pp. 1, 16, 3/21/56, p. 29; for other DDE's views on education and southern defiance, see *NYT,* 1/6, 9/6/56, and *WP,* 6/27/57; for other administration views, see position of Dr. Herold Hunt, undersecretary of HEW, *NYT,* 12/7/55, p. 31; Hunt's exchange of letters with CM, NAACP WB-71, LC; WB press release, 12/22/55, NAACP II A-274, LC; WB annual report, 1955, DW Files; on defiance by Louisiana, Mississippi, and Georgia, see CM statement to the House Subcommittee on General Education, 2/26/57, MP; CM to McCormack, 1/25/56, on the stand by four southern governors, NAACP WB-71, LC; see also *NYT,* 1/25/56, p. 1; RW letter to NAACP branches on Lucy, NAACP III B-96, LC; *Adams* v. *Lucy,* 228 F.2d 619 (1955); *Sweatt* v. *Painter,* 339 U.S. 629 (1950); *NAACP Annual Report,* 1956, p. 5; CM speech at NAACP mass meeting in Chicago, 9/14/56, DW Files; for decisions on Florida and North Carolina university cases, see *NYT,* 3/6/56, p. 1, 3/12/56, p. 1, respectively; *(Board of Trustees of the University of North Carolina* v. *Frasier,* and *Hawkins* v. *Board of Control);* Fred Rodell, "The Pattern of Defiance," *Look,* 4/3/56, pp. 25 ff.

15. CM testimony on "Proposed Amendments to Public Laws 815 and 874," *Hearings,* Subcommittee of the House Committee on Education, 84th Cong., 2d sess., 4/11/56, p. 195; CM draft statement, 1/25/56, op. cit., note 9; CM letter to Powell on Committee of the Whole strategy, 4/18/56, WB-71; NAACP press release, 4/13/56, NAACP III B-96, LC; CM letter to Bolling on fight against closed rule, 1/20/56, and other materials, NAACP WB-71, LC; House support for Powell Amendment, see letter to DDE, 2/10/56, from Democrats Thomas Ludlow Ashley (Ohio), Charles A. Boyle (Ill.), Frank M. Clark (Pa.), James M. Quigley (Pa.), Edith Green (Ore.), Don Hayworth (Mich.), Henry S. Reuss (Wis.), and George M. Rhodes (Pa.), NAACP III B-96, LC.

16. CM to *WP,* 7/3/56, responding to a "School Encumbrance" editorial, copy of letter, as well as of another letter on 1/27/56, in NAACP WB-71, LC; John Morsell to *NYT,* 5/21/56, NAACP III B-96, LC.

17. WB, "Statement on Powell Amendment to the School Construction Bill," 7/6/56, NAACP WB-71, LC; WB annual report, 1956, NAACP III B-241, LC; WB report, 11/7/56, NAACP III B-241, LC; WB report, 5/9/57, NAACP III B-241, LC; Bolling, "Who Killed the School Bill?," *The New Republic* (7/16/56), pp. 7–8; *CQ,* 7/6/56, pp. 801, 808, and 7/13/56, pp. 824, 827–828.

18. CM speech, 9/13/56, in St. Louis, DW Files; CM speech, 10/30/56, DW Files; CM testimony, *Hearings,* Subcommittee of the House Committee on Education, 85th Cong., 1st sess., 2/26/57, pp. 568 ff.

CHAPTER TWELVE

1. CM letter to Truman, NAACP WB-45, LC; CM interview, CUOH, p. 34; White, *America's Town Meeting of the Air,* first broadcast, 1947, *Town Meeting Bulletin* (11/20/55).

2. CM letter to White, 12/2/52, NAACP WB-11, LC; NAACP press release,

1/3/53, NAACP WB-157, LC; assessment on 83rd Congress (no date or title), and other materials in NAACP WB-111, LC; DW interview with CM; Anderson, *Eisenhower, Brownell,* pp. 138–139.

3. Anderson, op. cit., pp. 13, 78–79; Pohlhaus's memo to CM, 12/30/54, NAACP II A-187, LC; "A Report from Washington," NAACP II A-298, LC; WB press release, 11/30/53, NAACP WB-157, LC; Pohlhaus's memoranda to Mitchell, 12/30, 12/27/54, NAACP WB-111, LC; "A Summary of the Civil Rights Record of the 83rd Congress," 8/21/54, MP; CLSA Reports (Commission on Law and Social Action), 2/5/53, NAACP II A-188, LC.

4. CM speech, 4/9/54, NAACP II A-577, LC.

5. CM speech, 11/7/54, NAACP II A-526, LC; election coverage, *NYT,* 11/3, 11/7/54; DW interview with CM; "McCarthy's Mississippi Friend," wire text of "Merry-Go-Round" column, 12/20/54, MP; CM speeches, 2/26, 11/7/54, 3/20, 5/8/55, 5/21/56, all in MP; "Report from a Freshman Senator," *NYT,* IV, 3/20/49, p. 10, 8/3/49, p. 17.

6. CM speech, 2/24/55, NAACP II A-526, LC.

7. See materials on electoral college struggle in NAACP WB-126, LC; quote from *NAACP Annual Report,* 1950 in WB highlights, 12/20/60, MP; *CR,* 7/17/50, pp. 10579, 10584–10585; WB reports, 7–8/50, 1950 annual report (MP), 6/14, 8/31/51, 2/8, 3/8, 4/6, 6/6, 9/8/55 (NAACP II A-656, LC), 4/15/56 (NAACP III B-241, LC); DW interview with John A. Davis; "Politics," *The Crisis* (5/55), p. 297; CM letter to RW, 4/27/55, NAACP WB-27, LC; CM speeches, 6/19, 7/20/56, MP; CM, "Civil-Rights Football," *The Nation* (7/7/56), 6.

8. CM speech, 6/22/55, MP; "Legislative Suggestions for Branches," 3/9/55, II A-298, LC.

9. CM speeches, 11/7/54, II A-526, LC, 11/25/55, MP; WB reports, 12/4/50, 2/6/52, 2/8, 4/6, 5/2, 9/8/55, 1955 and 1956 WB annual reports, NAACP II A-656, LC; see also, CM testimony, 1/2/51, before the Preparedness Subcommittee of the Senate Committee on Armed Services, 1/24/51 (NAACP WB-141, LC), 5/18/55, before Hennings Subcommittee on S. 626 and Powell's statement on H.R. 389, NAACP WB-111, LC; CM legislative report to RW, 8/2/55, NAACP II A-298, LC; "Armed Services," 1/18/56, MP; McGregor, *Integration,* pp. 392–395.

10. CM, LBJLOH, Tape 1, p. 10, Accession No. 73-24, LBJL; CM draft letter for RW to Eisenhower, 12/6/55, NAACP WB-112, LC; report on CM meeting with Brownell, 9/7/56, NAACP III B-241, LC; for CM's earlier association with Brownell, see also his confidential memo to White, 6/28/55, NAACP II A-208, LC; CM to Celler, 11/22/55, NAACP WB-45, LC; for report on 12/9/55 meeting, see Pohlhaus memo to CM, 12/14/55, NAACP WB-28, LC; CM letter to Leonora Leach, 12/7/55, NAACP WB-71, LC; WB reports, 11/9, 12/7/55, NAACP II A-656, LC; CM speech, 9/14/56, MP; CM's "My dear Congressman" letter, 12/29/55, NAACP WB-112, LC; for another account of the December 9 meeting of House members, see also Bolling, *House Out of Order,* p. 178.

11. *CQ,* 12/21/56, p. 1455; CM letter to James Roosevelt, 2/21/55,

NAACP WB-112, LC; CM telephone memo to NAACP public relations department in N.Y., NAACP III B-62, LC; Carr, *Federal Protection*, pp. 28, 45–46, 48–54, the La Follette committee was a subcommittee of the Senate Committee on Education and Labor, authorized by S.R. 266, 75th Cong., 2d sess., 6/6/36—see also *NYT*, 2/4/39, for further background; CM report on 1/12/56 meeting with Brownell, 1/18/56, NAACP WB-28, LC; Bolling, *House Out of Order*, pp. 76–80; DW interview with Bolling, 7/12/82.

12. CM, *The Nation* (7/7/56), p. 5; for materials on opposition to Eastland, see NAACP WB-175, WB-201, LC, and *NYT*, 2/14, 3/2, 3/3/56; CM speech, 2/11/56, NAACP III B-207, LC; see also *The Carolina Times*, 3/13/56, for correct meaning of the metaphor; Radley, *Coleridge*, p. 64; Hartley, *The Complete Works*, pp. 186–209; CM telegram to Lehman and Morse, NAACP WB-112, LC; CM letter, 3/7/56, to J.H. Calhoun, NAACP III B-150, LC; WB reports, 3/8, 10/4/56, NAACP WB-241, LC; NAACP news release, 2/11/56, NAACP WB-28, LC; Eastland speech excerpts, 8/13/56, NAACP WB-134, LC.

13. WB report, 3/8, 4/5/56, NAACP WB-241, LC; Branch, *Parting the Waters*, pp. 180–183; for administration's civil rights proposals, see NAACP WB-28, and NAACP III C-3, LC; DW interview with CM; Anderson, op. cit., pp. 40, 58; for a detailed discussion within the administration on Brownell's proposals, see minutes and record of 3/19/56 cabinet meeting, DDE, Cabinet Series, Box 6, DDEL, also Adams, *First-Hand Report*, pp. 335–343; Sundquist, *Policy and Policy*, pp. 221–237; Morgan memo, 3/24/56, to Ann Whitman, DDEL.

14. *NYT*, 4/10, 4/11/55, p. 27; DW interview with David Brody of the ADL.

15. See materials on National Delegates Assembly for Civil Rights in NAACP III B-64, LC; CM letter, 7/9/56, to Carl Johnson, WB-71, LC; CM paper, "Racial Attitudes in the North," given to Powell, NAACP WB-154, LC.

16. NNPA dispatch by Louis Lautier, *BAF*, 5/1/56; DW interview with CM; Bolling, op. cit., pp. 82, 174–194; CM, *The Nation* (7/7/56), p. 5; Herman Edelsberg and David Brody, Washington Office of Anti-Defamation League of B'nai B'rith, "Civil Rights in the 84th Congress," 10/29/56, article in Office Files of George Reedy, Cont. 418, LBJL; CM memo to RW, 3/21/56, NAACP WB-112, LC; *CQ*, 6/15/56, p. 708; *WP*, 6/22/56; CM to Hugh Scott, 7/19/56, NAACP WB-111, LC; WB letter, 5/2/56, NAACP WB-112, LC.

17. Even the liberal ADA was sharply split on the Powell Amendment. Only by a vote of 128 to 123 did it endorse an antisegregation proposal offered by Lehman to withhold funds from state and school districts known or found to be in defiance of the courts on segregation. The ADA rejected the stronger Powell Amendment that called for an outright ban on aid to school districts that failed to comply with *Brown, NYT*, 5/13/56, p. 75; CM to Carl Johnson, op. cit., n. 15; CM speech, 7/20/56, MP; WB annual report, 1956, NAACP III B-241, LC; CM memo to RW and Moon, 7/23/56, NAACP III B-210, LC; Edelsberg and Brody, op. cit., n. 16; *NYT*, 5/15/56, p. 24; DW interview with CM; CM speech, 6/5/56, MP.

18. For Douglas's account of the battle see his *Memoirs*, pp. 282–283; *CQ*,

5/6/60, p. 768; CM letter to T.G. Nutter, 8/1/56, NAACP WB-111, LC; WB report, 9/6/56, and 1956 annual report, DW Files; *CR,* 7/27/56; WB press release, 7/29/56, MP; CM telegram to Douglas, 7/25/56, and Douglas to CM, 8/7/56, both in NAACP WB-111, LC; *NYT,* 3/3/56; DW interview with CM; CM column, *BS,* 3/1/82, op-ed page.

19. WB report, 9/6/56, and 1956 annual report, DW Files; WB "Legislative Suggestion for NAACP Branches," 6/56, NAACP WB-124, LC; CM speech, 6/5/56, MP; Woodward, *Commentary* (10/57), p. 283; Herbert Hoover, "Racial Tension and Civil Rights," 3/1/56, DDE Diary Series, Box 33, DDEL; CM interview, CUOH, pp. 52–53; WB press release, 2/11/56, NAACP III B-249, LC; *NYT,* 2/6, 2/11, 2/12, 2/13, 2/14, 2/15/56; NAACP statement on "Civil Rights Planks of Republican and Democratic Parties," 8/29/56, NAACP III B-169, LC.

20. CM speech, 9/9/56, MP; *CQ,* 10/19/56, p. 1243, 12/21/56, p. 1455; Washington City News Service, 3/1/57, copy of dispatch in FBI files on Mitchell, #1000-425685; DW interview with Bolling, 7/12/82.

21. CM letter to Kuchel, 3/16/56, NAACP WB-112, LC; CM speech, 10/21/56, MP; DW interview with CM; *CQ,* 4/30/56, p. 2.

22. CM speeches, 9/9, 11/11, 11/20, 11/30/56, MP; an article in *Look* (7/24/56) showed that Democratic leaders were worried over defection by black voters.

CHAPTER THIRTEEN

The following, not all cited below, were essential readings: Edelsberg, *The ADL Bulletin* (10/57); Carter, *The Reporter* (9/5/57); Woodward, *Commentary* (11/57), pp. 283–291; "Civil Rights," *NYT,* 7/28/57, IV, p. E-1, 8/4/57, IV, p. E-1; Coffin, *The New Leader* (8/57); Bolling, *House Out of Order;* Douglas, *Memoirs,* pp. 274–303; Stewart, "Independence and Control"; Lewis, *Portrait of a Decade.*

1. NAACP WB news releases, 11/9/56, NAACP III B-170, "Mitchell Cites Government at 'Worst' and at Best," NAACP III B-241, both at LC; *Detroit News,* 6/29/57; Anderson, *Eisenhower, Brownell,* pp. 137–139; Sundquist, *Politics and Policy,* p. 230; CM speech, 11/11/56, MP; Moon, *Journal of Negro Education* (Summer 1957), pp. 219–230; *CQ,* 12/21/56, p. 1455; RW to DDE, 4/21/59, NAACP III B-162, LC.

2. *CQ,* 4/26/57, p. 506; Jim Rowe memo to LBJ, 4/4/56, Office Files of George Reedy, Cont. 418, LBJL; Richard L. Neuberger, "Democrats' Dilemma: Civil Rights," *NYT Magazine* (7/7/57); Robert Allen Jablon, "A Study of the Commission on Civil Rights," unpublished paper submitted to American University in partial fulfillment of the requirements of the Washington Semester Program, Lehigh University, 5/25/59; CM column, *BS,* 9/28/80; DW interview with CM.

3. CM to Arthur Watkins, 12/20/56, NAACP WB-111, LC; Douglas, p. 284; Stewart, "Independence and Control," p. 97; CM memo to White,

12/22/53, NAACP WB-111, LC; NAACP press release, "Taft Rejects Plea to Curb Filibuster," 1/3/53, MP; *CQ,* 1/6/62, p. 22; NAACP press release, "To Continue Effort to Curb Filibuster," 1/8/53, NAACP II A-188, LC; other background materials in NAACP WB-33, LC; *WP,* 1/14/53; *CQ,* 11/30/56, p. 1392.

4. Coffin, *The New Leader,* pp. 3–4; *CQ,* 1/4/57, p. 29; Carter, *The Reporter,* pp. 9–13; Arthur Krock, "Five Political Figures with a Single Thought," *NYT,* 7/7/57, IV, p. E-3.

5. *CQ,* 1/4/57, p. 29, 1/11/57, pp. 55–58, 1/6/67, p. 22; WB annual report, 1957, DW.

6. Memo, Office Files of George Reedy, Cont. 420, LBJL; WB, "Civil Rights and the Filibuster in the 85th Congress," NAACP WB-27, LC.

7. *CQ,* 3/1/57, p. 268; CM speech, 4/28/57, MP; CM interview, CRDP; Carter, op. cit.; *FAS Reports,* University of Pennsylvania newsletter, 11/81; *CQ,* 1/11/57, p. 61; *CR,* 1/9/57, p. 312.

8. CM letter, 4/30/57, and other communication to NAACP branches, NAACP WB-124, LC; *Washington Star,* 6/21/57; *CQA,* 1957, p. 555; interview with JM.

9. Douglas, *Memoirs,* p. 285; "Statement of the Attorney General on the Proposed Civil Rights Legislation Before the Committee of the Judiciary of the House of Representatives," 85th Cong., 1st sess., 2/4/57, DW Files; WB annual report, 1957, DW Files; Brownell interview, CUOH.

10. CM night letter, 2/17/57, to Kefauver, O'Mahoney, Wiley, Jenner, Dirksen, Butler, Hruska, with copies to Watkins and Hennings (not sent to Neely and Langer because they were ill) MP; DW interview with Bolling; Bolling, *House Out of Order,* pp. 179–180.

11. DW interview with CM; CM speeches, 3/1, 3/20/57, MP.

12. DW interview with CM; CM speech, 3/1/57, MP; *CQ,* 3/1/57, p. 269; "Dixie's Jester-Knight," Man in the News, *NYT,* 3/25/57; WB background review, NAACP WB-27, LC; testimonies of Gus Courts, A.T. Walden, and Rev. W.H. Borders before Hennings Subcommittee, *BAF,* 2/23/57; CM statement, 2/20/57, before the Subcommittee on Constitutional Rights, 85th Cong., 1st sess., and other materials in NAACP III B-204, LC; CM column, *BS,* 6/7/81, op-ed page; *Hearings,* Subcommittee on Constitutional Rights of the Committee on the Judiciary, the U.S. Senate, 85th Cong., 1st sess., 2/14, 2/15, 2/16, 2/18/57, pp. 1–273.

13. RW testimony, Subcommittee on Constitutional Rights, *Hearings,* 2/19/57, pp. 291–324.

14. For statement by Gov. Coleman, see excerpts of CM's exchange with Ervin, 3/5/57, NAACP III B-204, LC.

15. Materials on NAACP criticisms of Ervin in NAACP WB-28, LC; *Carolina Times,* 2/23/57; "Senator Ervin and the Rights to Vote," 2/23/57, attached to letter from CM to Tobias, NAACP III B-249, LC; "Trial by Jury in Contempt Cases in Southern States," NAACP WB-55, LC; "Civil Rights and Injunctions," NAACP WB-58, LC.

16. For Senate Judiciary Committee record on civil rights bills, *CQ*, 2/15/57, p. 205; *NYT*, 3/6/57, p. 1; "Further Amendments to the Civil Rights Bill," 3/22/57, NAACP WB-113, LC; WB report, 3/7, 5/9/57, DW Files; *CQ*, 5/24/57, p. 620, 4/26/57, p. 506, 5/3/57, p. 529, 3/22/57, p. 364; DW interviews with CM, Rauh, and Bolling; Bolling, op. cit., pp. 183–185; CM, 4/30/57, letter to NAACP branches, NAACP WB-124, LC.

17. Morgan, ABC-Radio, 4/30/57, transcript attached to LCCR memo, 5/7/57, DW Files.

18. CM speech, 4/28/57, DW Files.

19. Chronology of DDE's hazy responses on bill, *Jackson Daily News*, 7/5/57; NAACP WB reports, 6/7, 5/9/57, DW Files; *CQ*, 6/7/57, p. 690.

20. RW to Dr. C. B. Powell, 6/4/57, explaining origins of Prayer Pilgrimage, NAACP III B-169, LC; *CQ*, 4/26/57, p. 506; CM interview, CRDP, p. 58; *CQ*, 5/3/57, p. 529; telephone messages from CM to RW's office, 4/29, 5/1/57, NAACP III B-57, LC; WB report, 5/9/57, 6/7/57, DW Files; CM interview, CRDP, p. 58.

21. WB, "Civil Rights Legislation in the 85th Congress," 6/21/57, MP; *CQ*, 6/7/57, p. 690; WB report, 6/7/57, DW Files.

22. *CQ*, 7/12/57, p. 847; WB report, 6/7/57; *NYT*, 11/6/52, p. 21; *CR*, 1957, pp. 9103, 9619, 9780–9715; Douglas, *Memoirs*, pp. 286–287; DW interview with CM; CM column, *BS*, 7/3/83, op-ed page; Javits to RW, 7/24/57, NAACP III B-57, LC; CM to Morse, 6/24/57, MP; CM telegram, 7/11/57, to Douglas and Knowland, NAACP III B-57, LC; *CQ*, 6/21/57, p. 736.

23. *CR*, 7/2/57, pp. 10771–10777, 11312, 7/22/57, p. 12304; *CQ*, 7/26/57, p. 904; *NYT*, 7/3/57, p. 1; DDE's news conference, *NYT*, 7/4/57; *NYT*, 7/5/57, editorial; William S. White story, *NYT*, 7/6/57, p. 1; Arthur Krock column, *NYT*, 7/11/57, op-ed page.

24. CM to Knowland, 7/13/57, NAACP WB-113, LC; CM telegram to Knowland and Douglas, 7/11/57, NAACP III B-57, LC; WB's refutation of Russell's charges, 7/17/57, NAACP III B-55, LC; RW to Powell, 9/19/57, quoted in Wilkins, *Standing Fast*, pp. 250–252; Ervin, *CR*, 7/22/57, pp. 12305–12306; WB's "Part III of H.R. 6127," 7/17/57, MP.

25. *CR*, 7/8/57, pp. 10986, 10991–10993, 7/11/57, p. 11312; *CQ*, 7/12/57, p. 847; Knowland 7/3/57, announcement that he would move for Senate to proceed to consider civil rights bill, reprint in MP; *CQ*, 7/19/57, p. 854; CM to RW, 7/13/57, NAACP WB-103, LC; Wilkins, op. cit.; DW interview with CM in which he corrects erroneous report by Carter in *The Reporter*, op. cit., and others that it was Wilkins who escorted Knowland into the meeting; in a 7/16/57 letter, Knowland assured RW he would support his motion to bring H.R. 6127 before the Senate and oppose Morse's effort to send the bill to the Senate Judiciary Committee, NAACP III B-57, LC; "Senate Votes 71-18 to Take Up the Civil Rights Bill," *CQ*, 7/7/57, p. 854.

26. RW's handwritten letter to John Morsell, 7/23/57, NAACP III B-55, LC; *CQ*, 7/26/57, pp. 904, 907; *CR*, 7/22/57, p. 12304.

27. CM speech, 7/21/57, DW Files; *CQ,* 7/26/57, p. 904.

28. Morse's office press release, 7/23/57, NAACP III B-55, LC; *CQ,* 7/29/57, p. 904; DW interview with Rauh, 11/30/81.

29. Edelsberg, *The ADL Bulletin;* Carter, op. cit.; Coffin, op. cit.; Woodward, *Commentary,* 1/57, pp. 285–295; WB 1957 annual report, DW Files; CM, interview, LBJLOH; Reedy memo (n.d.), and 7/29/57, to LBJ, Office Files of George Reedy, Cont. 420, LBJL; *CQ,* 8/2/57, p. 938.

30. Carter, op. cit., p. 12; WB 1957 annual report, op. cit.; CM, interview, Tape 1, pp. 11, 13, 30, 74, Acc. No. 73-24, LBJLOH; Rauh, "First Clarence Mitchell, Jr., Lecture," 10/30/85, MLK, Jr., Library; DW interviews with CM and Rauh; *CR,* 8/7/57, reprint of Morse's speech in NAACP III B-55, LC; see also, RW's "Memorandum on Civil Rights Bill," 8/13/57, WB-112, LC, "Fact Sheet on H.R. 6127," MP, and materials in NAACP WB-27, LC.

31. News releases, 8/7/57, from civil rights group and LBJ's office, "U.S. Senate 49-61 Collection," Civil Rights Act 1957 folder, LBJL; Bolling, op. cit., pp. 186–187; WB's "Civil Rights and the Filibuster Rule," NAACP WB-27, LC; *CQ,* 8/9/57, pp. 963–965.

32. "Thurmond's Filibuster Record," *CQ,* 8/30/57, p. 1057; Payne, *Chicago Defender,* 5/31/58; *Ebony,* Vol. XIII (11/57); DW interview with Rauh; see correspondence between Johnson and his constituents in "U.S. Senate 49-61 Collection", Cont. 2, Legislative-Civil Rights folder, LBJL; *CQ,* 8/23/57, p. 1006, 8/30/57, p. 1057.

33. CM, interview, Tape 1, p. 13, LBJLOH; CM telegram to Nixon, 8/30/57, NAACP WB-112, LC; CM to Joseph Martin, 8/13/57, and to RW, 8/14/57, NAACP III B-57, LC; DW interview with CM; Lewis, *Portrait of a Decade,* p. 81.

CHAPTER FOURTEEN

1. Earl Warren, "Equal Justice Under Law" (a condensation of Supreme Court's decision on denying the Little Rock School board's petition seeking a postponement of its desegregation program), *The Progressive* (11/58), pp. 23–25; *NYT,* 9/10/57, p. 1; CM statement, "Report of Proceedings, Summit Meeting of Negro Leaders" (sponsored by the National Newspaper Publishers Association), Washington, D.C., 5/12–13/58; WB reports, 2/5/58, NAACP III B-216, LC, 9/6/57, DW Files; *Evening Eagle* (Wichita, Kan.), 10/22/57, p. 6-A; CM speech, 2/2/58, NAACP III B-216, LC; WB report, 10/10/57, and 1957 annual report, DW Files.

2. For Rogers's plans on civil rights, see *WP,* 12/10/57; RW response to Rogers, letter, 12/12/57, NAACP III B-57, LC; see also *NYT,* 12/30/57, for Javits's response to Roger's "cooling off" call; Warren, op. cit., p. 24; Daisy Bates speech to Detroit NAACP, 5/2/58, NAACP III B-205, LC; CM speech, 1/1/58, MP.

3. CM letter to RW, 5/14/58, MP; "Negro Rights Official Heckles Mitchell," *WP,* 5/14/58. NAACP press release, "President's Patience Plea Deplored by

NAACP Leaders," 5/15/58, NAACP III B-157, LC; editorial, *Pittsburgh Courier*, 5/24/58; RW letter to Diggs, 5/28/58, NAACP III B-159, LC; DW interview with JM; Ethel Payne, *Chicago Defender*, 5/31/58; Paul Douglas speech introducing the 1959 civil rights bill, 1/29/59, NAACP WB-28, LC; WB report, 5/8/59, MP; CM speech, 5/17/58, NAACP WB-138, LC.

4. WB reports, 11/8, 12/6/57, 2/5/58, NAACP III B-216, LC; CM speech, 5/12/58, NAACP WB-138, LC; CM letter to RW, 4/2/58, NAACP III B-69, LC; WB 1957 annual report, DW Files; CM speeches, 4/27/58, NAACP III B-216, LC, 10/12/58, MP.

5. WB reports, 2/5/58, NAACP III B-216, 3/6, 5/9, 9/4/58, NAACP III B-241, LC; WB press release, 12/11/58, NAACP III B-61, LC; Knowland's White House Conference on Tiffany and White, CM memo to RW, 5/2/58, MP; CM memo, "Conference with FBI and the Department of Justice," 3/19/58, and other materials, NAACP III B-61, LC; CM speech, 4/27/58, op. cit.; WB reports, 2/5/58, NAACP III B-216, LC, 3/6, 4/11/58, NAACP III B-241, LC; Wofford, *Of Kennedys*, pp. 462, 466–467; *CQ*, 2/19/60, pp. 249, 399; WB "Highlights of 1960," DW Files; CM memo to Gordon Tiffany, 6/12/58, NAACP III B-61, LC; CM letter to Wilson White, 2/7/58, NAACP WB-97, LC; WB's "Memorandum on S. 1617 (86th Congress)," 6/16/57, NAACP WB-28, LC; WB statement, "Voting Record of Rep. Victor L. Anfuso," 9/58, attached to WB report, 10/9/58, DW Files.

6. Excerpts from Report of U.S. Civil Rights Commission, 1959 (Washington, D.C.: Government Printing Office); *CQ*, 2/19/60, p. 255; CM memo to Gordon Tiffany, 6/12/58, and other materials in NAACP III B-61, LC; WB report, 11/6/59, DW Files; CM draft, 3/10/59, of testimony for Wilkins to deliver 3/12/59, MP.

7. WB reports, 3/6, 5/9, 4/11, 6/5, 9/4, 11/6/58, and 1958 annual report, all in DW Files; CM speeches, 2/4/58, MP, 4/27/58, NAACP III B-216, LC; *WP*, 6/28/56, 3/25, 4/2/58.

8. Rauh, "The Truth About Congress and the Court," *The Progressive* (12/58), 30–33; *Pennsylvania* v. *Nelson*, 350 U.S. 497 (1956); *Mallory* v. *United States*, 354 U.S. 449 (1957); *NAACP* v. *Alabama*, 357 U.S. 449 (1958); CM column, *BS*, 7/12/81; CM letters to Roman L. Hruska and Arthur V. Watkins, 4/28/58, and other materials in NAACP III B-228, LC; WB reports, 3/6, 5/9, 9/4, 11/6, 12/4/58, all in NAACP III B-241, LC; *WSJ*, 5/9/58.

9. WB report, 2/5/59, DW Files; WB Analysis of Civil Rights Legislation, 3/4/59, NAACP WB-112, LC; ADA press release, "Civil Rights Groups Favor Douglas-Javits-Celler Bill," 4/8/59, attached to Rauh's testimony before the Senate Subcommittee on Constitutional Rights, 4/8/59, NAACP WB-28, LC; NAACP statement (no date or title), 1959: "The power and authority of the United States Government are indispensable to genuine desegregation progress. The provision of pending bills authorizing the Attorney General to obtain injunctive relief for Negro children denied their rights is basic to any civil rights legislation. Therefore, we remain firmly and unequivocally committed to the Douglas-Javits-Celler bill, S. 810, which contains such a provision—the substance

of Title III," MP; *WP,* 4/3/59; WB report, 4/10/59, DW Files; "Civil Rights Legislation," 7/10/59, NAACP III B-69, LC; CM, interview, p. 12, Acc. No. 734-24, LBJOH.

10. *CQ,* 1/8/60, p. 41; RW testimony, *Hearings,* Subcommittee on Constitutional Rights, Senate Judiciary Committee, 86th Cong., 1st sess., 4/8/59, pp. 225–275, 302.

11. 1960 *CQA,* p. 190; NAACP WB report, 9/11/59, and 1959 annual report, DW Files; statement of the attorney general, 1/26/59, NAACP III A-305, LC; CM letter to RW, 8/27/59, NAACP III B-69, LC; CM letter to Kelly Alexander, Sr., 1/8/60, outlining intention of seeking Part III, NAACP WB-114, LC; "Civil Rights Act of 1960," 3/26/60, MP.

12. "Federal Voting Registrar Bills," 1/13/60, and other materials in NAACP WB-114, LC. WB 1958 annual report, DW Files; CM letter to Kelly Alexander, Sr., 1/8/60, explaining interest in registrar proposal, NAACP WB-114, LC; DW interview with Rauh; WB report, 2/5/60, DW Files; Person's influence, *WP,* 3/20/60; CM letter, 3/19/60, to Rev. Ford Gibson, enlisting help from the Indiana NAACP in the battle for the voting registrar and Part III provisions, NAACP WB-114, LC.

13. "Memorandum on Germaneness of Proposed Amendments in the House of Representatives," and memo, 3/9/60, from William L. Taylor, MP; WB annual report, 1960, DW Files; CM letter to RW, 1/8/60, NAACP III B-305, LC.

14. "Statement of Attorney General William P. Rogers, in Support of a Bill to Amend the Civil Rights Act of 1957 by Providing for Court Appointment of United States Referees, and for Other Purposes," 1/26/60, NAACP III A-305, LC; memo from Pohlhaus to Ken Peterson, 3/10/60: "The administration has withdrawn support for Part III on the ground that the situation in the South has improved to such an extent that it is not now necessary. The opposite is true," NAACP WB-114, LC; *CQ,* 3/18/60, p. 435; WB assessment of Rogers's position, 3/9/59, NAACP WB-112, LC; Pohlhaus, "Additional Segregation Legislation," 3/14/59, NAACP WB-28, LC.

15. *CQ,* 2/19/60, p. 249; CM letter to RW, 3/2/60, NAACP III B-305, LC; Civil Rights Fact Sheets, NAACP WB-114, LC; 1960 *CQA,* p. 190; CM as Independent, see CM memo to the files, 4/23/62, MP.

16. CM, "From the Work Bench" column, *BAF,* 3/8/60; WB report, 3/12/60, DW Files.

17. *CQ,* 3/11/60, p. 399, 3/25/60, p. 467.

18. *NYT,* 3/5, p. 1, 5/6, p. 1, 5/7/60, p. 12; WB annual report, 12/22/59, DW Files; 1960 *CQA,* p. 185; *CR,* 3/3/60, p. 3955; WB reports, 3/12, 4/9/60, DW Files.

19. *CQ,* 8/12/60, p. 1434, 8/26/60, p. 1486; Nixon letter to CM, 9/25/1960, MP; *WP,* 8/22/60; CM interview, pp. 1–49, CUOH; "Chronology of NAACP Accomplishments—1960," MP; Thomas Kuchel, reprint of speech, *CR,* 2/15/60, MP; CM column, *BS,* 10/25/81; Hays, *A Southern Moderate;* WB "NAACP Highlights of 1960," DW Files.

20. 1960 *CQA,* p. 801; *WP,* 7/21/60; *NYT,* 7/26/60, p. 19; WB report,

9/9/60, DW Files; CM speech, 10/29/60, NAACP WB-138, LC; CM JFKLOH, interview by John Stewart, p. 4; Rauh interview, JFKLOH; CM interview, CRDP; Nixon letter to CM, 9/25/60, MP; CM letter to the editor, *WP*, 3/4/59; Branch, *Parting the Waters*, pp. 316, 321; DW interview with CM; CM speech, 10/29/60, NAACP WB-138, LC; WB report, 2/10/61; CM statement before the New Jersey Community Relations Conference, 10/22/60; WB report, 11/11/60, DW Files.

21. RW paper at National Conference on Political Parties, Hayden Lake, Idaho, 4/11/58, DW Files; Morrison and Commager, *The Growth*, pp. 622–627.

22. DW interviews with JM.

CHAPTER FIFTEEN

The following sources are not all cited below: Evers, *For Us the Living;* Farmer, *Freedom—When?;* Farmer, *Lay Bare the Heart;* Garrow, *Bearing the Cross;* Lewis, *Portrait of a Decade;* Luper, *Behold the Walls;* Meir, *CORE;* Peck, *Freedom Ride;* Pigee, *The Struggle of Struggles;* Viorst, *Fire in the Streets;* Zinn, *SNCC.*

1. DW interviews with Current and other NAACP executives, 1971–1988; *The Crisis* (8–9/60), pp. 405–409; *NAACP Annual Report,* 1960, p. 25; *NYT,* 3/23/60, p. 4; *Time* (8/30/63), p. 11; *NAACP Annual Report,* 1958, pp. 17, 32–33; ———, 1959, pp. 37–8; *Browder* v. *Gayle,* 352 U.S. 903 (1956); *NYT,* 5/14, 5/21/61; see Chs. 3, 4 of *Lion in the Lobby;* Harris L. Wofford, Jr., sec., Pennsylvania Department of Labor and Industry/chairman, White House Sub-cabinet Group on Civil Rights, 1961–62, "Dream and Reality: The Modern Black Struggle for Freedom and Equality," presentation at a conference sponsored by Hofstra University, 2/20/88; Wofford, *Of Kennedys and Kings,* pp. 119–120; *Ebony,* 4/57; Marshall interview, JFKLOH, p. 41.

2. DW interviews with Clarence III and JM; CM letter to Rogers, 1/15/60, NAACP WB-98, LC; *United States* v. *Raines,* 362 U.S. 17 (1960); "A Tribute to Our Senator Clarence M. Mitchell, III," booklet published by the Mitchell family; *Bell* v. *Maryland,* 378 U.S. 226 (1964).

3. CM interview, JFKLOH; Beverly Gary, "Closeup" column, *NY Post,* 8/21/62; CM memo to RW on his views concerning the sit-ins, 4/18/60, NAACP III B-435, LC.

4. *CQ,* 4/21/61, p. 667; Burns, *NYT Magazine* (1/14/62), pp. 70 ff; CM memo (n.d.) to RW on his 9/20/60 meeting, MP; DW interview with Tyler, 6/18/89; White House press release, 3/6/61, along with text of Executive Order 10925, NAACP WB-65, LC; White House memo to heads of all executive departments and agencies, 4/20/61, NAACP WB-65, LC; CM memo to the files, "Civil Rights Division of the Department of Justice," 12/9/60, NAACP III B-305, LC; *CQ,* 4/21/61, p. 667; statement on Lockheed by JFK, 5/25/61, *PPP,* p. 397; *NYT,* 5/6/61; "Race Relations in the South," A Tuskegee Institute Report, Tuskegee, Ala.; Wofford, op. cit., pp. 143–144.

5. Interview with CM; WB report, 9/11/64, MP; Pohlhaus memo to CM, 12/9/60, copy to Robert L. Carter, NAACP general counsel, NAACP WB-115,

LC; Pohlhaus memo to RW, converted to brochure, "Executive Power and Civil Rights," NAACP WB-27, LC; Pohlhaus's letter to RW, 1/16/61, NAACP WB-104, LC; *CQ,* 1/20/61, p. 68.

6. Draft paper, "A Federal Civil Rights Program," 1/5/61, NAACP III A-305, LC; Wofford outlined a White House strategy that reinforced the President's "minimum legislation, maximum executive action" mandate—see Wofford, op. cit., pp. 136 ff.

7. CM discrimination complaints, 4/7/61, and other materials in NAACP WB-65, LC; WB report, 3/10/61, NAACP III B-305, LC; DOJ press release, 10/13/60, WB-98, LC; *United States* v. *Thomas,* 362 U.S. 58 (1960); Burke Marshall interview, JFKLOH, p. 63; *CQ,* 4/21/61, p. 668; Burke Marshall to CM, 10/30/61, and other materials in NAACP WB-98, LC; CM speech, 4/9/61, MP; *CQ,* 4/14/61, p. 640, 4/21/61, p. 668; Wofford, op. cit., p. 136.

8. *CQ,* 4/14/61, pp. 630–631; Burke Marshall interview, JFKLOH, p. 60.

9. "Federal Action and Civil Rights," *Current,* 12/61 (NAACP reprint of section with 1961 Civil Rights Commission report); "Congress 1961, Special Report," an addendum to *CQ,* 1961, p. 12; *CQ,* 2/24/61, 319, 3/17/61, p. 422, 4/21/61, pp. 308, 667, 6/30/61, p. 1198; CM statement before the Senate Subcommittee on Education, 3/10/61, MP, also *Hearings* 87th Cong., 1st sess., p. 429; WB reports, 3/10/61, 4/4/62, MP; memo for Larry O'Brien, 12/10/62, Kennedy Papers, JFKL; WB 1958 annual report, MP.

10. *CQ,* 1/15/60, p. 98, 1/20/61, pp. 67–68, 4/21/61, p. 668, 6/16/61, p. 985, 9/21/62, p. 1580; Burke Marshall interview, 6/13/63, JFKLOH, pp. 47–49; WB reports, 9/4, 10/4, WB 1962 annual report; CM memo on Prince Georges County desegregation, 10/1/62, NAACP WB-98, LC; CM memo to files, "Conversations with Lester Banks Concerning Conversation with Mr. St. John Barnett of the DOJ," 8/22/62, NAACP WB-98, LC; DOJ press release, 9/17/62, NAACP WB-98, LC; CM speech, 9/23/62, MP; *NYT,* 5/6/61.

11. WB report, 6/6/63, MP; Louis Lautier, "Time for a Change for NAACP," "Capital Spotlight" column, *BAF,* 7/6/54; McGregor, *Integration,* pp. 9–12.

12. DW interview with CM; WB report, 8/25/61, in which CM quotes State Department press release, 8/15/61, on Rowan, MP; see also "Freedom Train" materials in NAACP WB-40, LC.

13. *WP,* 7/23/61, p. 38; *CQ,* 4/14/61, pp. 630–631, 4/21/61, p. 667; *NYT,* 1/18/62.

14. CM speech, 3/24/62, MP; WB reports, 2/2, 2/10/61, MP; CM, interview, JFKLOH, p. 27; *CQ,* 2/10/61, p. 218, 5/19/61, p. 852, 1/26/62, p. 99, 127, 1/12/62, p. 30; 2/2/62, p. 179; WB report, 10/27/62, and 1962 annual report, MP; *Jet* (6/28/62), p. 12; CM "From the Work Bench" column, *BAF,* 1/17/61.

15. *WP,* 9/25, 10/1, 11/1/61; CM speech, 8/14/61, WB-138, LC; WB reports, 8/25, 10/4/61, and 1961 annual report, MP.

16. DW interviews with CM, Harold Tyler, Myrlie Evers, and Dr. Gilbert R. Mason; CM speech, 5/17/60, and other materials in NAACP III B-435, LC; DW

interview with Tyler; Department of Agriculture letter to Javits, 9/9/60, and other materials in NAACP WB-1, LC; CM speech, 4/9/61, MP; *Catlette* v. *United States*, 132 F.2d. 902 (1943); WB 1959 annual report, MP.

17. "Working Draft of LCCR Project on Affirmative Action," MP; CM to Charles J. Waller, 5/15/61, NAACP WB-138, LC; In re *Debs*, 158 U.S. 564 (1895).

18. *Morgan* v. *Virginia*, 328 U.S. 373 (1946); *Browder* v. *Gayle*, 352 U.S. 903 (1956); *NYT*, 5/7/61, p. 10-E, 5/14, 5/16/61, and editorial 5/22/61; CM speech, 10/29/60, NAACP, WB-138, LC; WB report, 6/19/61, MP; Burke Marshall interview, 6/13/69, JFKLOH, p. 49; CM speech, 4/9/61, MP; *The Crisis* (12/56), p. 613; *CQ*, 6/9/61, p. 945; re attacks on the Court in 1962, see CM to Congressman Kenneth J. Gray, 6/21/62, WB-36.

19. *CQ*, 1/5/62, p. 27; *NYT*, 5/20, 5/21/61; Burke Marshall interview, 6/13, 6/14/64, JFKLOH, pp. 40, 43, 48, 67, 85.

20. *NYT*, 1/17/62, p. 15; "Race Relations in the South, 1962," op. cit., note 4; exchange of correspondence among CM, RFK, and Burke Marshall, NAACP WB-27, also NAACP WB-98, LC.

21. "Report of the Attorney General to the President on the Department of Justice's Activities in the Field of Civil Rights," NAACP WB-98, LC; *NYT*, 1/16/62; Burke Marshall, 5/29/64, JFKLOH, pp. 40, 41; ———— interview, 10/28/68, LBJLOH; CM interview, CRDP, p. 71; WB reports, 2/2, 3/7, 6/7/62, MP; CM, "From the Work Bench," column draft, 1961, MP; *CQ*, 11/23/62, p. 2203; CM letter to Kenneth Keating, 1/8/62, NAACP WB-138, LC; Burke Marshall, 5/29/64, JFKLOH, pp. 18, 40; Zinn, *SNCC*, pp. 196, 199.

22. *WP*, 4/24/62; *CQ*, 1/5/62; "Report of the Attorney General," op. cit.; CM letter to Javits, 8/2/62, and other materials, NAACP WB-115, LC; memo, 8/2/62, NAACP WB-98, LC; WB 1962 annual report, MP.

23. *NYT*, 8/2/62; CM, "From the Work Bench," column draft, late 1962 or early 1963, MP.

24. CM quoted in story, "Wilkins Sees Possibility of Shift to GOP by Negroes," *WP*, 5/30/63; CM to Keating, 1/8/62, NAACP WB-138, LC; "Eyes on the Prize, America's Civil Rights Years, 1954–1965," a 1986 public television series, Henry Hampton, producer, Blackside, Inc.; Evers, *For Us, the Living*, p. 244; Dr. James Wesley Silver speech, *NYT*, 11/8/63; Burke Marshall interview, 6/14/64, JFKLOH, p. 78; Sorensen interview, 5/3/64, JFKLOH; Mississippi field Sec. monthly report, 10/5/62, DW Files; CM telegram to all senators except those from Alabama, Arkansas, Florida, Georgia, Louisiana, North and South Carolina, Virginia, 9/27/62, NAACP WB-135, LC; WB report, 6/7/62, MP; CM, "From the Work Bench," column draft, 1961, MP.

25. DW interview with Rauh; *Scales* v. *United States*, 367 U.S. 203 (1964); Rauh letter to editor, *WP*, 12/28/62; Mississippi Advisory Committee to the United States Commission on Civil Rights, "Report on Mississippi" (Washington, D.C.: GSA), 1/63.

26. CM interview, CRDP, p. 71; CM interview, JFKLOH, pp. 30–31.

CHAPTER SIXTEEN

1. CM, "From the Work Bench" column, *BAF* (1961), MP; Evers, *For Us, the Living;* James W. Silver, excerpts from address to the annual meeting of the Southern Historical Society, *NYT,* 11/8/63; DW interviews with Myrlie Evers and Dr. Aaron Henry; Medgar Evers letter to RW, 4/1/58, NAACP III B-184, LC; "The Piney Woods Country Life School," a brochure, and other materials obtained from the Piney Woods School, Miss.

2. Medgar Evers letters to MLK and RW, 8/20/57, NAACP III B-184, LC; "Medgar Evers," a special issue, *Ebony* (9/63), p. 145; DW interviews with Current, Myrlie Evers, Henry, Dr. Gilbert C. Mason, CM; CM on Percy Greene's opposition to civil rights, WB report, 6/3/59, MP; Evers, *For Us, the Living,* pp. 151, 232, 238, 248, 250, 282; RW to Henry, 12/11/62, NAACP WB-1, LC; *Jet,* 7/11/63, p. 19; WB report, 3/8/63, MP; NAACP WB-135, LC; Current's book message to NAACP branches, 6/1/63, MP; "Violence Flares After Rites for Evers in Tense Jackson," *BAF,* 6/18/63, p. 20; *NY Daily News,* 7/23/63, p. 24; WB memo (n.d.) re Evers advising the route of the march, MP; "Widow Says She Will Keep Promise to Battle Bias," *Jet,* 7/11/63, pp. 18–22; CM telegram to JFK, 6/21/63, MP; *Ebony,* 6/28/63; CM on visit to Jackson, WB report, 6/6/63, MP; Wallace defies, see *NYT,* 6/2, p. 1, 6/12/63, p. 1; *Newsweek* (6/24/63), p. 32.

3. Drew Pearson on Byron de La Beckwith, "Washington Merry-Go-Round" column (n.d.), a copy in NAACP III B-435, LC; Pohlhaus memo to CM, 10/1/62, NAACP WB-131, LC.

4. "Negroes Ask Protection Law," *WP* article (n.d.), MP; *NYT,* 5/22/61; Stewart, "Independence and Control," p. 31; Edelsberg, "Civil Rights in the 87th Congress."

5. Stewart, "Independence and Control," pp. 31, 104–111; for Knowland's views, Edelsberg memo to RW, 5/2/28, MP; Collins, *NYT Magazine* (7/30/61); *CQ,* 1/4/63, p. 12; *Newsweek* (11/18/63); Mansfield's defense of his style, *CR,* 11/27/63, p. 22858; Rauh's brief on Rule XXII reform, *CR,* 1/2/59, pp. 133–141, subsequently, 12/30/60, WB-33, LC; "Why Kennedy's Program Is in Trouble with Congress," *U.S. News & World Report* (9/17/62); WB report, 12/4/58, NAACP III B-241, LC; WB annual report, 1958, DW Files; RW letter to Douglas, Case, Humphrey, Javits, 1/15/59, MP; "Civil Rights in the 86th Congress," a WB review, MP; *CQ,* 1/4/63, p. 12; CM statement to the NAACP annual convention in 1959 at Columbus Circle, N.Y.C., MP.

6. WB report, 2/10/61, MP; *CQ,* 1/6/61, pp. 23–24; Stewart, op. cit., pp. 113–119; Edelsberg, "Civil Rights in the 87th Congress," pp. 6–7, 50–56.

7. CM speech, 10/27/62, MP; WB reports, 11/9/62, 2/5/63, and WB "Highlights," 1963, both in MP; Stewart, op. cit., pp. 119–123; "Rayburn Shifts in Rules Battle," *NYT,* 1/18/61; CM memo to the files on meeting with Johnson, 1/25/63, MP; *CQ,* 1/4/63, pp. 9–12, 1/11/63, pp. 12, 31, 1/18/63, p. 73; 2/15/63, p. 192, 1/6/67, p. 22; Pohlhaus 1964 review, DW Files; for "History, Techniques of Senate Filibusters," see *CQ,* 4/27/62, pp. 660–662.

8. *CQ,* 1/4/63, pp. 9–11; see materials in NAACP WB-39, LC; Editorial, *WP,* 2/9/63; CM letter to the editor, *WP,* 2/14/63.

9. CM, "From the Work Bench," column draft, MP; *CR,* 2/11/63, p. 1974; Stewart, op. cit., pp. 120–122; CM speech, 4/9/61, MP; LCCR report, 1/15/63, NAACP WB-106, LC; *CQ,* 1/4/63, p. 10, 1/11/63, p. 31; *Legislators and the Lobbyists,* a book by Congressional Quarterly Service, 1965, p. 16; Pierre Salinger, *NYT,* 5/16/61, p. 1.

10. Pohlhaus letter to Donald F. Sullivan, 5/6/64, NAACP WB-151, LC; *CQA,* 1962, pp. 81, 292, 392; 1961 *CQ,* Appendix, p. 19; *CQ,* 5/12/61, p. 792; *CQA,* 1961, p. 81.

11. *CQ,* 1961, Appendix, p. 19; WB report, 2/2/62, MP; *CQ,* 4/27/62, p. 659; Burke Marshall interview, 5/29/64, JFKLOH, pp. 64–65; Edelsberg and Brody, op. cit.; WB report, 4/4/62, MP; RW testimony, Subcommittee on Constitutional Rights of the Senate Judiciary Committee, 4/6/62, MP; Ex parte *Siebold,* 100 U.S. 371 (1879); Ex parte *Yarborough,* 100 U.S. 651 (1884).

12. Testimony by RFK before the House Judiciary Committee, 3/15/62, MP; *CQ,* 4/27/62, p. 659, 5/4/62, p. 751, 5/18/62, p. 835; *CQA,* 1961, p. 395.

13. CM testimony before Subcommittee No. 5, House Judiciary Committee, 3/14/62, NAACP WB-136, LC; WB report, 2/2/62, MP; WB report, 5/10/82, MP; *CQ,* 5/4/62, p. 751, 5/18/62, p. 835; White House reaction, *Jet* (5/24/62), p. 6.

14. *NYT,* 8/2/62, p. 1, 6/2/63, IV, p. 8-E; DW interview with Nicholas Katzenbach; WB report, 9/4/62, and annual 1962 report, MP; Edelsberg and Brody, op. cit., p. 5; *CQ,* 8/17/62, p. 1358.

15. WB reports, 4/4, 9/4/62, and 1962 annual report, MP; CM speech, 9/12/62, MP; CM letter and memo to Kelly M. Alexander, 10/24/62, MP; for additional background, see WB report 2/5/60, MP; *CQA,* 1962, p. 404; *NYT,* 11/13, 11/16/43, 5/21/44; editorial, *Cleveland Plain Dealer,* 5/21/44; White to senators, 7/28/48, NAACP II A-465, LC; White to Philip Murray, president of CIO, 5/26/49, NAACP II A-466, LC; Pohlhaus's memo to CM, 12/22/55, NAACP II A-466, LC; CM to Arthur V. Watkins and all other senators, 2/14/55, NAACP II A-466, LC.

16. CM speech, 3/10/61, MP; *WP,* 1/24/63.

17. DW interview with CM; Farmer, *Lay Bare the Heart;* DW interview with Delbert Woods, Kelly M. Alexander, Sr., Rev. I. DeQuincey Newman; CM column, *BS,* 11/13/83, op-ed page.

18. William Taylor, "Executive Action to Enforce Civil Rights," MP; DW interviews with CM and Rauh; "George Meany Blasted," *Jet* (11/29/62), pp. 6–8; CM interview, JFKLOH, p. 36; "Black America on the March" series, *NY Daily News,* 7/25/63, p. 34.

19. CM memo, "Some Comments on Racial Practices in U.S. Churches," 9/5/62, submitted to Burke Marshall 9/6/62, NAACP WB-98, LC; James Baldwin, for example, declared that he was raised in the Christian Church but had abandoned it because it was the "worst place to learn about Christianity." *NYT,* 6/3/63; Pohlhaus to the National Catholic Conference on Interracial Justice, 7/27/63, NAACP WB-151, LC.

20. "Religion and Race Conference," *America* (1/12/63), 32, (2/2/63), p. 150; "Marking 100 Years of Freedom," *The Christian Century* (1/16/63), pp. 68–69, (1/30/63), pp. 133–135, (3/27/63), p. 412, (6/19/63), p. 797; *The Commonweal* (1/18/63), p. 426 (2/8/63), p. 518; *Liberation* (6/63), pp. 10–14; *NYT*, 6/8/63, "A Call to Racial Justice, from the Commission on Social Action of Reform Judaism," MP.

21. See materials in "Legislative Activity Folder, 1958–1960," NAACP WB-104, LC; minutes of LCCR steering committee, 3/12/52, NAACP II A-195, LC; LCCR press release, 7/25/63, NAACP WB-106, LC; in addition to CM, Rauh, and Aaronson, the LCCR's steering committee was composed of Jack Conway, exec. dir. of UAW-DC, Jake Clayman, exec. dir. of AFL-CIO Industrial Unions Department, James Hamilton, exec. dir. of National Council of Churches, and Thomas Donahue, nominal Republican and White House liaison, "strictly confidential" memorandum, "Democratic Strategy in Dealing with Republicans on the Civil Rights Bill of 1963," 8/30/63, MP; DW interview with Aaronson; LCCR statement of purpose for 1967, 1/30/68, NAACP WB-107, LC; RW speech, 4/11/58, DW Files.

22. CM interview, CUOH, pp. 19–20; FBI special inquiry on CM, 7/15/75, FBI Communications Section, FOI #44-10030.

CHAPTER SEVENTEEN

Not always cited below are CM personal recollection notes, MP, an unpublished article by Rauh, and Stewart's "Independence and Control: The Challenge of Senatorial Party Leadership."

1. *Freedom to the Free,* a report of the U.S. Civil Rights Commission, Washington, D.C.: U.S. Government Printing Office, 1963; *CQ,* 1/11/63, p. 30, 2/15/63, p. 192; WB report, 2/5/63, MP; Edelsberg and Brody, "Civil Rights in the 87th Congress."

2. DW interview with John Lindsay; CM personal recollections; Stewart, "Independence and Control," pp. 187, 192; *CQ,* 2/15/63, p. 191; press release from Sen. Joseph Clark, 2/63, NAACP WB-116, LC; Republicans' press release (William McCulloch, Lindsay, William T. Cahill of N.J., Clark MacGregor of Minn., Charles Mathias of Md., James E. Bromwell of Iowa, and Pat Minor Martin of Calif.), 1/31/63, NAACP WB-116, LC.

3. Assessment of Kennedy's 2/28/63 bill, WB report, 4/2/63, MP; text of Kennedy message, *CQ,* 3/8/63, pp. 292–293, 303–306; "GOP Challenges," WP, 3/29/63; Pohlhaus memo to CM, 3/12/63, "President's Civil Rights Message," MP; Pohlhaus memo to RW, "President's Civil Rights Program," MP; Pohlhaus, "Evaluation of Administrative Program," DW Files.

4. CM's personal recollections, MP; CM testimony before the House General Subcommittee on Education, 4/24/63, NAACP WB-139, LC; also *Hearings,* Committee on Education and Labor, 88th Cong., 1st sess., 4/26/63, p. 627; CM letter to Carl D. Perkins in which he complains that a check in four states showed that nearly two thousand retraining opportunities would be offered but fewer than

two hundred would be for blacks; WB press release, 5/6/63, NAACP WB-106, LC; also, WB "Evaluation of Administrative Program" (n.d.), MP; *CQ*, 4/5/63, p. 527; CM, "From the Work Bench" column, *BAF*, 4/2/63; CM telegrams to Clifford Case, Hiram Fong, Jacob Javits, Kenneth Keating, Thomas Kuchel, Hugh Scott, J. Glenn Beall, and Leverett Saltonstall, 3/28/63, NAACP WB-116, LC; CM letter to Hugh Scott, 4/5/53, NAACP WB-116, LC.

5. CM, "From the Work Bench," op. cit., note 4.

6. Republicans' press release, 3/28/63, NAACP WB-116, LC; WB report, 4/2/63, MP; *NYT*, 6/6/63; CM 3/28/63 telegrams, op. cit.

7. Rustin, "From Protest to Politics: The Future of the Civil Rights Movement," *Commentary* (2/63); David Danzig, "The Meaning of Negro Strategy," *Commentary* (2/64), pp. 41–45; WB report, 5/10/63, MP; James MacGregor Burns, "The Four Kennedys of the First Year," *NYT Magazine* (1/14/62); *NYT*, 5/9/63, p. 1, 16; weekly review and James Reston column, *NYT*, 6/9/63, both in IV, p. E-1, op-ed; *NYT*, 7/22/63, p. 1 ff; *NYT*, 7/23/63, p. 1, 7/26/63, p. 14; Pohlhaus to Lindsay, 2/15/6ɔ, NAACP WB-116, LC; Andrew Biemiller letter to Humphrey, 6/7/63, with memo, "Labor Views on Administration Civil Rights Package," NAACP WB-116, LC; *WP*, 5/20/63.

8. *CQ*, 5/10/63, p. 727, 5/24/63, p. 820; *NYT*, 7/22/63, p. 12; re SNCC testimony, CM letter to Celler, 6/6/63, NAACP WB-111, LC; *Davis* v. *East Baton Rouge School Board* is cited as *Bush* v. *Orleans Parish School Board*. Bolling, *House Out of Order*, p. 191; CM telegram to Carl Albert, Charles Halleck, McCormack, Celler, and McCulloch, 4/12/63, NAACP WB-116, LC; Celler, press release, 4/28/63, MP; *NYT*, 6/12/63, p. 1; CM personal recollections, MP.

9. *CQ*, 6/21/63, pp. 97–99, 7/26/63, pp. 1319–1320; LCCR Memo No. 1, 7/25/63, MP; *NYT*, 6/23/63, IV, pp. E-1, E-5; White House press release, "Message on Civil Rights and Job Opportunities," 6/19/63, NAACP III B-305, LC; CM, *Hearings*, Subcommittee No. 5, House Judiciary Committee, 88th Cong., 1st sess., 1963, p. 1266.

10. *CQ*, 6/21/63, pp. 997–1000; RFK statement on H.R. 7152 before the House Judiciary Committee, 6/26/63, MP; LCCR Memo No. 1, 7/5/63, MP.

11. LCCR Memo No. 1, op. cit.; Pohlhaus memo to RW reviewing President's program, 7/19/63, MP; DW interview with Katzenbach.

12. NAACP press release, 7/27/63, NAACP III B-305, LC; *WP*, 6/20/63; *NYT*, 6/23/63, IV, p. 1; Rauh's unpublished article; CM speech, 6/20/63, MP; CM interview, LBJLOH, p. 15.

13. *Life* (8/23/63), pp. 84 ff; "Black America on the March" series, *NY Daily News*, 7/22/63, p. 22; *NYT*, 6/23/63; NAACP legislative conference and other materials in MP and NAACP WB-27, LC; organizations participating in the conference listed in WB report, 9/6/63, were Alpha Phi Alpha Fraternity, ADA, American Nurses Association, CORE, American Friends Service Committee, Hadassah, Catholic Council on Civil Liberties, National Council of Jewish Women, Japanese American Citizens League, National Council of Churches, National Council of Catholic Women, National Education Association, National Students Association, National Association of Colored Women's Clubs, National

Council of Catholic Men, NAIRO, National Consumers League, National Conference of Christians and Jews, Prince Hall Masons, UAHC Religious Action Center, UAW, United Packinghouse Workers, Southern Regional Council, Social Action Committee of the Unitarian Church of Arlington, Va., Women's Division of the Methodist Church, YWCA; *WP,* 8/6, 8/7, 8/8, 8/9/63; Pohlhaus 1964 review of the struggle (no date or title), DW Files; Pohlhaus speech, Catholic Interracial Council, 6/27/63, NAACP WB-151, LC; Stewart, op. cit., p. 178.

14. LCCR Memo No. 5, 8/30/63, MP; *Time* (9/6/63), p. 14; *NYT,* 8/29/63, pp. 1, 17; DW interviews with CM, Rustin, Aaronson; CM interview, JFKLOH, p. 38; sec. report, NAACP Bd. reports, 9/9/63; materials in NAACP WB-127, LC, and MP; Garrow, *Bearing the Cross,* pp. 287–302; *BS,* 9/13/61; Sorensen interview, JFKLOH; DW interview with CM; *Time* (8/30/63), pp. 9, 11.

15. CM column, *BS,* 8/28/83, op-ed page; Pohlhaus 1964 review, note 13; LCCR Memo No. 6, 9/13/63; *WSJ,* 9/17/63; *CQ,* 8/2/63, p. 1374; DW interviews with CM, Jane O'Grady, Aaronson, Rauh; LCCR Memo No. 6, 9/13/63, NAACP WB-106, LC; James Reston, *NYT,* 8/30/63, op-ed page; Marquis Childs, "Churches and Negroes," *NY Post,* 9/5/63.

16. Wilkins, *Hearings,* on S. 1732, Senate Commerce Committee, 88th Cong., 1st sess., 7/22/63, pp. 655 ff; RW, "Humiliation Stalks Them," copy in DW Files; *Liberation* (6/63); *NYT,* 8/21/63, IV, p. E-5.

17. RFK statement on H.R. 7152 to Subcommittee No. 5, House Judiciary Committee, 6/26/63, MP; *CQ,* 7/26/63, p. 1318, 8/9/63, p. 1404.

18. RFK, *Hearings,* Subcommittee No. 5, House Judiciary Committee, 88th Cong., 1st sess., p. 1379; *CQ,* 7/26/63, p. 1318, 8/9/63, p. 1404; RFK statement before Senate Commerce Committee, 7/1/63, President's Office Files, RFK Papers, JFKL; *NYT,* 7/23/63, p. 1; LCCR's "Suggested Position Concerning Commerce-Clause-Fourteenth-Amendment Controversy as Preferable Basis for Public Accommodations Bill" and other materials in MP; Rauh, statement to Subcommittee of Senate Commerce Committee, 7/30/63, MP; Javits, excerpts from testimony before Senate Commerce Committee, 6/9/63, "Congressional Digest," MP; *Civil Rights Cases,* 109 U.S. 3 (1883); *Shelley* v. *Kraemer,* 334 U.S. 1 (1948); *Boynton* v. *Virginia,* 364 U.S. 454 (1960); *Burnton* v. *Wilmington Parking Authority,* 365 U.S. 715 (1961); re National Labor Relations Act, see *Meat Cutters* v. *Fairlawn Meats,* 353 U.S. 20 (1957); re farmers, *Wickard* v. *Filburn,* 317 U.S. 111 (1942); re regulation of property rights, see *Nebbis* v. *New York,* 291 U.S. 902 (1939).

19. DW interview with Katzenbach; Rauh, "First Clarence Mitchell, Jr., Memorial Lecture," Martin Luther King, Jr., Library, Atlanta, 10/30/85; CM similarly charged that the administration's strategy was to get a bill in the House Judiciary Committee that was so restricted it would sail through both houses with only token opposition. But it would not work, he said—not "even on a bill to reaffirm our belief in the Ten Commandments or the Bill of Rights." CM speech, 9/20/63, MP; LCCR "strictly confidential" memo, "Democratic Strategy in Dealing with Republicans on the Civil Rights Bill of 1964," 8/30/63, MP.

20. WB report, 10/9/63, MP; DW interview with Rauh; Evans, *The Exercise*

of Power; CM's recollection, MP; Pohlhaus 1964 review, op. cit. note 13; Rowland Evans and Robert Novak, "The Extremists," syndicated "Inside Report" column, 8/28/62; *CQ,* 9/20/63, p. 1632; CM speech, 9/20/63, MP; CM interview, JFKLOH; CM, *Hearings,* Senate Subcommittee No. 5, House Judiciary Committee, 88th Cong., 1st sess., p. 1263.

21. Lord, *The Past,* p. 113; *Jet* (11/9/63), p. 6; Rauh, "First CM Memorial Lecture," note 18; *WSJ,* 11/7/63; *WP,* 7/31/63; *CQ,* 10/11/63, p. 1749; Pohlhaus 1964 review, note 13.

22. Bolling, op. cit., p. 192; *WSJ,* 11/7/63; CM interview, JFKLOH, p. 41; *NYT,* 10/17/63; *WP,* 10/17/63; CM speech, 10/13/63, MP.

23. CM letter to Celler, 10/16/63, MP; RFK statement before the House Judiciary Committee (in executive session), 10/15/63, pp. 12–16, MP; *CQ,* 10/18/63, p. 1814; Garrow, op. cit., pp. 287–304; minutes, NAACP Executive Committee, 10/14/63; Pohlhaus memo to CM, 10/16/63, DW Files.

24. CM speech, 10/5/63, MP.

25. CM to Mathias, 10/8/63, and to Lindsay, 10/18/63, NAACP WB-116, LC; *CQ,* 11/1/63, p. 1879; Pohlhaus 1964 review, note 13.

26. WB report, 11/8/63, MP; Pohlhaus 1964 review, op. cit. note 13.

27. WB report, 11/8/63, MP.

28. *Jet* (12/13/63), pp. 19, 26; WB report, 12/6/63, MP; CM, "confidential" memos to the files, 12/3, 12/5/63, MP.

29. DW interview with CM; Pohlhaus 1964 review, note 13; LCCR Memo No. 17, 12/9/63, MP; LCCR Memo No. 19, 12/23/63, MP; CM interview, JFKLOH, p. 55; Burns, *NYT Magazine* (1/14/62); see also *Jet* (11/7), pp. 6–8, (11/14/63), pp. 8–15, for debate between RW and Robert Kennedy on civil rights bill.

CHAPTER EIGHTEEN

Not necessarily cited below are CM's personal recollection notes, and CM's detailed "Memorandum on Civil Rights Act of 1964," both in MP; an unpublished article by Rauh; a collection of "Bipartisan Newsletters," 1964, LCCR-31, LC; WB report, 5/5/64, detailing organizational responsibilities, MP; WB report, 4/10/64, re Dirksen's opposition to FEPC, MP; WB report, 5/8/64, on the maneuvering in the Senate, and WB 1964 annual report, MP. This chapter was also considerably strengthened by insights on the personalities of Mansfield and Dirksen provided by Stewart, "Independence and Control."

1. CM telegram to LBJ, 1/9/64, and letter, 1/30/64, LBJL, LE/HU2; CM interview, JFKLOH, p. 10; Viorst, *Fire in the Streets,* p. 239; *CQ,* 11/29/63, p. 2089; *Washington Evening Star,* 1/8/64; Evans, *The Exercise of Power,* p. 349; CM interview, CRDP, pp. 80, 81.

2. CM interview, LBJLOH, pp. 16 ff; WB report, 12/6/63, MP.

3. Bolling, *House Out of Order,* p. 80; CM, "From the Work Bench," column draft (n.d.), MP; CM interview, JFKLOH, pp. 13, 39, 44; CM interview, LBJLOH, pp. 22 ff.; CM interview, CUOHC, p. 45; RFK interview, JFKLOH,

p. 524; WB report, 12/19/63, MP; Evans, op. cit., p. 268; Johnson, *From the Vantage Point*, p. 158.

4. DW interview with CM; CM, "Civil Rights and Economic Rights," *The Crisis* (4/68), p. 118; LBJ speech, 5/26/61, statements, Cont. 54, LBJL; *U.S. News & World Report* (8/21/61), pp. 56–58; "Johnson Back in the Headline," *U.S. News & World Report* (8/20/62), p. 37; "Vice President Tours Colored World," *Ebony* (8/61); "U.S. Vice President Johnson Visits South and Southeast Asia," *Current History* (9/61), pp. 171–177; Ben H. Bagdikian, "New Lyndon Johnson," *The Saturday Evening Post,* 2/24/62; "Johnson and Civil Rights," *The New Republic* (9/10/62), p. 6; *NYT,* 10/11/61, p. 12; CM, LBJLOH, pp. 22–23; CM interview, CRDP, pp. 82–83; Johnson, op. cit., p. 157.

5. CM interview, JFKLOH, p. 13; Lawrence F. O'Brien memo to the President, 11/29/63, and White House memo, "Equality of Races," both in LE/HU2, LBJL; internally, LBJ set up a subcabinet group on civil rights to review and accelerate action—see Lee C. White memo to the President, 4/15/64, HU2, FG1; CM interview, LBJLOH, p. 21.

6. Viorst, op. cit.; DW interview with Rauh; Chalmers M. Roberts, "Courtship of Johnson and Rauh Lifts Some Political Eyebrows," *WP,* 2/6/64; Douglas, *In the Fullness of Time,* p. 295.

7. DW interviews with CM, Rauh, and Biemiller; Bolling, op. cit., p. 100; *CQ,* 1/24/64, pp. 157, 163, 2/7/64, p. 250, 2/14/64, p. 294; Memo to the President, 1/21/64, Executive, LE/HU2, LBJL; CM, "Special Memorandum on Civil Rights Bill," 1/24/64, MP.

8. Report of the exec. sec., 2/10/64, NAACP Bd. reports; CM interview, LBJLOH; Garrow, op. cit., pp. 322–324; *NYT,* IV, p. 1, 6/23/63.

9. CM recollections, MP; DW interviews with CM, Rauh, and Jane O'Grady.

10. CM speech, 5/11/65, MP; DW interview with Katzenbach; CM, "From the Work Bench," column draft (n.d.), MP; *CR,* 2/8/64, pp. 2548, 2577.

11. WB advisory, 2/12/64, NAACP WB-27, LC; WB memo, "House-Passed Civil Rights Bill," 2/13/64, DW Files; WB memo, "Amendments to H.R. 7152, the Civil Rights Bill," DW Files; sec. report, NAACP Bd. reports, 3/9/64; CM recollections, MP; *CQ,* 2/14/64, p. 293.

12. CM recollections; DW interview with CM; CM letter to RW, 2/18/64, NAACP WB-197, LC: except in one interview where he states that it was Rauh who took the call from LBJ, CM gives the impression that it was with him whom LBJ had spoken; so Rauh's version, differing somewhat from CM's, is used here; Rauh, "First Clarence Mitchell, Jr., Memorial Lecture," Martin Luther King, Jr., Library, Atlanta, 10/30/85; NAACP executive committee minutes, 2/10/64.

13. CM interview, LBJLOH, p. 31; "Like a Lone Tree," *Time* (6/7/63), p. 24; CM letter to RW, 2/18/64, NAACP WB-197, LC; CM, "From the Work Bench," column draft (n.d.), MP.

14. DW interviews with CM and Rauh; Stewart, "Independence and Control"; Rauh, "First CM Memorial Lecture"; CM interview, LBJLOH, pp. 33–34.

15. DW interview with CM.

16. Ibid; Stewart, op. cit., pp. 175, 180, 182, 183, 378; DW interview with

CM; Humphrey, *The Education of a Public Man*, p. 274; *CQ*, 5/15/64, p. 947; CM article submitted to Ray Boon, *BAF*, 1/24/78, MP.

17. DW interview with CM; CM, "Memorandum on Civil Rights Act of 1964"; Humphrey, op. cit., p. 276.

18. Humphrey, op. cit., p. 279; Stewart, op. cit., pp. 186, 193–195; CM interview, LBJLOH, p. 35; Rauh, "First CM Memorial Lecture."

19. *NYT*, 6/23/63, p. 1; Bill Moyers memo to the President, 6/1/64, LE/HU2, LBJL, *NYT*, 4/26, IV, p. E-6, 4/26, p. 25, 4/29/64, pp. 1, 29; *NYT*, 3/27/64, p. 10; CM recollections, MP.

20. Rauh, JFKLOH, p. 15; CM report recommending the LCCR send a telegram to Senate leaders, 2/26/64, NAACP WB-106, LC; *CQ*, 2/28/64, p. 385; minutes of NAACP executive committee, 3/9/64; Stewart, op. cit.; Pohlhaus memo, "Civil Rights Bill; Parliamentary Procedures" (n.d.), MP; LCCR Memo No. 31, 3/31/64, NAACP WB-106, LC.

21. "Bipartisan Newsletter," No. 5, 3/14/64, MP; LCCR Memo. No. 31, op. cit.

22. *WP*, 3/20/64; *NYT*, 3/20/64; *CQ*, 3/27/57; *BS*, 3/20/64; DW interview with CM; LCCR Memo No. 31, op. cit.

23. Rauh's unpublished article; DW interview with CM; CM, "From the Work Bench" column draft (n.d.), MP; CM letter to RW, 3/12/64, with an analysis of the House-passed bill, NAACP WB-97, LC.

24. *Bipartisan Newsletter*, 6/19/64, MP; Stewart, op. cit., pp. 207, 219; *CQ*, 4/17/64, p. 717, 6/12/64, p. 1170; Humphrey, op. cit., pp. 274–276; Stewart, op. cit.; DW interview with Katzenbach.

25. *Bipartisan Newsletter*, No. 30, 4/15/64; CM recollections, MP.

26. Humphrey, op. cit., p. 276; CM recollections, MP; DW interview with Katzenbach.

27. CM, ibid; *NYT*, 4/26/64, IV, p. E-6, 5/6, 5/17/64, IV; Talmadge jury trial amendment, *CQ*, 6/26/64, p. 1274; WB report, 5/8/64, MP; Farmer, *Lay Bare the Heart*, pp. 256–259; Garrow, op. cit., pp. 331–332; Viorst, op. cit., pp. 140, 235–240; Johnson, op. cit., p. 159.

28. *NYT*, 4/28/64; Solberg, *Hubert Humphrey*, pp. 221–227; DW interviews with Joseph R.L. Sterne, ed., editorial pages, *BS*, Katzenbach, Stewart, and Rauh; Marvin Caplan report on 5/11/64 meeting with Humphrey, MP; *CQ*, 5/15/64, p. 947.

29. DW interview with Rauh; Rauh's unpublished article; *CQ*, 5/15/64, p. 947; Caplan's 5/11/64 report, op. cit.

30. *CQ*, 5/29/64, p. 1032; LCCR statement, 5/14/64, carried in Memo No. 38, 5/8/64, MP; CM letter to RW, 5/15/64, NAACP WB-197, LC; memo from John H. Beidler to Andrew J. Biemiller, 5/15/64, MP.

31. CM, "From the Work Bench," column draft (n.d.), MP; *CQ*, 6/12/64, p. 1169; *BS*, 6/11/64; LCCR Memo No. 41, 6/10/64; *BAF*, 6/13/64; also see *BAF*, 2/8/64, p. 6, for earlier stories on CM's attitude on the filibuster; Garrow, op. cit., pp. 331–332; CM interview, LBJLOH, p. 34; Humphrey, op. cit., p. 283.

32. "Enforcement of Title VI of the Civil Rights Act," an analysis, MP; CM

speeches at lawyers' breakfast, 1979 NAACP Annual Convention in Louisville, Ky., on 7/26/64, and 8/8/65, DW Files and MP; CM's recollection; *NYT,* 6/21/63, p. 1; CM interview, CRDP, p. 70.

33. Humphrey, op. cit., p. 285; WB memo, "Civil Rights Bill," 6/24/64, MP; *CQ,* 6/19/64, pp. 1199–1206, 7/3/64, pp. 1221–1222; Bolling, op. cit., p. 196; WB memo, 6/24/64, NAACP WB-41, LC; *WP,* 6/23/64, p. 6; Farmer, op. cit., pp. 272–278.

34. CM, "From the Work Bench," column draft (n.d.), MP; Farmer, op. cit., pp. 272–278; Garrow, op. cit., p. 337; RW report to annual meeting, 1/4/65, NAACP Bd. reports; CM recollections, MP.

35. DW interview with CM; CM article submitted to Ray Boon, op. cit.; CM speech, 10/31/64, MP; *NYT,* 7/1/64; CM interview, CRDP.

36. "Statement of Civil Rights Organization Leaders," 7/29/64, issued by RW, NAACP III B-305, LC; DW interview with CM.

37. CM, *Nebraska Law Review,* 1968, pp. 91–128.

CHAPTER NINETEEN

1. Memo to the files, Files of Lee C. White, LE/HU2, LBJL; Minutes, NAACP Bd., 9/64; minutes, NAACP executive committee, 2/8/65; *Jet* (10/31/63), p. 4; *CQ,* 4/9/65, pp. 617–624; WB 1965 annual report; CM speech, 5/19/65, MP.

2. CM speech, 7/26/64; CM, "From the Work Bench," column draft (n.d.), MP.

3. *NYT,* 7/21/64, p. 19, 8/1/64, p. 1; RW memo, 8/12/64, to NAACP branch presidents, "Support for Mississippi Freedom Party at Democratic Convention in Atlantic City, 8/12/64, NAACP WB-3, LC; memo from MFDP to "All Friends of MFDP," a report explaining its role at the convention, DW Files; White, *The Making 1964,* pp. 329–336; *WP,* 7/25/63, 2/6, 5/25, 8/23, 8/25, 8/26, 8/27/64; *NYT,* 8/23/64, IV, p. 1; *The Congress and the Nation,* p. 8; *Jet* (10/31/63), p. 16, (9/3/64), pp. 6–8; CM column, *BS,* 5/29/83, op-ed page; "Memorandum on the Possibility of Unseating the Mississippi Congressional Delegation," 1/56, DW Files; "The Mississippi Freedom Democratic Party," a mimeographed booklet, DW Files; "Fannie Lou Hamer, Prophet of Freedom," *Sojourners,* a special issue (12/82); Ronald L. Goldfarb, "Aaron Henry's Unending Quest for Equality," *WP,* 6/27/77, op-ed page; letter from David L. Lawrence, chairman, special committee of DNC, inviting CM to testify at the convention, MP; "Mississippi Challenge," "Christianity and Crisis," Vol. XXIV, No. 24, 1/24/65, a newsletter; CM, "From the Work Bench," column draft (n.d.), MP.

4. Pohlhaus letter to John Morsell, 2/19/65, NAACP WB-135, LC; WB report, 2/5/65, MP; Morsell memo to NAACP field leaders, "Challenge to Mississippi," 3/22/65, NAACP WB-135, LC; press release, "Statement Concerning Plan to Dismiss Mississippi Seating Challenge," from Commission on Religion and Race, National Council of Churches, 9/12/65, NAACP WB-135, LC; Current memo to RW and Henry Lee Moon, 8/3/65, NAACP WB-135, LC; *Birmingham*

News, 9/23/65, p. 11; memo from MFDP executive committee re "Mississippi House Delegation's Motion to Dismiss Challenge," 9/10/65.

5. *WP,* 9/18/64; Pohlhaus, "Looking at the Record," *Community* (10/64), p. 10; RW letter to Aaron Henry, 12/11/62, NAACP WB-1, LC; WB 1964 annual report, p. 6, MP; CM to RW, 10/23/64, and other materials in NAACP WB-197, LC; CM speech, 4/19/65, MP; "Rights Aide Backs Johnson-Humphrey," *WP,* late 6/64 (copy of article in MP).

6. CM speeches, 5/19, 6/17/65, MP; CM column, *BS,* 6/27/83, op-ed page; WB report, 11/6/64, MP; statement by Robert L. Carter, NAACP general counsel, 4/2/65, at annual conference of Civil Liberties Clearing House, MP; NAACP Bd. minutes, 7/2/65; DW interview with JM; "Nation's Youngest Lawmaker," *Ebony* (6/63), p. 135; *Heart of Atlanta Hotel, Inc.* v. *United States,* 379 U.S. 241 (1964); also Pohlhaus review on constitutionality of poll tax as applicable to Texas (n.d.), MP.

7. Katzenbach statement on the proposed voting rights act, House Judiciary Committee, 3/18/65, MP; for additional background on Selma, see Garrow, *Bearing the Cross.*

8. RW, like CM, relying strongly on the NAACP's existing voter registration program in the South, told his 1965 annual meeting that "other civil rights organizations were just now regarding political activity as a primary program," NAACP Bd. minutes, 1/65; CM memo of review with cover letter to RW, 3/19/68, NAACP III B-377, LC; CM speech, 3/19/65, MP; see also "Differences between Administration's February and June 1963 Voting Proposals and Title I of the Civil Rights Act of 1964" in Files of Lee C. White, LBJL.

9. Katzenbach 3/18/65 statement; for DDE's DOJ's opposition to stronger voting registrar proposal, see Chapter 14; *CQ,* 2/12/65, p. 253, 2/19/65, pp. 269–271; CM memo to RW, "Meeting with Senator Paul Douglas, Long and Rauh," 2/4/65, NAACP III B-376, LC; CM 5/19/65 speech, MP.

10. CM column, *BS,* 1/3/82; Pohlhaus memo to CM, "DSG Meeting with Vice President and Attorney General," on 2/24, NAACP WB-99, LC; CM, "From the Work Bench" column, *BAF,* 2/23/65; CM 2/4/65 memo to RW, op. cit., and RW response, 2/9/65, MP; CM memo to files, "Meeting at Justice Department Today," 3/11/65, NAACP WB-99, LC; Russell Long said, on 2/17/65, that a decision had not been made to wage a filibuster against the voting bill because "President Johnson might send us a bill that the southerners could support." He said that "a majority of the people in the South feel that the Negro people should be able to vote. . . . My own feeling is that under certain circumstances federal registrars might be justified." In contrast, Long had supported the filibuster against the 1964 act, see *CQ,* 2/19/65, p. 271, 2/19/65, pp. 449–450; CM, "From the Work Bench," *BAF,* 5/11/65.

11. *CQ,* 3/19/65, pp. 445–447; CM speech, 3/19/65, MP; "Quick Passage Seen on Voting Rights Bill," *WP,* 3/16/65.

12. WB report, 4/9/65, MP; *WP,* 3/16/65; memo to "All Participating Groups in the American Civil Rights Movement," from MFDP executive committee, 2/21/65, NAACP WB-106, LC; memo to all Participating Groups from

Farmer, Foreman, King, and Guyot, 2/27/65, NAACP WB-106, LC; memo to LCCR from King (n.d.—follow-up to 2/27/65 memo), NAACP WB-106, LC; Katzenbach 3/18/65 statement.

13. DW interview with CM; WB memo, "Urgent Call to Action," 9/14/65, MP.

14. CM speech, 4/19/65, MP.

15. Pohlhaus memo on 2/24/65 DSG meeting, op. cit., n. 10; CM, memo to files on "Meeting at Justice Department Today," 3/11/65, NAACP WB-99, LC; minutes, NAACP executive committee, 3/8/65; WB 1965 highlights, MP.

16. CM letter to RW with S. 1517, 3/17/65, MP; WB report, 4/9/65, NAACP WB-2, LC; excerpts of RW's testimony before House Judiciary Subcommittee No. 5, WB report 4/9/65, MP; WB memo, 4/6/65, MP; *CQ*, 4/2/65, p. 287; CM interview, LBJLOH, p. 5 of tape 2.

17. *WP*, 4/21/65; LCCR Memo No. 64, 5/31/65, MP; *CQ*, 3/26/65, p. 558; see also, *CQ*, 3/19/65, p. 435, 4/2/65, p. 588, 4/16/65, pp. 685–687; WB report, 4/9/65, NAACP WB-2, LC; editorial, *NYT*, 4/18/65.

18. *CQA*, 1962, p. 404; Herbert Reid, "Memorandum in Support of Power of Congress to Abolish the Poll Tax as a Prerequisite for Voting in State Elections," NAACP WB-154, LC; Rauh to Gilbert A. Harrison, editor in chief, *The New Republic*, 4/22/65, NAACP WB-154, LC; CM, "From the Work Bench," *BAF*, 3/23/65; "Senate Unit Majority Backs Vote Bill," *WP*, 4/21/65; CM interview, LBJLOH.

19. WB press release, 4/22/65, MP; CM letter, 4/22/65, to LBJ, and 4/30/65 response from Lee C. White, General Office Files, HU2, LBJL; *CQA*, 1965, p. 546; *CQ*, 4/30/65, p. 824, 7/2/65, p. 1299; CM speech, 5/11/65, MP; *Harman* v. *Forssenius*, 380 U.S. 528 (1964); *WP*, 4/21, 5/13/65; minutes, NAACP executive committee, 5/10/65; report of the executive sec., NAACP Bd. reports, 5/10/65; memo for Marvin Watson from Harold F. Reiss, office of attorney general, 5/21/65, re "Reasons Why the Justice Department Has Favored the Mansfield-Dirksen Approach to Elimination of the Poll Tax," LE/HU2, LBJL; WB press release, 4/22/65, MP; CM, "From the Work Bench," *BAF*, 5/11/65; memo from Larry O'Brien to the President, 4/26/65, Executive, LE/HU2, LBJL.

20. *NYT*, 4/18/65, editorial; CM speech, 5/3/65, MP; LCCR press release, 5/6/65, and statement on "The Right of Congress to Outlaw State and Local Poll Taxes," NAACP WB-106, LC; *CQ*, 5/14/65, p. 899; CM interview, CUOH, p. 60; CM speeches, 5/3, 5/11, 5/19/65, MP; CM, "From the Work Bench," *BAF*, 4/27/65.

21. *CQ*, 5/7/65, p. 857, 5/21/65, pp. 962–963, 5/28/65, pp. 1007–1009, 6/4/65, pp. 1052–1057, 6/11/65, pp. 1123–1124, 7/9/65, p. 1324, 7/16/65, p. 1361; LCCR Memo No. 64, 5/31/65, No. 68, 7/12/65, and other materials in NAACP WB-106, LC; *BS*, 4/6/65.

22. CM interview, LBJLOH; LCCR summary of the 1965 Voting Rights Act, Author's Files—other materials can be found in NAACP WB-119, LC; *CQ*, 8/6/65, pp. 1539–1540; CM speech, 6/17/65, MP.

23. DW interview with Katzenbach; DOJ press release, 8/7/65, announcing

filing of suit against Mississippi, MP; in *South Carolina* v. *Katzenbach*, 383 U.S. 301 (1966), decided by the Supreme Court 3/7/66, the state sought to upset parts of the 1965 Voting Rights Act. The Court generally followed the reasoning offered by Katzenbach and Archibald Cox, former solicitor general, in upholding the federal government's program for carrying out the aims of the Fifteenth Amendment. On 3/24/66, in *Harper* v. *Virginia State Board of Electors*, 383 U.S. 663 (1966), and *Butts* v. *Harrison* (decided as one), the Supreme Court struck down the poll taxes in Virginia and Mississippi. Federal district courts also declared unconstitutional poll taxes in Texas (*U.S.* v. *Texas,* 2/9/66) and in Alabama (*U.S.* v. *Alabama,* 3/3/66). Vermont abolished its poll tax by legislation on 2/23/66. Cases all cited in *CQA,* 1966, pp. 96–197.

24. CM to RFK, 6/14/65, MP; see also *Jet* (7/1/65), p. 9; *NYT,* 4/26, 12/4/65, p. 1; *NAACP Annual Report,* 1965, p. 76.

25. CM, "From the Work Bench," *BAF,* 8/31/65.

CHAPTER TWENTY

1. CM speeches, 6/17, 9/18/65, MP; *CQ,* 9/24/65; Jack Langguth, "Political Fun and Games in California," *NYT Magazine* (10/16/66), pp. 27 ff; WB 1965 highlights; *National Advisory Commission,* pp. 35–42; DW interview with Ramsey Clark; memo, to LCCR re ACLU's "Outline of a Proposed Federal Statute to Ensure Fair Selection of Juries in Federal and State Courts," 12/18/65, NAACP WB-118, LC.

2. LBJ daily diary, 3/18/66, Container No. 6, LBJL; DW interview with CM and Ramsey Clark; DW interview with Weaver; CM letter to LBJ, 8/12/66, White House Name File, LBJL; Johnson, *From the Vantage Point,* pp. 176–177; see also, Garrow, *Bearing the Cross,* pp. 357–451.

3. "Report on Mississippi," Mississippi Advisory Committee to the United States Commission on Civil Rights, 1/63, p. 23; CM speech, 11/20/65, MP; *The Crisis* (2/66), p. 103, (5/66), p. 266; *NYT,* 3/12/65, p. 1, 4/26/65, p. 1, 12/11/65, p. 1; WB 1965 highlights; RW LCCR statement before Subcommittee No. 5 of the House Judiciary Committee, 5/17/66, MP.

4. CM speech, 9/18/65.

5. Rauh and Pohlhaus memo for the LCCR, "Potential Avenues of Federal Legislation to Prevent and Deter Anti-Civil Rights Violence in the South," 10/29/65, NAACP WB-117, LC; RW 5/17/66 statement, NAACP WB-117, LC; *Screws* v. *United States,* 325 U.S. 91 (1945); see also Houston and Ransom, *The Nation* (7/4/34), pp. 18 ff.

6. WB 1965 highlights; WB reports, 2/11, 3/11/66, 9/67, MP; *United States* v. *Price,* 383 U.S. 787 (1966); *United States* v. *Guest,* 383 U.S. 745 (1966); *NYT,* 3/29/66, p. 1.

7. *CQ,* 5/6/66, pp. 943–946.

8. CM speeches, 5/12, 5/15/66, MP.

9. Katzenbach statements before Subcommittee No. 5 on H.R. 14765, 5/5, 6/6/66, MP; WB memo, "Proposed Amendment to Title IV of H.R. 14765,"

806

NOTES

NAACP WB-117, LC; RW 5/17/66 statement, op. cit.; see also CM speech, 6/19/66, MP; *CQ,* 7/22/66, p. 1586.

10. CM telegram to Drew Pearson, 4/4/66, and copy of Pearson-Anderson column, 4/4/66, in *WP,* NAACP III B-376, LC; *CQ,* 5/13/66, pp. 959–960; *Jet* (1/11/68), pp. 56–57; CM telegram to Mansfield, 8/23/66, NAACP WB-117, LC; Katzenbach urges passage, *CQ,* 5/13/66, p. 959.

11. *WSJ,* 6/13/66; DW interview with Mathias; Mathias amendment, *CQ,* 7/1/66, p. 1378, 7/15/66, p. 1463, 7/22/66, p. 1585, 8/12/66, p. 1719.

12. *CQ,* 5/13/66, p. 992, 5/20/66, p. 992, 7/1/66, p. 1378, 7/15/66, p. 1463.

13. *CQ,* 8/5/66, pp. 1687–1713.

14. *CQ,* 8/12/56, p. 1720.

15. CM letter to LBJ, 8/12/66, White House Name File, LBJL; CM letters to Horton, 8/18/66, and to Rodino, 8/23/66, NAACP WB-117, LC; WB report, 9/1/66, MP; CM memo to NAACP state conference and branch presidents, 10/19/66, NAACP III B-376, LC; CM letter to RW, 8/11/66, with analysis of H.R. 14765 as passed by the House, MP.

16. *CQ,* 9/16/66, p. 2179; *NYT,* 10/17/66, pp. 1, 24; Garrow, op. cit., p. 536; Walter White, "Disgrace in Cicero," *NY Herald Tribune,* 1951, copy in DW Files; CM telegram to Mansfield, 8/23/66, NAACP WB-117, LC; DW interview with CM.

17. CM memo, 9/7/66, "Meeting with Senator Kuchel and other Republican Senators, Tuesday, 9/6/66," MP; CM letter to Ella Anderson, 9/2/66, NAACP WB-117, LC; CM to Morsell, 9/1/66, and to RW, 9/6/66, NAACP III B-376, LC; CM telegram to LBJ assessing House and Senate votes, 9/19/66, White House Name File, LBJL; *WP,* 9/1/66; CM review, "Civil Rights and Congress—1966," DW Files; LCCR statement to Senate Press Gallery, NAACP III B-376, LC; Mansfield, "Statement on Parliamentary Procedure for Handling H.R. 14765," 8/11/66, NAACP WB-117, LC; *CQ,* 9/23/66, pp. 2199–2200.

18. CM speeches, 9/24, 10/13, 11/5/66, 1/11/67, MP; *Jet* (10/6/66), p. 4; press release from John J. Rhodes, Republican Policy Committee statement on Civil Rights Act of 1966, 8/1/66, NAACP WB-117, LC.

19. *CQ,* 3/1/68, p. 378; CM letter to Mathias, 5/1/68, MP; CM speech, 2/4/67; Katzenbach interview, LBJLOH, p. 27; *United States* v. *Price,* 383 U.S. 787 (1866).

20. CM memo to RW, 2/2/67, NAACP III B-376, LC.

21. CM letter to RW, 2/28/67, LCCR's "Notes on Meeting with Phil Hart 2/21/67," to CM prepared by Marvin Caplan, CM memo to RW, 2/28/67, re discussions with Ramsey Clark, all three attached in NAACP III B-376, LC; *CQ,* 3/31/67, p. 482; DW interview with CM.

22. *Newsweek,* 5/15/67, p. 27; *CQ,* 6/30/67, p. 1113, 8/4/67, p. 1350, 9/29/67, p. 1970, 10/13/67, p. 2059; *NYT,* 8/17/67, p. 1; WB report, 9/67, MP; CM speech, 10/7/67.

23. *CQ,* 10/27/67, p. 2174; *NYT,* 10/26/67; *WP,* 10/26/67.

24. CM interview, LBJLOH, tape 2, p. 15; Garrow, op. cit., pp. 578–593.

25. Garrow, op. cit., p. 575; CM speech, 11/18/67, MP.

26. *CQ,* 4/26/68, p. 931; CM letter to RW, 1/4/68, NAACP III B-377, LC.

27. DW interview with CM and Clark; CM letter to RW, 1/24/68, NAACP III B-376, LC; *CQ,* 2/2/68, p. 169, 4/26/68, p. 932.

28. *CQA,* 1968, p. 37-A; CM letter to LBJ, 1/18/68, NAACP WB-46, LC; CM telegram to NAACP branch presidents, 1/24/68, NAACP III B-377, LC.

29. LCCR, "Memorandum on New Version of Civil Rights Protection Bill Drafted at the Justice Department" (n.d.), MP.

30. DW interview with Rauh; *CQ,* 2/9/68, pp. 208–209.

31. CM memo dictated 2/23/68, NAACP III B-376, LC; CM telegram to LBJ, 2/24/68, General Office Files, LE/HU2, LBJL; *CQ,* 2/28/68, p. 4574; Mike Manatos to the President, memo 3/5/68, Executive, LE/HU2, LBJL.

32. *CQ,* 4/26/68, p. 932; Dirksen, *CR,* 2/26/68, pp. 4049–4060, 2/28/68, pp. 4568–4570, 4574–4575.

33. Memo from Louis Martin to Joseph Califano, 3/1/68, with copy of RW day letter to all senators, 2/29/68, LE/HU2, LBJL; see also CM letter to Nixon on House-phase of battle, 3/22/68, NAACP III B-377, LC.

34. *CQ,* 3/8/68, p. 469, 3/15/68, p. 509; CM letter to Harold Holliday, 3/8/68, NAACP WB-46, LC.

35. *CQ,* 3/1/68, p. 380, 3/22/68, p. 578; Barefoot Sanders memo to the President, 3/9/68, Executive, LE/HU2, LBJL; CM letter to Leonard Carter, 3/20/68, NAACP WB-46, LC; CM letter to NAACP branch presidents, 3/29/68, MP; CM letter to Nixon, 3/22/68, NAACP III B-377, LC.

36. *CQ,* 3/11/68, p. 509; CM memo to files, 3/20/68, NAACP WB-46, LC; CM review of GOP activities with copy to RW and letter 3/19/68, NAACP III B-377, LC; CM historical review of Republican party stand on civil rights, memo to "Republican congressmen," 8/2/68, NAACP WB-117, LC; CM letter to Stewart Udall, 4/26/68, NAACP WB-46, LC; CM letter to Rep. John P. Saylor, 3/18/68, NAACP III B-377, LC; *CQ,* 3/22/68, p. 579.

37. CM memo to files re House action on Senate version of bill, 3/20/68, NAACP WB-46, LC.

38. Abernathy telegram to CM, 4/21/68, LE/HU2, LBJL; *CQ,* 4/26/68, p. 933.

39. CM memo to files, "Meeting with Gerald Ford," 4/8/68, NAACP WB-46, LC; *CQ,* 4/12/68, pp. 791–793; CM, "Civil Rights and Economic Rights," *The Crisis* (4/68), p. 117; CM, *BS,* 3/16/80.

40. CM letter to Bolling, 4/24/68, NAACP WB-46, LC.

41. DW interview with CM; article by Harriet Douty reprinted from *WP,* in *Los Angeles Times,* 2/12/69, G, p. 2; CM press statement 4/11/68, NAACP WB-45, LC; CM letter to LBJ, 4/12/68, with 4/11/68 statement attached, Executive, LE/HU2, LBJL; editorial, *WP,* 4/14/68, p. B-5; article, *WP,* 4/28/68; *CQ,* 4/26/68, pp. 931–934.

42. DW interviews with Clark and CM.

43. DW interview with Clark and CM.

CHAPTER TWENTY-ONE

1. CM, "From the Work Bench," column draft (n.d.), MP.

2. *Time* (8/30/63), p. 9; CM speech, 5/5/69, MP; *Newsweek* (5/15/67), p. 30; *WSJ*, 4/23/69; CM speeches, 3/16, 8/2/67, 4/19/68, MP; CM interview, CUOH, pp. 26, 27.

3. CM speech, 6/19/66, MP, quoted in *BS*, 6/20/66; RW, "Black Power," *The Crisis* (8–9/66), p. 313; *The Christian Science Monitor*, 7/11/66; *CQ*, 7/8/66, pp. 1431, 10/28/66, pp. 2179, 2665–2666, 12/23/66, pp. 2870, 3025, 3067.

4. DW interview with CM.

5. DW interview with CM and Ramsey Clark.

6. Beverly Gray, "Close Up," *NY Post*, 8/21/63; DW interview with CM; CM interview, CRDP, pp. 86–87; Garrow, *Bearing the Cross*, pp. 546–565, 591, 593.

7. *CQ*, 4/21/67, pp. 647–648, 4/28/67; *Newsweek*, op. cit., n. 2; DW interviews with CM, JM, and Rauh; CM speech, 6/6/69, MP.

8. CM interview, CUOH.

9. CM speeches, 6/15, 7/21/68, MP; Martin Arnold, "Roy Wilkins," *NYT Magazine* (9/28/69); CM, statement on the Economic Opportunity Act before the Poverty Task Force of the House Committee on Education and Labor, MP.

10. CM speech, 10/7/67, MP; *NAACP Annual Report*, 1962, p. 37; DW interview with CM; WB report, 10/4/62, MP; *CQ*, 6/16/67, p. 1030; CM interview, CRDP.

11. LBJ remarks, 12/17/68, *PPP*, pp. 1200 ff; CM letter to LBJ, 4/1/68, SP3-236/FG 216, LBJL.

12. CM letter to Eugene Taylor, 7/19/68, NAACP WB-45, LC; DW interview with CM.

13. CM, "Spotlight on Political Conventions," *The Crisis* (10/68), pp. 276–294; CM speeches, 9/21, 11/24/68, MP.

14. CM letter to LBJ, 12/20/72, MP.

EPILOGUE

1. CM interview, by Ruth Campbell, 4/7/83, Mississippi ETV.

2. CM speech, 7/1/69, MP, excerpts, *The Crisis* (8–9/69), p. 277; Evans and Novak, *Nixon in the White House*, p. 136; CM speech, 12/5/69, MP.

3. CM, "A Personal View of Eight Presidents: Franklin D. Roosevelt to Jimmy Carter," Morgan State University lecture, 10/25/78, MP; CM letter to Rep. William Clay, 3/2/71, MP; Nixon letter to CM, 3/30/68, MP; DW interviews with CM, Rauh, and Kenneth Young; Evans and Novak, op. cit., pp. 129–134; *CQ*, 1/8/71, p. 37; CM address to Lawyers' Breakfast, NAACP Annual Convention, July 1979; Ehrlichman, *Witness to Power*, pp. 220–241; CM interview, CRDP; CM to William R. Ming, 6/20/69, MP; DW interviews with Rauh and Kenneth Young.

4. CM, MSU lecture; DW interview with CM.

5. CM memo, "Meeting with Attorney General Griffin Bell," 4/12/77, MP.

6. CM MSU lecture.

7. DW report on Congressional Black Caucus dinner.

8. DW interview with CM.

9. McGregor, *Integration,* pp. 10–11, 168, 169, 292, 412, 413, 500–522, 549, 579, 590–608; CM letter to RW, 6/22/67, MP; RW day letter to McNamara, 2/29/68.

10. WB reports, 2/5/65, WB 1966 highlights, reports 2/8/67, WB 1967 annual report, 3/31/78, all in MP; LCCR Memo No. 4-75, 3/11/75, MP; CM letter to RW, 1/16/67, NAACP III B-376, LC; *CQ,* 1/6/67, pp. 22, 23, 41, 1/20/67, pp. 87–88, 2/12/71, p. 366, 2/19/71, p. 415, 2/26/71, p. 450, 3/5/71, p. 509, 5/6/78, p. 1100; CM column, *BS,* 8/3/80; DW interview with CM; *WP,* 10/10/78, p. 1; CM letter to RW, 1/16/67, NAACP III B-396, LC.

11. Du Bois, *Autobiography,* pp. 399, 404.

Bibliography

SELECTED BOOKS AND PAMPHLETS

Adams, Sherman. *First-Hand Report.* New York: Harper & Brothers, 1961.

Anderson, J. W. *Eisenhower, Brownell, and the Congress: The Tangled Origins of the Civil Rights Bill of 1956–1957.* Published for Inter-University Case Program, Inc., Kingsport, Tenn., by University of Alabama Press, 1964.

Bailey, Stephen Kemp. *Congress Makes a Law.* New York: Columbia University Press, 1950, 1965.

Berman, William C. *The Politics of Civil Rights in the Truman Administration.* Columbus: Ohio State University Press, 1970.

Bland, Randall W. *Private Pressure on Public Law: The Legal Career of Justice Thurgood Marshall.* Port Washington, N.Y.: Kennikat Press, 1973.

Bolling, Richard. *House Out of Order.* New York: E. P. Dutton & Co., 1965.

Branch, Taylor. *Parting the Waters: America in the King Years, 1954–63.* New York: Simon and Schuster, 1988.

Carr, Robert K. *Federal Protection of Civil Rights.* Ithaca, N.Y.: Cornell University Press, 1947.

Carter, Dan T. *Scottsboro: A Tragedy of the American South.* New York: Oxford University Press, 1969.

Cash, W. J. *The Mind of the South.* New York: Alfred A. Knopf, 1941.

Chadbourn, James Harmon. *Lynching and the Law.* Chapel Hill: University of North Carolina Press, 1933.

Clark, Charles B. *The Eastern Shore of Maryland and Virginia,* Vol. 1. New York: Lewis Historical Publishing Co., 1950.

Congress and the Nation, 1945–1964. Washington, D.C.: Congressional Quarterly, 1965.

Congress and the Nation, 1965–1968. Washington, D.C.: Congressional Quarterly, 1969.

Crawford, Kenneth G. *The Pressure Boys.* New York: Julian Messner, 1939.

Dalfiume, Richard M. *Desegregation of the U.S. Armed Forces.* Columbia: University of Missouri Press, 1969.

Division of Review and Analysis. *FEPC: How It Operates.* Washington, D.C.; Government Printing Office, 1944.

810

Dixon, Thomas, Jr. *The Leopard's Spots.* New York: Doubleday, Page & Company, 1904.

———. *Clansman.* New York: Doubleday, Page & Co., 1905.

Douglas, Paul H. *In the Fullness of Time: Memoirs.* New York: Harcourt Brace Jovanovich, 1972.

Du Bois, W.E.B. *The Souls of Black Folk.* Greenwich, Conn.: Fawcett Publications, 1961.

———. *The Autobiography of W.E.B. Du Bois.* New York: International Publishers Co., 1968.

———. *Dusk of Dawn.* New York: Schocken Books, 1968.

———. *The Philadelphia Negro.* Millwood, N.Y.: Kraus-Thompson Organization, 1973.

Ehrlichman, John. *Witness to Power: The Nixon Years.* New York: Simon and Schuster, 1982.

Eisenhower, Dwight D. *Mandate for Change, 1953–1956.* Garden City, N.Y.: Doubleday & Co., 1963.

Evans, Rowland, and Robert Novak. *Lyndon B. Johnson: The Exercise of Power.* London: George Allen and Unwin, 1967.

———. *Nixon in the White House: The Frustration of Power.* New York: Random House, 1971.

Evers, Mrs. Medgar, with William Peters. *For Us, the Living.* Garden City, N.Y.: Doubleday & Co., 1967.

Fairbanks, W. L., and W. S. Hamill. *A Statistical Analysis of the Population of Maryland.* Baltimore: Maryland Development Bureau of the Baltimore Association of Commerce, 1937.

Farmer, James. *Freedom—When?* New York: Random House, 1965.

———. *Lay Bare the Heart: An Autobiography of the Civil Rights Movement.* New York: Arbor House, 1985.

Final Report. Washington, D.C.: Fair Employment Practices Committee, July 28, 1946.

First Report. Washington, D.C.: Fair Employment Practices Committee, July 1943–December 1944.

Foner, Philip S. *American Socialism and Black Americans: From the Age of Jackson to World War II.* Westport, Conn.: Greenwood Press, 1977.

Franklin, John Hope. *From Slavery to Freedom,* 5th ed. New York: Alfred A. Knopf, 1980.

Frazier, E. Franklin. *Black Bourgeoisie.* New York: The Free Press, 1957.

Garfinkel, Herbert. *When Negroes March.* Glencoe, Ill.: The Free Press, 1959.

Garrow, David J. *Bearing the Cross: Martin Luther King, Jr., and the Southern Christian Leadership Conference.* New York: William Morrow & Company, 1986.

Graham, Hugh Davis. *Huey Long.* Englewood Cliffs, N.J.: Prentice Hall, 1970.

Hamby, Alonzo L. *Beyond the New Deal: Harry S. Truman and American Liberalism.* New York: Columbia University Press, 1973.

Hays, Brooks. *A Southern Moderate Speaks.* Chapel Hill: University of North Carolina Press, 1959.

Hill, Herbert. *Black Labor and the American Legal System*. Washington, D.C.: Bureau of National Affairs, 1977.

Hofstadter, Richard. *The Age of Reform*. New York: Alfred A. Knopf, 1955.

Humphrey, Hubert. *The Education of a Public Man*. Garden City, N.Y.: Doubleday & Company, 1976.

Inventory of the Records of the War Manpower Commission. Record Group 211. Washington, D.C.: National Archives and Records Service, General Services Administration, 1973.

Israel, Fred L., ed. *The State of the Union Messages of the Presidents, 1790–1966*, Vol. III. New York: Chelsea House, 1966.

Johnson, Lyndon Baines. *From the Vantage Point*. New York: Holt, Rinehart and Winston, 1971.

Kellogg, Charles Flint. *NAACP*, Vol. 1 (1909–1920). Baltimore: Johns Hopkins Press, 1967.

Kesselman, Louis C. *The Social Politics of FEPC: A Study in Reform Pressure*. Chapel Hill: University of North Carolina Press, 1948.

Kluger, Richard. *Simple Justice*. New York: Alfred A. Knopf, 1976.

Konvitz, Milton. *The Constitution and the United States*. New York: Columbia University Press, 1946.

Kuntsler, William M. *Deep in My Heart*. New York: William Morrow & Company, 1966.

Lee, R. Alton. *Truman and Taft-Hartley: A Question of Mandate*. Lexington: University of Kentucky Press, 1966.

Legislators and the Lobbyists. Washington, D.C.: Congressional Quarterly, 1965.

Lewis, Anthony, and *The New York Times*. *Portrait of a Decade: The Second American Revolution*. New York: Random House, 1964.

Logan, Rayford W. *What the Negro Wants*. Chapel Hill: University of North Carolina Press, 1944.

Luccock, Alfred E., and Paul Hutchinson. *The Story of Methodism*. New York: Abingdon Press (n.d.).

Luper, Clara. *Behold the Walls*. Published by Jim Wire, 1979. Orders to Clara Luper, 1609 N. Eastern, Oklahoma City, Okla. 73111.

Lynch, Hollis R. *The Black Urban Condition: A Documentary History, 1866–1971*. New York: Thomas Y. Crowell Co., 1973.

McGregor, Morris J., Jr. *Integration of the Armed Forces, 1940–1965*. Washington, D.C.: Center of Military History, U.S. Army, 1981.

McNeil, Genna Rae. *Groundwork: Charles Hamilton Houston and the Struggle for Civil Rights*. Philadelphia: University of Pennsylvania Press, 1983.

Meir, August, and Elliott Rudwick. *CORE: A Study in the Civil Rights Movement, 1942–1968*. New York: Oxford University Press, 1973.

Meyer, Howard N. *The Amendment That Refused to Die*. Radnor, Pa.: Chilton Book Co. 1973.

Moon, Henry Lee. *Balance of Power: The Negro Vote*. New York: Kraus Reprint Co., 1969. Originally published in Garden City, N.Y.: Doubleday & Company, 1948.

————. *The Emerging Thought of Du Bois.* New York: Simon and Schuster, 1972.

Morgan, Ruth P. *The President and Civil Rights.* New York: St. Martin's Press, 1970.

Morison, Samuel Eliot, and Henry Steele Commager. *The Growth of the American Republic,* Vol. 2. New York: Oxford University Press, 1962.

Morrow, E. Frederick. *Way Down South Up North.* Philadelphia: United Church Press, 1973.

Northrup, Herbert R. *Organized Labor and the Negro.* New York: Harper, 1944.

Ottley, Roi. *Black Odyssey: The Story of the Negro in America.* New York: Charles Scribner's Sons, 1948.

Parris, Guichard, and Lester Brooks. *Blacks in the City: A History of the National Urban League.* Boston: Little, Brown & Co., 1971.

Peck, James. *Freedom Ride.* New York: Simon and Schuster, 1962.

Pigee, Vera. *The Struggle of Struggles,* Part One. Vera Pigee, 14110 Steele, Detroit, Mich. 48227, 1975.

Public Papers of the Presidents. Washington, D.C.: Government Printing Office, 1963.

Race Relations in the South—1961. Tuskegee, Ala.: Tuskegee Institute, January 31, 1961.

Raper, Arthur F. *The Tragedy of Lynching.* New York: Dover Publications, 1970.

Report of the National Advisory Commission on Civil Disorders. New York: Bantam Books, 1968.

Ross, Malcolm. *All Manner of Men.* New York: Reynal & Hitchcock, 1948.

Ruchames, Louis. *Race, Jobs and Politics: The Story of the FEPC.* New York: Harcourt, Brace & Co., 1946.

Schlesinger, Arthur M., Jr. *The Politics of Upheaval.* Boston: Houghton Mifflin Company, 1960.

Sinkler, George. *The Racial Attitudes of American Presidents, from Abraham Lincoln to Theodore Roosevelt.* New York: Doubleday & Co., 1971.

Solberg, Carl. *Hubert Humphrey: A Biography.* New York: W. W. Norton & Co., 1984.

Spangler, Earl. *The Negro in Minnesota.* Minneapolis, Minn.: T. S. Denison & Co., 1961.

Sundquist, James L. *Politics and Policy: The Eisenhower, Kennedy and Johnson Years.* Washington, D.C.: The Brookings Institution, 1968.

To Secure These Rights: The Report of the President's Committee on Civil Rights, with an introduction by Charles E. Wilson, committee chairman. New York: Simon and Schuster, 1947.

Viorst, Milton. *Fire in the Streets: America in the 1960s.* New York: Simon and Schuster, 1979.

Walsh, Richard, and William Lloyd Fox, eds. *Maryland: a History.* Annapolis, Md.: Hall of Records Commission, Department of General Services, 1983.

Weaver, Robert C. *Negro Labor: A National Problem.* New York: Harcourt, Brace & Co., 1946.

Weiss, Nancy J. *Farewell to the Party of Lincoln.* Princeton, N.J.: Princeton University Press, 1983.

White, Walter. *A Rising Wind*. Garden City, N.Y.: Doubleday, Doran & Co., 1945.

———. *A Man Called White*. Bloomington: Indiana University Press, 1948.

———. *How Far the Promised Land?* New York: Viking Press, 1955.

Wilkins, Roy. *Standing Fast*. New York: Viking Press, 1982.

Wofford, Harris. *Of Kennedys and Kings*. New York: Farrar, Straus & Giroux, 1980.

Wolseley, Roland E. *The Black Press*. Ames: Iowa University Press, 1971.

Zaid, Charles. *Preliminary Inventory of the Records of the Committee on Fair Employment Practices*, Record Group 228. Washington, D.C.: National Archives, and Records Service, General Services Administration, 1962.

Zangrando, Robert L. *The NAACP Crusade Against Lynching, 1909–1950*. Philadelphia: Temple University Press, 1980.

Zinn, Howard. *SNCC: The New Abolitionists*. Boston: Beacon Press, 1964.

SELECTED ARTICLES AND SCHOLARLY WORKS

Birnie, William A. H. "Black Brain Trust." *The American Magazine* (January 1943), pp. 36–37, 94.

Bunche, Ralph J. "A Critique of New Deal Social Planning As It Affects Negroes." *The Journal of Negro History* (January 1936), pp. 59–65.

Burns, James MacGregor. "The Four Kennedys of the First Year." *The New York Times Magazine* (January 14, 1962), pp. 9 ff.

Carter, Douglas. "How the Senate Passed the Civil Rights Bill." *The Reporter* (September 5, 1957), pp. 9–13.

Clark, Kenneth B. "The Civil Rights Movement: Momentum and Organization." *Daedalus*, Vol. 95 (Winter 1966), pp. 239–267.

Coffin, Tris. "How Lyndon Johnson Engineered Compromise on Civil Rights Bill." *The New Leader* (August 5, 1957), pp. 3–4.

Coleman, McAlister. "Who Are the Socialists?" *The World Tomorrow* (October 12, 1932), pp. 347–349.

Collins, Frederick W. "How to Be a Leader Without Leading." *The New York Times Magazine* (July 30, 1961), p. 9 ff.

Danzig, David. "The Meaning of Negro Strategy." *Commentary* (February 1964), pp. 41–46.

Davis, John A. "Educational Programs for the Improvement of Race Relations: Organized Labor and Industrial Organizations." *Journal of Negro Education*, Vol. XIII (1944), pp. 340–348.

"Declaration of Principles." *The American Socialist Quarterly* (July 1934), pp. 3–57.

Doerfler, Ernest. "Socialism and the Negro Problem." *The American Socialist Quarterly* (Summer 1933), pp. 23–36.

Edelsberg, Herman. "The New Civil Rights Law: How It Happened." *The ADL Bulletin* (October 1957), pp. 1–3, 8.

———, and David Brody. "Civil Rights in the 87th Congress." A printed review (January 1, 1961).

Frazier, E. Franklin. "Ethnic Minority Groups in Wartime, with Special Reference to the Negro." *The American Journal of Sociology,* Vol. 48 (November 1942), pp. 369–377.

Gressman, Eugene. "The Unhappy History of Civil Rights Legislation." *Michigan Law Review,* Vol. 50 (1952), pp. 1323–1358.

Hardin, Frances Anne. "The Role of Presidential Advisors, Roosevelt Aides and the FEPC, 1941–1943." A thesis presented to the faculty of the Graduate School of Cornell University for the degree of Master of Science, June 1975.

Henson, Francis A. "Socialism's Contribution to Christianity." *The World Tomorrow* (June 1932), pp. 182–184.

Hill, Herbert. "Race, Ethnicity and Organized Labor: The Opposition to Affirmative Action." *New Politics* (Winter 1987–88), pp. 31–82.

Hill, T. Arnold. "The Plight of the Negro Industrial Worker." *The Journal of Negro Education* (January 1936), pp. 40–47.

Ickes, Harold L. "To Have Jobs or to Have Not." *Negro Digest* (January 1946), pp. 73–75.

Kellogg, Peter J. "Civil Rights Consciousness in the 1940s." *The Historian,* Vol. 42, No. 79, pp. 18–41.

McWilliams, Carey. "Race Relations and the Law." *Science and Society* (Winter 1945), pp. 1–22.

Marshall, Thurgood. "The Supreme Court as Protector of Civil Rights: Equal Protection of the Laws." *The Annals of the American Academy of Social and Political Science* (May 1951), pp. 101–110.

Maslow, Will. "Fair Employment State by State." *The Nation* (April 14, 1945), pp. 410–411.

———. "The Law and Race Relations." *The Annals of the American Academy of Social and Political Science* (March 1946), pp. 75–81.

———. "FEPC—A Case History in Parliamentary Maneuver." *The University of Chicago Law Review* (June 1946), pp. 407–444.

———, and Joseph B. Robinson. "Civil Rights Legislation and the Fight for Equality, 1862–1952." *The University of Chicago Law Review,* Vol. 20, No. 3 (Spring 1953), pp. 363–413.

Miller, Sally M. "The Socialist Party and the Negro, 1901–20." *Black Scholar* (February 1974), pp. 220–229.

Mitchell, Clarence, Jr. "Democrats Versus Dixiecrats." *The Nation,* Vol. 175 (September 27, 1952), pp. 268–271.

———. "The Status of Racial Integration in the Armed Services." *The Journal of Negro Education* (Summer 1954), pp. 208–213.

———. "The Warren Court and Congress: A Civil Rights Partnership." Booklet reprinted from *Nebraska Law Review,* Vol. 48, No. 1 (1968), pp. 91–128.

Moon, Henry Lee. "The Negro Vote in the Presidential Election of 1956." *The Journal of Negro Education* (Summer 1957), pp. 219–230.

———. "The Negro Voter." *The Nation* (September 17, 1960), pp. 155–157.

Morrison, Allan. "A. Philip Randolph: Dean of Negro Leaders." *Ebony* (November 1958), pp. 103–114.

Myers, A. Howard. "The Negro Worker Under NRA." *The Journal of Negro Education* (January 1936), pp. 48–53.

"National Conference on the Economic Crisis and the Negro, The." *Journal of Negro Education* (January 1936), pp. 1–87.

Randolph, A. Philip. "The Trade Union Movement and the Negro." *The Journal of Negro Education* (January 1936), pp. 54–58.

Ransom, Leon A. "Combatting Discrimination in the Employment of Negroes in War Industries and Government Agencies." *Journal of Negro Education,* Vol. XII (1943), pp. 405–416.

Rauh, Joseph L., Jr. "First Clarence Mitchell, Jr., Lecture." Martin Luther King, Jr., Center for Social Change (October 30, 1985).

Roosevelt, Eleanor. "The Negro and Social Change." *Opportunity* (January 1936), pp. 22–23.

Ross, B. Joyce. "Mary McLeod Bethune and the National Youth Administration." *The Journal of Negro History,* Vol. LX, No. 1 (January 1975), pp. 1–29.

"Socialist Party Comes Alive, The." *The World Tomorrow* (June 14, 1934), p. 3.

Sosna, Morton. "The South in the Saddle: Racial Politics During the Wilson Years." *Wisconsin Magazine of History* (Autumn 1970), pp. 30–49.

Stewart, John Gilman. "Independence and Control: The Challenge of Senatorial Party Leadership." Dissertation for Ph.D. at University of Chicago, 1968.

Thomas, Norman. "The Campaign of 1934." *The American Socialist Quarterly,* Vols. 3–5 (1934–35), pp. 3–8.

Waring, Thomas S. "The Southern Case Against Desegregation." *Harper's Magazine* (January 3, 1956), pp. 39–45.

Weaver, Robert C. "The New Deal and the Negro." *Opportunity* (July 1935), pp. 200–202.

———. "An Experiment in Negro Labor." *Opportunity* (October 1936), pp. 295–298.

———. "Racial Employment Trends in National Defense." *Phylon* (Fourth Quarter, 1941), pp. 3–23.

———. "The Negro Comes of Age in Industry." *Atlantic Monthly* (September 1943), pp. 54–56.

———. "Recent Events in Negro Union Relationships." *Journal of Political Economy,* Vol. LII, No. 3 (September 1944), pp. 234–249.

———. "Housing in a Democracy." *The Annals of the American Academy of Political and Social Science* (March 1946), pp. 95–105.

———. "Negro Labor Since 1929." *The Journal of Negro History* (January 1950), pp. 20–38.

White, Walter. "I Investigate Lynchings." *The American Mercury,* Vol. 16 (January 1929), pp. 77–84.

———. "It's Our Country, Too." *The Saturday Evening Post* (October–December 1940), p. 58 ff.

———. "Why I Remain a Negro." *Saturday Review of Literature* (October 11, 1947), NAACP reprint, DW Files.

———. "Has Science Conquered the Color Line?" Reprinted from *Look* in *Negro Digest* (December, 1949), pp. 37–40.

———. "How Washington's Color Line Looks to Me." *The Saturday Evening Post* (April 3, 1954), pp. 32–33 ff.

Woodward, C. Vann. "The Great Civil Rights Debate." *Commentary* (October 1957), pp. 285–295.

ORAL HISTORIES

Kennedy, Robert F. Interview by Anthony Lewis, December 4, 6, 1964. John F. Kennedy Library Oral History Program.

King, Martin Luther, Jr. Interview by Berl I. Bernhard, March 4, 1964. John F. Kennedy Library Oral History Program.

Marshall, Burke. Interviews by Louis Oberdorfer, May 29, 1964; Anthony Lewis, June 13, 14, 20, 1964; Larry J. Hackman, January 19–20, 1970. John F. Kennedy Library Oral History Program.

Mitchell, Clarence, Jr. Interview by John Stewart, February 9, 1957. John F. Kennedy Library Oral History Program.

————. Interview by Robert Martin, December 6, 1968. Civil Rights Documentation Project, Ralph J. Bunche Oral History Collection, Manuscript Department, Moorland-Spingarn Research Center, Howard University.

————. Interview by Thomas Baker, November 7, 1972. Lyndon Baines Johnson Oral History Collection, Accession No. 73-24.

————. Interview by Charles Wagandt, February 12, 1977 (OH 8209). Maryland Historical Society Oral History.

————. Interview by Ed Edwin, July 24, 1981. Columbia University Oral History Collection.

Mitchell, Juanita. Interviews by Charles Wagandt, July 25, 1975 (OH 8095), December 9, 1976 (OH 8183). Maryland Historical Society Oral History.

Rauh, Joseph L., Jr. Interview by Charles T. Morrissey, December 23, 1965. John F. Kennedy Library Oral History Program.

Sorensen, Theodore. Interview by Carl Kaysen, May 3, 1964. John F. Kennedy Library Oral History Program.

Wilkins, Roy. Interview by Joe Wall, June 4, 1957. Columbia University Oral History Collection.

Wofford, Harris. Interviews by Berl I. Bernhard, November 29, 1965; Larry Hackman, November 22, 1968. John F. Kennedy Library Oral History Program.

Principal Cases Cited

Adams v. *Lacy*, 228 F.2d 619 (1955).

Adams v. *Richardson*, 356 F.Supp. 92 (D.D.C. 1973).

Bell v. *Maryland*, 378 U.S. 226 (1964).

Board of Trustees of University of North Carolina v. *Frasier*, 350 U.S. 979 (1956); 134 F.Supp. 589.

Bouie v. *Columbia*, 378 U.S. 347 (1964).

Boynton v. *Virginia*, 364 U.S. 454 (1960).

Briggs v. *Elliott*, 98 F.Supp. 529 (1951); 347 U.S. 497 (1954).

Browder v. *Gayle*, 352 U.S. 903 (1956).

Brown v. *Board of Education*, 347 U.S. 483 (1954); 349 U.S. 294 (1955).

Brunson v. *Board of Trustees of School District No. 1 of Clarendon County, South Carolina*, 311 F.2d 107, cert. den., 373 U.S. 933 (1963).

Buchanan v. *Warley*, 245 U.S. 60 (1917).

Burr v. *Columbia*, 378 U.S. 146 (1964).

Burton v. *Wilmington Parking Authority*, 365 U.S. 715 (1961).

Bush v. *Orleans Parish School Board (Harry K. Williams* v. *Jimmie H. Davis)*, 187 F.Supp. 42 (1960).

Catlette v. *United States*, 132 F.2d. 902 (1943).

City of Birmingham v. *Monk*, 184 F.2d 859, cert. den., 341 U.S. 940 (1951).

Civil Rights Cases, 109 U.S. 3 (1883).

In re *Debs*, 158 U.S. 564 (1895).

Detroit Housing Commission v. *Lewis*, 226 F.Supp. 180 (1955).

Gon Lum v. *Rice*, 275 U.S. 78 (1927).

Griffin v. *Maryland*, 378 U.S. 130 (1964).

Harman v. *Forssenius*, 380 U.S. 528 (1964).

Harmon v. *Tyler*, 273 U.S. 668 (1927).

Harper v. *Virginia State Board of Electors*, 383 U.S. 663 (1966).

Hawkins v. *Board of Control*, 350 U.S. 413 (1956).

Heart of Atlanta Hotel, Inc. v. *United States*, 379 U.S. 241 (1964).

Hirabayshi v. *United States*, 320 U.S. 81 (1943).

Holmes v. *City of Atlanta*, 350 U.S. 879 (1955).

James v. *Marineship Corp.*, 25 Cal.2d 721, 155 P.2d 329, 15 **LRRM** 798 (1945).

John R. Thompson Co. v. *District of Columbia*, 203 F.2d. 579 (1953).

Korematsu v. *United States*, 323 U.S. 214 (1944).

McLaurin v. *Oklahoma State Regents of Higher Education*, 339 U.S. 637 (1950).

Mallory v. *United States*, 345 U.S. 449 (1957).

Meat Cutters v. *Fairlawn*, 353 U.S. 20 (1957).

Morgan v. *Virginia*, 328 U.S. 373 (1946).

Murray v. *Maryland*, 182 A 590 (1936); 169 Md. 478 (1937).

NAACP v. *Alabama*, 359 U.S. 449 (1958).

Nebbis v. *New York*, 291 U.S. 902 (1939).

New Negro Alliance v. *Sanitary Grocery Company*, 303 U.S. 552 (1938).

Norris v. *Alabama*, 294 U.S. 589 (1935).

Pennsylvania v. *Nelson*, 350 U.S. 497 (1956).

Piper v. *Big Pine School District*, 193 Cal. 664 (1924).

Plessy v. *Ferguson*, 163 U.S. 537 (1896).

Richmon v. *Deans*, 281 U.S. 704 (1930).

Robinson v. *Florida*, 378 U.S. 153 (1964).

Scales v. *United States*, 367 U.S. 203 (1964).

Screws v. *United States*, 325 U.S. 91 (1945).

Shelley v. *Kraemer*, 333 U.S. 1 (1948).

Ex parte *Siebold*, 100 U.S. 371 (1880).

Smith v. *Allwright*, 321 U.S. 649.

South Carolina v. *Katzenbach*, 383 U.S. 301 (1966).

Steele v. *Louisville and Nashville Railroad Company*, 323 U.S. 192 (1944).

Sweatt v. *Painter*, 339 U.S. 629 (1950).

Sweezy v. *New Hampshire*, 354 U.S. 234 (1957).

Terry v. *Adams*, 345 U.S. 461 (1953).

Tunstall v. *Brotherhood of Locomotive Firemen & Enginemen*, 323 U.S. 210 (1944).

United States v. *Alabama*, 252 F.Supp. 95 (1966).

United States v. *Guest*, 383 U.S. 745 (1966).

United States v. *Price*, 383 U.S. 787 (1966).

United States v. *Raines*, 362 U.S. 17 (1960).

United States v. *Texas*, 252 F.Supp. 234 (1966), 384 U.S. 155 (1966).

United States v. *Thomas*, 362 U.S. 58 (1960).

Urciolo v. *Hodge*, 334 U.S. 24 (1948).

Ex parte *Virginia*, 100 U.S. 339 (1879).

Watkins v. *United States*, 354 U.S. 178 (1957).

Wickard v. *Filburn*, 353 U.S. 111 (1942).

Williams v. *Louisville and Nashville Railroad Company*, 27 Cal.2d 586, 165 P.2d 903, 17 LRRM 771 (1946).

Ex parte *Yarborough*, 100 U.S. 651 (1884).

Yick Wo v. *Hopkins*, 118 U.S. 356 (1886).

Index

821

radical, 187, 381
Urban Affairs Department proposal and,
    466–467
voting rights and, 646, 649–650
Reserve Officer Training Corps, 250
Resnick, Joseph, 646
restaurants and lunch counters, segregation
    of, 83–84, 105, 226, 441, 443,
    447–448, 457
Reuther, Walter, 178, 274, 294, 304, 309,
    495, 527, 531, 554, 561, 632–633
Reynolds, Grant, 165
Ribicoff, Abraham, 460–461
Richardson, John, 33
Ridgely, K., 45
right-to-work amendment, 373, 375, 378
Rime of the Ancient Mariner, The (Coleridge),
    338
riots, 41, 147, 154, 660–661, 671,
    676–677, 698
Risher, John T., 162
Rising Wind, A (White), 236
Ritchie, Albert C., 41–42, 44, 50, 99,
    100
Robertson, Willis, 603
Robins, John B., 33–34, 42, 44
Robinson, Jackie, 409
Robinson, Rev. James H., 108
Rockefeller, Nelson A., 431, 435, 693,
    743
Rodino, Peter, 363, 571, 593–594,
    675–676, 735
Rogers, Byron G., 593–594
Rogers, William P., 239, 374, 401, 415,
    421, 422, 425, 447, 461–462, 476
Rolph, James, 44
Roman Catholic Church, 121, 181, 328,
    528, 529, 558, 601
Roosevelt, Eleanor, 128, 155, 304, 305
Roosevelt, Franklin D., Jr., 194, 206
Roosevelt, Franklin D., Sr., 51, 102, 122,
    128, 130, 207–208, 223, 320, 329
in election of 1934, 98–99, 101
Executive Order 8802 and, 127, 131,
    133, 146, 147, 148, 165–166
FEPC and, 131–135, 141, 142, 144,
    148, 156
Truman compared with, 173, 176
White (Walter) and, 132–133, 134
see also New Deal
Roosevelt, James, 336, 337, 343, 372,
    461, 571–572
Rosenau, William, 47
Rosenberg, Anna M., 237, 242
Ross, Malcolm, 137, 143

Ross, Mike, 137
Rowan, Carl, 464
Ruff, Charles (grandfather), 70
Ruff, Elsie Davis, see Mitchell, Elsie Davis
    Ruff
Ruff, Grace Davis (grandmother), 76
Rummel, Francis, 328
Russell, Richard B., 148, 174, 179,
    189–190, 199, 212, 213, 341,
    347, 357–360, 506, 587–588,
    643
civil rights bills and, 375, 378–379,
    381–387, 391–392, 398, 425,
    427, 602, 608, 610, 615, 616,
    620, 680
Russell amendment, 166, 189
Russwurm, John, 76
Rustin, Bayard, 105, 557–558, 693

St. Katherine's Episcopal Church, 68
St. Paul Urban League, 113, 114,
    120–121, 122, 140
Salinger, Pierre, 516
Salter, John, 502
Saltonstall, Leverett, 374, 388, 544, 679
Sanders, Barefoot, 685
satellite bill, 521
Scales, Junius, 483
Schaefer, William Donald, 26
Schlesinger, Arthur M., Jr., 495
school construction bill (H.R. 7535),
    314–315, 344–345
schools, see education; specific schools
Schuyler, George S., 37, 89, 153
Schwellenbach, Lewis B., 160, 162
Schwerner, Michael Henry, 667
Schwerner, Rita, 630
Scott, Dred, 120, 390
Scott, Hugh, 336, 344, 351, 479, 524,
    544–545, 648n, 650n, 679, 684,
    688, 701
Scott, W. Kerr, 327
Scottsboro Defense Committee, 58
Scottsboro trial, 40, 49–60
Scott v. Sanford, 395
Screws v. United States, 666
Seale, Bobby, 708
segregation, 133, 202, 203, 219–258
in Baltimore, 64, 68–69, 78, 79, 81–86
cost of, 219–220
discrimination linked with, 205
of education, 72, 78, 210–211, 221,
    241–244, 248
of housing, 68–69, 78, 81, 250–252
religion and, 105–106, 527–529